Harappa Script & Language

Data mining of Corpora, *tantra yukti* & knowledge discovery of a civilization

S. Kalyanaraman

Sarasvati Research Center 2016

ISBN-10:0-9911048-7-0
ISBN-13:978-0-9911048-7-1
Library of Congress Control Number 2016915600

Harappa Script & Language

- *Data mining of Corpora, tantra yukti & knowledge discovery of a civilization*

Table of contents

Definition of terms: *tantra, yukti*	4
Methodology for knowledge discovery through data mining	20
Rebus method to signify phonetic sounds of words, a logo-phonetic writing system	21
Annex A Harappa Script inscriptions found in temple area of Mohenjo-daro (and Harappa?)	277
Annex B *Dharma saṁjñā* Corporate badges of Harappa Script Corpora, ceramic (stoneware) bangles, seals, fillets	305
Annex C Form and function of inscribed tablets, miniature tablets	347
Annex D Ligatures to *ayo, aya* 'fish' rebus: *aya* 'iron' *ayas* 'metal', *meḍ* 'body' rebus: *meḍ* 'iron' semantic modifiers as hypertexts and Harappa Script inscriptions on 240 copper tablets	365
Annex E Clustering 'temple' hieroglyph, pictorial narratives of kneeling adorant, together with markhor and offering on a stool	422
Annex F Multiple tablets with same inscription in Harappa signify work-in-process in circular platforms	458
Annex G *kulā* 'hood of snake' as tail and Harappa Script hypertext	470
Annex H Black ant hieroglyph and *cīmara kāra* 'coppersmith'	478
Annex I Hieroglyphs of animal clusters. Mohenjo-daro m0304 (Reconstructed) Seal. A person is shown seated in 'penance' may signify *Triśiras*, son of *Tvaṣṭā*, कुबेर	484
Annex J Crocodile, scorpion, disheveled hair in Harappa Script hieroglyphs signify work in *bica* 'haematite stone ore'	529
Annex K Structure, form, function and significance of *caṣālḥ* चषालः on Yūpa in a *yajna* and carburization	535
Annex L List of Harappa Script 'text signs'	561
Select inscriptions of Harappa Script Corpora	566
Bibliography	764
Index	767
End Notes	780

Prelude

Tantra yukti is a research documentation doctrine together with *data mining* of Harappa Script Corpora and lexis (vocabulary) of ancient languages of Bharata. The process has resulted in many lessons learnt from a historical narrative of the Bronze Age Revolution. It was a technological revolution when copper could be alloyed with other minerals such as tin, zinc, antimony to create hard alloys of utilitarian value to societies. This revolution changed the economic form of social organizations, resulting in Corporate forms of guilds of workmen and merchants working for a common cause. The revolution also changed the *weltanschauung* by the brilliant principle of *dharma-dhamma* which was deemed inexorable. In one form, *dharma-dhamma* meant the discharge of one's responsibilities according to one's proclivities and talents.

Dharma-dhamma saṁjñā – Corporate badges of responsibility were written down and inscribed as tokens, veritable reminders of the wearer's responsibilities for *abhyudayam*, 'social welfare' coupled with his or her own life imperative moving from being to becoming, to attain *nihs'reyas*, union of the *atman* with the *paramaatman.* This was a breath-taking innovation. It resulted in the dominant doctrine of treating the workplace as a place of worship. *kole.l* 'smithy, forge' as an economic form to cope with the Bronze Age Revolution expanded the semantics of the expression to *kole.l* 'temple' (root: *kol* 'working in iron, metal'). This active life-doctrine provides a significant lesson of history of a civilization: work results in creation of wealth and a person's conduct changes in relation to the Supreme Divinity, metaphored as the Cosmic Dancer. The imperative of trade necessitated the invention of a Harappa Script writing system with tokens of *dharma-dhamma saṁjñā* – Corporate badges of responsibility.

Ancient Bharata accounted for 32.9% of world Gross Domestic Product (GDP) in 0 CE thanks mainly to the contributions of the workforce of explorers searching for minerals and artisans working with the minerals to produce exquisite works of art and of utility (pots, pans, tools, implements, weapons) which resulted in trade transactions across space and time, using geographical matrix of history and economic opportunities provided by discoveries of resources of Mother Earth and Sovereign Ocean.

This treatise as the story of a civilization documents the nature of work performed as people moved from rural to urban living coping with the industrial society formed by the Bronze Age Revolution and conduct of guilds as incipient economic forms of states called *janapada*-s. I agree with Will Durant that history is "an industry, an art and a philosophy -- a search for perspective and enlightenment." The story of Ancient Bharata Civilization revealed in the knowledge discoveries of data mining using *tantra yukti* doctrine describes the historical panorama in one expression: *dharma-dhamma, esha dhammo sanantano*, as Gautama the Buddha avers. This is thus a treatise on *dharma*, deciphering *dharma-dhamma saṁjñā* of Harappa Script Corpora. The lesson of this history narrative is declaration of a future possibility, an inspiration for youth to regain status of Bharat to its 0 CE level in world GDP governed by *dharma-dhamma*: work is worship and source of wealth of a nation. This will be a recital in *chandas*, a prayer to Vagdevi Sarasvati who proclaimed: अहं राष्ट्री संगमनी वसूनां 'I am the Rashtra, mover of wealth'. This prayer governed lives of the ancient people on the Vedic Sarasvati River Basin in over 2000 settlements (80% of the total settlement of the civilization). -- S. Kalyanaraman

Harappa Script & language

Data mining of Corpora, *tantra yukti* & knowledge discovery of a civilization

This is a treatise, a formal and systematic written discourse on knowledge discovery of a civilization in two domains of knowledge: 1. Archaeo-metallurgical advances during Bronze Age Revolution; and 2. Invention of a writing system to document, in Meluhha (Harappa) language, technical details of these advances anchored on the imperative of supporting long-distance trade transactions by seafaring artisans and merchants.

The objective of the treatise is to unravel the semantics of *Dharma saṁjñā or Bharatiya hieroglyphs* using a method of data mining. The method of data mining of Harappa Script Corpora of over 7000 inscriptions is based on the principles of *tantra yukti*. The doctrine of *tantra yukti* provides a scientific basis for reconstructing the lexis of an ancient Bharata language, Meluhha (Mleccha). The lexis (vocabulary) matches both the hieroglyphs/hypertexts and the metalwork catalogues signified by the Corpora. Since the Bronze Age Revolution increased interactions among people across space and time, many of the 25+ ancient languages of Bharata retain all spoken (*parole*) words and expressions in Meluhha lexis related to metalwork. This reinforces the linguistic identification of areal languages features within a linguistic union, Bharata *sprachbund*. Meluhha artisans are attested in cuneiform texts and as language on Shu-ilishu cylinder seal. Mleccha (cognate) language is attested in Manu (*mleccha vAcas* or *mlecccha* speech) and Mahabharata. The Great Epic also refers to mleccha rulers and people from many *janapada-s* of Ancient Bharata and many contact regions in Ancient Near East and Ancient Far East. It is notable that rebus expressions *milakkhu* 'copper' *mleccha-mukha* 'copper ingot' are attested in Pali and Samskrtam. Old Bible *Harosheth hagoyim* 'smithy of nations' is cognate Meluhha *kharoṣṭī* खरोष्ठी *goya,* 'blacksmith lip + guild'. The association of Meluhha with metalwork is thus traceable to ancient times of the Bronze Age Revolution.

Tantra yukti doctrine is precisely defined for linguistic analyses and is applied to delineate the origin and formation of ancient languages of Bharata. This is a more analytical doctrine than the 'Aryan Invasion Theory' (AIT) which is an article of faith subjected to polemics. AIT has been treated as a 'linguistic doctrine' by many linguists and researchers of Bharata civilization and the theory has yielded limited or no success in deciphering the Harappa Script.

Exeutive summary. *Tantra yukti doctrine* is an exercise in general semantics, a data mining method

Definition of terms: *tantra, yukti*[1]

Tantra can be termed as that which discusses and details subjects and concepts; yukti is "... that which removes blemishes like impropriety, contradiction, etc., from the intended meaning and thoroughly joins the meanings together." The expression, *Tantra-yukti* denotes those devices that aid the composition of a text in a systematic manner to convey intended ideas clearly. Cakrapāṇi lists 40 distinct devices of tantra yukti; 32 or more of these devices are exemplified in the treatises of Suśruta, Caraka, Vāgbhaṭa, Kautilya, Panini on knowledge domains of Ayurveda, Arthas'Astra and grammar of Samskrtam. Caraka notes: तंत्रे समासव्यासोक्ते भवन्त्येता हि क्रत्स्नशः एकदेशने दृश्यन्ते समासाभिहिते तथा 'all these *tantrayukti*-s occur in a scientific work in brief and in detail. But only some of them occur in a work written in brief."

A characteristic feature of the structure and form of Harappa script is crispness of expression. This is governed by the cardinal principle of *tantra yukti* : स्फुटता न पदैरपाकृता न च न स्वीकृत मर्थगौरवम् 'Crispness (of an expression) is not obliterated by verbosity, nor is the depth of meaning that is intended to be conveyed compromised (to attain crispness).

Precision of speech expression is achieved by unambiguously orthographed devices of hieroglyphs signified by images of wild and domestic animals (tiger, elephant, rhinoceros, boar, buffalo, zebu, ox, goat, markhor, ram, serpent hood), narratives such as a tiger or an antelope with head turned backwards, an archer or person seated in penance, a worshipper, tumblers, drummer, *ficus religiosa* leaf, claws of crab, rice-plant sprout, pincers, harrow, comb, scarf, lid of jar, rim of jar, rimless pot, ladle, stool, hayrick, platform, crocodile, frog, turtle, fish, fish-eye, quail, duck or aquatic birds, black ant, svastika, fire-altar, hillock, mountain-range, twig or sprig, numerical markers – one, two, three, four to signify numeral words. Semantic expansion to signify speech expressions is achieved by the 'crispness' feature of ligaturing combining animal heads, animal parts, infixed or circumscribed or superscripted hieroglyph multiplexes creating hypertexts. Such hypertexts have been matched with words and expressions of Harappa language (Meluhha) using the lexis of *Indian Lexicon*. Such words and expressions of animals, etc. hieroglyph-muliplexes have homonyms (rebus, similar sounding words) in the *parole* (speech forms) of Meluhha (again using the lexis of *Indian Lexicon*). All the homonyms for words and expressions so discovered relate to metalwork catalogues.

Some typical *tantra yukti* devices in the narratives of Harappa Script Corpora are: *upamAnam* (or **दृष्टान्त *dRṣṭA***nta or analogy), *vAkyaviśesha* (completion of a sentence meaningfully even in the absence of a word which is understood), *pUrvapakṣa* (objections, *prima facie* or provisional view), *uttarapakṣa* (correct view or answers). These devices are among 32 devices in *Arthas'Astra* list of *Tantra yukti.*

The significance of some *tantra yukti* devices are presented, as an executive summary, in the context of Harappa Script Corpora. These devices will be elaborated further by specific illustrations gleaned from the Corpora.

1. *Adhikaraṇa (subject matter)* The subject matter of Harappa script Corpora relates to metalwork in the Bronze Age across Eurasia, from Hanoi, Vietnam to Haifa, Israel
2. Yoga (arrangement) The Corpora is arranged in about 7000 inscriptions presented on seals, tablets, copper plates, metal implements, ivory rods, potsherds or as writing on pendants or sculptures in the round (e.g. gold pendant with inscription painted and statue of 'priest' with Harappa script hieroglyphs of dotted circle and *uttarIyam* 'shawl' worn by the priest.)
3. *Hetvārtha (extension of argument)* The purpose achieved by the Corpora is to covey messages about the technical specifications of products (packages or cargo) which are authenticated by the messages

4. *Padārtha (import of words)* The import of words conveyed by the hieroglyphs read rebus is to specify the resources used: e.g. minerals, furnaces or smelters used in creating the product (either an ingot or alloy of minerals or implement or weapon or a *cire perdue* casting in metal)
5. *Pradeśa (poetic adumbration)* Some inscriptions are composed of narratives as semantic determinants (e.g. a tiger looking backwards connotes *kola* 'tiger' rebus: *kol* 'working in iron' PLUS *krammara* 'look backwards' rebus: *kamar* 'artisan, smith'; thus signifying an artisan working in iron).
6. *Uddeśa (concise statement)* Some inscriptions are just composite heads of animals joined to an animal or bovine body. The concise statement intends to signify three minerals which compose the product or package or cargo (e.g. combined animal with bovine body and heads of antelope, one-horned young bull, ox each signifying *ranku* 'antelope' rebus: *ranku* 'tin' PLUS *konda* 'young bull' Rebus: *kondar* 'turner' PLUS *barad, barat* 'ox' rebus: *bharat* 'alloy of pewter, copper, tin').
7. *Nirdeśa (amplification)* Some inscriptions contain phonetic or semantic orthographic deteminatives to amplify the message conveyed (e.g. body of a person with legs spread out signifies two rebus renderings: *meD* 'body' rebus: *meD* 'iron, copper' *karNika* 'legs spread out' rebus: *karNI* 'supercargo, engraver, scribe, account'
A Supercargo is a representative of the ship's owner on board a merchant ship, responsible for overseeing the cargo and its sale. Thus, the Supercargo is signified as in control of iron/metal merchandise on a seafaring ship.
8. *Vākyaśeṣa (supply of ellipsis -- the omission from speech or writing of a word or words that are superfluous or able to be understood from contextual clues.)* Some inscriptions signify 'fish' as a hieroglyph. In the context of Supercargo's responsibility, the 'fish' hieroglyph may have orthographic accent on 'fins' of fish which signify: *khambhaṛā* 'fish fin' rebus: *kammaṭa* 'portable furnace to melt metals, mint, coiner, coinage' PLUS *ayo, aya* 'fish' rebus: *aya* 'iron' *ayas* 'metal'.
9. *Prayojana (purpose)* The purpose of the entire Harappa script Corpora is to document the products which are merchandise for exchange with contact areas and provide explanatory messages to the trade representatives such as Meluhha colonies in Ancient Near East or along the Persian Gulf metalwork sites.
10. *Upadeśa (instruction)* An example may be cited to explain how the instruction is achieved on Harappa script Corpora. A statue of a priest of Mohenjo-daro is shown wearing a fillet (dotted circle PLUS string) on the forehead and on right-shoulder. The message signified is: *dhăvaḍ* 'iron-smelter' with Harappa script hieroglyphs signifies पोतृ,'purifier' of *dhāū, dhāv* 'red stone minerals'. The compound phrase is broken up into two segments: *dhăv* 'strand' rebus: *dhăv, dhAtu* 'mineral' PLUS -*vaḍ* 'string' rebus: వడగ 'clever, skilful' i.e. a person skilled in smelting minerals, hence an iron (red ore) smelter.
11. *Apadeśa (advancement of reason)* The choice of hieroglyphs in Harappa script Corpora is to avoid ambiguities in expressions. Thus, hieroglyphs such as elephant, rhinoceros, tiger, buffalo, fish are incorporated in inscriptions to signify: *karabha* 'trunk of elephant' rebus: *karba* 'iron' *ibha* 'elephant' rebus: *ib* 'iron', *gaNDa* 'rhinoceros' rebus: *khaNDA* 'implements', *kola* 'tiger' rebus: *kol* 'working in iron', *kolle* 'blacksmith' *kolhe* 'smelter', *ranga* 'buffalo' rebus: *ranga* 'pewter', *ayo, aya* 'fish' rebus: *aya* 'iron' *ayas* 'metal'. These are further complemented by other hieroglyphs such as standing person with legs spread, rim-of-jar to signify *meD* 'body' rebus: *meD* 'iron' PLUS *karNika* 'legs spread out' rebus: *karNIka* 'helmsman, engraver, scribe, account'; *kanka, karNika* 'rim of jar' rebus: *karNI* 'Supercargo' *karNIka* 'engraver, scribe, account' PLUS *kanda* 'pot' rebus: *kanda* 'fire-altar' *khaNDa* 'implements'.

12. *Atideśa (indication or application)* On some inscriptions, an additional orthographic device is used to indicate that a metal implement is the product being managed by a Supercargo. Thus, on a Chanhudaro seal, the double-axe signifies a metal axe. It also signifies *kuThAru* 'armourer'.

Double-axe found in a Mesopotamian site. Comparable to the double-axe shown on Chanhudaro seal C-23. Pictorial motif of a double-axe is a Sarasvati hieroglyph (Pict-133).

13. *Arthāpatti (implication)* The fact that these

hieroglyph compositions occur on bronze artifacts imply that competence in metalcasting, bronze metalwork is signified.

14. *Nirṇaya (decision)*

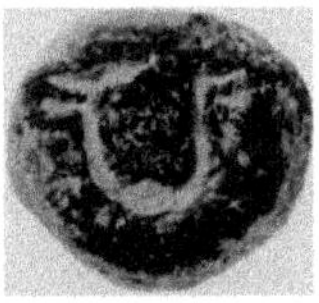

A simple seal of Daimabad which merely shows the 'rim of jar' hieroglyph is a decisive signifier of the rebus message: kanka 'rim of jar' rebus: karNika 'Supercargo'.

15. *Prasaṅga (restatement)* A remarkable device in orthography on Harappa script Corpora is duplication. For example, a markhor is reduplicated back-to-back on a gold artifact.

Proceedings of the First International Conference on the Archaeology of the U.A.E.

Fig. 96f: Failaka no. 260 Double-antelope at the belly in the Levant similar doubling occurs for a lion.

16 Ekānta (categorical statement or invariable rule)

On this pectoral, emphasis is on the overflowing pot (in addition to other hieroglyphs such as standard device and one-horned young bull). The categorical message relates to *lo* ‘overflowing’ *kaNDa* ‘pot’ rebus: *lokhanda* ‘metal implements’. The invariable rule of Harappa script Corpora is that inscriptions are metalwork catalogues, metalwork proclamations.

17 *Naikānta / anekānta / anekārtha (comprising statement)* Using the pectoral example this tantrayukti can be demonstrated. The message conveyed: kan.d. kan-ka 'rim of jar'(Santali)karn.aka 'ear or rim of jar' (Sanskrit) kan.d. 'pot' (Santali)Rebus: karan.ika 'writer' (Telugu). kan.d.'fire-altar' (Santali).করণিক [karaṇika] n an office-clerk, a clerk. কারণিক [kāraṇika] a pertaining to cause, causal; ex amining, judging. n. an examiner; a judge; a clerk (Bengali). खनक [Monier-Williams lexicon, p= 336,3]m. one who digs , digger , excavator MBh. iii , 640 R.

18 *Apavarga / apavarja (exception or restriction of a pervasive rule)* While many seals and tablets are incised, the writing also occurs in paint (perhaps ferrous oxide on metal) on a gold pendant.

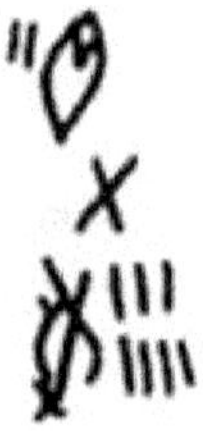

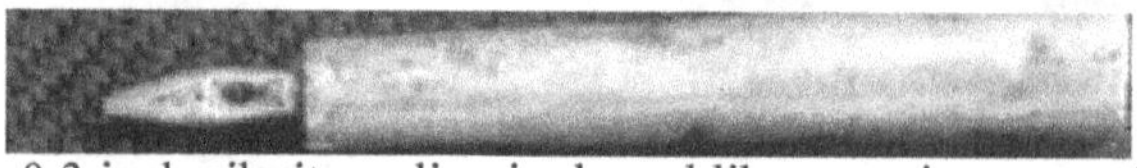

This 2.5inch long gold pendant has a 0.3 inch nib; its ending is shaped like a sewing or netting needle. It bears an inscription painted in Harappa script. This inscription is deciphered as a proclamation of metalwork competence.

19. *Viparyaya (opposite)* I need not elaborate on the objections raised to reject over 150 decipherment claims. My submission is that the orthography is NOT intended to signify syllables but full words, hence the script is logographic. Second point is that it is an error to exclude pictorial motifs from the decipherments and focus only on ‘signs’. Both signs and pictorial motifs have to signify TOGETHER a message of the Bronze Age. Most decipherments prejudge that names or titles should be signified by ‘signs’. This prejudgement leads to erroneous results. The possibility that all hieroglyphs (both signs and pictorial motifs) signify metalwork catalogues should NOT be ruled out because of the imperative created by the Bronze Age revolution which resulted in surplus goods which were bartered by seafaring merchants.

20. *Pūrvapakṣa (objection) The* previous arguments also relate to this device of *tantra yukti*. There are, in Harappa Script Corpora words which signify functionaries like Supercargo and also minerals such as magnetite (*poLa* ‘zebu’ rebus: *poLa* ‘magnetite ferrous ore’).

21. *Vidhāna (right interpretation)* The right interpretation should relate to the Bronze Age economic imperative. Wealth was created by metalwork and mintwork and artifacts were created like the Nahal Mishmar *cire perdue* artifacts which were proclaimed in processions (as evidenced by Jasper cylinder seal).

22. *Anumata (concession or agreement)* There is general consensus that Harappa script Corpora is related to trade since many seals also had exact replicas as seal impressions. So, the logical extension is to review the Corpora as metalwork catalogues for trade transactions.

23. *Vyākhyāna (explanation)* The explanation is provided in the decipherment of almost all 7000 inscriptions in 16 volumes which also include explanations of some pictorial motifs as Harappa script hieroglyphs on Ancient Near East and Persian Gulf (Dilmun) seals.

24. *Samśaya (doubt)* There are linguistic arguments which raise doubts about the Meluhha (Mleccha) language. It is possible that this was the spoken version of Prakrtam which co-existed with the *chandas* which is the literary version of Samskrtam or Vedic diction. There is general consensus that Ancient Bharata was a *sprachbund* (language union or linguistic area) wince many features of languages of ancient Bharatam Janam 'metalcaster folk' as self-identification by Visvamitra in Rigveda (3.53.12) are common, such as the feature of reduplication to convey semantics, e.g. *kandAnmuNDAn* 'bits and pieces'.

25. *Atītāpekṣaṇa /atītavekṣaṇa (retrospective reference; atikrAntAveksana 'reference to a past statement')* The occurrence of Harappa Script hieroglyphs on Dong Son bronze drums is also explained by the occurrence of Yupa inscriptions in East Borneo and occurrence of S'ivalingas in the Ancient Far East. This suggests the possibility of a Maritime Tin Route from Hanoi to Haifa because the largest tin belt of the globe is in the Far East, along the Mekong delta.

26. *Anāgatāvekṣaṇa (prospective reference)* The continued use of Harappa script hieroglyphs on early punch-marked coins from Takshasila to Eran to Karur to Anuradhapura are indicative of an Age of Symbols coterminous with the Bronze Age organizations of mints. Many hieroglyphs signify mintwork catalogues and in many cases together with Brahmi or Kharoshthi inscriptions which signify names or titles using the syllabic scripts which are distinct from the logographic Harappa script hieroglyphs.

27. *Svasaṁjñā (technical nomenclature)* The entire Harappa script Corpora of about 7000 inscriptions provide many examples of technical nomenclature such as *poLa* (zebu) 'magnetite ore', *maraka* (peacock) 'a type of steel', *rango* (buffalo) 'pewter, an alloy of copper, zinc and tin', *sattva* 'svastika hieroglyph' rebus: *sattva, jasta* 'zinc'.

28. *Ūhya (deduction or what is understood)* When a string of, say, five hieroglyphs signify minerals and operations in a furnace, the inference is that the signified is the

metalworker or artisan working with such minerals and furnaces (in a workshop or mint).

29. *Samuccaya (specification or combination, collection of ideas)* A typical example of collection of related messages occurs in hieroglyph-multiplexes or hypertexts, say, of a composite animal.

Orthographic components explained by Dennys Frenez and Massimo Vidale.

30. *Nidarśana (illustration)* The illustration of the devices of *tantra yukti* occurs on a cylinder seal from Ancient Near East, the seal of Sharkali-Sharri.

Cylinder Seal of Ibni-Sharrum Agade period, reign of Sharkali-Sharri (c. 2217-2193 BCE) Mesopotamia Serpentine H. 3.9 cm; Diam. 2.6 cm Formerly in the De Clercq collection; gift of H. de Boisgelin, 1967 AO 22303 The signifiers: *rango* 'buffalo' rebus: *rango* 'pewter' *lo* 'overflow' *kanda* 'pot' rebus: *lokhanda* 'metal implements' *baTa* 'six' rebus: *bhaTa* 'furnace' *meD* 'curl' rebus: *meD* 'iron'. Thus, Ibni-Sharrum is a smelter working with pewter and metal implements.

31. *Nirvacana (definition or derivation or etymology of terms)* An *Indian Lexicon* provides etyma which include most of the 25+ ancient languages of Indian *sprachbund.* Many metalwork terms used in Harappa script Corpora are traceable to one or more of the etyma of the *sprachbund.*

32. *Niyoga / sanniyoga (injunction)* The occurrence of Harappa script hieroglyphs on 21 stoneware ceramic bangles is a pointer to the 21 types of functions (within a guild) identified during the Bronze Age for metalwork.

33. *Vikalpana (option)* It is possible to indicate alternative rebus readings for some select inscriptions. Thus, a standing person may signify *meD* 'body' rebus*: meD* 'iron' and also 'legs spread out': *karNika* rebus: 'Supercargo, helmsman' or *karNaka* 'scribe, engraver'

34. *Pratyutsāra / pratyucāra (rebuttal)* The decipherment of Harappa Script Corpora as metalwork catalogues is a rebuttal of arguments made that the people who created the writing system were 'illiterates' who engaged in some rituals. The rebuttal alternative argument is that the writing system was necessitated by the Bronze Age revolution to document trade exchange or barter transactions of products of surplus metal artifacts of Meluhha metalwork guilds..

35. *Uddhāra (reaffirmation)* Inscription after inscription continues to refer to technical terms of metalwork, furnace/smelter work, mint work. This rebus rendering occurs for over 500 hieroglyphs (called signs) and over 100 hieroglyphs (called pictorial motifs)

36. *Sambhava (possibility)* The Harappa Script Cipher as rebus reading of ancient Prakritam (Meluhha) words points to the possibility that the Vedic Sarasvati River Basin was the epicentre of trade and production activity along the Maritime Tin Route from Hanoi to Haifa which predated the Silk Road by over 2 millennia. This constitutes a hypothesis for further researches.

37. *Pariprasna (question and answer)* A paripras'na is: why would even wild animals be shown in front of feeding troughs, unless both the animal and the trough are hieroglyphs? Why was the water-carrier shown in parenthesis together with star hieroglyphs on a circular Gadd seal?

Seal impression, Ur (Upenn; U.16747); dia. 2.6, ht. 0.9 cm.; Gadd, PBA 18 (1932), pp. 11-12, pl. II, no. 12; Porada 1971: pl.9, fig.5; Parpola, 1994, p. 183; water carrier with a skin (or pot?) hung on each end of the yoke across his shoulders and another one below the crook of his left arm; the vessel on the right end of his yoke is over a receptacle for the water; a star on either side of the head (denoting supernatural?). The whole object is enclosed by 'parenthesis' marks. The parenthesis is perhaps a way of splitting of the ellipse (Hunter, G.R., *JRAS*, 1932, 476). An unmistakable example of an 'hieroglyphic' seal.

38. *Vyākaraṇa (grammar)* Since the writing system is logophonetic and composed of lists of 0 to 5 terms (glosses), there is no need for grammatical expressions in the writing system on Harappa Script Corpora or to explain symbols used on early punch-marked and cast coins.

39. *Vyutkrāntabhidāna (transgression)* The presence of trefoils on the base of a s'ivalinga is a transgression of the *adhyatmika* connotations of the divine iconography of linga as a fiery pillar of light and fire. The base with trefoil may signify tri-*dhAtu* 'three strands' rebus: 'three minerals' which were subjected to smelting operations. The presence of a *mukha* 'human face' or Bhuteswar s'ivalinga atop a smelter is indicative of rebus: *muha* 'quantity produced from a furnace, ingot'

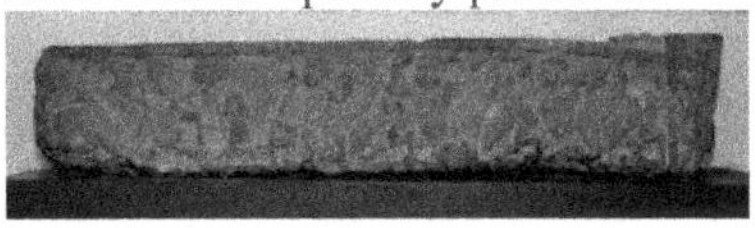

40. *Hetu (purpose)* The *tantra yukti* devices have demonstrated the purpose of the Harappa Script Corpora. They are metalwork catalogues as proclamations to promote trade. Such proclamations also occur on procession tablets or on a monolithic signboard of Dholavira.

Ten hieroglyphs on Dholavira signboard

m0490At m0490B

Mohenjodaro Tablet

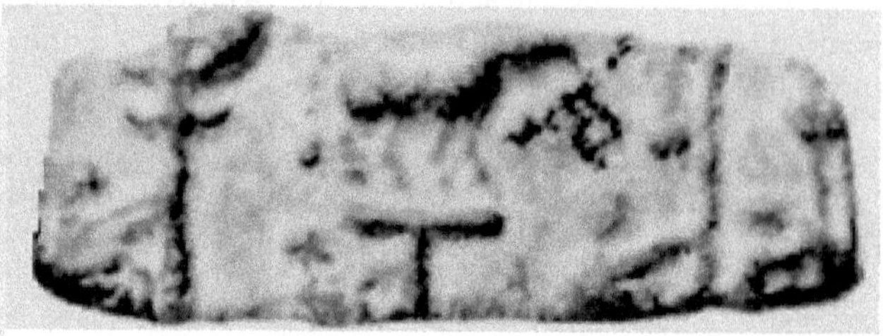

showing Meluhha combined standard. Four standards carried in a procession, comparable to Tablet m0491. m0491 Tablet. Line drawing (right). This tablet showing four hieroglyphs may be called the Meluhha standard. Combined reading for the joined or ligatured glyphs.

Rebus reading of m0490 is: *dhatu kõdā sangaḍa* 'mineral, turner, stone-smithy guild'.

Dawn of the bronze age is best exemplified by this Mohenjo-daro tablet m0491 which shows a procession of four hieroglyphs carried on the shoulders of four persons. The hieroglyphs are: 1. *eraka* 'knave of wheel' rebus: *erako* 'moltencast, copper' *arA* 'spoke' rebus: *Ar̤a* 'brass'.2. *dhat*u, 'scarf' carried on a pole (rebus: *dhatu, '* mineral ore'); 3. A young bull carried on a stand *kõdā* Rebus: turner; 4. Portable standard device (Top part: lathe-gimlet; Bottom part: portable furnace *sãgāḍ* rebus: stone-cutter *sangatarāśū*). *sanghāḍo* (Gujarati) cutting stone, gilding (Gujarati); *sangsāru karaṇu* = to stone (Sindhi) *sanghāḍiyo*, a worker on a lathe (Gujarati) *samgraha, samgaha* 'arranger, manager'.

The procession is a celebration of the graduation of a stone-cutter as a metal-turner in a smithy/forge. A *sangatarāśū* 'stone-cutter' or lapidary of neolithic/chalolithic age had graduated into a metal turner's workshop (*koḍ*), working with metallic minerals (*dhatu*) of the bronze age.

Three professions are described by the three hieroglyphs: scarf, young bull, standard device *dhatu kõdā sãgāḍī* Rebus words denote: ' mineral worker; metals turner-joiner (forge); worker on a lathe' – associates (guild). The guild organization caused by the Bronze Age Revolution, necessitating work-in-process controls in workshops, smithy, forge is exemplified by the rebus reading of *samgraha, samgaha* 'arranger, manager'.

Set theory Venn diagram set-intersection explains Harappa script cipher. Harappa script Corpora are *chitrakāvya sangara*, proclamations of metalwork

Set Theory in Mathematics is used to demonstrate a Venn Diagram intersection for Harappa script cipher as an intersection between a hieroglyph set signifying pictures and a set of Meluhha words signifying metalwork. The intersections subset yields Harappa script Corpora as *catalogus catalogorum* of metalwork. This is demonstrated using examples of processions of hieroglyph-multiplexes on Mohenjo-daro tablets.

Hieroglyphs signifying 'lathe' or 'joined animals --*sãghāṛɔ* (Gujarati) *sãgaḍ* (Marathi) linked together' are signifiers of *sangara* a proclamation by the artisans/traders, *samgraha, samgaha* 'arranger, managers' of Sarasvati-Sindhu civilization through Harappa Script Corpora.

Such *sangara* 'proclamations' are demonstrated using examples from Harappa script Corpora: Procession tablets of Mohenjo-daro

These are proclamations of metalwork competence of Meluhha artisans presented as SETS.

The processions of hieroglyph-multiplexes are announcements of SETS which is a foundational theory of mathematics. What was achieved in mathematics by ancient Bharata was also achieved in the delineation of sets on Harappa script Corpora.

The SETS of Harappa script Corpora relate to ONLY one category: metalwork.

Venn diagram, in mathematics, illustrates the intersection of two sets. Set A is hieroglyphs of Harappa Script Corpora (both 'pictorial motifs' and 'text signs'). Set B is Lexis of *Bharata sprachbund* provided by the *Indian Lexicon.*

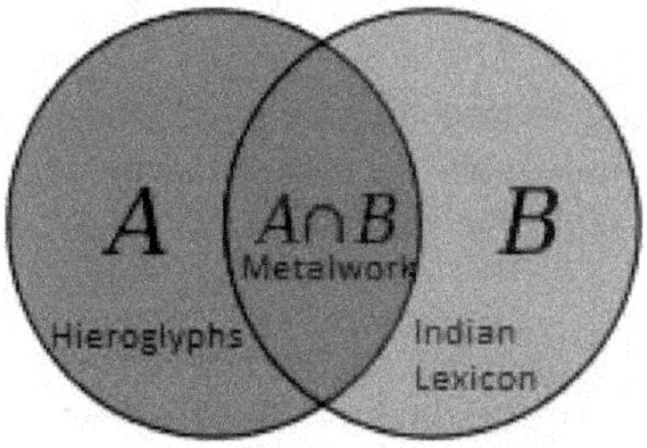

Set A is Harappa Script lexis of hieroglyphs which signify the pictorial motifs and text signs...

Intersection of two sets $A \cap B$ is the metalwork lexis of the Bronze Age which provide matching rebus words which signify metalwork.[2]

Cantor's proof was that there are more real numbers than integers and the 'infinity of infinities' which is explained as 'Cantor's paradise'. Cantor obtained a paradox by asking the question: 'What is the cardinal number of the set of all sets?' This was elaborated further in Russel's paradox by Bertrand Russel which noted: 'the set of all sets that are not members of themselves...leads to a paradox that it must be a member of itself, and not a member of itself.'

This paradox is resolved when a variable of language is used to describe the members of a set. This description is achieved on Harappa script Corpora. Artisans who designed the writing system chose hieroglyphs to signify 'tiger', 'elephant', 'zebu', 'crocodile' etcetera words which constituted a set of animals (both wild and

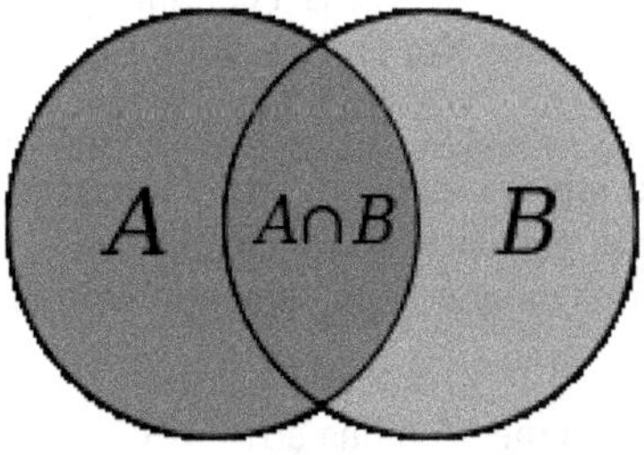

ed). Meluhha had similar sounding words s sounding similar to *kola* 'tiger'; *karabha* lephant', *poLa* 'zebu', *karA* 'crocodile'). These imilar sounding words of Meluhha (Proto-Prakritam) constituted a set: metalwork set during the evolving Bronze Age: *kol* working in iron'; *karba* 'iron'; *poLa* agnetite, ferrite ore'; *khAr* 'blacksmith'.

iagram results in the intersecting set : set of

animal hieroglyphs intersecting (A) with a set of metalwork semantics (B).

This intersection $A \cap B$ creates the Harappa script Corpora.

Databases of Harappa Script[3] inscriptions (which may also be called: *Dharma saṁjñā or Bharatiya hieroglyphs)* narrate the cultural, socio-economic history of a civilization. It is called Harappa Script since the first discovery reported was of an inscription on a seal from Harappa.[4]

First seal with Harappa script discovered in Harappa by Major Clarke before 1872; given to the British Museum (1892-12-10, 1) in 1886 by Alexander Cunningham. The hieroglyphs of the historic Harappa seal signify: arranger, manager, turner with dhow, seafaring vessel for cargo of ingots, implements, metal castings bronze workshop. The number of Harappa script inscriptions total over 7000 (as of 2016). The entire corpora constitute metalwork catalogues. This monograph details data mining method of knowledge discovery to achieve a breakthrough to resolve the 144-year challenge of deciphering the script.

Harappa Script Corpora: background

Seafaring Meluhha merchants used Harappa Writing in trade transactions; artisans created metal artifacts, lapidary artificats of terracotta, ivory for trade. Glosses of the Proto-Indic or Harappa language are used to read rebus the Harappa script inscriptions.

The hieroglyphs of the Harappa script or Harappa Writing include both pictorial motifs and signs and both categories of hieroglyphs are read rebus. As a first step in delineating the Harappa language, an *Indian lexicon5* provides a resource, compiled semantically cluster over 1240 groups of glosses from ancient Bharata languages as a Proto-Indic substrate dictionary.

The evidence is remarkable that many single glyphs or glyptic elements of the Harappa writing can be read rebus using the repertoire of artisans (lapidaries working with precious shell, ivory, stones and terracotta, mine-workers, stone-masons, metal-smiths working with a variety of minerals, furnaces and other tools) who created the inscribed objects and used many of them to authenticate their trade transactions. Many of the inscribed objects are seen to be calling cards of the professional artisans, listing their professional skills and repertoire. Many are veritable mining- and metal-work catalogs.

Continuing legacies of glyptic art noted by Huntington: "There is a continuity of composite creatures demonstrable in Indic culture since Kot Diji ca. 4000 BCE."[6]

The identification of glosses from the present-day languages of India on Sarasvati river basin is justified by the continuation of culture evidenced by many artifacts evidencing civilization continuum from the Vedic Sarasvati River basin, since language and culture are intertwined, resulting in a unique, logo-semantic writing system. .

Harappa writing in Ancient Near East is a tribute to the Meluhha artisans who have established an expansive contact area in Eurasia and left for posterity the bronze-age *harosheth hagoyim*, 'the smithy of nations.'

Concordance lists for epigraphs

Abbreviations and references to heiroglyphs and text transcripts

m-Mohenjodaro

h-Harappa

ABCDE at the end of a reference number indicate side numbers of an inscribed object. Multiple seal impressions on the same object are numbered 1 to 4.

At the end of the reference number:

'a' sealing; 'bangle' inscription on bangle or bangle fragment; other objects: shell, ivory stick, ivory plaque, ivory cube, faience ornament, steatite ornament; 'ct' copper tablet; 'Pict-' Pictorial motifs (0 to 145) described as illustrations of field-symbols in Appendix III of Mahadevan corpus (pp. 793 to 813); 'it' inscribed tablet; 'si' seal impression; 't' tablet.

Illegible inscribed objects are excluded in the following tabulations. Many potsherds Rahmandheri and Nausharo are excluded since the 'signs' are considered to be potters' marks; only those inscriptions which appear to have parallels of field symbols or 'signs' in the corpora are included.

Based on a number of resources and from the collections of inscribed objects held in many museums of the world, such as the Metropolitan Museum of Art, the Harappa Writing Corpora include Sarasvati heiroglyphs, representing many facets of glyptic art of Sarasvati Civilization. The corporas also includes many texts of inscriptions, corresponding to the epigraphs inscribed on objects. The compilation is based mostly on published photographs in archaeological reports right from the days of Alexander Cunningham who discovered a seal at Harappa in 1875, of Langdon at Mohenjodaro (1931) and of Madhu Swarup Vats at Harappa (1940). The corpus includes objects collected in India, Pakistan, other countries and the finds of the excavations at Harappa by Kenoyer and Meadow during the seasons 1994-1995 and 1999-2000.

Framework for decoding epigraphs of Sarasvati Sindhu Civilization

This is also intended to serve as a pictorial and text index to Mahadevan Concordance and to the three volumes published so far of pictorial corpus of Parpola et al.

Many texts are indexed to the text numbers of Mahadevan concordance. The choice of this concordance is based on four factors: (a) the concordance is priced at a reasonable cost; (b) it is a true concordance for every sign of the corpus to facilitate an analysis of the frequency of occurrence of a sign and the context of other sign clusters/ sequences in relation to a sign and for researchers to cross-check on the basic references for the inscribed objects; (c) the exquisite nature of orthography is notable and 'readings' are authentic, even for very difficult to read inscriptions; and (d) signs and variants of signs have been delineated with cross-references to selected text readings.

Mahadevan concordance excludes inscribed objects which do not contain 'texts'; for example, this concordance excludes about 50 seals inscribed with the 'svastikā' pictorial motif and a pectoral which contains the pictorial motif of a one-horned bull with a device in front and an over-flowing pot. Parpola concordance has been used to present such objects which also contain valuable orthographic data which may assist in decoding the inscriptions. Many broken objects are also contained in Parpola concordance which are useful, in many cases, to count the number of objects with specific 'field symbols', a count which also provides some valuable clues to support the decoding of the messages conveyed by the 'field symbols' which dominate the object space.

Cross-references to excavation numbers, publications, photographs and the museum numbers based on which these texts have been compiled are provided in Appendix V: List of Inscribed Objects (pages 818 to 829) in Iravatham Mahadevan, 1977, *The Indus Script: Texts, Concordance and Tables*, Memoirs of the Archaeological Survey of India No. 77, New Delhi, Archaeological Survey of India, Rs. 250. In most cases, these text numbers are matched with the inscribed objects after Asko Parpola concordance [Two volumes: Rs. 21,000: 1. Jagat Pati Joshi and Asko Parpola, eds., 1987, *Corpus of Indus Seals and Inscriptions: 1. Collections in India*, Memoirs of the Archaeological Survey of India No. 86, Helsinki, Suomalainen Tiedeakatemia; 2. Sayid Ghulam Mustafa Shah and Asko Parpola, eds., 1991, *Corpus of Indus Seals and Inscriptions: 2. Collections in Pakistan*, Memoirs of the Department of Archaeology and Museums, Govt. of Pakistan, Vol. 5, Helsinki, Suomalainen Tiedeakatemia]. *Memoir of ASI No. 96 Corpus of Indus Seals and Inscriptions, Vol. II* by Asko Parpola, B.M. Pande and Petterikoskikallio (containing copper tablets) is in press (December 2001).

The debt owed to Iravatham Mahadevan, Asko Parpola, Archaeological Survey of India, Department of Archaeology and Museums, Govt. of Pakistan and Finnish Academy for making this presentation possible is gratefully acknowledged. I am grateful to Iravatham Mahadevan who made available to me his annotated personal copy of a document which helped in collating the texts with the pictures of inscribed objects. [Kimmo Koskenniemi and Asko Parpola, 1980, Cross references to Mahadevan 1977 in: *Documentation and Duplicates of the Texts in the Indus Script, Helsinki*, pp. 26-32].

Four epigraphs from Bhirrana from ASI website http://asi.nic.in and five epigraphs from Bagasra (Gola Dhoro) reported by VH Sonawane in *Puratattva*, Number 41, 2011 have also been included.

Pitfalls of normalising orthography of some glyphs

Parpola (1994) identifies 386 (+12?) signs (or graphemes) and their variant forms. Mahadevan (1977) identifies 419 graphemes; out of these 179 graphemes have variants totalling 641 forms.

Parpola observes: "...the grapheme count might be as low as 350...The total range of signs once present in the Indus script is certain to have been greater than is observable now, for new signs have kept turning up in new inscriptions. The rate of discovery has been fairly low, though, and the new signs have more often been ligatures of two or more signs already known as separate graphemes than entirely new signs." (Parpola, 1994, p. 79)

Many 'signs' are ligatures of two or more 'signs'.

In the process of normalizing the orthography of some glyphs to identify the core 'signs' of the script, some information is lost and at times, the process itself impedes the possibility of decoding the writing system. This can be demonstrated by (1) the 'identification' of a 'squirrel' glyph and (2) the failure to identify 'dotted circle' or 'stars' as glyphs.

It is, therefore, necessary to view the inscribed object as a composite message composed of glyphs: pictorial motifs and signs alike. Many scholars have noted the contacts between the Mesopotamian and Sarasvati Sindhu (Indus) Civilizations, in terms of cultural history, chronology, artefacts (beads, jewellery), pottery and seals found from archaeological sites in the two areas.

An outstanding contribution to the study of the script problem is the publication of the Corpus of Indus Seals and Inscriptions (CISI) Three volumes have been published so far:

> *Corpus of Indus Seals and Inscriptions, 1. Collections in India, Helsinki, 1987 (eds. Jagat Pati Joshi and Asko Parpola)*
>
> *Corpus of Indus Seals and Inscriptions, 2. Collections in Pakistan, Helsinki, 1991 (eds. Sayid Ghulam Mustafa Shah and Asko Parpola)*
>
> *Corpus of Indus Seals and Inscriptions, 3. 1 Supplement to Mohenjo-daro and Harappa, 2010 (eds. Asko Parpola, B.M. Pande and Petteri Koskikallio) in collaboration with Richard H. Meadow and Jonathan Mark Kenoyer. (Annales Academiae Scientiarum Fennicae, B. 239-241.) Helsinki: Suomalainen Tiedeakatemia.*

These volumes in which Asko Parpola is the co-author constitute the photographic corpus. The CISI contains all the seals including those without any inscriptions, for e.g. those with the geometrical motif called the 'svastika'. Parpola's initial corpus (1973) included a total number of 3204 texts. After compiling the pictorial corpus, Parpola notes that there are approximately 3700 legible inscriptions (including 1400 duplicate inscriptions, i.e. with repeated texts). Both the concordances of Parpola and Mahadevan complement each other because of the sort sequence adopted. Parpola's concordance was sorted according to the sign following the indexed sign. Mahadevan's concordance was sorted according to the sign preceding the indexed sign. The latter sort ordering helps in delineating signs which occur in final position. With the publication of CISI Vol. 3, Part 1, the total number of inscriptions from Mohenjo-daro totals 2134 and from Harappa totals 2589; thus, these two sites alone accounting for 4,723 bring the overall total number of inscriptions to over 6,000 from all sites (even after excluding comparable inscriptions on 'Persian Gulf type' circular seals from the total count).

Compendia of the efforts made since the discovery by Gen. Alexander Cunningham, in 1875, of the first known Indus seal (British Museum 1892-12-10, 1), to decipher the script appear in the references cited in the Bibliography.

Harappa Script is a corpus of symbols constituting a logo-phonetic writing system which was used in Harappa (also known as Sarasvati-Sindhu) Civilization, during the Bronze Age from ca. 3300 BCE [7] to 600 BCE[8] in the doab of Vedic Rivers Sarasvati and Sindhu (also called Meluhha in ancient cuneiform texts), in the Persian Gulf (also called Magan and Dilmun in ancient cuneiform texts) and also in contact areas of Mesopotamia (Ancient Near East) and Dong Son Bronze Culture areas of the Ancient Far East (L'Extrême-Orient pace George Coedes[9])

Meluhha-Magan-Dilmun=Mesopotamia[10]

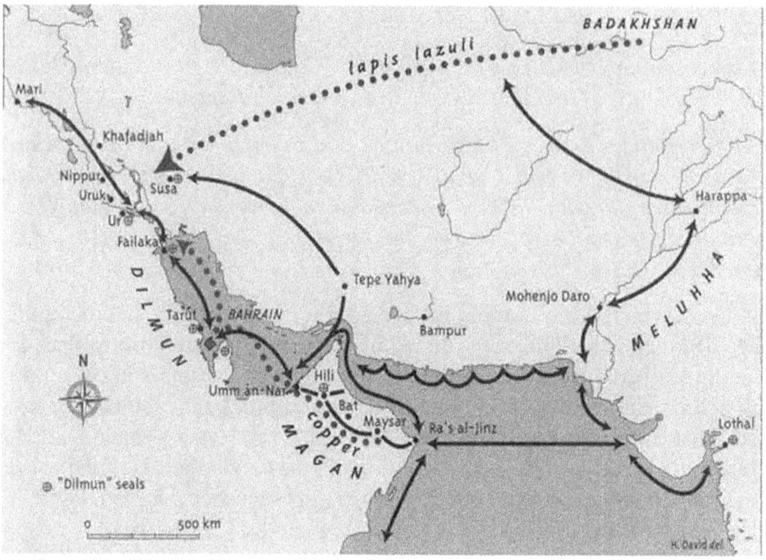

Gregory Possehl has provided a bibliography of attempts at decipherment of Harappa Script.[11]

Harappa Script inscriptions are very short. The average number of 'text signs' is 5 with or without pictorial motifs or field symbols on seals and tablets. The short texts and the 400+ symbols on 'sign list' are pointers to the logo-phonetic nature of the Script. These 'signs' are NOT pictograms but logograms because they represent words in Harappa language. Unfortunately, many attempts at decipherment were premised on a conjecture of alphabetical or syllabic nature of the Script and searching for 'names or titles or sentences composed of morphemes and grammatical units such as prepositions' on the assumption that the seals and tablets should have recorded names or titles or even poems of prayer. Such assumptions ignored the essentially pictorial nature of the Script composed of hieroglyphs both as 'text signs' and as 'pictorial motifś and pictorial narratives such as a tiger looking back and a person sitting on a tree branch. An approach framed on the hypothesis that Harappa Script was necessitated for trade transactions to cope with the Bronze Age Revolution, provides a framework for the use of rebus method evidenced on Egyptian hieroglyphs which are rebus renderings of consonants in words (See

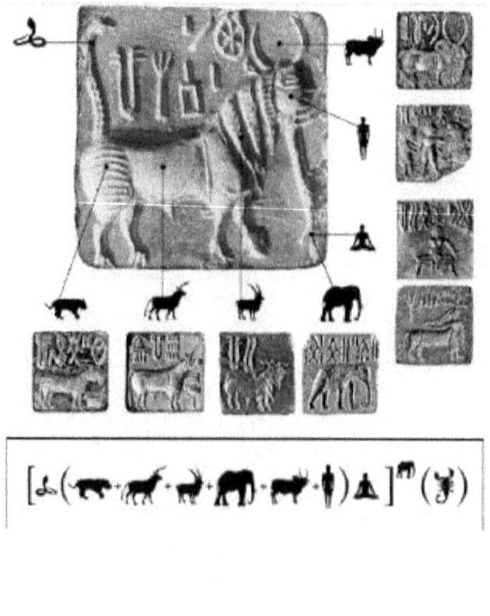

discussions on rebus readings of hieroglyphs which are complete messages on Narmer palette and on Ivory tags with one to four hieroglyphs, from U-J of Abydos tomb dated to ca. 32nd cent. BCE). Thus, it will be a futile and speculative exercise to look for long texts in Harappa Script which has achieved comprehensive messaging to render utterances in Harappa language, using rebus principle to compose hypertexts in Meluhha cipher (pairs of homonymous words, one set signifying logograms and another set ssignifying similar sounding metalwork catalogue items).

Received wisdom about Aryan Invasion as a 'linguisticdoctrine'[12] is also a principal reason for the polemics of dubious decipherment claims. It is heartening no note that many linguists now recognize the nature of the Bharata sprachbund. A language X is also proposed to explain the nature of lexical, semantic structures with common features noticed in many ancient Bharata languages explained by sustained sustained cultural contacts among the people of Bhāratam. While attempts are ongoing to unravel the true import of the metaphors in Chandas of Vedic texts, laudable efforts of many scholars have resulted in the compilation of Harappa Script Corpora..

Since Harappa Script is NOT syllabic, long texts of inscriptions are NOT necessary for decipherment. Now that over 7000 inscriptions are available, there is enough evidence to unravel the cipher of Harappa Script. Recognizing the metalwork catalogues of Harappa Script Corpora, the contributions of *Bhāratam Janam* to the Bronze Age Revolution and as intermeḍiaries along the Maritime Tin Route which preceded the Silk Road by 2 millennia, can be re-evaluated and the Bronze Age interaction maps can be re-drawn.

It is a leap of faith to rush to judgement that Harappa Script is NOT based on language because the length of inscriptions is very short (composed of upto 5 symbols). It has been demonstrated from the evolution of Egyptian hieroglyphs from ca. 32nd cent. BCE that short texts as inscriptions are read rebus. If each symbol or hieroglyph is logo-phonetic, words and combinations of words are identifiable on hypertexts created by Harappa Script. See Annex G.

As Bhartṛhari (c. 5th century) notes, in *Vākyapadīya* ("[treatise] on words and sentences"). Act of speech is made of three stages which can be completed with just one or upto 5 symbol hypertexts as demonstrated by over 7000 inscriptions of Harappa Script Corpora: Conceptualization by the speaker (*Paśyantī* "idea");Performance of speaking (*Madhyamā* "meḍium"); Comprehension by the interpreter (Vaikhārī "complete utterance"). These principles of language govern the identification of hieroglyphs as hypertexts, word expressions of Meluhha (Harappa language) read rebus – comprehended by the interpreters of Harappa Script inscriptions.

Decipherment of Harappa Script results in knowledge discovery of the contributions made by artisans of ancient India with metallurgical advances, during the Bronze Age Revolution.

Data mining is defined as 'the process of collecting, searching through, and analyzing a large amount of data in a database, as to discover patterns or relationships'[13].

Such patterns or relationships or knowledge discovery from data mining are in two groups of databases, orthographic and lexical: Harappa Script inscriptions with photographic corpora resources; and 2. *Indian Lexicon*[14] of over 25 ancient languages of Bharata *sprachbund* organized in over 8000 semantic data base clusters.

Based on a number of resources and from the collections of inscribed objects held in many museums of the world, such as the Metropolitan Museum of Art, the Harappa Script Corpora include hieroglyphs, representing many facets of glyptic art of Harappa Civilization. The corpora also include many texts of inscriptions, corresponding to the epigraphs inscribed on objects themselves. The compilation is based mostly on published photographs in archaeological reports right from the days of Alexander Cunningham who discovered a seal at Harappa in 1875, of Langdon at Mohenjodaro (1931) and of Madhu Swarup Vats at Harappa (1940). The corpus includes objects collected in India, Pakistan, other and the finds of the excavations at Harappa by Kenoyer and Meadow during the seasons 1994-1995 and 1999-2000.

Methodology for knowledge discovery through data mining

The resources provided by Harappa Script Corpora of over 7000 inscriptions are clustered together using the following contexts for a reconstruction of proto-history reporting on the cultural markers (such as invention of a writing system, organization of guilds as corporate forms) of the civilization – in response to the Bronze Age Revolution: a stunning evidence for the use of Harappa Script to describe metalwork cargo comes from hieroglyphs of ox-hide ingots shown as cargo on a boat on a Mohenjo-daro seal. The following are data mining clusters discovered:

1. space or locus of script discoveries;
2. artisans as functionaries in guilds;
3. orthographic devices of 'hieroglyph' modifiers;
4. action narratives signified pictorially;
5. significance of scores of duplicates of inscriptions;
6. significance of combining body parts in pictorials;
7. impact of Bronze Age revolution on emergence of specialist professionals;
8. clusters of animals as cultural activity signifiers;
9. archaeometallurgical advances signified in hypertexts;
10. Semantics of over 400 hypertext 'signs'.

These clusters of data archives from the Corpora are presented in the following Annexes:

Annex A Harappa Script inscriptions found in temple area of Mohenjo-daro (and Harappa?)

Annex B *Dharma saṁjñā* Corporate badges of Harappa Script Corpora, ceramic (stoneware) bangles, seals, fillets

Annex C Form and function of inscribed tablets, miniature tablets

Annex D Ligatures to *ayo, aya* 'fish' rebus: *aya* 'iron' *ayas* 'metal', *meḍ* 'body' rebus: *meḍ* 'iron' semantic modifiers as hypertexts and Harappa Script inscriptions on 240 copper tablets

Annex E Clustering 'temple' hieroglyph, pictorial narratives of kneeling adorant, together with markhor and offering on a stool

Annex F Multiple tablets with same inscription in Harappa signify work-in-process in circular platforms

Annex G *kulā* 'hood of snake' as tail and Harappa Script hypertext

Annex H Black ant hieroglyph and *cīmara kāra* 'coppersmith'

Annex I Hieroglyphs of animal clusters. Mohenjo-daro m0304 (Reconstructed) Seal. A person is shown seated in 'penance' may signify *Triśiras*, son of *Tvaṣṭā*, कुबेर

Annex J Crocodile, scorpion, disheveled hair in Harappa Script hieroglyphs signify work in *bica* 'haematite stone ore'

Annex K Structure, form, function and significance of *caṣālḥ* चषालः on Yūpa in a *yajna* and carburization

Annex L List of Harappa Script 'text signs'[15]

Rebus method to signify phonetic sounds of words, a logo-phonetic writing system

The writing system seems to use the rebus principle to phonetize its hieroglyphs. Such a rebus principle is seen in ca. 3100 BCE Egyptian hieroglyphs of Narmer and Abydos tomb.[16] At Tomb UJ at Abydos in Upper Egypt (dated to ca. 3250 BCE), Dreyer found place names written in Egyptian hieroglyphs (up to four in number) recognizable as hieroglyphs which persisted and were employed during later periods and which are written and read phonetically.[17] The rebus principle may explain the pictorial motifs of some cylinders of Ancient Near East of ca. 3100 BCE.

Ivory tags from tomb UJ at Abydos

Hieroglyphs: N'r M'r (N'r 'cuttle fish' M'r 'awl') rebus: Narmer (king's name of 33rd cent. BCE in Egypt).

"Linguistic terminology makes it psosible to identify the various units of language that helped to transform communication in early Egypt from merely pictorial expression to speech writing, which is important in identifying the nature of early graphic material:

"1) Logograms: symbols representing specific words

"2) Phonograms: symbols representing specific sounds

"3) Determinatives: symbols used for classifying words

"Moreover, writing on the tags shows that the Egyptian writing system had adopted the rebus principle, which broadened the meaning of symbols to include their homophones—words with the same sound but different definitions..." (Elise V. Macarthur,2010)[18]

It is remarkable that the writing systems of Egyptian hieroglyphs, cuneiform texts on cylinder seals with pictorial motifs which include Harappa Script hieroglyphs were invented ca. 3000 BCE almost simultaneously with the invention of Harappa Script ca. 3300 BCE.

Ox-hide ingots shown as cargo on a boat on a Mohenjo-daro seal

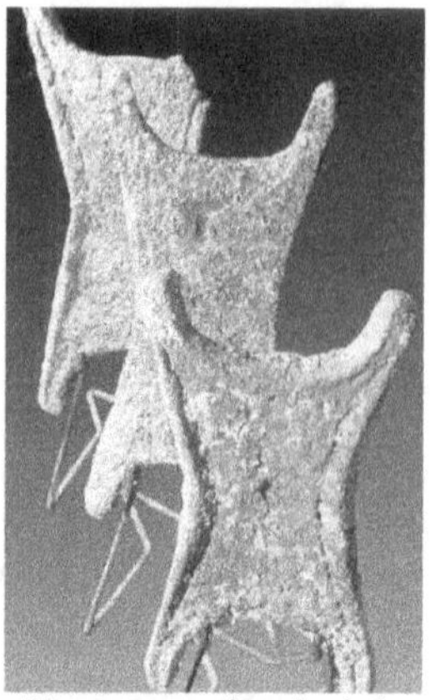

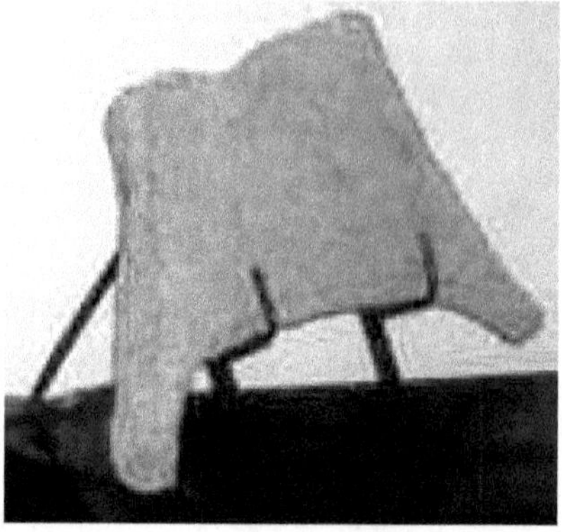

Copper ingotsTin ingot19

While 354 oxhide ingots discovered in a shipwreck in Uluburn were copper ingots, it should be noted that oxhide shaped tin ingots were also discovered

The ox-hide shape of the copper and tin ingots is the key to Harappa script decipherment because such ox-hide shaped symbols have been shown on a Mohenjo-daro tablet in the context of a cargo on a seafaring boat.

What was the cargo carried on the boat from Mohenjo-daro? I suggest that the cargo signified by two oxhide ingots on the boat was Meluhha metalwork. The shape of the pair of ingots on the boat (shown on the tablet) is comparable to following figures: 1.

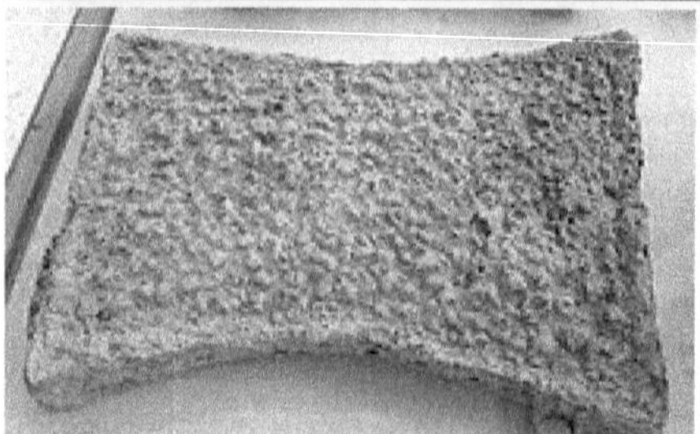

the ingot on which stands the horned, helmeted Ingot-god (Enkomi) holding a spear and a shield; 2. Copper ingot from Zakros, Crete, displayed at the Heraklion Archaeological Museum But the script used on the Mohenjo-daro tablet is NOT Cypro-Minoan or Cretan or Minoan but Meluhha: While the Uluburn shipwreck is dated to 14th cent. BCE, the Mohenjo-daro tablet is from the Mature Harappa period of ca. 2500 BCE. It is a surprising fact indeed that oxhide ingots are signified as cargo on a boat depicted on a Mohenjo-daro tablet.

m1429 Prism tablet with Indus inscriptions on 3 sides. Fired clay L.4.6 cm W. 1.2 cm Mohenjo-daro,MD 602, Harappa,ca 2600 -1900 B.C E Islamabad Museum, Islamabad NMP 1384, Pakistan.

Decipherment of hieroglyphs of Harappa Script on Mohenjo-daro tablet m1429 as metalwork cargo, shipment

bagalo = an Arabian merchant vessel (Gujarati) *bagala* = an Arab boat of a particular description (Ka.); *bagalā* (M.); *bagarige, bagarage* = a kind of vessel (Kannada) Rebus: *bangala* = *kumpaṭi* = *angāra śakaṭī* = a chafing dish a portable stove a goldsmith's portable furnace (Telugu) cf. *bangaru bangaramu* = gold (Telugu) *karaṇḍa* 'duck' (Sanskrit) *karaṛa* 'a very large aquatic bird' (Sindhi)

Rebus: करडा [*karaḍā]* Hard from alloy--iron, silver &c. (Marathi) NOTE: A hieroglyph to signify *bagalo* 'shipping vessel' is *bagala* 'Pleiades'. Such a hieroglyph showing 6 or 7 women as Pleiades is signified on three inscriptions of Harappa Script Corpora.

A pair of palm trees flanking a pair of oxhide ingots. Hieroglyph: **tāḍa3* ' fan -- palm ', *tāḍī* -- 2 f. in *tāḍī* -- *puṭa* -- ' palm -- leaf ' Kād., *tāla* -- 2 m. ' *Borassus flabelliformis* ' Mn., *tālī* -, °*lakī* -- f. ' palm -- wine ' W. [Cf. hintāla-]Pa. *tāla* -- m. ' fan -- palm ', Pk. *tāḍa* -- , *tāla* -- , *tala* -- m., *tāḍī* -- , *tālī* -- f., K. *tāl* m., P. *tāṛ* m., N. *tār* (*tāṛ* ← H.), A. *tāl*, B. *tāṛ*, Or. *tāṛa*, *tāri*, *tāḷa*, Bi. *tār*, *tāṛ*, OAw. *tāra*, H. G. *tāṛ* m., M. *tāḍ* m., Si. *tala.* -- Gy. gr. *taró* m., *tarí* f. ' rum ', rum. *tari* ' brandy ', pal. *tar* ' date -- spirit '; S. *tāṛī* f. ' juice of the palmyra '; P. *tāṛī* ' the fermented juice '; N. *tāṛī* ' id., yeast ' (← H.); A. *tāri* ' the fermented juice ', B. Or. *tāṛi*, Bi. *tārī*, *tāṛī*, Bhoj. *tāṛī*; H. *taṛi* f. ' the juice, the fermented juice '; G. *tāṛī* f. ' the juice ', M. *tāḍī* f. <-> X hintāla -- q.v. tālavr̥nta -- ; *madatāḍikā -- .Addenda: *tāḍa* -- **3:** S.kcch. *tāṛ* m. ' palm tree '.(CDIAL 5750) Ta. *kara tāḷam* palmyra palm.

Ka. *kara-tāḷa* fan-palm, *Corypha umbraculifera* Lin.

Tu. *karatāḷa* cadjan. Te. (B.) *kara-tāḷamu* the small-leaved palm tree.(DEDR 1270) Ka. *tāṟ* palmyra or toddy palm, *Borassus flabelliformis. Tu. tāri, tāḷi id. Te. tāḍu,* (inscr., Inscr.2) of or belonging to the palmyra tree; *tāṭi ceṭṭu* palmyra tree; *tāṭ-āku* palmleaf. Kol. (Kin.) *tāṭi māk* palmyra tree. Nk. *tāṛ* māk/śeṭṭ toddy palm. *Nk. (Ch.) tāṛ id. Pa. tāṛ id. Ga. (S.3) tāṭi* palmyra palm. *Go. (G. Ma. Ko.) tāṛ, (S.) tāṛi, (A.) tāḍi* toddy palm; (SR.) *tādī kal* palm liquor (Voc.1709). Konḍa *ṭāṛ maran, ṭāṭi maran* palmyra tree. Pe. *tāṛ mar* toddy palm. *Kuwi (Su.) tāṭi mārnu, (S.) tāti id. Kur. tāṛ* palm tree. Malt. *tálmi Borassus flabelliformis. /* Cf. Skt. tāla-, Pkt. tāḍa-, tāla-; Turner, CDIAL, no. 5750 (some of the Dr. items may be < IA)(DEDR 3180) tāl 2 ताल् m. the palmyra tree or fan palm, *Borassus flabelliformis*. (Kashmiri). Hieroglyph: ढाळा (p. 204) *ḍhāḷā* m A small leafy branch, sprig. 2 A plant of gram, sometimes of वाटाणा, or of लांक. ढाळी (p. 204) *ḍhāḷī* f A branch or bough. தளம்³ *taḷam, n.* < *dala.* 1. Leaf; இலை. (சூடா.) 2. Petal; பூவிதழ். (சூடா.) Rebus: *ḍhālako* = a large metal ingot (Gujarati) ढाळ (p. 204) Cast, mould, form (as of metal vessels, trinkets &c.)

ढाल (p. 204) *ḍhāla* f (S through H) A shield. ढालपट्टा (p. 204) *ḍhālapaṭṭā* m (Shield and sword.) A soldier's accoutrements comprehensively. ढाल्या (*p. 204*) *ḍhālyā* a ढाल Armed with a Shield. *ḍhāla* n. ' shield ' lex. 2. *ḍhāllā -- 1. Tir. (Leech) "*dàl*" ' shield ', Bshk. *ḍāl*, Ku. *ḍhāl*, gng. *ḍhāw*, N. A. B. *ḍhāl*, Or. *ḍhāḷa*, Mth. H. *ḍhāl* m.2. Sh. *ḍal* (pl. °*lẹ*) f., K. *ḍāl* f., S. *ḍhāla*, L. *ḍhāl* (pl. °*lā̃*) f., P. *ḍhāl* f., G. M. *ḍhāl* f.Addenda: *ḍhāla --* . 2. **ḍhāllā --* : WPah.kṭg. (kc.) *ḍhā`l* f. (obl. -- *a*) ' shield ' (a word used in salutation), J. *ḍhāl* f CDIAL 5583) தளவாய் *taḷa-vāy*, n. prob. தளம்³ + வாய். *[T. daḷavāyi, K. dalavāy.]* Military commander, minister of war; படைத்தலைவன். ஒன்னலரைவென்று வருகின்ற தளவாய் (திருவேங். சத. 89).Rebus: *ḍhālako* = a large metal ingot (G.) *ḍhālakī* = a metal heated and poured into a mould; a solid piece of metal; an ingot (Gujarati) ढाळ (p. 204) Cast, mould, form (as of metal vessels, trinkets &c.)

करण्ड m. a sort of duck L. కారండవము (p. 274) [*kāraṇḍavamu*] *kāraṇḍavamu.* [Skt.] n. A sort of duck. (Telugu) *karaṭa*1 m. ' crow ' BhP., °aka -- m. lex. [Cf. *karaṭu --* , *karkaṭu* -- m. ' Numidian crane ', *karēṭu --* , °*ēṭavya --* , °*ēḍuka* -- m. lex., *karaṇḍa*2 -- m. ' duck ' lex: see kāraṇḍava --]Pk. *karaḍa* -- m. ' crow ', °*ḍā* -- f. ' a partic. kind of bird '; S. *karaṛa -- ḍhī̃gu* m. ' a very large aquatic bird '; L. *karṛā* m., °ṛī f. ' the common teal'(CDIAL 2787) Rebus: *karaḍā* 'hard alloy'

tamar 'palm' (Hebrew) Rebus: *tam(b)ra* 'copper' (Santali) *dula* 'pair'
Rebus: dul 'metal casting' (Santali)

kāru a wild crocodile or alligator (Telugu) *ghariyal* id. (Hindi) கராம் *karām*, n. prob. *grāha.* 1. A species of alligator; முதலைவகை. முதலையு மிடங்கருங் கராமும் (குறிஞ்சிப். 257). 2. Male alligator; ஆண் முதலை. (திவா.) కారుమొసలి a wild crocodile or alligator. (Telugu) Rebus: *kāru* 'artisan' (Marathi) *kāruvu* 'artisan' (Telugu) *khār* 'blacksmith' (Kashmiri)
Hieroglyph fish = *aya* (Gujarati); crocodile = *kāru* (Telugu)
Rebus: *ayakāra* 'ironsmith' (Pali)

khār 1 खार् । लोहकारः m. (sg. abl. khāra 1 खार; the pl. dat. of this word is *khāran* 1 खारन्, which is to be distinguished from *khāran* 2, q.v., s.v.), a blacksmith, an iron worker (cf. *bandūka-khār*, p. 111b, l. 46; K.Pr. 46; H. xi, 17); a farrier (a smith who shoes horses).

अयोगू: A blacksmith; Vāj.3.5. अयस् a. [इ-गतौ-असुन्] Going, moving; nimble. n. (-यः) 1 Iron
(एति चलति अयस्कान्तसंनिकर्षं इति तथात्वम्; नायसोल्लिख्यते रत्नम् Śukra4.169. अभितप्तम योऽपि मार्दवं भजते कैव कथा शरीरिषु R.8.43. -2 Steel. -3 Gold. -4 A metal in general. *ayaskāṇḍa* 1 an iron-arrow. -2 excellent iron. -3 a large quantity of iron. Pāṇ. gaṇ. viii.3.48 cf. Lat. *aes* , *aer-is* for *as-is* ; *Goth. ais , Thema aisa; Old Germ. eir , iron ;Goth. eisarn* ; Mod. Germ. *Eisen.*

;Text 3246 on the third side of the prism tablet.

Forge: stone, minerals, gemstones

khaḍā 'circumscribe' (M.); Rebs: *khaḍā* 'nodule (ore), stone' (M.) *kolom* 'cob'; *kolmo* 'seedling, rice (paddy) plant' (Munda.) *kolma hoṛo* = a variety of the paddy plant (Desi)(Santali.) *kolmo* 'rice plant' (Mu.) Rebus: *kolimi* 'furnace,smithy' (Telugu) Thus, the ligatured glyph reads: *khaḍā* 'stone-ore nodule' *kolimi* 'furnace,smithy'. Alternatives: 1. *koṛuŋ* young shoot (Pa.) (DEDR 2149) Rebus: *kol* 'metal, iron, working in iron, blacksmith' (Tamil) *kollan* blacksmith, artificer (Malayalam) *kolhali* to forge (DEDR 2133).2. *kaṇḍe* A head or ear of millet or maize (Telugu) Rebus: *kāṇḍa* 'stone (ore)(Gadba)' *Ga. (Oll.) kanḍ, (S.) kanḍu (pl. kanḍkil)* stone (DEDR 1298).

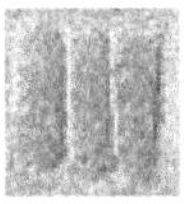

kolom 'three' Rebus: *kolimi* 'furnace, smithy'. Thus, the pair of glyphs may denote lapidary work – working with stone, mineral, gemstones and smithy.

a*yo, aya* 'fish' rebus: *aya* 'iron' *ayas* 'metal' *khambhaṛā* 'fish fin' rebus: *kammaṭa* 'mint, coiner, coinage'.

kanka, karṇaka 'rim of jar' Rebus: *karṇaka* 'account scribe'. *kārṇī* m. 'super cargo of a ship '(Marathi)

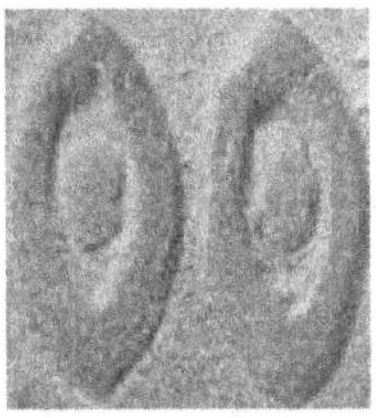

Cast alloy ingots

A pair of ingots with notches in-fixed as ligatures.

ḍhālako 'large ingot'. खोट [*khōṭa*] 'ingot, wedge'; A mass of metal (unwrought or of old metal melted down)(Marathi) *khoṭ* f 'alloy (Lahnda) Thus the pair of ligatured oval glyphs read: *khoṭ ḍhālako* 'alloy ingots PLUS *dula* 'pair' Rebus: *dul* 'cast metal'. PLUS खाडा [*kāṇḍā*] 'A jag, notch, or indentation (as upon the edge of a tool or weapon)' Rebus: *kāṇḍa* 'implements (Santali). Thus, the hypertext signifies cast alloy ingots and implements.

kanka, karṇaka 'rim of jar' Rebus: *karṇaka* 'account scribe'. *kārṇī* m. 'super cargo of a ship '(Marathi)

कर्णक *kárṇaka, kannā* 'legs spread', rebus: *karaṇī* 'scribe', *kañi-āra* 'helmsman'.

Dholavira advertisement-board using many hieroglyphs signified on metal tool inscriptions

Deciphered advertisement-board of Dholavira which proclaims a variety of metallurgical services

Each sign made up of mineral gypsum pieces, is about 37 cm (15 in) high. The board on which hieroglyphs were inscribed was about 3 m (9.8 ft) long. Mounted on a Northern gateway, the message board should have been visible to mariners on seafaring vessels navigating from across the Persian Gulf to the West and the Indian Ocean to the South.

Metalwork repertoire of seafaring merchantsand artisans of Kotda (Dholavira]

Segment 1: Working in ore, copper, brass metal castings, lathe (work) *eraka* 'knave of wheel' Rebus: *eraka* 'copper' (Kannada) *eraka* 'molten cast (metal)(Tulu) *arā* 'spoke' rebus: *Ara* 'brass *dula* 'two' rebus: *dul* 'metal casting' *ḍato* 'claws or pincers of crab' (Santali) rebus: *dhatu* 'ore' (Santali) *kAru* 'pincers' rebus: *kAru* 'artisan'

Segment 2: Bronze, native metal tools, pots and pans, metalware, engraving (molten cast copper) *eraka* 'knave of wheel' Rebus: *eraka* 'copper' (Kannada) *eraka* 'molten cast (metal)(Tulu) *arā* 'spoke' rebus: *Ara* 'brass *koṇḍa* bend (Ko.); *kanac* 'corner' rebus: *kancu* 'bronze' Tu. *kōḍi* corner; *kōṇṭu* angle, corner, crook. Nk. *kōnṭa* corner (DEDR 2054b) G. *khũṭrī* f. 'angle' Rebus: *kõdā* 'to turn in a lathe'(B.) कोंद kōnda 'engraver, lapidary setting or infixing gemś (Marathi) *aḍaren, ḍaren* lid, cover (Santali) Rebus: *aduru* 'native metal' (Ka.) *aduru = gan.iyinda tegadu karagade iruva aduru* = ore taken from the mine and not subjected to melting in a furnace (Kannada).[20] खांडा [*khāṇḍā*] m A jag, notch, or indentation (as upon the edge of a tool or weapon). (Marathi) Rebus: *khāṇḍā* 'tools, pots and pans, metal-ware'.

Segment 3: Coppersmith, brass mint, smelter, furnace, workshop (molten cast copper)[21] eraka 'knave of wheel' Rebus: *eraka* 'copper' (Kannada) *eraka* 'molten cast (metal)(Tulu) *arā* 'spoke' rebus; *Ara* 'brass; khuṇṭa 'peg'; *khũṭi* = pin (M.) rebus: *kuṭi*= furnace (Santali) *kūṭa* 'workshop' *kuṇḍamu* 'a pit for receiving and preserving consecrated fire' *loa* 'fig leaf; Rebus: *loh* '(copper) metal' PLUS *karNa* 'ear' rebus: *karṇī* 'supercargo' *kAru* 'artisan'.

Terms borrowed from an otherwise unknown language include those relating to cereal-growing and bread-making (bread, ploughshare, seed, sheaf, yeast), water-works (canal, well), architecture (brick, house, pillar, wooden peg), tools or weapons (axe, club), textiles and garments (cloak, cloth, coarse garment, hem, needle) and plants (hemp, cannabis, mustard, Soma plant).[22] Lubotsky pointed out that the phonological and morphological similarity of 55 loanwords in Proto-Indo-Iranian and in Sanskrit indicates that a substratum of Indo-Iranian and a substratum of Indo-Aryan represent the same language, or perhaps two dialects of the same language. He concludes that the language of the original population of the towns of Central Asia, where Indo-Iranians must have arrived in the second millennium BCE, and the language spoken in Punjab (see Harappa below) were intimately related.[23] However an alternative interpretation is that 55 loanwords entered common Proto-Indo-Iranian during its development in the Sintashta culture in distant contact with the Bactria–Margiana Archaeological Complex, and then many more words with the same origin enriched Old Indic as it developed among pastoralists who integrated with and perhaps ruled over the declining BMAC.[24]

Orthography of Harappa Script

Long distance trade by seafaring merchants and caravans of the Bronze Age is the principal reason for the invention of Harappa Script as a logo-phonetic writing system.

The entire Script Corpora are metalwork catalogues to document such trade, create data archive records of technical details of work-in-process transactions and metalwork cargo/shipments produced during the Bronze Age Revolution.

A unique characteristic of Harappa Script is the presentation of narratives in pictorial motifs which are very specific and unambiguous. Such pictorials are clearly intended to convey cultural expressions of ideas (in thought as in the case of Chinese hieroglyphs) or *lingua franca* (spoken words/morphemes/sememes used to signify the pictorials as in the case of Egyptian hieroglyphs evidenced in N'r M'r palette and ivory tags ofTomb UJ at Abydos).

An insightful observation was recorded by CL Fabri[25] in 1935 following data mining clusters provided by Theobald[26] to compare Harappa Script pictorials with 'devices or symbols' on punch-marked coins from ca. 6th cent. BCE. Thes observations provide a framework to advance efforts to decipher the script.

'Symbols' of punch-marked coins are a Harappa Script tradition of hieroglyphs.[27]

Tree shown on a tablet from Harappa. *kuṭi* 'tree' *rebus: kuṭhi* 'smelter'.

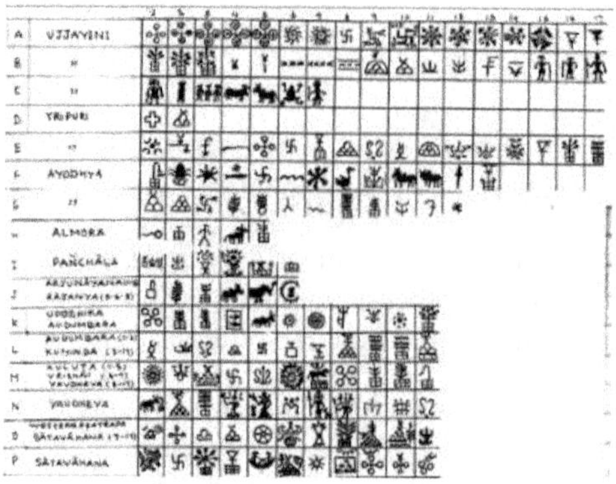

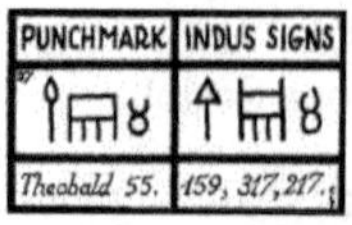

The three 'hieroglyphs' sequence on punch-marks –a tradition of continuum from Harappa Script are deciphered from r. to l.: *meḍhā* m. 'curl, snarl, twist or tangle in cord or thread' Rebus: *mẽṛhẽt, meḍ* 'iron' (Santali.Mu.Ho.) *ranku* 'antelope' rebus: *ranku* 'tin' *kāṇḍa, kā̃ṛ* stalk, arrow' Rebus: *khāṇḍa, '*implements'

Punch-marked coin symbols (hieroglyphs in Harappa Script tradition).[28]

M428 Mohenjo-daro seal. Sun's rays

c. 5th-4th century BCEWeight: 3.08 gm., Dim: 26 x 24 mm. Five punches: sun, 6-arm, and three others, plus banker's marks / Banker's marks. Ref: GH 36.

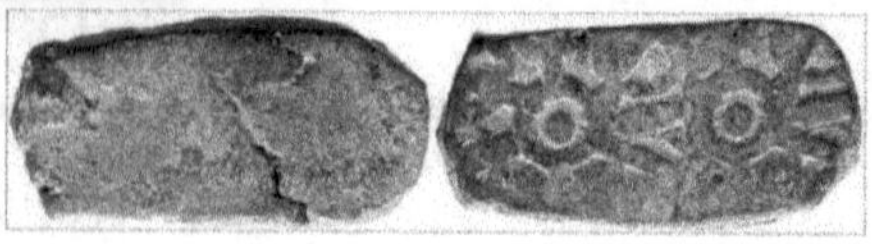

Bent-bar punch-marked coin. Sun's rays, star, stalk, doted circle.

Seal from Rahman Dheri with the motif of 'rays around concentric circles'.[29]

'Sun' in 'four quadrants', painted on faiz Mohammad style grey ware from Mehrgarh, period VI (c. 3000-2900 BCE), Kacchi plain, Pakistan.[30] *arka* 'sun' rebus: *arka, eraka* 'gold, copper, molten cast'

The entire Harappa Script Corpora consist of hieroglyph multiplexes -- using hieroglyphs as components -- and hence, the comparison with hypertexts[31] should cover both 'text signs' and 'pictorial motifs or field symbols' of Harappa Script inscriptions. Punch-marked coin 'symbols' were signified in hundreds of mints which extended from Takshasila to Purola to Eran to Karur to Anuradhapura and constitute a continuum of the Harappa Script tradition of signifying cultural markers or indicators as hieroglyphs. The closest parallel to this method is provided by N'r M'r palette of Egyptian hieroglyphs.

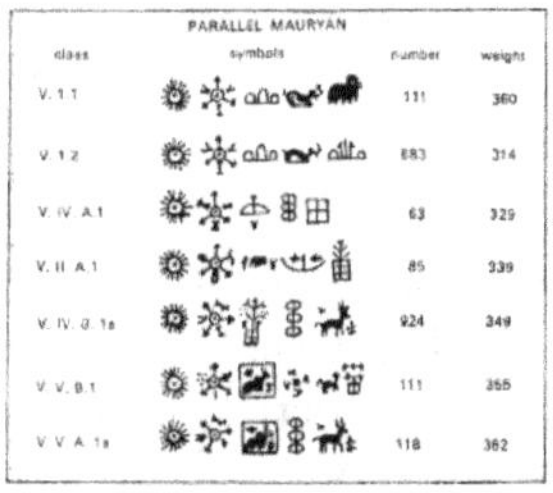

PARALLEL MAURYAN

class	symbols	number	weight
V.1.1		111	360
V.1.2		883	314
V.IV.A.1		63	329
V.II.A.1		85	339
V.IV.Ø.1a		924	349
V.V.B.1		111	355
V.V.A.1a		118	362

Failaka, Persian Gulf; no. 174 impression; two bull heads emanating from a chequered square [see m0296 seal, a Harappa Script motif of heads of two one-horned bulls emanating from a brazier]; two persons drinking; altar and sun; bull in the lower register. *kuṭi* 'drink' *rebus: kuṭhi* 'smelter' *kāṇḍa* 'water' rebus: *kaṇḍa* 'implements.'

khāṇḍa 'divisions'; rebus: *kaṇḍa* 'implements' dula 'pair' rebus: dul 'metal casting' *dhangar* 'bull' Rebus: *ḍangar* 'blacksmith' (Hindi) *dhangar*, *ṭhākur* 'blacksmith' (Maithili)(CDIAL 5488). Thus,metal casting blacksmith, implements *arka* 'sun' rebus: *arka, eraka* 'gold, copper, molten cast' Bun ingot: **mũh**, muhã 'ingot' or muhã 'quantity of metal produced at one time in a native smelting furnace.' The form of iron ingots is attested in Santali *expressions:* ***mũhã mẽṛhẽt*** = iron smelted by the Kolhes and formeḍ into an equilateral lump a little pointed at each of four ends; *kolhe tehen mẽṛhẽt ko mũhã akata* = the Kolhes have to-day produced pig iron (Santali) Dotted cicle as eye: *dhAu* 'strand' rebus: *dhAtu* 'mineral'. Thus, the inscription on the Failaka seal signifies blacksmith's metalwork repertoire.

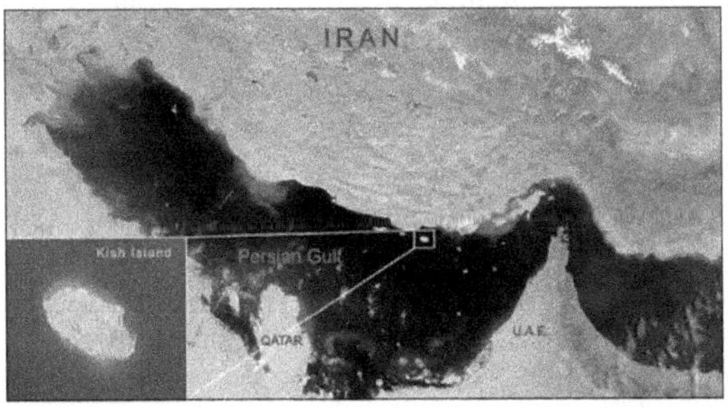

Many seals were used to impress clay sealings on packages to authenticate documents and shipment cargo. The seal impression of a seal from Mohenjo-daro mint found at  Kish (an island in the Persian Gulf) had the text message together with lathe+one-horned young bull: *ayo* 'fish' rebus: *aya* 'metal' *khambhaṛā* 'fish fin' rebus: *kammaTa* 'mint, coiner, coinage' *bhaTa* 'six' rebus: *baTa* 'iron' *kole.l* 'temple'

rebus: *kole.l* 'smithy' *kanka* 'rim of jar' rebus: *karNI* 'supercargo'. *sangaḍa*, 'lathe-brazier' rebus: *konda* 'young bull' Rebus: *kondar* 'turner' *sangar* 'fortification', *sangaḍa*, 'catamaran' *koḍiya* 'young bull' rebus: *koTiya* 'dhow, seafaring vessel'.

A seal inscribed with Harappa Scrpt found in Kish by Oxford Field Museum, (Chicago) Expedition. This is evidence of use of Harappa Script to authenticate long-distance trade by seafaring merchants of Meluhha.

The continuity in the writing tradition as an 'Age of hieroglyphs' into historicl periods is a principal justification for choosing Bharata *sprachbund* of the Bronze Age to signify pictorial and metalwork words of the underlying Harappa language.

Orthography of Harappa Script is unique among ancient writing systems which include Cuneiformj script and Egyptian hieroglyphic writing. Hypertexts in Harappa Script inscriptions are orthographed by combining hieroglyph components into hypertext. This orthographic style results in the data archiving of detailsd technical specifications of metallurgical work in inscriptions of very small sizes with upto 5 or 6 pictorial motifs and text 'signs'. Examples of hypertexts or hieroglyph-multiplex are fig+crab/pincers (shown as Sign 124 Parpola concordance) occurs on other Harappa Script inscriptions as shown in the following examples, with variant orthographic renderings of the hypertext components:

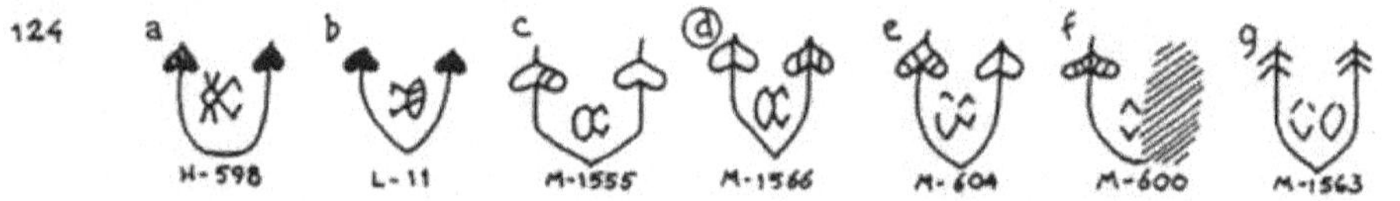

Variants of Sign 124 Parpola concordance.[32] Ficus leaves and arrows are ligatured to a rimless pot and duplicated to signify: *dula* 'pair' rebus: *dul* 'metal casting' *loa* 'ficus religiosa' rebus: *loha* 'copper' PLUS *bāṭi*'cup,'*varti* f. 'projecting rim'. [√*vṛt1*] Pa. *vaṭṭi -*, °*ikā* --'rim, brim'(CDIAL 1136) rebus: *bhatti* 'furnace, forge'.

On the hypertext shown on h 598, the hieroglyph 'pincers" is ligatured to a 'black ant' hieroglyph. 2623 *Te. cīma ant. Kol. si·ma, (SR.) sime id. Nk. śīma id. Konḍa sīma id. Kuwi (F. Su.) sīma, (P.) hīma id.* (DEDR 2623) This hypertext signifies a particular type of metalworker, one who is a coppersmith working in: cīmara -- 'copper. The pincers signify: *kāru* rebus: *khār* 'smith'. hence, *cīmara kāra* 'coppersmith' -- an expression cited in *Saṁghāṭa sutra.*

The hypertext on h598 is *dul bhatti cīmarakāra* 'metal casting furnace coppersmith; the hypertexts on l-14, m-1555, m-1566, m-604, m-600, are *dul bhatti lohakara* 'metal casting furnace metalsmith'; and the hypertext on m-1563 in *dul bhatti loha-khāṇḍa-kara* 'metal casting furnace metal implements artisan'. Evidence is presented and analysed in Annex H Black ant hieroglyph and *cīmara kāra* 'coppersmith'. Many such hypertext signs may be seen in Annex I List of Harappa Script 'signs'.

ayo, aya 'fish' rebus: *aya* 'iron' ayas 'metal' PLUS Hieroglyph: ढाळ (p. 204) *ḍhāḷa* Slope, inclination of a plane. Rebus: *ḍhālako* = a large metal ingot . Thus, large metal or iron ingot.

Just as 'text signs' are ligatured with modifiers, a unique orthographic device is used on Harappa Scrip inscriptions. This orthographic device may be called 'hypertexting'. Such hypertexting is a principal reason for the number of 'text signs' to total over 400.

On the stamp seal, this orthographic device can be seen as hieroglyphs of 'rings on neck', 'one horn' (on the young bull), 'rings on neck', pannier on shoulder. All these hieroglyphs constitute a hypertext. Similarly, the standard device shown in front of the hypertext 'one-horned young bull' is a combination of two major components: top register signifying a lathe with gimlet and the bottom register held on a flagpost signifying a bowl or portable furnace with smoke emanating from the surface and with the hieroglyphs of dotted circles on the bottom bowl.

Many scholars (e.g., Knorozov, Parpola, Mahadevan) see this sign as a fish. The accent is on 'fin' hieroglyph ligature. *ayo, aya* 'fish' rebus: *aya* 'iron' *ayas* 'metal' PLUS *khambhaṛā* 'fish fin' rebus: *kammaṭa* 'mint, coiner, coinage'. Thus, iron metal mint

Modifiers are added to signs, for e.g. the 'fish' hieroglyph is superscripted with a ^ symbol to create a hypertext such as the following 'text sign':

ayo, aya 'fish' rebus: *aya* 'iron' *ayas* 'metal' PLUS *khambhaṛā* 'fish fin' rebus: *kammaṭa* 'mint, coiner, coinage' PLUS *adaren* 'lid' rebus: *aduru* 'native metal' *d.aren-mund.i* 'lid of pot'; *d.aren, ad.aren* to cover up pot with lid (Bond.a); *d.arai* to cover (Bond.a.Hindi) Rebus: *mund* 'iron'. Thus, native metal mint.

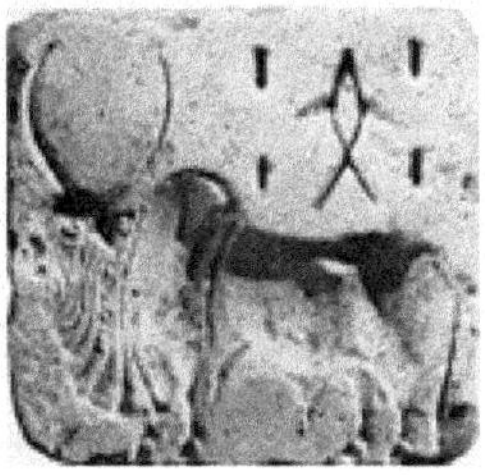

Mohenjo-daro Seals m1118 and Kalibangan 032, glyphs used are: Zebu (*bos taurus indicus*), fish, four-strokes (allograph: arrow). *ayo, aya* 'fish' (Mu.) + *kāṇḍa* 'arrow' (Skt.) *ayaskāṇḍa* 'a quantity of iron, excellent iron' (Pāṇ.gaṇ) *aya* = iron (G.); *ayah, ayas* = metal (Skt.) *gaṇḍa*, 'four' (Santali); Rebus: *kaṇḍa* 'fire-altar', 'furnace'), *kaṇḍa* 'arrow' read rebus in mleccha (Meluhha) as a reference to a guild of artisans working

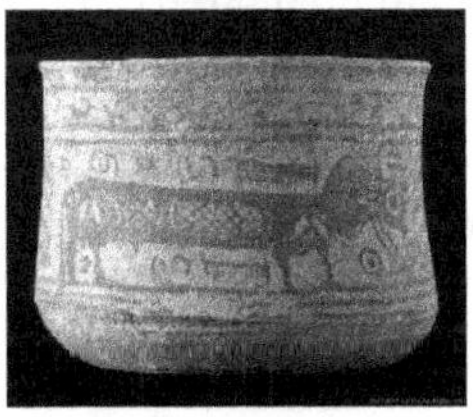

with *ayaskāṇḍa* 'excellent quantity of iron' (Pāṇini) is consistent with the primacy of economic activities which resulted in the invention of a writing system, now referred to as Harappa Script Writing.

पोळ *pōḷa* 'zebu' See: *bolad* 'steel' (Russian) *folad* 'steel' (Old Persian). It is possible that the word *bolad* (Russian) was cognate with पोळ (p. 305) *pōḷa* m A bull dedicated to the gods, marked with a trident and discus, and set at large. पोळा (p. 305) *pōḷā* m (पोळ) A festive day for cattle, the day of new moon of श्रावण or of भाद्रपद. Bullocks are exempted from labor; variously daubed and decorated; and paraded about in worship rebus: पोळ *pōḷa* 'magnetite (a ferrite ore)'.

Large storage pot. Nausharo? Smith working in magnetite, ferrite ore *poLa* 'zebu' rebus: *poLa* 'magnetite' *ayo* 'fish' rebus: *aya* 'iron' *ayas* 'metal; *ḍhaṁkhara* — m.n. 'branch without leaves or fruit' (Prakrit) (CDIAL 5524) Rebus: dhangar 'blacksmith' (Maithili) *kUdI* 'twig', *kuTi* 'tree' rebus: *kuThi* 'smelter' *meDh* 'polar star', *meRh* 'tied rope' rebus: *meD* 'iron' *med* 'copper' *khareḍo* = a currycomb (G.) Rebus: *kharādī* ' turner' (Gujarati)

Fish-eye stones from Meluhha are ferrite ores (magnetite, haematite, laterite) signified on Harappa Script hypertext inscriptions

కండె [*kaṇḍe] kaṇḍe.* [Tel.] n. A head or ear of millet or maize. జొన్నకండి. Mth. *kā̃ṛ* stack of stalks of large millet' (CDIAL 3023). Rebus: *kaṇḍ* 'furnace, fire-altar, consecrated fire'. Rebus: *khāṇḍā* 'tools, pots and pans, and metal-ware'. By shaping the tablets in fish-shapes, the intent is to convey the definitive message that the *khāṇḍā* 'implements are made of metal (*ayo* 'fish' rebus: *ayas* 'metal')

h337, h338 Texts 4417, 4426 with two glyphs each on lea

fish-shaped, miniature Harappa tablets.

A miniature, incised tablet from Harappa h329A has a fish-shaped tablet with two signs: fish + arrow (which combination was also pronounced as *ayaskāṇḍa* on a *bos indicus taurus* seal Kalibangan032.

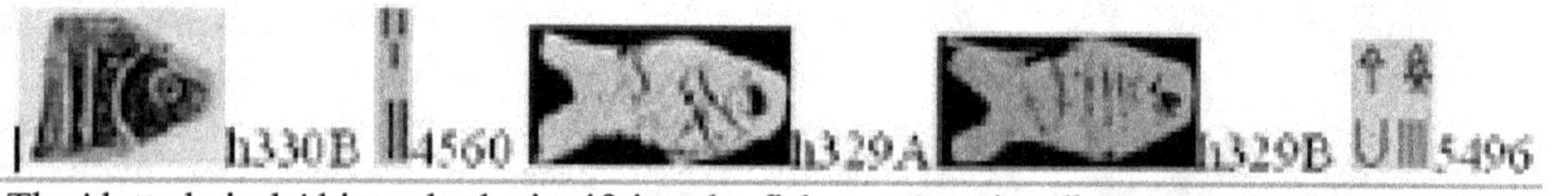

The 'dotted circle' hieroglyph signifying the fish-eye may be *dhAu* 'strand' rebus: *dhAu* 'mineral'.

Reference to 'fish-eye' in cuneiform texts may signify 'dotted circle' hieroglyph of Harappa Script.

The 'dotted circle' hieroglyph is referred to in cuneiform texts as 'fish-eye or fish-eye stones'. I suggest that this reference to 'fish-eye' is in fact, a reference to the cargo of ores, sand ores, stone ores of copper and ferrite ores (magnetite, haematite, laterite) imported through seafaring merchnts from Meluhha, Magan, Dilmun.[33]

The 'dotted circle' as a Harappa Script hieroglyph is read rebus: Pa. *dhātu* -- m. ' element, ashes of the dead, relic '; KhārI. *dhatu* ' relic '; Pk. *dhāu* -- m. ' metal, red chalk '; N. *dhāu* ' ore (esp. of copper) '; Or. *ḍhāu* ' red chalk, red ochre ' (whence *ḍhāuā* ' reddish '; M. *dhāū, dhāv* m.f. ' a partic. soft red stone ' (whence *dhā̆vaḍ* m. ' a caste of iron -- smelters ', *dhāvḍī* 'composed of or relating to iron')(CDIAL 6773) Thus, the 'fish-eye' in cuneiform texts may be a reference to this rebus semantics.

[Quote] The suggestion that 'fish-eyes' (IGI.HA, IGI-KU6), imported through Ur, may have been pearls has been advanced by a number of scholars. 'Fish-eyes' were among a number of valuable commodities (gold, copper, lapis lazuli, stone beads) offered in thanksgiving at the temple of the Sumerian goddess Ningal at Ur by seafaring merchants who had returned safely from Dilmun and perhaps further afield. Elsewhere they are said to have been bought in Dilmun. Whether 'fish-eyes' differed from 'fish-eye stones' (NA4 IGI.HA, NA4 IGI-KU6) and from simply 'eye-stones' is not entirely clear. The latter are included among goods imported from Meluhha (NA4 IGI-ME-LUH-HA) ca. 1816-1810 BCE and ca. 1600-1570 BCE. Any pearls from Meluhha – probably coastal Baluchistan-Sind – would have been generally inferior to those from Dilmun itself. It has been strongly argued that 'fish-eyes', 'fish-eye stones' and 'eye-stones' in Old Babylonian and Akkadian texts were not in fact pearls, but rather (a) etched cornelian beads, imported from India and/or (b) pebbles of banded agate, cut to resemble closely a black/brown pupil and white cornea. The nearest source of good agate is in northwest India, which would accord with supplies obtained from Meluhha. 'Eye-stones' of agate were undoubtedly treasured: some were inscribed and used as amulets, others have been found in votive deposits. Perhaps pearls were at times included among 'fish-eyes,' if not 'fish-eye stones'. More likely, however, the word for 'pearl' is among the 'more than 800 terms in the lexical lists of stones and gems [that] remain to be identified. [unquote][34]

With the decipherment of Harappa Script, 'eye-stones', 'fish-eyes', 'fish-eye stones' become unambiguously identified as related to ferrite ore stones, which are signified by 'dotted circle' 'blob' hieroglyphs. The fish miniature tablets indicate dotted circles as fish-eyes. The dotted circle is deciphered as dhAu 'strand' rebus: dhAu 'mineral, ore, red ores' or tri-dhAtu which are: *poLa, bica, goTa* (magnetite, haematite, laterite ferrite ores). The artisan processing such ores is: *dhāvaḍ* m. ' a caste of iron -- smelters ', *dhāvḍī* 'composed of or relating to iron') (CDIAL 6773).

Susa pot is a 'Rosetta stone' for Harappa Script

One of the 'Rosetta' stones for validating any Harappa Script decipherment is a clay storage pot discovered in Susa (Acropole mound), Old Elamite period, ca. 2500-2400 BCE (H. 20 1/4 in. or 51 cm.) now in Musee du Louvre, Paris which displayed three Harappa script hieroglyphs on the rim: fish, quail, running water. The pot which also had a lid, contained metal tools, and weapons. Hieroglyph: *aya* 'fish' Rebus: *aya* 'iron' (Gujarati) *ayas* 'metal' (Rigveda).

That Susa had used *turbinella pyrum* columella to create cylinder seals has been noted by JM Kenoyer and TR Gensheimer.35 This shows that there was trade interaction between Meluhha and Susa since *turbinella pyrum* is a signature tune of the Sarasvati_Sindhu civilization, with turbinella pyrum habitat restricted to the coastline of the Indian Ocean. It should, therefore, be seen as a reinforcement that Meluhha settlements existed in Susa. Meluhha artisans created the Harappa Script artifacts of a painted pot and cylinder seal with Harappa Script hieroglyphs.

It is a remarkable 'rosetta stone' because it validates the expression used by Panini: *ayaskāṇda* अयस्--काण्ड [p= 85,1] m. n. " a quantity of iron " or " excellent iron " , (g. कस्का*दि q.v.). The early semantics of this expression is likely to be 'metal implements compared with the Santali expression to signify iron implements: *med'* 'copper' (Slovāk), *mẽṛhẽt,khaṇḍa* (Santali) मृदु *mṛdu*,'soft iron' (Samskrtam).

Mĕrhĕt. **Iron.**

Mĕṛhĕt icena. The iron is rusty.
Ispat mĕṛhĕt. Steel.
Dul mĕṛhĕt. Cast iron.
Mĕṛhĕt khanḍa. Iron implements. Santali glosses.

It is a remarkable 'rosetta stone' because it provides archaeo-metallurgical and also epigraphic evidence of metal implements by holding them as contents of the storage pot, describes them with a 'fish' hieroglyph of Harappa Script as a painting on the pot itself.

The vase a la cachette, shown with its contents. Acropole mound, Susa. Old Elamite period, ca. 2500 - 2400 BCE. Clay. H 201/4 in. (51 cm) Paris.[36]

Harappa Script hieroglyphs painted on the jar are: fish, quail and streams of water;

aya 'fish' (Munda) rebus: *aya* 'iron' (Gujarati) *ayas* 'metal' (Rigveda)

baṭa 'quail' Rebus: *bhaṭa* 'furnace'.

kāṇḍa 'water' Rebus: *kāṇḍa* 'implements'.

karaṇḍa 'duck' (Sanskrit) *karaṛa* 'a very large aquatic bird' (Sindhi) Rebus: करडा karaḍā 'Hard from alloy--iron, silver &c'. (Marathi) PLUS *meRh* 'tied rope' *meṛh* f. ' rope tying oxen to each other and to post on threshing floor ' (Lahnda)(CDIAL 10317) Rebus: *mũhā mẽṛhẽt* = iron smelted by the Kolhes and formeḍ into an equilateral lump a little pointed at each end; *mẽṛhẽt, meḍ* 'iron' (Mu.Ho.)

Thus, read together, the proclamation on the jar by the painted hieroglyphs is: *baṭa meṛh karaḍā ayas kāṇḍa* 'hard alloy iron metal implements out of the furnace (smithy)'.

A Susa pot with metal implements and Harappa Script hieroglyphs as hypertext inscription A quail or aquatic bird painted on water flow, on the top register of the jar. Fish painted on the rim and top segment of the storage pot.

Jarre et couvercle

Terre cuite peinte

H. : 51 cm. ; D. : 26 cm.

Sb 2723, Sb 2723 bis

Antiquités orientales

Aile Richelieu Rez-de-chaussée

Iran, Suse au IIIe millénaire avant J.-C.Salle 8Vitrine 2 : Le Vase à la Cachette. Suse IVA (vers 2450 avant J.-C.). Fouilles Jacques de Morgan, 1907, tell de l'Acropole.Notes by Nancie Herbin (Translated) on the treasure of copper and bronze objects:

[quote]This jar covered with a bowl contained, and a second pottery, buried treasure by its owner on the tell of the Acropolis of Susa. The set includes objects of various shapes and materials typical of an era when Susa, dominated by its Mesopotamian neighbors, kept numerous exchanges with areas ranging from the Gulf to the Indus.

A treasure hidden in a jar

This is a jar closed with a ducted bowl. The treasure called "vase in hiding" was

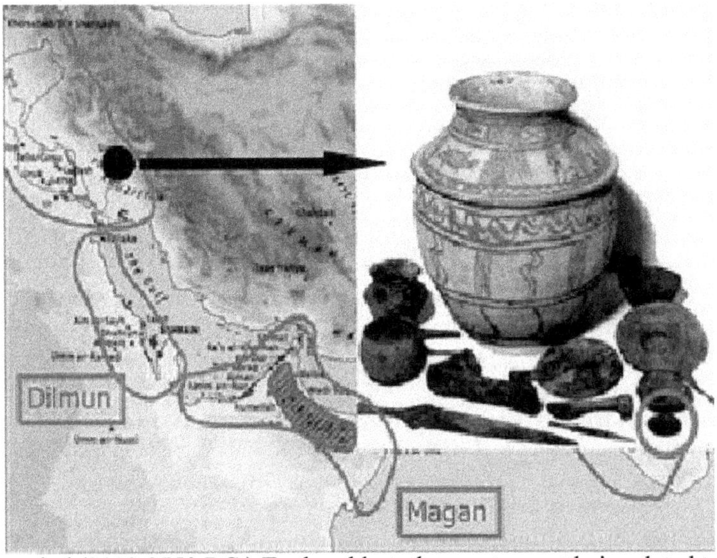

initially grouped in two containers with lids. The second ceramic vessel was covered with a copper lid. It no longer exists leaving only one. Both pottery contained a variety of small objects form a treasure six seals, which range from proto-Elamite period (3100-2750 BC.) To the oldest, the most recent being dated to 2450 BC. AD (First Dynasty of Ur). Therefore it is possible to date these objects, this treasure. Everything included 29 vessels including 11 banded alabaster, mirror, tools and weapons made of copper and bronze, 5 pellets crucibles copper, 4 rings with three gold and a silver, a small figurine of a frog lapis lazuli, gold beads 9, 13 small stones and glazed shard. Metal objects, including tools used may have weight or exchange currency. For some reason we do not know, this treasure has been hidden by its owner but may not get it back. According to Pierre Amiet, it may have been a vassal tribute to the local prince.

A wide variety of shapes and materials

The large number and variety of copper objects testify to the importance of this metal in the middle of the 3rd millennium BC. J-C. The shapes are inspired by the craftsmanship of the neighboring regions such as Luristan and Mesopotamia. The presence of four bronze objects indicates that this alloy began to be controlled by the artisans of the region. However, the small number of objects in precious metals and stones contrast with the richness of the materials used in the Sumerians. Copper came from Oman while lapis lazuli was mined Afghan mountains. The alabaster vases imported objects are either Sistan or Lut desert, the Susian artisans using a coarser material. Such vases were found in large numbers in the city of Ur and show a taste for the exotic which is found until the beginning of the second millennium.

A new cultural momentum

At that time, the Susa region is successively under the aegis of the Mesopotamian kingdoms of Sumer and Akkad. Suse likely begins to emerge from the isolation in which she was to enter a new cultural phase. Although still on the fringes of commercial circuits, a network of exchanges, particularly with regard to materials, is set up with neighboring regions such as Southeast Iran and the Gulf countries, or slightly more distant as the Indus valley. [unquote]

"In the third millennium Sumerian texts list copper among the raw materials reaching Uruk from Aratta and all three of the regions Magan, Meluhha and Dilmun are associated with copper, but the latter only as an emporium. Gudea refers obliquely to receiving copper from Dilmun: 'He (Gudea) conferred with the divine Ninzaga (= Enzak of Dilmun), who transported copper like grain deliveries to the temple builder Gudea...' (Cylinder A: XV, 11-18, Englund 1983, 88, n.6). Magan was certainly a land producing the metal, since it is occasionally referred to as the 'mountain of copper'. It may also have been the source of finished bronze objects."*37*

Daniel T. Potts discounts the possibility that Meluhha was the source of tin. His arguments, however, do not exclude the possibility that ancient Meluhha traders may have acted as intermediaries to the suppliers of tin from the largest tin belt of the globe in the Mekong River delta in the Ancient Far East.

"Tin. The sources of Mesopotamia's tin...have been sought from Southeast Asia to Cornwall. With regard to the former possibility, it has always proved difficult to establish any sort of an archaeological link between Burma, Thailand or any other part of mainland Southeast Asia and the Bharata sub-continent, supposing that this was the location of Meluhha from which Gudea (Cyl B XIV.13) claims to have imported tin. As the Bharata subcontinent has no tin itself, Meluhha's tin must have been acquired elsewhere and then trans-shipped to Mesopotamia, just as Dilmun's copper was acquired in Magan during the early second millennium BCE. With a view to examining the evidence for a connection between the tin-rich regions of Southeast Asia and the Indus Valley, it is interesting to note that some years ago the claim was made that etched carnelian beads, a particularly diagnostic type fossil of the Harappa civilization, had been found at the early tin-bronze producing site of Ban Chiang in Thailans. This made the likelihood that Meluhha tin was southeast Asian in origin less far-fetched than previously thought. In fact, however, scholars who have actually seen the Ban Chiang beads have confirmed that they are not Harappa at all, but date rather to the last centuries BCE or first centiries CE when different types of etched carnelian beads, clearly distinct from those of the earlier Harappa period, were manufactured. For the time being, therefore, we should not consider southeast Asia a likely tin source based on this now discredited piece of evidence...Since lapiz lazuli, which certainly originated in Afghanistan (Badakshan), is said by Gudea to have been acquired from Meluhha, it is quite probable that the tin which he received from that country originated in Central Asia as well."[38]

Three hieroglyphs of Harappa Script on Susa pot which contained metal implements, weapons, pots and pans.

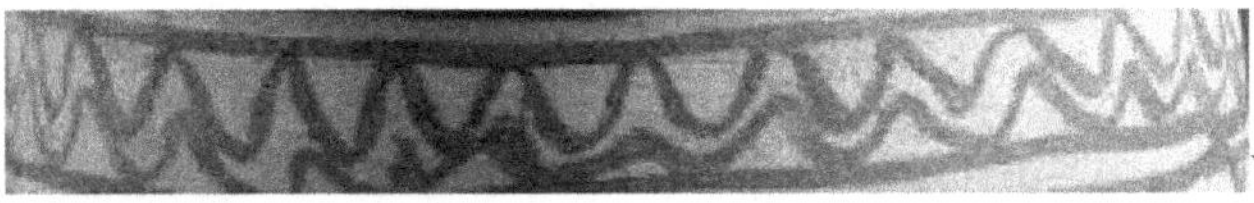
Water (flow)

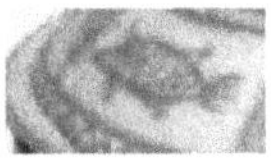
Fish fish-fin

aquatic bird on wave (indicating aquatic nature of the bird), tied to rope, water kāṇḍa 'water' rebus: kāṇḍa 'implements

ayo, aya 'fish' rebus: *aya* 'iron' *ayas* 'metal' *khambhaṛā* 'fin' rebus: *kammaṭa* 'mint' Thus, together *ayo kammaṭa*, 'metals mint'

Duck on wave tied to a rope:

కరడము (p. 250) karaḍamu or కరడు or కరుడు karaḍamu. [Tel.] n. A wave. అల. Parij. ii. 59.

करण्ड m. a sort of duck L. కారండవము (p. 274) [*kāraṇḍavamu*] *kāraṇḍavamu.* [Skt.] n. A sort of duck. (Telugu) karaṭa1 m. ' crow ' BhP., °aka -- m. lex.

[Cf. *karaṭu* -- , *karkaṭu* -- m. 'Numidian crane ', *karēṭu* -- , °*ēṭavya* -- , °*ēḍuka* -- m. lex., *karaṇḍa*2 -- m. ' duck ' lex: see kāraṇḍava --]Pk. *karaḍa* -- m. ' crow ', °*ḍā* -- f. ' a partic. kind of bird '; S. *karaṛa* -- *ḍhī̃gu* m. ' a very large aquatic bird '; L. *karṛā* m., °ṛī f. ' the common teal'(CDIAL 2787) Rebus: *karaḍā* 'hard alloy'

Remarkable evidence for traded metalwork: 3 pure tin ingots with Harappa Script

Tin ingots in the Museum of Ancient Art of the Municipality of Haifa, Israel (left #8251, right #8252).

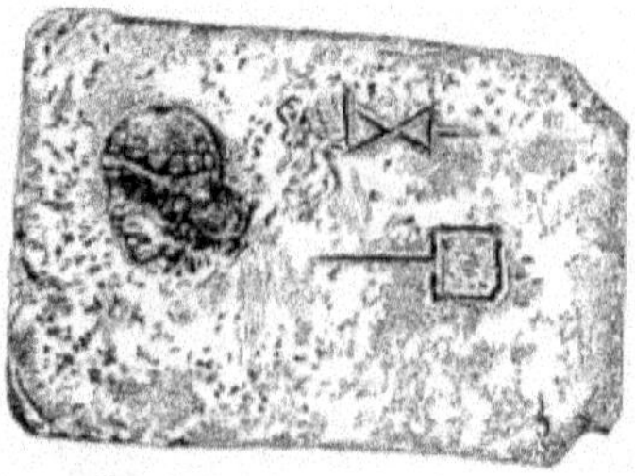

Three pure tin ingots each bear inscribed Harappa Script hieroglyphs; I have argued in a monograph in *Journal of Indo-Judaic Studies*, that the inscriptions were Meluhha hieroglyphs (Harappa Script writing)[39]. A third ingot was found inscribed with an added huieroglyph: moulded head, hieroglyph: *mũhe* 'face' (Santali) Rebus: *mũh* 'ingot'. Thus, the inscriptions on the tingots signify *ranku dhatu mũh,* 'tin mineral ingot'.

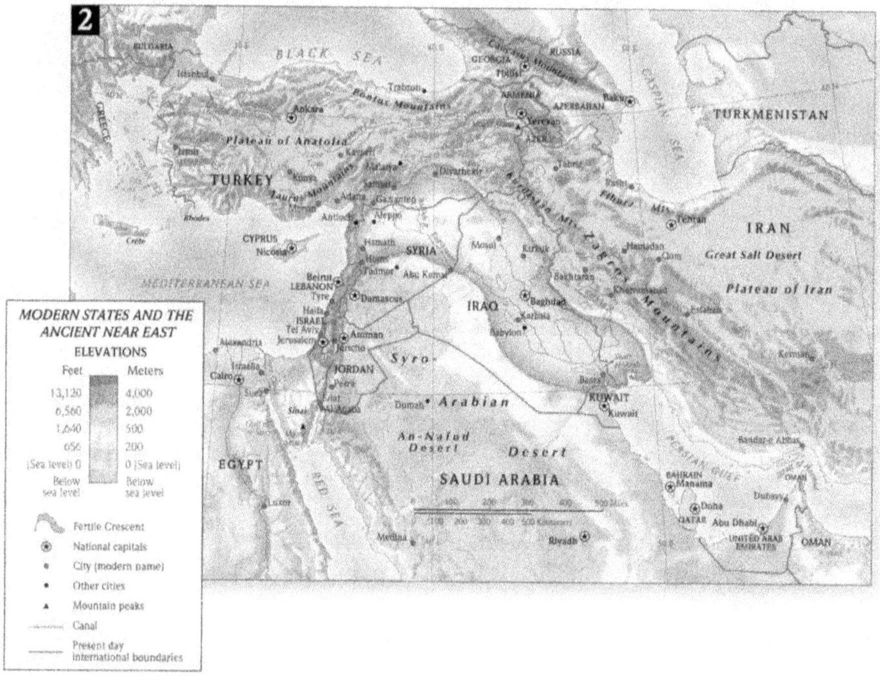

Map showing location of Haifa port where a shipwreck yielded two pure tin ingots with Harappa Script inscriptions.

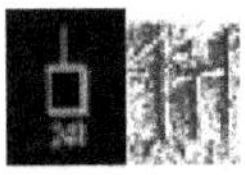

The other hieroglyphs are: *ran:ku* = liquid measure (Santali) *ran:ku* a species of deer; ran:kuka (Skt.)(CDIAL 10559). Rebus: *ranku* 'tin' (Santali)

dāṭu = cross (Te.); *dhatu* = mineral (Santali) Hindi. *dhāṭnā* 'to send out, pour out, cast (metal)' (CDIAL 6771) PLUS खाडा [*khāṇḍā*] 'A jag, notch, or indentation (as upon the edge of a tool or weapon)' Rebus: *khaṇḍa* 'implements (Santali). Thus, tin mineral ingots are implements-grade.

It is significant that the largest tin belt of the globe is in Mekong delta in Ancient Far East. The availability of tin was critical to produce tin-bronzes since naturally occurring arsenical copper (or arsenical bronze) was limited. A hypothesis for testing is hat tin for the Bronze Age Revolution was resourced from the Ancient Far East with seafaring merchants of Harappa (Sarasvati-Sindhu) Civilization acting as intermediaries to reach tin supplies to the Ancient Near East through the Maritime Tin Route40 using navigable waterways and through the Persian Gulf. Framing this hypothesis is justified by the evidence of Dong Son Bronze Drums with Harappa Script hieroglyphs inscribed using cire perdue (lost-wax) technology.

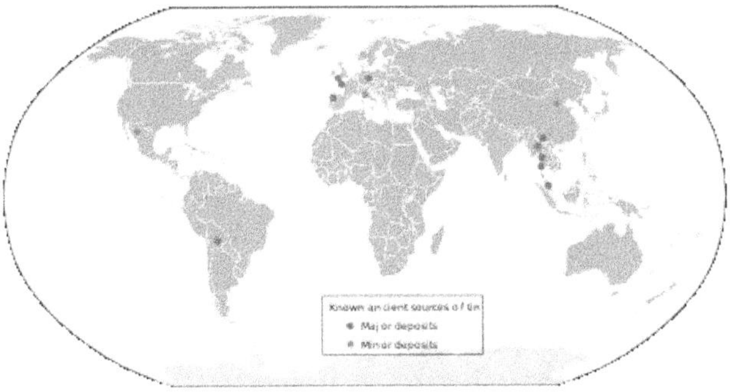

Map showing the location of known tin deposits exploited during ancient times

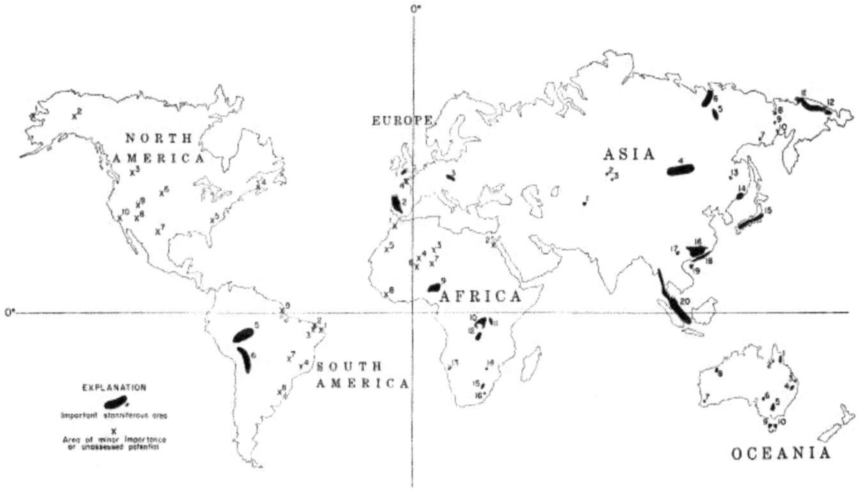

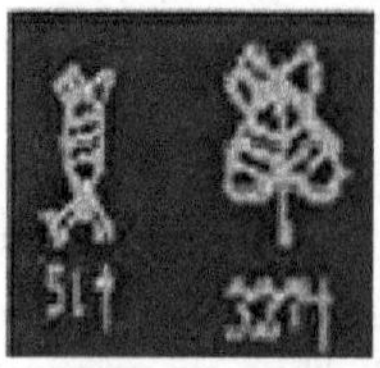

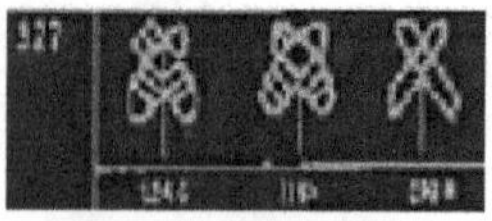

Text signs 51 and 327 are two hypertext 'signs' of the script with unique superscripted ligatures; such a pair created with unique ligatures does not occur on any other ligatured hieroglyph in the entire Harappa Script Corpora.

Sign 51 variants, Sign 327 variants These two signs have characteristically unique ligatures like 'ears'. The underlying hieroglyphs are, respectively, *bica* 'scorpion' and *loa 'ficus religiosa'*. I suggest that the 'ears" ligatured like superscripts are intended to convey a hypertext. The diacritics suffix may read: *-kAra* 'artisan' to yield: *bicakAra* 'stone ore artisan' *lohakAra* 'copper smith'.

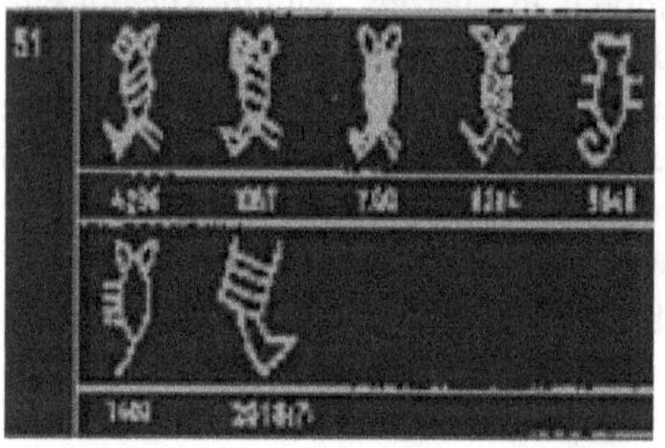

kárṇa m. ' ear, handle of a vessel ' RV., ' end, tip (?) ' RV. ii 34, 3. [Cf. *kāra -- 6]
Pa. *kaṇṇa* -- m. ' ear, angle, tip '; Pk. *kaṇṇa*--, °*aḍaya*<-> m. ' ear ', Gy. as. pal. eur. *kan* m., Ash. (Trumpp) *karna* NTS ii 261, Niṅg. *kõ*, Woṭ. *kanə*, Tir. *kana;* Paš. *kan, kaṇ(ḍ)* -- ' orifice of ear ' IIFL iii 3, 93; Shum. *kȭṛ* ' ear ', Woṭ. *kan* m., Kal. (LSI) *kuṛȭ*, rumb. *kuŕũ*, urt. *kŕãdotdot;* (< **kaṇ*), Bshk. *kan*, Tor. *k**lṇ, Kand. *kōṇi*, Mai. *kaṇa*, ky. *kān*, Phal. *kāṇ*, Sh. gil. *kọn* pl. *kọṇí* m. (→ Ḍ *kon* pl. *k**lṇ*a*), koh. *kuṇ*, pales. *kuāṇə*, K. *kan* m., kash. pog. ḍoḍ. *kann*, S. *kanu* m., L. *kann* m., awāṇ. khet. *kan*, P. WPah. bhad. bhal. cam. *kann* m., Ku. gng. N. *kān*; A. *kāṇ*' ear, rim of vessel, edge of river '; B. *kāṇ* ' ear ', Or. *kāna*, Mth. Bhoj. Aw. lakh. H. *kān* m., OMarw. *kāna* m., G. M. *kān* m., Ko. *kānu* m., Si. *kaṇa, kana.* -- As adverb and postposition (*ápi kárṇē* ' from behind ' RV., *karṇē* ' aside ' Kālid.): Pa. *kaṇṇē* ' at one's ear, in a whisper '; Wg. *ken* ' to ' NTS ii 279; Tir. *kõ* ' on ' AO xii 181 with (?); Paš. *kan* ' to '; K. *kàni* with abl. ' at, near, through ', *kani* with abl. or dat. ' on ', *kun* with dat. ' toward '; S. *kani* ' near ', *kanā̃* ' from '; L. *kan* ' toward ', *kannũ* ' from ', *kanne* ' with ', khet. *kan*, P. ḍog. *kanē* ' with, near '; WPah. bhal. *k**lṇ, °*ṇi, keṇ, °ṇi* with obl. ' with, near ', *kiṇ, °ṇiā̃, k*ṇiā̃, keṇ°* with obl. ' from '; Ku. *kan* ' to, for '; N. *kana* ' for, to, with '; H. *kane, °ni, kan* with *ke* ' near '; OMarw. *kanai* ' near ', *kanā̃ sā̃* ' from near ', *kā̃nī̃* ' towards '; G. *kan*e ' beside '.
kárṇaka -- , kárṇikā -- , karṇín -- ; karṇakaṇḍū -- , *karṇakāṣṭhaka -- , *karṇakīla -- , karṇadhāra -- , karṇapattraka -- , karṇapuṭa -- , *karṇapuṣya -- , *karṇamarda -- , karṇamūla -- , *karṇavaṭikā -- , karṇavēdha -- , *karṇavyādhikā -- , karṇaśūlá -- , *karṇasphōṭikā -- , *karṇākṣi -- ; ākarṇayati, utkarṇa -- ; ajakarṇa -- , gōkarṇa -- , catuṣkarṇa -- , lambakarṇa -- .Addenda: *kárṇa* -- **:** S.kcch. *kann* m. ' ear ', WPah.kṭg. (kc.) *kān*, poet. *kanṛu* m. ' ear ', kṭg. *kanni* f. ' pounding -- hole in barn floor '; J. *kā'n* m. ' ear ', Garh. *kān*; Md. *kan* -- in *kan -- fat*' ear ' < karṇapattraka -- , *kan -- huḷi* (+ cūḍa -- 1) ' side -- burns '. (CDIAL 2830). The lexeme expands semantically: As adverb and postposition (*ápi kárṇē* ' from behind ' RV., *karṇē* ' aside ' Kālid.): Pa. *kaṇṇē* ' at one's ear, in a whisper '

Similary, it is suggested that the two ligatured signs Sign 51 and Sign 327 may be read as: *bicha kárṇi* and *loha kárṇi* 'haematite sandstone supercargo' and 'copper supercargo' respectively, or *bicha kAru* 'haematite ore worker' or *loha kAru* 'copper ore worker' – expressions in which supercargo is the merchant's representative responsible for handling the cargo of products or iron (haematite) and copper mineral smelters and iron/copper metal workers.

The Harappa Script hieroglyphs -- squirrel, lathe/portable furnace, one-horned young bull -- which signify two functionaries of the guild of metalworkers/merchants are:

śrēṣṭhin 'guild master'

samgaha, saṁgraha '*a* 'manager, arranger' कोंद *kōnda* 'engraver'. These two signifiers also indicate that the artisans working on the circular platforms were required to consign the metalwork products into the temple for accounting and trade transactions.

Harappa script cipher (methodology) and decipherment

A method suggested for decipherment of Harappa Script as a logo-phonetic structure read rebus in Meluhha (Harappa language) may be gleaned from the following example. Each hieroglyph or hypertext is read as words or expressions in Meluhha.

Writing instruments/devices and pigments

Many Harappa Script inscriptions are incised using a sharp stylus. Some inscriptions are hypertexts composed as raised script on metal. Some inscriptions on metal (for e.g. on a gold pendant) are written in some form of ink of ferric oxide or carbon black as pigment (perhaps using a writing brush). Some inscriptions are created with dotted orthography as on a gold fillet signifying the standard device which normally occurs in front of a one-horned young bull on many inscriptions. Hard metal styluses have been used to create over 240 copper plate Harappa Script inscriptions. Many copper inscriptions in bas-relief, raised script may have been used to created printed copies using ferric oxide ink. Evidence for writing in paint is provided by an inscription on a gold pendant and on pots wih painted with Harappa Script hieroglyphs, for e.g. Susa pot with 'fish' hieroglyph and Nausharo pot showing a zebu tied to a post.

Methodology

Methodology of Harappa script is exemplified by the following square-shaped stamp seal with inscriptions composed of two broad categories of hieroglyphs which are often identified in Harappa Script Corpora as 'pictorial motif or field symbol' and 'text signs'. There are over 100 pictorial motifs or field symbols and over 400 'text signs'. A vivid portrayal of the two categories may be seen on the following stamp seal from Harappa discovered by HARP (Harappa Archaeological Research Project of Harvard University).[41]

Harappa stamp seal inscription: *kōḍiya* 'young bull' Hieroglyph 2: *koḍiyum* 'ring on neck' (Gujarati) Rebus: *koṭiya* 'dhow seafaring vessel' *sãgaḍ,* 'lathe' Rebus: *sãgaḍa* 'double-canoe, catamaran'. Dhatu सं-ग्रह *saṁgraha, samgaha* 'a guardian , ruler , manager , arranger'of minerals. Text message:

कुटिल kuṭila, *katthīl*

'curve' *kuṭila* 'bent' (CDIAL 3230) rebus: *kuṭila*, katthīl = bronze (8 parts copper and 2 parts tin) *dāṭu* = cross rebus: *dhatu* 'mineral' *sal* 'splinter' rebus: *sal* 'workshop' *dula* 'two' rebus: *dul* 'metal casting' *ayo* 'fish' rebus: *aya* 'iron' *aDaren* 'lid' rebus *aduru* 'native metal' PLUS *ayo* 'fish' rebus: *aya* 'iron' *pajhar* 'sprout' rebus: *pasra* 'smithy' PLUS *mũhã mẽṛhẽt* 'iron ingot' *kolom* 'three' rebus: *kolimi* 'smithy, forge' *kuṭila*, katthīl = bronze (8 parts copper and 2 parts tin) *dula* 'two' rebus: *dul* 'metal casting' ranku 'liquid measure' rebus:ranku 'tin' *pajhar* 'sprout' rebus: *pasra* 'smithy' *kanka* 'rim of jar' rebus: *karNI* 'supercargo'. Thus the inscription signifies: supercargo responsible for copper-tin minerals for bronze metal castings, mineral, iron, native metal, iron ingot smithy, bronze smithy, tin metal castings smithy.

Person kneeling under a tree facing a tiger. [Chanhudaro Excavations, Pl. LI, 18]

See: Annex E Clustering 'temple' hieroglyph, pictorial narratives of kneeling adorant, together with markhor and offering on a stool

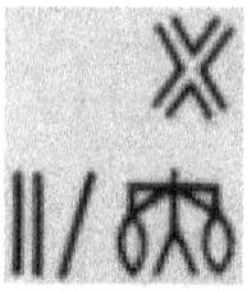

6118 Hieroglyph: *dāṭu* = cross (Telugu) Rebus: *dhatu* = mineral (Santali)

kuṭi 'water-carrier' rebus: *kuṭhi* 'smelter'

Hypertext composed of slanted stroke PLUS two linear strokes: *dhal* 'slant' rebus: *dhALako* 'large ingot' PLUS *dula* 'two' rebus: *dul* 'metal casting' Thus, metalcasting ingot.

kuṭi 'tree' rebus: *kuṭhi* 'smelter' *kuThAru* 'tree' rebus: *kuThAru* 'armourer'

kola 'tiger' rebus: *kol* 'working in iron' *kolhe* 'smelter' *kolle* 'blacksmith' *kol* 'furnace, forge'

eragu 'bow' rebus: *erako* 'moltencast, copper'. *bhaṭa* 'worshipper' rebus: *bhaṭa* 'furnace'. The sitting pose of the worshipper is that of an archer: *kamāṭhiyo* 'archer' rebus: *kammaṭa* 'mint, coiner, coinage'

Thus, the inscription with hypertexts on the seal signifies *dharma saṁjñā* 'responsibility indicators": armourer, smelter working in iron, copper, metalcastings, ingots (with) furnace, forge, mint.

The methodology of the form, structure and function of Harappa Script is demonstrated with three hieroglyphs signified on Harappa Script inscriptions read rebus to decipher the script and read the plain texts of the messages.

Hieroglyph (three meanings): *bāṭi* 'cup', 'stone', 'wick'.

These three meanings of the word suggest three hieroglyphs read rebus: *bhaṭṭī* 'furnace, forge' *bhāṭi* ' kiln ' *bhaṭhī, bhaṭṭī ' bhāṭhā* ' kiln '; H. *bhaṭṭhā* m. ' kiln', *bhaṭ* f. 'kiln'. Thus, metal furnace, (metals) turner.

Hieroglyph set 1: stone (round pebble), dotted circle, fire-altar

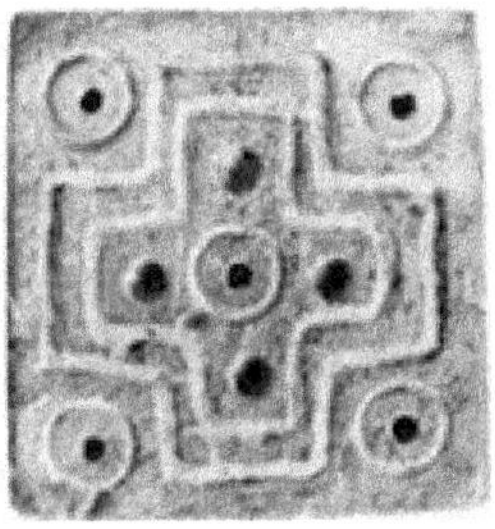

m0352 Mohnjo-daro seal Some furnaces (fire-altars) are shown with 'pebbles, or round stones' and dotted circles. Dotted circles signify *dhAi* 'strand' rebus: *dhAu, dhAtu* 'mineral, ore'. The + shaped structure is: *kaṇḍa* 'fire-altar' or *kāṇḍa* 'implements'. *goTa* 'stone' rebus: *goTa* 'laterite ore' *khōṭaa* 'ingot'. Thus, the rebus reading of this hypertext on m0352 is the message*:* *kaṇḍa* 'fire-altar' (for) *dhAtu* 'mineral' *khōṭaa* 'ingots' *kāṇḍa* 'implements'.

Hieroglyph set 2: wick (lamp)

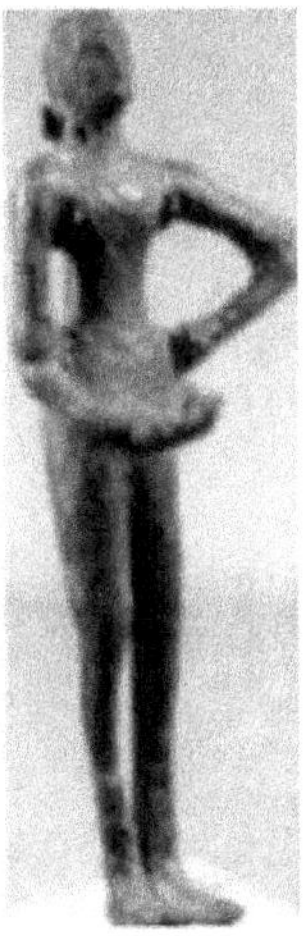

Lost-wax casting. Bronze statue, Mohenjo-daro. Bronze statue of a woman holding a small bowl, Mohenjo-daro; copper alloy made using *cire perdue* method (DK 12728; Mackay 1938: 274, Pl. LXXIII, 9-11)

Both women in the cire perdue (lost-wax) cast bronze sculptures, seem to hold a lamp (bowl) wick in a hand. *karā̃* n. pl. ' wristlets, bangles ' (Gujarati) Rebus: *khār* 'blacksmith'. *bāṭi* 'cup' *bāṭi* 'wick' rebus: *bhaṭṭī* 'furnace, forge' *kola* 'woman' rebus: k*ol* 'working in iron' One is shown with a dance-step: *meḍ* 'dance step' rebus: *meḍ* 'iron'. Thus, iron furnace blacksmith.

loh 'copper, iron, metal' PLUS *bhaṭṭī* 'furnace, forge' *bhāṭi* ' kiln ' *bhaṭhī, bhaṭṭī ' bhāṭhā* ' kiln '; H. *bhaṭṭhā* m. ' kiln', *bhaṭ* f. 'kiln'. Thus, metal furnace turner

Hieroglyph set 3: *bāṭi* 'cup'

Harappa. Tablets with script. *kolmo* 'three' rebus: *kolimi* 'smithy, forge' PLUS *baṭa* 'rimless pot' rebus: *baṭa* 'iron' *bhaṭa* 'furnace'. Thus furnace (of) smithy/forge; *bhaṭṭī* 'furnace, forge'

baṭa 'rimless pot' rebus: *baṭa* 'iron' *bhaṭa* 'furnace'. Thus furnace (of) smithy/forge. That is, iron (metal) furnace.

Rebus: *bhaṭṭī* 'furnace, forge' *bhāṭi* ' kiln ' bhaṭhī, bhaṭṭī ' *bhāṭhā* ' kiln '; H. *bhaṭṭhā* m. ' kiln', *bhaṭ* f. 'kiln'

Hieroglyph: one-horned young bull: खोंड (p. 216) [*khōṇḍa*] m A young bull, a bullcalf. Rebus: कोंद *kōnda* 'engraver, lapidary setting or infixing gemś (Marathi)खोदगिरी [*khōdagirī*] f Sculpture, carving, engraving.

loa 'ficus religiosa' rebus: l*oh* 'copper, iron, metal' PLUS *varti* f. ' projecting rim '. [√vṛt1] Pa. *vaṭṭi* -- °*ikā* -- f. ' rim, brim '(CDIAL 1136) rebus: *bhatti* 'furnace, forge' PLUS *karṇaka, kanka* 'rim of jar' rebus: *karṇī* 'Supercargo' *karṇika* 'scribe, account'

Etyma from Bharata *sprachbund* from which a pair of matching, similar sounding words -- homonyms are culled to read hieroglyphs using rebus method:

**varta2* ' circular object ' or more prob. ' something made of metal ', cf. *vartaka* -- 2 n. ' bell -- metal, brass ' lex. and *vartalōha* -- . [√vṛt?]Pk. *vaṭṭa* -- m.n., °*aya* -- m. ' cup '; Ash. *waṭā'k* ' cup, plate '; K. *waṭukh*, dat. °*ṭakas* m. ' cup, bowl '; S. *vaṭo* m. ' metal drinking cup '; N. *bāṭā,* ' round copper or brass vessel '; A. *bāṭi* ' cup '; B. *bāṭā* ' box for betel '; Or. *baṭā* ' metal pot for betel ', *bāṭi* ' cup, saucer '; Mth. *baṭṭā* ' large metal cup ', *bāṭī* ' small do. ', H. baṭrī f.; G. M. *vāṭī* f. ' vessel '(CDIAL 11347)

**varta3* ' round stone '. 2. **vārta* -- . [Cf. Kurd. *bard* ' stone '. -- √vṛt1]
1. Gy. eur. *bar*, SEeur. *baj* ' stone ', pal. *wăṭ*, *wŭṭ* ' stone, cliff '; Ḍ. *boṭ* m. ' stone ', Ash. Wg. *wāṭ*, Kt. *woṭ*, Dm. *bɔ̄'ṭ*, Tir. *baṭ*, Niṅg. *bōt*, Woṭ.*baṭ* m., Gmb. *wāṭ*; Gaw. *wāṭ* ' stone, millstone '; Kal.rumb. *bat* ' stone ' (*bad* -- *váṣ* ' hail '), Kho. *bort*, Bshk. *baṭ*, Tor. *bāṭ*, Mai. (Barth) "*bhāt*" NTS xviii 125, Sv. *bāṭ*, Phal. *bā̆ṭ*; Sh.gil. *băṭ* m. ' stone ', koh. *băṭṭ* m., jij. *baṭ*, pales. *baṭ* ' millstone '; K. *waṭh*, dat. °*ṭas* m. 'round stone ', *vüṭüf*. ' small do. '; L. *vaṭṭā* m. ' stone ', khet. *vaṭ* ' rock '; P. *baṭṭ* m. ' a partic. weight ', *vaṭṭā*, *ba*° m. ' stone ', *vaṭṭī* f. ' pebble '; WPah.bhal. *baṭṭ* m. ' small round stone '; Or. *bāṭi* ' stone '; Bi. *baṭṭā* ' stone roller for spices, grindstone '. -- With unexpl. -- *ṭth* -- : Sh.gur. *baṭṭh* m. ' stone ', gil.*baṭhā'* m. ' avalanche of stones ', *baṭhúi* f. ' pebble ' (suggesting also an orig. **vartuka* -- which Morgenstierne sees in Kho. place -- name*bortuili*, cf. *vartu -- , vartula --).2. Paš.lauṛ. *wāṛ*, kuṛ. *wō* ' stone ', Shum. *wāṛ*. (CDIAL 11348)

várti1 (and *vartí* --) f. ' wick ' MBh., ' small compress ' Suśr., ' lamp ' lex., °*ikā* -- f. ' wick ' KālP. [√vṛt1]Pa. *vaṭṭi* -- , °*ikā* -- f. ' wick ', Pk. *vaṭṭī̆* -- , °*ṭiā* -- , *vatti* -- f.; Sh. *baṭī'* ' unlit native lamp, candle, wick of European lamp ' (← H.?); S. *vaṭi* f. ' wick '; L. *vaṭṭ* f. ' roll of grass, wick ', awāṇ. *vaṭ* ' wick ', P. *vaṭṭī*, *ba*°, *battī* f.; N. *bāti* ' lamp ' (*bati* ← H.), A. *bāti*; B. *bāti* ' wick, lamp, candle '; Or. *bati* ' lamp ' (← H.), Bi. Mth. Bhoj. *bātī*; OAw. *bātī̆* ' wick ', H. *bātī*, *battī* f. (→ N. Or. and prob. Sh.); G. *vāṭ* f. ' lamp ', *vātī* f. ' perfumed match or taper '; M. *vāt* f. ' wick ', Ko. *vāti*; Si. *väṭ* -- *a* ' lamp ', *väṭi* -- *ya* ' wick '; Md. *vo'* ' lamp '; -- with -- *o* as from an orig. masculine: Ku. *bāto* m. ' wick, lamp '; N. *bāto* ' rope of twisted cane (to tie down thatch) '.dīpavarti -- , *pādavarti -- , *saṁdhyāvartikā -- .Addenda: várti -- 1: S.kcch. *batī*, *bhatī* f. ' lamp, torch ' ← H.; WPah.kṭg. *batti*, kc. *baṭe* f. ' wick, lamp, light ', J. *bāṭī* f. (CDIAL 11359) varti2 f. ‘ projecting rim ’. [√vṛt1]Pa. *vaṭṭi* -- , °*ikā* -- f. ‘ circumference, rim, brim ’; vártikā f. ‘ quail ’ RV. 2. vārtika -- m. lex. 3. var- takā -- f. lex. (eastern form ac. to Kātyāyana: S. Lévi JA 1912, 498), °*ka* -- m. Car., *vārtāka* -- m. lex. [Cf. *vartīra* -- m. Suśr., °*tira* -- lex., *vartakara --]1. Ash. *uwŕe*/ ‘ partridge ’ NTS ii 246 (connexion denied NTS v 340), Paš.snj. *waṭī′*; K. *hāra* -- *wüṭü* f. ‘ species of waterfowl ’ (*hāra* -- < śā′ra --).2. Kho. *barti* ‘ quail, partridge ’ BelvalkarVol 88.3. Pa. *vaṭṭakā* -- f., °*ka* -- in cmpds. ‘ quail ’, Pk. *vaṭṭaya* -- m., N. *baṭṭāi* (< *vārtāka* -- ?), A. *batā* -- *sarāi*, B. *batui*, *baṭuyā*; Si. *vaṭuvā* ‘ snipe, sandpiper ’ (ext. of **vaṭu* < *vartakā* --). -- With unexpl. *bh* -- : Or. *bhāṭoi*, °*ṭui* ‘ the grey quail Cotarnix communis ’, (dial.) *bhāroi*, °*rui* (< early MIA. **vāṭāka* -- < *vārtāka* -- : cf. *vāṭī* -- f. ‘ a kind of bird ’ Car.)Addenda: vartikā -- [Dial. *a* ~ *ā* < IE. non -- apophonic *o* (cf. Gk. o)/rtuc and early EMIA. *vāṭī* -- f. ‘ a kind of bird ’ Car. < **vārtī* --) T. Burrow BSOAS xxxviii 71] (CDIAL 11361)

bhráṣṭra n. ‘ frying pan, gridiron ’ MaitrS. [√bhrajj]Pk. *bhaṭṭha* -- m.n. ‘ gridiron ’; K. *büṭhü* f. ‘ level surface by kitchen fireplace on which vessels are put when taken off fire ’; S. *baṭhu* m. ‘ large pot in which grain is parched, large cooking fire ’, *baṭhī* f. ‘ distilling furnace ’; L. *bhaṭṭh* m. ‘ grain -- parcher's oven ’, *bhaṭṭhī* f. ‘ kiln, distillery ’, awāṇ. *bhaṭh*; P. *bhaṭṭh* m., °*ṭhī* f. ‘ furnace ’, *bhaṭṭhā* m. ‘ kiln ’; N. *bhāṭi* ‘ oven or vessel in which clothes are steamed for washing ’; A. *bhaṭā* ‘ brick -- or lime -- kiln ’; B. *bhāṭi* ‘ kiln ’; Or. *bhāṭi* ‘ brick -- kiln, distilling pot ’; Mth. *bhaṭhī*, *bhaṭṭī* ‘ brick -- kiln, furnace, still ’; Aw.lakh. *bhāṭhā* ‘ kiln ’; H. *bhaṭṭhā* m. ‘ kiln ’, *bhaṭ* f. ‘ kiln, oven, fireplace ’; M. *bhaṭṭā* m. ‘ pot of fire ’, *bhaṭṭī* f. ‘ forge ’. -- X bhástrā -- q.v.bhrāṣṭra -- ; *bhraṣṭrapūra -- , *bhraṣṭrāgāra -- .Addenda: bhráṣṭra -- : S.kcch. *bhaṭṭhī keṇī* ‘ distil (spirits) ’ *bhraṣṭrāgāra ‘ grain parching house ’. [bhráṣṭra -- , agāra --]P. *bhaṭhiār*, °*ālā* m. ‘ grainparcher's shop ’. (CDIAL 9656, 9658)

Inference in choosing ancient phonetic forms and alternative rebus renderings of Harappa language

In the following example of a seal, the decipherment of a hypertext ‘duck in a circle’ is read as *vartaka* because the phonetic form is closest to the form attested in Rigveda: *vartika* ‘quail’ and the word *varti* signifies a ‘round circle’. It is thus inferred that the lexeme *vartaka* is the spoken form of Harappa language and signified as *vartaka* ‘merchant’ on Harappa Script. It is also possible that *baṭṭai[i]* ’quail’ rebus: *bhāṭi* ‘kiln’ were spoken forms in the vernacular or *parole* of Harappa language.

Similarly, the young bull hieroglyph is read: कोंड *[kōṇḍa]* ‘young bull’ rebus: *kundār* turner (A.)(CDIAL 3295). Since *sangaḍa*, 'lathe-brazier' rebus: *sangar* ‘fortification’, *sangaḍa*, 'catamaran' is NOT shown on this seal, it is inferred that the intention of the scribe is to signify *koḍiya* 'young bull' rebus: *koTiya* ‘dhow, seafaring vessel’.

Mohenjodaro MIC, Pl. CVI,93 *eka-shingi* 'one horn' rebus: 'single-masted dhow' *koḍiya* 'young bull' rebus: *koTiya* 'dhow, seafaring vessel'. Text message of inscription: Line 1:: *baṭṭai[i]* quail (N.) *vartaka* = a duck (Samskrtam) *baṭak* = a duck (G.) *vartikā* = quail (RV.); *wuwrc* partridge (Ash.); *barti* = quail, partridge (Kho.); *vaṭṭaka_* quail (Pali); *vaṭṭaya* (Pkt.) (CDIAL 11361). Rebus 1: *bhāṭi* 'kiln, funace' Rebus 2: *vartaka* 'merchant' (Skt.) *dula* 'two 'rebus: *dul* 'metal casting' *kanka, karṇaka*, 'rim of jar' rebus: *karṇī* 'supercargo, a representative of the ship's owner on board a merchant ship, responsible for overseeing the cargo and its sale.' karṇika 'scribe, account'. Thus, a metal castings merchant.

Line 2: *ayo, aya* 'fish' rebus: *aya* 'iron', ayas 'metal' PLUS *khambharā* 'fish **fin' rebus: *kammaṭa*** 'mint, coiner, coinage'. *dula* 'pair' rebus: *dul* 'metal casting' PLUS *kolmo* 'rice plant' rebus: *kolimi* 'smithy, forge' *kol* 'furnace, forge'. *kanka, karṇika* 'rim of jar' rebus: *karṇika* 'scribe, account'.

Thus, the message is: merchant supercargo with seafaring vessel with cargo of metal castings from smithy, forge, furnace.

If the hypertext within a circle is a 'quail' an alternative rebus reading is suggested: *bat.t.ai* 'quail' rebus: *bhāṭi* 'kiln, furnace'.

bat.a = a quail, or snipe, coturuix coturnix cot; *bon.d.e bat.a* = a large quail; *dak bat.a* = the painted stripe, *rostraluta benghalensis bengh; gun.d.ri bat.a* = a small type, coloured like a *gun.d.ri* (quail); *ku~k bat.a* = a meḍium-sized type; *khed.ra bat.a* = the smallest of all; *lan.d.ha bat.a* = a small type (Santali) *bat.ai* (Nag.); *bat.er* (Has.); [H. *bat.ai* or *bat.er perdix olivacea*; Sad. *bat.ai*] *coturnix coromandelica*, the black-breasted or rain-quail; two other kinds of quail are called respectigely: *hur.in bat.ai* and *gerea bat.ai* (Mundari *vartaka* = a duck (Samskrtam) *baṭak* = a duck (Gujarati) *vartika_* = quail (RV.); *wuwrc* partridge (Ash.); *barti* = quail, partridge (Kho.); *vat.t.aka_* quail (Pali); *vat.t.aya* (Pkt.); *bat.t.ai* (N.)(CDIAL 11361). varta1 m. ' *turning round', ' livelihood ' lex. [√vr̥t]
S. *vaṭu* m. ' twist '; H. *baṭṭā* m. ' exchange '; -- Si. *vaṭa* ' subsistence, livelihood '(CDIAL 11346) **vartakara* ' making turns (of the quail) '. [Pop. etym. for vártikā -- (*vartīra* -- m. Suśr., °*tira* -- m. lex.)? -- varta -- 1, kará-- 1] Ku. B. *baṭer* ' quail '; Or. *baṭara, baṭara* ' the grey quail '; Mth. H. *baṭer* f. ' quail '; -- →
P. *baṭer*, °*rā* m., °*rī* f., L. *baṭērā* m., S. *baṭero* m.; K.*bāṭuru* m. ' a kind of quail ', *baṭēra* m. ' quail '.)(CDIAL 11350).

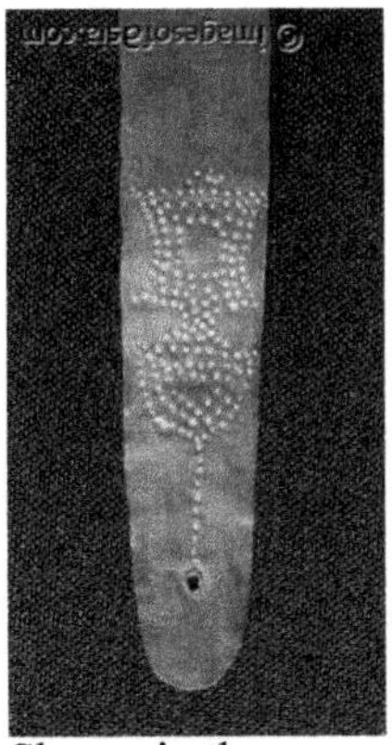

Gold fillet with standard device figure with punctuated design of dots shaping the hieroglyph-hypertext

Shown in the middle is the standard device in the round (ivory) with dotted circles on the bottom register. Top register hypertext: sangada 'lathe' PLUS bottom register hypertext: sangada 'portable furnace' PLUS dotted circles are hieroglyph-multiplexes shown on gold fillets. What do the dotted circles signify? A dotted circle is read in Meluhha (Bharata *sprachbund*) Hieroglyph: dhāī 'strand or wisp of fibre' rebus: dhā̆vaḍ 'iron smelter'.

I have suggested that N. *dhāu* ' ore (esp. of copper) '; Or. *ḍhāu* ' red chalk, red ochre ' (whence *ḍhāuā* ' reddish '; M. *dhāū, dhāv* m.f. ' a partic. soft red stone ' (whence *dhā̆vaḍ* m. ' a caste of iron -- smelters ', *dhāvḍī* ' composed of or relating to iron ') is related to the hieroglyph: strand of rope: S. *dhāī* f. ' wisp of fibres added from time to time to a rope that is being twisted ', L. *dhāī̃* f.(CDIAL 6773) తాడు [tāḍu] or [తాడు *tādu.* [Tel.] n. A cord, thread, string. दामन् n. [दो-मनिन्] 1 A string, thread, fillet, rope. A cross-sectional orthography of a strand is the 'dottedcircle'.

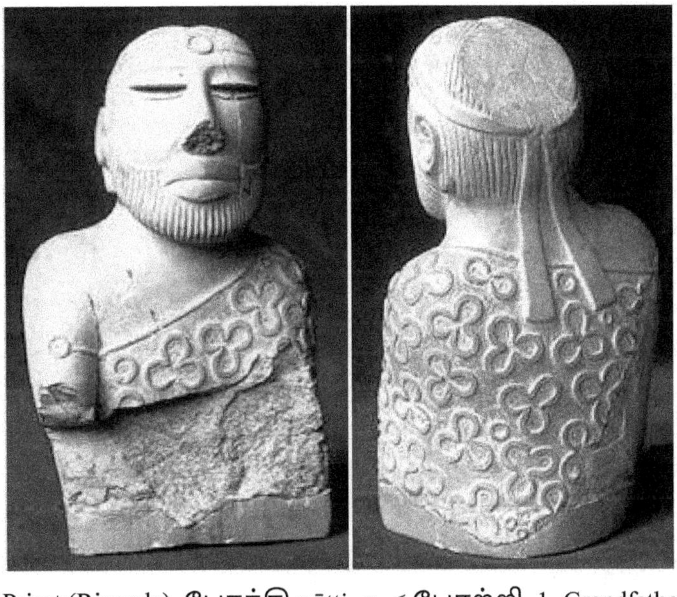

The fillet worn on the forehead and on the right-shoulder signifies one strand; while the trefoil on the shawl signifies three strands. A hieroglyph for two strands is also signified.

The shawl worn by him is: potī f. 'shawl'
Rebus: *Potṛ*, पोतृ 'purifier'

Priest (Rigveda). போத்தி *pōtti* , n. < போற்றி. 1. Grandfather; பாட்டன். Tinn. 2. Brahman temple- priest in Malabar; மலையாளத்தி

லுள்ள கோயிலருச்சகன்.

पोतदार (p. 303) *pōtadāra* m (P) An officer under the native governments. His business was to assay all money paid into the treasury. He was also the village-silversmith. (Marathi) पोतृ [p= 650,1] प/ओतृ or पोतृ, m. " Purifier " , N. of one of the 16 officiating priests at a sacrifice (the assistant of the Brahman ; = यज्ञस्यशोधयिट्रि Saly.) RV. Br. S3rS. Hariv. शोधयितृ [p= 1092,1] *mfn.* (fr. id.) purifying, a purifier L.

The *potti* 'priest' is engaged in an economic activity of the Bronze Age Revolution, purification of metals through smelting process. Hence, *dhā̆vaḍ* 'iron smelter' is *Potṛ,* पोतृ 'purifier *Potti* 'priest', पोतदार (p. 303), in semantic evolution, later a *pōtadāra* m (P) an officer under the native governments who assays all money paid into the treasury. He was also the village-silversmith. (Marathi)

Sanchi sculptural frieze. Two smelters flanking vedi, sacred fire-altar.

Thus, the statue is an Harappa Script hieroglyph signifier of *dhā̆vaḍ* 'iron smelter' is *Potṛ,* पोतृ 'purifier' working with three ferrite ores: *pōḷa* 'zebu' rebus: *pōḷa* 'magnetite'; *bica* 'scorpion' rebus: *bica* 'haematite' *gōṭā* 'round pebble' rebus: *gōṭā* 'laterite'. This explains why all three hieroglyphs are evidenced on the Harappa Script Corpora which are metalwork catalogues.

The purifier, smelter is signified by the semantic determinant *dāuṇī* f. ' gold ornament worn on forehead rebus: *dhāvḍī* 'related to iron smelting work'.

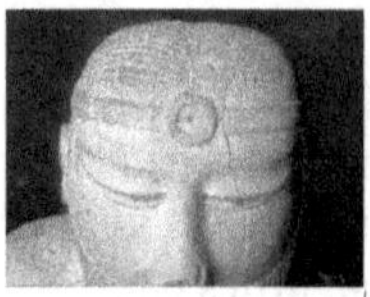

Semantics of single strand of rope and three strands of rope are: 1. Sindhi *dhāī* f. ' wisp of fibres added from time to time to a rope that is being twisted ', Lahnda *dhāī̃* id.; 2. *tridhā́tu* -- ' threefold ' (RigVeda).

 Single strand (one dotted-circle)

 Two strands (pair of dotted-circles)

 Three strands (three dotted-circles as a trefoil)

These orthographic variants provide semantic elucidations for a single: *dhātu, dhāū, dhāv* 'red stone mineral' or two minerals: *dula* 'two' PLUS *dhātu, dhāū, dhāv* 'cast minerals' or *tri- dhātu, -dhāū, -dhāv* 'three minerals' to create metal alloys'. The artisans producing alloys are *dhā̆vaḍ* m. 'a caste of iron -- smelters', *dhāvḍī* 'composed of or relating to iron' (CDIAL 6773).

An evidence for the continuum of the Harappa Script traditions is seen in the Pillar of Boatmen Pilier des Nautes of ca. 1st cent. BCE. On this pillar, Karnonou (Cernunnos) is depicted with stalks as hair-dress horns strung with stoneware bangles (dhamma samjna 'responsibilitiy indicators"). It has been shown that the significance of Karnonou is cognate with kāraṇī 'helmsman, scribe, supercargo' of Harappa Script.[42]

Cernunnos (of Gundestrup Cauldron) is a Celtic inscription written in Greek characters at Montagnac, Hérault (as καρνονου, karnonou, in the dative case)[43]

Panel A of the Gundestrup Cauldron: Cernunnos surrounded by animals, including a ram-headed snake.[44]

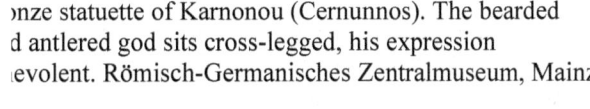

ᵖ ›nze statuette of Karnonou (Cernunnos). The bearded d antlered god sits cross-legged, his expression ıevolent. Römisch-Germanisches Zentralmuseum, Mainz

ıe sound k in Samskrtam is not lost in Celtic, would it be onable to hypothesise a Prakritam (Proto-Indo-Aryan) as cognate: कारणी prime minister of a state, the rgo of a ship -- a representative of the ship's owner on ant ship, responsible for overseeing the cargo and its (Marathi. Molesworth)?

Note: I use the language as Prakritam -- as distinct from संस्कृत [p=1121,1]

mfn. (or सं/अं-स्कृत) put together, constructed, well or completely formed, perfected Lalit. -- as a proto-form of Samskrtam. Surely, some proto-form of Prakritam should have been the *lingua franca* in Bharata *sprachbund* (language union) which may also have been referred to as Meluhha or Mleccha?]

My hypothesis is that the early word expressed in Greek letters ın an inscription at Montagnac, Herault (southern France) as KARNONOU- is cognate with

kāraṇī कारणी the supercargo of a ship (Marathi. Molesworth) and *kāraṇīka* 'helmsman'. The two torcs depicted on Karnonou (Kernunnos) of the Pillar of Boatmen are comparable to the धम्म संज्ञा dhamma saṁjñā 'duty signifiers" described in Harappa Script Corpora on stoneware ceramic bangles.

A similar cultural continuum is seen in the traditions of Vedic culture evidenced in Ancient Germany. *Tvaṣṭṛ, Meluhha* of *Bhāratam Janam* (Rigveda) is Tuisto, divine ancestor of Germanic peoples (Tacitus), legacy of Proto-Indo-Aryan superstrate & Mitanni Treaty.[45]

Chandas, 'prosody' was the diction for the chanting of prayers and philosophical inquiries in Rigveda using *Arya vācas*, also of dasyu (*daha* 'people'), while Mleccha (cognate Meluhha), 'parole' was the spoken form of *dasyu* (*daha* 'people'), *mleccha vācas* of Proto-Indo-Aryan or Prakrits, which constituted the *lingua franca* of the civilization of the early Bronze Age and advances in *cire perdue* (lost-wax) casting methods using metal alloys. *Mleccha vācas* was so-called because of use of ungrammatical forms and incorrect pronunciations which did not meet the grammatical and literary rigour required for sacred sounds of mantras rendered in *chandas*, 'prosody'. It is notable that *mleccha* was called *milakkhu* (as in *milakkhu rajanam*, 'copper coloured' in Pali) cognate with *Meluhha* and meant 'copper'. Another expression was *mleccha mukha* 'copper', more precisely, 'copper ingot (*muh*)' Both *Arya* and *mleccha* were called *Bhāratam janam*, a compound derived from the parole: भरत [*bharata*] n 'a factitious metal compounded of copper, pewter, tin &c.' भरताचें भांडें [bharatācē mbhāṇḍēṃ] n A vessel made of the metal भरत. भरती [*bharatī*] a Composed of the metal भरत. (Marathi) L. *bhāraṇ* ' to spread or bring out from a kiln '(Lahnda)(CDIAL 9463). *baran, bharat* 'mixed alloyś (5 copper, 4 zinc and 1 tin) (Punjabi).

A hypothesis is that the Harappa Script writing is related to smithy-guild. The hypothesis is validated by reading rebus, the *mleccha* [*milakkhu* 'copper' (Pali), cognate *meluhha*] homonym glosses.

The early smith not only invented alloying but also a writing system to create smithy-guild tokens and documentation to authenticate the trade transactions over an extensive area extending from Ropar in Sarasvati River basin, Punjab to Ur in Mesopotamia. The trade imperative was the mother of invention of a writing system; trade necessitated authentication of the smelting, forging, casting, ingot, moulding metalwork using a range of mineral ores. This is the function performeḍ by over 400 pictorial glyphs (so-called signs)) and over 100 pictorial motifs (so-called field symbols) of the Harappa Script writing system which encoded mleccha speech (referred to as *mlecchitavikalpa* by Vatsyayana included in the list of 64 arts in vidyaasamuddesha, objective of vidyaa, education).

1. There are inscriptions on metal tools, evidencing the competence of the smith as a scribe (karṇaka, the most-frequently used glyph, which means: rim of jar).

2. There are over 240 copper tablets inscribed with Harappa Script writing (see appended epigraphs), again evidencing the competence of the smith as a scribe.

3. Over 10 metal tools and metal weapons of Kalibangan, Chanhu-daro, Harappa and Mohenjo-daro are inscribed.

4. Mesopotamian texts evidence trade with Harappa (Meluhha or Sarasvati-Sindhu civilization area) in metals such as gold, silver, copper, tin and alloys such as bronze which are high-value products of the times.

5. The legacy of the Indus mint continues into the historical periods with the vivid use of Indus glyphs on early punch-marked coins (cf. Theobald sign-list of punch-mark signs), Sohgaura copper-plate, Rampurva copper bolt between ca. 6th and 3rd cent. BCE.

6. An average of 5 glyphs (both pictorial motifs and signs) are used on Indus epigraphs. An average of 5 glyphs (both pictorial motifs and signs) are used on punch-marked coins produced by metal-smith-guilds/mints of janapadas (peoples' republics), consistent with the repertoire of early smithy-guilds.

7. The tradition of use of copper tablets to record property/trade transactions and rajashasana continues in India during the historical periods.

8. The cultural continuum is also evidenced by the continued use of cire perdue (lost wax) technique used for making bronze images (as in Mohenjodaro dancing girl) of utsavabera made even today in Swamimalai and other parts of India.

9. Bronze-age iron is evidenced in many archaeological sites and 3 sites of Malhar, Lohardewa and Raja-nal-ki-tila on Ganga basin have shown evidence of iron smelters ca. 1800 BCE. The areas of austro-asiatic speakers is correlated with the areas where early mineral-smelting, iron-smelting have been located.

10. The standards of metrology (particulary weights) are used in the civilization contact area (e.g. Magan, Dilmun) as evidenced by the recent archaeological finds of weights and use of Harappa Script writing system in Persian Gulf states.

11. Three pure tin ingots found in a shipwreck at Haifa contained inscriptions using Harappa Script glyphs. The glyphs have been decoded as tin mineral (*ranku dhatu*).

Identification of underlying Harappa language of Harappa script

The idea of a Linguistic Area is linked with the term *sprachbund* which was introduced in April 1928 in the 1st Intl. Congress of Linguists by Nikolai Trubetzkoy. He made a distinction between Sprachfamilien and Sprachbunde: the distinction in classifying languages was suggested by Trubetzkoy in order to avoid 'missverstandnisse und fehler' (trans. misunderstandings and errors).

The metaphor of a 'family' gets expanded to an area of intense cultural contacts among people resulting in the formation of a *sprachbund.*

What is a *sprachbund*?

"First, the languages of a *sprachbund* show certain similarities in the field of phonetics, morphology, syntax and lexis. Secondly, the languages of a *sprachbund* belong to different families. They are neighbouring geographically, as Trubetzkoy has shown, using the example of the *Balkansprachbund*...In contrast to the genetically defined family of languages (*genus proximum*), the *sprachbund* comprises a typologically defined group of geographically neighbouring languages whose common features are derived from mutual influences (*differentia specifica*)."[46] R. Jakobson published in 1931 three articles about the question of *sprachbund.* He also noted that the phonological system of Serbo-Croatian is a remnant of proto-slavic language features.

“Ancient texts from India confirm this linguistic area.[47] An ancient text called Manusmrti refers to two categories of speakers of languages: Mleccha vaacas and Arya vaacas. This is explained as those who speak ungrammatical, colloquial tongues and those who speak grammatically correct speech. Both *mleccha vaacas* and *arya vaacas* (that is, mleccha speakers and arya speakers) are referred to as the same people: *dasyu* (cognate: *daha*). The choice of the Bharata linguistic area and its substrate dictionary is justified on the following grounds: 1) there is substantial evidence for the essential continuity of the culture of the civilization into historical periods; 2) Akkadian is ruled out as a possible underlying language because a cuneiform cylinder seal showing a seafaring Meluhha merchant (carrying an antelope) required an interpreter, Shu-ilishu, confirming that the Meluhhan's language was not Akkadian; and 3) there is substantial agreement among scholars pointing to the Bharata civilization area as Meluhha mentioned in Mesopotamian texts of 3rd-2nd millennium BCE. That meluhha and mleccha are cognate and that mleccha is attested as a mleccha vaacas (mleccha speech) distinguished from arya vaacas (arya speech) indicates that the linguistic area had a colloquial, ungrammatical mleccha speech and a grammatically correct arya speech. The substrate glosses of the Indian lexicon are thus reasonably assumed to be the glosses of mleccha vaacas, the speech of the artisans who produced the artifacts and the inscribed objects with the writing system. This assumption is further reinforced by the fact that about 80% of archaeological sites of the civilization are found on the banks of Vedic River Sarasvati leading some scholars to rename the Indus Valley civilization as Sarasvati-Sindhu civilization.

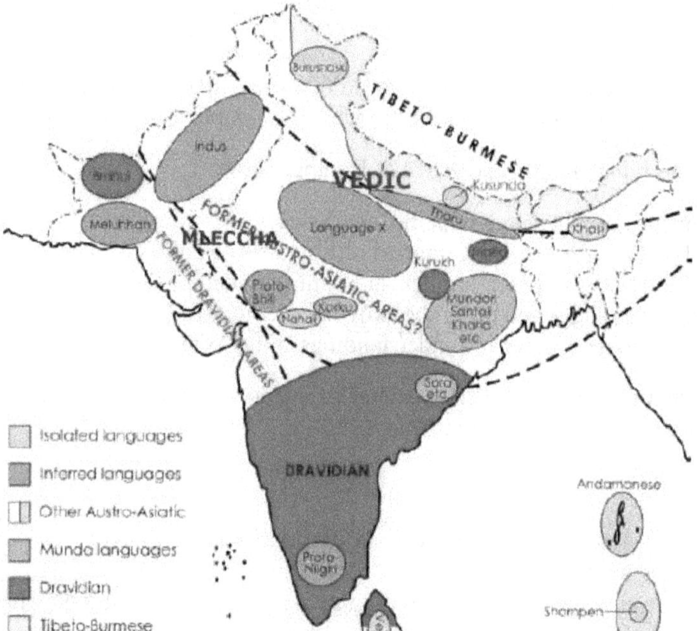

After F. Southworth, 2005 **(added VEDIC)**

Since what Southworth calls ‘*Meluhha’* was referred to as *mleccha* in the Bharata linguistic area and since he omits ‘vedic’, I have added VEDIC & MLECCHA on the adapted map to hypothesise on the sprachbund (map) of Sarasvati civilization ca. 5th millennium BCE, consistent with a Proto-Vedic continuity theory of Bharatiya languages. Linguistic methodological advances have now made it possible to isolate and identify the substratum language of a linguistic area of the civilization. Speakers of meluhha (cognate: mleccha) had contact areas which stretched from Alamgirpur (in Uttar Pradesh, India) to Haifa (port in Israel).

"...a very considerable amount (say some 40%) of the New Indo-Aryan vocabulary is borrowed from Munda, either via Sanskrit (and Prakrit), or via Prakrit alone, or directly from Munda; wide-branched and seemingly native, word-families of South Dravidian are of Proto-Munda origin; in Vedic and later Sanskrit, the words adopted have often been Aryanized, resp. Sanskritized. "In view of the intensive interrelations between Dravidian, Munda and Aryan dating from pre-Vedic times even individual etymological questions will often have to be approached from a Pan-Indic point of view if their study is to be fruitful. It is hoped that this work may be helpful to arrive at this all-embracing view of the Bharata languages, which is the final goal of these studies." (Kuiper, opcit., p. 9)

Emeneau, Masica and Kuiper have shown that language and culture had fused for centuries on the Bharata soil resulting in structural convergence of four language families: Indo-Aryan, Dravidian, Munda and Tibeto-Burman. This concept explains the essential semantic unity (or, *Bharatiyata*) of underlying variegated cultural and linguistic patterns.[48]

The artefacts with the Harappa Script (such as metal tools/weapons, dholavira signboard, copper plates, gold pendant, silver/copper seals/tablets etc.) are *mleccha* smith guild tokens -- a tradition which continues on mints issuing punch-marked coins from ca. 6th cent. BCE.

The justification for the presence of Bharata *sprachbund* words in Ancient Near East and Ancient Far East is provided by an ancient text. All indications point to Vedic people performing their fire worship on the banks of River Sarasvati. The river basin has revealed 80% or over 2000 of the 2600 archaeological sites of Sarasvati-Sindhu (Hindu) civilization. Language, astronomical, and archaeological pointers refer to 7th millennium BCE as the date for the formation of language and activities of Vedic people on this doab of Sarasvati-Sindhu rivers.

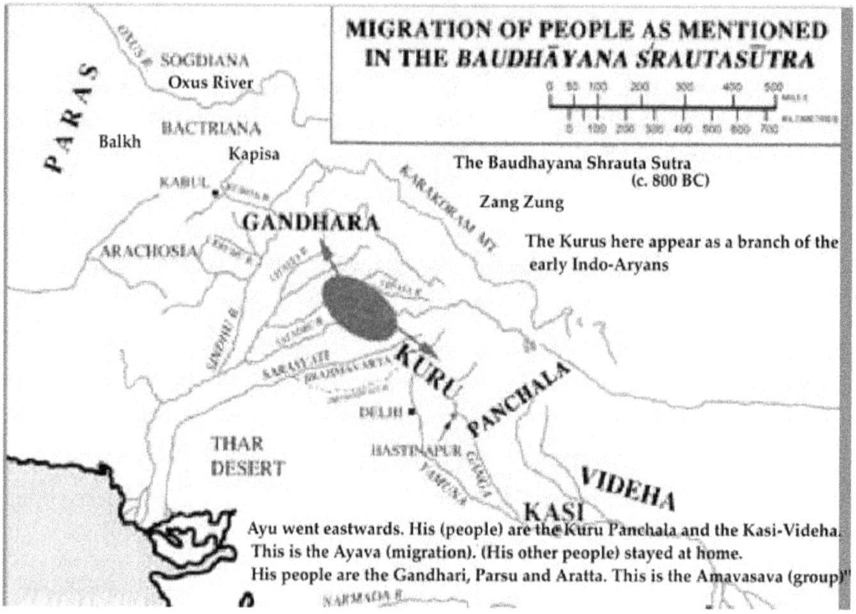

Baudhāyana Śrautasūtra belongs to *Taittiriya Shakha* school of the *Krishna Yajurveda.* This Vedic text has the following statement:

pran Ayuh pravavraja. tasyaite Kuru-Pancalah Kasi-Videha ity. etad Ayavam pravrajam. Pratyan amavasus. Tasyaite Gandharvarayas Parsavo 'ratta ity. Etad Amavasavam. (BSS18.44:397.9 sqq)

Translation: Ayu migrated eastwards. His (people) are the Kuru-Pancalas and the Kasi-Videhas. This is the Ayava (migration). Amavasu migrated westwards. His (people) are the Ghandhari, Parsu and Aratta. This is the Amavasu (migration).

This Sutra provides evidence for two historical narratives: 1. Both Ayu and Amavasu were indigenous Vedic people located on the Sarasvati-Sindhu river basins and hence, provides ZERO evidence for any mythical Aryan Invasion/Migration theory; 2. the movements of people away from Kurukshetra on the banks of River Sarasvati attest to the formation of the Bharata *sprachbund* in Gangetic basin, Gujarat and beyond including areas west of River Sindhu (Indus).

The memory recorded in the *Baudhāyana Śrautasūtra* refers to an ancient Itihasa of *Bhāratam Janam*, in the context of narratives related to philosophers of fire, worshippers of fire. That the legend is mentioned as a received memory in Rigveda points to the possibility of this narrative related to Ayu and Amavasu being dated earlier than 7th millennium BCE. The passage is part of a dialogue between Pururava and Urvasi. Their sons were Ayu and Amavasu who were associated with two twin groups formed as they wandered forth: Ayava (eastern) kin group and Amavasava (western) kin group.

Yes, there were migrations but the text in *Baudhāyana Śrautasūtra* emphatically declares the directions of earlier migrations of Ayu and Amavasu who are memories from events in bygone millennia, perhaps earlier to the 7th millennium BCE which is the date posited for Rigveda by other evidences such as the archaeologically attested pit-dwellings of Bhirrana, a site which is dated to 7th millennium BCE. Nicholas Kazanas a scholar in Indo-European studies dates the bulk of Rigveda to the fourth millennium BCE based on hiseorical linguistic analyses.[49] After affirming that Indo-Aryans were indigenous to India from at least the 7th millennium BCE, Kazanas also notes that Vedic is much older than any other IE language and suggests a fresh start to IE studies and to studies on Proto-Indo-European mother tongue. In all his studies spanning many IE branches, comparing evidences from the linguistic, literary, anthropological and archaeological fields (and from Genetics), Vedic inheritance emerges as the oldest of all IE traditions, older than even the Near Eastern cultures; the bulk of the Rgveda hymns appear to have been composed with Indo-Aryans residing in North-West India (and Pakistan) since about 5000 BCE.

BB Lal's work[50] notes that the Rigveda (10.75, 5-6) refers to Vedic people occupying the entire territory from the Indus on the west to the upper reaches of the Ganga-Yamuna in the east and only one civilization that existed in the same region: Harappa Civilization. Lal concludes that the Civilization and Vedas are but two faces of the same coin (pp.122-23) and adds that evidence from Kunal and Bhirrana (pp. 54-55) trace the roots of the civilization to the 6th-5th millennia BCE, indicating that Harappas were the 'sons of the soil' and not aliens. Thus, according to Lal, the Vedic people who were themselves the Harappas, were indigenous and neither 'invaders" nor 'immigrants'.

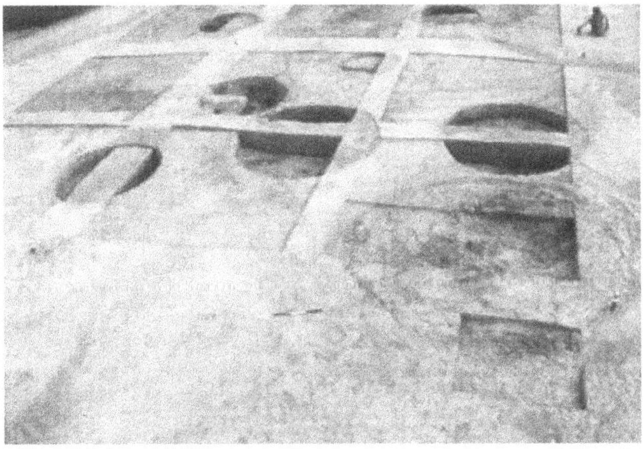

After Fig. 6.1 Bhirrana: Dwelling-pits, Stage I "These pits measured from 2.3 m to 3.4 m in diameter and from 34 cm to 58 cm in depth...The walls were plastered with mud and the same treatment was also given to the floor. The excavators have stated that they did not come across any holes along the edges of these pits, which could have carried posts to support a peripheral wall. However, in one of the pits they did find a chunk of clay bearing reed-impressions, which has suggested to them that, in all probability, there was some kind of covering of wattle-and-daub...the inhabitants had well stepped into 'Copper Age', as clearly estabished by the occurrence in these strata of a bangle and an arrowhead of copper. In fact, in one of the pits fragments of crucibles with specks of molten copper still sticking to them have also been found indicating local manufacturing activity...there occurred beads of semi-precious stones such as agate, carnelian, jasper and even lapis lazuli, the last-named material having had its source far away in the west."[51]

What language did the Harappa (Sarasvati-Sindhu) civilization people speak? To attempt an answer to this question, with all humility, I add a footnote that scholars of historical linguists accept (pace FBJ Kuiper, MB Emeneau, Colin Masica, Southworth) that a language union (linguistic area) existed, called Bharata *sprachbund.* Georges Pinault pointed to the concordance between Vedic and Tocharian: *amśu ~~ ancu*, 'iron' (Tocharian). Amśu is a synonym for Soma (as Louis Renou noted that Rigveda is present *in nuce*, 'nutshell' in the themes related to Soma). The direction of borrowing *amśu ~~ ancu* is a matter to be studied further in historical linguistic studies, but is relatable to a date prior to 1800 BCE, the date of the Tarim mummies in Tushara (Tocharian). Tushara are mleccha (meluhha)[52]. This work demonstrates that Meluhha, parole of the Vedic people was a Proto-Indo-Aryan language.

A remarkable archaeological evidence validates the Vedic culture and provides an indication of the spoken language of the people who invented and used Harappa Script. The evidence is from Binjor (near Anupgarh) in an archaeological site called 4MSR. At this site, agni kunda with aSTAsri Yūpa was found evidencing the performance of a Soma Yaga. Vajapeya is one of 7 samstha (profession) for processing/smelting soma (a mineral, NOT a herbal): सोमः [सू-मन् Uṇ.1.139]-संस्था a form of the Soma-sacrifice; (these are seven:- अग्निष्टोम, अत्यग्निष्टोम, उक्थ, षोढशी, अतिरात्र, आप्तोर्याम and वाजपेय). The Vajapeya performed in Binjor and Kalibangan should have been related to the *Soma-samstha*: सोमः संस्था specified as वाजपेय with the shape of the *Yūpa* with eight- or four-angles. For every *Soma Yaga* such a Yūpa is installed. 19 such Yūpas have been found in Rajasthan, Allahabad, Mathura and East Borneo.[53] At the Vājapeya, the *yūpa* is eight-angled (as in Binjor), corresponding to the eight quarters (Sat.Br. V.2.1.5 *aṣṭāśrir yūpo bhavati*) अश्रि [p= 114,2] f. the sharp side of anything , corner , angle (of a room or house) , edge (of a sword) S3Br. Ka1tyS3r.often ifc. e.g. अष्टा*श्रि , त्रिर्-/अश्रि , च्/अतुर्-श्रि , शता*श्रि q.v. (cf. अश्र) ;([cf. Lat. acies , acer ; Lith. assmu3]). "The first *Yūpa* inscription of Mulavarman (in East Borneo) was erected to commemorate a *bahu-suvarnaka* sacrifice,'that on which gold is spent (used?) in profusion'."[54] I suggest that *bahu-suvarNaka* refers to the many wealth-giving metals worked in a *Soma Yaga.*

Binjor. The fire altar, with a yasti made of an octagonal brick. Photo: Subhash Chandel, ASI

Binjor seal

Binjor (4MSR) seal decipherment.

Binjor Seal Text of Inscription

Fish + scales, *aya ãs (amśu)* 'metallic stalks of stone ore'. Vikalpa: *badhoṛ* 'a species of fish with many bones' (Santali) Rebus: *baḍhoe* 'a carpenter, worker in wood'; *badhoria* 'expert in working in wood'(Santali) *khambhaṛā* 'fish fin' rebus: *kammaTa* 'mint, coiner, coinage'

gaṇḍa 'four' Rebus: *khaṇḍa* 'metal implements. Together with cognate ancu 'iron' the message is: native metal implements mint

Thus, the hieroglyph multiplex reads: *aya ancu khaṇḍa kammaṭa* 'metallic iron alloy implements, mint, coiner, coinage'.

koḍi 'flag' (Ta.)(DEDR 2049). Rebus 1: *koḍ* 'workshop' (Kuwi) Rebus 2: *khŏḍ* m. 'pit', *khöḍü f.* 'small pit' (Kashmiri. CDIAL 3947)

The bird hieroglyph: *karaḍa* करण्ड m. a sort of duck L. కారండవము (p. 274) [*kāraṇḍavamu*] *kāraṇḍavamu.* [Skt.] n. A sort of duck. (Telugu) *karaṭa*1 m. ' crow ' BhP., °aka -- m. lex. [Cf. *karaṭu -- , karkaṭu* -- m. ' Numidian crane ', *karēṭu -- , °ēṭavya -- , °ēḍuka* -- m. lex., *karaṇḍa*2 -- m. ' duck ' lex: see *kāraṇḍava* --]Pk. *karaḍa* -- m. ' crow ', *°ḍā* -- f. ' a partic. kind of bird '; S. *karaṛa -- ḍhī̃gu* m. ' a very large aquatic bird '; L. *karṛā* m., °ṛī f. ' the common teal' (CDIAL 2787) Rebus: *karaḍā* 'hard alloy'

Thus, the text of Harappa Script inscription on the Binjor Seal reads: 'metallic iron alloy implements mint, hard alloy workshop' PLUS the hieroglyphs of one-horned young bull PLUS standard device in front read rebus:

kõda 'young bull, bull-calf' rebus: *kõdā* 'to turn in a lathe'; *kōnda* 'engraver, lapidary'; *kundār* 'turner'.

Hieroglyph: *sãghāṛɔ* 'lathe' (Gujarati) Rebus: *sangara* 'proclamation. सं-ग्रह *saṁgraha, samgaha* 'a guardian , ruler , manager , arranger' R. BhP.

Together, the message of the Binjor Seal with inscribed text is a proclamation, 'a metalwork catalogue (of) manager, turner of metallic iron alloy implements, hard alloy workshop'

This is a clear, unambiguous evidence of the spoken language (Mleccha or proto-Prakritam of Bharata *sprachbund*) which is a continuum of the Vedic culture exemplified by chandas of 10,800 Rigveda rica-s.

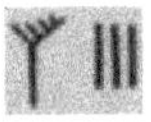

8024

Kalibangan cylinder seal impression.Pict-104 Composition: A tree; a person with a composite body of a human (female?) in the upper half and body of a tiger in the lower half, having horns, and a trident-like head-dress, facing a group of three persons consisting of a woman (?) in the middle flanked by two men on either side throwing a spear at each other (fencing?) over her head. *kuṭi* 'tree' *kuṭhi* 'smelter' tagaraka 'tabernae montana' rebus: tagara 'tin' *kolom* 'three' rebus: *kolimi* 'smithy, forge' *dhatu* 'scarf' rebus: *dhatu* 'mineral, ore' *kola* 'woman' *kola* 'tiger' rebus: *kol* 'furnace, forge' *kol* 'metal, working in iron'. Headdress of the woman: kūṭī = bunch of twigs (Skt.)The bunch of twigs = *kūḍī, kūṭī* (Samskrtam) *kūḍī* (also written as kūṭī in manuscripts).[55] Rebus: *kuṭhi* 'smelting furnace'; koṭe 'forged metal' (Santali) *karat.i, karut.i, kerut.i* fencing, school or gymnasium where wrestling and fencing are taught (Ta.); *garad.i, garud.i* fencing school (Ka.); *garad.i, garod.i (Tu.); garid.i, garid.i_* id., fencing (Te.)(DEDR 1262). Rebus 1: करडा [*karaḍā*] Hard from alloy--iron, silver &c. Rebus 2: *khara_di_* = turner (Gujarati) Thus, the inscription reads: Tin smelter, iron smelter, furnace, forge, smithy PLUS hard metal alloy. The narrative of fencers with a woman in between: *kola* 'woman' rebus: *kola*, 'metal' PLUS *karaḍā* 'hard alloy' – thus, hard metal alloy.

Knowledge discovery from database mining is in five unique facets of cultural continuum from ca. 7th millennium BCE:

1. *kolc.l* 'smithy, forgc' is *kole.l* 'temple'. The *adhyatmika* significance attached to a workplace of artisans is governed by the *waltenschauung* of performance of one's responsibilities for advancing a common cause, *dharma-dhamma* of Vedic culture;

2. Harappa Script as a knowledge system creates data archives --documented records of metallurgical technical advances matching the Bronze Age Revolution exemplified by *cire perdue* metal castings, inventions and uses of metal alloys to create wealth; There are indications that seal impressions were created on cargo shipments/packages to validate the contents. Miniature tablets with Harappa Script were used ro record metal work-in-process of metal pots, implements, weapons and to subsequently copy & incorporate the documented tablet information on to seals used to authenticate metalwork cargo.

3. Incipient state formation with corporate forms of metalwork-lapidary guilds as social organizations with assigned responsibilities to guild-corporate functionaries, to cope with wealth creation and trade exchanges by seafaring artisan and merchants across a Maritime Tin Route from Hanoi to Haifa;

4. Databases – orthographic and lexical – validate the Bharata *sprachbund* (language union) which explains the formation and evolution of over 25 ancient languages of *Bhāratam Janam* 'metalcaster folk'.

5. Over 7000 Harappa Script inscriptions (*mlecchita vikalpa* or Meluhha ciper) in *parole* (Meluhha vernacular) of the Harappa civilization match and constitute a continuum from Vedic culture, from the 10,800 rica-s of Rigveda in *langue* (Chandas prosody) of pre-Bronze Age periods.

Some examples of Harappa Script hieroglyphs with rebus readings of metalwork, which recur on Ancient Near and Ancient Bharata seals of the Bronze Age

The following is lexis (vocabulary) from Bharata *spcachbund* matching words which signify hieroglyphs and homonyms which are catalogues of metalwork:

bull-man, bull *ḍangar* 'bull' read rebus *ḍhangar* 'blacksmith'; *ṭagara* 'ram' Rebus: *damgar* 'merchant' (Akkadian) *ṭhakkura,* 'idol', *ṭhākur* ' blacksmith ', *ṭhākur* m. 'master'. *ḍhangar* 'blacksmith'.
tiger *kol* 'tiger' Rebus: *kol* 'working in iron' 'furnace, forge'

kick *kolsa* 'to kick' Rebus: *kol* working in iron, blacksmith *kol* 'furnace, forge'
lion *arye* 'lion' *āra* 'brass
aquatic bird *karaḍa* 'aquatic bird, duck' Rebus: *karaḍa* 'hard alloy'
eagle *eraka* 'eagle' Rebus: *erako* 'moltencast copper
buffalo கண்டி *kaṇṭi* , n. 1. Buffalo bull Rebus: Pk. *gaḍa* -- n. 'large stone'? (CDIAL 3969) ranga 'buffalo' rebus: rango 'pewter, tin'
six hair-curls *āra* 'six curls' Rebus: *āra* 'brass
face *mũh* 'face' Rebus: *mũh* 'ingot'.
stag *karuman* 'stag' k*armara* 'artisan'
antelope *melh* 'goat' Rebus: *milakkhu* 'copper'
calf *khoṇḍ* 'young bull-calf' Rebus *khuṇḍ* '(metal) turner'.
scorpion *bica* 'scorpion' (Assamese) Rebus: *bica* 'stone ore, haematite'
stalk *daṭhi, daṭi* 'stalks of certain plants Rebus: *dhatu* 'mineral.

kandə Rebus: *khaṇḍa.* A portion of the front hall, in a temple khāṇḍa 'implements'

kāṇḍa काण्डः m. the stalk or stem of a reed. Rebus: *kāṇḍa* 'tools, pots and pans and metal-ware'.

kāṇḍa काण्डः m. stem of a reed. Rebus: *kāṇḍa* 'tools, pots and pans and metal-ware'
twig *kūdī* 'twig' Rebus: *kuṭhi* 'smelter'
fish *ayo* 'fish' Rebus: a*yo, ayas* 'metal'.
overflowing pot lo 'pot to overflow' *kāṇḍa* 'water'. Rebus: लोखंड *lokhaṇḍ* Iron tools, vessels, or articles in general.
spear మేడెము [*mēḍemu*] or మేడియము *mēḍemu.* [Tel.] n. A spear or dagger. Rebus: *meḍ* 'iron'.
ring, bracelet *kaḍum* a bracelet, a ring (G.) Rebus: *kaḍiyo* [Hem. Des. *kaḍaio* = Skt. sthapati a mason] a bricklayer; a mason; *kAru*'wristlets,bracelets'rebus: khAr 'blacksmith'

kAru ‘pincers’ rebus: *khAr* ‘blacksmith’
star मेढ [*mēḍha*] The polar star (Marathi). [cf.The eight-pointed star Rebus: *meḍ* 'iron' (Mundari. Remo.)
safflower *karaḍa* -- m. ‘safflower’ Rebus: करडा [*karaḍā*] Hard from alloy--iron, silver &c. (Marathi)
twig *kūdī* ‘twig’ Rebus: *kuṭhi* ‘smelter’
frond (of palm), palm *tamar*, ‘palm tree, date palm’ Rebus: *tam(b)ra*, ‘copper’ (Prakrit)

dAla ‘leaf,sprig’ rebus: *dhAla* ‘ingot’
tree *kuṭhāru* 'tree' Rebus: *kuṭhāru* ‘armourer or weapons maker’(metal-worker)
ram, ibex, markhor 1. ram मेंढा [*mēṇḍhā*] m (मेष S through H) A male sheep, a ram or tup.(Marathi) *meḍ* 'iron' (Mundari. Remo.)
goat *melh* 'goat' Rebus: *milakkhu* 'copper'
knot (twist) *meḍ*, ‘knot, curl’ Rebus: 'iron'
reed, scarf *dhaṭu* m. (also *dhaṭhu*) m. ‘scarf’ (WPah.) (CDIAL 6707) Rebus: *dhatu* ‘minerals’ (Santali); *dhātu* ‘mineral’ (Pali) mountain डोंगर [ḍōṅgara] m A hill. डोंगरकणगर or डोंगरकंगर [*ḍōṅgarakaṇagara or ḍōṅgarakaṅgara*] m (डोंगर & कणगर form of redup.) Hill and mountain; hills comprehensively or indefinitely. डोंगरकोळी [*ḍōṅgarakōḷī*] m A caste of hill people or an individual of it. (Marathi) *ḍāngā* = hill, dry upland (B.); *ḍā̃g* mountain-ridge (H.)(CDIAL 5476). Rebus: *dhangar* ‘blacksmith’ (Maithili) *dhokra* 'cire perdue metallurgist'
wing *eraka* 'wing' *eṟaka, ṟekka, rekka, neṟaka, neṟi* ‘wing’ (Telugu)(DEDR 2591). Rebus: *erako* 'moltencast copper'.
snake *nāga* 'snake' *nāga* 'lead'

sā̃gāḍa 'lathe, portable brazier’ rebus: *sangar* ‘fortification, *sā̃gāḍa ‘catamaran’*
frame of building *sā̃gāḍā* m. ‘ frame of a building ’ (M.)(CDIAL 12859) Rebus: *sangāth* संगाठ् । सामग्री m. (sg. dat. *sangāṭas* संगाटस्), a collection (of implements, tools, materials, for any object), apparatus, furniture, a collection of the things wanted on a journey, luggage (Kashmiri) *jangaḍ* 'entrustment note' (Gujarati) सं-ग्रह *saṁgraha* ‘a guardian , ruler , manager , arranger’ R. BhP.
monkey *kuṭhāru* = a monkey (Sanskrit) Rebus: *kuṭhāru* ‘armourer or weapons maker’(metal-worker), also an inscriber or writer.
foot . *khuṭo* ‘ leg, foot ’ Rebus: *khũṭ* ‘community, guild’ (Santali)
penance kamadha ‘penance’ Archer kamAThiyo ‘archer’

copulation (mating) *kamḍa, khamḍa* 'copulation' (Santali) Rebus: *kampaṭṭa* ‘mint, coiner’
adultery *ṛanku, ranku* = fornication, adultery (Telugu) *ranku* 'tin'

goTa ‘stone’ rebus: *goTa* ‘laterite ore’ *khōṭaa ‘ingot’*

dhal ‘slant’ rebus: *dhALa* ‘ingot’

maraka ‘peacock’ rebus: *marakaka loha* ‘special type of copper’ मारक *loha* 'a kind of calcining metal' (Samskritam)

arye ‘lion’ rebus: *Ara* ‘brass’

kuranga ‘antelope’ (MBh.) *kulaṅgá* -- MaitrS., *kuluṅgá* -- TS.Pa. *kuraṅga* -- , *kuruṅga* -- m., Pk. *kuraṁga* -- m., P. *kuraṅg* m., OG. *karaṁgī* f.,

G. *kurãg* m., °*gī*, °*gṇī* f.; Si. *kuruňga* ' antelope ', *kiraňgu* ' the elk Rusa aristotelis ' (CDIAL 3320) rebus: *kuraga* 'anvil, apparatus of goldsmith'.

Early intimations of state formation with corporate forms of guild organizations

*_śrēṇiḥ_*श्रेणि [p=1102,2] is attested in Rigveda: *f.* (_L._also m. ; according to Un2._iv , 51 , fr. √ श्रि ; connected with श्रेटी above) a line , row , range , series , succession , troop , flock , multitude , number RV._&c. (Monier-Williams). The semantics expand in corporate forms of guild organizations to signify: a company of artisans following the same business, a guild or association of traders dealing in the same articles Mn._MBh._&c. This fom of organization is exemplified in Rigveda Sukta 10.125 which explains the role of राष्ट्री the State personified as *Vāgdevi, devatā ātmā*.अहं राष्ट्री संगमनी वसूनां says *Vāgdevi, devatā ātmā*, proclaiming her sovereignty as gatherer, mover of treasures. Following this Rigveda proclamation dated to many (indeterminate) millennia prior to the Bronze Age civilizational advances, the gathering and exchanges of treasures are the dominant feature of the Bronze Age Revolution from ca. 5th millennium BCE.

(**8**) **125** (म.**10**, अनु.**10**)

ऋषिः वाक् आम्भृणी	छन्दः त्रिष्टुप् **1,3-8**, जगती **2**	देवता आत्मा

अहं रुद्रेभिर्वसुभिश्चराम्यहमादित्यैरुत विश्वदेवैः ।
अहं मित्रावरुणोभा बिभर्म्यहमिन्द्राग्नी अहमश्विनोभा ॥ **1** ॥
अहं सोममाहनसं बिभर्म्यहं त्वष्टारमुत पूषणं भगम् ।
अहं दधामि द्रविणं हविष्मते सुप्राव्ये यजमानाय सुन्वते ॥ **2** ॥
अहं राष्ट्री संगमनी वसूनां चिकितुषी प्रथमा यज्ञियानाम् ।
तां मा देवा व्यदधुः पुरुत्रा भूरिस्थात्रां भूर्यावेशयन्तीम् ॥ **3** ॥
मया सो अन्नमत्ति यो विपश्यति यः प्राणिति य ईं शृणोत्युक्तम् ।
अमन्तवो मां त उप क्षियन्ति श्रुधि श्रुत श्रद्धिवं ते वदामि ॥ **4** ॥
अहमेव स्वयमिदं वदामि जुष्टं देवेभिरुत मानुषेभिः ।
यं कामये तंतमुग्रं कृणोमि तं ब्रह्माणं तमृषिं तं सुमेधाम् ॥ **5** ॥
अहं रुद्राय धनुरा तनोमि ब्रह्मद्विषे शरवे हन्तवा उ ।
अहं जनाय समदं कृणोम्यहं द्यावापृथिवी आ विवेश ॥ **6** ॥
अहं सुवे पितरमस्य मूर्धन्मम योनिरप्स्वन्तः समुद्रे ।
ततो वि तिष्ठे भुवनानु विश्वोतामूं द्यां वर्ष्मणोप स्पृशामि ॥ **7** ॥
अहमेव वातइव प्र वाम्यारभमाणा भुवनानि विश्वा ।
परो दिवा पर एना पृथिव्यैतावती महिना सं बभूव ॥ **8** ॥

RV 10.125 Griffith translation:

1. I TRAVEL with the Rudras and the Vasus, with the Adityas and All-Gods I wander. I hold aloft both Varuna and Mitra, Indra and Agni, and the Pair of Asvins. 2 I cherish and sustain high-swelling Soma, and Tvastar I support, Pusan, and Bhaga. I load with wealth the zealous sdcrificer who pours the juice and offers his oblation 3 I am the Queen, the gatherer-up of treasures, most thoughtful, first of those who merit worship. Thus Gods have stablished me in many places with many homes to enter and abide in. 4 Through me alone all eat the food that feeds them, each man who sees, brewhes, hears the word outspoken They know it not, but yet they dwell beside me.

Hear, one and all, the truth as I declare it. 5 1, verily, myself announce and utter the word that Gods and men alike shall welcome. I make the man I love exceeding mighty, make him a sage, a Rsi, and a Brahman. 6 I bend the bow for Rudra that his arrow may strike and slay the hater of devotion. I rouse and order battle for the people, and I have penetrated Earth and Heaven. 7 On the world's summit I bring forth the Father: my home is in the waters, in the ocean. Thence I extend o'er all existing creatures, and touch even yonder heaven with my forehead. 8 I breathe a strong breath like the wind and tempest, the while I hold together all existence. Beyond this wide earth and beyond the heavens I have become so mighty in my grandeur.

The spoken form of the language of Vedic people was *mleccha* (cognate Meluhha) and their writing system was *mlecchita vikalpa*, 'Meluhha cipher' (attested in a 6th cent. BCE work by Vatsyayana on *Vidya Samuddes'a*) which means 'Mleccha (Meluhha) cipher' and is listed as one of 64 arts taught to youth together with *des'abhāṣājnānam* and *akṣara muṣṭika kathanam*. Patanjali elaborates on *mleccha* as a dialect characterized by mispronunciations and ungrammatical utterances. There is a lot of textual data on *parole*, 'spoken form, vernacular' as distinct from *language* 'grammatically correct language'-- both *mleccha* and *ārya* as *dasyu* (cf. cognate OIr. *Daha* 'people') and as *dwīpavāsinah* 'island dwellers.

The writing system is attested on ca. 7000 inscriptions on Harappa Script Corpora, almost all of which constitute metalwork catalogues by *Bhāratam Janam*, 'metalcaster folk'. This compound *Bhāratam Janam* is attested by Viśvāmitra in Rigveda (RV 3.53.12)

A significant aspect of Harappa Script during the Bronze Age Revolution is the presence of many clearly identifiable hieroglyphs of the Script in many ancient sites, in many parts of Eurasisa – in Ancient Near East and in Ancient Far East. This points to the extensive nature of trade contacts of Meluhhas necessitated by the surplus production of bronze artifacts available for trade exchanges and the civilizational imperative explorations for new mineral resources to sustain and enhance the impact of the Bronze Age Revolution. Closely connected to the industrial nature of metalwork is the emergence of organized workshops and trade/professional organizations called guilds, śreni with the newly acquired knowledge of metallurgical techniques such as smelting, furnace blasting, smithy and forge to create metal tools, implements, weapons and artistic sculptural artifacts such as the dancing girl made by cire perdue (lost-wax) technique.

By the 5th millennium BCE, armlets of copper plus added lead, were cast at Mehergarh by lost-wax process.[56]

It is suggested that a narrative based on archaeo-metallurgical researchers documenting lost-wax casting techniques and bronze drum artifacts from Dong Son (Hanoi) to Nahal Mishmar (Haifa) along the Maritime Tin Route is likely to be a riveting narrative. The narrative will certainly herald the contributions made by artisans of the Bronze Age reinforced by the metalwork catalogues of Harappa Script Corpora which have documented the technological splendour.

This splendour will be matched by utsava bera which are taken in processions all over *Bhāratam*, that is India, even today, during days of temple festivities attesting the abiding nature of the awe-inspiring cire perdue bronze or brass metal castings.[57]

The organizations of guilds of the Bronze Age also necessitated the invention of writing systems to cope with the imperative of trade exchanges. Three writing systems were invented between 3300 to 3100 BCE: Harappa Script, Egyptian Hieroglyphs, Cuneiform Writing and are directly related to two phenomena: evolution and expansion of Tin-Bronze cultures and incipient state formation through guilds for organized production workshops.

Bronze Age was a revolution -- a quantum leap from the earlier chalcolithic phase and so was the writing system necessitated by this revolution which resulted in extensive contacts among cultures in Ancient Far East and Ancient Near East. The metal products of usage value (such as metal alloy *cire perdue* castings, metal alloy tools, implements, weapons, pots and pans) were produced in excess of the needs of local consumption and were available for trade exchanges and barter by seafaring merchants and trade caravans. A writing system as data archiving was an imperative to facilitate such trade transactions by guilds.

Guilds श्रेणि: *śrēṇiḥ* were early corporate forms of the 4th-3rd millennium BCE.

Incipient state formation is exemplified in a Rigveda *sukta* (also called Devi or *vāgdevi suktam*), where, in a soliloquy, *vāk*, 'speech' refers to herself and her role as: राष्ट्री संगमनी वसूनाम् 'sovereign moving wealth'.

Writing systems provided the vehicles for transmission of knowledge gained in Tin-Bronze Age metallurgical techniques and production of metal artifacts of utilitarian value for emerging civilizations and urban settlements of people. Many cultural groups were involved in the interactions along the Maritime Tin Route from Hanoi to Haifa. The extensive and long-distance exchanges of Bronze Age artifacts are exemplified by the Uluburun, Gelidonya, Haifa shipwrecks which revealed large cargo of copper, tin, bronze artifacts. Discovery of over 200 Dong Son/Karen bronze drums in Ancient Far East also points to the emergence of Bronze Age cultures in Ancient Far East coterminous with the emergence of such cultures in Ancient Near East dated to ca. 4th millennium BCE (cf. evidence of *cire perdue* techniques gleaned by archaeometallurgical investigations of Nahal Mishmar artifacts, inscribed Dong Son/Karen bronze drums, metal sculptures in the round). In the *cire perdue* method, duplicate metal sculpture (often silver, gold, brass or bronze) is cast from an original sculpture. The earliest evidence is from Cave of the Treasure (Nahal Mishmar) hoard in southern Israel, and which belongs to the Pre-Bronze Age, Chalcolithic period (4500–3500 BCE).

***kole.l* signifies 'smithy, forge', the same word *kole.l* also signifies 'temple' (Kota)**

kol sangaḍi 'fortified place for metal (& ore stone) workers. *sangar* S سنګر *r*, sm. (2nd) A breastwork of stones, etc., erected to close a pass or road; lines, entrenchments. Pl. سنګرونه*sangarūnah*. See باره (Pashto). Annex A details the Harappa Script inscription found at the temple area of Mohenjo-daro which is a smithy, forge.

This *sangaḍi* 'fortified place' is signified by a standard device shown in front of one-horned young bull. The standard is: *sangaḍa*, 'lathe-brazier' rebus: *sangar* 'fortification'. सं-ग्रह *saṁgraha* 'a guardian , ruler , manager , arranger' R. BhP.

kol 'metal', 'working in iron' is semantically expanded to *kole.l* 'smithy, forge'. The artisan's place of work, of life-activity, *kole.l* is a temple. The *weltanschauung* which makes *Bhāratam Janam* 'metalcaster folk' treat the workplace in a metals workshop (smithy, forge) as a temple. This is the *raison d'etre* for the *utsava bera* 'procession idols' from a temple carried on festive days in villages of ancient *Bhāratam*, India. *kole.l* 'smithy, forge' as *kole.l* 'temple' is complemented by the dance-step as a hieroglyph (evidence Chandi Sukuh dance step of *Ganesa* -- *meḍ* 'dance step' rebus: *meḍ* 'iron'). The dance-step is also seen in the cosmic dance of *Siva* as *Nataraja* when the aniconic skambha or *Yūpa* signified on *Soma samsthA soma yAga* is signified on human form.

The cosmic dance is a metaphor to signify the phenomenon of mere earth and stone getting transformeḍ into wealth-giving metals out of a smelter meḍiated by the *skambha*, the cosmic pillar of light and fire. The चषाल: *caṣāla* atop the *skambha* or *Yūpa* is the *jaTa* of *godhuma*, wheat chaff. The fumes from चषाल: caṣāla in the burning fire of the smelter or furnace infuse into the ores to carburize the minerals to create hard metal and metal alloys which get transformeḍ into implements, pots and pans and weapons of utility to the society in an evolving Bronze Age Revolution. Annex K details the structure, form, function and significance of *caṣālḥ* चषाल: on *Yūpa* in a *yajna* and carburization-cum-pyrolysis.

Data mining techniques are appliedto ancient artifacts, of ca. 3rd millennium BCE, demonstrated by hieroglyphic cipher (phonetic picture writing) signified on 250 deciphered metal tablets, tools, gold pendant, gold fillets of Harappa (Sarasvati-Sindhu) Civilization. All these inscriptions of the Harappa Script Corpora are *catalogus catalogorum* of metalwork -- a veritable data mine for advances in computational and data encryption processes relatable to knowledge discovery of archaeo-metallurgical inventions and processes and of civilizational transformations in social organizations.

Four significant features of the discovery sites of Harappa Script Corpora of inscriptions may be outlined:

1. The extensive area from which inscriptions of Harappa Script Corpora have been found which covered sites of Shortugai (Bactria) in the North to Daimabad (Narmada river, southern Bhārat), Tepe Gawra in the Northwest (Ancient Near East) beyond the Caspian Sea to Alamgirpur in Yamuna Basin.

2. In all the inscriptions, there is consistent use of the same hieroglyphs (subject, of course, stylistic vriations in writing or inscribing styles) which are composed of 'pictorial motifś (sun's rays, tiger, elephant, buffalo, zebu, goat, composite animals with animal components as hypertexts relatable rebus to metalwork) and 'pictographs' (called 'signs' such as rim of jar, rimless-widemouthed pot, fish, fish-fin, arrow, standing person with spread legs, water-carrier). Such remarkable consistency in the use of hieroglyphs from a repertoire of about 100+ 'pictorial motifs and 500+ 'pictographs' shows that some mechanisms existed to transmit the main principles of the writing system to all the lapidaries who prepared the inscriptions which constitute the Harappa Script Corpora which now contains over 7000 inscriptions (about 6000 from India and Pakistan, about 1000 from Persian Gulf sites and scores from Ancient Near East sites). There are also over 200 Dong Son bronze drums of Ancient Far East which also contain Harappa Script hieroglyphs (such as sun's rays, frog, heron, peacock, antelope, elephant)

3. Small sizes of the seals and tablets used to create inscriptions may be seen from these photographs. Some tablets of Harappa are miniature incised tablets of the size of thumbnails. Within the short space of inscribed objects, remarkably precise hieroglyphs are signified attesting to the artistic excellence of the artisans who created the inscriptions. Most of the hieroglyphs are rendered with such orthographic fidelity that every feature of a pictorial motif or a pictograph is recognizable without any ambiguity. Annex C details the form and function of tablets, miniature tablets.

4. The underlying words which signify the pictorial motifs and pictographs and homonymous parole (speech) words which render rebus readings of metalwork are based on a common Prakrtam lexis (words and phrases of Bharata *sprachbund*) used across the extensive area in which the writing system was used by *Bhāratam Janam* who were Prakrtam speakers (also called *Meluhha/Mleccha*). Hence, Vātsyāyana calls this writing system as mlecchita vikalpa (cipher of Meluhha).

A brilliant invention evidenced by Harappa Script is the use of stoneware ceramic bangles as *Dharma saṁjñā*[58], corporate badges as 'responsibility indicators" for participants in guilds of artisans and merchants. This breakthrough in incipient corporate forms of guilds resulted in dramatic changes in social organization, corporate management and control of Bronze Age production and trade exchange activities for material wealth, in particular of metalwork resources which constituted the dominant wealth-creation activity of the Bronze Age Revolution.

This 'responsibility signifier' process is central to the *weltanshauung* governed by the inexorable, inviolable principle of *dharma-dhamma* which are manifest in the life-activities and *samājam* (society) of *Bhāratam Janam*.

Sharply defined inscriptions on each of the 21 ceramic (stoneware) bangles indicate 21 sharply assigned responsibilities within the guild for metalwork, for e.g.,

 Sign 403 (Balakot-6) 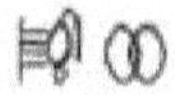 Squirrel + Sign 403 (Mohenjo-daro m1634).

Phal. *šẽ̄ṣṭrī̃* 'flying squirrel'?(CDIAL 12723) Rebus:k *śrēṣṭhin* m.'distinguished man' AitBr.'foreman of a guild'.

Sign403: *bārī*,'small ear-ring' Rebus: *bārī* 'merchant' *vāḍhī, bari, barea* 'merchant'

bārakaśa 'seafaring vessel'. *karā̃* n. pl.'wristlets, bangles'.(Gujarati) (CDIAL 2779) Rebus: *khār* खार् । लोहकारः m. 'a blacksmith, an iron worker'.

21 functional allocations of responsibilitie delineated for artisans/merchants in a Vedic village:

1. iron smelting, furnace work (m1659)
2. metal casting, engraving, documenting supercargo (m1647)
3. bronze (casting)(m1646)
4. *gōṭā* (laterite) (m1641)
5. Seafaring merchant, magnetite ingot workshop (m1643)
6. Smithy, forge (m1641)
7. Moltencast copper, brass (m1640)
8. Alloy metal mint, weapons, implements workshop, guild master workshop (m1639)
9. Bronze ingots, implements, magnetite ingots (m1638)
10. Metalcasting workshop (*cire perdue*?) (m1637)
11. Metal implements, weapons, smithy, forge (m1636)
12. Blacksmith, seafaring merchant (m1634)
13. Helmsman for supercargo boat, iron furnace work, metals workshop (m1633)
14. Metal casting, alloy mixing workshop (m1632)
15. *dhā̆vaḍ* 'smelter', supercargo of implements (m1631)
16. Magnetite ingots, furnace work, supercargo engraver (m1630)

17. Iron furnace work, metal casting of tin, helmsman supercargo of metals, *bharat* 'mixed alloyś metalworker (m1629)
18. Minerals workshop guild (h2576)
19. Magnetite ingots, smelter (h1010)
20. *dhǎvaḍ* 'smelter' *tri-dhAtu*, "three minerals (H98-3516/8667-01)
21. Seafaring merchant, supercargo engraver(Blkt-6)

The brilliant and original techniques for manufacturing stoneware ceramic bangles was a complex process and was carefully controlled. The form and function of these badges in the context of Harappa Script as a knowledge system are discussed in Annex B.

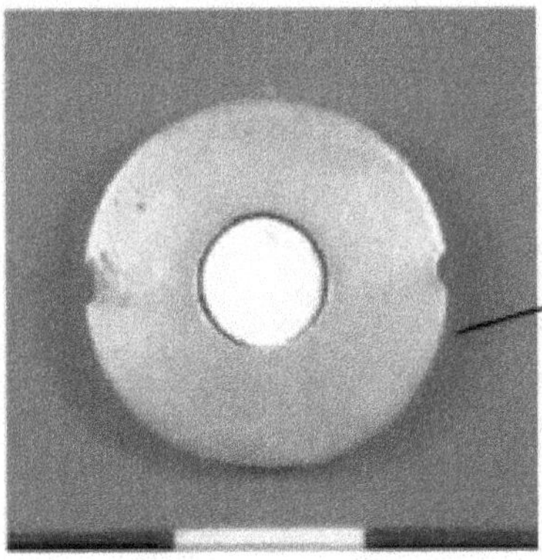

Gold Disc

The central ornament worn on the forehead of the famous "priest-king" sculpture from Mohenjo-daro appears to represent an eye bead, possibly made of gold with steatite inlay in the center.

A ceramic stoneware bangle and a fillet worn on the forehed and shoulder of a priest in Mohenjo-daro. It has been demonstrated that the 'dotted circle' on the fillet is a Harappa Script hieroglyph and the person wearing it as a signifier is *potṛ*, पोतृ 'purifier', (later historical periods *pōtadāra* 'precious metal assayer'), also *dhǎvaḍ* 'iron smelter'. In Rigveda, *dhā´tu* means 'a strand' rebus: *dhāū*, *dhāv* 'a partic. soft red stone', *dhā´tu* 'mineral, ore'. The 'strand' is signified by a dotted circle, as a cross-sectional orthographic device.

Bronze Age was a revolution in the story of civilization heralded by the invention of tin-bronze alloy to produce hard metal for implements, tools, weapons, pots and pans. This meant a sea-chage in trade interactions in extensive civilizational contact areas from the Ancient Far East to the Ancient Near East through Ancient India. Biblical harosheth hagoyim 'smithy of nations' is indicative of travels by ancient artisans/smiths in Eurasia searching for mineral resources and working in metals, evidenced by Nahal Mishmar arsenical *cire perdue* hoards.

Data mining results in a hypothesis, the story of Maritime Tin Route source from the largest tin belt of the globe in the delta of a Himalayan River Mekong River. The Tin Route predated the Silk Road by about 2 millennia. Annex D presents *ayo, aya* 'fish' rebus: *aya* 'iron' *ayas* 'metal', hieroglyph modifiers and Harappa Script inscriptions on 240 copper tablets.

A parallel is seen in multi-layered metaphors in Vedic texts, for e.g. on *Yūpa* and चषालः *caṣāla* which signify smelting processes using wheat chaff for caburizing/pyrolysis (infusion of carbon fumes in ores) to harden metals produced in smelters and furnaces. The idea of multi-layering which is brilliantly evidenced in the orthography of Harappa Script (unparalleled in any other ancient writing system) is likely to be a key component in further strengthening encryption systems for data security.

Data security systems devised by ancient artisans of India could help improve present-day data security systems with tight encryptions of data which are crucial for cyber security.

Notable is the varieties of writing techniques by metalworkers, *Bhāratam Janam*. Many variant writing devices are used, for e.g., raised script on copper/bronze tablets, incisions on hard surfaces and free-hand writing on metal surfaces with herbal/metallic paint (perhaps ferric oxide pigment). Hieroglyphs of Harappa Script are also signified – in addition to inscriptions on seals and tablets -- on sculptures in the round and on reliefs.

Data mining techniques of computer science widely used in Information Technology and Wi-Fi cellular/mobile communication system of the present day can be paralleled by the techniques demonstrated by artisans who created and used the Harappa Script writing. The techniques used on Harappa Script could be of value to enhance data security through advanced cipher systems in cryptology, the study of codes, or the art of writing and solving them.

"Data mining is an interdisciplinary subfield of computer science. It is the computational process of discovering patterns in large data sets ("bigdata") involving methods at the intersection of artificial intelligence, machine learning, statistics, and database systems."[59]

Applying data mining to Harappa Script is appropriate because the pre-existing data bases relate to an ancient period starting from ca. 3300 BCE and to a vast expansive space from Hanoi in Vietnam to Haifa in Israel in Eurasia with evidences of over 7000 inscriptions from over 2600 archaeological sites of the Bronze Age Revolution.

Harappa Script hieroglyphs are signified not only on seals, tablets and sealings related to trade exchanges and metalwork processing stages in workshops, but also on sculptures in the round, reliefs and paintings.

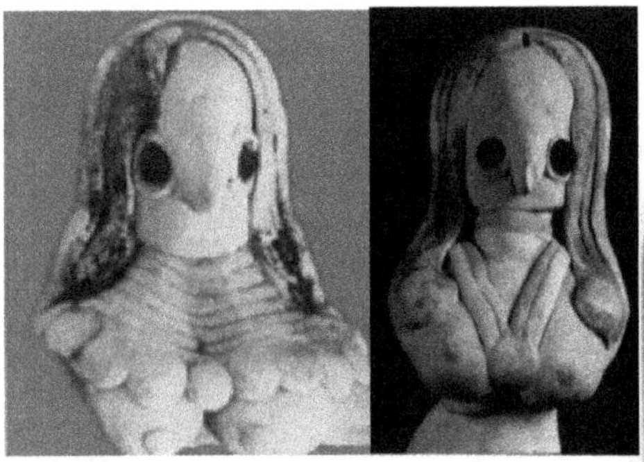

Nausharo (Mehrgarh): female figurines. Gold ornaments are painted yellow, hair is painted black and at the parting of the hair red pigment sindhur is signified.

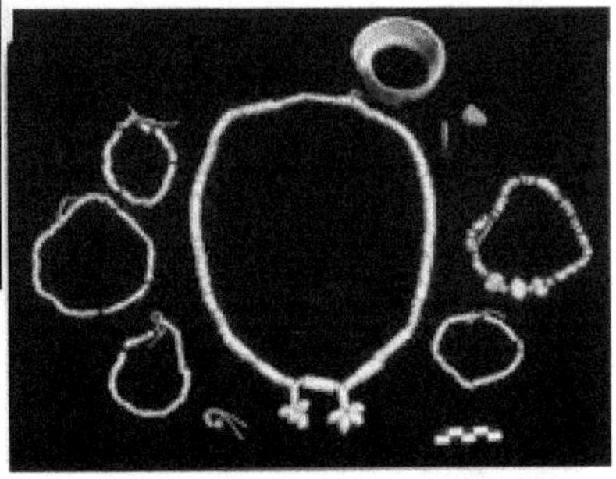

Emphatic evidence of Vedic culture continuing into historical periods and practiced even today in *Bhāratam*. 2800 – 2600 BCE. 11.6 x 30.9 cm.[60]

Wide bangle made from a single conch shell found in a woman's burial dated to ca. 6500 BCE[61] and carved with a chevron motif, Harappa; marine shell, *Turbinella pyrum* which is a signature tune of provenance from the Indian Ocean along the coastline of Bhāratam.

The lapidary work of making śankha bangles using a bronze sword continues even today.

A lapidary, bangle-maker in West Bengal.

Harappa Script hieroglyphs constitute knowledge systems of the Bronze Age Revolution. From these databases, cultural, socio-economic history of a civilization can be narrated from proto-historic times.

A terracotta *linga* from Kalibangan (2600 BCE)

Tre-foil inlay decorated

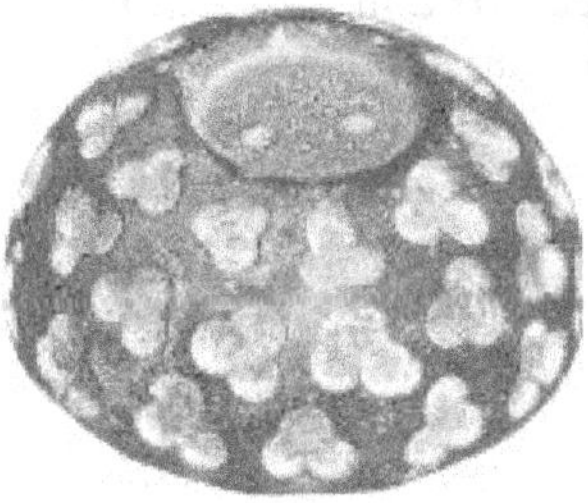

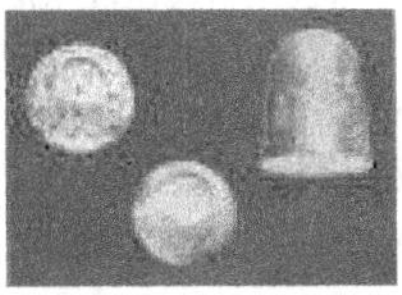

base (for linga icon?); smoothed, polished pedestal of dark red stone; National Museum of Pakistan, Karachi.[62]

Veneration of Sivalinga is signified atop smelters during the historical periods. This is the emphatic evidence of linga signifying smelting, metallurgical process.

Worship of *linga* by *gandharva*, Shunga period.Bhuteshwar, Mathura Museum.

Architectural fragment with relief showing winged dwarfs (or *gaNa* or *khārva* signifier of *nidhi* of *Kubera*) worshipping with flower garlands, *linga*. Bhuteshwar, ca. 2nd cent BCE. *Linga* is on a platform with wall under a pipal tree encircled by railing. The tree is a phonetic determinant of the smelter indicated by the railing around the linga: *kuṭa, °ṭi* -- , *°ṭha* -- 3, *°ṭhi* -- m. ' tree ' Rebus: *kuṭhi* 'smelter'. *kuṭa, °ṭi* -- , *°ṭha* -- 3, *°ṭhi* -- m. ' tree ' lex., *°ṭaka* -- m. ' a kind of tree ' Kauś.Pk. *kuḍa* -- m. ' tree '; Paš. lauṛ. *kuṛā´* ' tree ', dar. *kaṛék* ' tree, oak ' ~ Par. *kōṛ* ' stick ' IIFL iii 3, 98. (CDIAL 3228).[63] H. *dām* m.f. ' rope, string, fetter ', *dāmā* m. ' id., garland '(Si. *dama* ' chain, rope ', (SigGr) *dam* ' garland '(CDIAL 6283) rebus: *dhAu* 'metal; (Prakrtam) *dhAI* 'wisp of fibres' (S.) dhā´tu n. ' substance ' RV., m. ' element ' MBh., ' metal, mineral, ore (esp. of a red colour) ' Mn., ' ashes of the dead ' lex., ' *strand of rope ' (cf. *tridhā´tu* -- ' threefold ' RV., *ayugdhātu* -- ' having an uneven number of strands ' KātyŚr.). [√dhā]

Pa. *dhātu* -- m. ' element, ashes of the dead, relic '; KhārI. *dhatu* ' relic '; Pk. *dhāu* -- m. ' metal, red chalk '; N. *dhāu* ' ore (esp. of copper) '; Or. *ḍhāu* ' red chalk, red ochre ' (whence*ḍhāuā* ' reddish '; M. *dhāū, dhāv* m.f. ' a partic. soft red stone ' (whence *dhā̆vaḍ* m. ' a caste of iron -- smelters ', *dhāvḍī* ' composed of or relating to iron '); -- Si. *dā* ' relic '; -- S. *dhāī* f. ' wisp of fibres added from time to time to a rope that is being twisted ', L. *dhāī̃* f.(CDIAL 6773) the *staff* or *stay*. मेढेजोशी (p. 665) [mēḍhējōśī] *m* A stake-जोशी; a जोशी who keeps account of the तिथि &c., by driving stakes into the ground: also a class, or an individual of it, of fortune-tellers, diviners, presagers, seasonannouncers, almanack-makers &c. They are Shúdras and followers of the मेढेमत q. v. 2 Jocosely. The hereditary or settled (quasi fixed as a stake) जोशी of a village.मेंधला (p. 665) [mēndhalā] *m* In architecture. A common term for the two upper arms of a double चौकठ (door-frame) connecting the two. Called also मेंढरी & घोडा. It answers to छिली the name of the two lower arms or connections. (Marathi)मेंढा [*mēṇḍhā*] A crook or curved end rebus: *meḍ* 'iron, metal' (Ho. Munda) Since Sivalinga as aniconic forms are also signified by चतुर्श्रि, अष्टाश्रि quadrangular, octagonal components and as iconic connotations appear with *ekamukha linga* (*linga* with one face ligatured), it is surmised that *linga* is *Yūpa skambha*, as a multi-layered, metallurgical metaphor. One layer relates to the rebus reading of the *ekamukha.* The surmise of Sivalinga as Yūpa Skambha is frameḍ on the extraordinary metaphors of the philosophical tractus in Atharva veda called *Skambha Sukta* (AV X.7,8). *Skambha*, *Yūpaskambha* 'pillar' and *kangar*, 'brazier' respectively are attested as hieroglyphs on Harappa Script inscriptions and on early punch-marked/cast coins of Ancient Bhāratam. A variant pronunciation *stambha* is read rebus in Pali and Bihari: *tā̃bā* 'copper' (Bihari) *Tamba* (nt.) [Sk. *tāmra*, orig. adj.=dark coloured, leaden; cp. Sk. adj. *taŋsra* id., to *tama*] copper ("the dark metal"); usually in combinations, signifying colour of or made of (cp. loha bronze), e. g. *lākhātamba* (adj.) Th 2, 440 (colour of an ox); °*akkhin* Vv 323 (*timira*°) Sdhp 286; °*nakhin* J vi.290; °*nettā*

(f.)ibid.; °*bhājana* DhA i.395; °*mattika* DhA iv.106; °*vammika* DhAiii.208; °loha PvA 95 (=loha). *tāmrá* ' dark red, copper -- coloured ' VS., n. ' copper ' Kauś., *tāmraka* -- n. Yājñ. [Cf. tamrá -- . -- √tam?]Pa. *tamba* -- ' red ', n. ' copper ', Pk. *taṁba* -- adj. and n.; Dm. *trāmba* -- ' red ' (in *trāmba -- laçuk* ' raspberry ' NTS xii 192); Bshk. *lām* ' copper, piece of bad pine -- wood (< ' *red wood '?); Phal. *tāmba* ' copper ' (→ Sh.koh. *tāmbā*), K. *trām* m. (→ Sh.gil. gur. *trām* m.), S. *ṭrāmo* m., L. *trāmā*, (Ju.) *tarāmā̃* m., P. *tāmbā* m., WPah. bhad. *ṭḷām* n., kiũth. *cāmbā*, sod. *cambo*, jaun. *tā̃bō*, Ku. N. *tāmo* (pl. ' young bamboo shoots '), A. *tām*, B. *tā̃bā*, *tāmā*, Or. *tambā*, Bi *tā̃bā*, Mth. *tām*, *tāmā*, Bhoj. *tāmā*, H. *tām* in cmpds., *tā̃bā*, *tāmā* m., G. *trā̃bũ*, *tā̃bũ* n.;M. *tā̃bẽ* n. ' copper ', *tā̃b* f. ' rust, redness of sky '; Ko. *tāmbe* n. ' copper '; Si. *taṁba* adj. ' reddish ', sb. ' copper ', (SigGr) *tam*, *tama.* -- Ext. -- *ira* -- : Pk. *taṁbira* -- ' coppercoloured, red ', L. *tāmrā* ' copper -- coloured (of pigeons) '; -- with -- *ḍa* -- : S. *ṭrāmiṛo* m. ' a kind of cooking pot ', *ṭrāmiṛī* ' sunburnt, red with anger ', f. ' copper pot '; Bhoj. *tāmrā* ' copper vessel '; H. *tā̃bṛā*, *tāmṛā*' coppercoloured, dark red ', m. ' stone resembling a ruby '; G. *tā̃baṛ* n., *trā̃bṛī*, *tā̃bṛī* f. ' copper pot '; OM. *tāṁbaḍā* ' red '. -- X trápu -- q.v.tāmrika -- ; tāmrakāra -- , tāmrakuṭṭa -- , *tāmraghaṭa -- , *tāmraghaṭaka -- , tāmracūḍa -- , *tāmradhāka -- , tāmrapaṭṭa -- , tāmrapattra -- , tāmrapātra -- , *tāmrabhāṇḍa -- , tāmravarṇa -- , tāmrākṣa -- .Addenda: tāmrá -- [< IE. **tomró* -- T. Burrow BSOAS xxxviii 65]S.kcch. *trāmo*, *tām(b)o* m. ' copper ', *trāmbhyo* m. ' an old copper coin '; WPah.kc. *cambo* m. ' copper ', J. *cāmbā* m., kṭg. (kc.) *tambɔ* m. (← P. or H. Him.I 89), Garh. *tāmu*, *tā̃bu.*(CDIAL 5779)

A striking result of the data mining process is that there are many duplicate inscriptions, that hypertexts of Harappa Script do NOT inscribe names of invividuals but document – in a logo-phonetic script -- knowledge systems of the metals age and trade exchanges signified by the Bronze Age Revolution.

Kalibangan terracotta cake hieroglyphs deciphered. *Yūpa-skambha*, Vedic religion in Bronze Age of Sarasvati-Sindhu civilization

Harappa script Corpora and archaeological excavations of 'fir-altars" provide evidence for continuity of Vedic religion of fire-worship in many sites of Sarasvati-Sindhu civilization.

The metalwork catalogues of deciphered Harappa script Corpora are consistent with the fire-altars found in almost every single site of the civilization consistent with the documentation of yajna, fire-worship, in ancient texts of the Veda. The continuity of Vedic religion, veneration of Ruda-Siva among Bronze Age *Bhāratam Janam*, 'metalcaster folk' is firmly anchored.

In Hindu civilization tradition, Yūpa associated with smelter/furnace operations in fire-altars as evidenced in Bijnor, Kalibangan, Lothal and in many Yūpa pillars of Rajasthan of the historical periods, assume the aniconic form of linga venerated as Jyotirlinga, fierly pillars of light.

A 10th-century four-headed stone lingam (Mukhalinga) from Nepal. The 'mukha' or face on the linga is a hieroglyph read rebus muh 'ingot'. Hieroglyph: *mũh* 'face' (Hindi) rebus:

mũhe 'ingot' (Santali) *mũhā̃* = the quantity of iron produced at one time in a native smelting furnace of the Kolhes; iron produced by the Kolhes and formeḍ like a four-cornered piece a little pointed at each end; mūhā mẽṛhẽt = iron smelted by the Kolhes and formeḍ into an equilateral lump a little pointed at each of four ends; *kolhe tehen mẽṛhẽt ko mūhā akata* = the Kolhes have to-day produced pig iron (Santali)

"The worship of the lingam originated from the famous hymn in the *Atharva-Veda Samhitâ* sung in praise of the *Yūpa-Skambha*, the sacrificial post. In that hymn, a description is found of the beginningless and endless *Stambha* or *Skambha*, and it is shown that the said *Skambha* is put in place of the eternal Brahman. Just as the Yajna (sacrificial) fire, its smoke, ashes, and flames, the *Soma* , and the ox that used to carry on its back the wood for the Vedic sacrifice gave place to the conceptions of the brightness of Shiva's body, his tawny matted hair, his blue throat, and the riding on the bull of the Shiva, the *Yūpa-Skambha* gave place in time to the *Shiva-Linga*. In the text *Linga Purana*, the same hymn is expanded in the shape of stories, meant to establish the glory of the great Stambha and the superiority of Shiva as Mahadeva. Jyotirlinga means "The Radiant sign of The Almighty". The Jyotirlingas are mentioned in the *Shiva Purana*."[64]

Roots of the world-views are traced into the database of archaeological evidences.

Kalibangan. Fire-altar

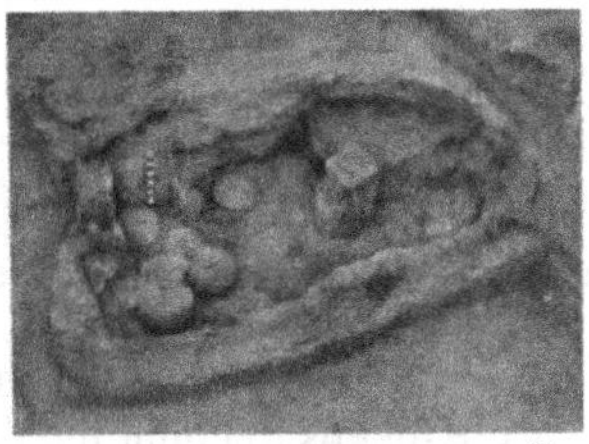

with stele 'linga' and terracotta cakes. Plate XXA. "Within one of the rooms of amost each house was found the curious 'fire-altar', sometimes also in successive levels, indicating their recurrent function."[65]

Pl. XXII B. Terracotta cake with incised figures on obverse and reverse, Harappa. On one side is a human figure wearing a head-dress having two horns and a plant in the centre; on the other side is an animal-headed human figure with another animal figure (feline), the latter being dragged by the former.

Decipherment of hieroglyphs on the Kalibangan terracotta cake:

The tiger is being pulled to be tied to a post, pillar. Hieriglyph: *meṛh* rope tying to post, pillar: mēthí m. ' pillar in threshing floor to which oxen are fastened, prop for supporting carriage shafts ' AV., *°thī* -- f. KātyŚr.com., *mēdhī* -- f. Divyāv. 2. mēṭhī -- f. PañcavBr.com., *mēḍhī* -- , *mēṭī* -- f. BhP.1. Pa. *mēdhi* -- f. ' post to tie cattle to, pillar, part of a stūpa '; Pk. *mēhi* -- m. ' post on threshing floor ', N. *meh(e)*, *miho*, *miyo*, B. *mei*, Or. *maï* -- *dāṇḍi*, Bi. *mēh*, *mēhā* ' the post ', (SMunger) *mehā* ' the bullock next the post ', Mth. *meh*, *mehā* ' the post ', (SBhagalpur)*mīhā̃* ' the bullock next the post ', (SETirhut) *mēhi bāṭi* ' vessel with a projecting base '.2. Pk. *mēḍhi* -- m. ' post on threshing floor ', *mēḍhaka*<-> ' small stick '; K. *mīr*, *mīrü* f. ' larger hole in ground which serves as a mark in pitching walnuts ' (for semantic relation of ' post -- hole ' see *kūpa* -- 2); L. *meṛh* f. ' rope tying oxen to each other and to post on threshing floor '; P. *mehṛ* f., *mehaṛ* m. ' oxen on threshing floor, crowd '; OA *meṛha*, *mehra* ' a circular construction, mound '; Or. *meṛhī*, *meri* ' post on threshing floor '; Bi. *mēṛ* ' raised bank between irrigated beds ', (Camparam) *mēṛhā* ' bullock next the post ', Mth. (SETirhut) *mēṛhā* ' id. '; M. *meḍ(h)*, *meḍhī* f., *meḍhā* m. ' post, forked stake '.mēthika -- ; mēthiṣṭhá -- . mēthika m. ' 17th or lowest cubit from top of sacrificial post ' lex. [mēthí --]Bi. *mēhiyā* ' the bullock next the post on threshing floor' *mēthiṣṭhá* 'standing at the post' TS. [mēthí -- , stha --] Bi. (Patna) *mĕhṭhā* ' post on threshing floor ', (Gaya) *mehṭā*, *mēhṭā* ' the bullock next the post '(CDIAL 10317 to, 10319) Rebus: *meḍ* 'iron' (Ho.); *meḍ* 'copper' (Slavic)

bhaṭa 'warrior' rebus: *bhaṭa* 'furnace'

kolmo 'rice plant' rebus: *kolimi* 'smithy, forge'

koḍ 'horn' rebus: *koḍ* 'workshop'

kola 'tiger' rebus: *kolle* 'blacksmith', *kolhe* 'smelter' *kol* 'working in iron'

Thus, the terracotta cake inscription signifies a iron workshop smelter/furnace and smithy.

The recording of an inscription on a terracotta cake used in a fire-altar continues as a tradition with inscriptions recorded on *Yūpa*, 'pillars" of Rajasthan indicating the type of *Soma yajna*-s performeḍ using those *Yūpa.*[66]

These terracotta cakes are like Ancient Near East tokens used for accounting, as elaborated by Denise Schmandt-Besserat67 in her pioneering researches.

The context in which an incised terracotta cake was found at Kalibangan is instructive. I suggest that terracotta cakes were tokens to count the ingots produced in a 'fire-altar' and crucibles, by metallurgists of Sarasvati civilization. This system of incising is found in scores of miniature incised tablets of Harappa, incised with Harappa Script writing. Some of these tablets are shaped like bun ingots, some are triangular and some are shaped like fish. Each shape should have had some semantic significance, e.g., fish may have connoted ayo 'fish' as a glyph; read rebus: ayas 'metal (alloy)'. A horned person on the Kalibangan terracotta cake described herein might have connoted: *kōṭu* 'horn'; rebus: खोट *khōṭa* 'A mass of metal (unwrought or of old metal melted down); an ingot or wedge. Hence 'A lump or solid bit'; खोटसाळ *khōṭasāḷa* 'Alloyed--a metal'(Marathi) A stake associated with the fire-altar was ढांगर [*ḍhāṅgara*] n 'A stout stake or stick as a prop to a Vine or scandent shrub]' (Marathi); rebus: *ḍhaṅgar* 'smith' (Maithili. Hindi) *Tu. kandůka, kāṇḍaka* ditch, trench. *Te.* kāṇḍakamu id. *Konḍa kāṇḍa* trench made as a fireplace during weddings. *Pe. kāṇḍa* fire trench. *Kui kāṇḍa* small trench for fireplace. *Malt. kandri* a pit. (DEDR68 1214) *Ka. kunda* a pillar of bricks, etc. *Tu. kunda* pillar, post. *Te. kunda* id. *Malt. kunda* block, log. ? Cf. Ta. *kantu* pillar, post. (DEDR 1723)

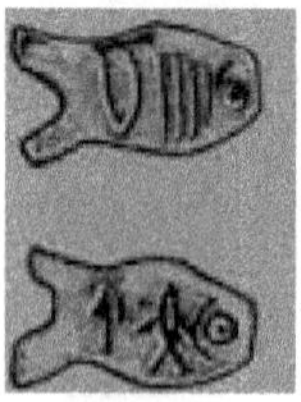

Harppa. Two sides of a fish-shaped, incised tablet with Harappa Script writing. Hundreds of inscribed texts on tablets are repetitions; it is, therefore, unlikely that hundreds of such inscribed tablets just contained the same 'names' composed of just five 'alphabets or 'syllables', even after the direction of writing is firmeḍ up as from right to left. *gaṇḍa* 'four' rebus: *khaṇḍa* 'implements *kaṇḍa 'fire-altar' baṭa* 'rimless pot' rebus: *bhaṭa* 'furnace' *kāṇḍa* 'arrow' rebus: *khaṇḍa* 'implements *ayo, aya* 'fish' rebus: *aya* 'iron' *ayas* 'metal'. The incised, miniature tablet of Harappa is also a good illustration of the function of tablets. Tablets are tokens of metal work assignments to artisans working on circular platforms. The products made by the artisans are consolidated and seals are inscribed based on the tablet-token information, by the *samgara, samgraha*, 'manager' of the guild to be handed over to supercargo for shipment.

At Kalibangan, fire Vedic altars have been discovered, similar to those found at Lothal which S.R. Rao thinks could have served no other purpose than a ritualistic one. These altars suggest fire worship or worship of Agni, the Vedic, Hindu divinity of fire.

Within the fortified citadel complex, the southern half contained many (five or six) raised platforms of mud bricks, mutually separated by corridors. Stairs were attached to these platforms. Vandalism of these platforms by brick robbers makes it difficult to reconstruct the original shape of structures above them but unmistakable remnants of rectangular or oval kuṇḍas or fire-pits of burnt bricks for Vedi (altar)s have been found, with a yūpa or sacrificial post (cylindrical or with rectangular cross-section, sometimes bricks were laid upon each other to construct such a post) in the middle of each kuṇḍa and sacrificial terracotta cakes (piṇḍa) in all these fire-pits. Houses in the lower town also contain similar altars. Burnt charcoals have been found in these fire-pits. The structure of these fire-altars is reminiscent of (Vedic) fire-altars, but the analogy may be coincidental, and these altars are perhaps intended for some specific (perhaps religious) purpose by the community as a whole. In some fire-altars remnants of animals have been found, which suggest a possibility of animal-sacrifice."[69]

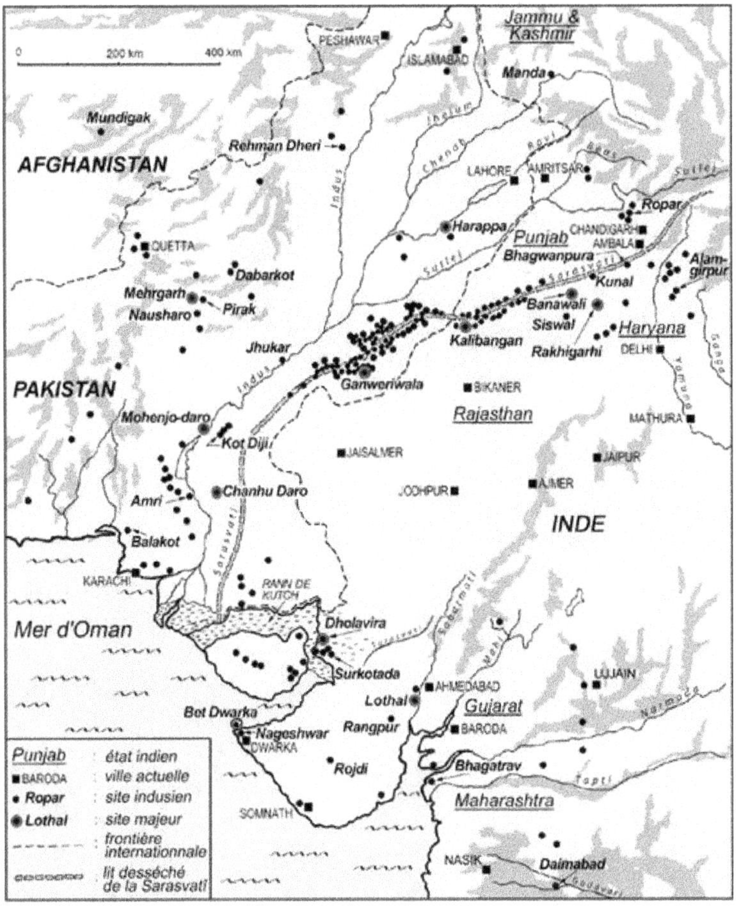

Over 2000 archaeological sites (80% of the over 2600 sites) of the civilization are on the banks of Vedic River Sarasvati. Binjor is an archaeological site at the forking of the river near Anupgarh, one channel flows southwards to Jodhpur, Jaisalmer and another flows westward to Ganwerivala, Bahalpur, Cholistan.

Binjor fire-altar evidences performance of a *Soma Yaga*

Binjor is a remarkable archaeological site (called 4MSR) excavated in April 2015. This site on the bnks of Vedic River Sarasvati. Binjor seal with Harappa script together with a *yajna kunda*, fire-altar attests Vedic River Sarasvati as a Himalayan navigable channel en route to Persian Gulf and attests the signature tune of an octagonal pillar to signify that a *Soma SamsthA, Soma Yaga* was performed ca. 2500 BCE.

The fire altar, with a *yasti* or *Yūpa* made of an octagonal brick.

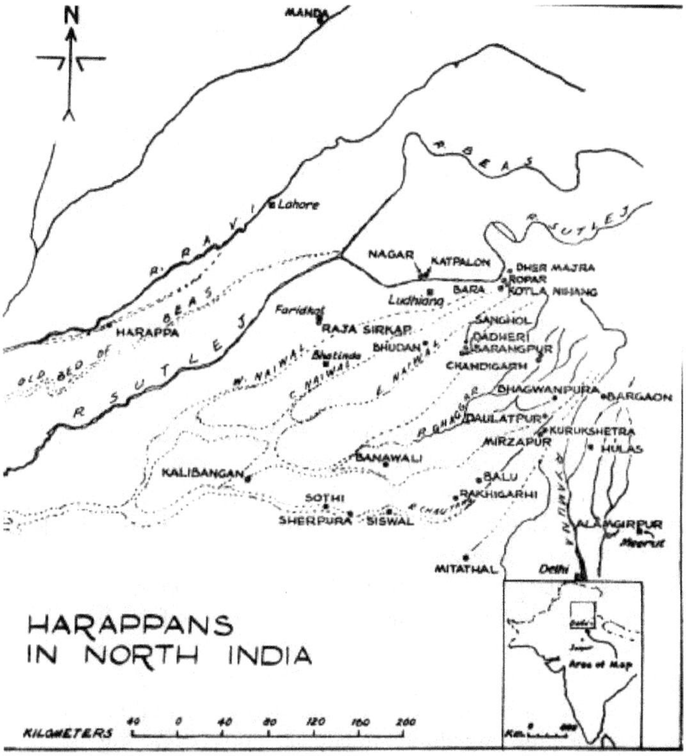
N
MANDA
R. BEAS
R. SUTLEJ
R. RAVI
Lahore
NAGAR
KATPALON
DHER MAJRA
ROPAR
BARA
KOTLA NIHANG
Ludhiana
Faridkot
HARAPPA
RAJA SIRKAP
SANGHOL
DADHERI
SARANGPUR
BHUDAN
Bhatinda
CHANDIGARH
OLD BED OF BEAS
W. NAIWAL
C. NAIWAL
E. NAIWAL
BHAGWANPURA
BARGAON
R. GHAGGAR
DAULATPUR
KURUKSHETRA
MIRZAPUR
HULAS
BANAWALI
KALIBANGAN
BALU
RAKHIGARHI
SOTHI
SHERPURA
SISWAL
R. CHAUTANG
YAMUNA
ALAMGIRPUR
Meerut
MITATHAL
Delhi
Area of Map
HARAPPANS
IN NORTH INDIA
KILOMETERS
40
0
40
80
120
160
200

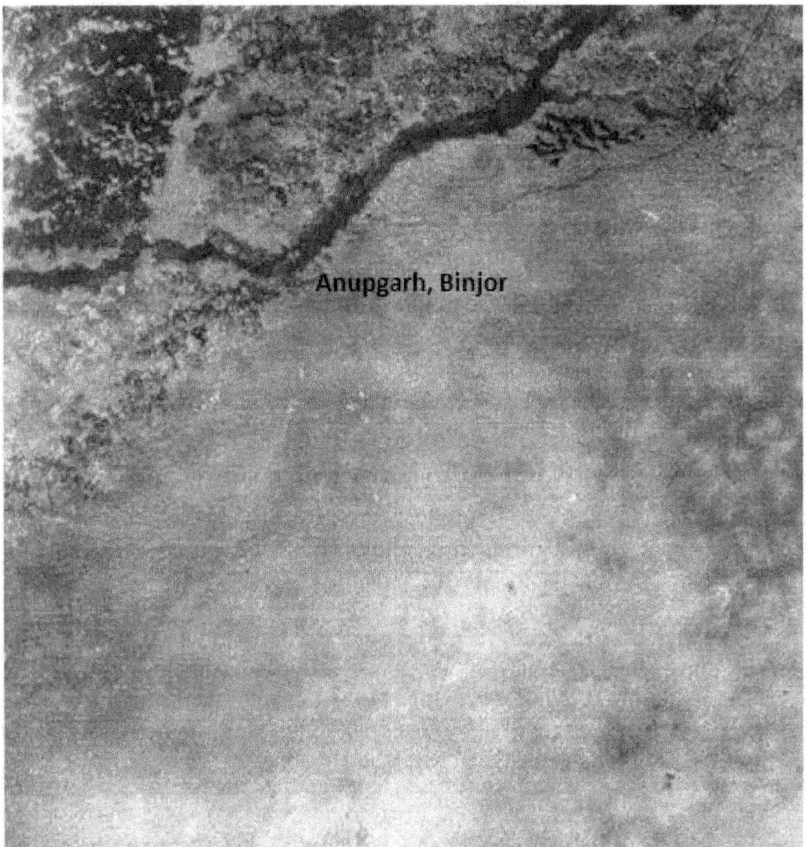
Anupgarh, Binjor

Binjor is downstream Vedic River Sarasvati southwestof Kalibangan as may be seen from the Landsat satellite image which shows Anupgarh/Binjor.

Landsat image of paleo-channels about 6 kms. wide. Anupgarh, Binjor on the banks of Vedic River Sarasvati. At this place, the river forks, with one channel going westwards into Bahawalpur province and another southwards to Jodhpur, Jaisalmer. At Binjor, a yajna kunda and evidence for performance of a Soma Yaga have been discovered establishing the roots of Vedic culture for Harappa civilization.

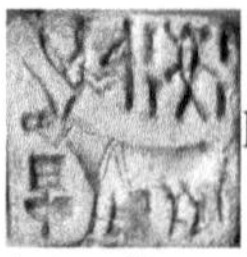
Binjor (4MSR) seal Binjor Seal Text. Ayo, aya 'fish' rebus: aya 'iron' ayas 'metal'

Fish + scales, *aya ā̃s (amśu)* 'metallic stalks of stone ore'. Vikalpa: *badhoṛ* 'a species of fish with many bones' (Santali) Rebus: *baḍhoe* 'a carpenter, worker in wood'; *badhoria* 'expert in working in wood'(Santali)
*skambha2 ' shoulder -- blade, wing, plumage '. [Cf. **skapa* -- s.v. *khavāka --] S. *khambhu*, *°bho* m. ' plumage ', *khambhuṛi* f. ' wing '; L. *khabbh* m., mult. *khambh* m. ' shoulder -- blade, wing, feather ', khet. *khamb* ' wing ', mult. *khambhaṛā* m. ' fin '; P. *khambh* m. ' wing, feather '; G. *khā̆m* f., *khabhɔ* m. ' shoulder '.(CDIAL 13640) *khambhaṛā* 'fish fin' rebus: *kammaṭa* 'mint, coiner, coinage' *gaṇḍa* 'four' Rebus: *khaṇḍa* 'metal implements Together with cognate *ancu* 'iron' the message is: native metal implements. Thus, the hieroglyph multiplex reads: *aya ancu kammaṭa khaṇḍa* 'metallic iron alloy implements, mint'. *koḍi* 'flag' (Ta.)(DEDR 2049). Rebus 1: *koḍ* 'workshop' (Kuwi) Rebus 2: *khŏḍ* m. 'pit', *khŏḍü* f. 'small pit' (Kashmiri. CDIAL 3947).
The bird hieroglyph: करण्ड m. a sort of duck L. కారండవము (p. 274) [*kāraṇḍavamu*] *kāraṇḍavamu.* [Skt.] n. A sort of duck. (Telugu) karaṭa1 m. ' crow ' BhP., °aka -- m. lex. [Cf. *karaṭu -- , karkaṭu* -- m. ' Numidian crane ', *karēṭu -- , °ēṭavya -- , °ēḍuka* -- m. lex., *karaṇḍa2* -- m. ' duck ' lex: see kāraṇḍava --]Pk. *karaḍa* -- m. ' crow ', *°ḍā* -- f. ' a partic. kind of bird '; S. *karaṛa -- ḍhī̃gu* m. ' a very large aquatic bird '; L. *karṛā* m., °ṛī f. ' the common teal'(CDIAL 2787) Rebus: *karaḍā* 'hard alloy'

Thus, the text of Harappa script inscription on the Binjor Seal reads: 'metallic iron alloy implements, hard alloy workshop' PLUS the hieroglyphs of one-horned young bull PLUS standard device in front read rebus: *kõda* 'young bull, bull-calf' rebus: *kõdā* 'to turn in a lathe'; *kõnda* 'engraver, lapidary'; *kundār* 'turner'. Hieroglyph: *sãghāṛɔ* 'lathe'.(Gujarati) Rebus: *sangara* 'proclamation', 'fortification'. सं-ग्रह *saṁgraha* 'a guardian , ruler , manager , arranger' R. BhP.

Together, the message of the Binjor Seal with inscribed text is a proclamation, a metalwork catalogue (of) 'mint, metallic iron alloy implements, hard alloy workshop (of) *sangara* 'fortification'. सं-ग्रह *saṁgraha, samgaha* 'a guardian , ruler , manager , arranger' R. BhP.

Exchanges and movements of metalwork treasures produced during the Bronze Age by caravans and seafaring merchants were the *raison d'etre* for the invention and use of Harappa Script. Early evidence of use of Harappa Script is on an inscribed potsherd dated to ca. 3300 BCE in archaeological context in Harappa.

Three ‘text signs’: “…three primitive inscriptions found on pottery may pre-date all other known writing.”[Richard Meadow, an excavator for Harappa Archaeological Research Project of Harvard University(HARP)].

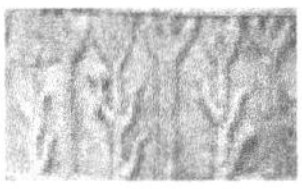

Tabernae montana on a register on Warka vase (Late Uruk period 3600 to 3200 BCE). If a Meluhha artisan had rendered the art-work, he would have conveyed in writing: tagaraka, tabernae montana. Rebus: tagara ‘tin’ (Ka.); tamara id. (Skt.) Allograph (alternative hieroglyph): ṭagara ‘ram’.

Harappa Script is a logo-phonetic writing system based on Meluhha [milakkhu ‘dialect’ (Pali)] parole to document the spoken words of Meluhha (mleccha) speakers among *Bhāratam Janam* (an expression used by Rishi Visvamitra in Rigveda 3.53.12 which identifies Meluhha speakers as metal workers and metal merchants.) (Note: Langue, ‘language’ and parole ‘speaking’ are linguistic terms in French defined by Ferdinand de Saussure in his Course in General Linguistics[70] published in 1916.) Language is a product of social interaction. Meluhha as a language exemplifies this as may be seen from the lexis (vocabulary) of Bharata sprachbund (language union or linguistic area). Almost all ancient Bharatiya languages have retained metalwork words from the ancient Meluhha which was recognized and recorded in cuneiform texts as the language of the people from Meluhha (Harappa or Sarasvati-Sindhu Civilization). This Meluhha language required an Akkadian translator and hence Meluhha is distinct from Akkadian.

The rollout of Shu-ilishu's Cylinder seal. Courtesy of the Department des Antiquites Orientales, Musee du Louvre, Paris. Shu-ilishu, interpreter for Meluhha Cuneijbrm inscription in Old Akkadian Scrpentinc II. 2.9 cm (1% 1'n.); Diam. 1.8tm (3/4 in.) Mesopotamia. A personal cylinder seal of Shu-ilishu, a translator of the Meluhha language with cuneiform writing.

Akkadian calls himself *eme-bal mel-u-h-ha-ki* ‘Meluhha translator’.

"The presence in Akkad of a translator of the Meluhha language suggests that he may have been literate and could read the undeciphered Harappa Script. This in turn suggests that there may be bilingual Akkadian/Meluhha tablets somewhere in Mesopotamia. Although such documents may not exist, Shu-ilishu's cylinder seal offers a glimmer of hope for the future in unraveling the mystery of the Harappa Script."71 The Meluhha carries a goat as his dharma samjna 'responsibility identifier': *mēḻh* (Brahui), *mṛēka* (Telugu) 'goat' rebus: *mleccha, milakkhu* 'copper'. It is also notable that Vatsyayana includes an expression *mlecchita vikalpa* 'Meluhha cipher' as one of the 64 arts to be learnt by youth.

This work identifies the vocabulary of Meluhha related to metalwork with identification and rebus readings of pictorial motifs signified as hieroglyphs/hypertexts on over 7000 Harappa Script inscriptions.

Since the epigraphs or inscriptions of Harappa Script are sangara 'proclamations सं-ग्रह *saṁgraha* 'a guardian , ruler , manager , arranger' R. BhP. they become catalogues conveying to the receivers of the messages information on technical specifications of innovative metalwork accomplishments. These accomplishments were a life-activity of *Bhāratam Janam*, metalcaster people (RV 3.53.12: Visvamitra).

Rishi Visvamitra in Rigveda (RV 3.53.12) reads in Chandas: *viśvāmitrasya rakṣati brahmeḍam bhārataṃ janam* Translation: "This mantra (brahma) of Visvāmitra protects the people of Bhāratam." This is an emphatic Rigvedic self-identification of the people.

Bhāratam Janam refers to artisans working with *baran, bharat* 'mixed alloy' (5 copper, 4 zinc and 1 tin) (Punjabi) *bhārata* 'a factitious alloy of copper, pewter, tin' (Marathi). An expression in parole is: भरताचें भांडें (p. 353) *bharatācē mbhāṇḍēṃ* n A vessel made of the metal bharata.(Marathi).

Decipherment of Harappa Script also demonstrates 1. the continuum of Vedic culture in Bharata sprachbund exemplified by a Meluhha lexis (vocabulary); and 2. the continuum of metallurgical competence of the Bronze Age Revolution into the historical periods evidenced by the continued use of Harappa Script hieroglyphs in hundreds of mints from Takshasila to Karur to Anuradhapura and on the sculptural friezes of Sanchi and Bharhut.

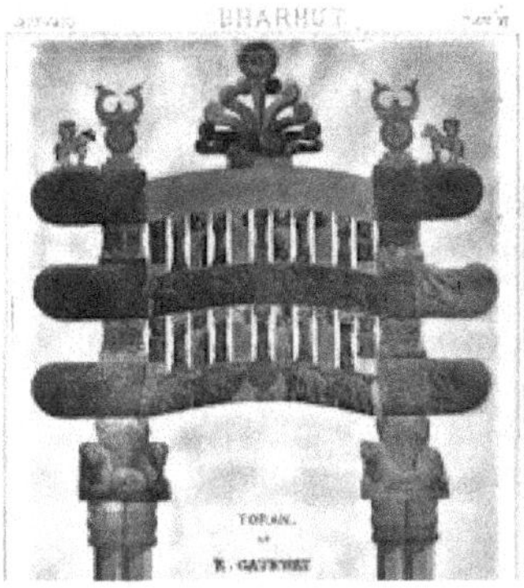

Sanchi and Bharhut stupa toranas (gateway arches) show a hypertext of two fish-fins fused together. This is deciphered in the Harappa Script tradition.

ayo, aya 'fish' rebus: *aya* 'iron' ayas 'metal', *khambhaṛā* 'fish-fin' rebus: *kammaṭa* 'mint, coiner, coinage'. *dula* 'pair' rebus: *dul* 'metal casting'. Thus, the hypertext proclaims *ayo kammaṭa* 'metalwork mint'. This expression is attested in an ancient text: *ayo-kammaṭa dvāra* = *aya* 'iron' PLUS *kammaṭa* 'mint' PLUS *dvāra* 'gateway'. The words *ayo*, and *kammaṭa* are used in the Mahavamśa expression (Mahavamśa, XXV, 28)72. I submit that this expression proclaims the nature of metallurgical artisanal work of the settlements in Sanchi and Bharhut. The torana (gateway) inscribed with Harappa Script hieroglyphs is an advertisement hoarding comparable to the advertisement board on the northern Gateway of Dholava with Harappa Script inscription.

m1431A Pictorial: From R.—a person holding a vessel; a woman with a platter (?); a kneeling person with a staff in his hands facing the woman; a goat with its forelegs on a platform under a tree. [Or, two antelopes flanking a tree on a platform, with one antelope looking backwards?]

mṛeka, melh 'goat' (Telugu. Brahui) Rebus: *melukkha milakkha,* 'copper'. Dula 'pair' rebus: dul 'metal casting'. Thus, copper metal casting.

kuṭi 'tree' rebus: *kuṭhi* 'smelter'

loa 'ficus religiosa' rebus: *loha* 'copper'

Kol. (SR.) *meṭṭā* hill; (Kin.) *meṭṭ, (*Hislop) *met* mountain. *Nk. meṭṭ* hill, mountain. *Ga.* (S.3, *LSB* 20.3) meṭṭa high land. *Go.* (Tr. W. Ph.) maṭṭā, (Mu.) *maṭṭa* mountain; (M. L.) *meṭā* id., hill; (A. D. Ko.) *meṭṭa,* (Y. Ma. M.) *meṭa* hill; (SR.) *meṭṭā* hillock (*Voc.* 2949). *Koṇḍa meṭa id. Kuwi* (S.) *metta* hill; (Isr.) *meṭa* sand hill. (DEDR 5058) Rebus: *mẽd, mēd* 'iron'.

The narrative in the middle signifies a turner working with a lathe:

kũdār 'turner' *kõdā* 'to turn in a lathe' (B.) कोंद *kōnda* 'engraver, lapidary setting or infixing gems' (Marathi) कोंडण [*kōṇḍaṇa*] f A fold or pen. (Marathi)

baṭa 'rimless pot' rebus: *baṭa* 'iron' *bhaṭa* 'furnace'.

The hypertext signifies: engraver, turner lapidary work, furnace for metal castings of copper, iron and smelter work.

m1431B

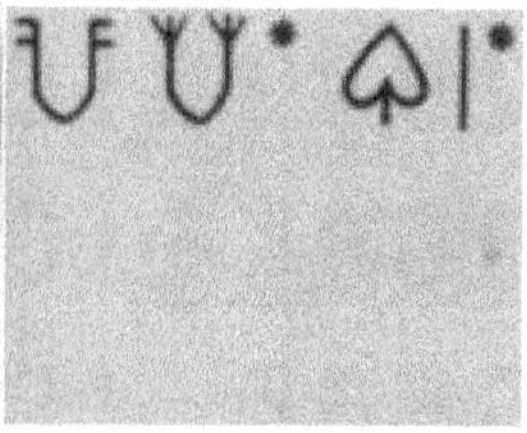

2805 *kola* 'tiger' Rebus: *kol* 'working in iron' 'furnace, forge'.

heraka 'spy' Rebus: *eraka* 'copper' erako 'molten cast'. *khōṇḍa* 'leafless tree' (Marathi). Rebus: *kõdār*'turner' (Bengali) *dhamkara* 'leafless tree' Rebus: *dhangar* 'blacksmith'

Looking back: *krammara* 'look back' Rebus: *kamar* 'smith, artisan'

ḍāḷ= a branch of a tree (G.) Rebus: *ḍhāḷako* = a large ingot (G.) *ḍhāḷakī* = a metal heated and poured into a mould; a solid piece of metal; an ingot (G.)

Hypertext Side B: *koḍa* 'one' rebus: *koḍ* 'workshop'

loa 'ficus religiosa' rebus: *loh* 'copper'

k*olom* 'rice plant' rebus: *kolimi* 'smithy, forge' *dula* 'pair' rebus: *dul* 'metal casting' *kanka, karṇaka* 'rim of jar' rebus: *karṇī* 'supercargo' 'scribe, account'.

Thus, Side B message is: coppersmith with furnace, forge and with metal castings, large ingots.

m1431E

पोळ *pōḷa,* 'zebu' rebus: पोळ *pōḷa,* 'magnetite, ferrite ore'

m1431 prism tablet with inscription on 4 sides shows the association of hieroglyphs tiger + person on tree as one glyphic set (Side B) and crocodile + 3 animals as another glyphic set (Side C).

m1431C

The procession of a tiger, an elephant and a rhinoceros (with fishes (or perhaps, crocodile) on top?) This hieroglyph set describes artisans:

kāru 'crocodile' (Telugu). Rebus: artisan (Marathi) Rebus: *khār* 'blacksmith' (Kashmiri) *ayakāra* 'ironsmith' (Pali)[fish = *aya, ayo* (Munda. Gujarati); crocodile = kāru (Te.)] *baṭṭai* quail (N.Santali) Rebus: *bhaṭa* = an oven, kiln, furnace (Santali) Annex J provides examples of crocodile, scorpion, disheveled hair in Harappa Script hieroglyphs to signify work in *bica* 'haematite stone ore' together with other metalwork.

koḍe 'young bull' (Telugu) खोंड [khōṇḍa] m A young bull, a bullcalf. Rebus: *kõdā* 'to turn in a lathe' (B.) कोंद *kōnda* 'engraver, lapidary setting or infixing gemś (Marathi) कोंडण [*kōṇḍaṇa*] f A fold or pen. (Marathi) *koTiya* 'dhow seafaring vessel'

ibha 'elephant' Rebus ibbo 'merchant'; ib 'iron' karibha 'trunk of elephant' rebus: karba 'iron'.

kāṇḍa 'rhinoceroś Rebus: *khāṇḍa* 'tools, pots and pans, and metal-ware'. ayaskāṇḍa is a compounde word attested in Panini.

Thus, Side C provides four categories of artisans: metalsmith, worker in iron, smith working in a forge to produce tools, pots and pans and metalware.

It is possible that the broken portions of set 2 (h1973B and h1974B) showed three animals in procession: tiger looking back and up + rhinoceros + tiger.

Hieroglyph: *heraka* 'spy'. Rebus: eraka, arka 'copper, gold'; eraka 'moltencast, metal infusion'; *era* 'copper'. *āra* 'spokes' Rebus: *āra* 'brass. Hieroglyph: हेर [*hēra*] m (हेरक S through or H) A spy, scout, explorator, an emissary to gather intelligence. 2 f Spying out or spying, surveying narrowly, exploring. (Marathi) **hērati* ' looks for or at '. 2. *hēraka* -- , °*rika* -- m. ' spy ' lex., *hairika* -- m. ' spy ' Hcar., ' thief ' lex. [J. Bloch FestschrWackernagel 149 ← Drav., *kuiēra* ' to spy ', Malt. *ére* ' to see ', DED 765]

Pk. *hēraï* ' looks for or at ' (vihīraï ' watches for '); K.ḍoḍ. *hērūō* ' was seen '; WPah.bhad. bhal. he_rnū ' to look at ' (bhal. *hirāṇū* ' to show '), pāḍ. *hēraṇ, paṅ. hēṇā,* cur. *hērnā,* Ku. *herṇo,* N. *hernu,* A. *heriba,* B. *herā,* Or. *heribā* (caus. herāibā), Mth. *herab,* OAw. *heraï,* H. hernā; G. *hervũ* ' to spy ', M. *herṇẽ* 2. Pk. *hēria* -- m. ' spy '; Kal. (Leitner) "*hériu*" ' spy '; G. *herɔ* m. ' spy ', *herũ* n. ' spying '. Addenda: *hērati: WPah.kṭg. (Wkc.) *hèrnõ, kc. erno* ' observe '; Garh. *hernu* ' to look' (CDIAL 14165) Ko. *er uk- (uky-)* to play 'peeping tom'. Kui *ēra (ēri-)* to spy, scout; n. spying, scouting; pl action *ērka (ērki-).* ? Kuwi (S.) *hēnai* to scout; *hēri kiyali* to see; (Su. P.) *hēnḍ- (hēṭ-)* id. Kur. *ērnā (īryas)* to see, look, look at, look after, look for, wait for, examine, try; ērta'ānā to let see, show; ērānakhrnā to look at one another. Malt. *ére* to see, behold, observe; érye to peep, spy. Cf. 892 Kur. ēthrnā. / Cf. Skt. *heraka-* spy, Pkt. *her-* to look at or for, and many NIA verbs; Turner, CDIAL, no. 14165(DEDR 903)

The most characteristic and unique feature of Harappa Script is the orthography of creating composite hieroglyphs. One vivid example is cited and explained on 3 molded tablets. A narrative on molded tablets and seals shows a one-eyed woman thwarting two rearing tigers. The woman is orthographed with one eye.

Leftmost figure is a seal, to the right are two seals and corresponding sealings made.

The leftmost seal shows the ligatured face, as a hypertext, of the woman holding back two rearing tigers73:

Hieroglyphs to signify *kol* 'furnace, forge' (Kuwi)

kola 'woman' (Nahali.Assamese)

kul 'tiger' (Santali); *kōlu* id. (Te.) *kōlupuli* = Bengal tiger (Te.)Pk. *kolhuya* -- , *kulha* -- m. ' jackal ' < **kōḍhu* -- ; H.*kolhā,* °*lā* m. ' jackal ', adj. ' crafty '; G. *kohlũ,* °*lũ* n. ' jackal ', M. *kolhā,* °*lā* m. *krōṣṭŕ̥* ' crying ' BhP., m. ' jackal ' RV. = *krṓṣṭu* -- m. Pāṇ. [√*kruś*] Pa. *koṭṭhu* -- , °*uka* -- and *kotthu* -- , °*uka* -- m. ' jackal ', Pk. *koṭṭhu* -- m.; Si. *koṭa* 'jackal', *koṭiya* 'leopard' GS 42 (CDIAL 3615). कोल्हा [*kōlhā*] कोल्हें [*kōlhēṃ*] A jackal (Marathi) *kol* 'tiger, jackal' (Konkani.) Rebus: *kol* 'iron', working in iron (Tamil) 'furnace, forge' (Kuwi) k*ol* alloy of five metals, pañcaloha' (Tamil) *kolhe* 'smelters" (See rebus readings of *kulāi*, 'hare' hieroglyph').

Hieroglyph components in the hypertext are: face in profile, one eye, circumfix (circle) and 6 curls of hair.

Note explaining the semantics *kan* 'copper': கன்மம் *kaṉmam,* n. < *karman.* See கருமம். கன்மமன் றெங்கள்கையிற் பாவை பறிப்பது (திவ். திரு வாய். 6, 2, 7). கன்[1] kaṉ, n. perh. கன்மம். 1. Workmanship; வேலைப்பாடு. கன்னார் மதில்சூழ் குடந்தை (திவ். திருவாய். 5, 8, 3). 2. Copper work*; கன்னார் தொழில். (W.) 3. Copper; செம்பு. (ஈடு, 5, 8, 3.) 4. See கன்னத்தட்டு. (நன். 217, விருத்.) I suggest that the expression *karmAra* 'artisan' has this variant in Tamil. **karmán* 'working'. [√kr̥1]Sh. *kramōn̥u* ' hardworking ', m. ' labourer, farmer ' (< *karmāṇaka --); Si. (SigGr) *kamuṇa* ' artisan '.(CDIAL 2893) *karmaśālā* f. ' workshop ' MBh. [kárman -- 1, śā´lā --]Pk. kammasālā -- f.; L. *kamhāl* f. ' hole in the ground for a weaver's feet '; Si. kamhala 'workshop', kamala 'smithy'(CDIAL 2896)

Hieroglyph: circle around the 'eye': Pa. *vaṭṭi -- , °ikā* -- f. 'circumference'(CDIAL 11360) **vartu --* 'something round '. [Cf. *trivártu --* ' threefold ' RV.](CDIAL 11364). *bāṭā,* ' round copper or brass vessel '(Nepali)(CDIAL 11347)

The compound expression Ta. *kampaṭṭam* coinage, coin. Ma. *kammaṭṭam, kammiṭṭam*

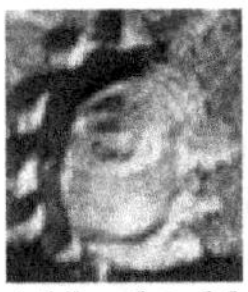

coinage, mint. Ka. *kammaṭa* id.; *kammaṭi* a coiner. (DEDR 1236) is composed of: *ka(n) + (p)aṭṭa*. This is signified orthographically as hieroglyphs signifying semantics: *kāṇa* 'one eye' PLUS *vaṭṭa* 'circumference'. The head of the person is dotted with six pebbles: *baṭa* 'pebble' *baṭa* 'six' Rebus: *bhaṭṭī* 'furnace, forge' *bhāṭi* ' kiln ' *bhaṭhī, bhaṭṭī ' bhāṭhā '* kiln '; H. *bhaṭṭhā* m. ' kiln', *bhaṭ* f. 'kiln'

Thus, the artist scribe orthographically presents a compound expression using the signifiers of *bhaṭṭhā* ' furnace' (for) *kan* (*karman*) 'copperwork' for the message: *kammaṭa* 'mintwork'.

kaṇga 'eye' (Pe.) Rebus: *kang* m. ' brazier, fireplace '?(Kashmiri)(CDIAL 2999) When a 'fish-eye' is mentioned in cuneiform texts, it possibly signified *kang* 'portable brazier'. Other rebuses are: *kan* 'copper'; *dhAu* 'strand' rebus: *dhAI* 'mineral, ore'.

kāṇa -- 'blind of one eye, blind' (Prakrtam.Pali) (CDIAL 3019) *kaṇ* 'eye' (Tamil.Kannada), *kanu, kannu,* 'eye' (Telugu)(DEDR 1159) rebus: Ta. *kaṉ* copper work, copper, workmanship; *kaṉṉāṉ* brazier. Ma. *kannān* id. (DEDR 1402) Alternative: கண்வட்டம்

kaṇ-vaṭṭam 'eye PLUS circumfix' rebus: கண்வட்டம் *kaṇ-vaṭṭan* 'mint'; *baṭa* 'six' rebus: *baṭa* 'iron' *bhaṭa* 'furnace' PLUS *meḍh* 'curl' rebus: *meḍ* 'iron' (Mu.Ho.) *meḍ* 'copper' (Slavic) Thus, the message is: mint with furnace for iron, copper. Tigers: *dula* 'two' rebus: *dul* 'cast metal' *kola* 'tiger' rebus: *kol* 'furnace, forge, working in iron' *kolhe* 'smelter' *kolle* 'blacksmith' *kariba* 'elephant trunk' *ibha* 'elephant' rebus: *karba* 'iron' *ib* 'iron' *eraka* 'nave of wheel' rebus: *erako* 'moltencast, copper' arā 'spoke' rebus: āra 'brass.

The hypertext also signifies *mũh* 'face' for the rebus message: *mũhe* 'ingot' (Santali) *mũhã̄* 'quantity of metal produced at one time in a native smelting furnace'. Thus, the message is amplified: a mint producing iron, copper metal ingots from smelting furnace and brazier.

The lexical evidence is that கண்வட்டம் *kaṇ-vaṭṭam* 'mint' has a synonym (demonstrably, a phonetic variant in *mleccha/meluhha*) The pun intended is conveyed in a Begram ivory hypertext: *khambhaṛā* 'fish-fin' (Lahnda) rebus: *kammaṭa* 'mint' and these two expressions are combined in the Begram ivory (Plate 389)

Begram ivories. Plate 389 Reference: Hackin, 1954, fig.195, no catalog N°. கண்வட்டம் *kaṇ-vaṭṭam*, n. < id. +. 1. Range of vision, eye-sweep, full reach of one's observation; கண்பார்வைக்குட்பட்ட இடம். தங்கள் கண்வட்டத்திலே உண்டுடுத்துத்திரிகிற (ஈடு, 3, 5, 2). 2. Mint; நாணயசாலை.

Bronze Age Revolution and *cire perdue* method of metal casting

Bronze Age Revolution (from ca. 4th millennium BCE) was characterized by the use of tin to create a bronze alloy which was a harder metal than malleable copper and hence, bronze could be used for creating metal statues using cire perdue (lost-wax) technique and to produce cast metal implements and weapons. This revolutionary moment in civilization also necessitated a writing system to document shipments of surplus bronze artifacts and implements to contact areas. In Ancient Near East three writing systems were invented: Egyptian hieroglyphs (ca. 33rd cent. BCE), Cuneiform script (ca. 31st cent. BCE) and Harappa script (c. 34th cent. BCE).

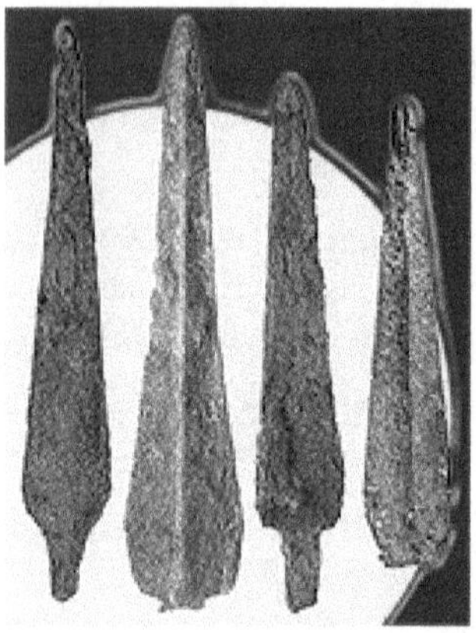

Poliochni. Copper daggers from the "treasure" of the Red period. Early Bronze Age.

"The processing of copper, silver and lead from the mines of the Cyclades (Siphnos, Kythnos), is attested on the Aegean already from the beginning of the 3rd millenium. During the same period the mixing of copper and arsenic (a metal which occurs in copper metals) is ascertained. It aims at the easier processing of copper and at the manufacture of more resistant tools. But the early presence of bronze jewellery and tools on Troy, Poliochni and Thermi does not imply that bronze metallurgy, of copper and tin was developed on these islands. According to archaeometallurgical surveys, the bronze alloy reached the islands in this form from Central Asia through Asia Minor, since sources of tin do not exist in the Aegean. The islands were occupied only with its formation into tools, etc. The knowledge of the preciousness of tin is expressed by the treasuring up of bronze tools in Thermi IVB (Potter's pool), Poliochni Red, Troy IIg and Kythnos, as well as by the presence of a tin bracelet in Thermi IIIA. The bronze alloys were promoted around the middle of the 3rd millenium from the islands of the northeastern Aegean to the Cyclades and the south Aegean. Poliochni seems to have an important role in marine trade and the promotion of the raw material and new technology. The reference to Lemnos in the legend of the expedition of the Argonauts that sailed to Colchis to get the "golden fleece" reflects nothing more than the organized sea trips to obtain precious raw materials for the practice of metallurgy."[74]

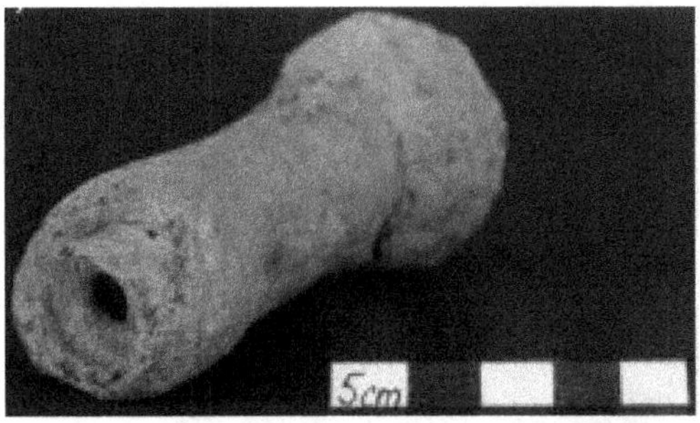

Lost-wax mould, showing layered construction, from Tell edh-Dhiba'i, suburb of Baghdad, excavated in 1965 where a coppersmith's workshop was found (Photo: CJ Davey)[75]"...lost-wax casting was a common process in much of the ancient world from the time that copper metallurgy was first developed. The development of the process begins with solid wax models in the late 5th millennium and ends with skin of wax models for life-size statuary formed by the 'sloshing' method in the classical period. Its origins are therefore much older than previously thought and its geographical spread is broader...Tell edh-Dhiba'I mould...the use of fine and coarse clays reveal that the practices described by the Sanskrit and medieval texts were established by 1700 BCE in Mesopotamia. The attention to the quality of the casting's surface represents an advance in the technology of lost-wax casting...Nahal Mishmar hoard...the mace-heads were made over a wooden stick, the standards had clay cores and the crowns were formed from slabs of wax...Polinchini lost-wax mould[76]...Early Bronze Age lost-wax mould...the mould is for an axe-head and was broken before it was used. It is made from coarse clay and is reddish on the exterior and black on the interior...The mould appears to have been found in a metalworking context...The mould is about 1,000 years earlier than that of Tell edh-Dhiba'i...Benoit Mille has drawn attention to copper alloy 'amulets discovered in the early Chalclithic (late 5th millennium) levels of Mehrgarh in Baluchistan, Pakistan. He reported that metallographic examination established that the ornaments were cast by the lost-wax method.77 The amulets were made from copper alloyed with lead...Mille also draws attention to the 'Leopard Weights from Baluchistan, dating to about 3000 BCE, which were made using a complex core keyed into the investment mould. "

To you, O Aswins, that fly betrayed the soma: RV 1.119.9[78]

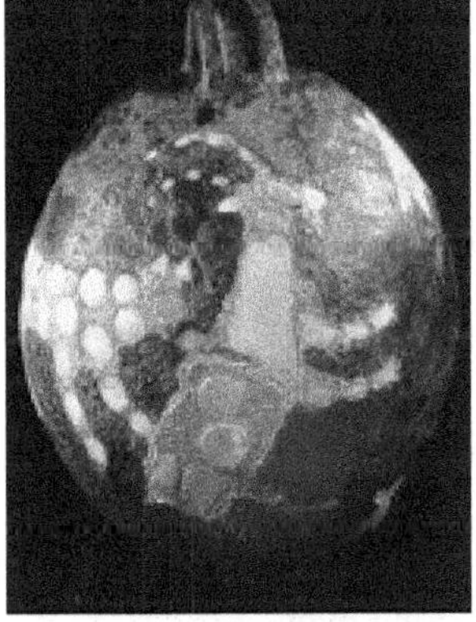

A remarkable *cire perdue* artifact called 'lead or leopard weight' has been found in Shahi Tump which mirrors the Rigvedic metaphor of 'fly betrying the soma'. The fly signifies bees' wax used for *cire perdue* production of ally metal artifacts and sculptures. Such 'bees' are signified together with other hieroglyphs on this lead weight.

Sample of Shahi Tump lead weight with Harappa Script hieroglyphs. Beginning of 3rd millennium BCE. Leopard weight from Shahi-Tump (Baluchistan).

"The artefact was discovered in a grave, in the Kech valley, in eastern Balochistan. It belongs to the Shahi Tump - Makran civilisation (end of 4th millennium -- beginning of 3rd millennium BCE). Ht. 200 mm. weight: 13.5 kg. The shell has been manufactured by lost-wax foundry of a copper alloy (12.6%b, 2.6%As), then it has been filled up through lead (99.5%) foundry. The shell is engraved with figures of leopards hunting wild goats, made of polished fragments of shellfishes. No identification of the artefact's use has been given. (Scientific team: B. Mille, D. Bourgarit, R. Besenval, Musee Guimet, Paris)."

Hieroglyphs of Harappa Script Cipher are signified on the Shahi Tump leopard weight

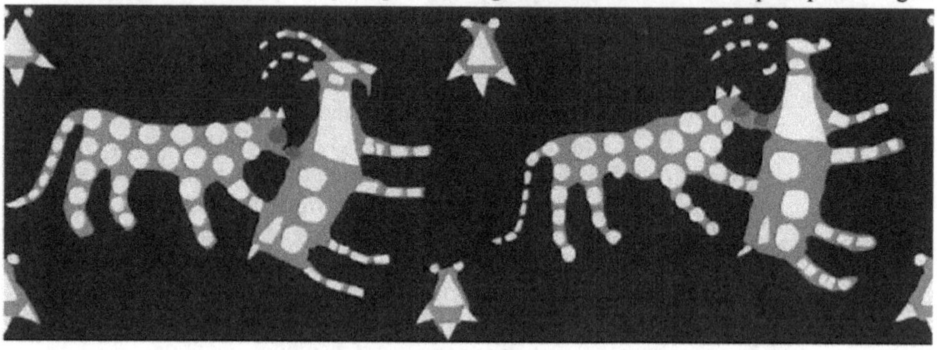

which has been produced using the lost-wax casting method.

The hieroglyphs are: 1. leopard; 2. ibex or antelope; 3. bees (flies).

The rebus-metonymy readings in Meluhha are:

Rebus reading 1: Si. *koṭa* ' jackal ', *koṭiya* ' leopard ' GS 42 (CDIAL 3615). Rebus: *koṭiya* 'dhow, seafaring vessel'

Rebus reading 2: *karaḍa* 'panther'; karaḍa tiger (Pkt); खरडा [*khāraḍā*] A leopard. खरड्या [*khāraḍyā*] m or खरड्यावाघ m A leopard (Marathi). Kol. *keḍiak* tiger. Nk. *khaṛeyak* panther Go. (A.) *khaṛyal* tiger; (Haig) *kariyāl* panther Kui *kṛāḍi, krānḍi* tiger, leopard, hyena. Kuwi (F.) *kṛani* tiger; (S.) *klā'ni* tiger, leopard; (Su. P. Isr.) *kṛa'ni* (pl. *-ŋa*) tiger. / Cf. Pkt. (DNM) *karaḍa-* id. (DEDR 1132). Rebus: करडा [*karaḍā*] Hard from alloy--iron, silver &c. (Marathi) *khārādī* ' turner, a person who fashions or shapes objects on a lathe' (Gujarati)

Hieroglyph: *miṇḍāl* 'markhor' (Tōrwālī) *meḍho* a ram, a sheep (Gujarati)(CDIAL 10120) Rebus: *mẽṛhẽt, meḍ* 'iron' (Santali.Munda.Ho.) *mṟeka, melh* 'goat' (Telugu. Brahui) Rebus: *melukkha milakkhu*, 'copper'. If the animal carried on the right hand of the Gudimallam hunter is an antelope, the possible readings are: *ranku* 'antelope' Rebus: *ranku* 'tin'.

Ka. *mēke* she-goat; mē the bleating of sheep or goats. Te. *mēka, mēka* goat. Kol. *me·ke* id. Nk. *mēke* id. Pa. *mēva*, (S.) *mēya* she-goat. Ga. (Oll.) *mēge,* (S.) *mēge* goat. Go. (M) *mekā*, (Ko.) *mēka* id. ? Kur. *mēxnā (mīxyas)* to call, call after loudly, hail. Malt. *méqe* to bleat. [Te. *mṟēka* (so correct) is of unknown meaning. Br. *mēl̤h* is without etymology; see MBE 1980a.] / Cf. Skt. (lex.) *meka-* goat. (DEDR 5087). *Meluhha, mleccha* (Akkadian. Samskrtam). *Milakkha, Milāca* 'hillman' (Pali) *milakkhu* 'dialect' (Pali) rebus: *mleccha* 'copper' (Prakritam), *milakkhu* 'copper' (Pali).

The bees are metaphors for wax used in the lost-wax casting method.

Hieroglyph: माक्षिक [p= 805,2] mfn. (fr. मक्षिका) coming from or belonging to a bee Rebus: 'pyrites': माक्षिक [p= 805,2] n. a kind of honey-like mineral substance or pyrites MBh. उपधातुः An inferior metal, semi-metal. They are seven; सप्तोपधातवः

स्वर्णं माक्षिकं तारमाक्षिकम् । तुत्थं कांस्यं च रातिश्च सुन्दूरं च शिलाजतु ॥ उपरसः uparasḥउपर सः 1 A secondary mineral, (red chalk,
bitumen, माक्षिक, शिलाजित &c).(Samskritam) मक्षिकः मक्षि (क्षी) का A fly, bee; भो उपस्थितं नयनमधु संनिहिता मक्षिका च M.2. -Comp. -मलम् wax. (Apte)

माक्षिक n. a kind of honey-like mineral substance or pyrites MBh.

माक्षिक, the fly, betrays Soma. RV 1.119.9 There is a pun on the word माक्षिक which also signifies 'pyrites' (secondary ores). An ancient alchemy text refers to the processing of pyrites: uta syaa vaam madhuman maakshikaarapan madey somasyausijo huvanyati (To you, O Aswins, that fly betrayed the soma: RV 1.119.9); maakshika = pyrite ores; fly. cf."maakshikam (pyrites), digested hundred times with juice of plantain leaves, andthen steeped for three days in oil, clarified butter and honey, and then heated strongly in a crucible yields its essence."[79]

(10) **119** (म.1, अनु.17)

ऋषिः कक्षीवान् दैर्घतमसः औशिजः	छन्दः जगती	देवता अश्विनौ

आ वां रथं पुरुमायं मनोजुवं जीराश्वं यज्ञियं जीवसे हुवे ।
सहस्रकेतुं वनिनं शतद्वसुं श्रुष्टीवानं वरिवोधामभि प्रयः ॥ 1 ॥
ऊर्ध्वा धीतिः प्रत्यस्य प्रयामन्यधायि शस्मन्त्समयन्त आ दिशः ।
स्वदामि घर्मं प्रति यन्त्यूतय आ वामूर्जानी रथमश्विनारुहत् ॥ 2 ॥
सं यन्मिथः पस्पृधानासो अग्मत शुभे मखा अमिता जायवो रणे ।
युवोरह प्रवणे चेकिते रथो यदश्विना वहथः सूरिमा वरम् ॥ 3 ॥
युवं भुज्युं भुरमाणं विभिर्गतं स्वयुक्तिभिर्निवहन्ता पितृभ्य आ ।
यासिष्टं वर्तिर्वृषणा विजेन्यं१ दिवोदासाय महि चेति वामवः ॥ 4 ॥
युवोरश्विना वपुषे युवायुजं रथं वाणी येमतुरस्य शर्ध्यम् ।
आ वां पतित्वं सख्याय जग्मुषी योषावृणीत जेन्या युवां पती ॥ 5 ॥
युवं रेभं परिषूतेरुरुष्यथो हिमेन घर्मं परितप्तमत्रये ।
युवं शयोरवसं पिप्यथुर्गवि प्र दीर्घेण वन्दनस्तार्यायुषा ॥ 6 ॥
युवं वन्दनं निर्ऋतं जरण्यया रथं न दस्रा करणा समिन्वथः ।
क्षेत्रादा विप्रं जनथो विपन्यया प्र वामत्र विधते दंसना भुवत् ॥ 7 ॥
अगच्छतं कृपमाणं परावति पितुः स्वस्य त्यजसा निबाधितम् ।
स्वर्वतीरित ऊतीर्युवोरह चित्रा अभीके अभवन्नभिष्टयः ॥ 8 ॥

उत स्या वां मधुमन्मक्षिकारपन्मदे सोमस्यौशिजो हुवन्यति ।
युवं दधीचो मन आ विवासथोऽथा शिरः प्रति वामश्व्यं वदत् ॥ 9 ॥
युवं पेदवे पुरुवारमश्विना स्पृधां श्वेतं तरुतारं दुवस्यथः ।
शर्यैरभिद्युं पृतनासु दुष्टरं चर्कृत्यमिन्द्रमिव चर्षणीसहम् ॥ 10 ॥

Griffith translation: RV 1.119.1-10:1. HITHER, that I may live, I call unto the feast your wondrous car, thought-swift, borne on by rapid steeds. With thousand banners, hundred treasures, pouring gifts, promptly obedient, bestowing ample room. 2 Even as it moveth near my hymn is lifted up, and all the regions come together to sing praise. I sweeten the oblations; now the helpers come. Urjani hath, O Asvins, mounted on your car. 3 When striving man with man for glory they have met, brisk, measurcless, eager for victory in fight,Then verily your car is seen upon the slope when ye, O Asvins, bring some choice boon to the prince. 4 Ye came to Bhujyu while he struggled in the flood, with flying birds, self-yoked, ye bore him to his sires. Ye went to the far-distant home, O Mighty Ones; and fameḍ is your great aid to Divodisa given. 5 Asvins, the car which you had yoked for glorious show your own two voices urged directed to its goal. Then she who came for friendship, Maid of noble birth, elected you as Husbands, you to be her Lords. 6 Rebha ye saved from tyranny; for Atri's sake ye quenched with cold the fiery pit that compassed him. Ye made the cow of Sayu stream refreshing milk, and Vandana was holpen to extended life. 7 Doers of marvels, skilful workers, ye restored Vandana, like a car, worn out with length of days. From earth ye brought the sage to life in wondrous mode; be your great deeds done here for him who honours you. 8 Ye went to him who mourned in a far distant place, him who was left forlorn by treachery of his sire. Rich with the light ofheaven was then the help ye gave, and marvellous your succour when ye stood by him. 9 To you in praise of sweetness sang the honey-bee: Ausija calleth you in Soma's rapturous joy. Ye drew unto yourselves the spirit of Dadhyac, and then the horse's head uttered his words to you. 10 A horse did ye provide for Pedu, excellent, white, O ye Asvins, conqueror of combaṭants, Invincible in war by arrows, seeking heaven worthy of fame, like Indra, vanquisher of men.

A reference to *mAkshika* in RV 1.119.9 is a pun on the word: *mAkshika* 'fly' *mAkshika* 'pyrites'. It is suggested that the 'bees' signified as hieroglyphs on the leopard weight are an intimation of the nature of the metal alloy used to create the weight: the alloy was a copper pyrite. (copper + lead). It appears that the processing of Soma involved the purification processes to isolate such pyrites by processes of carburization and oxidation in processing/purifying Soma (which may have been compounded with pyrites), through fire-altars.

Replica of bronze sceptre from the Nahal Mishmar Hoard. The double ibex was made using a complicated wax and ceramic mold. Standard (scepter) with ibex heads.Dm. mraṅ m. 'markhor' Wkh. merg f. 'ibex' (CDIAL 9885) Tor. miṇḍ 'ram', miṇḍā́l 'markhor' (CDIAL 10310) Rebus: meḍ (Ho.); mẽṛhet 'iron' (Munda.Ho.) dula 'pair' Rebus: *dul* 'cast metal'. *Āra* 'six' 'spokes' Rebus: *āra* 'brass.

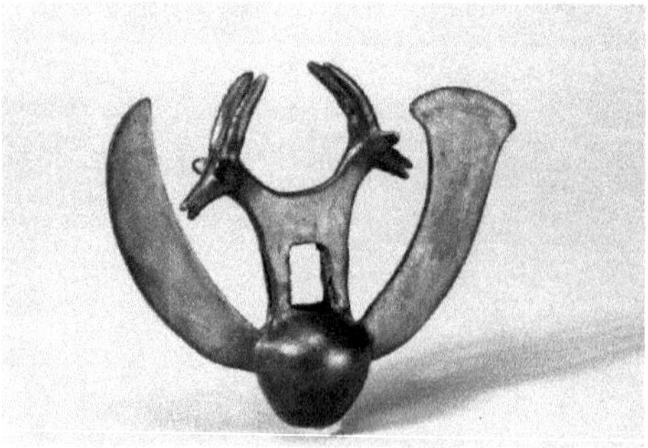

Late Cycladic (17th century BC) gold ibex sculpture about 10 cm long with lost-wax cast feet and head and repoussé body, from an excavation on Santorini, an island in the southern Aegean Sea, about 200 km (120 mi) southeast of Greece's mainland.

Akkadian head made by lost-wax cassting method found at Nineveh 2300-2159 BCE (from Iraq 3 pl.6 British School of Archaeology in Iraq)

First recorded use of wax for casting by sculptors (After figure in LB Hunt80 document)

The First Recorded Use of Lost Wax Casting

The earliest known written reference to lost wax casting comes from the Babylonian city of Sippar and is dated 1 789 B.C., during the reign of the great King Hammurabi. Written in cuneiform on a clay tablet, this is a receipt for a small quantity of wax issued to a metal worker and is composed in the typically bureaucratic manner of the period.

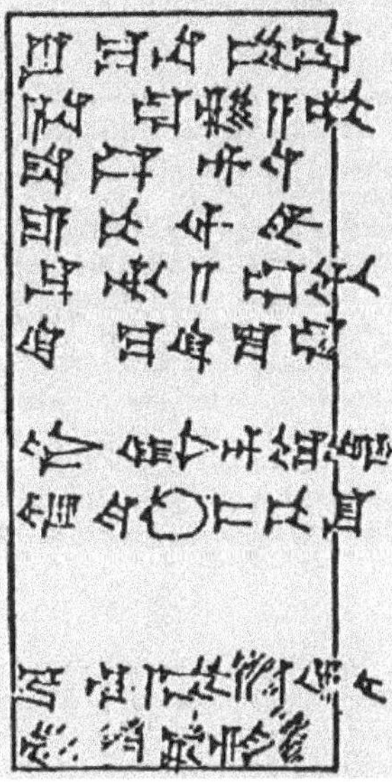

'Two thirds of a mina of wax to make a bronze key for the temple of Shamash received by the metal worker from the temple treasury

In the presence of Silli-nin-karrak and of the storekeeper, his colleagues

On the nineteenth day of the month of Arabsammu in the year of building the temple wall'

Sumerian metalworkers were practicing lost-wax casting from approximately c. 3500–3200 BCE81 The earliest example from Harappa civilization is that of a dancing girl bronze statue which dates to the period c. 3300 to 1300 BCE.82 There is evidence for Meluhha dhokra-kamar metalwork in Harappa civilization; the word dhokra refers to lost-wax method of metal castings. This professional title, dhokra kamar, is evidenced by Meluhha hieroglyphs on a seal from Mohenjo-daro and on a tablet from Dholavira of the Sarasvati-Sindhu (Harappa) Civilization. In ancient Bharata texts, the cire perdue technique is referred to as madhucchiṣṭa vidhānam. मधु madhu -उच्छिष्टम्,-उत्थम्,-उत्थितम् 1 bees'-wax; शस्त्रासवमधूच्छिष्टं मधु लाक्षा च बर्हिषः Y.3.37; मधूच्छिष्टेन केचिच्च जध्नुरन्योन्यमुत्कटाः Rām.5.62.11.-2 the casting of an image in wax; Mānasāra; the name of 68th chapter. This technique was clearly attested in the Epic Rāmāyaṇa. मधुशिष्ट madhuśiṣṭa 'wax' (Monier-Williams, p. 780).

At the end of 5th millennium BCE, Shahi Tump evidences lost-wax casting83 on the lead weight with Harappa Script hieroglyphs of bees, leopard and goat.

Muhly speculates on the possible reason for using of hard alloy for lost-wax castings:"…perhaps arsenical copper was used at Nahal Mishmar not because it was harder, more durable metal but because it would have facilitated the production of intricate lost-wax castings." (Muhly, J., 1986, The beginnings of metallurgy in the old world. In Maddin R, ed., The beginning of the use of metals and alloys, pp. 2-20. Zhengzhou: Second International conference on the beginning of the use of metals and alloys.)

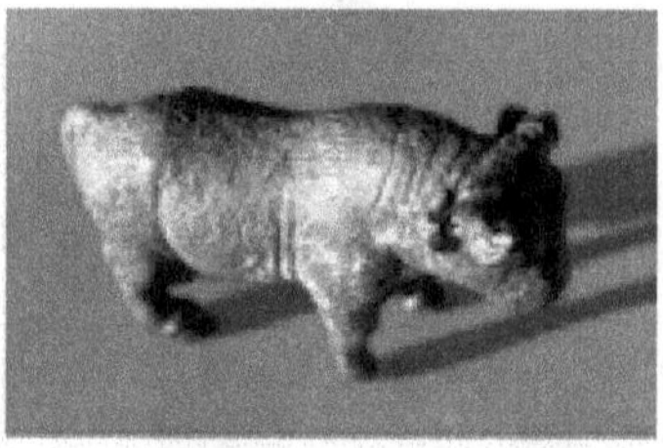

Dancing girl. Mohenjo-daro. Now displayed at National Museum, New Delhi.Lost-wax copper alloy casting. c. 2500 BCE.

Dancing girl of Sarasvati civilization. 4.3 in. h. Mohenjo-Daro. "Metallurgists smelted silver, lead, and copper and worked gold too. Coppersmiths employed tin bronze as in Sumer, but also an alloy of copper with from 3.4 to 4.4 per cent of arsenic, an alloy used also at Anau in Transcaspia. They could cast cire perdue (lost wax) and rivet, but never seem to have resorted to brazing or soldering." (Childe, Gordon, 1952, New light on the most ancien East, New York, Frederick A. Praeger)

'Dancing girl' 10.8 cm. from Mohenjo-daro of Sarasvati civilization dates to the early 2nd millennium BCE. (Marshall, 1931, Mohenjo-daro and the Indus civilization, Vol. I, London, Arthus Probsthain, p. 345; pl. 94). It is unclear if the following artefacts were also made by the cire perdue (lost-wax) casting technology: a bronze foot and anklet from Mohenjo-daro; and a bronze figurine of a bull (Kalibangan). (Courtesy: ASI) "Archaeological excavations have shown that Harappa metal smiths obtained copper ore (either directly or through local communities) from the Aravalli hills, Baluchistan or beyond. They soon discovered that adding tin to copper produced bronze, a metal harder than copper yet easier to cast, and also more resistant to corrosion."

Dance-step as hieroglyph on a potsherd, Bhirrana. Hieroglyph: meṭ sole of foot, footstep, footprint (Ko.); meṭṭu step, stair, treading, slipper (Te.)(DEDR 1557). Rebus: meḍ

'iron'(Munda); मेढ meḍh'merchant's helper'(Pkt.) meḍ iron (Ho.) meṛed-bica = iron stone ore, in contrast to bali-bica, iron sand ore (Munda)

मेढो vi. 138 वणिक्सहायः, one who helps a merchant.

Des'īnāmamālā Glossary, p. 71

Desinamamala of Hemacandra ed. R. Pischel (1938) meḍ 'iron'(Munda); मेढ meḍh'merchant's helper'(Prakrtam) meḍho 'one who helps a merchant' (Desi) meḍ iron (Ho.) meṛed-bica = iron stone ore, in contrast to bali-bica, iron sand (Santali.Munda)

Yuval Gorden notes:"While the traditional manifestation of the technology has vanished from many parts of the world, it has survived in some areas of India. The tradition is carried on in the manufacture of small pieces by tribal groups or by Hindu metalworkers. These tribal people live in the districts of Bankura, Burdwan, and Midnapore in West Bengal...The Dhokra apply two or more layers of clay on top of the wax model. First, a thin clay paste is added and allowed to dry; then a layer of rougher clay mixed with rice husks is added and also allowed to dry. A hole is sometimes cut through the top of the clay coverings to allow for the entrance of the molten metal. Likewise, a channel is made in the bottom to let the wax flow out of the mold. Metal wires are then tied around the whole construction to keep it intact. The mold is heated until the wax is melted and poured out...Once the mold mixture has set hard, the molds are placed in a furnace and heated until the wax is melted and integrated into the rather spongy fabric of the mold. Then the heating continues until the metal is melted, made evident by a green tinge of the fire, at which point the molds are turned upside down and filled with the liquid metal from the flask. This point is extremely important for our discussion, because it indicates that crucibles are not necessarily used in the process of lost wax casting, in contrast to open casting, where their use is mandatory."

Apart from Dong Son drums, which come from the Dong Son, and Phung Nguyen cultures, bracelets and rings, were made by cire perdue at Non Nok Tha and Ban Chiang, Thailand.[84]

1357

Mohenodaro seal. Pict-103 Horned (female with breasts hanging down?) person with a tail and bovine legs standing near a tree fisting a horned tiger rearing on its hindlegs.

Rebus Meluhha readings of hieroglyphs/hypertext:

kuṭi 'tree' rebus: *kuṭhi* 'smelter'*kola* 'tiger' rebus: *kol* 'working in iron''furnace, forge' *kūdā* 'jumping' rebus: *kūdār* 'turner' PLUS *dhokra* 'decrepit woman' rebus: *dhokra* '*cire perdue* metal casting artisan' PLUS *ḍhaṅgaru, ḍhiṅgaru* m. 'lean emaciated beast'(Sindhi) Rebus: *dhangar* 'blacksmith' (Maithili) Thus, the pictorial motif narrative signifies a cire perdue blacksmith with smelter and working in iron.

Text signs: *dhAtu* 'strands of rope' Rebus: *dhAtu* 'mineral, metal, ore'

ḍato 'claws or pincers (chelae) of crabś rebus: *dhAtu* 'mineral ore' PLUS *ḍhāḷā* m. 'sprig' rebus: *ḍhāḷa* m. 'large ingot' *dula* 'two' rebus: *dul* 'metal casting'. Thus, the three hieroglyphs as hypertext reinforce the working with minerals (ores), metals, metal castings.

A comment is warranted on the following Fig. 16 of Parpola's paper85:

Fig. 16 Two-faced tablet from Dholavira, Kutch, Gujarat, suggesting child sacrifice (lower picture) connected with crocodile cult (upper picture).86

Even assuming that a seated person on the lower sketch figure with raised arms carries 'children' I do not see how Asko Parpola (AP the sketch-maker) can jump to the conclusion of 'suggested child sacrifice'. The pair of children are hieroglyphs of Harappa script: *dula* 'pair' rebus: *dul* 'metal casting'

Hieroglyph Alternative 1: B. *polā* ' child, son '; M. *poḷ* m. ' bull dedicated to the gods '; Si. pollā ' young of an animal '.4. Pk. *pōāla* -- m. ' child, bull '; A. *powāli* ' young of animal or bird '. (CDIAL 8399) Rebus: पोळ *pōḷa* 'magnetite, ferrite ore'. The adorant carrying two children may signify: *bhaTa* 'worshipper' rebus: *bhaTa* 'furnace' PLUS dula 'two' rebus: dul 'metal casting' PLUS *pōḷa* 'child' rebus: *pōḷa* 'magnetite, ferrite ore'. Thus, furnace work for magnetite castings (a special type of cast iron).

Hieroglyph Alternative 2: **kuḍa*1 ' boy, son ', °*ḍī* ' girl, daughter '. [Prob. ← Mu. (Sant. Muṇḍari *koṛa* ' boy ', *kuṛi* ' girl ', Ho *koa, kui*, Kūrkū *kōn, kōnjē*); or ← Drav. (Tam. *kuṟa* ' young ', Kan. *koḍa* ' youth ') T. Burrow BSOAS xii 373. Prob. separate from RV. *kŕ̊tā* -- ' girl ' H. W. Bailey TPS 1955, 65. -- Cf. *kuḍáti* ' acts like a child ' Dhātup.]NiDoc. *kuḍ'aġa* ' boy ', *kuḍ'i* ' girl '; Ash. *kū'ṛə* ' child, foetus ', *istrimalī* -- *kuṛä´* ' girl '; Kt. *kŕū, kuŕuk* ' young of animals '; Pr. *kyúru* ' young of animals, child ', *kyurú* ' boy ', *kurī´* ' colt, calf '; Dm. *kúŕa* ' child ', Shum. *kuṛ*; Kal. *kūŕ**1*k* ' young of animals '; Phal. *kuṛī̃* ' woman, wife '; K. *kūrü* f. ' young girl ', kash. *kōṛī*, ram. *kuṛhī*; L. *kuṛā* m. ' bridegroom ', *kuṛī* f. ' girl, virgin, bride ', awāṇ. *kuṛī* f. ' woman '; P. *kuṛī* f. ' girl, daughter ', P. bhaṭ. WPah. khaś. *kuṛi*, cur. *kuḷī*, cam. *kŏḷā* ' boy ', *kuṛī* ' girl '; -- B. *ā̃ṭ* -- *kuṛā* ' childless ' (*ā̃ṭa* ' tight ')? -- X pṓta -- 1: WPah. bhad. *kō* ' son ', *kūī* ' daughter ', bhal. *ko* m., *koi* f., pāḍ. *kuā, kōī*, paṅ. *koā, kūī.* (CDIAL 3245) rebus: *kuṭhi* 'smelter'. Thus, metal casting (using) smelter. *kuṛī* 'girl, child' Rebus: *kuṭhi*

'smelter furnace' (Santali) *kuṛī* f. 'fireplace' (H.); *krvṛi* f. 'granary (WPah.); *kuṛī, kuṛo house,* building'(Ku.)(CDIAL 3232) *kuṭi* 'hut made of boughs' (Skt.) *guḍi* temple (Telugu). A narrative seen as a rebus metonymy is an alternative to the speculation of some type of child sacrifice which is not consistent with the social organization evidenct from archaeological reports of hundreds of ancient sites.

To compare the details provided by AP's sketch on this Fig. 16, I a photograph of the tablet is presented. The seated person holding two children may signify smelting and casting of पोळ *pōḷa* 'magnetite (a ferrite ore)' since the hieroglyphs of Harappa Script signify:1. *dula* 'pair' (of children) rebus: *dul* 'metal casting' PLUS 2. *polā* 'child, son'. It will be an article of faith if any interpretation of 'child sacrifice' is read in the inscription of the Dholavira terracotta tablet. The overall message has to be consistently read for both pictorial motifs and narratives and the text signs documenting *dhamma samjna* 'responsibilty indicators" and detailing metalwork technical details.]

Harappa script hieroglyphs on Dholavira terracotta tablet

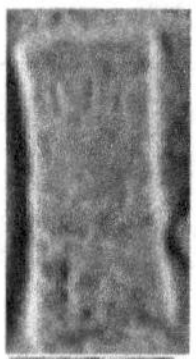

poḷy sacred dairy (Toda) Alternative: *kole.l* 'temple' Rebus: *kole.l* 'smithy, forge' where iron smelting/working involves पोळ *pōḷa* 'magnetite (a ferrite ore)' (cognate with *bolad* 'steel' (Russian).

kuṭi 'curve; rebus: कुटिल *kuṭila, katthīl* (8 parts copper, 2 parts tin) PLUS *sal* 'splinter' rebus: *sal* 'workshop'. Thus, *kuṭila sal*,'bronze workshop'.

dula 'pair' rebus: *dul* 'metal casting' PLUS खांडा [*khāṇḍā*] m A jag, notch, or indentation (as upon the edge of a tool or weapon). (Marathi) Rebus: *khāṇḍā* 'tools, pots and pans, implements PLUS *aḍaren, ḍaren* lid, cover (Santali) Rebus: *aduru* 'native metal' (Ka.) *aduru* = *gan.iyinda tegadu karagade iruva aduru* = ore taken from the mine, unsmelted. Thus, native metal cast implements

Hieroglyph: *kanka, karṇaka,* 'rim of jar' rebus: *karṇī* 'supercargo, a representative of the ship's owner on board a merchant ship, responsible for overseeing the cargo and its sale'. Thus, the Dholavira terracotta tablet inscription is a proclamation of a dhokra kamar 'cire perdue metal caster artisan' and the text signs as hypertext declare his profession or responsibility indicators as iron worker with native metal, metal caster, working in a smithy, forge (temple).

Dholavira molded terracotta tablet with Meluhha hieroglyphs written on two sides.

Hieroglyph: *eraka* 'upraised arm' rebus: *eraka* 'molten cast, copper'

Hieroglyph: *dula* 'pair' rebus: *dul* 'metal casting' PLUS *karA* 'crocodile' rebus: *khār* 'blacksmith'

Hieroglyph: *Ku. ḍokro, ḍokhro ' old man '; B. ḍokrā ' old, decrepit ', Or. ḍokarā; H. ḍokrā ' decrepit '; G. ḍokɔ m. ' penis ', ḍokrɔ m. ' old man ', M. ḍokrā m. -- Kho. (Lor.) duk ' hunched up, hump of camel '; K. ḍǒku ' humpbacked ' perh. < *ḍōkka -- 2. Or. dhokaṛa ' decrepit, hanging down (of breasts) '*.(CDIAL 5567). M. *ḍhẽg n. ' groin ', ḍhẽgā* m. ' buttock '. M. *dhõgā* m. ' buttock '. (CDIAL 5585). Glyph: Br. *kōṇḍō* on all fours, bent double. (DEDR 204a) Rebus: *kunda* 'turner' *kundār* turner (A.); *kũdār, kũdāri (B.); kundāru (Or.); kundau* to turn on a lathe, to carve, to chase; *kundau dhiri* = a hewn stone; *kundau murhut* = a graven image (Santali) *kunda* a turner's lathe (Skt.)(CDIAL 3295) Tiger has head turned backwards. క్రమ్మర *krammara.* adv. క్రమ్మరిల్లు or క్రమరబడు Same as క్రమ్మరు (Telugu). Rebus: *krəm* back'(Kho.)(CDIAL 3145) *karmāra* 'smith, artisan' (Skt.) *kamar* 'smith' (Santali)

Pa. kōḍ (pl. kōḍul) horn; Ka. kōḍu horn, tusk, branch of a tree; kōr horn Tu. kōḍů, kōḍu horn Ko. kṛ (obl. kṭ-)((DEDR 2200) *Paš. kōṇḍā 'bald', Kal. rumb. kōṇḍa 'hornless'.(CDIAL 3508). Kal. rumb. khōṇḍ a 'half'* (CDIAL 3792). Rebus: *koḍ* 'workshop' (Gujarati)

kāruvu 'crocodile' Rebus: *khār* 'blacksmith' (Kashmiri)

kola 'tiger' Rebus: *kol* 'metal, working in iron', '*pañcaloha*, alloy of five metals. *kōlal* m. ' name of a degraded tribe ' Hariv. Pk. *kōla* -- m.; B. *kol* ' name of a Muṇḍā tribe'(CDIAL 3532).

Hieroglyph: *dhokra* 'decrepit woman with breasts hanging down'. Rebus: *dhokra kamar* 'artisan caster using lost-wax technique'.

Hieroglyph: **dhōkkal ' sacking, matting '. 2. *dhōkha -- . 3. *dhōṅga -- 2. 4. *ḍhōkka* -- 1. [Cf. *ṭōkka -- 1]1. Ext. -- *ḍ* -- : N. *dhokro* ' large jute bag ', B. *dhokaṛ*; Or. *dhokaṛa* ' cloth bag '; Bi. *dhŏkrā* ' jute bag '; Mth. *dhokṛā* ' bag, vessel, receptacle '; H. *dhukṛī* f. ' small bag '; G.*dhokṛũ* n. ' bale of cotton '; -- with -- *ṭṭ* -- : M. *dhokṭī* f. ' wallet '; -- with -- *n* -- : G. *dhokṇũ* n. ' bale of cotton '; -- with -- *s* -- : N. (Tarai) *dhokse* ' place covered with a mat to store rice in '.2. L. *dhohẽ* (pl. *dhūhī̃*) m. ' large thatched shed '.
3. M. *dhõgḍā* m. ' coarse cloth ', *dhõgṭī* f. ' wallet '.4. L. *ḍhok* f. ' hut in the fields '; Ku. *ḍhwākā* m. pl. ' gates of a city or market '; N. *ḍhokā* (pl. of **ḍhoko*) ' door '; -- OMarw. *ḍhokaro* m. ' basket '; -- N. *ḍhokse* ' place covered with a mat to store rice in, large basket '..(CDIAL 6880) Rebus: dhokra 'cire perdue' casting metalsmith.

Plate II. Chlorite artifacts referred to as 'handbagś f-g (w 24 cm, thks 4.8 cm.); h (w 19.5 cm, h 19.4 cm, thks 4 cm); j (2 28 cm; h 24 cm, thks 3 cm); k (w 18.5, h 18.3, thks 3.2) Jiroft IV. Iconography of chlorite artifacts.[87]

Mehergarh. 2.2 cm dia. 5 mm reference scale. Perhaps coppper alloyed with lead. [quote]Bourgarit and Mille (Bourgarit D., Mille B. 2007. Les premiers objets métalliques ont-ils été fabriqués par des métallurgistes ? L'actualité Chimique .

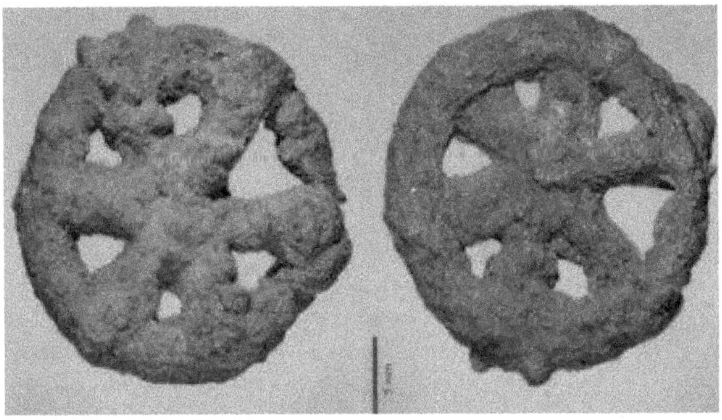

Octobre-Novembre 2007 - n° 312-313:54-60) have reported the finding (probably in the later still unreported excavation period) of small Chalcolithic "amulets" which they claim to have been produced by the process of Lost

Wax. According to them, "The levels of the fifth millennium Chalcolithic at Mehrgarh have delivered a few amulets in shape of a minute wheel, while the technological study showed that they were made by a process of lost wax casting. The ring and the spokes were modelled in wax which was then coated by a refractory mould that was heated to remove the wax. Finally, the molten metal was cast in place of the wax. Metallographic examination confirmed that it was indeed an object obtained by casting (dendrite microstructure). This discovery is quite unique because it is the earliest attestation of this technique in the world." They then, further on, state that "The development of this new technique of lost wax led to another invention, the development of alloys...Davey (Davey C. 2009.The Early History of Lost-Wax Casting, in J. Mei and Th. Rehren (eds), Metallurgy and Civilisation: Eurasia and Beyond Archetype, pp. 147-154. London: Archetype Publications Ltd.) relies only upon these Mehrgarh findings, as well as on the Nahal Mishmar hoard, to claim that Lost Wax casting began in the Chalcolithic period before 4000 BCE."
[unquote][88] (Shlomo Guil)

Cire perdue method was used in Uruk, ca.3500 BCE. to make a recumbent ram in silver which is mounted on pins and dowelled into the center of a cylinder seal. This was a hieroglyph, tagged to cylinder seal method of writing by impressing an agreement to a transaction or to indicate ownership. This cylinder seal is carved with figures of cattle. Ashmolean Museum, Univ. of Oxford. "The Ashmolean Museum describes this item as a cylinder seal showing a herd of cattle and reed huts containing calves and vessels. The seal itself is made of magnesite ($MgCO_3$) with small (a few centimeters) cast silver ram-shaped finial. No claim is made by the museum that it was produced by the Lost Wax process and it is dated by the museum to the Late Uruk period or "around 3200 BCE". The item has been purchased by the museum but its provenance is unknown and therefore cannot be precisely dated." (Shlomo Guil)[89]

Bull figure with a vertical hole Maykop kurgan (Oshad) Middle of the 4th millenium B.C.E. Silver Bull figure with a vertical hole Maykop kurgan (Oshad)Middle of the 4th millenium B.C.E.Gold.[90]

"Maykop culture (also spelled Maikop), ca. 3700 BC—2500 BC, was a major Bronze Age archaeological culture in the Western Caucasus region of Southern Russia. It extends along the area from the Taman Peninsula at the Kerch Strait to near the modern border of Dagestan and southwards to the Kura River."[91]- "The skeleton of a chief, thickly covered with cinnabar, (red mercury sulphide) lay in the southern half of the chamber. Ten objects, made of arsenical copper were placed on a woven mat along with three stone objects. Also found were about twenty silver and gold vessels, kettles, a bucket and bowls all made of arsenical copper. Next to the body lay hollow rods of silver and gold compound, some of which were inserted into gold and silver bull figures of approximate height of 8 cm. There were four bulls in all, two of gold and two of silver. There is no doubt that the bull statuettes were produced by the Lost Wax technique." (Shlomo Guil)[92]

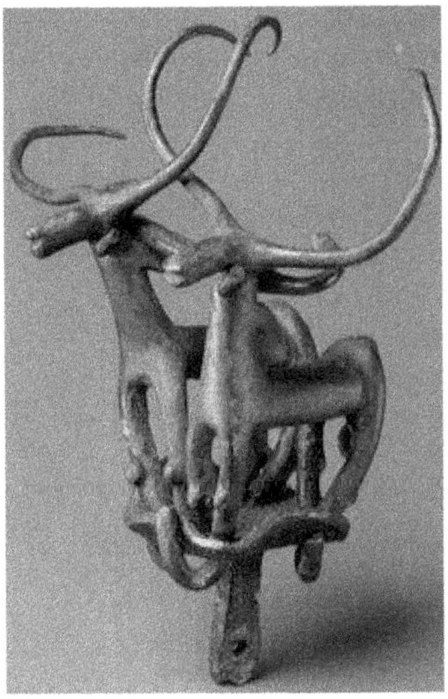

Rhyton in shape of a Zebu, Eastern Iran/Western Central Asia, late 3rd to early 2nd millennium B.C.E.[93]

Standard with two long–horned bulls, 2400–2000 BCE;[94] Early Bronze Age III North central Anatolia Arsenical copper; H. 6 1/4 in. (15.9 cm) This pair of long-horned bulls probably served as a finial for a religious or ceremonial standard. Cast separately, they are held together by extensions of their front and back legs, bent around the plinth. A pierced tang at the base suggests that the pair was connected to another objectBronze bull. 5 in. h. X 7 in. l. Empty eye-sockets possibly held semiprecious stones. The small hump on its back, amove the forelegs, identifies this as a "Zebu bull" (Bos indicus), a species that originated in India, but which was present in the Near East as early as the fourth millennium B.C.E. Prof. Amihai Mazar, 1983, Bronze Bull Found in Israelite "High Place" from the Time of the Judges, BAR 9:05, Sep/Oct 1983 notes that the discovery was made on the summit of a hill in northern Samaria. Meluhha rebus readings:

khũṭ 'zebu'. Rebus: *khũṭ* 'guild, community'; *adar ḍaṅgra* 'zebu or humped bull'; rebus: *aduru* 'native metal' (Kannada); *dhangar* 'blacksmith' (Hindi) *pōḷa* 'zebu' rebus: *pōḷa* 'magnetite, ferrite ore'.

Migrations of hieroglyphs and the significance of hieroglyphs of Harappa Script

Analyzing artifacts from Jiroft, Jean Perrot makes an interesting observation: "Significance. The interpretation of images is a risky enterprise. Decorative themes are transmitted, but they sometimes end up expressing an ideology that is different from the one that was initially symbolized. Images have a life of their own, and when they travel in space and time, their meaning may undergo a change. Our interpretations are a function of our culture and of our myths. Moreover, when dealing with the Middle East and its ancient spirituality, we tend to be content with notions found in late Mesopotamian literature, but such notions are anachronistic. Whatever the case, the iconography of the Iranian plateau should not be viewed through the prism of the Mesopotamian civilization. In the same fashion as there is a certain logic between the containing and the contained in the ornamentation of the vases, there may be another between that of an object and its end-use. Since the vases and objects of Jiroft are known to have come from tombs, their ornamentation may relate to funerary rites. This is what the bucolic scenes decorating the high cups suggest, where ibexes of all ages are harmoniously mixing with 'blooming bushes."[95]

Ibexes and bushes (After Fig. 5 in Jean Perrot, opcit.)

miṇḍā'l ' markhor ' Pa. meṇḍa -- m. ' ram ', °aka -- ' made of a ram's horn (e.g. a bow) '; Pk. meḍḍha -- ,meṁḍha -- (°ḍhī -- f.), °ṁḍa -- , miṁḍha -- (°dhiā -- f.), °aga -- m. ' ram '(CDIAL 10310) rebus: *mẽṛhẽt, meḍ* 'iron' (Santali.Mu.Ho.)
meḍhA 'dhanam, wealth'; *medha* 'yajna' *meḍh* 'merchant's .helper. Thus, iron worker, merchant.

Following this insightful note of Jean Perrot, it is reasonable to hypothesise that the images presented such as those of ibexes, zebu may also relate to the 'responsibility signifiers" *dhamma samjna*, which are clear and unambiguous from Harappa Script hieroglyphs. These images of Jiroft may thus represent the professions and functions with which the deceased ancestors were associated during the Bronze Age Revolution.

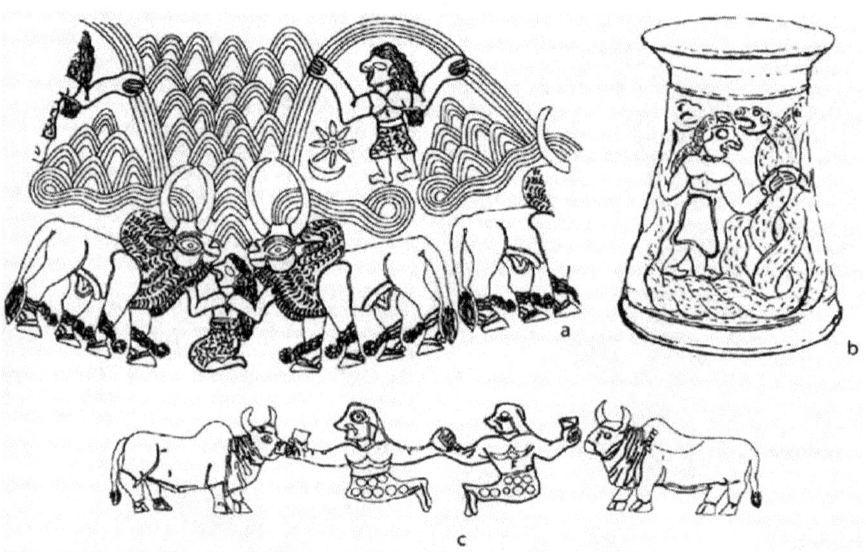

a. mountains landscape and waers; (upper part) a man under an arch with sun and crescent moon symbols; (lower part) man seated on his heels holding zebus; b. man holding a snake; c. two men (drinking) and zebus, on a small cylindrical vessel; d. Head of woman protruding from jar, and snakes; 3. man falling from a tree to the trunk of which a zebu is tied; f. man with clas and bull-man playing with cheetahs, and a scorpion in the center (on a cylindrical vessel).[96]

These are hieroglyph narratives rendering rebus metalwork catalogues: *poLa 'zebu' rebus: poLa 'magnetite, ferrite ore' bica 'scorpion' rebus: bica 'haematite, ferrite ore' kola 'woman', kulA 'serpent hood' rebus: kol 'working in iron' karaDa 'leopard'*

rebus: karaDa 'hard alloy' tALa 'palm' rebus: dhALa 'large ingot' ayo 'fish' rebus: aya 'iron', ayas 'metal'..

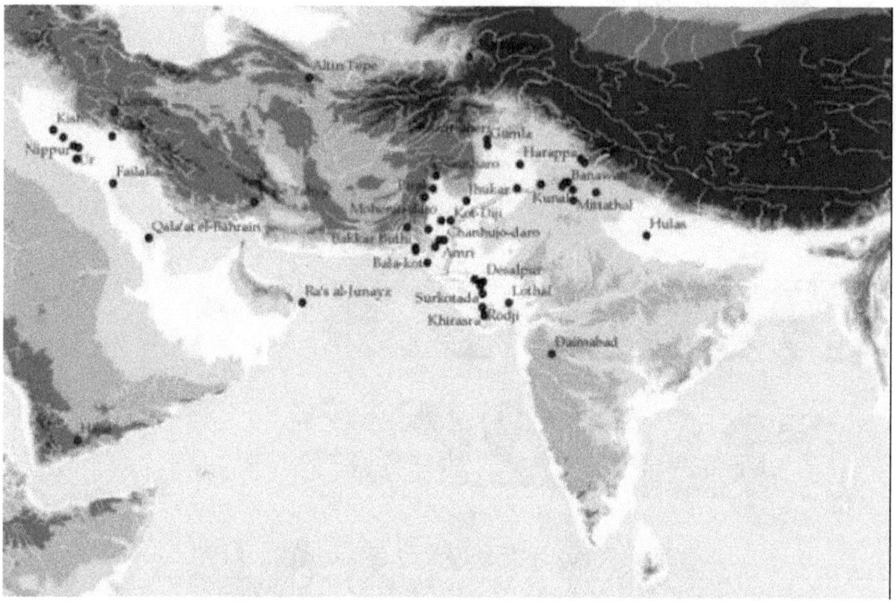

Some discovery sites of Harappa Script Corpora in Bhāratam (Ancient India), Persian Gulf and Ancient Near East

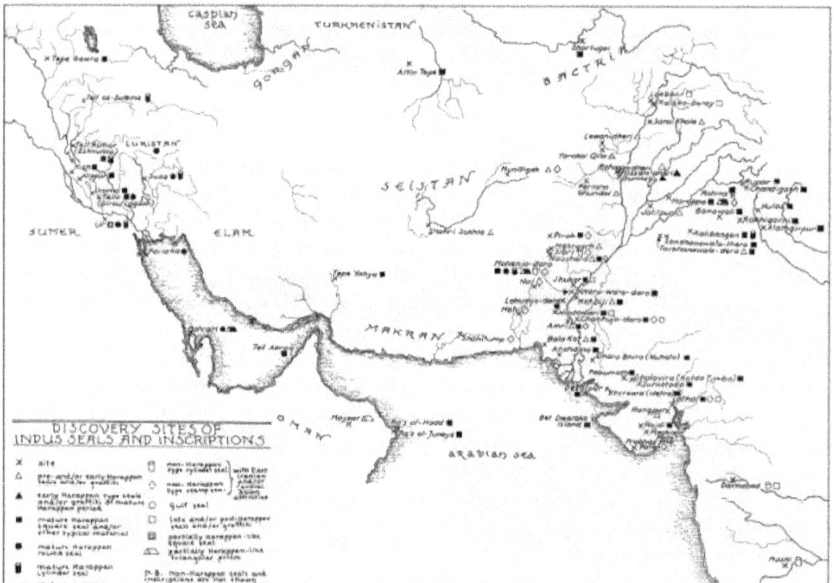

Discovery sites of over 7000 inscriptions of Harappa Script Corpora (After CISI 2:448) New discovery sites such as Ganweriwala, Bet Dwaraka, Kanmer, Farmana, Bhirrana, Gola Dhoro, Haifa, Assur, Bogazkhoy have to be added to the ma

Harappa Script hieroglyphs on images of processions of animals and of persons carrying flagposts.

Clusters are presented in Harappa Script Corpora in three orthographic styles:

Processions of animals/symbols (also called signs) 2. Galleries/Collages of animals and 3. Hieroglyph-multiplexes (hypertexts) combining signifier components (say, makara combining trunk of elephant with horns of zebu or fin of fish or crocodile body) as in composite animals and composite 'signs.' There is a word in Meluhha to signify such combinations of hypertext components: the word is सांगड (p. 840) [sāṅgaḍa] A body formed of two or more (fruits, animals, men) linked or joined together.

One reasonable surmise about the significance of over 400 artifacts of Nahal Mishmar is that many would have been carried in processions. This is not unlike the utsava bera carried in processions on festive days in Ancient Bhāratam, a practice which continues even today.[97]

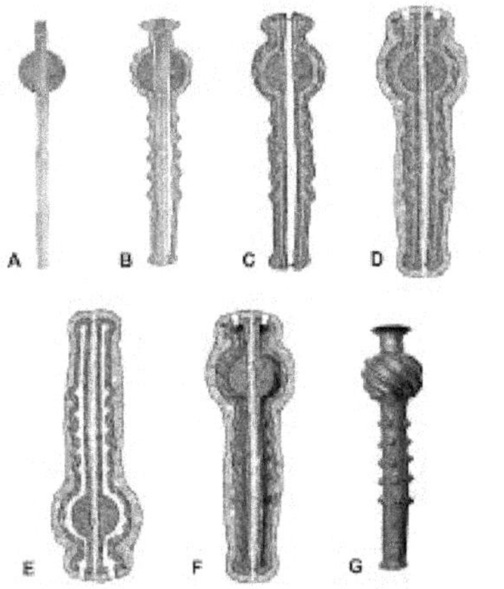

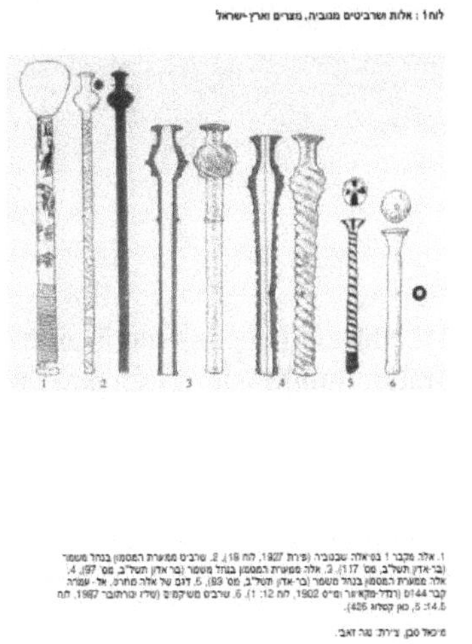

240 maceheads of Nahal Mishmar are indicative of the widely prevalent name for a blacksmith of the *Harosheth Hagoyim* Biblical *Judges* 4-5 is home of General Sisera, 'smithy of nations'; rebus: khār gōya 'artisan guild' (Prākṛtam). If taken in a procession on flagposts, these would have recollected the memories of the metalsmiths of yore and paying respects to the memories of ancestors. Hieroglyph: *ḍā̃g* m. ' club, mace '(Kashmiri) Rebus: K. *ḍangur* (dat. °garas) m. ' fool '; P. *ḍaṅgar* m. ' stupid man '; N. *ḍā̃ro* ' term of contempt for a blacksmith ', ḍā̃re ' large and lazy '; A.*ḍaṅurā* ' living alone without wife or children '; H. *ḍā̃gar, ḍā̃grā* m. ' starveling '.N. *ḍiṅgar* ' contemptuous term for an inhabitant of the Tarai '; B. *ḍiṅgar* ' vile '; Or. *ḍiṅgara* ' rogue ', °rā ' wicked '; H. *ḍiṅgar* m. ' rogue '; M. *ḍī̃gar* m. ' boy '(CDIAL 5524)

If carried on processions, these standards or flagposts are comparable to the procession shown on two Mohenjo-daro tablets as proclamations of metallurgical competence.

Haematite manufacture finds its echo in the three classifications evidenced by Harappa Script Corpora of magnetite, haematite and laterite signified by three hieroglyphs: zebu, scorpion and round raised dot.

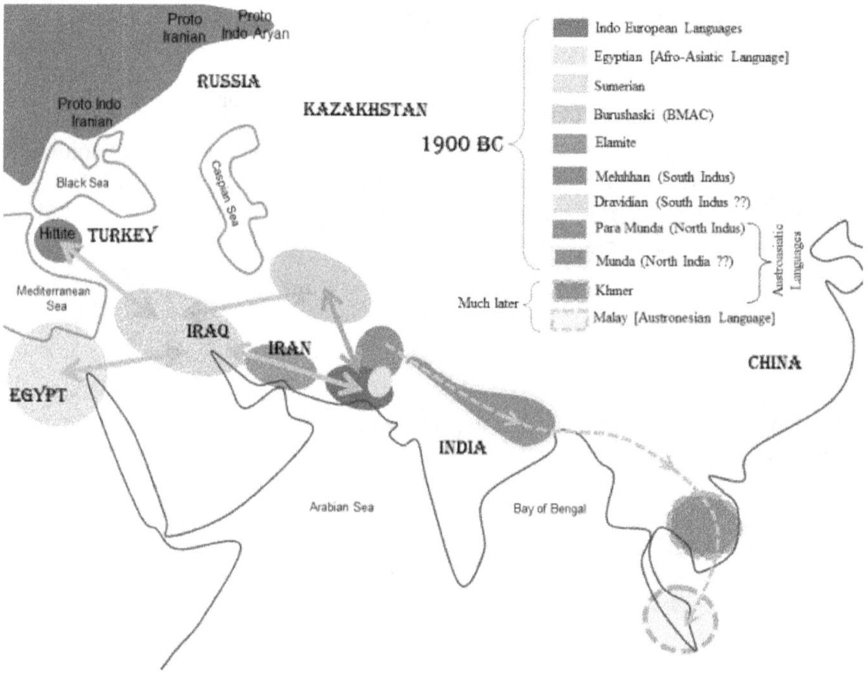

Languages of Meluhha (Mleccha) and Marhashi are the same98See: Potts, Daniel T. (2004). "Exit Aratta: Southeastern Iran and the Land of Marhashi". Name-ye Iran-e Bastan 4/1: 1–11.

"Not very far from the BMAC, to its south along the coast of Arabian Sea, are the Indus Valley, Elamite and Sumerian settlements stretching from east to west. The Sumerian name for the southern Indus Valley settlement (Mohenjo-daro) in Sind and Baluchistan is Meluhha. To its west is an area referred to as Marhashi by the Sumerians. Further west is the Elamite settlement of Shimashki (refer to the diagram below). The languages of Meluhha and Marhashi are believed to be the same - we call it Meluhha. The language of Shimashki is Elamite. BMAC artifacts have been found in all these places and also in the northern Indus areas (Harappa). This implies that there were trade links between these areas. Hence the languages of these areas are likely to have some common loan words between them. As the Indo Aryans were present in Central Asia for a considerable amount of time before moving into India it's likely that their language (Rig Vedic Sanskrit) would have substrates from all these older native languages from the areas around."

"The Ninevite Gigamesh Epic, composed probably at the end of the second millennium BC, has Utnapishtim settled "at the mouth of the rivers", taken by all commentators to be identical with Dilmun."[99] The mouth of the rivers may relate to the Rann of Kutch/Saurashtra lying at the mouth of the Sindhu and Sarasvati rivers. In the Sumerian myth Enki and Ninhursag, which recounts a Golden Age, paradise is described: "The crow screams not, the dar-bird cries not dar, the lion kills not... the ferry-man says not 'it's midnight', the herald circles not round himself, the singer says not elulam, at the outside of the city no shout resounds." The cry of the sea-faring boatmen in Bharata languages on the west-coast is: e_le_lo!

The contact area of the metalworkers extended beyond Persian Gulf into Mesopotamia as demonstrated by Dilmun seal finds with Harappa Script from sites along the Persian Gulf and also on the banks of the doab: Tigris-Euphrates in Mesopotamia:

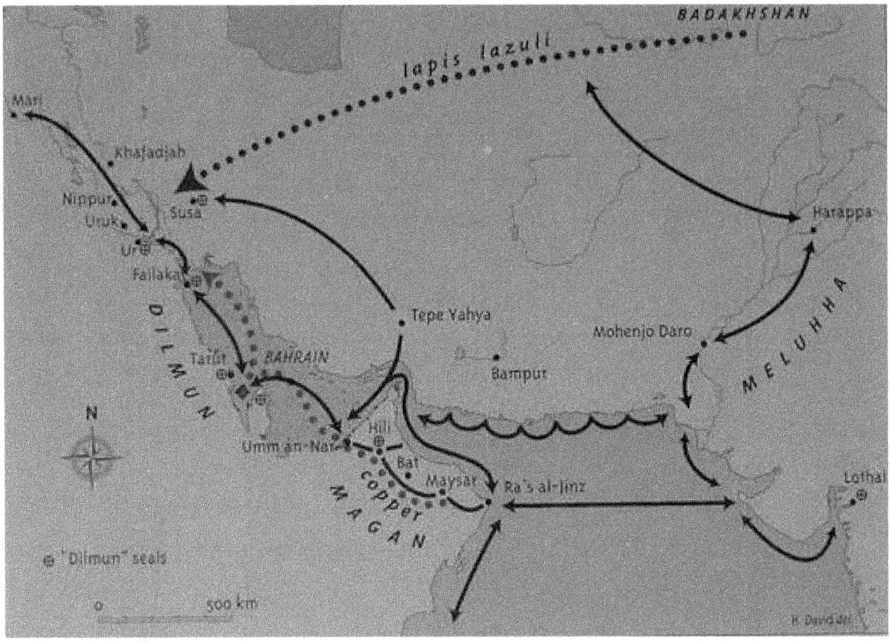

Dilmun Seals: Persian Gulf find sites. "Dilmun is understood to embrace the eastern coastline of Arabia including the island of Failaka opposite Kuwait to the island of Bahrain (cf. p. 15. Harriet Crawford & Michael Rice, editors. Traces of Paradise, the Archaeology of Bahrain, 2500 B.C -300 A.D. London. Published by the Dilmun Committe for an exhibit from the Bahrain National Museum. Printed June 2000)."[100]

Lines 123-129; and interpolation UET VI/1:
"Let me admire its green cedars. The (peole of the) lands Magan and Dilmun, Let them come to see me, Enki! Let the mooring posts beplaced for the Dilmun boats! Let the magilum-boats of Meluhha transport of gold and silver for exchange...The land Tukriś shall transport gold from Harali, lapis lazuli and bright... to you. The land Meluhha shall bring cornelian, desirable and precious sissoo-wood from Magan, excellent mangroves, on big ships The land Marhashi will (bring) precious stones, dushia-stones, (to hang) on the breast. The land Magan will bring copper, strong, mighty, diorite-stone, na-buru-stones, shumin-stones to you. The land of the Sea shall bring ebony, the embellishment of (the throne) of kingship to you. The land of the tents shall bring wool... The city, its dwellin gplaces shall be pleasant dwelling places, Dilmun, its dwelling place shall be a pleasant dwelling place. Its barley shall be fine barley, Its dates shall be very big dates! Its harvest shall be threefold. Its trees shall be ...-trees."101
I suggest that Shahdad and Tepe Yahya were important settlements (which included Meluhha settlements) of Marhashi). The inscriptional evidence of Harappa Script writing in these settlements attest to the trade contacts between Meluhha and ancient Elam (souh-eastern Iran), close to Baluchistan.

Researchers have suggested various locations for Marhashi. It refers to the lands situated to the east of Ur, during the period of Ur III state. It has also been called Old Akkadian Barahshum. Some place it in 'the perimeter of Kerman and eastern Fars"

(Stein Keller 1982: 255) or in Iranian Baluchistan (Vallat 1993: CXIII). Karl Lamberg-Karlovsky suggests that the size of Shahdad (over 100 ha.)in Kerman makes Shahdad a possible capital of Marhashi; Tepe Yahya, a site in Kerman might have been one of the smaller towns of Marhashi (Lamberg-Karlovsky 2001: 278-279). As DT Potts notes102, Sharkalisharri or his son went to Marhashi and married a Marhashian (Westenholz 1987: nos. 133 and 154). In the 18th year of Shulgi's reign, Shulgi's daughter became queen of Marhashi. 'The water buffaloes so beloved by the Sargonic seal cutters must have come to Babylonia as diplomatic gifts from Meluhha.' (Westenholz 199: 102; Boehmer 1975:4). DT Potts adds: "A well-known Old Babylonian inscription of Ibbi-Sin's from Ur (Sollberger 1965: 8, UET 8.34) records the dedication to Nanna of a statue of an ur gun-a Me-luhha-ki which the king had originally received a a gift from Marhashi and which he named 'let him catch' or 'may he catch'." (p.346) Elamites and soldiers are referred to as 'Elamites of Marhashi' (Steinkeller 1982: 262, n. 97). Ur and Marhashi had always enjoyed friendly diplomatic relationships, sometimes fortified by royal marriages. Steinkeller suggests that the ur gun-a Meluhha-ki was a spotted feline given to Ibbi-Sin, it was 'most likely a leopard (*Panthera pardus*) (Steinkeller 1982: 253 and n. 61). It could also have been a cheetah (*Acinonyx jubatus vernaticus*). In Hindi chita means 'spotted' (Yule and Burnell 1886: 187).

Gold foil feline from Tal-i Malyan, Banesh period (courtesy of WM Sumner).

It is possible that the cheetah from Meluhha was the animal given to Ibbi-Sin with the legend 'let him catch'.[103] As a Harappa hieroglyph, it may also signify: *karaḍa* 'panther' Rebus: *karaḍa* 'hard alloy' -- the *ur gun-a Meluhha-ki* given to Ibbi-Sin who reigned from 1963 to 1943 BCE in Sumer and Akkad.

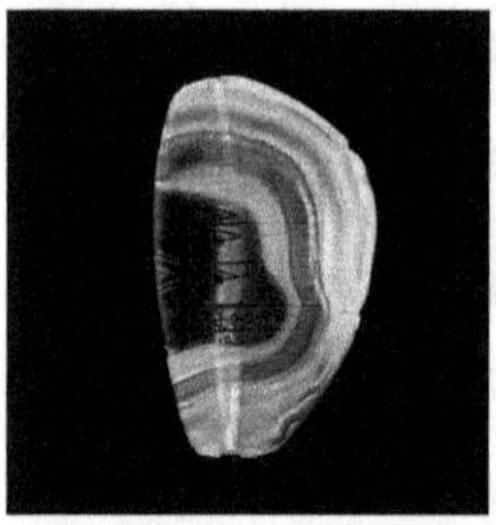

Votive bead dedicated to the Moon god Nanna (Sin) by Ibbi-Sin, god-king of Ur, in recognition for saving his life. Text in Sumerian language: "To (the god) Nanna, his master, Ibbi-Sin, god of his country, strong king, king or Ur, king of the four regions, has, for his life, dedicated this bead."[104] The bead was agate, a possible import from Meluhha.

Late (600 BCE) Hittite God / warrior with sword and mace. Source: Photographed at the Karatepe / Turkey open-air museum.105 The kid (young goat) carried on his shoulders is a signature tune of the nature of the metal used for the mace head and the sword (which is a hard alloy):

Hieroglyph: करडूं or करडें [*karaḍū* or *ṅkaraḍēṃ*] n A kid (young goat).

Rebus: करडा [*karaḍā*] Hard from alloy--iron, silver &c.

Rebus: करडा *[karaḍā*] m The arrangement of bars or embossed lines (plain or fretted with little knobs) raised upon a तार of gold by pressing and driving it upon the अवटी or grooved stamp. Such तारis used for the ornament बुगडी, for the hilt of a पट्टा or other sword &c. Applied also to any similar barform or line-form arrangement (pectination) whether embossed or indented; as the edging of a rupee &c.

Buffalo bull. *meTTu* 'hill' Rebus: meḍ 'iron' *kolmo* 'three' Rebus: *kolimi* 'smithy, forge' *karava* 'narrow pot' Rebus: *khārva* 'nidhi, wealth' *karba* 'iron' karṇika 'rim of jar' Rebus: *karṇī* 'supercargo' *karṇika* 'scribe'.

Fig. 25.4 : A buffalo with both the horns. The face is identical to that of Fig. 1.

Hieroglyph: *rā̃go* 'buffalo' Rebus: *rāṅgā* 'zinc alloy, spelter, pewter'.

Hieroglyhph: buffalo: Ku. N. *rā̃go* ' buffalo bull ' (or < *raṅku* -- ?).(CDIAL 10538, 10559)
Rebus: *raṅga*3 n. ' tin ' lex. [Cf. *nāga* -- 2, *vaṅga* -- 1] Pk. *raṁga* -- n. ' tin ';
P. rā̃g f., rā̃gā m. ' pewter, tin ' (← H.);
Ku. rāṅ ' tin, solder ', gng. *rā̃k; N. rāṅ, rāṅo* ' tin, solder ', *A. B. rāṅ; Or. rāṅga* ' tin ', *rāṅgā* ' solder, spelter ', *Bi. Mth. rā̃gā, OAw. rāṁga; H. rā̃g f., rā̃gā* m. ' tin, pewter '; *Si. raṅga ' tin '.(CDIAL 10562) B. rāṅ(g)tā* ' tinsel, copper -- foil '(CDIAL 10567) తుత్తము [tuttamu] or తుత్తరము *tuttamu.* [Tel.] n. sulphate of zinc. మైలతుత్తము sulphate of copper, blue-stone.తుత్తినాగము [*tuttināgamu*] *tutti-nāgamu.* [Chinese.] n. Pewter. Zinc. లోహవిశేషము (Telugu)

Note on spelter: "Spelter, while sometimes used merely as a synonym for zinc, is often used to identify a zinc alloy. In this sense it might be an alloy of equal parts copper and zinc, i.e. a brass, used for hard soldering and brazing, or as an alloy, containinglead, that is used instead of bronze. In this usage it was common for many 19th-century cheap, cast articles such as candlesticks and clock cases...The word "pewter" is thought to be derived from the word "spelter". Zinc ingots formeḍ by smelting might also be termeḍ spelter."[106] French Bronze is a form of bronze typically consisting of 91% copper, 2% tin, 6% zinc, and 1% lead.[107] "The term French bronze was also used in connection with cheap zinc statuettes and other articles, which were finished to resemble real bronze, and some older texts call the faux-bronze finish itself "French bronze". Its composition was typically 5 parts haematite powder to 8 parts lead oxide, formeḍ into a paste with spirits of wine. Variations in tint could be obtained by varying the proportions. The preparation was applied to the article to be bronzed with a soft brush, then polished with a hard brush after it had dried."[108] "The term latten referred loosely to the copper alloys such as brass or bronze that appeared in the Middle Ages and through to the late 18th and early 19th centuries. It was used for monumental brasses, in decorative effects on borders, rivets or other details of metalwork (particularly armour), in livery and pilgrim badges or funerary effigies. Metalworkers commonly formed latten in thin sheets and used it to make church utensils. Brass of this period is made through the calamine brass process, from copper and zinc ore. Later brass was made with zinc metal from Champion's smelting process and is not generally referred to as latten. This calamine brass was generally manufactured as hammered sheet or "battery brass" (hammered by a "battery" of water-powered trip hammers) and cast brass was rare. "Latten" also refers to a type of tin plating on iron (or possibly some other base metal), which is known as white latten; and black latten refers to laten-brass, which is brass milled into thin plates or sheets. The term "latten" has also been used, rarely, to refer to lead alloys. In general, metal in thin sheets is said to be latten such as gold latten; and lattens (plural) refers to metal sheets between 1/64" and 1/32" in thickness."[109]

Water-buffalo on artefacts of Ancient Near East

Seal. Mohenjo-daro. Hieroglyph: *rāngo* 'water buffalo bull' (Ku.N.)(CDIAL 10559) Rebus: *rango 'pewter'. ranga, rang* pewter is an alloy of tin, lead, and antimony (anjana) (Santali)

Hieroglyphs: *dula* 'two'; *ayo* 'fish'; *kāṇḍa* 'arrow': rebus: *dula* 'cast' *ayo* 'iron, metal' (Gujarati. Rigveda); *kāṇḍa* 'metalware, pots and pans, tools' (Marathi) Hieroglyph: Rings on neck: *koḍiyum* (Gujarati) *koṭiyum* = a wooden circle put round the neck of an animal; *koṭ* = neck (Gujarati)Rebus: *koḍ* 'artisan's workshop'(Kuwi) *koḍ* = place where artisans work (Gujarati) *koṭe* 'forge' (Mu.) koṭe meṛed = forged iron, in contrast to dul meṛed, cast iron (Mundari) koTiya 'dhow, seafaring vessel'.

rango 'buffalo' rebus: *rango* 'pewter'*pattar* 'feeding trough' rebus: *pattharaka* 'merchant' pattar 'guild of goldsmiths *bhaṭa* 'warrior' rebus: *bhaṭa* 'furnace' gōṭā 'round' (Parenthesis) rebus: *gōṭā* 'laterite ore' *baṭa* 'quail' rebus: *bhaṭa* 'furnace' *kanka* 'rim of jar' rebus: *karṇī* 'supercargo, scribe' *dATu* 'crosś rebus: *dhatu* 'mineral, ore' *khaṇḍa* 'notch' rebus: *khaṇḍa* 'implements PLUS *dhALa* 'slope' rebus: *dhALa* 'large ingot'

Buffalo. Mohenjo-daro.

Buffalo. Daimabad bronze. Prince of Wales Museum, Mumbai.

ran:gā 'buffalo'; *ran:ga* 'pewter or alloy of tin (*ran:ku*), lead (*nāga*) and antimony (*añjana*)'(Santali)

Trough in front of wild-buffalo, B007. *kanac* 'corner' rebus: *kancu* 'bronze' *sal* 'splinter' rebus: *sal* 'workshop' *rango* 'buffalo' rebus: *rango* 'pewter'

Bisons face-to-face. Person throwing a spear at a bison and placing one foot on the head of the bison; a hooded serpent at left.

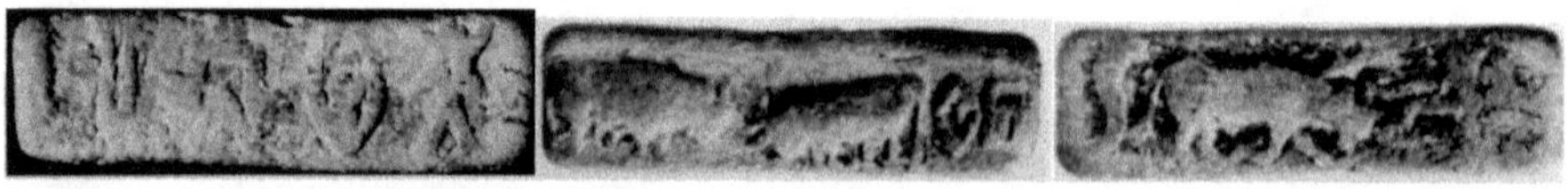

m0492 2835 Pict-99: *dula* 'pair' rebus: *dul* 'metal casting' *barad, balad* 'ox' rebus: *bharata* 'alloy of copper, pewter, tin' *kulā* 'hood of serpent' rebus: *kol* 'working in iron' 'furnace, forge' *kolsa* 'to **kick**' Rebus: *kol* 'metal', 'working in iron, blacksmith' *kol* 'to kill' Text of inscription: *kole.l* 'temple' rebus: *kole.l* 'smithy' *kanac* 'corner' rebus: *kancu* 'bronze' ayo, *aya* 'fish' rebus: *aya* 'iron' *ayas* 'metal' *khambhaṛā* 'fish **fin**' rebus: *kammaṭa* 'mint, coiner, coinage' *gōṭā* 'round' Rebus: *khōṭa* 'ingot' PLUS *kolom* 'rice plant' rebus: *kolimi* 'smithy, forge' Thus ingot smithy; *kanka* 'rim of jar' rebus: *karṇī* 'supercargo' *khāreDo* '**currycomb**' rebus: Rebus: *khārādī* ' turner' (Gujarati.) *kāmsako, kāmsiyo* = a large sized comb (Gujarati.) Rebus: *kaṁsa* 'bronze' (Telugu)

The following ANE seals with Harappa Script hieroglyphs may indicate Meluhha merchants settled in the region handling cargo from Meluhha; hence, the rebus readings suggested.

ca. 2254-2220 BC (mature); ceramic; cat. 79; two groups in combat. A naked, bearded hero wrestles with a water buffalo, and a bull-man wrestles with a lion. In the centre: inscription (unread). Appears to be recut. Girdled nude hero attacking water buffalo; bullman attacking lion; inscription. Kafaje, Akkadian (ca. 2300 - 2200 BC)

Frankfort, Henri: Stratified Cylinder Seals from the Diyala Region. Oriental Institute Publications 72. Chicago: University of Chicago Press, no. 396.

Gilgamesh and Enkidu struggle of the celestial bull and the lion (cylinder seal-print Approx. 2,400 BC, Walters Art Gallery, Baltimore)

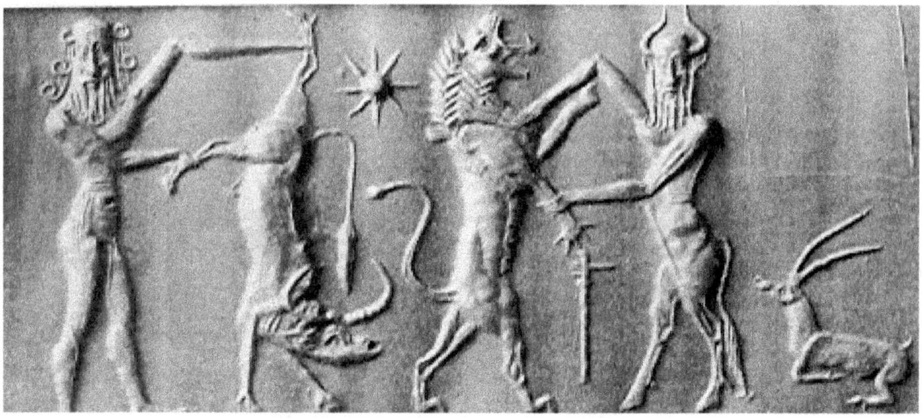

Akkadian Cylinder Seal (c. 2200 B.C. showing Gilgamesh slaying the bull of heaven, with Enkidu? Also from Dury; both in British Museum)[110]

In the two scenes on this cylinder seal, a heroic figure with heavy beard and long curls holds off two roaring lions, and another hero struggles with a water buffalo. The inscription in the panel identifies the owner of this seal as "Ur-Inanna, the farmer."

Cylinder seal and modern impression: bull-man combatting lion; nude hero combatting water buffalo; inscription ara 'lion' rebus: Ara 'brass *rango* 'buffalo' rebus: *rango* 'pewter' miṇḍāl 'markhor' (Tōrwālī) *meḍho* a ram, a sheep (Gujarati)(CDIAL 10120) Rebus: *mẽṛhẽt, meḍ* 'iron' (Munda.Ho.) meḍ 'copper' (Slavic languages). मेढ (p. 662) [*mēḍha*] 'polar' star' Rebus: *mẽṛhẽt, meḍ* 'iron' (Ho.Munda)

Period: Akkadian Date: ca. 2250–2150 B.C.E
Geography: Mesopotamia
Culture: Akkadian Meḍium: Albite
Dimensions: H. 15/16 in. (3.4 cm); Diam. 7/8 in. (2.3 cm)
Classification: Stone-Cylinder Seals-Inscribed Accession Number: 1999.325.4 Metmuseum

William Hayes Ward Seal No. 26[111].

Cylinder Seal of Ibni-Sharrum Agade period, reign of Sharkali-Sharri (c. 2217-2193 BCE) Mesopotamia Serpentine/chlorite H.

Seal of Ibni-Sharrum, the scribe of King Sharkali-Sharri son of Naram-Sin - 2,250 B.C.

26

3.9 cm; Diam. 2.6 cm Formerly in the De Clercq collection; gift of H. de Boisgelin, 1967 AO 22303 The inscription reads "O divine Shar-kali-sharri, Ibni-sharrum the scribe is your servant." "A scene testifying to relations with distant lands Buffaloes are emblematic animals in glyptic art in the Agade period. They first appear in the reign of Sargon, indicating sustained relations between the Akkadian Empire and the distant country of Meluhha, that is, the present Indus Valley, where these animals come from. These exotic creatures were probably kept in zoos and do not seem to have been acclimatized in Iraq at the end of the 3rd millennium BC. Indeed, it was not until the Sassanid Empire that they reappeared. The engraver has carefully accentuated the animals' powerful muscles and spectacular horns, which are shown as if seen from above, as they appear on the seals of the Indus."112

*<lo->(*B) {V} ``(pot, etc.) to ^overflow". See *<lo->* `to be left over'. @B24310. #20851. *Re<lo->(*B) {V} ``(pot, etc.) to ^overflow". See *<lo->* `to be left over'. (Munda) Rebus: *loh* 'copper' (Hindi) Glyph of flowing water in the second register: காண்டம் *kāṇṭam* , n. < *kāṇḍa.* 1. Water; sacred water; நீர்; *kāṇṭam* 'ewer, pot' கமண்டலம். (Tamil) Thus the combined rebus reading: Ku. *lokhaṛ* 'iron tools '; H. *lokhaṇḍ* m. ' iron tools, pots and pans '; G. *lokhãḍ* n. 'tools, iron, ironware'; M. lokhãḍ n. ' iron '(CDIAL 11171). The kneeling person's hairstyle has six curls. *bhaṭa* 'six'; rebus: *bhaṭa* 'furnace'. मेढा *mēḍhā* A twist or tangle arising in thread or cord, a curl or snarl. (Marathi) Rebus: *meḍ* 'iron' (Ho.) Thus, the orthography denotes meḍ bhaṭa 'iron furnace'.

rango 'buffalo' rebus *rango* 'tin, pewter'

Zinc alloys include: spelter, solder, pewter, tin, copper-foil, latten, French bronze. The Meluhha Prakritam gloss rāṅgā signified these zinc alloys with varying proportions of mineral constituents deploying *rā̃go* 'water-buffalo' hieroglyph.

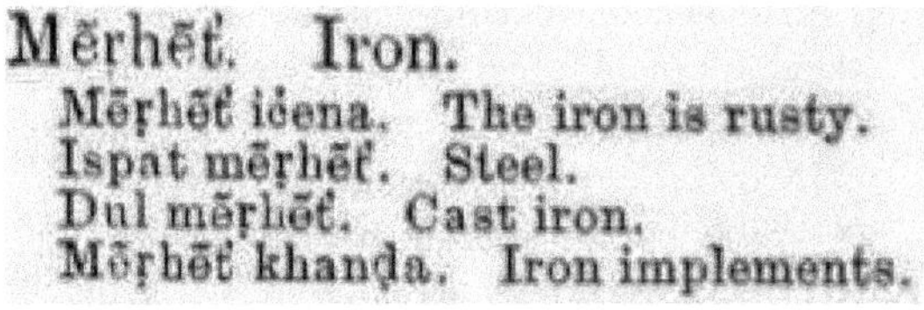
Mĕrhĕt. Iron.
Mĕṛhĕt idena. The iron is rusty.
Ispat mĕṛhĕt. Steel.
Dul mĕṛhĕt. Cast iron.
Mĕṛhĕt khanḍa. Iron implements.

Santali glosses. On many hierolyph multiplexes, water-buffalo (rā̃go) is associated with kāṇḍa 'overflowing water'. The rebus renderings are: rāṅgā khaṇḍa 'zinc alloy implements. The semantics of *khaṇḍa* 'implements is attested in Santali: *me~r.he~t khaṇḍa* 'iron implements.

"A copper trade down the Euphrates is extremely ancient; the river's original name was Urudu or 'copper river'. (Hawkes, J. (ed.), 1977, The First Civilizations, London, Pelican: 159, 167-8). The whole purpose of sending Assyrian merchants to Anatolia was to ensure a steady supply of Anatolian silver and some gold. In exchange they gave cloth and tin, 'transported by caravans of black donkeys bred in Assyria'. They made a profit on the cloth of 100% and on the tin of 75-100%. The quantities traded could be considerable; a cargo of 410 talents of tin (more than 12 t) is once mentioned, though for some curious reason tin prices are never recorded. Trade with Kanesh continued until ca. 1757 BC when Hammurabi of Babylon destroyed Mari (900 km. up the Euphrates) and a period of wars followed which reduced 'central Anatolia, once rich, to a land of ruins. The Kanesh tablets give no indicatin of where Assyrian tin came from. The texts from Mari show a way out of the difficulty by also recording tin being shipped up the Euphrates, presumably from the Persian Gulf, pointing to a distant origin involving maritime trade. The Arab geographer Muqadasi stated that tin occurred at Hamadan, 560 km south-west of Tehran. As Muhly wrote, 'a mineral zone running roughly from Hamadan to Tabriz seems to fit all the evidence for the Near Eastern tin trade'. (Muhly, J.D., 1973, Copper and Tin: the distribution of mineral resources and the nature of the metals trade in the Bronze Age, Hamden, Connecticut, Archon Books, p.409).

"Tin from 'Meluhha'. According to the Larsa texts, merchants were there (in Mari and Larsa) to purchase copper and tin: the copper came from Magan in Oman, via Tilmun (Bahrain), but the origin of the tin is left in question. Tin mines in north-west Iran or the Transcaucasus are highly unlikely. Fortunately, there is evidence for another tin source in texts from Lagash. Lagash, about 50 km east of Larsa, was of minor importance except under the governorship of Gudea (ca. 2143-2124 BC). His inscriptions indicate extensive trade: gold from Cilicia in Anatolia, marble from Amurra in Syria, and cedar wood from the Amanus Mountains between these two countries, while up through the Persian Gulf or 'Southern Sea' came more timber, porphyry (strictly a purplish rock), lapis lazuli and tin.[113] One inscription has been translated:

Copper and tin, blocks of lapis lazuli and ku ne (meaning unknown), bright carnelian from Meluhha.

"This is the only reference to tin from Meluhha. Either Meluhha was a name vague enough to embrace Badakhshan (the northernmost province of Afghanistan) as well as some portion of the Bharata subcontinent including the Indus valley, or 'tin from Meluhha' means that the metal came from some port in Meluhha -- just as 'copper from Tilmun' means copper from elsewhere shipped through the island of Bahrain. Whichever interpretation is correct, the result is the same. Tin must have come from somewhere in India, or from elsewhere along a trade route down the Indus valley. India is not without its tin locations, rare though they are. The largest deposits in India proper are in the Hazaribagh district of Bihar. 'Old workingś are said to exist.[114] Tin bronzes from Gujarat are at the southernmost limit of Indus influence. The copper could have come from Rajasthan, though copper ingots at the port of Lothal, at the head of the Gulf of Cambay, suggest imports from Oman or some other Near Eastern copper mining district. Tin supplying Harappa and Mohenjo-daro, most famous of the Indus cities, may have been sent overland to Lothal for export, though the scarcity of tin in the Indus cities makes this idea unconvincing.

"At Harappa, three copper alloys were used in the period 2500-2000 BC: copper and up to 2% nickel; copper and up to 5% nickel; copper with ca. 10% tin and a trace of arsenic. Ingots of tin as well as of copper were found at Harappa.[115] Ingots of tin bronze have also been found at Chanhu-daro. Yet in spite of its scarcity, tin bronze was widely used. Its occasional abundance and, in the case of the bronzes from Luristan in southern Iran, the high quality of the tin bronzes produced, equally underline the fact that rich source of tin existed somewhere.

"The archaeological evidence from Afghanistan is not unequivocal. What is surprising is the discovery in 1962 of corroded pieces of sheet metal bearing traces of an embossed design and made of a low tin content bronze (5.15%). The uncorroded metal is thought to have contained nearer 7% tin.[116] These fragments came from the deepest level in the Snake Cave, contemporary with the earliest occupation dated by 14C to around 5487 and 5291 BCE[117]. If this dating is acceptable, not only is this metal the earliest tin bronze known from anywhere, but it is also an isolated occurrence of far older than its nearest rival and quite unrelated to the main development of bronze age metallurgy.

"Even more exciting is the evidence from Shortugai. Since the discovery of the first Indus finds at Harappa in 1921, the sphere of influence of this civilization has been greatly extended, first southwards to Gujarat and the Makran coast of Baluchistan, and now into northern Afghanistan. In 1975, French archaeologists discovered on the surface at Shortugai, sherds of Indus pottery extending over more than a millennium -

the whole span of the Indus civilization.[118] The sites are clustered above the confluence of the Amur Darya and the Kokcha. Finds also included gold and, nor expectedly, much lapis lazuli. Particularly important is a Harappa seal bearing an engraved rhinoceros and an inscription which reinforces the belief that the site was a trading post. Shortugai is only 800 km from Harappa, as the crow flies, though the journey involves hundreds of kilometres of mountainous terrain through the Hindu Kush. Lyonnet's conclusion was that the most likely explanation for their existence was an interest in 'the mineral resources of the Iranian Plateau and of Central Asia', to which can now be added those of Afghanistan itself. Indus contacts extended well into Turkmenia where the principal bronze age settlements, such as Altin-depe and Namasga-depe, lie close to the Iranian border. Imports here include square and oval gaming-counters of Bharata ivory, and decorated sticks, numerous at Mohenjo-daro, related to types described in Sanskrit texts as being used in fortune-telling. The flat daggers of southern Turkmenia also closely resemble Harappa types.

"A fine copper axe-adze from Harappa, and similar bronze examples from Chanhu-daro and, in Baluchistan, at Shahi-tump, are rare imports of the superior shaft-hole implements developed initially in Mesopotamia before 3000 BCE. In northern Iran examples have been found at Shah Tepe, Tureng Tepe, and Tepe Hissar in level IIIc (2000-1500 BCE). Tin was more commonly used in eastern Iran, an area only now emerging from obscurity through the excavation of key sites such as Tepe Yahya and Shahdad. In level IVb (ca. 3000 BCE) at Tepe yahya was found a dagger of 3% tin bronze[119;] perhaps the result of using a tin-rich copper ore. However, in later levels tin bronze became a 'significant element in its material culture' comparatble with other evidence from south-east Iran where at Shadad bronze shaft-hole axes and bronze vessels were found in graves dated to ca. 2500 BCE[120]. The richness of Tepe Yahha, Shahr-i-Sokhta, and Shadad, are all indicative of trade and 'an accumulation of wealth unsuspected from the area'.[121] Namazga-depe and neighbouring sites are a long way from the important tin reserves of Fergana. The origin of Near Eastern tin remains unproven; the geological evidence would favour the deposits of Fergana and the Tien Shan range."[122]

Clay sealing from private collection with water buffalo, crescent-star, apparently Akkadian period

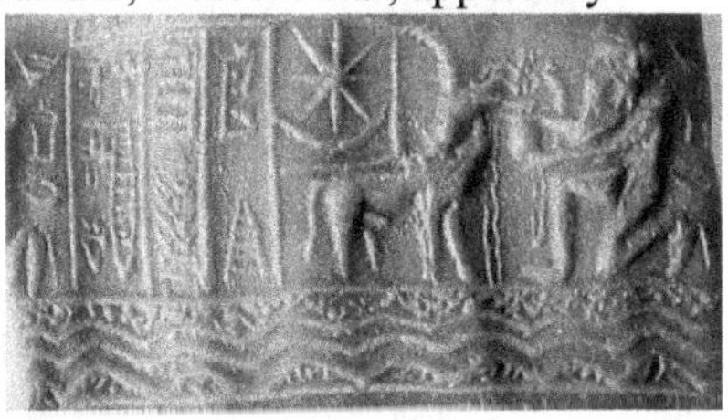

Signs of a house.[123] Hieroglyph: house: *Ta. kuṭi* house, abode, home, family, lineage,

town, tenants; *kuṭikai* hut made of leaves, temple; kuṭical hut; *kuṭicai, kuṭiñai* small hut, cottage; *kuṭimai* family, lineage, allegiance (as of subjects to their sovereign), servitude; *kuṭiy-al* tenant; *kuṭiyilār* tenants; *kuṭil* hut, shed, abode; *kuṭaṅkar* hut, cottage; *kaṭumpu* relations. *Ma. kuṭi* house, hut, family, wife, tribe; *kuṭima* the body of landholders, tenantry; *kuṭiyan* slaves (e.g. in Coorg); *kuṭiyān* inhabitant, subject, tenant; *kuṭiññil* hut, thatch; *kuṭil* hut, outhouse near palace for menials. *Ko. kuṛjl* shed, bathroom of Kota house; *kuṛm* family; *kuḍḷ* front room of house; *kuṛḷ* hut; *guṛy* temple. *To. kwïṣ* shed for small calves; kuṣ room (in dairy or house); *kuḍṣ* outer room of dairy, in: *kuḍṣ* waṣ fireplace in outer room of lowest grade of dairies (cf. 2857), *kuḍṣ* moṇy bell(s) in outer section of ti· dairy, used on non-sacred buffaloes (cf. 4672); *kuṛy* Hindu temple; ? *kwïḏy* a family of children. *Ka. kuḍiya, kuḍu* śūdra, farmer; *guḍi* house, temple; *guḍil, guḍalu, guḍisalu, guḍasalu, guḍasala,* etc. hut with a thatched roof. *Koḍ. kuḍi* family of servants living in one hut; *kuḍië* man of toddy-tapper caste. *Tu. guḍi* small pagoda or shrine; *guḍisalů, guḍisilů, guḍsilů, guḍicilů* hut, shed. *Te. koṭika* hamlet; guḍi temple; *guḍise* hut, cottage, hovel. *Kol.* (SR) *guḍī* temple. *Pa. guḍi* temple, village resthouse. *Ga.* (Oll.) *guḍi* temple.

Go. (Ko.) *kuṛma* hut, outhouse; (Ma.) *kurma* menstruation; (Grigson) *kurma* lon menstruation hut (*Voc.* 782, 800); (SR.) *guḍi, (Mu.) guḍḍi, (S. Ko.) guṛi* temple; *guḍḍī* (Ph.) temple, (Tr.) tomb (*Voc.* 1113). *Kui guḍi* central room of house, living room. / Cf. Skt. *kūˇṭa-, kuṭi-, kūˇṭī-* (whence Ga. (P.) *kuṛe* hut; Kui *kūṛi* hut made of boughs, etc.; Kur. *kuṛyā* small shed or outhouse; Malt. *kuṛya* hut in the fields; Br. *kuḍ(ḍ)ī* hut, small house, wife),*kuṭīkā-, kuṭīra-, kuṭuṅgaka-, kuṭīcaka-, koṭa-* hut; *kuṭumba-* household (whence Ta. Ma. *kuṭumpam id.; Ko. kuṛmb [? also kuṛm* above]; To. *kwïḍb, kwïḍbïl* [-ïl from *wïkïl*, s.v. 925 Ta. *okkal*]; Ka., Koḍ., Tu. *kuṭumba; Tu. kuḍuma; Te. kuṭumbamu; ? Kui kumbu* house [balance word of *iḍu*, see s.v. 494 Ta. il]). See Turner, *CDIAL*, no. 3232, *kuṭī-*, no. 3493, *kōṭa-*, no. 3233, *kuṭumba-*, for most of the Skt. forms; Burrow, *BSOAS* 11.137. (DEDR 1655) Rebus: *kuṭhi* 'smelter'. *karṇaka* 'spread legś rebus: karNI 'supercargo', *karṇaka* 'helmsman'. Thus, supercargo helmsman molten copper smelter, pewter alloy.

Gaur. H176A *rango* 'buffalo' rebus: *rango* 'pewter' *kanka* 'rimof jar' rebus: *karṇī* 'supercargo' *dula* 'pair' rebus: *dul* 'metal casting' *eraka* 'nave of wheel' rebus: *erako* 'moltencast copper' *arA* 'spokes' rebus: *Ara* 'brass.

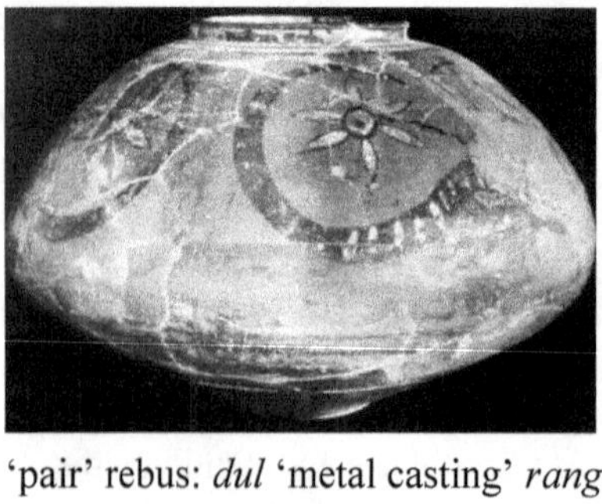

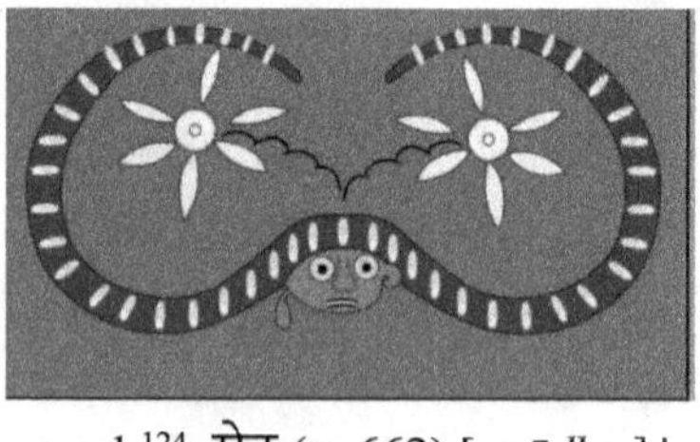

Kotdiji burial vessel.[124] मेढ (p. 662) [*mēḍha*] **'polar' star'** Rebus: *mẽṛhẽt, meḍ* 'iron' (Ho.Munda) dula 'pair' rebus: *dul* 'metal casting' *rango* 'buffalo' rebus: *rango* 'pewter'.

A vivid Meluhha hieroglyph 'overflowing pot' has rebus-metonymy reading: metal tools, pots and pans

m1656 Mohenjodro Pectoral.

Hieroglyph: *sãghāṛɔ* 'lathe'.(Gujarati). Rebus: सं-ग्रह *saṁgraha, samgaha* 'a guardian , ruler , manager , arranger' R. BhP. *Vajra Sanghāta* 'binding together' (Varahamihira) **saṁgaḍha* ' collection of forts '. [*gaḍha --]L. *sãgaṛh* m. ' line of entrenchments, stone walls for defence '.(CDIAL 12845).

Hieroglyph: खोंड (p. 216) [*khōṇḍa*] m A young bull, a bullcalf; खोंडा [*khōṇḍā*] m A कांबळा of which one end is formed into a cowl or hood. खोंडरूं [*khōṇḍarūṃ*] n A contemptuous form of खोंडा in the sense of कांबळा-cowl (Marathi. Molesworth[125]); *kōḍe dūḍa* bull calf (Telugu); *kōṛe* 'young bullock' (Konda)Rebus: *kõdā* 'to turn in a lathe' (Bengali) Rebus 2: koTiya 'dhow, seafaring vessel'.
kāṇḍam காண்டம்² *kāṇṭam*, n. < *kāṇḍa*. 1. Water; sacred water; நீர். துருத்திவா யதுக்கிய குங்குமக் காண் டமும் (கல்லா. 49, 16). Rebus: *khāṇḍā* 'metal tools, pots and pans' (Marathi) (B) {V} *lo* ``(pot, etc.) to ^overflow''. See `to be left over'. @B24310. #20851. Re(B) {V} ``(pot, etc.) to ^overflow''. See `to be left over'. (Munda) Rebus: *loh* 'copper' (Hindi) The hieroglyph clearly refers to the metal tools, pots and pans of copper.

Some examples of 'overflowing pot' metaphors on Ancient Near East artifacts, cylinder seals:

Akkadian Cylinder Seal of Adda (c. 2250 B.C.) with, left to right, Ninurta, Ishtar, Shamash, and Ea. From Dury, Art of the Ancient Near and Middle East, Abrams, NY Enki walks out of the water to the land attended by his messenger, Isimud who is readily identifiable by his two faces looking in opposite directions (duality). Dhangar 'bull' rebus: dhangar 'blacksmith' dhanga 'mountain range' rebus: dhangar 'blacksmith' *ayo, aya* 'fish' rebus: *aya* 'iron' *ayas* 'metal' *kāṇḍa* 'overflowing water' rebus: *khaṇḍa* 'implements eruvai 'kite' rebus: *eruvai* 'copper'. *kāmṭhiyɔ* 'archer' rebus: *kammaṭa* 'mint, coiner, coinage' ara 'lion' rebus: *Ara* 'brass *kuṭi* 'tree' rebus: *kuṭhi* 'smelter' *meḍ* 'foot' rebus: *meḍ* 'iron' *khaṇḍa* 'sword' rebus: *khaṇḍa* 'implements.

Bull men contesting with lions. Cylinder seal and impression. Akkadian period. ca. 2334-2154 BCE. Marble. 28X26 mm. Seal No. 167 Morgan Library and Museum.[126] A variant narrative adds hieroglyphs of an aquatic bird in flight. Hieroglyph: *karaṭa*1 m. ' crow ' BhP., °*aka* -- m. lex. [Cf. *karaṭu* -- , *karkaṭu* -- m. ' Numidian crane ', *karēṭu* -- , °*ēṭavya* -- , °*ēḍuka* -- m. lex., *karaṇḍa*2 -- m. ' duck ' lex: see kāraṇḍava --]

Pk. *karaḍa* -- m. ' crow ', °*ḍā* -- f. ' a partic. kind of bird '; S. *karaṛa* -- *ḍhī̃gu* m. ' a very large aquatic bird '; L. *karṛā* m., °*ṛī* f. ' the common teal '..(CDIAL 2787). Allograph: *karaṭa*2 m. ' Carthamus tinctorius ' lex.Pk. *karaḍa* -- m. ' safflower ', °*ḍā* -- f. ' a tree like the karañja '; M. *karḍī*, °*ḍaī* f. ' safflower, Carthamus tinctorius and its seed '. CDIAL 2788). Rebus: karaḍā 'hardalloy of metals' (Marathi) ara 'lion' rebus: *Ara* 'brass *dhangar* 'bull' rebus: *dhangar* 'blacksmith'. *kolmo* 'rice plant' rebus: *kolimi* 'smithy, forge'.

This unique mold-made faience tablet or standard (H2000-4483/2342-01) was found in the eroded levels west of the tablet workshop in Trench 54. On one side is a short inscription under a rectangular box filled with 24 dots. The reverse has a narrative scene with two bulls fighting under a thorny tree. *kuṭi* 'tree' rebus: *kuṭhi* 'smelter' *dula* 'pair' rebus: *dul* 'metal casting' barad, balad 'ox' rebus: *bharata* 'alloy of pewter, copper, tin' Thus, pewter alloy metal casting smelter.

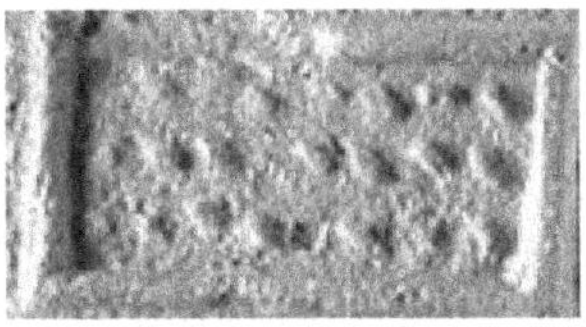

Hieroglyph: cartouche with 24 dots: rectangle with pair of 12 dots.

gōṭā 'pebble' rebus: *gōṭā* 'laterite' *khōṭa* 'ingot' PLUS कारु [kāru] 'twelve' Rebus: 'artisan' *dula* 'pair' rebus: *dul* 'cast metal' Thus, the 24 dots signify: ingot, laterite metalcasting artisan.

dula 'pair' Rebus: *dul* 'cast metal' PLUS *baroṭi* 'twelve' Rebus: *bharata* 'alloy of copper, pewter, tin'. Thus together, copper-pewter-tin-alloy metal casting. PLUS कारु [*kāru* 'artisans'. Thus, *bharata* 'alloy' metal casting artisans.

Hieroglyph: A pair of twelve dots: dula 'pair' Rebus: dul 'cast metal' PLUS कारु [*kāru*] *m* (S) A common term for the twelve बलुतेदार q. v. Also कारुनारु *m pl* q. v. in नारुकारु. Rebus: कारु [*kāru*] *m* (S) An artificer or artisan. बाराकारू (p. 576) [bārākārū] *m pl* The twelve कारू or बलतेदार. See बलुतेदार.बलोतें, बलोतेदार, बलोता or त्या (p. 567) [*balōtē, mbalōtēdāra, balōtā or tyā*] Commonly बलुतें &c. *karuvu* n. Melting: what is melted (Telugu).

kharoṣṭhī a script of Ancient Near East and ancient India is relatable to *kāru* 'An artificer or artisan' and *khār* 'blacksmith'. खरोष्टी [p= 337,3] *f.* a kind of written character or alphabet Lalit. x, 29; °रोष्ट्रि is a compound expression: *khār* + ओष्ठ that is, rebus: *khār* 'blacksmith' PLUS 'lip' which is metonymy for blacksmith speech. This is also an indicator that early writing systems were invented and used by *kāru* 'artisans, blacksmiths' of ancient India. Similarly, *brahmi,* name of another ancient script relates to ब्राह्मी [p= 742,1] speech or the goddess of speech (= सरस्वती) MBh. i, 19 *mfn.* ब्राह्मि (fr. ब्र्/अह्मन्) holy, divine VS. becomes the framework for writing systems of all languages in India and many languages in Ancient Far East.

Hieroglyph: गोटा [*gōṭā] m* A roundish stone or pebble. 2 A marble (of stone, *lac,* wood &c.) Rebus 1: खोट (p. 212) [*khōṭa*] *f* A mass of metal (unwrought or of old metal melted down); an ingot or wedge. Rebus 2: gōṭā 'laterite (ferrous ore)' [*khōṭasāḷa*] *a* (खोट & साळ from शाला) Alloyed--a metal. (Marathi) Bshk. *khoṭ* ' embers ', Phal. *khūṭo* ' ashes, burning coal' (CDIAL 3931)

ayo, aya 'fish' rebus: *aya* 'iron' rebus: *ayas* 'metal' baraDo 'spine' rebus: *bharata* 'alloy of pewter, copper, tin' *kanka* 'rim of jar' rebus: *karṇī* 'supercargo, scribe' *khāreDo* '**currycomb**' rebus: Rebus: *khārādī* ' turner' (Gujarati) *kāmsako, kāmsiyo* = a large sized comb (Gujarati) Rebus: *kaṁsa* 'bronze' (Telugu)

Note on: ancient lexemes and expressions to signify artisans of Bronze Age.

कारु [*kāru*] m (S) Affixed as an honorary designation to the names of Barbers, and sometimes of सुतार, गवंडी, & चितारी. 3 Used laxly as adj and in the sense of Effectual, availing, effective of the end. बलुतें [*balutēṃ*] n A share of the corn and garden-produce assigned for the subsistence of the twelve public servants of a village, for whom see below. 2 In some districts. A share of the dues of the hereditary officers of a village, such as पाटील, कुळकरणी &c. बलुतेदार or बलुता [*balutēdāra* or *balutā*] or त्या m (बलुतें &c.) A public servant of a village entitled to बलुतें. There are twelve distinct from the regular Governmentofficers पाटील, कुळकरणी &c.; viz. सुतार, लोहार, महार, मांग (These four constitute पहिली or थोरली कास or वळ the first division.

Of three of them each is entitled to चार पाचुंदे, twenty bundles of Holcus or the thrashed corn, and the महार to आठ पाचुंदे); कुंभार, चाम्हार, परीट, न्हावी constitute दुसरी orमधली कास or वळ, and are entitled, each, to तीन पाचुंदे; भट, मुलाणा, गुरव, कोळी form तिसरी or धाकटी कास or वळ, and have, each, दोन पाचुंदे. Likewise there are twelve अलुते or supernumerary public claimants, viz. तेली, तांबोळी, साळी, माळी, जंगम, कळवांत, डवऱ्या, ठाकर, घडशी, तराळ, सोनार, चौगुला. Of these the allowance of corn is not settled.

The learner must be prepared to meet with other enumerations of the बलुतेदार (e. g. पाटील, कुळ- करणी, चौधरी, पोतदार, देशपांड्या, न्हावी, परीट, गुरव, सुतार, कुंभार, वेसकर, जोशी; also सुतार, लोहार, चाम्हार, कुंभार as constituting the first-class and claiming the largest division of बलुतें; next न्हावी, परीट, कोळी, गुरव as constituting the middle class and claiming a subdivision of बलुतें; lastly, भट, मुलाणा, सोनार, मांग; and, in the Konkaṇ̤, yet another list); and with other accounts of the assignments of corn; for this and many similar matters, originally determined diversely, have undergone the usual influence of time, place, and ignorance.

Of the बलुतेदार in the Indápúr pergunnah the list and description stands thus:--First class, सुतार, लोहार, चाम्हार, महार; Second, परीट, कुंभार, न्हावी, मांग; Third, सोनार, मुलाणा, गुरव, जोशी, कोळी, रामोशी; in all fourteen, but in no one village are the whole fourteen to be found or traced. In the Panḍharpúr districts the order is:--पहिली or थोरली वळ (1st class); महार, सुतार, लोहार, चाम्हार, दुसरी or मधली वळ(2nd class); परीट, कुंभार, न्हावी, मांग, तिसरी or धाकटी वळ (3rd class); कुळकरणी, जोशी, गुरव, पोतदार; twelve बलुते and of अलुते there are eighteen. According to Grant Duff, the बलतेदार are सुतार, लोहार, चाम्हार, मांग, कुंभार, न्हावी, परीट, गुरव, जोशी, भाट, मुलाणा; and the अलुते are सोनार, जंगम, शिंपी, कोळी, तराळ or वेसकर, माळी, डवऱ्यागोसावी, घडशी, रामोशी, तेली, तांबोळी, गोंधळी. In many villages of Northern Dakhaṇ̤ the महार receives the बलुतें of the first, second, and third classes; and, consequently, besides the महार, there are but nine बलुतेदार. The following are the only अलुतेदार or नारू now to be found;-- सोनार, मांग, शिंपी, भट गोंधळी, कोर- गू, कोतवाल, तराळ, but of the अलुतेदार & बलुते- दार there is much confused intermixture, the अलुतेदार of one district being the बलुतेदार of another, and vice lls. (The word कास used above, in पहिली कास, मध्यम कास, तिसरी कास requires explanation. It means Udder; and, as the बलुतेदार are, in the phraseology of endearment or fondling, termed वासरें (calves), their allotments or divisions are figured by successive bodies of calves drawing at the कास or under of the गांव under the figure of a गाय or cow.) (Marathi)kruciji 'smith' (Old Church Slavic)

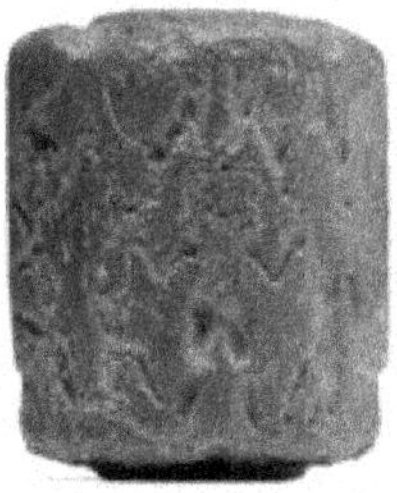

One-Eyed Hero with Lions Flanked by Enclosures Iran (?) (ca. 3100 B.C.E) 50 x 40 mm Seal No. 4 "Seal 4 presents as its central figure a cyclopic hero holding lions. The rest of the scene includes animals, pots, and other types of containers, as well as a human figure and two lion-headed eagles, all apparently meant to be within an enclosure indicated by two stockade-like frames. A related theme is found in a fragment of a vase from Khafajah.... The nude bearded hero seen in 4 remained a stock figure of the Mesopotamian repertory, aapearing for the most part in contst scenes. The cyclopic version of this figure in 4 is paralleled in only one other instance, an Early Dynastic seal impression from Fara (ancient Shuruppak). A plaque from Khafajah of some thousand years later shows a cyclopic demon whose head has the form of a sun. Because of the wide gap in time, however, there is no assurance that the hero in 4 is to be associated in any manner with this figure."--Porada, CANES, p. 3 Center: nude one-eyed hero holding two reversed lions, two more lions forming pyramid above him -- Left: section of inclosure containing sheep, latter between two pots, with lion-headed eagle perched on head of sheep; basket, pouch(?), fish, and bird in upper field -- Right: sheep-headed demon grasping pole of second section of inclosure; within latter, human figure(?) with upturned curls holding in outstretched hands indefinable curved object marked by vertical incisions; lion-headed eagle above horns of sheep-demon; crib(?) in upper field. Hieroglyp:one-eyed: *kANA, kanga* 'one-eyed' rebus: *kanga* 'brazier' *ara* 'lion' rebus: *Ara* 'brass'.

Cylinder unperforated; in both top and bottom shallow central cavity and outer circle of small depressions. "Seal 4 presents as its central figure a cyclopic hero holding lions. The rest of the scene includes animals, pots, and other types of containers, as well as a human figure and two lion-headed eagles, all apparently meant to be within an inclosure indicated by two stockade-like frames. A related theme is found in a fragment of a vase from Khafajah.... The nude bearded hero seen in 4 remained a stock figure of the Mesopotamian repertory, aapearing for the most part in contst scenes. The cyclopic version of this figure in 4 is paralleled in only one other instance, an Early Dynastic seal impression from Fara (ancient Shuruppak). A plaque from Khafajah of some thousand years later shows a cyclopic demon whose head has the form of a sun. Because of the wide gap in time, however, there is no assurance that the hero in 4 is to be associated in any manner with this figure."[127]

Rakhigarhi seals

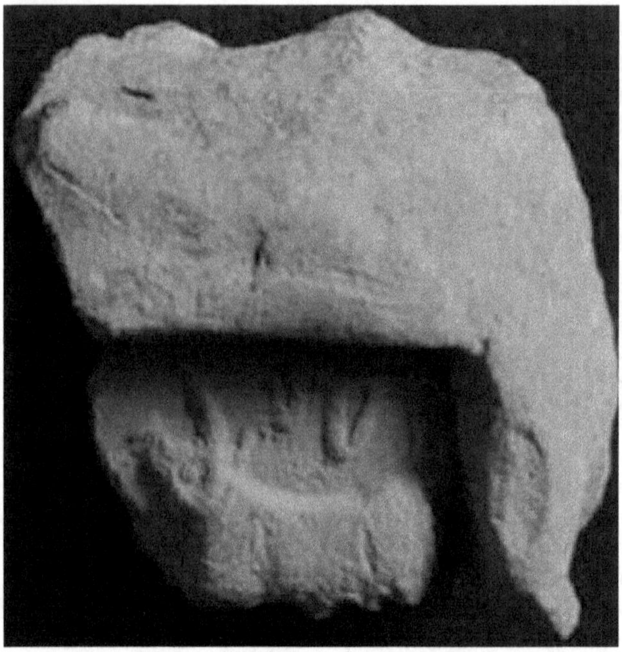

Hieroglyph: one-horned young bull

kõdā खोंड [*khōṇḍa*] m A young bull, a bullcalf. (Marathi) Rebus 1: *kǒnḍu or konḍu* l कुण्डम् m. a hole dug in the ground for receiving consecrated fire (Kashmiri) Rebus 2: *A. kundār, B. kũdār, °ri, Or. kundāru; H. kũderā* m. ' one who works a lathe, one who scrapes ', *°rī f., kũdernā* ' to scrape, plane, round on a lathe '.(CDIAL 3297).

Hieroglyph: 'rim-of-jar': Phonetic forms: *kan-ka* (Santali) k*arṇika* (Sanskrit) Rebus: *karṇī,* supercargo for a boat shipment. *karṇīka* 'account (scribe)'.

Hieroglyph: sprout ligatured to rimless pot: *baṭa* = rimless pot (Kannada) Rebus: *baṭa* = a kind of iron; *bhaṭa* 'furnace; *dula* 'pair' Rebus: *dul* 'cast (metal) *kolmo* 'sprout' Rebus: *kolimi* 'smithy/forge' Thus the composite hieroglyph: furnace, metalcaster smithy-forge

Hieroglyph: मेंढा *[mēṇḍhā*] A crook or curved end (of a stick) Rebus: *meḍ* 'iron'.

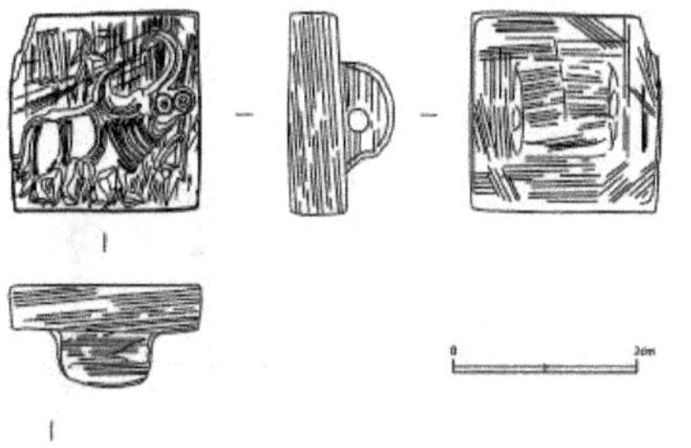

(After Fig. 68. Steatite seal and terracotta seal impression from Structure No. 1)

The following three examples from Mehrgarh, Mohenjo-daro and Banawali show acrobats in bull-jumping or buffalo-leaping.

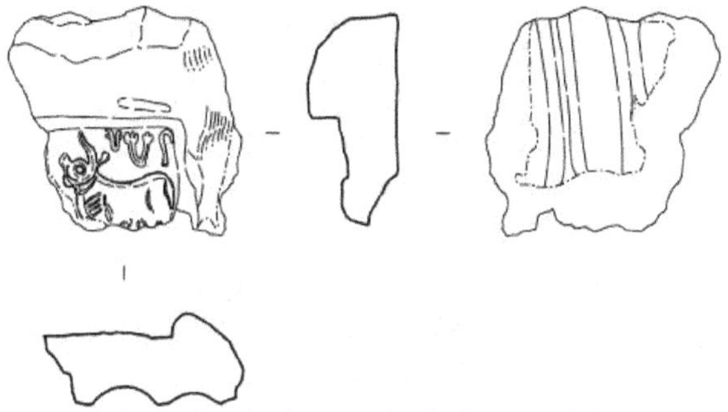

Mehrgarh. Terracotta circular button seal. (Shah, SGM & Parpola, A., 1991, Corpus of Indus Seals and Inscriptions 2: Collections in Pakistan, Helsinki: Suomalainen Tiedeakatemia, MR-17. A humped bull (water buffalo?) and abstract forms (one of which is like a human body) around the bull. The human body is tossed from the horns of the bovine.

m0312 Persons vaulting over a water buffalo. The water buffalo tosses a person on its horns. Four or five bodies surround the animal. Rounded edges indicate frequent use to create clay seal impressions.

Impression of a steatite stamp seal (2300-1700 BCE) with a water-buffalo and acrobats. Buffalo attack or bull-leaping scene, Banawali (after UMESAO 2000:88, cat. no. 335). A figure is impaled on the horns of the buffalo; a woman acrobat wearing bangles on both arms and a long braid flowing from the head, leaps over the buffalo bull. The action narrative is presented in five frames of the acrobat getting tossed by the horns, jumping and falling down.Two Harappa Script glyphs are written in front of the buffalo. (ASI BNL 5683).

Rebus readings of hieroglyphs: '1. arrow, 2. jag/notch, 3. buffalo, 4. acrobatics:

1. *kāṇḍa* 'arrow' (Skt.) H. *kãḍerā* m. ' a caste of bow -- and arrow -- makers

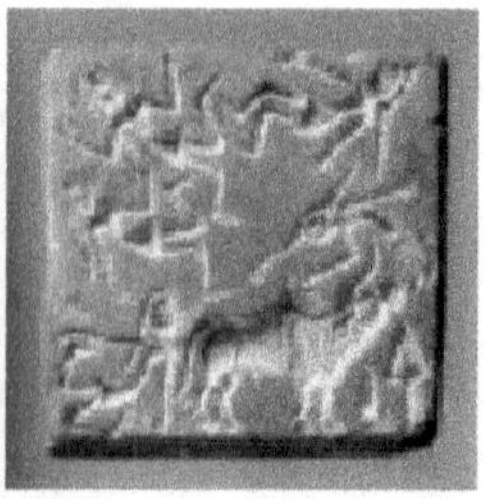

(CDIAL 3024). Or. *kāṇḍa, kā̃ṛ* ‘stalk, arrow ’(CDIAL 3023). *ayaskāṇḍa* ‘a quantity of iron, excellent iron’ (Pāṇ.gaṇ) *sal* ‘splinter’ rebus: *ssl* ‘workshop’

2. खांडा [*khāṇḍā*] m A jag, notch, or indentation (as upon the edge of a tool or weapon). (Marathi) Rebus: *khāṇḍā* ‘tools, pots and pans, metal-ware’.

3. *rāngo* ‘water buffalo bull’ (Ku.N.)(CDIAL 10559) Rebus: *rango* ‘pewter’. *ranga, rang* pewter is an alloy of tin, lead, and antimony (*anjana*) (Santali).

4. *ḍullu* to fall off; *ḍollu* to roll over (DEDR 2698) Te. *ḍul(u)cu, ḍulupu* to cause to fall; *ḍollu* to fall; *ḍolligillu* to fall or tumble over (DEDR 2988) డొలుచు [*ḍolucu*] or *ḍoluṭsu.* [Tel.] v. n. To tumble head over heels as dancing girls do (Telugu) Rebus 1: *dul* ‘to cast in a mould’; *dul mẽṛhẽt, dul meṛeḍ,* 'cast iron'; *koṭe meṛeḍ* ‘forged iron’ (Santali) Bshk. ḍōl ‘ brass pot (CDIAL 6583). Rebus 2: WPah. *ḍhō`ḷ* m. ‘stone’, *ḍhòḷṭɔ* m. ‘big stone or boulder’, *ḍhòḷṭu* ‘small id.’ Him.I 87(CDIAL 5536). Rebus: K. *ḍula* m. ‘ rolling stone’(CDIAL 6582).

baṭi trs. To overturn, to overset or ovethrow; to turn or throw from a foundation or foothold (Santali) *baṭi* to turn on the ground to any extent, or roll; uaurbaṭi, to upset or

overthrow by shoving or pushing; mabaṭi to overturn by cutting, to fell trees; *baṭi*-n rflx. v., to lay oneself down; *ba-p-aṭi* repr. V., to throw each other; baṭi-o to be overturned, overthrown; ba-n-at.i vrb.n., the extent of the overturning, falling down or rolling; *baṭi*-n rflx.v., to lie down; baṭi-aṛagu to bring or send down a slope by rolling; *baṭi bar.a* to roll again and again or here and there; *baṭi-bur* to turn over by rolling (Mundari) Rebus: *baṭi, bhaṭi* ‘furnace’ (H.) Rebus: *baṭa* = a kind of iron (G.) *bhaṭa* (G.) *baṭa* = kiln (Santali). *bhaṭa* = an oven, kiln, furnace (Santali) *baṭhi* furnace for smelting ore (the same as *kuṭhi*) (Santali)

m1406A m1406B

‘furnace’

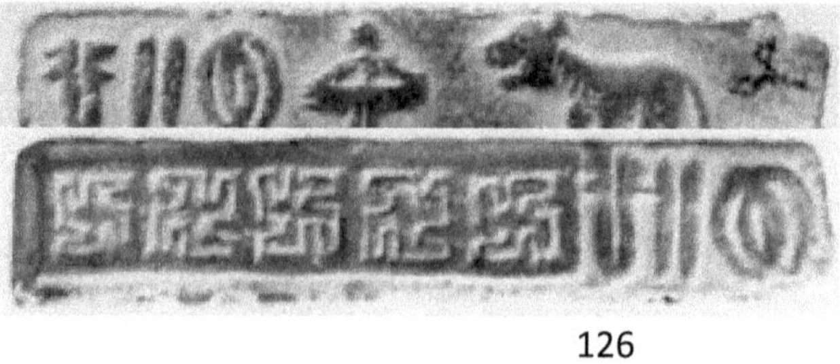

h182A, h182B The drummer hieroglyph is associated with svastika glyph on this tablet (har609) and also on h182A tablet of

Harappa with an identical text.

dhollu 'drummer' (Western Pahari) Rebus: *dul* 'cast metal'

kola 'tiger' Rebus: *kolle* 'blacksmith' *kol* 'working in iron' ‘furnace, forge’

kolimi 'smithy, forge' *jasta, dasta* 'five' (Kafiri) *jasta, sattva* 'zinc'. Thus, five ‘svastika’ hieroglyphs are phonetic determinatives of the lexeme *sattva*, ‘zinc’.

Text message: *karā̃* n. pl. ‘ wristlets, bangles ’ (Gujarati) Rebus: *khār* 'blacksmith'. The pair of ‘ovals’ are ingot-shaped: *mũh* ‘ingot’ (Santali) *dula* 'pair' Rebus: *dul* 'cast metal' Thus, cast metal ingot. *kanka, karṇaka* ‘rim of jar’ rebus: *karṇī* ‘supercargo, script’. The message of the inscription is: cargo of zinc ingots and metal castings.

Zinc (Pewter)

jasta'h, Pewter, Pl. ئي *ey.* جس *jas*, s.m. (6th) Pewter. Sing. and Pl. See also HI جست *jast*, s.m. (6th) Pewter. Sing. and Pl.(Pashto) These glosses are cognate with *jasta* 'zinc' (Hindi) *svastika* pewter (Kannada); *jasta* = zinc (Hindi) *yasada* (Jaina Prakritam)

hasta 'hand' (Rigveda); Kafiri. **dasta* -- < **jasta* -- is a Meluhha homonym: *jasta, dasta* 'five' (Kafiri) Rebus: *jasta, sattva* 'zinc, pewter, sphalerite'. The semantics 'hand' and 'five' are meanings signified by *hath, ath* ‘ hand, five ’(Gypsy). Thus, it is reasonably deduced that Proto-Prakritam (Meluhha) *jasta* signified numeral 'five'.

Thus, the tablets denote blacksmith's alloy cast metal accounting including the use of alloying mineral zinc -- *satthiya* 'svastika' glyph.

I suggest that it reads sattva. Its rebus rendering and meaning is zastas 'spelter or sphalerite or sulphate of zinc.'
Zinc occurs in sphalerite, or sulphate of zinc in five colours.

The Meluhha gloss for 'five' is: *taṭṭal* Homonym is: *ṭhaṭṭha* ‘brass’ (i.e. alloy of copper + zinc). The scribe has thus clearly indicated the competence of Bharatam janam to create an alloy of brass mixing copper with zinc and points to the invention of brass ca. 2500 BCE, given the evidence of rebus rendering of lexeme for ‘brass’ signified by the Harappa Script hieroglyph of 5 svastika hieroglyph displayed in sequence.

dhollu ‘drummer’ (Western Pahari) Rebus: *dul* ‘cast metal’

Lexically attested glosses for zinc are: *sattu (Tamil), satta, sattva* (Kannada) *jasth* जसथ् ।रपु m. (sg. dat. *jastas* ज्तस), zinc, spelter; pewter; *zasath* ◌़ ज़स्◌़थ् ◌़or *zasuth* ज़सुथ ◌़। रप m. (sg. dat. *zastas* ◌ु ज़्तस),◌़ zinc, spelter, pewter (cf. Hindī jast). *jastuvu*; । रपूभवः adj. (f. *jastüvü*), made of zinc or pewter (Kashmiri). Hence the hieroglyph: svastika repeated five times. Five svastika thus read: *taṭṭal sattva* Rebus: zinc (for) brass (or pewter).

**ṭhaṭṭha*1 'brass'. [Onom. from noise of hammering brass?]N. *ṭhaṭṭar* 'an alloy of copper and bell metal'. **ṭhaṭṭhakāra* ' brass worker '. 1.*Pk. ṭhaṭṭhāra -- m., K. ṭhö̃ṭhur m., S. ṭhã̄ṭhāro m., P. ṭhaṭhiār, °rā m.2. P.* ludh. *ṭhaṭherā m., Ku. ṭhaṭhero m., N. ṭhaṭero, Bi. ṭhaṭherā, Mth. ṭhaṭheri, H. ṭhaṭherā* m. (CDIAL 5491, 5493).

Tammuz, alabaster (Gypsum?) relief from Ashur, c. 1500 BCE; in the Staatliche Museen zu Berlin, Germany Foto Marburg/Art Resource, New York. Two goats flank the person feeding them with leafy twigs. In the lower register, two women carry jars with overflowing streams of water. This is a Meluhha hieroglyph, as is the pair of twigs emanating from the waist of the standing person. Tham·muz (tä'mʊz) n. The tenth month of the year in the Jewish calendar. [Hebrew tammūz, akin to Iraqi Arabic tabbūz, July, both ultimately from Sumerian dumu-zi, Dumuzi, a dying and rising shepherd divinity (Inanna's husband): dumu, son, offspring + zi, true, effective.]

Meluhha hieroglyphs read rebus:

mṛeka, melh 'goat' Rebus: *milakkhu* 'copper'. *kūdī, kūṭī* 'bunch of twigś (Sanskrit) Rebus: *kuṭhi* 'smelter furnace' (Santali) *kūdī* (also written as *kūṭī* in manuscripts) occurs in the Atharvaveda (AV 5.19.12) and *Kauśika Sūtra.*[128]

dula 'pair' Rebus: *dul* 'cast (metal)'.

lo 'pot to overflow'; *kāṇḍa* 'water'. Rebus: लोखंड *lokhaṇḍ* Iron tools, vessels, or articles in general.

kola 'woman' Rebus: *kol* 'smithy, working in iron' 'furnace, forge'.

Kalibangan 067 Antelope with long tail + two glyphs of ficus religiosa. *mẽḍha* 'antelope'; rebus: *meḍ* 'iron' (Mu.) *meḍho* 'merchant'. Alternative: *tagara* 'antelope' Rebus: *tagara*'tin'; *damgar*

'merchant'. *dula* 'two' rebus: *dul* 'metal casting' PLUS *loa* 'fig leaf' (Santali): Rebus: *lo* 'iron' (Assamese, Bengali); *loa* 'iron' (Gypsy) Glyph: *lo* = nine (Santali); *no*= nine (B.) *on-patu* = nine (Ta.) The message of the inscription is: *dul meḍ* 'cast iron' *meḍho* 'merchant'.

Meluhha is added to the list of languages by first written accounts of Ancient Near East. Harappa Script decipherment pushes Samskrta Bharati lexis with Meluhha metalwork words to ca. 3300 BCE.

Deployment of a Harappa Script cipher during the Bronze Age is most likely to be by Meluhha speakers who were itinerant Bronze Age explorers for minerals along the Tin Route from Hanoi to Haifa, producing metals, alloys and metal castings AND documenting them using the Prakrtam Sanskrta Bharati (Meluhha) cipher. The data mining provided in over 7000 inscriptions of the Harappa Script Corpora by this Tvaṣṭā of a karmā́ra 'blacksmith' tradition is datable to (indeterminate) Rigvedic times and dhokra kamar 'cire perdue artificer' tradition datable to Nahal Mishmar times of ca. 5th millennium BCE.

Gaullic Travos Trigaranus on Pilier des Nautes (Pillar of Boatmen) is a signifier of the profession of a blacksmith in a smithy-forge, using three braziers; kolom 'three' rebus: *kolimi* 'smithy, forge' PLUS *kangu* 'crane, heron' rebus: *kang* 'brazier'. The crane, egret, heron is also a hieroglyph signified on Dong Son bronze drum. That the smith is also a seafaring merchant is signified by other hieroglyphs including that of *Karnonou* (Greek inscription spelling), *kañi-āra* 'helmsman (navigator)' *kāraṇī* 'helmsman, scribe, supercargo' of Harappa Script~~*Karnonou, Kernunno, Cernunnos* of Pilier des Nautes

kāraṇī 'helmsman, scribe, supercargo' of Harappa Script is *Karnonou* of Pilier des Nautes

Ancient near Eastern cylinder seal, Marcopoli Collection (Beatrice Teissier, 1985, Univ. of California Press).

Ta. *kōṭaram* monkey. Ir. *kōḍa* (small) monkey; *kūḍag* monkey. Ko. *ko·ṛṇ* small monkey. To. *kwṛṇ* monkey. Ka. *kōḍaga* monkey, ape. Koḍ. *ko·ḍë* monkey. Tu. koḍañji, koḍañja, koḍaṅgů baboon. (DEDR 2196). *kuṭhāru* = a monkey (Sanskrit) Rebus: *kuṭhāru* 'armourer or weapons maker'(metal-worker), also an inscriber or writer. Rebus: *koḍ* = the place where artisans work (Gujarati)

Monkeys shown with Phoenicians thus represent the role of Phoenicians as sellers of weapons and hence, read rebus as hieroglyphs or semantic identifiers of the resources traded:

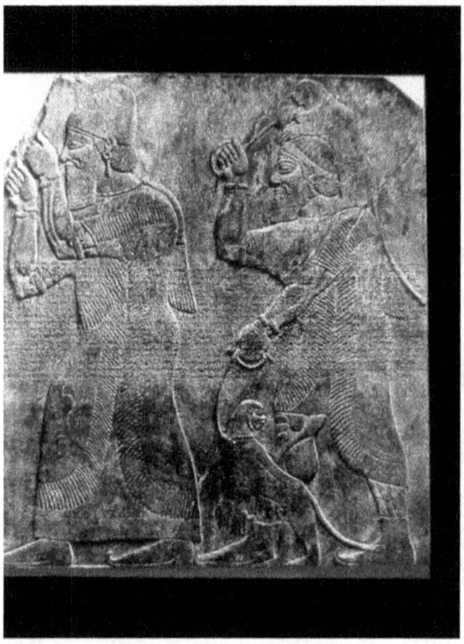

Neo-Assyrian, Nimrud, NW Palace of Assurnasirpal, Room D, Phoenicians with monkeys.[129]

kuThAru 'monkey' rebus: *kuThAru* 'armourer'.

Meṇḍa [dial., cp. Prk. mĕṇṭha & miṇṭha: Pischel, Prk. Gr. § 293. The Dhtm (156) gives a root meṇḍ (meḍ) in meaning of "*koṭilla*," i. e. crookedness. (Pali) M. mẽḍhā m. ' crook or curved end (of a horn, stick, &c.) '. Glyph: 'ram with curling horns': H. *mẽṛā, mẽḍā* m. ' ram with curling horns ', °ḍī f. ' she -- goat do. ' (CDIAL 10120)

mēṭu, mēṭa, mēṭi stack of hay; (Inscr.) (Telugu)

meṛā m. (Bihari) *meṇḍa* -m. ' ram ' (Pali) *miṇḍā'l* ' markhor ' (Tōrwālī) मेंढा [*mēṇḍhā*] m A crook or curved end (of a stick, horn &c.) and attrib. such a stick, horn, bullock.

मेंढका or क्या [*mēṇḍhakā or kyā*] a (मेंढा) A shepherd. मेंढा [mēṇḍhā] m (मेष S through H) A male sheep, a ram or tup. (Marathi) **mēṇḍharūpa* ' like a ram '. [mēṇḍha -- 2, rūpá --]Bi. *mẽṛhwā* ' a bullock with curved horns like a ram's '; M. *mẽḍhrũ* n. ' sheep '(CDIAL 10311). *mēṇḍha2* m. ' ram ', °*aka* -- , *mēṇḍa* -- 4, *miṇḍha* -- 2, °*aka* -- , *mēṭha* -- 2, *mēṇḍhra* -- , *mēḍhra* -- 2, °*aka* -- m. lex. 2. *mēṇṭha- (*mēṭha* -- m. lex.). 3. *mējjha -- . [*r* -- forms (which are not attested in NIA.) are due to further sanskritization of a loan -- word prob. of Austro -- as. origin (EWA ii 682 with lit.) and perh. related to the group s.v. bhēḍra --]1. Pa. *meṇḍa* -- m. ' ram ', °*aka* -- ' made of a ram's horn (e.g. a bow) '; Pk. *meḍḍha* -- , *meṁḍha* -- (°*ḍhī* -- f.), °*ṁḍa* -- , *miṁḍha* -- (°*dhiā* -- f.),°*aga* -- m. ' ram ', Dm.
Gaw. *miṇ* Kal.rumb. *amŕn/aŕə* ' sheep ' (*a* -- ?); Bshk. *mināʹl* ' ram '; Tor. *miṇḍ* ' ram ', *miṇḍā'l* ' markhor '; Chil.*mindh*l*l* ' ram ' AO xviii 244 (*dh*!), Sv. *yēṛo -- miṇ*; Phal. *miṇḍ, miṇ* ' ram ', *miṇḍṓl* m. ' yearling lamb, gimmer '; P. *mẽḍhā* m., °*ḍhī* f., ludh.*mīḍḍhā, mī̃ḍhā* m.; N. *meṛho, meṛo* ' ram for sacrifice '; A. *mersāg* ' ram ' (-- *sāg* < *chāgya -- ?), B. *meṛā* m., °*ṛi* f., Or. *meṇḍhā*, °*ḍā* m., °*ḍhi*f., H. *meṛh, meṛhā, mẽḍhā* m., G. *mẽḍhɔ*, M. *mẽḍhā* m., Si. *mäḍayā.*
2. Pk. *meṁṭhī* -- f. ' sheep '; H. *meṭhā* m. ' ram '.3. H. *mejhukā* m. ' ram '.*mēṇḍharūpa -- , mēḍhraśr̥ṅgī -- .Addenda: *mēṇḍha* -- 2: A. also *mer* (phonet. *mer*) ' ram ' AFD 235. (CDIAL 10310).

**mēṭṭa2* ' lump '. 2. **mēṇḍa* -- 2. [See list s.v. **maṭṭha* -- 2. -- Cf. **mēṭṭa* -- 1, **mēṇḍa* -- 1 ' defective ' s.v. *miḍḍa --]1. Or. *meṭṭā* ' hillock '. 2. Or. *meṇḍā* ' lump, clot '.(CDIAL 10308)

Tablet with seal impression of a horned animal and a plant. Clay. H. 2 ½ in. (6.4 cm); W. 1 ¾ in. (4.5 cm) Proto-Elamite period, ca 3100-2900 BCE Sb 4841. Excavated by Morgan[130]

Based on MDP 16 (1921), pl. 8, no. 125, Holly Pittman notes about this seal impression: "This tablet is inscribed with Proto-Elamite script and impressed by a seal…The seal would have had one caprid and a plant engraved on its surface, but because of multiple rollings there are repeated impressions of the animal. As is obvious from this example, seals were applied to the still-soft tablets first and the inscriptions added afterwards." The 'inscription' added afterwards on this tablet is a hieroglyph of 'two linear strokes' which is a common Harappa Script hieroglyph. The inscription reads in Meluhha: *miṇḍāl* 'markho**r**' (Tōrwālī) *meḍho* a ram, a sheep (Gujarati)(CDIAL 10120) Rebus: *mẽṛhẽt, meḍ* 'iron' (Santali.Munda.Ho.) *mṟeka, melh* 'goat' (Telugu. Brahui) Rebus: *milakkhu* 'copper' (Pali) *dula* 'two' rebus: *dul* 'metal casting' *tagaraka* '*tabernae montana*' rebus: *tagara* 'tin' Thus, the inscription reads: tin metal castings, iron, copper work.

Animals in procession: Two gazelles (antelopes?), stalks, two tigers

Two eagles, sprout between.

Base for a ritual offering, carved with

animals Elamite period, mid-3rd millennium BCE. Tell of the Acropolis, Susa, Iran Bituminous rock H. 19 cm; Diam. 11 cm Jacques de Morgan excavations, 1908 Lions and gazelles passant; eagles protecting their young Sb 2725.

This base for a ritual offering is made of bitumen. This material was plentiful throughout the Middle East, but only in Susa was it used in sculpture. The object is carved with big cats, gazelles, and eagles. The theme of the eagle spreading its wings to protect its young was found only in Iran and also features on painted ceramics of the same period. *eruvai* 'kite' rebus: *eruvai* 'copper'. *khambhaṛā* 'fin', *kambha*'wing' rebus: *kammaTa* 'mint, coiner, coinage' *kāṇḍa* 'stalk' rebus: *kāṇḍa* 'implement'. *kola* 'tiger' rebus: *kol* 'metal' 'working in iron' 'furnace, forge' *mṛeka,* melh 'goat' (Telugu. Brahui) Rebus: *milakkhu* 'copper' (Pali). Thus,the inscription reads: copper mint, implements, working in iron, furnace, forge.

Late Uruk and Jemdet Nasr seal; ca. 3200-3000 (?) BC; marble; cat.3; loop bore; an antelope with two tigerss, one with head turned. *kola* 'tiger' Rebus: *kol* 'working in iron'. *tagara* 'antelope' Rebus: *tagara* 'tin'. *krammara* 'head turned back' Rebus: *kamar* 'smith, artisan'

Cylinder seal and impression: cattle herd at the cowshed. White limestone,

Mesopotamia, Uruk Period (4100 BC–3000 BC). Louvre Museum.

Bronze dish found by Layard at Nimrud: circular objects are decorated by consecutive chains of animals following each other round in a circle. A similar theme occurs on the famous silver vase of Entemena. In the innermost circle, a troop of gazelles (similar to the ones depicted on cylinder seals) march along in file; the middle register has a variety of animals, all marching in the same direction as the gazelles. A one-horned bull, a winged griffin, an ibex and a gazelle, are followed by two bulls who are being attacked by lions, and a griffin, a one-horned bull, and a gazelle, who are all respectively being attacked by leopards. In the outermost zone there is a stately procession of

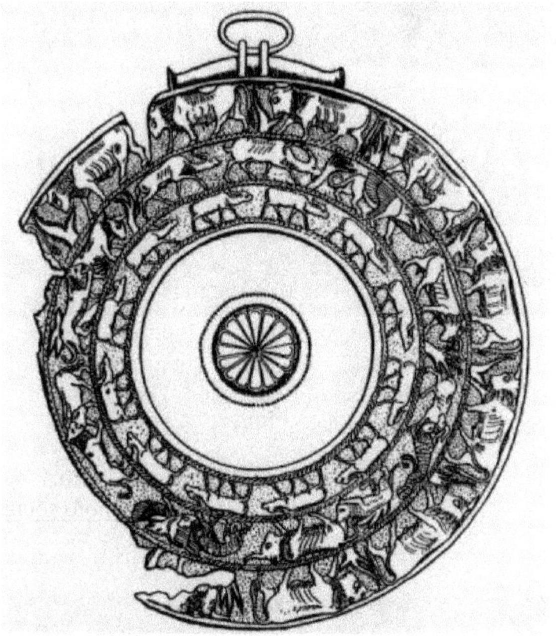

realistically conceived one-horned bulls marching in the opposite direction to the animals parading in the two inner circles. The dish has a handle.[131]

Cylinder seal and impression: cattle herd in a wheat field. Limestone, Mesopotamia, Uruk Period (4100 BC–3000 BC). *kuṇḍa* n. 'clump' (Samskrtam) A phonetic determinant of the young bull *kõdā* खोंड [*khōṇḍa*] m 'A young bull, a bullcalf'. (Marathi) read rebus: *kũderā* m. 'one who works a lathe'. Alternative: The cob is *kolmo* 'seeding, rice-plant'(Munda) rebus: *kolimi* 'smithy' (Telugu)

Mudhif and three reed banners. A cow and a stable of reeds with sculpted columns in the background. Fragment of another vase of alabaster (era of Djemet-Nasr) from Uruk, Mesopotamia. Limestone 16 X 22.5 cm. AO 8842, Louvre, Departement des Antiquites Orientales, Paris, France. Six circles decorated on the reed post are semantic determinants of Glyph: *bhaṭa* 'six'. Rebus: baTa 'iron', *bhaṭa* 'furnace'. काँड् । काण्डः m. the stalk or stem of a reed, grass, or the like, straw. In the compound with dan 5 (p. 221a, l. 13) the word is spelt *kāḍ*. The rebus reading of the pair of reeds in Sumer standard is: *khāṇḍa* 'tools, pots and pans and metal-ware'.

Uruk trough, Uruk, c. 3000 BCE. This cult drinking trough recovered from a stable consecrated to the great goddess Inanna. Notice traditional reed structure 'mudhif' common in Southern Iraq, depicted centre. The mudhif (Toda mund) is shown symbolised by a a prif of reeds with a hanging scarf atop either side of the roof.

Sumerian mudhif facade, with uncut reed fonds and sheep entering, carved into a gypsum trough from Uruk, c. 3200 BCE (British Museum WA 120000). Photo source.

Reedhut shrine with flagposts.and cattle with calves[132]

Quadrupeds exiting the mund (or mudhif) are *pasaramu, pasalamu* 'an animal, a beast, a brute, quadruped' (Telugu) పసరము [*pasaramu*] or పసలము *pasaramu.* [Tel.] n. A beast, an animal. గోమహిషహాతి.

One frame of the cybrus bronze stand showing a bronze ingot bearer. A reed post is signified. A male carrying a scarf on his right hand and fish on his left. *ayo* 'fish' *ayas* 'metal (bronze)'. *dhatu* 'scarf'. *dhatu* 'mineral'.

Rebus: *pasra* = a smithy, place where a black-smith works, to work as a blacksmith; *kamar pasra* = a smithy; *pasrao lagao akata se ban:?* Has the blacksmith begun to work? *pasraedae* = the blacksmith is at his work (Santali.lex.) *pasra meṛed, pasāra* meṛed = syn. of *koṭe meṛed* = forged iron, in contrast to *dul meṛed*, cast iron (Mundari) పసారము [*pasāramu*] or పసారు pasārdmu. [Tel.] n. A shop. అంగడి. Allograph: *pacar* = a wedge driven ino a wooden pin, wedge etc. to tighten it (Santali.lex.) Allograph: *pajhar* 'eagle'.

A cow and a stable of reeds with sculpted columns in the background. Fragment of another vase of alabaster (era of Djemet-Nasr) from Uruk, Mesopotamia. Limestone 16 X 22.5 cm. AO 8842, Louvre, Departement des Antiquites Orientales, Paris, France. Six circles decorated on the reed post are semantic determinants of Glyph: *bhaṭa* 'six'. Rebus: *bhaṭa* 'furnace'.

A Toda temple in Muthunadu Mund near Ooty, India. For example, on a cylinder seal from Uruk, a professional group of workers in a smithy are shown as a procession of

young bull calves and other quadrupeds emerging out of the smithy. *kole.l* 'temple' rebus: *kole.l* 'smithy, forge'

Kur. *xolā* tail. Malt. *qoli* id.(DEDR 2135) Rebus: *kolle* 'blacksmith' *kol* 'working in iron'. The 'tail' atop the reed-structure banner glyph is a phonetic determinant for *kole.l* 'temple, smithy'. Alternative: *pajhaṛ* = to sprout from a root (Santali); Rebus: *pasra* 'smithy, forge' (Santali)

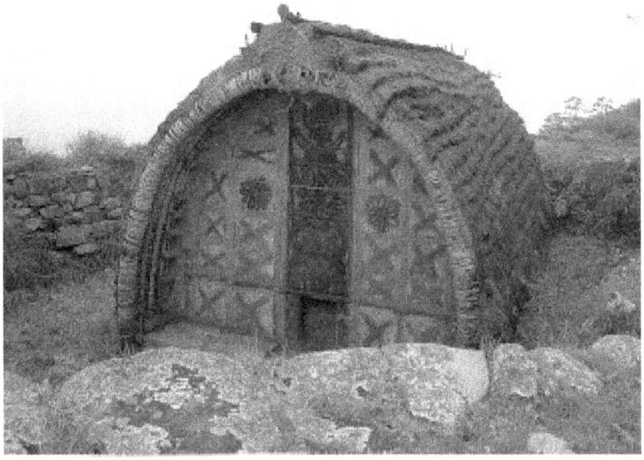

Ta. kuṭi house, abode, home, family, lineage, town, tenants; kuṭikai hut made of leaves, temple; *kuṭical* hut; *kuṭicai, kuṭiñai* small hut, cottage; kuṭimai family, lineage, allegiance (as of subjects to their sovereign), servitude; kuṭiy-āḷ tenant; kuṭiyilār tenants; kuṭil hut, shed, abode; *kuṭaṅkar* hut, cottage; *kaṭumpu* relations. *Ma. kuṭi* house, hut, family, wife, tribe; *kuṭima* the body of landholders, tenantry; kuṭiyanslaves (e.g. in Coorg); kuṭiyān inhabitant, subject, tenant; kuṭiññil hut, thatch; kuṭil hut, outhouse near palace for menials. *Ko. kuṛjl* shed, bathroom of Kota house; *kuṛm* family; *kuḍḷ* front room of house; *kuṛḷ* hut; *guṛy* temple. *To. kwïṣ* shed for small calves; *kuṣ* room (in dairy or house); *kuḍṣ* outer room of dairy, in: kuḍṣ waṣ̱ fireplace in outer room of lowest grade of dairies (cf. 2857), *kuḍṣ* moṇy bell(s) in outer section of ti· dairy, used on non-sacred buffaloes (cf. 4672); kuṛy Hindu temple; ? *kwïḍy* a family of children. *Ka. kuḍiya, kuḍu* śūdra, farmer; guḍihouse, temple; *guḍil, guḍalu, guḍisalu, guḍasalu, guḍasala,* etc. hut with a thatched roof. *Koḍ. kuḍi* family of servants living in one hut; kuḍië man of toddy-tapper caste. *Tu. guḍi* small pagoda or shrine; *guḍisalů, guḍisilů, guḍsilů, guḍicilů* hut, shed. *Te. koṭika* hamlet; guḍitemple; guḍise hut, cottage, hovel. *Kol.* (SR) *guḍī* temple.

Pa. guḍi temple, village resthouse. *Ga.* (Oll.) *guḍi* temple. *Go.* (Ko.) *kuṛma* hut, outhouse; (Ma.) *kurma* menstruation; (Grigson) kurma lon menstruation hut (*Voc.* 782, 800); (SR.) guḍi, (Mu.) *guḍḍi*, (S. Ko.) *guṛi* temple; *guḍḍī* (Ph.) temple, (Tr.) tomb (*Voc.* 1113). *Kui guḍi* central room of house, living room. / Cf. Skt. *kū̆ṭa-, kuṭi-, kū̆ṭī-* (whence Ga. (P.) kuṛehut; Kui kūṛi hut made of boughs, etc.; Kur. *kuṛyā* small shed or outhouse; Malt. *kuṛya* hut in the fields; Br. *kuḍ(ḍ)ī* hut, small house, wife), *kuṭīkā-, kuṭīra-, kuṭuṅgaka-, kuṭīcaka-, koṭa-* hut; *kuṭumba-* household (whence Ta. Ma. *kuṭumpam* id.; Ko. *kuṛmb* [? also *kuṛm* above]; To. *kwïḍb, kwïḍbïl* [-ïl from wïkïl, s.v. 925 Ta. *okkal*]; Ka., Koḍ., Tu. *kuṭumba*; Tu. *kuḍuma*; Te. *kuṭumbamu*; ? Kui *kumbu* house [balance word of iḍu, see s.v. 494 Ta. il]). See Turner, *CDIAL*, no. 3232, *kuṭī-*, no. 3493, *kōṭa-*, no. 3233, *kuṭumba-*, for most of the Skt. forms; Burrow, *BSOAS* 11.137. (DEDR 1655) Rebus: *kuṭhi* 'smelter' (Santali).

m0702 Text 2206 Glyph 39, a glyph which compares with the Sumerian mudhif or Toda munda structure.

[Kannada. *kōḍu*]tusk; யானை பன்றிகளின் தந்தம். மத்த யானையின் கோடும் (தேவா. 39, 1). Rebus: खोट [*khōṭa*] A lump or solid bit (as of phlegm, gore, curds, inspissated milk); any concretion or clot. (Marathi) Rebus: L. *khoṭ* f. ' alloy, impurity ', °ṭā ' alloyed ', awāṇ. *khoṭā* ' forged '; P. *khoṭ* m. ' base, alloy ' M. *khoṭā* 'alloyed' (CDIAL 3931) *kole.l* = smithy (Ko.) Rebus: Kuwi (F.) *kolhali* to forge. Koḍ. *kollë* blacksmith. (DEDR 2133).

Reading 1: *kole.l* = smithy, temple in Kota village (Ko.) Rebus 1: Ta. *kol* working in iron, blacksmith; *kollan̲* blacksmith. Ma. *kollan* blacksmith, artificer. Ka. *kolime, kolume, kulāme, kulime, kulume, kulme* fire-pit, furnace; (Bell.; U.P.U.) *konimi* blacksmith (Gowda) *kolla*

id. Koḍ. *kollë* blacksmith. Te. *kolimi* furnace. Go. (SR.) *kollusānā* to mend implements; (Ph.) *kolstānā, kulsānā* to forge; (Tr.) *kōlstānā* to repair (of ploughshares); (SR.) *kolmi* smithy (Voc. 948). Kuwi (F.) *kolhali* to forge. (DEDR 2133). Rebus 2: Ko. *kole·l* smithy, temple in Kota village.To. *kwala·l* Kota smithy (DEDR 2133).

Reading 2: *goṭ* = the place where cattle are collected at mid-day (Santali); goṭh (Brj.)(CDIAL 4336). *goṣṭha* (Skt.); cattle-shed (Or.) *koḍ* = a cow-pen; a cattlepen; a byre (G.) कोठी cattle-shed (Marathi) कोंडी[*kōṇḍī*] A pen or fold for cattle. गोठी [*gōṭhī*] f C (Dim. Of गोठा) A pen or fold for calves. (Marathi) Cattle Byres c.3200-3000 B.C. Late Uruk-Jemdet Nasr period. Magnesite. Cylinder seal. In the lower field of this seal appear three reed cattle byres. Each byre is surmounted by three reed pillars topped by rings, a motif that has been suggested as symbolizing a male god, perhaps Dumuzi. Within the huts calves or vessels appear alternately; from the sides come calves that drink out of a vessel between them. Above each pair of animals another small calf appears. A herd of enormous cattle moves in the upper field. Cattle and cattle byres in Southern Mesopotamia, c. 3500 BCE. Drawing of an impression from a Uruk period cylinder seal.[133]

Text 1330 (appears with zebu glyph – not illustrated). Shown as exiting the *kole.l* 'smithy' are *kol* 'blaksmiths' and *kũderā* 'lathe-workers.' *kolA* 'tail' rebus: *kol* 'working in iron' *sal* 'splinter' rebus: *sal* 'workshop' *ayo, aya* 'fish' rebus: *aya* 'iron' ayas 'metal'.

The young bulls emerging from the smithy. *kõdā* खोंड [*khōṇḍa*] m A young bull, a bullcalf. (Marathi) Rebus 1: *kǭndu* or *konḍu* । कुण्डम् m. a hole dug in the ground for receiving consecrated fire (Kashmiri)Rebus 2: *A. kundār, B. kũdār, °ri, Or. kundāru; H. kũderā* m. ' one who works a lathe, one who scrapes ', °rī f., *kũdernā* ' to scrape, plane, round on a lathe '.(CDIAL 3297).

खांडा [*khāṇḍā*] m A jag, notch, or indentation (as upon the edge of a tool or weapon). Rebus: *khāṇḍa* 'tools, pots and pans, and metal-ware'. *kole.l* = smithy (Ko.) Rebus: Kuwi (F.) *kolhali* to forge. Koḍ. *kollë* blacksmith. (DEDR 2133). *kol* 'furnace, forge'

kuṭila 'bent'; rebus: *kuṭila, katthīl* = bronze (8 parts copper and 2 parts tin) [cf. āra-kūṭa, 'brass (Skt.) (CDIAL 3230) *kuṭi—* in cmpd. 'curve' (Skt.)(CDIAL 3231).

kanka 'rim of jar' Rebus: *karṇika* 'accountant'. *kul -- karṇī* m. 'village accountant' (Marathi); karṇikan id. (Tamil) கணக்கு *kaṇakku*, n. cf. *gaṇaka. [M. kaṇakku]* 1. Number, account, reckoning, calculation, computation (Tamil)

Rebus: 'to engrave, write; lapidary': <*kana-lekhe*>(P) {??} ``??''. |. Cf. <kana->. %16123. #16013. <lekhe->(P),,<*leke-*>(KM) {VTC} ``to ^write''. Cf. <kana-lekhe>. *Kh.<*likhae*>, H.<*lIkhAna*>, O.<*lekhIba*>, B.<*lekha*>; Kh.<*likha*>(P),

Mu.<*lika*>. %20701. #20541. (Munda etyma) Kashmiri:khanun खनुन् । खननम् conj. 1 (1 p.p. *khonu* for 1, see s.v.; f. *khüñü* to dig (K.Pr. 155, 247; L. 459; Śiv. 59, 746, 994, 143, 1197, 1214, 1373, 1754; Rām. 343, 958, 1147, 1724; H. xii, 6); to engrave (Śiv. 414, 671, 176; Rām. 1583). khonu-motu खनुमतु; । खातः perf. part. (f. *khüñümütsü*) dug (e.g. a field, or a well); engraved. *mŏhara-khonu* म्वहर-खनु; or (Gr.M.) *mŏhar-kan* । मुद्राखननकारुः m. a seal-engraver, a lapidary (El. *mohar-kand*). -wöjü । *अङ्गुलिमुद्रा f. a signet-ring.

DEDR 1170 Ta. *kaṇṭam* iron style for writing on palmyra leaves. Te. *gaṇṭamu* id.

DEDR 1179 Kur. *kaṇḍō* a stool. Malt. kanḍo stool, seat. గడమంచె *gaḍa-manche.* n. A wooden frame like a bench to keep things on. గంపలు మొదలగువాటిని ఉంచు మంచె.

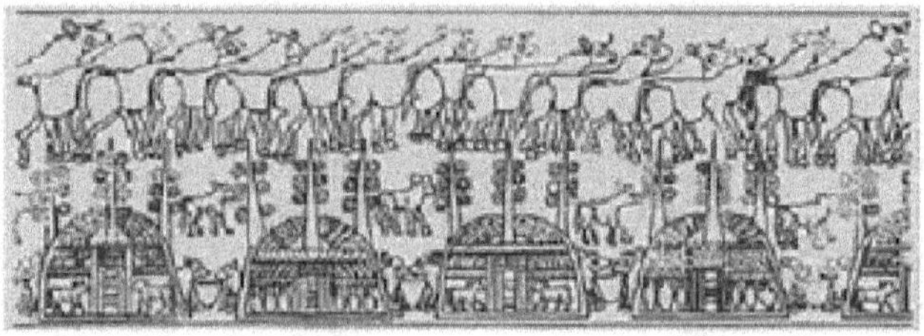

There three reed decorations atop the mudhif (or, Toda mund). *kā̃ḍ* 1 काँड् । काण्डः m. the stalk or stem of a reed, grass, or the like, straw. In the compound with dan 5 (p. 221a, l. 13) the word is spelt *kāḍ*. Rebus: *khāṇḍa* 'tools, pots and pans, and metal-ware'.

Sumerian mudhif facade, with uncut reed fonds and sheep entering, carved into a gypsum trough from Uruk, c. 3200 BCE. This trough was found at Uruk, the largest city so far known in southern Mesopotamia in the late prehistoric period (3300-3000 BC). The carving on the side shows a procession of sheep (a goat and a ram)

Carved gypum trough from Uruk. Two lambs exit a reed structure. A bundle of reeds (Inanna's symbol) can be seen projecting from the hut and at the edges of the scene.

The British Museum. WA 120000, neg. 252077 Part of the right-hand scene is cast from the original fragment now in the Vorderasiatisches Museum, Berlin

A cylinder seal with zebu and lion, Sibri

{Jarrige) पोळ *pōḷa* 'zebu' पोळ *pōḷa* 'magnetite (a ferrite ore)' kola 'tiger' rebus: kol 'metal' kol 'working in iron' खांडा [*khāṇḍā*] m A jag, **notch**, or indentation (as upon the edge of a tool or weapon). (Marathi) Rebus: *khāṇḍā* 'tools, pots and pans, metalware'.

Hieroglyphs: *kulā 'A* 'serpent hood', *kola* 'tiger' rebus: *kol* 'working in iron' *kolhe* 'smelter', *kolle* 'blacksmith' *kol* 'furnace, forge' Annex G presents examples of ligature *kulā* 'hood of snake' as tail

Hieroglyph: *nāga* 'serpent' Rebus: *nāga* 'lead'

Hieroglyph: *dhanga* 'mountain range' Rebus: dhangar 'blacksmith'

mēḍu 'height, rising ground, hillock' rebus: *meḍ* 'iron', *meḍ* 'copper' (Slavic).

Nahal Mishmar procession
The procession[134] is complemented by explaining the pair of birds perched on the edge of the crown, as Meluhha hieroglyphs:

dula 'pair' *rebus: dul* 'cast metal'
Glyph: *karaḍa* 'aquatic bird, duck'

Rebus: करडा *[karaḍā]* Hard from alloy--iron, silver &c. (Marathi) khārādī ' turner' (Gujarati) karaḍo –kār : an artisan-turner who works on a lathe – on hard alloys (Gujarati)

Fig

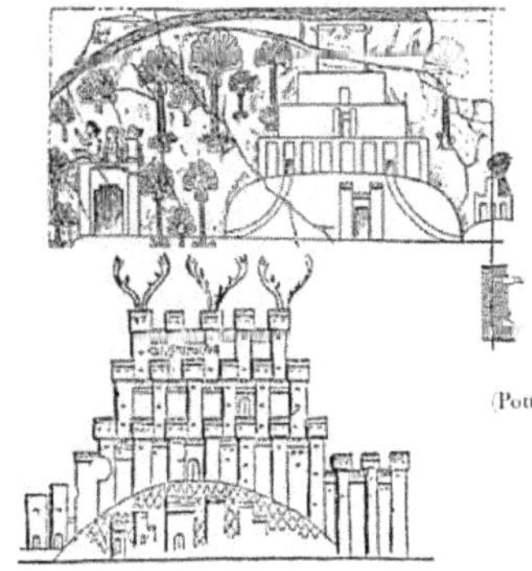

(Potts 1990, fig. 2)

Figure 6. Siege of Kišesim, Khorsabad (Amiet 1987, fig. 4)

Figure 5. Late Uruk cylinder seal impression from Choga Mish showing war scene near a stepped building (Amiet 1987, fig. 3)

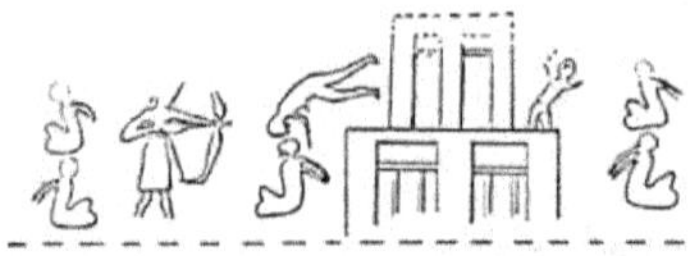

Figure 4. Late Uruk cylinder seal impression showing war scene with stepped ing (Amiet 1987, fig. 2)

2. Cult stand/altar made of superimposed crowns, as reconstructed by Amiran an 1985, fig. 1)

Figure 1. Copper crown with gate-like projections (Amiran 1985, fig. 1)

Two remarkable sets of bronze artifacts were found at Daimabad:

Daimabad bronze chariot. c. 1500 BCE. 22X52X17.5 cm. related to a metalwork guild.

A repertoire of four hieroglyphs (cart, buffalo, rhinoceros and elephant) are read rebus as related to the guild of artisans engaged in metal casting and in

1. stone-work, 2. alloy metal tools, pots and pans and 3. merchants of iron ore.

Buffalo on four-legged platform attached to four solid wheels 31X25 cm.; elephanton four-legged platform with axles 25 cm.; rhinoceros on axles of four solid wheels 25X19 cm. (MK Dhavalikar, 'Daimabad bronzes' in: Harappa civilization, ed. by GL Possehl, New Delhi, 1982, pp. 361-6; SA Sali, Daimabad 1976-1979, New Delhi, 1986).

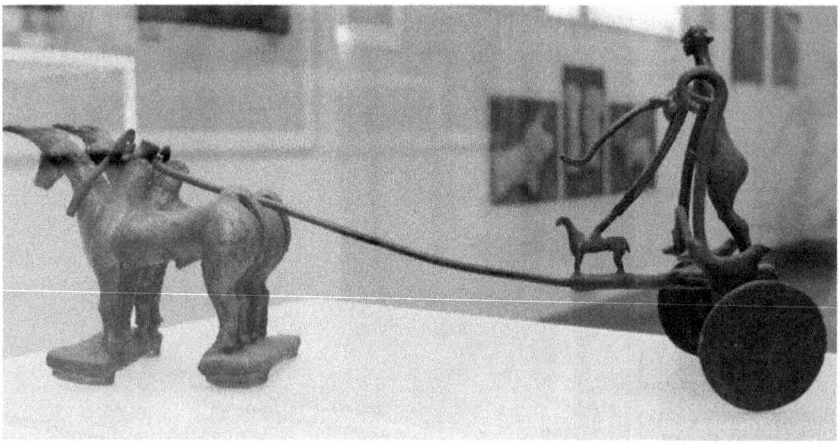

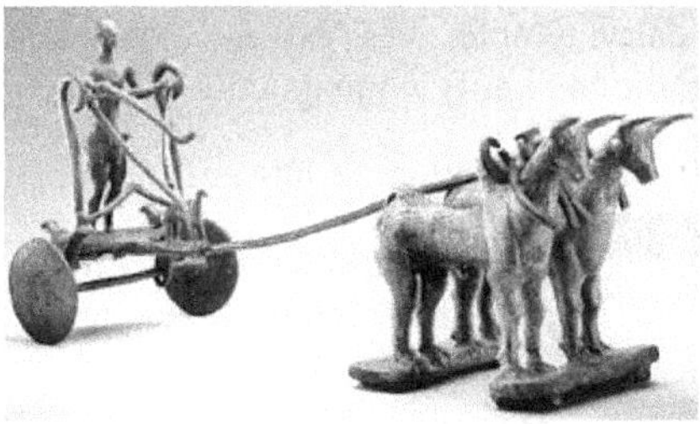

Daimabad bronze chariot. c. 1500 BCE. 22X52X17.5 cm.

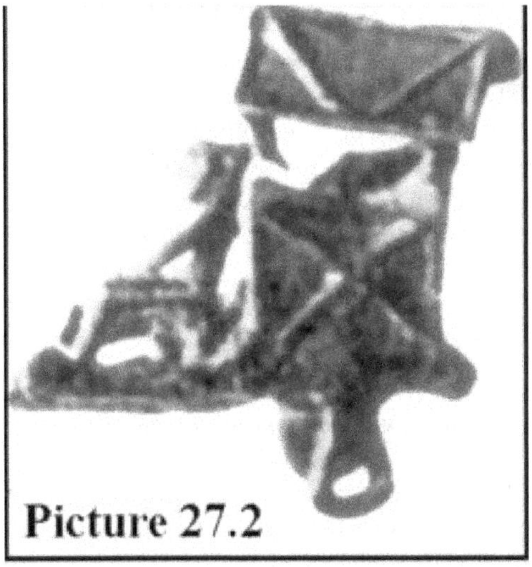

Picture 27.2

Copper chariot was found by M.S. Vats, the Director of the ASI, at Harappa. Dates back to 3000 BCE "(Vats) found several pieces of a small copper chariot, about two inches in height. Hreconstructed it from those several pieces or parts. The wheels are missing, so are the yoke and the axle. The man sitting inside has braided his long hair into a knot. Mr. Vats claims this to be the first miniature model of a chariot in the worlld."[135]

Copper model of a passenger box on a cart, Chanhudaro, ca. 2,000 BCE

Blacksmith Guild engaged in hard alloy casting

ḍangar 'bull' Rebus *ḍhangar* 'blacksmith'.

kāṭhī = body, person; *kāṭhī* the make of the body; the stature of a man (Gujarati) Rebus: *khāṭī* 'wheelwright' (H.)

dula 'pair' (Kashmiri); rebus: *dul* 'cast metal' (Mu.)

Hieroglyph: <*barad*>(D) {NA} ``^bullock used for carrying or dragging carts'. *@. #2631.Kh<*barad*>(D) {NA} ``^bullock used for carrying or dragging carts'.

Rebus: *barada, barda, birada* = a vow (Gujarati) Rebus: *baran, bharat* (5 copper, 4 zinc and 1 tin)(P.B.)

1. stone-work, 2. alloy metal tools, pots and pans and 3. merchants of iron ore.

Pola festival in *Bhāratam*, buffalo in sacred dairy, temple, zebu, *bos indicus* dedicated to the gods in Harappa Script hieroglyphic tradition signifying magnetite

Nausharo: céramique de la période I (c. 2500 BCE) cf. Catherine Jarrige136

After the domestication of the zebu, bos indicus, deployment of the hierolyph of zebu on Harappa Script Corpora is a significant advance in archaeometallurgy documentation.

The writing system depicting a hieroglyph multiplex of a zebu tied to a post with a bird perched on top is based on the rebus rendering of the Prakritam glosses: Hieroglyph: पोळ [*pōḷa*], 'zebu' Rebus: magnetite, citizen. *baṭa* 'quail' Rebus: *bhaTa* 'furnace'. The messaging on Nausharo pots of a magnetite furnace for metalwork continues on seals and tablets including copper plates as metalwork catalogues.

The Prakritam gloss पोळ [*pōḷa*], 'zebu' as hieroglyph is read rebus: *pōḷa*, 'magnetite, ferrous-ferric oxide'; *poliya* 'citizen, gatekeeper of town quarter'.

The early Prakritam form of the word signifying a village, temple, sacred dairy may be *poḷ* m. ' bull dedicated to the gods ': *poḷy* sacred dairy (Toda) since the related gloss pōḷa signifies a bull set at liberty. B. *polā* ' child, son '; M. *poḷ* m. ' bull dedicated to the gods '; Si. pollā ' young of an animal '.4. Pk. *pōāla* -- m. ' child, bull '; A. *powāli* ' young of animal or bird '. (CDIAL 8399)

Hieroglyph: पोळ [*pōḷa*] m A bull dedicated to the gods, marked with a trident and discus, and set at large. பொலியெருது *poli-y-erutu* , n. < பொலி- +. 1. Bull kept for covering; பசுக்களைச் சினையாக்குதற் பொருட்டு வளர்க்கப்படும் காளை. (பிங்.) கொடிய பொலியெருதை யிருமூக்கிலும் கயி றொன்று கோத்து (அறப். சத. 42). 2. The leading ox in treading out grain on a threshing-floor; களத்துப் பிணையல்மாடுகளில் முதற்செல்லுங் கடா. (W.) பொலி முறைநாகு poli-muṟai-nāku, n. < பொலி + முறை +. Heifer fit for covering; பொலியக்கூடிய பக்குவமுள்ள கிடாரி. (S. I. I. iv, 102.)

Rebus 1: *pōḷa* 'magnetite, ferrous-ferric oxide Fe3O4'.

Rebus: cattle festival: पोळा [*pōḷā*] m (पोळ) A festive day for cattle,--the day of new moon of श्रावण or of भाद्रपद. Bullocks are exempted from labor; variously daubed and decorated; and paraded about in worship. "Pola is a bull-worshipping festival celebrated by farmers mainly in the Bharata state of Maharashtra (especially among the Kunbis). On the day of Pola, the farmers decorate and worship their bulls. Pola falls on the day of the Pithori Amavasya (the new moon day) in the month of Shravana (usually in August)."[137] Festival held on the day after Sankranti (= *kANum*) is called *pōlāla paNDaga* (Telugu).

FIGURES OF ANIMALS MADE FOR POLA FESTIVAL.

Toy animals made for the Pola festival especially celebrated by the Dhanoje Kunbis. (Bemrose, Colo. Derby - Russell, Robert Vane (1916). The Tribes and Castes of the Central Provinces of India: volume IV. Descriptive articles on the principal castes and tribes of the Central Provinces. London: Macmillan and Co., limited. p. 40).

Some artifacts of Sarasvati-Sindhu Civilization point to the possibility that the celebration of pola cattle festival may be traced to the cultural practices of 3rd millennium BCE.

Harappa Chariot toy kept at the Brooklyn University Museum[138]

A person is a standard bearer of a banner holding aloft the one-horned young bull which is the signature glyph of Harappa Script writing. The banner is comparable to the banner shown on two Mohenjo-daro tablets.[139]

Ancient Near East bronze-age legacy: Processions depicted on Narmer palette, Harappa Script writing denote artisan guilds

Ancient near East lapidary guilds graduate into bronze-age metalware *kōḍu* horn (Kannada. Tulu. Tamil) खोंड [*khōṇḍa*] m A young bull, a bullcalf. (Marathi) Rebus: कोंड [kōṇḍa] A circular hamlet; a division of a मौजा or village, composed generally of the huts of one caste. खोट [*khōṭa*] Alloyed--a metal (Marathi).

Frieze of a mosaic panel Circa 2500-2400 BCE Temple of Ishtar, Mari (Tell Hariri), Syria Shell and shale André Parrot excavations, 1934-36 AO 19820[140]

maṇḍa = a branch; a twig; a twig with leaves on it (Telugu) rebus: *maṇḍā* = warehouse, workshop (Konkani) . A twig upholds the one-horned young bull held aloft as the standard by a priest leading the procession. Is it the k*oDiya* 'young bull' rebus: *koTiya* 'dhow, seafaring vessel' carrying the cargo from the warehouse?

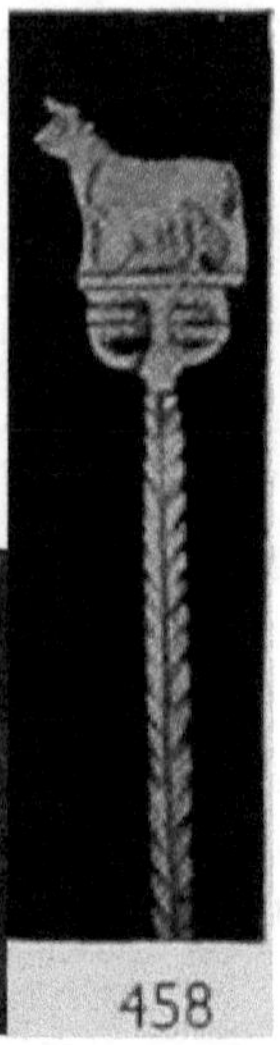

The post holding the young bull banner is signified by a stalk. kāṇḍa, kā̃ṛ 'stalk, arrow ' (CDIAL 3998) PLUS koḍe, koḍiya 'young bull' rebus: koṭiya 'dhow, seafaring vessel'.

Frise d'un panneau de mosaïque Vers 2500 - 2400 avant J.-C. Mari, temple d'Ishtar Coquille, schiste

Fouilles Parrot, 1934 – 1936 AO 19820 Louvre reference

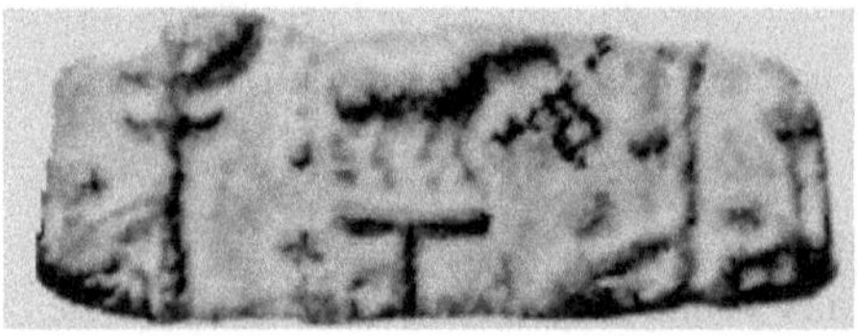

In front of a soldier, a Sumerian standard bearer holds a banner aloft signifying the one-horned young bull which is the signature glyph of Harappa Script writing. Detail of a victory parade, from the Ishtar temple, Mari, Syria. 2400 BCE Schist panel inlaid with mother of pearl plaques. Louvre Museum. It is also a Meluhha standardd shown on two tablets with Harappa Script (together with other dharma samjnA (responsibility signifiers).

It is possible that the hypertexts of the one-horned young bull and the standard device signify: కోడియ (p. 326) kōḍiya Same as koḍe కోడె (p. 326) kōḍe kōḍe. [Tel.] n. A bullcalf. కోడెదూడ. A young bull.

కాడిమరపదగినదూడ. Plumpness, prime. తరుణము. జోడుకోడయలు a pair of bullocks. కోడె adj. Young. కోడెత్రాచు a young snake, one in its prime. "కోడెనాగముం బలుగుల రేడుతన్ని కొని పోవుతెరంగు" రామా. vi. కోడెకాడు kōḍe-kāḍu. n. A young man. పడుచువాడు. A lover విటుడు. కారుకోడె (p. 275) kārukōḍe karu-koḍe. [Tel.] n. A bull in its prime.

Hieroglyph: *kōḍiya* 'young bull' Hieroglyph 2: *koḍiyum* 'ring on neck' (Gujarati) Rebus: *koṭiya* 'dhow seafaring vessel'

sãgaḍ, 'lathe' Rebus: *sãgaḍa* 'double-canoe, catamaran'. सं-ग्रह *saṁgraha* 'a guardian , ruler , manager , arranger' R. BhP.

m1656. Mohenjo-daro pectoral with two streams of water flowing out of pot. Hieroglyphs: overflowing pot, young bull, standard device. koḍe, koḍiya 'young bull' 'rings on neck' with koḍ 'horn' rebus 1: koṭiya 'dhow, seafaring vessel' eka-shingi, 'a dhow, single-masted seafaring vessel' khōṇḍī 'pannier sack' खोंडी (p. 216) [khōṇḍī] f An outspread shovelform sack (as formed temporarily out of a कांबळा, to hold or fend off grain, chaff &c.)

khOnda 'young bull' rebus 2: kOnda 'lapidary, engraver' rebus 3: kundār 'turner' (CDIAL 3295) कोंड [kōṇḍa] A circular hamlet; a division of a मौजा or village, composed generally of the huts of one caste. खोट [khōṭa] Alloyed--a metal

2. sangaDa 'lathe' sanghaṭṭana 'bracelet' rebus 1: .sanghāṭa 'raft' sAngaDa 'catamaran, double-canoe'rebusčaṇṇāḍam (Tu. ജംഗാല, Port. Jangada). Ferryboat, junction of 2 boats, also rafts. 2 jangaḍia 'military guard accompanying treasure into the treasury' ചങ്ങാതം čaṇṇāδam (Tdbh.; സംഘാതം) 1. Convoy, guard; responsible Nāyar guide through foreign territories. rebus 3: जाकड़ ja:kaṛ जांगड़ jāngāḍ'entrustment note' जखडणें tying up (as a beast to a stake) rebus 4: sanghāṭa 'accumulation, collection' rebus 5. sangaDa 'portable furnace, brazier' rebus 6: sanghAta 'adamantine glue' rebus 7: sangara 'fortification' rebus 8: sangara 'proclamation'. सं-ग्रह *saṁgraha* 'a guardian , ruler , manager , arranger' R. BhP.

Gundestrup cauldron hieroglyphs

Meluhha smiths' Gundestrup cauldron[141]

The cauldron was discovered in a bog near Gundestrup, Denmark. Dimensions: 9 kg. silver, 14 in. high, 28 in. dia., seven outer plates, five inner plates. Was the cauldron worked on by five or more Thracian artisans?

No special pleading is needed to explain the glyptic themes of Gundestrup cauldron. The themes were simply metal-smiths' inventory of a mint. The glyphs on Gundestrup cauldron are hieroglyphs, read rebus, as metal-smiths' repertoire in a mint or metal-smith (viśvākarma) artisans' workshops. The language was Meluhha, mleccha – a language attested as *vyavaha_ra bha_s.a* (*lingua franca*) by Manu and as the dialect of island-dwellers attested in Mahabharata. Two dialects are identified by Manu: mleccha *va_cas, a_rya va_cas* (mleccha speech, *a_rya* speech). *A_rya* speech is a refined (aha, metallurgical idiom!) form of *mleccha* and is also called Samskr.tam; *mleccha* is a Pra_kr.tam, Proto-Indic. This explains why Vidura and Yudhishthira could converse in mleccha as attested in the Mahabharata since both mleccha and samskr.tam dialects were in vogue in the linguistic area of ancient times, between c. 3300 to 1900 BCE.

Let us review some glyptic themes common to both Gundestrup cauldron and Sarasvati hieroglyphs (of the epigraphic corpus of over 4000 inscribed objects).:

Why is a horned-person seated in yogic posture shown on the cauldron?

To depict *kammat.a* 'mint, gold furnace' (Te.) is to depict a yogi seated in a yogic posture, that is in penance. The lexeme for penance is: *kamad.ha, kamat.ha, kamad.haka,*

*kamad.haga, kamad.*haya = a type of penance (Prakrtam)

Ta. kampaṭṭam coinage, coin. *Ma. kammaṭṭam, kammiṭṭam* coinage, mint. *Ka. kammaṭa* id.; kammaṭi a coiner (DEDR 1236) *kamat.amu, kammat.amu* = a portable furnace for melting precious metals; *kammat.i_d.u* = a goldsmith, a silversmith (Telugu) *ka~pr.aut., kapr.aut.* jeweller's crucible made of rags and clay (Bi.); *kapr.aut.i_* wrapping in cloth with wet clay for firing chemicals or drugs, mud cement (H.)[cf. modern compounds: kapar.mit.t.i_wrapping in cloth and clay (H.); *kapad.lep* id. (H.)](CDIAL 2874). *kapar-mat.t.i* clay and cowdung smeared on a crucible (N.)(CDIAL 2871). *kompat., kompa_t., kumpa_t.* adj. with *mund.a*, a genuine *munda*, one of those generally called *mundas* simply, in contrast to *mahali mund.a, ho_ mund.a, birur.u mund.*a etc. (Mu.lex.)

Other *glyptic homonyms:*

*kamar.*kom = fig leaf (Santali.lex.) *kamarmar.a_* (Has.), *kamar.kom* (Nag.); the petiole or stalk of a leaf (Mundari.lex.)

kama_t.hiyo = archer; *ka_mat.hum* = a bow; *ka_mad.i_, ka_mad.um*= a chip of bamboo (G.) *ka_mat.hiyo* a bowman; an archer.

Notes on orthography and significance of Seal m0296

The joining of parts in orthography, constructing hypertext is: *sãghāṛɔ* 'lathe'. 'brazier' (Gujarati) सांगड [*sāṅgaḍa*] m f (संघट्ट S) f A body formeḍ of two or more (fruits, animals, men) linked or joined together (Marathi). Rebus: *sangara* 'proclamation'. सं-ग्रह *saṁgraha* 'a guardian , ruler , manager , arranger' R. BhP.

What is proclaimeḍ in the metalwork catalogue? Signifying a gimlet creating perforations on beads? -- *kandi* 'beadś Rebus: *kaṇḍa 'fire-altar'.*

Two heads of bull-calves are joined together with other hieroglyph components: one horn, rings on neck completing the hieroglyph-multiplex as 'orthographed hypertext'.

All are hieroglyph components and each component is read rebus using the lexis of Meluhha (Bharata *sprachbund*). *koḍiyum* 'rings on neck' koḍ `horn' (Kuwi); rebus: koḍ `artisan's workshop' (Gujarati). खोंड [*khōṇḍa*] m A young bull, a bullcalf.(Marathi) Rebus: *kõdā* 'to turn in a lathe'(B.) कोंद *kōnda* 'engraver, lapidary setting or infixing gemś (Marathi). I would like to add two points: 1. Bronze Age discovery of tin-bronzes and ability to produce metal implements necessitated a writing system; and 2. the sources for tin could have extended into the Ancient Far East, the largest mineral tin belt of the world. See evidences at the URL cited in an extensive area from Dong Son to Nahal Mishmar through Shahi Tump, Nausharo and Mohenjo-daro.

Any one or more Bharata languages provide homonymous glosses for the reconstruction of ancient lexis of metalwork, lapidary work expressed in Prakritam, the speech form of the Bharata language union called sprachbund in linguistic studies. Mleccha is mispronunciations in speech. Mleccha speakers are attested in most of the *janapada's* of ancient India.

What is the device in front of the young bull hieroglyph-multiplex? It is also a symbolic hypertext with joined parts: 1. Lathe (gimlet) on top; 2. Portable brazier on bottom; 3. Dotted circles.

The fire-altar message is in front of the workshop (koḍ) of कोंद *kōnda* 'engraver, lapidary (Marathi). This combination ofhieroglyph-multiplexes: 'one-horned young bull with pannier, rings on neck' PLUS 'lathe, brazier, dotted circles' is thus a proclamation, a catalogue of work performeḍ by a metalworker, engraver.

Text of inscription on m0296: *kanac* 'corner' rebus: *kancu* 'bronze' PLUS *eraka* 'nave of wheel' rebus: *erako* 'moltencast, copper' *arA* 'spokes' rebus: *Ara* 'brass' Thus, together, the hypertext reads: bronze, brass metal castings. खाडा [*khāṇḍā*] 'A jag, notch, or indentation (as upon the edge of a tool or weapon)' Rebus: *kāṇḍa* 'implements (Santali). ḍāla 'slant' rebus: ḍhāla 'large ingot'. Thus, together, the hypertext reads: ingots, implements. a*yo, aya* 'fish' rebus: *aya* 'iron' *ayas* 'metal' PLUS *khambhaṛā* 'fish fin' rebus: *kammaṭa* 'mint, coiner, coinage'. *kāṇḍa* 'arrow' rebus: *khāṇḍa* 'implements'. *kole.l* 'temple' rebus: *kole.l* 'smithy, forge' *kol* 'furnace, forge'.

Thus, the text message reads: bronze, brass metal castings, implements, large ingots, mint, coiner, coinage from *kole.l* 'smithy, forge, furnace'.

ḍāla'branch, sprig' rebus: *ḍhāla* 'large ingot'.

Vikalpa: *kamaṛkom* = fig leaf (Santali.lex.) *kamarmaṛā (Has.), kamaṛkom (Nag.)*; the petiole or stalk of a leaf (Mundari.lex.) *kamat.ha* = fig leaf, religiosa (Skt.) *kammaTa* 'mint, coiner, coinage'. *lo* = nine (Santali) [Note the count of nine fig leaves on m0296] *loa* = a species of fig tree, *ficus glomerata,* the fruit of *ficus glomerata* (Santali)
Rebus: *loha lut.i* = iron utensils and implements (Santali) *lauha* = made of copper or iron (Gr.Śr.); metal, iron (Skt.); *lo_haka_ra* = coppersmith, ironsmith (Pali); *lo_ha_ra* = blacksmith (Pt.); *lohal.a* (Or.); *lo_ha* = metal, esp. copper or bronze (Pali); copper (VS.); *loho, lo_* = metal, ore, iron (Si.)

வடம்[1] *vaṭam* , n. < *vaṭa* 'chain of a necklace' rebus: *bhatti* 'furnace, forge' *dula* 'pair' rebus: *dul* 'metal casting'. Thus, metal casting furnace.

Or. *kāṇḍa, kā̃ṛ* 'stalk, arrow '(CDIAL 3023) Pa. *kāṇḍa* -- m.n. joint of stalk, lump. काठ: A rock, stonc. *kāṭha* m. ' rock ' lcx. [Cf. *kānta* -- 2 m. ' stonc ' lex.]Bshk. *kōr* ' large stone ' AO xviii 239(CDIAL 3018). অয়সঠন [*aẏaskaṭhina*] as hard as iron; extremely hard (Bengali) *kāṇḍa* 'implements'. *goṭā* 'stones, pebbles' rebus: *goṭā* 'laterite, ferrite ore' *khoṭā* 'wedge, ingot' *baṭi* 'round vessel' rebus: *bhaṭṭi* 'furnace, forge'

Hypertext: two heads of young bulls: Hieroglyph: *damra* 'young bull calf' Rebus: *tam(b)ra* = copper (Skt.) *damr.i, dambr.i, damt.i* 'one-eighth of a pice (copper)';

damha = a fireplace (Santali) *damad.i, dammad.i* = a ka_su, the fourth part of a *dud.d.u* or *paisa* (Ka.M.); *damad.i_ (H.) damr.i, dambr.i* = one eighth of a pice (Santali) *dammid.i* = pice (Telugu.) *mũh* 'face'rebus: *mũhã̄, mũhe* 'ingot' (Santali) *mũhã̄* the quantity of iron produced at one time in a native smelting furnace of the Kolhes; iron produced by the Kolhes and formed like a four-cornered piece a little pointed at each end (Santali). *koḍiyum* = a wooden circle put round the neck of an animal; *kot.* = neck (Gujarati) [cf. the orthography of rings on the neck of one-horned young bull]. *ko_d.iya, ko_d.e* = young bull; *ko_d.elu* = plump young bull; *ko_d.e* = a. male as in: *ko_d.e du_d.a* = bull calf; young, youthful (Telugu) Rebus: *koTiya* 'dhow, seafaring vessel' Rebus 2: B. *kõdā* 'to turn in a lathe'; Or. *kū̃nda* 'lathe', *kũdibā, kū̃d* 'to turn' (→ Drav. Kur. *kū̃d* 'lathe') (CDIAL 3295)] *kõdār, kū̃dar* 'turner, lapidary'. *ko_t.u* = horns (Ta.) Go. *ko_r* (pl. *ko_hk*)(DEDR 2200). खोंड (p. 216) [*khōṇḍa*] *m* A young bull, a bullcalf. [2] Rebus: *koḍ.* = place where artisans work (Gujarati) *koḍ* = a cow-pen; a cattlepen; a byre (Gujarati) Vikalpa: *khad.a_i_* a heifer (used in the Sorat.h Pra_nt)(Gujarati) Rebus: *kad.iyo* [Hem. Des. *kad.a i o* = Skt. sthapati a mason] a bricklayer; a mason; *kad.iyan.a, kad.iyen.a* a woman of the bricklayer caste; a wife of a bricklayer (G.)

Hieroglyph: *erga* = act of cleaning jungle (Kui)

Hieroglyph (allograph): *era, er-a* = *eraka* =?nave; *erako_lu* = the iron axle of a carriage (Ka.M.); cf. irasu (Ka.)

Hieroglyph (allograph): *er-aka* = upper arm, wing (Te.) [Note the glyptic theme of upper arm lifted up of a standing person.] rebus: erako 'moltencast'.

Rebus: Molten metal: *akka, aka* (Tadbhava of arka) metal; *akka* metal (Te.) *arka* = copper (Skt.) *erka* = ekke (Tbh. of *arka*) *aka* (Tbh. of *arka*) copper (metal); crystal (Ka.) *erako* molten cast (Tu.) *agasa_le, agasa_li, agasa_lava_d.u* = a goldsmith (Telugu)] *eraka, er-aka* any metal infusion (Ka.Tu.); *urukku* (Ta.); *urukka* melting; *urukku* what is melted; fused metal (Ma.); *urukku* to melt (Ta.Ma.); *eragu* to melt (Tu.); *eraka* molten state, fusion; *erakaddu* any cast thing; *eraka hoyi* to pour melted metal into a mould, to cast; erako_lu the iron axle of a carriage (Ka.); *er-e* to pour any liquids; to pour (Ka.); to cast as metal (Ka.) *erande* sp. fruit, red in colour (Ka.); *re_cu, re_cu-kukka* a sort of ounce or lynx said to climb trees and to destroy tigers; a hound or wild dog (Te.)(DEDR 817). *eruvai* copper, blood (Ta.); *ere* a dark-red or dark-brown colour (Ka.)(DEDR 817). *ere* black soil (Ka.)(DEDR 820). *ke~r.e~ ko~r.e~* an aboriginal tribe who work in brass and bell-metal (Santali) *ker.e sen:gel* fire in a pit (Santali) *eru_* = copper (?), bronze *[eru_* = engrave, carve]; *urudu_* = bronze (Akkadian)

Other (allograph) glyptic homonyms (similar sounding lexemes):

eru_, aru = eagle (Akkadian. Assyrian) *eruvai* = a kind of kite whose head is white and whose body is brown; eagle (Ta.); eruva = eagle, kite (Ma.)(DEDR 819).

ero = watering place for cattle (G.)

eru = a serpent (G.)

*aru_* = lion (As god of devastation, Nergal is called *A-ri-a*) (Akkadian)

a_ru = offspring, child (Akkadian)

Why an eagle?

pasra = a smithy, a place where a blacksmith works; to do a blacksmith's work; kamar *pasrat.hene sen akantalea* = our man has gone to the smithy; *pasrao lagao* (or *ehop*) *akata* = he (the blacksmith) has started his work (Santali); pasra (Mundari)(Santali.Bodding) *pasra, pasa_ra* (Sad.; Or. *pasra_,* a blacksmith's implements) = a blacksmith's forge; the place where a brazier (t.ent.era, malar.a) makes his bowls, armlets; *ne pa_l t.apuakana pasarate idiime* = this ploughshare is blunt, take it to the smithy; the set of a blacksmith working in his forge; *pasra o* = of the blacksmith's work in the forge; *pa nasra* = the length of a blacksmith's work in the forge; *pasraili* = rice beer offered for sale; *pasra mer.ed, pasa_ra mer.ed* = syn. of *kot.emer.ed* = forged iron, in contrast to *dul mer.ed*, cast iron (Mundari.lex.) *pan~ja_va_, pa~ja_va_ = brick kiln (P.); pa~_ja_* kiln (B.); paja_vo (G.)(CDIAL 7686). *paya_n* = potter's kiln (B.)(CDIAL 8023). *paja_vo* = a kiln; cf. *paca_vavum*, to digest in the stomach (Gujarati)

prasta_ra = a process in preparing minerals (Skt.); *prastara* = anything strewn, grass to sit on (RV); rock, stone (Skt.); *pa_thar* = stone (Ku.A.b.); *patthal* = hailstone (Bi.)(CDIAL 8857). *pathraut.i_* = clay mixed with fine gravel (Bi.)(CDIAL 8861). *pa_car-ai* = *pa_t.i vi_t.u*, i.e. town house or army house (Pur-ana_.) *pasa_re, pasa_ra* = a grocer's shop (Ka.Te.); *pasarike, pasara* = articles of a shop (Ka.) *pa_śo* = a silver ingot; *pa_śa_ta_n.iyo* = one who draws silver into a wire (G.) *pa_slo* = a nugget of gold or silver having the form of a die (G.)

pajhar = the Bharata tawny , the Bharata black eagle, the Bharata crested hawk; eagle, *buru pajhar*, the hill-eagle, *aquila imperialis*; *hako sat.i pajhar.* = a fish-eating eagle (also called *dak pajhar.); huru pajhar.* = the imperial eagle (Santali) *panji-il* = a certain feather in each wing of a vulture (Mundari)

Other glyptic homonyms:

pasaramu, pasalamu = an animal, a beast, a brute, quadruped (Telugu)

pajhar. = to sprout from a root; *pagra* = a cutting of sugar-cane used for planting (Santali)

panje, panjho = the hand opened out; a claw, a paw; the five on a dice in play; *pasli_* the hollow of the hand (G.) *pan~jali* = with outstretched hands, as token of reverence (Skt. *pra_n~jali)(*Pali) *pan~ja_* = the paw, the palm; the image of a hand worshipped and taken in procession during the Mohurrum festival (Telugu)

*pisera_* = a small deer brown above and black below (H.)(CDIAL 8365). *pr.s.ata* = spotted; spotted deer (VS.); *pr.s.ita* = spotted (n. 'rain' Gobh.); *pr.s.at* = spotted (AV); spotted antelope (R.); *pasata-miga* = spotted deer (Pali); *pasaya* = a kind of deer (Pkt.); *pusia* id. (Pkt.)(CDIAL 8364). *paha_ru (P.); pa_hr.a_* = stag (P.) *pa_ri_ (G.), paha_r, paha_ray* (M.) Spotted antelope *pa_r.ho* hogdeer or cervus porcinus (S.); *pa_hr.a_ (L.); pa_r.ha_* = spotted antelope, hogdeer (P.H.)

pasu_r.u, pasr.u = the condition of a man or boy with uncovered private parts; pasu_r.u n= of the loin cloth, to slip or be pulled aside; of the parts, to be rendered or become visible (Mundari) [Note the orthography of the seated person with horns and bangles on his arms surrounded by a rhinoceros, a buffalo, a jumping tiger and an elephant].

panjaramu = the body; skeleton (Telugu) *panjara* = skeleton, ribs (MBh.)(CDIAL 7685).

panjaramu = a cage for the birds (Te.) *pa_njarum* = a cage (G.)

Why a skull? Why present it reverentially?

*khāra_di_* = turner (G.) *khāra_di_* = a turner; *khāra_da* = a turner's lathe (Gujarati) *kara_d.i_* = a goldsmith's tool; *kara_d.o* = a carpenter's tool used in hewing down large pieces of wood (Used in the Surat district); *karad.o, kara_d.i_* a goldsmith's tool (Gujarati) Seller of earthenware, earthen goblets, smoking pipes etc. = *kara_d.iyo,kara_l.iyo* (G.)

karot.i = human skull (G.Skt.) Dh. Des. *karod.iya_* from Skt.*karot.ika_* the skull.

karaḍāmu = present to a superior (Telugu) *karet.um* = an annual offering and present to a godess or to an evil spirit (Gujarati) *karavr.tti(*Skt.)

samanom = an obsolete name for gold (Santali). [*hom* = gold (Ka.); *soma* = electrum (Old Egyptian) Glyph: *homa* = bison (Pengo)]

saman: = to offer an offering, to place in front of; front, to front or face (Santali) *samna samni* = face to face (Santali)[Note the glyph of short-horned bulls facing each other.]

Other glyptic homonym:

erugu = to bow, to salute or make obeisance (Te.) *er-agu* = obeisance (Ka.), *ir_ai* (Ta.) [Note image of an offering adorant]

eraka, erka = copper (Ka.)

Why a boar or rhinoceros?

kha~_g (H.) kha_g (B.H.Ku.N.); khagga = rhinoceros (Pkt.) rebus: *kan:g* = brazier, fireplace (K.)(IL 1332) Portable brazier; *ka~_guru, ka~_gar* (Ka.) whence, large brazier = *kan:gar (K.) kan:g* portable brazier (B.)

Other homonyms:

Why tiger's mane with on three faces of the seated yogi? And why does the seated person hold a torc on his hand? Why twigs on the head-dress of horns?

cu_l.ai = kiln; *cul.l.ai* = furnace (Ta.). *culli* = a fireplace, a cooking stove, *ole (Ka.) culli* = a fireplace, a hearth, a funeral pile (Te.) *cula_sagad.i_* = a portable hearth or stove of iron, clay etc. (G.) *culi_, culd.i_* = a small fireplace, a hearth; *culo, cu_l, cu_lo* = a fireplace, the hearth; a stove (G.) *culha* = a fireplace; *mit achia culha* = a fireplace with one opening; bar achia culha = a fireplace with two openings (Santali)

*cū́ḍa*1 m. ' protuberance on brick ' ŚBr., *cōḍa* -- 3 m. TS., *cūḍā* -- f. ' topknot on head ' Kālid., *cūlikā* -- f. ' cockscomb '. 2. *cōṇḍa -- 3. *cōṭṭa -- 1. 4. *cunda -- 2. [← Drav. EWA i 396 with lit. -- *cūlā* -- f. ' ceremony of tonsure ' (which leaves the topknot, cf. the full name *cūḍākaraṇa* -- n.) is the same word: derivation from *kṣurita* -- (Tedesco JAOS 74, 133, EWA i 397) is phonet. impossible. -- But it may belong eventually to the group of words for ' hair ' (PMWS 63 ← Mu.), including jūṭa -- and listed under jáṭā --]
1. Pa. *cūḷa* -- m. ' swelling, protuberance, knot, crest ', *cūḷā* -- f. ' topknot, cockscomb '; Pk. *cūḍā* -- , *cūlā* -- , *°liyā*<-> f. ' topknot, peacock's crest, cockscomb, tiger's mane '; Gy. SEeur. *čuṛiya* pl. ' curls ', rus. *čur* ' plait of hair ', gr. *čurn* f., wel. *čōrn* ' lock of hair '; Wg. *čuṛúk* ' long hair '; Kt. *čuŕ* ' point, tip '; Dm. *čṓŕu, čũŕ* ' peak, high mountain ', *čuŕwyéla* ' pheasant ' (< ' *crested '); Kal. rumb. *čũ̄ŕi* ' long hair '; Kho. *čuḷ* ' plait, woman's hair ' (→ Kal. *čul* NTS xv 269); S. *cūṛa* f. ' tenon ', *cūṛi* f. '

hip '; L. *cūṛ* f. ' tenon ', *cū̃ṛī* f. ' hair on temples ', awāṇ. *cūl*, pl. °*lã* f. ' tenon ';
P. *cūl* f. ' pivot of a hinge, tenon ', *cūlā* m. ' hipbone, upper part of ox -- plough ';
Ku. *culo* ' mountain peak ', gng. *cuī* ' topknot '; N. *cur* ' tenon ', *curo* ' central strand of hair ', *culi* ' mountain peak '; A. *suli* ' hair on head ', *sulā* ' knob on a wooden sandal, any knob or protuberance '; B. *cul* ' hair of head, curl ', *culā* ' hair of head, lock, headdress '; Or. *cūṛa* ' hump on bull or other animal ', *cūḷa* ' hair on head, lock, hump on certain animals ', *cūlā* ' dome on top of a building ', *cūḷi* ' conical peak of hill '; Bi. *cūr, cūl* ' pivot on door as hinge, wedge fastening segments of felly, end pieces of bedstead '; Bhoj. *curiyā* ' iron ring fastening blade of hoe ' (or < cū´ḍa -
- 2?); Mth. *cūṛ* ' crest, top, forehead '; H. *cūṛ* m. ' topknot, ceremony of tonsure ', *cūrā* m. ' topknot ', *cūl* f. ' tenon '; M. *čūḍ* f. ' tuft of rice plants ', *čuḷet,* °*ḷat* n. ' peg of a rowlock '; Ko. *cuḍi* f. ' torch of wisps '; Si. *siḷu* ' top, head, lock of hair, peacock's crest '.2. Paš. al. *čūn* ' knot of hair '; L. *cū̃ḍā* m. ' hair worn with plaits in front (by virgins) '; P. *cū̃ḍā* m. ' knot of hair, cockscomb '; H. *cõḍā, cõṛā* m. ' head, crest, topknot, coil of woman's hair '.(CDIAL 4883). *chur.* bangle, bracelet (P.) *chhura_ (P.) tsud.o, tsude.a_ (Kon.); suri, surye (*Kon:kan.i) [Note the glyph of a horned, seated person wearing bracelets from wrist to forearm]

Other glyptic homonyms :

cu_l.i = scales of fish (Ma.)(DEDR 2740).

cuila, coelo = sharp, pointed (Santali) *śu_la, śu_le, sul.a, su_la, su_l.a* = a sharp or pointed weapon: a pike, a spear, a lance; *śu_li* = spearman; *śu_lika* = piercing, killing (Ka.)

cul.li = dry twigs, small stick, branch (Ta.); a dry spray, sprig, brushwood (Ma.); *cul.l.ai* a chip, fuel stick; nul.l.i small sticks for firewood (Ma.); *cul.k* long pliable stick, stalk of plant (Ko.)(DEDR 2706).

Why a tiger?

kol 'working in iron, blacksmith (Ta.); *kollan-* blacksmith (Ta.); *kollan* blacksmith, artificer (Ma.)(DEDR 2133) *kolme* = furnace (Ka.) *kole.l* 'temple, smithy' (Ko.); *kolme* smithy' (Ka.) *kol = pan~calo_kam* (five metals); *kol* metal (Tamil) *pan~caloha* = a metallic alloy containing five metals: copper, brass, tin, lead and iron (Skt.); an alternative list of five metals: gold, silver, copper, tin (lead), and iron (*dha_tu*; Na_na_rtharatna_kara. 82; Man:gara_ja's Nighan.t.u. 498)(Ka.) *kol, kolhe,* 'the koles, an aboriginal tribe if iron smelters speaking a language akin to that of Santals(Santali) *kol = kollan-, kamma_l.an-* (blacksmith or smith in general)(Tamil) *kollar* = those who guard the treasure (Tamil) cf. golla (Telugu) *khol, kholi_* = a metal covering; a loose covering of metal or cloth (G.) *kolime, kolume, kulāme, kulime, kulume,* kulme fire-pit, furnace (Ka.); *kolimi* furnace (Te.); pit (Te.); *kolame* a very deep pit (Tu.); *kulume kāṇḍa_ya* a tax on blacksmiths (Ka.); *kol, kolla* a furnace (Ta.) *kole.l* smithy, temple in Kota village (Ko.); *kwala.l* Kota smithy (To.); *konimi* blacksmith; *kola* id. (Ka.); *kolle* blacksmith (Koḍ.); *kollusa_na_* to mend implements; *kolsta_na, kulsa_na_* to forge; *ko_lsta_na_* to repair (of plough-shares); *kolmi* smithy (Go.); *kolhali* to forge (Go.)(DEDR 2133).] *kolimi-titti* = bellows used for a furnace (Telugu) *kollu-* to neutralize metallic properties by oxidation (Tamil) *kol* brass or iron bar nailed across a door or gate; *kollu-t-tat.i-y-a_n.i* large nail for studding doors or gates to add to their strength (Tamil) *kollan–kamma_lai < + karmaśa_la_, kollan–pat.t.arai, kollan-ulai-k-ku_t.am* blacksmith's workshop, smithy (Tamil) cf. *ulai* smith's forge or furnace (Na_lat.i, 298); *ulai-k-kal.am* smith's forge; *ulai-k-kur.at.u* smith's tongs; ulai-t-turutti smith's bellows; *ulai-y-a_n.i-k-ko_l* smith's poker, beak-iron (Tamil) [*kollulaive_r-kan.alla_r*: nait.ata. na_t.t.up.); *mitiyulaikkollan- mur-iot.ir.r.an-n-a*: perumpa_)(Tamil) Temple; smithy: *kol-l-ulai* blacksmith's forge (*kollulaik ku_t.attin-a_l*: Kumara. Pira. Ni_tiner-i. 14)(Tamil) cf. *kolhua_r* sugarcane milk and boiling house (Bi.); *kolha_r* oil factory (P.)(CDIAL 3537). *kulhu* 'a hindu caste, mostly oilmen' (Santali) *kolsa_r* = sugarcane mill and boiling house (Bi.)(CDIAL 3538).

kola, kolum = a jackal (G.) *kolhuyo* (Dh.Des.); *kulho, kolhuo* (Hem.Des.) *ko_lupuli* = a big, huge tiger, royal or Bengal tiger; *ko_lu* = big, great, huge (Telugu)

Other Glyptic homonyms:

ko_lemu = the backbone (Te.)

ko_l 'woman' (Nahali); dual. *ko_lhilt.el (*Sudhibhushan Bhattacharya, Field-notes on Nahali, Ind. Ling. 17, 1957, p. 247); *kola* = bride, son's (younger brother's) wife (Kui) *ko_l* = woman, wife (Nahali); *ko_l-na kupra* = the wife's cloth (Nahali); *ko_lama* wife (Ko.); *kolay* wife (K.); *kulis* wife (Ta.Burgandi dialect); *khuliśi_* id. (Yerukala); khulsa_ *husband* (Malar); *kola* = bride, son's (younger brother's) wife (Kui)

*xola_* = tail (Kur.); *qoli* id. (Malt.)(DEDr 2135). [Note the rump of ox with tail depicted ligatured to horned, standing persons].

ko_le = a stub or stump of corn (Te.)(DEDR 2242). *kol.ake, kol.ke,* the third crop of rice (Ka.); *kolake, kol.ake* (Tu.)(DEDR 2154) *xo_l* = rice-sheaf (Kur.) *ko_li* = stubble of *jo_l.a* (Ka.); *ko_r.a* = sprout (Kui.) *kolma* = a paddy plant (Santali)

ko_l = stick (Ta.) *ulai-y-a_n.i-k-ko_l* smith's poker, beak-iron (Tamil) [Staff ligatured to a persin standing with legs spread out.]

kulāi = hare (Santali)

ko_la decoration (Ka.); *ko_lam* = form (Ta.Ma.)(DEDR 2240).

kola = killing, e.g. *a_d.ukola* = woman-slaying (Te.)

ko_lu = an orifice, hole (Te.) *kolo* = a hole in a wall (G.); *koravum* = to bore a hole (G.) *khol* = hollow (Santali)

kola foetus (OMarw.)(CDIAL 3607). *kola* = foetus; *kor.o* bosom, breast (S.); kurouru breast (Dm.); *kor.i_* breast of a quadruped (L.); *koli_* chest of an anim l (L.)(CDIAL 3607).a

Tub: *go_lemu* (Te.) *gollemu, gol.l.emu* (Te.)

ko_l. = a planet, navagraha; *ra_ku* (planet)[Skt. *ra_hu*] (Tamil)

Why a serpent?

na_ga = serpent (Skt.)

Rebus: *na_ga* = lead (metal) (Skt.)

Why a zebu or brahmani bull? Why the glyptic theme of a herd of animals? Why a lid sign graph? Why a splinter sign graph?

Rebus: *aduru* = *gan.iyinda tegadu karagade iruva aduru* = ore taken from the mine and not subjected to melting in a furnace (Ka. *Siddha_nti Subrahman.ya' Śastri's new interpretation of the Amarakośa*, Bangalore, Vicaradarpana Press, 1872, p. 330); *adar* = fine sand (Ta.); *ayir* – iron dust, any ore (Ma.) *aduru* = native metal (Ka.); *ajirda karba* = very hard iron (Tu.); *ayil* = iron (Ta.); *ayir, ayiram* any ore (Ma.)(DEDR 192). *darap* = metal, excluding iron, money, wealth (Santali) darja = property, house and stock; *khub darja menaktaea* = he is very well-to-do; *darja* = degree, rank, station (Santali) *daran:, daran: daran:* = white hot, blazing hot, glowing (Santali) *dr.śad* = a stone (Skt.G.) *ayas* metal, iron (RV.); ayo_ (Pali); *aya* iron (Pali.Pkt.); *ya* id. (Si.)(CDIAL 590). *yahun.u* iron filings (Si.)(CDIAL 589). *yakad.a* iron (Si.); *ayaska_n.d.a* a quantity of iron, excellent iron (Pa_n..gan..) *atar* = fine sand (Ta.); *adaru* = a sparkle (Te.); *at.a_r* = sand (in Kathiawa_d.)(G.); *adar* = the waste of pounded rice, broken grains (Kur.); *adru* = broken grain (Malt.)(DEDR 134).

adar, adar d.an:gra a brahmini bull, a bull kept for breeding purposes and not put to work (Santali) पोळ *pōḷa*, 'zebu' rebus: पोळ *pōḷa*, 'magnetite, ferrite ore'

d.aren-mund.i lid of pot; *d.aren, ad.aren* to cover up pot with lid (Bond.a); d.arai to cover (Bond.a.Hindi)

at.ar a splinter; *at.aruka* to burst, crack, slit off, fly open; *at.arcca* splitting, a crack; *at.arttuka* to split, tear off, open (an oyster)(Ma.);*ad.aruni* to crack (Tu.)(DEDR 66). *ad.aru* twig; *ad.iri* small and thin branch of a tree; *ad.ari* small branches (Ka.); *ad.aru* twig (Tu.)(DEDR 67).

ad.ar an attack (Ka.); *at.ar* to beat, strike, mould by beating (Ta.)(DEDR 77).

ad.ar = herd of cows (Kond.a); ad.er id. (Pe.)(DEDR 84). *da_yaro* (Persian da_yareh a circle fr. *da_yar* fr. der revolving, turning, round) an assemblage; a company; a group (G.)

Why a lizard?

kuduru = lizard (Te.); Rebus: *kuduru* = a goldsmith's portable furnace (Telugu) *kudru* top of fireplace (Kuwi)(DEDR 1709).

Why over-sized persons? Why a bull? Why a trough? Why an alligator?

*d.hagga_* small weak ox (L.); *d.han:garu, d.hin:garu* lean emaciated beast (S.)(CDIAL 5524). *d.han:gar* = bull, ox; *d.an:gra* = an ox, a bullock; *mun.d.ra d.an:gra* = a polled ox; a tiger; *ran:gia d.an:gra* = a red ox; fire; a tiger; *d.an:gri* = cattle in general, a cow (Santali)

*d.a_n:gra_* = a wooden trough just enough to feed one animal. cf.*id.ankar..i* = a measure of capacity, 20 *id.an:kar...i* make *a par-r-a* (Ma.lex.) *d.ha_kar* = a kind of large basket (N.)(CDIAL 5574). *da_gara* = a large flat basket woven of thin bamboo strips in which articles are fried or exposed to the sun; *d.a_gara, d.a_gara_* = a large winnowing basket; a large shallow, square tray of bamboo splints (Te.)

it.an·kar = a type of crocodile (*kur-in~ci*); crocodile (Tamil)

d.han:ga = tall, long shanked; maran: *d.han:gi aimai kanae* = she is a big tall woman (Santali.lex.)

Rebus: *d.han:gar* 'blacksmith' (WPah.): *d.a_n:ro* = a term of contempt for a blacksmith (N.)(CDIAL 5524) *t.ha_kur* = blacksmith (Mth.); *t.ha_kar* = landholder (P.); *t.hakkura* – Rajput, chief man of a village (Pkt.); *t.hakuri* = a clan of Chetris (N.); *t.ha_kura* – term of address to a Brahman, god, idol (Or.)(CDIAL 5488). *dha~_gar., dha_~gar* = a non-Aryan tribe in the Vindhyas, digger of wells and tanks (H.); *dha_n:gar* = young servant, herdsman, name of a Santal tribe (Or.); *dhan:gar* = herdsman (H.)(CDIAL 5524).

Why a person with long legs?

kan:kar., kan:kur. = very tall and thin, large hands and feet; *kan:kar dare* = a high tree with few branches (Santali)

Rebus: *kanka, kanaka* = gold (Skt.); *kan* = copper (Tamil)

Many scholars have noted the common glyptic themes of the cauldron and a seal from Mohenjodaro depicting a horned-person seated in yogic posture, surrounded by four animals and spread-out legs of a standing person.

Art historian Timothy Taylor (1992) notes about the glyptics of the Gundestrup cauldron: "A shared pictorial and technical tradition stretched from India to Thrace, where the cauldron was made, and thence to Denmark. Yogic rituals, for example, can be inferred from the poses of an antler-bearing man on the cauldron and of an ox-headed figure on a seal impress from the Bharata city of Mohenjo-Daro…Three other Bharata links: ritual baths of goddesses with elephants (the Bharata goddess is Lakshmi); wheel gods (the Bharata is Vishnu); the goddesses with braided hair and paired birds (the Bharata is Hariti)." He further speculates that members of an Bharata itinerant artisan class, not unlike the later Gypsies in Europe who also originate in India, must have been the creators of the cauldron.[142] Hindu Deities in Iron Age Denmark: The Religious Iconography and Ritual Context of the Gundestrup Cauldron This paper considers aspects of the second century BCE iconography of the Gundestrup cauldron in relation to the idea of death in various frameworks of thought and belief: Shamanistic, Mithraic, Pythagorean, Hindu, Celtic, Orphic, and Christian. Following from this, some general theoretical considerations about the relationship of iconographic, ritual, textual, and oral religious modes are presented. In the light of this, a precise context for the cauldron's production and use is suggested.[143]

Dong Son bronze drum hieroglyphs

Co Loa bronze drum surface. "The drum only has two warriors with spears, in contrast to that of the Ngọc Lũ drum. Another difference is that the ensemble of percussionists consists of three drummers, with one drum lying under the eaves of the house. Meanwhile, an extra person is depicted in the rice threshing process. The person has long hair and is winnowing grain into a bowl. The percussion ensemble is also depicted differently in that the drummers are not all drumming in synchronisation. Two of the drummers are depicted making contact with the drum, while the other two drummers have their batons in the raised position." (Higham, opcit., p.126)

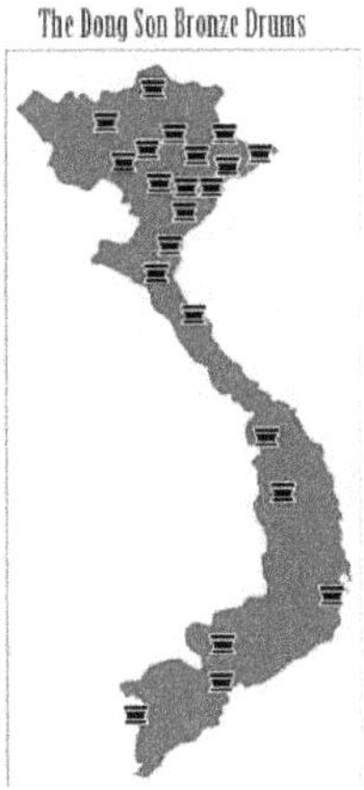

Image on Ngoc Lu bronze

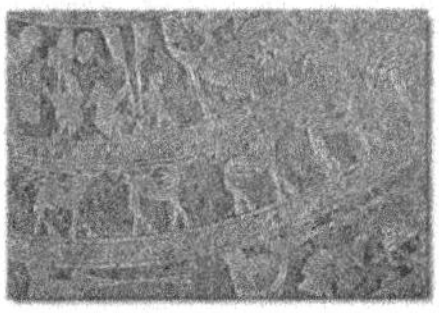

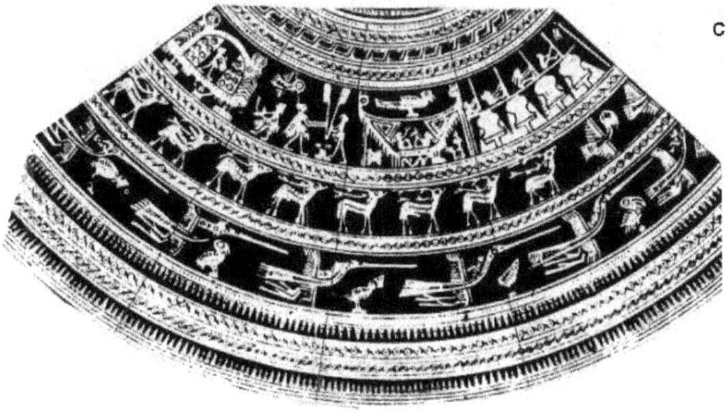

c

D

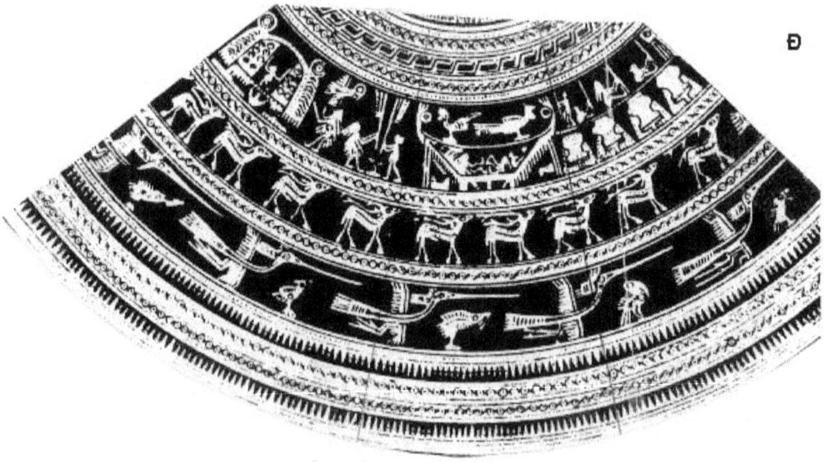

Đ

B

While the lost wax method of casting metals is well-documented in ancient texts of India, such documentation does NOT exist for the artifacts found in Ancient Near East and Ancient Far East, Vietnam, in particular where Dong Son Bronze Drum tradition is evidenced with the finds of over 200 ancient drums all over the Far East.

Image on the Ngoc Lu bronze drum's surface,Vietnam

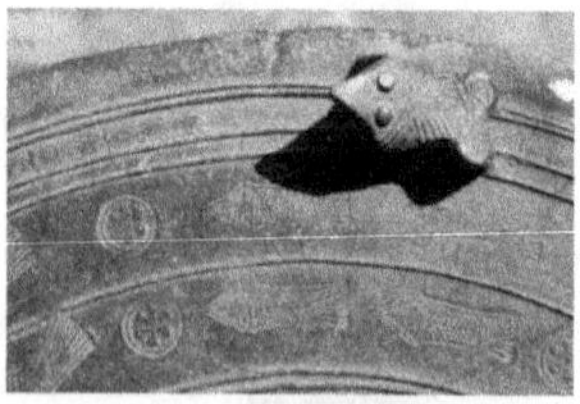

Cire Perdue technique to signify hieroglyphs on Karen bronze drum, Myanmar (Cire Perdue is a metallurgical process dated to ca. 5th millennium BCE, to cast duplicate bronze sculpture from an original made of wax. The wax model is coated with clay to form a mold. Molten bronze is poured through holes left in the mold. Wax melts and drains out. After cooling, molten bronze takes the shape of the wax sculpture).

Close-up view of design of a typical Đông Sơn drum

The depiction of frogs on the Dong Son drums is significant. I suggest that it is a hieroglyph signifying metal ingot: *Kur. mūxā frog. Malt. múqe* id. / Cf.

Skt. *mūkaka*- id. (DEDR 5023) Rebus: *mū̃h* 'ingot'. *muha.* The quantity of iron produced at one time in a native smelting furnace. (Santali)

It is possible that metalwork consignments accompanied the consignments of bronze drums as they were carried to different locations in the Far East.

miṇḍāl 'markhor' (Tōrwālī) *meḍho* a ram, a sheep (Gujarati)(CDIAL 10120) Rebus: *mẽṛhẽt, meḍ* 'iron' (Mu.Ho.)

Hieroglyph: *arka* 'sun' Rebus: *arka, eraka* 'copper, gold, moltencast'

kaṅká m. ' heron ' VS. [← Drav. T. Burrow TPS 1945, 87; onomat. Mayrhofer EWA i 137. Drav. influence certain in o of M. and Si.: Tam. Kan. Mal. *kokku* ' crane ', Tu. *koṛṅgu, Tel. koṅga, Kuvi koṅgi, Kui kohko] Pa. kaṅka* -- m. ' heron ', *Pk. kaṁka -- m., S. kaṅgu* m. ' crane, heron ' (→ Bal. *kang*); B. *kā̃k* ' heron ', *Or. kāṅka; G. kā̃*kṛũ n. ' a partic. ravenous bird '; -- with o from Drav.: M. *kõkā* m. ' heron '; *Si. kokā, pl. kokku* ' various kinds of crane or heron ', *kekī* ' female crane ', *kēki* ' a species of crane, the paddy bird ' (ē?).(CDIAL 2595) Ta. kokku common crane, Grus cinerea; stork, paddy bird; *kuruku* heron, stork, crane, bird, gallinaceous fowl, aṉṟil bird. Ma. *kokku, kokkan, kocca, kuriyan* paddy bird, heron; *kuru* heron. To. k*ošk* heron. Ka. *kokku, kokkare*

crane; *kukku* heron, crane. Tu. *koṛṅgu* crane, stork. Te. *koṅga, kokkera, kokkarāyi* crane; *pegguru, begguru* (< *peru-kuru*) adjutant crane. Kol. (Kin.) *koŋga*

crane. *Pa.kokkal (pl. kokkacil) id. Ga. (S) kokkāle (pl. kokkāsil)* heron; (S.2) *koŋalin (pl. koŋasil),* (S.3) *kokalin* crane. Go. (L.) *koruku* id. (Voc. 921); (Mu.) *kokoḍal* heron, duck (Voc. 870); (Ma. Ko.) *koŋga* crane (Voc. 874). Kui *kohko* paddy bird. Kuwi (S.) *kongi,(T.) kokoṛa* crane.

Br. *xāxūr* demoiselle crane. / Cf. Skt. *kaṅka*- heron; Turner, CDIAL, no. 2595.(DEDR 2125) కొంగ (p. 0313) [*koṅga] konga.* [Tel.] n. A bird of the heron or stork kind. బకము (Telugu)

Hieroglyph: *maraka* 'peacock' (Santali. Mu.) Rebus: मारक *loha* 'a kind of calcining metal' (Samskritam)

Writing in the National Geographic Magazine (March 1971). Dr. Wilhelm G Solheim II, professor of Anthropology of the University of Hawaii gave an account of how excavations at Nok Nok Tha in northern Thailand resulted in the discovery of bronze tools of advanced design including bronze axes cast in double sand-stone moulds pre-dating Dong-son culture by at least 2,000 years, suggesting that South East Asian bronze industry began around 3,000 BC or even earlier. This would put it some 500 years earlier than the first known bronze casting in India and some 1,000 years before any known in China.144

The unique arhaeometallurgical method of casting exquisite arsenical and tin-bronze artifacts holds the key to evaluate links between the Ancient Far East and Ancient Near East during the early Bronze Age.

Evaluating bronze age metalwork exemplified by 'Ram in the Thicket' and 'Maikop gold bull' and placing the art works in the context of a universal art idiom -- across time and space --, Editors, Neil Collins and Áine Ni Muireadhaigh present a veritable

Encyclopaedia of Visual Arts.[145] In the context of this universal art idiom, it is apposite to trace the roots of Dian Bronze Art, starting with an evaluation presented by TzeHuey Chiou-Peng. In an archaeometallurgical framework, Dian culture is dated to ca. 4th century BCE and located not far from the famẹd Dong Son culture famẹd for the bronze drums of Ancient Vietnam which were cast using thecire perdue (lost-wax) method.

I suggest that the art idiom of Dian culture (Yunnan) and Dong Son culture (Vietnam) are a Meluhha metalwork hieroglyph continuum. The hieroglyphs used such as humped bull, tiger, multi-pointed star (sun), rhinoceros are read rebus, related to Meluhha metalwork, with particular reference to tin-bronzes which were produced in the world's larges Tin Belt of the Far East (Vietnam-Thai-Malay Peninsula). This indicates that Meluhha speakers from the Bharata *sprachbund* had established a Trans-Asiatic network to spread 1) cire perdue (lost-wax) casting methods and 2) tin-bronzes as the contributory material resources which made the Bronze Age revolution possible in an extended Eurasian zone extending from Hanoi to Haifa. These are evidenced by the metaphors of Nahal Mishmar cire perdue metal castings (using arsenical copper) and by the presence of Harappa Script writing on pure tin ingots discovered in a shipwreck at Haifa.[146]

Munda people are perhaps descendants of Austroasiatic migrants from southeast Asia. The relationship between Munda languages which may explain many Austro-asiatic language features and lexis, is an area of ongoing research.[147]

The largest tin belt of the globe in Ancient Far East is posited as the source of Bronze Age tin in Eurasia, which indicates a Maritime Tin Route from Hanoi to Haifa, a hypothesis to be tested by further researches to explain the relationship among Austroasiatic languages and Munda languages of Bharatam Janam.

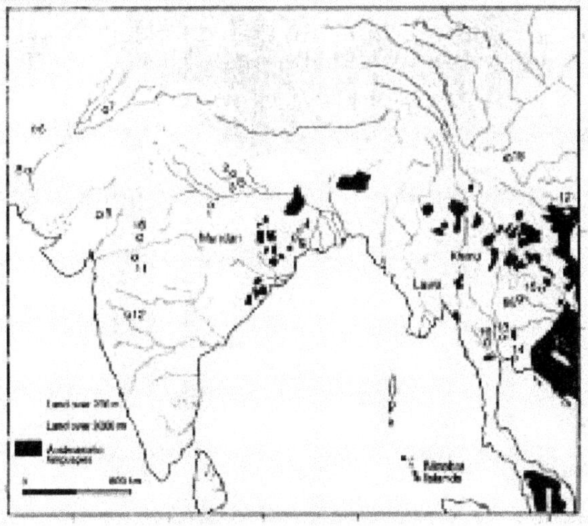

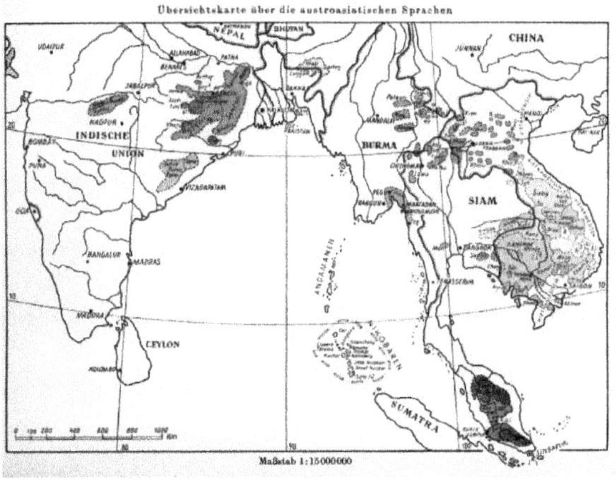

Bronze Age sites of eastern Bha_rata and neighbouring areas: 1. Koldihwa; 2. Khairdih; 3. Chirand; 4. Mahisadal; 5. Pandu Rajar Dhibi; 6. Mehrgarh; 7. Harappa; 8. Mohenjo-daro; 9. Ahar; 10. Kayatha; 11. Navdatoli; 12. Inamgaon; 13. Non Pa Wai; 14. Nong Nor; 15. Ban Na Di and Ban Chiang; 16. Non Nok Tha; 17. Thanh Den; 18. Shizhaishan; 19. Ban Don Ta Phet[148] Pinnow-map of Austro-Asiatic language speakers[149]

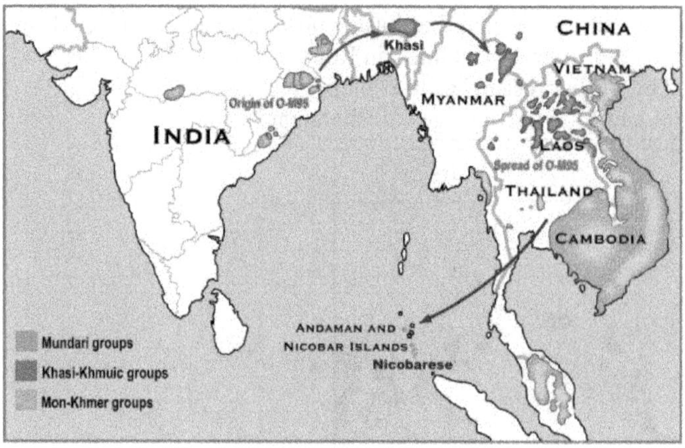

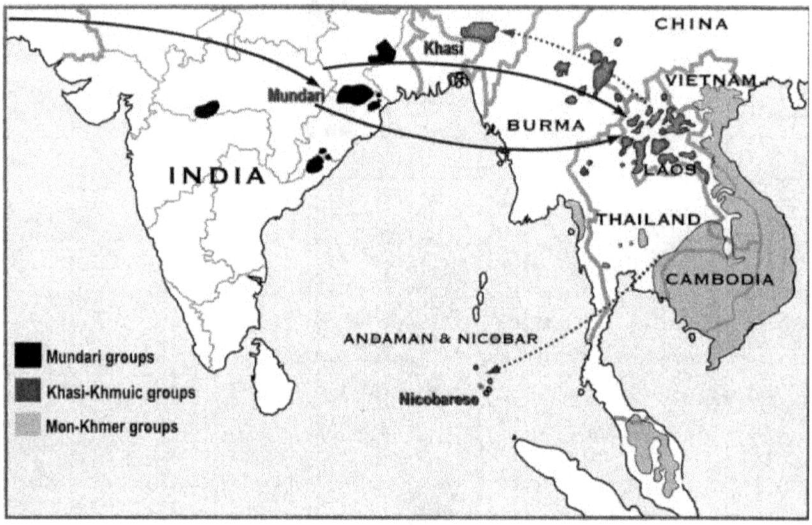

Fig. 4. Map showing present-day distribution of Austro-Asiatic groups (as depicted in van Driem, 2001) and schematic representation of routes of migration of different Austro-Asiatic linguistic subgroups of India. Dotted arrows indicate back-migration.

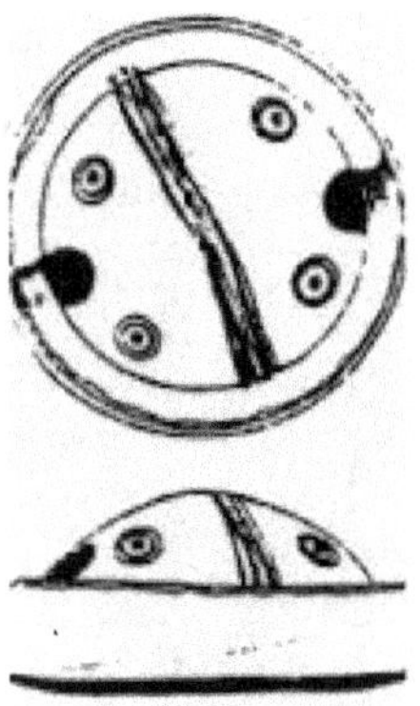

Dilmun seal from Barbar; six heads of antelope radiating from a circle; similar to animal protomes in Failaka, Anatolia and Indus. Obverse of the seal shows four dotted circles.150 A tree is shown on this Dilmun seal.

Glyph: 'tree': *kuṭi* 'tree'. Rebus*:* *kuṭhi* 'smelter furnace' (Santali). *baṭa* 'six' rebus: *bhaṭa* 'furnace' PLUS *mẽḍha* 'antelope'*miṇḍāl* 'markhor' (Tōrwālī) *meḍho* a ram, a sheep (Gujarati)(CDIAL 10120) Rebus 1: *mẽṛhẽt, meḍ* 'iron' (Santali.Munda.Ho.) Rebus 2: *meḍh* 'helper of merchant' (Pkt.) *meṛha, meḍhi* 'merchant's clerk (Des'i).

Izzat Allah Nigahban, 1991, Excavations at Haft Tepe, Iran, The University Museum, UPenn, p. 97. furnace' Fig.96a.

There is a possibility that this seal impression from Haft Tepe had some connections with Dharma saṁjñā or Bharatiya hieroglyphs. This requires further investigation. "From Haft Tepe (Middle Elamite period, ca. 13th century) in Ḵūzestān an unusual pyrotechnological installation was associated with a craft workroom containing such materials as mosaics of colored stones frameḍ in bronze, a dismembered elephant skeleton used in manufacture of bone tools, and several hundred bronze arrowpoints and small tools. "Situated in a courtyard directly in front of this workroom is a most unusual kiln. This kiln is very large, about 8 m long and 2 and one half m wide, and contains two long compartments with chimneys at each end, separated by a fuel chamber in the middle. Although the roof of the kiln had collapsed, it is evident from the slight inturning of the walls which remain in situ that it was barrel vaulted like the roofs of the tombs. Each of the two long heating chambers is divided into eight sections by partition walls. The southern heating chamber contained metallic slag, and was apparently used for making bronze objects. The northern heating chamber contained pieces of broken pottery and other material, and thus was apparently used for baking clay objects including tablets . . ."[151]

Many of the bronze-age manufactured or industrial goods were surplus to the needs of the producing community and had to be traded, together with a record of types of goods and types of processes such as native metal or minerals, smelting of minerals, alloying of metals using two or more minerals, casting ingots, forging and turning metal into shapes such as plates or vessels, using anvils, cire perdue technique for creating bronze statues – in addition to the production of artifacts such as bangles and ornaments made of śankha or shell (turbinella pyrum), semi-precious stones, gold or silver beads. Thus writing was invented to maintain production-cum-trade accounts, to cope with the economic imperative of bronze age technological advances to take the artisans of guilds into the stage of an industrial production-cum-trading community.

Tablets and seals inscribed with hieroglyphs, together with the process of creating seal impressions took inventory lists to the next stage of trading property items using bills of lading of trade loads of industrial goods. Such bills of lading describing trade loads were created using tablets and seals with the invention of writing based on phonetics and semantics of language – the hallmark of Dharma saṁjñā or Bharatiya hieroglyphs.

Tell Asmar Boar or rhinoceros in procession. Cylinder seal impression: Rhinoceros, elephant, lizard (gharial?).Tell Asmar (Eshnunna), Iraq. IM 14674; glazed steatite. Frankfort, 1955, No. 642; Collon, 1987, Fig. 610. 152

kāru a wild crocodile or alligator (Te.) కారు mosale 'wild crocodile or alligator. S. *gharyālu* m. ' long — snouted porpoise '; N. *ghaṛiyāl* ' crocodile' (Telugu)'; A. B. *ghā̃ṛiyāl* ' alligator ', *Or. ghaṛiāḷa, H. ghaṛyāl, ghariār* m. (CDIAL 4422) கரவு² *karavu*, n. < கரா. Cf. *grāha*. Alligator; முதலை. கரவார்தடம் (திவ். திருவாய். 8, 9, 9). 1. A species of alligator; முதலை. கராவதன் காலினைக்கதுவ (திவ். பெரியதி. 2, 3, 9). 2. Male alligator; ஆண்முதலை. (பிங்.) கராம் *karām n. prob. grāha. 1.* A species of alligator ; முதலைவகை. முதலையு மிடங்கருங் கராமும் (குறிஞ்சிப். 257). 2. Male alligator; ஆண் முதலை. (திவா.)

kāru a wild crocodile or alligator (Te.) Rebus: *khār* a blacksmith, an iron worker (cf. *bandūka-khār*) (Kashmiri)

karbha, 'trunk of elephant' *ibha* 'elephant' Rebus: *karba* 'iron' *ib* 'iron', *ibbo* (merchant of ib 'iron') *kāṇḍā* 'rhinoceroś Rebus: *khāṇḍa* 'tools, pots and pans, and metal-ware'. *kāṇḍa* 'furnace, fire-altar, consecrated fire'.

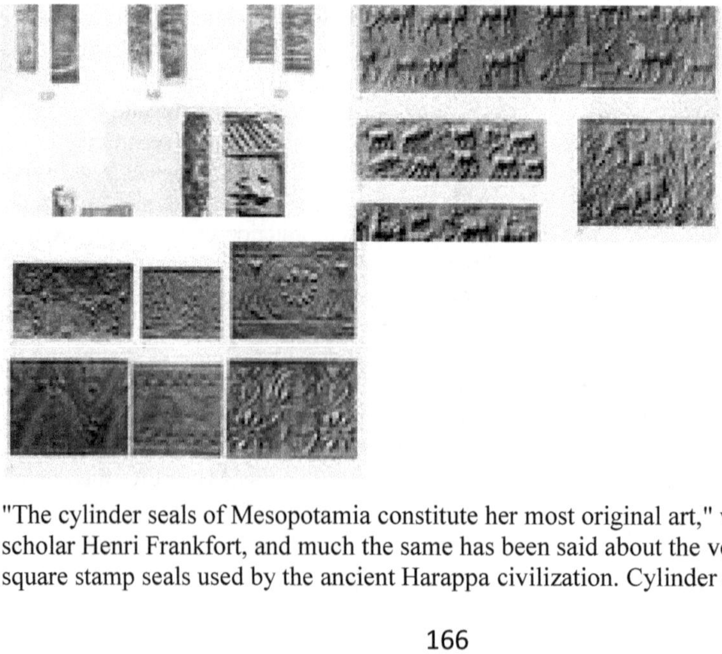

"The cylinder seals of Mesopotamia constitute her most original art," wrote the scholar Henri Frankfort, and much the same has been said about the very different square stamp seals used by the ancient Harappa civilization. Cylinder seals are "small, barrel-shaped stone object[s] with a hole down the center, rolled on clay when soft to indicate ownership or to authenticate a document . . . used chiefly in Mesopotamia from the late 4th to the 1st millennium BCE." Many of the handful of cylinder seals found at ancient Indus sites or Mesopotamian ones with Harappa themes are clustered.

1. Impression of a Harappa cylinder seal from Kalibangan (K-65). "Two warriors, distinguished by the hair worn in a divided bun at the back of the head, are spearing each other, while they are both being held by the hand by a goddess wearing a head-dress with a long pendant (comparable to the ones decorated with cowry shells and turquoise that are worn by the women of Ladakh and Chitral), bangles on the arms, and a skirt. Next to the combat scene (where space appears to have prevented the depiction of those details), her body merges with that of the tiger (later the Hindu goddess of war) and her head-dress is elaborated with animal horns and a tree branch," writes Asko Parpola.[153]

2. "The most reliable evidence of the date of the upper levels of Mohenjo-daro still continues to be Dr. Frankfort's seal. This seal is cylindrical in form and of a totally different shape from the majority of the seals found in the Indus valley; but as three cylindrical specimens have been found at Mohenjo-daro, all of them, it should be noted, in the upper levels of that city, it is probably that they also were sometimes used by the inhabitants. The Tell Asmar seal is, however, certainly of Bharata workmanship. Not only are the animals upon it Bharata, the elephant, rhinoceros, and gharial, or fish-eating crocodile, none of which ever appears on Sumerian or Akkadian seals, but the style of the carving is undoubtedly Bharata."[154]

3. Imported Bharata seal from Tell Asmar. "The Indus civilization used the signet, but knew the cylinder seal. Whether the five tall ivory cylinders [4] tentatively explained as seals in Sir John Marshall's work were used for that purpose remains uncertain. They have nothing in common with the seal cylinders of the Near East. In the upper layers of Mohenjo Daro, however, three cylinder seals were found [2,3]. The published specimen shows two animals with birds upon their backs, a snake and a small conventional tree. It is an inferior piece of work which displays none of the characteristics of the finely engraved stamp-seals which are so distinctive a feature of early Bharata remains. Another cylinder of glazed steatite was discovered at Tell Asmar in Iraq, but here the peculiarities of design, as well as the subject, show such close resemblances to seals from the Indus valley that its Bharata origin is certain. The elephant, rhinoceros and crocodile (gharial), foreign to Babylonia, were obviously carved by an artist to whom they were familiar, as appears from the faithful rendering of the skin of the rhinoceros (closely resembling the plate-armour) and the sloping back and bulbous forehead of the elephant. Certain other peculiarities of style connect the seal as definitely with the Indus civilisation as if it actually bore the signs of the Harappa Script. Such is the convention by which the feet of the elephant are rendered and the network of lines, in other Bharata seals mostly confined to the ears, but extending here over the whole of his head and trunk. The setting of the ears of the rhinoceros on two little stems is also a feature connecting this cylinder with the Indus valley seals."[155]

4. John Marshall wrote: "Seals of this group [cylinder seals, although Mackay above is not sure they are true cylinder seals]], if indeed they are seals, are very rarely found at Mohenjo-daro, only five specimen being obtained in all. They are all made of ivory and differ from the cylinder seals of other countries in being very long and thing; nor are they perforated for suspension on a cord. It is possible that these so-called seals are not true seals at all. They incised characters upon them might conceivably be identification marks for a game or something similar. On the other hand, they are

certainly suitable for use a seals and in this account they are included in this chapter For the sake of clearness the actual seal is shown side by side with each impression.[156]

5 and 6. These are not Indus seals, but appear in Frankfort as seals from Mesopotamia, and bear some resemblance to the Mackay seals above [2, 3] and point to some of the similarities between the contemporaneous Mesopotamian and Indus civilizations.

Galleries or processions of hieroglyphs are also achieved orthographically by combining (ligaturing) elements of signifiers of a set

m1177, m1175, m3

M-1181 K-50 H-1951 B

7. Different personages and creatures depicted on Indus seals and tablets with both arms entirely covered by bangles: male deity or man in yogic position over a throne with bovine hoofs, centaur-like creature with tiger body and human fore-body and deity or man/woman standing within a pipal tree (from Parpola's CISI volumes – see notes 2 and 3; not to scale).

Shahi Tump. Kech valley, Makran division, Baluchistan, Pakistan[157]

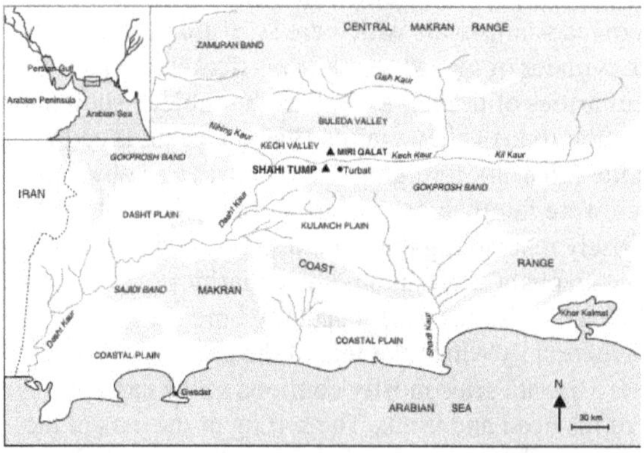

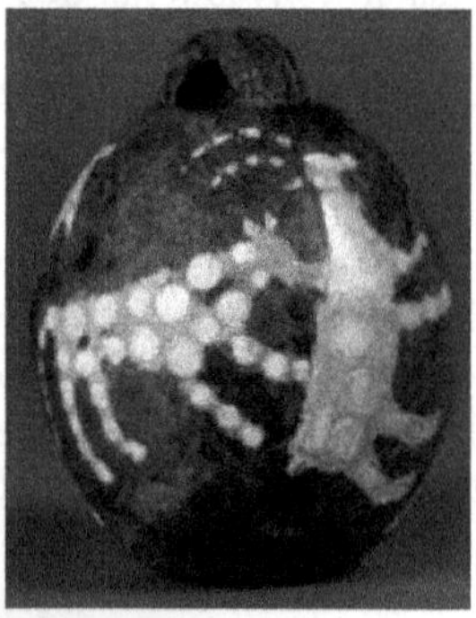

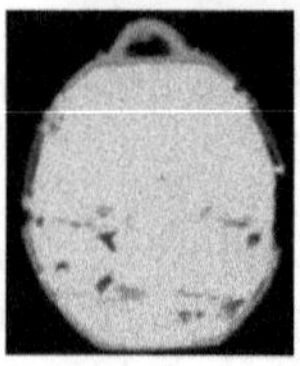

Leopards weight from Shahi Tump - Photography and The 30 MeV accelerator tomodensimetry showing the copper shell and the lead filling. (Science for Cultural Heritage: Technological Innovation and Case Studies in Marine and Land Archaeology in the Adriatic Region and Inland: VII International Conference on Science, Arts and Culture ; August 28-31, 2007, Veli Lošinj, Croatia, World Scientific, 2010. The aim of the conference was to discuss the contribution of physics and other sciences in archaeological research and in the preservation of cultural heritage.)

Leopards weight of Shahi Tump (Balochistan), National Museum, Karachi. The artefact was discovered in a grave, in the Kech valley, in Balochistan. ca. 4th millennium BCE. 200 mm. h. 13.5kg wt. The shell has been manufactured by lost-wax foundry of a copper alloy (12.6% Pb, 2.6% As), then it has been filled up through lead (99.5%) foundry. The shell is engraved with figures of leopards hunting wild goats, made of polished fragments of shellfishes. No identification of the artefact's use has been given. (Scientific team: B. Mille, D. Bourgarit, R. Besenval, Musee Guimet, Paris.[158]

Meluhha hieroglyphs:

karaḍa 'panther' Rebus: *karaḍa* 'hard alloy'. *mēḻh (Brahui), mṟēka (Telugu)* 'goat' Rebus: milakkhu 'copper' (Pali)

Ka. *mēke* she-goat; mē the bleating of sheep or goats. Te. *mẽka, mēka* goat. Kol. *me·ke*

id. *Nk. mēke id. Pa. mēva, (S.) mēya* she-goat. *Ga. (Oll.) mēge, (S.) mēge goat. Go. (M) mekā, (Ko.) mēka id. ? Kur. mēxnā (mīxyas) to call, call after loudly, hail. Malt. méqe to bleat. [Te. mṟēka (so correct) is of unknown meaning. Br. mēḻh* is without etymology; see MBE 1980a.] / Cf. Skt. (lex.) *meka-* goat. (DEDR 5087)

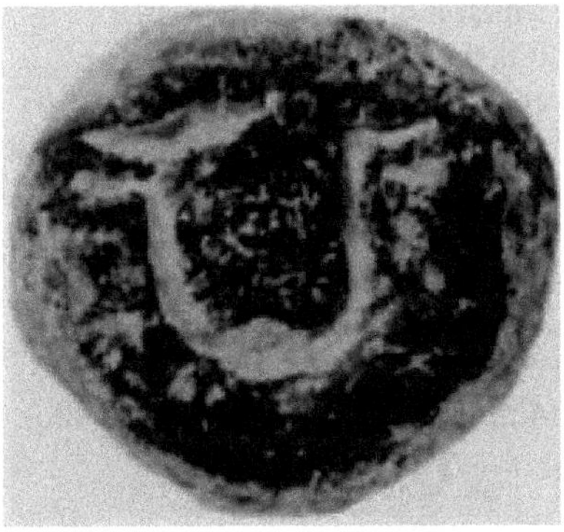

Daimabad seal. Glyph is decoded: *kaṇḍ karṇaka, kaṇḍ kan-ka* 'rim of jar'. Rebus: 'furnace scribe, *karṇī* supercargo'. Harappa Script Corpora includes this seal with just one 'text sign' which is the most frequently occurring hieroglyph on inscriptions. The hieroglyph signifies 'rim of jar' as on a Daimabad seal: The act of speech is complete: *kanka, karṇika* 'rim of jar' rebus: *karṇī* 'supercargo, a representative of the ship's owner on board a merchant ship, responsible for overseeing the cargo and its sale'. With accent on the rim of the jar (in many instances narrow-necked), Vaikhārī or complete utterance is signified on Harappa Script.

Given the function and form of the Harappa Script, it is not necessary to look for long texts to statistically derive possible syllables in the expressions composed as messages. Even small-sized seals and tablet tokens serve the purpose of unambiguously conveying messages of technical specifications of metalwork products of the Bronze Age Revolution – in over 200 instances even without any 'text sign' from a Sign List (see one example of Harappa Script sign list) in Annex L.

Bet Dwaraka seal. Turbinella pyrum (śankha) seal without any 'text sign' but with a composition combing three animal faces (ox, one-horned young bull, antelope) to a bovine body. In such orthographic rendering, the message obviously is that the three animals constitute the hypertext together with with the word: sangaDa 'joined animal parts rebus: sangara 'fortification'. सं-ग्रह *saṁgraha, samgaha* 'a guardian , ruler , manager , arranger' R. BhP. barad, balad 'ox' rebus: bharata 'mixed alloy of copper, pewter, tin'. kundar 'young bull' rebus: kundār 'turner'. ranku 'antelope' rebus:ranku 'tin'.. Thus, the message is turner's work with tin, and copper-pewter-tin alloy.

Two contextual aspects of Harappa Script need to be highlighted:

1. Inventions of tin-bronzes to substitute for scarcity of naturally-occurring arsenical copper.

2. Maritime Tin Route linking the largest tin belt of the world in Mekong River delta in Ancient Far East with the archaeometallurgically-attested artifacts including cylinder seals in Ancient Near East.

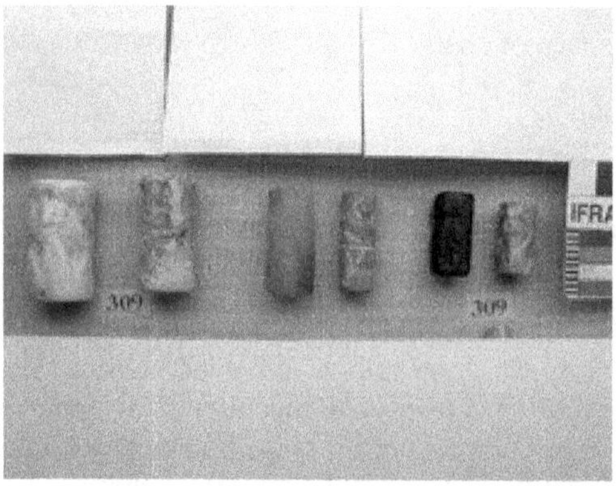

Products made of tin-bronzes constituted a revolutionary advance of the Bronze Age and led to long-distance maritime trade exchanges across Eurasia. A good example of the antiquity of artisanal competence in using material resources is provided byturbinella pyrum, śankha which is a signature resource indigenous to the Indian Ocean coastline. Columella of this conch-shell was also used to create cylinder seals.159

Examples of seals made of turbinella pyrum or sea shell:
Six cylinder seals of various materials including marble, shell, agate, chlorite, and steatite. N. Syria and Mesopotamia, ca. late 4th to early 3rd millennium BCE. The large shell seal, second from the left, was carved from the columella of Turbinella pyrum, the Bharata śankha shell. Yale Peabody Museum of Natural History Catalog Number YPM ANT 295376

The entire Harappa Script Corpora are inscriptions which are signifiers of धम्म संज्ञा *dhamma saṁjñā* 'responsibility indicators"160. This explains why, for example, a pectoral which is worn as a pendant by a seafaring artisan also contains Harappa Script hieroglyphs. The overflowing pot on the pectoral signifies: lo-*khāṇḍā* 'metal tools, pots and pans.' Hypertext of pictorial motif created as hieroglyphs signify the locus: sangara 'a fortified settlement', सं-ग्रह *saṁgraha, samgaha* 'a guardian , ruler , manager , arranger' R. BhP. *kundār* a turner, metal artisan (with) *koḍe, koḍiya, 'eka-shinga,* single-masted dhow or seafaring vessel'.

kāṇḍam காண்டம்[2] *kāṇṭam, n. < kāṇḍa.* 1. Water; sacred water; நீர். துருத்திவா யதுக்கிய குங்குமக் காண் டமும் (கல்லா. 49, 16). Rebus: *lokhāṇḍā* 'metal tools, pots and pans' (Marathi*)<lo->(B) {V} ``(pot, etc.) to ^overflow". See <lo-> `to be leftover'. @B24310. #20851. Re<lo->(*B) {V} ``(pot, etc.) to ^overflow". See *<lo->* `to be left over'. (Munda) Rebus: *loh* 'copper' (Hindi)

"The origins of lost wax or investment casting, often known as *cire perdue*, and still the most accurate and reliable means of reproducing complex shapes in gold or other metals with all the fine detail of an original pattern, go back to the very first civilisations in the Near East and to a combination of primitive art, religion and metallurgy. The historical development of the process and its several variations are reviewed here as well as its transmission to other parts of the world."[161]

Cire perdue (lost-wax) method of casting metal alloys was used in Uruk, ca. 3500 BCE. to make a recumbent ram in silver which is mounted on pins and dowelled into the center of a cylinder seal with Harappa Script hieroglyph. This was a hieroglyph, tagged to cylinder seal method of writing by impressing an agreement to a transaction or to indicate ownership. This cylinder seal is carved with figures of cattle. Ashmolean Museum, Univ. of Oxford. "The Ashmolean Museum describes this item as a cylinder seal showing a herd of cattle and reed huts containing calves... The seal itself is made of magnesite ($MgCO_3$) with small (a few centimeters) cast silver ram-shaped finial. No claim is made by the museum that it was produced by the Lost Wax process and it is dated by the museum to the Late Uruk period or "around 3200 BCE". The item has been purchased by the museum but its provenance is unknown and therefore cannot be precisely dated."[162] (Shlomo Guil)

Chalcolithic Period 4th-3rd millennium BCE- culture unknown. Ibex headed scepter created by the lost wax technique. From the Nahal Mishmar Cave Hoard in Ein Gedi Israel. The hoard contains 240 mace heads, 80 sceptres and 10 crowns - all copper except for a few ivory objects. Collections of Israel Museum, Jerusalem. Chalcolithic Levant Nahal Mishmar treasure: Model of a building. Shaped like a copper crown.

Nahal Mishmar. Crown with building facade decoration and birds. The birds on the Nahal Mishmar artifact are comparable to the birds shown on Mohenjo-daro tablet which shows two birds perched on a boat flanked by a pair of palm trees.

karaṇḍa 'duck' (Sanskrit) *karaṛa* 'a very large aquatic bird' (Sindhi)

Rebus: करडा [*karaḍā*] Hard from alloy--iron, silver &c. (Marathi) *dula* 'pair' Rebus: *dul* 'metal casting'.

sã̄gāḍā m. ' frame of a building ' (M.)(CDIAL 12859) Rebus: *jaṅgaḍ* 'entrustment articles' *sã̄gaṛh* m. ' line of entrenchments, stone walls for defence ' (Lahnda).(CDIAL 12845) Allograph: *saṅgaḍa* 'lathe'. 'potable furnace'. सं-ग्रह *saṁgraha,samgaha* 'a guardian , ruler , manager , arranger' R. BhP. *sang* 'stone', *gaḍa* 'large stone'. *dula* 'pair' Rebus: dul 'cast metal'. *koḍ* 'horns' Rebus: *koḍ* 'artisan's workshop'.

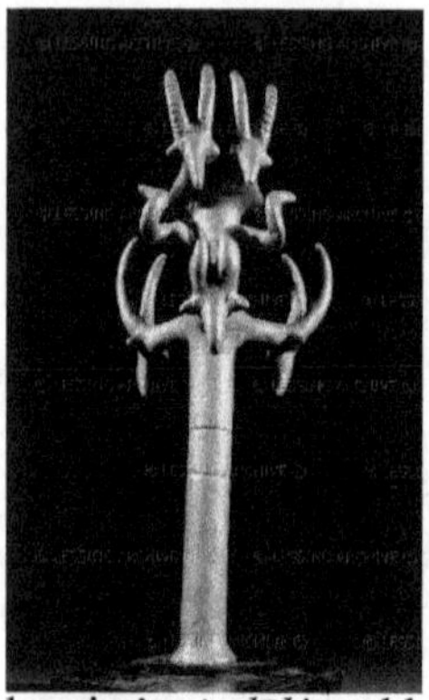

Some seal impressions have been found indicating the use of seals with Harappa Script inscriptions to authenticate trade transactions during the Bronze Age. Hieroglyph: *karabha* 'trunk of elephant' *ibha* 'elephant' rebus: *karba, ib* 'iron' Kur. mūxā frog. Malt. *múqe* id. / Cf. Skt. *mūkaka*- id. (DEDR 5023). *muka* 'ladle' (Tamil)(DEDR 4887) Rebus: *mū̃h* 'ingot' Hieroglyph: *maraca, mora* 'peacock' rebus: *morakkhaka loha, marakaka loha*, a kind of copper, grouped with pisācaloha (Pali). मारक *loha* 'a kind of calcining metal' (Samskritam) *moraka* "a kind of steel" *arka* 'sun' rebus: *eraka* 'moltencast, copper' *kangu,* कंक [*kaṅka*] m S A heron or curlew. (Marathi) *rebus: kanga* 'portable furnace, brazier' *miṇḍāl* 'markhor' (Tōrwālī) *meḍho* a ram, a sheep' Rebus: *mẽṛhẽt, meḍ* 'iron' (Munda.Ho.) *meḍ* 'iron' meḍ 'copper' (Slavic)

Peacocks as Harappa Script hieroglyph hypertext on Samarra bowl

Samarra, Iraq. Eight fish, four peacocks holding four fish, slanting strokes surround. The Samarra bowl (ca. 4000 BCE) on exhibit at the Pergamon museum, Berlin. The bowl was excavated as Samarra by Ernst Herzfeld in the 1911-1914 campaign, and described in a 1930 publication. The design consists of a rim, a circle of eight fish, and four fish swimming towards the center being caught by four birds. At the center is a swastika symbol.[163]

satthiya 'svastika glyph'; rebus: *satthiya* 'zinc', *jasta* 'zinc' (Kashmiri), *satva*, 'zinc' (Pkt.)

ayo 'fish'; rebus: *ayas* 'metal'

mora peacock; *morā* 'peafowl' (Hindi); rebus: *morakkhaka loha*, a kind of copper, grouped with pisācaloha (Pali). *moraka* "a kind of steel" (Samskrtam)

Limestone Kish tablet from Sumer with pictographic writing; may be the earliest known writing, 3500 BCE. AshmoleanMuseum This may be a precur to the system of tokens and bullae for account keeping in Sumer. This link is provided to indicate the relative dates in chronology of evolution of writing systems during the Bronze Age which necessitated increased congtacts aong people of Eurasia..

Tabernae montana hieroglyph is shown together with zebu and a thorny object, on a Mesopotamian cylinder seal.

Other hieroglyphs shown on the cylinder seal: ran:ga ron:ga, ran:ga con:ga = thorny, spikey, armed with thorns; edel dare ran:ga con:ga dareka = this cotton tree grows with spikes on it (Santali)) Rebus: ran:ga, ran: pewter is an alloy of tin lead and antimony (añjana) (Santali).Alternative: *adar ḍangar* 'bull, zebu' *aduru* = *gan.iyinda tegadu karagade iruva aduru* ಗಣಿಯಿಂದ ತೆಗದು ಕರಗದೆ ಇರುವ ಅದುರು = ore taken from the mine and not subjected to smelting in a furnace.164 *ădar* = fine sand (Tamil) *aduru* native metal (Ka.); *ayil* iron (Ta.) *ayir, ayiram* any ore (Ma.); *ajirda karba* very hard iron (Tu.)(DEDR 192). *pōḷa* 'zebu' rebus: pōḷa 'magnetite, ferrite ore'; *bica* 'scorpion' rebus: *bica* 'haematite, ferrite ore'. *kulā* 'hood of snake' rebus: *kol* 'metal, working in iron' *kolle* 'blacksmith' *ḍhan:ga* = tall, long shanked; maran: *ḍhan:gi aimai kanae* = she is a big tall woman (Santali)

S. *ḍhaṅgaru* m. 'lean emaciated beast'; L. (Shahpur) *ḍhaggā* ' small weak ox '(CDIAL 5324) Ku. ḍhā̃go ' lean ', m. ' skeleton '; Ku. *ḍā̃go* ' lean (e.g. of oxen) '; N. ' male (of animals) '; Psht. Orm. *ḍaṅgar* ' lean '(CDIAL 5524) Rebus: ḍhan:gar 'blacksmith' (WPah.); N. ḍāṅro ' term of contempt for a blacksmith '(CDIAL 5524) Mth. *ṭhākur* ' blacksmith ' (CDIAL 5524).

Examples from Bharata *sprachbund*:[165]

♣ Skt. amsu- `Soma plant'; Av. asu- 'Haoma plant'

♣ Skt. *atharvan-* : Av. *aerauuan-/araurun-* `priest'

♣ Skt. *bhisaj-* m. `physician'; Av. *bi-* `meḍicine', LAv. *biaziia-* 'to cure'

♣ Skt. *chaga-* : Oss. *saeg / saegae* `billy-goat'

♣ Skt. *dursa-* `coarse garment' : Wakhi *dərs* `wool of a goat or a yak'

♣ Skt. *gandha-* `smell' : LAv. *gainti-* `bad smell'

♣ Skt. *gandharva-* : LAv. *ganedərəva-* `a mythical being'

♣ Skt. *Indra-* name of a god; LAv. *Indra-* name of a daeva

♣ Skt. *istaka-* f. (VS+); LAv. *istiia-* n., OP *isti-* f., MiP xist 'brick'

♣ Skt. *jahaka-* : LAv. *duzuka-*, Bal. *jajuk, duzux*, MoP *zuza* `hedgehog'

♣ Skt. *kesa-* `hair' : LAv. *gaesa-* `curly hair'

♣ Skt. *nagnahu-* (AVP+) m. `yeast, ferment'; PIr. **nagna-* `bread'

♣ Skt. *phala-* : MoP *supar* `ploughshare'

♣ Skt. *seppa-,* but Prkrit *cheppa-* : LAv. *xsuuaepa-* `tail'

♣ Skt. *sikata-* : OP *sika-* `sand'

♣ Skt. *suco-* : LAv. *suka-* `needle'

♣ Skt. *ustra-*; Av. *ustra-*, 'camel'

♣ Skt. *yavya- /yaviya/* `stream, canal'; OP *yauviya-* `canal'.

One intriguing semantic may be cited, again, in the context of the bronze-age. There are two compounds: *milakkhu rajanam* 'copper-coloured' (Pali), *mleccha mukha* 'copper' (Samskrtam).

Mleccha mukha, knowledge discovery of Bharata *sprachbund*

Why mleccha mukha? I think the lexeme *mukha* is a substrate lexeme *mūh* 'face, ingot' (Munda. Santali etc.); it is possible that *mleccha mukha* may refer to 'copper ingot'. *mũhã* = the quantity of iron produced at one time in a native smelting furnace (Santali) *Mleccha*, language. *Mleccha,* copper. The other meaning of *mūh* 'face' (CDIAL 10158) explains why a face glyph gets ligatured in Harappa Script writing to clear composite hieroglyphs to create *mlecchitavikalpa* (cipher mentioned by Vātsyāyana).

m1179

m1186A

m0302

A reference to mleccha as language, *bhāṣā,* occurs in Bharata's Nāṭyaśāstra:

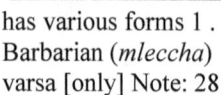

XVIII. 80] Rules on the use of languages. The Common Language

28. The Common Language prescribed for use [on the stage] has various forms 1 . It contains [many] words of Barbarian (*mleccha*) origin and is spoken in Bharata-varsa [only] Note: 28 (C.26b-27a; B. XVII.29b-30a). 'Read *vividha-jatibhasa* ; *vividha (ca, da in B.) for dvividha.*

'The common speech or the speech of the commoners is distinguished here from that of the priests and the nobility by describing it as containing words of Barbarian (mleccha) origin. These words seem to have been none other than vocables of the Dravidian and Austric languages. They entered Indo-Aryan pretty early in its history.[166]

1 4 | I.11 - 12 {6/8} *mlecchaḥ ha vai eṣaḥ yat apaśabdaḥ .*

1 4 | I.11 - 12 {7/8} *mlecchāḥ mā bhūma iti adhyeyam vyākaraṇam .~*

V.118.5 - 119.12 {20/36} *mlecchitam vispaṣṭena iti eva anyatra tasmāt brāhmaṇena na mlecchitavai na apabhāṣitavai .*

Patanjali explains in the context of ungrammatical mleccha with *apaśabdaḥ* (Patanjali: *Mahābhāṣya*).

The acculturation of Meluhhas (probably, Indus people) residing in Mesopotamia in the late third and early second millennium BC, is noted by their adoption of Sumerian names.[167]

"The adaptation of Harappa motifs and script to the Dilmun seal form may be a further indication of the acculturative phenomenon, one indicated in Mesopotamia by the adaptation of Harappa traits to the cylinder seal."[168]

One example can be presented to show how convergences occurred to form lexis of Indo-European languages, in the context of archaeo-metallurgy of the Bronze Age since the invention of tin bronzes was a revolutionary advance in industrialization.

I have suggested, based on the fact the the largest tin belt of the globe is in Mekong river delta, that a cultural *sprachbund* of tin bronzes and related metalcastings as cultural markers can be traced along the Tin Maritime Route from Hanoi to Haifa which predates the Silk Road by about 2 millennia -- from Dong Son bronze drums to Nahal Mishmar *cire perdue* arsenical bronze artifacts of 5th millennium BCE.

In the context of the Bronze Age advances along the Maritime Tin Route from Hanoi to Haifa, identification of the Meluhha language and *soma* of Rigveda, decryption of Harappa Script are some of the major challenges. Harappa Script writing can be described as corpus of inscriptions of professional guild calling cards. This is consistent with the cultural tradition attested in the historical periods of the contributions made *śrēṇiḥ* (guilds), and institutions such as *gana, samgha, nigama, jati* in socio-economic organization. Harappa Script writing thus describes the corporate life of ancient India with particular reference to the smith guilds who created mineral and metal artefacts and traded them over an extensive interaction area of the civilization.

Emeneau who has done remarkable work with Burrow in compiling a Dravidian Etymological Dictionary and Toda etyma refers to Aryan Invasion Theory as a 'linguistic doctrine', to explain many cognate lexemes in language streams of India. The polemics of the invasion or migration or of directions of migration or invasion need not detain us here.

Trubetzkoy and Jakobson are early founders of a phonological method called *sprachbunds*. Emeneau applied the method to Bharata languages and identified an Bharata sprachbund. Trubetzkoy first suggested in 1923 in "Vavilonskaja basnja i smesenie jazykov" and proposed in 1928 in the First International Congress of Linguists in The Hague the term 'sprachbund' to add to language families and groups. Trubetzkoy states: "Viele Missverstandnisse und Fehler entstehen dadurch, das die Sprachforscher die Ausdrucke Sprachgruppe und Sprachfamilie ohne genugende Vorsicht und in zu wenig bestimmter Bedeutung gebrauchen."[169]

This statement can be translated: "Many misunderstandings and errors arise because the linguists use the expression language group and language family without enough caution and in the end to little specific meaning." Trubetzkoy went on to delineate a *sprachbund* as a group of languages with parallels in syntax, morphology, cultural vocabulary and phonetics (even without systematic sound correspondences or shared basic vocabulary).

In Ancient India, Dravidian andIndo-Aryan languages shared a number of features that were not inherited from a common source, but were areal features, the result of diffusion during sustained contact.[170]

The delineation of Bharata sprachbund of the Bronze Age is based on the metallurgical vocables and expressions so diffused during sustained contacts along the Maritime Tin Route.

In the context of Indo-European language family, a comparable profundity in understanding semantics is made by MB Emeneau, a co-author of Dravidian Etymological Dictionary with T. Burrow. Identifying an Bharata *sprachbund*, Emeneau proposed in 1956 in his paper, 'India as a Linguistic Area' based on his observation that Dravidian and Indo-Aryan languages shared a number of language areal structural language features caused by sustained contact among Indo-Aryan, Dravidian, Munda and Tibeto-Burma language families. One such shared feature was reduplication of words in sentences or phrases. Within Autro-Asiatic language family for which an Etymological Dictionary is under construction in University of Hawii,

Khmer (Mon–Khmer), Cham (Austronesian) and Lao (Kadai) languages have almost identical vowel systems. Sumerian and Akkadian have shared features. (Deutscher, Guy, 2007, Syntactic changes in Akkadian. Sumerian has substratum words which have parallels in Bharata languages, words such as sanga 'priest' [sanghvi 'leader of pilgrimś (Gujarati)]; nangar 'carpenter', ashgab 'leather worker'.[171] This linguistic exploration of *sprachbunds* should go on to delineate with reasonable precision the Bharata *sprachbund* relatable to Harappa Script Corpora.

Identifying an Bharata *sprachbund* can also be advanced by using archaeological evidences of artifacts and epigraphs. One set of epigraphs has emerged for Bharata *sprachbund* which is composed as about 7000 epigraphs in Harappa Script Corpora. For example, Brunswig et al have identified some epigraphs with or without cuneiform inscriptions which share features with Harappa Script epigraphs of the corpora, say, compiled by Marshall, Mahadevan, Parpola.

Bharatiya *sprachbund* or language union. "(*Sprachbun*d or linguistic area is) an area which includes languages belonging to more than one family but showing traits in common which are found not to belong to the other members of (at least) one of the families."[172] For Emeneau, it is a 'multi-familial convergence (or diffusion) area'. "In Language in India (9, Jan, 2002), G. Sankaranarayanan observes how repeating words and forms is a significant feature that extends across the Bharata subcontinent and includes not only the Sanskrit and Tamil derivatives but also Munda and languages from the Tibetan-Burmese group."

Many researchers have reached a consensus that ancient India constituted a linguistic area[173], that is, an area wherein specific language-speakers absorbed features from other languages and made the features their own. To delineate such a linguistic area and the glosses that might have been used in that area, the glosses are chosen from all Bharata languages. Bharata language glosses are compared because there is evidence for cultural continuum of the civilization which produced the objects inscribed with Harappa Script.[174]The glosses are semantically-phonetically clustered together in an Indian lexicon [175]which helps construct a subset of lexemes as substrate dictionary of the linguistic area. The assumption is that one or more languages of this lexicon could hold the legacy of the ancient phonetic forms of words used by the authors of the civilization who also invented the writing system. This is the reason why no attempt has been made to reconstruct hypothetical phonetic forms of the lexemes which might have constituted the parole of the Bronze Age in Bharata sprachbund. On the premise that one or more languages retain the proto-forms of words, the homonyms identified serve as counter-checks to affirm the ancient phonetic forms of parole (spoken words) of metalwork and related catalogue entries documented on Harappa Script hieroglyphs/hypertexts.

This lexicon clusters together, semantically, lexemes from over 25 Bharata languages with surface resemblances (äussere Ähnlichkeit) in the sound system. This lexicon demonstrates a large amount of shared cultural vocabulary in the three streams.

The field of inquiry is to delineate how this sharing occurred. In some semantic clusters of the lexicon, a hypothesized common substrate may explain the surface resemblances in the sound system.

One possibility is that the three streams descend from a community which lived and worked together in a transition from chalcolithic age to bronze age.

Determination of the direction of 'borrowingś from among the substratum words of a linguistic area is governed by faith of the investigator.

Substratum words Bharata *sprachbund* could be culled from the Bronze Age social experience recorded in the data archives of Harappa Script Corpora and hypothesised to constitute lexemes of 'Harappa language' of the Bronze Age. The 4th millennium BCE heralded the arrival of a veritable revolution in technology -- the making of tin bronzes to complement scarce arsenical bronzes. Contemporaneous with this metallurgical revolution was the invention of writing systems which evolved from early tokens and bullae to categorise commodities and provide for their accounting systems using advanced tokens with writing as administrative devices.

Substratum words are likely to have been retained in more than one language of the Bharata *sprachbund*, irrespective of the language-family to which a particular language belongs. This is the justification for the identification, in comparative lexicons, of sememes with cognate lexemes from languages such as Gujarati, Marathi, Kannada, Santali, Munda or Toda or Kota. The underlying assumption is that the substratum words were absorbed into the particular languages either as borrowings or as morphemes subjected to phonetic changes – as *tatsama, tadbhava* -- over time. There is no linguistic technique available to 'date' a particular sememe and relate it to the technical processes which resulted in naming, for example, the metalware or furnaces/smelters used to create metals and cast the metals or alloys and forge them. It is remarkable, indeed, that hundreds of cognate lexemes have been retained in more than one language to facilitate rebus readings of Harappa Script hieroglyphs.

An example can be cited to elucidate the point made in this argument. The word attested in Rigveda is *ayas*, often interpreted as 'metal or bronze'. The cognate lexemes are *ayo* 'iron' (Gujarati. Santali) *ayaskāṇḍa* 'excellent quantity of iron' (Panini), *kāṇḍā* 'tools, pots and pans of metalware' (Marathi). अयोगूः A blacksmith; Vāj.3.5. अयस् a. [इ-गतौ-असुन्] Going, moving; nimble. N. (-यः) 1 Iron (एति चलति अयस्कान्तसंनिकर्षं इति तथात्वम्; नायसोल्लिख्यते रत्नम् Śukra 4.169. अभितप्तमयो$पि मार्दवं भजते कैव कथा शरीरिषु R.8.43. -2 Steel. -3 Gold. -4 A metal in general. Ayaskāṇḍa 1 an iron-arrow. -2 excellent iron. -3 a large quantity of iron. – क_नत_(अयसक_नत_) 1 'beloved of iron', a magnet, load-stone; 2 a precious stone; °मजण_ a loadstone; ayaskāra 1 an iron-smith, blacksmith (Skt.Apte) ayas-kāntamu. [Skt.] n. The load-stone, a magnet. *Ayaskāruḍu*. n. A black smith, one who works in iron. ayassu. N. *ayō-mayamu.* [Skt.] adj. made of iron (Telugu) *áyas*— n. 'metal, iron' RV. Pa. *ayō* nom. Sg. N. and m., *aya*— n. 'iron', Pk. *Aya*— n., Si. *Ya. AYAŚCŪRṆA—*, AYASKĀṆḌA—, *AYASKŪṬA—. Addenda: áyas— : Md. Da 'iron', dafat 'piece of iron'. ayaskāṇḍa— m.n. 'a quantity of iron, excellent iron' Pāṇ. Gaṇ. Viii.3.48 Si. *yakaḍa* 'iron'.* — 'iron hammer'. *[ÁYAS—, KUU'ṬA— 1] Pa. ayōkūṭa—, ayak* m.; Si. *Yakuḷa* 'sledge —hammer', *yavuḷa (< ayōkūṭa)* (CDIAL 590, 591, 592). Cf. Lat. *Aes , aer-is for as-is ; Goth. Ais , Thema aisa; Old Germ. E7r , iron ;Goth. Eisarn ; Mod. Germ. Eisen. aduru* native metal (Ka.); *ayil iron (Ta.) ayir, ayiram* any ore (Ma.); ajirda karba very hard iron (Tu.)(DEDR 192). Ta. *ayil* javelin, lance, surgical knife, lancet.Ma. *ayil* javelin, lance; *ayiri* surgical knife, lancet. (DEDR 193). *aduru = gan.iyinda tegadu karagade Iruva aduru* – ore taken from the mine and not subjected to melting in a furnace (Ka. *Siddhānti Subrahmaṇya' Śastri's new interpretation of the Amarakośa*, Bangalore, Vicaradarpana Press, 1872, p.330); adar = fine sand (Ta.); *ayir* – iron dust, any ore (Ma.) Kur. *adar* the waste of pounded rice, broken grains, etc. Malt. *adru* broken grain (DEDR 134). Ma. *aśu* thin, slender; *ayir, ayiram* iron dust.Ta. ayir subtlety, fineness, fine sand, candied sugar; ? atar fine sand, dust. அய.ர[3] ayir, n. 1. Subtlety, fineness; நணசம. (த_வ_.) 2. [M. *ayir.]* Fine sand; நணமணல. (மலசலப. *92.) ayiram,* n. Candied sugar*; ayil, n. cf. ayas. 1. Iron; 2*. Surgical knife, lancet; Javelin, lance; *ayilavaṉ*, Skāṇḍa, as bearing a javelin

(DEDR 341).Tu. *gadarů* a lump (DEDR 1196) *kadara*— m. 'iron goad for guiding an elephant' lex. (CDIAL 2711).

It will be a highly speculative exercise to determine how a*duru* became *ayas*.

Fish hieroglyph on anthropomorph from Sheorajpur, shaped like a person with spread legs and horns of a ram.

कर्णक *kárṇaka, kannā* 'legs spread', rebus: *karaṇī* 'scribe, supercargo', *kañi-āra* 'helmsman' PLUS hieroglyph, 'markhor'. *miṇḍāl* 'markhor' (Tōrwālī) *meḍho* a ram, a sheep (Gujarati)(CDIAL 10120) Rebus: *mẽṛhẽt, meḍ* 'iron' (Santali.Mu.Ho.) PLUS *ayo, aya* 'fish' rebus: *aya* 'iron' *ayas* 'metal. Thus, supercargo for metal and iron.

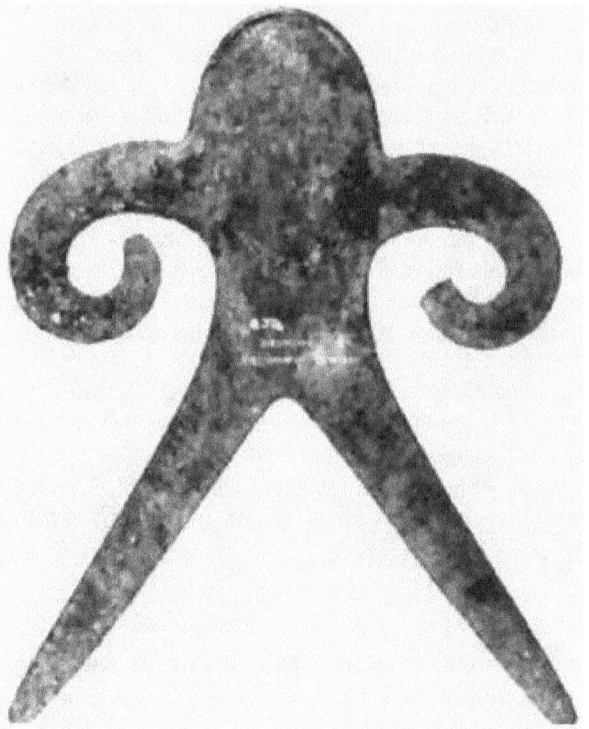

Sanjay Manjul of ASI reports a variant anthropomorph with variant Harappa Script hieroglyphs: Fish is replaced by 'one-horned young bull' and the head is ligatured with a 'boar' hieroglyph.

Hieorglyph of one-horned bull inscribed on chest of anthropomorph:

First reading: *khoṇḍ, kõda* 'young bull-calf' Rebus: *kũdār* 'turner'. कोंद *kōnda* 'engraver, lapidary setting or infixing gems' (Marathi) *miṇḍāl* markhor (Tor.wali) *meḍho* a ram, a sheep (G.)(CDIAL 10120) Rebus: *meḍh* 'helper of merchant' (Gujarati) *mẽṛhẽt, meḍ* 'iron' (Mu.Ho.) *meḍ* 'copper' (Slavic) meṛed-bica = iron stone ore, in contrast to bali-bica, iron sand ore (Munda)

Second reading: Hieroglyph: *kōḍiya* 'young bull' Hieroglyph 2: *koḍiyum* 'ring on neck' (Gujarati) Rebus: *koṭiya* 'dhow seafaring vessel'

The rebus reading is provided by the fish hieroglyph which reads in Munda languages:

*<ayu?>(A) {N} ``^fish''. #1370. <yO>\\<AyO>(L) {N} ``^fish''. #3612. <kukkulEyO>,,<kukkuli-yO>(LMD) {N} ``prawn''. !Serango dialect. #32612. <sArjAjyO>,,<sArjAj>(D) {N} ``prawn''. #32622. <magur-yO>(ZL) {N} ``a kind of ^fish''. *Or.<>. #32632. <ur+Gol-Da-yO>(LL) {N} ``a kind of ^fish''. #32642.<bal.bal-yO>(DL) {N} 'smoked fish'. #15163. Vikalpa: Munda: <aDara>(L) {N} ``^scales of a fish, sharp bark of a tree''.#10171. So<aDara>(L) {N} ``^*scales of

a fish, sharp bark of a tree''. Bharata mackerel Ta. *ayirai, acarai, acalai* loach, sandy colour, Cobitis *thermalis; ayilai* a kind of fish. Ma. *ayala* a fish, mackerel, scomber; *aila, ayila* a fish; ayira a kind of small fish, loach (DEDR 191)

A composite copper anthropomorphic figure along with a copper sword was found by Dr. Sanjay Manjul, Director, Institute of Archaeology at the Central Antiquity Section, ASI, Purana Qila in 2005. This composite copper Anthropomorph is a solitary example in the copper hoard depicting a Varah head. The Anthropomorphic figure, its inscription and animal motif that it bears, illustrate the continuity between the Harappa and Early Historical period. *varāhá -- , varā'hu -- m. ' wild boar ' RV.Pa. Pk. varāha -- m. ' boar '; A. B. barā ' boar ' (A. also ' sow, pig '), Or. barāha, (Sambhalpur) barhā, (other dial.) bǎrihā, bāriā, H. bǎrāh m., Si. varāvarāhamūla* n. ' name of a place in Kashmir ' Rājat. [*varāhá -- , mū'la -- ?]K. warahmul* ' a town at west end of the valley of Kashmir '.(CDIAL 11325, 11326) *baḍhia* = a castrated boar, a hog; rebus: *baḍhi* 'a caste who work both in iron and wood'; *baḍhoe* 'a carpenter, worker in wood'; *badhoria* 'expert in working in wood'(Santali) 'Rebus: *bari* 'merchant'. *barea* 'merchant' (Santali) বরাহ *barāha* 'boar' Rebus: *bāṛaï* 'carpenter' (Bengali)

Tablet Sb04823: receipt of 5 workers(?) and their monthly(?) rations, with subscript and seal depicting animal in boat; excavated at Susa in the early 20th century; Louvre Museum, Paris (Image courtesy of Dr Jacob L. Dahl, University of Oxford) Cited in an article on Reflectance Transformation Imaging (RTI) System. The animal in boat may be a boar and may signify supercargo of wood and iron products. Meluhha rebus readings: *baḍhia* = a castrated boar, a hog; rebus: *baḍhi* 'a caste who work both in iron and wood'.
baḍhoe 'a carpenter, worker in wood'; *badhoria* 'expert in working in

वाढी vii. 53 वणिक्सहायः, one who helps a merchant.

wood'(Santali) वराह *barāha* 'boar'Rebus: *bāṛaï* 'carpenter' (Bengali) *bari* 'merchant' barea 'merchant' (Santali) बारकश or बारकस [*bārakaśa* or *bārakasa*] *n* (P) A trading vessel, a merchantman.

*kamaṛkom (*Nag.); the petiole or **stalk** of a **leaf** (Mundari) rebus: *kammaṭa* 'mint, coiner, coinage'

kāṇḍa 'arrow' rebus: *khaṇḍa* 'implements'. Thus, a *vADhI*, 'merchant' with a trading vessel (merchantman) with a cargo of implements.

Bowl with a boar, and decorated with a tree on a Mountain. Gold, ht. 11.6 cm. Musée National d'Afghanistan– MK 04.29.3 *kuṭi* 'tree' rebus: *kuṭhi* 'smelter' *dhanga* 'mountain range' Rebus: *dhangar* 'blacksmith' *dhanga* 'mountain range' Rebus: *dhangar* 'blacksmith'.

miṇḍāl markhor (Tor.wali) *meḍho* a ram, a sheep (Gujarati)(CDIAL 10120) Rebus: *meḍh* 'helper of merchant' (Gujarati*) mẽṛhẽt, meḍ* 'iron' (Mu.Ho.) *meḍ* 'copper' (Slavic) *meṛed-bica* = iron stone ore, in contrast to *bali-bica*, iron sand ore (Munda).

Tepe Fullol hoard: boar vessel. redrawn by Eric Olijdam after Dupree et al 1971. Vessel 5.

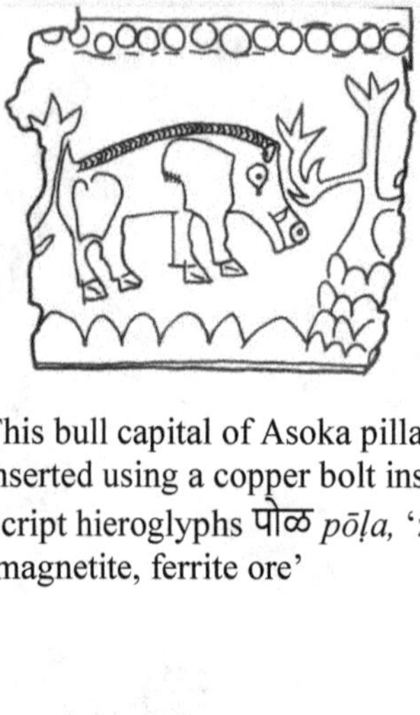

"On the Fullol vessel at least two boars were depicted…since boars are very rarely depicted in late 2nd millennium Mesopotamia but are characteristic of Bactrian iconography, the 'boar vessel' is probably a local Bactrian product inspired upon Middle Assyrian seals or more likely sealings…"[176]

An evidence for the continued use of Harappa Script hieroglyphs comes from Rampurva copper bolt.

This bull capital of Asoka pillar at Rampurva was inserted using a copper bolt inscribed with Harappa Script hieroglyphs पोळ *pōḷa,* 'zebu' rebus: पोळ *pōḷa*, 'magnetite, ferrite ore'

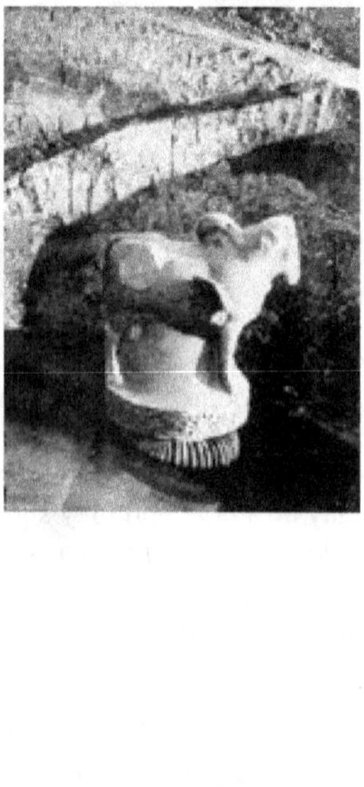

Rampurva copper bolt "The starting place for the inquiry is the Rampurva copper bolt at present in the Indian Museum, Calcutta. This was discovered in 1880 by Cunningham and H.B. Garrick. It was buried beside the fallen southerly pillar on which was engraved a set of Asoka's pillar edicts. The pillar and its lion capital were subsequently fully excavated by Daya Ram Sahni. The more northerly Rampurva pillar is that associated with the famous bull capital. The bolt was examined by Cunningham who concluded that there could be n doubt of its being original and that it must have served to hold the lion capital in place upon its pillar. It is probable that other Asokan pillars and capitals bear mortises for similar bolts. This one is described as barrel shaped, of pure copper measuring 2 ft. ½ in. in length, with a diameter of 4 5/16 in. in the centre, and 3 5/8 in. at each end. Cunningham makes no mention of any marks upon the bolt, but Durga Prasad published an impression of four marks. They are made of lines of impressed dots and include the hill-with-crescent, the taurine or Nandipada, and the open cross:

Here then these signs occur upon an object which must have been made by craftsmen working for Asoka or one of his predecessors."[177]

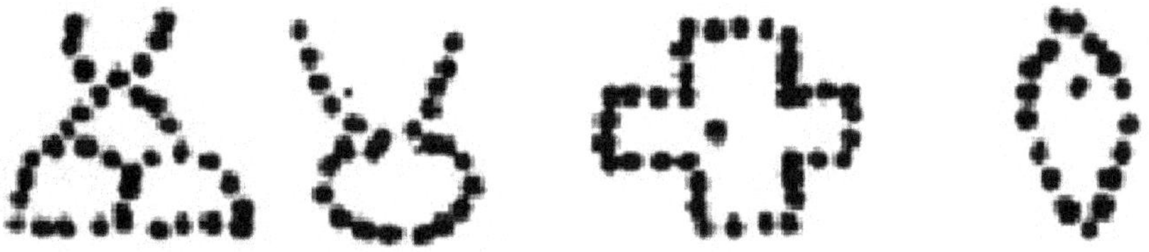

Hieroglyphs:

goT 'seed' Rebus: *khōṭa* 'alloy ingot'. खोट (p. 212) [*khōṭa*] f A mass of metal (unwrought or of old metal melted down); an ingot or wedge. (Marathi) kaṇḍa 'fire-altar' Rebus: *khaṇḍa* 'metal implements; *goT* 'round object' Rebus: *khōṭa* 'alloy ingot' PLUS *bhaṭa* 'rimless pot' Rebus: *bhaṭa* 'furnace'; *dhanga* 'mountain-range' Rebus: *dhangar* 'metalsmith' PLUS *bhaṭa* 'rimless pot' Rebus: *bhaṭa* 'furnace'. Thus, the inscription on the Rampurva copperbolt provides technical specification on the metal object, the copper bolt: that it was made of an alloy ingot (from) furnace, (made by) metal implements metalsmith.

Some devices used on punch-marked coins also occur as the first line of the Sohgaura copper plate inscription.[178]

Gruppen, bestehend aus Sprachen, die eine große Ähnlichkeit in syntaktischer Hinsicht;

eine Ähnlichkeit in den Grundsätzen des morphologischen Baues aufweisen; und eine große Anzahl gemeinsamer Kulturwörter bieten, manchmal auch äussere Ähnlichkeit im Bestande der Lautsystem, — dabei aber keine systematischen Lautentsprechungen keine Übereinstimmung in der lautlichen Gestalt der morphologischen Elemente, und keine gemeinsamen Elementarwörter besitzen, — solche Sprachgruppen nennen wir Sprachbünde.[179] Translation: Groups consisting of languages which are very similar syntactically; have a similarity in the principles of the morphological building; and a large number of common words culture offer, sometimes external similarity as a part of the sound system - thereby however no systematic sound correspondences no match in the phonetic form of the morphological elements, and have no common elementary words - those language groups we call *sprachbund.*

Language studies of the last two centuries point to an Bharata Sprachbund (language union or linguistic area) coterminous with over 2000 (i.e. 80% of all 2600 archaeological sites of the civilization) on the banks of Vedic River Sarasvati in northwest Bhratam. The inference is that all languages of the Harappa (Sarasvati-Sindhu) civilization area absorbed language features from one another and have made them their own. Thus, Munda family of languages spoken in parts of Ganga Basin and Eastern Bharat are also related to some Austro-Asiatic languages of Ancient Far East and many Munda words are also found in other languages of Bharata *sprachbund.*

Remarkable progress has been made ever since Kuiper identified a stunning array of glosses which were found in early Samskrtam and which were not explained by Indo-Aryan or Indo-European language evolution chronologies. On Munda lexemes in Sanskrit Kuiper presents a detailed list.[180]

Kuiper's brilliant exposition begins: "Some hundred Sanskrit and Prakrit words are shown to be derived from the Proto-Munda branch of the Austro-Asiatic source. The term 'Proto-Munda' is used to indicate that the Munda languages had departed considerably from the Austro-Asiatic type of language as early as the Vedic period... a process of 'Dravidization' of the Munda tongues... contributing to the growth of the Bharata linguistic league (sprachbund)."

Thus, vocabulary of almost all languages such as Prakritam, Samskritam, Dravidian or Indo-Aryan languages are likely to retain cognates from the Harappa language. Using the rebus method, homonyms of words which signify hieroglyphs may yield plain textual meanings of the Harappa Script inscriptions. Thus the hieroglyph karibha 'trunk of elephant' yields a close phonetic homonym karba 'iron' which is attested in Tulu language vocabulary. An Akkadian cylinder seal signifies in cuneiform text a Meluhha translator. That there was trade contact between Mesootamia and Meluhha is attested in ancient cuneiform texts. General consensus is that Meluhha was the Harappa (Sarasvati-Sindhu) Civilization area. Meluhha language is attested in Mahabharata identifying Meluhha speakers from many regions of Bhāratam. Thus, the decipherment can be premised on a hypothesis that the ancient Harappa language was Meluhha which can be identified in the glosses of ancient Bharatiya languages, Desi and Prakritam language dictionaries, and in the language repertoire of Munda language speakers, in particular.

Ancient Near East evidence for mleccha (meluhha) language from ancient texts

Evidence for Meluhha as a language comes from Mahabharata which cite conversation between Vidura'a emissary Kanaka and Dhrtarashtra about the impending dangers from non-metallic weapons embedded in Jatugrha (lac palace)

which would be in flames if Duryodhana's evil plans fructify. The conversation is in mleccha (cognate: meluhha).

Decipherment of inscription on the gold pendant-needle

2.5 inch long Mohenjo-daro gold pendant has a 0.3 inch nib; its ending is shaped like a nib of a stylus pen or sewing or netting needle. It bears an inscription painted (perhaps with ferric oxide pigment) in Harappa Script. This inscription is deciphered as a proclamation of metalwork competence.

Hieroglyh: *ṭáṅkati1, ṭaṅkáyati* ' ties ' Dhātup. 2. **ṭañcati.* 1. S. *ṭākaṇu* ' to stitch ', *ṭā̃ko* m. ' a stitch '; Ku. *ṭā̃ko* ' sewing, joining, patch '; N. *ṭā̃knu* ' to join, tack, button up ', *ṭā̃ko* ' stitch, seam '; A. *ṭākiba* ' to tie loosely '; B. *ṭā̃kā* ' to stitch ', Or. *ṭāṅkibā, ṭāk* ' hand -- stitching '; Bhoj. *ṭā̃kal* ' to sew '; H. *ṭā̃knā* ' to stitch, join, rivet, solder ', *ṭā̃kā* m. ' stitch, join '; G. *ṭā̃kvũ* ' to stitch ', *ṭā̃kɔ* m., M. *ṭā̃kā, ṭākā* m.2. G. *ṭā̃cvũ* ' to stitch ', *ṭā̃cṇī* f. ' small pin '; M. *ṭā̃ċṇẽ, ṭāċ°* ' to sew lightly ', *ṭā̃ċṇī, ṭāċ°* f. ' pin '.**ṭaṅkat*i2 ' chisels '. [ṭaṅka -- 2]Pa. *ṭaṅkita -- mañca --* ' a stone (i.e. chiselled) platform '; G. *ṭā̃kvũ* ' to chisel ', M. *ṭā̃kṇẽ. (*CDIAL 5432, 5433)

ṭaṅkaśālā -- , *ṭaṅkakaś°* f. ' mint ' lex. [ṭaṅka -- 1, śā´lā --]N. *ṭaksāl, °ār,* B. *ṭāksāl, ṭā̃k°, ṭek°,* Bhoj. *ṭaksār,* H. *ṭaksāl, °ār* f., G. *ṭā̃ksāḷ* f., M. *ṭā̃ksāl,*

ṭāk°, ṭā̃k°, ṭak°. -- Deriv. G. *ṭaksāḷī* m. ' mint -- master ', M. *ṭāksāḷyā* m. Addenda: *ṭaṅkaśālā* -- : Brj. *ṭaksāḷī, °sārī* m. ' mint -- master ' CDIAL 5434)

A painted inscription occurs on a Mohenjo-daro gold pendant:

The gold pendant is made from a hollow cylinder with soldered ends and perforated point. Museum No. MM 1374.50.271; Marshall 1931: 521, pl. CLI, B3. [After Fig. 4.17a, b in: JM Kenoyer, 1998, p. 196]. A fish sign, preceded by seven short numeral strokes, also appears on a gold Golden pendant with inscription from jewelry hoard at Mohenjo-daro. Drawing of inscription that encircles the gold ornament. Needle-like pendant with cylindrical body. Two other examples, one with a different series of incised signs were found together. The pendant is made from a hollow cylinder with soldered ends and perforated point. Museum No. MM 1374.50.271; Marshall 1931: 521, pl. CLI, B3[181]

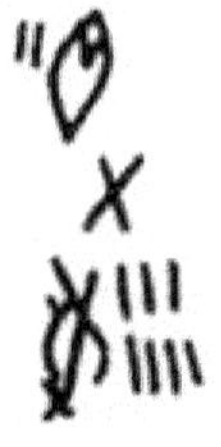

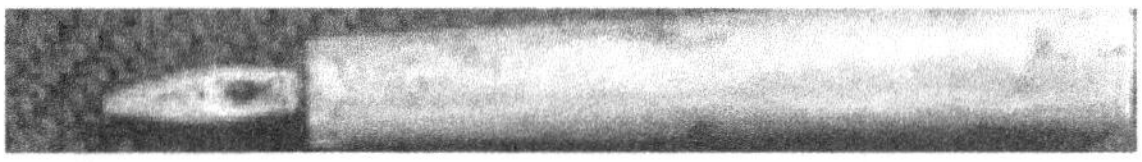

kanac 'corner' Rebus: *kancu* 'bronze'; *sal* 'splinter' Rebus: *sal* 'workshop'; *dāṭu* 'crosś(Telugu) *bāṭa* 'cross road' Rebus: *dhatu* 'mineral'; *bhaṭa* 'furnace'; *gaṇḍa* 'four' Rebus: *khaṇḍa* 'implements; *kolmo* 'three' Rebus: *kolimi* 'smithy, forge'; Vikalpa: *?ea* 'seven' (Santali); rebus: ?eh-ku 'steel' (Te.)

aya, ayo 'fish' Rebus: *aya* 'iron'(Gujarati) *ayas* 'metal' (Rigveda)
Thus, the inscription is: *ṭaksāḷī* m. *ṭāksāḷyā* 'mint master' PLUS *kancu sal* (bronze workshop), *dhatu aya kaṇḍ kolimi* mineral, metal, furnace/fire-altar smithy.

The inscription is a professional calling card -- describing professional competence of *ṭaksāḷī* m. *ṭāksāḷyā* m. 'mint master' (Gujarati.Marathi) and ownership of specified items of property -- of the wearer of the pendant.

Three such needles are identified by John Marshall, in the excavation report.

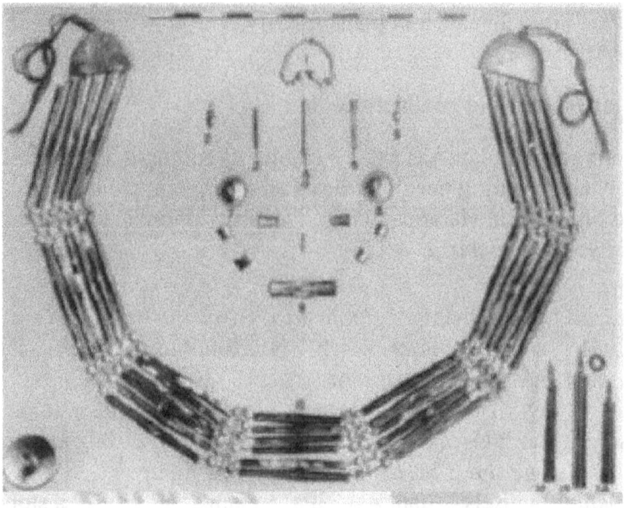

pries

The comments made by John Marshall on three curious objects at bottom right-hand corner of Pl. CLI, B3: "Personal ornaments…Jewellery and Necklaces…Netting needles (?) Three very curious objects found with the studs and the necklace appear to be netting needles of gold. They are shown just above the ear-studs and also in the lower right-hand corner of Pl. CLI, B, 3-5 and 12-14. The largest of these needles (E 2044a) is 2.5 inches long. The handle is hollow and cylindrical and tapers slightly, being 0.2 inch in diameter at the needle-end. The needle point is 0.5 inch long and has a roughly shaped oval eye at its base. The meḍium sized needle (E 2044b) is 2.5 inches long and of the same pattern: but the cap that closed the end of the handle is now missing. The point which has an oval eye at its base is 0.3 inch long. The third needle (E 2044c) is only 1.7 inches long with the point 0.3 inch in length. Its handle, which is otherwise similar to those of the other two needles, is badly dented. The exact use of these three objects is open to question, for they could have been used for either sewing or netting. The handles seem to have been drawn, as there is no sign of a soldered line, but the caps at either end were soldered on with an alloy that is very little lighter in colour than the gold itself. The two smaller needles have evidently been held between the teeth on more than one occasion." (p.521)

Evidently, Marshall has missed out on the incription written in paint, as a free-hand writing, over one of the objects: Pl. CLI, B3.

This is an extraordinary evidence of the Harappa Script writing system written down, with hieroglyphs inscribed using a coloured paint, on an object.

What could these three objects be? Sewing needles? Netting needles?

I surmise that all the three gold objects could be pendants tagged to other jewellery such as necklaces. The pendants were perhaps worn with a thread of fibre passing through the eye of the needle-like ending of the pendants.

Why needle-like endings? Maybe, the pendants were used as 'writing' devices 1) either to engrave hieroglyphs into objects; 2) or to use the needle-ending like a metal nib to dip into a colored ink or liquid or zinc-oxide paste or cinnabar-paste. This possibility is suggested by the use of cinnabar in ancient China to paint into lacquer plates or bowls. Cinnabar or powdered mercury sulphide was the primary colorant lof lacquer vessels. "Known in China during the late Neolithic period (ca. 5000–ca. 2000 B.C.E), lacquer was an important artistic meḍium from the sixth century B.C.E to the second century CE and was often colored with minerals such as carbon (black), orpiment (yellow), and cinnabar (red) and used to paint the surfaces of sculptures and vessels...a red lacquer background is carved with thin lines that are filled with gold, gold powder, or lacquer that has been tinted black, green, or yellow."[182]

The decipherment of the inscription on one of these three gold pendants points to the function of the writing system as a catalogue proclaiming the profession and metalwork competence of the pendant wearer.

I would, therefore, suggest that the three gold pendants with needle-like endings were 'writing' instruments to engrave or paint Harappa Script hieroglyphs.

Fired steatite beads appear to have been extremely important to the Indus people because they were incorporated into exquisite ornaments, such as this "eye bead" made of gold with steatite inlay found in 1995 at Harappa [Harappa Phase].

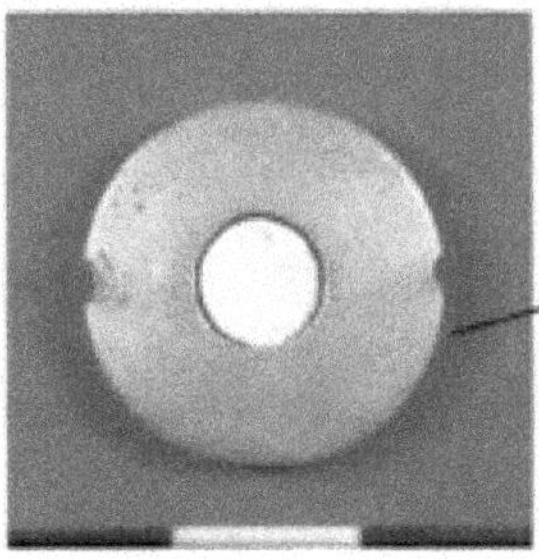

Gold Disc

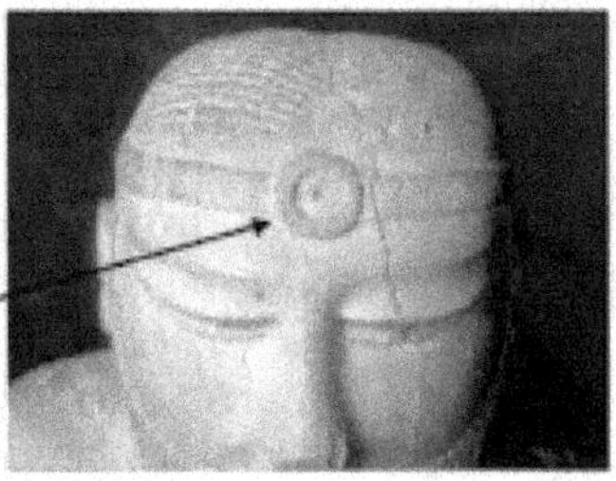

The central ornament worn on the forehead of the famous "priest-king" sculpture from Mohenjo-daro appears to represent an eye bead, possibly made of gold with steatite inlay in the center.

It is possible that the ceramic stoneware bangles (22 discovered in the civilization at Harappa, Mohenjodaro and Balakot) were also used as fillets similar to the 'eye beadś noted by Kenoyer and Meadow. These rings are NOT bangles because of their small size, they were perhaps used as badges tied with bandages on shoulders and foreheads as paTa, 'band' signifying function of importance in the guild. It is likely that such ceramic stoneware bangles or badges or rings were called paTTaDi 'neck ornament', a torc worn by Karnonou (Kernunnos) or hung on the twig horns of the person seated in penance Karnonou (Cernunnos aka *karaNIka* 'helmsman' and kuṭhi 'smelter') on Pillar of Boatmen. कारणी or कारणीक (p. 159) [*kāraṇī or kāraṇīka*] a (कारण S) That causes, conducts, carries on, manages. Applied to the prime minister of a state, the supercargo of a ship &c *kūdī* 'bunch of twigś (Sanskrit) Rebus: *kuṭhi* 'smelter furnace'

Stone bas-relief from the boatmen's guild pillar from Paris

"Ancient Bharata literature has even recorded a breakthrough in zinc extraction in those days. Such process included high temperature distillation that was developed and then applied in future zinc extraction and purification from their metal ore sources. Zinc ores were broken with the use of iron hammers or pestles. Then, such broken ores were again crushed by larger pestles. Then, the ore would have to be thoroughly roasted in order to reduce the levels of sulphur. After which, a high proportion of calcined dolomite was mixed with the crushed and roasted ores. An interesting ingredient in this process is the addition of common salt. This is for the reason that salt would help in the distillation process, thereby, producing soda vapor that assists in amassing calcium and magnesium oxides. This allows zinc vapor to freely flow and increasing zinc yield. This zinc yield was poured on clay containers for heating."

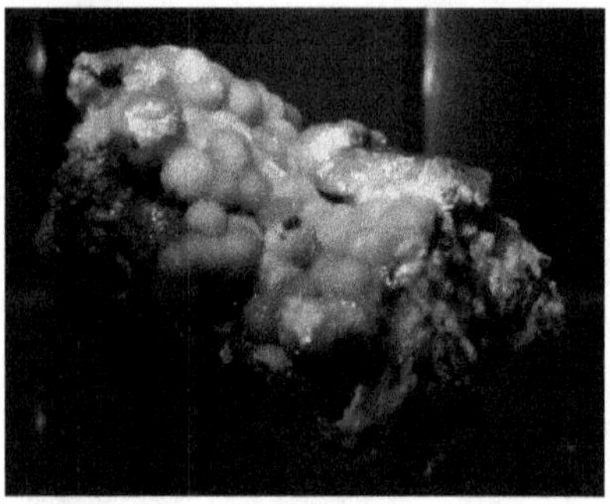

Bright-blue velvety rosasite mass lining a cavity, from 79 mine, Winkelman, Arizona, USA. Photograph taken at the Natural History Museum, London.[183] Rosasite is a carbonate mineral with minor potential for use as a zinc and copper ore. Chemically, it is a copper zinc carbonatehydroxide with a copper to zinc ratio of 3:2, occurring in the secondary oxidation zone of copper-zinc deposits.

Rosasite forms in the oxidation zones of zinc-copper deposits. It typically is found as crusts and botryoidal masses or nodules. Crystals are fibrous and found in tufted aggregates. The color is an attractive bluish green. Rosasite is associated with red limonite and other such colorful minerals as aurichalcite, smithsonite and hemimorphite. Nodules of rosasite certainly add color to what are termed "landscape" specimens.[184]

Example of Rosasite. Minor ore of zinc and copper and as a mineral specimen. Colour: Blue to green. Rosasite forms in the oxidation zones of zinc-copper deposits. It typically is found as crusts and botryoidal masses or nodules. Crystals are fibrous and found in tufted aggregates. The color is an attractive bluish green. Rosasite crystals are harder than aurichalcite; 4 versus 1 - 2 respectively. Rosasite is associated with red limonite and other such colorful minerals as aurichalcite, smithsonite and hemimorphite. Nodules of rosasite certainly add color to what are termed "landscape" specimens.[185]

It will be necessary to test the greenish layers of clay found in the circular platform for the presence of such alloying mineral clays. Annex F presents multiple tablets with same inscription in Harappa leading to the possible identification of the functions served by circular platforms. Is it possible that the working platforms were also used by the smiths to work on their anvils to forge metal artifacts, using portable furnaces?[186]

As of 1927, 558 objects with inscriptions had been found.

Discussing 80 copper tablets found, Mackay notes (p. 398): "The rectangular pieces are of various sizes, ranging from 1.2 by 0.5 in. to 1.5 by 1.0 in. The square pieces, which are rare, average 0.92 by 0.92 in. in size. These tablets vary greatly in thickness, from 0.07 in. to 0.12 in. One especially substantial tablet (HR 4799) measures 0.85 in. square by 0.23 in. thick...On most of the tablets there is the figure of an animal on one side, and on the other three or more signs forming an inscription. The figures and signs were in every case carefully cut with a burin...Below is a list of the animals on the legible tablets with the numbers found, up to the present, of each: elephant (6), antelope (5), hare (5), rhinoceros (4), buffalo(?)(4), short-horned bull (4), human figure (3), goat (2), brahmani bull (2), tiger (2), two-headed animal (2), composite animal (1), monkey (?)(1)...The above list shows that most of the animals that appear on the seals are also represented on the copper tablets...composite animal...It has the hind-quarters of a rhinoceros and the fore-quarters of a leopard or tiger. It has the unicorn's horn, and a manger stands before it. (Pl. CXVIII,2). A very curious animal on two sides of the tablets appears to have the body of an antelope with a head at either end. The fact that more than one example has been found of this animal proves that it is not a vagary of the engraver (Pl. CXVII,3). The tablet bearing the figure of a man dressed in what seems to be a costume of leaves is exceptionally interesting (Pl. CXVII, 16). He is apparently a hunter armed with a bow and arrow...The antelope appears on five of the tablets, represented in a typical attitude with his head turned to look behind him (Pl. CXVII, 1 and 2; Pl. CXVIII,1). This attitude is very common in Elamitic art, especially on the pottery and seals. The position is also well known on both the archaic seals and pottery of Mesopotamia. For the present, the elephant appears to take first place amongst the animals on these copper tablets. An excellent example is seen in Pl. CXVII,11, of which the original was found at a depth of 1 foot below the surface in House XXVI, VS Area...The exceptionally powerful-looking animal with long curling horns (Pl. CXVII, 8 and 12, and Pl. CXVIII, 4 and 6), and with a manger placed in front of it, does not appear on any of the seals. The long tail of the animal with a tuft at the end is carried well in the air, as if the creature were about to charge...The rope pattern on the obverse of Tablet No. 5 in Pl. CXVIII is unique at Mohenjo-daro...The fact that all of the tablets bearing the representation of a hare have the same inscription on the obverse (Pl. CXVII, 5 and 6), and that the animals with long curling horns and long tail also bear the same inscription – different, however, from the inscription on the tablet refers in some way to the animal on the tablet. Of three tablets, each with an elephant engraved upon it, all bear the same inscription (Pl. CXII, 11), and lastly those with the figures of antelopes looking backwards over their shoulders all have the same characters on the reverse (Pl. CXVII, 1 and 2; Pl. CXVIII,1). Some, if not all the animals on the copper tablets were possibly dedicated to certain gods. As on some of the seals, we find a manger placed before certain of them, as, for instance, the unicorn, the rhinoceros, antelope, and Brahmani bull. This suggests that these animals were kept in captivity, and, if so, it is likely to have been for religious purposes; a rhinoceros is obviously quite useless for any domestic purpose. A manger is placed before the composite animal on the tablet illustrated in Pl. CXVIII,2, despite the fact that such an animal could never have existed."[187] (pp. 400-401).

h2219A First side of three-sided tablet

h2219B Second side of three-sided tablet

h2219C Third side of three-sided tablet

The two glyphs which appear on the h2219A example also appear on a seal. "In a street deposit of similar age just inside the wall, a seal was found with two of the same characters as seen on one side of the tablets."

Kalibangan048

Kalibangan 048 Seal

This pictorial motif gets normalized in Harappa Script writing system as a hieroglyph sign: *baraḍo* = spine; backbone (Tulu) Rebus: *baran, bharat* 'mixed alloyś (5 copper, 4 zinc and 1 tin) (Punjabi) Tir. *mar -- kaṇḍḗ* ' back (of the body) '; S. *kaṇḍo* m. ' back ', L. *kaṇḍ f., kaṇḍā* m. ' backbone ', awāṇ. *kaṇḍ,* °*ḍī* ' back *'H. kā̃ṭā m. ' spine ', G. kā̃ṭɔ m., M. kā̃ṭā m.; Pk. kam̐ḍa* -- m. ' backbone '.(CDIAL 2670) Rebus: *kaṇḍ* 'fire-altar' (Santali) The hieroglyph ligature to convey the semantics of 'bone' and rebus reading is: 'four short numeral strokes ligature' |||| Numeral 4: *gaṇḍa* 'four' Rebus: *kanda* 'furnace, fire-altar' (Santali)

Copper tablet (H2000-4498/9889-01) with raised script found in Trench 43[188]

The obvious purpose of such a seal with raised script is to create multiple seal impressions, not unlike the printing demonstrated by the finds of copper tablets by Rick Willis.[189]

Kalibangan 039 Text 8011

gaṇḍá 'rhinoceros' Rebus: *kāṇḍā* 'metalware, tools, pots and pans'

ranku 'liquid measure'; *ranku* 'antelope' Rebus: *ranku* 'tin' (Santali)

kolmo 'sprout' Rebus: *kolimi* 'smithy, forge' *koṭi* 'flag' Rebus: *koḍ* 'workshop' (Detailed Meluhha etyma annexed)

Text 8011 is on a Kalibangan pink terracotta object with a boss on the reverse. Text is on two lines. The field symbol of a rhinoceros looking left and the inscription are in relief indicating that the seal was made from a mould. This is referred to as a 'raised seal'. Fig. 27 in PI. II (p. 803). (Mahadevan, 1977, p.25)

K039 is a seal with raised script. This method of writing script is comparable to the raised script found on a copper molded tablet at Harappa: Copper tablet (H2000-4498/9889-01) with raised script found in Trench 43.

Ras-al-Junayz. Copper seal.

Harappa. Raised script. H94-2198. [After Fig. 4.14 in JM Kenoyer, 1998]. Eight inscribed copper tablets were found at Harappa and all were made with raised script, a technique quite different from the

The inscription on the cast copper tablet is read as: dul 'cast metal', *khōṭa* 'alloy ingot', bharata, 'alloy of coper, pewter, tin'. Hieroglyphs: *dula* 'pair' Rebus: *dul* 'cast metal';

goT 'seed' Rebus: *khōṭa* 'alloy ingot'. खोट (p. 212) [khōṭa] f A mass of metal (unwrought or of old metal melted down); an ingot or wedge. (Marathi) *baraDo* 'spine' Rebus: भरत (p. 603) [*bharata*] n A factitious metal compounded of copper, pewter, tin &c. (Marathi) *karava* 'pot' Rebus: *khārva* 'wealth'; *karba* 'iron'; *karṇaka* 'rim of jar' Rebus: *karṇī* 'supercargo'; *karṇika* 'scribe'.

"For example, the characteristic square steatite seals with animal motifs and short inscriptions begins in late Period 2 as noted above, is found in 3A and continues into Period 3C, but the carving style for both the animal motifs, and the inscriptions shows stylistic changes. The greatest variation and widespread use of such seals appears to be during Period 3B. Small rectangular inscribed tablets made from steatite begin to appear at the beginning of Period 3B and by the end of 3B there is a wide variety of tiny tablets in many different shapes and materials. They were made of fired steatite or of molded terracotta or faience. Some of the steatite tablets were decorated with red pigment and the faience tablets were covered with a thick blue-green glaze. These various forms of inscribed tablets continued on into Period 3C where we also find evidence for copper tablets all bearing the same raised inscription."[190] Kenoyer and Meadow date the Period 3 between c.600 BCE – 1900 BCE(Period 3A c.2600BCE - 2450BCE; Period 3B c.2450BCE – c. 2200BCEl Period 3C c. 2200BCE -1900BCE) This particular inscription on the tablet is one of the most frequently occurring texts in Harappa Script corpora, in particular the hieroglyphs of 'back-hone + rim-of-jar'

gōṭā 'round' Rebus: khōṭa 'ingot' goTa 'laterite, ferrite ore' *DhALako* 'large metal ingot' (Gujarati) *kana, kanac* = corner (Santali); Rebus: *kañcu* = bronze (Telugu). *dula* 'pair' rebus: *dul* 'cast metal' Thus Copper tablet (H2000-4498/9889-01) is deciphered: *dul kañcu DhALako* bronze cast ingot PLUS *bharat* 'alloy of copper, zinc, tin'.

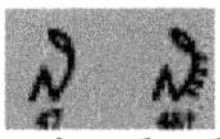

bharaḍo 'spine' backbone (Tulu); Rebus: *bharan* 'to spread or bring out from a kiln' (P.) *baran, bharat* (5 copper, 4 zinc and 1 tin)(P.B.) *baraḍo* = spine; backbone; the back; *baraḍo thābaḍavo* = lit. to strike on the backbone or back; hence, to encourage; *baraḍo bhāre thato* = lit. to have a painful backbone, i.e. to do something which will call for a severe beating (G.lex.) Sign 47 may signify *kaśēru* rebus: metal worker. Sign 48 may signify भरत *bharata* n A factitious metal compounded of copper, pewter, tin &c

A third glyph on these tablets is an oval sign -- like a metal ingot -- and is ligatured with an infixed sloping stroke: *ḍhāḷiyum* = adj. sloping, inclining (G.) The ligatured glyph is read rebus as: *ḍhālako* = a large metal ingot (G.) *ḍhālakī* = a metal heated and poured into a mould; a solid piece of metal; an ingot (G.) The inscription on these tablets is in bas-relief:

h232A
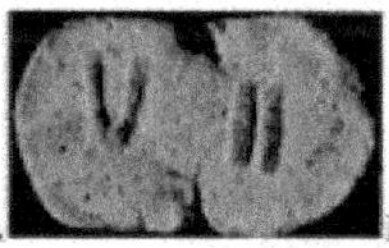
h232B tablet in bas relief

4368 Inscribed object in the shape of a double axe.

h233A
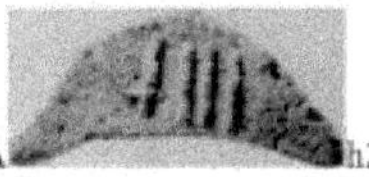
h233B

4387 Tablet in bas-relief. Sickle-shaped. Pict-131: Inscribed object in shape of a crescent?

m1449Act

m1449Bct (obverse of inscription) Incised copper tablet (two sides) Markhor with head turned ba

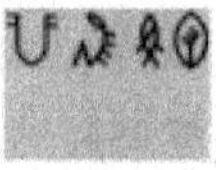
1801

m1450Act

m1450Bct
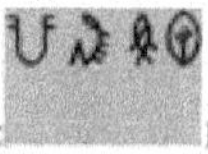
1701

m1452Act

m1452Bct
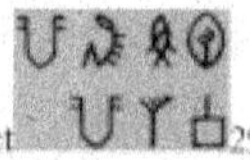
2912

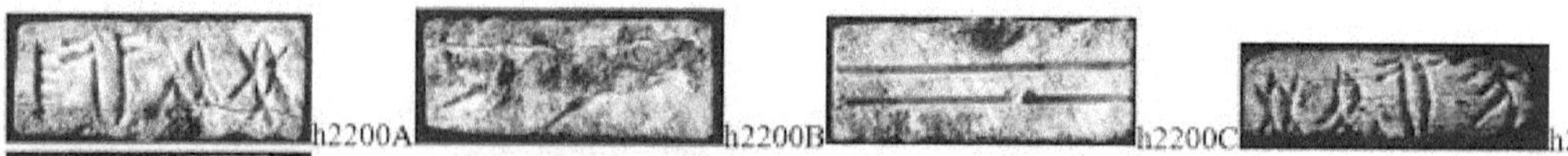
h2200A h2200B h2200C h220

h2201B h2201C

h2028A

h2029A

h2029B

h2029C

h2029D

h2030A

h2030C

h2030D

h2031A

h2031B

h2031C

h2031D

h2023A

h2023B

h2023C

h2024A

h2024B

h2024C

h2025C

h2026A

h2026B

h2026C
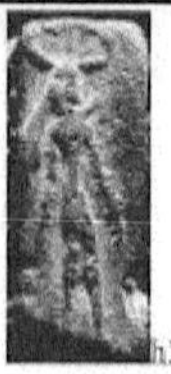
h2026D

h2027A

h2027B

h2027C

h2027D

h2028A

h2028B

h2028C

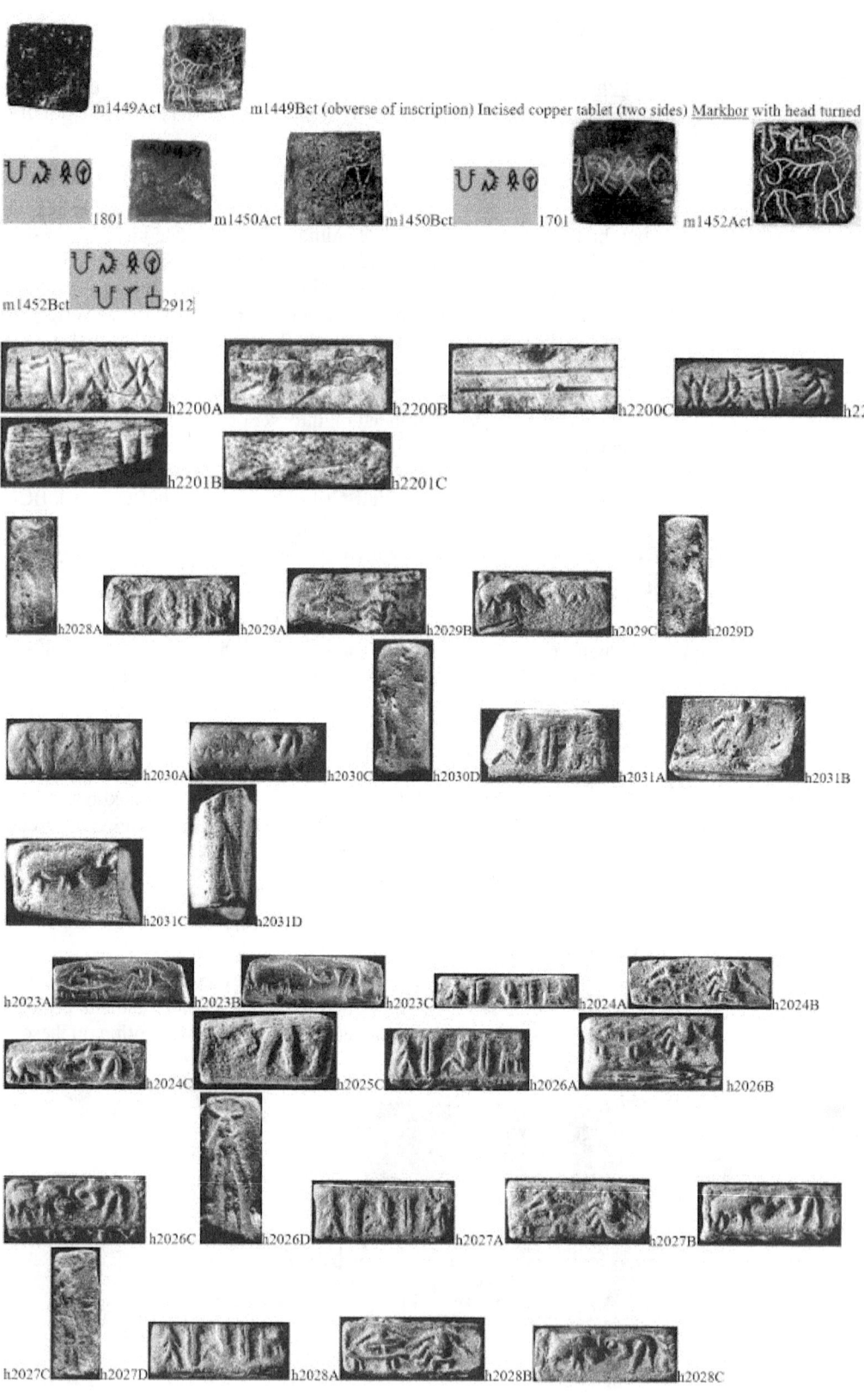

h1997A

h1997B

h1825A h1825B h1826A h1826B

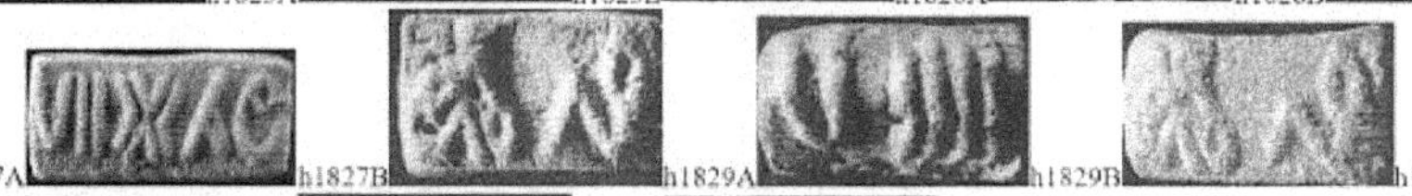
h1827A h1827B h1829A h1829B h1830A

h1830B h1831A h1831B

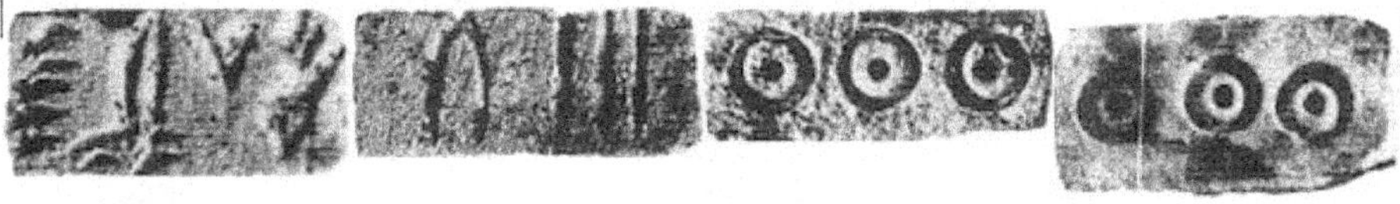
h1344C

h1344A h1344B h1345A h1345B

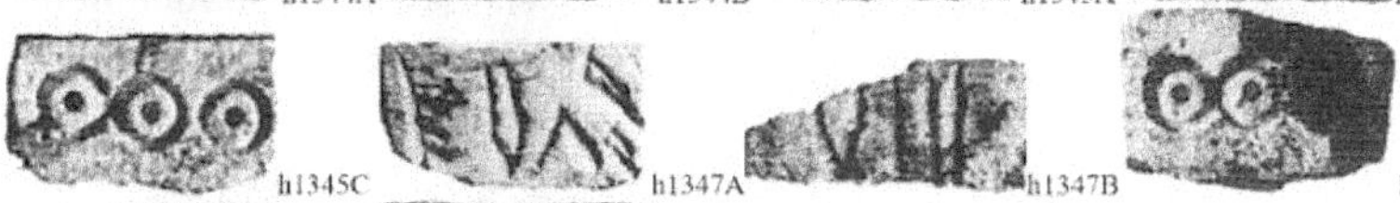
h1345C h1347A h1347B h1347C

h1348A h1348B h1348C

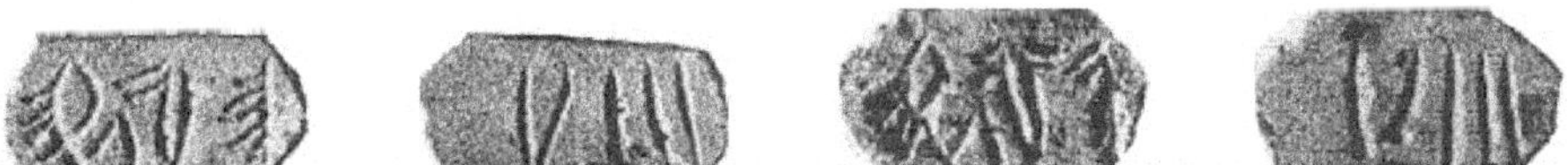
h1302A h1302B h1303A h1303B

h1304A h1304B

h1322B

h1323A h1323B h1324A h1324B h1325A

 h987Ait  h987Bit  h987Cit  4586

 h978Ait  h978Bit  h978Cit  5412

 h979Ait  h979Bit  h979Cit

 h980Ait  h980Bit 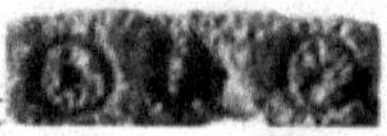 h980Cit

 h981Ait  h981Bit  h981Cit  5415

Hieroglyph of Harappa Script. Dancing-girl on potsherd, Bhirrana. ca 4th millennium BCE

Dancing girl statue. 3rd millennium BCE. Mohenjo-daro. National Museum. Delhi

Glyph: *meḍ* 'to dance' (F.)[reduplicated from *me*-]; me id. (M.) in Remo (Munda)(Source: D. Stampe's Munda etyma) *meṭṭu* to tread, trample, crush under foot, tread or place the foot upon (Te.); meṭṭu step (Ga.); *mettunga* steps (Ga.). *maḍye* to trample, tread (Malt.)(DEDR 5057) మెట్టు (p. 1027) [*meṭṭu*] *meṭṭu*. [Tel.] v. a. &n. To step, walk, tread. అడుగుపెట్టు, నడుచు, త్రొక్కు. "మెల్ల మెల్లన మెట్టుచుదొలగి అల్లనల్లనతలుపులండకు జేరి." BD iv. 1523. To tread on, to trample on. To kick, to thrust with the foot. మెట్టిక *meṭṭika*. n. A step , మెట్టు, సోపానము (Telugu)

Rebus: *meḍ* 'iron' (Mundari. Remo). *bāti* 'wick, lamp, candle' *rebus: vaṭloi* 'brass *baṭa* 'iron' *bhaṭa* 'furnace'. Hem. Des. *koḍiyam* fr. Skt. *kos.t.ha* the inner part] *koḍ.iyum* an earthen cup holding oil and a wick for a light (G.) Rebus: *koTiya* 'dhow, seafaring vessel'. Thus, the hypertext on the Bhirrana potsherd reads: seafaring vessel (cargo) iron ore.

An example of hypertexting on a bas-relief fragment is that of a spinning lady of Susa:

Hieroglyphs of a spinner bas-relief fragment from Susa dated to 8th cent. BCE (now in Louvre Museum) are identified. The Elamite lady spinner bas-relief is a composition of hieroglyphs depicting a guild of wheelwrights or 'smithy of nations' (harosheth hagoyim). The hieroglyphs are read rebus using lexemes of Bharata sprachbund given the archeological evidence of Meluhha settlers in Susa.

Such a *khati* 'spinner' rebus: *khati* 'wheelwright' is shown on a sculptural frieze in Louvre Museum. Louvre Excerpt Fragment of the bas-relief called "The spinner" H 9.3 cm; L 13 cm Sb 2834

Technical description
Bas-relief fragment, called "The Spinner"
Bitumen J. de Morgan excavations Sb 2834 Near Eastern Antiquities Sully wing Ground floor Iran in the Iron Age (14th–mid-6th century BC) and during the Neo-Elamite dynasties

A fragment of a relief 'The spinner' made of Bitumen mastic of Neo-Elamite period (8th cent. BCE - middle of 6th cent. BCE) was found in Susa. This fragment displayed a well-coiffured woman being fanned by an attendant while the woman wearing bangles on both arms -- seated on a stool with feline legs -- held what may be a spinning device before a table with feline legs with a bowl containing a whole fish with six blobs assembled on top of the fish.

Hieroglyphs: curls on hair, fan, feline-legged stools, six round objects, fish, arms with bangles, headband, hair-knot, spindle, circles on scarf.

Hieroroglyph: *aya* 'fish' Rebus: *aya* 'iron' (Gujarati) *ayas* 'metal' (Rigveda)
kola 'tiger' Rebus: *kolle* 'blacksmith' *kol* 'metal, working in iron'; *kolhe* 'smelter' kole.l 'smithy, temple'; *kolimi* 'smithy, forge' Hieroglyph: *bhaṭa* 'six' Rebus: *bhaṭa* 'furnace'.

karttr̥2 m. ' spinner ' MBh. [√kr̥t2]H. kātī f. ' woman who spins thread '; -- Or. *kā̃tiā* ' spinner ' with ã from verb *kā̃tibā* (CDIAL 2861) See: khātrī m. ' member of a caste of Hindu weavers '(Gujarati)(CDIAL 3647) *kātī* 'spinner' Rebus: *khātī* m. ' member of a caste of wheelwrights '(Hindi) *kṣattŕ̥* m. ' carver, distributor ' RV., ' attendant, door-keeper ' AV., ' charioteer ' VS., ' son of a female slave ' lex. [√kṣad]Pa. khattar -- m. ' attendant, charioteer ' (CDIAL 3647)

bīcā, bīcī. vījana n. ' fanning ' Kāv., ' fan ' Bhpr. 2. *vyajana* -- n. ' fan ' Mn (CDIAL 12043) Rebus: *bica* 'haematite, ferrite ore'.

Harappa Scripthieroglyphs on Warka Vase

Hieroglyph: eruvai 'European reed' European bamboo reed. See கொறுக்கச்சி. (குறிஞ்சிப். 68, உரை.) Species of Cyperus. See பஞ்சாய்க்கோரை.

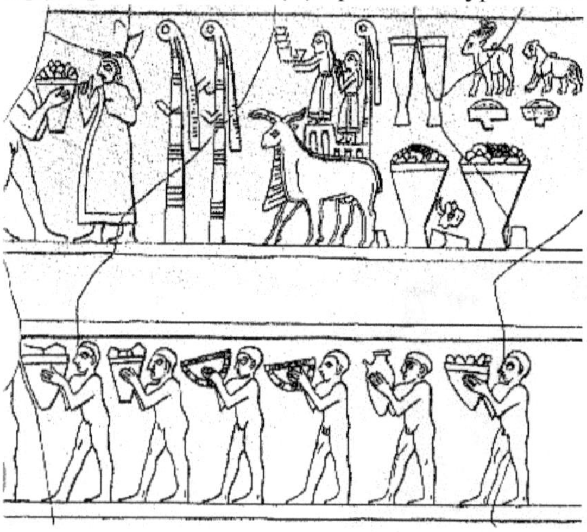

எருவை செருவிளை மணிப்பூங் கருவிளை (குறிஞ்சிப். 68). Straight sedge tuber; கோரைக்கிழங்கு. மட் பனை யெருவைதொட்டி (தைலவ. தைல. 94).

Rebus: eruva 'copper' எருவை eruvai Copper; செம்பு. எருவை யுருக்கினா லன்ன குருதி (கம்பரா. கும்பக. 248). dhatu 'scarf' rebus: dhatu 'minerals'

kola 'tiger' rebus: *kol* 'metal, working in iron'

mēl̠h (Brahui), mṛēka (Telugu) 'goat' rebus: *milakkhu* 'copper'

miṇḍāl 'markhor' (Tōrwālī) *meḍho* a ram, a sheep (Gujarati)(CDIAL 10120) Rebus: *mẽṛhẽt, meḍ* 'iron' *meḍ* 'copper' (Slavic languages)

Bogazkoy seal impression with 'twisted rope' hieroglyph (ca. 18th cent. BCE) *dhAI* ‘strand’ rebus: *dhAtu* ‘mineral’ *tri-dhAtu* ‘three strandś rebus: three minerals’ *eru*vai ‘kite’ rebus: *eruvai* ‘copper’ *khambhaṛā* 'fish fin' *khamba* ‘wing’ rebus: *kammaṭa* ‘mint, coiner, coinage’ *dula* ‘two’ rebus: *dul* ‘metal casting’.

Hittite, seal, bird, Boğazköy, 1800 BCE, Museum of Anatolian Civilisations, Ankara *eruvai* ‘kite’ rebus: *eruvai* ‘copper’ *khambhaṛā* 'fish fin' *khamba* ‘wing’ rebus: *kammaṭa* ‘mint, coiner, coinage’ *dula* ‘two’ rebus: *dul* ‘metal casting’. mēḍha 'the polar star'. Rebus: *mẽṛhẽt, meḍ* 'iron' (Santali.Ho.Munda) *meḍ* ‘copper’ (Slavic languages).

Harappa Script data archive, knowledge system inscriptions signify sphalerite (zinc-ferrite) alloys191

An indication of the knowledge system linking to sphalerite as an alloy of zinc and iron ores comes from the fact that some inscriptions signify 'svastika' and 'endless knot' hieroglyphs together and in sequence. Hieroglyph '*svastika*' signifies zinc. Hieroglyph 'endless knot' signifies 'iron'. It also signifies *dhAtu* 'ore, mineral'.

See: Two Ravi phase settlements mentioned by JEM Kenoyer of Rajanpur and Hissaka located approx. 75 to 83 kms. northeast of Harappa on the opposite bank of the Ravi river.

A tablet surface find from Rajanpur (site first reported by Muhammad Hassan during the Punjab Survey of 1986) 70 km. northeast of Harappa is a revelation of a Bronze Age knowledge system. It signifies the alloying and metalcasting by Meluhha artisans using zinc and iron ores (*bici* 'haematite, stone ore') and a large portable furnace: *kanga.*

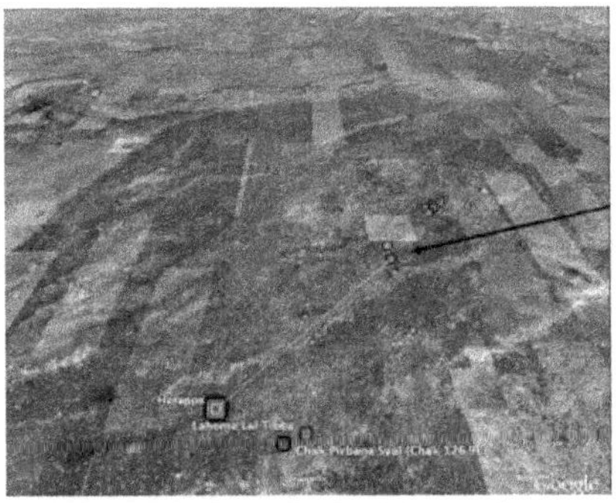

Rajanpur, 77 km. northeast of Harappa, on west bank of Ravi river.

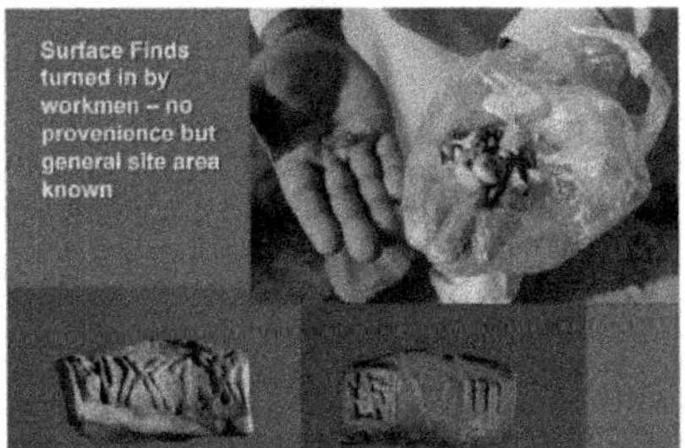

Rajanpur surface find tablet. Rajanpur is 70 km. northeast of Harappa. (Courtesy: Kenoyer, JEM)

Rajanpur Tablet Side A *sattva* 'svastika' rebus: *sattva, jasta* 'zinc' *baṭa* 'rimless pot'

rebus: *bhaṭa* 'furnace' *baṭa* 'iron' *gaṇḍa* 'four' Rebus: *khaṇḍa* 'implements’. Alternative: *kolmo* 'three' rebus: *kolimi* 'smithy, forge'. Thus, zinc and iron implements (smithy)

Rajanpur Tablet Side B *khāreḍo* = a currycomb (Gujarati) खरारा [*khārārā*] m (H) A currycomb. *kangsi* ‘comb’ rebus: *kamsa* ‘bronze’ 2 Currying a horse. (Marathi) Rebus: 1. करडा [*karaḍā*] Hard alloy. *khārādī* ' turner' (Gujarati) *karṇaka, kanka* 'rim of jar'; rebus: *karṇī* 'Supercargo' *karṇika* 'scribe, account' *dATu* 'crosś rebus: *dhatu* 'mineral'

Crook मेंढा [*mēṇḍhā*] A crook or curved end (of a stick) Rebus: *meḍ* 'iron' Scorpion *bica* 'scorpion' Rebus: *bica* 'stone ore, haematite ferriteore' Thus, a turner working as supercargo (responsible for shipment of) minerals, ferrite haematite ore. Thus, both sides of Rajanpur tablet show zinc and iron haematite ore metalwork implements.

Hieroglyphs and decipherment:

Four Linear strokes *gaṇḍa* 'four' Rebus: *khaṇḍa* 'implements
Rimless pot *baṭa* 'rimless pot' Rebus: *baṭa* 'iron' *bhaṭa* 'furnace'
svastika *sattva* 'svastika glyph' Rebus: *sattva, jasta* 'zinc'

Scorpion *bica* 'scorpion' Rebus: *bica* 'stone ore' *bica* 'haematite (iron ore)'
Crook मेंढा [*mēṇḍhā*] A crook or curved end (of a stick) Rebus: *meḍ* 'iron'
Crossing *dATu* 'crosś Rebus: *dhatu* 'mineral'
Rim of jar *karṇika* 'rim of jar' Rebus: *karṇī* 'supercargo' *karṇika* 'scribe'
Comb कंकवा (p. 123) [*kaṅkavā*] m A sort of comb. See कंगवा. कोंगें (p. 180) [*kōṅgēṃ*] n A long sort of honeycomb.Rebus: *kanga* 'portable furnace' Rebus: *kangar* 'large brazier': **kāṅgārikā* 'poor or small brazier'. Rebus: kamsa 'bronze'

The tablet is thus a metalwork catalog: alloy implements with zinc, haematite, iron ore, portable furnace supercargo. A documentation of the metallurgical competence of the artisan (guild) and an advancement in the knowledge systems conveyed by Harappa Script inscriptions signifying knowledge of a mineral which was zinc iron sulfide. This mineral is called sphalerite ((Zn,Fe S) is a mineral -- zinc iron sulfide-- that is the chief ore of zinc. It consists largely of zinc sulfide in crystalline form but almost always contains variable iron.

Sphalerite on dolomite from the Tri-State District, Jasper County, Missouri, US Spelter is a solder or other alloy in which zinc is the main constituent. Spelter is impure zinc, usually containing

about 3 per cent of lead and other impurities. Spelter is generally in the form of ingots cast in slabs.

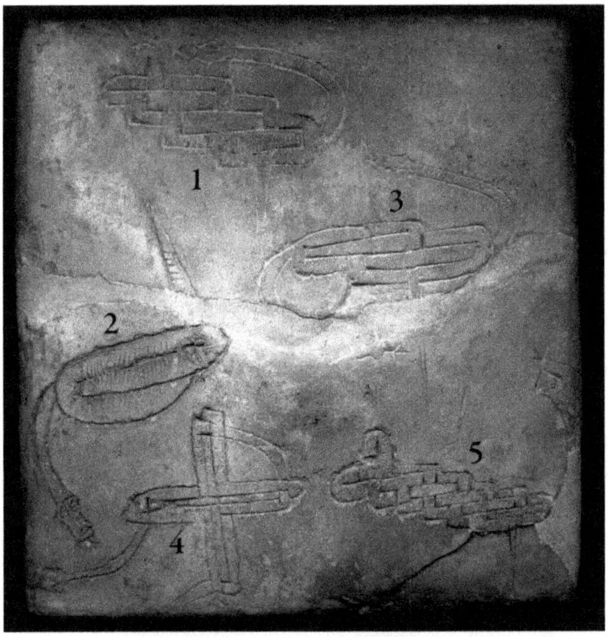

பித்தளை *pittaḷai, n.* < *pittalā.* [K. *hittaḷē.*] Brass, Aurichalcum; செம்பும் நாகமுங் கலந்த உலோகவகை. ஈயம் செம்பிரும் பிரசித மென்பவும் புணர்ப்பாற் றோயும் பித்தளை (திருவிளை. இரசவாத. 23). spelter zinc XVII; zinc alloy XIX. corr. to OF. espeautre, MDu. speauter (Du. spiauter), LG. spialter; rel. to PEWTER. Thus, spelter may relate to either pewter or to *pital. pittala2* n. ' brass ' lex. [*pītala* -- 2 n. ' brass ' lex. -- Cf. *pītala* -- *Pk. pittala* -- n. ' brass '; P. *pittal* m. (→ *S. pitalu m.), Ku. pĩtal, N. A. B. pital, Or. pitaḷa, Bi. Bhoj. pītar, H. pītal m., G. pĩtaḷ n., M. pitaḷ n. -- Deriv.: P. pitlī, °līā ' brazen '; A. pitalīyā ' made of brass '; -- Ku. pitlaiṇo* ' tasting of brass, rather bitter '; H. *pitrāī* f. ' verdigris '*paittala* ; *pittalagandha* -- .Addenda: *pittala* -- 2: S.kcch. *pittar* m. ' brass ', WPah.kṭg. *pitəḷ* m., J. *pitḷ* m.(CDIAL 8184) H. *pitarāĩdh* f. ' smell or taste of brass '

Soldering at a red heat by means of spelter is calledbrazing.."Spelter, while sometimes used merely as a synonym for zinc, is often used to identify a zinc alloy. In this sense it might be an alloy of equal parts copper and zinc, i.e. a brass, used for hard soldering and brazing, or as an alloy, containing lead,..Zinc ingots formed by smelting might also be termed spelter"

.https://en.wikipedia.org/wiki/SpelterShuruppak tablet knots, hooded snake, are allographs of trefoils deciphered as metalwork catalogues. Trefoils are cross-section orthographic signifiers of *dhāī* 'strands of rope' rebus: *dhāv* 'a partic. soft redstone; *dhātu* 'mineral ore'. Reverse of Sumerian tablet VAT 09130 EDIIIA ca. 2600-2500 BCE Shuruppak (mod. Fara).[192]

Hagan Brunke interprets this diagram as a set of knots. "While the drawings 1, 2, 4, and 5 show one knotted snake each, entangled in itself (i.e., a one-component knot), there are two snakes entangled with each other (i.e., a two-component knot) in drawing 3. "Hagan Brunke, Embedded structures: two Mesopotamian examples.[193]

An alternative interpretation is possible in the context of metalwork signified on Harappa Script Corpora using 'endless knot' hieroglyph-multiplexes. Interactions of Meluhha artisans and Sumer are well attested archaeologically.

Strands of rope or entangled strings are displayed as hieroglyph-multiplexes on a number of inscriptions of Harappa Script Corpora. All these inscriptions have been deciphered as metalwork catalogues.

Trefoil is a set of three cross sections of three strands. This is read as tri-dhātu 'three-fold'. Rebus: tri-dhāv 'three soft red stone mineral ores'.

Creating the knotted structures of strings as 'endless knot' motifs is explained by the gloss: मेढा [*mēḍhā*] A twist or tangle arising in thread or cord, a curl or snarl (Marathi). Rebus: *meḍ* 'iron, copper' (Munda. Slavic) *mẽṛhẽt, meḍ* 'iron' (Munda).

The + hieroglyph on Shuruppak tablet knots set signifies a fire-altar as do similar hieroglyphs on Harappa Script Corpora. The gloss is: kanda 'fire-altar'.

The 'snake' hieroglyph on Shuruppak tablet knots set signifies *kulā* 'hood of snake' Rebus: *kolle* 'blacksmith'; *kolhe* 'smelter', kol 'metal, working in iron;'.

dhāī wisp of fibers added to a rope (Sindhi) Rebus: *dhātu* 'mineral ore' (Samskritam) *dhāū, dhāv* m.f. 'a partic. soft red stone' (whence *dhā̆vaḍ* m. ' a caste of iron -- smelters ', *dhāvḍī* 'composed of or relating to iron'(Marathi) धवड [*dhavaḍa*] m (Or धावड) A class or an individual of it. They are smelters of iron. धावड [*dhāvaḍa*] m A class or an individual of it. They are smelters of iron. धावडी [*dhāvaḍī*] a Relating to the class धावड. Hence 2 Composed of or relating to iron. (Marathi.Molesworth)

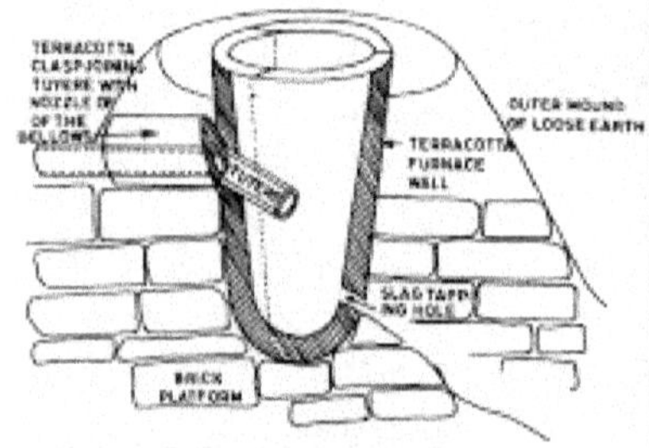

Assembled smelting furnaces, copper: Singhbum, Aravalli; zinc: Zawarmala.194

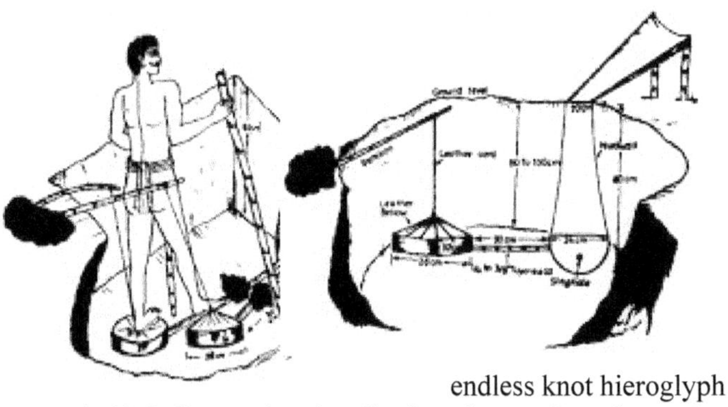

Rojdi. Ax-head or knife of copper, 17.4 cm. long (After Possehl and Raval 1989: 162, fig. 77. The

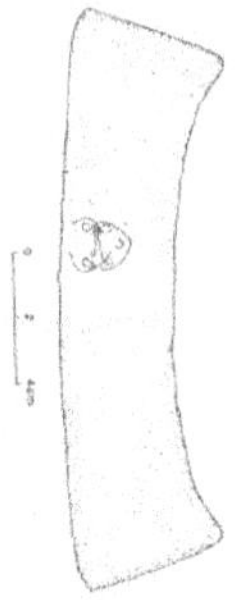

endless knot hieroglyph on the copper knife indicates that the alloying element is: red ore of copper: *meḍ* 'copper', *dhāu* 'metal'.

In Harappa Script Corpora, 'endless knot' hieroglyph can be read with two hieroglyph components: 1. strand of rope or string; 2. twist: *dām* 'rope, string' rebus: *dhāu* 'ore' rebus: मेढा [*mēḍhā*] A twist or tangle arising in thread or cord, a curl or snarl (Marathi). Rebus: *meḍ* 'iron, copper' (Munda. Slavic) *mẽṛhẽt, meḍ* 'iron' (Munda).

Dotted-circle and trefoil hieroglyphs on the shawl of the statue of Mohenjo-daro priest are interpreted as orthographic signifiers, respectively, of: 1. single strand of string or rope; 2. three strands of string or rope. The glosses these hieroglyphs signify are, respectively: 1. Sindhi *dhāī* f. ' wisp of fibres added from time to time to a rope that is being twisted ', Lahnda *dhāī̃* id.; 2. *tridhā́tu* -- ' threefold ' (RigVeda).

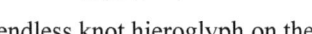

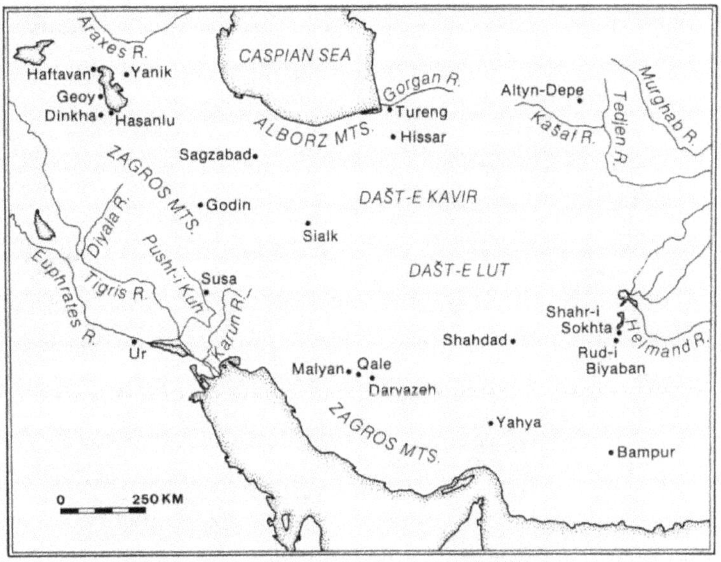

Figure 29. Bronze Age sites in Iran and Afghanistan

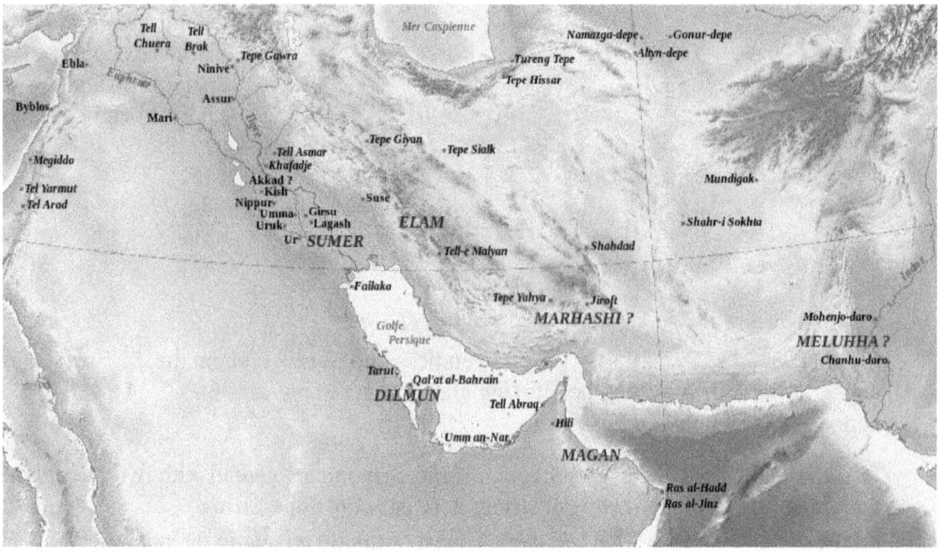

Map of bronze age sites.[195] Meluhha, Magan, Dilmun, Marhashi, Elam, Sumer

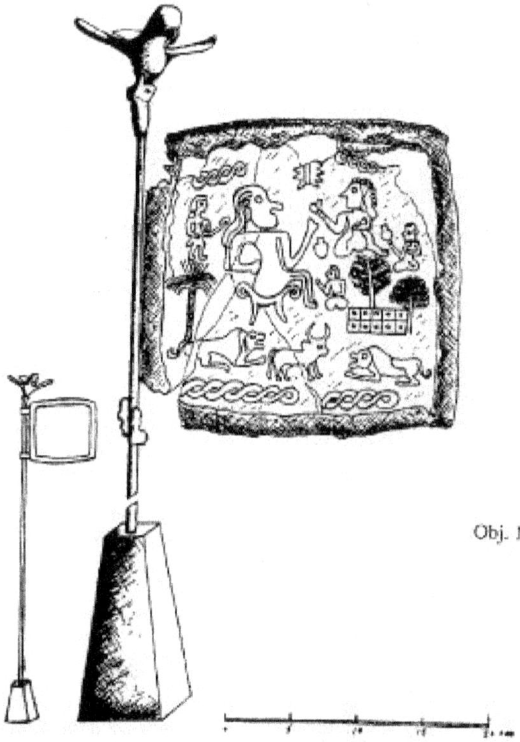

Obj. No. 1049

Shahdad standard. 23.4 in 23.4 centimetres in size, mounted on a 128-centimeter metal axle

Oldest standard in the world. Shahdad standard, 2400 BCE (Prof. Mahmoud Rexa Maheri, Prof. Dept. of Civil Engineering, Shiraz University, dates this to ca. 3000 BCE Oct. 15, 2015 "Following an archeological survey of the South-East Iran in 1930's by Sir Auriel Stein, in 1960's and 1970's a number of archeological expeditions spent a few seasons digging at different locations through theKerman province. Of these, three teams are worthy of mention; one team from Harvard University lead by Professor Lamberg-Karlovsky focused on different layers of the 7000 years old Tape-Yahya at Sogan valley; another team from Illinois University lead by Professor Joseph Caldwell worked on the remains of Tal-i-Iblis, another 7000 years old settlement and a third team by Iranian Department of Archaeology, lead by Mr Hakemi, dug the rich graveyards of the 6000 years old Shahdad near the great Lut desert. The wealth of discoveries though great, went almost unnoticed by the public in the pursuant academic research in the form of Doctorate theses and expedition reports and scientific journal papers. Little attempt was also made to correlate the findings at different sites."[196]

Shahdad standard is a Meluhha (mleccha) metalware catalog describing the repertoire of a smithy in Shahdad, Marhashi:

pajhaṛ 'kite'. Rebus: *pasra* 'smithy' (Santali)

Three pots are shown of three sizes in the context of kneeling adorants seated in front of the person seated on a stool. *meṇḍā* 'kneeling position' (Gondi) Rebus: *meḍ* 'iron' (Munda) *kōla* = woman (Nahali) Rebus: *kol* 'furnace, forge' (Kuwi) *kol* 'alloy of five metals, pañcaloha' (Tamil) *kol* 'metal, working in iron' (Tamil)

kaṇḍō a stool. Malt. *kanḍo* stool, seat. (DEDR 1179) Rebus: *kaṇḍ* = a furnace, altar (Santali) *khaṇḍa* 'implements'.

tāḷa 'palmyra palm' rebus: Rebus: *ḍhāḷako* = a large ingot (G.) ḍhāḷakī = a metal heated and poured into a mould; a solid piece of metal; an ingot (G.) If the date palm denotes *tamar* (Hebrew language), 'palm tree, date palm' the rebus reading would be: *tam(b)ra,* 'copper' (Pkt.)

kaṇḍ kan-ka 'rim of jar' (Santali). *kanka* 'rim (of jar, *kaṇḍ*)' (Santali) *kárṇa*— m. 'ear, handle of a vessel' RV., 'end, tip (?)' RV. ii 34, 3. [Cf. **kāra*—6] Pa. *kaṇṇa*— m. 'ear, angle, tip' (CDIAL 2830). Rebus: 'scribe'. Pk. *kaṁḍa* -- m. ' piece, fragment '; -- Deriv. Pk. *kaṁḍārēi* ' scrapes, engraves'; M. *kā̃ḍārṇẽ, karā̃ḍṇẽ* ' to gnaw ', *kā̃ḍārṇẽ* n. ' jeweller's hammer, barber's nail -- parer '. (CDIAL 2683) कंडारणें [*kaṇḍāraṇēṃ*] n An instrument of goldsmiths, the iron spike which is hammered upon plates in reducing them to shape (Marathi) khanaka m. one who digs , digger , excavator MBh. iii , 640 R. ; a miner L. ; a house-breaker , thief L. ; a rat L. ; N. of a friend of Vidura MBh. i , 5798 f. ; (%{I}) f. a female digger or excavator Pāṇ. 3-1 , 145 Pat. ; iv , 1 , 41 Ka1s3.

kaṇḍ 'jar' (Santali) Rebus: *kāḍ* 'stone'. Ga. (Oll.) *kanḍ,* (S.) *kanḍu* (pl. *kanḍkil*) stone (DEDR 1298). *maypoṇḍi kanḍ* whetstone; (Ga.)(DEDR 4628). (खडा) Pebbles or small stones: also stones broken up (as for a road), metal. खडा [*khaḍā*] m A small stone, a pebble. Rebus: *kaṇḍ* = a furnace, altar (Santali)

kul 'tiger' (Santali); *kōlu* id. (Te.) *kōlupuli* = Bengal tiger (Te.) *krōṣṭŕ̥* ' crying ' BhP., m. ' jackal ' RV. = *krṓṣṭu* -- m. Pāṇ. [√kruś] Pa. *koṭṭhu* -- , °*uka* -- and *kotthu* -- , °*uka* -- m. ' jackal ', Pk. *koṭṭhu* -- m.; Si. *koṭa* ' jackal ', *koṭiya* ' leopard ' GS 42; -- Pk. *kolhuya* -- , *kulha* -- m. ' jackal ' < **kōḍhu* -- ; H. *kolhā,* °*lā* m. ' jackal ', adj. ' crafty '; G. *kohlũ,* °*lũ* n. ' jackal ', M. *kolhā,* °*lā* m. (CDIAL 3615). कोल्हा [kōlhā] कोल्हें [kōlhēṃ] A jackal (Marathi) Rebus: *kol* 'furnace, forge' (Kuwi) *kol* 'alloy of five metals, pañcaloha' (Ta.)

पोळ *pōḷa*, 'zebu' rebus: पोळ *pōḷa*, 'magnetite, ferrite ore'

adar ḍangra 'zebu or humped bull'; *ḍangar* 'bull' Rebus: *adar ḍhangar* 'native metal-smith'. Rebus: *ḍangar* 'blacksmith'; *aduru* native metal (Kannada). Tu. *ajirda karba* very hard iron (DEDR 192). *aduru* =*gaṇiyinda tegadu karagade iruva aduru* = ore taken from the mine and not subjected to melting in a furnace (Ka. *Siddhānti Subrahmaṇya śastri's New interpretation of the Amarakośa*, Bangalore, Vicaradarpana Press, 1872, p. 330) *aduru* 'native metal' (Kannada); *ḍhangar* 'blacksmith' (Hindi)

kuṭi 'tree'. Rebus: *kuṭhi* 'smelter' (Santali). The two trees are shown ligatured to a rectangle with ten square divisions and a dot in each square. The dot may denote an ingot in a furnace mould.

Glyph of rectangle with divisions: *baṭai* = to divide, share (Santali) [Note the glyphs of nine rectangles divided.] Rebus: *bhaṭa* = an oven, kiln, furnace (Santali) *ḍāḷ*= a branch of a tree (G.) Rebus: *ḍhāḷako* = a large ingot (G.) ḍhāḷakī = a metal heated and poured into a mould; a solid piece of metal; an ingot (G.)

Three sets of entwined 'glyphs (like twisted ropes) are shown around the entire narrative of the Shahdad standard.

meṛhao = v.a.m. entwine itself; wind round, wrap round roll up (Santali); *maṛhnā* cover, encase (Hindi) (Santali.Bodding) Rebus: *meḍ* 'iron' (Mu. Ho.) *meṛed-bica* = iron stone ore, in contrast to *bali-bica*, iron sand ore (Munda) *mẽṛhẽt* 'iron'; *mẽṛhẽt icena* 'the iron is rusty'; *mẽṛhẽt khaṇḍa* 'iron implements (Santali) meḍ. (Ho.)(Santali.Bodding) *meṛed, mṛed, mṛd* iron; *enga meṛed* soft iron; *sanḍi meṛed* hard iron; *ispāt meṛed* steel; *dul meṛed* cast iron; i *meṛed* rusty iron, also the iron of which weights are cast; bica meṛed iron extracted from stone ore; bali meṛed iron extracted from sand ore (Mu.)

měď (copper)(Czech) *mid' (copper, cuprum, orichalc)(Ukrainian) meḍ' (copper, cuprum, Cu), meḍnyy (copper, cupreous, brassy, brazen, brass), omeḍnyat' (copper, coppering), sul'fatmeḍi (Copper), politseyskiy (policeman, constable, peeler, policemen, redcap), pokryvat' meḍ'yu (copper), payal'nik (soldering iron, copper, soldering pen, soldering-iron), meḍnyy kotel (copper), meḍno-krasnyy (copper), meḍnaya moneta (copper). медь (copper, cuprum, Cu), медный (copper, cupreous, brassy, brazen, brass), омеднять (copper, coppering), Сульфатмеди (Copper), полицейский (policeman, constable, peeler, policemen, redcap), покрывать медью (copper), паяльник (soldering iron, copper, soldering pen, soldering-iron), медный котел (copper), медно-красный (copper), медная монета* (copper).(Russian)

Soap stone bowl, Shahdad, 3000 BC Clay figurine, Shahdad, 3rd Millennia BCE

A drummer, in the context of hieroglyphs of tumblers on Seal m1406 has been deciphered: *mēd*, 'boatman, one who plays drums at ceremonies' Rebus: *mẽṛhẽt*, meḍ 'iron (metal)'Alternative: *dhollu* 'drummer'

(Western Pahari) *dolutsu* 'tumble' Rebus: *dul* 'cast metal'.

karaḍa 'double-drum' Rebus: *karaḍa* 'hard alloy'.

mẽṛhẽt, meḍ 'iron (metal)' and a cognate word,मृदु *mṛdu* 'iron' (Samskritam) is signified by a number of hieroglyphs मेढा [*mēḍhā*] curls of hair on cylinder seals; मेढा [*mēḍhā*]twist (rope) on a Bogazkoy seal; मेढ (p. 662) [*mēḍha*]

meḍha 'polar star' Rebus: *mẽṛhẽt, meḍ* 'iron' (Mu.Ho.) PLUS *kuṭi* 'water-carrier' (Telugu); Rebus: *kuṭhi* 'smelter furnace' (Santali) *kuṛī f. 'fireplace' (H.); krvṛI f. 'granary (WPah.); kuṛī, kuṛo house, building'(Ku.)(*CDIAL 3232) kuṭi 'hut made of boughs' (Skt.) *guḍi* temple (Telugu) A comparable glyptic representation is provided in a Gadd seal found in an interaction area of the Persian Gulf. Gadd notes that the 'water-carrier' seal is is an unmistakable example of an 'hieroglyphic' seal. Seal impression, Ur (Upenn; U.16747); [After Edith Porada, 1971, Remarks on seals found in the Gulf States. Artibus Asiae 33 (4): 331-7: pl.9, fig.5]; water carrier with a skin (or pot?) hung on each end of the yoke across his shoulders and another one below the crook of his left arm; the vessel on the right end of his yoke is over a receptacle for the water; a star on either side of the head (denoting supernatural?). The whole object is enclosed by 'parenthesis' marks. The parenthesis is perhaps a way of splitting of the ellipse (Hunter, G.R., *JRAS*, 1932, 476).

Gadd has demonstrated how an ellipse may be broken into parenthesis marks contituting hieroglyph component pair. His insight is that an ellipse split into parenthesis of two curved lines ( ) signifies hieroglyph writing. I suggest that the hieroglyph components signify the orthography which matches an 'ingot' formation -- a four-cornered ellipse a little pointed at each end.

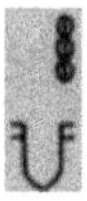

The polar star. on Water-carrier seal impression, Ur (Upenn; U.16747.

m1406 Hieroglyphs: thread of three stands + drummer + tumblers

dhollu 'drummer' (Western Pahari) *dolutsu* 'tumble' Rebus: *dul* 'cast metal'

karaḍa 'double-drum' Rebus: *karaḍa* 'hard alloy'.
dhAtu, dhAv 'strands of rope' Rebus: *dhAtu* 'mineral, metal, ore'

Kalibangan seal. k020 Text 8047: Hieroglyphs: thread of three strands + water-carrier + one-horned young bull. *kuṭi* 'water-carrier' Rebus: *kuṭhi* 'smelter'. *dhAv* 'strands of rope' rebus: d*hAv* 'element, ore'; *dhAtu* id.

kõdā खोंड *khōṇḍa]* m A young bull, a bullcalf. (Marathi) Rebus 1: *kọṇḍu or konḍu* । कुण्डम् m. a hole dug in the ground for receiving consecrated fire (Kashmiri) Rebus 2: *A. kundār, B. kũdār, °ri, Or. kundāru; H. kũderā* m. ' one who works a lathe, one who scrapes ', *°rī f., kũdernā* ' to scrape, plane, round on a lathe '(CDIAL 3297).

The broken portion of the seal should have shown a 'standard device'.

Hieroglyph: *sãghāṛɔ* 'lathe'.(Gujarati. Desi)) Purport of Harappa Script corpora. Rebus: Vajra Sanghāta 'binding together': Mixture of 8 lead, 2 bell-metal, 1 iron rust constitute adamantine glue. *sangāṭh* संगाठ् । सामग्री m. (sg. dat. *sangāṭas* संगाटस्), a collection (of implements, tools, materials, for any object), apparatus, furniture, a collection of the things wanted on a journey, luggage, and so on. -- karun -- करुन् । सामग्रीसंग्रहः m.inf. to collect the ab. (L.V. 17)(Kashmiri). सं-ग्रह *saṁgraha* 'a guardian , ruler , manager , arranger' R. BhP.

Examples of acrobats as hieroglyphs:

A set of tumblers (sometimes accompanied by a drummer as on m1406), or persons tossed by the horns of a buffalo is a definitive hieroglyph-multiplex on Harappa Script Corpora as seen from the following examples:

Mehrgarh. Terracotta circular button seal.[197] A humped bull (water buffalo?) and abstract forms (one of which is like a human body) around the bull. The human body is tossed from the horns of the bovine. Meluhha lexis. Deciphered 5 Harappa Script inscriptions with drummer-tumbler hieroglyphs: मृदु mṛdu, mẽṛhẽt, meḍ 'metal' *sangāṭas* संगाटस् 'collection of implements, tools'

- Five inscriptions from Harappa Script Corpora with hieroglyphs of drummer-tumbler are deciphered as metal-work/-implements from smelter/smithy/forge.

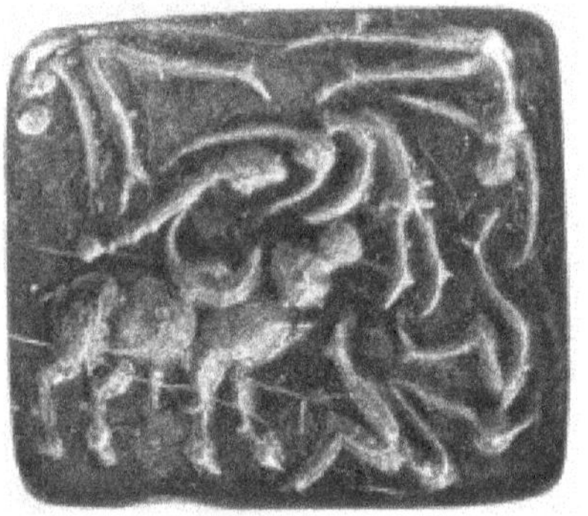

Together, the five selected inscriptions from Harappa Script Corpora signify mẽṛhẽt, meḍ 'iron or copper (metal)' *sangāṭas* संगाटस् 'collection of implements, tools' from smeter/smithy/forge. The context is definitive: affirming Harappa Script Corpora as catalogus catalogorum of metalwork.

The deciphered words which signify hieroglyphs and rebus metalwork are from Meluhha lexis.

The decipherment validates the identification of the lingua franca of the Sarasvati-Sindhu civilization as Meluhha (mleccha or spoken form of Prakritam) of Bharata sprachbund. This is consistent with the identification in an Akkadian cuneiform text on a cylinder seal of Shu-ilishu who is described as a translator of 'Meluhha language'.[198]

Rebus readings of hieroglyphs: '1. arrow, 2. jag/notch, 3. buffalo, 4. acrobatics:

m0312 Persons vaulting over a water buffalo. The water buffalo tosses a person on its horns. Four or five bodies surround the animal. Rounded edges indicate frequent use to create clay seal impressions.

Impression of a steatite stamp seal (2300-1700 BCE) with a water-buffalo and acrobats. Buffalo attack or bull-leaping scene, Banawali (after UMESAO 2000:88, cat. no. 335). A figure is impaled on the horns of the buffalo; a woman acrobat wearing bangles on both arms and a long braid flowing from the head, leaps over the buffalo bull. The action narrative is presented in five frames of the acrobat getting tossed by the horns, jumping and falling down. Two Harappa Script glyphs are written in front of the buffalo. (ASI BNL 5683).

Rebus readings of hieroglyphs: '1. arrow, 2. jag/notch, 3. buffalo, 4.acrobaticś:

Mohenjodaro seal m0312 depicts people jumping over a water buffalo. The action represented is *khamd.a, khamd.ao* = to gambol, to sport (Santali) Rebus: *kammat.a* 'mint' (Te.)

1. *kāṇḍa* 'arrow' (Skt.) H. *kā̃ḍerā* m. ' a caste of bow -- and arrow -- makers (CDIAL 3024). Or. *kāṇḍa, kā̃ṛ* 'stalk, arrow '(CDIAL 3023). *ayaskāṇḍa* 'a quantity of iron, excellent iron' (Pāṇ.gaṇ)

2. खांडा [*khāṇḍā*] m A jag, notch, or indentation (as upon the edge of a tool or weapon). (Marathi) Rebus: *khāṇḍā* 'tools, pots and pans, metal-ware'.

3. *rāngo* 'water buffalo bull' (Ku.N.)(CDIAL 10559)

Rebus: *rango* 'pewter'. *ranga, rang* pewter is an alloy of tin, lead, and antimony (anjana) (Santali).

4. *ḍullu* to fall off; *ḍollu* to roll over (DEDR 2698) Te. *ḍul(u)cu, ḍulupu* to cause to fall; *ḍollu* to fall; ḍolligillu to fall or tumble over (DEDR 2988) డొలుచు [*ḍolucu*] or *ḍoluṭsu* [Tel.] v. n. To tumble head over heels as dancing girls do (Telugu) Rebus 1: *dul* 'to cast in a mould'; *dul mẽṛhẽt, dul meṛeḍ,* 'cast iron'; koṭe meṛeḍ 'forged iron' (Santali) Bshk. *ḍōl* ' brass pot (CDIAL 6583). Rebus 2: WPah. *ḍhō`ḷ* m. 'stone', *ḍhò̄ḷṭɔ* m. 'big stone or boulder', *ḍhò̄ḷṭu* 'small id.' Him.I 87(CDIAL 5536). Rebus: K. *ḍula* m. ' rolling stone'(CDIAL 6582).

Hieroglyph: धातु [p= 513,3] m. layer , stratum Ka1tyS3r. Kaus3. constituent part , ingredient (esp. [and in RV. only] ifc. , where often = " fold " e.g. त्रि-धा/आतु , threefold &c ; cf.त्रिविष्टि- , सप्त- , सु-) RV. TS. S3Br. &c (Monier-Williams) *dhā´tu* n. ' substance ' RV., m. ' element ' MBh., ' metal, mineral, ore (esp. of a red colour) ' Mn., ' ashes of the dead ' lex., ' *strand of rope ' (cf. *tridhā´tu* -- ' threefold ' RV., *ayugdhātu* -- ' having an uneven number of strands ' KātyŚr.). [√dhā] Pa. *dhātu* -- m. ' element, ashes of the dead, relic '; KharI. *dhatu* ' relic '; Pk. *dhāu* -- m. ' metal, red chalk '; N. *dhāu* ' ore (esp. of copper) '; Or. *ḍhāu* ' red chalk, red ochre ' (whence*ḍhāuā* ' reddish '; M. *dhāū*, *dhāv* m.f. ' a partic. soft red stone ' (whence *dhă̄vaḍ* m. ' a caste of iron -- smelters ', *dhāvḍī* ' composed of or relating to iron '); -- Si. *dā* ' relic '; -- S. *dhāī* f. ' wisp of fibres added from time to time to a rope that is being twisted ', L. *dhāī̃* f (CDIAL 6773) *tántu* m. ' thread, warp ' RV. [√tan] Pa. *tantu* -- m. ' thread, cord ', Pk. *taṁtu* -- m.; Kho. (Lor.) *ton* ' warp ' < **tand* (whence *tandeni* ' thread between wings of spinning wheel '); S. *tandu* f. ' gold or silver thread '; L. *tand*(pl. °*dū̃*) f. ' yarn, thread being spun, string of the tongue '; P. *tand* m. ' thread ', *tanduā*, °*dūā* m. ' string of the tongue, frenum of glans penis '; A. *tā̃t* ' warp in the loom, cloth being woven '; B. *tā̃t* ' cord '; M. *tā̃tū* m. ' thread '; Si. *tatu*, °*ta* ' string of a lute '; -- with -- *o*, -- *ā* to retain orig. gender: S. *tando* m. ' cord, twine, strand of rope '; N. *tā̃do* ' bowstring '; H.*tā̃tā* m. ' series, line '; G. *tā̃tɔ* m. ' thread '; -- OG. *tāṁtaṇaü* m. ' thread ' < **tāṁtaḍaü*, G. *tā̃tṇɔ* m. (CDIAL 5661)

Rebus: धातु primary element of the earth i.e. metal , mineral, ore (esp. a mineral of a red colour) Mn. MBh. &c element of words i.e. grammatical or verbal root or stem Nir. Pra1t. MBh. &c (with the southern Buddhists धातु means either the 6 elements [see above] Dharmas. xxv ; or the 18 elementary spheres [धातु-लोक] ib. lviii ; or the ashes of the body , relics L. [cf. -गर्भ]) (Monier-Williams. Samskritam).

मृदु *mṛdu* : (page 1287) A kind of iron.-कार्ष्णायसम्,-कृष्णायसम् soft-iron, lead. (Apte. Samskritam) This gloss could link with the variant lexis of Bharata **sprachbund** with the semantics 'iron'*: Bj. <i>merhd</i>(Hunter) `iron'. Sa. <i>mE~R~hE~'d</i> `iron'. ! <i>mE~RhE~d</i>(M).*

Mërhët. Iron.
Mërhët icena. The iron is rusty.
Ispat mërhët. Steel.
Dul mërhët. Cast iron.
Mërhët khanda. Iron implements.

.meḍ 'copper' (Slavic languages)

Origin of the gloss meḍ 'copper' in Uralic languages may be explained by the word meḍ (Ho.) of Munda family of Meluhha language stream:

Sa. <i>mE~R~hE~'d</i> `iron'. ! <i>mE~RhE~d</i>(M).

Ma. <i>mErhE'd</i> `iron'.

Mu. <i>mERE'd</i> `iron'.

~ <i>mE~R~E~'d</i> `iron'. ! <i>mENhEd</i>(M).

Ho <i>meḍ</i> `iron'.

Bj. <i>merhd</i>(Hunter) `iron'.

KW <i>mENhEd</i>

@(V168,M080)*199*

— Slavic glosses for 'copper'200

Мeд [Meḍ]Bulgarian

Bakar Bosnian

Медзь [meḍz']Belarusian

Měď Czech

Bakar Croatian

KòperKashubian

Бакар [Bakar]Macedonian

Miedź Polish

Медь [Meḍ']Russian

Meď Slovāk

BakerSlovenian

Бакар [Bakar]Serbian

Мідь [mid'] Ukrainian[unquote]

Miedź, meḍ' (Northern Slavic, Altaic) 'copper'.

One suggestion is that corruptions from the German "Schmied", "Geschmeide" = jewelry. Schmied, a smith (of tin, gold, silver, or other metal)(German) result in meḍ 'copper'.

Votive relief of Dudu, priest of Ningirsu, in the days of King Entemena of Lagash.

Mésopotamie, room 1a: La Mésopotamie du Néolithique à l'époque des Dynasties archaïques de Sumer. Richelieu, ground floor.

Votive bas-relief of Dudu, priest of Ningirsu in the time of Entemena, prince of Lagash C. 2400 BCE Tello (ancient Girsu) Bituminous stone H. 25 cm; W. 23 cm; Th. 8 cm De Sarzec excavations, 1881 AO 2354

This work is part of the collections of the Louvre (Department of Near Eastern Antiquities).Louvre Museum1881: excavated by Ernest de Sarzec.
Place: Girsu (modern city of Telloh, Iraq). Musée du Louvre, Atlas database: entry 11378 Votive relief of Dudu, priest of Ningirsu, in the days of King Entemena of Lagash. Oil shale, ca. 2400 BC. Found in Telloh, ancient city of Girsu. |H. 25 cm (9 ¾ in.), W. 23 cm (9 in.), D. 8 cm (3 in.)

Hieroglyph: *ḍhAi* 'rope strand' Rebus: *dhAtu* 'mineral element'
Alternative: मेढा [*mēḍhā*] 'a curl or snarl; twist in thread' (Marathi) Rebus: *mẽṛhẽt, meḍ* 'iron' (Mu.Ho.) *eruvai* 'eagle' Rebus: *eruvai* 'copper'.

eraka 'wing' Rebus: *erako* 'moltencast copper'.

Hieroglyph: *arye* 'lion' (Akkadian) Rebus: *Ara* 'brass

Hieroglyph: *damya* ' tameable ', m. ' young bullock to be tamed ' Mn. [~ *dāmiya -- . -- √dam]Pa. *damma* -- ' to be tamed (esp. of a young bullock) '; Pk. *damma* -- ' to be tamed '; S. *ḏamu* ' tamed '; -- ext. -- *ḍa* -- : A. *damrā* ' young bull ', *dāmuri* ' calf ';

B. *dāmṛā* ' castrated bullock '; Or. *dāmaṛī* ' heifer ', *dāmaṛiā* ' bullcalf, young castrated bullock ', *dāmuṛ*, *°ṛi* ' young bullock '.Addenda: *damya* -- : WPah.kṭg. *dām* m. ' young ungelt ox ' CDIAL 6184). This is a phonetic determinative of the 'twisted rope' hieroglyph: *dhāī̃* f. *dā́man*1 ' rope ' (Rigveda)

Alternative: *kōḍe, kōḍiya.* [Tel.] n. A bullcalf. Rebus: *koḍ* artisan's workshop (Kuwi) kunda 'turner' kundār turner (Assamese) मेढा [*mēḍhā*] A twist or tangle arising in thread or cord, a curl or snarl (Marathi)(CDIAL 10312).L. *meṛh* f. 'rope tying oxen to each other and to post on threshing floor'(CDIAL 10317) Rebus: *mẽṛhẽt, meḍ* 'iron' (Mu.Ho.)

Hieroglyph: endless knot motif

After Fig. 52, p.85 in Prudence Hopper opcit. Plaque with male figures, serpents and quadruped. Bitumen compound. H. 9 7/8 in (25 cm); w. 8 ½ in. (21.5 cm); d. 3 3/8 in. (8.5 cm). ca. 2600-2500 BCE. Acropole, temple of Ninhursag Sb 2724. The scene is described: "Two beardless, long-haired, nude male figures, their heads in profile and their bodies in three-quarter view, face the center of the composition…upper centre, where two intertwined serpents with their tails in their mouths appear above the upraised hands. At the base of the plaque, between the feet of the two figures, a small calf or lamb strides to the right. An irregular oblong cavity or break was made in the centre of the scene at a later date."

The hieroglyphs on this plaque are: kid and endless-knot motif (or three strands of rope twisted).

Hieroglyph: 'kid': करडूं or करडें (p. 137) [*karaḍū or ṅkaraḍēṃ*] n A kid. कराडूं (p. 137) [karāḍūṃ] n (Commonly करडूं) A kid. Rebus: करडा (p. 137) [*karaḍā*] Hard from alloy--iron, silver &c.(Marathi)

I suggest that the center of the composition is NOT set of intertwined serpents, but an endless knot motif signifying a coiled rope being twisted from three strands of fibre.

Bogazkoy Seal impression: Two-headed eagle, a twisted cord below. From Bogazköy.

18th c. BCE (Museum Ankara). *eruvai* 'kite' Rebus: *eruvai* 'copper' *dhAtu* 'strands of rope' Rebus: *dhAtu* 'mineral' (Note the three strands of the rope hieroglyph on the seal impression from Bogazkoy; it is read: *tridhAtu* 'three mineral elements). It signifies copper compound of three minerals; maybe, arsenic copper? or arsenic bronze, as distinct from tin bronze?

Copper and arsenic ores: Arsenopyrigte is FeAsS in chemical formula.

Sulfide deposits frequently are a mix of different metal sulfides, such as copper, zinc, silver, lead, arsenic and other metals. (Sphalerite (ZnS2), for example, is not uncommon in copper sulfide deposits, and the metal smelted would be brass, which is both harder and more durable than bronze.) The metals could theoretically be separated out, but the alloys resulting were typically much stronger than the metals individually.

There are two Railway stations in India called Dharwad and Ib. Both are related to Prakritam words with the semantic significance: iron worker, iron ore.

dhāvaḍ m. ' a caste of iron -- smelters ', *dhāvḍī* ' composed of or relating to iron ' (Marathi)(CDIAL 6773)

The evolution of Brahmi syllable for ma- is comparable deciphered hieroglyphs from Harappa Script Corpora to affirm the continuum of the writing tradition of *Bhāratam Janam*, 'metalcaster folk'.

Thus, together, four consonants ḍha- dha-, ka-, ma- signified by Brahmi syllables are traceable to the tradition of Harappa Script Corpora which is a catalogus catalogorum of metalwork.

Brahmi syllabic orthography and evolution over time from ca. 300 BCE is presented in the following table[201]:

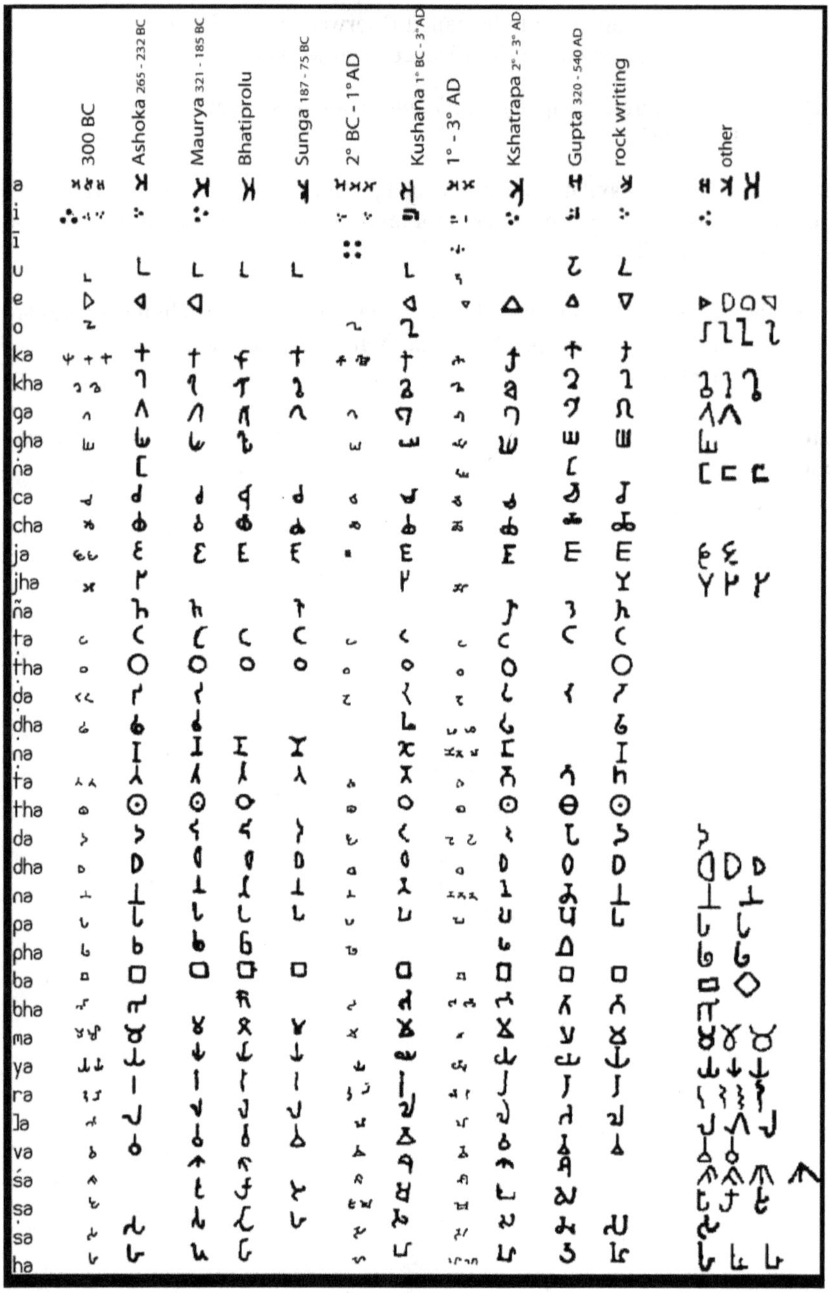
300 BC
Ashoka 265 - 232 BC
Maurya 321 - 185 BC
Bhatiprolu
Sunga 187 - 75 BC
2° BC - 1°AD
Kushana 1° BC - 3°AD
1° - 3° AD
Kshatrapa 2° - 3° AD
Gupta 320 - 540 AD
rock writing
other
a
i
ī
u
e
o
ka
kha
ga
gha
ṅa
ca
cha
ja
jha
ña
ṭa
ṭha
ḍa
ḍha
ṇa
ta
tha
da
dha
na
pa
pha
ba
bha
ma
ya
ra
la
va
śa
ṣa
sa
ha

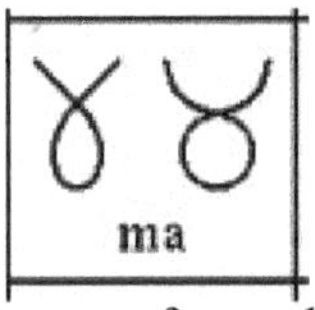

Brahmi syllable ma- is a 'knot' hieroglyph, a continuum fom Harappa Script Corpora wherein the 'knot' hieroglyph signified meḍ 'iron, copper, metal'.

The orthography of ma- syllable was possibly identified as ma- for meḍ, 'iron, copper, metal'.

Svastika hieroglyph multiplex is a remarkable hypertext of Harappa Script Corpora, which signify catalogus catalogorum of metalwork.
Svastika signifies zinc metal, spelter. This validates Thomas Wilson's indication -- after a wide-ranging survey of migrations of the hieroglyph across Eurasia and across continents -- that svastika symbol connoted a commodity, apart from its being a hieroglyph, a sacred symbol in many cultures.
"Spelter, while sometimes used merely as a synonym for zinc, is often used to identify a zinc alloy. In this sense it might be an alloy of equal parts copper and zinc, i.e. a brass, used for hard soldering and brazing, or as an alloy, containing lead, that is used instead of bronze."[202]

Hieroglyph: sattva 'svastika' glyph Rebus: sattu, satavu, satuvu 'pewter' (Kannada) సత్తుతపెల a vessel made of pewter त्रपुधातुविशेषनिर्मितम् jasth जस्थ । त्रपु m. (sg. dat. jastas जस्तस्), zinc, spelter; pewter.

A Gold Rhyton with two tigers; svastika incised on thigh of tiger; found in historical site of Gilan[203]

sattu (Tamil), satta, sattva (Kannada) jasth जसथ् ।रपु m. (sg. dat. jastas ज्तस), zinc, spelter; pewter; zasath ◌़ ज़स्◌़थ् ◌़or zasuth ज़सुथ ◌़। रप m. (sg. dat. zastas ◌ु ज़्तस),◌़ zinc, spelter, pewter (cf. Hindī jast). jastuvu; । रपूभवः adj. (f. jastüvü), made of zinc or pewter.(Kashmiri). Hence the hieroglyph: svastika repeated five times. Five svastika are thus read: taṭṭal sattva Rebus: zinc (for) brass (or pewter*ṭhaṭṭha1 ' brass '. [Onom. from noise of hammering brass? -- *ṭhaṭṭh --]N. *ṭhaṭṭar* ' an alloy of copper and bell metal ' **ṭhaṭṭhakāra* ' brass worker '. 2. *ṭhaṭṭhakara [*ṭhaṭṭha -- 1, kāra -- 1]1. Pk. *ṭhaṭṭhāra* -- m., K. *ṭhö̃ṭhur* m., S. *ṭhã̄ṭhāro* m., P. *ṭhaṭhiār*, °*rā* m.2. P. ludh. *ṭhaṭherā* m., Ku. *ṭhaṭhero* m., N. *ṭhaṭero*, Bi. *ṭhaṭherā*, Mth. *ṭhaṭheri*, H. *ṭhaṭherā* m. (CDIAL 5491, 5493).

Mohejodaro, tablet in bas relief (M-478)

The first hieroglyph-multiplex on the left (twisted rope):

m478a tablet

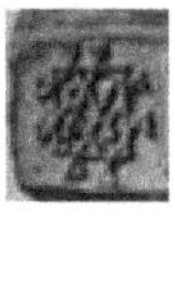

The hieroglyph may be a variant of a twisted rope.

dhāu 'rope' rebus: dhāu 'metal' PLUS मेढा [mēḍhā] 'a curl or snarl; twist in thread' rebus: mẽṛhẽt, meḍ 'iron'. Thus, metallic ore.

Hieroglyph: मेढा [mēḍhā] A twist or tangle arising in thread or cord, a curl or snarl (Marathi). Rebus: *meḍ* 'iron, copper' (Munda. Slavic) mẽṛhẽt, meḍ 'iron' (Mu.Ho.Santali)

meď 'copper' (Slovāk)

Santali glosses:

Mẽṛhẽt́. Iron.
Mẽṛhẽt́ ićena. The iron is rusty.
Ispat mẽṛhẽt́. Steel.
Dul mẽṛhẽt́. Cast iron.
Mẽṛhẽt́ khaṇḍa. Iron implements.

Wilhelm von Hevesy wrote about the Finno-Ugric-Munda kinship, like "Munda-Magyar-Maori, an Bharata link between the antipodes new tracks of Hungarian origins" and "Finnisch-Ugrisches aus Indien". (DRIEM, George van: Languages of the Himalayas: an ethnolinguistic handbook. 1997. p.161-162.) Sumerian-Ural-Altaic language affinities have been noted. Given the presence of Meluhha settlements in Sumer, some Meluhha glosses might have been adapted in these languages. One etyma cluster refers to 'iron' exemplified by meḍ (Ho.). The alternative suggestion for the origin of the gloss meḍ 'copper' in Uralic languages may be explained by the word meḍ (Ho.) of Munda family of Meluhha language stream:

Sa. <i>mE~R~hE~'d</i> `iron'. ! <i>mE~RhE~d</i>(M).

Ujjain, ca. 200 BCE, Copper, 1.81g, Multi-symbols with Swastika to left. Association of 'svastika' hieroglyph with 'dotted circle' indicates that the scribe intends to show that 'svastika' signifying zinc is a metal out of a smelter, kāṇḍa 'fire-altar'.

Saurashatra (Gujarat), ca. 100 BCE, Copper, 5.83g, Double Swastika with Nandi-pad arms.[204]

The svastika hieroglyph on Saurashtra (ca. 100 BCE) coin shows a variant with a 'twist' hieroglyph ligatured to each of the four arms of the svastika glyph.

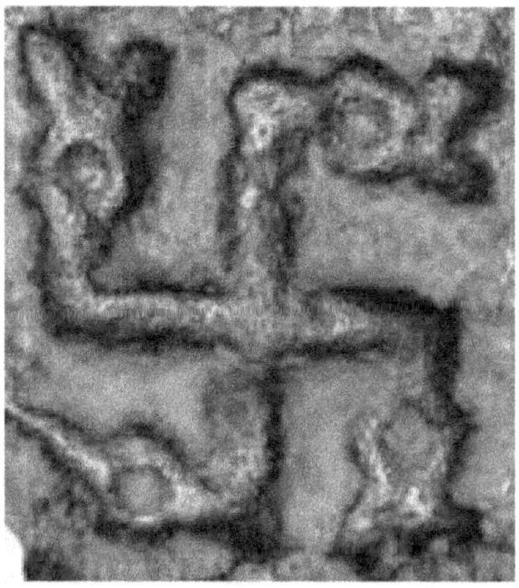

This is an orthographic determinant of the nature of the object denoted by svastika, spelter, zinc ore. The tagged 'twist' glyph denotes: meḍ 'twist' rebus: meḍ 'iron, copper, metal'. Thus, zinc/spelter is identified as a metallic ore and signified as such on this hieroglyph variant on Saurashtra coin of ca. 100 BCE.

A corollary result of this exposition is that the so-called 'nandipada' symbol of historical period epigraphs has to be explained as 'twist' hieroglyph: meḍ 'twist' rebus: meḍ 'iron, copper, metal'.

Harappa Script hieroglyph svastika signifies zinc metal

Hieroglyph: मेढा [*mēḍhā*] 'a curl or snarl; twist in thread' (Marathi) .L. meṛh f. 'rope tying oxen to each other'. मेढा [*mēḍhā*] A twist or tangle arising in thread or cord, a curl or snarl.(Marathi) mer.ha = twisted, crumpled, as a horn (Santali.lex.) meli, melika = a turn, a twist, a loop, entanglement; meliyu, melivad.u, meligonu = to get twisted or entwined (Telugu)) [Note the endless knot motif]. Rebus: *meḍ.* 'iron' (Mu.) sattva 'svastika glyph' Rebus: *sattva, jasta* 'zinc'.

The 'endless knot' hieroglyph can be interpreted as composed of two related semantics: 1. strand of rope or string; 2. twist or curl

Twisted rope as hieroglyph:

dhā̆vaḍ m. ‘ a caste of iron -- smelters ’

The suffix -vaḍ is relatable to the semantics of *vaTam* ‘string’.(as may be seen in the expressions in vogue in Tamil) Thus, dhā̆vaḍ can be elaborated as a compound made of dhA PLUS vaTam, i.e. layers of minerals or elements in the smelting process.

அணிவடம் *aṇi-vaṭam*, n. < அணி- +. Ornamental string of jewels, necklace; கழுத் திலணியு மாலை.

அரைவடம் *arai-vaṭam*, n. < id. +. String of beads round the waist, worn by little children; அரைச்சதங்கை.அரைவடங்கள் கட்டி (திருப்பு. 2).

ஈர்வடம் īr-vaṭam , n. < ஈர்[3] +. Rope made of the ribs of the palmyra leaf; பனை யீர்க்குக்கயிறு. (J.) ஏகவடம் ēka-vaṭam , n. < id. +. Necklace of a single string.
See ஏகாவலி. பொங்கிள நாகமொரேகவடத்தோடு (தேவா. 350, 7)

கால்வடம் *kāl-vaṭam*, n. < கால்[1] +. Foot- ornament strung with pearls; காலணிவகை. திருக்கால்வடமொன்றிற் கோத்த (S.I.I. ii, 397, 205).

சபவடம் capa-vaṭam , n. < சபம்[1] +. String of beads for keeping count in prayer, rosary; செபமாலை. சபவடமும்வெண்ணூல் மார்பும் (திருவாலவா. 27, 51).

தாழ்வடம் t*āḻ-vaṭam, n. < id. +. 1. [M. tāḻvaṭam.]* Necklace of pearls or beads; கழுத் தணி. தாவி றாழ்வடம்தயங்க (சீவக. 2426).

தேர்வடம் *tēr-vaṭam ,* n. < id. +. Cable, thick rope for drawing a car; தேரிழுத்தற்குரிய பெரிய கயிற்றுவடம்.மணலையு மேவுதேர் வட மாக்க லாம் (அருட்பா, vi, வயித்திய. 4).

வடம்[1] *vaṭam , n. < vaṭa.* 1. Cable, large rope, as for drawing a temple-car; கனமான கயிறு. வடமற்றது (நன். 219, மயிலை.). 2. Cord; தாம்பு. (சூடா.) 3. A loop of coir rope, used for climbing palm-trees; மரமேறவுதவுங் கயிறு. Loc. 4. Bowstring; வில்லின் நாணி. (பிங்.) 5. String of jewels; மணிவடம்.

வடங்கள் அசையும்படி உடுத்து(திருமுரு. 204, உரை). (சூடா.) 6. Strands of a garland; chains of a
necklace; சரம். இடை மங்கை கொங்கைவட

மலைய (அஷ்டப். திருவேங்கடத் தந். 39). 7. Arrangement; ஒழுங்கு.

தொடங்கற் காலை வடம்படவிளங்கும் (ஞானா. 14, 41).

m478a tablet

கோலம்[1] kōlam, n. [T. kōlamu, K. kōla, M. kōlam.] 1. Beauty, gracefulness, handsomeness; அழகு. கோலத் தனிக்கொம்பர் (திருக் கோ. 45). 2. Colour; நிறம். கார்க்கோல மேனி யானை (கம்பரா. கும்பக. 154). 3. Form, shape, external or general appearance; உருவம். மானுடக் கோலம். 4. Nature; தன்மை. 5. Costume; appropriate dress; attire, as worn by actors; trappings; equipment; habiliment; வேடம். உள்வரிக் கோலத்து (சிலப். 5, 216). 6. Ornament, as jewelry; ஆபரணம். குறங்கிணை திரண்டன கோலம் பொறாஅ (சிலப். 30, 18). 7. Adornment, decoration, embellishment; அலங்காரம். புறஞ்சுவர் கோலஞ்செய்து (திவ். திருமாலை, 6). 8. Ornamental figures drawn on floor, wall or sacrificial pots with rice-flour, white stone-powder, etc.; மா, கற்பொடி முதலியவற்றாலிடுங் கோலம். தரை மெழுகிக் கோலமிட்டு (குமர. மீனாட். குறம். 25). Rebus: kol 'metal, working in iron'

Harappa tablet.

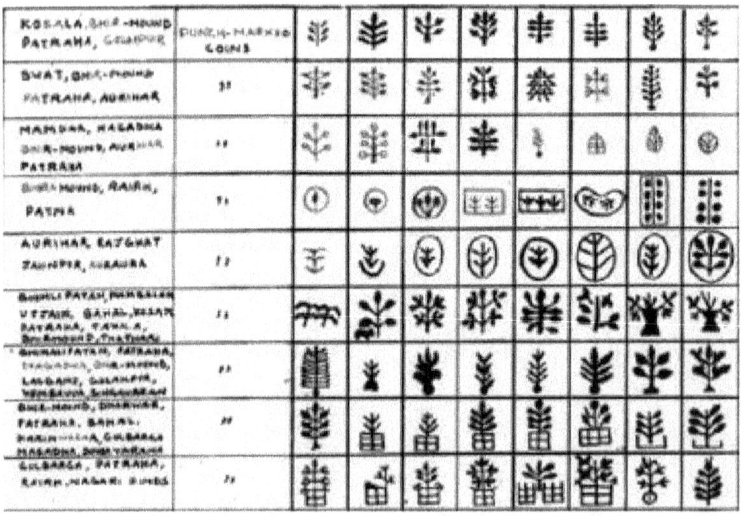

After Pl. 30 C in: Savita Sharma, 1990, Early Indian symbols, numismatic evidence, Delhi, Agama Kala Prakashan; cf. Shah, UP., 1975, Aspects of Jain Art and Architecture, p.77)

Hieroglyph: *kuṭi* 'tree' Rebus: *kuṭhi* 'smelter, furnace'.

kuṭire bica duljad.ko talkena, 'they were feeding the furnace with ore'. (Santali) This use of bica in the context of feeding a smelter clearly defines bica as 'stone ore, mineral', in general.

The hieroglyphs on m478a tablet are read rebus:

kuṭi 'tree'Rebus: *kuṭhi* 'smelter'

bhaṭa 'worshipper' Rebus: *bhaṭa* 'furnace' *baṭa* 'iron' (Gujarati) This hieroglyph is a phonetic determinant of the 'rimless pot': *baṭa* = rimless pot (Kannada) Rebus: *baṭa* = a kind of iron (Gujarati) *bhaṭa* 'a furnace'. Hence, the hieroglyph-multiplex of an adorant with rimless pot signifies: 'iron furnace' *bhaṭa.*

bAraNe ' an offering of food to a demon' (Tulu) Rebus: *baran, bharat* (5 copper, 4 zinc and 1 tin) (Punjabi. Bengali) The narrative of a worshipper offering to a tree is thus interpretable as a smelting of three minerals: copper, zinc and tin.

Numeral four: *gaṇḍa* 'four' Rebus: *kand* 'fire-altar'; Four 'ones': *koḍa* 'one' (Santali) Rebus: koḍ 'artisan's workshop'. Thus, the pair of 'four linear strokes PLUS rimless pot' signifies: 'fire-altar (in) artisan's wrkshop'.

Circumscript of two linear strokes for 'body' hieroglyph: *dula* 'pair' Rebus: *dul* 'cast metal' *koḍa* 'one'(Santali) Rebus: *koḍ* 'artisan's workshop'. Thus, the circumscript signifies 'cast metal workshop'. *meḍ* 'body' Rebus: *meḍ* 'iron'.

khāreḍo = a currycomb (G.) Rebus: *khārādī* 'turner' (Gujarati)

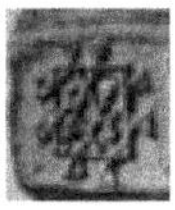

The hieroglyph may be a variant of a twisted rope.

dhāu 'rope' rebus: *dhāu* 'metal' PLUS मेढा [*mēḍhā*] 'a curl or snarl; twist in thread' rebus: *mẽṛhẽt, meḍ* 'iron'. Thus, metallic ore.

kōlam, n. [T. kōlamu, K. kōla, M. kōlam.] 'ornamental figure' Rebus: *kol* 'working in iron'

The inscription on m478 thus signifies, reading hieroglyphs from r.:

Tree: *kuṭhi* 'smelter'

Worshipper: *bhaṭa* 'furnace'

Four linear strokes + rimless pot: *kāṇḍa baṭa* 'fire-altar for iron'

Circumscript two linear strokes + body: *meḍ koḍa* 'metal workshop'

Currycomb: *khāreḍo* 'currycomb' rebus: *khārādī* 'turner'; dhāu 'metal'

PLUS *mẽṛhẽt, meḍ* 'iron'; *kol* 'working in iron'. Together, the two hieroglyphs

signify metalworker, ironsmith turner.

A note on ancient rope-making with two/three strands

Three rope-makers working in the marshes making a two strand rope.

Above the labourers are depicted the tools of their trade, a bundle of raw material, and four finished coils of rope. The same three-men technique

was still in use in the 20th century CE

Tomb of Ti Quibell 1896, Pl.32

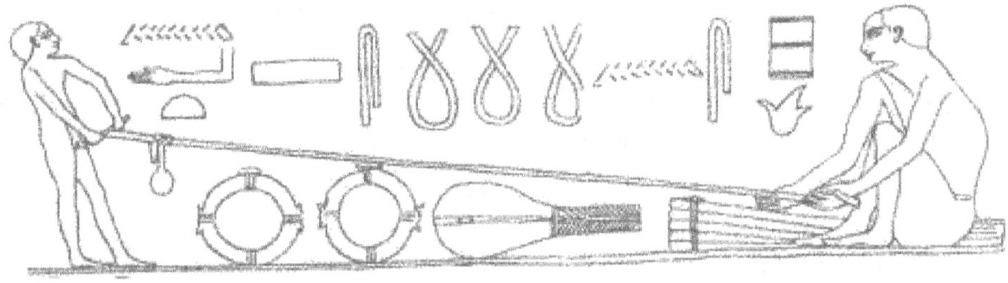

At times a worker would tie the rope around his waist using the weight of his body to keep the rope taught, freeing his hands for manipulating it. Source: Maude 1862, p.375

Fragment of papyrus rope, Late Period, length: 42 cm, diameter: 9 cm

Cordage was occasionally made by braiding three strands of material together, but the main manufacturing technique consisted in twisting two or more yarns of the same thickness individually in the same direction and then combining the strands by twisting them together in the opposite direction. The resulting cord could be twisted together with similar chords to form a rope of even greater girth. The ends of twisted rope were tied up to keep them from unravelling. The finished rope was

beaten with a wooden implement or

brushed.
Three-strand twisted natural fibre rope.[205]

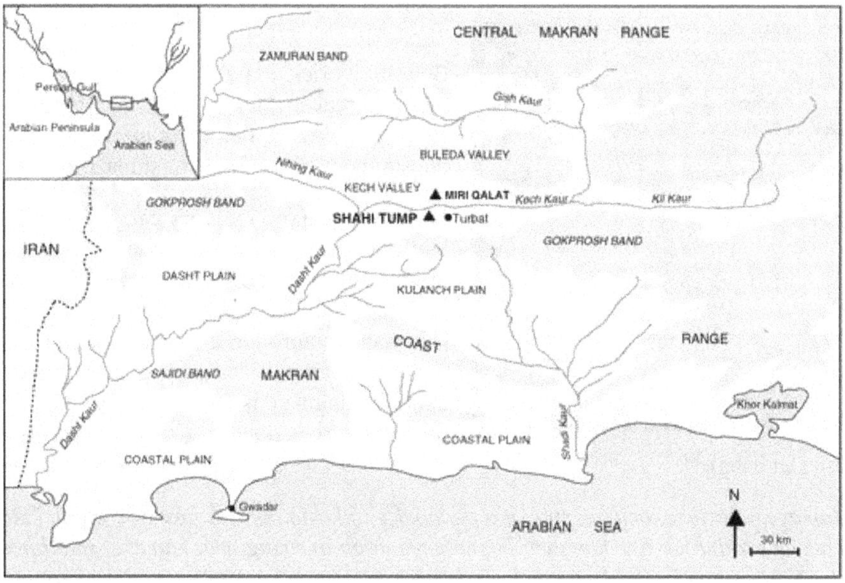

dhā̆vaḍ m. ' a caste of iron -- smelters '

The suffix *-vaḍ* is relatable to the semantics of *vaTam* 'string'.(as may be seen in the expressions in vogue in Tamil) Thus, *dhā̆vaḍ* can be elaborated as a compound made of *dhA* + *vaTam*, i.e. layers of minerals or elements in the smelting process.

In the historical periods, starting from ca. 3rd cent. BCE, some hieroglyphs of Harappa Script get venerated as sacred symbols. This cultural phenomenon is explained by the occurrence -- in Jaina Ananta gumpha of Khaṇḍagiri caves -- of svastika hieroglyph together with 'lathe/furnace standard device' and 'mollusc' component in hieroglyph-multiplex variously designated by art historians as śrivatsa/nandipada /triratna.

Why did Harappa Script hieroglyphs -- e.g., svastika, portable furnace, pair of fish, fish tied to a pair of molluscs, safflower, pair of fish, fish tail -- get venerated as sacred symbols, displayed on homage tablets, say, on the Jaina *AyagapaTTa* अयागपट्ट of Kankali Tila, Mathura, ca. 1st or 3rd century BCE?

The context is clear and unambiguous from a pair of glosses of Bharata sprachbund attested in Kota *language: kole.l* 'smithy' kole.l 'temple'. Harappa Script hieroglyphs which signified products and resources of a smithy (e.g., minerals, metals, alloys, smelters, furnaces, supercargo) also signified the cosmic phenomenon held in awe by the *Bhāratam Janam*, metlcaster folk that mere dhatu 'minerals or earth stones or sand' could upon smelting yield metal implements, and weapons. The operations in a smithy/forge became a representation of a cosmic dance. Hence, *kole.l* signified both a smithy and a temple.

Srivatsa with kanka, 'eyes' (Kui).

Begram ivories. Plate
389 Reference: Hackin, 1954, fig.195, no catalog N°. According to an inscription on the southern gate of Sanchi stupa,

It has been carved by ivory carvers of Vidisha.Southern Gateway panel information: West pillar Front East Face has an inscription. Vedisakehi dantakarehi rupa-kammam katam - On the border of this panel – Epigraphia Indica vol II – written in Brahmi, language is Pali – the carving of this sculpture is done by the ivory carvers of Vedisa (Vidisha).[206]

Ta. kaṇ eye, aperture, orifice, star of a peacock's tail. Ma. kaṇ, kaṇṇu eye, nipple, star in peacock's tail, bud. Ko. kaṇ eye. To. koṇ eye, loop in string. Ka. kaṇ eye, small hole, orifice. Koḍ. kaṇṇï id. Pe. kaṇga (pl. -ŋ, kaṇku) id. Manḍ. kan (pl. -ke) id. Kui kanu (pl. kan-ga), (K.) kanu (pl. kaṛka) id. Kuwi (F.) kannū (S.) kannu (pl. kanka), (Su. P. Isr.) kanu (pl. kaṇka) id. (DEDR 1159).

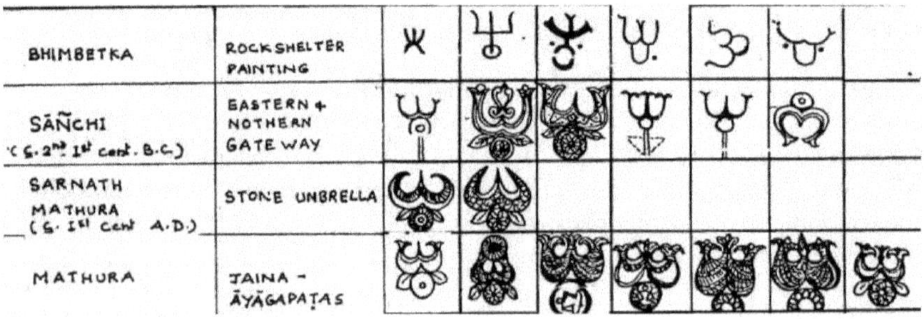

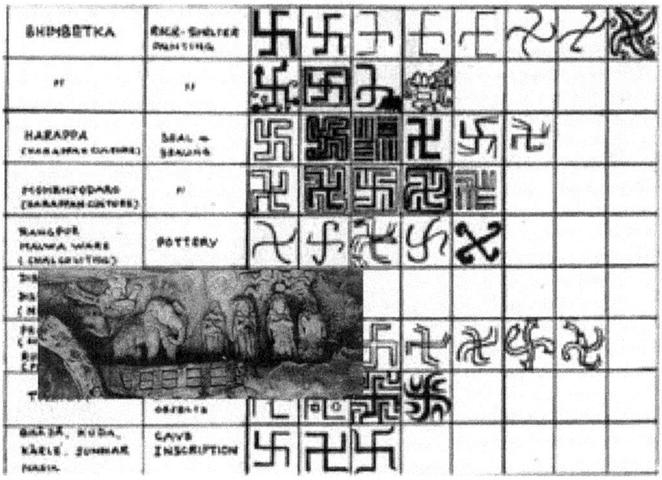

śrivatsa symbol [with its hundreds of stylized variants, depicted on Pl. 29 to 32] occurs in Bogazkoi (Central Anatolia) dated ca. 6th to 14th cent. BCE on inscriptions Pl. 33, Nandipāda-Triratna at: Bhimbetka, Sanchi, Sarnath and Mathura] Pl. 27, Svastika symbol: distribution in cultural periods] The association of śrivatsa with 'fish' is reinforced by the symbols binding fish in Jaina āyāgapaṭas (snake-hood?) of Mathura (late 1st cent. BCE). śrivatsa symbol seems to have evolved from a styli□ed glyph showing 'two fishes'. In the Sanchi stupa, the fish-tails of two fishes are combined to flank the 'śrivatsa' glyph. In a Jaina āyāgapaṭa, a fish is ligatured within the *śrivatsa* glyph, emphasizing the association of the 'fish' glyph with *śrivatsa* glyph.

(After Plates in: Savita Sharma, 1990, Early Bharata symbols, numismatic evidence, Delhi, Agama Kala Prakashan; cf. Shah, UP., 1975, Aspects of Jain Art and Architecture, p.77)
Khaṇḍagiri caves (2nd cent. BCE) Cave 3 (Jaina Ananta gumpha). Fire-altar?, śrivatsa, svastika

(hieroglyphs) (King Khāravela, a Jaina who ruled Kalinga has an inscription dated 161 BCE) contemporaneous with Bharhut and Sanchi and early Bodhgaya.

Kushana period, 1st century C.E.From Mathura Red Sandstone 89x92cm[207]

Ayagapatta, Kankali Tila, Mathura.

"Jain homage tablet. The tablet was

set up by the wife of Bhadranadi, and it was found in December 1890 near the centre of the mound of the Jain stupa at Kankali Tila. Mathura has extensive archaeological remains as it was a large and important city from the middle of the first millennium onwards. It rose to

particular prominence under the Kushans as the town was their southern capital. The Buddhist, Brahmanical and Jain faiths all thrived at Mathura, and we find deities and motifs from all three and others represented in sculpture. In reference to this photograph in the list of photographic negatives, Bloch wrote that, "The technical name of such a panel was ayagapata [homage panel]." The figure in the centre is described as a Tirthamkara, a Jain prophet."[208]

Hieroglyph: arye 'lion' Rebus: arya 'person of noble character'

cakra, cakka 'wheel' Rebus: dhamma cakka 'wheel of dharma' (Pali.Prakrit).

Wheel in Hindu, Jaina and Bauddham is a metaphor of consciousness-cosmic ordering in cyclical rythm of time and space, which is dharma-dhamma.

Vishnu Sandstone Relief From Meerut India Indian Civilization 10th Century Dharma chakra. Srivatsa. Gada.

Rebus: *dhamma 'dharma'* (Pali) Hieroglyphs: *dām* 'garland, rope':

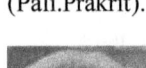

Hieroglyphs: *hangi*, 'mollusc' tied to a fish: *ayira* 'fish' Rebus; *ariya*, *ayira* 'person of noble character'.

Hieroglyphs: *hangi* 'mollusc' + *dām* 'rope, garland' *dā̃u* m. 'tying'; *puci* 'tail'
Rebus: *puja* 'worship'

Rebus: *ariya sanghika dhamma puja* 'veneration of arya sangha dharma'

Hieroglyph: *khambhaṛā* 'fish fin' rebus: *kammaTa* 'mint, coiner, coinage'

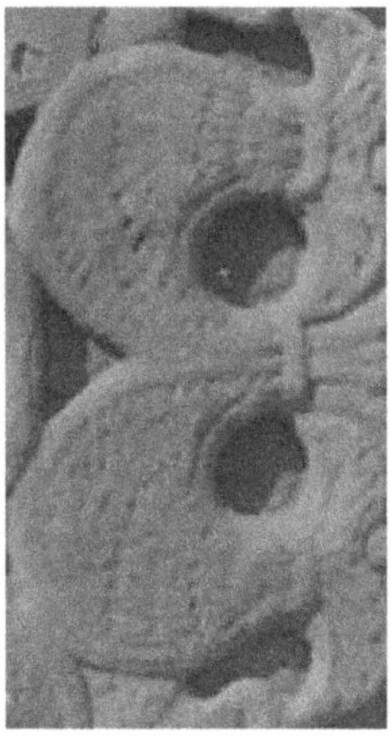

Four hieroglyphs are depicted. Fish-tails pair are tied together. The rebus readings are as above: *ayira (ariya) dhamma puja* 'veneration of arya dharma'.

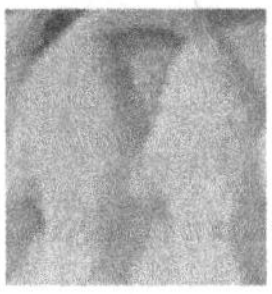

aya 'fish' rebus: *aya* 'metal' dula 'two' rebus: dul 'metal casting'

ayira 'fish' Rebus: *ayira, ariya, 'person of noble character'.* युगल *yugala 'twin' Rebus:* जुळणें *(p. 323)* *[juḷaṇēṃ]* v c & i (युगल S through जुंवळ) To put together in harmonious connection or orderly disposition (Marathi). Thus an arya with orderly disposition.

sathiya 'svastika glyph' Rebus: Sacca (adj.) [cp. Sk. satya] real, true D i.182; M ii.169; iii.207; Dh 408; nt. saccaŋ truly, verily, certainly Miln 120; saccaŋ kira is it really true? D i.113; Vin i.45, 60; J (Pali) Rebus: jasta 'zinc'

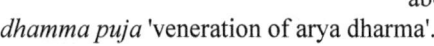

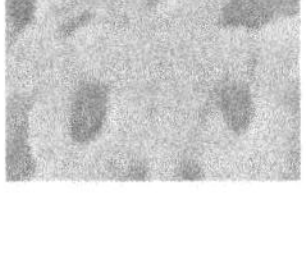

सांगाडा [*sāṅgāḍā*] m The skeleton, box, or frame (of a building, boat, the body &c.), the hull, shell, compages. 2 Applied, as Hulk is, to any animal or thing huge and unwieldy.

सांगाडी [*sāṅgāḍī*] f The machine within which a turner confines and steadies the piece he has to turn. Rebus: samgaha 'manager' सांगाती [*sāṅgātī*] a (Better संगती) A companion, associate, fellow.Buddha-pada (feet of Buddha), carved on a rectangular slab. The margin of the slab was carved with scroll of acanthus and rosettes. The foot-print shows important symbols like triratna, svastika, srivatsa, ankusa and elliptical objects, meticulously carved in low-relief. From Amaravati, Andhra Pradesh, being assignable on paleographical grounds to circa 1st century B.C --2nd century CE,

The piece is now in the Lucknow Museum.[209]

An ayagapata or Jain homage tablet, with small figure of a tirthankara in the centre and inscription below, from Mathura. "Photograph taken by Edmund William Smith in 1880s-90s of a Jain homage tablet. The tablet was set up by the wife of Bhadranadi, and it was found in December 1890 near the centre of the mound of the Jain stupa at Kankali Tila. Mathura has extensive archaeological remains as it was a large and important city from the middle of the first millennium onwards. It rose to particular prominence under the Kushans as the town was their southern capital. The Buddhist, Brahmanical and Jain faiths all thrived at Mathura, and we find deities and motifs from all three and others represented in sculpture. In reference to this photograph in the list of photographic negatives, Bloch wrote that, "The technical name of such a panel was ayagapata [homage panel]." The figure in the centre is described as a Tirthamkara, a Jain prophet. The piece is now in the Lucknow Museum."[210]

Dr. Anton Führer (to the right of the statue) at the Kankali Tila site in 1886–87. The original photograph was removed from the photographic records of his Archaeological Survey Department after his forced resignation (from the frontispiece of *The Jain Stupas and Other Antiquities of Mathura* by Vincent A. Smith, 1901).

View of the Jaina stupa excavated at Kankali Tila, Mathura.

Manoharpura. Svastika. Top of āyāgapaṭa. Red Sandstone. Lucknow State Museum. (Scan no.0053009, 0053011, 0053012)[211]

Ayagapata (After Huntington)

Jain votive tablet from Mathurå. From Czuma 1985, catalogue number 3. Fish-tail is the hieroglyph together with svastika hieroglyph, fish-pair hieroglyph, safflower hieroglyph, cord (tying together molluscs and arrow?) hieroglyph multiplex, lathe multiplex (the standard device shown generally in front of a one-horned young bull on Harappa Script corpora), flower bud (lotus) ligatured to the fish-tail. All these are venerating hieroglyphs surrounding the Tirthankara in the central meḍallion.

Pali etyma point to the use of 卐 with semant. 'auspicious mark'; on the Sanchi stupa; the cognate gloss is: *sotthika, sotthiya* 'blessed'.

Harappa Script Inscriptions on metal (copper plates, implements/weapons)[212]

Rick Willis and Vasant Shinde hypothesise the possibility that copper plate printing (i.e. transfer of pigment) might also have been used with such writing on metal tablets.[213] “The principles of printing were perhaps known to Indus Valley artisans through the ancient technique of ajrakh, printing fabric with woodblock designs. It is possible that the copper plates were created firstly to maintain a permanent record of the standard designs on seals and tablets, and furthermore provide a cheap and portable means to distribute standard designs to craftsmen that carved seals in the Indus Valley region. To test this idea, an experimental trial printing was carried out with the plates by Marco Luccio, an artist and master printer based in Melbourne, Australia. Two printing inks were tested: 1) a water-based ink with ferric oxide as the pigment, and 2) an oil-based ink with carbon black. Prints were first trialled with rag paper, but then were printed on tussah silk cloth and parchment, materials which were likely available in the third millennium BC. Almost no organic materials, such as cloth, leather or wood have survived from Indus civilisation, although impressions of woven fabric have been found on terracotta vessels.[214]"

Rick Willis and Vasant Shinde demonstrate the printing on tussah silk from a copper template of the types found in Sarasvati-Sindhu Civilization:

Simple ferric oxide and carbon black inks print on tussah silk taken from an inscribed copper plate. Demonstration in 2012 (After Fig. 13 in Willis & Shinde, opcit.) One possibility is that such prints from inscriptions on metal were taken on birch-bark documents as demonstrated in ancient epigraphical evidence. This lends credence to the manuscript discussed in a thesis. (Zuberbühler, L. (2009). A comparison of a manuscript with the Harappa Script. Unpublished Bachelor Thesis in: Department of Linguistics and Literary Studies Institute of Linguistics, University of Bern.)

Historical periods also evidence of printing on textiles using such transferance of pigments from templates.

meḍ(h), meḍhī f., meḍhā ‘ post, forked stake ’; meṛh f. ‘ rope tying oxen to each other and to post on threshing floor ’ (See the rope tied to a tiger on Kalibangan terracotta cake found in a fire-altar; *kola* 'tiger' rebus: *kol* 'working in iron'; *kolhe* 'smelters’.)

Binjor octagonal brick as a skambha, pillar *mēthí* m. ‘ pillar in threshing floor to which oxen are fastened, prop for supporting carriage shafts ’ AV., °*thī* -- f. KātyŚr.com., *mēdhī* -- f. Divyāv. 2. ***mēṭhī*** --f. PañcavBr.com., *mēḍhī* -- , *mēṭī* -- f. BhP. 1. Pa. *mēdhi* -- f. ‘ post to tie cattle to, pillar, part of a stūpa ’; Pk. *mēhi* -- m. ‘

post on threshing floor ', N. *meh(e), miho, miyo*, B. *mei*, Or. *maï -- dāṇḍi*, Bi. *mẽh, mẽhā* ' the post ', (SMunger) *mehā* ' the bullock next the post ', Mth. *meh, mehā* ' the post ', (SBhagalpur) *mīhā̃* ' the bullock next the post ', (SETirhut) *mẽhi bāṭi* ' vessel with a projecting base '.
2. Pk. *mēḍhi* -- m. ' post on threshing floor ', *mēḍhaka*<-> ' small stick '; K. *mīr, mīrü* f. ' larger hole in ground which serves as a mark in pitching walnuts ' (for semantic relation of ' post -- hole ' see kūpa -- 2); L. *meṛh* f. ' rope tying oxen to each other and to post on threshing floor '; P. *mehṛ* f., *mehaṛ* m. ' oxen on threshing floor, crowd '; OA*meṛha, mehra* ' a circular construction, mound '; Or. *meṛhī, meri* ' post on threshing floor '; Bi. *mẽṛ* ' raised bank between irrigated beds ', (Camparam) *mẽṛhā* ' bullock next the post ', Mth. (SETirhut) *mẽṛhā* ' id. '; M. *meḍ(h), meḍhī* f., *meḍhā* m. ' post, forked stake '*mēthika* -- ; *mēthiṣṭhá* -- . *mēthika* m. ' 17th or lowest cubit from top of sacrificial post ' lex. [mēthí --] Bi. *mẽhiyā* ' the bullock next the post on threshing floor '.*mēthiṣṭhá* ' standing at the post ' TS. [mēthí -- , stha --]Bi. (Patna) *mĕhṭhā* ' post on threshing floor ', (Gaya) *mehṭā, mẽhṭā* ' the bullock next the post '(CDIAL 10317 to, 10319) Rebus: मृदु *mṛdu, mẽṛhẽt,* meḍ 'iron, metal'

Thanks to Benoy Behl for disseminating the photograph of an exquisite gold disc now in al-Sabah collection of Kuwait National Museum. This gold disc is a veritable metalwork catalogue, consistent with the entire Harappa Script Corpora as catalogus catalogorum of metalwork. The uniqueness of the collection of hieroglyph-multiplexs on this gold disc is that a large number of metalwork catalogue items (more than 12) have been presented on a circular space with 9.6 cm diameter validating the Maritime Tin Route which linked Hanoi to Haifa through the Persian Gulf.

Phoen., MH and Assyr.; in the latter damgaru or tamkaru, Syr. taggara, {2} = merchant, Del. Ass. HWB, 222.[215]

—Sumerian damgar, Babylonian tamkarum—usually is translated as "merchant" or, by Babylonian times,"entrepreneur."[216]

Cognate with tamkāru, dam-gar '(mint) merchant' Bharata sprachbund glosses: *ṭhakkura* m. ' idol, deity (cf. *ḍhakkārī* --), ' lex., ' title ' Rājat. [Dis- cussion with lit. by W. Wüst RM 3, 13 ff. Prob. orig. a tribal name EWA i 459, which Wüst considers nonAryan borrowing of *śākvará* -- : very doubtful]Pk. *ṭhakkura* -- m. ' Rajput, chief man of a village '; Kho. (Lor.) *takur* ' barber ' (= *ṭ*° ← Ind.?), Sh. *ṭhăkŭr* m.; K. *ṭhôkur* m. ' idol ' (← Ind.?); S. *ṭhakuru* m. ' fakir, term of address between fathers of a husband and wife '; P. *ṭhākar* m. ' landholder ', ludh. *ṭhaukar* m. ' lord '; Ku. *ṭhākur* m. ' master, title of a Rajput '; N. *ṭhākur* ' term of address from slave to master ' (f. *ṭhakurāni*), *ṭhakuri* ' a clan of Chetris ' (f. *ṭhakurni*); A. *ṭhākur* ' a Brahman ', *ṭhākurānī* ' goddess '; B. *ṭhākurāni, ṭhākrān,* °*run* ' honoured lady, goddess '; Or. *ṭhākura* ' term of address to a Brahman, god, idol ', *ṭhākurāṇī* ' goddess '; Bi. *ṭhākur* ' barber '; Mth. *ṭhākur* ' blacksmith '; Bhoj. Aw.lakh. *ṭhākur* ' lord, master '; H. *ṭhākur* m. ' master, landlord, god, idol ', *ṭhākurāin, ṭhăkurānī* f. ' mistress, goddess '; G. *ṭhākor,* °*kar* m. ' member of a clan of Rajputs ', *ṭhakrāṇī* f. ' his wife ', *ṭhākor* ' god, idol '; M. *ṭhākur* m. ' jungle tribe in North Konkan, family priest, god, idol '; Si. mald. "*tacourou*" ' title added to names of noblemen ' (HJ 915) prob. Garh. *ṭhākur* ' master '; A. *ṭhākur* also ' idol ' AFD 205.(CDIAL 5488)

Homonym: *tagara*1 n. 'the shrub *Tabernaemontana coronaria* and a fragrant powder obtained from it' Kauś., °aka<-> VarBṛS. [Cf. *sthagara* -- , *sthakara* -- n. ' a partic. fragrant powder ' TBr.] (CDIAL 5622).

Hieroglyph: Ta. *takar* sheep, ram, goat, male of certain other animals (yāḷi, elephant, shark). Ma. *takaran* huge, powerful as a man, bear, etc. Ka. *tagar, ṭagaru, ṭagara, ṭegaru* ram. *Tu. tagaru, ṭagarů id. Te. tagaramu, tagaru id. / Cf. Mar. tagar* id. (DEDR 3000).

Substantive (in the context of a merchant's business): Ta. *takaram* tin, white lead, metal sheet, coated with tin. Ma. *takaram* tin, tinned iron plate. Ko. *tagarm (obl. tagart-)* tin. Ka. *tagara, tamara, tavara id. Tu. tamarů, tamara, tavara id. Te. tagaramu, tamaramu, tavaramu id. Kuwi (Isr.) ṭagromi* tin metal, alloy. / Cf. Skt. *tamara-* id. (DEDR 3001).

Decoding 'ram' glyph of Harappa Script, meḍh: rebus: 'helper of merchant'

An aspect of metalwork of the Bronze Age which should receive detailed attention of archaeo-metallurgical researchers is the competence demonstrated by artisans of Sarasvati-Sindhu civilization to inscribe on metal.

Such evidences of inscriptions on metal presented in this note, reinforce the validity of decipherment of almost the entire set of 7000 inscriptions on Harappa Script Corpora as catalogus catalogorum of metalwork.

Such inscriptions on metal are not merely those found on copper plates but also on metal objects themselves such as silver seals, axes, chisels, knives, spearheads, daggers, tin ingots, copper alloy ingots, celts.

m0317 Silver seal *bica* 'scorpion' rebus: *bica* 'sand stone ore, haematite ore' *dATu* 'crosś rebus: *dhatu* 'mineral' *khāreDo* 'currycomb' rebus: Rebus: *khārādī* ' turner' (Gujarati) *kāmsako, kāmsiyo* = a large sized comb (Gujarati) Rebus: *kaṁsa* 'bronze' (Telugu) *kōḍiya* 'young bull' rebus *kōṭiya* 'dhow, seafaring vessel' *sãgaḍa* 'lathe, brazier' rebus: *sangara* 'fortification'. सं-ग्रह *saṁgraha, samgaha* 'a guardian , ruler , manager , arranger' R. BhP.

m1199 Silver seal Mackay 1938, vol. 2, Pl. XC,1; XCVI, 520

ayo, aya 'fish' rebus: aya 'iron' *ayas* 'metal' *ḍato* 'claws or pincers (chelae) of crabś rebus: *dhatu* 'mineral, ore' *kanka* 'rim of jar' rebus: *karṇī* 'supercargo' *kōḍiya* 'young bull' rebus *kōṭiya* 'dhow, seafaring vessel' *sãgaḍa* 'lathe, brazier' rebus: *sangara* 'fortification'. सं-ग्रह *saṁgraha, samgaha* 'a guardian , ruler , manager , arranger' R. BhP.

seal. 2520 *adaren* 'lid' + *ayo* 'fish' rebus: *aduru ayas* 'native metal, iron' *gaNDa* 'four' rebus: *khaNDa* 'implements' PLUS *kolom* 'three' rebus: *kolimi* 'smithy' Thus, smithy implements. Kanka 'rim of jar' rebus: *karNI* 'supercargo'

Slide 209 (Harappa.com). harappa.com Inscribed lead celt or ingot fragment from the Trench 54 area (H2000-4481/2174-321). The object was apparently chiseled to reduce its size. Lead may have been used as an alloy with copper, for making pigments, or as meḍicine.

Altyn-depe. Silver seal. Pictograph of ligatured animal with three heads. Hieroglyph: *sangaDa* 'joined animals' (Marathi) Rebus: sangāṭh संगाठ् । सामग्री m. (sg. dat. *sangāṭas* संगाटस्), a collection (of implements, tools, materials, for any object), apparatus. *samgaha* 'manager' Given examples of similar joined animals, it may be surmised that the three animal hieroglyphs are: *ranku* 'antelope' Rebus: *ranku* 'tin'; *krammara* 'look backwardś Rebus: *kamar* 'smith'; *barad* 'ox' Rebus: *bharat* 'alloy of copper, pewter, tin'; *kondh* 'one-horned young bull' Rebus: *kondh* 'turner'.

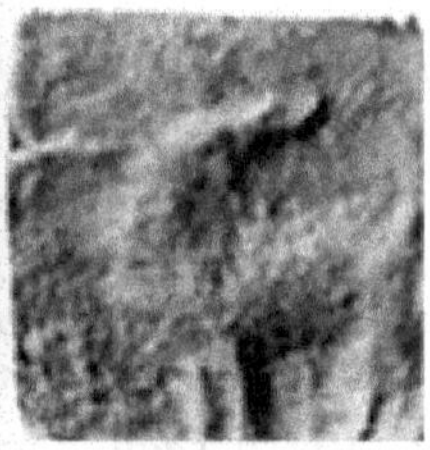

m0438, m1449, m1452, m1486, m1493, m1498, m1501; m0582 (123 copper tablets)

A list of Inscribed metal tools

Broken axe, Chanhu-daro (C-40) inscribed on both sides.
Ingot. Chanhu-daro (C-39)
Chisel. Kalibangan (K-121). Wt. 210 g.
Parallels broken chisel (tang) Mohenjo-daro (DK-7856). Wt. 165/343 g/
Axe. Kaibangan (K-122). Wt. 476 g.
Parallels axe Mohenjo-daro (DK-7835). Wt. 1910.030 g.
Knife. DK-7800
Spearhead DK-7857
Axe. DK-7855. Wt. 262 g.

(Note: Of the five metal objects from Mohenjo-daro, four were found 'at the low level 24.4 ft.[and one (copper knife) was found 18.4 ft. below datum. (Mackay 1938: 454; Vol. II. Pl. CXXVI #2.3 and 5, Pl. CXXVII #1, Pl. CXXXI; Vol. II. Pl. CXXXIII#1).Mackay 1938: Vol. 1, p. 348, Vol. 2, Pl. XC,1; XCVI, 520.[217]

Chanhu-daro Pl. LXXIV and Mohenjo-daro: copper and bronze tools and utensils (an inscriptions line mirrored on a zebu seal)

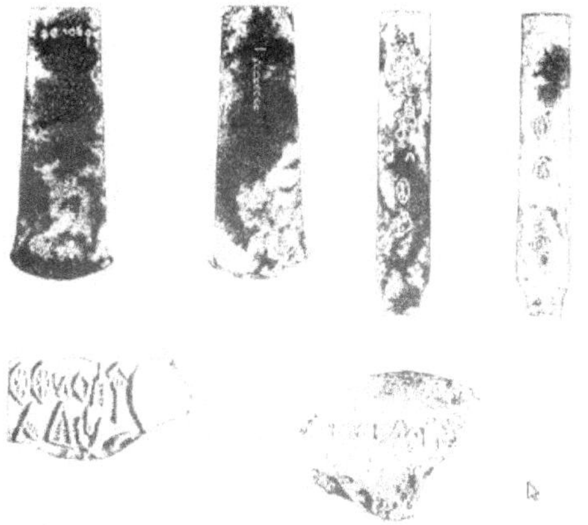

2925 Inscribed bronze implement (MIC Plate CXXVI-5)

2903 Incised copper tablet

2923 Inscribed bronze implement (MIC PlatCXXVI-2)

2924 Inscribed bronze implement (MIC Plate CXXVI-3)

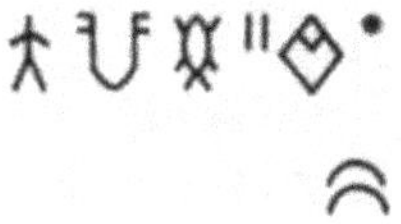

Chanhu-daro, Pl. LXXIV & Mohenjo-daro: copper and bronze tools and utensils (an inscription line mirrored on a zebu seal)

A report from an archaeological excavation at Banawali indicates that a seal with the inscription with hieroglyphs such as: horned tiger, standard device and other hieroglyphs such as body, fish was found in a silversmith's residence: Banawari. Seal 17. Text 9201. Hornd tiger PLUS lathe + portable furnace. Banawali 17, Text 9201 Find spot: "The plan of 'palatial building' rectangular in shape (52 X 46 m) with eleven units of rooms…The discovery of a tiger seal from the sitting room and a few others from the house and its vicinity, weights ofchert, and lapis lazuli beads and deluxe Harappa pottery indicate that the house belonged to a prominent merchant."[218]

Message on metalwork: *kol* 'tiger' (Santali); *kollan* 'blacksmith' (Ta.) *koḍ.* 'horn'; *koḍ.* 'artisan's workshop' PLUS *śagaḍī*= lathe (Gujarati) *san:gaḍa,* 'lathe, portable furnace'; rebus: sanga th संगथ् । संयोगः f. (sg. dat. *sangüʦü* association, living together, partnership (e.g. of beggars, rakes, members of a caravan, and so on); (of a man or woman) copulation, sexual union. sangāṭh संगाठ् । सामग्री m. (sg. dat. *sangāṭas* संगाटस्), a collection (of implements, tools, materials, for any object), apparatus, furniture, a collection of the things wanted on a journey, luggage, and so on. --karun -- करुन् । सामग्रीसंग्रहः m.inf. to collect the ab. (L.V. 17).(Kashmiri) सं-ग्रह *saṁgraha, samgaha* 'a guardian , ruler , manager , arranger' R. BhP. *gaNDa* 'four' rebus: *khaNDa* 'implements' PLUS *ayo* 'fish' rebus: *aya* 'metal' PLUS *aDaren* 'lid' rebus: *aduru* 'native metal'. Thus, native metal implements. *dhAu* 'strands' rebus: *dhAu, dhAtu* 'minerals' Hieroglyph: *karNaka* 'spread legs' rebus: *karNaka* 'helmsman'

The Technique -
Most plates that are classed as engraved start out by having parts of the main design etched first. Etching gives a greater freedom and ease in laying down bold areas of design, the finishing and detail then being added by pure engraving.

The engraver used a burin (illustration above), or graver, which was a prism shaped bar of hardened steel with a sharp point and wooden handle. This was pushed across the surface of the plate away from the artist, the palm was used to push the burin and it was guided by the thumb and forefinger. The action of engraving produced thin strips of waste metal and left thin furrows in the plate's surface, to take the ink. Any burr left on the edge of the engraved lines was removed with a 'scraper'.[unquote]219

That the artisans had the competence to create such inscriptions in bas relief (as raised script), on copper is also evidenced by the multiple solid copper tablets found in Harappa and reported by HARP. An example is provided by Kenoyer who was in the HARP project team:

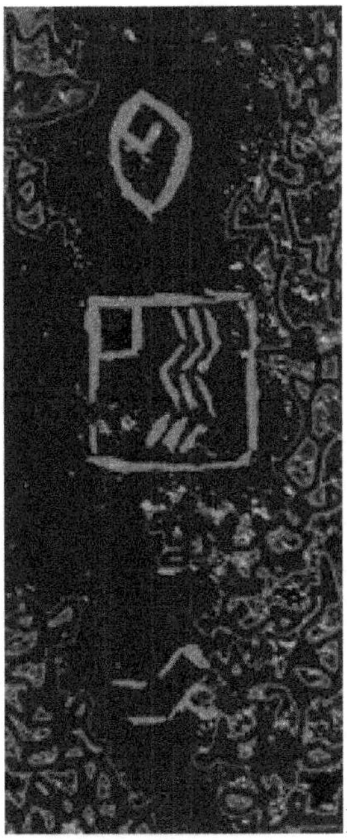

Kalibangan 122A

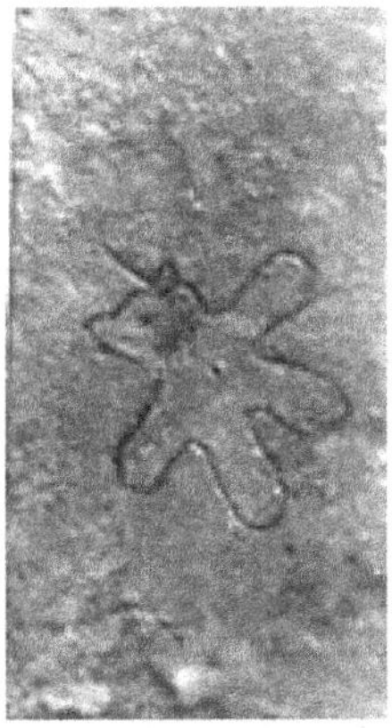

m0475 Inscribed metal place (One-horned young bull PLUS octopus)

"Rendered in strict profile, standing before what might be an altar, the bull is by far the most popular motif in the Indus Valley glyptic art; there is virtually no v ariation in either the style or the iconographic details among the individual examples. The shoulder of the bull is emphasized by an upside-down doubly outlined heart shape that has been interpreted as painted decoration on the body of the bull, but is more likely an artistic convention for representing the muscles of the bull's shoulder." [After Fig. 38 in Holly Pittman, 1984, p. 84].

Mohenjo-daro. Silver seal (After Mackay 1938, vol. 2, Pl. XC,1; XCVI, 520). Two silver seals at Mohenjo-daro, two copper seals at Lothal and at Ras al-Junayz in Oman are rare uses of metal for making seals.

Stamp seal and a modern impression: unicorn or bull and inscription,, Mature Harappa period, ca. 2600–1900 B.C. Indus Valley Burnt steatite; 1 1/2 x 1 1/2 in. (3.8 x 3.8 cm)

http://www.metmuseum.org/toah/ho/02/ssa/ho_49.40.1.htm

An evidence for the continued use of Harappa Script hieroglyphs comes from Ramurva copper bolt.

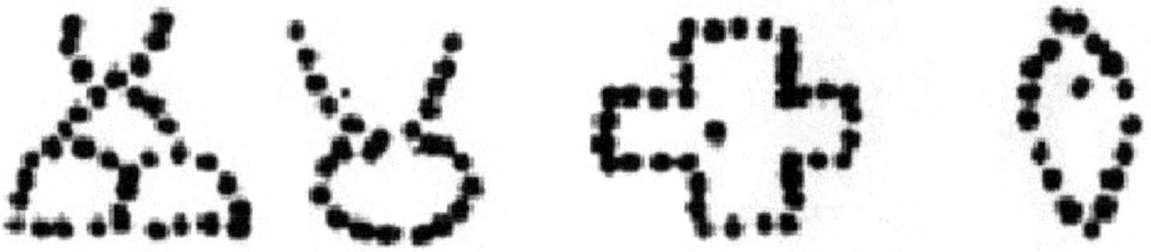

Hieroglyphs:

goT 'seed' Rebus: *khōṭa* 'alloy ingot'.goTa 'laterite, ferrite ore'. खोट (p. 212) [*khōṭa*] f A mass of metal (unwrought or of old metal melted down); an ingot or wedge. (Marathi) *kāṇḍa* 'fire-altar' Rebus: *khaṇḍa* 'metal implements; *goT* 'round object' Rebus: *khōṭa* 'alloy ingot' PLUS *bhaṭa* 'rimless pot' Rebus: *bhaṭa* 'furnace'; *dhanga* 'mountain-range' Rebus: *dhangar* 'metalsmith' PLUS *bhaṭa* 'rimless pot' Rebus: *bhaṭa* 'furnace'. Thus, the inscription on the Rampurva copperbolt provides technical specification on the metal object, the copper bolt: that it was made of an alloy ingot (from) furnace, (made by) metal implements metalsmith.

Who knows? The metalsmith might have worked for Asoka or Asoka's predecessors (earlier than 3rd cent. BCE), as Allchin surmises.

Rampurva copper bolt "The starting place for the inquiry is the Rampurva copper bolt at present in the Indian Museum, Calcutta. This was discovered in 1880 by Cunningham and H.B. Garrick. It was buried beside the fallen southerly pillar on which was engraved a set of Asoka's pillar edicts. The pillar and its lion capital were subsequently fully excavated by Daya Ram Sahni. The more northerly Rampurva pillar is that associated with the famous bull capital. The bolt was examined by Cunningham who concluded that there could be n doubt of its being original and that it must have served to hold the lion capital in place upon its pillar. It is probable that other Asokan pillars and capitals bear mortises for similar bolts. This one is described as barrel shaped, of pure copper measuring 2 ft. ½ in. in length, with a diameter of 4 5/16 in. in the centre, and 3 5/8 in. at each end. Cunningham makes no mention of any marks upon the bolt, but Durga Prasad published an impression of four marks. They are made of lines of impressed dots and include the hill-with-crescent, the taurine or Nandipada, and the open cross:

Here then these signs occur upon an object which must have been made by craftsmen working for Asoka or one of his predecessors."[220]

Sohgaura copper plate inscription as a survival of Sarasvati hieroglyphs and writing system

The

Sohgaura copper plate refers to a pair of kos.t.ha_ga_ra (dva_ra kot.t.haka); the two storehouses described as tri-*garbha (*i.e. having three rooms) are illustrated on line 1. (Fleet, JRAS, 1907). The illustrations indicate that the three rooms are in three storeys, with supporting pillars clearly seen. The inscription refers to the junction of three highways named Manavati, in two villages called Dasilimita and Usagama. The storehouses were made at this junction for the goods of people using the highways, which are indicated in line 3 by mentioning the three places to and from which they led. One of the names give is reognized by Fleet as Chanchu.[221] Some glyphs on line 1: *kut.hi* = tree; rebus: *kut.hi* = smelting furnace; *kos.t.ha_ga_ra* = storehouse; *śu_la* = spear; *cu_l.a* = kiln; *kan.d.kanka* = rim of jar; rebus: copper furnace; *bat.a* = quail; rebus: kiln.

The top line is a set of hieroglyphs (from left to right).

Tree = *kut.i*; rebus: *kut.hi* 'smelter, furnace'
Warehouse = *kot.* (*kos.t.hagara*)
Spear = *cu_la;* rebus: *cu_lha* 'furnace'
Mountain-summit = *ku_t.amu* ; rebus : *ku_t.a* 'workshop'
Wide-mouthed pot on mountain-summit = *bat.i;* rebus: *bat.hi* 'furnace')
Rim of jar = *kan.d.*; rebus: *kand.* 'fire-altar'
Tree = *kut.i;* rebus: *kut.hi* 'smelter, furnace'
Bird on branch: *bat.a* 'quail'; rebus: *bat.a* 'furnace'; *d.a_l.* 'branch of tree'; rebus: *d.ha_l.ako* 'large metal ingot' [The glyptic composition refers to a kut.hi which can produce metal ingots]
Warehouse = *kot.* (*kos.t.hagara)*)

The brahmi epigraph on the lines following the top line refers to two kos.t.hagara set up for itinerant merchants (smiths?) at the junction of three roads. Some devices used on punch-marked coins also occur as the first line of the Sohgaura copper plate inscription.[222]

Sohgaura or Soghaura is a village on the right bank of River Rapti, about fourteen miles south-east from Gorakhpur. The plate measures 2 ½ X 1 7/8 inches. The copper plate was cast in a mould. The writing is NOT incised, but in bold, high relief. (JRAS 1907, p. 527). "In the first place, this archaeological find affords the oldest known and clear example of the use of a copper-plate as a material for writing, especially for inscribing a record in Brahmi characters…Secondly, the record has its uniqueness and importance for the standard of Brahmi characters which it presents, the standard which, in the opinion of Dr. Fleet, 'refers it to at any rate an early date in the Maurya period, BC 320 to about [180]'…

Non-religious nature of sign graphs on Sohgaura copper plate

"Lastly, with regard to its subject-matter, the inscription is found to be a public notification about the judicious use of certain things in two storehouses by persons carrying on traffic along the high roads leading to Śra_vasti, or it may be, by persons carrying on traffic by all the three kinds of vehicles along the high roads, in times of urgent need…What we owe to Dr. Fleet's study of the nature of the devices (used on the top line of the copper plate) is the recognition in all of them a significance other than that of religious symbols. To quote him in his words: 'Two of them obviously represent the storehouses themselves, which are shown as shed with double roofs. The lower roof in each case is supported by four rows of posts; and these perhaps stand for four rows of posts, the front posts hiding, those behind them. In the other devices I recognize, not religious emblems, Buddhist or otherwise, -- (I mean, not religious emblems employed here as such), -- nor Mangalas, auspicious symbols, but the arms of the three towns mentioned in L3 of the record.'[223]

The text of the inscription (which is considered by some to of pre-Mauryan days, i.e. circa 4th century BCE) refers to some famine relief measures and notifies the establishment of two public storehouses at a junction of three great highways of vehicular traffic to meet the needs of persons (apparently merchants and metal-workers) using these roads. The first line which is full of glyphs or devices should relate to the inscription and the facilities provided to the traders. Next to the symbol of the *kos.t.haagaara* is a *śu_la* (spear). This is phonetically *cuula* 'kiln' for metals to be heated and copper/bronze/brass vessels and tools, worked on by metalsmiths. Similarly, the first glyph of a tree on a platform can be read as *kuṭi* 'tree'; another word *kuṭhi* in Santali means a 'furnace' for melting metals. The other devices are: three peaks mounted by a rimless pot, a rim of a jar, a tree branch with a bird perched on top. These can also be explained in the context of Sarasvati heiroglyphs and the context of metals/minerals-trade.

The second symbol from the left and the second symbol from the right may refer to a *kos.t.haagaara. Ko.s.thaagaara* is a pair of storehouses are referred to by this name in the Sohgaura plaque inscription, and illustrated on the same plaque (Fleet, The tradition about the corporeal relics of Buddha, JRAS, 1907, pp. 341-363: I find a mention of a place named Chanchu, which I take to be the same one, in the Sohgaura plate (JASB, 63, 1894. proceedings, 86, plate; IA, 25. 262). That record, as I understand it, is a public notification relating to three great highways of vehicular traffic…It notifies that at the junction, named Manavasi, of the three roads, in two villages named Dasilimata and Usagama, storehouses were made for the goods of people using the roads. It indicates the roads by mentioning in line 3, the three places to and from which they led; as regards the junction of them.). They are described as trigarbha, having three rooms; Fleet discusses this at length, but it is evident from the illustrations that these rooms are on three storeys, for the storehouses are represented as small three-storeyed pavilions; it is true that the roof of the top storey is "out of the picture," but its supporting pillars can be clearly eeen. Another use of garbha designates chambers of a many-storeyed building,[224]

The devices on the top line of the Sohgaura copper plate can be read rebus as hieroglyphs, as in the case of Sarasvati hieroglyphs: 1. tree, kut.i (as smelting furnace); 2. tree twigs, *kut.i* (as smelting furnace); 3. cup, *bat.i* (as a furnace for melting iron ore); 4. bird, *bat.a* (as iron or metal); 4. two *kos.t.ha_ga_ra* (as storehouses), comparable to a sign graph with four posts used on Harappai epigraphs (so called Indus inscriptions); three mountains with a U graph on top summit. The presence of furnace facilities for working with metal tools in the two warehouses can be explained in the context of the types of conveyances, parts of which may require mending and to work/tinker on metallic articles and wares of itinerant merchants who need such publicly provided facilities in times of emergency as the *śa_sana* in Brahmi writing notes.

kut.hi kut.a, kut.i, kut.ha a tree (Kauś.); kud.a tree (Pkt.); kur.a_ tree; kar.ek tree, oak (Pas;.)(CDIAL 3228). kut.ha, kut.a (Ka.), kudal (Go.) kudar. (Go.) kut.ha_ra, kut.ha, kut.aka = a tree (Skt.lex.) kut., kurun: = stump of a tree (Bond.a); khut. = id. (Or.) kut.a, kut.ha = a tree (Ka.lex.) gun.d.ra = a stump; khun.t.ut = a stump of a tree left in the ground (Santali.lex.) kut.amu = a tree (Telugu)

kut.i, 'smelting furnace' (Mundari). *kut.hi, kut.i (Or.; Sad. kot.hi)* (1) the smelting furnace of the blacksmith; *kut.ire bica duljad.ko talkena*, they were feeding the furnace with ore; (2) the name of e_kut.i has been given to the fire which, in lac factories, warms the water bath for softening the lac so that it can be spread into sheets; to make a smelting furnace; *kut.hi-o* of a smelting furnace, to be made; the smelting furnace of the blacksmith is made of mud, cone-shaped, 2' 6" dia. At the base and 1' 6" at the top. The hole in the centre, into which the mixture of charcoal and iron ore is poured, is about 6" to 7" in dia. At the base it has two holes, a smaller one into which the nozzle of the bellow is inserted, and a larger one on the opposite side through which the molten iron flows out into a cavity (Mundari) cf. *kan.d.a* = furnace, altar (Santali)

kut.i = a woman water-carrier (Telugu) *kut.i* = to drink; drinking, beverage (Ta.); drinking, water drunk after meals (Ma.); *kud.t-* to drink (To.); *kud.i* to drink; drinking (Ka.); *kud.i* to drink (Koḍ.); *kud.i* right, right hand (Te.); *kut.i_* intoxicating liquor (Skt.)(DEDR 1654).

The bunch of twigs = *ku_di_, ku_t.i_* (Skt.lex.) *ku_di_* (also written as *ku_t.i_* in manuscripts) occurs in the Atharvaveda (AV 5.19.12) and Kauśika Su_tra (Bloomsfield's ed.n, xliv. cf. Bloomsfield, American Journal of Philology, 11, 355; 12,416; Roth, Festgruss an Bohtlingk, 98) denotes it as a twig. This is identified as that of Badari_, the jujube tied to the body of the dead to efface their traces. (See Vedic Index, I, p. 177).
Bird on the tree: *baṭa* 'quail' rebus: *bhāṭi* 'kiln, furnace'

bat.i = a metal cup or basin; bhat.i = a still, a boiler, a copper; *dhubi bhat.i* = a washerman's boiler; jhuli *bhat.i* = a trench in the ground used as a fireplace when cooking has to be done for a large number of people (Santali)

This note has presented two continuities from Sarasvati civilization: 1. use of punches to mark devices on punch-marked coins and 2. use of copper plate to convey message related to an economic transaction.

This continuity of tradition is linked by the metallurgical tradition of śreni/artisan guilds working with metals, minerals and furnaces to create copper/bronze artifacts and terracotta or śankha bangles and ornaments of silver, copper or semi-precious stones such as agate, carnelian or lapis lazuli. The code of the writing system which was employed on Sarasvati hieroglyphs with 5 or 6 sign graphs constituting an inscription, is the same code which was employed on devices of punch-marked coins (produced in mints belonging to guilds) and on copper plate *śa_śana-s* or historical periods of pre-mauryan times in India, like the evidence presented by Sohgaura copper plate. Since this plate contains a Brahmi inscription, this constitutes a Rosetta stone to explain the meanings of the sign graphs or glyphs employed on the top line of the plate in the context of the facilities provided in two warehouses to traveling caravan merchants or rive-faring merchants.

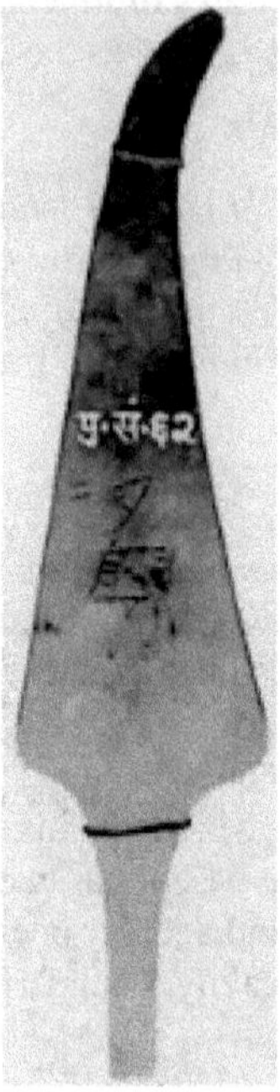

h380, h381 Bronze dagger inscribed in Harappa Script *kuṭi* 'curve; rebus: कुटिल *kuṭila, katthīl* (8 parts copper, 2 parts tin) *kole.l* 'temple' rebus: *kole.l* 'smithy, forge' *kanac* 'corner' rebus: *kancu* 'bronze' PLUS *sal* 'splinter' rebus: *sal* 'workshop'.

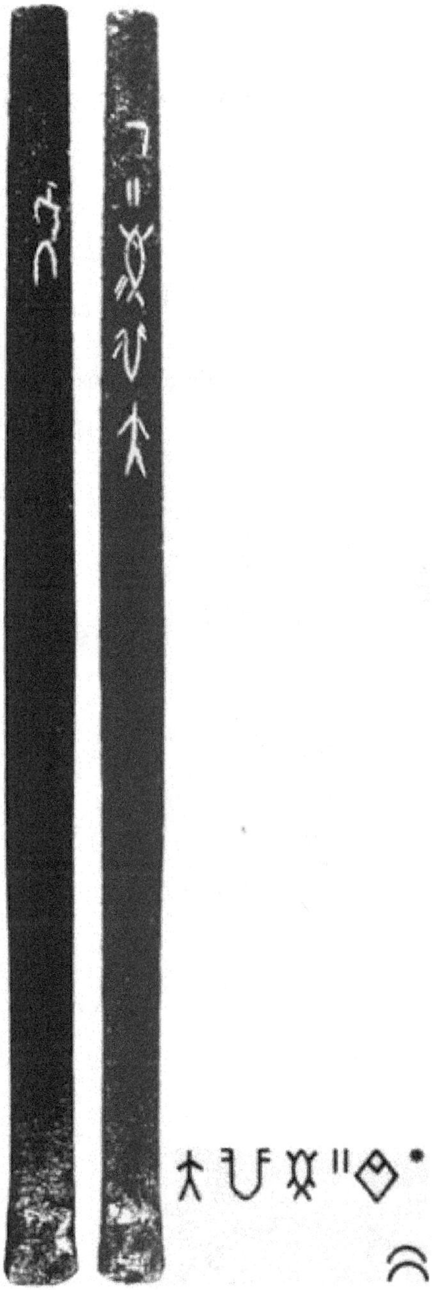

Kalibangan. Inscribed bronze rod (Mahadevan 1977:7)

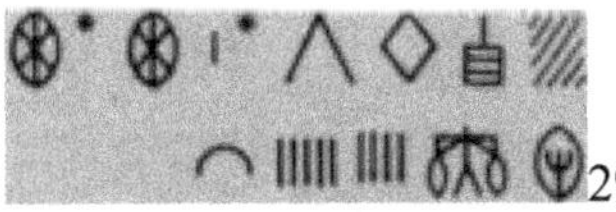2923 Inscribed bronze implement (MIC Plate CXXVI-3)

2924 Inscribed bronze implement (MIC Plate CXXVI-3)

2925 Inscribed bronze implement (MIC Plate CXXVI-5)

2903 Inscribed copper tablet

Inscribed weapons are further reported from Harappa Vats 1940: 384ss, Pl. CXX, 5,19), Chanhu Daro (Mackay 1943: 178, Pl. LXXIV, 1-1a,8)

Chanhu-daro, Pl. LXXIV & Mohenjodaro: copper and bronze tools and utensils (an inscription line mirrored on a zebu seal)

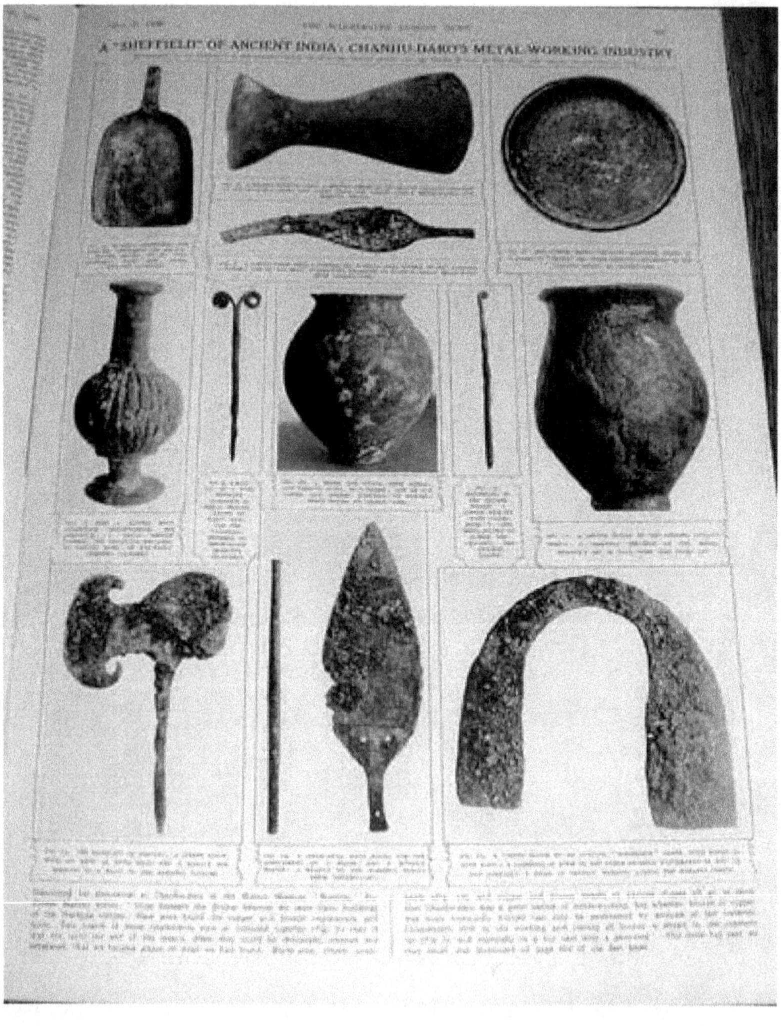
A "SHEFFIELD" OF ANCIENT INDIA: CHANHU-DARO'S METAL-WORKING INDUSTRY

Chanhudaro. Sheffield of Ancient Near East. Metalware catalog in London News Illustrated, November 21, 1936.

A 'Sheffield

of Ancient India: Chanhu-Daro's metal working industry 10 X photos of copper knives, spears, razors, axes and dishes. The words used in the *lingua franca*of such tin-processing families constitute the words invented to denote the Bronze Age products and artifacts such as tin or zinc or the array of metalware discovered in the Sheffied of the Ancient East, Chanhu-daro as reported in the London News Illustrated by Ernest Mackay.

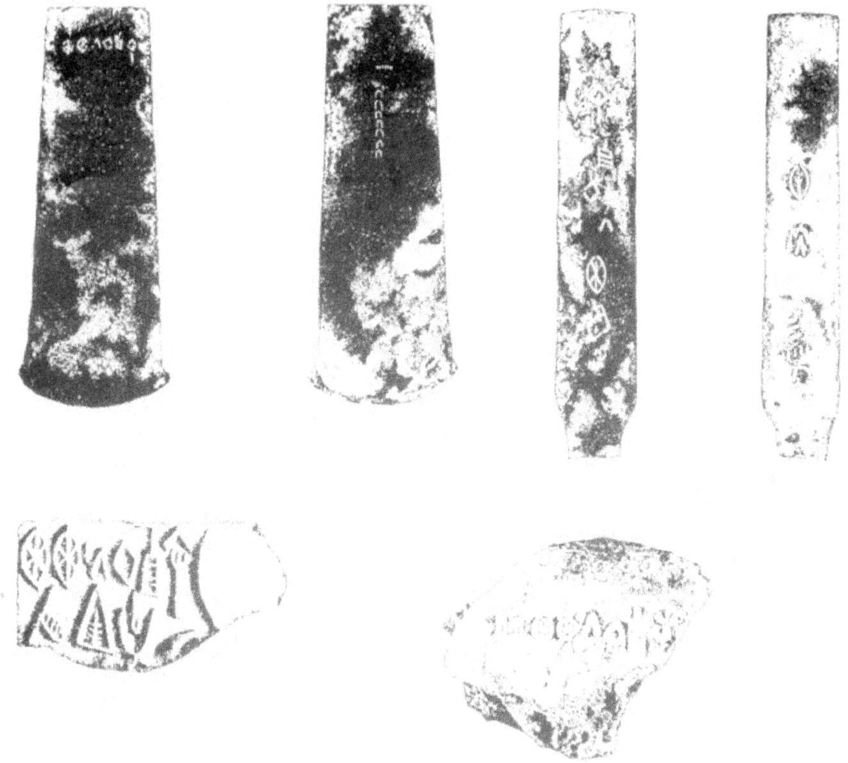

Axe-head of brown schist (L 15 cm) with the head of a leopard or lioness on the butt. From the palace of Mallia, destroyed in LM I B ca. 1450 BCE. After Plate 90 in: Sinclair Hood, 1971, The Minoans, New York, Praeger Publishers

Shaft-hole axhead with a bird-headed demon, boar,and dragon, late 3rd–early 2nd millennium BCE Central Asia (Bactria-Margiana) Silver, gold foil; 5 7/8 in. (15 cm) "Western Central Asia, now known as Turkmenistan, Uzbekistan, and northern Afghanistan, has yielded objects attesting to a highly developed civilization in the late third and early second millennium B.C. Artifacts from the region indicate that there were contacts with Iran to the southwest. Tools and weapons, especially axes, comprise a large portion of the metal objects from this region. This shaft-hole axhead is a masterpiece of three-dimensional and relief sculpture. Expertly cast in silver and gilded with gold foil, it depicts a bird-headed hero grappling with a wild boar and a winged dragon. The idea of the heroic bird-headed creature probably came from western Iran, where it is first documented on a cylinder seal impression. The hero's muscular body is human except for the bird talons that replace the hands and feet. He is represented twice, once on each side of the ax, and consequently appears to have two heads. On one side, he grasps the boar by the belly and on the other, by the tusks. The posture of the boar is contorted so that its bristly back forms the shape of the blade. With his other talon, the bird-headed hero grasps the winged dragon by the neck. The dragon, probably originating in Mesopotamia or Iran, is represented with folded wings, a feline body, and the talons of a bird of prey."

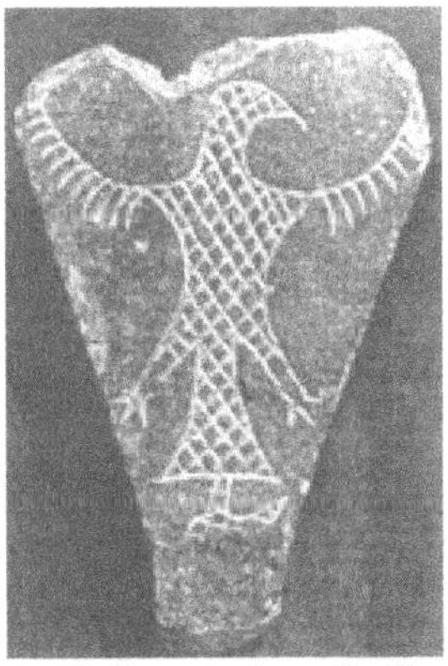

Eagle incised on a ceremonial axe made of chlorite. Tepe Yahya. (After Fig. 9.6 in Philip H. Kohl, 2001)

Rebus readings are: *eruvai* 'kite' rebus: *eruvai* 'copper' PLUS kambha 'shoulder, wing' rebus: *kammaṭa* 'mint'; thus, copper mint.

kola 'tiger' rebus: *kol* 'working in iron' *kolhe* 'smelter' PLUS *kambha* 'wing' rebus: k*ammaṭa* 'mint'; thus, iron smelter's mint.

badhi 'boar' rebus: *badhi* *dhangar* 'bull' rebus: carpenter, worker in 'carpenter, worke in iron' and *dhangar* 'blacksmith'. *baḍhoe* 'a wood'; badhoria 'expert in working in wood'(Santali) বরাহ *barāha* 'boar'Rebus: *bāṛaï* 'carpenter' (Bengali) bari 'merchant' *barea* 'merchant' (Santali) बारकश or बारकस [*bārakaśa* or *bārakasa*] *n* (P) A trading vessel, a merchantman.

Bactrian bronze axe-head

The narrow blade decorated with incised chevrons, cut-away socket with banded edges, the shaft decorated with two squatting figures each wearing short tunic, one wrestling a seated feline the other with arms around the feline and a standing quadruped (perhaps bull). Rebus readings: *kola* 'tiger' rebus: *kolhe* 'smelter' *dhangar* 'bull' rebus: *dhangar* 'blacksmith'.

2nd Millennium BCE L. 6 3/4 in. (17.2 cm.) Ex London art market, late 1990s. Published: J. Eisenberg, Art of the Ancient World, 2012, no. 251.[225]
Gold sheet and silver, Late 3rd/early 2nd millennium B.C.E.
L. 12.68 cm. Ceremonial Axe Bactria, Northern Afghanistan[226] "The whole cast by the lost wax process. The boar covered with a sheet of gold annealed and hammered on, some 3/10-6/10 mm in thickness, almost all the joins covered up with silver. At the base of the mane between the shoulders an oval motif with irregular indents. The lion and the boar hammered, elaborately chased and polished. A shaft opening - 22 holes around its edge laced with gold wire some 7/10-8/10 mm in diameter - centred under the lion's shoulder; between these a hole (diam: some 6.5 mm) front and back for insertion of a dowel to hold the shaft in place, both now missing.

Ceremonial axe (inscribed with name) of king Untash-Napirisha, from his capital Tchoga Zambil. Back of the axe adorned with an electrum boar; the blade issues from a lion's mouth. Silver and electrum, H: 5,9 cm Sb 3973

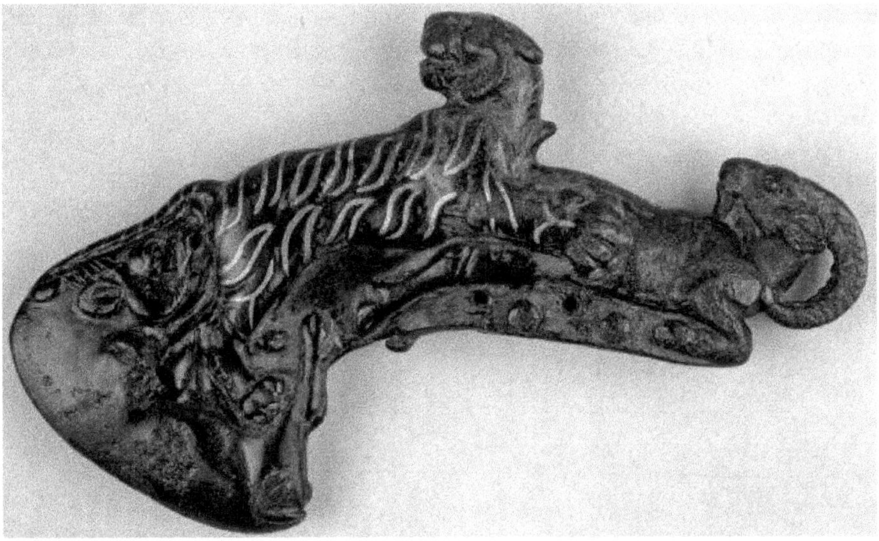

Cast axe-head; tin bronze inlaid with silver; shows a boar attacking a tiger which is attacking an ibex.ca. 2500 -2000 BCE Bactria-Margiana Archaeological Complex. Length: 17.8 cm (7 in). Weight: 675.5 g (23.82 oz). British Museum.ME 123628 (1913,0314.11913,0314.1)[227]

Decipherment: There are three hieroglyphs: ram (markhor), tiger, boar. The rebus renderings are: coppersmith (merchant's helper), smelter, worker in wood and iron.

Tor._*miṇḍ* 'ram',_*miṇḍā́l*_'markhor' (CDIAL 10310) Rebus:_*meḍh* 'helper of merchant' (Gujarati) *mẽṛhẽt, meḍ* 'iron' (Mu.Ho.) *meḍ* 'copper' (Slavic) *meṛed-bica* = iron stone ore, in contrast to bali-bica, iron sand ore (Munda) Thus, coppersmith, helper of merchant.

kola 'tiger' rebus: *kolle* 'blacksmith', *kolhe* 'smelter' kol 'working in iron'. Thus, a smelter.

badhi 'boar' rebus: *badhi* 'carpenter, worke in iron' and *dhangar* 'bull' rebus: *dhangar* 'blacksmith'. *baḍhoe* ‘a carpenter, worker in wood’; badhoria ‘expert in working in wood’(Santali) বরাহ *barāha* 'boar'Rebus: *bāṛaï* 'carpenter' (Bengali) bari 'merchant' *barea* 'merchant' (Santali) बारकश or बारकस [*bārakaśa* or *bārakasa*] *n* (P) A trading vessel, a merchantman.

h1518 copper axe sal ‘splinter’ rebus: sal ‘workshop’ kanac ‘corner’ rebus:kancu ‘bronze’ kole.l ‘temple’ rebus:kole.l ‘smithy, forge’

Mohenjo-daro seal m297a: Harappa h1018a copper plate. Head of one-horned bull ligatured with a four-pointed star-fish (Gangetic octopus?)

The hieroglyphs are explained as fortified enclosures of *mleccha* smithy guild workshops. *veṛhā* 'octopus, said to be found in the Induś (Jaṭki lexicon of A. Jukes, 1900) Rebus: *beṛɔ* m. ‘palace’, *beṛā* m. id. *beṛā* ‘building with a courtyard’ (Western Pahari) *vāṛo* m. ‘ cattle enclosure ’ (Sindhi) *baTi* ‘cup’ rebus: *baThi* ‘furnace’ PLUS *sal* ‘splinter’ rebus: *sal* ‘workshop’. மேடை mēṭai, *n.* [T. *mēḍa.*] 1. Platform, raised floor; தளமுயர்ந்த இடப்பகுதி. 2. Artificial mound; செய்குன்று. (W.) *meḍh* ‘helper of merchant’ (Pkt.) *meṛha, meḍhi* ‘merchant’s clerk (Gujarati) *ayo, aya* ‘fish’ rebus: *aya* ‘iron’ *ayas* ‘metal’ *khambhaṛā* 'fish **fin**' rebus: *kammaṭa* ‘mint, coiner, coinage’ *kanka* ‘rim of jar’ rebus: *karṇī* ‘supercargo’ *karṇaka* ‘spread legś rebus: *karṇika* ‘helmsman’ *meḍ* ‘body’ rebus: *meḍ* ‘iron’ (Mu.Ho.) *meḍ* ‘copper’ (Slavic languages) *koḍe, koḍiya* ‘young bull’ *koḍ* ‘horn’ rebus: *koTiya* ‘dhow, seafaring vessel’.

Kuwait cylinder seal. Gold. Possibly southeastern Iran, mid 3rd millennium BCE. Ht. 2.21 cm. dia. 2.74 cm. Fabricated from gold sheet with chased decoration. Inv. No. LNS 4517J

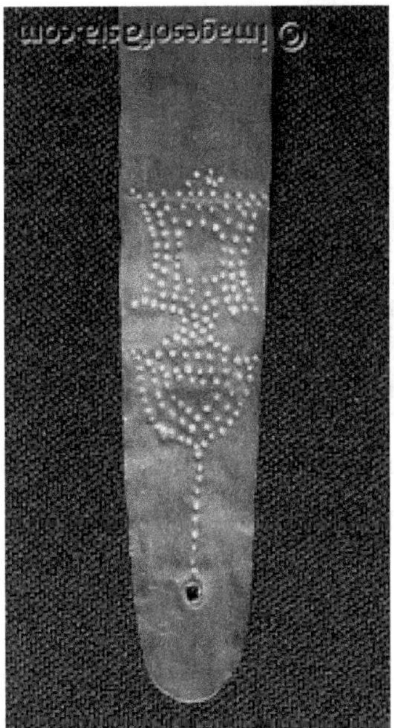

Gold fillet. Punctuated design on both ends. Mohenjodaro.228

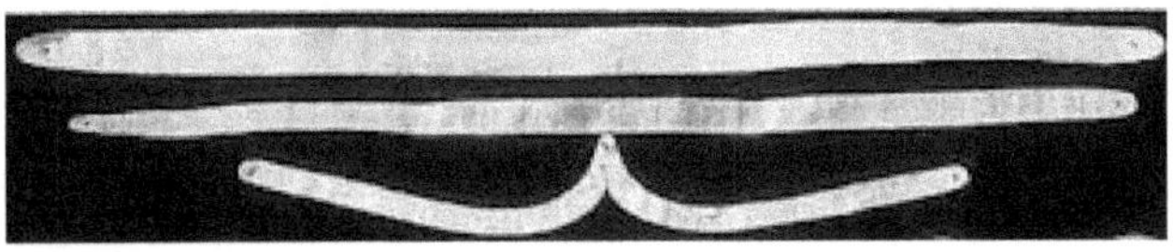

Gold fillet. Punctuated design on both ends.
Mohenjodaro. http://www.imagesofasia.com/html/mohenjodaro/gold-fillet.html

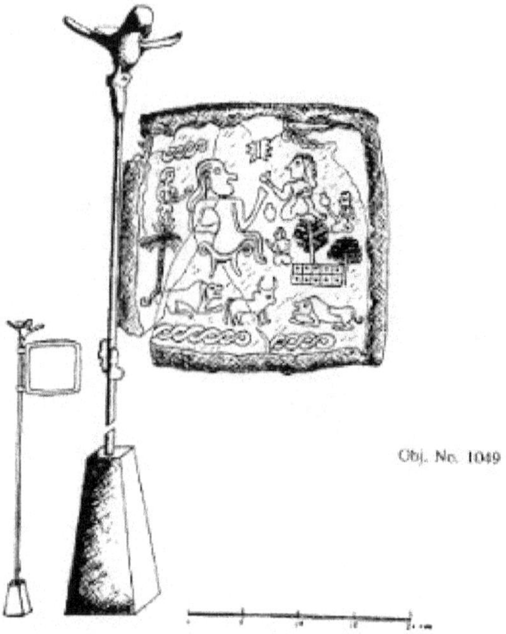

Shahdad Standard. Bronze. Drawing.

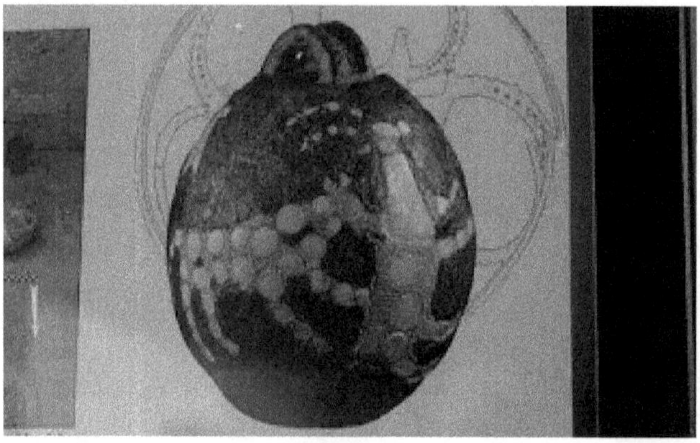

Lead weight. Shahi Tump. Ornamental ball (lead weight) discovered from Shahi Tump, Makran. It is 15 cm high and 15 kg in weight made by pure lead and wrapped in copper using cire perdue technique of casting.

Deciphered A4 to A11 sets of copper plate inscriptions

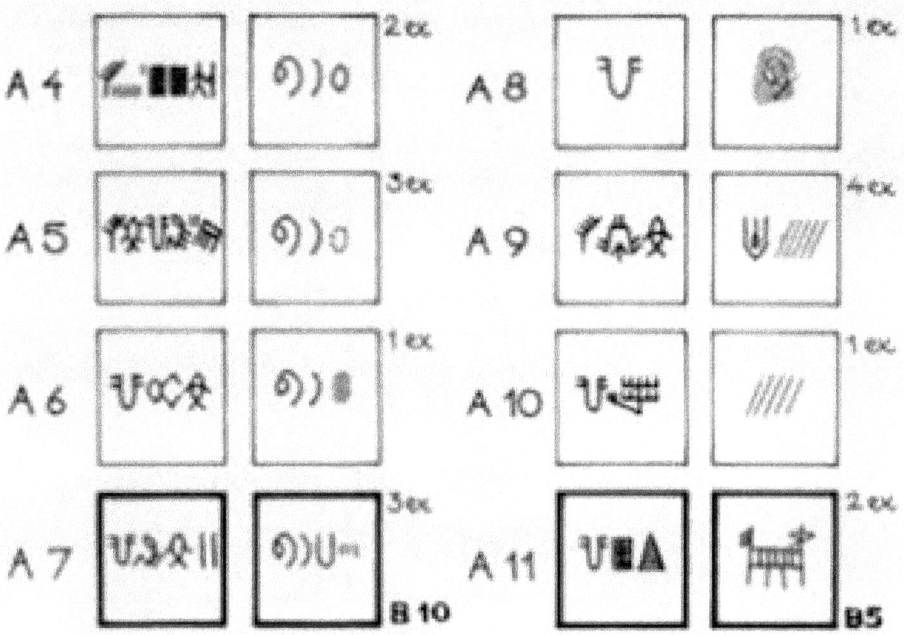
A 4
2 ex
A 8
1 ex
A 5
3 ex
A 9
4 ex
A 6
1 ex
A 10
1 ex
A 7
3 ex
B 10
A 11
2 ex
B5

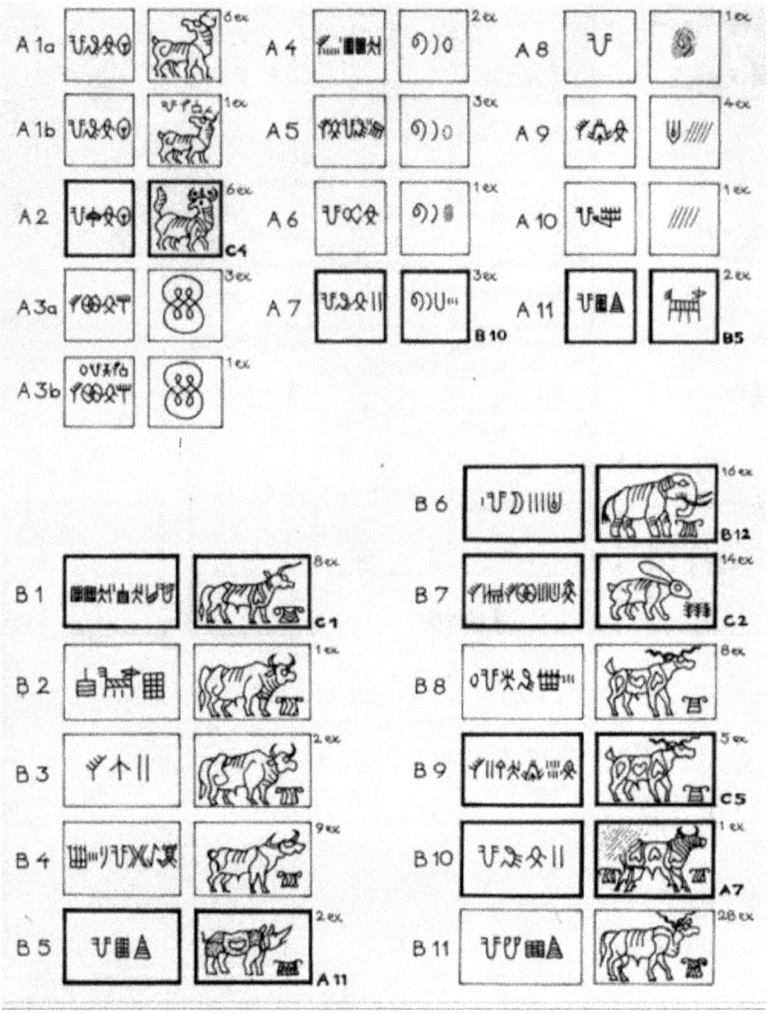
A 1a
6ex
A 1b
1ex
A 2
6ex
C4
A 3a
3ex
A 3b
1ex
A 4
2ex
A 5
3ex
A 6
1ex
A 7
3ex
B 10
A 8
1ex
A 9
4ex
A 10
1ex
A 11
2ex
B5
B 1
8ex
C1
B 2
1ex
B 3
2ex
B 4
9ex
B 5
2ex
A 11
B 6
16ex
B12
B 7
14ex
C2
B 8
8ex
B 9
5ex
C5
B 10
1ex
A7
B 11
28ex

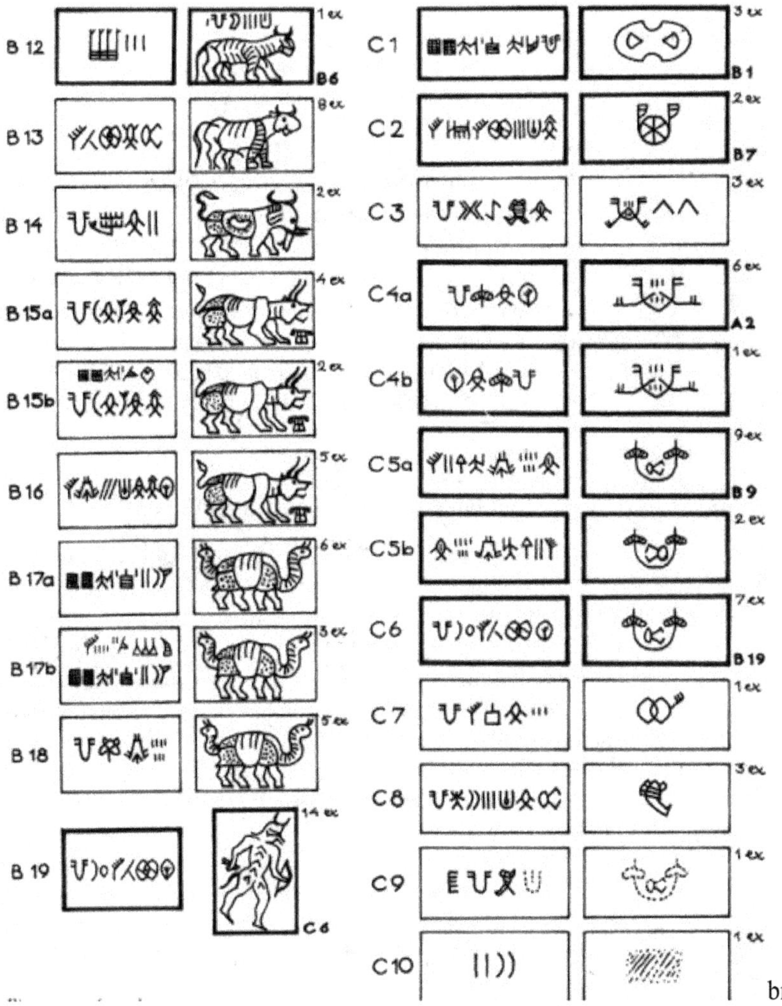

B 12
B 13
B 14
B 15a
B 15b
B 16
B 17a
B 17b
B 18
B 19
1 ex
8 ex
2 ex
4 ex
2 ex
5 ex
6 ex
3 ex
5 ex
14 ex
B6
C6
C 1
C 2
C 3
C 4a
C 4b
C 5a
C 5b
C 6
C 7
C 8
C 9
C 10
3 ex
2 ex
3 ex
6 ex
1 ex
9 ex
2 ex
7 ex
1 ex
3 ex
1 ex
1 ex
B 1
B 7
A 2
B 9
B 19

bronz

h1018copperobject Head of one-horned bull ligatured with a four-pointed star-fish (Gangetic octopus?).

koḍiyum 'rings on neck' koḍ `horn' (Kuwi); rebus: koḍ `artisan's workshop' (Gujarati). खोंड [khōṇḍa] m A young bull, a bullcalf.(Marathi) Rebus: kõdā 'to turn in a lathe'(B.) कोंद kōnda 'engraver, lapidary setting or infixing gemś (Marathi). The joined animal is a Gangetic octopus.veṛhā octopus, said to be found in the Indus (Jaṭki lexicon of A. Jukes, 1900) Rebus: . vēḍa 'boat'(Prakritam) Alternative:

Rebus: beṛhī 'warehouse';

beṛā building with a courtyard (WPah.)

9308 bēḍā f. ' boat ' lex. 2. vēḍā, vēṭī -- f. lex. 3. bhēḍa -- 3 m., bhēla -- 1, °aka -- m.n. lex.1. Pk. bēḍa -- , °aya -- m., bēḍā -- , °ḍiyā -- f. ' boat ', Gy. eur. bero, S. ḇeṛo m., °ṛī ' small do. '; L. bēṛā (Ju. ḇ --) m. ' large cargo boat ', bēṛī f. ' boat ', P. beṛā m., °ṛī f.; Ku. beṛo ' boat, raft ', N. beṛā, OAw. beḍā, H. beṛā m., G. beṛɔ m., beṛi f., M.beḍā m.2. Pk. vēḍa -- m. ' boat '.3. Pk. bhēḍaka -- , bhēlaa -- m., bhēlī -- f. ' boat '; B. bhelā ' raft ', Or. bheḷā. *bēḍḍa -- , *bēṇḍa -- ' defective ' see *biḍḍa -- .Addenda: bēḍā -- . 1. S.kcch. beṛī f. ' boat ', beṛo m. ' ship '; WPah.poet. beṛe f. ' boat ', J. beṛī f.3. bhēḍa -- 3: A. bhel ' raft ' (phonet. bhel) ' raft ' AFD 89.

h1518copperaxe

beṛhī 'warehouse'; beṛā building with a courtyard (WPah.) Alternative: kole.l 'temple' rebus: kole.l 'smithy, forge'

kanac 'corner' rebus:kancu 'bronze' āra 'spokes' rebus: āra 'brass sal 'splinter' rebus: sal 'workshop'

maṁḍaya -- ' adorning ' (Prakritam) rebus: mā̃ḍ m. ' array of instruments . (Marathi)(CDIAL 9736) The inscription on the copper axe signifies: array of brass instruments workshop and warehouse.

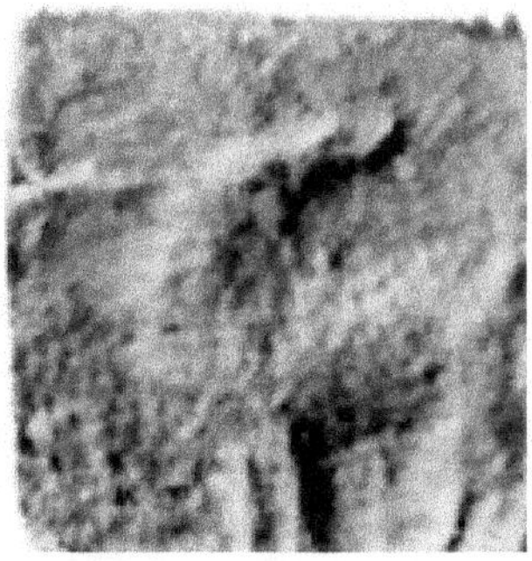

m0438 copper tablet

krammara 'look back' (Telugu) rebus: kamar 'blacksmith' mē̱ḻh (Brahui), mṟēka (Telugu) 'goat' rebus: milakkhu 'copper' mleccha 'copper'. thus, coppersmith.

Inscribed weapons are further reported from Harappa Vats 1940: 384ss, Pl. CXX, 5,19), Chanhu Daro (Mackay 1943: 178, Pl. LXXIV, 1-1a,8)

Chanhu-daro, Pl. LXXIV & Mohenjodaro: copper and bronze tools and utensils (an inscription line mirrored on a zebu seal)

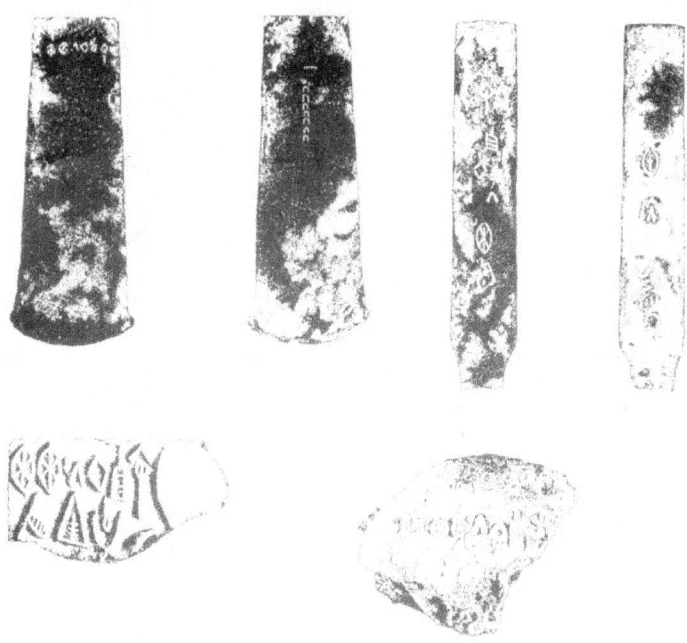

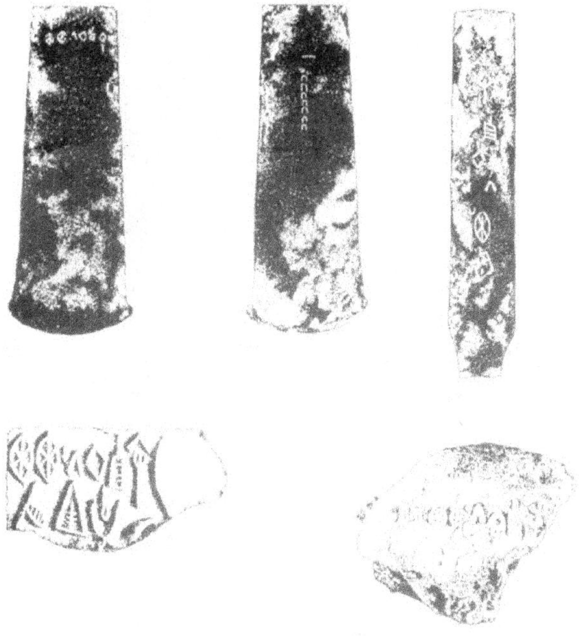

m0317 Silver seal

m1199 Silver seal

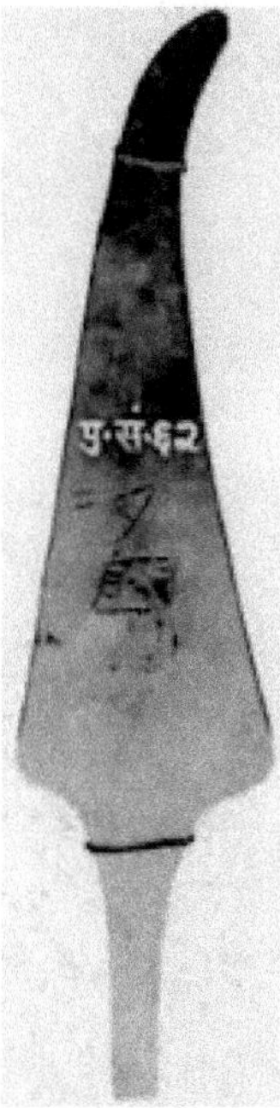
h381 Bronze dagger

h380 Bronze dagger

Kalibangan. Inscribed bronze rod (Mahadevan 1977:7)

h1018copperobject Head of one-horned bull ligatured with a four-pointed star-fish (Gangetic octopus?)

koḍiyum 'rings on neck' koḍ `horn' (Kuwi); rebus: koḍ `artisan's workshop' (Gujarati). खोंड [*khōṇḍa*] m A young bull, a bullcalf.(Marathi) Rebus: *kõdā* 'to turn in a lathe'(B.) कोंद *kōnda* 'engraver, lapidary setting or infixing gemś (Marathi). The joined animal is a Gangetic octopus. *veṛhā* octopus, said to be found in the Indus (Jaṭki lexicon of A. Jukes, 1900) Rebus: . *vēḍa* 'boat'(Prakritam) Alternative:

Rebus 1: *bari, barea* 'merchant'

Rebus 2: *beṛhī* 'warehouse';

beṛā building with a courtyard (WPah.)

bēḍā f. ' boat ' lex. 2. vēḍā, *vēṭī* -- f. lex. 3. *bhēḍa* -- 3 m., *bhēla* -- 1, °*aka* -- m.n. lex. 1. Pk. *bēḍa* -- , °*aya* -- m., *bēḍā* -- , °*ḍiyā* -- f. ' boat ', Gy. eur. *bero*, S. *ḇeṛo* m., °*ṛī* ' small do. '; L. *bēṛā* (Ju. *ḇ* --) m. ' large cargo boat ', *bēṛī* f. ' boat ', P. *beṛā* m., °*ṛī* f.; Ku.*beṛo* ' boat, raft ', N. *beṛā*, OAw. *beḍā*, H. *beṛā* m., G. *beṛɔ* m., *beṛi* f., M. *beḍā* m.2. Pk. *vēḍa* -- m. ' boat '.3. Pk. *bhēḍaka* -- , *bhēlaa* -- m., *bhēlī* -- f. ' boat '; B. *bhelā* ' raft ', Or. *bheḷā.**bēḍḍa -- , *bēṇḍa -- ' defective ' see *biḍḍa -- .Addenda: bēḍā -- . 1. S.kcch. *beṛī* f. ' boat ', *beṛo* m. ' ship '; WPah.poet. *beṛe* f. ' boat ', J. *beṛī* f.3. *bhēḍa* -- 3: A. *bhel* ' raft ' (phonet. *bhel*) ' raft ' (CDIAL 9308)

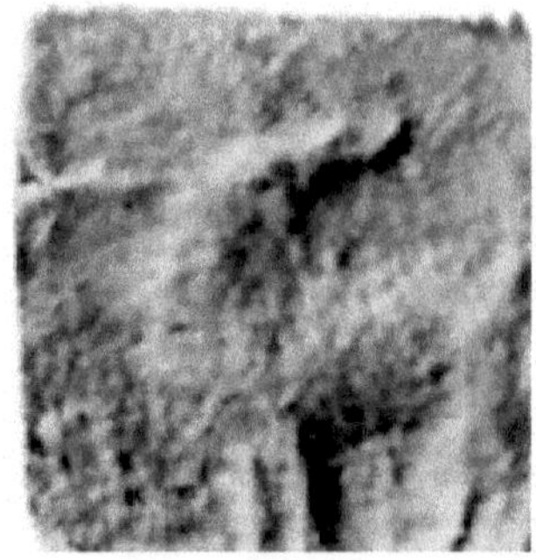

m0438 copper tablet

krammara 'look back' (Telugu) rebus: *kamar* 'blacksmith' *mēl̠h (Brahui), mṛēka* (Telugu) 'goat' rebus: *milakkhu* 'copper' mleccha 'copper'. thus, coppersmith.

arka 'sun' rebus: *eraka* 'moltencast, copper' *arka* 'gold, copper'

<u>Ancient Near East Harappa Script metalwork catalogues 1.Tablet of Shamash, 2.Sit Shamshi bronze, 3.Susa Ritual Basin, 4.Napirisha stele</u>

Stone tablet BM or ME 90922, published as BBSt XXVIII. Sun-divinity, Shamash,its canopy, a human-headed snake divinity, supported on a date-palm column; bottom register of Apsû waters, punctuated by stars; celestial bodies, sun, moon, and Venus, throne as the gate of sunrise with doors held apart by two bison men.

Inscription reads: mdNábû-ápla-iddinana[i 2] or mdNábû-apla-íddina,[i 3] = ca. 888 – 855 BCE, 6th king of the dynasty of E of Babylon, contemporary of Aššur-nāṣir-apli II. The tablet portrays him being led by Nabû-nadin-shum, the priest and descendant of Ekur-šum-ušabši, and the goddess Aa, facing the seated Šamaš. "The inscription celebrates Nabû-apla-iddina's victory over the Sutû, the "evil foe," being the first Babylonian king in over two centuries (since Nabû-kudurrī-uṣur I, ca. 1126–1103 BC) to claim a military title, “heroic warrior .. who bears an awe-inspiring bow ...,” for their overthrow."[229]

Another artefact of bronze also celebrates the worship of sun-divinity, the Sit Shamshi bronze in Louvre Museum.

Model of a temple, called the Sit-shamshi, made for the ceremony of the rising sun

12th century BCE Tell of the Acropolis, Susa Bronze J. de Morgan excavations, 1904-05

Sb 2743[230] ढांगर [*ḍhāṅgara*] n 'A stout stake or stick as a prop to a Vine or scandent shrub]' (Marathi); rebus: *ḍhaṅgar* 'smith' (Maithili. Hindi)

Bassssin cultuel orné de poissons-chèvres This limestone basin dates from the 13th or 12th century BC. It was used for ritual libations. The decoration depicts goatfish figures around a sacred tree in reference to the Mesopotamian god Enki/Ea. Sacred palm. Apsu, the body of fresh water lying beneath the earth and feeding all the rivers and streams, links this artefact to the bronze model called Sit-Shamshi (Louvre, Sb2743). The sacred tree also links to Napirisha stele.[231]

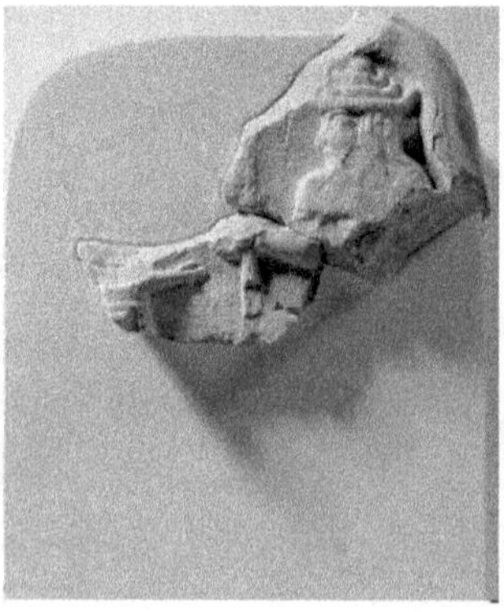

Stele representing King Untash Napirisha, "King of Anzan and Susa"

C. 1340-1300 BCE This stele with four registers was commissioned by the Elamite king Untash-Napirisha for the city of Chogha Zanbil. It was later moved to Susa by one of his successors, probably Shutruk-Nahhunte I. The four registers depict the god Inshushinak acknowledging the monarch's power, two priestesses accompanying the king to the temple, minor deities - half-women, half-fish - holding streams of water, and two creatures - half-men, half-mouflons - who are guardians of the sacred tree. Sandstone J. de Morgan excavations Sb 12[232]

I suggest that the four artefacts: Tablet of Shamash of Nábû-apla-íddina; Sit Shamshi bronze; Susa Ritual basin; and Napirisha stele are celebrations of one thme: Bronze Age smithy, consistent with the Meluhha cultural idiom. Hieroglyph: *kole.l* 'temple' rebus: *kole.l* 'smithy, forge' (Kota).

The Harappa Script hieroglyphs on both the artefacts -- 1. Tablet of Shamash of Nábû-apla-íddina and 2. Sit Shamshi bronze; 3. Susa Ritual Basin; 4. Napirisha stele are read rebus as metalwork catalogues, making them part of Harappa Script Corpora.

1. Hieroglyphs of Tablet of shamash

mēḍha 'polar' star' Rebus: *mẽṛhẽt, meḍ* 'iron' (Ho.Munda) *meḍ* 'copper' (Slavic languages)

arka 'sun' rebus: *arka, eraka* 'copper, moltencast'

kuThari 'crucible' Rebus: *kuThari* 'storekeeper, treasury' . Rebus: *kuThAru* 'armourer'

barad, balad 'ox' rebus: *bharata* 'alloy of copper, pewter, tin'. The expression '*Bhāratam Janam*' in RV 3.53.12 has been interpreted as 'metalcaster folk'

2. Hieroglyphs of Sit Shamshi bronze

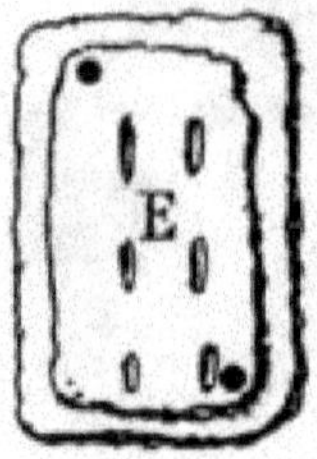

Six hollows for offerings in front of the ziggurat. *baṭa* 'six' Rebus: *baṭa* 'furnace'. Also, षष् 'six' षडशीतिः 'passages of the sun'.

This large bronze platform shows a religious ceremony. In the center are two men in ritual nudity, surrounded by religious furnishings: vases for libations, perhaps bread for offerings, steles; in a stylized urban landscape: a multi-tiered tower, a temple on a terrace, a sacred wood. Middle-Elamite period (15th-12th century B.C.)

षष् num. a. (used in pl., nom. षट्; gen. षण्णाम्) Six; तेषां त्ववयवान् सूक्ष्मान् षण्णामप्यमितौजसाम् Ms.1.16;8.43. अशीतिः f. (-षडशीतिः) 1 eighty-six. -2 N. of the four passages of the sun from one zodiacal sign to the other. शोषयित्नुः [शुष्-इत्नुच् Uṇ.3.29] The sun.शोषिणी Ether. Fire; शुचि a. [शुच्-कि] 1 Clean, pure, clear; the sun शुचीनां हृदयं शुचिः Mb.12.193.18. शाश्वत a. (-ती f.) 1 [शश्वद् भवः अण्] 1 Eternal, per- petual, everlasting; शाश्वतीः समाः Rām.1.2.15 (= U.2. 5) 'for eternal years", 'ever more', 'for all time to come'; श्रेयसे शाश्वतो देवो वराहः परिकल्पताम् U.5.27 (v. l.); R.14.14. -2 All. -तः 1 N. of Śiva. -2 Of Vyāsa. -3 The sun.

In Vedic tradition of education which is a life-long continuum, are the prayers offered annually on upakarma day, include the key componentsof: *kāmokarsheet Japam:2. Brahma Yagnam3. Maha Sankalpam4. Yajnopaveeta dharanam5. Kāṇḍarishi tarpaṇam 6. Kāṇḍarishi Homam (includes Veda reciting)7. Acharya Sambhavana.*

Who is काण्ड--ऋषि who is remembered, invoked and veneration on this upakarma day? He is the sage who performeḍ the yajna, like Jaimini who performeḍ Atiratra Soma yajnam. The word काण्ड is a hieroglyph, a stalk. The word काण्ड in metalwork is a metal implement; The word कण्ड is a sword.

Another hieroglyph (allograph) to signify काण्ड metal implement is: काण्ड 'water'; காண்டம்² *kāṇṭam, n. < kāṇḍa.* 1. Water; sacred water; நீர்.

துருத்திவா யதுக்கிய குங்குமக் காண் டமும் (கல்லா. 49, 16). कद a. 1 Giving water.

The invocation also includes the japam कामोकार्षीत् मन्युरकार्षीत् नमो नमः This is an extraordinary self-introspection and explanations for the deviations from the path of dharma caused by anger, grief or desire, passion. The japam is a resolve to stay firm on the path of dharma seeking prayascittam for past mistakes or deviations, while venerating the ancestors, the Pitr-s.

काण्ड--ऋषि [p= 269,2] m. the ऋषि of a particular काण्ड of the वेद TA1r. i , 32 , 2. ऋषिः ṛṣiḥ A sanctified sage, saint, an ascetic, anchorite; (there are usually three classes of these saints; देवर्षि, ब्रह्मर्षि and राजर्षि; sometimes four more are added; महर्षि, परमर्षि, श्रुतर्षि and काण्डर्षि. (Samskritam. Apte) काण्डः kāṇḍḥ ण्डम् ṇḍam Any division of a work, such as a chapter of a book; as the seven Kāṇḍas of the Rām. - A section, a part in general. -2 The portion of a plant from one knot to another. काण्डात्काण्ड-त्प्ररोहन्ती Mahānār.4.3. काण्डः ण्डम् -ऋषिः A class of sages including Jaimini. -

कार्ष [p= 276,3]m. (√कृष् ; g. छत्त्रा*दि) , " one who ploughs " , a peasant , husbandman DivyA7v.कार्षी f. » गोमय-कृ°.कार्षि [p= 276,3]mfn. (cf. कर्ष/इ) drawing , ploughing VS. vi , 28 ([v.l. कार्ष् इन् MaitrS. Ka1t2h.])m. fire Comm.. on Un2. iv , 128f. drawing , ploughing , cultivation W.

काम b[p= 271,3]m. (fr. √2. कम् ; once काम्/अ VS. xx , 60), wish , desire , longing (कामो मे भुञ्जीत भवान् , my wish is that you should eat Pa1n2. 3-3 , 153), desire for , longing after (gen. dat. , or loc.) , love , affection , object of desire or of love or of pleasure RV. VS. TS. AV. S3Br. MBh. R. &cLove or Desire personified AV. ix , xii , xix (cf. RV. x , 129 , 4) VS. Pa1rGr2.

मन्यु a [p=786,3]m. (L. also f.) spirit , mind , mood , mettle (as of horses) RV. TS. Br.high spirit or temper , ardour , zeal , passion RV. &crage , fury , wrath , anger , indignation ib. (also personified , esp. as अग्नि or काम or as a रुद्र ;मन्युं √ कृ , with loc. or acc. with प्रति , " to vent one's anger on , be angry with ")grief , sorrow , distress , affliction MBh. Ka1v. &c

kāmokarsheet manyurakārsheet namo namah is the japam.

kāṇḍarishi tarpanam is a veneration of seeking blessings from the rishis and ancestors who are he authors of the kāṇḍas of the Veda and protectors of dharma tradition.

Shilhak-in-Shushinak and ceremony of the sun mentioned on the Akkadian inscription dates the inscription to 12th century BCE. It is possible that the model itself might have been made at an earlier date. One adorant sprinkles water on the palms of another also kneeling in adoration in front. It is a process of purification paralleling the purification of metals in a smelter and a furnace or crucible.

There are two ziggurats: one is a dagoba (dhatugarbha) in three tiers, the other is a kuṭhi 'smelter'. Two linga stambhas flank the ziggurat. In front of the ziggurat is a table with six narrow hollows, perhaps to hold flagposts or bronze standards comparable to those taken on processions shown on cylinder seals or Harappa Script tablets. The ziggurat is flanked by 8 round objects, 4 on either side as offerings of bronze bun-ingots to the divine. Also flanking the ziggurat are two linga stambhas.

Behind one of the adorants are the following objects:

a big jar (H), a water reservoir,

two square tubs (I,J),

three tree stalks without branches (K),

a stèle connected to a platform (M) with raised edges.

Sit Shamshi model. Two sivalinga flanking the ziggurat.

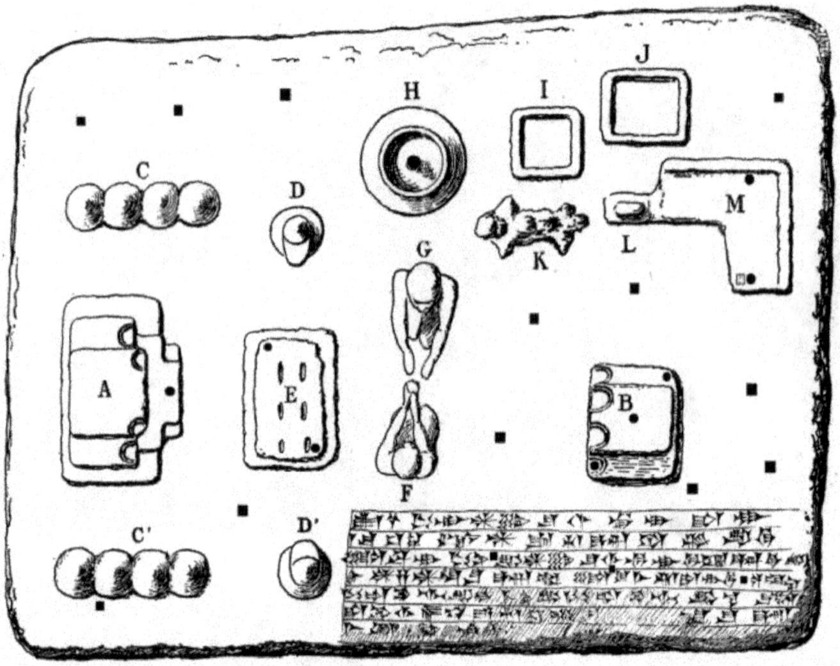

Fig. 200

Gautier 1911: 145, fig. 200 + F.W. König, *Corpus Inscriptionum Elamicarum*, no. 56, Hannover 1926 + Tallon & Hurtel 1992: 140, fig. 43. The base measures 60 x 40 cm.

Tallon 1992

 Ziggurat model. Sit Shamshi bronze. Ziggurat. Mohenjo-daro. *kolmo kāṇḍa* 'three stalks' Rebus: *kolimi kāṇḍa* 'smithy/forge implements'. 3 stalks. Sit Shamshi model. *kolom* 'three' Rebus: *kolimi* 'smithy, forge' *kole.l* 'temple' *kolle* 'blacksmith' कांडें (p. 151) [*kāṇḍēṃ*] n (कांड S) A joint or knot, an articulation. 2 The portion included between two knots, an internodation. 3 A piece (as of sugarcane or bamboo) comprising three or four knots. 4 The whole stem or trunk of a plant, or esp. up to the shooting of the branches. 5 fig. A measure of length,--a pole, stick, straw, thread, any thing (of definite or indefinite length) taken to measure with: also the measure so taken. v घे. Hence A section or defined portion (of a long wall, of an elevated platform sometimes appended to a draw-well, of a raised पाट or plantation-watercourse, of any long line of masonry). 6 A creeping plant old, dry, and stiff. 7 Stalks and heads of corn once trodden or thrashed (as thrown or reserved for a second treading or thrashing). 8 A young plant (of नाचणी, वरी &c.) fit to be transplanted. 2 A disease attacking the finger-joints. अडचा कांड्यावर येणें (Because two large and one small कांडीं or joints are the amount of a stalk of wheat.) To be ready to throw out the ear (to shoot the hose)--wheat. 2 fig. To be nubile or ready for a spouse;--said of a boy or a girl. कांडें पेरें लावणें or लावून पाहणें To compare together the foot of a person (suspected to be a murderer, thief &c.) with a footprint. And कांडे पेरें मिळणें, कमीज्यास्त होणें &c. expresses their agreement or disagreement. Hence ह्याचें त्याचें कांडें पेरें मिळालें Said of two persons of mutual resemblance. कांडें पेरें घेणें to take the measurement of. कांडें पेरें पाहून After observing the joints and points. Said in purchasing cattle &c.

Mẽṛhẽt́. Iron.
Mẽṛhẽt́ ićena. The iron is rusty.
Ispat mẽṛhẽt́. Steel.
Dul mẽṛhẽt́. Cast iron.
Mẽṛhẽt́ khaṇḍa. Iron implements.

Rebus: Santali glossed. See: khaṇḍa 'implements

Rebus: लोखंडकाम [*lōkhaṇḍakāma*] n Iron work; that portion (of a building, machine &c.) which consists of iron. 2 The business of an ironsmith. (Marathi)

Vorderasiatisches Museum, Berlin
Symbolizing Nusku, the god of light, a thin, bright rod elicits the adoration of the Assyrian king Tukulti-Ninurta in this relief, carved on one side of a stone altar dating from the 13th century B.C.E.Veneraton of the stalk. Ishtar temple. Altar for fire-god karaṇḍi (of Tukulti-Ninurta I, Assur).करडा (p. 137) [*karaḍā*] Hard from alloy--iron, silver &c (hieroglyph: *karaḍi* 'safflower' had been deified. Veneration of the stmbha.

करडा (p. 137) [*karaḍā*] m The arrangement of bars or embossed lines (plain or fretted with little knobs) raised upon a तारof gold by pressing and driving it upon the अवटी or grooved stamp. Such तार is used for the ornament बुगडी, for the hilt of aपट्टा or other sword &c. Applied also to any similar barform or line-form arrangement (pectination) whether embossed or indented; as the edging of a rupee &c. The embossed lines of 4+4 (8) balls flank the ziggurat on Sit Shamshi bronze

Sivalinga Harappa compares with sivalinga, linga stambhas on Sit Shamshi bronze model.

Linga worship relief. Bhutesvara, Mathura. 1st cent. BCE (Fig. 5.1)

Ekamukha linga. Udayagiri caves. Vidisa. Cave 4.

Ekamukha linga Uttar Pradesh, Mathura, India, Asia 1st century CE Sandstone 30 3/4 x 7 x 8 1/2 inches (78.1 x 17.8 x 21.6 cm). Philadelphia Museum of Art

Sivalinga, linga stambhas atop a smelter and tree kuṭi in background, rebus: kuṭhi 'smelter'. khārva 'dwarf' Rebus: khārva 'nidhi of Kubera' karba 'iron'. Relief with Ekamukha linga. Mathura. 1st cent. CE (Fig. 6.2). This is the most emphatic representation of linga as a pillar of fire. The pillar is embedded within a brick-kiln with an angular roof and is ligatured to a tree. Hieroglyph: kuṭi 'tree' rebus: kuṭhi 'smelter'. In this composition, the artists is depicting the smelter used for smelting to create *mũh* 'face' (Hindi) rebus: *mũhe* 'ingot' (Santali) of *mēḍha* 'stake' rebus: meḍ 'iron, metal' (Ho. Munda). मेड (p. 662) [mēḍa] f (Usually मेढ q. v.) मेडका m A stake, esp. as bifurcated. मेढ (p. 662) [*mēḍha*] f A forked stake. Used as a post. Hence a short post generally whether forked or not. मेढा (p. 665) [*mēḍhā*] m A stake, esp. as forked. 2 A dense arrangement of stakes, a palisade, a paling. मेढी (p. 665) [*mēḍhī*] f (Dim. of मेढ) A small bifurcated stake: also a small stake, with or without furcation, used as a post to support a cross piece. मेढ्या (p. 665) [*mēḍhyā*] a (मेढ Stake or post.) A term for a person considered as the pillar, prop, or support (of a household, army, or other body), the staff or stay. मेढेजोशी (p. 665) [*mēḍhējōśī*] m A stake-जोशी; a जोशी who keeps account of the तिथि &c., by driving stakes into the ground: also a class, or an individual of it, of fortune-tellers, diviners, presagers, seasonannouncers, almanack-makers &c. They are Shúdras and followers of the मेढेमत q. v. 2 Jocosely. The hereditary or settled (quasi fixed as a stake) जोशी of a village. मेंधला (p. 665) [mēndhalā] m In architecture. A common term for the two upper arms of a double चौकठ (door-frame) connecting the two. Called also मेंढरी & घोडा. It answers to छिली the name of the two lower arms or connections. (Marathi)

मेंढा [*mēṇḍhā*] A crook or curved end rebus: meḍ 'iron, metal' (Ho. Munda)

Susa Sit Shamshi 'sunrise' is Vedic काण्डर्षि.tarpaṇam, purification by water & the Sun, veneration of ancestors

3. Hieroglyphs of Susa Ritual Basin

The hieroglyph components of the Susa Ritual Basin hieroglyph-multiplex, the centre-piece (together with goat-fish hieroglyph-multiplex) of Susa ritual basin are: mollusc, goat (kid), reed, spathe (palm, sprout)

Mollusc

śāṅkhika ' relating to a shell ' W. 2. **śāṅkhinī* -- (*śaṅkhinī* -- f. ' mother -- of -- pearl ' Bālar.). [śaṅkhá -- 1]1. K. *hāngi* ' snail '; B. *sā̃khī* ' possessing or made of shells '. 2. K. *hõgiñ* f. ' pearl oyster shell, shell of any aquatic mollusc '.CDIAL 12380) Rebus: *saṁghá* m. ' association, a community ' Mn. [√han1]Pa. *saṅgha* -- m. ' assembly, the priesthood '; Aś. *saṁgha* -- m. ' the Buddhist community '; Pk. *saṁgha* -- m. ' assembly, collection '; OSi. (Brāhmī inscr.) *saga*, Si. *saṅga* ' crowd, collection '. -- Rather < saṅga -- : S. (CDIAL 12854).

Goat, kid

करड़ूं or करडें [*karaḍū or ṅkaraḍēṃ*] n A kid. (Marathi) Rebus: *karaḍā* 'hard alloy'. *aya* 'fish' Rebus: *aya* 'iron' *ayas* 'metal' (Rigveda) Thus the hieroglyph-multiplex of goat-kid-fish reads: *aya* करडें 'fish kid' Rebus: *ayaskaraḍ*ā 'metal alloy' (comparable to ayaskāṇḍa mentioned by Panini for excellent metal implements. khaṇḍa 'implements (Santali)

Reed

Reeds on Susa ritual basin. Compare with the reed posts PLUS scarves of Warka vase *eruvai* 'reed' + d*hatu* 'scarf' + *dula* 'pair' Rebus: *eruvai* 'copper' + *dhatu* 'mineral' + dul 'cast metal'.

Hieroglyph: *eruvai* 'European reed' European bamboo reed. See கொறுக்கச்சி. (குறிஞ்சிப். 68, உரை.) Species of Cyperus. See பஞ்சாய்க்கோரை. எருவை செருவிளை மணிப்பூங் கருவிளை (குறிஞ்சிப். 68). Straight sedge tuber; கோரைக்கிழங்கு. மட் பனை யெருவைதொட்டி (தைலவ. தைல. 94).

Rebus: *eruva* 'copper' எருவை eruvai Copper; செம்பு. எருவை யுருக்கினா லன்ன குருதி (கம்பரா. கும்பக. 248).

Spathe (palm)

Hieroglyph: गाभा (p. 233) [*gābhā*] m (गर्भ S) The heart, core, pith, interior substance (of wood, stalks, roots &c.) 2 The spadix or fruit-receptacle (of the Palm or Plantain) whilst yet unevolved. 3 The crop or bush (of a Palm).

Dagoba is the Sinhalese name for the Buddhist Stupa, a mound-like structure with relics, used by Buddhist monks to meḍitate. This is a compound comprising: *dhatu* + *garbha* 'mineral core' 'containing dhatu, mineral'. dhAtugarbha m. (with Buddh.) receptacle for ashes or relics , a Dagaba or Dagoba (Sinhalese corruption of Pali Dhatu-gabbha) MWB. xxxv {-kumbha} m. a relic-urn.[233]

Rebus: गाभारा (p. 227) [*garbhārā*] m (गर्भ S) The innermost apartment of a temple; penetralia, adytum, sanctuary.(Marathi) Gabbha [Vedic garbha, either to *gelbh, as in Lat. galba, Goth. kalbo, Ohg. kalba, E. calf, or *gu̯e bh, as in Gr. delfu/s womb, adelfo/s sharing the womb, brother, de/lfacyoung pig; cp. *gelt in Goth. kilpei womb. Ags. cild, Ger. kind, E. child. Meaning: a cavity, a hollow, or, seen from its outside, a swelling] 1. interior, cavity (loc. gabbhe in the midst of: angāra° J iii.55).[234]

This trough was found at Uruk, the largest city so far known in southern Mesopotamia in the late prehistoric period (3300-3000 BC). The carving on the side shows a procession of sheep (a goat and a ram) approaching a reed hut (of a type still found in southern Iraq) and two lambs emerging. The decoration is only visible if the trough is raised above the level at which it could be conveniently used, suggesting that it was probably a cult object, rather than of practical use. It may have been a cult object in the Temple of Inana (Ishtar), the Sumerian goddess of love and fertility; a bundle of reeds (Inanna's symbol) can be seen projecting from the hut and at the edges of the scene. Later documents make it clear that Inanna was the supreme goddess of Uruk. Many finely-modelled representations of animals and humans made of clay and stone have been found in what were once enormous buildings in the center of Uruk, which were probably temples. Cylinder seals of the period also depict sheep, cattle, processions of people and possibly rituals. Part of the right-hand scene is cast from the original fragment now in the Vorderasiatisches Museum, Berlin

melh, mṛeka 'goat'; rebus: *milakkhu* 'copper' (Pali). *pasara* 'domestic animals'. *pasra* 'smithy, forge'.

4. Hieroglyphs of Napirisha stele

tamar 'palm tree, 'date palm' (Hebrew) Rebus: *tAm(b)ra* 'copper' (Pali. Samskritam)

kulā 'hood of serpent' Rebus: *kolle* 'blacksmith', *kol* 'working in iron', *kolhe* 'smelters", *kolimi* 'smithy, forge'

Hieroglyph: overflowing pot: *lo* 'overflowing' PLUS *kand* 'pot'
Rebus: *lōkhaṇḍa* लोहोलोखंड 'copper tools, pots and pans' (Marathi) N. *lokhār* ' bag in which a barber keeps his tools '; H. *lokhār* m. ' iron tools, pots and pans '; --
X *lauhabhāṇḍa* -- : Ku. *lokhaṛ* ' iron tools '; H. *lokhaṇḍ* m. ' iron tools, pots and pans '; G. *lokhā̃ḍ* n. ' tools, iron, ironware '; M. *lokhā̃ḍ* n. ' iron ' (LM 400 < -- *khaṇḍa* --)(CDIAL 11171).

The abiding hieroglyphic tradition to signify artisanal competence of the Bronze Age Revolution is the framework to use the tantra yukti doctrine and present clusters of metalwork catalogues across an expansive civilizational contact area. Examples of such catalogues are presented in Annexed A to L of this treatise.

Annex A

Harappa Script inscriptions found in temple area of Mohenjo-daro (and Harappa?)

Definition and function of *kole.l* 'smithy, forge,' from 12 Harappa Script inscriptions found in and layout of House 1 (with several rooms) HR Area, Mohenjo-daro, ivory/bone stick cylinder seals of Mohenjo-daro and Harappa. The workplace of the artisans was a *kole.l* 'temple' where the products for sale by artisans were assembled and prepared as cargo to be entrusted to seafaring merchants.

The large house H1 (HR Area) with many rooms on the upper storey was a temple. The 12 Harappa Script inscriptions found in this temple which was a smithy-fore are metalwork catalogues.

Prof. Chakrabarti provides an overview of the civilization in the magnum opus -- distribution and features mirrored in an essay.[235]

The word is *kole.l* which signifies a temple in a Kota village. It also means 'smithy, forge'.

This house and the finds of Harappa script inscriptions are conclusive archaeological evidence validating the *weltanschauung* of the civilization which treated work as worship and deemeḍ the smithy, forge to be a temple, an offering to the paramaatman.

Complementary evidence comes from the hieroglyphs deciphered on 22 ceramic stoneware bangles defining functions in metalwork guild.

This monograph confirms that the House 1 in HR Area of Mohenjo-daro was NOT a palace but a smithy, forge organized in several rooms surrounding the upper storey courtyard. In Kota village tradition a *kole.l* is not merely a smithy but also a temple. This explains the discovery of a stone sculpture of a person wering a cloak on the left shoulder (comparable to the vestment of the Mohenjo-daro priest wearing a trefoil decorated cloak and fillets on forehead and right shoulder. The hieroglyphs have been deciphered as signifying *dhǎvaḍ* 'smelter'). If the sculpture shown wearing a cloak also had a ribbon or fillet on his forehead, such ornamentation would signify *śrēṣṭhin* 'merchant guild-master'

kole·l smithy, temple in Kota village: *Ta. kol* metal, working in iron, blacksmith; *kollan̲* blacksmith. *Ma. kollan* blacksmith, artificer. *Ko. kole·l* smithy, temple in Kota village. *To. kwala·l* Kota smithy. *Ka. kolime, kolume, kulāme, kulime, kulume, kulme* fire-pit, furnace; (Bell.; U.P.U.) konimi blacksmith (Gowda) *kolla* id. *Koḍ. kollë* blacksmith.

ಕೊಲಿಮೆ, ಕೊಲುಮೆ.=ಕುಲಿಮೆ. k. *n.* A forge. ಕುಲುಮೆ, ಕುಲ್ಮೆ k. *n.* A fire-pit or furnace.

కుల s. n. A race, family, tribe, caste. 2, a crowd, herd, troop, multitude. 3, a noble family. 4, a house. -క.

Te. kolimi furnace. *Go.* (SR.) *kollusānā* to mend implements; (Ph.) *kolstānā, kulsānā* to forge; (Tr.) *kōlstānā* to repair (of ploughshares); (SR.) *kolmi* smithy (*Voc.* 948). *Kuwi* (F.) kolhali to forge. (DEDR 2133) Based on the decipherment of 12 inscriptions found in the rooms of the courtyard to be metalwork catalogues, it is suggested that the House 1 in HR Area was *kole.l* 'smithy, temple'. *kúla* n. 'herd, troop ' RV., ' race, family ' Pāṇ., ' noble family ' Mn., ' house ' MBh.
Pa. *kulā* -- n. ' clan, household ', Pk. *kulā* -- n.m. ' family, house '; Dm. *kul* ' house '; Sh. (Lor.) *d**l*da* -- *kul* ' grandfather's relations '; K. *kŏl* m. ' family, race '; S. *kuru* m. ' tribe, family ', L. *kull* m., P. *kul* f.; WPah. bhad. *kul* n. ' sub -- caste, family '; N. A. B. *kul* ' clan, caste, family ', Or. *kuḷa*, OMth. *kulā*; H. *kul* m. ' herd, clan, caste, family ', Marw. *kul*; G. *kuḷ* n. ' family, tribe ', M. *kūḷ* n., °*ḷī* f.; OSi. -- *kolaṭ* dat. ' family '; -- Si. *kulāya* ' family, caste ' ← Pa. or Sk. -- Deriv. Or. *kuḷā* ' of good family ', *akuḷā* ' illegitimate (of birth) '.(CDIAL 3330)

HR area refers to the area excavated in Mohenjo-daro by Hargreaves. HR Area is located southeast of the citadel mound. Large areas of the mound have not yet been excavated and are covered with eroding brick structures and pottery.
House I, HR area

House A1 may have been a temple or palace of an important leader. Two doorways lead to a narrow courtyard at a lower level. A double staircase leads to an upper courtyard surrounded by several rooms. This house had numerous seals and fragments of a stone sculpture depicting a seated man wearing a cloak over the left shoulder.

The 3 L-Area Mohenjo-daro Statues: The Seated Nobleman, The Stern Male, The Unknown Woman.

"In January 1927, Mackay began working in L-Area, ca. 28 meters south of the Stupa on the Mound of the Great Bath. He uncovered the so-called 'Assembly Hall' and other architectural remains that are not well understood, even today. He also found three pieces of limestone sculpture: a seated torso (L-950), a reasonably well-preserved bust (L-898) and a very poor, abraded head, possibly of a woman (L-127)." (Indus Age, p. 78)

1. The Seated Nobleman of L-Area as it was excavated. "Seated male figure with head missing (45, 46). On the back of the figure, the hair style can be partially reconstructed by a wide swath of hair and a braided lock of hair or ribbon hanging along the right side of the back. A cloak is draped over the edge of the left shoulder and covers the folded legs and lower body, leaving the right shoulder and chest bare. The left arm is clasping the left knee and the hand is visible peeking out from underneath the cloak. The right hand is resting on the right knee which is folded beneath the body." (Gregory Possehl, Indus Age: The Beginnings, p. 78)." (Plate 2.29 in the book, facing p. 92.)

2. Male Statue . "[The Seated Nobleman was] found above pavement in N.E. corner of Chamber 75 in L-Area. (its datum was 2.5 feet below datum.) Late Period. Material, veined grey alabaster. The figure, which is 11.5 inches high, is obviously that of a male and is dressed in a thin kilt-like garment fastened round the waist. (It is not clear how Mr. Mackay infers the existence of this kilt beneath the outer garment.–[ED.].) Another garment or shawl of thin material is worn over the left shoulder and under the right arm, and appears to hang down over the kilt. The left knee of the figure is raised, but there is nothing to indicate the position of the right foot beneath it. The sculptor, and not subsequent weathering, is responsible for this lack of detail. The left arm is carried around the side of the left knee, so that the hand clasps the front of the knee. This hand is only roughly indicated, and the sculptor evidently was not clear how it should be arranged. Indeed, it is difficult to believe that the same man carved both the arms and hands, for the right arm, though of rough workmanship, shows some power of modeling, whereas the left arm and hand are positively shapeless. (It should not be forgotten that the left arm is hidden beneath the mantle or shawl, while the right arm is bare. It is not to be expected, therefore, that there should be much definition in the modeling of the left arm. Probably the mantle itself was painted, and this would have made a great difference to the apparent uncouthness of the lower part of the figure.) A squarish projection at the back of the head is evidently intended to represent a knot of hair. It is, however, unfinished and shows the chisel marks of the preliminary dressing. There is somewhat more finish about what may be a rope of hair hanging down the back." (John Marshall, Mohenjo-daro, Plate C, 1-3 (L 950), pp. 358-9)

Western Staircase, House I, HR area

Many houses had stairs leading to upper courtyards of the building or to a second floor. This house in HR area had a double staircase that would allow people to enter and exit the upper courtyard in an orderly fashion. Some scholars feel this may have been a palace or a temple.

"A house in the HR area (numbered House 1) has been interpreted as a temple mainly because of its approach through a large gateway and he find of two stone male figures in its precincts." (DK Chakrabarti, opcit.)

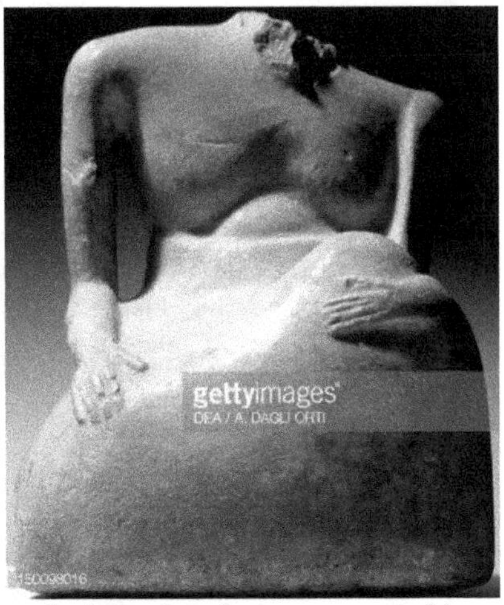

Man sitting, hed broken at beard, alabaster statue Mohenjo-daro (See comparable images from L-Area showing a man seated in the same posture with a cloak over the left shoulder and with a ribbon (fillet) tied on the forehead).

Mohenjo-daro, a seated male figure with head missing. On the back of the figure, the hair style can be partially reconstructed by a wide swath of hair and a braided lock of hair. A cloak is draped over the edge of the left shoulder and covers the folded legs and lower body, leaving the right shoulder and chest bare. The left arm is clasping the left knee and the hand is visible peeking out from underneath the cloak. The right hand is resting on the right knee which is folded beneath the body.

If the head is comparable to that of other statues found in Mohenjo-daro, it is reasonable to assume that the missing head would have been adorned with a ribbon, fillet. If such a fillet had a dotted circle, the reading is: dhǎvaḍ'smelter' of dhāū, vaṭṭā 'red stone, mineral (iron ore)'.

The upper courtyard of House 1 was surrounded by several rooms from where many seals and tablets with Harappa Script inscriptions have been found and deciphered as metalwork catalogues.

Thus, the House 1 was a kole.l 'smithy, forge' and the assumption made by many scholars is resonable that such a smithy/forge was recognized as kole.l 'temple' where the Supercargo's worked as merchant's representatives to take charge of metalwork shipments. This inference is supported by the decipherment of 12 inscriptions found in House 1 of HR Area of Mohenjo-daro.

Steps at House I, HR area

In the lower courtyard was a circle of bricks (barely visible in the foreground), which might have been the site of a sacred tree. The walls in the right foreground may have been part of a large water tank.

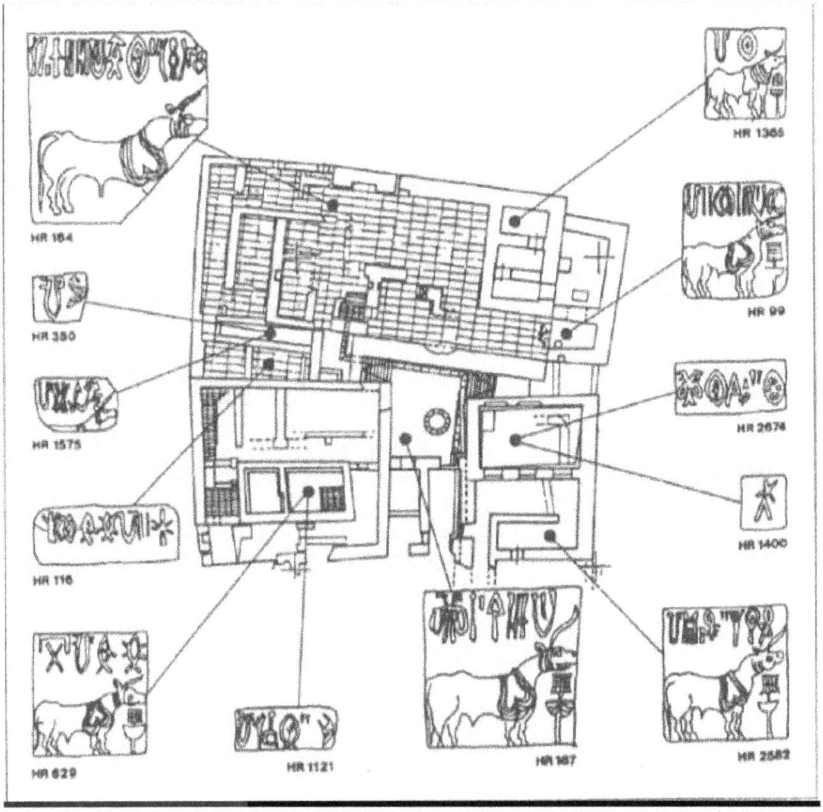

Distribution of seals/tablets within House AI, Block 1, HR at Mohenjodaro (After Jansen, M., 1987, Mohenjo-daro -- a city on the Indus, in Forgotten Cities on the Indus (M. Jansen, M. Mulloy and G. Urban Eds.), Mainz, Philip Von Zabern, p. 160). Jansen speculated that the house could have been a temple.

House I, HR-A area, Mohenjo-daro: Find spots of twelve seals together with many prestige objects, all from one house; Wheeler assumed that this was a temple; the house has rooms immediately adjacent to the exit, transit rooms having more than one door, terminal rooms with just one door; seals were found in all these rooms.236

Seals have been found in almost every exposed room excavated in Mohenjodaro. In room 85 in house IX of the HR-area in Mohenjodaro were found five unicorn selas. In this room 'a mass of shell-lay was found...along with...many waste pieces of sea-shells' indicating this to be a shell-cutter's room (Mackay, 1931a: I, 195).

HR area, corbelled arch drain

Many large covered drains were constructed with corbelled arches. These drains ran beneath streets and lanes and were large enough for workmen to enter and clear any obstructions.

Mohenjo-daro Lower Town: HR area and Stupa

This general view of houses in HR area shows the color of the brick walls prior to use of mud brick and clay slurry for conservation. The lower parts of the walls have the natural reddish color of fired brick.

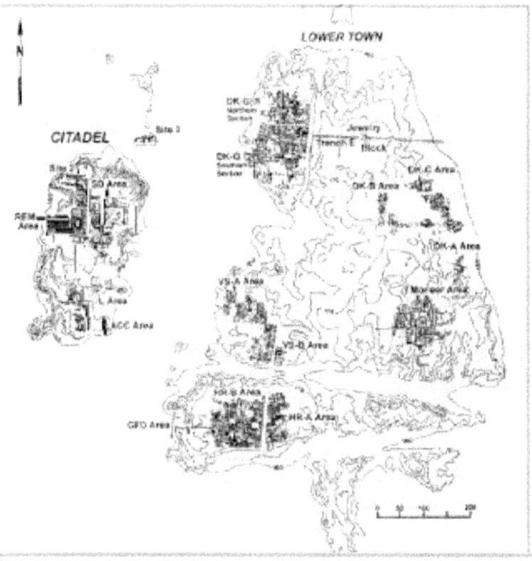
LOWER TOWN
CITADEL
N
SD Area
REM Area
ACC Area
DK-G Northern Section
DK-G Southern Section
Trench E
Jewelry Block
DK-C Area
DK-B Area
DK-A Area
VS-A Area
VS-B Area
Moneer Area
HR-B Area
HR-A Area
GFD Area

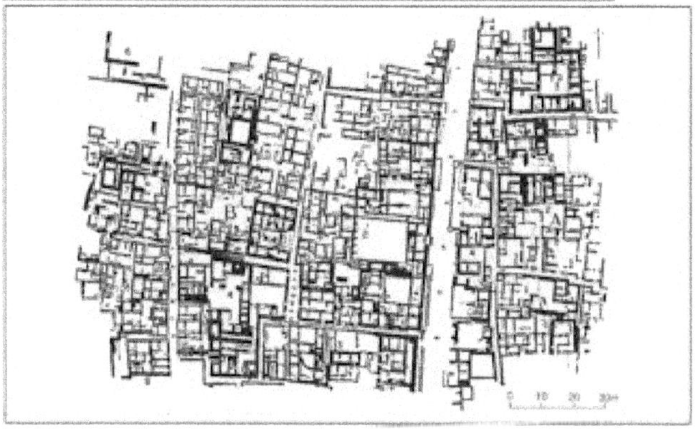

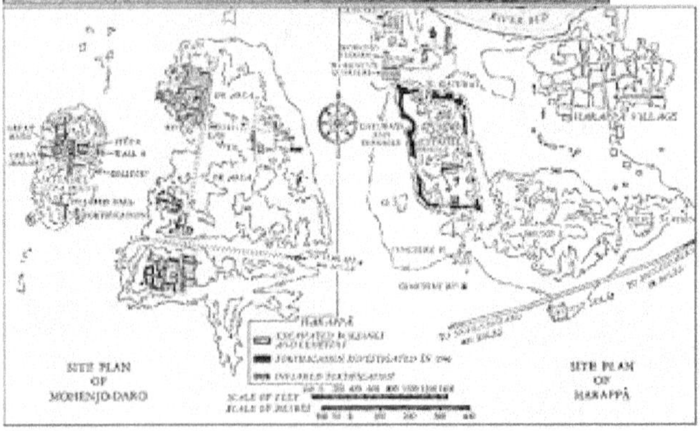

Lime stone sculpture

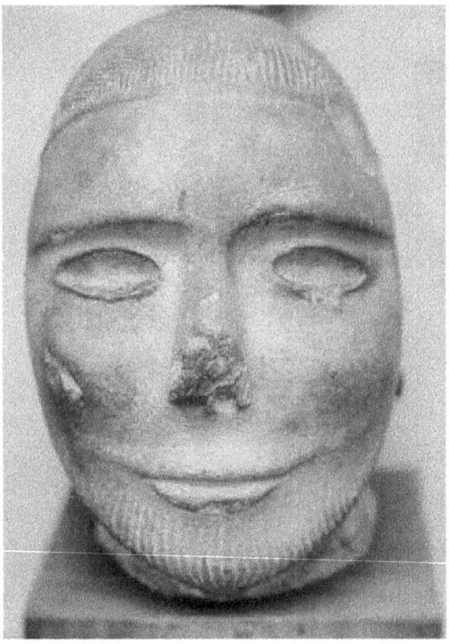

Priest head Mohenjo-daro

Clay Sculpture

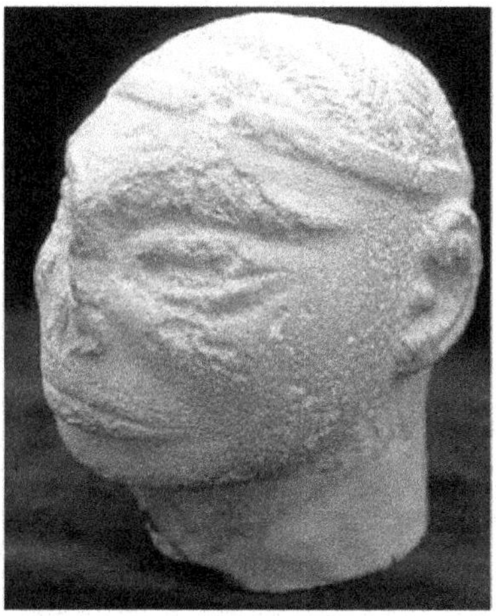

The 3 L Area Mohenjodaro Statues

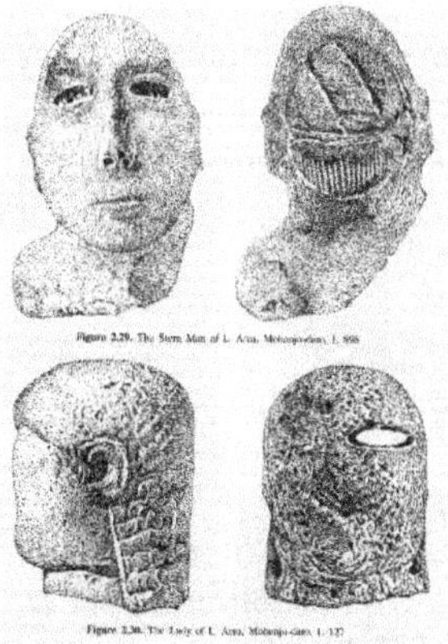

The stern man (top) and lady (bottom) of L-Area

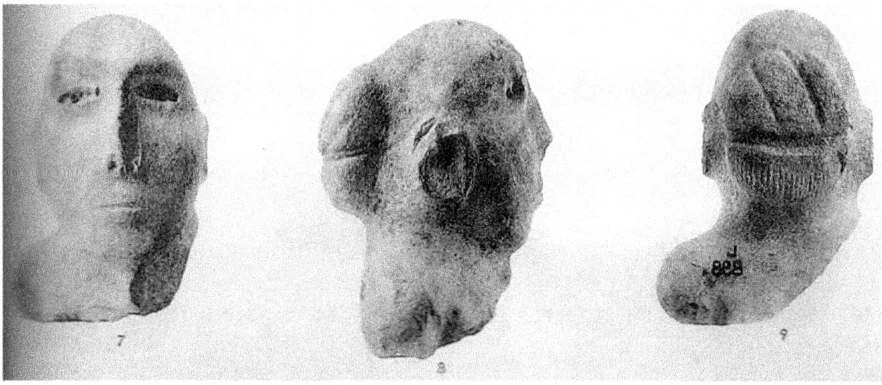

3. The Stern Man of L Area, Mohenjo-daro, L 898. The Lady of L Area, Mohenjo-daro, L 127. [Figures]

4. Chamber 7, L Area where L 950 Male Statue was found

5. Yellow limestone head. [Stern Man of L Area] "Found 2 feet below the surface of the ground in Chamber 77 of L-Area (Its datum level is minus 2.3 feet.) It belongs to the late period. Material, yellow limestone.
This head, which is 7.75 inches high, may present either a male or females, as there is no beard; but the hair is gathered up in a knot at the back of the head in a similar way to the obviously male figure shown in illustration no. 6. This may have been the customary fashion for hair-dressing for me–a fashion which still survives in many parts of India at the present day. A cord of fillet worn round the head serves to keep the know of hair at the back of the head in place.
The arrangement of the hair knot is curious. Two oblique depressions, which run from the right to left across its uppoer portion, apparently mark off three separate twists of hair. A number of vertical lines on the lower portion of the knot suggest strands of hair lying close together." (Marshall, Mohenjo-daro, Plate XCIX, 7-9 (L 898), p. 358)

6. Female head. [Lady of L Area] "Found just below the first pavement of Chamber 100 in L Area. Late Period. This is the badly weathered head of a statue in grey limestone, now 5.7 inches high. It apparently represents a female, for there is no beard, and the hair, which is slightly curly, hangs down the back of the head. The eye beneath the receding brows are long and narrow and the original inlay of the right eye, which is made of a whiter stone than the head, is still in place.
The nose, unfortunately, is missing and the mouth too weathered for us to discern its original shape. That there was once a necklace is suggested by the presence of two holes on each side of the neck, just in front of the hair. The ears are very primitive and a deep ear-hole is drilled in each. (These holes, which are found in all these heads, seem intended for the attachment of some ornament in the middle of the ear and perhaps explain why the ears themselves are left without structural definition.) It is unfortunate that this head is in such a bad state of preservation." (Marshall, Mohenjo-daro, Plate XCIX, 1-3 (L 127), p. 358)

Harappa Script hieroglyphs on priest statue of Mohenjo-daro signify dhă̄vaḍ 'iron-smelter', potṛ, पोतृ 'purifier'

The 'purifier' is also a *dhă̄vaḍ* 'iron-smelter'

The hieroglyph signifiers are related to some etyma of Bharata *sprachbund* in this addendum. vaṭa- string, rope, tie (Samskrtam) is signified by the string which ties the 'dotted circle' on the forehead and right-shoulder of the Priest. The rebus reading is: -vaḍ వటుగ 'clever, skilful' (Telugu).

Hieroglyph: string, wisp: S. *dhāī* f. ' wisp of fibres added from time to time to a rope that is being twisted ', L. *dhāī̃* f. Rebus: *dhāu* ' ore (esp. of copper) '; Or. *ḍhāu* ' red chalk, red ochre ' (whence *ḍhāuā* ' reddish '; dhā´tu n. ' substance ' RV., m. ' element

' MBh., ' metal, mineral, ore (esp. of a red colour) ' Mn., ' ashes of the dead ' lex., ' *strand of rope ' (cf.*tridhā'tu* -- ' threefold ' RV., *ayugdhātu* -- ' having an uneven number of strands ' KātyŚr.). [√dhā]

Thus, the 'dotted circle' *dhāī̃* PLUS vaṭa 'string' is read: dhā̆vaḍ 'smelter'.

The uttarIyam worn by the Priest is *potta* -- , °*taga* -- , °*tia* -- n. ' cotton cloth ' (Prakrtam) potti 'cloth' (Kannada) Rebus: Potṛ, पोतृ 'purifier' Priest (Rigveda). போத்தி pōtti

, *n*. < போற்றி. 1. Grandfather; பாட்டன். *Tinn*. 2. Brahman temple- priest in Malabar; மலையாளத்திலுள்ள கோயிலருச் சகன். पोतदार (p. 303) pōtadāra m (P) An officer under the native governments. His business was to assay all money paid into the treasury. He was also the village-silversmith. (Marathi)

The fillet worn on the forehead and on the right-shoulder signifies one strand; while the trefoil on the shawl signifies three-strands.

 Single strand (one dotted-circle)

 Two strands (pair of dotted-circles)

 Three strands (three dotted-circles as a trefoil)

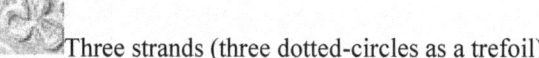

These orthographic variants provide semantic elucidations for a single: *dhātu, dhāū, dhāv* 'red stone mineral' or two minerals: dul PLUS dhātu, dhāū, dhāv 'cast minerals' or *tri- dhātu, -dhāū, -dhāv* 'three minerals' to create metal alloys'. The artisans producing alloys are *dhā̆vaḍ* m. 'a caste of iron -- smelters', *dhāvḍī* 'composed of or relating to iron')(CDIAL 6773)..
dām 'rope, string' rebus: *dhāu* 'ore' rebus: मेढा [*mēḍhā*] A twist or tangle arising in thread or cord, a curl or snarl (Marathi). Rebus: *meḍ* 'iron, copper' (Munda. Slavic) *mẽṛhẽt, meḍ* 'iron' (Munda).

Semantics of single strand of rope and three strands of rope are: 1. Sindhi *dhāī* f. ' wisp of fibres added from time to time to a rope that is being twisted ', Lahnda *dhāī̃* id.; 2. *tridhā'tu* -- ' threefold ' (RigVeda)

Evolution *ḍha-, dha-* in Brahmi script syllables are evocative of 'string' and 'circle, dotted circle' as may be seen from the following orthographic evidence of epigraphs dated from ca. 300 BCE:

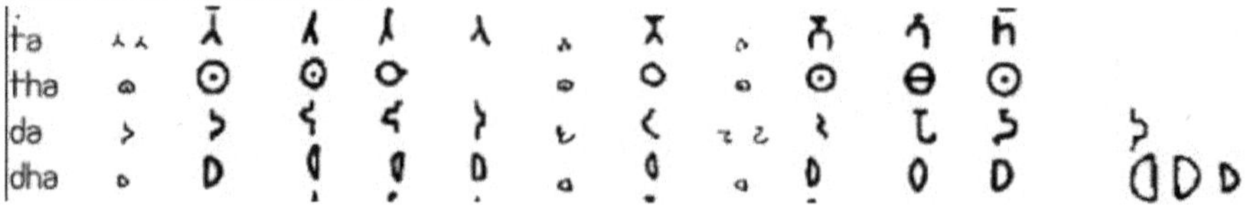

It may be seen from the table of evoution of Brahmi script orthography that

1. a circle signified the Brahmi syllable '*ṭh*a-' and a dotted circle signified the syllable '*tha-*';

2. a string with a twist signified the syllable '*da-*', a string ending in a circled twist signified the syllable '*ḍha-*' and a stepped string signified the syllable '*ḍa-*'.

Section 4: Orthograhy of Brahmi syllabary from ca. 300 BCE

వడము (p. 1124) vaḍamu vaḍamu. [Tel.] n. A very thick rope. మోకు. A garland, దండ. సమర్థతగల. తేరివడము a rope used to drag a car. vaṭa2 ' string ' lex. [Prob. ← Drav. Tam. *vaṭam*, Kan. *vaṭi*, *vaṭara*,] N. *bariyo* ' cord, rope '; Bi. *barah* ' rope working irrigation lever ', *barhā* ' thick well -- rope ', Mth. *barahā* ' rope '.vaṭāraka -- , vaṭin -- ; *karṇavaṭikā -- , *yantravaṭa -- .(CDIAL 11212) vaṭāraka -- , *varāṭaka* -- m. ' string ' MBh. [vaṭa -- 2]Pa. *sa -- vaṭākara* -- ' having a cable '; Bi. *baral -- rassī* ' twisted string '; H. *barrā* m. ' rope ', *barārā* m. ' thong '. (CDIAL 11217) *karṇavaṭikā ' side -- cord '. [kárṇa -- , vaṭa -- 2]WPah. bhal. *k*lnɔṛi* f. ' knots between upper and lower parts of a snow -- shoe, rope pegs to which the distaff in a spinning -- wheel is attached '.(CDIAL 2842) *yantravaṭa ' cord of a machine '. [Cf. Pa. *yantasutta-* n. -- yantrá -- , vaṭa -- 2]WPah.bhal. *jaṇṭlor* m. ' long string round spinning wheel '.(CDIAL 10413) *Ta.* vaṭam cable, large rope, cord, bowstring, strands of a garland, chains of a necklace; vaṭi rope; vaṭṭi (-pp-, -tt-) to tie. *Ma.* vaṭam rope, a rope of cowhide (in plough), dancing rope, thick rope for dragging timber. *Ka.* vaṭa, vaṭara, vaṭi string, rope, tie. *Te.* vaṭi rope, cord. *Go.* (Mu.) vaṭiya strong rope made of paddy straw (*Voc.*3150). Cf. 3184 Ta. tāṟvaṭam. / Cf. Skt. vaṭa- string, rope, tie; vaṭāraka-, vaṭākara-, varāṭaka- cord, string; Turner, *CDIAL*, no. 11212.(DEDR 5220) வடம்[1] vaṭam , *n.* < *vaṭa.* 1. Cable, large rope, as for drawing a temple-car; கனமான கயிறு. வடமற்றது (நன். 219, மயிலை.). 2. Cord; தாம்பு. (சூடா.) 3. A loop of coir rope, used for climbing palm-trees; மரமேறவுதவுங் கயிறு. *Loc.* 4. Bowstring; வில்லின் நாணி. (பிங்.) 5. String of jewels; மணிவடம். வடங்கள் அசையும்படி உடுத்து (திருமுரு. 204, உரை). (சூடா.) 6. Strands of a garland; chains of a necklace; சரம். இடை மங்கை கொங்கை வடமலைய (அஷ்டப். திருவேங்கடத் தந். 39). 7. Arrangement; ஒழுங்கு. தொடங்கற் காலை வடம்பட விளங்கும் (ஞானா. 14, 41). தாழ்வடம் tāḻ-vaṭam , *n.* < id. +. 1. [M. *tāḻvaṭam.*] Necklace of pearls or beads; கழுத் தணி. தாவி றாழ்வடம் தயங்க (சீவக. 2426). 2. String of Rudrākṣa beads; உருத்திராக்கமாலை.

மார்பின்மீதிலே தாழ்வடங்கள் மனதிலே கரவடமாம் (தண்டலை. சத. 29).

వటగ (p. 1122) vaṭaga , వటారి or వఠారి vaṭaga. [Tel.] adj. Clever, skilful, నేర్పుగల,

वराटक [p= 921,1] a rope , cord , string (only ifc. , with *f*(आ).) MBh. xii , 2488 v.l. वरारका वरारक [p= 923,2] *n.* a diamond L.

pōta2 m. ‘ cloth ’, *pōtikā* -- f. lex. 2. *pōtta -- 2 (sanskrit- ized as *pōtra* -- 2 n. ‘ cloth ’ lex.). 3. *pōttha -- 2 ~ *pavásta*<-> n. ‘ covering (?) ’ RV., ‘ rough hempen cloth ’ AV. T. Chowdhury JBORS xvii 83. 4. pōntī -- f. ‘ cloth ’ Divyāv. 5. *pōcca -- 2 < **pōtya* -- ? (Cf. *pōtyā* = *pōtānāṁ samūhaḥ* Pāṇ.gaṇa. -- *pṓta* -- 1?). [Relationship with *prōta* -- n. ‘ woven cloth ’ lex., plōta -- ‘ bandage, cloth ’ Suśr. or with *pavásta* -- is obscure: EWA ii 347 with lit. Forms meaning ‘ cloth to smear with, smearing ’ poss. conn. with or infl. by *pusta* -- 2 n. ‘ working in clay ’ (prob. ← Drav., Tam. *pūcu* &c. DED 3569, EWA ii 319)]
1. Pk. *pōa* -- n. ‘ cloth ’; Paš.ar. *pōwok* ‘ cloth ’, *pōg* ‘ net, web ’ (but lauṛ. dar. *pāwāk* ‘ cotton cloth ’, Gaw. *pāk* IIFL iii 3, 150).
2. Pk. *potta* -- , °*taga* -- , °*tia* -- n. ‘ cotton cloth ’, *pottī* -- , °*tiā* -- , °*tullayā* -- , *puttī* -- f. ‘ piece of cloth, man's dhotī, woman's sāṛī ’, *pottia* -- ‘ wearing clothes ’; S. *potī* f. ‘ shawl ’, *potyo* m. ‘ loincloth ’; L. *pot*, pl. °*tā̃* f. ‘ width of cloth ’; P. *potṛā* m. ‘ child's clout ’, *potṇā* ‘ to smear a wall with a rag ’; N. *poto* ‘ rag to lay on lime -- wash ’,*potnu* ‘ to smear ’; Or. *potā* ‘ gunny bag ’; OAw. *potaï* ‘ smears, plasters ’; H. *potā* m. ‘ whitewashing brush ’, *potī* f. ‘ red cotton ’, *potiyā* m. ‘ loincloth ’, *potṛā* m. ‘ baby clothes ’; G. *pot* n. ‘ fine cloth, texture ’, *potũ* n. ‘ rag ’, *potī* f., °*tiyũ* n. ‘ loincloth ’, *potṛī* f. ‘ small do. ’; M. *pot* m. ‘ roll of coarse cloth ’, n. ‘ weftage or texture of cloth ’, *potrẽ* n. ‘ rag for smearing cowdung ’.
3. Pa. *potthaka* -- n. ‘ cheap rough hemp cloth ’, *potthakamma* -- n. ‘ plastering ’; Pk. *pottha* -- , °*aya* -- n.m. ‘ cloth ’; S. *potho* m. ‘ lump of rag for smearing, smearing, cloth soaked in opium ’.
4. Pa. *ponti* -- ‘ rags ’.
5. Wg. *pōč* ‘ cotton cloth, muslin ’, Kt. *puč*; Pr. *puč* ‘ duster, cloth ’, *pū'čuk* ‘ clothes ’; S. *poco* m. ‘ rag for plastering, plastering ’; P. *poccā* m. ‘ cloth or brush for smearing ’, *pocṇā* ‘ to smear with earth ’; Or. *pucā̆ra*, *pucurā* ‘ wisp of rag or jute for whitewashing with, smearing with such a rag ’.
*maṣipōtta -- . pōta -- 3 ‘ boat ’ see *plōtra -- . pōta -- 4 ‘ foundation ’ see *pēnda -- . *pōtara -- ‘ young ’, pōtalaka -- see pṓta -- 1. Addenda: pōta -- 2. 2. *pōtta -- 2: S.kcch. *potyo* m. ‘ small dhoti ’.(CDIAL 8400) *Ta.* potti garment of fibres, cloth. *Ka.* potti cloth. *Te.* potti bark, a baby's linen, a sort of linen cloth; pottika a small fine cloth; podugu a baby's linen. *Kol.* (*SSTW*)pot sari. *Pa.* bodgid a short loincloth. / Cf. Skt. potikā-, Pkt. potti-, pottiā-, etc.; Turner, *CDIAL*, no. 8400. (DEDR 4515)

पोत (p. 303) pōta m f A bead of glass and, sometimes, of gold and of stone. 2 m A neck-ornament of females made of these beads.
58) पोत (p. 303) pōta m (or P) A link composed of rolls of coarse cloth. This portion, together with the विडी or iron handle, constitute the मशालor torch. 2 The head, end, point (of a tool, stick &c.): also the end or extreme portion (of a thing gen.) 3 m A seton; and fig. the hole of a फाळ or ploughshare.
59) पोत (p. 303) pōta n m (H Quality; or formed by redup. out of सूत with which word it is generally conjoined in use.) Weftage or texture (of cloth); quality as respects closeness, firmness, body. Ex. सूत- पोत पाहून धोत्र घ्यावें.
पोंत (p. 303) pōnta m (In Konkaṇ neuter.) A seton.

61) पोतडी (p. 303) pōtaḍī f पोतडें n (पोतें) A bag, esp. the circular bag of goldsmiths, shroffs &c. containing their weights, scales, coins &c.
62) पोतंडी (p. 303) pōtaṇḍī f A little thing (as a nut, a pebble,) or a small quantity (as of sugar, flour, grain) put up in a corner of a cloth and confined by a knot; thus forming a knob or ball. 2 Meḍicaments tied up in a corner of a cloth, to be dabbed on the eye or other part: also a cloth rolled up into a ball, heated, and applied to foment. v दे,लाव, also पोतंडीनें or पोतंडीचा शेक.
63) पोतदार (p. 303) pōtadāra m (P) An officer under the native governments. His business was to assay all money paid into the treasury. He was also the village-silversmith.
64) पोतदारी (p. 303) pōtadārī f (P) The office or business of पोतदार: also his rights or fees.
65) पोतनिशी (p. 303) pōtaniśī f (P) The office or business of पोतनीस.
66) पोतनीस (p. 303) pōtanīsa m (P) The treasurer or cash-keeper. पोतें (p. 303) pōtēṃ n (or P) A sack or large bag. 2 The treasury or the treasure-bags of Government. 3 The treasure-bag of a village made up for the district-treasury.
73) पोतेखाद (p. 303) pōtēkhāda f Wastage or loss on goods (as on sugar &c.) from adhesion to the containing sack or bag.
74) पोतेचाल (p. 303) pōtēcāla f (Treasury-currency.) The currency in which the public revenue is received. 2 Used as a Of that currency; as पोतेचालीचा (रूपया-पैसा- नाणें &c.) Coin or money admitted into or issued from the Government-treasury; sterling money of the realm.
75) पोतेझाडा (p. 303) pōtējhāḍā m Settlement of the accounts of the treasury.
76) पोतेरें (p. 303) pōtērēṃ n A clout or rag (as used in cowdunging floors &c.) 2 By meton. The smearing of cowdung effected by means of it. पो0 करून टाकणें To treat with exceeding slight and contumely. (Marathi)

धावड (p. 250) *dhāvaḍa* m A class or an individual of it. They are smelters of iron. In these parts they are Muhammadans. धावडी (p. 250) *dhāvaḍī* a Relating to the class धावड. Hence 2 Composed of or relating to iron.

धातु 1[p= 513,3]*m.* layer , stratum KaltyS3r. Kaus3.constituent part , ingredient (esp. [and in RV. only] ifc. , where often = " fold " e.g. त्रि-धा/आतु , threefold &c ; cf. त्रिविष्टि- ,सप्त- , सु-) RV. TS. S3Br. &celement , primitive matter (= महा-भूत L.) MBh. Hariv. &c (usually reckoned as 5 , viz. ख or आकाश , अनिल , तेजस् , जल , भू; to which is added ब्रह्म Ya1jn5. iii , 145 ; or विज्ञान Buddh.)a constituent element or essential ingredient of the body (distinct from the 5 mentioned above and conceived either as 3 humours [called also दोष] phlegm , wind and bile BhP. [cf. पुरीष , मांस , मनस् , ChUp. vi , 5 , 1] ; or as the 5 organs of sense , इन्द्रियाणि [cf. s.v. and MBh. xii , 6842 , where श्रोत्र , घ्राण , आस्य , हृदय and कोष्ठ are mentioned as the 5 धातु of the human body born from the either] and the 5 properties of the elements perceived by them , गन्ध , रस , रूप , स्पर्श andशब्द L. ; or the 7 fluids or secretions , chyle , blood , flesh , fat , bone , marrow , semen Sus3r. [L. रसा*दि or रस-रक्ता*दि, of which sometimes 10 are given , the above 7 and hair , skin , sinews BhP.])primary element of the earth i.e. metal , mineral , are (esp. a mineral of a red colour) Mn. MBh. &c element of wordsi.e. grammatical or verbal root or stem Nir. Pra1t. MBh. &c (with the southern Buddhists धातु means either the 6 elements [see above] Dharmas. xxv ; or the 18 elementary spheres [धातु-लोक] ib. lviii ; or the ashes of the body , relicsL. [cf. -गर्भ]). *dhā´tu* n. ‘ substance ’ RV., m. ‘ element ’ MBh., ‘ metal, mineral, ore (esp. of a red colour) ' Mn., ' ashes of the dead ' lex., ' *strand of rope ' (cf. *tridhā´tu* -- ' threefold ' RV., *ayugdhātu* -- ' having an uneven number of strands ' KātyŚr.). [√dhā] Pa. *dhātu* -- m. ' element, ashes of the dead, relic '; KhārI. *dhatu* ' relic '; Pk. *dhāu* -- m. ' metal, red chalk '; N. *dhāu* ' ore (esp. of copper) '; Or. *ḍhāu* ' red chalk, red ochre ' (whence *ḍhāuā* ' reddish '; M. *dhāū, dhāv* m.f. ' a partic. soft red stone ' (whence *dhā̆vaḍ* m. ' a caste of iron -- smelters ', *dhāvḍī* ' composed of or relating to iron '); -- Si. *dā* ' relic '; -- S. *dhāī* f. ' wisp of fibres added from time to time to a rope that is being twisted ', L. *dhāī̃* f.(CDIAL 6773).

Twelve Harappa Script imetalwork catalogues from one Mohenjo-daro house -- smithy/forge guild artisans of kole.l 'temple'

The decipherment of the seals and ivory inscriptions found in the temple area indicate the presence of: *śrēṣṭhin* 'master of guild' and *saṁgraha, samgaha* 'a guardian, ruler , manager , arranger', who is also an engraver. These functionaries seem to have had the responsibility to organize and control the products made on circular platforms and made available for shipments as cargo through seafaring merchants.

The Harappa Script hieroglyphs -- squirrel, lathe/portable furnace, one-horned young bull -- which signify these two functionaries are:

śrēṣṭhin 'guild master'

samgara, samgaha 'manager, arranger' कोंद *kōnda* 'engraver'. These two signifiers also indicate that the artisans working on the circular platforms were required to consign the metalwork products into the temple for accounting and trade transactions.

All seven seals out of the 12 inscriptions depicted the same animal 'one-horned young bull in front of a standard device'

Hieroglyph: *sãgaḍ*, 'lathe' (Meluhha) Rebus 1: *sãgaṛh* , 'fortification' (Meluhha). Rebus 2: *sanghAta* 'adamantine glue'. Rebus 3: *sangāṭh* *संगाठ़*'assembly, collection'. Rebus 4: *sãgaḍa* 'double-canoe, catamaran'. सं-ग्रह *saṁgraha, samgaha* 'a guardian, ruler , manager , arranger' R. BhP.

Hieroglyph: one-horned young bull: खोंड (p. 216) [*khōṇḍa*] *m* A young bull, a bullcalf.

Rebus: कोंद *kōnda* 'engraver, lapidary setting or infixing gems (Marathi) खोदगिरी *khondagiri* f Sculpture, carving, engraving.

The inscriptions on the seven seals and five tablets are:

dula 'two' rebus: dul 'metal casting' *khaṇḍa* 'notch' rebus*: khaṇḍa* 'implements
khaṇḍa 'arrow' rebus: *khaṇḍa* 'implements
muka 'ladle' rebus:*muhA* 'quantity of smelted metal produced from a furnace' PLUS *baṭa* 'rimless pot' rebus: *bhaṭa* 'furnace' *ayo, aya* 'fish' rebus: *aya* 'iron' *ayas* 'metal' PLUS *aDaren* 'lid' rebus: *aduru* 'unsmelte metal' muh 'ingot' PLUS *kolmo* 'rice plant' rebus: *kolimi* 'smithy, forge' *sal* 'splinter' rebus: *sal*

'workshop' *muh* 'ingot' PLUS *baṭa* 'quail' rebus: *bhaṭa* 'furnace'. Thus, the inscription on the seal signifies: workshop smithy/forge with furnace working to produce metal castings, ingots, implements, iron, unsmelted ore.

karṇaka, kanka 'rim of jar' rebus: *karṇī* 'supercargo' *karṇaka* 'scribe, account' कुटिल

HR 350

kuṭila, katthīl 'curve' kuṭila 'bent' CDIAL 3230 *Rebus: kuṭila* 'bronze' (8 parts copper, 2 parts tin).. Thus, a bronze worker handing over produce to the Supercargo as shipment.

HR 1575

karṇaka, kanka 'rim of jar' rebus: karṇī 'supercargo' *karṇaka* 'scribe, account' *dula* 'two' rebus: *dul* 'metal casting' Bshk. *sum -- taçh* ' hoe ' (< ' *earth -- scratcher '),*teçh* ' adze ' (< **takṣī* -- ?); Sh. *taçi* f. ' adze '; -- Phal. *tērçhi* ' adze ' (with "intrusive" *r*).Rebus: *takṣa* in cmpd. ' cutting ', m. ' carpenter ' VarBṛS., *vṛkṣa -- takṣaka --* m. ' tree -- feller ' R. [√takṣ]Pa. *tacchaka --* m. ' carpenter ', *taccha -- sūkara --* m. ' boar '; Pk. *takkha --* , °*aya --* m. ' carpenter, artisan' (CDIAL 5618) PLUS *khaṇḍa* 'arrow' rebus: *khaṇḍa* 'implements'. Thus, a carpenter artisan implements.

HR 116

kolom 'rice plant' rebus: *kolimi* 'smithy, forge' *karā̃* n. pl. wristlets, banglesRebus: *khār* 'blacksmith, iron worker' *ayo, aya* 'fish' rebus: aya 'iron' *ayas* 'metal' *karṇaka, kanka* 'rim of jar' rebus: *karṇī* 'supercargo' *karṇaka* 'scribe, account' *dula* 'two' rebus: *dul* 'metal casting' **śrēṣṭrī* ' clinger '. [√śriṣ1]Phal. *šẽṣṭrī̃* ' flying squirrel '?(CDIAL 12723) Rebus: guild master *khāra,* 'squirrel', rebus: *khār* खार् 'blacksmith' (Kashmiri). Thus, the inscription signifies: blacksmith guild-master working in iron in smithy/forge, metal castings handed over to Supercargo for shipment.

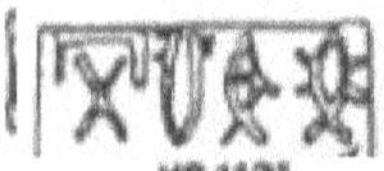

HR 1121

dATu 'cross' rebus: dhAtu 'element, mineral' *karṇaka, kanka 'rim* of jar' rebus: *karṇī* 'supercargo' *karṇaka* 'scribe, account' *ayo, aya* 'fish' rebus: *aya* 'iron' *ayas* 'metal' *khambhaṛā* 'fin' rebus: *kammaṭa* 'mint' *khaṇḍa* 'notch' rebus: *khaṇḍa* 'implements'. Thus, minerals, metal, alloys handed over to Supercargo for shipment.

karṇaka, kanka 'rim of jar' rebus: *karṇī* 'supercargo' *karṇaka* 'scribe, account' *ranku* 'liquid measure' rebus: *ranku* 'tin' *muh* 'ingot' PLUS *kolom* 'rice plant' rebus: *kolimi* 'smithy, forge' *sal* 'splinter' rebus: *sal* 'workshop' *baṭa* 'quail' rebus: *bhaṭa* 'furnace' Thus workshop smithy/forge (working with) furnace ingots, tin handed over to Supercargo for shipment.

kuṭi 'water carrier' rebus: *kuṭhi* 'smelter' PLUS *karṇaka, kanka* 'rim of jar' rebus: *karṇī* 'supercargo' karṇaka 'scribe, account' *koḍa* 'one' rebus: *koḍ* 'workshop' *kāṇḍa* 'notch' *kāṇḍa* 'arrow' rebus: kāṇḍa 'implements *kolom* 'three' rebus: *kolimi* 'smithy, forge' *baṭa* 'rimless pot' PLUS *muka* 'ladle' rebus: *muhA* 'quantity of metal produced from furnace, ingot'. Thus, Supercargo of smelter workshop produce, metal implements furnaced metal for smithy, forge.

karṇaka, kanka 'rim of jar' rebus: *karṇī* 'supercargo' karṇaka 'scribe, account' *kole.l* 'temple' *rebus:kole.l* 'smithy, forge' *kāṇḍa* 'backbone' rebus:*khaṇḍa* 'implements *baraDo* 'spine' rebus: *bharata* 'alloy of pewter, copper, tin' *sal* 'splinter' rebus: *sal* 'workshop' k*olom* 'rice plant' rebus:*kolimi* 'smithy, forge' *muh* 'ingot' Thus, Supercargo from smithy, forge, implements, ingots workshop of smithy/forge.

bhaṭa 'warrior' rebus: *bhaṭa* 'furnace' *karṇika* 'spread legs rebus:

karṇī 'Supercargo' Thus, furnace (produce) worker.and a Supercargo, merchant's representative responsible for the cargo.

kuṭi 'water carrier' rebus: *kuṭhi* 'smelter' PLUS *karṇaka, kanka* 'rim of jar' rebus: *karṇī* 'supercargo' *karṇaka* 'scribe, account' *muh* 'ingot' PLUS *kolom* 'rice plant' rebus: *kolimi* 'smithy, forge' *teçh* 'adze' rebus: *taksa* 'carpenter' *sal* 'splinter' rebus: *sal* 'workshop' *kanac* 'corner' rebus: *kancu* 'bronze'. Thus, Supercargo-carpente of smelter workshop, smithy, forge, bronze.

karṇaka, kanka 'rim of jar' rebus: *karṇī* 'supercargo' *karṇaka* 'scribe, account' *dula* 'two' rebus: dul 'metal casting' *karā̃* n. pl. wristlets, bangles Rebus: *khār* 'blacksmith, iron worker' *kolmo* 'three' *rebus: kolimi* 'smithy/forge' *baṭa* 'rimless pot' rebus: *bhaṭa* 'furnace' PLUS *khAṇḍa* **'notch'** rebus*: khaṇḍa* 'implements dhaTo 'claws of crab' rebus: dhatu 'mineral' Thus,Supercargo of metal castings, blacksmith, smithy/forge furnace implements.

karṇaka, kanka 'rim of jar' rebus: karṇī 'supercargo' *karṇaka* 'scribe, account' muh 'ingot' PLUS *khAṇḍa* 'notch' rebus: *khaṇḍa* 'implements'. Thus, Supercargo of metal ingots, implements.

Thus, it is seen that all the 12 inscriptions are metalwork catalogues of artisans of the guild preparing products (ingots, implements) for shipment to be handed to Supercargo responsible for the cargo.

The building HR1 was thus a smithy, forge. kole.l signified 'smithy/forge'. The same word kole.l also signified 'temple'. Thus, all the artisans at work documenting 12 inscriptions were members of the smithy/forge guild which was the temple.

A guild-master of the guild was *śrēṣṭhin*: śrēṣṭhin m. ' distinguished man ' AitBr., ' foreman of a guild ', °*nī* -- f. ' his wife ' Hariv. [śrḗṣṭha --]Pa. *seṭṭhin* -- m. ' guild -- master ', Dhp. *śeṭhi*, Pk. *seṭṭhi* -- , *siṭṭhi* -- m., °*iṇī* -- f.; S. *seṭhi* m. ' wholesale merchant '; P. *seṭh* m. ' head of a guild, banker ', *seṭhaṇ*, °*ṇī* f.; Ku.gng. *śēṭh* ' rich man '; N. *seṭh* ' banker '; B. *seṭh* ' head of a guild, merchant '; Or. *seṭhi* ' caste of washermen '; Bhoj. Aw.lakh. *sēṭhi* ' merchant, banker ', H. *seṭh* m., °*ṭhan* f.; G. *śeṭh*, *śeṭhiyɔ* m. ' wholesale merchant, employer, master '; M.*śeṭh*, °*ṭhī*, *śeṭ*, °*ṭī* m. ' respectful term for banker or merchant '; Si. *siṭu*, *hi*° ' banker, nobleman ' H. Smith JA 1950, 208 (or < śiṣṭá --2?)(CDIAL 12726).

Harappa Script inscriptions (22) on ivory and bone cylinder seals

Area excavated by Hargreaves is called HR Area; area excavated by K. N. Dikshit is called DK Area; area excavated by Madhu Swarup Vats is called VS Area.

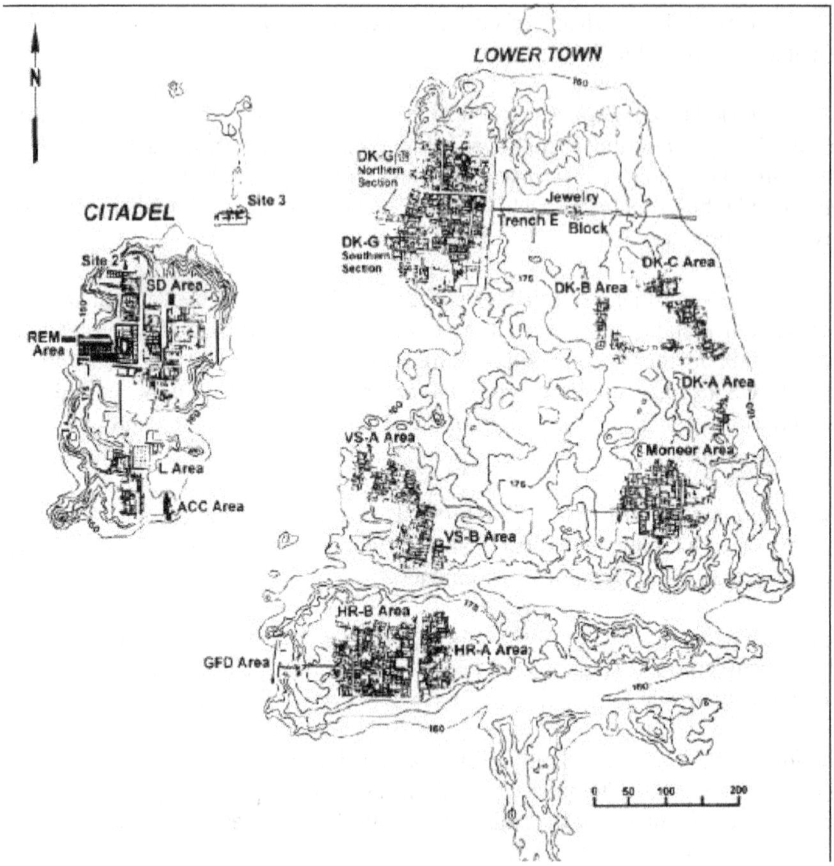

N
LOWER TOWN
CITADEL
Site 3
Site 2
SD Area
REM Area
L Area
ACC Area
DK-G Northern Section
DK-G Southern Section
Jewelry Block
Trench E
DK-C Area
DK-B Area
DK-A Area
Moneer Area
VS-A Area
VS-B Area
HR-B Area
HR-A Area
GFD Area
0 50 100 200

Definition of kole.l 'smithy, forge, temple' from 12 Harappa Script inscriptions found in and layout of House 1 (with several rooms) HR Area, Mohenjo-daro; a report on *kole.l*'smithy' found in HR Area House 1. This house had several rooms on the upper storey with two clear entry and exit stairways (Annex A).

In the same temple (*kole.l*) area, ivory/bone rods with Harappa Script inscriptions, possibly used as cylinder seals were found.

The 19 Harappa Script inscriptions on ivory rods, plaques and cubes of Mohenjo-daro and Harappa are presented in this monographs with their decipherment as metalwork catalogues.

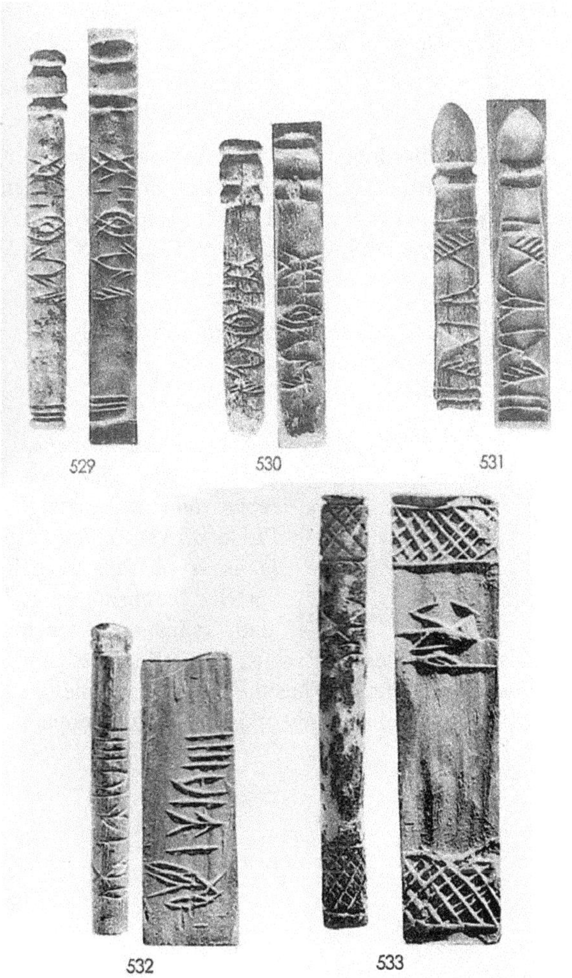

530 and 531 ivory rods are shaped like a meḍha 'stake' rebus: meḍha 'yajna' (Yūpa) with caSAla (as described in *Satapatha Brahmana* and Taittiriya Samhita) for a Soma yaga.

John Marshall wrote: "Seals of this group [cylinder seals, although Mackay is not sure they are true cylinder seals]], if indeed they are seals, are very rarely found at Mohenjo-daro, only five specimen being obtained in all. They are all made of ivory and differ from the cylinder seals of other countries in being very long and thing; nor are they perforated for suspension on a cord. It is possible that these so-called seals are not true seals at all. They incised characters upon them might conceivably be identification marks for a game or something similar. On the other hand, they are certainly suitable for use as seals and in this account they are included in this chapter For the sake of clearness the actual seal is shown side by side with each impression.

No 529 (Pl. CXIV, HR 5515). Ivory. 2.7 inches long by 0.25 in. in diameter. Double groove at one end for attachment of cord. The other end is decorated with three parallel grooves. Level, 4 feet below surface. Central Courtyard (30), House LIII, Block 7, HR Area.

No 530 (Pl. CXIV, HR 4985). Ivory. 2.05 inches long by 0.25 in. in diameter. Double groove at one end for a cord; the other end is broken. Level 3 feet below surface. Central Courtyard (30), House LIII, Block 7, HR Area.

No 531 (Pl. CXIV, DK 2666). Ivory. Now 2.05 inches long by 0.3 in. in diameter. Its polish shows that it has been much used. About one-half of the seal is covered with an inscription, deeply and roughly incised and bordered by two deep cut lines. One end of the seal is shaped into a conical head with a deep groove possibly intended for a cord. The seal is not bored; nor is it perfectly round. Level, 4 feet below surface. Street between Blocks 1 and 2, Section B, DK Area.

No 532 (Pl. CXIV, VS 875). Ivory. Now 2 inches long by 0.3 in. in diameter. One end is broken and a small piece is missing. The seal tapers slightly towards its complete end. Five deeply incised characters occupy a space of about two-thirds of the circumference of the seal. Level, 12 feet below surface. Found in front of Room 70, House XXVII, VS Area.

No 533 (Pl. CXIV, VS 958). Ivory. 2.75 inches long by 0.3 in. in diameter. Decorated at 0-.5 in. from each end with a deeply incised cross-hatched border. Towards one end of the intervening space are two deeply incised characters This seal is not perfectly round. Level, 10 feet below surface of the ground. From Room 69, House XXVIII, VS Area.237

The 5 ivory rod inscriptions (529 to 533 Marshall) are flipped left horizontally and presented with rebus readings:

Ivory inscription 1

kuTi 'water carrier' *rebus: kuThi* 'smelter' *dula* 'two' rebus: *dul* 'metal casting' PLUS *karNika* 'spread legs' rebus: *karNI* 'Supercargo' karNIka 'helmsman'; *meḍ* 'body' rebus: *meḍ* 'iron' meḍ 'copper' (Slavic) *baTa* 'rimless pot' rebus: *bhaTa* 'furnace' gaṇḍa 'four' rebus: *kaṇḍa* 'implements'. Thus the message is: smelter, metalcaster, supercargo, helmsman working with iron/copper implements and furnace.

Ivory inscription 2

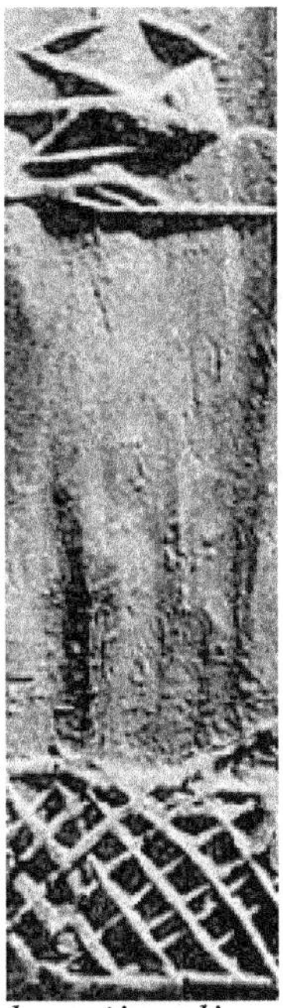

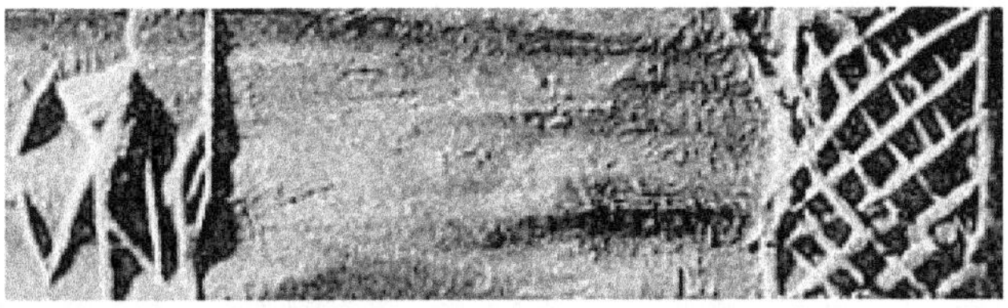

khāṇḍa 'divisions'; rebus: *kaṇḍa* 'implements' *dhAu* 'strand' *dhAv* 'string' rebus: *dhAvaD* 'smelter' *dhaTo* 'claws of crab' rebus: *dhatu* 'minerals' kAru 'pincrs' rebus: kAru 'artisan'. Thus the message is: smelter of minerals, (maker of metal) implements.'

Ivory inscription 3

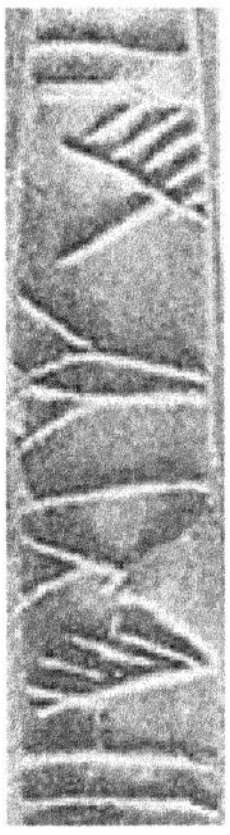

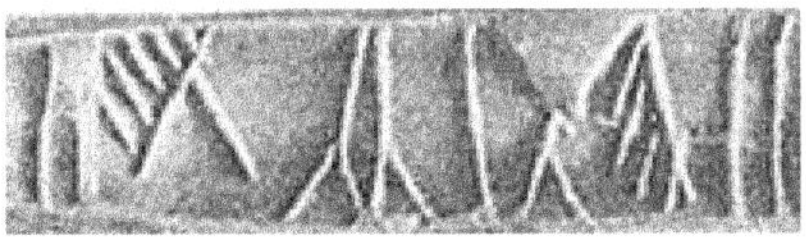

kangsi '*comb*' *kammaTa* 'mint, 'metal' *khāṇḍa* rebus: *aduru* is: Turner of (metal)

dula 'two' rebus: *dul* 'metal casting' *kharedo* = a currycomb (G.) Rebus: *kharādī* ' turner' (G.) rebus: *kancu* 'bronze' *kamaTha* 'bow and arrow' rebus: coiner, coinage' ayo, aya 'fish' rebus: *aya* 'iron' *ayas* 'notch' rebus: *kaṇḍa* 'implements'. *ad.ar* '*harrow*'; 'native metal, unsmelted' (Kannada) Thus, the message metal castings, native metal, mint-master-coiner, iron implements, ingots and metal (alloys) turner.

Ivory inscription 4

529 Marshall Ivory rod *kharedo* = a currycomb (G.) Rebus: *kharādī* ' turner' (G.) *kangsi* '*comb*' rebus: *kancu* 'bronze' *karNaka, kanka* 'rim of jar' rebus: k*arNI* 'Supercargo' *karNaka* 'scribe, account' *karā̃* 'wristlets, bangles' rebus: *khAr* 'blacksmith' *sal* 'splinter' rebus: *sal* 'workshop' PLUS *khāṇḍa* 'notch' rebus: *kaṇḍa* 'implements' Fish-fin: *ayo, aya* 'fish' rebus: *aya* 'iron' *ayas* 'metal' PLUS *khambhaṛā* 'fin' rebus: *kammaTa* 'mint, coiner, coinage'. Thus, the message is: blacksmith, turner, tupercargo bronze implements workshop, mint-master/coiner. (529 and 530 ivory rods have identical inscriptions; 530 has an additional hieroglyph: three linear strokes)

Ivory inscription 5

530 Marshall Ivory rod *kharedo* = a currycomb (G.) Rebus: *kharādī* ' turner' (G.) *kangsi* '*comb*' rebus: *kancu* 'bronze' *karNaka, kanka* 'rim of jar' rebus: k*arNI* 'Supercargo' *karNaka* 'scribe, account' *karā̃* 'wristlets, bangles' rebus: *khAr* 'blacksmith' *sal* 'splinter' rebus: *sal* 'workshop' PLUS *khāṇḍa* 'notch' rebus: *kaṇḍa* 'implements' Fish-fin: *ayo, aya* 'fish' rebus: *aya* 'iron' *ayas* 'metal' PLUS *khambhaṛā* 'fin' rebus: *kammaTa* 'mint, coiner,

coinage'. Thus, the message is: blacksmith, turner, tupercargo bronze implements workshop, mint-master/coiner. *kolom* 'three' rebus: *kolimi* 'smithy, forge'. Thus, the message is: Blacksmith, Turner, Supercargo (engraver) implements workshop, mint-master/coiner, (working in) smithy/forge..

Bone rod inscription 6

Incised bone rod discovered in Mohenjo-daro in the 1920s.
m1650 Ivory? stick Hypertext 3505

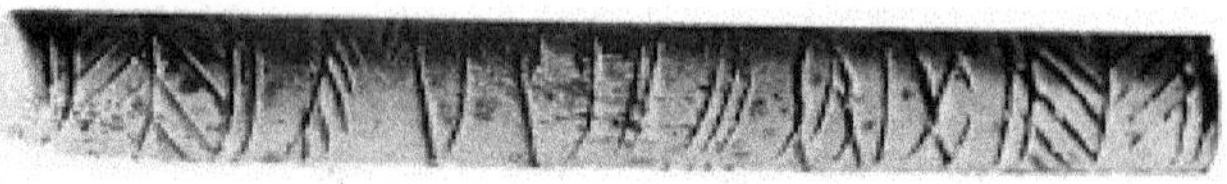

On either side of the hypertext inscription, two twigs with leaves are signified: *aḍaru twig*; aḍiri small and thin ***branch*** of a tree; *aḍari* m.n. 'branch without ***leaves*** or fruit' (Prakrit) (CDIAL 5524) Rebus: *aduru* 'unsmelted, native metal' *kAru* 'pincers' rebus: *kAru* 'artisan' *daTo* 'claws of crab' rebus: *dhatu* 'mineral' *kanac* 'corner' rebus: *kancu* 'bronze' *gaṇḍa* 'four' rebus: *kaṇḍa* 'implements' PLUS *kolom* 'three (sets of four)' rebus: *kolimi* 'smithy, forge'(thus, together,signify smithy,forge implements) *dula* 'two' rebus: *dul* 'metal casting' *kolmo* 'rice plant' rebus: *kolimi* 'smithy, forge' PLUS *dula* 'two' rebus: *dul* 'metal casting' PLUS *baTa* 'rimless pot' rebus: *bhaTa* 'furnace'. Thus, furnace for metal casting smithy. *karNaka, kanka* 'rim of jar' rebus: *karNI* 'Supercargo' *karNaka* 'scribe, account' *khareḍo* = a currycomb (G.) Rebus: *kharādī* ' turner' (G.) *kangsi* '*comb*' rebus: *kancu* 'bronze'. Thus, the message is: supercargo, (worker in) minerals, bronze implements, smithy/forge, metal caster, metals turner (alloys) using furnace.

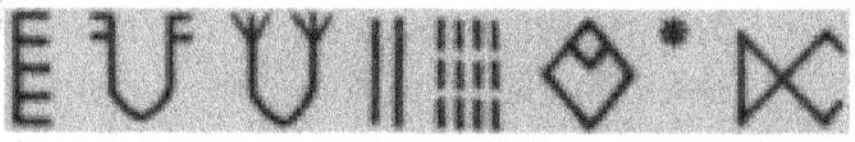

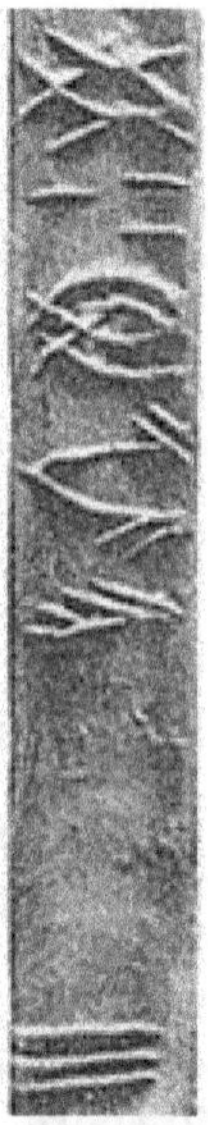

Ivory inscription 7

Pict-141 Geometrical pattern Hypertext 2942 *karNika* 'spread legs' rebus: *karNI* 'supercargo' *meḍ* 'body' rebus: *meḍ* 'iron' meḍ 'copper' (Slavic) PLUS dato 'scarf'rebus: dhatu 'mineral, ore'. Thus supercargo for iron ore shipment. *kanac* 'corner' rebus: *kancu* 'bronze' *sal 'splinter' rebus: sal 'workshop'.Thus, bronze workshop. khāṇḍa 'divisions'; rebus: kaṇḍa* 'implements'. Tus, the message is: Supercargo (working in) iron/copper, bronze implements workshop.

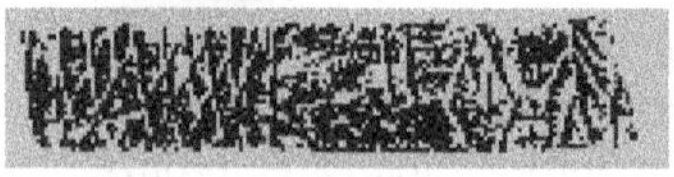

Ivory inscription 8

Pict 142 geometrical pattern Hypertext 2941 Ivory or bone rod geometrical pattern followed by inscription *koDa* 'one' rebus: *koD* 'workshop' *dula* 'two' rebus: *dul* 'metal casting'PLUS *baTa* 'rimless pot' rebus: *bhaTa* 'furnace' PLUS kolmo 'rice plant' rebus: smithy, forge'. Thus, smithy, forge furnace for casting metal. *karNaka, kanka* 'rim of jar' rebus: *karNI* 'Supercargo' *karNaka* 'scribe, account' *khareḍo* = a currycomb (G.)

Rebus: *kharādī* ' turner' (G.*)*. *kangsi* 'comb' rebus: *kancu, kamsa* 'bronze' Thus, the message is: turner, Supercargo in metal casting, bronze workshop (with) furnace

Ivory inscription 9

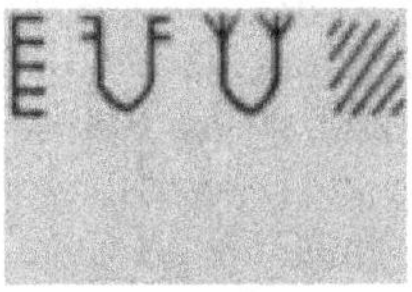

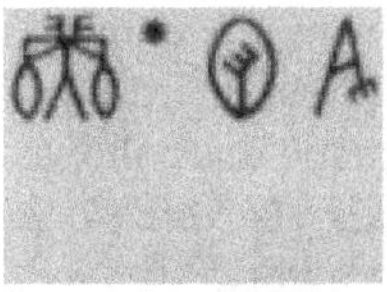

Hypertext 2943 is a duplication of the Hypertext 2941 on Pict-142: *koDa* 'one' rebus: *koD* 'workshop' *dula* 'two' rebus: *dul* 'metal casting'PLUS *baTa* 'rimless pot' rebus: *bhaTa* 'furnace' PLUS kolmo 'rice plant' rebus: smithy, forge'. Thus, smithy, forge furnace for casting metal. *karNaka, kanka* 'rim of jar' rebus: *karNI* 'Supercargo' *karNaka* 'scribe, account' *khareḍo* = a currycomb (G.) Rebus: *kharādī* ' turner' (G.*)*. *kangsi* 'comb' rebus: *kancu, kamsa* 'bronze' Thus, the message is: turner, Supercargo in metal casting, bronze workshop (with) furnace

Ivory inscription 10

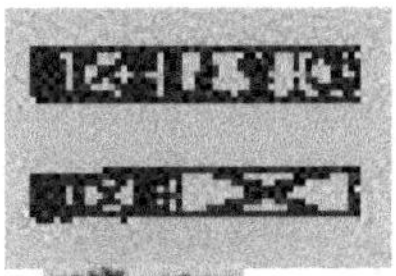

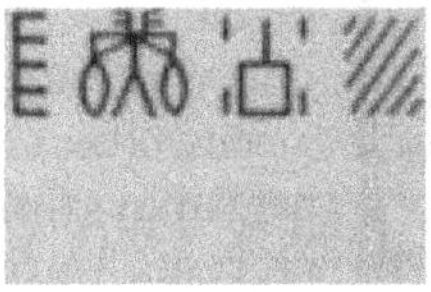

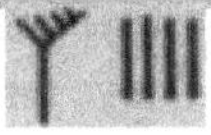

Pict 143 Geometrical pattern Hypertext 2948 *dATu* 'cross' rebus: *dhatu* 'mineral, ore' *gaṇḍa* 'four' rebus: *kaṇḍa* 'implements' *ranku* 'liquid measure' rebus: *ranku* 'tin' (thus, tin implements) *kuTi* 'water carrier' rebus: *kuThi* 'smelter' *PLUS karNaka, kanka* 'rim of jar' rebus: *karNI* 'Supercargo' *karNaka* 'scribe, *account' khareḍo* = currycomb (G.) Rebus: *kharādī '* turner' (G.) *kangsi* 'comb' rebus:*kamsa, kancu* 'bronze' (thus, Supercargo, engraver working with minerals, bronze, tin and smelter, turner (of metal alloys) working with furnace and engraving.

Ivory inscription 11

Hypertext 2944 Ivory or bone rod Phal. *tērçhi* ' adze ' (with "intrusive" r).Rebus: *takṣa* in cmpd. ' cutting ', m. ' carpenter ' VarBr̥S PLUS *kolom* 'three' rebus: *kolimi* 'smithy, forge' (Thus, carpenter working with smithy/forge). Oval shape: *muh* 'ingot' PLUS *kolmo* 'rice plant' rebus: *kolimi* 'smithy, forge' (Thus smithy/forge ingots) *kuTi* 'water carrier' rebus: *kuThi* 'smelter' PLUS kanka, karNaka 'rim of jar' rebus: *karNI* 'supercargo' *karNaka* 'scribe, account' Thus the message is: Carpenter working with smithy/forge, ingots for smithy and supercargo working with smelter and engraving.

Ivory inscription 12

Hypertext 2945 Ivory or bone rod *gaṇḍa* 'four' rebus: *kaṇḍa* 'implements' kaṇḍa 'fire-altar' *kolmo* 'rice plant' rebus: *kolimi* 'smithy, forge' Thus, the message is: (Maker of) implements in smithy/forge.

Ivory inscription 13

Ivory rod, ivory plaques with dotted circles. Mohenjo-daro (Musee National De Arts Asiatiques, Guimet, 1988-1989, *Les cites oubliees de l'Indus Archeologie du Pakistan.*] *dhātu* 'layer, strand'; *dhāv* 'strand, string' Rebus: *dhāu, dhātu* 'ore'. *dATu* 'cross' rebus: *dhatu* 'mineral'. Thus, the message signified by dotted circles and phonetic determinant X hieroglyph refers to *dhā̆vaḍ* priest of 'iron-smelters'. The aquatic duck shown atop an ivory rod is: *karaṇḍa* 'duck' (Sanskrit) *karaṛa* 'a very large aquatic bird' (Sindhi) Rebus: करडा [*karaḍā*] Hard from alloy--iron, silver &c. (Marathi) Thus, the metalworker (smelter) works with hard alloys (using carburization process). Three dotted circles: *kolom* 'three' rebus: *kolimi* 'smithy, forge'. Thus working with minerals and hard alloys for smithy, forge.

Ivory inscription 14

m1652 Ivory stick *sal* 'splinter' rebus: *sal* 'workshop' PLUS d*aTo* 'claws of crab' rebus: *dhatu* 'mineral' kAru 'pincers' rebus: kAru 'artisan' *ayo, aya* 'fish' rebus: *aya* 'iron' *ayas* 'metal' k*oDa* 'one' rebus: *koD* 'workshop' PLUS *dula* 'two' rebus: *dul* 'metal casting'. Thus the message is: workshop for minerals, metals and metal caster.

Ivory inscription 15 m1651 Ivory stick A, D, F

Hypertext 2947 Dotted circle hieroglyphs at the ends of the rod: *dhātu* 'layer, strand'; **d***hāv* 'strand, string' Rebus: *dhāu, dhātu* 'ore'.(smelter) *dATu* 'cross' rebus: *dhatu* 'mineral'. Fish-fin: *ayo,* aya 'fish' rebus: *aya* 'iron' *ayas* 'metal' PLUS *khambhaṛā* '**fin**' rebus: *kammaTa* 'mint, coiner, coinage'.Oval shape: *muh* 'ingot' PLUS *khāṇḍa* 'notch' rebus: *kaṇḍa* 'implements' (Thus, ingot implements) *koḍa* 'sluice'; Rebus: *koḍ* 'artisan's workshop (Kuwi) karNaka, kanka 'rim of jar' rebus: *karNI* 'Supercargo' karNaka 'scribe, account' *khareḍo* = a currycomb (G.) Rebus: *kharādī* ' turner' (G.) kangsi 'comb' rebus: kams, kancu 'bronze'. thus the message is: Working with dhatu (minerals), mint (coiner), ingot implements bronze workshop, Supercargo (scribe, account), Turner (alloys) of metal, Smelter

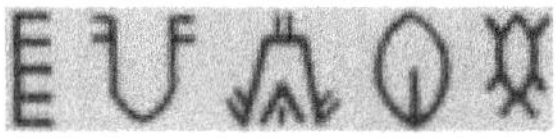

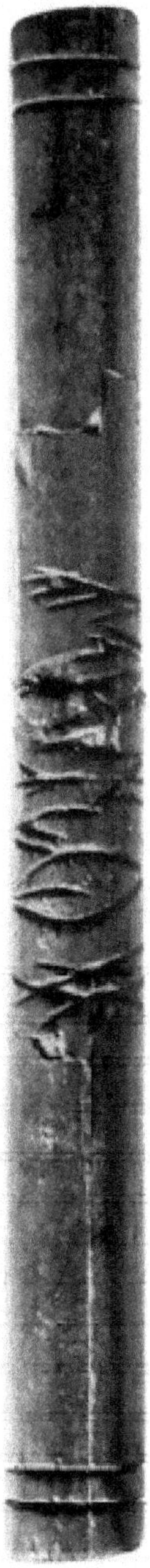

Ivory inscription 16

Hypertext 2940 Ivory or bone rod dula 'two' rebus: dul 'metal casting' arA 'spokes' rebus: *Ara* 'brass' *eraka* 'nave of wheel' rebus: *erako* 'molten cast, copper'.*kamaTha* 'bow and arrow' rebus: *kammaTa* 'mint, coiner, coinage' *karNaka, kanka* 'rim of jar' rebus: *karNI* 'Supercargo' *karNaka* 'scribe, account' *khareḍo* = a currycomb (G.) Rebus: k*harādī* ' turner' (G.) kangsi 'comb' rebus: kamsa, kancu 'bronze'. Thus, the message is: Supercargo (scribe, account), Turner (of alloys) of metal, mint-master, working with bronze and metal casting.

Ivory inscription 17

m1653 ivory plaque Hypertext

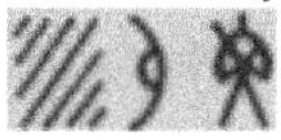

1905 *bhaTa* 'warrior' rebus: *bhaTa* 'furnace' *kuṭila* 'bent' CDIAL 3230) Rebus: *kuṭila, katthīl* = bronze (8 parts copper and 2 parts tin).Thus, a bronze furnace worker.

Ivory inscription 18

m1654 Ivory cube with dotted circles Dotted circle hieroglyphs on each side of the cube (one dotted circle surrounded by 7 dotted circles): *dhātu* 'layer, strand'; *dhāv* 'strand, string' Rebus: *dhāu, dhātu* 'ore'.(smelter).

Ivory inscription 19

Ivory is also used to record an inscription in Harappa:
h101 Ivory stick Hypertext 4561 *dhātu* 'layer, strand'; *dhāv* 'strand, string' Rebus: *dhāu, dhātu* 'ore'.(smelter) kAru 'pincers' rebus: kAru 'artisan' *ḍhāla 'slanted' rebus: ḍhāla 'ingot'l koDa* 'one' rebus: *koD* 'workshop' khāṇḍa 'notch' rebus: *kaṇḍa* 'implements'. Thus, Smelter (ores), ingots and implements workshop.

Ivory inscription 20

m1652A ivory stick *sal* 'splinter' rebus: *sal* 'workshop' *dhāv* 'strand, string' Rebus: *dhāu, dhātu* 'ore'.(smelter) *kAru* 'pincers' rebus: *kAru* 'artisan' ayo, aya 'fish' rebus: aya 'iron' ayas 'metal' *koDa* 'one' rebus: *koD* 'workshop' *dula* 'two' rebus: *dul* 'metal casting'. Thus, workshop minerals, metal, metal casting.

Cone inscription 21

m1649Acone

m1649Bcone

3253

ayo, aya 'fish' rebus: *aya* 'iron' *ayas* 'metal' *kaṇḍa* 'arrow' rebus:kaṇḍa 'implements' *aDaren* 'lid' rebus: *aduru* 'unsmelted,native metal'. Thus, nativemetal implements.

Bone inscription 22

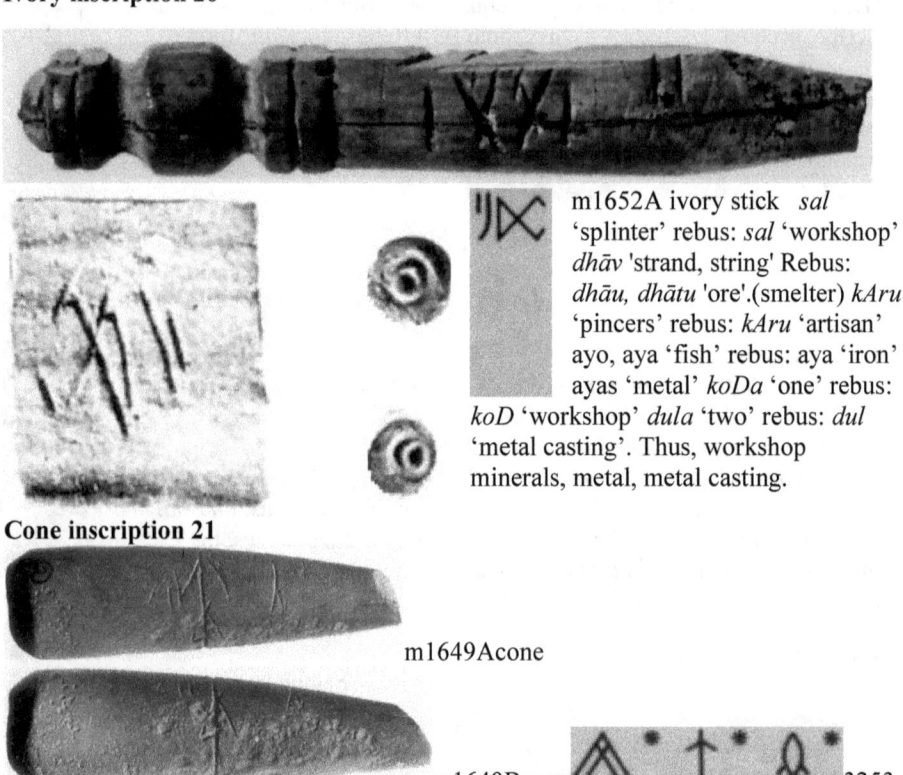

h2570Abone *gaṇḍa* 'four' rebus: *khāṇḍa* 'implements' *kaṇḍa* 'fire-altar' *baTa* 'rimless pot' rebus: *bhaTa* 'furnace'.

Annex B

Dharma saṁjñā Corporate badges of Harappa Script Corpora, ceramic (stoneware) bangles, seals, fillets

Data mining of Harappa Script Corpora reveal the purpose of ceramic (stoneware) bangles (22), seals, fillets as *dharma saṁjñā,* 'badges of responsibility'. They are Corporate badges, with deciphered Harappa Script inscriptions. Socio-cultural framework of a workshop (smithy-forge as a temple) for a cluster of Vedic villages unravels organization of artisanal-seafaring merchant society as a Corporation with ancient guilds.

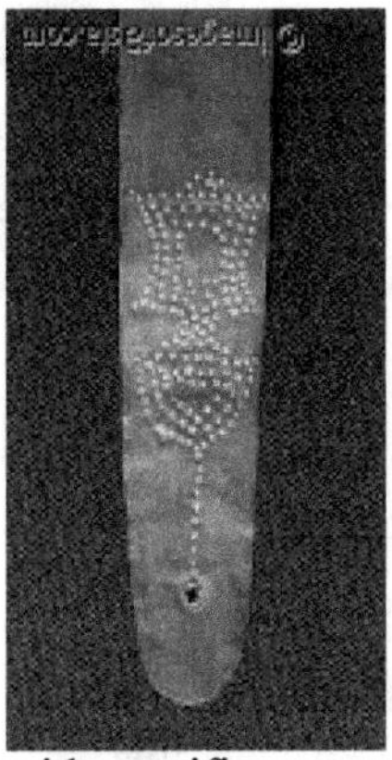

Gold *paṭa,* 'fillet'. Punctuated design on both ends. Mohenjodaro. *sãghāṛɔ* 'lathe, brazier' rebus: *samgraha, samgaha* 'arranger, manager'.

Executive summary: Socio-cultural framework of Vedic village clusters of Bronze Age

The workshops evidenced by circular platforms are Corporations of the Bronze Age, with the emergence of guilds of artisans with specific functions and responsibilities to promote the Corporation as a commonwealth. It was a smiths' guild at work on circular platforms of Harappa using tablets as category 'tallies' for the final shipment of package with a seal impression. each functionary in the guild had a recognizable *paṭa* 'badge' (Corporate badge of dharma, of responsibility assigned in a socio-cultural organization of the samajam). A Bronze Age village of Bhāratam Janam or a cluster of such villages was a janapada, a Corporation of artisan guilds.

Three *paṭa* 'badges' are shown on the stone statue of the so-called 'priest-king' who wears a fillet on his forehead and also on hi right shoulder. A third badge is signified on his uttariyam (shawl) which is embellished with the hieroglyphs of 'trefoils' signifying tri-dhAtu 'three mineral' strands of *dhā̆vaḍ* 'smelter', with assigned functional responsibility.of a Potr 'purifier'.

It is suggested that many such badges were worn by artisans of a Vedic village of the Bronze Age; such badges were ceramic (stoneware) bangles.

An "eye bead" made of gold with steatite inlay, Harappa. Fired steatite beads appear to have been extremely important to the Indus people because they were incorporated into exquisite ornaments, such as this "eye bead" made of gold with steatite inlay found in 1995 at Harappa [Harappa

Phase]. https://www.harappa.com/slide/gold-disc
The central ornament worn on the forehead of the famous "priest-king" sculpture from Mohenjo-daro appears to represent an eye bead, possibly made of gold with steatite inlay in the center. https://www.harappa.com/slide/priest-king-forehead

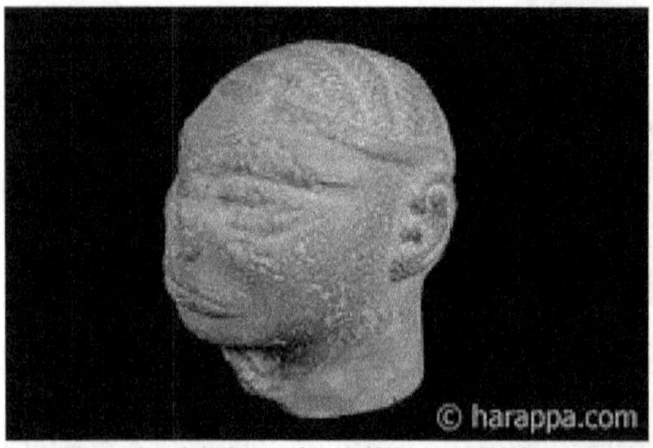

The weltanchauung, 'world perception' of artisans in a Vedic village was governed by 1. dharma, assigned responsibilities and 2. the metaphor of a kole.l 'smithy-forge' as a kole.l 'temple'. Male head probably broken from a seated sculpture. Finely braided or wavy combed hair tied into a double bun on the back of the head and a plain fillet or headband with hanging ribbons falling down the back. The upper lip is shaved and a closely cropped and combed beard lines the pronounced lower jaw. Male head shows the typical arrangement of the hair in a double bun, held in place by a thin fillet (badge) tied on the forehead.

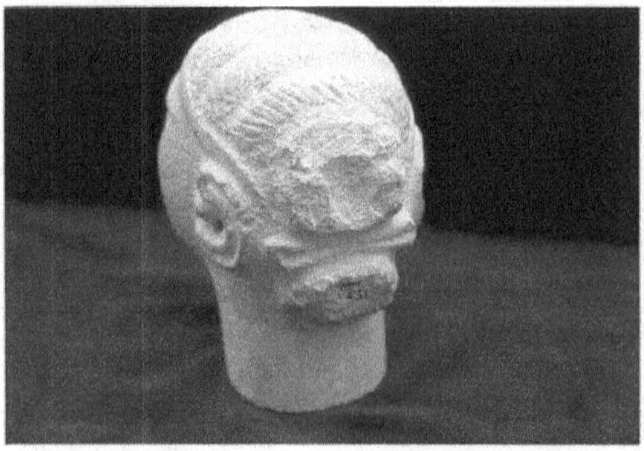

Functions assigned were recognized by distribution of ceramic (stoneware) bangles worn as *paṭa,* 'socio-cultural honour-badges'. Such a *paṭa* m. ' slab, tablet, metal plate ',was distinct from the seals and tablets.

Such a *paṭa* was a gold fillet with the inscribed *sā̃gāḍā°ḍī* 'lathe, portable furnace' hieroglyph-multiplex .

Hieroglyph: सांगड [*sāṅgaḍa*] That member of a turner's apparatus by which the piece to be turned is confined and steadied. सांगडीस धरणें To take into linkedness or close connection with, lit. fig.Rebus 1: *sangara* [fr. saŋ+gṛ1 to sing, proclaim, cp. gāyati & gīta] 1. a promise, agreement J iv.105, 111, 473; v.25, 479; sangaraŋ karoti to make a compact Vin i.247; J (Pali) Rebus 2: *śā̃gaḍa* 'catamaran'. Such a सांगड [*sāṅgaḍa*] is alsoa hieroglyph-multiplex, *f* A body formeḍ of two or more (fruits, animals, men) linked or joined together. सं-ग्रह *saṁgraha* 'a guardian , ruler , manager , arranger' R. BhP.

Such a *paṭa* were two anthropomorphs of copper/bronze with spread legs of a human body. The rebus reading of the hieroglyph-multiplex (hypertext) on the badges: 1. helmsman, merchantman, (metal) suercargo, engraver, merchant, worker in wood and iron; 2. helmsman, (metal) supercargo, iron worker

Spread legs on both anthropomorphs signify कर्णक 'spread legś rebus: 'helmsman'

This is an apparent link of the 'fish' or 'boar' broadly with the profession of 'metal-, wood-work' and 'seafaring merchantman'. The 'fish' sign is apparently related to the copper object which seems to depict a 'fighting ram' symbolized by its in-curving horns. The 'fish' sign may relate to a copper furnace. The underlying imagery defined by the style of the copper casting is the pair of curving horns of a fighting ram ligatured into the outspread legs (of a warrior). The badge was shaped like a person with ram's (or markhor's) horns, with spread legs and inscribed with hieroglyph-multiplexes or metaphors.

The script inscriptions indicate a set of modifiers or ligatures to the hieroglyph indicating that the metal, *aya*, was worked on during the early Bronze Age metallurgical processes -- to produce *aya* ingots, *aya* metalware,*aya* hard alloys.

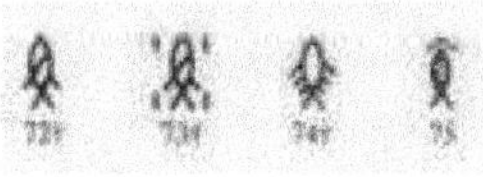

Fish hieroglyph in its vivid orthographic form is shown in a Susa pot which contained metalware -- weapons and vessels.

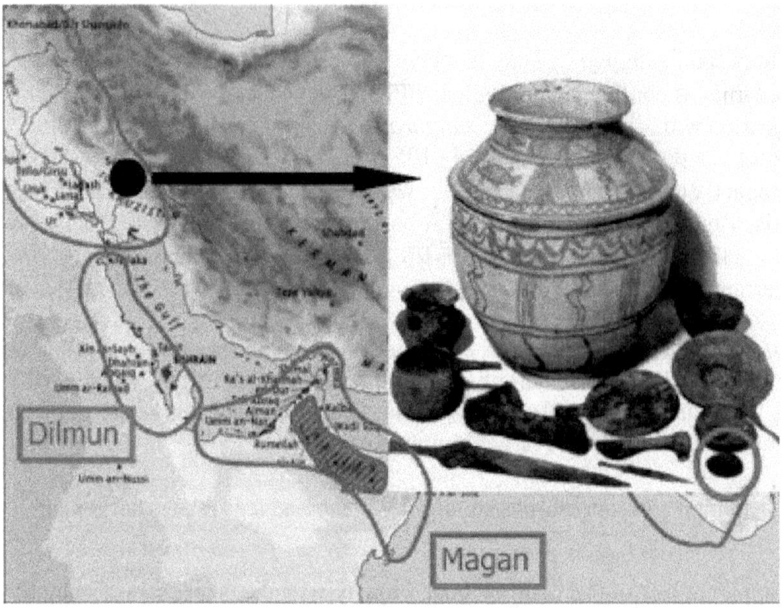

Context for use of 'fish' glyph. This photograph of a fish and the 'fish' glyph on Susa pot are comparable to the 'fish' glyph on Indus inscriptions.

Read on the arguments at: http://bharatkalyan97.blogspot.com/2011/11/decoding-fish-and-ligatured-fish-glyphs.html

The modifiers to the 'fish' hieroglyph which commonly occur together are: slanted stroke, notch, fins, lid-of-pot ligatured as superfix:

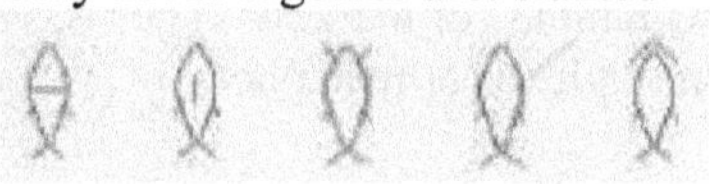

For determining the semantics of the messages conveyed by the script. Positional analysis of 'fish' glyphs has also been presented in: *The Harappa Script: A Positional-statistical Approach* By Michael Korvink, 2007, Gilund Press.

Mahadevan notes (Para 6.5 opcit.) that 'a unique feature of the 'fish' signs is their tendency to form clusters, often as pairs, and rarely as triplets also. This pattern has fascinated and baffled scholars from the days of Hunter posing problems in interpretation.' One way to resolve the problem is to interpret the glyptic elements creating ligatured fish signs and read the glyptic elements rebus to define the semantics of the message of an inscription.

karaṇḍa 'duck' (Sanskrit) *karaṛa* 'a very large aquatic bird' (Sindhi) Rebus: करडा [*karaḍā]* Hard from alloy--iron, silver &c. (Marathi) Rebus: fire-god: @B27990. #16671. Remo <*karandi*>E155 {N} ``^fire-^god".(Munda) Rebus:. *khārādī* ' turner' (Gujarati)

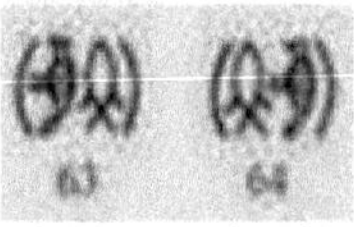

The 'parenthesiś modifier is a circumfix for both 'fish' and 'duck' hieroglyphs, the semantics of () two parenthetical modifiers are: kuṭilá— 'bent, crooked' KātyŚr., °*aka*— Pañcat., n. 'a partic. plant' [√kuṭ 1] Pa. *kuṭila*— 'bent', n. 'bend'; Pk. *kuḍila*— 'crooked', °*illa*— 'humpbacked', °*illaya*— 'bent'DEDR 2054 *(a) Ta.* koṭu curved, bent, crooked; koṭumai crookedness, obliquity; koṭukki hooked bar for fastening doors, clasp of an ornament. A pair of curved lines: *dol* 'likeness, picture, form' [e.g., two tigers, two bulls, sign-pair.] Kashmiri. dula दुल । युग्मम् m. a pair, a couple, esp. of two similar things (Rām. 966). Rebus: dul meṛeḍ cast iron

(Mundari. Santali) *dul* 'to cast metal in a mould' (Santali) pasra meṛed, pasāra meṛed = syn. of koṭe meṛed = forged iron, in contrast to dul meṛed, cast iron (Mundari.) Thus, *dul kuṭila* 'cast bronze'.
The parenthetically ligatured fish+duck hieroglyphs thus read rebus: *dul kuṭila ayas karaḍā* 'cast bronze *ayas*or cast alloy metal with *ayas* as component to create *karaḍā* ''hard alloy with *ayas'.*

Ligatures to fish: parentheses + snout *dul kuṭila ayas* 'cast bronze *ayas* alloy with *tuttha*, copper sulphate*'*

Modifier hieroglyph: 'snout' Hieroglyph: WPah.kṭg. *ṭōṭ* ' mouth '.WPah.kṭg. *thótti* f., *thótthəṛ* m. ' snout, mouth ', A. *ṭhõṭ*(phonet. *thõṭ*) (CDIAL 5853). Semantics, Rebus:

tutthá n. (m. lex.), *tutthaka* -- n. ' blue vitriol (used as an eye ointment) ' Suśr., *tūtaka* -- lex. 2. *thōttha -- 4. 3. *tūtta -- . 4. *tōtta -- 2. [Prob. ← Drav. T. Burrow BSOAS xii 381; cf. *dhūrta* -- 2 n. ' iron filings ' lex.]1. N. *tutho* ' blue vitriol or sulphate of copper ', B. *tuth.*2. K. *thŏth*, dat. *°thas* m., P. *thothā* m.3. S.*tūtio* m., A. *tutiyā*, B. *tũte*, Or. *tutiā*, H. *tūtā*, *tūtiyā* m., M. *tutiyā* m.
4. M. *totā* m.(CDIAL 5855) *Ka.* tukku rust of iron; tutta, tuttu, tutte blue vitriol. *Tu.* tukků rust; mair(ů)suttu, (*Eng.-Tu. Dict.*) mairůtuttu blue vitriol. *Te.* t(r)uppu rust; (*SAN*) trukku id., verdigris. / Cf. Skt. tuttha- blue vitriol (DEDR 3343).

Decipherment of Var̲āha anthropomorph: বরাহ *barāha*'boar' Rebus: *bāṛaï*'carpenter' *barea*'merchant', कोंद *kōnda* 'engraver, lapidary setting or infixing gemś
PLUS Tor.*miṇḍ* 'ram',*miṇḍā́l*'markhor' (CDIAL 10310)
Rebus:*meḍ* (Ho.);*mẽṛhet*'iron' (Munda.Ho.)*meḍ*'copper' (Slavic). *ayo,* 'fish' rebus: aya 'iron' ayas 'metal'

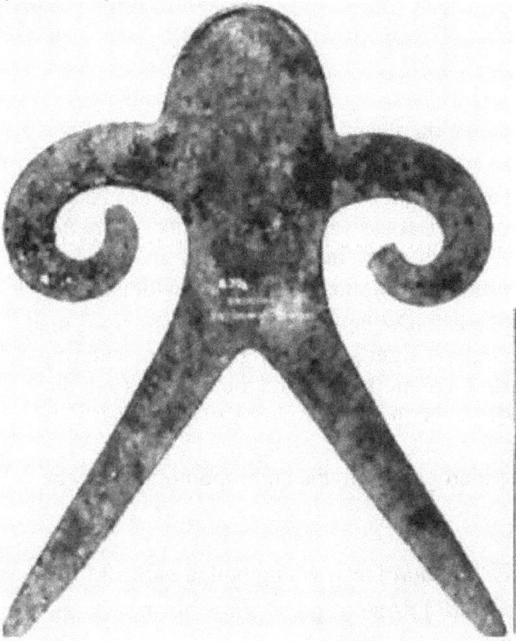

Such a *paṭa* was a seal with distinct pictorial motifs (such as one-horned young bull, tiger, elephant, rhinoceros, ox, zebu, further distinguished with the pattar 'trough'

hieroglyph. The *pattar*,'trough' signifies profession of *patthar*, 'merchant'. The animal hieroglyphs shown in front of these troughs on seals signify: kariba 'trunk of elephant' ibha 'elephant' rebus: karba 'iron' ib 'iron'; rango 'buffalo' rebus: rango 'pewter'; baDhi 'boar' rebus: baDhi 'merchant, worker in wood, iron'; barad 'ox' rebus: bharata 'alloy of pewter, copper, tin'; meḍ 'markhor' rebus: meḍ 'iron' meḍ 'copper' (Slavic); kola 'tiger' rebus: kol 'working in iron' kolhe 'smelter' kolle 'blacksmith'; kuṭi 'water-carrier' rebus: kuṭhi 'smelter'; karṇaka 'spread legś rebus: karṇaka 'helmsman'; meḍ 'body' rebus: meḍ 'iron'; eraka 'raised arm' rebus: eraka 'moltencast copper'.

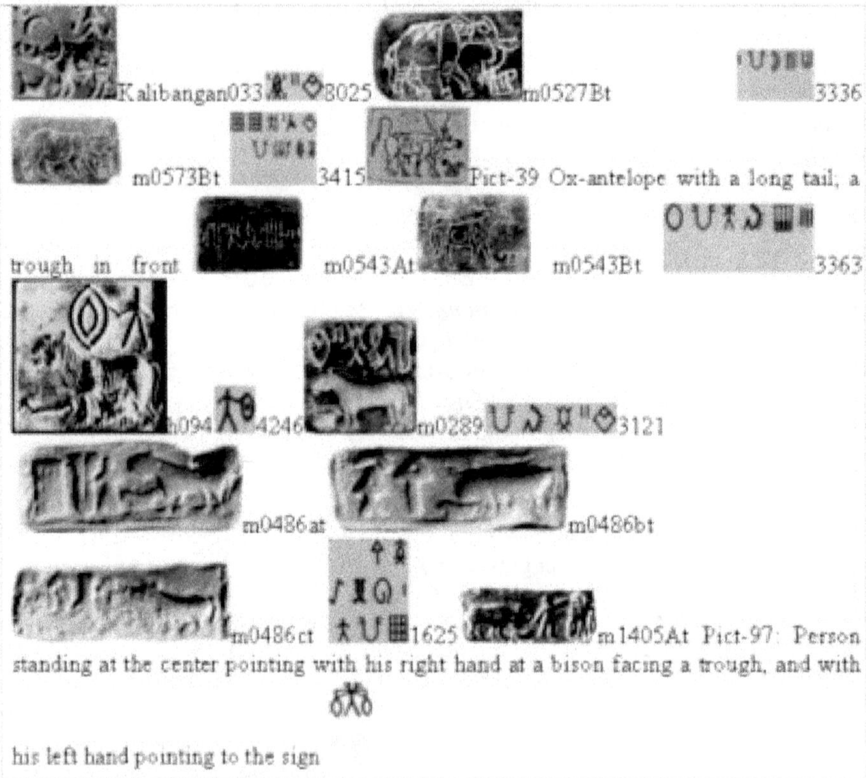

Rebus 'merchant, artisan': vartaka, pattar 'merchant' Pattharika [fr. patthara] a merchant Vin ii.135 (kaŋsa°). (Pali) பத்தர்² pattar , n. < T. battuḍu. A caste title of goldsmiths. Pattharika [fr. patthara] a merchant Vin ii.135 (kaŋsa°).(Pali) battuḍu. n. The caste title of all the five castes of artificers as vaḍla b*, carpenter. *battuḍu*. n. A worshipper (Telugu)It was a smiths' guild at work on circular platforms of Harappa using tablets as category 'tallies' for the final shipment of package with a seal impression. कर्णक 'helmsman' PLUS *mē̃d, mēd* 'body' rebus: *mē̃d, mēd* 'iron', meḍ 'copper' (Slavic). Thus the body hieroglyph signifies an iron helmsman seafaring merchant. The fish hieroglyph signifies a metallic mint and the boar hieroglyph signifies a merchantman.

The rebus readings of the composite hieroglyphs on the anthropomorphs may be suggested:

1. khoṇḍ, kõda 'young bull-calf' खोंड [*khōṇḍa*] m A young bull, a bullcalf. (Marathi) 'Pannier' glyph: खोंडी [*khōṇḍī*] *f* An outspread shovelform sack (as formeḍ temporarily out of a कांबळा, to hold or fend off grain, chaff &c.) Rebus: *kõdā* 'to turn in a lathe' (Bengali) *kũdār* 'turner, brass-worker'. कोंद *kōnda* 'engraver, lapidary setting or infixing gemś (Marathi) Tor.

miṇḍ 'ram', miṇḍāl 'markhor' (CDIAL 10310) Rebus: meḍ (Ho.); mẽṛhet 'iron' (Munda.Ho.) meḍ 'copper' (Slavic) कर्णक 'spread legś rebus: 'helmsman', karṇī 'supercargo'; meṛed 'iron' rebus: meḍh 'merchant' ayo 'fish' rebus: aya 'iron' ayas 'metal'; 2. कर्णक 'spread legś rebus: 'helmsman', karṇi 'supercargo' Indicative that the merchant is seafaring metalsmith. karṇadhāra m. ' helmsman ' Suśr. [kárṇa -- , dhāra -- 1]Pa. *kaṇṇadhāra* -- m. ' helmsman '; Pk. *kaṇṇahāra* -- m. ' helmsman, sailor '; H. *kanahār* m. ' helmsman, fisherman '.(CDIAL 2836) *baḍhia* = a castrated boar, a hog; rebus: *baḍhi* 'a caste who work both in iron and wood' baḍhoe 'a carpenter, worker in wood'; badhoria 'expert in working in wood'(Santali) বরাহ barāha 'boar'Rebus: *bāṛaï* 'carpenter' (Bengali) bari 'merchant' barea 'merchant' (Santali) बारकश or बारकस [bārakaśa or bārakasa] *n* (P) A trading vessel, a merchantman.

Sharply defined inscriptions on each of the 22 ceramic (stoneware) bangles indicate 22 sharply assigned responsibilities within the guild for metalwork, for e.g. 22 functional allocations of responsibilitie of artisans delineated in a Vedic village:

1. iron smelting, furnace work (m1659)
2. metal casting, engraving, documenting supercargo (m1647)
3. bronze (casting)(m1646)
4. *gōṭā* (laterite) (m1641)
5. Seafaring merchant, magnetite ingot workshop (m1643)
6. Smithy, forge (m1641)
7. Moltencast copper, brass (m1640)
8. Alloy metal mint, weapons, implements workshop, guild master workshop (m1639)
9. Bronze ingots, implements, magnetite ingots (m1638)
10. Metalcasting workshop (cire perdue?)(m1637)
11. Metal implements, weapons, smithy, forge (m1636)
12. Blacksmith, seafaring merchant (m1634)
13. Helman for supercargo boat, iron furnace work, metals workshop (m1633)
14. Metal casting, alloy mixing workshop (m1632)
15. *dhǎvaḍ* 'smelter', supercargo of implements (m1631)
16. Magnetite ingots, furnace work, supercargo engraver (m1630)
17. Iron furnace work, metal casting of tin, helmsman supercargo of metals, *bharat* 'mixed alloyś metalworker (m1629)
18. Minerals workshop guild (h2576)
19. Magnetite ingots, smelter (h1010)
20. *dhǎvaḍ* 'smelter' tri-dhAtu, "three minerals (H98-3516/8667-01)
21. Seafaring merchant, supercargo engraver(Blkt-6)

 Sign 403  Squirrel + Sign 403 These are two inscriptions on two ceramic (stoneware) bangles. What do they signify?

At the outset, thanks to Asko Parpola for the brilliant identification of 'squirrel' hieroglyph in Harappa Script Corpora. (www.harappa.com/script/indus-writing.pdf page 128). This orthogrraphic identification is accepted, but Parpola's decipherment of the hieroglyph as aNIl or aNilpiLLai [from caṇilů (Tulu) or variant] (http://www.harappa.com/script/script-indus-parpola.pdf) is, however, refuted.

Bharata palm squirrel, *Funambulus Palmarum*

Squirrel hieroglyph of Harappa Script: Nindowari Damb seal Nd-1; Mohenjo-daro seal m-1202; Harappa tablet h-771; Harappa tablet h-419.

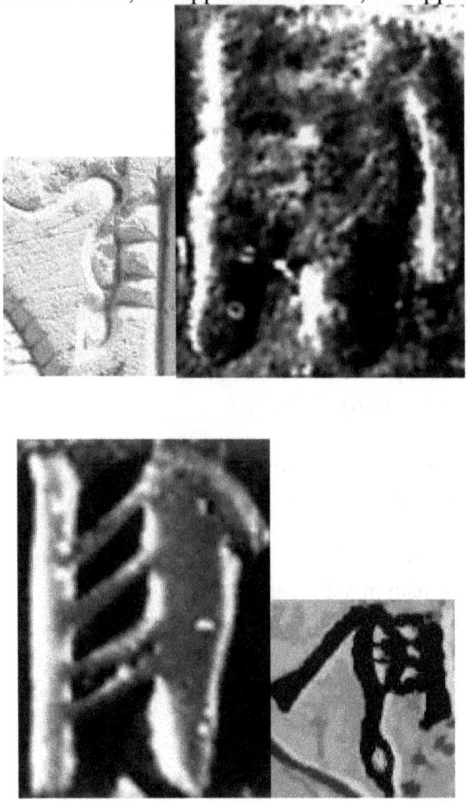

Nindowari seal Nd-1

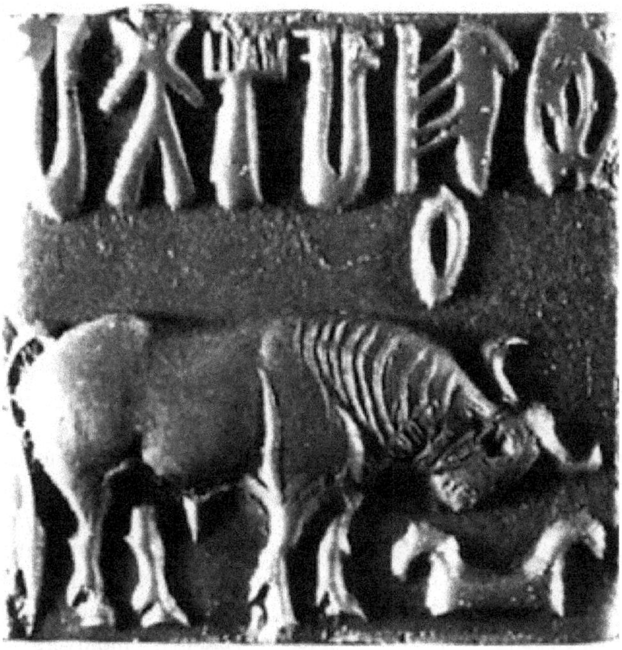

m1202

h771

h419

Hieroglyph: khāra, 'squirrel', rebus: *khār* खार् 'blacksmith' (Kashmiri). *śrēṣṭrī1 ‘ clinger ’. [√śriṣ1]Phal. *śẽṣṭrī̃* ‘ flying squirrel ’?(CDIAL 12723) Rebus: guild master: Pk. *sēḍhī̃* -- f. ‘ line, row ’ (cf. *pasēḍhi* -- f. ‘ id. ’. -- < EMIA. **sēṭhī* -- sanskritized as *śrēḍhī* -- , *śrēṭī* -- , *śrēḍī*<-> (Col.), *śrēdhī* -- (W.) f. ‘ a partic. progression of arithmetical figures ’); K. *hēr*, dat. °*ri* f. ‘ ladder ’.(CDIAL 12724) Rebus: śrḗṣṭha ‘ most splendid, best ’ RV. [śrī́ --]Pa. *seṭṭha* -- ‘ best ’, Aś.shah. man. *sreṭha* -- , gir. *sesṭa* -- , kāl. *seṭha* -- , Dhp. *śeṭha* -- , Pk. *seṭṭha* -- , *siṭṭha* -- ; N. *seṭh* ‘ great, noble, superior ’; Or. *seṭha* ‘ chief, principal ’; Si. *seṭa*, °*ṭu* ‘ noble, excellent ’. śrēṣṭhin m. ‘ distinguished man ’ AitBr., ‘ foreman of a guild ’, °*nī* -- f. ‘ his wife ’ Hariv. [śrḗṣṭha --]Pa. *seṭṭhin* -- m. ‘ guild -- master ’, Dhp. *śeṭhi*, Pk. *seṭṭhi* -- , *siṭṭhi* -- m., °*iṇī* -- f.; S. *seṭhi* m. ‘ wholesale merchant ’; P. *seṭh* m. ‘ head of a guild, banker ’, *seṭhaṇ*, °*ṇī* f.; Ku.gng. *śēṭh* ‘ rich man ’; N. *seṭh* ‘ banker ’; B. *seṭh* ‘ head of a guild, merchant ’; Or. *seṭhi* ‘ caste of washermen ’; Bhoj. Aw.lakh. *sēṭhi* ‘ merchant, banker ’, H. *seṭh* m., °*ṭhan* f.; G. *śeṭh*, *śeṭhiyɔ* m. ‘ wholesale merchant, employer, master ’; M. *śeṭh*, °*ṭhī*, *śeṭ*, °*ṭī* m. ‘ respectful term for banker or merchant ’; Si. *siṭu*, *hi*° ‘ banker, nobleman ’ H. Smith JA 1950, 208 (or < śiṣṭá -- 2?)(CDIAL 12725, 12726) See also hieroglyph: 'ladder' m1639 given below.

The prefix 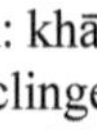 Sign403: Hieroglyph: *bārī* , 'small ear-ring': H. *bālā* m. ‘bracelet’ (→ S. *b̠ālo* m. ‘bracelet worn by Hindus’), *bālī*, *bārī* f. ‘small ear -- ring’, OMārw. *bālī* f.; G. *vāḷɔ* m. ‘ wire ’, pl. ‘ ear ornament made of gold wire ’; M. *vāḷā* m. ‘ ring ’, *vāḷī* f. ‘ nose -- ring ’.(CDIAL 11573) Rebus: *bārī* 'merchant'
vāḍhī, bari, barea 'merchant' *bārakaśa* 'seafaring vessel'.

Thus, the sequence of hieroglyphs  Squirrel + Sign 403 signifies two professional responsibilities/functions merchant, blacksmith.

Hieroglyph: squirrel (phonetic determinant): खार (p. 205) [khāra] A squirrel, Sciurus palmarum. खारी (p. 205) [khārī] *f* (Usually खार) A squirrel. (Marathi)

A homonymous hieroglyph or allograph: arms with bangles: karā̃ n.pl.'wristlets, bangles'.(Gujarati)(CDIAL 2779)

khār खार् । लोहकारः m. (sg. abl. khāra 1 खार; the pl. dat. of this word is khāran 1 खारन्, which is to be distinguished from khāran 2, q.v., s.v.), a blacksmith, an iron worker (cf. bandūka-khār, p. 111*b*,l. 46; K.Pr. 46; H. xi, 17); a farrier (El.). This word is often a part of a name, and in such case comes at the end (W. 118) as in Wahab khār, Wahab the smith (H. ii, 12; vi, 17). khāra-basta 'bellows of blacksmith'.

खडी (p. 193) [khaḍī] *f* खटी S) A squirrel खडू (p. 193) [khaḍū] *f* खडूळ *f* A squirrel.gilahári गिल्ह; or gilahári गिलह; f. a squirrel (Gr.M.). (Kashmiri)

खडी (p. 193) [khaḍī] *f* खटी S) A species of steatite used to rub over the writing-board, or to whitewash walls: also an unctuous and whitish stone, a sort of pipeclay. 2 A composition (of talc, gum &c.) for raising figures on cloth: also the figures raised.

Datamining of all inscriptions on bangles is presented in the following section. Consistent with the architecture of Harappa Script Corpora, there are between, number of hieroglyphs incised on each stoneware bangle range from one to five.

The bangles are from the sites of Balakot (1), Harapa (4 including 2 trefoil decorated bangle fragments) and Mohenjo-daro (18). The longest inscription with 5 hieroglyphs occurs on m1629 and m1639bangles.

Squirrel+bangles sequence  occurs on m1634bangle.

The ceramic (stoneware) bangles are of great significance because of the special care taken by the artisans to prepare the artifacts incised before firing. Massimo Vidale and others have done pioneering archaeo-research to reconstruct the processes involved in preparing these written artifacts, almos as data archiving of ancient times during the Bronze Age.

The descriptions of the processes to make the extraordinary ceramic artifacts provided by Massimo Vidale are gratefully acknowledged.

Distinction between terracotta bangles and ceramic (stoneware) bangles)

Excavated Bangle, Harappa. Terracotta bangles are of sizes wearable as wristlets or armlets.

Harappa. Kot Diji phase streets were filled with debris, including potsherds, charcoal, ash, animal bones, and occasional bangles and steatite beads.

A distinction has to be made between terracotta bangles and these inscribed ceramic (stoneware) bangles. Most terracotta bangles are uninscribed and are of sizes which are wearable by men and women. The ceramic (stoneware) bangles are of a very small size and NOT meant to be worn but perhaps used as centre-pieces of the fillet band of the type worn by Mohenjo-daro priest king on his forehead and right shoulder, as insignia, as professional titles or functions

Randall Law and Shamoon excavating a red stoneware bangle in Period 3C levels just below the surface in Trench 43.https://www.harappa.com/indus4/76.html

Red stoneware bangle (H2000-4490/9843-01) with no inscription. The lack of inscription may indicate that this may have been a place where the bangles were stored prior to inscribing them for distribution.

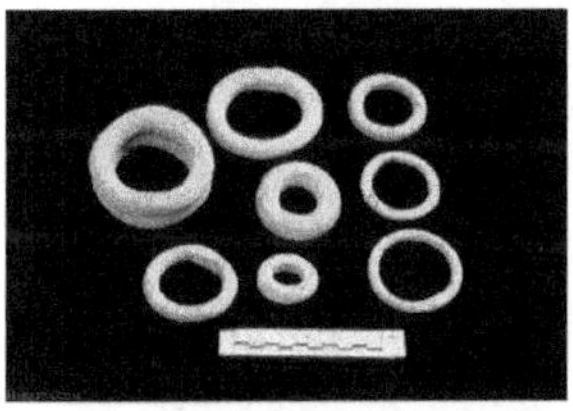

Many of the terra cotta bangles were originally painted with black or red designs. Such ornaments are found in the thousands and may have been worn, broken and discarded much as glass bangles are used today throughout the subcontinent. (Terracotta bangles were worn.Inscribed stoneware bangles are too small in size and which could have been worn not as bangles as writlets or armlets, but tied with bands like fillets worn by th priest-king of Mohenjo-daro or as pendants on necklaces).

Balakot 06 bangle

 Sign403: Hieroglyph: *bārī* , 'small ear-ring': H. *bālā* m. 'bracelet' (→ S. *ḇālo* m. 'bracelet worn by Hindus'), *bālī, bārī* f. 'small ear -- ring', OMārw. *bālī* f.; G. *vāḷɔ* m. ' wire ', pl. ' ear ornament made of gold wire '; M. *vāḷā* m. ' ring ', *vāḷī* f. ' nose -- ring '.(CDIAL 11573) Rebus: *bārī* 'merchant' *vāḍhī, bari, barea* 'merchant' *bārakaśa* 'seafaring vessel'.

 Sign 342 karṇī 'rim of jar' rebus: 'supercargo', 'engraver'

Terracotta bangle fragments decorated with red trefoils outlined in white on a green ground from late Period 3C deposits in Trench 43. This image shows both sides of the two fragments (H98-3516/8667-01 & H98-3517/8679-01).

Detail of terracotta bangle with red and white trefoil on a green background (H98-3516/8667-01 from Trench 43).

Trefoil motifs are carved on the robe of the so-called "priest-king" statuette from Mohenjo-daro and are also known from contemporary sites in western Pakistan, Afghanistan, and southern Central Asia. *dhā̆vaḍ* 'smelter' tri-dhAtu, "three minerals

h1010bangle  'magnetite ingot' PLUS 'twig' a stalk/twig, sprout (or tree branch) *kūdī, kūṭī* bunch of twigs (Sanskrit) kūdī (also written as kūṭī in manuscripts) occurs in the Atharvaveda (AV 5.19.12) and Kauśika Sūtra (Bloomsfield's ed.n, xliv. Cf. Bloomsfield, American Journal of Philology, 11, 355; 12,416; Roth, Festgruss an Bohtlingk, 98) denotes it as a twig. This is identified as

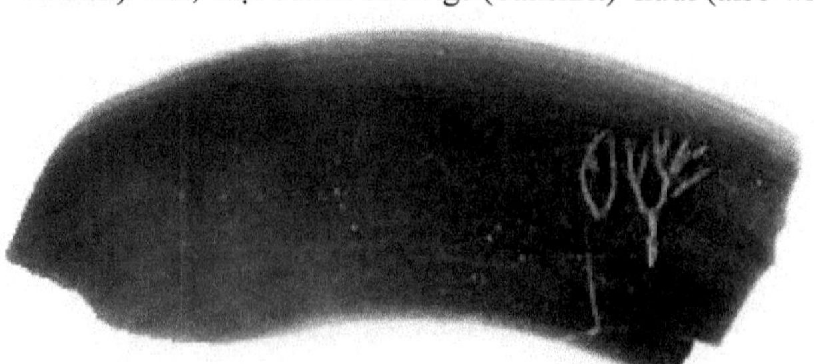

that of Badarī, the jujube tied to the body of the dead to efface their traces. (See Vedic Index, I, p. 177). Rebus: kuṭhi 'smelting furnace' (Santali) For the 'oval' hieroglyph, see: http://bharatkalyan97.blogspot.in/2015/08/decipherment-of-harappa-zebu-figurine.html The reading is: पोळ [*pōḷa*] खोट khōṭa, 'magnetite ingot or wedge'.

Slide 33. Early Harappa zebu figurine with incised spots from Harappa.पोळ [*pōḷa*], 'zebu' Rebus: magnetite, citizen.(See: http://bharatkalyan97.blogspot.in/2015/08/zebu-archaeometallurgy-legacy-of-india.html)

mūhā mẽṛhẽt = iron smelted by the Kolhes and formeḍ into an equilateral lump a little pointed at each of four ends (Santali) खोट (p. 212) [khōṭa] *f* A mass of metal (unwrought or of old metal melted down); an ingot or wedge. (Marathi)

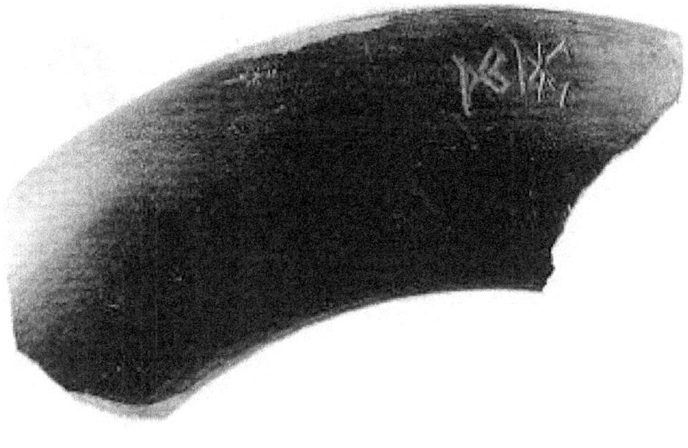

h2576Abangle

Sign 216

Sign 221 dhatu PLUS koḍ 'minerals workshop'

Sign 229 sanni 'smith's vice' rebus: seni 'guild'

The sequence of hieroglyphs Sign 221-Sign 229 is comparable to the sequence which occurs on the so-called Pasupati seal:

Text 2420 on m0304 Sign 216 (Mahadevan). *ḍato* 'claws or pincers (chelae) of crabś; *ḍaṭom, ḍiṭom* to seize with the claws or pincers, as crabs, scorpions; *ḍaṭkop* = to pinch, nip (only of crabs) (Santali) Rebus: *dhatu* 'mineral' (Santali) Vikalpa: *erā* 'clawś; Rebus: *era* 'copper'.

Sign 229. *sannī, sannhī* = pincers, smith's vice (P.) *śannī* f. ' small room in a house to keep sheep in ' (WPah.) *Bshk. šan, Phal.šān* 'roof' (Bshk.)(CDIAL 12326). *seṇi* (f.) [Class. Sk. *śreṇi* in meaning "guild"; Vedic= row] 1. a guild Vin iv.226; J i.267, 314; iv.43; Dāvs ii.124; their number was eighteen J vi.22, 427; VbhA 466. ° -- pamukha the head of a guild J ii.12 (text *seni* --). -- 2. a division of an army J vi.583; ratha -- ° J vi.81, 49; seṇimokkha the chief of an army J vi.371 (cp. *senā* and *seniya*). (Pali)

Long linear stroke:

Ko. ko·ṛ

line marked out (DEDR 2200) rebus: koḍ 'workshop'
Ma. *koṭṭil* cowhouse, shed, workshop, house. (DEDR 2058)

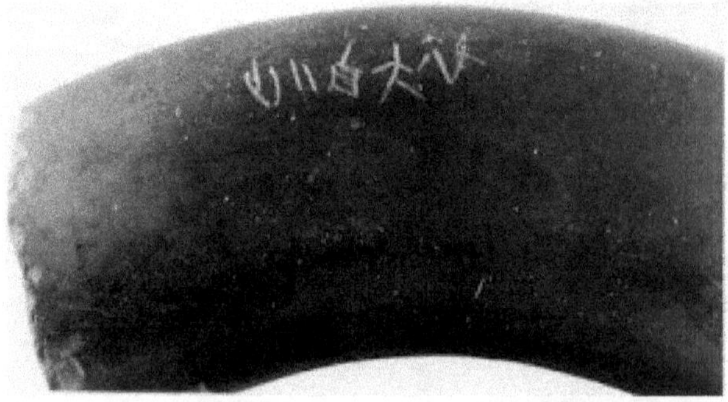

m1629bangle

Sign 47 kaśēru 'the backbone' (Bengali. Skt.); kaśēruka id. (Skt.) Rebus: kasērā' metal worker ' (Lahnda)(CDIAL 2988, 2989) *baraḍo* = spine; backbone (Tulu) Rebus: *baran, bharat* 'mixed alloyś (5 copper, 4 zinc and 1 tin) (Punjabi) +

gaṇḍa 'four' Rebus: *kaṇḍ* 'fire-altar'. Thus, Sign 48 reads rebus: *bharat kaṇḍ* 'fire-altar', furnace for mixed alloy called *bharat*(copper, zinc, tin alloy).

Faience tablet (H2001-5082/2920-02) made from two colors of faience was found eroding from the Trench 54 South workshop area. Identical tablets made from two colors of faience were recovered in Area J, at the south end of Mound AB, in the excavations of Vats during the 1930s. gaṇḍa 'four' rebus: kāṇḍa 'fire-altar' baṭa 'rimless pot' rebus: bhaṭa 'furnace' *baraḍo* = spine; backbone (Tulu) Rebus: *baran, bharat* ‘mixed alloyś (5 copper, 4 zinc and 1 tin) (Punjabi) ayo 'fish' rebus: aya 'iron' ayas 'metal'.

Signs:

47 48 261 373

Texts:

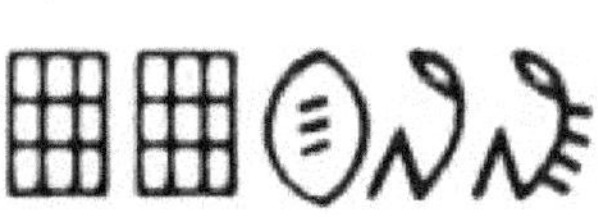

4589

5265

Copper tablet (H2000-4498/9889-01) with raised script found in Trench 43. Harappa. (Source: Slide 351. harappa.com) Eight such tablets have been found (HARP, 2005); these were recovered from circular platforms. This example of a uniquely scripted tablet with raised Harappa Script glyphs shows that copper tablets were also used in Harappa, while hundreds of copper tablets with Harappa script inscriptions were found in Mohenjo-daro. See also:http://bharatkalyan97.blogspot.com/2011/11/decoding-longest-inscription-of-indus.html The copper tablet with raised script contains a 'backbone' glyph; decoding: kaśēru 'the backbone' (Bengali. Skt.); kaśēruka id. (Skt.) Rebus: kasērā' metal worker ' (Lahnda)(CDIAL 2988, 2989)mũhā̃ = the quantity of iron produced at one time in a native smelting furnace of the Kolhes; iron produced by the Kolhes and formeḍ like a four-cornered piece a little pointed at each end (Santali).

'Backbone, spine' hieroglyph: *baraḍo* = spine; backbone; the back; baraḍo thābaḍavo = lit. to strike on the backbone or back; hence, to encourage; baraḍo bhāre thato = lit. to have a painful backbone, i.e. to do something which will call for a severe beating (Gujarati)bārṇe, bāraṇe = an offering of food to a demon; a meal after fasting, a breakfast (Tulu) barada, barda, birada = a vow (Gujarati)bharaḍo a devotee of Śiva; a man of the bharaḍā caste in the bra_hman.as (Gujarati) baraṛ = name of a caste of jat- around Bhaṭiṇḍa; bararaṇḍā melā = a special fair held in spring (Punjabi) bharāḍ = a religious service or entertainment performeḍ by a bharāḍi_; consisting of singing the praises of some idol or god with playing on the d.aur (drum) and dancing; an order of aṭharā akhād.e = 18 gosāyi_ group; bharād. and bhāratī are two of the 18 orders of gosāyi_ (Marathi).

 Sign 1 कर्णक*m. du.* the two legs spread out AV. xx , 133 , 3 karṇaka 'spread legś rebus: karṇaka 'helmsman' karṇī 'supercargo', engraver meḍ 'body' rebus: rebus: meḍ 'iron' meḍ 'copper' (Slavic)

 Sign 249 ranku 'liquid measure' rebus: ranku 'tin'

 Sign 87 dula 'pair'; rebus dul 'cast (metal)'

 Sign 336 baṭa 'rimless pot' rebus: baṭa 'iron' bhaṭa 'furnace' PLUS Te. garĩṭe, gaṇṭe, geṇṭe spoon, ladle rebus: *To.* ködm (*obl.* ködt-) live coal. *Ka.* keṇḍa id.; keṇḍavisu to put live coals on (for blasting rocks). *Tu.* keṇḍa, geṇḍa live coal. (DEDR 1950)
Thus, furnace worker, metal casting, tin supercargo helmsman, metal worker are signified.

m1630bangle

 Sign 17 bhaṭa 'warrior' rebus: bhaṭa 'furnace'

 Sign 342 karṇī 'rim of jar' rebus: 'supercargo', 'engraver'

 'magnetite ingot'

m1631bangle

 Sign 343 karṇī kāṇḍa 'supercargo implements

 *dhăvaḍ* 'smelter' Sign 180 Hieroglyph: tántu m. ' thread, warp ' RV. [√tan] Pa. *tantu* -- m. ' thread, cord ', Pk. *taṁtu* -- m.; Kho. (Lor.) *ton* ' warp ' < **tand* (whence *tandeni* ' thread between wings of spinning wheel '); S. *tandu* f. ' gold or silver thread '; L. *tand* (pl. °*dū̃*) f. ' yarn, thread being spun, string of the tongue '; P. *tand* m. ' thread ', *tanduā*, °*dūā* m. ' string of the tongue, frenum of glans penis '; A. *tā̃t* ' warp in the loom, cloth being woven '; B. *tā̃t* ' cord '; M. *tā̃tū* m. ' thread '; Si. *tatu*, °*ta* ' string of a lute '; -- with -- *o*, -- *ā* to retain orig. gender: S. *tando* m. ' cord, twine, strand of rope '; N. *tā̃do* ' bowstring '; H. *tā̃tā* m. ' series, line '; G. *tā̃tɔ* m. ' thread '; -- OG. *tāṁtaṇaü* m. ' thread ' < **tāṁtaḍaü*, G.*tā̃tṇɔ* m.(CDIAL 5661) Rebus: M. *dhāū*, *dhāv* m.f. ' a partic. soft red stone ' (whence *dhăvaḍ* m. ' a caste of iron -- smelters ', *dhāvḍī* ' composed of or relating to iron '); dhā́tu n. ' substance ' RV., m. ' element ' MBh., ' metal, mineral, ore (esp. of a red colour) '; Pk. *dhāu* -- m. ' metal, red chalk '; N. *dhāu* ' ore (esp. of copper) '; Or. *ḍhāu* ' red chalk, red ochre ' (whence *ḍhāuā* ' reddish '; (CDIAL 6773) धातु primary element of the earth i.e. metal , mineral, ore (esp. a mineral of a red colour) Mn. MBh. &c element of words i.e. grammatical or verbal root or stem Nir. Pra1t. MBh. &c (with the southern Buddhists धातु means either the 6 elements [see above] Dharmas. xxv ; or the 18 elementary spheres [धातु-लोक] ib. lviii ; or the ashes of the body , relics L. [cf. -गर्भ]) (Monier-Williams. Samskritam).

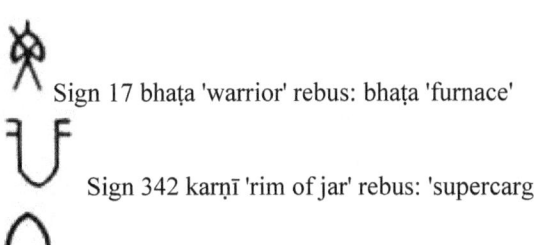

Sign 342 PLUS notch: Sign 342. kaṇḍa kanka 'rim of jar' (Santali): karṇaka rim of jar'(Skt.) Rebus: karṇaka 'scribe, accountant' (Te.); gaṇaka id. (Skt.) (Santali) copper fire-altar scribe (account)(Skt.) Rebus: kaṇḍ 'fire-altar' (Santali) Thus, the 'rim of jar' ligatured glyph is read rebus: fire-altar (furnace) scribe (account) karṇī 'supercargo' (Marathi) karṇaka 'helmsman' PLUS खाडा [khāṇḍā] 'A jag, notch, or indentation (as upon the edge of a tool or weapon)' Rebus: kāṇḍa 'implements (Santali).

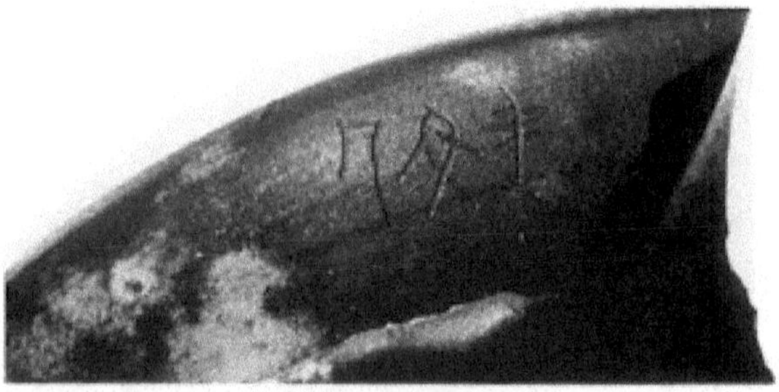

m1632bangle

 Sign 86 koḍ 'one' rebus: koḍ 'workshop'

 Sign 59 ayo 'fish' rebus: aya 'iron' ayas 'metal' **fish**

fins khambhaṛā '**fin**' rebus: kammaṭa '**mint**'

 Sign 87 dula 'pair'; rebus dul 'cast (metal)'

m1633bangle

 Sign 1 कर्णक *m. du.* the two legs spread out AV. xx , 133 , 3 karṇaka 'spread legś rebus: karṇaka 'helmsman' karṇī 'supercargo meḍ 'body' rebus: rebus: meḍ 'iron' meḍ 'copper' (Slavic)

 Sign 336 baṭa 'rimless pot' rebus: baṭa 'iron' bhaṭa 'furnace' PLUS Te. garĩṭe, gaṇṭe, geṇṭe spoon, ladle rebus: *To.* köḍm (*obl.* köḍt-) live coal. *Ka.* keṇḍa id.; keṇḍavisu to put live coals on (for blasting rocks). *Tu.* keṇḍa, geṇḍa live coal. (DEDR 1950)

 Sign 86 koḍ 'one' rebus: koḍ 'workshop' PLUS 'notch': खाडा [khāṇḍā] 'A jag, notch, or indentation (as upon the edge of a tool or weapon)' Rebus: kāṇḍa 'implements (Santali). Thus, implements workshop, furnace work, helmsman of supercargo signified.

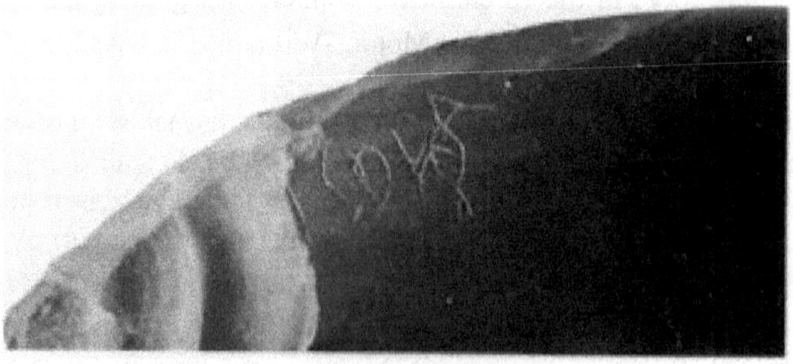

m1634bangle

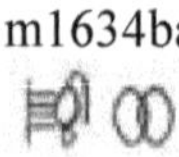 Read from r. to l.: The prefix 

Sign403: Hieroglyph: *bārī* , 'small ear-ring': H. *bālā* m. 'bracelet' (→ S. *b̠ālo* m. 'bracelet worn by Hindus'), *bālī*, *bārī* f. 'small ear -- ring', OMārw. *bālī* f.; G. *vāḷɔ* m. ' wire ', pl. ' ear ornament made of gold wire '; M. *vāḷā* m. ' ring ', *vāḷī* f. ' nose --

ring '.(CDIAL 11573) Rebus: *bārī* 'merchant' *vāḍhī, bari, barea* 'merchant' *bārakaśa* 'seafaring vessel'.

Hieroglyph: squirrel (phonetic determinant): खार (p. 205) [khāra] A squirrel, Sciurus palmarum. खारी (p. 205) [khārī] *f* (Usually खार) A squirrel. (Marathi)
A homonymous hieroglyph or allograph: arms with bangles: karā̃ n.pl.'wristlets, bangles'(Gujarati)(CDIAL 2779) Rebus: khār खार् । लोहकारः m. (sg. abl. khāra 1 खार; the pl. dat. of this word is khāran 1 खारन्, which is to be distinguished from khāran 2, q.v., s.v.), a blacksmith, an iron worker (cf. bandūka-khār, p. 111*b*,l. 46; K.Pr. 46; H. xi, 17); a farrier (El.). This word is often a part of a name, and in such case comes at the end (W. 118) as in Wahab khār, Wahab the smith (H. ii, 12; vi, 17). khāra-basta 'bellows of blacksmith'.

m1635bangle

Sign 244 kolmo 'three' rebus: kolimi 'smithy' kole.l 'smithy, forge' rebus: kole.l 'temple'

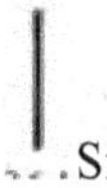

Sign 86 koḍ 'one' rebus: koḍ 'workshop' PLUS 'notch': खाडा [khāṇḍā] 'A jag, notch, or indentation (as upon the edge of a tool or weapon)' Rebus: kāṇḍa 'implements (Santali). Thus, implements workshop, furnace work, helmsman of supercargo signified.

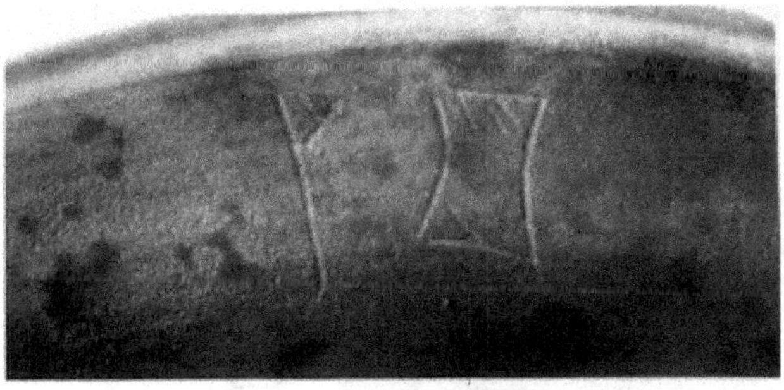

m1636bangle (Identical to m1635 inscription)

Sign 244 kolmo 'three' rebus: kolimi 'smithy' kole.l 'smithy, forge' rebus: kole.l 'temple'

Sign 86 koḍ 'one' rebus: koḍ 'workshop' PLUS 'notch': खाडा [khāṇḍā] 'A jag, notch, or indentation (as upon the edge of a tool or weapon)' Rebus: kāṇḍa 'implements (Santali). Thus, implements workshop, furnace work, helmsman of supercargo signified.

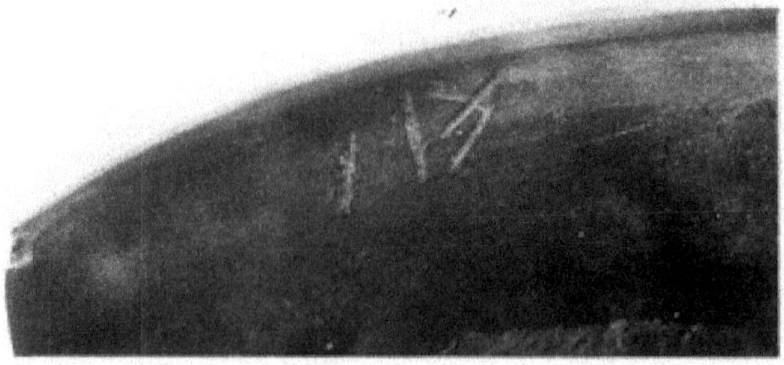

m1637bangle

Sign 99 sal 'splinter' rebus: sal 'workshop'

Sign 87 dula 'pair'; rebus dul 'cast (metal)'

m1638bangle

'magnetite ingot'

Sign 301 The 'curve' hieroglyph is a splitting of the ellipse. *kuṭila* 'bent' CDIAL 3230 kuṭi— in cmpd. 'curve', *kuṭika—* 'bent' MBh.

Rebus: कुटिल *kuṭila, katthīl* = bronze (8 parts copper and 2 parts tin) cf. āra-kūṭa, 'brass Old English *ār* 'brass, copper, bronze' Old Norse *eir* 'brass, copper', German *ehern* 'brassy, bronzen'. kastīra n. ' tin ' lex. 2. *kastilla -- .1. H. *kathīr* m. ' tin, pewter '; G. *kathīr* n. ' pewter '.2. H. (Bhoj.?) *kathīl*, °*lā* m. ' tin, pewter '; M. *kathīl* n. ' tin ', *kathlẽ* n. ' large tin vessel '.(CDIAL 2984) PLUS खाडा [khāṇḍā] 'A jag, notch, or indentation (as upon the edge of a tool or weapon)' Rebus: kāṇḍa 'implements (Santali).

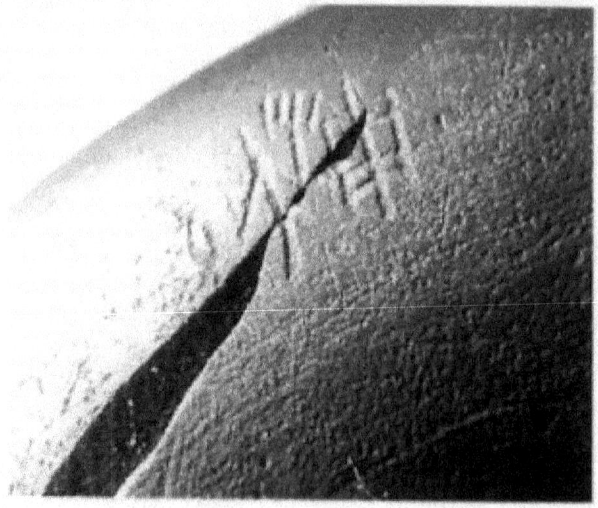

m1639 bangle

Sign 86 koḍ 'one' rebus: koḍ 'workshop' PLUS 'notch': खाडा [khāṇḍā] 'A jag, notch, or indentation (as upon the edge of a tool or weapon)' Rebus: kāṇḍa 'implements (Santali).

Sign 186 *śrētrī ' ladder '. [Cf. *śrētṛ* -- ' one who has recourse to ' MBh. -- See śrití -- . -- √śri]Ash. *ċeitr* ' ladder ' (< **ċaitr* -- dissim. from *ċraitr* -- ?).(CDIAL 12720)*śrēṣṭrī2 ' line, ladder '. [For mng. ' line ' conn. with √śriṣ2 cf. śrēṇi -- ~ √śri. -- See śrití -- . -- √śriṣ2]Pk. *sēḍhī̃* -- f. ' line, row ' (cf. *pasēḍhi* -- f. ' id. '. -- < EMIA. **sēṭhī* -- sanskritized as *śrēḍhī* -- , *śrēṭī* -- , *śrēḍī*<-

> (Col.), *śrēdhī* -- (W.) f. ' a partic. progression of arithmetical figures '); K. *hēr*, dat. *°ri* f. ' ladder '.(CDIAL 12724) Rebus: śrēṣṭha ' most splendid, best ' RV. [śrī́ --]Pa. *seṭṭha* -- ' best ', Aś.shah. man. *sreṭha* -- , gir. *sesṭa* -- , kāl. *seṭha* -- , Dhp. *śeṭha* -- , Pk. *seṭṭha* -- , *siṭṭha* -- ; N. *seṭh* ' great, noble, superior '; Or. *seṭha* ' chief, principal '; Si. *seṭa*, *°ṭu* ' noble, excellent '. śrēṣṭhin m. ' distinguished man ' AitBr., ' foreman of a guild ', *°nī* -- f. ' his wife ' Hariv. [śrēṣṭha --]Pa. *seṭṭhin* -- m. ' guild -- master ', Dhp. *śeṭhi*, Pk. *seṭṭhi* -- , *siṭṭhi* -- m., *°iṇī* -- f.; S. *seṭhi* m. ' wholesale merchant '; P. *seṭh* m. ' head of a guild, banker ', *seṭhaṇ*, *°ṇī* f.; Ku.gng. *śēṭh* ' rich man '; N. *seṭh* ' banker '; B. *seṭh* ' head of a guild, merchant '; Or. *seṭhi* ' caste of washermen '; Bhoj. Aw.lakh. *sēṭhi* ' merchant, banker ', H. *seṭh* m., *°ṭhan* f.; G. *śeṭh*, *śeṭhiyɔ* m. ' wholesale merchant, employer, master '; M. *śeṭh*, *°ṭhī*, *śeṭ*, *°ṭī* m. ' respectful term for banker or merchant '; Si. *siṭu*, *hi°* ' banker, nobleman ' H. Smith JA 1950, 208 (or < śiṣṭá -- 2?)(CDIAL 12725, 12726)

Sign 86 koḍ 'one' rebus: koḍ 'workshop' PLUS 'notch': खाडा [khāṇḍā] 'A jag, notch, or indentation (as upon the edge of a tool or weapon)' Rebus: kāṇḍa 'implements (Santali). Thus, implements workshop, furnace work, helmsman of supercargo signified.PLUS

Sign 99 sal 'splinter' rebus: sal 'workshop'

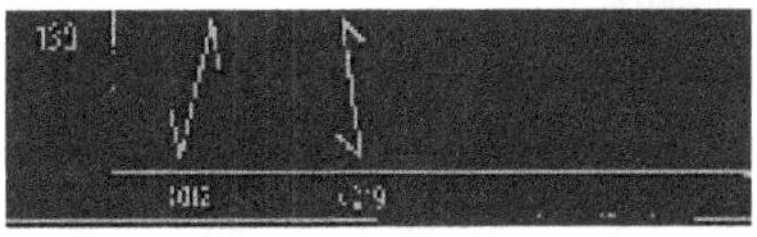

Mahadevan concordance Sign 130 variants. This hieroglyph may signify: tutta 'goad' Rebus: tuttha 'pewter-zinc alloy'

Allograph: tutta (goad) (Pali) tṓttra n. ' goad for cattle or elephants ' ŚBr. [√tud]

Pa. *tutta* -- n. (with *u* from tudáti?), Pk. *totta* -- , *tutta*<-> n.; Si. *tutta* ' elephant goad '.(CDIAL 5966) It is possible that one of the 500+ 'signs' or hieroglyph-multiplexes of Harappa Script Corpora signifies this etymon cluster: tutta 'goad' Rebus: tuttha 'pewter-zinc alloy'. A crook maybe signified by: मेंढा [mēṇḍhā] A **crook** or curved end rebus: meḍ 'iron' (Ho.Mu.)

Sign 59 ayo 'fish' rebus: aya 'iron' ayas 'metal' **fish fins** khambhaṛā '**fin**' rebus: kammaṭa '**mint**'

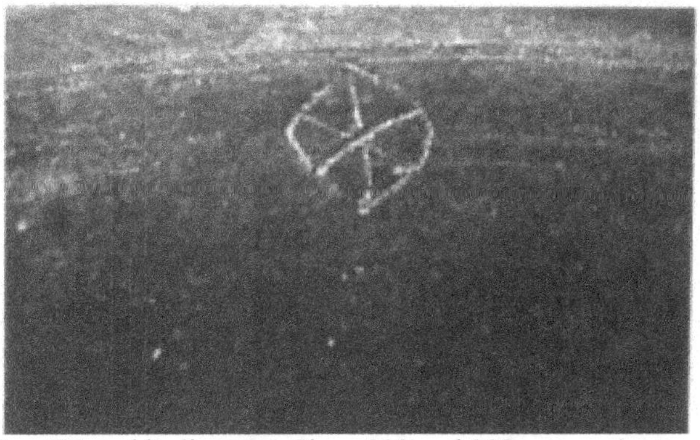

m1640bangle

Sign 391 Ligatured hieroglyph multiplex. arā 'spoke' rebus: ara 'brass'. **era, er-a** = eraka =?nave; erako_lu = the iron axle of a carriage (Ka.M.); cf. irasu (Ka.lex.)[Note Sign 391 and its ligatures Signs 392 and 393 may connote a spoked-wheel,nave of the wheel through which the axle passes; cf. **ara_**, spoke]**erka** = **ekke** (Tbh.of **arka**) **aka** (Tbh. of **arka**) **copper (metal);**crystal (Ka.lex.) cf. eruvai = copper (Tamil) **eraka, er-aka** = anymetal infusion (Ka.Tu.); **erako** molten cast

(Tu.lex.) Rebus: **eraka**= copper (Ka.)**eruvai** =copper (Ta.); **ere** - a dark-red colour (Ka.)(DEDR 817). **eraka, era, er-a**= syn. **erka**, copper, weapons (Ka.)Vikalpa: **ara, arā** (RV.) = spokeof wheel ஆரம்[2] āram , *n.* < *āra.* 1. Spokeof a wheel.See ஆரக்கால். ஆரஞ்சூழ்ந்தவயில்வாய் நேமியொடு (சிறுபாண். 253). Rebus: ஆரம் brass; பித்தளை.(அக. நி.) pittal is cognate with 'pewter'.

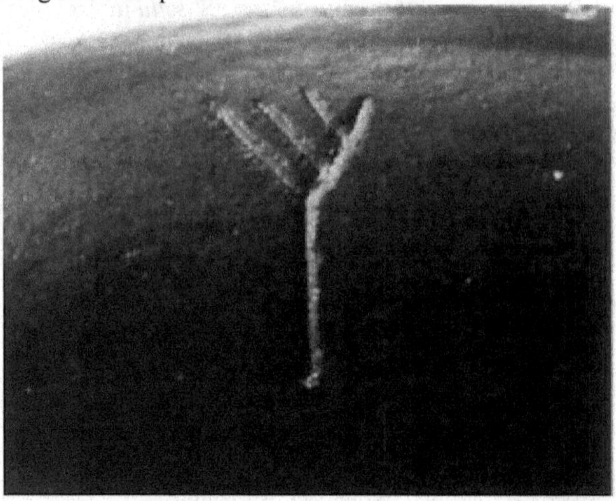

m1641bangle

Sign 169 kolom 'sprout, rice plant' Rebus: kolimi 'smithy, forge' Thus, ingot smithy Rebus: kol metal (Ta.) kol = pan~calōkam (five metals) (Tamil)
kolmo 'rice plant' (Mu.)
kolom = cutting, graft; to graft, engraft, prune; kolmahoṛo = a variety of the paddy plant (Desi)(Santali.)
kolime, kolume, kulāme, kulime, kulume, kulme fire-pit, furnace (Ka.); kolimi furnace (Te.); pit (Te.); **kolame** a very deep pit (Tu.); kulume kāṇḍa_ya a tax on blacksmiths (Ka.); **kol, kolla** a furnace (Ta.) *kole.l* smithy, temple in Kota village (Ko.); *kwala.l* Kota smithy (Tọ.); *konimi* blacksmith; *kola* id. (Ka.); *kolle*blacksmith (Koḍ.); *kollusa_na_* to mend implements; *kolsta_na, kulsa_na_* to forge;*ko_lsta_na_* to repair (of plough-shares); *kolmi* smithy (Go.); *kolhali* to forge (Go.)(DEDR 2133).] **kolimi-titti** = bellows used for a furnace (Telugu) **kollu-** to neutralize metallic properties by oxidation (Tamil) **kol** brass or iron bar nailed across a door or gate; kollu-t-tat.i-y-a_n.i large nail for studding doors or gates to add to their strength (Tamil) **kollan--kamma_lai** < + karmaśa_la_, kollan--pat.t.arai, kollan-ulai-k-ku_t.am blacksmith's workshop, smithy (Tamil) cf. ulai smith's forge or furnace (Na_lat.i, 298); ulai-k-kal.am smith's forge; ulai-k-kur-at.u smith's tongs; ulai-t-turutti smith's bellows; ulai-y-a_n.i-k-ko_l smith's poker, beak-iron (Tamil) [**kollulaive_r-kan.alla_r: nait.ata. na_t.t.up.); mitiyulaikkollan- mur-iot.ir.r.an-n-a: perumpa_**)(Tamil) Temple; smithy: kol-l-ulai blacksmith's forge (kollulaik ku_t.attin-a_l : Kumara. Pira. Ni_tiner-i. 14)(Tamil) cf. kolhua_r sugarcane milkl and boiling house (Bi.); kolha_r oil factory (P.)(CDIAL 3537). *kulhu* 'a hindu caste, mostly oilmen' (Santali) kolsa_r = sugarcane mill and boiling house (Bi.)(CDIAL 3538). Alternative reinforcing semantics:
pajhaṛ = to **sprout** from a root (Santali) Rebus: pasra 'smithy'

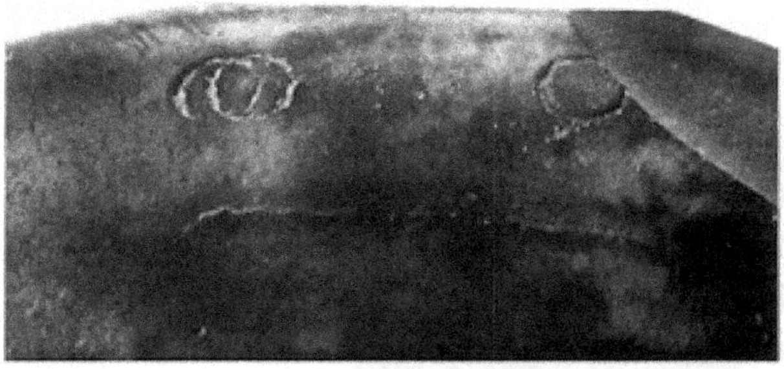

m1643bangle

'magnetite ingot'

Sign 99 sal 'splinter' rebus: sal 'workshop'

Sign403: Hieroglyph: *bārī* , 'small ear-ring': H. *bālā* m. 'bracelet' (→ S. *ḇālo* m. 'bracelet worn by Hindus'), *bālī, bārī* f. 'small ear -- ring', OMārw. *bālī* f.; G. *vāḷɔ* m. ' wire ', pl. ' ear ornament made of gold wire '; M. *vāḷā* m. ' ring ', *vāḷī* f. ' nose -- ring '.(CDIAL 11573) Rebus: *bārī* 'merchant' *vāḍhī,*

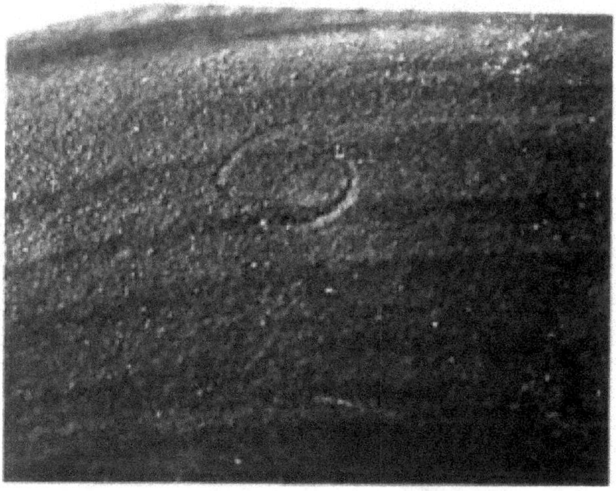

bari, barea 'merchant' *bārakaśa* 'seafaring vessel
m1641bangle
Kur. goṭā any seed which forms inside a fruit or shell. *Malt.* goṭa a seed or berry(DEDR 069) N. *goṭo* ' piece ', *goṭi* ' chess piece '; A. *goṭ* ' a fruit, whole piece ', °*ṭā* ' globular, solid ', *guṭi* ' small ball, seed, kernel '; B. *goṭā* ' seed, bean, whole '; Or. *goṭā* ' whole, undivided ', M. *goṭā* m. ' roundish stone ' (CDIAL 4271) <gōṭā>(P) {ADJ} ``^whole''. {SX} ``^numeral ^intensive suffix''. *Kh., Sa., Mu., Ho<gōṭā>,B.<gōṭā> `undivided'; Kh.<goThaG>(P), Sa.<gōṭāG>,~<gOTe'j>, Mu.<goTo>; Sad.<goT>, O., Bh.<gōṭā>; cf.Ju.<goTo> `piece', O.<gōṭā> `one'. %11811. #11721. <gōṭā>(BD) {NI} ``the ^whole''. *@. #10971. (Munda etyma) Rebus: *gōṭā* (laterite)

Rebus: <gōṭā> {N} ``^stone''. @3014. #10171. Note: The stone may be gōṭā, laterite mineral ore stone. *khoṭ* m. 'base, alloy' (Punjabi) Rebus: koṭe 'forging (metal)(Mu.) Rebus: goṭī f. 'lump of silver' (G.) goṭi = silver (G.) koḍ 'workshop' (Gujarati).

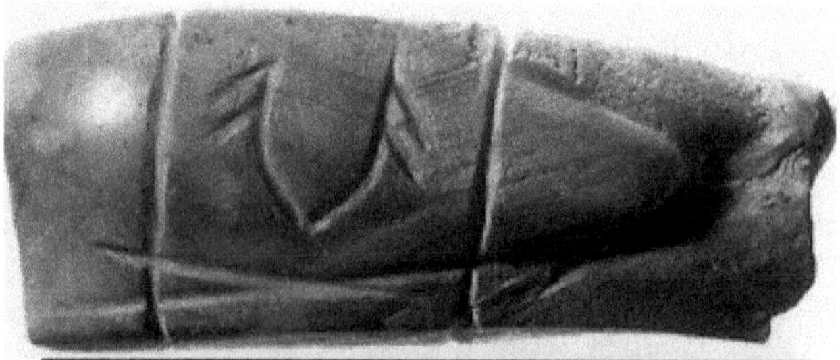

m1646bangle

Sign 261 kana, kanac = **corner** (Santali); Rebus: kañcu = bronze (Telugu).

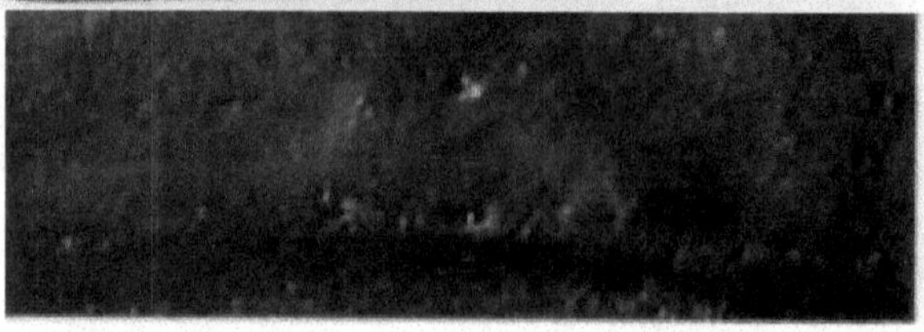

m1647bangle

Sign 87 dula ‘pair’; rebus dul ‘cast (metal)’

Sign 342 karṇī 'rim of jar' rebus: 'supercargo', 'engraver'

m1659bangle

Sign 336 baṭa 'rimless pot' rebus: baṭa 'iron' bhaṭa 'furnace' PLUS Te. gar̃ṭe, gaṇṭe, geṇṭe spoon, ladle rebus: *To.* köḍm (*obl.* köḍt-) live coal. *Ka.* keṇḍa id.; keṇḍavisu to put live coals on (for blasting rocks). *Tu.* keṇḍa, geṇḍa live coal. (DEDR 1950)

Sign 17 bhaṭa 'warrior' rebus: bhaṭa 'furnace'

The person performing the furnace operations to produce ceframic (stoneware) bangles is the person entitled to use the seal with the hieroglyph-multiplex of 'one-horned young bull' as demonstrated in the following reconstructed diagram of the apparatus.

Uniformity in the Harappa Script writing system enjoined by the ceramic (stoneware) bangles as insignia of authority to be scribes

This artisan was preparing ceramic (stoneware) bangles with inscriptions. He was clearly the standard-bearer for the Harappa Script writing system which was stunningly uniform across time and space over an extensive contact area on the Vedic Sarasvati river basin and extended along the maritime tin route from Hanoi to Haifa. If such an organizational structure is posited, it is possible to explain the uniformity maintained in the writing system on over 2600 sites of the civilization and also in contact areas where Meluhha merchants had established colonies. As an extended hypothesis, it is suggested that the recipient of the ceramic (stoneware) bangles in the work areas (sites) of the civilization are authorised to be scribed for documenting and archiving the metalwork catalogues.

Each ceramic (stoneware) bangle owner is authorised with specific functions in the guild, with the specific functional allocations of the joint community enterprise of the Bronze Age, as demonstrated by the decipherment of 22 unique functional categories of artisans.

खोंद [khōnda] *n* A hump (on the back): also a protuberance or an incurvation (of a wall, a hedge, a road). Rebus: खोदणें [khōdaṇēṃ] *v c & i* (H) To dig. 2 To engrave. खोद खोदून विचारणें or -पुसणें To question minutely and searchingly, *to probe.*गोट [gōṭa] *m* (H) A metal wristlet. An ornament of women. 2 Encircling or investing. *v* घाल, दे. 3 An encampment or camp: also a division of a camp. 4 The hem or an appended border (of a garment)*kõdā*'to turn in a lathe'(B.) कोंद kōnda 'engraver, lapidary setting or infixing gemś (Marathi) koḍ 'artisan's workshop' (Kuwi) koḍ = place where artisans work (G.) ācāri koṭṭya 'smithy' (Tu.) कोंडण [kōṇḍaṇa] f A fold or pen. (Marathi) B. kõdā 'to turn in a lathe'; Or.kũnda 'lathe', kũdibā, kũd 'to turn' (→ Drav. Kur. Kũd ' lathe') (CDIAL 3295) A. kundār, B. kũdār, ri, Or.Kundāru; H. kũderā m. 'one who works a lathe, one who scrapes', rī f., kũdernā 'to scrape, plane, round on a lathe'; kundakara—m. 'turner' (Skt.)(CDIAL 3297). कोंदण [kōndaṇa] n (कोंदणें) Setting or infixing of gems.(Marathi) খোদকার [khōdakāra] n an engraver; a carver. **খোদকারি** n. engraving; carving; interference in other's work. খোদাই [khōdāi] n engraving; carving. **খোদাই করা** v. to engrave; to carve. **খোদানো** v. & n. en graving; carving. খোদিত [khōdita] a engraved. (Bengali) खोदकाम [khōdakāma] n Sculpture; carved work or work for the carver. खोदगिरी [khōdagirī] f Sculpture, carving, engraving: also sculptured or carved work. खोदणावळ [khōdaṇāvaḷa] f (खोदणें) The price or cost of sculpture or carving. खोदणी [khōdaṇī] f (Verbal of खोदणें) Digging, engraving &c. 2 fig. An exacting of money by importunity. V लाव, मांड. 3 An instrument to scoop out and cut flowers and figures from paper. 4 A goldsmith's die. खोदणें [khōdaṇēṃ] v c & i (H) To dig. 2 To engrave. खोद खोदून विचारणें or -पुसणें To question minutely and searchingly, to probe. खोदाई [khōdāī] f (H.) Price or cost of digging or of sculpture or carving. खोदींव [khōdīṃva] p of खोदणें Dug. 2 Engraved, carved, sculptured. (Marathi)

Hieroglyphs: G. *sãghāṛɔ* m. ' lathe '; M. *sãgaḍ* f. ' a body formed of two or more fruits or animals or men &c. linked together, part of a turner's apparatus ', m.f. ' float made of two canoes joined together ' (LM 417 compares saggarai at Limurike in the Periplus, Tam.*śaṅgaḍam*, Tu.*jaṅgala* ' double -- canoe '), *sãgāḍā* m. ' frame of a building ', °*ḍī* f. ' lathe '; Si. *saṅgaḷa* ' pair ', *haṅguḷa, aṅg*° ' double canoe, raft '.(CDIAL 12859) Pa. *saṅghāta* -- m. ' killing, knocking together '; Pk. *saṁghāya* --

m. ' closeness, collection '; Or. *saṅghā, saṅgā* ' bamboo scaffolding inside triangular thatch, crossbeam of thatched house, copulation (of animals) '; -- adj. ' bulled (of a cow) ' < **saṁghātā* -- or *saṁhatā* -- ?(CDIAL 12862)
Rebus: *sangara [fr. saŋ+gṛ1 to* sing, proclaim, cp. gāyati & gīta] 1. a promise, agreement J iv.105, 111, 473; v.25, 479 सं-ग्रह *saṁgraha* 'a guardian , ruler , manager , arranger' R. BhP.
Rebus: s*aṁghāṭa* m. ' fitting and joining of timber ' R. [√ghaṭ](CDIAL 12859) संगत *saṅgata* Assembled, collected, convened, met together.संगतिः saṅgatiḥ Company, society, association, intercourse (Samskritam. Apte) Sangata [pp. of sangacchati] 1. come together, met Sn 807, 1102 (=samāgata samohita sannipātita Nd2 621);
nt. sangataŋ association Dh 207. -- 2. compact, tightly fastened or closed, well -- joined Vv 642 (=nibbivara VvA 275). *sangati* (f.) [fr. sangacchati] 1. meeting, intercourse J iv.98; v.78, 483. In defn of yajati (=service?) at Dhtp 62 & Dhtm 79. -- 2. union, combination M i.111; Sii.72; iv.32 sq., 68 sq.; Vbh 138 (=VbhA 188).
<-> 3. accidental occurrence D i.53; DA i.161. (Pali)

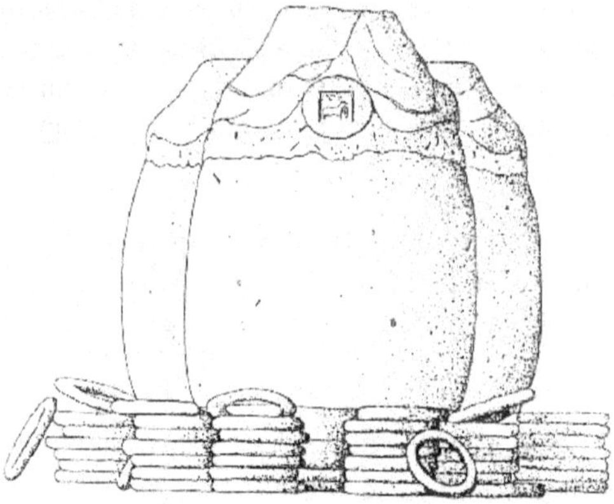

Fig. 9. Graphic reconstruction of an assembled apparatus for firing stoneware bangles inserted in the kiln.

Massimo Vidale
An article examining the construction of ceramic stoneware in the Indus Valley Civilization with a focus on Mohenjo-daro.[238]

Fragment of stoneware bangle bearing an exceptionally long micro-inscription of 5 signs (Dep. CS.Neg. 14756/27).

Fragment of stoneware bangle from the surface of Mohenjodaro with a short micro-inscription of 2 signs (Dep. CS.Neg. 14575/11).

Mohenjodaro detail of a vitrified block recovered on surface. The piece contains the remnants of a pile of sub-cylindrical saggars partially melted due to a firing accident. One of the saggars still contains a couple of superimposed stoneware bangles, showing the original arrangement of the products to be fired.

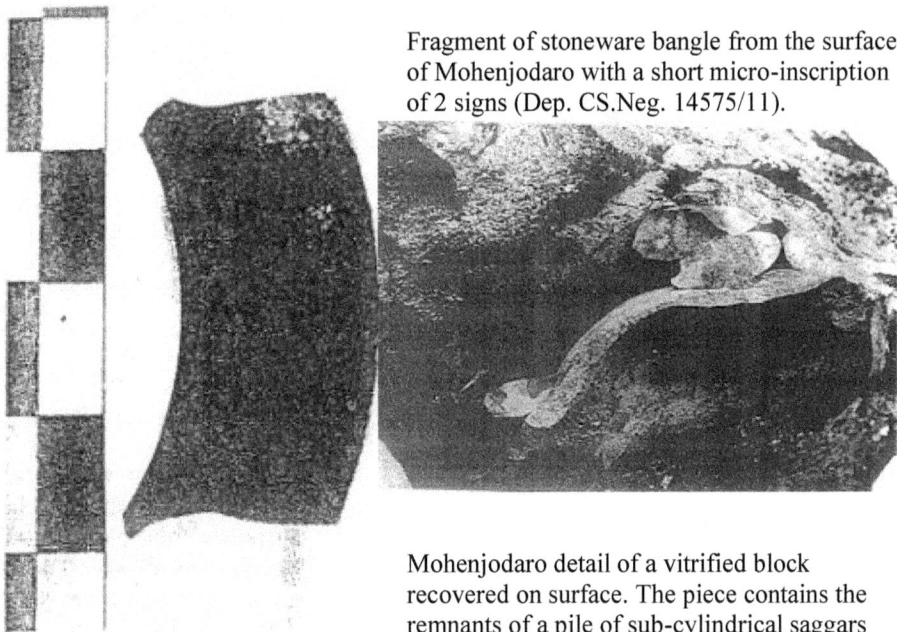

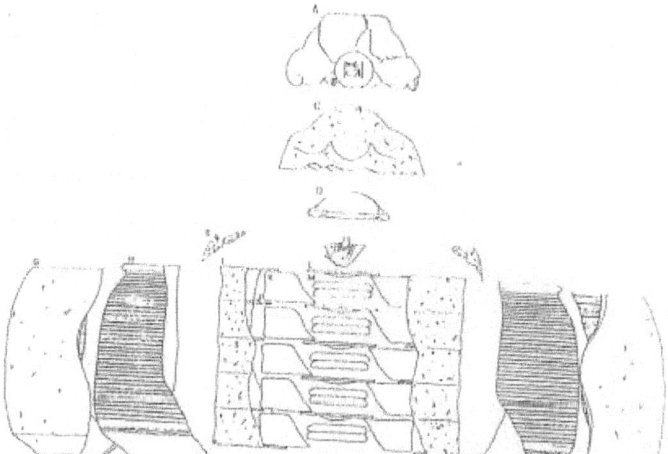

A: Upper capping in clay; B: Oval sealing with imprint of a Indus 'unicorn' stamp seal, applied in sets of three around the mouth of the closed saggars before firing; C: Intermeḍiate coating in chaff-tempered clay; D: Pottery semispherical lid; E,F: broken terracotta rings used to support the lid…K: Pile formeḍ by superimposed small saggars. This type of firing container was made by throwing a ceramic mixture very close to the stoneware of the bangles…M: Sets of stoneware bangles, inserted in couples with in each saggar of type K.[239]

Stoneware bangles are unique because they carry micro-inscriptions. "The term 'stoneware' was used by the early excavators to designate artifcts with a highly siliceous, partially sintered, homogeneous ceramic body, usually free from inclusions or voids visible to the naked eye, and characterized by a very low porosisity."[240]

How were stoneware bangles made?

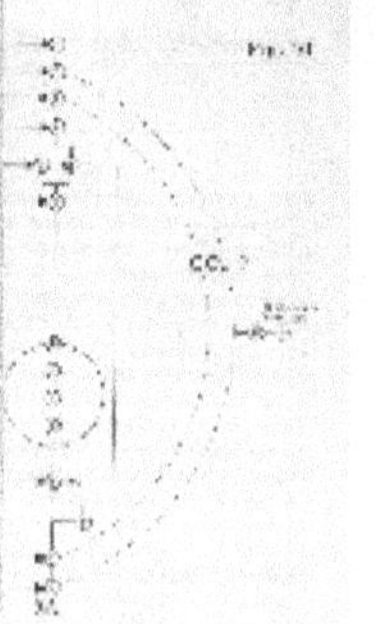

View of the slag with the coated sub-cylindrical bowl enclosing the stoneware bangles in a pile, in central position, Mohenjodaro.[241]

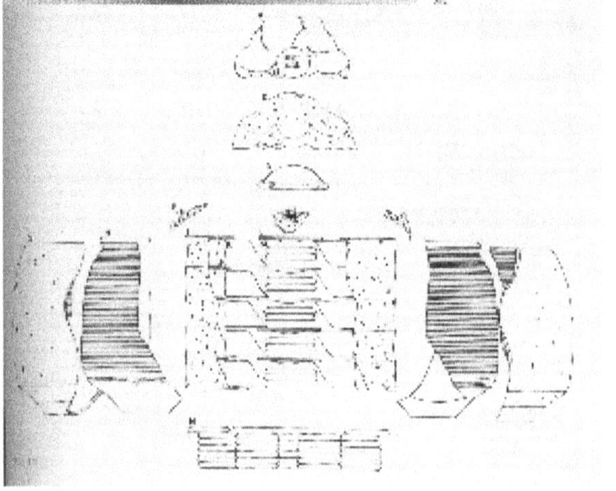

Kenoyer has shown that these bangles were formed by throwing clay cylinders on a fast wheel and trimming and burnishing them with sharp pointed tools which left distinctive, fine parallel marks on them. Smalll saggars or firing containers were used to stack these bangles for firing. *saṁgaḍha ' collection of forts '. [*gaḍha --]L. *sãgaṛh* m. ' line of entrenchments, stone walls for defence '.(CDIAL 12845) Reconstruction of the stoneware bangles' firing apparatus; stoneware bracelets are piled up in five pairs and enclosed in a coated carinated jar. The jar is given red-slipped, chaff-tempered outer coating. The apparatus is mounted on a network of supporting terracotta bangles. A unicorn seal impression is affixed on the upper capping.[242]

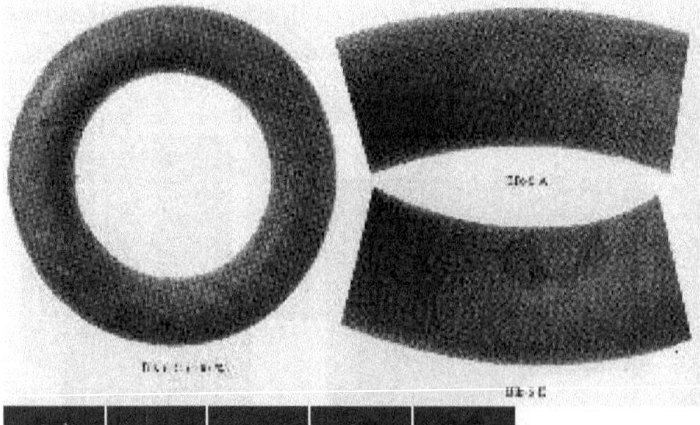

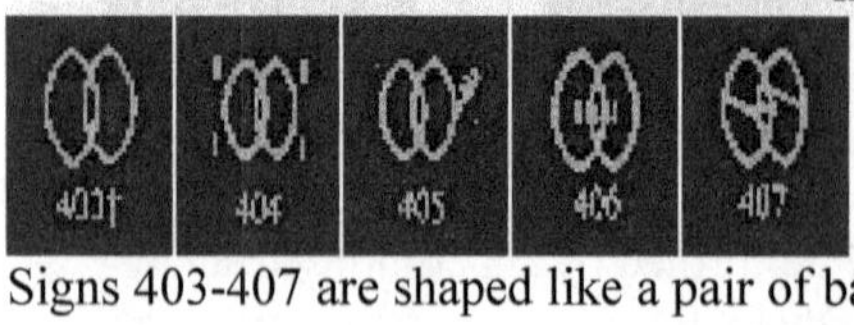

Signs 403-407 are shaped like a pair of bangles

Balakot, Stoneware bangle and fragments (Blk-6, Parpola)

The bangle has an inscription in red: 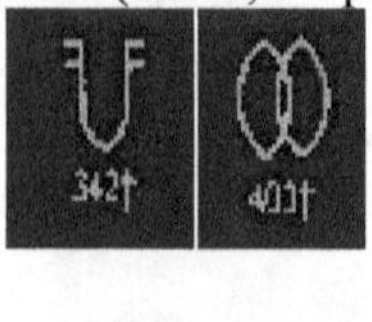

سنګر sangarS سنګر *sangar*, s.m. (2nd) A breastwork of stones, etc., erected to close a pass or road; lines, entrenchments. Pl. سنګرونه *sangarūnah*. See باره

Hieroglyph: wristlets, bangles *karā̃* n. pl. ' wristlets, bangles '(Gujarati)(CDIAL 2779) Rebus: khār 1 खार् । लोहकारः m. (sg. abl. khāra 1 खार; the pl. dat. of this word is khāran 1 खारन्, which is to be distinguished from khāran 2, q.v., s.v.), a blacksmith, an iron worker (Kashmiri)

Rebus: सांगड [sāṅgaḍa] *m f* (संघट्ट S) A float composed of two canoes or boats bound together: also a link of two pompions &c. to swim or float by. सांगडणी [sāṅgaḍaṇī] *f* (Verbal of सांगडणें) Linking or joining together.सांगडणें [sāṅgaḍaṇēṃ] *v c* (सांगड) To link, join, or unite together (boats, fruits, animals). 2 Freely. To tie or bind up or unto.सांगडी [sāṅgaḍī] *f* (Commonly सांगड) A float &c.सांगड्या [sāṅgaḍyā] *a* sometimes सांगडी *a* That works a सांगड or canoe-float.śā̃gaḍ 'chain' rebus: sanghāta 'vajra, metallic adamantine glue'. rebus: śā̃gaḍa 'catamaran' *śaṅgaḍam* 'double canoe'(Tamil) Cangavāra [cp. Tamil canguvaḍa a dhoney, Anglo-- Ind. ḍoni, a canoe hollowed from a log, see also doṇi] a hollow vessel, a bowl, cask M i.142; J v.186 (in similes). As °ka Miln 365 (trsl. Miln ii.278 by "straining cloth"). <-> Cp. cañcu "a box" Divy 131 (Pali) .saṁghāṭa m. ' fitting and joining of timber ' R. [√ghaṭ]Pa. *nāvā -- saṅghāṭa* -- , *dāru -- s°* ' raft '; Pk. *saṁghāḍa* -- , *°ḍaga* -- m., *°ḍī* -- f. ' pair '; Ku. *sĩgāṛ* m. ' doorframe '; N. *saṅār*, *siṅhār* ' threshold '; Or.*saṅghāṛi* ' pair of fish roes, two rolls of thread for twisting into the sacred thread, quantity of fuel sufficient to maintain the cremation fire '; Bi. *sĩghārā* ' triangular packet of betel '; H. *sĩghāṛā* m. ' piece of cloth folded in triangular shape '; G. *sā̃ghāṛɔ* m. ' lathe '; M. *sā̃gaḍ* f. ' a body formed of two or more fruits or animals or men &c. linked together, part of a turner's apparatus ', m.f. ' float made of two canoes joined together ' (LM 417 compares saggarai at Limurike in the Periplus, Tam. *śaṅgaḍam*, Tu.*jaṅgala* ' double -- canoe '), *sā̃gāḍā* m. ' frame of a building ', *°ḍī* f. ' lathe '; Si. *saṅgaḷa* ' pair ', *haṅguḷa,aṅg°* ' double canoe, raft '.Addenda: saṁghāṭa -- : Md. *aṅgoḷi* ' junction '?(CDIAL 12859) rebus: सं-ग्रह *saṁgraha* 'a guardian , ruler , manager , arranger' R. BhP.

ayakāṇḍa ''large quantity of stone (ore) metal' or *aya kāṇḍa,* 'metal fire-altar'. *ayo, hako* 'fish'; *ā̃s* = scales of fish (Santali); rebus: *aya* 'metal, iron' (G.); *ayah, ayas* = metal (Skt.) Santali lexeme, *hako* 'fish' is concordant with a Proto-Indic form which can be identified as *ayo* in many glosses, Munda, Sora glosses in particular, of the Bharata linguistic area.

beḍa hako (ayo) 'fish' (Santali); *beḍa* 'either of the sides of a hearth' (G.) Munda: So. *ayo* `fish'. Go. ayu `fish'. Go <ayu> (Z), <ayu?u> (Z),, <ayu?> (A) {N} ``^fish". Kh. kaDOG `fish'. Sa. Hako `fish'. Mu. hai (H) ~ haku(N) ~ haikO(M) `fish'. Ho haku `fish'. Bj. hai `fish'. Bh.haku `fish'. KW haiku ~ hakO |Analyzed hai-kO, ha-kO (RDM). Ku. Kaku`fish'.@(V064,M106) Mu. ha-i, haku `fish' (HJP). @(V341) ayu>(Z), <ayu?u> (Z) <ayu?>(A) {N} ``^fish". #1370. <yO>\\<AyO>(L) {N} ``^fish". #3612. <kukkulEyO>,,<kukkuli-yO>(LMD) {N} ``prawn". !Serango dialect. #32612. <sArjAjyO>,,<sArjAj>(D) {N} ``prawn". #32622. <magur-yO>(ZL) {N} ``a kind of ^fish". *Or.<>. #32632. <ur+GOl-Da-yO>(LL) {N} ``a kind of ^fish". #32642.<bal.bal-yO>(DL) {N} ``smoked fish". #15163. Vikalpa: Munda: <aDara>(L) {N} ``^scales of a fish, sharp bark of a tree".#10171. So<aDara>(L) {N} ``^scales of a fish, sharp bark of a tree".

Fish + corner, *aya koṇḍa*, 'metal turned or forged'

Fish, *aya* 'metal'

Fish + scales, *aya ãs (amśu)* 'metallic stalks of stone ore'. Vikalpa: *badhoṛ* 'a species of fish with many bones' (Santali) Rebus: *baḍhoe* 'a carpenter, worker in wood'; *badhoria* 'expert in working in wood'(Santali)

Fish + splinter, *aya aduru* 'smelted native metal'

Fish + sloping stroke, *aya ḍhāḷ* 'metal ingot'

Fish + arrow or allograph, Fish + circumscribed four short strokes

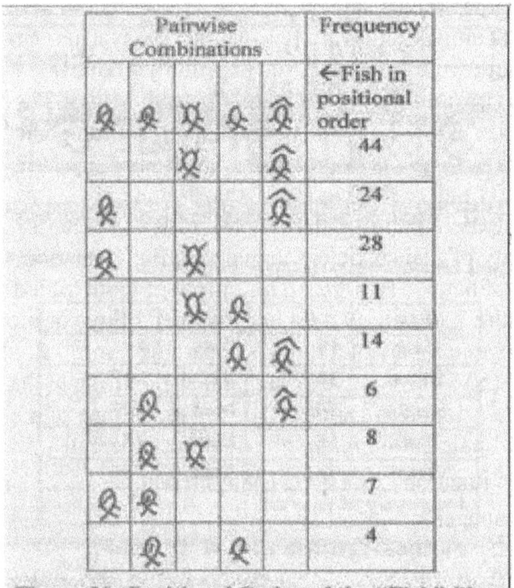

Figure 20: Positional Order of the "Fish" Signs

This indication of the occurrence, together, of two or more 'fish' hieroglyphs with modifiers is an assurance that the modifiers ar semantic indicators of how aya 'metal' is worked on by the artisans.

Hieorglyph: boar: baḍhia = a castrated boar, a hog; rebus: baḍhi 'a caste who work both in iron and wood'; baḍhoe 'a carpenter, worker in wood'; badhoria 'expert in working in wood'(Santali) 'Rebus: bari 'merchant'.barea 'merchant' (Santali)বরাহ barāha 'boar'Rebus: *bāṛaï* 'carpenter' (Bengali) bari 'merchant' barea 'merchant' (Santali) *Varāha is explained by* वाचस्पत्यम् Vācaspatyam: वराय अभीष्टाय मुस्तादिलाभाय आहन्ति खनति भूमिम् To represent a boon, (to obtain) wished, desired products (including species of grass) mined from the earth, by striking, hitting. Hieroglyph: Spread legs: कर्णक m. du. the two legs spread out AV. xx , 133 'spread legś; (semantic determinant) Rebus: karNa 'helmsman', karṇī 'scribe, account' 'supercargo'. Thus, the hieroglyphs on the anthropomorph Type 2 signify a helmsman, engraver who works with metals and mines to produce supercargo of mined products. (Note: I had suggested that the head ligature on the anthropomorph signifies a crocodile, but Dr. Sanjay Manjul's suggestion that it signifies head of a boar is consistent with the Vedic metaphor and tradition of *Varāha.* I correct my identification and read the Anthropomorph head as signifier of *Varāha.*)

*vaḍradaṇḍa ' large pole '. [vaḍra -- , daṇḍá --]Bi. *baṛẽṛā, °ṛī* ' upper iron bar of pillars supporting a smith's bellows ', *bẽriyā* (< **baṛẽṛiyā*? -- Other names are *ḍaṇḍā, ḍaṇṭā* Grierson BPL 414). 11211 vaṭa1 m. ' the banyan Ficus indica ' MBh.Pa. *vaṭa* -- m. ' banyan ', Pk. *vaḍa* -- , *°aga* -- m., K. *war* in *war -- kulu* m., S. *baṛu* m. (← E); P. *vaṛ, baṛ* m., *vohṛ, bohṛ* f. ' banyan ', *vaṛoṭā,ba°* m. ' young banyan ' (+?); N. A. *bar* ' banyan ', B. *baṛ*, Bi. *bar* (→ Or. *bara*), H. *baṛ* m. (→ Bhoj. Mth. *baṛ*), G. *vaṛ* m., M. *vaḍ* m., Ko.*vaḍu.**vaṭapadra -- , *vaṭapātikā -- .

Addenda: vaṭa -- 1: Garh. *baṛ* ' fig tree '.vaṭa 11212 vaṭa2 ' string ' lex. [Prob. ← Drav. Tam. *vaṭam*, Kan. *vaṭi, vaṭara*, &c. DED 4268]N. *bariyo* ' cord, rope '; Bi. *barah* ' rope working irrigation lever ', *barhā* ' thick well -- rope ', Mth. *barahā* ' rope '.(CDIAL 11227) తక్షకుడు (p. 0500) [takṣakuḍu] *takshakuḍu*. [Skt.] n. The name of mythological serpent ఒక సర్పరాజు. The name of a race of men called Takshakas. A carpenter వడ్లవాడు.వర్ధకి (p. 1142) [vardhaki] *vardhaki*. [Skt.] n. A carpenter. వడ్లవాడు.వడ్రంగి, వడ్లంగి, వడ్లవాడు (p. 1133) [vaḍraṅgi, vaḍlaṅgi, vaḍlavāḍu] or వడ్లబత్తుడు *vaḍrangi*. [Tel.] n. A carpenter. వడ్రంగము, వడ్లపని, వడ్రము or వడ్లంగితనము *vaḍrangamu*. n. The trade of a carpenter. వడ్లవానివృత్తి. వడ్రంగిపని. వడ్రంగిపిట్ట or వడ్లంగిపిట్ట *vaḍrangi-piṭṭa*. n. A woodpecker. దార్వాఘాటము. వడ్లకంకణము *vaḍla-kankaṇamu*. n. A curlew. ఉల్లంకులలో భేదము. వడ్లతor వడ్లది *vaḍlata*. n. A woman of the carpenter caste. वर्धक [p= 926,1]*mfn.* cutting , dividing , cutting off , shearing (» माष- and श्मश्रु-व्°)*m.* a carpenter R. 11371 *varddhṛ ' cutter, knife '. [√vardh] **varddhrī* -- : N. *bāṛ* ' blade of khukri '; Bi. *bāṛh* ' bookbinder's papercutter '; H. *bāṛh, bāṛ* f. ' edge of knife ', G. *vāḍh* f.; -- P. *vāḍh, bāḍh* f. ' cutting edge ' poss. < **vārddhrī* -- . **vardharī* -- , **vardhāra* -- : Bi. *badhrī, °riyā, °rā, badhārū* ' knife with a heavy blade for reaping with '; <-> WPah.bhad. *bardhāṇū* ' to shear sheep ' < **badhār -- ṇū*? 11372 vardha1 m. ' a cutting ' W. [√vardh] S. *vaḍhu* m. ' a cut '; L. *vaḍḍh* m. ' ears of corn remaining in a field after sheaves have been removed '; P. *vaḍḍh, ba°* m. ' a cut in a piece of wood, chip, stubble of grain (wheat, maize, &c.) ', *vaḍḍhā, ba°* m. ' cut, mark '; G. *vāḍh* m. ' cut, wound, reaping a field '; Si. *vaḍa -- ya* ' act of cutting off '; -- K. *broḍu* m. ' septum of nose '? 11374 vardhaka in cmpd. ' cutting ', m. ' carpenter ' R. [√vardh] Pa. *cīvara -- vaḍḍhaka* -- m. ' tailor '; Kho. *bardog, °ox* ' axe ' (early → Kal. *wadók* before *v* -- > *b* -- in Kho.); <-> Wg. *wāṭ* ' axe ', Paš.dar. *wā'ṭak* (*ṭ*?).

vardhaki 11375 vardhaki m. ' carpenter ' MBh. [√vardh] Pa. *vaḍḍhaki* -- m. ' carpenter, building mason '; Pk. *vaḍḍhaï* -- m. ' carpenter ', *°aïa* -- m. ' shoemaker '; WPah. jaun. *bāḍhōī* ' carpenter ', (Joshi) *bāḍhi* m., N. *baṛhaï, baṛahi*, A. *bāṛai*, B. *bāṛaï, °ṛui*, Or.*baṛhaï, °ṛhāi*, (Gaṛjād) *bāṛhoi*, Bi. *baṛahī*, Bhoj. H. *baṛhaī* m., M. *vāḍhāyā* m., Si. *vaḍu -- vā*. *vārdhaka -- . Addenda: vardhaki -- : WPah.ktg. *báḍḍhi* m. ' carpenter '; ktg. *bəṛhe\i, báṛhi*, kc. *baṛhe* ← H. beside genuine *báḍḍhi* Him.I 135), J. *bāḍhi*, Garh. *baṛhai*, A. also *bāṛhai* AFD 94; Md. *vaḍīn, vaḍin* pl. †*vardhakikarman -- . 11375a †*vardhakikarman -- ' carpentry '. [vardhaki -- , kár- man --] Md. *vaḍām* ' carpentry '.11385 *vardhira ' axe, hammer '. [Cf. *varddhṛ -- . - √vardh]Kho. *bəḍī'r* ' sledgehammer (?) ' (→ Gaw. *bāḍíl*), Bshk. *baḍī'r*; Phal. *buḍhī'r* ' axe (?), sledgehammer ' AO xviii 227: very doubtful.11381 vardhayati1 ' cuts, divides ' Dhātup., *vardhāpayati*1 Weber. [√vardh] Pa. *vaḍḍhāpēti* ' cuts (moustache) '; Kal.rumb. *badhém* ' I cut, shear '; Kho. (Lor.) *sōr -- bərdēk* ' custom of cutting an infant's original hair '; K.ḍoḍ. *baḍṇō* ' to cut ', S. *vaḍhaṇu*; L. *vaḍḍhaṇ* ' to cut, reap '; P.*vaḍḍhṇā, ba°* ' to cut, kill, bite '; WPah. (Joshi) *bāḍhṇu* ' to cut '; B. *bāṛā* ' to cut, mend, distribute food '; Or. *bāṛhibā* ' to serve out food '; H. *bāḍhnā* ' to cut, shear, divide '; G. *vāḍhvũ* ' to cut ', *vadhervũ* ' to cut, sacrifice '; M. *vāḍhṇẽ* ' to serve out (food) ' (in sense ' to fill (a lamp with oil) ' rather < vardháyati2). 11387 várdhra m. ' leather thong ' AV., *vardhrī* -- f. lex., *vadhra* -- m.n. MBh. 2. badhra -- (v.l.) MBh. (X √bandh?). [√vardh]1. Pa. Pk. *vaddha* -- m.n. ' thong '; S. *vaḍhī, vāḍhī̃* f.; L. *vaddhar* m., *vadhrī* f., (Shahpur) *vadhar* m. ' shoulder -- strap '; P. *vahdar, vaddhrī, baddharī* f., ludh. *baddhī* f. ' leather thong '; Or. *badhī* ' dog's collar, leather thong round a drum '; Bi. *bādhā* ' strings of a balance ', *bādhī* ' ties fastening bamboo poles to body of cart '; Bhoj. Aw.lakh. *bādh* ' rope, string '; OG. *vādhra* n. ' leather ', G. *varadhi, vādhar,vādhrī, vādharṛī* f. ' leather strap '; M. *vād, vād(h)ī* f. ' strap

', *vādā* m. ' whiplash '; Si. *vada* ' leather strap '; -- Kal. *badrí* ' leather belt ', Phal. *ḍāk -- badhrḗi* (rather than with NOPhal 34 < *baddhrikā --); -- Paš.weg. *walā´* ' tie, band ' IIFL iii 3, 185 (< *vardh -- tra -- ?). 2. Pa. *baddha* -- n. ' thong '.*vardhrya -- .Addenda: várdhra -- [< IE. **werdhro* -- ~ *vārdhrī* -- f. ' strap ' < IE. **wordhrī* -- T. Burrow BSOAS xxxviii 65, but rather like *vā´rdhra* -- ' fit for strap ' Pāṇ., n. ' strap ' vṛddhi of *várdhra* --] Md. *vadu* ' strap '.
வராகபுடம் varāka-puṭam, *n.* < id. +. Calcining metals with 20 or 50 cakes of cowdung; 20 அல்லது 50 எருவிட்டுப் போடப் படும் புடம். (மூ. அ.)
warāh वराह॒ । सूकरः m. a boar, pig (wild or domesticated); the third, or boar, incarnation of Vishnu (Śiv. 856).(Kashmiri)বরা² (p. 0721) [barā²] n the boar, the hog.বরাহ (p. 0721) [barāha] n the boar, the hog; the third incar nation of Vishnu (বিষ্ণু) when he slew Bara (বরা) the demon. *fem.* বরাহী the sow.
(Bengali) வாராகன் vārākaṉ, *n.* < *Vārāha*. Viṣṇu, as having assumeḍ the form of a boar; பன்றி யவதாரமெடுத்த திருமால். வாராக வாமனனே (அஷ் டப். திருவரங்கத்தந். 60).வாராகி vārāki, *n.* < *vārāhī*. 1. Vārāhi, Sakti of the Boar-form of Viṣṇu, one of *catta-mātar*, q.v.; சத்தமாதரில் வராகாவதாரத்தின் சத்தி. 2. Sow; பெண்பன்றி. (யாழ். அக.) 3. Earth; பூமி. (யாழ். அக.) 4. A bulbous plant; ஒருவகைக் கிழங்குச்செடி. (யாழ். அக.)*வாராகம் vārākam*
, *n.* < *Vārāha*. 1. Viṣṇu's Boar-incarnation; திருமாலின் பன்றியவ தாரம். வாராகமதாகி யிம்மண்ணை யிடந்தாய் (திவ். பெரியதி. 4, 7, 8). 2. A Sanskrit astronomical treatise by Varākamikirar; வடமொழியில் வராக மிகிரராற் செய்யப்பட்ட ஒரு சோதிடக்கணிதநூல். நாராயணீயம் வாராக முதலிய கணதங்களும் (தொல். பொ. 75, உரை).
வராககற்பம் varāka-kaṟpam, *n.* < *Varāha* +. The age when Viṣṇu assumeḍ His boar-incarnation; திருமால் வராகாவதாரங் கொண்ட காலம். (பரிபா. 2, 16, உரை.) வராகம்¹ varākam, *n.* < *varāha*. 1. Boar, swine; பன்றி. கோலமேனி வராகமே (திருவாச. 30, 5). 2. The boar-incarnation of Viṣṇu, one of *tacāvatāram*, q.v.; திருமாலின் தசாவதாரத்துள் பன்றியுருக்கொண்ட அவதாரம். (பிங்.) 3. (Šaiva.) See வராகாதனம். மாநிருத்தங் குஞ்சிதம் வராகம் (தத்துவப். 108). 4. An Upaniṣad, one of 108; நூற் றெட்டுபநிடதங்களுள் ஒன்று. 5. A chief Purāṇa. See வராகபுராணம். 6. The region at the foot of Mt. Malayam; மலயபர்வதத் தடிவாரத்துள்ள பிரதேசம். (சிவதரு. கோப. 48.) 7. A mathematical treatise; ஒரு கணித நூல். (கலித். கடவு. உரை.) 8. cf. வராகி. Moosly or weevil root. See நிலப்பனை. (சங். அக.) వరహా [varahā] or వరా *varahā*. [from Skt. వరాహము.] n. The gold coin bearing the impression of a boar (వరాహము.) and termeḍ a pagoda. equal to 3 1/2 rupees. కరుకువరహా a coin equal to four rupees. కంఠీరవరాయ వరహాలు Kanterai pagodas, 105 of which are equal to rupees 305-7-4. The weight called వరహాయెత్తు is equal to 52.56. grains avoirdupois. తొమ్మిదిచిన్నములయెత్తు బంగారపుముద్రిక.వరాహము [varāhamu] *varāhamu*. [Skt.] n. A boar or hog. అడవిపంది. వరాహావతారము the third incarnation of Vishnu in the shape of a boar. వరాహకూర్చము (or, vulgarly వరాకట్లె) *varāha-kūrchamu*. n. A brush made of hog's bristles. సూకరము (p. 1353) [sūkaramu] *sūkaramu*. [Skt.] n. A hog. అడవిపంది, వరాహము. A pig, పంది. సూకరి *sūkari*. n. A sow. varāhá -- , *varā´hu* -- m. ' wild boar ' RV.Pa. Pk. *varāha* -- m. ' boar '; A. B. *barā* ' boar ' (A. also ' sow, pig '), Or. *barāha*, (Sambhalpur) *barhā*, (other dial.) *bărihā*, *bāriā*, H. *bărāh* m., Si. *varā*varāhamūla n. ' name of a place in Kashmir ' Rājat. [varāhá -- , mū´la -- ?]K. *warahmul* ' a town at

west end of the valley of Kashmir '.(CDIAL 11325, 11326) वराह (p. 734) [varāha] *m* (S) A boar. 2 The boar-avatár of Vishṇu.(Marathi) वराह [p= 923,2] *m.* (derivation doubtful) a boar , hog , pig , wild boar RV. &c (ifc. it denotes , " superiority , pre-eminence " ; » g. व्याघ्रा*दि); a bull Col.; a ram L.; N. of विष्णु in his third or boar-incarnation cf. वराहा*वतार) TA1r.
MBh. &c; of the son of a guardian of a temple Ra1jat.(Samskrtam) पोत्रम् pōtramपोत्रम् [पू-त्र] 1 The snout of a hog; धृतविधुरधरं महा- वराहं गिरिगुरुपोत्रमपीहितैर्जयन्तम् Bk.1.6; Ki.13.53.-2 A boat, ship.-3 A plough share.-4 The thunderbolt. -5 A garment.-6 The office of the Potṛi.-Comp. -आयुधः a hog,varāhḥ वराहः [वराय अभीष्टाय मुस्तादिलाभाय आहन्ति भूमिम् आ-हन्-ड Tv.] 1 A boar, hog; विस्रब्धं क्रियतां वराहततिभिर्मुस्ताक्षतिः पल्वले Ś.2.6. -2 A ram. -3 A bull. -4 A cloud. -5 A crocodile. -6 An array of troops in the form of a boar. -7 N. of Viṣṇu in the third or boar incarna- tion; cf. वसति दशनशिखरे धरणी तव लग्ना शशिनि कलङ्ककलेव निमग्ना । केशव धृतशूकररूप जय जगदीश हरे Gīt.1. -8 A parti- cular measure. -9 N. of Varāhamihira -1 N. of one of the 18 Purāṇas. -11 A mountain; L. D. B. -12 A coin; L. D. B. -13 A kind of grass; L. D. B. -Comp. -अवतारः the boar or third incarnation of Viṣṇu. -कन्दः a kind of esculent root.-कर्णः a kind o arrow; वराह- कर्णैर्नालोकैविकर्णैश्चाभ्यवीवृषत् Mb.7.166.24. -कर्णिका a kind of missile. -कल्पः the period of the boar incarnation, the period during which Viṣṇu assumeḍ the form of a boar. -क्रान्ताthe sensitive plant. -द्वादशी a festival held on the 12th day in the bright half of Māgha in honour of Viṣṇu. -नामन् *n.* an esculent root. -पुराणम् N. of one of the 18 major purāṇas. -मिहिरः N. of a celebrated astronomer, author of बृहत्संहिता (supposed to be one of the 'nine gemś at the court of king Vikrama). -शृङ्गः N. of Śiva.वराहुः Ved. A boar, hog.vārāha वाराह *a.* (-ही *f.*) [वराहस्येदं प्रियत्वात् अण्] Relating to a boar; वाराहीमात्मयोनेस्तनुमवनविधावास्थितस्यानुरूपाम् Mu.7. 19; Y.1.259; शक्तिः साप्याययौ तत्र वाराहीं विभ्रती तनुम् Devīmāhātmya. -हः 1 A boar. -2 A kind of tree. -Comp. -कर्णी Physalis Flexuosa (अश्वगन्धा). -कल्पः N. of the present *Kalpa* (that in which we are at present living). -पुराणम् N. of one of the 18 Purāṇas.vārāhīवाराही 1 A sow. -2 The earth. -3 The Śakti of Viṣṇu in the form of a boar. -4 A measure. -Comp. -कन्दः N. of a bulbous plant (Mar. डुकरकंद).
वराह पुस्त्री० वराय अभीष्टाय मुस्तादिलाभाय आहन्ति

खनति भूमिम् आ + हन--ड । १ शूकरे अमरः स्त्रियां ङीष् । २ यज्ञवराहाख्ये भगवतोऽवतारभेदे पु० ३ पर्वत-भेदे ४ मुस्तके ५ मानभेदे मेदि० । ६ शिशुमारे ७ वाराही- कन्दे पु० राजनि० ८ अष्टादशद्वीपमध्ये द्वीपभेदे च ।"गन्धर्वो वरुणः सौम्यो वराहः कङ्क एव च । कुमु-दस कसेरुश्च नागो भद्रारकस्तथा । चन्द्रेन्द्र मलयाःशङ्ख यवाङ्क गभस्तिपान् । ताम्राङ्गस कुमारी च तत्रद्वीपा दशाष्टभिः" शब्दमा० ।

वराहकन्द पु० वराहप्रियः कन्दः शा० त० । स्वनामख्याते वृक्षभेदे राजनि० ।

वराहकान्ता स्त्री वराहाणां कान्ताऽभीष्टा । वराहकन्दे शब्दर० ।

वराहक्रान्ता स्त्री वराहेण क्रान्तेव । १ लज्जालुलतायाम् शब्दच० २ वाराह्यां (चामरालु) सुभूतिः ।

वराहिका स्त्री वराहो भक्षकत्वेनास्त्यस्याः ठन् । कपिकच्छ्वाम् राजनि० ।

वराही स्त्री वराहो भक्षकत्वेनास्त्यस्या अच् गौरा० ङीष् । १ भद्रमुस्तायाम् २ वराहकन्दे च राजनि० ।

वाराह पु० वराहस्येदं प्रियत्वात् अण् । १ महापिण्डीतकवृक्षे राजनि० । २ वराहसम्बन्धिनि त्रि० ।

वाराहकर्णी स्त्री वराहस्यायं वाराह इव कर्णः पत्त्र-मस्याः ङीप् । अश्वगन्धायाम् राजनि० ।

वाराहपत्री स्त्री वाराहस्तत्कर्ण इव धत्त्रमस्याः ङीप् अश्वगन्धायाम् राजनि० ।

वाराहाङ्गी स्त्री वाराहमिवाङ्गमस्याः ङीप् । दन्तीवृक्षे भावप्र० ।

वाराही स्त्री वराहस्येयमण् ङीप् । अष्टमातृकामध्ये १ वराहशक्तौ "यज्ञवराहमतुलं रूपं या विभ्रता हरेः । शक्तिः साप्याययौ तत्र वाराहीं विभ्रती तनुम्" देवीमा० "वाराही नारसिंही च" श्यामास्तवः । २ योगिनीभेदे वृहन्नन्तिकेश्वरपु० । ३ वराहक्रान्तायाम् अमरः ४ वराह- योषिति च ५ श्याभाखगे राजनि० ।

वाराहीकन्द पु० (चामरालु) ख्याते कन्दभेदे "वाराहीकन्द एवान्यैश्चर्म्मकार लुको मतः । अनूपे स भवेद्देशे वराहैव लोमवान्" भावप्र० ।

https://sa.wikisource.org/wiki/वाचस्पत्यम्

वराहः, पुं, (वरान् आहन्ति इति दुर्गः ।कृत्० ४ । ३ । ४९ । हन् + डः ।) पशु-विशेषः । वरा इति भाषा । तत्पर्य्यायः ।शूकरः २ घृष्टिः ३ कोलः ४ पोत्री ५ किरिः ६किटिः ७ द्रंष्ट्री ८ घोणी ९ स्तब्धरोम्रा १०क्रोडः ११ भूदारः १२ । इत्यमरः ॥ किरः १३मुस्तादः १४ मुखलाङ्गूलः १५ । इति जटा-धरः ॥ स्थूलनासिकः १६ दन्तायुधः १७ वक्र-वक्त्रः १८ दीर्घतरः १९ आखनिकः २०भूक्षित् २१ बहुसूः २२ । इति शब्दरत्ना-वली ॥ अस्य मांसस्य गुणाः । वृष्यत्वम् ।वातघ्नत्वम् । बलवर्द्धनत्वञ्च । इति राजवल्लभः ॥बद्धमूत्रत्वम् । विरूक्षणत्वञ्च । इति तत्रैव

पाठान्तरम् । अन्यत् शूकरशब्दे द्रष्टव्यम् ॥ * ॥ तन्मांसं विष्णवे न देयम् । यथा । "नाभक्ष्यंनैवेद्यार्थे भक्ष्येष्वजामहिषीक्षीरं वर्ज्जयेत् ।पञ्चनखमत्स्यवराहमांसानि चेति ।" इत्याह्निक-तत्त्वधृतविष्णुसूत्रम् ॥ * ॥ वराहमांसं भुक्त्वाविष्णुपूजादिनिषेधो यथा, --वराह उवाच ।"भुक्त्वा वाराहमांसन्तु यो वै मामुपसर्पति ।
पतनं तस्य वक्ष्यामि यथा भवति सुन्दरि ! ॥वराहो दश वर्षाणि भूत्वा तु चरते वने ।व्याधो भूत्वा महाभागे समाः सप्त च सप्ततिः ॥कृमिर्भूत्वा समाः सप्त तिष्ठते तस्य पुष्कले ।अथोच्चैर्म्मूषिको भूत्वा वर्षाणाञ्च चतुर्द्दश ॥एकोनविंशवर्षाणि यातुधानश्च जायते ।शल्लकश्चाष्टवर्षाणि जायते भवने बहु ॥व्याघ्रस्त्रिं शतिवर्षाणि जायते पिशिताशनः ।एष संसारिताङ्गत्वा वाराहामिषभक्षकः ॥जायते विपुले सिद्धे कुले भागवतस्तथा ।हृषीकेशवचः श्रुत्वा सर्व्वसम्पूर्णलक्षणम् ॥शिरसा चाञ्जलिं कृत्वा वाक्यञ्चेदमुवाच ह । एतन्मे परमं गुह्यं तव भक्तसुखावहम् ।वाराहमांसभक्षास्तु येन मुच्यन्ति किल्वि-षात् ॥ वाराह उवाच ।तरन्ति मानवा येन तिर्य्यक्संसारसागरात् ।गोमयेन दिनं पञ्च कणाहारेण सप्त वै ॥
पानीयन्तु ततो भुक्त्वा तिष्ठेत् सप्तदिनं ततः ।अक्षारलषणं सप्त शक्तुभिश्च तथा त्रयः ॥तिलभक्षो दिनान् सप्त सप्त पाषाणभक्षकः ।पयो भुक्त्वा दिनं सप्त कारयेच्छुद्धिमात्मनः ॥शान्तदान्तपराः कृत्वा अहङ्कारविवर्ज्जिताः ।दिनान्येकोनपञ्चाशच्चरेत कृतनिश्चयः ॥प्रमुक्तः सर्व्वपापेभ्यः ससंज्ञो विगतज्वरः । कृत्वा तु मम कर्म्माणि मम लोकाय गच्छति ॥"इति वाराहमांसभक्षणापराधप्रायश्चित्तम् ।इति वाराहपुराणम् ॥ * ॥वन्यवराहमांसं श्राद्धादौ विहितम् । यथाअश्नन्तीत्यनुवृत्तौ हारीतः । महारण्यवासि-
नश्च वराहांस्तथेति । एवञ्च विवदन्ते अग्रा-म्यशूकरांश्चेति वशिष्ठोक्तं श्वेताश्वेतया व्यव-स्थितम् । कल्पतरुस्तु । श्राद्धे नियुक्तानि युक्त-तयेति । विष्णूपासकस्य सर्व्वथा निषेधः । यथावाराहे भगवद्वाक्यम् ।

"भुक्त्वा वाराहमांसन्तु यस्तु मामुपसर्पति ।वराहो दशवर्षाणि भूत्वा वै चरते वने ॥"इत्येकादशीतत्त्वम् ॥ * ॥याज्ञवल्क्यः ।"हविष्यान्नेन वै मासं पायसेन च वत्सरम् ।मास्त्यहारिणकौरभ्रशाकुनिच्छानपार्षतैः ॥
ऐणरौरववाराहशशैर्मांसैर्यथाक्रमम् ।मासवृद्ध्याभितृप्यन्ति दत्तेनेह पितामहाः ॥"इति श्राद्धतत्त्वम् ॥ * ॥
विष्णोरवतारविशेषः । यथा, --सायम्भुव उवाच ।"कुत्र प्रजाः स्थास्यन्ति पृथिवी तावत् प्रलया-
र्णवे मग्ना तस्या उद्धरणे यत्नं कुरु । इति श्रुत्वाब्रह्मा भगवन्तं ध्यातवान् । ध्यायतस्तस्य नासाविवरात् अङ्गुष्ठप्रमाणो वराहपोतो निरगात् ।स च आकाशस्थः सन् क्षणमात्रेण पर्व्वतोपमो
बभूव । तं विष्णुं मत्वा ब्रह्मा तुष्टाव । स च तेन स्तुतः प्रलयार्णवजलमध्ये प्रविश्य दन्ताग्रेण
पृथ्वीमुद्धृत्य निजधारणशक्त्या संस्थाप्य अन्त-र्हितो बभूव । ततः पृथिव्यां राजा सायम्भुव-
मनुरासीत् ।" इति श्रीभागवतमतम् ॥ * ॥ तद-वतारकर्त्तृकहिरण्याक्षवधो यथा, --
"वराहपर्व्वतो नाम यः पुरा हरिनिर्म्मितः ।स एव भूतो भगवानाजगामासुरान्तिकम् ॥ततश्चन्द्रप्रतीकाशमगृह्णाच्छङ्खमुत्तमम् ।
सहस्रारं ततश्चक्रं सूर्य्यवह्निसमप्रभम् ॥यो वैकुण्ठः सुरेन्द्राणामनन्तो भोगिनामपि ।विष्णुर्यो योगविदुषां यो यज्ञो यज्ञकर्म्मणाम् ॥विश्वे यस्य प्रसादेन सवनस्था दिवौकसः ।आज्यं महर्षिभिर्द्दत्तमश्नुवन्ति सुधाहुतम् ॥
ततो दैत्यद्रवकरं पुराणं शङ्खमुत्तमम् ।वक्त्रेण दध्मौ वेगेन विक्षिपन् दैत्यजीवितम् ॥ततः संरक्तनयनो हिरण्याक्षो महासुरः ।कोऽयन्त्विति वदन् रोषान्नारायणमुदैक्षत ॥वाराहरूपिणं देवं स्थितं पुरुषविग्रहम् ।
शङ्खचक्रोद्यतकरं देवानामार्त्तिनाशनम् ॥रराज शङ्खचक्राभ्यां ताभ्यामसुरसूदनः ।सूर्य्याचन्द्रमसोर्मध्ये पौर्णमास्यामिवाम्बुदः ॥ततो हिरण्याक्षमुखाश्च सर्व्वेसमाद्रवन् दैत्यगणाः सुरेशम् ।निहन्तुकामाः सहसा वराहं
गृहीतशस्त्रा बलपूर्णदर्पाः ॥तैर्व्वध्यमानोऽतिशयेन शस्त्रै-र्दैत्यासुरैर्दानवपुङ्गवैश्च ।नासौ चचालासुरवृन्द हा वै
मेघैः सुवृष्टा इव मन्दराद्रिः ॥दैत्यस्ततोऽसौ नृवराहमाहवेनिपातयामास रुषा ज्वलन्तीम् ।शक्तिं यथा विद्युतमाशु कुञ्जेप्रवर्षमाणोऽपि गिरिं सुमेघः ॥स हन्यमानो गदयाप्रमेयःप्रोवाच दैत्यं नृवराहमूर्त्तिः ।
प्रजापतेः सेतुमिमं निहत्यव्रजेच्च क्व स्वस्ति यथा सुरेन्द्रः ॥बलं समासाद्य परैरजेयंविनाशयिष्याम्यहमेवमाजौ ।दैत्यांस्त्वया साकमतो हि देवान्हृतस्वकीयान् सुनयोपपन्नान् ॥संस्थापयिष्यामि न संशयोऽत्र
दैत्येन्द्रदर्पः क्व नु मत्समीपे ॥एवं ब्रुवति वाक्यन्तु विष्णोर्वक्षस्यपातयत् ।स बाहुशतमुद्यम्य सर्व्वप्रहरणं रणे ॥
दानवाश्चापि समरे मयतारपुरोगमाः ।उद्यतायुधनिस्त्रिंशाः सर्व्वे तं समुपाद्रवन् ॥स ताड्यमानोऽतिबलैर्दैत्यैः सन्नायुधोद्यतैः ।न चचाल वराहस्तु गैनाक इव पर्व्वतः ॥क्रोधसंरक्तनयनः शङ्खचक्रधरो हरिः ।
व्यवर्द्धत स वेगेन व्याप्नुवन् सर्व्वतो दिशम् ॥तं जयायासुरेन्द्राणां वर्द्धमानं नभस्तले ।ऋषयः सह गन्धर्व्वैस्तुष्टुवुर्मधुसूदनम् ॥दीप्ताग्निसदृशं घोरं दर्शनीयसुदर्शनम् ।सुवर्णरेणुपर्य्यन्तं वज्रनाभं भयावहम् ॥
मेदोऽस्थिमज्जारुधिरैः सिक्तं दानवसम्भवैः ।अद्वितीयं प्रहारैस्तु क्षुरपर्य्यन्तमण्डलम् ॥स्रग्दाममालाविततं कामगं कामरूपिणम् ।चक्रमुद्यम्य समरे वाराहः स्वेन तेजसा ॥चिच्छेद बाहूंश्चक्रेण हिरण्याक्षस्य कं तथा ॥

स छिन्नबाहुर्विशिरा न प्राकम्पत दानवः ।कवन्धवत्स्थितः संख्ये विशाख इव पादपः ॥ततः स्थितस्यैव शिरस्तस्य भूमावपातयत् ।हिरण्मयं रुक्मचित्रं मेरोः शृङ्गमिवोत्तमम् ॥हिरण्याक्षे हते दैत्या ये शेषाश्चैव दानवाः ।सर्व्वे तस्य भयात् त्रस्ता जग्मुरार्त्ता दिशोदश ॥"इति वह्निपुराणम् ॥अथ वराहावतारकारणम् । शरभरूपिमहा-
देवकर्त्तृकतच्छरीरनाशश्च ।"त्रैलोक्यमखिलं दग्धं यदा कालाग्निना तदा ।अनन्तः पृथिवीं त्यक्त्वा विष्णोरन्तिकमागतः ॥तेन त्यक्ता तु पृथिवी क्षणमात्रादधोगता ।ततो वराहरूपेण निमग्नां पृथिवीं जले ।मग्नां समुद्धाराशु न्यधात् तत्सलिलोपरि ॥वराहोऽपि स्वयं गत्वा लोकालोकाह्वयं गिरिम् ।वाराह्या सह रेमे स पृथिव्या चारुरूपया ॥स तया रममाणस्तु सुचिरं पर्व्वतोत्तमे ।नावाप तोयं लोकेशः पोत्री परमकामुकः ॥पृथिव्याः पोत्रिरूपाया रमयन्त्यास्ततः सुताः ।त्रयो जाता द्विजश्रेष्ठास्तेषां नामानि वै शृणु ॥

दुर्वृत्तः कनको घोरः सर्व्व एव महाबलाः ।स तैः पुत्रैः परिवृतो वाराहो भार्य्यया स्वया ॥रममाणस्तदा कायत्यागं नैवागणद्धिया ।इतस्ततश्च शिशुभिः क्रीडद्भिः पोत्रिभिस्तदा ॥जगन्ति तत्र भग्नानि नदीः कल्पतरूंस्तथा ।त्तो देवगणाः सर्व्वे सहिता देवयोनिभिः ॥शक्रेण सहिता मन्त्रं चक्रुः सम्यक् जगद्धितम् ॥

ततो निश्चित्य ते सर्व्वे शक्राद्या मुनिभिः सह ।शरण्यं शरणं जग्मुर्नारायणमजं विभुम् ॥तं समासाद्य गोविन्दं वासुदेवं जगत्पतिम् ।प्रणम्य सर्व्वे त्रिदशास्तुष्टुवुर्गरुडध्वजम् ॥देवा ऊचुः ।नमस्ते देवदेवेश ! जगत्कारणकारण ।कालस्वरूपिन् भगवन् प्रधानपुरुषात्मक ॥इति स्तुतो देवदेवो भूतभावनभावनः ।

सेन्द्रैर्देवगणैरूचे तान् सर्व्वान् मेघनिस्वनः ॥श्रीभगवानुवाच ।यदर्थमागता यूयं यद्वो भयमुपस्थितम् ।यत्र यद्वा मया कार्य्यं तद्देवास्तूर्णमुच्यताम् ॥देवा ऊचुः ।शीर्य्यते वसुधा नित्यं क्रीडया यज्ञपोत्रिणः ।लोकाश्च सर्व्वे संक्षुब्धा नाप्नुवन्त्युपशान्तिताम् ॥इति तेषां निगदतां श्रुत्वा वाक्यं जनार्द्दनः ।उवाच शङ्करं देवं ब्रह्माणञ्च विशेषतः ॥यत्कृते देवताः सर्व्वाः प्रजाश्च सकला इमाः ।प्राप्नुवन्ति महद्दुःखं शीर्य्यते सकलं जगत् ॥

वाराहं तदहं कायं त्यक्तुमिच्छामि शङ्कर ।निदेशशक्तं तत् त्यक्तुं स्वेच्छया नहि शक्यते ॥त्वं त्याजयस्व तत् कायं यत्रात्मा शङ्कराधुना ।त्वमाप्यायस्व तेजोभिर्ब्रह्मन् स्मरहरं मुहुः ॥आप्यायन्तु तदा देवाः शङ्करो हन्तु पोत्रिणम् ।रजस्वलायाः संसर्गात् विप्राणां मारणात् तथा ॥कायः पापकरो भूतस्तं त्यक्तुं मुह्यतेऽधुना ।

प्रायश्चित्तैरुपेतैर्यः प्रायश्चित्तमहं ततः ।चरिष्यामि तदर्थं मे तनुर्यत्नेन पात्यताम् ॥प्रजा पाल्या मम सदा या हि सीदति नित्यशः ।मत्कृते प्रत्यहं तस्मात् त्यक्ष्ये कायं प्रजाकृते ॥श्रीमार्कण्डेय उवाच ।

इत्युक्तौ वासुदेवेन तदा च ब्रह्मशङ्करौ ।त्वया यथोक्तं तत् कार्य्यमिति गोविन्दमूचतुः ॥वासुदेवोऽपि तान् सर्व्वान् विसृज्य त्रिदशां-स्तदा ।वाराहं तेजसा हर्त्तुं स्वयं ध्यानपरोऽभवत् ॥शनैः शनैर्यदा तेज आहरत्येष धवः ।तदा देहन्तु वाराहं सत्त्वहीनं व्यजायत ॥ब्रह्माद्यास्त्रिदशाः सर्व्वे महादेवमुमापतिम् ।अनुजग्मुस्तथा ज आधातुं स्मरनाशने ॥ततः सर्व्वैर्देवगणैः स्वं स्वं तेजो वृषध्वजे ।आदधे तेन बलवान् सोऽतीव समजायत ॥

ततः शरभरूपी स तत्क्षणाद्गिरिशोऽभवत् ।ऊर्द्ध्वाधोभावतश्चाष्टपादयुक्तः सुभैरवः ॥द्विलक्षयोजनोच्छ्रायः सार्द्धलक्षैकविस्तृतः ॥ऊर्द्ध्वं वराहकायस्तु लक्षयोजनविस्तृतः ॥लक्षार्द्धविस्तृतः पार्श्वे वर्द्धमानस्तदाभवत् ।

तमायान्तं ततो दृष्ट्वा क्रोधाद्धावन्तमञ्जसा ॥मुवृत्तः कनको घोर आसेदुः क्रोधमूर्च्छिताः ।उच्चिक्षिपुस्तं युगपत् पोत्रघातैर्महाबलाः ॥ततस्तुण्डप्रहारेण शरभः कण्ठमध्यतः ।भित्त्वा वपुर्वराहस्य पातयाभास तज्जले ॥

तं पातयित्वा प्रथमं सुवृत्तं कनकं तथा ।घोरञ्च कण्ठदेशेषु भित्त्वा भित्त्वा जघान ह ॥त्यक्तप्राणास्तु ते सर्व्वे पेतुस्तोये महार्णवे ।जलशब्दं वितन्वानाः कालानलसमर्च्चिषः ॥पतितेषु वराहेषु ब्रह्मा विष्णुर्हरस्तथा ।

सृष्ट्यर्थं चिन्तयामासुः पुनरेव समागताः ॥"इति कालिकापुराणीयाष्टाविंशत्यूनत्रिंशाध्यायात् सङ्कलितः ॥ * ॥ विष्णुः । मानभेदः ।पर्व्वतभेदः । मुस्ता । इति मेदिनी । हे, २२ ॥(पर्व्वतार्थे उदाहरणम् । यथा, महाभारते ।२ । २१ । २ ।"वैहारो विपुलः शैलो वराहो वृषभस्तथा ।तथा ऋषिगिरिस्तात शुभाश्चैत्यकपञ्चमाः ॥")शिशुमारः । वाराहीकन्दः । इति राज-निर्घण्टः ॥ अष्टादशद्वीपान्तर्गतक्षुद्रद्वीपविशेषः ।यथा, --

"गन्धर्व्वो वरुणः सौम्यो वराहः कङ्क एव च ।कुमुदश्च कसेरुश्च नागो भद्रारकस्तथा ॥चन्द्रेन्द्रमलयाः शङ्खयवाङ्कगभस्तिमान् ।ताम्राकुश्च कुमारी च तत्र द्वीपाः दशाष्टभिः ॥"इति शब्दमाला ॥

(कृष्णपिण्डीरः । तत्पर्य्यायो यथा, --"वराहः कृष्णपिण्डीरः कृष्णपिण्डीतकस्तु सः ॥"इति वैद्यकरत्नमालायाम् ॥)वराहकन्दः, पुं, (वराहप्रियः कन्दो यस्य ।)वाराही । इति राजनिर्घण्टः ॥

खदिरी ११ । इति रत्नमाला ॥ लज्जालुका १२अञ्जलिकारिका १३ कृताञ्जलिः १४ गण्डकारी१५ समीच्छदा १६ । इति ग्रन्थान्तरम् ॥वाराही । चामारालु इति ख्याते । इतिसुभूतिः । इत्यमरटीकायां भरतः ॥

क्ली, तीर्थभेदः । यथा, महाभारते । ३ । ८३ । १८ ।"ततो गच्छेत धर्म्मज्ञ ! वाराहं तीर्थमुत्तमम् ।

विष्णुर्वराहरूपेण पूर्ब्बं यत्र स्थितोऽभवत् ॥"पुराणविशेषः । यथा, देवीभागवते । १ । ३ । ८ ।

"चतुर्व्विंशतिसाहस्रं वाराहं परमाद्भुतम् ॥")

वाराहकर्णी, स्त्री, (वाराहकर्ण इव पत्रमस्त्यस्याः ।वाराहकर्ण + अच् । गौरादित्वात् ङीष् ।)अश्वगन्धा । इति राजनिर्घण्टः ॥

वाराहपत्री, स्त्री, (वाराहस्तत्कर्ण इव पत्र-मस्त्यस्याः । अच् । गौरादित्वात् ङीष् ।)अश्वगन्धा । इति राजनिर्घण्टः ॥

वाराहाङ्गी, स्त्री, (वाराहमिवाङ्गमस्याः । ङीष् ।)दन्तीवृक्षः । इति भावप्रकाशः ॥

वाराही, स्त्री, (वाराह + ङीष् ।) ब्रह्माण्या-द्यष्टमातृकान्तर्गतमातृकाविशेषः । यथा, --"वराहरूपधारी च वराहोपम उच्यते ।वाराहजननी चाथ वाराही वरवाहना ॥"इति देवीपुराणे देवीनिरुक्ताध्यायः ४५ ॥योगिनीविशेषः । यथा, --"दुर्गा चण्डेश्वरी चण्डी वाराही कार्त्तिकी

तथा ।हरसिद्धा तथा काली इन्द्राणी वैष्णवी तथा ॥भद्रकाली विशालाक्षी भैरवी कामरूपिणी ।

एताः सर्व्वाश्च योगिन्यो भृङ्गारैः स्नापयन्तु ते ॥"तीर्थविशेषः । यथा, --"वाराही यमुना गङ्गा करतोया सरस्वती ।कावेरी चन्द्रभागा च सिन्धुभैरवसागराः ।पशुस्नानविधानाय सान्निध्यमिह कल्पय ॥"इति बृहन्नन्दिकेश्वरपुराणोक्तदुर्गापूजापद्धतिः ॥वराहदेवस्य शक्तिः । यथा, --

"यज्ञवाराहमतुलं रूपं या बिभ्रतो हरेः ।शक्तिः साप्याययौ तत्र वाराहीं विभ्रतीतनुम् ॥" इति चण्डी ॥अपि च ।"वाराहरूपिणीं देवीं दंष्ट्रोद्धृतवसुन्धराम् ।शुभदां सुप्रभां शुभ्रां वाराहीं तां नमाम्यहम् ॥"इति बृहन्नन्दिकेश्वरपुराणोक्तदुर्गापूजापद्धतिः ॥वराहक्रान्ता । चामालु इति ख्यातः । तत्-पर्य्यायः । विष्वक्सेनप्रिया २ घृष्टिः ३ वदरा४ । इत्यमरः ॥ गृष्टिः ५ । इति भरतः ॥ शूकरी

६ क्रोडकन्या ७ विष्वक्सेनकान्ता ८ वराही ९कौमारी १० त्रिनेत्रा ११ ब्रह्मपुत्त्री १२ क्रोडी१३ कन्या १४ गृष्टिका १५ माधवेष्टा १६शूकरकन्दः १७ क्रोडः १८ वनवासी १९ कुष्ठ-नाशनः २० बल्यः २१ अमृतः २२ महावीर्य्यः२३ महौषधम् २४ शम्बरकन्दः २५ वराह-कन्दः २६ वीरः २७ ब्राह्मीकन्दः २८ सुककन्दः२९ वृद्धिदः ३० व्याधिहन्ता ३१ । अस्य गुणाः ।तिक्तत्वम् । कटुत्वम् । विषपित्तकफकुष्ठप्रमेह-क्रिमिनाशित्वम् । वृष्यत्वम्

। बल्यत्वम् । रसा-यणत्वञ्च । इति राजनिर्घण्टः ॥ अन्यच्च ।"वाराहीकन्द एवान्यैश्चर्म्मकारालुको मतः ।अनूपे स भवेद्देशे वाराह इव लोमवान् ॥" इति भावप्रकाशः ॥श्यामापक्षी । इति राजनिर्घण्टः ॥ मेदिनीमतेपवर्गीयबकारादिरयं शब्दः ॥

https://sa.wikisource.org/wiki/शब्दकल्पद्रु

Sign 15 occurs togethe with a notch-in-fixed fish hieroglyph on Harappa 73 seal:

H-73 a

Harappa seal (H-73)[Note: the hieroglyph 'water carrier' pictorial of Ur Seal Impression becomes a hieroglyph sign] Hieroglyph: fish + notch: aya 'fish' + khāṇḍā *m* A jag, notch Rebus: aya 'metal'+ *khāṇḍā* 'tools, pots and pans, metal-ware'. *kuṭi* 'water-carrier' Rebus: *kuṭhi* 'smelter'. खोंड (p. 216) [*khōṇḍa*] *m* A young bull, a bullcalf; खोंडा [khōṇḍā] *m* A कांबळा of which one end is formed into a cowl or hood. खोंडरूं [khōṇḍarūṃ] *n* A contemptuous form of खोंडा in the sense of कांबळा-cowl (Marathi); *kōḍe dūḍa*bull calf (Telugu); *kōṛe* 'young bullock' (Konda) rebus: *kõdā* 'to turn in a lathe' (Bengali) [The characteristic pannier which is ligatured to the young bull pictorial hieroglyph is a synonym खोंडा 'cowl' or 'pannier').खोंडी [khōṇḍī] *f* An outspread shovelform sack (as formed temporarily out of a कांबळा, to hold or fend off grain, chaff &c.)] खोंड (p. 216) [khōṇḍa] *m* A young bull, a bullcalf.(Marathi) खोंडरूं [khōṇḍarūṃ] *n* A contemptuous form of खोंडा in the sense of कांबळा-cowl.खोंडा [khōṇḍā] *m* A कांबळा of which one end is formed into a cowl or hood. खोंडी [khōṇḍī] *f* An outspread shovelform sack (as formed temporarily out of a कांबळा, to hold or fend off grain, chaff &c.) Hieroglyph: kōḍ 'horn' Rebus: kōḍ 'place where artisans work, workshop' কুঁদন, কোঁদন [kuṅdana, kōṅdana] n act of turning (a thing) on a lathe; act of carving (Bengali) कातारी or कांतारी (p. 154) [kātārī or kāntārī] *m* (कातणें) A turner.(Marathi)

Rebus: खोदकाम [khōdakāma] *n* Sculpture; carved work or work for the carver.

खोदगिरी [khōdagirī] *f* Sculpture, carving, engraving: also sculptured or carved work.खोदणें [khōdaṇēṃ] *v c* & *i* (H) To dig. 2 To engraveखोदींव [khōdīṃva] *p* of खोदणें Dug. 2 Engraved, carved, sculptured. http://bharatkalyan97.blogspot.in/2015/04/excavations-at-dholavifra-1989-2005-rs.html The intimations of a metals turner as a scribe are also gleaned from the gloss: खोडाखोड or डी [khōḍākhōḍa or ḍī] *f* (खोडणें) Erasing, altering, interlining &c. in numerous places: also the scratched, scrawled, and disfigured state of the paper so operated upon; खोडींव [khōḍīṃva] *p* of खोडणें *v c* Erased or crossed out.Marathi). खोडपत्र [khōḍapatra] *n* Commonly खोटपत्र.खोटपत्र [khōṭapatra] *n* In law or in caste-adjudication. A written acknowledgment taken from an offender of his falseness or guilt: also, in disputations, from the person confuted. (Marathi) Thus, *khond* 'turner' is also an engraver, scribe.

That a metals turner is engaged in metal alloying is evident from the gloss: खोट [khōṭa] *f* A mass of metal (unwrought or of old metal melted down); an ingot or wedge. Hence 2 A lump or solid bit (as of phlegm, gore, curds, inspissated milk); any concretion or clot. खोटीचा Composed or made of खोट, as खोटीचें भांडें.

Signifying a trough in front of a tiger (m290), a wild animal is a signal that hieroglyphs constitute a cipher, that the hieroglyph-multiplex should be read rebus in Harappa Script.

Seal m 290 Mohenjo-daro Hieroglyphs and rebus Meluhha readings:

Seal m 71

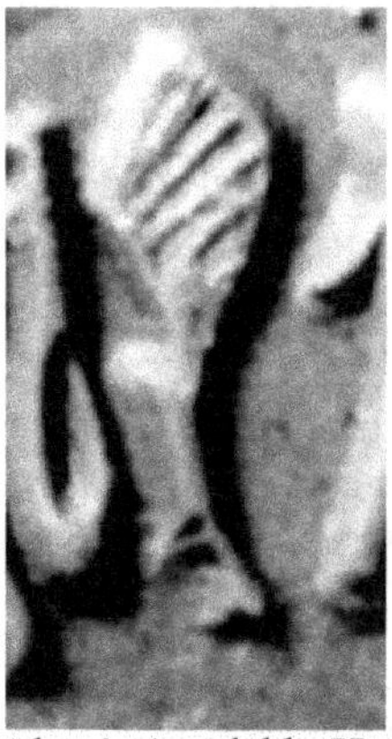

Mohenjo-daro. Hind leg hieroglyph: Pk. *ṭaṁka* -- m., °*kā* -- f. ‘ leg ’, S. *ṭaṅga* f., L. P. *ṭaṅg* f., Ku. *ṭā̃g*, N. *ṭāṅ*; Or. *ṭāṅka* ‘ leg, thigh ’, °*ku* ‘ **thigh**, buttock ’. 2. B. *ṭāṅ*, *ṭeṅri* ‘ leg, thigh ’; Mth. *ṭā̃g*, *ṭā̃gri* ‘ leg, foot ’; Bhoj. *ṭāṅ*, *ṭaṅari* ‘ leg ’, Aw. lakh. H. *ṭā̃g* f.; G. *ṭā̃g* f., °*gɔ* m. ‘ leg from hip to foot ’; M. *ṭā̃g* f. ‘ leg ’(CDIAL 5428) Rebus: stamped coin, mint: टंक (p. 335) [ṭaṅka] *m* S A stone-cutter's chisel. 2 A weight equal to four माष &c. टंकारी (p. 336) [ṭakārī or ṭaṅkārī] *m* (टंक) A caste or an indivi, dual of it. They are workers in stone, makers of handmills &c. **ṭaṅkaśālā --** , *ṭaṅkakaś°* f. ‘ mint ’ lex. [ṭaṅka -- 1, śā´lā --] N. *ṭaksāl*, °*ār*, B. *ṭāksāl*, *ṭā̃k°*, *ṭek°*, Bhoj. *ṭaksār*, H. *ṭaksāl*, °*ār* f., G. *ṭā̃ksāḷ* f., M. *ṭā̃ksāl*, *ṭāk°*, *ṭā̃k°*, *ṭak°*. -- Deriv. G. *ṭaksāḷī* m. ‘ mint -- master ’, M. *ṭāksāḷyā* m. Addenda: **ṭaṅkaśālā -- :** Brj. *ṭaksāḷī*, °*sārī* m. ‘ mint -- master ’.(CDIAL 5433, 5434).

Hieroglyph: **khāra**1 m. ‘ donkey ’ KātyŚr., °*rī* -- f. Pāṇ.NiDoc. Pk. *khāra* -- m., Gy. pal. *ḳăr* m., *kắri* f., arm. *xari*, eur. gr. *kher*, *kfer*, rum. *xerú*, Kt. *kur*, Pr. *korū'*, Dm. *khār* m., °*ri* f., Tir. *kh*lr*, Paš. lauṛ. *khār* m., *khär* f., Kal. urt. *khār*, Phal. *khār* m., *khári* f., K.*khār* m., *khürü* f., pog. kash. ḍoḍ. *khār*, S. *khāru* m., P. G. M. *khār* m., OM. *khāri* f.; -- ext. (CDIAL 3818) *khārun - khalun* transform attested in Kashmiri. So, too khura - khulan 'wild asś (Skt. -- Mongolian) **khaḍ 1** खड् m. an **ass**, i.q. **khār 1.** This is the form that the word takes towards Islāmābād (El.). **khār 1** खर् खरः m. (f. **khürü** ; or **khāriñ** खरिञ्), a donkey, an **ass** (L.V. 88; K.Pr. 26, 73, 14-5, 166, 174, 19, 215, 235, 262; H. iii, 8, 9; v, 7; K. 224); often used ° -- , to indicate the commonest, largest, or coarsest of the kind, like 'horse' in our 'horse-radish', 'a horse-laugh', etc.; cf. **khār-bādām,** bel., and **khārkhasun,** s.v. Towards Islāmābād the word is pronounced **khaḍ** (El.). **-āhang** -आहंग् f. an asśs bray (K.Pr. 235). Rebus: **khār 1** खार् । लोहकारः m. (sg. abl. **khāra 1** खार; the pl. dat. of this word is **khāran 1 खारन्,** which is to be distinguished from **khāran 2,** q.v., s.v.), a blacksmith, an iron worker **kõda khārüñü,** to raise a kiln; met. to raise or make a really good kiln in which only perfect bricks are baked (Śiv. 133; cf. **kõda khasüñü,** p. 384*b,* l. 28) (Kashmiri)

Comb कंकवा (p. 123) [kaṅkavā] m A sort of comb. See कंगवा. कोंगें (p. 180) [kōṅgēṃ] n A long sort of honeycomb.Rebus: *kanga* 'portable furnace' Rebus: *kangar* 'large brazier': *kāṅgārikā 'poor or small brazier'.

Hieroglyph: కోలు (p. 0329) [kōlu] *kōlu.* [Tel.] adj. Big, great, huge పెద్ద. కోలుపులి or కోల్పులి a royal tiger. kul 'tiger' (Santali) Pk. *kolhuya* -- , *kulha* -- m. ' jackal ' < **kōḍhu* -- ; H. *kolhā,* °*lā* m. ' jackal ', adj. ' crafty '; G. *kohlũ,* °*lũ* n. ' jackal ', M. *kolhā,* °*lā* m. (CDIAL 3615) Rebus: kolhe 'smelter' kol 'working in iron' kolle 'blacksmith'

Hieroglyph: *பத்தர்*[1] *pattar, n. 1. See பத்தல், 1, 4, 5. 2. Wooden trough for feeding animals; தொட்டி. பன்றிக் கூழ்ப்பத்தரில் (நாலடி, 257). 3. Cocoanut shell or gourd used as a vessel; குடுக்கை. கொடிக்காய்ப்பத்தர் (கல்லா. 40, 3).*

a. pātti bathing tub, watering trough or basin, spout, drain; pattal wooden bucket; **pattar** id., wooden trough for feeding animals. *Ka.* pāti basin for water round the foot of a tree. *Tu.* pāti trough or bathing tub, spout, drain. *Te.* pādi, pādu basin for water round the foot of a tree. (DEDR 4079) **pā´tra** n. ' drinking vessel, dish ' RV., °*aka* -- n., *pātrī´*- ' vessel ' GṛŚrS. [√pā1] Pa. *patta* -- n. ' bowl ', °*aka* -- n. ' little bowl ', *pātī̆* -- f.; Pk. *patta* -- n., °*tī* -- f., amg. *pāda* -- , *pāya* -- n., *pāī* -- f. ' vessel '; Sh. *păṭi̯* f. ' large long dish ' (← Ind.?); K. *pāthar*, dat. °*tras* m. ' vessel, dish ', *pôturu* m. ' pan of a pair of scales '(CDIAL 8055) Rebus: *பத்தர்*[2] ***pattar*** , *n.* < T. *battuḍu.* A caste title of goldsmiths; தட்டார் பட்டப்பெயருள் ஒன்று.

பத்தர்&sup5; pattar **బత్తుడు** *battuḍu.* n. A worshipper. భక్తుడు. The caste title of all the five castes of artificers as వడ్లబత్తుడు a carpenter. కడుపుబత్తుడు one who makes a god of his belly. L. xvi. 230.

Ancient ceramics from Sarasvati civilization.
पोळ *pōḷa*, 'zebu' rebus: पोळ *pōḷa*, 'magnetite, ferrite ore'ayo 'fish' rebus: aya 'iron' ayas 'metal; kuṭi 'tree' rebus: kuṭhi 'smelter' meRh 'tied rope' rebus: meḍ 'iron' meḍ 'copper'
khāreḍo = a **currycomb** (G.) Rebus: khārādī ' turner' (Gujarati)
saṁjñā´ f. ' agreement, understanding ' ŚBr., ' sign ' MBh. [√jñā]
Pa. *saññā* -- f. ' sense, sign ', Pk. *saṁṇā* -- f.; S. *sañaṇu* ' to point out '; WPah.jaun. *sān* ' sign ', Ku. *sān* f., N. *sān*; B. *sān* ' understanding, feeling, gesture '; H. *sān* f. ' sign, token, trace '; G. *sān* f. ' sense, understanding, sign, hint '; M. *sā̃j* f. ' rule to make an offering to the spirits out of the new corn before eating it, faithfulness of the ground to yield its usual crop ', *sā̃jẽ* n. ' vow, promise '; Si. *sana, ha*° ' sign '; -- P. H. *sain* f. ' sign, gesture ' (in mng. ' signature ' ← Eng. *sign*), G. *sen* f. are obscure. hastasaṁjñā -- .Addenda: **saṁjñā -- :** WPah.J. *sā'n* f. ' symbol, sign '; kṭg. *sánku* m. ' hint, wink, coquetry ', H. *sankī* f. ' wink ', *sankārnā* ' to hint, nod, wink ' Him.I 209.(CDIAL 12874)

Annex C

Form and function of inscribed tablets, miniature tablets

Tablets and miniature tablets were used to record work-in-process in metallurgical workshops. The data archived on the tablets were incorporated in the inscriptions on seals to validate shipments of cargo.[243]

A Bronze Age revolution necessitated organization of metalwork in workshops with specific functional assignments.This is clearly seeni in the documentation of tiny

steatite tablets of Harappa which indicate guild sub-organizations within smithy-forge workshops for 1. smelter work, 2.smithy or furnace work, 3. alloy (bronze) work. Such a functional organization also resulted in a writing system which could detail works in process at different stages of production in workshops before the supercargo consignments are readied, packed and sealed for shipment handed over to seafaring merchants or trade caravans.
This decipherment of 22 tiny steatite tablets discovered in Harappa 1991-1995 (HARP), demonstates how a sequence of hieroglyphs shown on such tablets is used as a hypertext, message string on a seal h1682. (Meadow, Richard H. and Jonathan Kenoyer, 1997, The 'tinysteatite seals' (incised steatitetablets) of Harappa: Some observations ontheir context and dating in: Taddei, Maurizio and Giuseppe de Marco, 2000, *South Asian Archaeology, 1997*, Rome, Istituto Italiano per l'Africa e l'Oriente.)

This is a string of hieroglyphs on 22 tiny steatite tablets of Harappa.

Rebus readings: kolmo 'three' rebus: kolimi 'smithy' PLUS *kuṭhi kaṇḍa kanka* 'smelting furnace account (scribe), *karNI*, supercargo'. In short, String 1: 'smelter-smithy supercargo'. This hieorlgyph-string is entered on the seal which technically documents the shipment with product catalogues included in a shipment.

h1682A (color) The messages of two strings are r. to l.: String 1: The smelter-smithy supercargo (taken from the product descriptions on tiny steate tablets) PLUS String 2: smithy cast implements. "Of great interest in this regard is a unicorn seal (Fig. 4.1) that was found inside the perimeter wall in the approximate location marked…The last two signs of this seal are the same as those on one side of the 22 tablets (taking the three strokes as a single sign). These are preceded by three additional signs (reading left to right on the seal as opposed to on the tablets which we assume are meant to be read right to left because they were not meant to be uimpressed…) It is rare to find the same sign sequence on a seal and on tablets, and the situation is that much more compelling because the street deposits from which the seal comes contain the same ceramic corpus as the dump deposits from which the tablets come, suggesting that both were originally formed at about the same time." (Meadow and Kenoyer, 1997, p.16)

This shows that tiny steatite tablets were documentation of work in process (say, from smelters, furnaces, circular platforms) which are brought into the storeroom (documentatin centre) to create a consolidated technical consignment note or metalwork catalogue on a seal. The supercargo is ready for despatch after the cargo is packed and the package sealed with the seal impression. For deciphered hieroglyphs of one-horned young bull PLUS standard device on the seal, see: http://bharatkalyan97.blogspot.in/2016/04/one-horned-young-bull-seal-standard.html

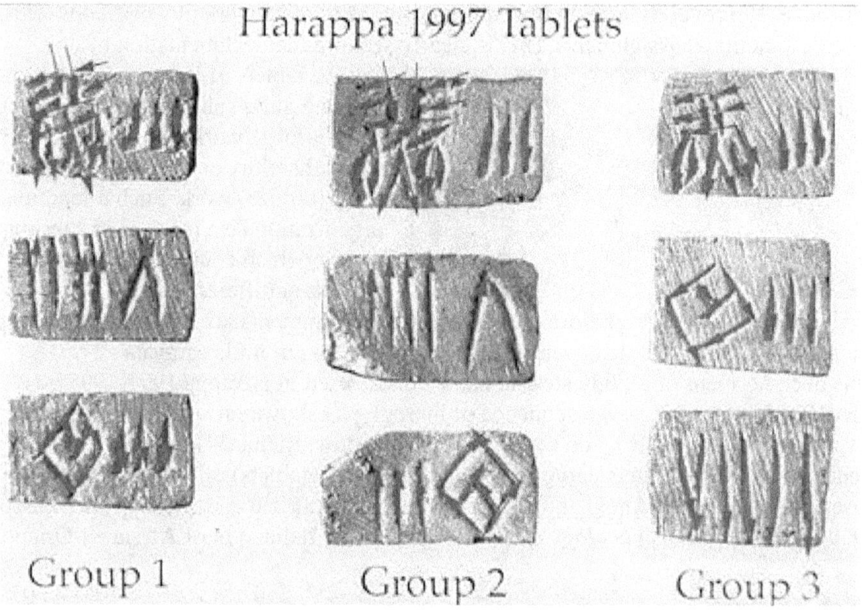

Three groups of tablets discovered at Harappa in 1997. 22 tablets were clustered in 3 groups to show styles of writing/incision indicating three distinct scribes at work. "Group of incised baked steatite tablets. A group of 16 three-sided incised baked steatite tablets, all with the same inscriptions, were uncovered in mid- to late Period 3B debris outside of the curtain wall. (See 146). These tablets may originally been enclosed in a perishable container such as a small bag of cloth or leather."

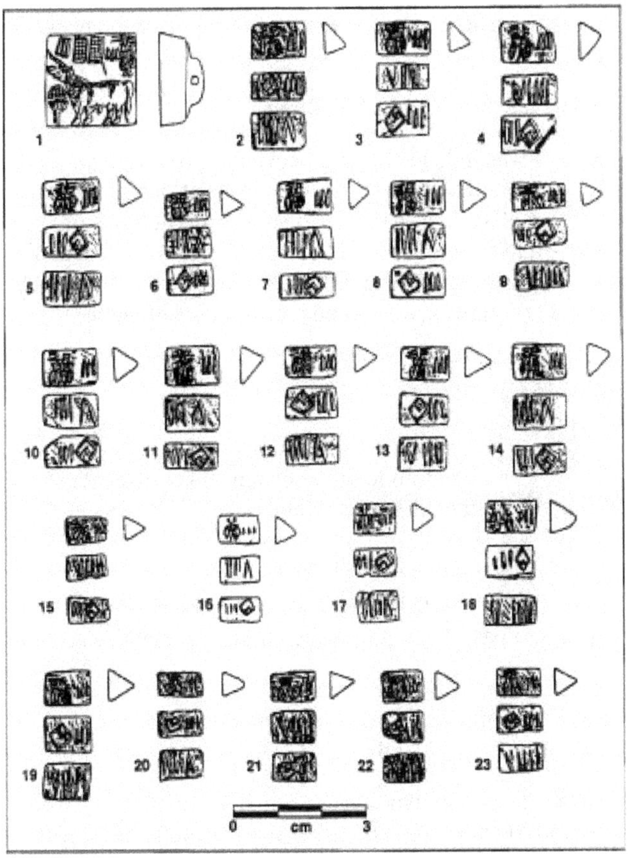

.Harappa 1995-7: MoundE, HARP Trench 11: steatite seal and incised steatite tablets (After Fig. 4. Harappa 1995-1997: Mounds E and ET; Trench 11: steatite seal H96-2796/6874-01 and incised steatite tablets (22) with the same inscriptions). "The last 2 signs of this seal are the same as those on one side of the 22 tablets (taking three strokes as a single sign)...Each tablet is three-sided with the inscription on each side comprising a single more complex sign accompanied by three or four simple strokes." The tablets are "incised with script that was to be read directly from the tablet." (Note by J. Mark Kenoyer & Richard H. meadow on Inscribed objects from Harappa excavations: 1986-2007 in: Asko Parpola, BM ande and Petteri Koskikallio eds., 2010, CISI, Vol.3: New material, untraced objects, and collections outside India and Pakistan, Part 1: Mohenjo-daro and Harappa, Helsinki, Suomalainen Tiedeakatemia, (pp.xliv to lviii), p. xliv http://www.harappa.com/indus/Kenoyer-Meadow-2010-HARP.pdf)

Harappa Script tablets are workshop product account tokens. Seals are technical aggregation of supercargo for shipment (caravan).

Tablets are account tokens of products produced in workshops. Seals consolidate or aggregate the information provided on tablets to prepare technical details for bills of lading.

The Harappa Script inscriptions on tiny tablets are linked to an identical segment of inscription on a Harappa seal (h1682A) with hieroglyphs of young bull + lathe. The tablets with inscriptions denote consignments coming out of furnace, smelter or smithy. These inscriptions are aggregated to signify as inscriptions on a seal (particularly the seals with hieroglyphs of young bull + lathe), an aggregation of supercargo metalwork, lapidary work (tools, implements, etc.) to be assigned to a sea-faring Meluhha merchant caravan.

This process of 'collection of consignments to constitute 'supercargo' shipment. This completes the technical specifications in a bill of lading process coming out of the fortification metalcaster, turner workshop.

Thus, the purport of tablets and seals is explained as an accounting process to provide information to prepare a bill of lading, handed over to the caravan leader by sealing the packages with the seal inscription as a technical recor of contents of the packages or shipment.

The discovery thanks to HARP (Kenoyer and Meadow)

A remarkable accounting process was indicated by the archaeologists Kenoyer and Meadow who unearthed a set of 22+6 tablets with identical inscriptions and a seal recording a part of this inscription. This seal (h1682A) also had hieroglyphs of young bull + lathe, together with five 'signs' composed of two signs from the tablets and three other signs. The first two signs on the seal (read from right) are taken from the inscriptions on one side of the 22+6 tablets (which had three sides with three inscriptions).

खांडा

h1682A

Three additionals signs on Seal h1682A, in addition to the two signs taken from 22+6 tiny tablets are read rebus:

[khāṇḍā] A division of a field. (Marathi) खंडणें (p. 192) [khaṇḍaṇēṃ] *v c* (खंडन S) To break; to reduce into parts (Marathi) Rebus: *khāṇḍā* 'metal tools, pots and pans' (Marathi)

Ku. *lokhaṛ* 'iron tools '; H. *lokhaṇḍ* m. ' iron tools, pots and pans '; G. *lokhā̃ḍ* n. 'tools, iron, ironware'; M. *lokhā̃ḍ* n. ' iron '(CDIAL 11171).

dula 'two' Rebus: dul 'cast metal'. Thus, the two divisions of field denoted by two rectangles with divisions are read together: *dul khāṇḍā* 'castings, metal tools, pots and pans'

kolmo 'three' Rebus: kolimi 'smithy'.

The first two signs read from right are explained as follows, since they are taken from the inscriptions on one side of 22+6 tiny tablets:*kuṭhi kaṇḍa kanka* 'smelting furnace account (scribe), supercargo' PLUS kolimi 'smithy'

Together, the five signs on the seal read: *dul khāṇḍā kolimi* 'castings, metal tools, pots and pans -- smithy' PLUS *kuṭhi kaṇḍa kanka kolimi* 'smelting furnace account (scribe) supercargo -- smithy'.

Hieroglyphs: lathe PLUS young bull rebus: 'caravan' PLUS turner: sã̄ghāṛɔ 'lathe', Rebus: sanghāta 'caravan'_सं-ग्रह *saṁgraha* 'a guardian , ruler , manager , arranger' R. BhP. खोंड [khōṇḍa] m A young bull, a bullcalf. (Marathi) గోద [gōda] gōda. [Tel.] n. An ox. A beast. kine, cattle.(Telugu) koḍiyum (G.) rebus: koḍ 'workshop' (G.) B. kõdā 'to turn in a lathe'; Or. kũnda 'lathe', kũdibā, kũd 'to turn' (→ Drav. Kur. kũd 'lathe') (CDIAL 3295)

Hieroglyph: *sãgaḍ*, 'lathe' (Meluhha) Rebus 1: *sãgaṛh* , 'fortification' (Meluhha). Rebus 2:*sanghAta* 'adamantine glue'. Rebus 3: *sangāṭh* संगाठ्'assembly, collection'. Rebus 4: *sãgaḍa* 'double-canoe, catamaran'. सं-ग्रह *saṁgraha* 'a guardian , ruler , manager , arranger' R. BhP.

Hieroglyph: one-horned young bull: खोंड (p. 216) [khōṇḍa] *m* A young bull, a bullcalf. Rebus: **कोंद** kōnda 'engraver, lapidary setting or infixing gemś (Marathi)

Hieroglyph: one-horned young bull: खोंड (p. 216) [khōṇḍa] *m* A young bull, a bullcalf.
Rebus: **कोंद** kōnda 'engraver, lapidary setting or infixing gemś (Marathi) **खोदगिरी** [khōdagirī] f Sculpture, carving, engraving.
ko_d.iya, ko_d.e = young bull; ko_d.elu = plump young bull; ko_d.e = a. male as in: ko_d.e du_d.a = bull calf; young, youthful (Telugu)
Hieroglyph: ko_t.u = horns (Ta.) ko_r (obl. ko_t-, pl. ko_hk) horn of cattle or wild animals (Go.); ko_r (pl. ko_hk), ko_r.u (pl. ko_hku) horn (Go.); kogoo a horn (Go.); ko_ju (pl. ko_ska) horn, antler (Kui)(DEDR 2200). Homonyms: kohk (Go.), gopka_ = branches (Kui), kob = branch (Ko.) gorka, gohka spear (Go.) gorka (Go)(DEDR 2126).
खोंड (p. 216) [khōṇḍa] *m* A young bull, a bullcalf. [2]

koḍ. = place where artisans work (G.lex.) koḍ. = a cow-pen; a cattlepen; a byre (G.lex.) gor.a = a cow-shed; a cattleshed; gor.a orak = byre (Santali.lex.) got.ho [Skt. kos.t.ha the inner part] a warehouse; an earthen vessel in wich indigo is stored (G.lex.) kot.t.amu = a stable (Telugu)

kot.iyum = a wooden circle put round the neck of an animal; kot. = neck (G.lex.) [cf. the orthography of rings on the neck of one-horned young bull].खोंड (p. 216) [khōṇḍa]A variety of जोंधळा.खोंडरूं (p. 216) [khōṇḍarūṃ] *n* A contemptuous form of खोंडा in the sense of कांबळा-cowl.खोंडा (p. 216) [khōṇḍā] *m* A कांबळा of which one end is formeḍ into a cowl or hood. 2 fig. A hollow amidst hills; a deep or a dark and retiring spot; a dell. 3 (also खोंडी & खोंडें) A variety of जोंधळा.खोंडी (p. 216) [khōṇḍī] *f* An outspread shovelform sack (as formeḍ temporarily out of a कांबळा, to hold or fend off grain, chaff &c.) Rebus: koTiya 'dhow, seafaring vessel'.

koḍ. = place where artisans work (G.lex.) koḍ. = a cow-pen; a cattlepen; a byre (G.lex.) gor.a = a cow-shed; a cattleshed; gor.a orak = byre (Santali.lex.) कोंड (p. 180) [kōṇḍa] A circular hedge or field-fence. 2 A circle described around a person under adjuration. 3 The circle at marbles. 4 A circular hamlet; a division of a मौजा or village, composed generally of the huts of one caste.कोंडडाव (p. 180) [kōṇḍaḍāva] *m* Ring taw; that form of marble-playing in which lines are drawn and divisions made:--as disting. from अगळडाव The play with holes.कोंडवाड (p. 180) [kōṇḍavāḍa] *n f* C (कोंडणें & वाडा) A pen or fold for cattle.कोंडाळें (p. 180) [kōṇḍāḷēṃ] *n* (कुंडली S) A ring or circularly inclosed space. 2 fig. A circle made by persons sitting round.

The Tiny tablets of Harappa

kuṭi 'water carrier' (Te.) Rebus: kuṭhi 'smelter furnace' (Santali) kuṛī f. 'fireplace' (H.); krvṛI f. 'granary (WPah.); kuṛī, kuṛo house, building'(Ku.)(CDIAL 3232) kuṭi 'hut made of boughs' (Skt.) guḍi temple (Telugu)

kaṇḍa kanka 'rim of jar' (Santali); rebus: furnace scribe. *kaṇḍa kanka* may be a dimunitive form of *kan-khār 'copper smith' comparable to the cognate gloss: kaṉṉār 'coppersmiths, blacksmiths' (Tamil) If so, kāṇḍa kan-khār connotes: 'copper-smith furnace.' *kāṇḍa* 'fire-altar (Santali); *kan* 'copper' (Ta.) Rebus: khaṇḍa 'a trench used as a fireplace when cooking has to be done for a large number of people' (Santali) kárṇaka m. ' projection on the side of a vessel, handle ' ŚBr. [kárṇa --]Pa. *kaṇṇaka* -- ' having ears or corners '; Wg. *kaṇə* ' ear -- ring ' NTS xvii 266; S. *kano* m. ' rim, border '; P. *kannā* m. ' obtuse angle of a kite ' (→ H. *kannā* m. ' edge, rim, handle '); N. *kānu* ' end of a rope for supporting a burden '; B. *kāṇā* ' brim of a cup ', G. *kānɔ* m.; M. *kānā* m. ' touch -- hole of a gun '.(CDIAL 2831).

kanka 'Rim of jar' (Santali); *karṇaka* rim of jar'(Skt.) Rebus: *karṇaka* 'scribe' (Te.); gaṇaka id. (Skt.) (Santali) kāraṇika m. ' teacher ' MBh., ' judge ' Pañcat. [kā- raṇa --] Pa. *usu* -- *kāraṇika* -- m. ' arrow -- maker '; Pk. *kāraṇiya* -- m. ' teacher of Nyāya '; S. *kāriṇī* m. ' guardian, heir '; N. *kārani* ' abettor in crime '; M. *kārṇī* m. ' prime minister, supercargo of a ship ', *kul* -- *karṇī* m. ' village accountant '.(CDIAL 3058). karṇadhāra m. ' helmsman ' Suśr. [kárṇa -- , dhāra -- 1]

Pa. *kaṇṇadhāra* -- m. ' helmsman '; Pk. *kaṇṇahāra* -- m. ' helmsman, sailor '; H. *kanahār* m. ' helmsman, fisherman '.(CDIAL 2836).

Thus, the 'rim-of-jar' glyph connotes: furnace account (scribe), supercargo.

Together with the glyph showing 'water-carrier', the ligatured glyphs of 'water-carrier' + 'rim-of-jar' can be read as: *kuṭhi kaṇḍa kanka* 'smelting furnace account (scribe), supercargo'.

Hieroglyph: kolom 'three' Rebus: kolimi 'smithy'

Pk. kaṇṇiā -- f. ' corner, pericarp of lotus '; Paš. kanī́ ' corner '(CDIAL 2849) kana, kanac 'corner' Rebus: kancu 'bronze, bellmetal' (Telugu) kaṁsá1 m. ' metal cup ' AV., m.n. ' bell -- metal ' Pat. as in S., but would in Pa. Pk. and most NIA. lggs. collide with kā́ṁsya -- to which L. P. testify and under which the remaining forms for the metal are listed. 2. ***kaṁsikā -- .**1. Pa. *kaṁsa* -- m. ' **bronze** dish '; S. *kañjho* m. ' bellmetal '; A. *kā̃h* ' gong '; Or. *kā̃sā* ' big pot of bell -- metal '; OMarw. *kāso* (= *kā̃* -- ?) m. ' bell -- metal tray for food, food '; G. *kā̃sā* m. pl. ' cymbals '; -- perh. Woṭ. *kasṓṭ* m. ' metal pot ' Buddruss Woṭ 109.

gaṇḍaka m. ' a coin worth **four** cowries ' lex., ' method of counting by fours ' W. [← Mu. Przyluski RoczOrj iv 234]S. *gaṇḍho* m. ' four in counting '; P. *gaṇḍā* m. ' four cowries '; B. Or. H. *gaṇḍā* m. 'a group of four, four cowries '; M. *gaṇḍā* m. ' aggregate of four cowries or pice '.With *du -- 2: OP. *dugāṇā* m. ' coin worth eight cowries '.(CDIAL 4001). Rebus: *kāṇḍa* 'fire-altar (Santali)

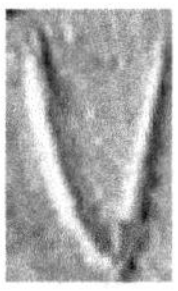

baṭa = wide-mouthed pot Rebus: *bhaṭ* 'kiln, furnace' (Hindi.Maithili) bhráṣṭra n. ' frying pan, gridiron ' MaitrS. [√bhrajj]Pk. *bhaṭṭha* -- m.n. ' gridiron '; K. *büṭhü* f. ' level surface by kitchen fireplace on which vessels are put when taken off fire '; S. *baṭhu* m. ' large pot in which grain is parched, large cooking fire ', *baṭhī* f. ' distilling furnace '; L. *bhaṭṭh* m. ' grain -- parcher's oven ', *bhaṭṭhī* f. ' kiln, distillery ', awāṇ. *bhaṭh*; P. *bhaṭṭh* m., °*ṭhī* f. ' furnace ', *bhaṭṭhā* m. ' kiln '; N. *bhāṭi* ' oven or vessel in which clothes are steamed for washing '; A. *bhaṭā* ' brick -- or lime -- kiln '; B. *bhāṭi* ' kiln '; Or. *bhāṭi* ' brick -- kiln, distilling pot '; Mth. *bhaṭhī*, *bhaṭṭī* ' brick -- kiln, furnace, still '; Aw.lakh. *bhāṭhā* ' kiln '; H. *bhaṭṭhā* m. ' kiln ',*bhaṭ* f. ' kiln, oven, fireplace '; M. *bhaṭṭā* m. ' **pot** of fire ', *bhaṭṭī* f. ' forge '.S.kcch. *bhaṭṭhī keṇī* ' distil (spirits) '.(CDIAL 9656).

The identical inscriptions on three sides of the following tablets: Side 1. *kuṭhi kaṇḍa kanka* 'smelting furnace account (scribe), supercargo' PLUS kolimi 'smithy'. Side 2. *bhaṭ* 'kiln, furnace' PLUS kāṇḍa 'fire-altar' Side 3. kanac 'bronze, mellmetal' PLUS kolimi 'smithy'.

The metalwork products are coming out of 'smithy' or 'furnace'. These products are aggregated as consignments which together constitute the supercargo. The consignments so received through accounting on tablets are consolidated into an inscription on a seal to constitute the supercargo, that is, cargo meant to be carried on a caravan on boat, by seafaring merchants. This intent is indicated by the 'lathe PLUS portable furnace' read rebus as: *sãghāṛɔ* 'lathe' Rebus: सं-ग्रह *saṁgraha* 'a guardian , ruler , manager , arranger' R. BhP. sangāṭa 'a collection of implement, tools, materials, apparatus, furniture OR collectively, metalwork, lapidary work'. That the metalwork or lapidary work is an aggregation of the work in a workshop by a turner, brassworker, engraver, joiner is indicated by the pictorial motif: young bull: *godhɔ* m. ' bull ', °*dhũ* n. ' **young bull** '(Gujarati)(CDIAL 4315) खोंड [khōṇḍa] m A young bull, a bullcalf. (Marathi) గోద [gōda] gōda. [Tel.] n. An ox. A beast. kine, cattle.(Telugu) koḍiyum (G.) rebus: koḍ 'workshop' (G.) B. kõdā 'to turn in a lathe'; Or. kũnda 'lathe', kũdibā, kũd 'to turn' (→ Drav. Kur. kũd 'lathe') (CDIAL 3295). The one horn ligatured to the young bull is a signifier (also a phonetic determinant) that the turner is at work in a workshop: koḍ. 'one horn'; rebus: koḍ. 'artisan's workshop' (Kuwi)

Hieroglyph: *sãghāṛɔ* m. 'lathe '(Gujarati); M. *sãgaḍ* f. 'part of a turner's apparatus'; *sãgāḍī* f. 'lathe' (Tulu) Rebus: सं-ग्रह *saṁgraha* 'a guardian , ruler , manager , arranger' R. BhP. sangāṭh संगाठ् । सामग्री m. (sg. dat. sangāṭas संगाटस्), a collection (of implements, tools, materials, for any object), apparatus, furniture, a collection of the things wanted on a journey, luggage, and so on. --karun -- करुन् । सामग्रीसंग्रहः m.inf. to collect the ab. (L.V. 17). (Kashmiri) saṁghaṭayati ' strikes (a musical instrument) ' R., ' joins together ' Kathās. [√ghaṭ] Pa. *saṅghaṭita* -- ' pegged together '; Pk. *saṁghaḍia*<-> ' joined ', caus. *saṁghaḍāvēi*; M. *sãgaḍṇẽ* ' to link together '. (CDIAL 12855).saṁghātá m. ' close union, mass ' TS., ' closing (a door) ' VS., ' dashing together ' MBh. [Cf. *saṁhata*<-> with similar range of meanings. -

- ghāta --]Pa. *saṅghāta* -- m. ' killing, knocking together '; Pk. *saṁghāya* -- m. ' closeness, collection '(CDIAL 12862).

"In the last four editions of South Asian Archaeology, we have given accounts of the different seasons of excavation at Harappa from 1989 to 1995 (4th season: Dales & Kenoyer 1992; 5th season: Kenoyer 1993; 6th season: Mcadow & Kenoyer 1994; 7th and 8th seasons: Meadow & Kenoyer 1997; see also Mcadow, ed. 1991: 1st through 5th seasons). In this edition we continue the tradition for the 9th and 10th seasons but focus on two specific areas of the site - the north end of Mound AB test trenched in 1996 (Kenoyer & Meadow, this volume) and the eastern margin of Mound E excavated since the 1993 season (this paper). Only partially covered in these reports is a particularly significant aspect ofthe work ofthe Harappa Archaeological Research Project (HARP) carried out during the 9th and 10th seasons. This involves an effort to re-investigate previously excavated parts of Harappa (Vats 1940; Wheeler 1947)"

Life and death of Harappa seals and tablets. An additional six copies of these tablets, again all with the same inscriptions, were found elsewhere in the debris outside of perimeter wall [250] including two near the group of 16 and two in debris between the perimeter and curtain walls. Here all 22 tablets are displayed together with a unicorn intaglio seal from the Period 3B street inside the perimeter wall, which has two of the same signs as those found on the tablets. (See also145, 146, 147, 148, 149, 150). Quoting from R.H. Meadow and J.M. Kenoyer's article in South Asian Archaeology 1997 (Rome, 2001): "It is tempting to think that the evident loss of utility and subsequent discard of the tablets is related to the "death" of the seal. Seals are almost always found in trash or street deposits (and never yet in a grave) indicating that they were either lost or intentionally discarded, the latter seeming the more likely in most instances. The end of the utility of a seal must relate to some life event of its owner, whether change of status, or death, or the passing of an amount of time during which the seal was considered current. A related consideration is that apparently neither seals nor tablets could be used by just anyone or for any length of time because otherwise they would not have fallen out of circulation. Thus the use of seals -- and of tablets -- was possible only if they were known to be current. Once they were no longer current, they were discarded. This would help explain why a group of 16 (or 18) tablets with the same inscriptions, kept together perhaps in a cloth or leather pouch, could have been deposited with other trash outside of the perimeter wall of Mound E."

Period 3B debris related to: c. 2450 BCE - c. 2200 BCE.

Examples of 22 duplicates steatite triangular tablets h-2218 to h-2239

h2219A First side of three-sided tablet

h2219B Second side of three-sided tablet

h2219C Third side of three-sided tablet

The two glyphs which appear on the h2219A example also appear on a seal. "In a street deposit of similar age just inside the wall, a seal was found with two of the same characters as seen on one side of the tablets."

While the 22 tablets were meant to help in 'tallying' the products produced by the artisans, the seal was meant to be used in preparing a bill of lading for the products to be couriered through containers.

h1682A. The seal which contained the set of hieroglyphs used on the 'tally' three-sided tablets. The seal showed a one-horned heifer + standard device and two segments of inscriptions: one segment from the 'tally' tablet; the other segment showing hieroglyphs of a pair of 'rectangle with divisions' + 'three long linear strokes'.

Decoding a pair of glyphs, a pair of 'rectangle with divisions': khaṇḍ 'field, division' (Skt.); Rebus: kaṇḍ 'furnace' (Skt.) Thus, reduplicated glyph connotes dul kaṇḍ 'casting furnace'. Vikalpa: khonḍu 'divided into parts (Kashmiri)khonḍu I खण्डितः, विकलावयवः adj. (f. khünḍü 1, sg. dat. khanjĕ 1 खंज्य), broken, divided into parts; hence, deprived of a part or limb or member, maimeḍ, mutilated; unevenly formeḍ, irregularly angled. (Kashmiri) A pair of such glyphs divided into parts, may thus be decoded as: dul kaṇḍ khonḍu khonḍ 'casting furnace workshop'. Vikalpa 1: jaṇḍ khaṇḍ = ivory (Jat.ki) khaṇḍi_ = ivory in rough (Jat.ki_); gaṭī = piece of elephant's tusk (S.) Vikalpa 2: Pa.kandi (pl. -l) necklace, beads. Ga. (P.) kandi (pl. -l) bead, (pl.) necklace; (S.2)kandiṭ bead (DEDR 1215). kandil, kandīl = a globe of glass, a lantern (Ka.lex.) The pair of glyphs 'rectangle with divisions' may thus also connote 'cast beads'. If so, the seal text inscription connotes two sets of products assembled for despatched through a courier: furnace metal products + furnace bead products.

Both sets of products are from the sanga turner's workshop.

Decoding the glyph, 'three long linear strokes': 'three'; rebus: 'smithy' (Santali)

Glyph of standard device in front of the one-horned heifer: sā~gāḍī lathe (Tu.)(CDIAL 12859). sāṅgaḍa That member of a turner's apparatus by which the piece to be turned is confined and steadied. सांगडीस धरणें To take into linkedness or close connection with, lit. fig. (Marathi) सांगाडी [sāṅgāḍī] f The machine within which a turner confines and steadies the piece he has to turn. (Marathi)सगडी [sagaḍī] f (Commonly शेगडी) A pan of live coals or embers. (Marathi) san:ghāḍo, saghaḍī (G.) = firepan;

saghaḍī, śaghaḍi = a pot for holding fire (G.)[culā sagaḍī portable hearth (G.)] rebus: सं-ग्रह *saṁgraha* 'a guardian , ruler , manager , arranger' R. BhP.

Thus, the entire set of glyphs on the h1682A seal [denoting the heifer + standard device] can be decoded: koḍiyum 'heifer'; [kōḍiya] kōḍe, kōḍiya. [Tel.] n. A bullcalf. . k* దూడA young bull. Plumpness, prime. తరుణము. జోడుకోడయలు a pair of bullocks. kōḍe adj. Young. kōḍe-kāḍu. n. A young man.పడుచువాడు. [kārukōḍe] kāru-kōḍe. [Tel.] n. A bull in its prime. खोंड [khōṇḍa] m A young bull, a bullcalf. (Marathi) గోద [gōda] gōda. [Tel.] n. An ox. A beast. kine, cattle.(Telugu) koḍiyum (G.) rebus: koḍ 'workshop' (G.) B. kõdā 'to turn in a lathe'; Or. kŭnda 'lathe', kũdibā, kũd 'to turn' (→ Drav. Kur. kũd 'lathe') (CDIAL 3295)

The two glyphs (heifer + lathe) together thus refer to a turner's workshop with a portable hearth. The two sets of the text of the inscription refer to the products assembled together (perhaps on the circular working platforms) by this workshop of the guild. The sets of products denoted by the two sets of glyphic sequences can be explained rebus:

The inscription on seal h1682A can be explained in the context of the tablets used as tally tokens to account for the despatch of the assembled products (delivered by the guild artisans) using the impression of the seal as a bill of lading.

"...these inscribed steatite tablets which Vats (1940) called 'tiny steatite seals', are not seals at all but are incised with script that was to be read directly from the tablet. And along with the steatite tablets are found terracotta and glazed faience tablets with molded bas-relief script, motifs and narrative cenes, which also start appearing in mid-Period 3B and continue into Period 3C (ca. 2400 to ca. 2000 BCE)...Unlike seals, almost all of which are unique, an important aspect of tablets is that, at Harappa (as well as at Mohenjo-daro), there are numerous instances of (1) incised steatite tablets with copies of the same signs and/or motifs and (2) duplicate bas-relief tablets of faience or terracotta made from the same mold...Copies of incised tablets and duplicates of molded tablets have been found in large numbers in two noteworthy instances of Harappa: script copies incised into 22 rectangular steatite tablets, triangular in section, from secondary deposits of Period 3B on the outside of the perimeter wall in Trench 11 on the East side of Mound E...H-2218 through H-2239."

Numeral strokes and miniature tablets

A characteristic feature of objects with Harppa Script is that they are of very small size. Many miniature tablets found at Harappa, for example, are thumb-nail sized. Within such a small space, remarkable messaging is accomplished using hypertexts.

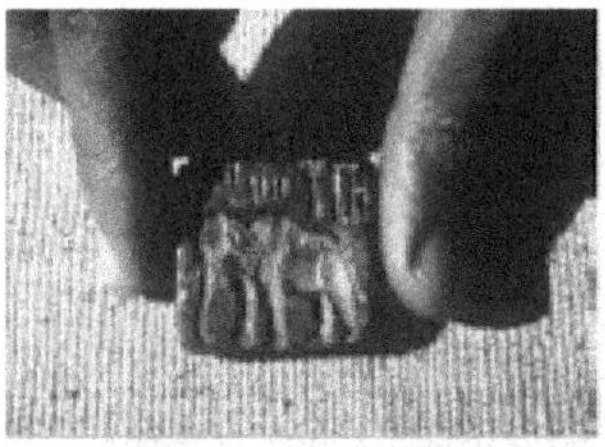

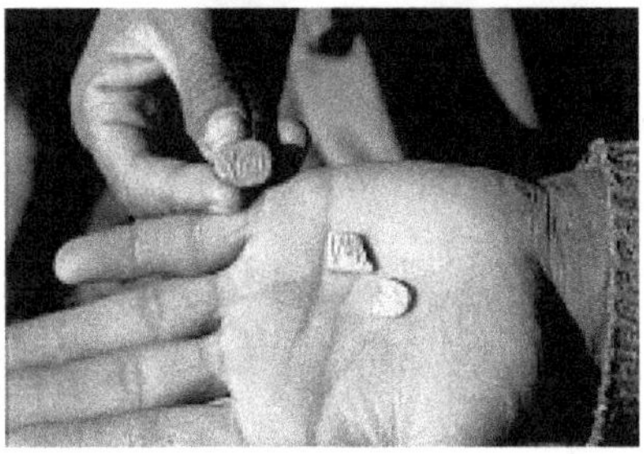

Data mining of Harappa Script Corpora (about 7000 objects with inscriptions) yields a remarkable feature of Harappa tablets (i.e. sealings as multiples and tablets both on tiny steate tablets and other multi-sided tablets). The feature is occurrence of multiple hypertexts (strings of hieroglyph-multiplexes).

Many tiny steatite inscised tablets also, as prism tablets add on one side three dotted circles, tridhAtu 'three strandś rebus: tri-dhAtu 'three minerals' to confirm that the product descriptions relate to baraDo 'an alloy of three minerals, copper, pewter and perhaps zinc'. On h979, for example, the rebus readings are: Side C: *tridhAtu* 'three dotted circles' rebus: *tridhAtu* 'three minerals' PLUS Side A khāreḍo = a **currycomb** (G.) Rebus: khārādī ' turner' (G.) *karṇika, kanka* 'rim of jar' rebus: kaṇḍa kanka 'smelting furnace account (scribe), *karNI*, supercargo' *baraDo* 'spine' Rebus: भरत 'alloy of pewter, copper, tin'.(Frequency of occurrence 41) *kolmo* 'three' rebus: *kolimi* 'smithy, forge' PLUS *baṭa* 'rimless pot' rebus: *bhaṭa* 'furnace'.

Note: Frenquency of hypertext string Signs 176, 342 and 48 (centre-piece oval in venn diagram) is in reference to Mahadevan corpus. The occurrences will be more if HARP discoveries are reckoned. The string of three hieroglyphs signifies भरत 'alloy of pewter, copper, tin' ready as supercargo (for seafaring merchants) and for turners in smithy.

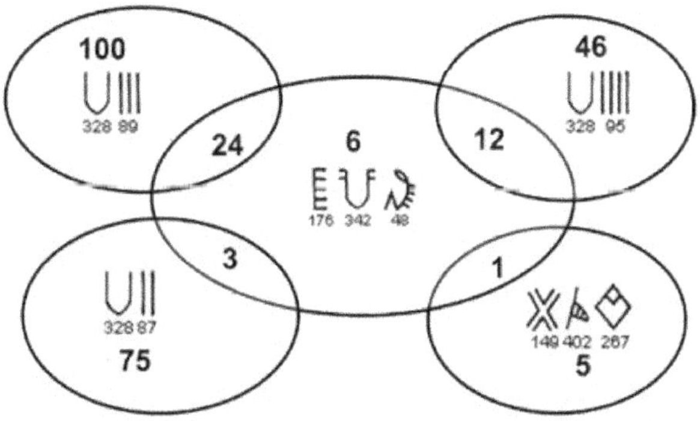

Figure 12. Venn diagram of the four most frequent texts in M77. The number of times a pair of texts appears on different sides of objects is marked in the overlapping region of the Venn diagram.

h978Aith978Bith978Cit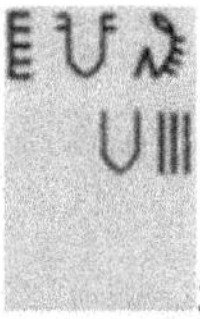5412

h979Aith979Bith979Cit

h980Aith980Bith980Cit

khāreḍo = a **currycomb** (G.) Rebus: khārādī ' turner' (G.) karṇika, kanka 'rim of jar' rebus: kaṇḍa kanka 'smelting furnace account (scribe), **karNI**, supercargo' **baraDo** 'spine' Rebus: भरत 'alloy of pewter, copper, tin'.(Frequency of occurrence 41) Note: Frenquency is in reference to Mahadevan corpus. The occurrences will be more if HARP discoveries are reckoned. The string of three hieroglyphs signifies भरत 'alloy of pewter, copper, tin'.ready as supercargo (for seafaring merchants) and for turners in smithy.

Many examples of such smultiple inscriptions on Harappa tablets have been noted by Meadow and Kenoyer (Meadow, Richard H. and Jonathan Kenoyer, 1997, The 'tinysteatite seals' (incised steatitetablets) of Harappa: Some observations ontheir context and dating in: Taddei, Maurizio and Giuseppe de Marco, 2000, *South Asian Archaeology, 1997*, Rome, Istituto Italiano per l'Africa e l'Oriente.After Fig. 3, p.12 Harappa 1995-1997: Mounds E and ET; molded terracotta tablets)

Mint, workshop (for) native metal, furnace, smithy

kalibangan 059a shows structural groups of numeral strokes, together with a 'bow' glyph.

kamāt.hiyo = archer; *kāmaṭhum* = a bow; *ka_mad.i_, ka_mad.um* = a chip of bamboo (G.) *ka_maṭhiyo* a bowman; an archer (Skt.lex.) Rebus: *kammaṭa* = portable furnace (Te.) *kampaṭṭam* coiner, mint (Ta.)

One short numeral stroke: sal stake, spike, splinter, thorn, difficulty (H.); rebus: sal 'workshop' (Santali)

One long numeral stroke with superscripte of two short strokes: *koḍ.a* = in arithmetic, one (Santali) Together with pairing sign Sign 99 : at.ar a splinter; at.aruka to burst, crack, slit off, fly open;at.arcca splitting, a crack; at.arttuka to split, tear off, open (an oyster)(Ma.); *ad.aruni* to crack (Tu.)(DEDR 66) Rebus: *koḍ.* 'workshop' (G.); *aduru* 'native metal' (Ka.)

The numeral strokes should be read as: 3+2 (non-superscript). *kolmo* 'three'; rebus: *kolimi* 'forge' (Te.); *dula* 'pair'; rebus: *dul* 'cast' as in *dul mer.ed* 'cast iron' (Santali). Thus 3+2 are decoded as: forging, casting (smithy)] *asta, dasta* 'five' (Kafiri) Rebus: *jasta, sattva* 'zinc'.

Examples of miniature tablets which are an expansion of the token shapes of ancient Near East may be seen with Harappa Script writing on the following 7 clusters of images. The writing deploys hieroglyphs. On one stream of evolution, the wedge-shape becomes a glyphic component of cuneiform writing; on another stream of evolution, the token-shapes get deployed with Harappa Script writing. That this deployment is closely related to the bronze-age revolution of tin- and zinc-bronzes and other metal alloys has been demonstrated by the cipher using rebus readings of hieroglyphs with the underlying sounds of lexemes evidenced from lexemes of Bharata sprachbund:

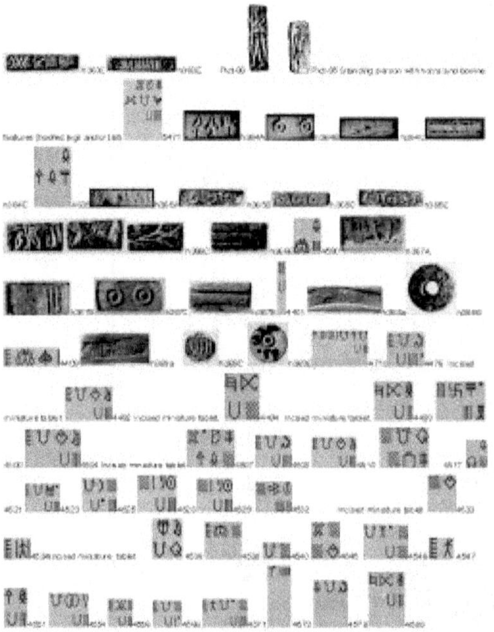

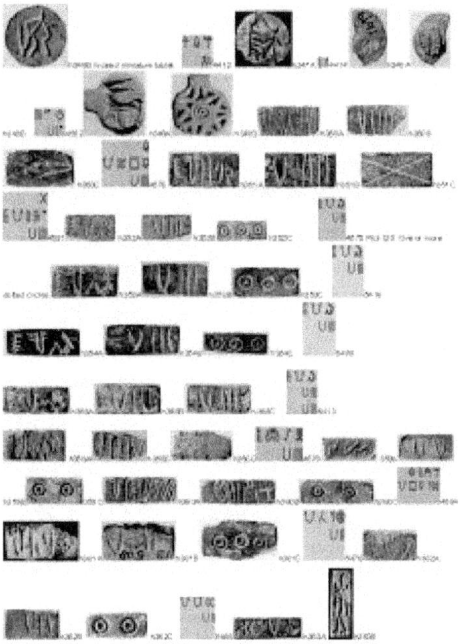

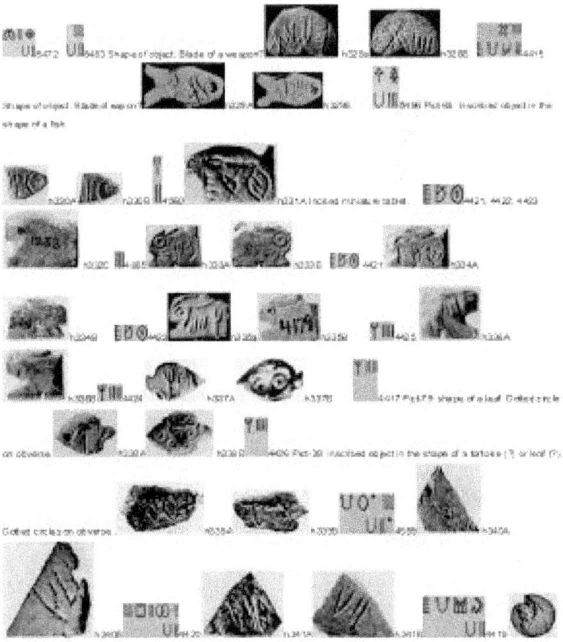

Shape of object: Blade of a weapon?
Incised object in the shape of a fish.
Incised miniature tablet.
4421, 4422, 4423
shape of a leaf. Dotted circle on obverse.
Incised object in the shape of a tortoise (?) or leaf (?)
Dotted circles on obverse.

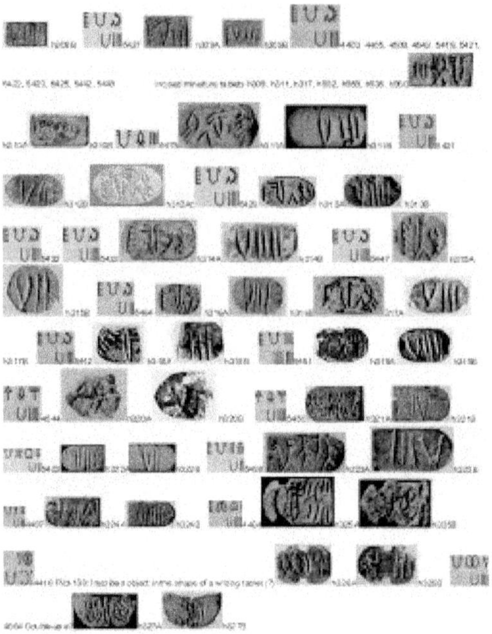

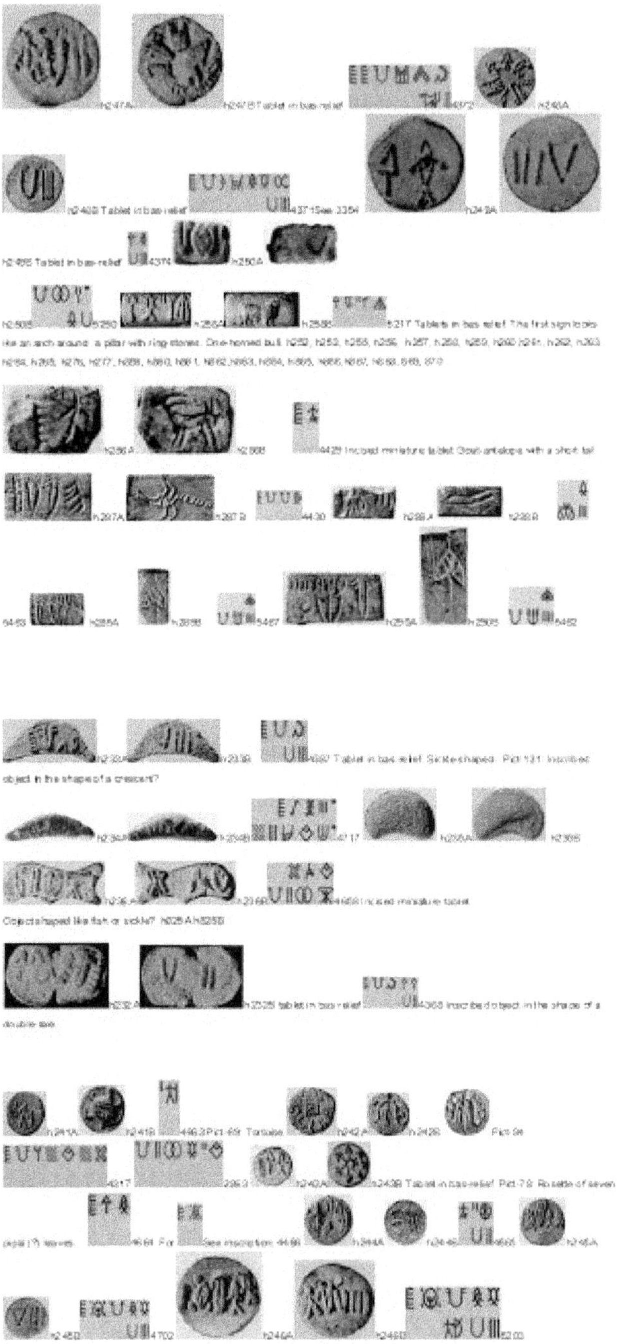

Most of the hieroglyphs on these tablets have been read rebus using the underlying sounds of substratum lexemes in Bharata sprachbund languages which are veritable substratum meluhha/mleccha lexemes. Further language studies on the sprachbundwill help identify the cluster of glosses related to metalware starting from ca. 4th millennium BCE in the linguistic area. It has been demonstrated in the context of HARP discoveries that the tablets could have been used to document metallurgical accounting transactions from furnace/ smelter to working platforms and from working platforms into the warehouse for further documentation on seals and documentation of jangaḍ 'entrustment articles' transactions through jangaḍiyo 'couriers, military guards who accompany treasure into the treasury' (Gujarati).

Short and long linear strokes also occur on inscriptions associated with other 'text signs'. These numeral signifiers may signify quantities or may also be treated as hypertexts signifying in words the number signified. For e.g., two short numeral strokes (like double-parenthesis) which often occur as superscripts may signify sal 'splinter' rebus: sal 'workshop'; a short numeral stroke (like single parenthesis) which occurs as superscript may signify: खाडा [khāṇḍā] 'A jag, notch, or indentation (as upon the edge of a tool or weapon)' Rebus: kāṇḍa 'implements (Santali). Three long linear strokes may signify kolom 'three' rebus: kolimi 'smithy, forge'.

Annex D

Ligatures to *ayo, aya* ‘fish’ rebus: *aya* ‘iron’ *ayas* ‘metal’, *meḍ* ‘body’ rebus: *meḍ* ‘iron’ semantic modifiers as hypertexts and Harappa Script inscriptions on 240 copper tablets

B19 and C6 are two categories of 21 copper plate inscriptions in Harappa Script. Are they allographs (hieroglyphs with identical lexemes and meanings)? Evidence of many multiples of inscriptions points to the messages being work-in-process accounts of artisans working in multiple circular platforms, for example, of Harappa.

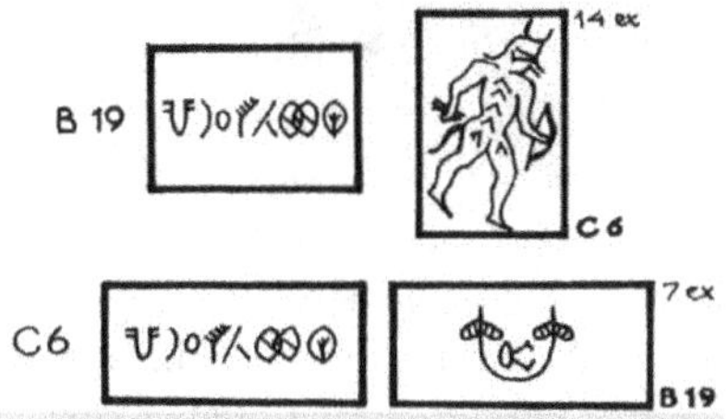

After Fig. 21.15 Parpola, 2015 opcit. A ‘pictorial translation’ of an Indus sign: the identical inscriptions on the obverse sides correlate the ‘horned archer’ on the reverse of the type B-19 (there are fourteen identical tablets of this type) and the ‘fig+crab’ sign on the reverse of the type C-6 (there are seven identical tablets of this type) among the copper tablets from Mohenjo-daro.[244] Countering the apparent correlation of two hypertexts, the decipherment has shown that C6 hypertext is *kauṭilikḥ* कौटिलिकः 1 A hunter.-2 A blacksmith; while the B19 hypertext is *dul lohakAru/lōhāra* ‘metal casting coppersmith’ (perhaps a *dhokra kamar* ‘*cire perdue* metal casting artisan’).

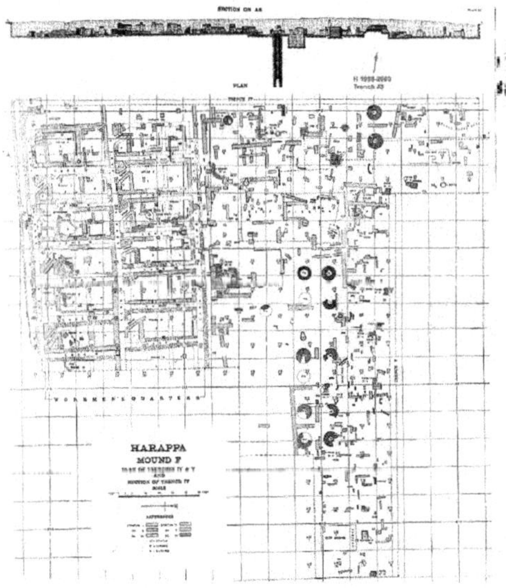

Plan of Vat's excavations showing circular platforms. In some cases remnants of the baked brick walls that probably surrounded each platform can be seen on the plan, although earlier and later walls are also shown. From M.S. Vats (1940) Excavations at Harappa. These could be called *pathār*, °*rɔ* ‘expanse’ *paTTaDe* ‘anvils’ set in the centre, of the platform where *pattharaka,* ‘merchants’ proclaimeḍ, traded their metal wares.

Different sizes and colors of ringstones from upper Harappa phase levels of Mound AB, Trench 39N. The smaller rings may have been used to make decorative columns while the larger ones were probably column bases.[245] Such ringstones may have been used on a stone or metal pillar (to hold the anvil steady) in the centre of the circular platforms for metal forge work by *sangatarAsu* 'stone cutters' and *kondar* 'turners, lapidaries'. The set of circular platforms may constitute Harappa Script hieroglyphs *pattar* 'trough' rebus: *pattar* 'guild' and *sal* 'splinter' rebus: *sal* 'workshop'.

Guild of workmen: ringstone pillar + awning

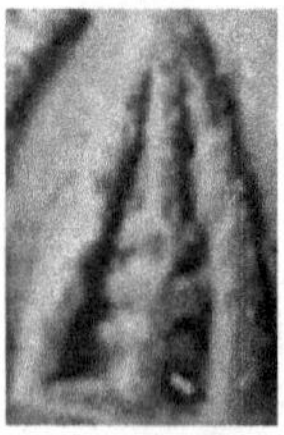

The importance of these circular platforms in the life activities of people of the civilization is evident from 31 multiples of inscriptions signifying a unique hieroglyph, an anvil with an awning. This is NOT a triangle with horizontal lines parallel to the base but stone rings on a stone pillar or metal rod and the area of the circular platform covered by an awning or roof. The awning or tent is: *śrēṇikā* -- f. ' tent ' (Samskrtam) *seṇi* 'row of rafters in a thatched roof' (CDIAL 12718) rebus: *śrēṇi* 'guild'. Thus, together, *pattharaka seni* 'guild of merchants'. This unique hieroglyph may be read as *paṭṭaṭai,* n. prob. படு¹- +அடை¹-. 1. [*Ta. paṭṭika, Ka. paṭṭaḍe.*] Anvil Rebus: *pattar* 'guild of goldsmiths'. *Ta. paṭaṅku* tent, awning, curtain; *paṭaṅkam* tent. *Ma. paṭaṅṅu* tent, awning (DEDR 3839). Thus, a total of 21 copper plates and 31 inscriptions on tablets with multiple inscriptions of the same text message may relate to smiths' work in a forge, beating metalware to shape using the anvils. Such a workplace organization along the major street of Harappa signifies பட்டறை² *paṭṭaṛai, n.* < K. *paṭṭale.* 1. Community; சனக்கூட்டம். 2. Guild, as of workmen; தொழிலாளர் சமுதாயம். Lexis cognate with the orthography of the stone-ring anvil: *Ka. ēṇ, ēṇu edge*, border, point. *Te. (VPK, intro. p. 123) ēnu* one edge of a blade of hoe or spade. *Ta. ēṇ, ēṇam, ēṇai, ēṭci Ta. ēṇ, ēṇam, ēṇai, ēṭci* firmness, stability; eṇ strength; (Tinn.) *ēṇu* to support. *Ma. ēṇam* steadfastness; ēṇu energy, firmness, stability (DEDR 886, 887).

Meluhha (Bharata *sprachbund*) lexis: *lohakāra* a metal worker, coppersmith, blacksmith Miln 331 (Pali) *lōhakāra* m. ' iron -- worker ', °*rī* -- f., °*raka* -- m. lex., *lauhakāra* -- m. Hit. [lōhá -- , kāra -- 1]Pa. *lōhakāra* -- m. ' coppersmith, ironsmith '; Pk. *lōhāra* -- m. ' blacksmith ', S. *luhāru* m., L. *lohār* m., °*rī* f., awāṇ. *luhār*, P. WPah.khaś. bhal. *luhār* m., Ku. *lwār*, N. B. *lohār*, Or. *lohaḷa*, Bi.Bhoj. Aw.lakh. *lohār*, H. *lohār*, *luh*° m., G. *lavār* m., M. *lohār* m.; Si. *lōvaru* ' coppersmith '. Addenda: *lōhakāra* -- : WPah.kṭg. (kc.) *lhwā`r* m. ' blacksmith ', *lhwàri* f. ' his wife ', Garh. *lwār* m. (CDIAL 11159).

C6 and B19 are NOT allographs. One is a metal casting coppersmith while the othr is a blacksmith. C6 and B19 inscriptions are remarkable examples of unambiguous, precise rendering of technical specifications of metal work catalogues in Harapp Script.

Mirroring of images in the writing system is a device to signify that *cire perdue* (lost-wax) technique is used for casting metal objects or sculptures. A decipherment has been posited based on the functions served by the writing system. The functions are to document metalwork, listing resources, lapidary/turner/joiner techniques and metal casting techniques.

Databases of 240 copper tablets and scores of inscriptions on metal artifacts are veritable manuals of metallurgical processing. The entire Harappa Script Corpora are data archives of metalwork documented for data mining and knowledge discovery.

Harappa Script Corpora evidences document metalwork, mintwork, lapidary/turner/joiner work on 240 copper/bronze tablets, hieroglyphs painted on a gold pendant, incised gold fillet, raised script on gold filet, scores of implements/weapons -- all of which signify unique artisanal competence to write inscriptions on metal.

The catalogues of metalwork, include repeated references to मृदुकृष्णायसम् soft-iron, rendered in Prakritam phonetic forms as: *mẽṛhẽt*, *meḍ*, *meḍ* (Bharata *sprachbund* and Slavic languages).

The modifiers to the 'fish' hieroglyph which commonly occur together are: slanted stroke, notch, fins, lid-of-pot ligatured as superfix:

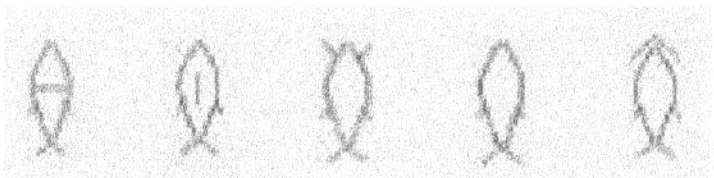

Each modified 'fish' hieroglyph constitutes a Meluhha expression. Two or three such expressions occur in sequence in Harappa Script inscriptions.

The meaning of 'ayaś in Rigveda has been uncertain and conjectures have been made from the texts as ex presentation by **Arthur Anthony Macdonell, and Arthur Berriedale Keith**

Ayas.—The exact metal denoted by this word when used by itself, as always in the Rigveda,[1] is uncertain. As favouring the sense of 'bronze' rather than that of 'iron' may perhaps be cited with Zimmer[2] the fact that Agni is called *ayo-daṃṣṭra*, 'with teeth of Ayas,'[3] with reference to the colour of his flames, and that the car-seat of Mitra and Varuṇa is called *ayaḥ-sthūṇa*,[4] 'with pillars of Ayas' at the setting of the sun.[5] Moreover, in the Vājasaneyi Saṃhitā,[6] Ayas is enumerated in a list of six metals: gold (*hiraṇya*), Ayas, Śyāma, Loha, lead (*sīsa*), tin (*trapu*). Here *śyāma* ('swarthy') and *loha* ('red') must mean 'iron' and 'copper' respectively; *ayas* would therefore seem to mean 'bronze.' In many passages in the Atharvaveda[7] and other books, the Ayas is divided into two species—the *śyāma* ('iron') and the *lohita* ('copper' or 'bronze'). In the Śatapatha Brāhmaṇa[8] a distinction is drawn between Ayas and *lohāyasa*, which may either be a distinction between iron and copper as understood by Eggeling,[9] or between copper and bronze as held by Schrader.[10] In one passage of the Atharvaveda,[11] the sense of iron seems certain. Possibly, too, the arrow of the Rigveda,[12] which had a tip of Ayas (*yasyā ayo mukham*), was pointed with iron. Copper, however, is conceivable, and bronze quite likely.

Iron is called *śyāma ayas* or *śyāma* alone.[13] See also **Kārṣṇāyasa**. Copper is **Lohāyasa** or **Lohitāyasa**.

The smelting (*dhmā* 'to blow') of the metal is frequently referred to. The Śatapatha Brāhmaṇa[14] states that if 'well smelted' (*bahu-dhmātam*) it is like gold, referring evidently to bronze. A heater of Ayas is mentioned in the Vājasaneyi Saṃhitā,[15] and bowls of Ayas are also spoken of.[16]

[1] Rv. i. 57, 3; 163, 9; iv. 2, 17; vi. 3, 5.

[2] *Altindisches Leben*, 52.

[3] Rv. i. 88, 5; x. 87, 2.

[4] Rv. v. 62, 8 (*cf.* 7).

[5] But this is not convincing, as in the same verse it is said to be 'of golden appearance at the flush of dawn.'

[6] xviii. 13.

[7] xi. 3, 1, 7; Maitrāyaṇī Saṃhitā, iv. 2, 9.

[8] v. 4, 1, 2.

[9] *Sacred Books of the East*, 41, 90.

[10] *Prehistoric Antiquities*, 189.

[11] v. 28, 1.

[12] vi. 75, 15.

[13] Av. ix. 5, 4.

[14] vi. 1, 3, 5. *Cf.* vi. 1, 1, 13; v. 1, 2, 14; xii. 7, 1, 7; 2, 10, etc.

[15] xxx. 14; Taittirīya Brāhmaṇa, iii. 4, 10, 1.

[16] Av. viii. 10, 22; Maitrāyaṇī Saṃhitā, iv. 2, 13.

Aya-sthūṇa.—He was Gṛhapati ('householder,' the sacrificer at sacrificial sessions) of those whose Adhvaryu was Śaulvāyana, and taught the latter the proper mode of using certain spoons.[1]

[1] Śatapatha Brāhmaṇa, xi. 4, 2, 17 *et seq.*

Ayāsya Āṅgirasa.—This sage appears to be mentioned in two passages of the Rigveda,[1] and the Anukramaṇī ascribes to him several hymns of the Rigveda (ix. 44-46; x. 67; 68). In the Brāhmaṇa tradition he was Udgātṛ at the Rājasūya or Royal Inauguration Sacrifice, at which Śunaḥśepa was to have been slain,[2] and his Udgītha (Sāmaveda chant) is referred to elsewhere.[3] He is also referred to several times as a ritual

[1] x. 67, 1; 108, 8. Perhaps x. 92, 15 also refers to him, but not i. 62, 7; x. 138, 4.

[2] Aitareya Brāhmaṇa, vii. 16.

[3] Jaiminīya Upaniṣad Brāhmaṇa, ii. 7, 2, 6; 8, 3. *Cf.* Chāndogya Upaniṣad, i. 2, 12.

authority.[4] In the Vaṃśas, or Genealogies of the Bṛhadāraṇyaka Upaniṣad,[5] he is named as the pupil of Ābhūti Tvāṣṭra.

[4] Pañcaviṃśa Brāhmaṇa, xiv. 3, 22; xvi. 12, 4; xi. 8, 10; Bṛhadāraṇyaka Upaniṣad, i. 3, 8. 19. 24; Kauṣītaki Brāhmaṇa, xxx. 6.

[5] ii. 6, 3; iv. 6, 3 (in both recensions).

Cf. Ludwig, Translation of the Rigveda, 3. 136; Hillebrandt, *Vedische Mythologie*, 2, 159; Weber, *Indische Studien*, 1, 255, n.; Pischel, *Vedische Studien*, 3, 204.

Source: Arthur Anthony Macdonell, Arthur Berriedale Keith (eds.),

Vedic Index of Names and Subjects, Volume 1 Motilal Banarsidass Publisher, 1995

A more precise understanding of the gloss *'ayas'* comes from the frequent use of a hieroglyph on Harappa Script inscriptions.

A Munda gloss for fish is '*aya*'. Read rebus: *aya* 'iron' (Gujarati) *ayas* 'metal' (Vedic).

Hieroglyph of Harppa Script: *beḍa hako (ayo)* 'fish' (Santali); *beḍa* 'either of the sides of a hearth' (G.) Munda: So. *ayo* `fish'. *Go. ayu `fish'. Go <ayu> (Z), <ayu?u> (Z),, <ayu?> (A) {N} ``^fish''. Kh. kaDOG `fish'. Sa. Hako `fish'. Mu. hai (H) ~ haku(N) ~ haikO(M) `fish'. Ho haku `fish'. Bj. hai `fish'. Bh.haku `fish'. KW haiku ~ hakO |Analyzed hai-kO, ha-kO (RDM). Ku. Kaku`fish'.@(V064,M106) Mu. ha-i, haku `fish' (HJP). @(V341) ayu>(Z), <ayu?u> (Z) <ayu?>(A) {N} ``^fish''. #1370. <yO>\\<AyO>(L) {N} ``^fish''. #3612. <kukkulEyO>,,<kukkuli-yO>(LMD) {N} ``prawn''. !Serango dialect. #32612. <sArjAjyO>,,<sArjAj>(D) {N} ``prawn''. #32622. <magur-yO>(ZL) {N} ``a kind of ^fish''. *Or.<>. #32632. <ur+GOl-Da-yO>*(LL) {N} ``a kind of ^fish''. #32642.*<bal.bal-yO>*(DL) {N} ``smoked fish''. #15163. Vikalpa: Munda: *<aDara>*(L) {N} ``^scales of a fish, sharp bark of a tree''.#10171. So*<aDara>*(L) {N} ``^scales of a fish, sharp bark of a tree''.

Munda: So. *ayo* `fish'. Go. *ayu* `fish'. Go *<ayu>* (Z), *<ayu?u> (Z),, <ayu?> (A) {N} ``^fish''. Kh. kaDOG `fish'. Sa. Hako `fish'. Mu. hai (H) ~ haku(N) ~ haikO(M) `fish'. Ho haku `fish'. Bj. hai `fish'. Bh.haku `fish'. KW haiku ~ hakO |Analyzed hai-kO, ha-kO (RDM). Ku. Kaku`fish'.@(V064,M106) Mu. ha-i, haku `fish' (HJP). @(V341) ayu>(Z), <ayu?u> (Z) <ayu?>(A) {N} ``^fish''. #1370. <yO>\\<AyO>(L) {N} ``^fish''. #3612. <kukkulEyO>,,<kukkuli-yO>(LMD) {N}* ``prawn''. !Serango dialect. #32612. *<sArjAjyO>,,<sArjA*j>(D) {N} ``prawn''. #32622. *<magur-yO>*(ZL) {N} ``a kind of ^fish''. *Or.<>. #32632. *<ur+GOl-Da-yO>*(LL) {N} ``a kind of ^fish''. #32642.*<bal.bal-yO>*(DL) {N} ``smoked fish''. #15163. Vikalpa: Munda: *<aDara>*(L) {N} ``^scales of a fish, sharp bark of a tree''.#10171. So*<aDara>*(L) {N} ``^scales of a fish, sharp bark of a tree''.[246]

Bharata mackerel Ta. *ayirai, acarai, acalai* loach, sandy colour, Cobitis thermalis; ayilai a kind of fish. Ma. a*yala* a fish, mackerel, scomber; *aila, ayila* a fish; ayira a kind of small fish, loach (DEDR 191)

Rebus: *aduru* native metal (Ka.); *ayil* iron (Ta.) *ayir, ayiram* any ore (Ma.); *ajirda karba* very hard iron (Tu.)(DEDR 192). Ta. *ayil* javelin, *lance, surgical knife, lancet.Ma. ayil javelin, lance; ayiri surgical knife, lancet. (DEDR 193). aduru = gan.iyinda tegadu karagade iruva aduru* = ore taken from the mine and not subjected to melting in a furnace (Ka. Siddhānti Subrahmaṇya' Śastri's new interpretation of the AmarakoŚa, Bangalore, Vicaradarpana Press, 1872, p.330); *adar* = fine sand (Ta.); ayir – iron dust, any ore (Ma.) Kur. *adar* the waste of pounded rice, broken grains, etc.

Malt. *adru* broken grain (DEDR 134). Ma. *aśu* thin, slender; *ayir, ayiram* iron dust.Ta. ayir subtlety, fineness, fine sand, candied sugar; ? atar fine sand, dust. அய.ர[3] ayir, n. 1. Subtlety, fineness; நணசம. (த_வ_.) 2. [M. *ayir]* Fine sand; நணமணல. (மலசலப. 92.) *ayiram*, n. Candied sugar; *ayil*, n. cf. *ayas*. 1. Iron; 2. Surgical knife, lancet; Javelin, lance; *ayilavaṉ*, Skāṇḍa, as bearing a javelin (DEDR 341).Tu. *gadarů* a lump (DEDR 1196) *áyas* n. ' metal, iron ' RV.Pa. *ayō* nom. sg. n. and m., *aya* -- n. ' iron ', Pk. *aya* -- n., Si. *ya.ayaścūrṇa* -- , *ayaskāṇḍa* -- , **ayaskūṭa* -- .Addenda: *áyas* -- : Md. *da* ' iron ', *dafat* ' piece of iron '.*ayaskāṇḍa* m.n. ' a quantity of iron, excellent iron ' Pāṇ. gaṇ. [*áyas* -- , *kā´ṇḍa* --]Si. *yakaḍa* ' iron '.(CDIAL 590, 591).

English meaning: `metal (copper; iron)'
German meaning: `Metall', under zw. probably `Kupfer ('brandfarbig'?), Bronze'; im Arischen also `Eisen'
Note:
Root / lemma: *ai̯os-* : `metal (copper; iron)' derived from Root / lemma: *eis-1* : `to move rapidly, *weapon, iron'.
Material:
Old Indian *áyas-* n., av. *ayaŋh-* n. `metal, iron';
lat. *aes*, g. *aeris*; got. *aiz* (proto germ. **a(i̯)iz-* = idg. **ai̯es-*) `copper ore, and the alloy of copper, bronze. Transf., anything made of bronze; a vessel, statue, trumpet, kettle', ahd. *ēr* `ore', anord. *eir* n. `ore, copper'.
thereof av. *ayaŋhaēna-* `metallic, iron', lat. *aēnus* (\**ai̯es-no-* = umbr. *ahesnes* `of copper, of bronze'), *aēneus*, ags. *ǣren*, as. ahd. mhd. *ērīn*, nhd. *ēren* (*ehern*). despite Pokorny KZ. 46, 292 f. is not idg. *ai̯os* old borrowing from *Ajasja*, older*Ałas(ja)*, the old name of Cyprus, as lat. *cuprum* : Κύπρος, there according to D. Davis (BSA. 30, 74-86, 1932) the copper pits were tackled in Cyprus only in late Mycenaean time.
Note:
Ajasja, older *Ałas(ja)* (Cyprus) : Hittite PN *Wilusa* (gr. reading *Ilios*) [common phonetic mutation of the old laryngeal *ḫ-* > *a-*, *i-*] : gall. *Isarno-* PN, ven. FlN'I σάρας, later *Īsarcus*, nhd. *Eisack* (Tirol); urir. PN *I(s)aros*, air. *Īär*, balkanillyr. *iser*, messap. *isareti* (Krahe IF. 46, 184 f.); kelt. FlN *Isarā*, nhd. *Isar, Iser*, frz. *Isère*; **Isiā*, frz. *Oise*; **Isurā*, engl. *Ure*, etc. (Pokorny Urillyrier 114 f., 161); nhd. FlN *Ill, Illach, Iller*, lett. FlN *Isline, Islīcis*, wruss. *Isła*, alb. VN *Illyrii.*
Here lat. *aestimō*, old *aestumō* `to appraise, rate, estimate the value of; to assess the damages in a lawsuit; in a wider sense, to value a thing or person; hence, in gen., to judge', Denomin. from \**ais-temos* `he cuts the ore' (to *temnō*).[247]

The script inscriptions indicate a set of modifiers or ligatures to the hieroglyph indicating that the metal, *aya*, was worked on during the early Bronze Age metallurgical processes – to produce *aya* ingots, *aya* metalware, *aya* hard alloys. The following etyma of Bharata sprachbund provide resources for data mining to identify the phonetic form of the word to signify 'fish' in the Bronze Age:

aya 'metal, iron' (G.); *ayah, ayas* = metal (Skt.) Santali lexeme, *hako* 'fish' is concordant with a Proto-Indic form which can be identified as *ayo* in many glosses, Munda, Sora glosses in particular, of the Bharata linguistic area.

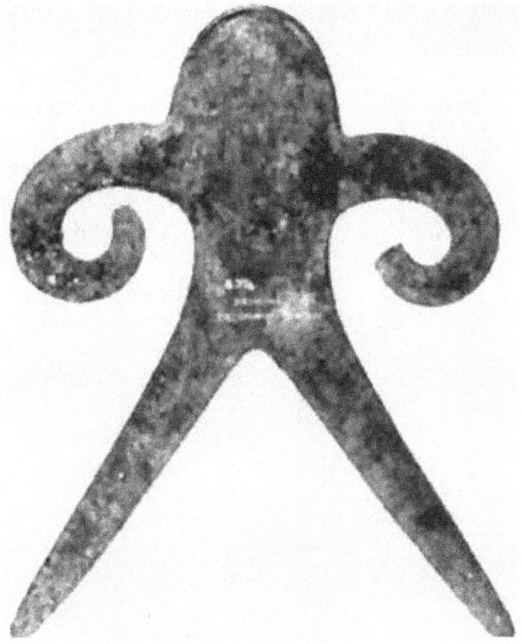

'Fish' hieroglyph on the chest of the anthropomorph is instructive. Oxford English Dictionary defines anthropomorphic: "a. treating the deity as anthropomorphous, or as having a human form and character; b. attributing a human personality to anything impersonal or irrational."One anthropomorph had fish hieroglyph incised on the chest of the copper object, Sheorajpur, upper Ganges valley, ca. 2nd millennium BCE, 4 kg; 47.7 X 39 X 2.1 cm. State Museum, Lucknow (O.37) Typical find of Gangetic Copper hoards.[248]

miṇḍāl markhor (Tor.wali) meḍho a ram, a sheep (G.)(CDIAL 10120) Rebus: meḍh 'helper of merchant' (Gujarati) meḍ iron (Ho.) meṛed-bica = iron stone ore, in contrast to bali-bica, iron sand ore (Munda) *ayo* 'fish' Rebus: *ayo, ayas* 'metal. Thus, together read rebus: *ayo meḍh* 'iron stone ore, metal merchant.'

अयोगूः A blacksmith; Vāj.3.5. अयस् a. [इ-गतौ-असुन्] Going, moving; nimble. n. (-**यः**) 1 Iron (एति चलति अयस्कान्तसंनिकर्षं इति तथात्वम्; नायसोल्लिख्यते रत्नम् Śukra4.169. अभितप्तमयो$पि मार्दवं भजते कैव कथा शरीरिषु R.8.43. -2 Steel. -3 Gold. -4 A metal in general. ayaskāṇḍa 1 an iron-arrow. -2 excellent iron. -3 a large quantity of iron. -क_नत_(अयसक_नत_) 1 'beloved of iron', a magnet, load-stone; 2 a precious stone; °मजण_ a loadstone; ayaskāra 1 an iron-smith, blacksmith (Skt.Apte) ayas-kāntamu. [Skt.] n. The load-stone, a magnet. ayaskāruḍu. n. A black smith, one who works in iron. ayassu. n. ayō-mayamu. [Skt.] adj. made of iron (Te.) áyas— n. 'metal, iron' RV. Pa. ayō nom. sg. n. and m., aya— n. 'iron', Pk. aya— n., Si. ya. AYAŚCŪRṆA—, AYASKĀṆḌA—, *AYASKŪṬA—. Addenda: áyas—: Md. da 'iron', dafat 'piece of iron'. ayaskāṇḍa— m.n. 'a quantity of iron, excellent iron' Pāṇ. gaṇ. viii.3.48 [ÁYAS—, KAA´ṆḌA—]Si.yakaḍa 'iron'.*ayaskūṭa— 'iron hammer'. [ÁYAS—, KUU´ṬA—1] Pa. ayōkūṭa—, ayak m.; Si. yakuḷa'sledge —hammer', yavuḷa (< ayōkūṭa) (CDIAL 590, 591, 592). cf. Lat. *aes , aer-is for as-is ; Goth. ais , Thema aisa; Old Germ. e7r , iron ;Goth. eisarn ; Mod. Germ. Eisen.*

For determining the semantics of the messages conveyed by the script the positional analysi presented by Korvink also constitutes a checklist to validate any decipherment of a sequence or expression as hypertext, containing 'fish' hieroglyph.

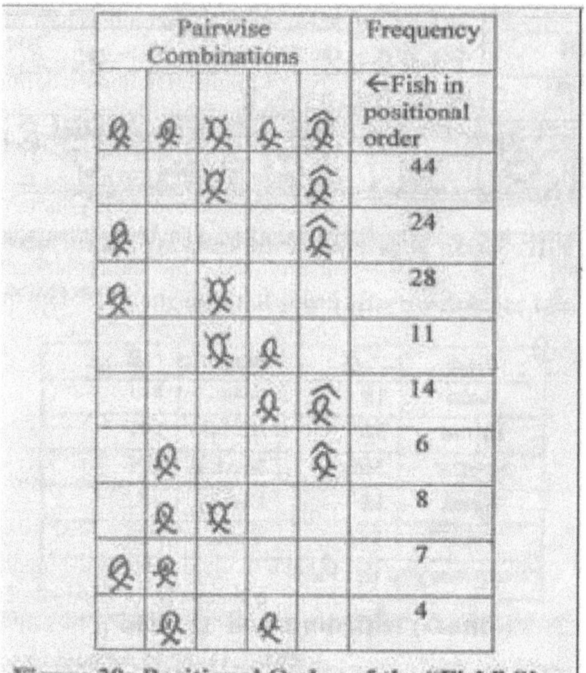

Figure 20: Positional Order of the "Fish" Signs

Positional analysis of 'fish' hieroglyphs. After Korvink[249]. This indication of the occurrence, together, of two or more 'fish' hieroglyphs with modifiers is an assurance that the modifiers ar semantic indicators of how aya 'metal' is worked on by the artisans.

Another hypertext orthographed by modified 'fish' hieroglyph expressions is circumscript, for e.g., fish+aquatic bird hypertext:

karaṇḍa 'duck' (Sanskrit) *karaṛa* 'a very large aquatic bird' (Sindhi) Rebus: करडा *[karaḍā]* Hard from alloy--iron, silver &c. (Marathi) Rebus: fire-god: @B27990. #16671. Remo <*karandi*>E155 {N} ``^fire-^god".(Munda) Rebus:. *khārādī* 'turner' (Gujarati)

The 'parenthesiś modifier is a circumfix for both 'fish' and 'duck' hieroglyphs, the semantics of () two parenthetical modifiers are: kuṭilá— 'bent, crooked' KātyŚr., °*aka*— n. 'a partic. plant' [√kuṭ 1] Pa. *kuṭila*— 'bent', n.

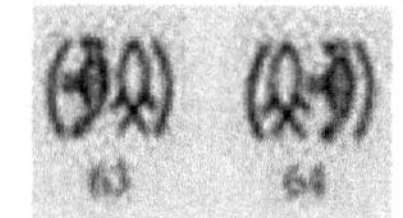

Pañcat., 'bend'; Pk. *kuḍila*— 'crooked', °*illa*— 'humpbacked', °*illaya*— 'bent' (DEDR 2054).Rebus: *kuṭila, katthīl* = bronze (8 parts copper and 2 parts tin) cf. āra-kūṭa, 'brass Old English *ār* 'brass, copper, bronze' Old Norse *eir* 'brass, copper', German *ehern* 'brassy, bronzen'. kastīra n. ' tin ' lex. 2. *kastilla -- .1. H. *kathīr* m. ' tin, pewter '; G. *kathīr* n. ' pewter '.2. H. (Bhoj.?) *kathīl*, °*lā* m. ' tin, pewter '; M. *kathīl* n. ' tin ', *kathlẽ* n. ' large tin vessel '(CDIAL 2984).

In these hypertexts (Signs 63, 64), a compound expression is signified:

In the orthographed compound expression: 'fish' hieroglyph reads: ayo, aya 'fish' rebus: aya 'iron' ayas 'metal' PLUS *karaṛa* 'a very large aquatic bird' (Sindhi) Rebus: करडा *[karaḍā]* 'Hard from alloy--iron, silver &c.' The compound expression aya + *karaḍā* signifies Hard alloy metal--iron,silver &c. The circumscript signifies: *kuṭila, katthīl* = bronze (8 parts copper and 2 parts tin). Thus, the compound expression orthographed as Signs 63,64 signify: hard metal alloy, bronze. Since two parentheses are signified, the reading is: dula 'pair' rebus: dul 'metal casting'. Thus, the Signs 63,64 signify, metal castings of hard metal alloy, bronze.

The message of Signs 63, 64 is deciphered: *dul kuṭila ayas karaḍā* 'cast bronze *ayas* or cast alloy metal with *ayas* as component to create metal castings of *karaḍā* ''hard alloy with *ayas'*.

The parentheses as expression modifiers of hieroglyphs is also seen in the hypertext Sign 62:

In this hypertext Sign 62, 'fish' hieroglyph is circumscribed by parentheses and a ligature 'horn' or 'tooth'or 'snout' is affixed.

Kannada. *kōḍu*]tusk; யானை பன்றிகளின் தந்தம். மத்த யானையின் கோடும் (தேவா. 39, 1). Rebus: खोट [*khōṭa*] A lump or solid bit (as of phlegm, gore, curds, inspissated milk); any concretion or clot. (Marathi) Rebus: L. *khoṭ* f. ' alloy, impurity ', °ṭā ' alloyed ', awāṇ. *khoṭā* ' forged '; P. *khoṭ* m. ' base, alloy ' M. *khoṭā* 'alloyed' (CDIAL 3931)

Alternative: The affixed 'snout' hieroglyph is read rebus: WPah.kṭg. *ṭōṭ* ' mouth '.WPah.kṭg. *thótti* f., *thótthər* m. ' snout, mouth ', A. *ṭhõt*(phonet. *thõt*) (CDIAL 5853). Semantics, Rebus: tutthá n. (m. lex.), *tutthaka* -- n. ' blue vitriol (used as an eye ointment) ' Suśr., *tūtaka* -- lex. 2. *thōttha -- 4. 3. *tūtta -- . 4. *tōtta -- 2. [Prob. ← Drav. T. Burrow BSOAS xii 381; cf. *dhūrta* -- 2 n. ' iron filings ' lex.]1. N. *tutho* ' blue vitriol or sulphate of copper ', B. *tuth*.2. K. *thŏth*, dat. °*thas* m., P. *thothā* m.3. S.*tūtio* m., A. *tutiyā*, B. *tũte*, Or. *tutiā*, H. *tūtā*, *tūtiyā* m., M. *tutiyā* m. 4. M. *totā* m.(CDIAL 5855) *Ka.* tukku rust of iron; *tutta, tuttu, tutte* blue vitriol. *Tu. tukků* rust; mair(ů)suttu, (*Eng.-Tu. Dict.*) mairůtuttu blue vitriol. *Te. t(r)uppu* rust; (*SAN*) trukku id., verdigris. / Cf. Skt. *tuttha-* blue vitriol (DEDR 3343).

Thus, the expression signified by Sign 62 is read: *dul kuṭila ayas tutta* 'metal casting bronze metal with tuttha, 'copper sulphate'. *dul kuṭila ayas kōḍu (khoṭ)* 'cast bronze metal alloy'.

Consistent with the orthographic method of signifying compound expressions in Meluhha, the modified 'fish' hieroglyphs can be read rebus:

Fish — *ayo, aya* 'fish' rebus: *aya* 'iron' *ayas* 'metal'

Figh+crocodile — *aya* 'fish' rebus: *aya* 'iron' *ayas* 'metal' PLUS *karA* 'crocodile rebus: *khār* 'blacksmith' Together, the expression is *ayakara* 'metalsmith'

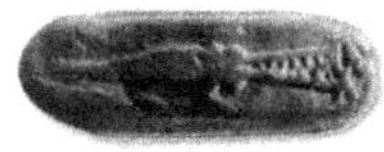
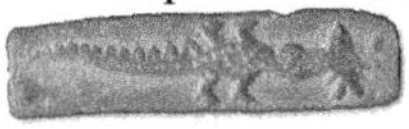

Fish + lid — *aya adaren* rebus: *aya aduru* 'iron metl/native unsmelted metal'

Fish+ slanted stroke — *aya* dhal rebus: *aya DhALako* 'iron/metal ingot'

Fish + scales — *aya ãs (amśu)* 'metallic stalks of stone ore' (Since *amśu* is cognate with ancu 'iron' (Tocharian)—pace research of Georges Pinault[250], the expression *aya ãs (amśu)* signifies iron ore [containing *assem*, 'electrum' (Old Egyptian); soma maNal 'sand containing silver ore' (Tamil)].

Fish+notch

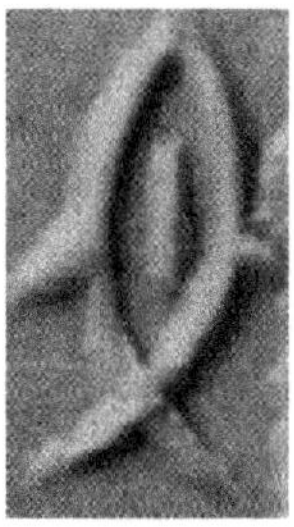

aya kāṇḍā 'metal (iron) implements खाडा [khāṇḍā] 'A jag, notch, or indentation (as upon the edge of a tool or weapon)' Rebus: kāṇḍa 'implements (Santali) khāṇḍā 'tools, pots and pans, metal-ware' (Marathi). The expression ayaskāṇḍa 'a quantity of iron, excellent iron' is attested in Panini. In the parole of Bharata *sprachbund*, लोखंडकाम [lōkhaṇḍakāma] *n* Iron work; that portion (of a building, machine &c.) which consists of iron. 2 The business of an

ironsmith (Marathi) **अयस्--कान्त [p= <u>85</u>,1]**
m. (g. कस्का*दि) , " iron-lover " , the loadstone
(cf. कान्ता*यस) <u>Ragh.</u> xvii , 63 (Monier-Williams)

Fish + III (three linear strokes) smithy/forge' — *aya kolom* Rebus:*aya kolimi* 'iron/metal smithy/forge'

Fish+ (3+3) short strokes — *aya baṭa* rebus: ayo bhaṭa 'iron/metal furnace'

Fish+(4+3) short strokes — *aya gaṇḍa kolom* rebus: *aya khaṇḍa kolimi* 'metal/iron implements smithy/forge'

Fish + 2 linearstrokes — *dul ayo* rebus: *dul ayo* 'metal casting'

dula tridhAtu 'two+three strands of rope' Rebus: *dul kolom dhatu* 'cast metal of three mineral ores'

aya tridhAtu 'fish+three strands of rope' Rebus: *aya kolom dhatu* 'metal/iron, three mineral ores'

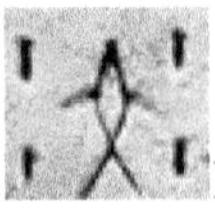

Fish+circumscript (4 strokes)

ayo gaṇḍa rebus: *aya khaṇḍa* 'metal/iron implements *aya kāṇḍa* 'metal/iron furnace, fire-altar'

ayo 'fish'; *kāṇḍa* 'arrow'
See: अयस्कांत [*ayaskānta*] *m* S (The iron gem.) The loadstone. (Molesworth. Marathi) Fish + circumgraph of 4 (gaṇḍa) notches: *ayaskāṇḍa* 'a quantity of iron, excellent iron' (Pāṇ.gaṇ) The gloss *kāṇḍa* may also signify 'metal implements'. A cognate compound in Santali has: *mẽṛhẽt khaṇḍa* 'iron implements'.

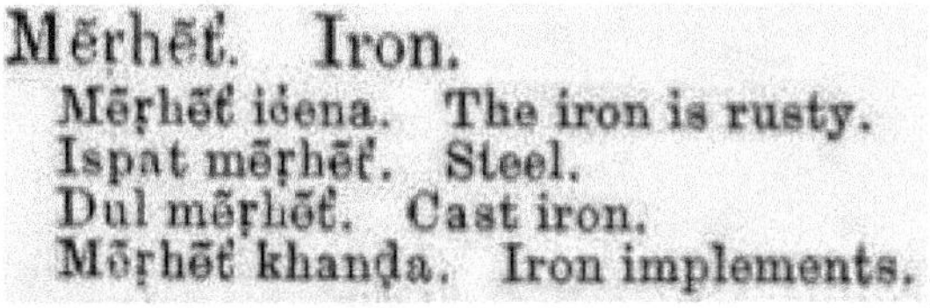
Mĕrhĕt̕. Iron.
Mĕṛhĕt̕ iċena. The iron is rusty.
Ispat mĕṛhĕt̕. Steel.
Dul mĕṛhĕt̕. Cast iron.
Mĕṛhĕt̕ khanḍa. Iron implements.

Santali glosses.

Seal. Mohenjo-daro
gaṇḍa ‘four’ rebus: *khaṇḍa* ‘implements PLUS hieroglyph: double parenthesis as circumflex: Oval shaped like a bun ingot; rebus: *mūhā* 'ingot' PLUS *kolmo* 'rice-plant' rebus: *kolimi* 'smithy, forge'. Thus, smithy, forge ingot

aya dhal ‘fish+slant’ rebus: *aya DhALako* 'iron/metal ingot'
aya kāṇḍā ‘metal (iron) implements
barad, balad ‘ox’ rebus:*bharata* ‘alloy of pewter, copper, tin’
pattar ‘trough’ rebus: *pattar* ‘guild’ *pattharaka* ‘merchant’

m 305 Seal. Mohenjo-daro.

Fish + scales, *aya ãs (amśu)* ‘metallic stalks of stone ore’. ayo, aya ‘fish’ rebus: aya ‘iron’ ayas ‘metal’
gaṇḍa 'four' Rebus: khaṇḍa 'metal implements Together with cognate ancu 'iron' the message is: native metal implements. Pictorial hypertext or hieroglyph-multiplex: *kamDha* ‘penance’ rebus: *kammaṭa* ‘mint, coiner, coinage’ muh ‘face’ rebus: muhA ‘quantity of metal taken out of furnace’ muh *‘ingot’ kuṭi* 'twig' Rebus: kuṭhi 'smelter' thattAr 'buffalo horn' Rebus: taTThAr 'brass worker' meḍha 'polar star' (Marathi). meḍ 'iron' (Ho.Mu.) Pictorial hieroglyph-multiplex: karã̄ n. pl. ‘ wristlets, bangles ’ (Gujarati) Rebus: *khār* 'blacksmith'(Kashmiri) sal ‘splinter’ rebus: sal ‘workshop’. dhatu ‘scarf’ rebus: dhatu ‘mineraś Thus, blacksmith working with iron smelter and metal implements of native metal.

It is remarkable that the hieroglyphs ayo, aya ‘fish’ rebus: aya ‘iron’ and meD ‘body’ rebus: meD ‘iron’ get ligatured with modifierso create hypertexts to signify specific duties related to iron metalwork. The following 48 ‘text signs’ are ligatures to the hieroglyph meD ‘body’, kAti ‘stature of body’. These 48 ‘text signs’ are thus, hypertexts conveying the specific responsibilities or functions performed by the artisan in the guild activities.

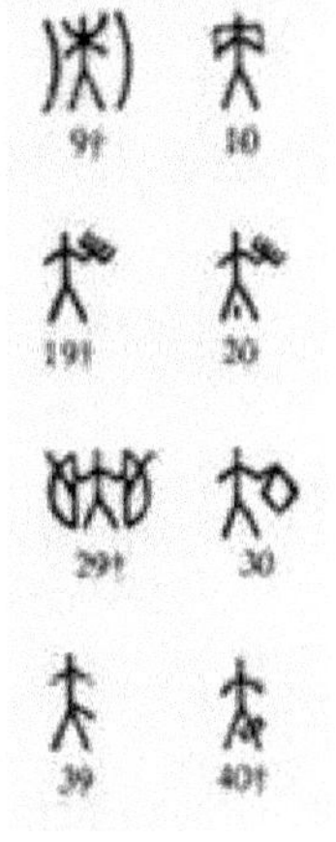

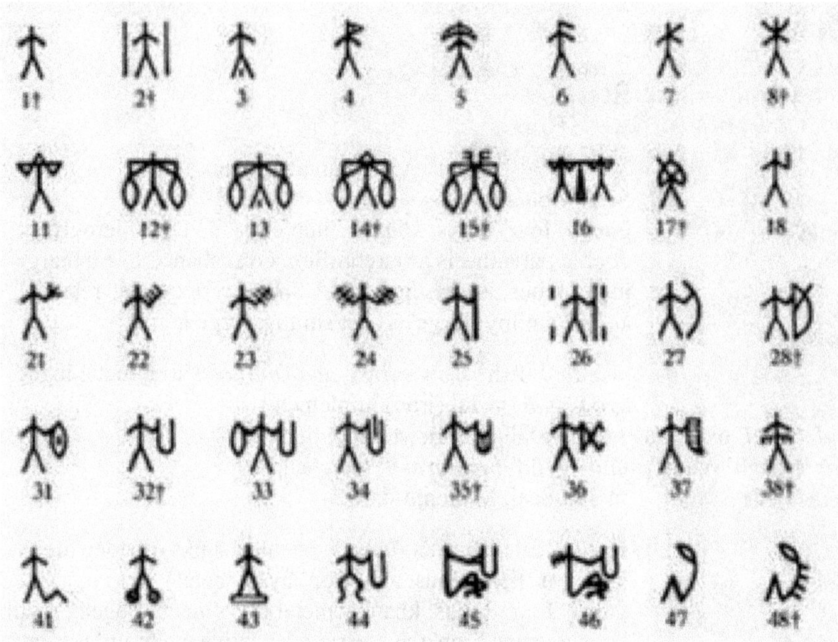

Sign 3*:* *mēd* 'body' (Kur.)(DEDR 5099) Rebus: *meḍ* 'iron' (Ho.) खांडा [*khāṇḍā*] m A jag, notch, or indentation (as upon the edge of a tool or weapon)(Marathi). Rebus: *kāṇḍa* 'tools, pots and pans and metal-ware' (Marathi) Thus, *meḍ kāṇḍa* 'iron implements'.

Ligature: Stool or plank/seat Sign 43: Kur. *kaṇḍō* a stool. Malt. *kanḍo* stool, seat. (DEDR 1179) Rebus: *kaṇḍ* 'fire-altar' (Santali) *kāṇḍa* 'tools, pots and pans and metal-ware' (Marathi) + *kāṭi* 'body stature; Rebus: fireplace trench. Thus, furnace for metals in mint. Thus, fire-altar metalware furnace.

Alternative: PLUS *mēd* 'body' (Kur.)(DEDR 5099) Rebus: *meḍ* 'iron' (Ho.) Thus, *meḍ kāṇḍa*,'iron implements'.

Ligature: crab, claws kAru 'pincers' rebus: kAru 'artisan' Sign 36: : *mēd* 'body' (Kur.)(DEDR 5099); *meḍ* 'iron' (Ho.) Thus, *meḍ dhātu* 'iron ore' , *meD kAru* 'iron artisan'

Alternative Sign 36: *kāṭi* 'body stature; Rebus: fireplace trench. Thus, furnace for metals in mint + *kamaḍha* 'crab' Rebus: *kammaṭa* 'mint, coiner'. *ḍato* = claws of crab (Santali) Rebus: *dhAtu* 'mineral' Thus mineral ore mint, coiner.

kamaḍha 'archer, bow' Rebus: *kammaṭa* 'mint, coiner'. *dula* 'two' Rebu: *dul* 'cast metal'. Thus metal castings mint. + *kāṭi* 'body stature; Rebus: fireplace trench. Thus, furnace for metal castings in mint. Alternative reading could be: *mēd* 'body' (Kur.) Rebus: *meḍ* 'iron' (Ho.) PLUS *dul* 'cast metal' PLUS *kammaṭa* 'mint' Thus, together, cast iron mint.

Similarly, in all the following hieroglyph-multiplexes, the 'body' hieroglyph can be deciphere and explained:as

mēd 'body' (Kur.) Rebus: *meḍ* 'iron' (Ho.) PLUS + *kāṭi* 'body stature'; Rebus: fireplace trench

Sign 28: Archer. Ligature one bow-and-arrow hieroglyph *kamaḍha* 'archer, bow' Rebus: *kammaṭa* 'mint, coiner'. + *kāṭi* 'body stature; Rebus: fireplace trench. Thus, furnace for metals in mint.

Ligature hieroglyph: 'lid of pot' *aḍaren* 'lid of pot' Rebus: *aduru* 'unsmelted, native metal' + *kāṭi* 'body stature; Rebus: fireplace trench. Thus furnace for aduru, unsmelted, native metal. Ligatures: water-carrier + lid of pot. *d.aren-mund.i* lid of pot; *d.aren, ad.aren* to cover up pot with lid (Bond.a); *d.arai* to cover (Bond.a.Hindi) rebus: *munda* 'iron'

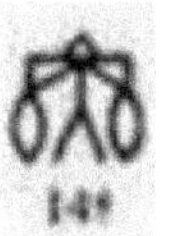

Sign 14: kuṭi 'water-carrier' Rebus: kuṭhi 'smelter/furnace'+ + *kāṭi* 'body stature; Rebus: fireplace trench +aḍaren'lid of pot' Rebus: aduru 'unsmelted, native metal' + kāṭi 'body stature; Rebus: fireplace trench. Thus furnace for aduru, unsmelted, native metal. Thus, furnace-smelter for unsmelted, native metal. d.aren-mund.i lid of pot; d.aren, ad.aren to cover up pot with lid (Bond.a); d.arai to cover (Bond.a.Hindi) munda 'iron'

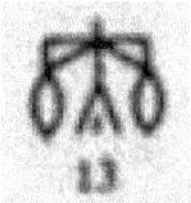

Ligature: water-carrier Sign 12: *kuṭi* 'water-carrier' Rebus: *kuṭhi* 'smelter/furnace'+ *kāṭi* 'body stature; Rebus: fireplace trench. Thus, smelter furnace.

Ligatures: water-carrier + notch Sign 13: *kuṭi* 'water-carrier' Rebus: *kuṭhi* 'smelter/furnace'+ *kāṭi* 'body stature; Rebus: fireplace trench. + खांडा [*khāṇḍā]* m A jag, notch, or indentation (as upon the edge of a tool or weapon)(Marathi). Rebus: *kāṇḍa* 'tools, pots and pans and metal-ware' (Marathi) + *kāṭi* 'body stature; Rebus: fireplace trench. + kāṭi 'body =stature; Rebus: fireplace trench. Thus, smelter-furnace metalware.

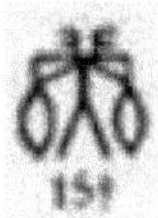

Ligatures: water-carrier (as in Sign 12) + rim of jar *kuThi kANDa karNI*, 'smelter, fire-altar supercargo'.

Ligature: rim of jar Rebus: *kaṇḍa kanka* 'fire-trench account, *karṇi* supercargo'

Tu. *kandůka, kāṇḍaka* ditch, trench. Te. *kāṇḍakamu* id. Koṇḍa *kāṇḍa* trench made as a fireplace during weddings. Pe. *kāṇḍa* fire trench. Kui *kāṇḍa* small trench for fireplace. Malt. *kandri* a pit. (DEDR 1214).'rim-of-jar' hieroglyph Rebus: *kanka* (Santali) *karṇika* 'scribe'(Sanskrit) *kuṭi* 'water-carrier' Rebus: *kuṭhi* 'smelter/furnace'.+*kāṭi* 'body stature; Rebus: fireplace trench. Thus, smelter furnace account, supercargo.

Ligature 'two spoked wheels' Spokes-of-wheel, nave-of-wheel *āra* 'spokes' Rebus: *āra* 'brass'. cf. *erka* = *ekke* (Tbh. of *arka*) *aka (Tbh. of arka)* copper (metal); crystal (Kannada) Glyph: *eraka* 'nave of wheel' Rebus: *eraka* 'copper'; cf. *erka* = ekke *(Tbh. of arka) aka (Tbh. of arka)* copper (metal); crystal (Kannada) *dula* 'two' Rebus: *dul* 'cast metal'. Thus, moltencast copper castings ++ *kāṭi* 'body stature; Rebus: fireplace trench. Thus, furnace for copper metal castings.

Ligature hieroglyph 'corner'

kanac 'corner' Rebus: kañcu 'bronze' + kāṭi 'body stature; Rebus: fireplace trench. Thus, furnace for bronze castings.

Ligatures: corner + notch

Sign 31: *kana, kanac* = corner (Santali); Rebus: *kañcu* = bronze (Telugu) PLUS खांडा [*khāṇḍā*] m A jag, notch, or indentation (as upon the edge of a tool or weapon). Rebus: *kāṇḍa* 'tools, pots and pans and metal-ware' Thus, bronze

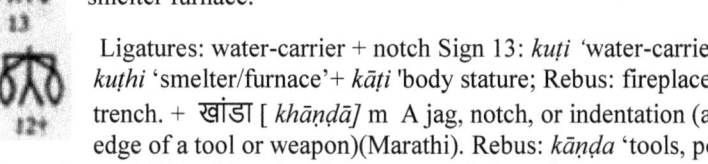

metalware. + *kāṭi* 'body stature; Rebus: fireplace trench. Thus, furnace bronze metalware castings.

Ligature hieroglyph: 'stick' or 'one'

Sign1 Hieroglyph: काठी [*kāṭhī*] f (काष्ट S) (or शरीराची काठी) The frame or structure of the body: also (viewed by some as arising from the preceding sense, Measuring rod) stature (Marathi) B. *kāṭhā* ' measure of length '(CDIAL 3120). H. *kāṭhī* 'wood' f. G. *kāṭh* n. ' wood ', °*ṭhī* f. ' stick, measure of 5 cubits '(CDIAL 3120). + *kāṭi* 'body stature; Rebus: fireplace trench.The 'stick' hieroglyph is a phonetic reinforcement of 'body stature' hieroglyph. Alternatively, *koḍ* 'one' Rebus: *koḍ* 'workshop'+ *kāṭi* 'body stature; Rebus: fireplace trench.. Thus, workplace of furnace fire-trench.
Rebus: G. *kāṭɔṛɔ* m. ' dross left in the furnace after smelting iron ore '.(CDIAL 2646)
Rebus: *kāṭi* , n. < U. *ghāṭī*. 1. Trench of a fort; அகழி. 2. A fireplace in the form of a long ditch; கோட்டையடுப்பு காடியடுப்பு *kāṭi-y-aṭuppu* , n. < காடி&sup6; +. A fireplace in the form of a long ditch used for cooking on a large scale; கோட்டையடுப்பு.
Rebus: S.kcch. *kāṭhī* f. ' wood 'Pa. Pk. *kaṭṭha* -- n. ' wood '(CDIAL 3120).
Sign 37 Hieroglyph: WPah.ktg. *ṭōṭ* ' mouth '. WPah.ktg. *thótti f., thótthəṛ* m. ' snout, mouth ', A. *ṭhõt* (phonet. *thõt)* (CDIAL 5853).
Rebus: tutthá n. (m. lex.), tutthaka -- n. ' blue vitriol (used as an eye ointment) ' Suśr., tūtaka -- lex. 2. *thōttha -- 4. 3. *tūtta -- . 4. *tōtta -- 2. [Prob. ← Drav. T. Burrow BSOAS xii 381; cf. dhūrta -- 2 n. ' iron filings ' lex.]1. N. tutho ' blue vitriol or sulphate of copper ', B. tuth.2. K. thŏth, dat. °thas m., P. thothā m.3. S.tūtio m., A. tutiyā, B. tũte, Or. tutiā, H. tūtā, tūtiyā m., M. tutiyā m.4. M. totā m.(CDIAL 5855) Ka. tukku rust of iron; tutta, tuttu, tutte blue vitriol. Tu. tukků rust; mair(ů)suttu, (Eng.-Tu. Dict.) mairůtuttu blue vitriol. Te. t(r)uppu rust; (SAN) trukku id., verdigris. / Cf. Skt. tuttha- blue vitriol (DEDR 3343).

Sign 2: *dula* 'pair' Rebus: *dul* 'cast metal' + *kāṭi* 'body stature; Rebus: fireplace trench. Thus furnace for metal casting. koḍ 'one' Rebus: koḍ 'workshop'. Thus, furnace workshop.

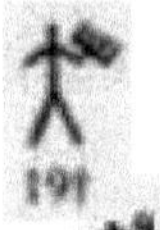

Ligature: harrow

Ligatures: harrow + notch (between legs) Allographs: Signs 18, 39

Sign 18: खांडा [*khāṇḍā]* m A jag, notch, or indentation (as upon the edge of a tool or weapon)(Marathi). Rebus: *kāṇḍa* 'tools, pots and pans and metal-ware' (Marathi) + *kāṭi* 'body stature; Rebus: fireplace trench. Thus, furnace for metalware castings of unsmelted, native metal.

Ligature component in hieroglyph 'harrow' Sign 19: *aḍar* 'harrow'; rebus: *aduru* 'native unsmelted metal' (Kannada) + *kāṭi* 'body stature; Rebus: fireplace trench. Thus, furnace for native metal. Sign 20: body+ notch: खांडा [*khāṇḍā*] m A jag, notch, or indentation (as upon the edge of a tool or weapon)(Marathi). Rebus: *kāṇḍa*

'tools, pots and pans and metal-ware' (Marathi) + *kāṭi* 'body stature; Rebus: fireplace trench. Thus, furnace for metalware castings of unsmelted, native metal.

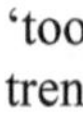

Ligature hieroglyph 'currycomb' Sign 38: *kharedo* = a currycomb (Gujarati) खरारा [*khārārā*] m (H) A currycomb. 2 Currying a horse. (Marathi) Rebus: करडा [*karaḍā*] Hard from alloy--iron, silver &c. (Marathi) *khārādī*' turner'

(Gujarati) *kāṭi* 'body stature; Rebus: fireplace trench. Thus, fireplace for hard alloy metal.

Ligature hieroglyph 'foot, anklet' Ligature is signifier of leg. Sign 40: toṭi bracelet (Tamil)(DEDR 3682). Jaina Skt. (IL 20.193) *toḍaka*- an anklet (Sanskrit) *khuṭo* ' leg, foot ', °*ṭī* ' goat's leg ' Rebus: *khōṭā* 'alloy' (Marathi) Rebus: *tuttha* 'copper sulphate' + *kāṭi* 'body stature; Rebus: fireplace trench. Thus smelted copper sulphate alloy.

Ligature hieroglyph 'rimless pot + ladle'

Sign 34: *muka* 'ladle' (Tamil)(DEDR 4887) Rebus: *mū̃h* 'ingot' (Santali) *baṭa* = a kind of iron (G.) *baṭa* = rimless pot (Kannada) Thus, iron ingot.+ *kāṭi* 'body stature; Rebus: fireplace trench. Thus, iron ingot furnace.

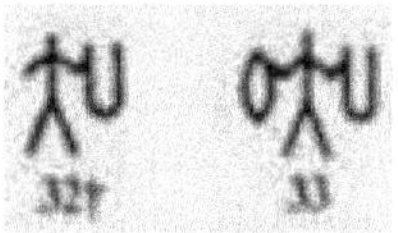

Ligatures: rimless pot + hollow or ingot Sign 32: baṭa = rimless pot (Kannada) Rebus: *baṭa* = a kind of iron (G.)+ *kāṭi* 'body stature; Rebus: fireplace trench. Thus, iron furnace

Sign 33: As for Sign 32 + *dulo* 'hole' Rebus: *dul* 'cast metal' goTa 'piece' rebus: goTa 'laterite, ferrite ore' Thus, furnace laterite iron castings.

Ligatures: rimless pot + dance step Sign 44: *meṭ* sole of foot, footstep, footprint (Ko.); *meṭṭu* step, stair, treading, slipper (Te.)(DEDR 1557). Rebus: *meḍ* 'iron'

(Munda); मेढ *meḍh* 'merchant's helper'(Pkt.) *meḍ* iron (Ho.) *meṛed-bica* = iron stone ore, in contrast to *bali-bica*, iron sand ore (Munda) + *kāṭi* 'body stature; Rebus: fireplace trench. Thus, iron merchant furnace.

Ligatures: rimless pot + wire mesh Sign 35: *baṭa* = rimless pot (Kannada) Rebus: *baṭa* = a kind of iron (G.)+ *kāṭi* 'body stature; Rebus: fireplace trench + *akho* m. 'mesh of a net' Rebus: L. P. *akkhā* m. ' one end of a bag or sack thrown over a beast of burden '; Or. *akhā* ' gunny bag '; Bi. *ākhā, ā̃khā* ' grain bag carried by pack animal '; H. *ākhā* m. ' one of a pair of grain bags used as panniers '; M. *ā̃khā* m. ' netting in which coco -- nuts, &c., are carried ', *ā̃khẽ* n. ' half a bullock -- load ' (CDIAL 17) అంకెము [aṅkemu] *ankemu.* [Telugu] n. One pack or pannier, being half a bullock load. Thus, a consignment or packload of furnace iron castings.

Ligature: warrior + *ficus religiosa* Sign 17: *loa* 'ficus religiosa' Rebus: *lo* 'iron' (Sanskrit) PLUS unique ligatures: लोखंड [lōkhaṇḍa] n (लोह S) Iron. लोखंडाचे चणे खावविणें or चारणें To oppress grievously.लोखंडकाम [*lōkhaṇḍakāma*] n Iron work; that portion (of a building, machine &c.) which consists of iron. 2 The business of an ironsmith. लोखंडी [*lōkhaṇḍī]* a (लोखंड) Composed of iron; relating to iron. (Marathi) *bhaṭa* 'warrior' (Sanskrit) Rebus: *baṭa* a kind of iron (Gujarati). Rebus: *bhaṭa* 'furnace' (Santali) Thus, together, th ligatured hieroglyph reads rebus: *loha bhaṭa* 'iron furnace'

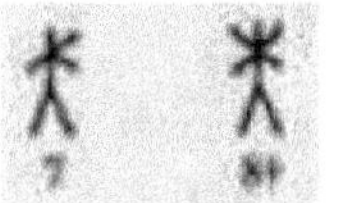

Ligature 'armeḍ body stature' or 'horned body stature'

Sign 8: *bhaṭa* 'warrior' (Sanskrit) Rebus: *baṭa* a kind of iron (Gujarati). Rebus: *bhaṭa* 'furnace' (Santali) + *kāṭi* 'body stature; Rebus: fireplace trench. Thus, furnace for a kind of iron.

Ligatures: two curved lines Sign 9: Read rebus as for Sign 8 PLUS Ligature hieroglyphs of two curved lines *dula* 'pair' Rebus: *dul* 'cast metal + () *kuṭila* 'bent' CDIAL *3230 kuṭi—* in cmpd. 'curve', *kuṭika—* 'bent' MBh. Rebus: *kuṭila, katthīl* = bronze (8 parts copper and 2 parts tin) [cf. *āra-kūṭa,* 'brass (Sanskrit) + *bhaṭa* 'warrior' (Sanskrit) Rebus: *baṭa* a kind of iron (Gujarati). Rebus: *bhaṭa* 'furnace' (Santali) + *kāṭi* 'body stature; Rebus: fireplace trench. Thus, bronze furnace castings.

Ligature hieroglyph: 'roof' bari 'thatched roof' rebus: bare 'merchant' meD 'body' rebus: meD 'iron' Allograph: Sign 10

Sign 5: *mūdh* ' ridge of roof ' (Assamese)(CDIAL 10247) Rebus: *mund* 'iron' + *kāṭi* 'body stature; Rebus: fireplace trench. Thus, furnace for iron

Ligature hieroglyph 'flag' Sign 4: *koḍi* 'flag' (Ta.)(DEDR 2049). Rebus 1: *koḍ* 'workshop' (Kuwi) Rebus 2: *khŏḍ* m. 'pit', *khŏḍü* f. 'small pit' (Kashmiri. CDIAL *3947). + kāṭi* 'body stature; Rebus: fireplace trench. Thus, furnace workshop.

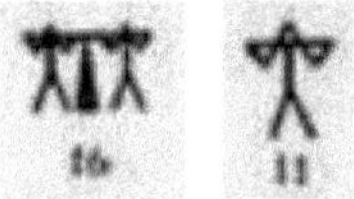

Sign 16: *dula* 'two' Rebus: *dul* 'cast metal' + *kāṭi* 'body stature; Rebus: fireplace trench + *koḍi* 'summit of mountain' (Tamil). Thus, furnace for metal casting. *mēḍu* height, rising ground, hillock (Kannada) Rebus: *mẽṛhẽt, meḍ* 'iron' (Munda.Ho.) Thus, iron metal casting. The ligaured hieroglyph of Sign 11 is a ligature with two mountain peaks. Hence *dul meḍ* 'iron casting'

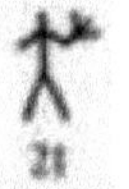

Ligature hieroglyph 'paddy plant' or 'sprout' *kolmo* 'paddy plant' Rebus: *kolimi* 'smithy, forge' Vikalpa: *mogge* 'sprout, bud' Rebus: *mū̃h* 'ingot' (Santali) *dolu* 'plant of shoot height' Rebus: *dul* 'cast metal' + *kāṭi* 'body stature; Rebus: fireplace trench. Thus furnace smithy or ingot furnace. *meḍ* 'body' rebus: *mẽṛhẽt, meḍ* 'iron' + *kolmo* 'rice plant' rebus: *kolimi* 'smithy'

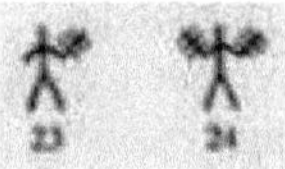

Ligature hieroglyph: 'three short strokes on a slanted stroke'

Signs 23, 24: *dula* 'two' Rebus: *dul* 'cast metal' *dhāḷ* 'a slope'; 'inclination of a plane' (G.); *ḍhāḷiyum* = adj. sloping, inclining (G.) Rebus: *ḍhālako* = a large metal ingot (G.) *ḍhālakī* = a metal heated and poured into a mould; a solid piece of metal; an ingot (Gujarati) + *kāṭi* 'body stature; Rebus: fireplace trench' Thus ingot furnace for castings. Three short strokes: *kolom* 'three' Rebus: *kolimi* 'smithy, forge'. Thus it is a place where artisans work with furnace for metal castings.

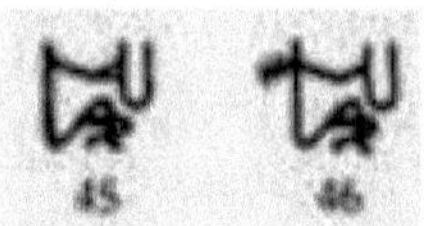

Ligatures: Worshipper + rimless pot + scarf (on pigtail)

Signs 45, 46: A variant of 'adorant' hieroglyph sign is shown with a *baTa* 'rimless, broad-mouthed pot' which is baṭa read rebus: *bhaṭa* 'furnace'. If the 'pot' ligature is a phonetic determinant, the gloss for the 'adorant' is *bhaṭa* 'worshipper'. If the 'kneeling' posture is the key hieroglyphic representation, the gloss is ***eragu*** 'bow' Rebus: *erako* 'moltencast copper'. Thus moltencast copper furnace. + *dhatu* m. (also *dhaṭhu*) m. 'scarf' (Western Pahari) (CDIAL 6707) Rebus: *dhatu* 'minerals' (Santali). Thus Sign 46 read rebus: moltencast copper minerals furnace.

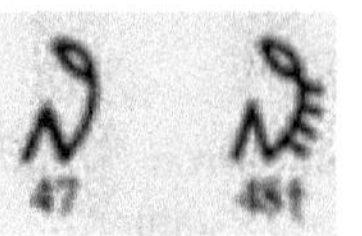

Hieroglyphs: backbone + four short strokes

Signs 47, 48: *baraḍo* = spine; backbone (Tulu) Rebus: *baran, bharat* 'mixed alloyś (5 copper, 4 zinc and 1 tin) (Punjabi) +

gaṇḍa 'four' Rebus: *kand* 'fire-altar'. Thus, Sign 48 reads rebus: *bharat kaṇḍ* 'fire-altar', furnace for mixed alloy called *bharat* (copper, zinc, tin alloy), or, *bharat* alloy implements.

'Backbone, spine' hieroglyph: baraḍo = spine; backbone; the back; baraḍo thābaḍavo = lit. to strike on the backbone or back; hence, to encourage; baraḍo bhāre thato = lit. to have a painful backbone, i.e. to do something which will call for a severe beating (Gujarati)bārṇe, bāraṇe = an offering of food to a demon; a meal after fasting, a breakfast (Tulu) barada, barda, birada = a vow (Gujarati)bharaḍo a devotee of Śiva; a man of the bharaḍā caste in the bra_hman.as (Gujarati) baraṛ = name of a caste of jat-around Bhaṭiṇḍa; bararaṇḍā melā = a special fair held in spring (Punjabi) bharāḍ = a religious service or entertainment performeḍ by a bharāḍi_; consisting of singing the praises of some idol or god with playing on the d.aur (drum) and dancing; an order of *aṭharā akhād.e* = 18 *gosāyi_* group; *bharād.* and *bhāratī* are two of the 18 orders of gosāyi_ (Marathi).

Harappa Script on Copper tablets

Brij Mohan Pande had analysed (1973) the importance and significance of copper tablets with unique sets of inscriptions. This contribution is just scintillating and was later (1992) followed up by Asko Parpola identifying 36 groups. The finds by HARP, of a copper tablet -- and duplicates -- (bas relief with raised script) in Harappa, together with 31 and 22 sets of duplicate tablets with identical inscriptions are significant developments which provide archaeometallurgical data archives.

Copper tablet (H2000-4498/9889-01) with raised script found in Trench 43. Harappa. (Source: Slide 351. harappa.com) Eight such tablets have been found (HARP, 2005); these were recovered from circular platforms. This example of a uniquely scripted tablet with raised Harappa Script glyphs shows that copper tablets were also used in Harappa, while hundreds of copper tablets with Harappa Script inscriptions were found in Mohenjo-daro. kāṇḍa 'backbone' rebus: khaṇḍa 'implements baraḍo = spine; backbone (Tulu) Rebus: baran, bharat 'mixed alloyś (5 copper, 4 zinc and 1 tin) (Punjabi) bhārata 'a factitious alloy of copper, pewter, tin' (Marathi) dula 'pair' Rebus: dul 'cast metal'. The cast metal is pewter. baraḍo = spine; backbone (Tulu) Rebus: baran, bharat 'mixed alloyś (5 copper, 4 zinc and 1 tin) (Punjabi) karaṁḍa -- m.n. ' bone shaped like a bamboo ', karaṁḍuya -- n. ' backbone '.(Prakrtam)(CDIAL 2670) rebus: karaḍa 'hard alloy'.

gōṭā 'round pebble' rebus: gōṭā 'laterite ferrous ore'. खोट (p. 212) [khōṭa] f A mass of metal (unwrought or of old metal melted down); an ingot or wedge. (Marathi) kanac 'corner' rebus: kancu 'bronze' PLUS dula 'pair' rebus: dul 'cast metal' PLUS muh 'ingot'. PLUS खाडा [khāṇḍā] 'A jag, notch, or indentation (as upon the edge of a tool or weapon)' Rebus: khaṇḍa 'implements'. (Santali). Thus, laterite, pewter and bronze ingots.

Thus, the inscription reads rebus: dul gōṭā PLUS bharata khaṇḍa, i.e., 'cast laterite PLUS pewter' implements. The obvious purpose of such a seal with raised script is to create multiple seal impressions, not unlike the printing demonstrated by the finds of copper tablets with Harappa Script inscriptions.[251]

h2249 to h2257 nine copper plates are duplicates of this inscription.

h2249A copper tablet

h2250A copper tablet

h2250A copper tablet (colour)

h2251 copper tablet

h2252A copper tablet

h253A copper tablet

h2254A copper tablet

h2255A copper tablet

h2256A copper tablet

h2257A copper tablet

Mohenjo-daro. Copper seal. National Museum, New Delhi. [Source: Page 18, Fig. 8A in: Deo Prakash Sharma, 2000, Harappa seals, sealings and copper tablets, Delhi, National Museum].

Comparable to the inscription on the bas relief inscribed copper tablet is the following inscribed copper tablet of Mohenjo-daro from Harappa Script Corpora:

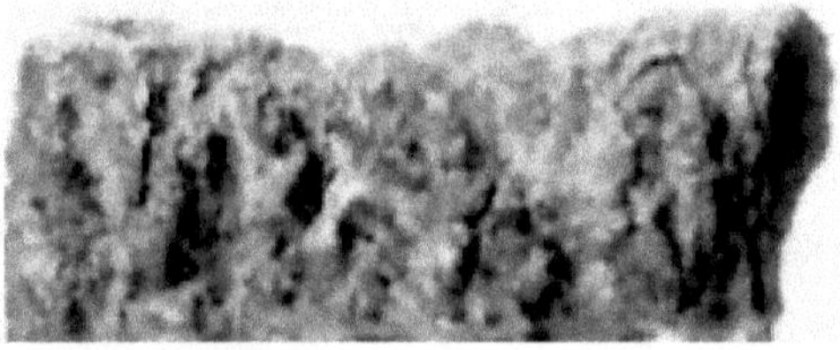
m0475Atcopper

3247 baraḍo = spine; backbone (Tulu) Rebus: baran, bharat 'mixed alloyś (5 copper, 4 zinc and 1 tin) (Punjabi) bhārata 'a factitious alloy of copper, pewter, tin' (Marathi) dula 'pair' Rebus: dul 'cast metal'. The cast metal is pewter.

gōṭā 'round pebble' rebus: gōṭā 'laterite ferrous ore'. dula 'pair' rebus: dul 'cast metal'

Thus, the inscription reads rebus: dul gōṭā PLUS bharat, i.e., 'cast laterite PLUS pewter'

Included in the analyses is a Mohenjo-daro tablet DK 11307 (Yule, Paul 1988)

The tablet shows mirror-duplicated oxen in front of two feeding troughs. dula 'pair' rebus: dul 'metal casting' barad,barat, 'ox' rebus:bharata 'alloy of pewter, copper, tin' pattar 'trough' rebus: pattar 'guild' See B10 category suggested by BM Pande, below

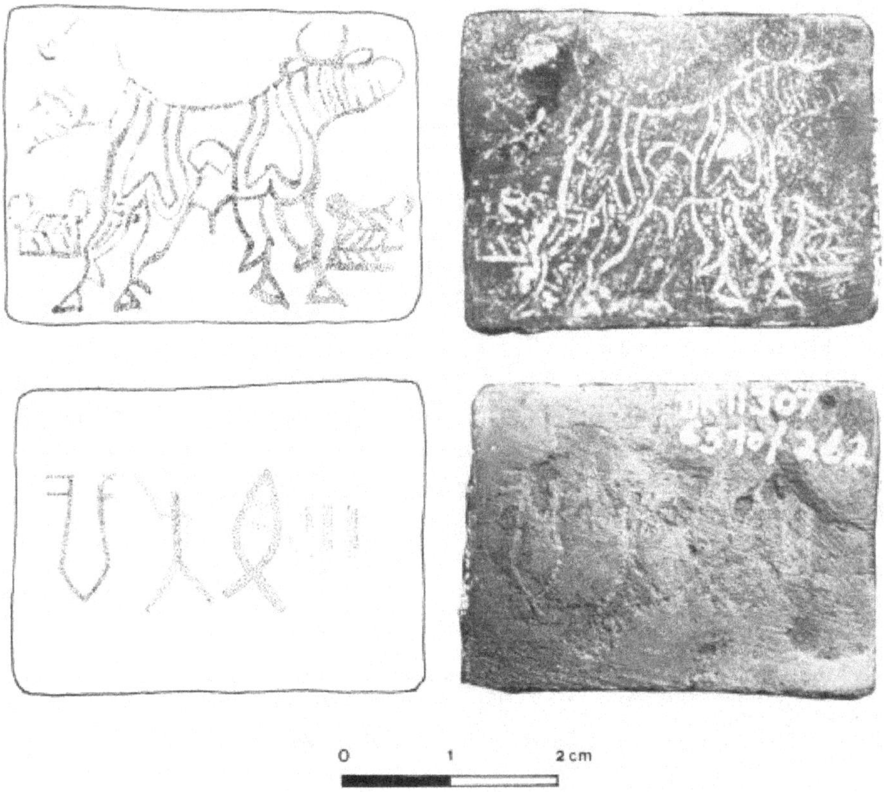

DK 11307

There are 240 such copper plate inscriptions in Harappa Script Corpora.

Semantic cluster 1: ranku ‘tin’ kolimi ‘smithy’ meḍha ‘yajna’ kammara ‘artisan’

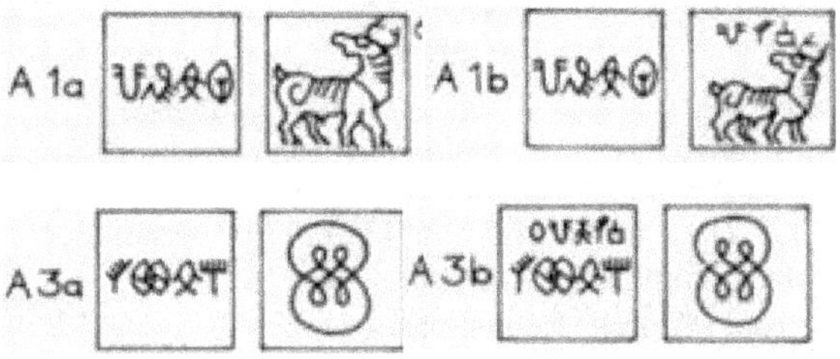

Hieroglyph on obverse of the inscription types A1, A2, A11:

krammara 'look back' (Te.); kamar 'smith' (Santali) PLUS mēḻh (Brahui), mṟēka (Telugu) 'antelope'; milakkhu 'copper' (Pali). Kur. xolā tail. Malt. qoli id.(DEDR 2135) rebus: kol ‘working in iron’ kolle ‘blacksmith’. Thus the artisan defines his or her profession as coppersmith.

A1 inscription

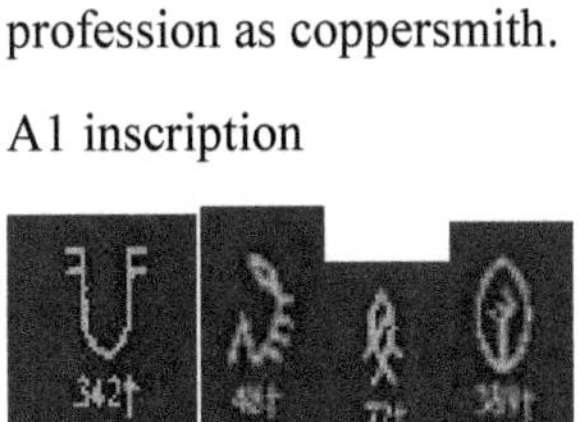

Deciphered from l.: supercargo, large metal (alloy) ingot, ingot for smithy,forge, bharat alloy of copper, zinc and tin

karṇika, kanka 'rim of jar' rebus: karṇī 'supercargo' karṇika 'account, scrobe' kaṇḍa kanka 'rim of jar' Rebus: karṇīka 'account (scribe)'karṇī'supercargo'.

aya 'fish' rebus: ayas, aya 'metal, iron' PLUS dhAL 'slanted' Rebus: DhALako 'large ingot'

double parenthesis as circumflex: Oval shaped like a bun ingot; rebus: mūhā 'ingot' PLUS kolmo 'rice-plant' rebus: kolimi 'smithy, forge'. Thus, smithy, forge ingot

baraḍo = spine; backbone (Tulu) Rebus: baran, bharat 'mixed alloyś (5 copper, 4 zinc and 1 tin) (Punjabi).baroṭi 'twelve' bhārata 'a factitious alloy of copper, pewter, tin' (Marathi)भरत (p. 603) [bharata] n A factitious metal compounded of copper, pewter, tin &c.भरताचें भांडें (p. 603) [bharatācē mbhāṇḍēṃ] n A vessel made of the metal भरत. 2 See भरिताचें भांडें.भरती (p. 603) [bharatī] a Composed of the metal भरत. (Molesworth Marathi Dictionary).

A3a and A3b

Text message of inscription A3b

A 3b Top line hypertext (in addition to the hypertext line on A3a): ranku 'liquid measure' rebus: ranku 'tin' kolmo 'rice plant' rebus: kolimi 'smithy, forge'

 Ligature hieroglyph 'currycomb' to meḍ 'body' rebus: meḍ 'iron' (Alternative: bhaṭa 'warrior' rebus: bhaṭa 'furnace') PLUS karaNika 'spread legś rebus: karṇī 'supercargo' karṇika 'scribe, account' PLUS Sign 38: khāreḍo = a currycomb (Gujarati) खरारा [khārārā] m (H) A currycomb. 2 Currying a horse. (Marathi) Rebus: करडा [karaḍā] Hard from alloy--iron, silver &c. (Marathi) khārādī ' turner' (Gujarati) kāṭi 'body stature; Rebus: fireplace trench. Thus, fireplace for hard alloy metal. karṇaka, kanka 'rim of jar' rebus: karṇī 'Supercargo' karṇika 'scribe, account';

kanac 'corner' Rebus: kancu 'bronze'

Line 2: aḍar 'harrow'; rebus: aduru 'native unsmelted metal; 'fish-fin 'khambharā', ayo, aya 'fish' rebus: aya 'iron' ayas 'metal' Thus, metal/iron mint karā̃ n. pl. ' wristlets, bangles ' (Gujarati) Rebus: *khār* 'blacksmith'. dula 'pair' rebus: dul 'metal casting'; *pajhaṛ* = to sprout from a root (Santali) Rebus: pasra 'smithy' (Santali) kolom,

Alternative: *kolmo* 'rice plant' rebus: *kolime* 'furnace' (Kannada) *kolimi* 'smithy, forge' (Telugu); *kolame* 'deep pit' (Tulu)

Hieroglyph: Endless knot

dhAtu 'strand of rope' Rebus: *dhAtu* 'mineral, metal, ore'धातु [p= 513,3] m. layer , stratum KaltyS3r. Kaus3. constituent part , ingredient (esp. [and in RV. only] ifc. , where often = " fold " e.g. त्रि-धा/आतु , threefold &c ; cf.त्रिविष्टि- , सप्त- , सु-) RV. TS. S3Br. &c (Monier-Williams) *dhā́tu* *strand of rope ' (cf. *tridhā́tu* -- ' threefold ' RV., *ayugdhātu* -- ' having an uneven number of strands ' KātyŚr.).; S. *dhāī* f. ' wisp of fibres added from time to time to a rope that is being twisted ', L. *dhāī̃* f.(CDIAL 6773)

मेढा [*mēḍhā*] A twist or tangle arising in thread or cord, a curl or snarl.(Marathi)(CDIAL 10312).L. *meṛh* f. 'rope tying oxen to each other and to post on threshing floor'(CDIAL 10317) Rebus: *meḍ* 'iron', *mẽṛhet* 'iron' (Mu.Ho.Santali)

Thus, together, a strand and a curl, the hieroglyph-multiplex of endless-knot signifies iron mineral. *mRdu dhAtu* (iron mineral).

C-49 A

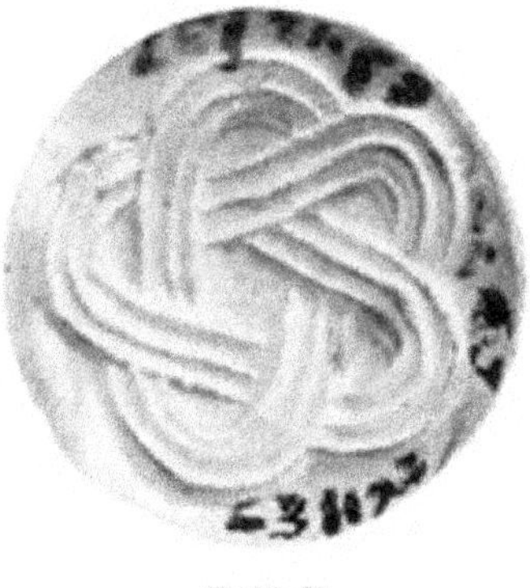

C-49 B

C-49 C

Chanhu-daro 49 a,b,c

+ hieroglyph in the middle with covering lines around/dots in corners पोळ *pōḷa*, 'zebu' rebus: पोळ *pōḷa*, 'magnetite, ferrite ore'; *dhAv. dhAtu* 'strand' rebus: *dhAvaD* 'smelter'; *kulā* 'hooded snake' rebus: *kolle* 'blacksmith' *kol* 'metal, working in iron' *kolhe* 'smelter'; *kolmo* 'three' *koḍ* 'horn' rebus: *kolimi* 'smithy' *koḍ* 'workshop'. *tri-dhAtu* 'three strands, threefold' rebus: *tri-dhAv* 'three mineral ores'.

mḗdha m. ' sacrificial oblation ' RV. Pa. *mēdha* -- m. ' sacrifice '; Si. *mehe, mē* sb. ' eating ' ES 69.(CDIAL 10327). *meḍhA* 'dhanam' (Nirukta)

Thus, *mḗdha* is a yajna. गृहम् grham मेध a. 1 one who performs the domestic rites or sacrifices; गृह- मेधास आ गत मरुतो माप भूतन Rv.7.59.1.-2 connected with the duties of a householder. (-धः) 1 a householder. -2 a domestic sacrifice; मेधः 1 A sacrifice, as in नरमेध, अश्वमेध, एकविंशति मेधान्ते Mb.14.29.18. (com. मेधो युद्धयज्ञः । 'यज्ञो वै मेधः' इति श्रुतेः ।). -2 A sacrificial animal or victim. -3 An offering, oblation. मेधा [मेध्-अञ्] (changed to मेधस् in Bah. comp. when preceded by सु, दुस् and the negative particle अ A sacrifice. -5 Strength, power (Ved.). मेध्य a. [मेध्-ण्यत्, मेधाय हितं यत् वा] 1 Fit for a sacrifice; अजाश्वयोर्मुखं मेध्यम् Y.1.194; Ms.5.54. -2 Relating to a sacrifice, sacrificial; मेध्येनाश्वेनेजे; R.13. 3; उषा वा अश्वस्य मेध्यस्य शिरः Bṛi. Up.1.1.1. -3 Pure, sacred, holy; भुवं कोष्णेन कुण्डोघ्नी मध्येनावमृथादपि R.1.84; 3.31;14.81 *Mejjha* (adj. -- nt.) [**meḍhya; fr. meḍha*] 1. (adj.) [to *meḍha*1] fit for sacrifice, pure; neg. a° impure Sdhp 363. *meḍha*

[Vedic meḍha, in *aśva, go°, puruṣa°* etc.] sacrifice only in *assa°* horse -- sacrifice (Pali)

मेढा [*mēḍhā*]'twist, curl'rebus: *meḍ* 'iron, copper, metal' *meḍha* 'yajna, *dhanam*'.(Nirukta)

Copper plate m1356 The set of hieroglyphs deciphered as: 1. zinc-pewter and 2. bronze:1. jasta, sattva, 'zinc, pewter' and 2. मेढा *mēḍhā* 'twist' *mẽṛhẽt, meḍ* 'iron (metal)'

Hieroglyph: *sattva* 'svastika hieroglyph'; *jasta, dasta* 'five' (Kafiri) Rebus: *jasta, sattva* 'zinc'.

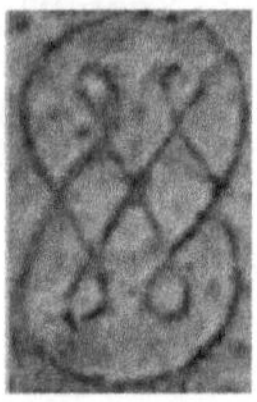

मेढा [*mēḍhā*] curls of hair on cylinder seals; मेढा [*mēḍhā*]twist rebus: *mẽṛhẽt, meḍ* 'iron (metal)' and a cognate word,मृदु *mṛdu* 'iron' (Samskritam) is signified by a number of hieroglyphs

Fatehpur Sikri (1569-1584 CE cf. RS Bisht

Dhruva II Inscription Gujarat Rashtrakuta 884 CE252

h613A

h613C *dhāu* 'rope' rebus: *dhāu* 'metal' PLUS मेढा [*mēḍhā*] 'a curl or snarl; twist in thread' rebus:

mẽṛhẽt, meḍ 'iron'.

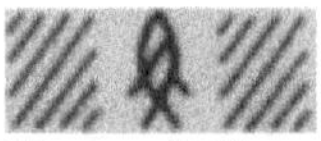

4259 *ayo, aya* 'fish' rebus: *aya* 'iron' ayas 'metal' PLUS *dhal* 'slope' rebus: *dhALako* 'large ingot (oxhide)'

Thomas Wilson curator of US National Museum had in 1894 presented a remarkable Annual Report on Swastika symbol and its migrations. This work is advanced further with the Harappa Script decipherment of the Meluhha glosses: sattva 'glyph' Rebus:sattu, satavu, satuvu 'pewter' (Kannada) In the context of archaeometallurgical indicators, the svastika hieroglyph multiplex seems to have connoted an alloying process of zinc with other minerals to create pewter or brasses of various kinds. Svastika hypertexts appear in remarkable contexts of Harappa Script Corpora which help prove the early significance of this hieroglyph related to metalcasters and turners" work involving creation of new alloys during the Bronze Age.

Focus of this note is on one hieroglyph: svastika evidenced on Harappa Script Corpora and deriving the semantics of the hieroglyph and rebus-metonymy rendering in Harappa Script cipher.

Svastika hieroglyph multiplex is a remarkable hypertext of Harappa Script Corpora, which signify catalogus catalogorum of metalwork.

Svastika signifies zinc metal, spelter. This validates Thomas Wilson's indication -- after a wide-ranging survey of migrations of the hieroglyph across Eurasia and across continents -- that svastika symbol connoted a commodity, apart from its being a hieroglyph, a sacred symbol in many cultures.

"Spelter, while sometimes used merely as a synonym for zinc, is often used to identify a zinc alloy. In this sense it might be an alloy of equal parts copper and zinc, i.e. a brass, used for hard soldering and brazing, or as an alloy, containing lead, that is used instead of bronze."[253]
Hieroglyph: *sattva* 'svastika' glyph Rebus: *sattu, satavu, satuvu* 'pewter' (Kannada) సత్తుతపెల a vessel made of pewter त्रपुधातुविशेषनिर्मितम् jasth जस्थ । त्रपु m. (sg. dat. jastas जस्तस्), zinc, spelter; pewter.

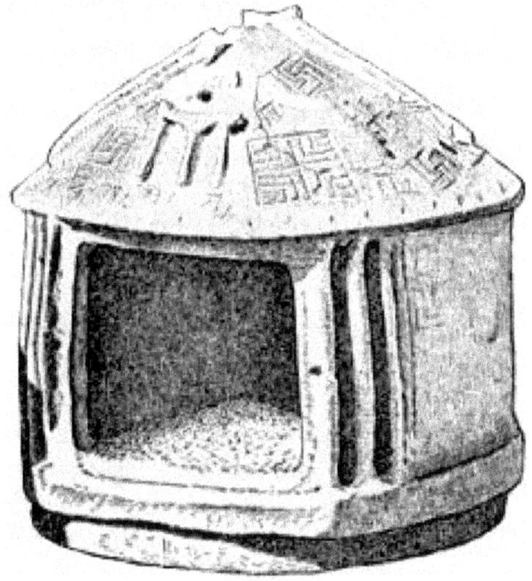

Fig. 183. (After T. Wilson opcit)[254]

Hut urn in the Vatican museum

"Burning altar" mark associated with Swastikas. Etruria (Bronze Age). "They belonged to the Bronze Age, and antedated the Etruscan civilization. This was demonstrated by the finds at Corneto-Tarquinii. Tombs to the number of about 300, containing them, were found, mostly in 1880-81, at a lower level than, and were superseded by, the Etruscan tombs. They contained the weapons, tools, and ornaments peculiar to the Bronze Age—swords, hatchets, pins, fibulæ, bronze and pottery vases, etc., the characteristics of which were different from Etruscan objects of similar purpose, so they could be satisfactorily identified and segregated. The hut urns were receptacles for the ashes of the cremated dead, which, undisturbed, are to be seen in the museum. The vases forming part of this grave furniture bore the Swastika mark; three have two Swastikas, one three, one four, and another no less than eight." (T. Wilson opcit p.857)

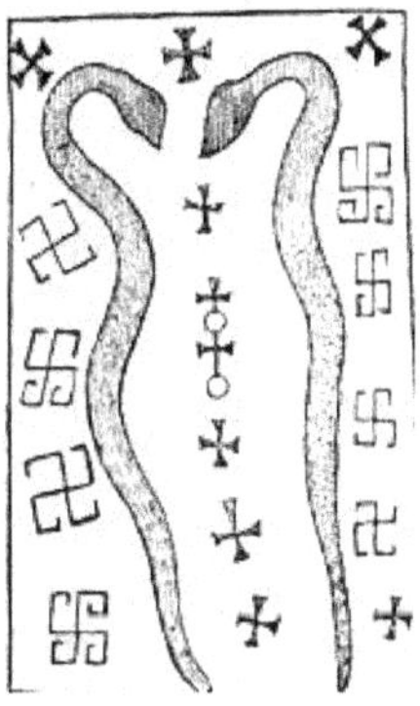

Fig. 175. (After T Wilson opcit)[255]

Detail of archaic Boeotian vase.

Serpents, crosses, and Swastikas (normal, right, left, and meander).[256]

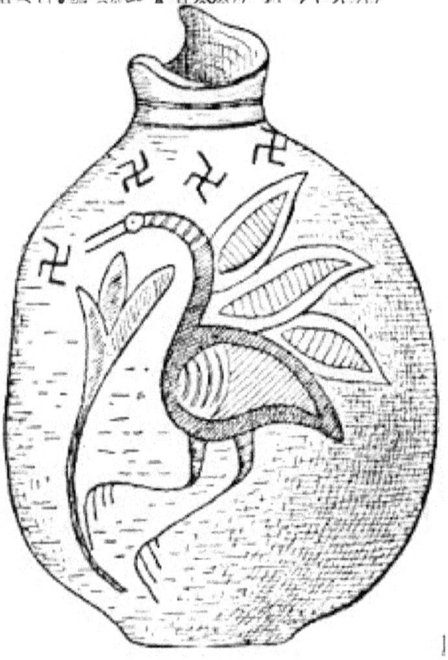

Fig. 174. (After T Wilson opcit)[257]

Archaic Greek vase with five svastiaks of four different forms.[258]

"The Swastika comes from India as an ornament in form of a cone (conique) of metal, gold, silver, or bronze gilt, worn on the ears (see G. Perrot: "Histoire de l'Art," iii, p. 562 et fig. 384), and nose-rings (see S. Reinach: "Chronique d'Orient," 3e série, t. iv, 1886). I was the first to make known the nose-ring worn by the goddess Aphrodite-Astarte, even at Cyprus. In the Indies the women still wear these ornaments in their nostrils and ears. The fellahin of Egypt also wear similar jewelry; but as Egyptian art gives us no example of the usage of these ornaments in antiquity, it is only from the Indies that the Phenicians could have borrowed them. The nose-ring is unknown in the antiquity of all countries which surrounded the island of Cyprus." (p.851, T Wilson opcit)

"The Swastika has been discovered in Greece and in the islands of the Archipelago on objects of bronze and gold, but the principal vehicle was pottery; and of these the greatest number were the painted vases. It is remarkable that the vases on which the Swastika appears in the largest proportion should be the oldest, those belonging to the Archaic period. Those already shown as having been found at Naukratis, in Egypt, are assigned by Mr. Flinders Petrie to the sixth and fifth centuries B. C., and their presence is accounted for by migrations from Greece." (p.839. T Wilson opcit)

"Whatever else the sign Swastika may have stood for, and however many meanings it may have had, it was always ornamental. It may have been used with any or all the above significations, but it was always ornamental as well. The Swastika sign had great extension and spread itself practically over the world, largely, if not entirely, in prehistoric times, though its use in some countries has continued into modern times." (T. Wilson, p.772)

Fig. 166. (After T Wilson opcit)[259]

Cyprian vase with svastikas and figures of birds.

Perrot and Chipiez, "History of Art in Phenicia and Cyprus," II, p. 300, fig. 237;

Goodyear, "Grammar of the Lotus," pl. 48, figs. 6, 12; Cesnola, "Cyprus, its Ancient Cities, Tombs, and Temples," Appendix by Murray, p. 412, pl. 44, fig. 34.[260]

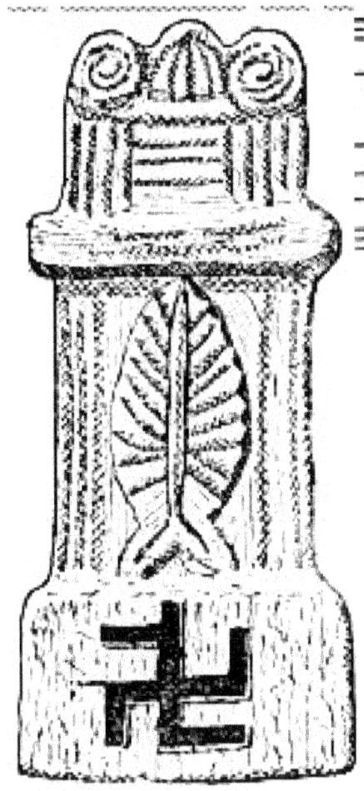

Syrian vase with lotus and svastikas and figure of bird Metropolitan Museum of Art, New York City.[261]

Musée St. Germain. Ohnefalsch-Richter, Bull.Soc. d'Anthrop., Paris, 1888, p. 674,

fig. 6.262

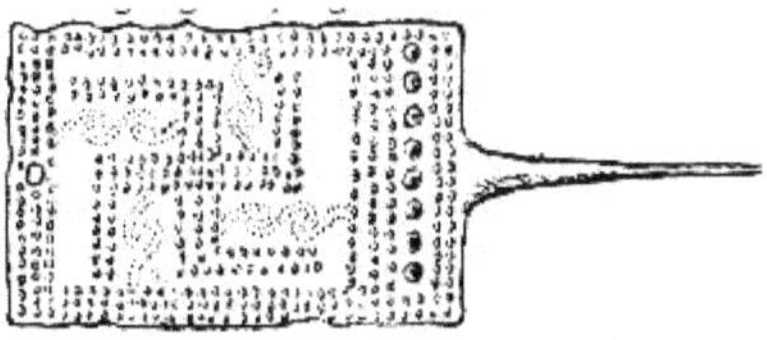

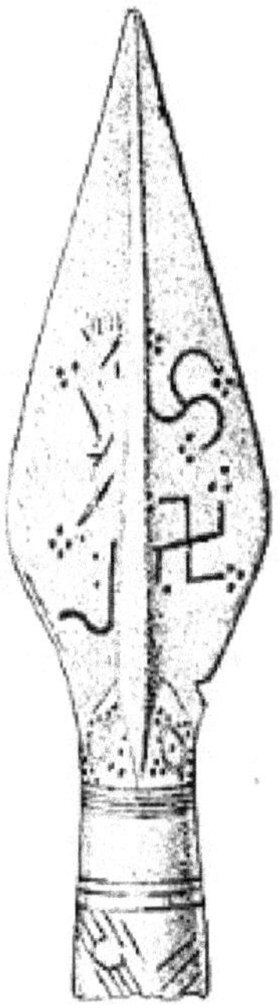

Fig. 202 (T. Wilson opcit)[263].

Bronze pin with svastika pointille from mound in Bavaria Chantre, Matériaux pour l'Histoire Primitive et Naturelle de l'Homme, 1854, pp. 14, 120.[264]

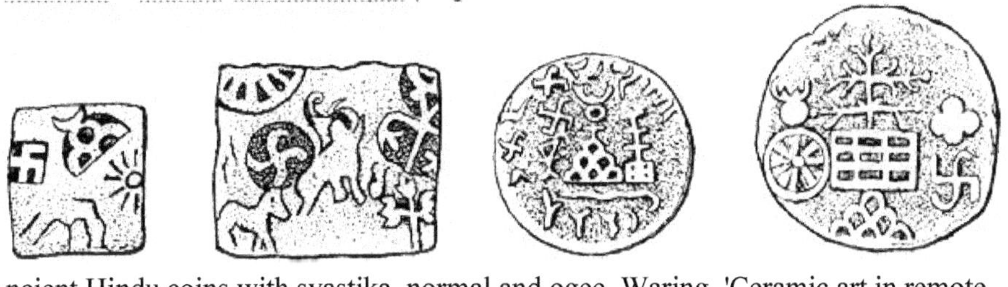

Ancient Hindu coins with svastika, normal and ogee. Waring, 'Ceramic art in remote ages,' pl. 41, figs. 20-24.265

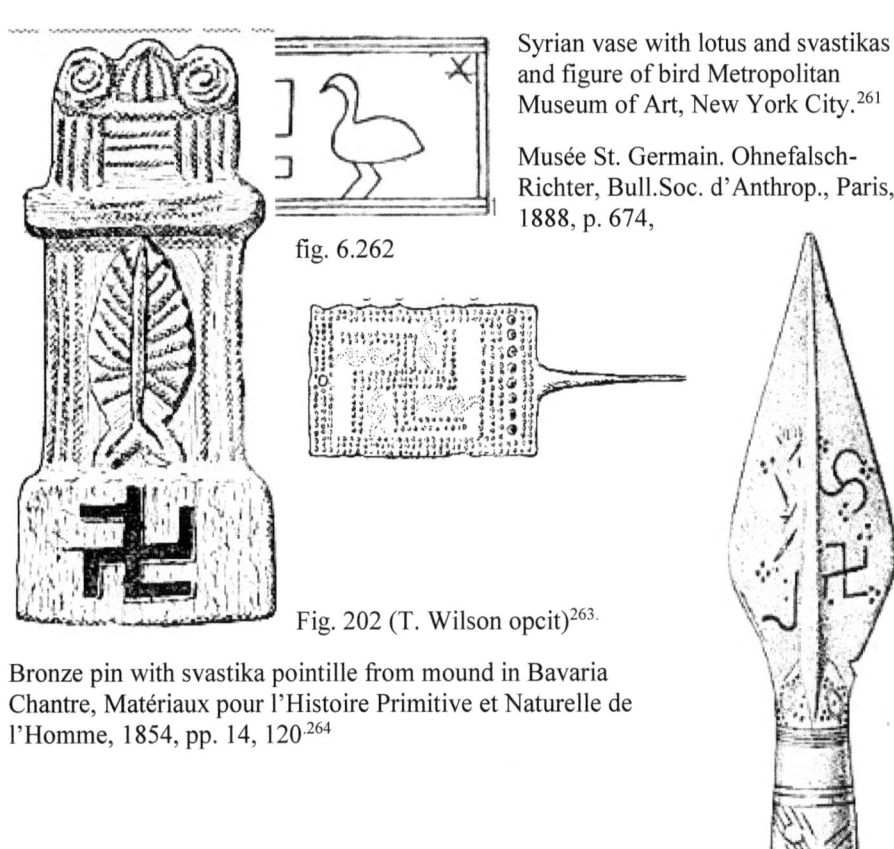

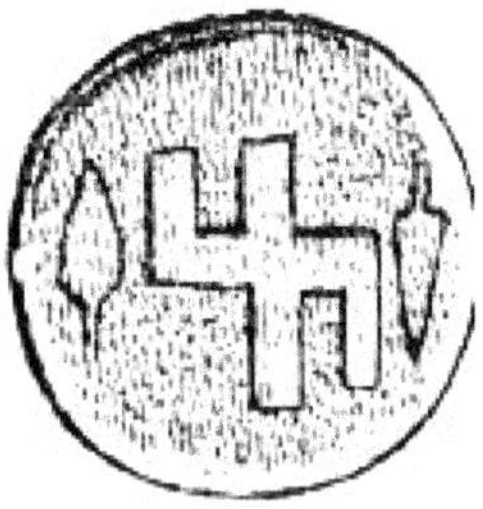

After Fig. 235 (T. Wilson opcit). Ancient coin with svastika. Gaza. Palestine. Waring 'Ceramic art in remote ages,' pl. 42, fig.6 [266]

Fig. 32. (After T Wilson opcit)

Footprint of Buddha with svastika, from Amaravati Tope..

From a figure by Fergusson and Schliemann.[267]

Plate 5. Buffalo with Swastika on Forehead. (After T. Wilson opcit)

Presented to Emperor of Sung Dynasty.

From a drawing by Mr. Li, presented to the U. S. National

Museum by Mr. Yang Yü, Chinese Minister, Washington, D. C. "In the Chinese language the sign of the Swastika is pronounced wan, and stands for “many,” “a great number,” “ten thousand,” “infinity,” and by a synecdoche is construed to mean “long life, a multitude of blessings, great happiness,” etc.; as is said in French, “mille pardons,” “mille remercîments,” a thousand thanks, etc." (T. Wilson opcit, p.800) “The possible migrations of the Svastika, and its appearance in widely separated countries and among differently cultured peoples, afford the principal interest in this subject to archæologists and anthropologists...The Swastika was certainly prehistoric in its origin. It was in extensive use during the existence of the third, fourth, and fifth cities of the site of ancient Troy, of the hill of Hissarlik; so also in the Bronze Age, apparently during its entire existence, throughout western Europe from the Mediterranean Sea to the Arctic Ocean...Professor Sayce is of the opinion that the Swastika was a Hittite symbol and passed by communication to the Aryans or some of their important branches before their final dispersion took place, but he agrees that it was unknown in Assyria, Babylonia, Phenicia, or among the Egyptians...Whether the Swastika was in use among the Chaldeans, Hittites, or the Aryans before or during their dispersion, or whether it was used by the Brahmins before the Buddhists came to India is, after all, but a matter of detail of its migrations; for it may be fairly contended that the Swastika was in use, more or less common among the people of the Bronze Age anterior to either the Chaldeans, Hittites, or the Aryans...Looking over the entire prehistoric world, we find the Swastika used on small and comparatively insignificant objects, those in common use, such as vases, pots, jugs, implements, tools, household goods and utensils, objects of the toilet, ornaments, etc., and infrequently on statues, altars, and the like. In Armenia it was found on bronze pins and buttons; in the Trojan cities on spindle-whorls; in Greece on pottery, on gold and bronze ornaments, and fibulæ. In the Bronze Age in western

Europe, including Etruria, it is found on the common objects of life, such as pottery, the bronze fibulæ, ceintures, spindle-whorls, etc."(ibid., pp. 950, 951)[268]
Thomas Wilson, Curator, Prehistoric Anthropology, US National Museum. His work on the Svastika (spelt swastika) presented in Annual Report 1894 (pp. 763 to 1011[269]

Thomas Wilson notes in the Preface: "The principal object of this paper has been to gather and put in a compact form such information as is obtainable concerning the Swastika, leaving to others the task of adjustment of these facts and their arrangement into an harmonious theory. The only conclusion sought to be deduced from the facts stated is as to the possible migration in prehistoric times of the Swastika and similar objects. No conclusion is attempted as to the time or place of origin, or the primitive meaning of the Swastika, because these are considered to be lost in antiquity. The straight line, the circle, the cross, the triangle, are simple forms, easily made, and might have been invented and re-invented in every age of primitive man and in every quarter of the globe, each time being an independent invention, meaning much or little, meaning different things among different peoples or at different times among the same people; or they may have had no settled or definite meaning. But the Swastika was probably the first to be made with a definite intention and a continuous or consecutive meaning, the knowledge of which passed from person to person, from tribe to tribe, from people to people, and from nation to nation, until, with possibly changed meanings, it has finally circled the globe." (ibid., p. 764). Harappa Script svastika hieroglyph is an object, it signifies 'zinc' mineral.

Semantic cluster 2: loha 'copper' meḍha 'yajna' kammara 'artisan'

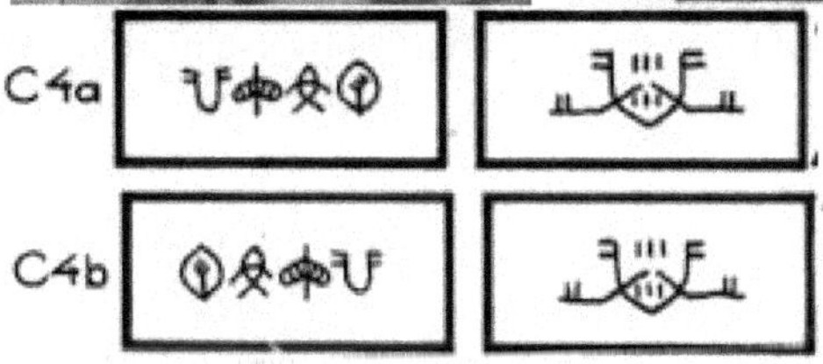

A2 obverse: hypertext

krammara 'look back' (Te.); *kamar* 'smith' (Santali) PLUS *mēl̠h* (Brahui), *mr̤ēka* (Telugu) 'antelope'; *milakkhu* 'copper' (Pali). Kur. *xolā* tail. Malt. *qoli* id. (DEDR 2135) rebus: *kol* 'metal, working in iron' *kolle* 'blacksmith'. Thus the artisan defines his or her profession as coppersmith.

A2 Text message of inscription is the same as the text messages on C4a and C4b (with reversal of the same set of sign sequences).

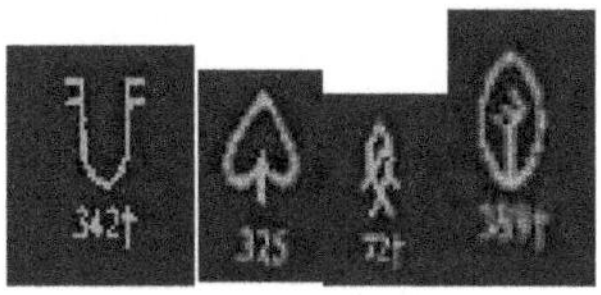

Deciphered from l: As in A1 decipherment but with the replacement of *baraDo* 'spine' hieroglyph with 'ficuś hieroglyph: *loa* 'ficuś rebus: *loh* 'copper, metal'. This hieroglyph substitution is significant: one indicates *bhārata* 'alloy of pewter, copper,tin' and another indicates *loha* 'metal alloy of copper, copper pyrites.'.

C4a Text

kaṇḍa kanka 'rim of jar' Rebus: *karṇīka* 'account (scribe)'*karṇī* 'supercargo'. *kaṇḍa* 'fire-altar', kaṇḍa 'implements'. Alternative: *kanka* 'rim of jar' rebus: *kan*ga 'brazier'.

loa 'ficuś rebus: *loh* 'copper'

aya 'fish' rebus: *aya, ayas* 'iron, metal' PLUS *dhal* 'slant' rebus: *dhALako* 'large ingot

Bun ingot shape: *mũh* 'ingot' (Santali) PLUS (infixed) *kolom* 'sprout, rice plant' Rebus: *kolimi* 'smithy, forge' Thus, ingot smithy. The text message thus reads: furnace, implements account, copper, metal, smithy, forge.

Notes: *dula* 'pair' Rebus: *dul* 'cast metal' Ellipse is split into two curves of parenthesis: ( ) Thus, *dul* 'cast metal' signified by the curves joined into an ellipses.

The oval shape is seen as two curves (parentheses): *dula* 'pair' rebus: *dul* 'metal casting' PLUS *kuṭi* 'curve; rebus: **कुटिल** *kuṭila, katthīl* tin-bronze (8 parts copper, 2 parts tin). Thus, the oval or rhombus shape may read: *dul kuṭila* 'metal casting of tin-bronze'. The Sign 359 may be read as a hypertext: *dul kuṭila kolimi* 'smithy for metal casting of tin-bronze'.

C4b Text is a reversal in sequence of the Text signs on C4a. Thus, the reading is the same as in C4a hypertext: *dul kuṭila kolimi* 'smithy for metal casting of tin=bronze'.

The obverse on both C4a and C4b provides another hypertext Sign 346. The 'rim of jar' hieroglyph is ligatured with six short linear strokes (a pair of 'three short linear strokes') (infixed) and two short linear strokes are signified on the edges of an extended tail. The extended tail compares with the orthography of tail ligatured to an antelope on h11 obverse hieroglyph:

The readings are of hypertext Sign 346:

Part 1 *kaṇḍa kanka* 'rim of jar' Rebus: *karṇīka* 'account (scribe)'*karṇī* 'supercargo' *kaṇḍa* 'fire-altar', *kaṇḍa* 'implements'. Alternative: *kanka* 'rim of jar' rebus: *kan*ga 'brazier' Part 2 *baTa* 'six' rebus: *bhaTa* 'furnace' PLUS sal 'splinter' rebus: sal 'workshop' PLUS dula 'pair' rebus: dul 'metal casting'. Reading the Parts 1 and 2 together, the message is: *kaṇḍa kanka dul kolimi, dul sal*: fire-altar furnace account of smithy metal casting and workshop metal casting.

Read with the hypertext on the obverse, the inscriptions on copper plates C4a, C4b both signify:

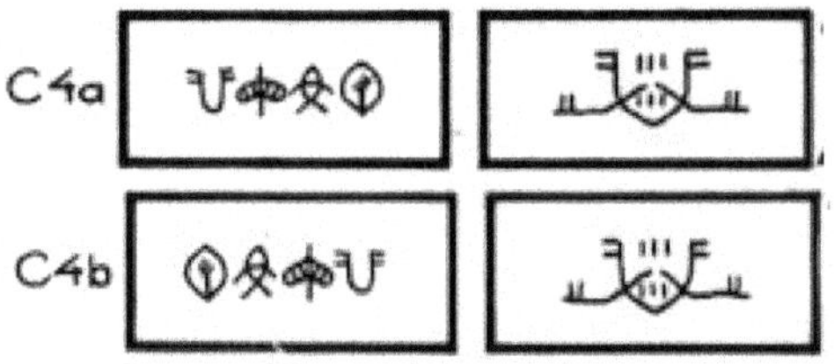

Reverse text message: furnace, implements account, copper, iron (metal), bronze, smithy, forge PLUS obverse: hypertext message: *kanka dul kolimi, dul sal*: fire-altar account of smithy metal casting and workshop metal casting PLUS (work done in) *dul kuṭila kolimi* 'smithy for metal casting of tin-bronze'. Thus, both hypertexts on the obverse and reverse convey the same message making a distinction between metalcasting work done in smithy and work done in workshop (maybe, forge as on circular platforms using an anvil).

Semantic cluster 3: *ranku* 'tin' *khaṇḍa* 'implements *kuThAru* 'axe' *bharata* 'alloy of pewter, copper, tin' *pattar* 'guild'

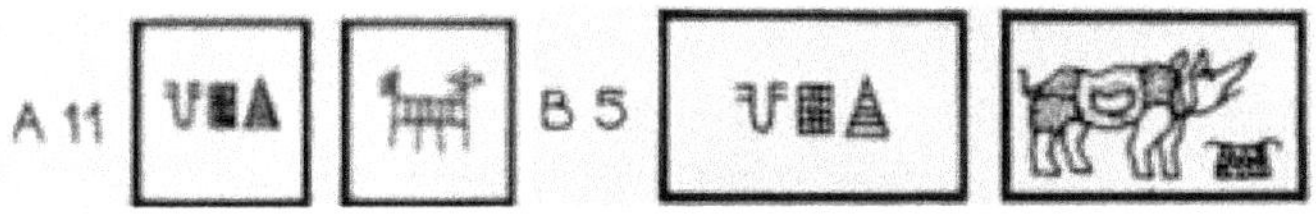

A11 Obverse Hypertext

krammara 'look back' (Te.); *kamar* 'smith' (Santali) PLUS *mē̱ḻẖ* (Brahui), *mṟēka* (Telugu) 'antelope'; *milakkhu* 'copper' (Pali). *ranku* 'antelope' rebus: *ranku* 'tin' Kur. *xolā* tail. Malt. *qoli* id.(DEDR 2135) rebus: *kol* 'metal, working in iron' *kolle* 'blacksmith'. Thus the artisan defines his or her profession as coppersmith, tinsmith.

A11, B5 The message is iron implements for supercargo. Hypertexts of pictorial motifs signify: tinsmith working in iron, smith guild working in iron implements.

Hieroglyph: B5 Hieroglyph: kāṇḍa 'rhinoceroś rebus: *khaṇḍa* 'implements PLUS pattar 'trough' rebus: *pattar* 'guild'

kaṇḍa kanka 'rim of jar' Rebus: *karṇīka* 'account (scribe)' *karṇī* 'supercargo'.

kaṇḍa 'fire-altar'. Alternative: *kanka* 'rim of jar' rebus: *kanga* 'brazier'.

khaṇḍa 'division' rebus: *khaṇḍa* 'implements

Hieroglyph: hillock: Te. *meṭṭa* raised or high ground, hill; (K.) meṭṭu mound; miṭṭa high ground, hillock, mound; high, elevated, raised, projecting; (VPK) *mēṭu, mēṭa, mēṭi* stack of hay; (Inscr.) *meṇṭa-cēnu* dry field (cf. meṭṭu-nēla, meṭṭu-vari). Kol. (SR.) *meṭṭā* hill; (Kin.) meṭṭ, (Hislop) *met* mountain. Nk. *meṭṭ* hill, mountain. Ga. (S.3, LSB 20.3) *meṭṭa* high land. Go. (Tr. W. Ph.) *maṭṭā*, (Mu.) *maṭṭa* mountain; (M. L.) *meṭā* id., hill; (A. D. Ko.) *meṭṭa, (Y. Ma. M.) meṭa hill; (SR.) meṭṭā* hillock (Voc. 2949). *Koṇḍa meṭa id. Kuwi (S.) metta* hill; (Isr.) *meṭa* sand hill. (DEDR 5058) Rebus*: mẽd, mēd* 'iron'.

Thus, the text message on A11 and C5 reads: iron implements scribe, account (for) supercargo.

Atides'a (indication or application in tantra yukti research method) On some inscriptions, an additional orthographic device is used to indicate that a metal implement is the product being managed by a Supercargo. Thus, on a Chanhudaro seal, the double-axe signifies a metal axe, rebus: *kuThAru*, 'armourer'.

Chanhu-daro seal C-23

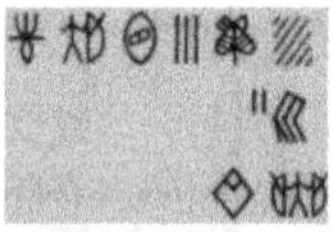

Text 6402 Goat-antelope with a short tail. The object in front of the *melh* 'goat-antelope' (rebus: milakkhu 'copper') is a double-axe.This *xolA, qoli* 'tail' hieroglyph signifies a *kol*, 'metal, working in iron' *kolle* 'blacksmith' working with copper/iron. The double-axe signifies that he is *kuThAru* 'armourer' कुठारु armourer.

Hypertext message: One standing person carries a bow on one hand. Another standing person carries bow and arrow on both hands.

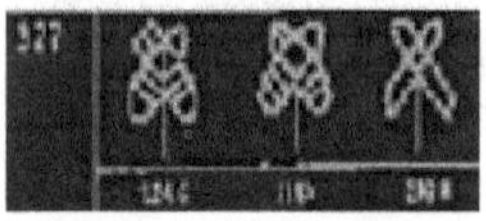

Sign 327 Hypertext 6402 is in three lines:

Line1

loa 'ficus religiosa' rebus: *loha* 'copper' PLUS signifier diacritics: modifying the expression to: *loḥakAr* 'coppersmith'. *khār* खार् । लोहकारः 'blacksmith' (Kashmiri)

kolom 'three' rebus: *kolimi* 'smithy, forge', *muh* 'ingot' PLUS *khaṇḍa* 'divisions' rebus: *khaṇḍa* 'implements *kāmṭhiyɔ* 'archer' rebus: *kammaṭa* 'mint, coiner, coinage' *baṭa* 'rimless pot' rebus: *bhaṭa* 'furnace' PLUS *muka* 'ladle' rebus: *muhA* 'quantity of metal taken out of furnace' PLUS *muh* 'ingot'

Line2

dhAI 'strandś rebus: *dhAtu* 'minerals' *sal* 'splinter' rebus: *sa*l 'workshop'

Line 3

dula 'pair' rebus: *dul* metal casting' *kāmṭhiyɔ* 'archer' rebus: *kammaṭa* 'mint, coiner, coinage' – thus, bronze metal casting mint. k*anac* 'corner' rebus: *kancu* 'bronze'PLUS

Pictorial of markhor with short tail: *miṇḍāl* 'markhor' (Tōrwālī) *meḍho* a ram, a sheep (Gujarati)(CDIAL 10120) Rebus: *mẽṛhẽt, meḍ* 'iron' (Munda.Ho.) *meḍ* 'copper' (Slavic languages) *meḍh* 'merchant's helper (Des'i) PLUS *Kur. xolā tail. Malt. qoli* id.(DEDR 2135) Rebus: கொல்லன் *kollaṉ*, n. < கொல்². [M. *kollan.]* Blacksmith.

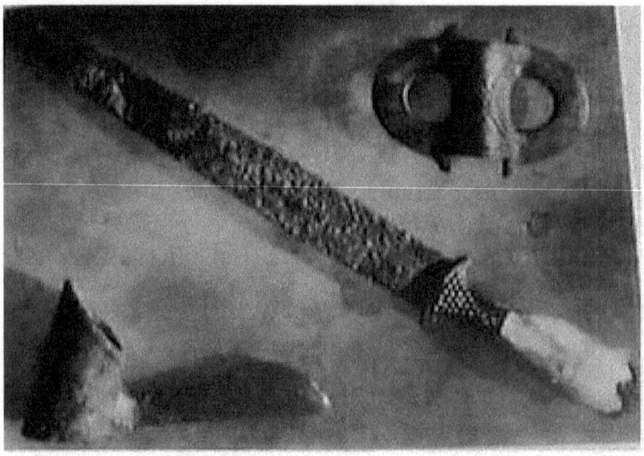

Double-axe found in a Mesopotamian site. Comparable to the double-axe shown on Chanhudaro seal C-23. Pictorial motif of a double-axe is a Harappa Script hieroglyph (Pict-133).

C1 obverse: double-axe hieroglyph Armourer, armoury

C1 Inscription
kuṭhāra m. ' axe ' R., °*raka* -- m. VarBṛS., °*rī* -- f. lex., °*rikā* -- f. Suśr. [*kuṭhātaṅka* -- m., °*kā* -- f. lex. Prob. ← Drav. and conn. with √kuṭṭ EWA i 223 with lit.]Pa. *kuṭhārī* -- f., Pk. *kuḍhāra* -- m., *kuhāḍa* -- m., °*ḍī* -- f. (for *ṭh* -- *r* ~ *h* -- *ḍ* see piṭhara --), S. *kuhāṛo* m., L. P. *kuhāṛā* m., °*ṛī* f., P. *kulhāṛā* m., °*ṛī* f., WPah. bhal. *kurhāṛi* f., Ku. *kulyāṛo*, gng. *kulyāṛ*, B. *kuṛā̆l*, °*li*, *kuṛul*, Or. *kuṛāla*, *kurāṛha*, °*ṛhi*, *kurhāṛi*, *kuṛāri*; Bi. *kulhārī* ' large axe for squaring logs '; H. *kulhāṛā* m., °*ṛī* f. ' axe ', G. *kuhāṛɔ* m., °*ṛī* f., *kuvāṛī* f., M. *kurhāḍ*, °*ḍī* f., Si. *keṇeri* Hettiaratchi Indeclinables 6 (connexion, if any, with *keṭeri*,°*ṭēriya* ' long -- handled axe ' is obscure).Addenda: kuṭhāra --: WPah.kṭg. *khəṛari*, *kəṛari* f. ' axe '.(CDIAL 3244) Rebus: *kuThAru* 'armourer' कुठारु [p= 289,1] an armourer L.

B1, C1 Text message of inscription

The hieroglyph is one-horned bull in front of trough. On C1 the same text has on obverse a double-axe hieroglyph.

dula  'pair' rebus: *dul* 'cast metal' *khaṇḍa* 'division' rebus: *khaṇḍa* 'implements, i.e. metal implement castings

 *koḍa* 'one' rebus: *koḍ* 'workshop' PLUS 'spreadlegś rebus: karṇaka 'helmsman'.

Hieroglyph: notch ' खाडा [khāṇḍā] 'A jag, notch, or indentation (as upon the edge of a tool or weapon)' Rebus: *kāṇḍa* 'implements (Santali). *meḍ* 'body' rebus: *meḍ* 'iron'

 ranku 'liquid measure' rebus: ranku 'tin'

 *mẽd, mēd* 'body'; BODY PLUS 'notch' rebus: *mẽd, mēd* 'iron'

PLUS खाडा [khāṇḍā] 'A jag, notch, or indentation (as upon the edge of a tool or weapon)' Rebus: *kāṇḍa* 'implements (Santali).

'hoof': Kumaon. *khuṭo* 'leg, foot', °*ṭī* 'goat's leg'; Nepalese. *khuṭo* 'leg, foot'(CDIAL 3894). S. *khuṛī* f. 'heel'; WPah. paṅ. *khūṛ* 'foot'. (CDIAL 3906). Rebus: *khũṭ* 'community, guild' (Santali) *khōṭa* 'wedge, ingot' *kūṭa*'workshop'

 *kaṇḍa kanka* 'rim of jar' Rebus: *karṇīka* 'account (scribe)' *karṇī* 'supercargo'.

kaṇḍa 'fire-altar'

B1 inscription
Hieroglyph: One horned young bull PLUS *pattar* 'trough' rebus: *pattar* 'guild'

Details of the work and produce are listed on the top register with four signs: *bhaṭa* 'warrior', rebus: *bhaṭa* 'furnace'; *ḍabu* 'an iron spoon' Rebus: *ḍab*, 'lump; *kolmo* 'paddy plant' Rebus: *kolimi* 'smithy, forge'; ranku 'liquid measure' Rebus: *ranku* 'tin'.

The word for the 'pannier' is: खोंडा [*khōṇḍā*] m A कांबळा of which one end is formed into a cowl or hood (Marathi). Hence, rebus: *kōnda* 'engraver, lapidary' (Meluhha. Bharata *sprachbund*).

The proclamation thus lists how the metallurgical work was done (to produce) tin mineral ingot from furnace and forge.

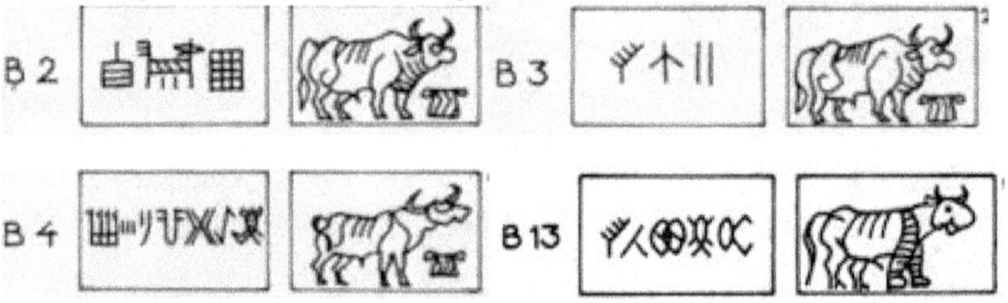

B2 inscription
Hieroglyph: Bull PLUS trough hieroglyph-multiplex
Hieroglyph: *barad, barat* 'ox' Rebus: भरत (p. 603) [*bharata*] n A factitious metal compounded of copper, pewter, tin &c.(Marathi) PLUS *pattar* 'trough' rebus: *pattar* 'goldsmith, guild'.

B2 text

ranku 'liquid measure' rebus: *ranku* 'tin'

mēḻh (Brahui), mṛēka (Telugu) 'goat' rebus: *milakkhu* 'copper' PLUS xol 'tail' rebus: kol 'metal, working in iron'

khaṇḍa 'division' rebus: *khaṇḍa* 'implements. Thus the inscription on B2 is: tin, copper, metal (iron), pewter-copper-tin alloy goldsmith-guild

B3 text

kolmo 'riceplant' rebus: *kolimi* 'smithy, forge' *pajhar* 'sprout' rebus: *pasra* 'smithy'

kāṇḍa 'arrow' rebus: *khaṇḍa* 'implements

dula 'two' rebus: *dul* 'cast metal'. Thus the inscription on B2 is: smithy implements, pewter-copper-tin alloy goldsmith-guild

B4 inscription

rango 'buffalo' rebus: *rango* 'pewter' PLUS *pattar* 'trough' rebus: *pattar* 'goldsmith, guild'

gaṇḍa 'four' rebus: *kaṇḍa* 'fire-altar' kaṇḍa 'implements'PLUS *kolmo* 'rice plant' rebus:

notch: *khāṇḍa* 'notch' rebus: *khaṇḍa* 'implements PLUS *kuṭi* = a. slice, a bit, a small piece (Santali.Bodding) Rebus: *kuṭhi* 'iron smelter furnace' (Santali)

kanka, karṇika 'rim of jar' rebus: *karṇī* 'supecargo, script'

dATu 'crosś rebus: *dhAtu* 'mineral'

ankaḍā 'crook, hook' rebus: *akhāḍā* 'comunity'

bicā 'scorpion' (Assamese) Rebus: *bica* 'haematite, stone ore' (Mu.) Thus, the B12 message reads: minerals, haematite, pewter, implements, smelter guild.

B13

Hypertext: *barad, balad* ‘ox’ rebus: *bharata* ‘alloy of pewter, copper, tin’ Ligatured with the face of ‘horned tiger’ *kola* ‘tiger’ rebus: *kol* ‘metal, working in iron’

Text message:

ḍato 'claws or pincers of crab' (Santali) rebus: *dhatu* 'ore' (Santali) Vikalpa: *erā* 'clawś; Rebus: era 'copper'. *kAru* ‘pincers’ rebus: *kAru* ‘artisan’

aya ‘fish’ rebus: *aya, ayas* ‘iron, metal’ PLUS B. *ā̃is ‘ scales of fish ’; Or. ā̃isa ‘* flesh, fish, fish scales ’ Thus phonetic determinative of *ayas* ‘metal (alloy)’ PLUS *khambhaṛā* m. ‘ fin ’; P. *khambh* m. ‘ wing, feather ’; G. *khā̆m* f., *khabhɔ* m. ‘ shoulder ’.(CDIAL 13640) khambhaṛā 'fish fin' rebus: *kammaṭa* ‘mint, coiner, coinage’

karā̃ n. pl. ‘ wristlets, bangles ’ (Gujarati) Rebus: *khār* 'blacksmith'. mū̃h ‘ingot’ (Santali) *dula* 'pair' Rebus: *dul* 'cast metal' Thus, cast metal ingot.

slant PLUS notch: *dhAL* 'slanted' Rebus: *DhALako* 'large ingot' PLUS खांडा (p. 202) [*khāṇḍā*] A jag, notch, or indentation (as upon the edge of a tool or weapon). Rebus: Rebus: *kāṇḍa* ‘tools, pots and pans and metal-ware’ (Marathi) *khaṇḍa* id. (Santali)

kolmo ‘rice plant’ rebus: *kolimi* ‘smithy, forge’

Semantic cluster 4: *kol* ‘working in iron’ *karba, ib* ‘iron’ *bhaṭa* ‘furnace’

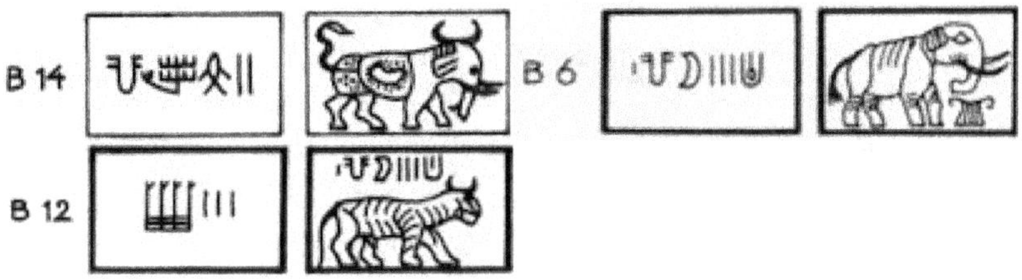

B14

Hieroglyph: horned elephant *karaba* ‘trunk of elephant’ *ibha* ‘elephant’ rebus: *karba* ‘iron’ *ib* ‘iron’ PLUS *koḍ* ‘horn’ rebus: *koḍ* ‘workshop’ *ibbo* ‘merchant’ Ligature with rhinoceros body: *kaṇḍa* ‘rhinoceros’ rebus: *kaṇḍa* ‘implements’.

kaṇḍa kanka ‘rim of jar’ Rebus: *karṇīka* ‘account (scribe)’*karṇī* ‘supercargo’. *kaṇḍa* ‘fire-altar’. Alternative: *kanka* 'rim of jar' rebus: *kanga* 'brazier'.

aDar 'harrow' rebus *aduru* 'native metal' PLUS *dula* ‘pair’ rebus: *dul* ‘cast metal’ PLUS *kolmo* ‘sprout’ rebus: *kolimi* ‘smithy, forge’ Thus smithy/forge for native metal castings

aya ‘fish’ rebus: *ayas, aya* ‘iron, metal’

dula ‘two’ rebus: *dul* ‘metal casting’

B6 inscription

Elephant hieroglyph

m1486B Text

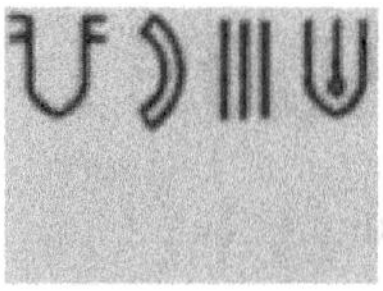

1711

karaba 'trunk of elephant' *ibha* 'elephant' Rebus: *karba* 'iron' *ib* 'iron' PLUS *pattar* 'trough' rebus: *pattar* 'goldsmith, guild'.

Reverse: Inscription of hypertext:

baṭa 'rimless pot' Rebus: *bhaṭa* 'furnace' PLUS *muka* 'ladle' rebus; *mū̃h* 'ingot', quantity of metal got out of a smelter furnace (Santali)

kolom 'three' Rebus: *kolimi* 'smithy, forge'

The lexis entry for bronze is signified by the hieroglyph 'curve' or 'right parenthesiś:

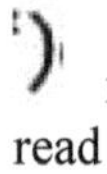 Doubling of this signifies *dula* 'pair' rebus: *dul* 'cast metal'. Thus doubling of the right parenthesis results in a hieroglyph-multiplex or hypertext This hypertext is read as: *kuṭilika* 'bent, curved' *dula* 'pair' rebus: *kuṭila, katthīl* = bronze (8 parts copper and 2 parts tin) cf. *āra-kūṭa,* ' brass Old English *ār* 'brass, copper, bronze' Old Norse *eir* 'brass, copper', German *ehern* 'brassy, bronzen'. *kastīra* n. ' tin ' lex. 2. **kastilla -- .1. H. kathīr* m. ' tin, pewter '; G. *kathīr* n. ' pewter '.2. H. (Bhoj.?) *kathīl, °lā* m. ' tin, pewter '; M. *kathīl* n. ' tin ', *kathlẽ* n. ' large tin vessel '.(CDIAL 2984)

 The 'curve' hieroglyph is a splitting of the ellipse. *kuṭila* 'bent' CDIAL 3230 *kuṭi*— in cmpd. 'curve', *kuṭika*— 'bent' MBh. Rebus: *kuṭila, katthīl* = bronze (8 parts copper and 2 parts tin)

Hieroglyphs: कौटिलिकः *kauṭilikḥ* कौटिलिकः 1 A hunter.-2 A blacksmith. कौटिलिक

[p= 315,2]m. (fr. कुटिलिका Pa1n2. 4-4 , 18) " deceiving the hunter [or the deer Sch.] by particular movements " , a deer [" a hunter " Sch.] Ka1s3. f. (Pa1n2. 4-4 , 18) कुटिलिका crouching , coming stealthily (like a hunter on his prey ; a particular movement on the stage) Vikr. कुटिलिक " using the tool called कुटिलिका " , a blacksmith ib. कुटिलक [p= 288,2] f. a tool used by a blacksmith Pa1n2. 4-4 , 18 Ka1s3.mfn. bent , curved , crisped Pan5cat.

The hieroglyph-multiplex may be a variant of split ellipse curves paired: *dula* 'pair' rebus: *dul* 'cast metal' PLUS *mū̃h* 'ingot' (Paired split ellipse or a pair of right parentheses) -- made of -- *kuṭila, katthīl* = bronze (8 parts copper and 2 parts tin)

karṇika 'rim of jar' rebus: *karṇī* 'supercargo'; *karṇaka* 'account'; Alternative: *kanka* 'rim of jar' rebus: *kanga* 'brazier'.

Thus, the entire inscription is a metalwork catalogue: supercargo of iron, cast bronze metal ingots, out of smithy furnace and forge.

Semantic cluster 5: *kulāi* 'hare' rebus *kol* 'metal, working in iron' *eraka* 'nave of wheel' rebus: *eraka* 'molten cast, copper'

B12

Hieroglyph: *kola* 'tiger' rebus: *kol* 'metal, working in iron' *kolle* 'blacksmith' *kolhe* 'smelter' *kolimi* 'smithy, forge'

kaṇḍa kanka 'rim of jar' Rebus: *karṇīka* 'account (scribe)' *karṇī* 'supercargo'. *kaṇḍa* 'fire-altar'. Alternative: *kanka* 'rim of jar' rebus: *kanga* 'brazier'.

kuṭilika 'bent, curved' dula 'pair' rebus: *kuṭila, katthīl* = bronze (8 parts copper and 2 parts tin) *dula* ‘pair’ rebus: *dul* ‘cast metal’ Thus, bronze casting

kolom ‘three’ rebus: *kolimi* ‘smithy, forge’

baṭa ‘rimless pot’ rebus: *bhaṭa* ‘furnace’ PLUS *muka* 'ladle' rebus; *mũh* 'ingot', quantity of metal got out of a smelter furnace (Santali)

gaṇḍa ‘four’ rebus: *kaṇḍa* ‘fire-altar’ PLUS *kolmo* ‘rice plant’ rebus: *kolimi* ‘smithy, forge’

kolom 'three' rebus: *kolimi* 'smithy, forge'

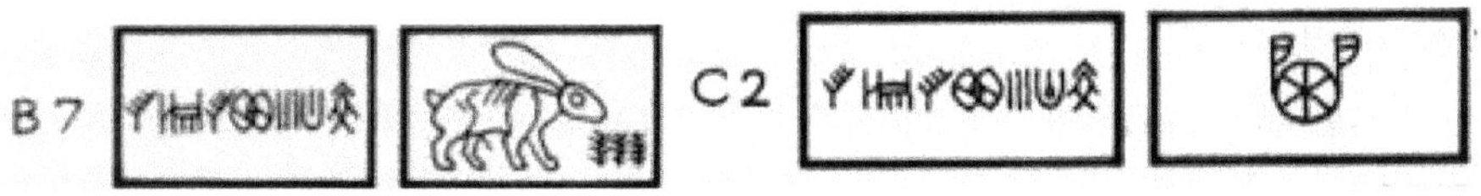

B7

Hieroglyph: *kulāi* ‘hare’ rebus: *kol* ‘metal, working in iron’ *kolle* ‘blacksmith’ *kolhe* ‘smelter’ PLUS *kolmo* ‘sprout’ rebus: *kolimi* ‘smithy, forge’ Alternative: Hieroglyph *kharā* 'hare' (Oriya*)* Rebus: *khār* खार् 'blacksmith' (Kashmiri) PLUS *kaṁṭiya* ‘thorny’ (Prakrit) Rebus: *kammaṭa* 'mint, gold furnace' (Telugu) Thus, *kaṁmaṭakAra* ‘mint master’. *kaṇḍɔ* m. ‘ thorn'; *kaṇṭa*l m. ‘ thorn ’ BhP. 2. *káṇṭaka* -- m. ‘ thorn ’ ŚBr., ‘ anything pointed ’ R. 1. Pa. *kaṇṭa* -- m. ‘ thorn ’, Gy. pal. *ḳand,* Sh. koh. gur. *kōṇ* m., Ku. gng. *kā̃ṇ*, A. *kāī̃ṭ* (< nom. **kaṇṭē*?), Mth. Bhoj. *kā̃ṭ,* OH. *kā̃ṭa.* 2. Pa. *kaṇṭaka* -- m. ‘ thorn, fishbone ’; Pk. *kaṁṭaya*<-> m. ‘ thorn ’, Gy. eur. *kanro* m., SEeur. *kaṭo*, Dm. *kā̃ṭa*, Phal. *kāṇḍu*, *kā̃ṛo*, Sh. gil. *kóṇŭ* m., K. *konḍu* m., S. *kaṇḍo* m., L. P. *kaṇḍā* m., WPah. khaś. *kaṇṭā* m., bhal. *kaṇṭo* m., jaun. *kā̃ḍā*, Ku. *kāno*; N. *kā̃ṛo* ‘ thorn, afterbirth ’ (semant. cf.śalyá --); B. *kā̃ṭā* ‘ thorn, fishbone ’, Or. *kaṇṭā*; Aw. lakh. H. *kā̃ṭā* m.; G. *kā̃ṭɔ* ‘ thorn, fishbone ’; M. *kā̃ṭā*, *kāṭā* m. ‘ thorn ’, Ko. *kāṇṭo*, Si. *kaṭuva.* kaṇṭala -- Addenda: kaṇṭa -- 1. 1. A. also *kā̃iṭ*; Md. *kaṙi* ‘ thorn, bone ’.2. káṇṭaka -- : S.kcch. *kaṇḍho* m. ‘ thorn ’; WPah.kṭg. (kc.) *kaṇḍɔ* m. ‘ thorn, mountain peak ’, J. *kā̃ḍā* m.; Garh. *kā̃ḍu* ‘ thorn ’. (CDIAL 2668) Rebus: kaṇḍa 'implements'. Thus, hare in front of thorn/bush signifies: khār खार् 'blacksmith' PLUS kaṇḍa 'implements', i.e. implements from smithy/forge.

C2

Hieroglyph: *eraka* ‘nave of wheel’ rebus: *eraka* ‘moltencast’ ‘copper’; *arā* ‘spoke’ rebus: *Ara* ‘brass. The ligature may signify: xola ‘tail’ rebus: kol ‘metal, working in iron’. Thus, together, *eraka kol* ‘copper, brass and iron’. Alternative: kAru ‘pincers’ rebus: kAru ‘artisan’. Thus, *eraka Ara kAru* ‘brass artisan’

Text: Same as on B7

kolmo ‘sprout’ rebus: *kolimi* ‘smithy, forge’ (for copper): *meḍ(h), meḍhī f., meḍhā* ‘ post, forked stake ’; *meṛh* f. ‘ rope tying oxen to each other and to post on threshing floor ’ rebus: *mēd* 'iron' PLUS *mē<u>l</u>ẖ (Brahui), mṛēka (Telugu)* 'goat' rebus: *milakkhu* 'copper''

kolmo ‘rice plant’ rebus: *kolimi* ‘smithy, forge’ (for bronze):

gaṇḍa ‘four’ rebus: *kaṇḍa* ‘fire-altar’

baṭa ‘rimless pot’ rebus: *bhaṭa* ‘furnace’ PLUS *muka* ‘ladle’ rebus: *muhA* ‘ingot’ *aya* ‘fish’ rebus: *aya, ayas* ‘iron,metal’ PLUS *aDaren* ‘lid’ rebus: *aduru* ‘unsmelted metal’

Semantic cluster 6: कुटिल *kuṭila, katthīl* (8 parts copper, 2 parts tin) dul ‘metal casting’ *pattar* ‘goldsmith guild’

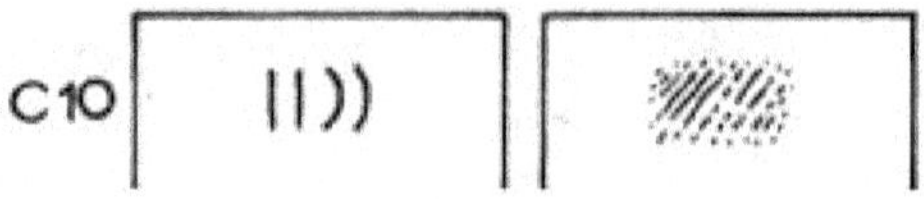

C10

Obverse: Illegible

Text: *dula* ‘two’ rebus: *dul* ‘cast metal’

The 'curve' hieroglyph is a splitting of the ellipse. kuṭila ‘bent’ CDIAL 3230 kuṭi— in cmpd. ‘curve’, *kuṭika—* ‘bent’ MBh. Rebus: *kuṭila, katthīl* = bronze (8 parts copper and 2 parts tin) cf. *āra-kūṭa,* 'brass Old English *ār* 'brass, copper, bronze' Old Norse *eir* 'brass, copper', German *ehern* 'brassy, bronzen'. *kastīra n. ‘ tin ’ lex. 2. *kastilla -- .1. H.* kathīr m. ‘ tin, pewter ’; G. *kathīr* n. ‘ pewter ’.2. H. (Bhoj.?) *kathīl, °lā* m. ‘ tin, pewter ’; *M. kathīl n. ‘ tin ’, kathlẽ* n. ‘ large tin vessel ’.(CDIAL 2984)

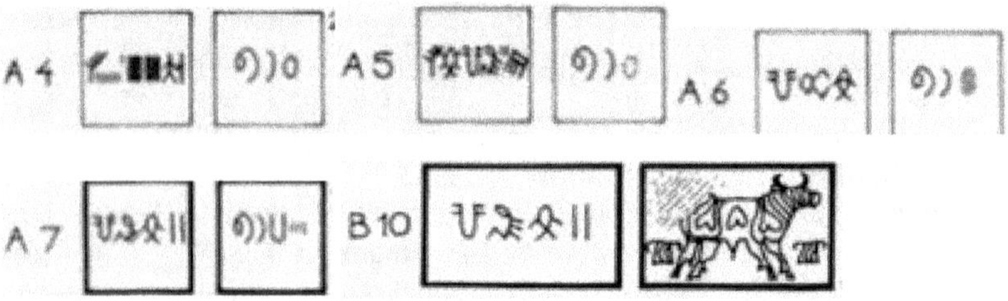

A4, A5, A6 reverse inscription:

This hieroglyph-multiplex or hypertext may be an oval as a circumflex with embedded 'notch' hieroglyph. If so, the rebus readings are: *muh* 'ingot' PLUS खांडा [khāṇḍā] 'A jag, notch, or indentation (as upon the edge of a tool or weapon)' Rebus: kāṇḍa 'implements (Santali). Thus, the hypertext signifies ingot (for) metal implements.

O *goṭ* 'seed, rounded object' Rebus: खोट (p. 212) [*khōṭa*] f A mass of metal (unwrought or of old metal melted down); an ingot or wedge (Marathi) *goTa* ‘laterite, ferrite ore’

) The 'curve' hieroglyph is a splitting of the ellipse. *kuṭila* ‘bent’ CDIAL 3230 kuṭi— in cmpd. ‘curve’, *kuṭika— ‘bent’* MBh.

Rebus: *kuṭila, katthīl* = bronze (8 parts copper and 2 parts tin)

A7 reverse inscription

muh 'ingot' PLUS खांडा [khāṇḍā] 'A jag, notch, or indentation (as upon the edge of a tool or weapon)' Rebus: kāṇḍa 'implements (Santali)

) The 'curve' hieroglyph is a splitting of the ellipse. *kuṭila* ‘bent’ CDIAL 3230 kuṭi— in cmpd. ‘curve’, *kuṭika—* ‘bent’ MBh.

Rebus: *kuṭila, katthīl* = bronze (8 parts copper and 2 parts tin)

U rimless pot: *baṭa* 'rimless pot' Rebus: *bhaṭa* 'furnace'

Numeral 3: *kolom* 'three' rebus: *kolimi* 'smithy, forge'.

A7 obverse Text message of inscription

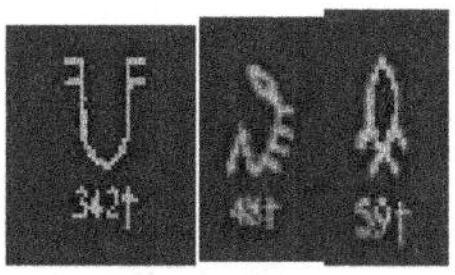 || (Two long linear strokes)

Deciphered from l. to r.:

karṇika, kanka 'rim of jar' rebus: *karṇī* 'supercargo' karṇika 'account, scrobe'

baraḍo = spine; backbone (Tulu) Rebus: *baran, bharat* 'mixed alloyś (5 copper, 4 zinc and 1 tin) (Punjabi).*baroṭi* 'twelve' *bhārata* 'a factitious alloy of copper, pewter, tin' (Marathi)भरत (p. 603) [*bharata*] n A factitious metal compounded of copper, pewter, tin &c.भरताचें भांडें (p. 603) [*bharatācē mbhāṇḍēṃ*] n A vessel made of the metal भरत. 2 See भरिताचें भांडें.भरती (p. 603) [*bharatī*] a Composed of the metal भरत. (Molesworth Marathi Dictionary).

aya 'fish' rebus: *ayas, aya* 'metal, iron'

dula 'two' rebus: *dul* 'cast metal'

B10

Hieroglyph: Back-to-back ligatured body of *barad*, 'ox' rebus: *bharata* 'aalloy of copper, pewter, tin'

PLUS *pattar* 'trough' rebus: *pattar* 'goldsmith, guild'

It is suggested that the back-to-back duplication of the body of an ox signifies *cire perdue* cesting technique used to produce metal castings. *sangaDa* 'joined animals' is a device used in front of the one-horned bull as sangada 'lathe, portable furnace' This technique of s*angaDa* signifies rebus *vajra sanghAta* 'damantine glue' to create alloys of metals by the turner. rebus: सं-ग्रह *saṁgraha, samgaha* 'a guardian , ruler , manager , arranger' R. BhP.

kaṇḍa 'fire-altar'. Alternative: *kanka* 'rim of jar' rebus: *kanga* 'brazier'.

baraḍo = spine; backbone (Tulu) Rebus: *baran, bharat* 'mixed alloyś (5 copper, 4 zinc and 1 tin) (Punjabi).*baroṭi* 'twelve' bhārata 'a factitious alloy of copper, pewter, tin' (Marathi)भरत (p. 603) [*bharata*] n A factitious metal compounded of copper, pewter, tin &c.भरताचें भांडें (p. 603) [*bharatācē mbhāndēm*] n A vessel made of the metal भरत. 2 See भरिताचें भांडें.भरती (p. 603) [*bharatī*] a Composed of the metal भरत. (Molesworth Marathi Dictionary).

aya 'fish' rebus: *aya, ayas* 'iron, metal'

dula 'two' rebus: *dul* 'cast metal'

A6 obverse text message of inscription

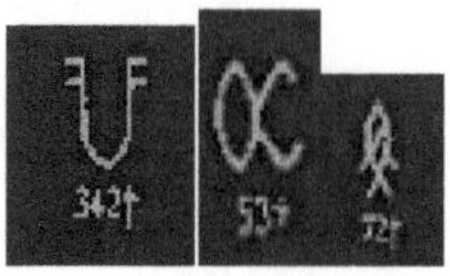

Deciphered from l. to r.:

karṇika, kanka 'rim of jar' rebus: *karṇī* 'supercargo' *karṇika* 'account, scrobe'

kamaḍha 'crab' Rebus: *kammaṭa* 'mint, coiner'.*ḍato* = claws of crab (Santali) *ḍato* = claws of crab (Santali) Rebus: *dhātu* 'mineral ore' *kAru* 'pincers' rebus: *kAru* 'artisan'

aya 'fish' rebus: *ayas, aya* 'metal, iron' PLUS *dhAL* 'slanted' Rebus: *DhALako* 'large ingot'

double parenthesis as circumflex: Oval shaped like a bun ingot; rebus: *mūhā* 'ingot' PLUS *kolmo* 'rice-plant' rebus: *kolimi* 'smithy, forge'.

A5 text message of inscription

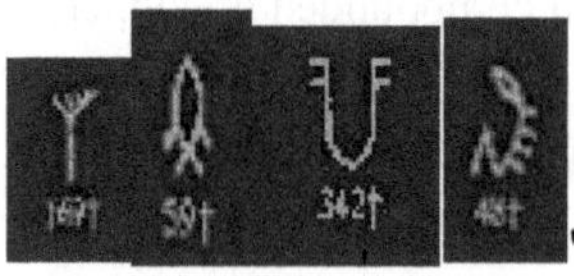" (splinter) (Variant platform) Deciphered from l. to r.:

kolmo 'rice-plant' rebus: *kolimi* 'smithy, forge' *pajhar* 'sprout' rebus: *pasra* 'smithy'

aya 'fish' rebus: *ayas, aya* 'metal, iron'

karṇika, kanka 'rim of jar' rebus: *karṇī* 'supercargo' *karṇika* 'account, scrobe'

baraḍo = spine; backbone (Tulu) Rebus: *baran, bharat* 'mixed alloyś (5 copper, 4 zinc and 1 tin) (Punjabi).*baroṭi* 'twelve' bhārata 'a factitious alloy of copper, pewter, tin' (Marathi)भरत (p. 603) [*bharata*] n A factitious metal compounded of copper, pewter, tin &c.भरताचें भांडें (p. 603) [*bharatācē mbhāṇḍēṃ*] n A vessel made of the metal भरत. 2 See भरिताचें भांडें.भरती (p. 603) [*bharatī*] a Composed of the metal भरत. (Molesworth Marathi Dictionary).

sal 'splinter' rebus: *sal* 'workshop' *kolmo* 'sprout' rebus: *kolimi* 'smithy, forge' PLUS double parenthesis as circumflex: Oval shaped like a bun ingot; rebus: *mūhā* 'ingot'

Platform: *Ta. mēṭai* platform, raised floor, artificial mound, terraced house. *Ma. mēṭa* raised place, tower, upper story, palace. Cf. Skt. (*lex.*) *meṭa-* whitewashed storied house; Pkt. *meḍaya-* id. (DEDR 4796)

Rebus 1: *mḗdha* m. ' sacrificial oblation ' RV.Pa. *mēdha* -- m. ' sacrifice '(CDIAL 10327) Rebus 2: *meḍ* 'iron' (Mu.Ho.) *mẽṛhẽt* iron; *dul m.* = cast iron (Mu.) *meṛed-bica* = iron stone ore, in contrast to bali-bica, iron sand ore (Munda) mẽṛhẽt'iron'; *mẽṛhẽt icena*'the iron is rusty';*ispat mẽṛhẽt*'steel', *dul mẽṛhẽt*'cast iron'; *mẽṛhẽt khaṇḍa*'iron implements (Santali) *meḍ.* (Ho.)(Santali.Bodding) *meṛed, mṛed, mṛd* iron; *enga meṛed* soft iron; *sanḍi meṛed* hard iron; *i meṛed* rusty iron, also the iron of which weights are cast; *bica meṛed* iron extracted from stone ore; *bali meṛed* iron extracted from sand ore (Mu.) *měď* (copper)(Czech) *mid'* (copper, cuprum, orichalc)(Ukrainian) *meḍ'* (copper, cuprum, Cu), *meḍnyy* (copper, cupreous, brassy, brazen, brass), *omeḍnyat'* (copper, coppering), *sul'fatmeḍi* (Copper), *politseyskiy* (policeman, constable, peeler, policemen, redcap), *pokryvat' meḍ'yu* (copper), *payal'nik* (soldering iron, copper, soldering pen, soldering-iron), *meḍnyy kotel* (copper), *meḍno-krasnyy (*copper), *meḍnaya moneta (*copper). *медь* (copper, cuprum, Cu), *медный* (copper, cupreous, brassy, brazen, brass), *омеднять* (copper, coppering), *Сульфатмеди* (Copper), *полицейский* (policeman, constable, peeler, policemen, redcap), *покрывать медью* (copper), *паяльник* (soldering iron, copper, soldering pen, soldering-iron), *медный котел* (copper), *медно-красный* (copper), *медная монета* (copper).(Russian)

A4 text message of inscription

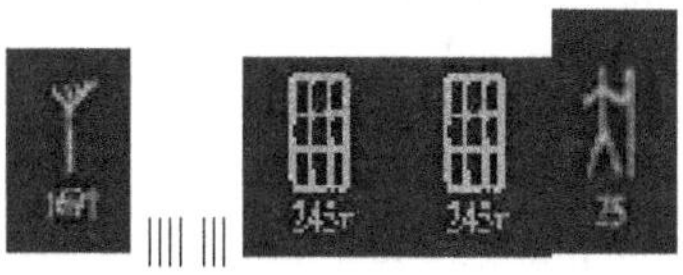

kolmo 'rice-plant' rebus: kolimi 'smithy, forge' pajhar 'sprout' rebus: pasra 'smithy'

khaṇḍa 'divisions' rebus: *khaṇḍa* 'implements PLUS *dula* 'pair' rebus: *dul* 'cast metal', i.e. cast metal implements

meḍ 'body' rebus: *meḍ* 'iron' PLUS *Yūpa* 'staff, pillar' in Prakritam: *meṇḍa* [dial., cp. Prk. *mĕṇṭha & miṇṭha*: Pischel, Prk. Gr. § 293. The Dhtm (156) gives a root *meṇḍ (meḍ)* in meaning of "koṭilla," i. e. crookedness. (Pali) M. *mẽḍhā* m. ' crook or curved end (of a horn, stick, &c.) (DIAL 10311) Rebus: *meḍ* 'iron' (Thus, phonetic determinative of the metal signified by the 'body' hieroglyph.) *koDa* 'one' rebus: *koD* 'workshop'

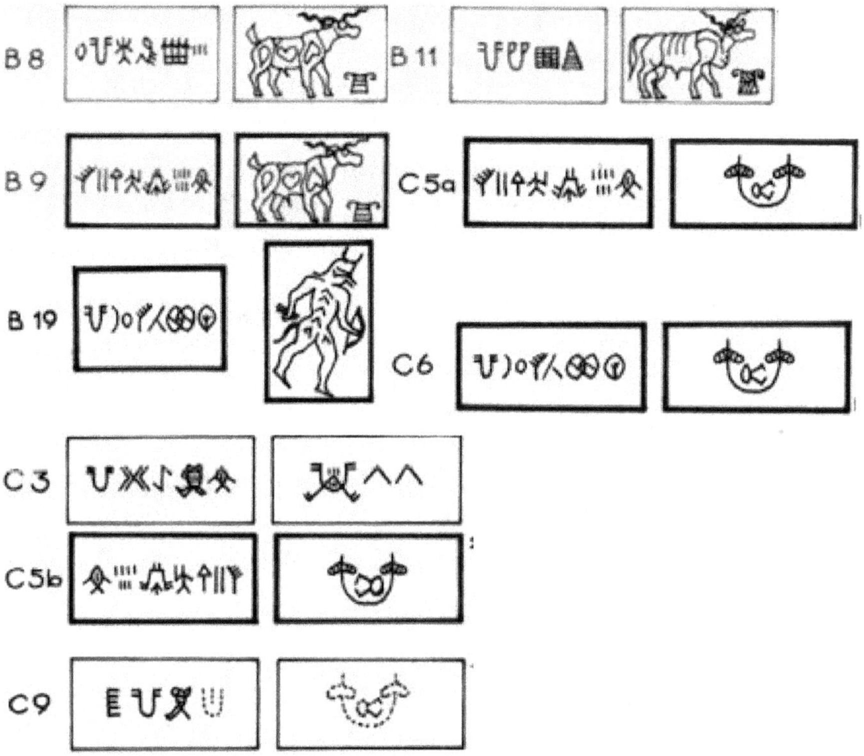

B8

Hieroglyph: *meḍho* a ram rebus: *mẽṛhẽt, meḍ* 'iron' (Mu.) *mRdu* 'iron' (Samskritam) PLUS *pattar* 'trough' rebus: *pattar* 'goldsmith-guild'

gōṭā 'round' rebus: *gōṭā* 'laterite, ferrite ore'

kaṇḍa kanka ‘rim of jar’ Rebus: *karṇīka* ‘account (scribe)’ *karṇī* ‘supercargo’. *kaṇḍa* ‘fire-altar’. Alternative: *kanka* 'rim of jar' rebus: *kanga* 'brazier'.

bhaṭa ‘warrior’ rebus: *bhaṭa* ‘furnace’

baraḍo = spine; backbone (Tulu) Rebus: *baran, bharat* ‘mixed alloyś (5 copper, 4 zinc and 1 tin) (Punjabi). *baroṭi* ‘twelve’ *bharata* ‘a factitious alloy of copper, pewter, tin’ (Marathi)भरत (p. 603) [*bharata*] n A factitious metal compounded of copper, pewter, tin &c.भरताचें भांडें (p. 603) [*bharatācē mbhāṇḍēṃ*] n A vessel made of the metal भरत. 2 See भरिताचें भांडें.भरती (p. 603) [*bharatī]* a Composed of the metal भरत. (Molesworth Marathi Dictionary).

gaṇḍa ‘four’ rebus: *kaṇḍa* ‘fire-altar’ PLUS kolmo ‘rice plant’ rebus: kolimi ‘smithy, forge’

kolom ‘three’ rebus: kolimi ‘smithy, forge’ (Phonetic determinant) kaṇḍa ‘implements’

B9, c5a Inscription

Text on incised copper tablet: Text Number 2901, 2903, 2911 Obverse: markhor These are possibly identical inscriptions on copper plates.

Line 1: Hieroglyph-multiplex or hypertext: *bāṭi* ‘cup,’*varti* f. ‘projecting rim’. [√*vr̥t1*] Pa. *vaṭṭi* - , °*ikā* --‘rim, brim’(CDIAL 1136) rebus: *bhatti* ‘furnace, forge’ PLUS *kāṇḍa* 'arrow' rebus: *khaṇḍa* 'implements *dula* 'pair' rebus: *dul* 'cast metal'. Thus, cast metal implements PLUS kAru ‘pincers’ rebus: kAru ‘artisan’ daTo ‘claws of crab’ rebus: dhatu ‘minerals’ *kamaḍha* 'crab' rebus: *kammaṭa* 'mint'. Thus the reading is: mint for cast metal implements.

as shown on c5a, c5b, c6, c9 copper plate types with hieroglyph-multiplex or hypertext of *loa* ‘ficus religiosa’ rebus: *loha* ‘copper’ PLUS *bāṭi*‘cup’ rebus: *bhaṭṭi*‘furnace’. *dula* ‘pair’ rebus: *dul* ‘metal casting’ Thus, furnaced copper metal castings.

Line 2: *aya* 'fish' rebus: *aya* 'iron' *ayas* 'metal' *gaṇḍa* 'four' rebus: kaṇḍa ‘fire-altar’ khāṇḍa 'implements’ kolmo 'three' rebus: kolimi 'smithy, forge'. Thus forged implements.

koḍa 'sluice'; Rebus: *koḍ* 'artisan's workshop (Kuwi)

meḍ 'body' rebus: meḍ 'iron' PLUS eṛaka 'upraised arm' (Tamil); rebus: eraka = copper (Kannada). Thus, copper and metal (alloy)

kāṇḍa 'arrowhead' 'arrowhead' Rebus: kaṇḍ 'fire-altar' (Santali) rebus: *kāṇḍa* 'tools, pots and pans and metal-ware' (Marathi) 'implements'

koDa ‘sluice’ rebus: *koD* ‘workshop’

kolmo 'rice-plant' rebus: *kolimi* 'smithy, forge'

mẽd, mēd 'body'; PLUS 'notch' PLUS खाडा [khāṇḍā] 'A jag, notch, or indentation (as upon the edge of a tool or weapon)' rebus: *mẽd, mēd* 'iron'

dula ‘two’ rebus: *dul* ‘metal casting’ *pajhar* ‘sprout’ rebus: *pasra* ‘smithy’. Thus metal casting smithy.

B11

Hieroglyph: *barad* ‘ox’ rebus: *bharat* ‘alloy of copper, pewter, tin’ PLUS *pattar* ‘trough’ rebus: *pattar* ‘goldsmith-guild’

kaṇḍa kanka ‘rim of jar’ Rebus: *karṇīka* ‘account (scribe)’karṇī‘supercargo’.

kaṇḍa ‘fire-altar’. Alternative: *kanka* 'rim of jar' rebus: *kanga* 'brazier'.

baṭa ‘rimless pot’ rebus: *bhaṭa* ‘furnace’ PLUS *dula* ‘pair’ rebus: *dul* ‘cast metal’ PLUS *koḍi* ‘flag’ rebus: *koḍ* ‘workshop’

khaṇḍa 'dividion' rebus: *khaṇḍa* 'implements

Te. *meṭṭa* raised or high ground, hill; (K.) meṭṭu mound; miṭṭa high ground, hillock, mound; high, elevated, raised, projecting; (VPK) *mēṭu, mēṭa, mēṭi* stack of hay; (Inscr.) *meṇṭa-cēnu* dry field (cf. meṭṭu-nēla, meṭṭu-vari). Kol. (SR.) *meṭṭā* hill; (Kin.) meṭṭ, (Hislop) *met* mountain. Nk. *meṭṭ* hill,
mountain. Ga. (S.3, LSB 20.3) *meṭṭa* high land. Go. (Tr. W. Ph.) *maṭṭā*, (Mu.) *maṭṭa* mountain; (M. L.) *meṭā* id., hill; (A. D. *Ko.) meṭṭa, (Y. Ma. M.) meṭa hill; (SR.) meṭṭā* hillock (Voc. 2949). *Koṇḍa meṭa id. Kuwi (S.) metta* hill; (Isr.) *meṭa* sand hill. (DEDR 5058) Rebus*: mẽd, mēd* 'iron'.

కమటము *kamaṭamu*. [Tel.] n. A portable furnace for melting the precious metals. అగసాలెవాని కుంపటి. Allograph: कमटा or ठा [*kamaṭā or ṭhā*] *m* (कमठ S) A bow (esp. of bamboo or horn) (Marathi). Allograph 2: *kamaḍha* ‘penance’ (Pkt.) This allograph 2 is seen on Mohenjo-daro sealing:

Mohenjo-daro. Sealing. Surrounded by fishes, lizard and snakes, a horned person sits in 'yoga' on a throne with hoofed legs. One side of a triangular terracotta amulet (Md 013); surface find at Mohenjo-daro in 1936, Dept. of Eastern Art, Ashmolean Museum, Oxford. [seated person penance, crocodile?] Brief memoranda: *kamaḍha* ‘penance’ Rebus: *kammaṭa* ‘mint, coiner’; *kaṇḍo* ‘stool, seat’ Rebus: *kāṇḍa* ‘metalware’ *kaṇḍa* ‘fire-altar’.
kAru 'crocodile' Rebus: kAru 'artisan'. *kuTo* ‘leg’ rebus: *khũṭ* ‘community, guild’. khōṭaa ‘wedge, alloy’. *kuThi* ‘smelter’. The bovine hoofs of the seat or stool or platform are hieroglyphs: Hieroglyph: ‘hoof’: Kumaon. *khuṭo* ‘leg, foot’, °*ṭī* ‘goat's leg’; Nepalese. *khuṭo* ‘leg, foot’(CDIAL 3894). S. *khuṛī* f. ‘heel’; WPah. paṅ. *khūṛ* ‘foot’. (CDIAL 3906). Rebus: *khũṭ* ‘community, guild’ (Santali)

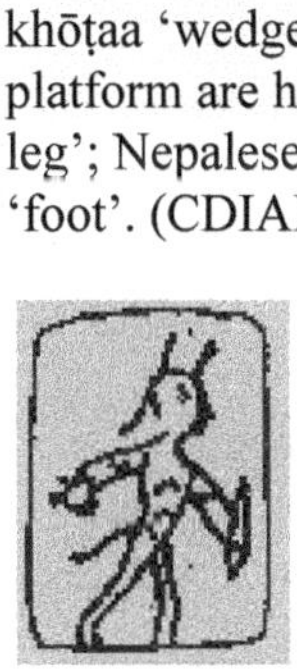

A line drawing rendering of the hieroglyph as Pict-89 pictorial motif on Mahadevan concordance.

m1540A कौटिलिकः kauṭilikḥ कौटिलिकः 1 A hunter. 2 A blacksmith. Archer. *kammaṭa 'coiner, mint'* signified by hieroglyph: *kamāṭhiyo*

'archer' (Rebus: *kammaTa* ‘mint, coiner, portable furnace) evolves as an iconic the aniconic ekamukhalinga on Batesvar frieze shown atop a smelter together with a background: *kuṭi* 'tree' rebus: *kuṭhi* 'smelter', reinforcing the association of *Yūpa Skambha* pillar of light as a metaphor for the smelting transmuting mere earth and stone into metal

coinage; metaphor of sculptural tree in the thus as a fiery processes heralding the inexorable processes of creation, destruction and rebirth exemplified by the Supreme divine -- a transformation from Being tio Becoming exemplified by the Cosmic Dancer emerging out of the Sivalinga. The process is mentioned as *gangga sudhi* on Candi Sukuh inscription on a linga signifying sudhi, 'purification' by *kanga* 'brazier'.

kuṭa, °ṭi -- , *°ṭha* -- 3, *°ṭhi* -- m. ' tree ' Rebus: *kuṭhi* 'smelter'. *kuṭa, °ṭi* -- , *°ṭha* -- 3, *°ṭhi* -- m. ' tree ' lex., *°ṭaka* -- m. ' a kind of tree ' Kauś.Pk. *kuḍa* -- m. ' tree '; Paš. lauṛ. *kuṛā´* ' tree ', dar. *kaṛék* ' tree, oak ' ~ Par. *kōṛ* ' stick ' IIFL iii 3, 98. (CDIAL 3228).

B 19 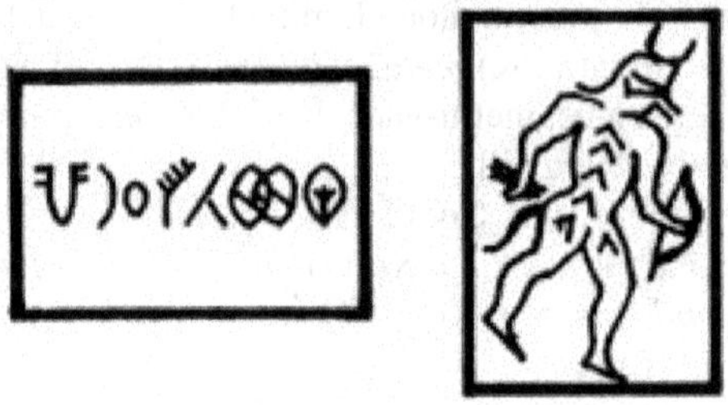 14 ex

While C6 signifies a *lohakAru* 'coppersmith', B19 signifies a 'pewtersmith'(*kuṭilika*)

B19 copper plate epigraph: hunter-blacksmith: कौटिलिकः kauṭilikḥ कौटिलिकः 1 A hunter 2 A blacksmith. कौटिलिक

[p= 315,2] m. (fr. कुटिलिका Paln2. 4-4 , 18) " deceiving the hunter [or the deer Sch.] by particular movements " , a deer [" a hunter " Sch.] Kals3. f. (Paln2. 4-4 , 18) कुटिलिका crouching , coming stealthily (like a hunter on his prey ; a particular movement on the stage) Vikr. कुटिलिक " using the tool called कुटिलिका " , a blacksmith ib. कुटिलक [p= 288,2] f. a tool used by a blacksmith Paln2. 4-4 , 18 Kals3.mfn. bent , curved , crisped Pan5cat.

Rebus 1: *kuṭila, katthīl* = bronze (8 parts copper and 2 parts tin) cf. āra-kūṭa, 'brass Old English *ār* 'brass, copper, bronze' Old Norse *eir* 'brass, copper', German *ehern* 'brassy, bronzen'. kastīra n. ' tin ' lex. 2. *kastilla -- .1. H. *kathīr* m. ' tin, pewter '; G. *kathīr* n. ' pewter '.2. H. (Bhoj.?) *kathīl*, *°lā* m. ' tin, pewter '; M. *kathīl* n. ' tin ', *kathlẽ* n. ' large tin vessel '(CDIAL 2984)

Rebus 2: *kAru* 'pincers' rebus: *kAru* 'artisan' *daTo* 'claws of crab' rebus: *dhatu* 'mineral' *kamaṭha* crab (Skt.) kamāṭhiyo=archer; *kāmaṭhum* =a bow; kāmaḍī ,kāmaḍum=a chip of bamboo (G.) *kāmaṭhiyo* bowman; an archer(Samskrtam) *kamaṛkom*= fig leaf (Santali) *kamarmaṛā* (Has.), *kamaṛkom*(Nag.); the petiole or stalk of a leaf (Mundari.lex.) *kamaṭha*= fig leaf, religiosa(Skt.) *dula* 'two' Rebus: *dul* 'cast metal 'Thus, *dul loha* 'copper casting' infurnace: *baṭa*= wide-mouthed pot; *bhaṭa*= kiln (Te.) *kammaṭa*=portable furnace(Te.) *kampaṭṭam* 'coiner,mint' (Tamil) kammaṭa (Malayalam)

Same inscription as on B19 sets of copper plates appears on C6 sets of copper plates but with a distinct hieroglyph-multiplex of ficus PLUS crab (pincers, tongs) on the obverse of the copper plate.

C6 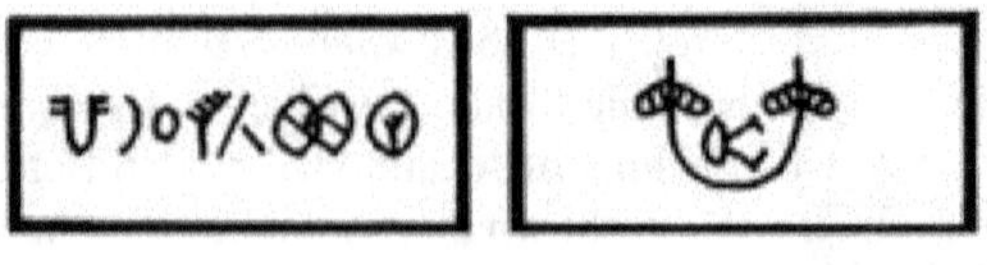 7ex

C6 copper plate epigraph: ficus PLUS pincers: metalsmith: लोह--कार [p= 908,3] m. a worker in iron , smith , blacksmith R. Hit. Hieroglyph component: *loa* 'ficus glomerata' Rebus: *loha* 'copper, iron' Hieroglyph component: *kāru* pincers, tongs. Rebus: khār खार् । लोहकारः 'blacksmith' (Kashmiri)

Variants of the 'crab' hieroglyph (sign).[270]

Since *loha* signifies 'copper' and kammaṭa signifies 'mint' this hieroglyph multiplex on the obverse of C6 set of copper plate inscriptions (ficus PLUS crab+pincers) should more precisely signify semantically: mint-master, coppersmith.

The text of the epigraph common to both sets of copper plates (B16, hunter and C9 ficus+crab/pincers) has hieroglyph-multiplexes or hypertexts.

C6 hypertext message

 Inscription message: Supercargo bronze cast metal, ingots (of different shapes), metal implements smithy/forge On C9 set of copper plates, these come from लोहकारः *lohakAra kammaṭa* the mint-master, coppersmith's workshop. On B16 set of copper plates, these come from कौटिलिकः kauṭilikḥ bronze worker's (smithy/forge).

 *mũh* 'ingot' (Santali) PLUS (infixed) kolom 'sprout, rice plant' Rebus: *kolimi* 'smithy, forge' Thus, ingot smithy

Notes: *dula* 'pair' Rebus: *dul* 'cast metal' Ellipse is split into two curves of parenthesis: ( ) Thus, *dul* 'metal casting' signified by the curves joined into an ellipse.

 mũh 'ingot' (Santali) *dula* 'pair' Rebus*: dul* 'metalcasting' Thus, cast metal ingot.

 *karã* n. pl. ' wristlets, bangles ' (Gujarati) Rebus: *khār* 'blacksmith'. *dula* 'pair' Rebus: *dul* 'metal casting' PLUS *kana, kanac* = corner (Santali); Rebus: *kañcu* = bronze (Telugu) Thus, cast bronze or bronze metal castings.

 This is a hieroglyph-multiplex: slant PLUS notch: *DhAL* 'slanted' Rebus: *DhALako* 'large ingot' PLUS खांडा (p. 202) [*khāṇḍā*] A jag, notch, or indentation (as upon the edge of a tool or weapon). Rebus: Rebus: *kāṇḍa* 'tools, pots and pans and metal-ware' (Marathi) *khaṇḍa* id. (Santali)

 *kolom* 'rice-plant, sprout' Rebus: *kolimi* 'smithy, forge' *pajhar* 'sprout' rebus; *pasra* 'smithy'.

 *goṭ* 'seed, rounded object' Rebus: खोट (p. 212) [*khōṭa*] f A mass of metal (unwrought or of old metal melted down); an ingot or wedge (Marathi) *goTa* 'laterite, ferrite ore'.

 The 'curve' hieroglyph is a splitting of the ellipse. *kuṭila* 'bent' CDIAL 3230 kuṭi— in cmpd. 'curve', *kuṭika—* 'bent' MBh. Rebus: *kuṭila, katthīl* = bronze (8 parts copper and 2 parts tin) cf. *āra-kūṭa*, 'brass Old English *ār* 'brass, copper, bronze' Old Norse *eir* 'brass, copper', German *ehern* 'brassy, bronzen'. *kastīra n. ' tin ' lex. 2. *kastilla -- .1. H. kathīr m. '* tin, pewter *'; G. kathīr n. '* pewter *'.2. H. (Bhoj.?) kathīl, °lā m. '* tin, pewter *'; M. kathīl n. ' tin ', kathlẽ* n. ' large tin vessel '.(CDIAL 2984)

 *kaṇḍa kanka* 'rim of jar' Rebus: *karṇīka* 'account (scribe)' *karṇī* 'supercargo'. *kaṇḍa* 'fire-altar' khāṇḍa 'implements'. Alternative: *kanka* 'rim of jar' rebus:

kanga 'brazier'. The text of the hypertext message is: laterite ore, bronze ingots, implements, smithy account.

C9 text

khāreḍo 'currycomb' rebus: *khārādī* 'turner' *kangsi* 'comb' rebus: *kamsa* 'bronze'

kaṇḍa kanka 'rim of jar' Rebus: *karṇīka* 'account (scribe)' *karṇī* 'supercargo'. *kaṇḍa* 'fire-altar' khāṇḍa 'implements'. Alternative: *kanka* 'rim of jar' rebus: kanga 'brazier'

bica 'scorpion' rebus: haematite, ferrite stone ore.

baṭa 'rimless pot' Rebus: *bhaṭa* 'furnace' PLUS *muka* 'ladle' rebus; *mū̃h* 'ingot', quantity of metal got out of a smelter furnace (Santali)

Semantic cluster: bica 'scorpion' rebus: bicha 'haematite, ferrite ore'

C8 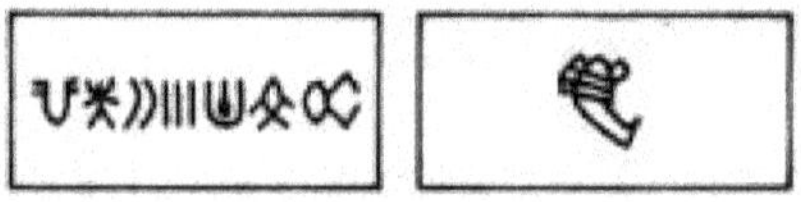

C8 Hieroglyph: Sting of scorpion:
bica 'scorpion' (Assamese) Rebus: *bica* 'stone ore' (Mu.) haematite ore. PLUS ligatures: *karNa* 'ear' rebus: *karNI* 'supercargo'

C8 hypertext

kaṇḍa kanka 'rim of jar' Rebus: *karṇīka* 'account (scribe)*'karṇī* 'supercargo'. *kaṇḍa* 'fire-altar'. Alternative: *kanka* 'rim of jar' rebus: kanga 'brazier'

bhaṭa 'warrior' rebus: *bhaṭa* 'furnace'

dula 'pair' Rebus: *dul* 'metal casting' Ellipse is split into two curves of parenthesis: ( ) Thus, *dul* 'metal casting' signified by the curves joined into an ellipse. The 'curve' hieroglyph is a splitting of the ellipse. kuṭila 'bent' CDIAL 3230 *kuṭi*— in cmpd. 'curve', *kuṭika*— 'bent' MBh. Rebus: *kuṭila, katthīl* = bronze (8 parts copper and 2 parts tin)

Sign 34: *muka* 'ladle' (Tamil)(DEDR 4887) Rebus: *mū̃h* 'ingot' (Santali) *baṭa* = a kind of iron (G.) *baṭa* = rimless pot (Kannada) Thus, iron ingot.+ *kāṭi* 'body stature; Rebus: fireplace trench. Thus, iron ingot furnace.

kolom 'three' rebus: *kolimi* 'smithy, forge'

aya 'fish' rebus: *aya, ayas* 'iron, metal'

kamaḍha 'crab' Rebus: *kammaṭa* 'mint, coiner'.

C3 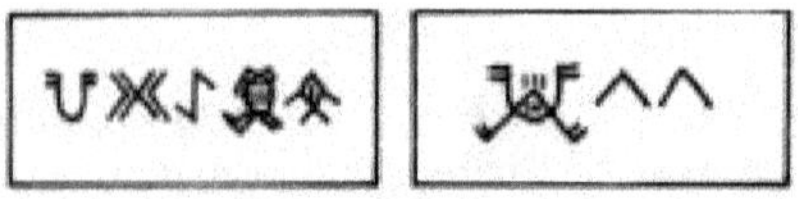

C3 hypertext hieroglyph-multiplex has additional duplicated hieroglyphs: ^^ *aDaren* 'lid' rebus: *aduru* 'native, unsmelted metal' PLUS *dula* 'pair' rebus: *dul* 'metal casting'. PLUS ligatured hieroglyph is comparable to the hypertext of C4a and C4b.

C4a, C4b hypertext: *dul kuṭila baTa kolimi* 'smithy furnace for metal casting of tin=bronze' PLUS *karNI* 'supercargo'.

The obverse on both C4a and C4b provides another hypertext Sign 346. The 'rim of jar' hieroglyph is ligatured with six short linear strokes (a pair of 'three short linear strokes') (infixed) and two short linear strokes are signified on the edges of an extended tail. The extended tail compares with the orthography of tail ligatured to an antelope on h11 obverse hieroglyph:

C3 Hypertext message:

kaṇḍa kanka 'rim of jar' Rebus: *karṇīka* 'account (scribe)' *karṇī* 'supercargo'. *kaṇḍa* 'fire-altar'. Alternative: *kanka* 'rim of jar' rebus: *kanga* 'brazier'.

dATu 'crosś rebus: *dhAtu* 'mineral'

ankaḍā 'crook, hook' rebus: *akhāḍā* 'comunity'. Thus, mineworker community.

bicā 'scorpion' (Assamese) Rebus: *bica* 'haematite ferrite ore, stone ore' (Mu.)

aya 'fish' rebus: *aya, ayas* 'iron, metal' PLUS खांडा [*khāṇḍā*] m A jag, notch, or indentation (as upon the edge of a tool or weapon)(Marathi). Rebus: *kāṇḍa* 'tools, pots and pans and metal-ware' (Marathi)

Semantic cluster: *karã̄* n. pl. ' wristlets, bangles ' (Gujarati) Rebus: *khār* 'blacksmith'. PLUS *xolā* 'tail' rebus: *kol* 'metal, working in iron'

C7 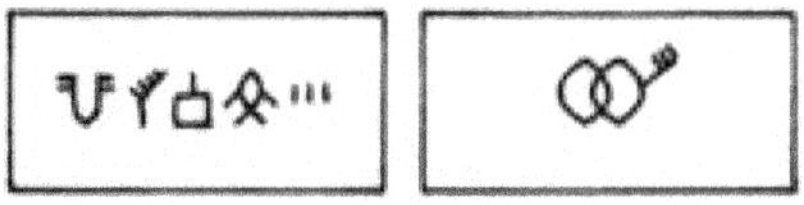

C7

Hieroglyph-multiplex: *kolmo* 'rice plant' rebus: *kolimi* 'smithy, forge' ligatured to: *dula* 'pair' Rebus: *dul* 'cast (metal)' PLUS *kana, kanac* = corner (Santali); Rebus: *kañcu* = bronze (Telugu) Thus, cast bronze or bronze casting. Alternative: *karã̄* n. pl. ' wristlets, bangles ' (Gujarati) Rebus: *khār* 'blacksmith'. PLUS *xolā* 'tail' rebus: *kol* 'metal, working in iron'

C7 text

kaṇḍa kanka 'rim of jar' Rebus: karṇīka 'account (scribe)' karṇī 'supercargo'. *kaṇḍa* 'fire-altar'. Alternative: *kanka* 'rim of jar' rebus: kanga 'brazier'

kolmo 'rice plant' rebus: *kolimi* 'smithy, forge'

ranku 'liquid measure' rebus: *ranku* 'tin'

aya 'fish' rebus: *aya, ayas* 'iron, metal'

kolmo 'three' rebus: *kolimi* 'smithy, forge'

Semantic cluster 8: *baḍhia* – a castrated boar, a hog; rebus: *baḍhi* 'a caste who work both in iron and wood'; *baḍhoe* 'a carpenter, worker in wood'; *badhoria* 'expert in working in wood'(Santali) 'Rebus: *bari* 'merchant'. *barea* 'merchant' (Santali) বরাহ *barāha* 'boar' Rebus: *bāṛaï* 'carpenter' (Bengali)

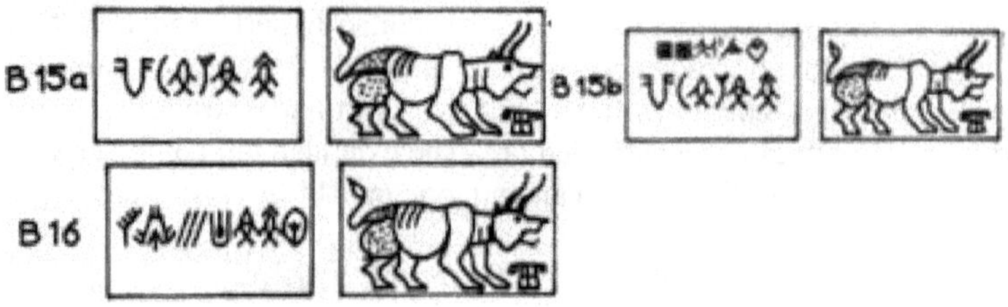

B15

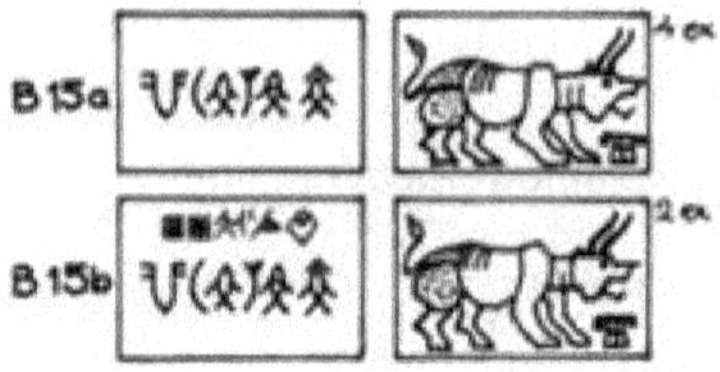

B15a, B15b

Hypertext hieroglyph-multiplex on B15a, B15b and B16 is a ligature of rhinoceros nd boar: *kāṇḍa* 'rhinoceroś rebus: khaṇḍa 'implement' PLUS *pattar* 'trough' rebus: *pattar* 'goldsmith-guild' PLUS বরাহ *barāha* 'boar' Rebus: *bāṛaï* 'carpenter' (Bengali)

Text

Line 1 B15b

khaṇḍa 'division' rebus: khaṇḍa 'implements PLUS dula 'pair' rebus: *dul* 'metal casting'; thus cast metal implements.

mẽd, mēd 'body'; PLUS STAFF is a phonetic
determinative: *meḍ(h), meḍhī f., meḍhā* ' post, forked stake'; *meṛh* f. ' rope tying oxen to each other and to post on threshing floor ' rebus: *mẽd, mēd* 'iron''

koḍi 'flag''rebus: *koḍ* 'workshop'

kanac 'corner' rebus: kancu 'bronze'. Thus, the text message is: iron, bronze workshop metal castings, implements.

Line 2 B15b; B15a

kaṇḍa kanka 'rim of jar' Rebus: *karṇīka* 'account (scribe)'karṇī'supercargo'. *kaṇḍa* 'fire-altar' khāṇḍa 'implements'. Alternative: *kanka* 'rim of jar' rebus: *kanga* 'brazier'

fish PLUS lid: *aya* 'fish' Rebus: *aya* 'iron, metal' *adaren* 'lid' Rebus: *aduru* 'native unsmelted metal' *d.aren-mund.i* lid of pot; *d.aren, ad.aren* to cover up pot with lid (Bond.a); *d.arai* to cover (Bond.a.Hindi) *munda* 'iron' Rebus: *aduru* 'unsmelted, native metal'.

fish PLUS notch: खांडा [*khāṇḍā*] m A jag, notch Rebus: *ayaskhāṇḍa* 'excellent implements: tools, pots and pans, metalware'

aya 'fish' rebus*: aya, ayas* 'iron, metal' PLUS circumflex of right- and left-parenthesis: *kuṭilaka* 'bronze' PLUS *koḍ* 'horn' rebus: *koḍ* 'workshop' Thus, bronze, metal (iron) implements workshop.

B16

kāṇḍa ‘rhinoceroś rebus: khaṇḍa ‘implement’ PLUS *pattar* ‘trough’ rebus: *pattar* ‘goldsmith-guild’ PLUS বরাহ *barāha* 'boar' Rebus: *bāṛaï* 'carpenter' (Bengali)

Text

kolmo ‘rice plant’ rebus: *kolimi* ‘smithy, forge’

koḍa 'sluice'; Rebus: *koḍ* 'artisan's workshop (Kuwi)

kolom ‘three’ rebus: *kolimi* ‘smithy, forge’ PLUS *dhal* ‘slant’ rebus: *dhALako* ‘large ingot’

baṭa ‘rimless pot’ rebus: *bhaṭa* ‘furnace’ PLUS *muka* 'ladle' rebus; *mũh* 'ingot', quantity of metal got out of a smelter furnace (Santali)

fish PLUS lid: *aya* 'fish' Rebus: *aya* 'iron, metal' *adaren* ‘lid’ Rebus: *aduru* 'native unsmelted metal' *d.aren-mund.i* lid of pot; *d.aren, ad.aren* to cover up pot with lid (Bond.a); *d.arai* to cover (Bond.a.Hindi) *munda* ‘iron’ Rebus: *aduru* ‘unsmelted, native metal’.

fish PLUS notch: खांडा [*khāṇḍā*] m A jag, notch Rebus: ayaskhāṇḍa 'excellent implements: tools, pots and pans, metalware'

fish PLUS oval as parenthesis circumscript PLUS horn: *aya* 'fish' Rebus: *aya* 'iron, metal' PLUS *gōṭā* 'round' Rebus: *khōṭa* 'ingot, alloy, wedge' koḍ 'horn' Rebus: *goTa* ‘laterite, ferrite ore’

mũh ‘ingot’ (Santali) PLUS (infixed) kolom 'sprout, rice plant' Rebus: *kolimi* 'smithy, forge' Thus, ingot smithy

Notes: *dula* 'pair' Rebus: *dul* 'metal casting' Ellipse is split into two curves of parenthesis: ( ) Thus, *dul* 'cast metal' signified by the curves joined into an ellipse.

Semantic cluster 9: *dula* ‘pair’ rebus: *dul* ‘metal casting’ *kamaṭha* 'turtle' rebus: *kãsā kammaṭa* 'bell-metal coiner, mint, portable furnace'.

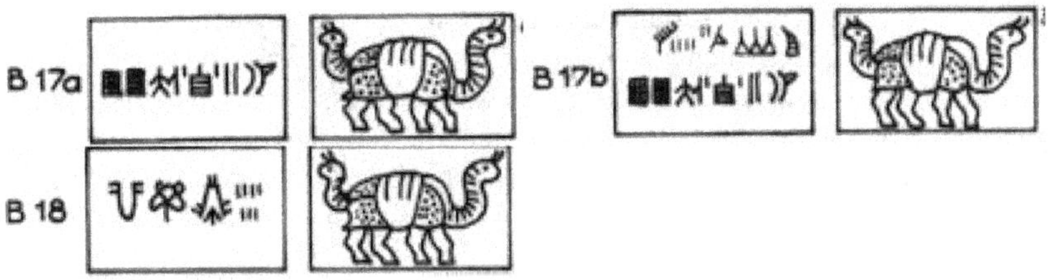

Identification of the hypertext hieroglyph-multiplex of two joined turtles

m1534b On this copper tablet, the correct identification of the animal heads will be turtle species comparable to *Meiolania,* a horned large turtle of New Guinea. m1532b On another copper tablet, the emphasis is clearly on the turtle's shell like that of Meiolania's shell.

dula 'pair' rebus: *dul* 'metal casting' PLUS *kassa* 'giant turtle' Rebus: *kamsA* 'bell-metal' Thus, bell-metal castings.

The hieroglyph multiplex on m1534b is now read rebus as: *dula* 'pair' rebus: *dul* 'cast metal' PLUS *kassa* 'turtle' rebus: *kãsā* 'bell-metal' *kamaṭha* 'turtle' rebus: *kãsā kammaṭa* 'bell-metal coiner, mint, portable furnace'.

கமடம், [**kamaṭam*] *s.* A turtle, a tortoise, ஆமை (Winslow Tamil) కమఠము [*kamaṭhamu*] *kamaṭhamu.* [Skt.] n. A tortoise. Rebus: కమటము [*kamaṭamu*] *kamaṭamu.* [Tel.] n. A portable furnace for melting the precious metals. అగసాలెవాని కుంపటి. Allograph: कमटा or ठा [*kamaṭā or ṭhā*] *m* (कमठ S) A bow (esp. of bamboo or horn) (Marathi). Allograph 2: *kamaḍha* 'penance' (Pkt.) Pictorial motif 69 (Mahadevan concordance). Tortoise.

Hieroglyph: *kacchapa [Sk. kacchapa, dial. fr. *kaśyapa, orig. Ep of kumma,* like magga of paṭipadā] a tortoise, turtle S iv.*177 (kummo kacchapo*); in simile of the blind turtle (*kāṇo k.)* M iii.169=S v.455; Th 2, 500 (cp.*J.P.T.S.* 1907, 73, 174). -- f. kacchapinī a female t. Miln 67. *கச்சபம் kaccapam, n. < kaccha-pa.* 1. Turtle, tortoise; ஆமை. 2. One of the nine treasures of Kubēra; நவநிதியு ளொான்று. कच्छ--प [p= 242,3] *m.* " keeping or inhabiting a marsh " , a turtle , tortoise MBh. Gaut. Mn. &can apparatus used in the distillation of spirituous liquor , a flat kind of still L. कच्छ--पी*f.* a kind of lute (so namẹd from being similar in shape to the tortoise ; cf. तेस्तुदो) *kacchapa* m. ' turtle, tortoise ' MBh. 2. **kacchabha* -- . [By pop. etym. through *kaccha* -- for *kaśyápa* -- VS. J. Charpentier MO xxvi 110 suggested equivalence in MIA. of *kassa* -- =*kaccha* -- to explain creation of *kacchapa* -- ~ *kassapa* -- . But K. *kochuwu*, unless a loan from Ind., points to **kakṣapa* -- , which would make the formation earlier.]1. Pa. *kacchapa* -- m. ' tortoise, turtle, °*pinī* -- f., Pk. *kacchava* -- m., °*vī* -- f., K. *kochuwu* m. (see above), S. *kachãũ*, °*chũ* m., L. *kachũ* m., P. *kacchū*, *kacchūkummã̄* m. (< kūrmá -- 1), N. *kachuwā*, A. *kācha*, B. *kāchim*,
Or. *kechu*, °*cho*, *kẽchu*, *kaĩ˜cha*, °*ca*, *kachima*, °*cima*, Mth. *kāchu*, Bhoj. Aw. lakh. *kachuā*; H. *kachuā*, °*chwā* m., °*uī*, °*wī* f. ' tortoise, turtle ', *kach* -- *mach* m. ' dwellers in the water ' (< mátsya --) whence *kacch*, *kach* m. ' turtle, tortoise ', M. *kāsav*, *kā̃s*° m., Ko. *kāsavu*.2. Pk. amg. *kacchabha* -- , °*aha* -- m., °*bhī* -- f.; Si. *käsum̆bu*, °*ubu* H. Smith JA 1950, 188; -- G. *kācbɔ* m., °*bī* f. with unexpl. retention of -- *b* -- and loss of aspiration in *c.*
Addenda: kacchapa -- . 1. A. *kācha* (phonet. -- *s* --) ' tortoise ' AFD 217.2. *kacchabha -- (with -- *pa* -- replaced by animal suffix -- *bha* --): Md. *kahan̆bu* ' tortoise -- shell '(CDIAL 2619)
Rebus: *kaccha m.* ' bank, shore, marshy ground ' MBh. [Conn. with kákṣa -- (EWA i 139) doubtful, but see kacchapa --]Pa. *kaccha* -- n. ' marshy land '; Pk. *kaccha* -- m. ' bank, shore, flooded forest, land near a river, garden to grow radishes &c. in ', *kacchara* -- m. ' mud, morass '; Sh. (Lor.) *k**lč with obl. ' beside, near ', *k**l*či* adv. ' near ', *k**l*čilo* adj.; P. *kāchaṛ*, °*al* f. ' river bank '; N. *kachār* ' hillside, foot of hill '; B. *kāchāṛ* ' steep slope '; Bi. *kāch* ' low marshy land '; H. *kachār* m. ' moist lowland

by a river ', *kāchī* m. ' caste of market gardener ' (< **kacchin* --), *kachiyānā, kachwārā*

m. ' vegetable plot '(CDIAL 2618).

Rebus: *kaṁsá*1 m. ' metal cup ' AV., m.n. ' bell -- metal ' Pat. as in S., but would in Pa. Pk. and most NIA. lggs. collide with kā´ṁsya -- to which L. P. testify and under which the remaining forms for the metal are listed. 2. **kaṁsikā* -- .
1. Pa. *kaṁsa* -- m. ' bronze dish '; S. *kañjho* m. ' bellmetal '; A. *kā̃h* ' gong '; Or. *kā̃sā* ' big pot of bell -- metal '; OMarw. *kāso* (= *kā̃* -- ?) m. ' bell -- metal tray for food, food '; G. *kā̃sā*m. pl. ' cymbals '; -- perh. Woṭ. *kasṓṭ* m. ' metal pot ' Buddruss Woṭ 109.
2. Pk. *kaṁsiā* -- f. ' a kind of musical instrument '; K. *k&ebrevdotdot;nzü* f. ' clay or copper pot '; A. *kā̃hi* ' bell -- metal dish '; G. *kā̃śī* f. ' bell -- metal cymbal ', *kā̃śiyɔ* m. ' open bellmetal pan '.kā´ṁsya -- ; -- *kaṁsāvatī -- ?Addenda: *kaṁsá* -- **1:** A. *kā̃h* also ' gong ' or < kā´ṁsya -- .CDIAL 2576) *kā´ṁsya* ' made of bell -- metal ' KātyŚr., n. ' bell -- metal ' Yājñ., ' cup of bell -- metal ' MBh., °*aka* -- n. ' bell -- metal '. 2. **kāṁsiya* -- . [kaṁsá -- 1]1. Pa. *kaṁsa* -- m. (?) ' bronze ', Pk. *kaṁsa* -- , *kāsa* -- n. ' bell -- metal, drinking vessel, cymbal '; L. (Jukes) *kā̃jā* adj. ' of metal ', awāṇ. *kāsā* ' jar ' (← E with -- *s* -- , not *ñj*); N. *kā̃so* ' bronze, pewter, white metal ', *kas* -- *kuṭ* ' metal alloy '; A. *kā̃h* ' bell -- metal ', B. *kā̃sā*, Or. *kā̃sā*, Bi. *kā̃sā*; Bhoj. *kā̃s* ' bell -- metal ', *kā̃sā* ' base metal '; H. *kās, kā̃sā* m. ' bell -- metal ', G. *kā̃sũ* n., M. *kā̃sẽ* n.; Ko. *kā̃śẽ* n. ' bronze '; Si. *kasa* ' bell -- metal '.2. L. *kā̃ihā̃* m. ' bell -- metal ', P. *kā̃ssī, kā̃sī* f., H. *kā̃sī* f.
*kāṁsyakara -- , kāṁsyakāra -- , *kāṁsyakuṇḍikā -- , kāṁsyatāla -- , *kāṁsyabhāṇḍa -- .
Addenda: *kā´ṁsya* -- **:** A. *kā̃h* also ' gong ', or < kaṁsá -- . **kāṁsyakara* ' worker in bell -- metal '. [See next: kā´ṁsya -- , kará -- 1]L. awāṇ. *kasērā* ' metal worker ', P. *kaserā* m. ' worker in pewter ' (both ← E with -- *s* --); N. *kasero* ' maker of brass pots '; Bi. H. *kaserā* m. ' worker in pewter '*kāṁsyakāra* m. ' worker in bell -- metal or brass ' Yājñ. com., *kaṁsakāra* -- m. BrahmavP. [kā´ṁsya -- , kāra -- 1]N. *kasār* ' maker of brass pots '; A. *kā̃hār* ' worker in bell -- metal '; B. *kā̃sāri* ' pewterer, brazier, coppersmith ', Or. *kā̃sārī*; H. *kasārī* m. ' maker of brass pots '; G. *kā̃sārɔ, kas°* m. ' coppersmith '; M. *kā̃sār, kās°* m. ' worker in white metal ', *kāsārḍā* m. ' contemptuous term for the same '. (CDIAL 2987-89)

Rebus: *காசு³ kācu, n. prob. kāš. cf. kāca. [M. kāšu.]* 1. Gold; பொன். (ஆ. நி.) 2. Necklace of gold coins; அச்சுத்தாலி. காசும் பிறப்புங் கலகலப்ப (திவ். திருப்பா. 7). 3. An ancient gold coin = 28 gr. troy; ஒரு பழைய பொன்னாணயம். (Insc.) 4. A small copper coin; சிறுசெப்புக்காசு. நெஞ்சே யுனையோர் காசா மதியேன் (தாயு. உடல்பொய். 72). 5. Coin, cash, money; ரொக்கம். எப்பேர்ப்பட்ட பல காசா யங்களும் (S.I.I. i, 89)

Tortoises as the supporting agent

An 1876 drawing of the world supported on the backs of four

elephants, themselves resting on the back

of a turtle. "The World Turtle in Hindu tradition is known as *Akupāra* (Sanskrit: अकूपार), or sometimes *Chukwa*. Example of a reference to the World Turtle in Hindu literature is found in *Jñānarāja* (the author of *Siddhāntasundara*, writing c. 1500): "A vulture, which has only little strength, rests in the sky holding a snake in its beak for a prahara [three hours]. Why can [the deity] in the form of a tortoise, who possesses an inconceivable potency, not hold the Earth in the sky for a *kalpa* [billions of years]?"The British philosopher John Locke made reference to this in his 1689 tract, *An Essay Concerning Human Understanding*, which compares one who would say that properties inhere in "substance" to the Indian, who said the world was on an elephant, which was on a tortoise, "but being again pressed to know what gave support to the broad-backed tortoise, replied—something, he knew not what."
Brewer's Dictionary of Phrase and Fable lists *Maha-pudma and Chukwa* as names from a "popular rendition of a Hindu myth in which the tortoise Chukwa supports the elephant Maha-pudma, which in turn supports the world" "In several cultures of the world, there is the concept of a gigantic turtle that holds up the Earth. Versions of the mtyh are found in India, China and North America, the last of which is known as "Turtle Island" to some tribes as a reference to the belief that the continent was resting on the back of a gigantic turtle. The European reduction of the myth is the island-beast, a creature so large that sailors take it to be an island and land upon it. When the creature submerges, the sailors are doomed. the Bestiary name for the Island-beast is Aspidochelone or snake-turtle but in some myths such as St. Brendan's voyage, it is called a "Whale"[271]

"The original for the gigantic turtle that is the World Turtle of Bharata myths is the giant fossil tortoise found in India, Colossochelys atlas, whose name actually means Giant Turtle That Holds Up The Earth (or The Sky)."[272]

"*Colossochelys atlas*, formerly known as *Testudo atlas*, and originally described as *Geochelone atlas*, is an extinct species of cryptodire turtle from the Pleistocene period, [as far back as] 2 million years ago. During the dry glacial periods [ie, *after* 2 million years ago-DD] it ranged from western India and Pakistan (possibly even as far west as southern and eastern Europe) to as far east as Sulawesi and Timor in Indonesia."

"Some more reconstructions and museum mounts for *Colossochelys*, which is something like double the dimensions of the Galapagoes or Seychelles tortoises of our times.

It would seem that the myth originates in the arera of Sundaland and adjoining-India, where pockets of *Colossochelys* survived and where they were not only economically exploiteed, they are indicated to have been of a particular religious and ritual status, along with the horned turtle *Meiolania* in Australia, New Guinea and Islands farther to the East."[273]

'Giant tortoises are characteristic reptiles of certain tropical islands. Often reaching enormous size—they can weigh as much as 300 kg (660 lbs) and can grow to be 1.3 m (4 ft) long—they live, or lived (some species are recently extinct), in the Seychelles, the Mascarenes and the Galapagos. ...Prior to the arrival of *Homo sapiens*, giant tortoises occurred in non-island locales as well. Between 200,000 to 10,000 years ago, tortoises on the mainland of Asia,in Indonesia,in Madagascar,in North and South America,and even the island of Malta became extinct.'

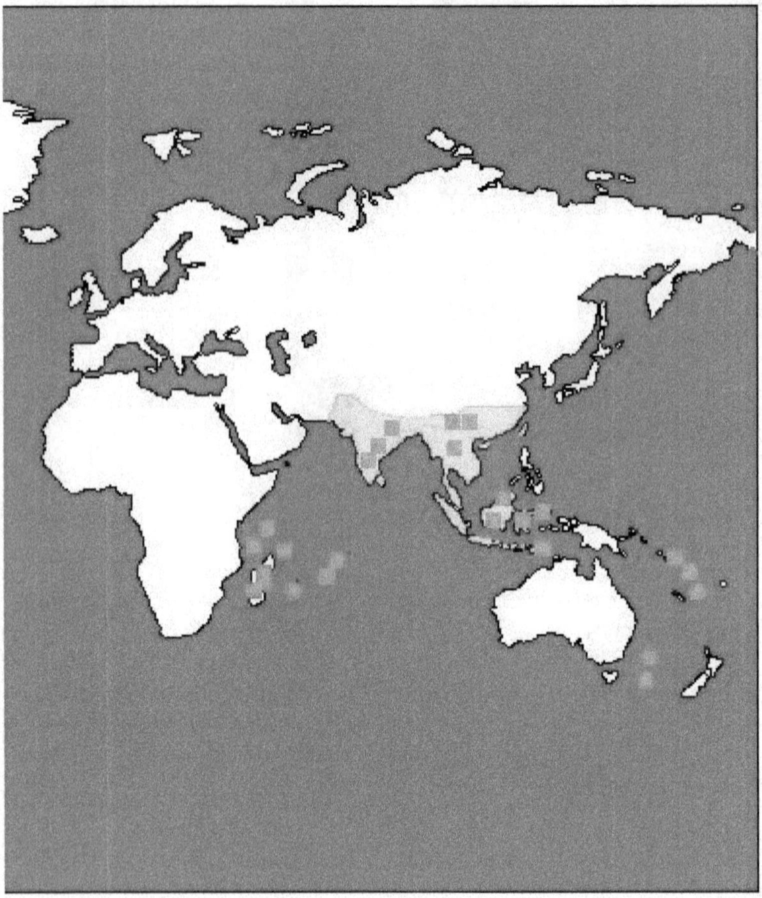

Map of Giant

Tortoises: light blue on South Asia for *Colossochelys* which seems to have persisted in pockets including in Indonesia

up to the end of the Ice Ages (Green Squares), plus the Madagscar area group of Tortoise islands, where some still survive, and *Meiolania* Islands offshore of Australia, where the turtles survived

into the postglacial period but were killed off in Ancient times.274

Rebus: कमठ [p= 252,1] *m.* (Un2. i , 102) a tortoise BhP. Pan5cat. &c Rebus: *kammaṭa* 'mint, coiner, coinage'. Thus, the hypertext of mirror-duplicated giant turtle signifies rebus: kamsA 'bell-metal' and also *kammaṭa* 'mint'. Thus, there are clear indications from Harappa Script that the roots of the tradition of mints to make money coins have to be found in the Bronze Age tradition of metalwork by Bharatam janam.

Three text messages on the mirror-duplicated 'giant turtle' inscriptions on copper tablets: Mirror-duplication signifies metal casting using *cire perdue* (lost-wax) technique of creating mirror image metal castings from wax casts.

B18 inscription

Obverse hypertext: mirror duplicated turtle: kamsa, kamaTha 'turtle' rebus: kamsA kammaṭa 'bell metal mint'

m1534A *gaṇḍa* 'four' rebus: *khaṇḍa* 'implements *kaṇḍa* 'fire-altar' *kolom* 'three' rebus: *kolimi* 'smithy, forge' *koḍa* 'sluice'; Rebus: *koḍ* 'artisan's workshop (Kuwi) Thus, workshop, smithy, forge for implements. *loa* 'ficus religiosa' rebus: *loha* 'copper' PLUS *kAru* 'hypertext superscript' rebus: *kAru* 'blacksmith'. Thus, blacksmith workshop, smithy, forge for implements. PLUS *kanka, karṇaka* 'rim of jar' rebus: *karṇī* 'supercargo, scribe'.

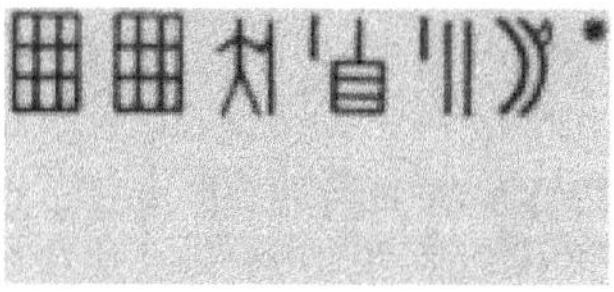

Text on inscription b17a and Line 2 of b17b *kuṭila* 'curve' rebus: *kuṭila* 'bronze' PLUS *koḍ* 'horn' *kODu* 'tusk' rebus: *koḍ* 'workshop' Thus, bronze workshop. खाडा [khāṇḍā] 'A jag, notch, or indentation (as upon the edge of a tool or weapon)' Rebus: *kāṇḍa* 'implements (Santali) PLUS *dula* 'two' rebus: *dul* 'metal casting'. Thus, cast metal implements. *ranku* 'liquid measure' rebus: *ranku* 'tin' PLUS खाडा [khāṇḍā] 'A jag, notch, or indentation (as upon the edge of a tool or weapon)' Rebus: *kāṇḍa* 'implements (Santali). Thus, tin metal castings. *meḍ* 'body' rebus: *meḍ* 'iron' meḍ 'copper' (Slavic languages) PLUS *koḍa* 'one' rebus: *koḍ* 'workshop' *dula* 'pair' rebus: *dul* 'metal casting' PLUS *khaṇḍa* 'division' rebus: khaṇḍa 'implements['.Thus the text message is: copper, tin, iron, bronz metal casting implements.

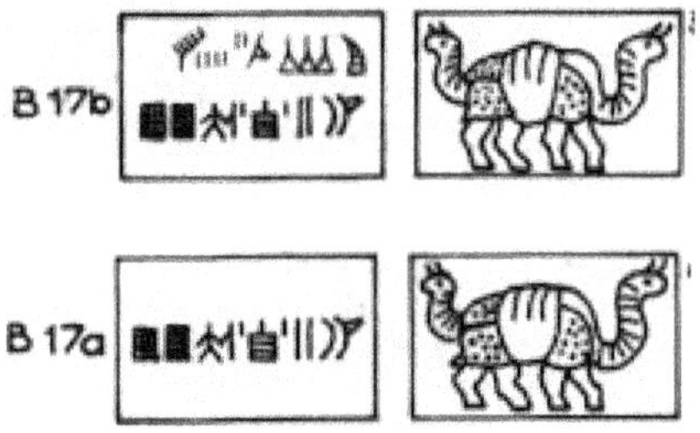

Text of Line 1 on B17b: *koḍ* 'horn' rebus: *koḍ* 'workshop' *dhanga* 'mountain range' rebus: *dhangar* 'blacksmith' *koḍi* 'flag' rebus: *koḍ* 'workshop' PLUS *sal* 'splinter' rebus: *sal* 'workshop' (Phonetic determinative) *gaṇḍa* 'four' rebus: *khaṇḍa* 'implements kaṇḍa 'fire-altar' PLUS *kolmo* 'rice plant' rebus: *kolimi* 'smithy, forge'. Thus, the text message of Line 1 on B17b is: blacksmith workshop (forge) implements.

A9 inscription

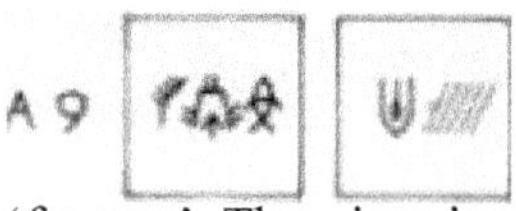

Hypertext on obverse of copper plate: muka 'ladle' (Tamil)(DEDR 4887) Rebus: *mũh* 'ingot' (Santali) *baṭa* = a kind of iron (G.) *baṭa* = rimless pot (Kannada) *bhaṭa* 'furnace'. Thus, iron ingot. Thus, iron ingot furnace.

Text of inscription on A9: *ayo, aya*, 'fish' rebus: *aya* 'iron' *ayas* 'metal' PLUS *dhAl* 'slope' rebus: *dhALaka* 'large ingot'

koḍa 'sluice'; Rebus: *koḍ* 'artisan's workshop (Kuwi)

kolmo 'rice-plant' rebus: *kolimi* 'smithy, forge' pajhar 'sprout' rebus: pasra 'smithy'

A10

A 10 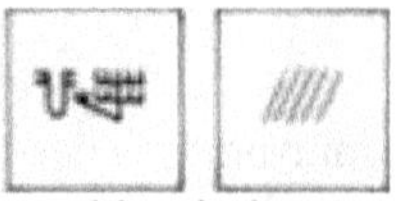 *aḍar* 'harrow' rebus: *aduru* ‘unsmelted metal’PLUS *dula* 'pair' rebus: *dul* 'metal casting' Thus, casting of unsmelted metal (meteorite iron?) PLUS *xolA* ‘tail’ rebus: *kol* ‘metal,working in iron’

 *kaṇḍa kanka* ‘rim of jar’ Rebus: *karṇīka* ‘account (scribe)’*karṇī* ‘supercargo’. *kaṇḍa* ‘fire-altar’. Alternative: *kanka* 'rim of jar' rebus: *kanga* 'brazier'.

Semantic cluster: metalwork cargo

A8 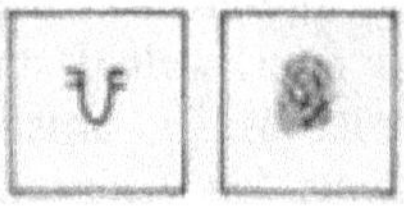

A8

 *kaṇḍa kanka* ‘rim of jar’ Rebus: *karṇīka* ‘account (scribe)’*karṇī* ‘supercargo’. *kaṇḍa* ‘fire-altar’. Alternative: *kanka* 'rim of jar' rebus: *kanga* 'brazier'.

 *muh* 'ingot' PLUS खाडा [*khāṇḍā*] 'A jag, notch, or indentation (as upon the edge of a tool or weapon)' Rebus*: kāṇḍa* 'implements (Santali) Thus the message of A8 inscription is: metal ingot, implements furnaceaccount

Furnace, smithy, anvil in Harappa Script hieroglyphs/hypertexts

Tepe Yahya. Seal impressions of two sides of a seal. Six-legged lizard and opposing footprints shown on opposing sides of a double-sided steatite stamp seal perforated along the lateral axis. Lamberg- Karlovsky 1971: fig. 2C Shahr-i-Soktha Stamp seal shaped like a foot.

Glyph: *aṭi* foot, footprint (Tamil) Rebus: *aḍe, aḍa, aḍi* the piece of wood on which the five artisans put the article which they happen to operate upon, a support (Kannada)

Glyph: *araṇe* 'lizard' (Tulu) அரணை Ta. *araṇai* typical lizard, Lacertidae; smooth streaked lizard, Lacerta interpunctula. Ma. *araṇa* green house lizard, L. interpunctula. Ka. *araṇe, rāṇe, rāṇi* greenish kind of lizard which is said to poison by licking, L. interpunctula. Tu. araṇe id. (DEDR 204). Rebus: a*rṇi* f. ‘ furnace, smithy ’(WPah.) a*raṇi* ‘anvil’ (Sindhi) *eraṇi* f. ‘ anvil ’ (Gujarati); *aheraṇ, ahiraṇ, airaṇ, airṇī, haraṇ* f. (Marathi)

The rebus readings are: *aḍi* 'anvil' airaṇ 'anvil' (for use in) *baṭa* 'iron working' or kiln/furnace-work.Glyph: *bhaṭa* ‘six’ (G.) rebus: *baṭa* = kiln (Santali*) baṭa* = a kind of iron (Gujarati) [Note: six legs shown on the lizard glyph]

kuduru = lizard (Te.); Rebus: *kuduru* = a goldsmith’s portable furnace (Telugu) *kudru* top of fireplace (Kuwi)(DEDR 1709). *kudur d.okka* = a kind of lizard (Pa.); kudur d.okke, kudur d.ekke = garden lizard; *kidri d.okke* house lizard (Go.)(DEDR 1712).

The Tepe yahya seal which shows a six-legged lizard also shows two soles of feet on the obverse, to indicate that an inventory of articles is the message conveyed; in this case, six portable, gold furnaces — *kuduru.*

talka sole of foot; *tala, tola* sole of shoe (Santali) *talka* = palm of the hand, ti talka (Santali.lex.) ti = the hand, arm (Santali.lex.) [A count of 12 phalanges on a palm, constitutes a palm of the hand]. Thus, the rectangle depicts, two talka-s or two palm-counts, i.e. two (*san:gad.a*) twelves or 24. *bar, barea* = two (Santali.lex.) *ba~r.ia~* = merchant (Santali)

talika = inventory, a list of articles, number, to count, to number; *hor.ko talkhaetkoa* = they are counting the people; *mi~hu~ merom reak talikako hataoeda* = they are taking the number of the cattle (Santali) The boxed count of 24 (on one side of tablet shown in Slide 205 represents an inventory of *san:gha_ta* or component articles, represented by the inscription of 4 glyphs: carpenter's axe (*badhor. hako*), anvil (*d.ha~go*), furnace (*kan.d.a kanka*), razor (bakhor.) (an instrument, with which tassar cocoons are cut into narrow strips for splicing purposes; teeth of a comb represented by E).

adhikaraṇī´ f. ' *anvil ', *adhikaraṇa* -- n. ' receptacle, support ' TUp. [√kr̥1]
Pa. *adhikaraṇī* -- f. ' smith's anvil '; Pk. *ahigaraṇī* -- f. ' a piece of apparatus for a smith '; K. *yīran*, dat. *yūrüñ* f. ' anvil ', S. *aharaṇi, araṇi* f., L. (Jukes) *ariṇ* f., awāṇ.. *aihran, airaṇ, ǟhraṇ* f., WPah. bhal. *arhini*; roh. *erṇe* ' smithy ', N. *āran;* H. *aheran, ǟhran* m. ' anvil '; -- H. Smith BSL 101, 115.
Addenda: *adhikaraṇī´* -- : S.kcch. *eṇ* f. ' anvil '; WPah.kṭg. n/*arəṇ*, n/*arṇi* f. ' furnace, smithy '; *ā´rəṇ* m. prob. ← P. Him.I 4; jaun. *āraṇ, airaṇ*; G. *eraṇi* f. ' anvil ', M. *aheraṇ, ahiraṇ,airaṇ, airṇī, haraṇ* f. (CDIAL 252)

The nine copper plates. Top row: Plates 1–3. Middle row: Plates 4–6. Bottom row: Plates 7–9. Scale in centimetres (Shinde & Willis 2014).

Annex E

Clustering 'temple' hieroglyph, pictorial narratives of kneeling adorant, together with markhor and offering on a stool

Rimless pot and rim of jar as Harappa Script hieroglyphs

On a Mohenjo-daro tablet m0478 with inscription on two sides, both hieroglyphs: 1. rimless pot and 2.rim of jar are signified.

meṇḍā 'kneeling position' (Gondi) Rebus: *meḍ* 'iron' (Munda) *baṭa* = rimless pot Rebus: *meḍ bhaṭa* 'iron furnace'

Same inscription is repeated on tablets m0479 and m0480.

M0478A smelter, furnace, furnace implements, turner, workshop supercargo, yajna, wealth

baṭa = rimless pot (Kannada) Rebus: *baṭa* = a kind of iron (Gujarati) *bhaṭa* 'a furnace'

bhaṭa 'worshipper in a temple' Rebus: *bhaṭa* 'furnace' Kneeling adorant hieroglyph: *eragu* 'bow' rebus: *erako* 'moltencast, copper'.

kuṭi 'tree' Rebus: *kuṭhi* = (smelter) furnace (Santali)

gaṇḍa 'four' rebus 1: *kaṇḍ* 'fire-altar' rebus 2: *khaṇḍa* 'implements PLUS *baṭa* = rimless pot (Kannada) Rebus: *baṭa* = a kind of iron (Gujarati) *bhaṭa* 'a furnace'

dula 'pair' rebus: *dul* 'metal casting' PLUS *koḍa* 'one' rebus; *koḍ* 'workshop' PLUS *karṇaka* 'spread legś rebus: *karṇika* 'helsman' PLUS *meḍ* 'body' rebus: *meḍ* 'iron' (Ho. Mu.) *meḍ* 'copper' (Slavic languages)

khāreḍo = a currycomb (Gujarati) Rebus: *khārādī* 'turner' (Gujarati)

mēḍhā 'twist' rebus *meḍ* 'iron' *meḍ* 'copper' (Slavic) *meḍhā* 'dhana, *yajna'*

m0478B tablet smelter, urnace, forge artisan for minerals iron, copper, moltencast

taṭu 'impeding, hindering'(Ta.) Rebus: dhatu 'mineral' (Santali) *erga* = act of clearing jungle (Kui) [Note image showing two men carrying uprooted trees].

eraka, hero = a messenger; a spy (Gujarati) *heraka* = spy (Skt.); *er* to look at or for (Pkt.); *er uk-* to play 'peeping tom' (Ko.) Rebus: *er-r-a* = red; *eraka* = copper (Kannada) *erka* = *ekke* (Tbh. of *arka*) *aka* (Tbh. of *arka*) copper (metal); crystal (Kannada) *erako* molten cast (Tulu) *agasa_le, agasa_li, agasa_lava_d.u* = a goldsmith (Telugu)

kōṭu branch of tree, Rebus: खोट [*khōṭa*] f A mass of metal (unwrought or of old metal melted down); an ingot or wedge.

kuṭi 'tree' Rebus: *kuṭhi* = (smelter) furnace (Santali)

Hieroglyph: Tiger looking back: *krammara* 'look back' (Telugu) *kamar* 'smith, artisan' (Santali)

kola 'tiger, jackal' (Kon.); rebus: kol 'working in iron, blacksmith, 'alloy of five metals, panchaloha' (Tamil) *kol* 'furnace, forge' (Kuwi) *kolimi* 'smithy' (Te.) kol 'furnace, forge'.

^ Inverted V, m478 (lid above rim of narrow-necked jar)

The rimmeḍ jar next to the tiger with turned head has a lid. Lid 'ad.aren'; rebus: aduru 'native metal' d.aren-mund.i lid of pot; d.aren, ad.aren to cover up pot with lid (Bond.a); d.arai to cover (Bond.a.Hindi) munda 'iron'

kanka, karṇika 'rim of jar' Rebus: *karṇī* 'supercargo' (Marathi) Thus, together, the jar with lid composite hieroglyhph denotes 'native metal supercargo'.

Hieroglyph of horned person in a wide pot with projecting base and adorned with ficus leaves

loa 'ficus religiosa' rebus: loha 'copperl

varti f. ' projecting rim '. [√vṛt1] Pa. *vaṭṭi* -- , °*ikā* -- f. ' rim, brim '(CDIAL 1136) rebus: *bhatti* 'furnace, forge' *bhaṭa* 'warrior' rebus: *bhaṭa* 'furnace' *karṇaka* 'spread legś rebus: *karṇaka* 'helmsman'

mṛeka, melh 'goat' (Telugu. Brahui) Rebus: *melukkha milakkha*, 'copper'.

bhaṭa 'worshipper' rebus: *bhaṭa* 'furnace'.

Executive summary of the message: The horned person is a helmsman with a workshop and a copper furnace, forge as signified by the Harappa Script hieroglyphs.

Some of the images such as a kneeling adorant (worshipper) shown on m0478A tablet is also signified on a Dholavira seal no. 56

'spread legś rebus: k*arṇika* 'helsman' PLUS *meḍ* 'body' rebus: *meḍ* 'iron' (Ho. Mu.) meḍ 'copper' (Slavic languages) PLUS horns: *koḍ* 'horns' rebus: *koḍ* 'workshop'. Thus copper workshop of helmsman.

bhaṭa 'worshipper in a temple' Rebus: *bhaṭa* 'furnace' Kneeling adorant hieroglyph: *eragu* 'bow' rebus: *erako* 'moltencast, copper'.

'markhor'. Hieroglyph*: miṇḍāl* 'markhor' (Tōrwālī) *meḍho* a ram, a sheep (Gujarati)(CDIAL 10120) Rebus: *mẽṛhẽt, meḍ* 'iron' (Munda.Ho.) *meḍh* 'merchant's helper (Des'i)

Hieroglyph: *loa* 'ficus religiosa' Rebus: *lo, loh* 'copper, metal' (Samskritam)Rebus: *lōhá* ' red, copper -- coloured ' ŚrS., ' made of copper ' ŚBr., m.n. ' copper ' VS., ' iron ' MBh. [*rudh --]Pa. *lōha* -- m. ' metal, esp. copper or bronze '; Pk. *lōha* -- m. ' iron ', Gy. pal. *li°*, *lihi*, obl. *elhás*, as. *loa* JGLS new ser. ii 258; Wg. (Lumsden) "*loa*" ' steel '; Kho. *loh* ' copper '; S. *lohu* m. ' iron ', L. *lohā* m., awāṇ. *lō`ā*, P. *lohā* m. (→ K.rām. ḍoḍ. *lohā*), WPah.bhad. *lɔ̃u* n., bhal. *lòtilde;*n., pāḍ. jaun. *lōh*, paṅ. *luhā*, cur. cam. *lohā*, Ku. *luwā*, N. *lohu*, *°hā*, A. *lo*, B. *lo*, *no*, Or. *lohā*, *luhā*, Mth. *loh*, Bhoj. *lohā*, Aw.lakh. *lōh*, H. *loh,lohā* m., G. M. *loh* n.; Si. *loho*, *lō* ' metal, ore, iron '; Md. *ratu* -- *lō* ' copper '.*lōhala -- , *lōhila -- , *lōhiṣṭha -- , lōhī -- , laúha -- ; lōhakāra -- , *lōhaghaṭa -- , *lōhaśālā -- , *lōhahaṭṭika -- , *lōhōpaskara -- ; vartalōha -- .Addenda: lōhá -- : WPah.kṭg. (kc.) *lóɔ* ' iron ', J. *lohā* m., Garh. *loho*; Md. *lō* ' metal '(CDIAL 11158) PLUS Pa. vaṭṭi 'projecting rim', rebus: bhāṭi 'furnce'. Thus, loha bhāṭi furnace for loha 'copper ore'.

varti2 f. ' projecting rim '. [√vr̥t1] Pa. *vaṭṭi* -- , *°ikā* -- f. ' circumference, rim, brim '; Pk. *vatti* -- f. ' edge, limit '; Si. väṭi -- ya ' edge of bank or river '(CDIAL 11360)

bhráṣṭra n. ' frying pan, gridiron ' MaitrS. [√*bhrajj]*Pk. *bhaṭṭha* -- m.n. ' gridiron ' (CDIAL 9656)

Variants of the hieroglyphs of kneeling adorant, arched pot on Harappa Script inscriptions

Comparable hieroglyph of kneeling adorant with outstretched hands occurs on a Mohenjo-daro seal m1186, m478A tablet and on Harappa tablet h177B:

Rebus readings: *maṇḍa* ' some sort of framework (?) '. [In *nau - maṇḍḗ* n. du. ' the two sets of poles rising from the thwarts or the two bamboo covers of a boat (?) ' ŚBr. Rebus: M. *mā̃ḍ* m. ' array of instruments &c. '; Si. *maḍa* -- *ya* ' adornment, ornament '. (CDIAL 9736) *kamaḍha* 'penance' (Pkt.) Rebus: *kampaṭṭam* 'mint' (Tamil) *battuḍu*. n. A worshipper (Telugu) Rebus: *pattar* merchants (Tamil), perh. *Vartaka* (Skt.)

bhaṭa 'worshipper' rebus: bhaṭa 'furnace' eragu 'bow' rebus: eraka 'moltencast, copper'

మేడ (p. 1034) [*mēḍa*] *mēḍa* 'platform' Rebus: *meḍ* 'iron' *meḍ* 'copper'

kamaḍha 'penance' rebus: *kammaṭa* 'mint, coiner, coinage'

bari 'roof' rebus: *bari* 'merchant'

kanka, karṇika 'rim of jar' rebus: *karṇī* 'supercargo' *karṇika* 'scribe, account'

khāreDo 'currycomb' rebus: Rebus: *khārādī* ' turner' (G.) karaḍā 'hard alloy' *kāmsako, kāmsiyo* = a large sized comb (G.) Rebus: kaṁsa 'bronze' (Te.)

Thus, the message is: bronze supercargo (on behalf of) copper moltencast, iron mint merchant

Ganweriwala tablet. Ganeriwala or Ganweriwala (Urdu: گنےریوالا Punjabi: گنیریوالا) is a Sarasvati-Sindhu civilization site in Cholistan, Punjab, Pakistan.

Glyphs on a broken molded tablet, Ganweriwala. The reverse includes the 'rim-of-jar' glyph in a 3-glyph text. Observe shows a person seated on a stool and a kneeling adorant below.

Ir. *bärī* roof. ĀlKu. *bari* thatched roof. Ko. *varj- (varj-)* to wrap, wind; *vayr* roof. To. *pary* roof of hut. Rebus: *baḍhi* 'worker in wood and iron' (Santali) *bāṛaï* 'carpenter' (Bengali) *bari* 'merchant' *barea* 'merchant' (Santali) *vāḍhī*, 'one who helps a merchant (Hemacandra Desinamamamala).

Hieroglyph: *kamaḍha* 'penance' Rebus: *kammaṭa* 'coiner, mint'.

1. *kuṭila* 'bent'; rebus: *kuṭila, katthīl* = bronze (8 parts copper and 2 parts tin) [cf. *āra-kūṭa,* 'brass (Skt.) (CDIAL 3230)

2. Glyph of 'rim of jar': *kárṇaka* m. ' projection on the side of a vessel, handle ' ŚBr. [*kárṇa --]Pa. kaṇṇaka* -- ' having ears or corners '(CDIAL 2831) *kaṇḍa kanka*; Rebus: furnace account (scribe). *kaṇḍ* = fire-altar (Santali); *kan* = copper (Tamil) *khanaka* m. one who digs , digger , excavator Rebus: karanikamu. Clerkship: the office of a Karanam or clerk. (Telugu) *káraṇa* n. ' act, deed ' RV. [√kr̥1] Pa. *karaṇa* -- n. 'doing'; NiDoc. *karana, kaṁraṁna* 'work'; Pk. karaṇa -- n. 'instrument'(CDIAL 2790). *karṇī* 'supercargo' karṇika 'account, scribe'.

Alternative: *kanka* 'rim of jar' rebus: *kanga* 'brazier'.

3. *khāreḍo* = a currycomb (G.) Rebus: *khārādī* ' turner' (G.)

kāṅga 'comb' Rebus: *kanga* 'brazier, fireplace'

kāmsako, kāmsiyo = a large sized comb (G.) Rebus: *kaṁsa* 'bronze' (Te.)

Ligatures: Worshipper + rimless pot + scarf (on pigtail)

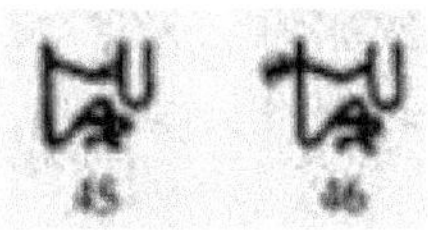

Signs 45, 46: A variant of 'adorant' hieroglyph sign is shown with a 'rimless, broad-mouthed pot' which is *baṭa* read rebus: *bhaṭa* 'furnace'. If the 'pot' ligature is a phonetic determinant, the gloss for the 'adorant' is *bhaṭa* 'worshipper'. If the 'kneeling' posture is the key hieroglyphic representation, the gloss is *eragu* 'bow' Rebus: *erako* 'moltencast copper'. Thus moltencast copper furnace. + *dhaṭu* m. (also *dhaṭhu*) m. 'scarf' (Western Pahari) (CDIAL 6707) Rebus: *dhatu* 'minerals' (Santali). Thus Sign 46 read rebus: moltencast copper minerals furnace.

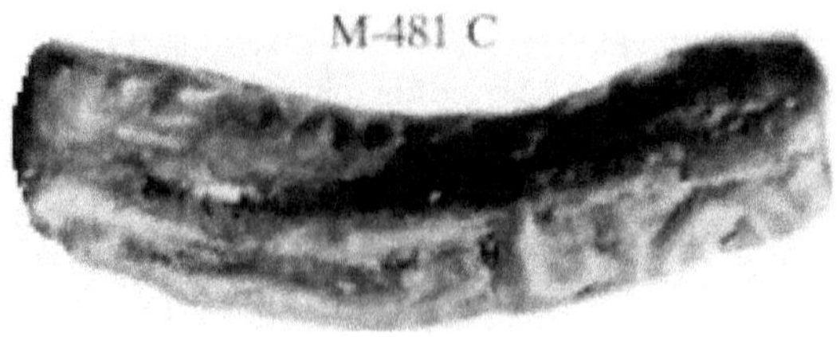

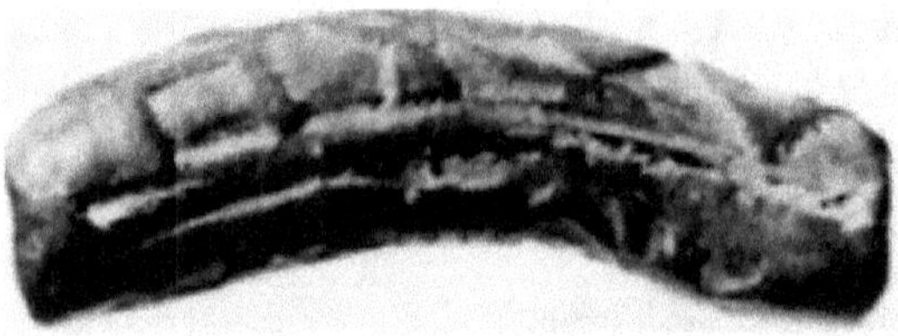

2846 Serpent, partly reclining on a low platform under a tree Pict-41

kāru pincers, tongs. Rebus: *khār* खार् l 'blacksmith' (Kashmiri)

P. (तक्षति, तक्ष्णोति, तष्ट) 1 To chop, cut off, pare, chisel, slice, split; rebus: taksa 'carpenter' PLUS खाडा [*khāṇḍā*] 'A jag, notch, or indentation (as upon the edge of a tool or weapon)' Rebus: *kāṇḍa* 'implements, furnace' (Santali).

kolom 'rice plant' rebus: *kolimi* 'smithy, forge' (circumscript): *mũh, muhe* 'ingot.' Thus, ingots for smithy/forge

kanka, karṇika 'rim of jar' rebus: *karṇī* 'supercargo' *karṇika* 'scribe, account'

bhaṭa 'warrior' rebus: *bhaṭa* 'furnace' karṇika 'spread legś rebus: *karṇī* 'supercargo' kuṭi 'curve; rebus: कुटिल *kuṭila, katthīl* (8 parts copper, 2 parts tin) *dula* 'pair' rebus: *dul* 'metal casting'. Thus bronze metal castings handed over to supercargo.

muhe 'ingot.' PLUS (infixed) *kāmsako, kāmsiyo* = a large sized comb (G.) Rebus: *kaṁsa* 'bronze' (Te.) Thus, bronze ingot.

Kumaon. *khuṭo* 'leg, foot', °ṭī 'goat's leg'; Nepalese. *khuṭo* 'leg, foot'(CDIAL 3894). S. *khuṛī* f. 'heel'; WPah. paṅ. *khūṛ* 'foot'. (CDIAL 3906). Rebus: *khũṭ* 'community, guild' (Santali)

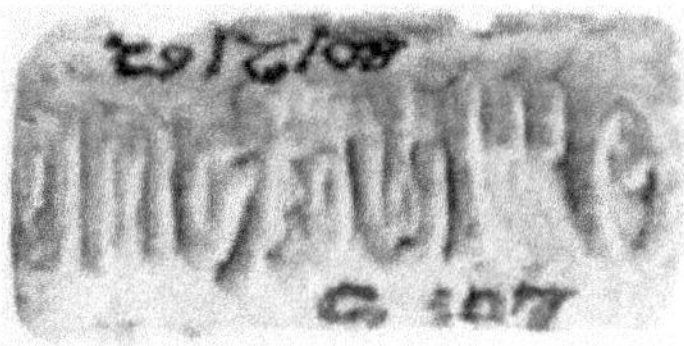

h177A

h177B

4316

Pict-115: From R.—a person standing under an ornamental arch; a kneeling adorant; a ram with long curving horns.

miṇḍāl 'markhor' (Torwali) *meḍho* 'ram' (Gujarati)(CDIAL 10120) Rebus: *me~Rhet, meḍ* 'iron' (Mu.Ho.Santali) *eragu* 'bow' rebus: *erako* 'moltencast, copper' *loa* 'ficus religiosa' rebus: *loh* 'copper' *bhaṭa* 'warrior' rebus: *bhaṭa* 'furnace'. Thus, the hypertext message is: copper, iron furnace for molten cast metalwork.

Text message complements this with additiona technical specifications: iron, bronze forge, furnace, workshop: *kanac* 'corner' rebus: *kancu* 'bronze' *koḍa* 'one' rebus: koḍ 'workshop' Thus, bronze workshop. *muka* 'ladle' rebus: *mũhe* 'ingot' (Santali) *mũhã* 'quantity of smelted metal produced from a furnace' PLUS *baṭa* 'rimless pot' rebus: *bhaṭa* 'furnace' *kuṭi* 'water-carrier' rebus: *kuṭhi* 'smelter' *kolmo* 'three' rebus: *kolimi* 'smithy, forge' *baṭa* 'rimless pot' rebus: *bhaṭa* 'furnace' baṭa 'iron'.

Four pictorial compositions of Pleiades (group of 6 or seven women) occur on: 4 inscriptions

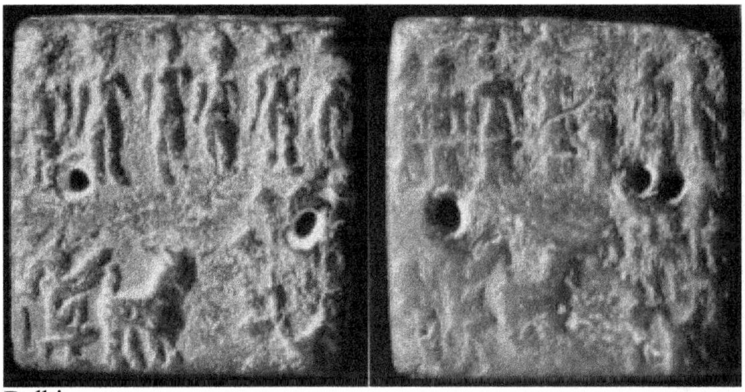

Mohenjo-daro HR 4161, now in the National Museum of India, New Delhi.

[Pleiades, (twigs as headdress) scarfed, framework, scarfed person, worshipper, markhor, *ficus religiosa*] On one side of the tablet, 7 women are shown, and on the obverse 6 women are shown. The narrative is in two registers.Top register shows 6 or 7 women Bottom register has a narrative which is a repeat from another seal h177B.

A comparable narrative comparable to h177b occurs on m488C

m488C This also compares with part of the narrative on m1186 with a kneeling adorant accompanied by a markhor (with short tail), with an offering on a stool, iin front of a warrior standing within a projecting base vessel ornamented as a pot ornamented with *ficus religiosa* leaves. *xolā* 'tail' of antelope and *kulā* hooded snake as tail rebus: *kol* 'furnace, forge' 'working in iron'

The bottom register message is: *miṇḍāl* 'markhor' (Torwali) *meḍho* 'ram' (Gujarati)(CDIAL 10120) Rebus: *me~Rhet, meḍ* 'iron' (Mu.Ho.Santali) *eragu* 'bow' rebus: *erako* 'moltencast, copper' *loa* 'ficus religiosa' rebus: *loh* 'copper' *bhaṭa* 'warrior' rebus: *bhaṭa* 'furnace'. Thus, the hypertext message is: copper, iron furnace for molten cast metalwork.

The top register message is: *bagala* 'pleiades' Rebus 1: *bagalo, bagala* 'Arabian merchant vessel' Rebus 2: *bangala* 'goldsmith's portable furnace'

Hieroglyph: మండ [*maṇḍa*] *manḍa.* [Tel.] n. A twig with leaves on it. Rebus 1: *mā̃ḍ* m. 'array of instruments &c.' (CDIAL 9736) maṇḍa 'iron dross, slag' Rebus 2: *maṇḍa* m. 'ornament' 'workshop, warehouse'. Thus, bagala seafaring vessel is a carrier of specialized cargo – array of instruments (made of molten cast metalwork, as detailed in the message of the bottom register of HR 4161..

Sa. <i>mE~R~hE~'d</i> `iron'. ! <i>mE~RhE~d</i>(M). Ma. <i>mErhE'd</i> `iron'.Mu. <i>mERE'd</i> `iron'. ~ <i>mE~R~E~'d</i> `iron'. ! <i>mENhEd</i>(M).Ho <i>meḍ</i> `iron'.Bj. <i>merhd</i>(Hunter) `iron'.KW <i>mENhEd</i> (Munda)

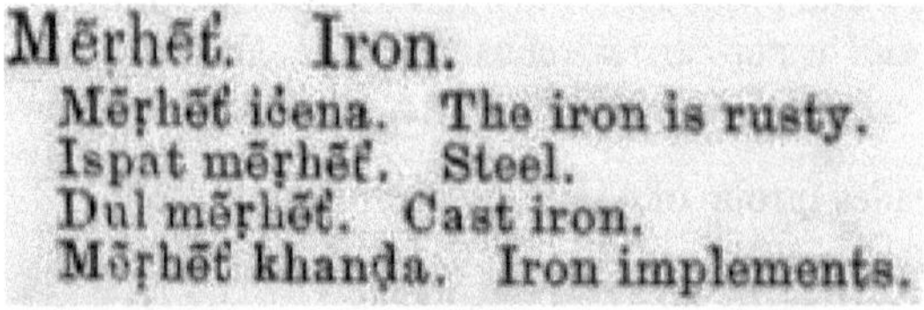
Mĕrhĕt. Iron.
Mĕṛhĕt iʗena. The iron is rusty.
Ispat mĕṛhĕt. Steel.
Dul mĕṛhĕt. Cast iron.
Mĕṛhĕt khanḍa. Iron implements.

h097 Pict-95 seven robed figures. Harappa tablet: *bagala* 'pleiades' Rebus: *bagalo* = an Arabian merchant vessel (G.) *bagala* = an Arab boat of a particular description (Kannada); *bagalā* (M.); *bagarige, bagarage* = a kind of vessel (Ka.)

kolmo 'three' *kole.l* 'temple' Rebus: *kole.l* 'smithy, forge' *kolimi* 'smithy, forge'

dhal '**slant**' rebus: *dhALako* 'large ingot' PLUS खांडा [*khāṇḍā*] m A jag, **notch**, or indentation (as upon the edge of a tool or weapon). (Marathi) Rebus: *khāṇḍā* 'tools, pots and pans, metalware'.

muka '**ladle**' rebus: *muhA* 'quantity of smelted metal produced from a furnace' PLUS *baTa* 'rimless **pot**' rebus: *bhaTa* 'furnace'

dula 'two' rebus: *dul* 'metal casting' PLUS kuṭi '**curve**; rebus: कुटिल kuṭila, katthīl (8 parts copper, 2 parts tin). Thus, bronze metal castings (perhaps *cire perdue* artifacts – bronze castings)..

m1186 seal

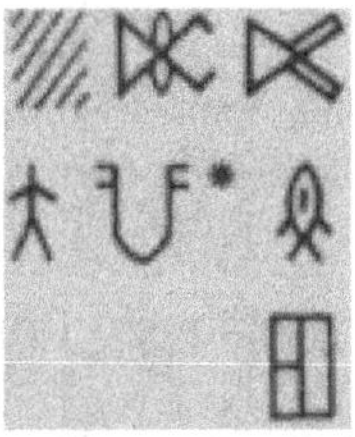

2430 Hypertext Composition of both pictorial motifs and text signs: horned person with a pigtail standing between the branches of a pipal tree; a low pedestal with offerings (? or human head?); a horned person kneeling in adoration; a ram with short tail and curling horns; a row of seven robed figures, with twigs on their pigtails.

The stool on which the bowl is placed is also a hieroglyph read rebus:

Text message of inscription on m1186:

kole.l 'temple' rebus: *kole.l* 'smithy, forge' *kol* 'furnace, forge'. A variant of the 'temple' hieroglyph also includes a U hieroglyph, i.e. 'rimless pot'. This is a reinforcement of the organization of the smithy, forge which includes a furnace: *baTi, baTa* 'rimless pot' rebus: *bhaTi, bhaTa* 'furnace, kiln'

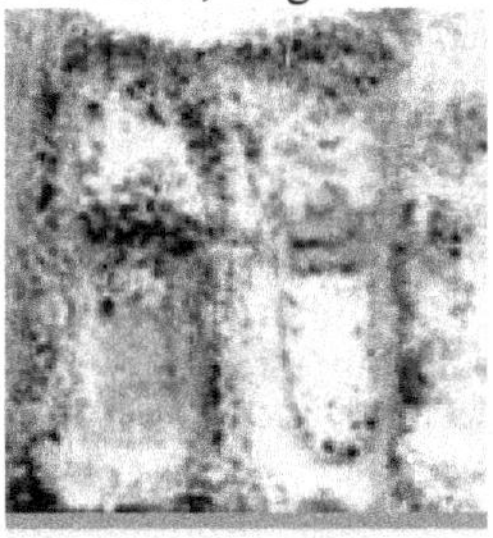

Sign 242

aya khāṇḍā 'fish+notch' Rebus: *aya khāṇḍā* 'iron tools, pots and pans, and metal-ware'.

kaṇḍa kanka 'rim of jar' Rebus: *karṇīka* 'account (scribe)' *karṇī* 'supercargo'. *kaṇḍa 'fire-altar'.*

कर्णक *kárṇaka, kannā* **'legs spread'**, कर्णक *kárṇaka,* 'helmsman'

kāru 'pincers, tongs' Rebus: *khār* खार् 'blacksmith'

ḍato 'claws or pincers (chelae) of crabs'; Rebus: *dhatu* 'mineral, ore'

The kneeling adorant is offering a bowl with a ladle on a stand.

loa 'ficuś Rebus: *loha* 'copper'

mẽhi bāṭi ' vessel with a **projecting base** ' Rebus: mẽṛhẽt, meḍ 'iron'. 'iron' (Mu.Ho.Santali) PLUS *bhaṭi* 'kiln, furnace'. *bhaṭa* 'warrior' rebus: *bhaṭā* 'kiln, furnace'.

bhaṭā (Gujarati) bhuvɔ m. ' worshipper in a temple ' rather < bhṛta --(CDIAL 9554) Yājñ.com., Rebus: *bhaṭā* 'kiln, furnace' *baṭa* 'iron' (Gujarati)

Kur. *kaṇḍō* a stool. Malt. *kanḍo* stool, seat. (DEDR 1179) Rebus: *kaṇḍ* 'stone (ore)' as in: *ayaskāṇḍ* 'excellent iron' (Panini)

saman 'make an offering (Santali) *samanon* 'gold' (Santali) *bAraNe* ' an offering of food to a demon' (Tulu) Rebus: *baran, bharat* (5 copper, 4 zinc and 1 tin) (Punjabi. Bengali)

muka '**ladle**' (Tamil)(DEDR 4887) *mũh* 'ingot'

maNDi 'kneeling position' *Rebus: mADa* 'shrine; mandil 'temple' (Santali)

miṇḍāl 'markhor' (Torwali) *meḍho* 'ram' (Gujarati)(CDIAL 10120) Rebus: mẽṛhẽt, meḍ 'iron'. 'iron' (Mu.Ho.Santali)

See the human face ligatured to a ram's body (an indication of the hieroglyphic nature of the orthographic composition):

mũh 'face' (Santali). Rebus: *mũh* metal ingot (Santali) *mũhã̄* = the quantity of iron produced at one time in a native smelting furnace of the Kolhes; iron produced by the Kolhes and formeḍ like a four-cornered piece a little pointed at each end; mūhā mẽṛhẽt = iron smelted by the Kolhes and formeḍ into an equilateral lump a little pointed at each end; kolhe tehen mẽṛhẽtko mūhā akata = the Kolhes have to-day produced pig iron (Santali.lex.)

miṇḍāl 'markhor' (Tor.wali) *meḍho 'a ram, a sheep' (G.)(CDIAL 10120)mēṇḍha 'ram'(CDIAL 9606). मेंढा [mēṇḍhā]* m (मेष S through H) A male sheep, a ram or tup. मेंढका or क्या [*mēṇḍhakā or kyā*] a (मेंढा) A shepherd (Marathi) Rebus: meḍ 'iron' (Ho.) *mēṇḍh* 'gold' as in: मेंढसर [*mēṇḍhasara*] m A bracelet of gold thread. (Marathi)

मेढ [mēḍha] f A forked stake. Used as a post. Hence a short post generally whether forked or not. Pr. हातीं लागली चेड आणि धर मांडवाची मेढ.

heraka 'spy' (Samskritam) Rebus: *erako* 'molten metal, copper'

maNDa 'branch, twig' (Telugu) Rebus: *maNDA* 'warehouse, workshop' (Konkani) *karibha* 'trunk of elephant' *ibha* 'elephant' Rebus: *karba, ib*, 'iron'

dhaṭu m. (also *dhaṭhu*) m. 'scarf' (WPah.) (CDIAL 6707) Allograph: *ḍato* = claws of crab (Santali) Rebus: *dhātu* = mineral (Skt.), *dhatu* id. (Santali)

The rice plant adorning the curved horn of the person (woman?) with the pig-tail is *kolmo*; read rebus, *kolime* 'smithy'. Smithy of what? *kol* 'pancaloha'. The curving horn is: *koḍ.u* = horn; rebus: *koḍ.* artisan's workshop (Kuwi)

bagaḷā 'pleiades' rebus: *bagala* 'dhow, Arab boat, seafaring vessel'. Glyph (seven women): *bahula_* = Pleiades (Skt.) *bagaḷā* = name of a certain godess (Te.) *bagaḷā ,bagaḷe, vagalā* (Ka.); *baka , bagaḷlā , vagaḷā* (Te.) *bakkulā* = a demon, uttering horrible cries, a form assumeḍ by the Yakkha Ajakalāpaka, to terrify the Buddha (Pali) *bahulā* f. pl. the Pleiades VarBṛS., likā -- f. pl. lex. *[bahulá --*] Kal. bahul the Pleiades , Kho. *ból,* (Lor.) *boul, bolh,* Sh. (Lor.) *b*lle* (CDIAL 9195) *bahule, bahulegal.* = the Pleiades or Kṛittikā-s (Kannada) *bahula_* (VarBr.S.); *bahul (*Kal.) six presiding female deities: *vahulā* the six presiding female deities of the Pleiades (Skt.); vākulāi id. (Tamil) Pleiades: bahulikā pl. pleiades; *bahula* born under the pleiades; the pleiades (Samskrtam) பாகுலம் **pākulām** , *n.* < *bāhula*. The month of Kārttikai = November-December; கார்த்திகை மாதம். (W.) పావడము [pāvaḍamu] *pāvaḍamu*. [Tel.] n. A present, gift. కానుక. *vākulēyan-* < *va_kulēya* Skāṇḍa (Tamil)

பாகுளி *pākuḷi,* n. perh. *bāhulī.* Full moon in the month of Puraṭṭāci; புரட்டாசி மாதத்துப் பௌர்ணமி. அதைப் பாகுளி யென்று (விநாயகபு. 37, 81). Glyph (twig on head on seven women): *adaru* 'twig'; rebus: aduru 'native metal'. Thus, the seven women ligatured with twigs on their heads can be read as: *bahulā* + *adaru*; rebus: *bangala* 'goldsmith's portable furnace' + aduru 'native metal'. *bāhulēya* Kārttikēya, son of Śiva; *bāhula* the month kārttika (Skt.Ka.) வாகுலை *vākulāi*, n. < *Vahulā.* The six presiding female deities of the Pleiades. Rebus: bagalo = an Arabian merchant vessel (Gujarati) *bagala* = an Arab boat of a particular description (Ka.); *bagalā* (M.); *bagarige, bagarage* = a kind of vessel (Kannada) cf. m1429 seal for the image of a boat from Mohenjo-daro. बहुल Born under the Pleiades; P.IV.3.33. An epithet of fire. -ला 1 A cow; कस्मात् समाने बहुलाप्रदाने सद्भिः प्रशस्तं कपिलाप्रदानम् Mb.13.77.9. The Pleiades (pl.) -लम् 1 The sky. बहुलिका (pl.) The Pleiades. बाहुल a. Manifold. -लः Fire; शीतरुजं समये च परस्मिन् बाहुलतो रसिका शमयन्ती Rām. Ch.4.99. -2 The month Kārtika. -लम् 1 Manifoldness. बाहुलेयः An epithet of Kārtikeya.बाहुल्यम् 1 Abundance, plenty, copiousness. -2 Manifoldness, multiplicity, variety. -3 The usual course or common order of things. (बाहुल्यात्, -ल्येन 1 usually, commonly. -2 in all probability.) बाह्लिः N. of a country (Balkh). -Comp. -ज, -जात a. bred in the Balkh country, of the Balkh breed.बाह्लकाः बाह्लिकाः बाह्लीकाः m. (pl.) N. of a people.-कम् 1 Saffron; ... प्रियाङ्गसंगव्यालुप्तस्तनतटबाह्लिक- श्रियो$पि दृश्यन्ते बहिरबलाः Rām. Ch.7.64. Amarakosha makes references to the Saffron of Bahlika and Kashmira countries (Amarkosha, p 159, Amarsimha.)

m488 three-sided tablet 2802 Prism: Tablet in bas-relief. Side b: Text +One-horned bull + standard. Side a: From R.: a composite animal; a person seated on a tree with a tiger below looking up at the person; a svastika within a square border; an elephant (Composite animal has the body of a ram, horns of a zebu, trunk of an elephant, hindlegs of a tiger and an upraised serpent-like tail). Side c: From R.: a horned person standing between two branches of a pipal tree; a ram; a horned person kneeling in adoration; a low pedestal with some offerings.

m488A *heraka* 'spy' rebus: *eraka* 'moltencast, copper' *kuṭi* 'tree' rebus: *kuṭhi* 'smelter' *kola* 'tiger' rebus: *kol* 'working in iron' 'furnace, forge' *kolhe* 'smelter' *krammara* 'look back' rebus: *kamar* 'artisan, smith' *sattva* 'svastika' rebus: *sattva, jasta* 'zinc' *karibha* 'trunk of elephant' *ibha* 'elephant' rebus: *karba* 'iron' *ib* 'iron'. Thus, the message on this side of the tablet is: artisan (working in) iron, zinc, furnace, forge, moltencast copper.

m488B *barad, balad* 'ox' rebus: bharata 'alloy of pewter, copper, tin' *bhaṭa* 'warrior' rebus: *bhaṭa* 'furnace' *karṇika* 'spread legś *meḍ* 'body' rebus: *karṇī* 'supercargo' *meḍ* 'iron' PLUS *khāreḍo* = a currycomb *(G.)* Rebus: *khārādī* 'turner'(Gujarati) *kāmsako, kāmsiyo* = a large sized comb (Gujarati) *Rebus: kaṁsa* 'bronze' (Te.) *bicha* 'scorpion' rebus: *bicha* 'haematite stone ore' मेंढा [*mēṇḍhā*] A crook or curved end rebus: *meḍ* 'iron' (Ho.Mu.) *dula* 'pair' rebus: *dul* 'metalcasting' PLUS *kolom* 'three' rebus: *kolimii* 'smithy, forge' Thus, metalcasting smithy. *dula* 'pair' rebus: *dul* 'metalcasting' PLUS khaṇḍa 'divisions' rebus: kāṇḍa 'implements, furnace' thus, cast metal implements. Thus, the message on this side of the tablet is: turner with furnace, working in bronze, brass, pewter, haematite ore, iron metal casting.

m488C *bhaṭa* 'warrior' rebus: *bhaṭa* 'furnace' *loa* 'ficus religiosa' rebus: *loh* 'copper' *miṇḍāl* 'markhor' (Torwali) *meḍho* 'ram' (Gujarati) (CDIAL 10120) Rebus: *me~Rhe~t, meḍ* 'iron' (Mu.Ho.Santali) dhaTa 'scarf' rebus: dhatu 'mineral' *eragu* 'bow' rebus: *erako* 'moltencast, copper' *dhata* 'scarf' rebus: *dhatu* 'mineral' *muka* 'ladle' rebus: *mũhe* 'ingot', *mũhā̃* 'quantity of metal produced from a furnace.' Kur. Kaṇḍō a stool. Malt. Kanḍo stool, seat. (DEDR 1179) Rebus: kaṇḍ = a furnace, altar (Santali). Thus, the message on this side of the tablet is: iron mineral, copper furnace for ingots.

The prism tablet m488 is a metalwork catalogue of a mint artisan providing technical details of metallurgical competence working with a variety of minerals, metals and alloys and metal castings.

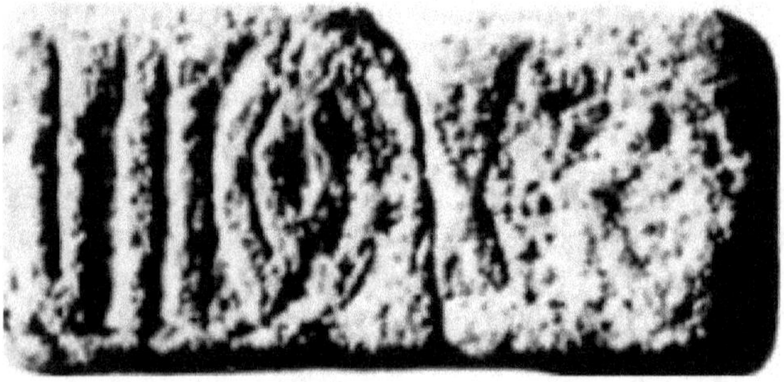

m453A *kanac* 'corner' rebus: *kancu* 'bronze' *sal* 'splinter' rebus: *sal* 'workshop' *ayo, aya* 'fish' rebus: *aya* 'iron' ayas 'metal' PLUS *khambhaṛā* 'fish-fin' rebus: *kammaṭa* 'mint, coiner, coinage' *karā̃* n. pl. wristlets, bangles' rebus: *khār* 'blacksmith' dula 'n. pl. wristlets, bangles' rebus: *khār* 'blacksmith' *kanka, karṇika* 'rim of jar' rebus: *karṇī* 'supercargo' 'scribe, account'. The two bangles suggest a mirror image technique of *cire erdue*. Thus, the message on the tablet: metal casting blacksmith & supercargo, a representative of the ship's owner on board a merchant ship, responsible for overseeing the cargo and its sale.

Mohenjo-daro seal

Deity Seal

Deity seal from Mohenjo-daro. E.J.H. Mackay writes of what he calls a "deity, seated in what may be a yogi attitude" where, in this case, "the stool is omitted, however, and the figure is apparently seated upon the ground. The headdress consists of two horn-like objects between which there appears to be a spike of flowers. A pigtail hangs down one side of the head which has one face only, in profile, facing to the right. Unfortunately this seal is badly broken, but enough remains to show that the figure was surrounded by pictographs arranged in a somewhat haphazard fashion." (Further Excavations at Mohenjo-daro, 1938, p. 334).

dhatu 'scarf' Rebus: *dhatu* 'mineral *khambhaṛā* 'fish **fin**' rebus: *kammaTa* 'mint, coiner, coinage' *gaṇḍa* 'four' rebus: *kaṇḍa* 'implements' *kaṇḍa* 'fire-altar' *sal* 'splinter' rebus: *sal* 'workshop' *ayo, aya* 'fish' rebus: *aya* 'iron' *ayas* 'metal' *kanac* 'corner' rebus: *kancu* 'bronze'

m453B. Scarf as pigtail of seated person.Kneeling adorant and serpent on the field.

khaṇḍiyo [cf. *khaṇḍaṇī* a tribute] tributary; paying a tribute to a superior king (Gujarti) Rebus: *khaṇḍaran, khaṇḍrun* 'pit furnace' (Santali)
paṭa. 'serpent hood' Rebus: *pata* 'sharpness (of knife), tempered (metal). *padm* 'tempered iron' (Kota) *kulA* 'hood of serpent' rebus: *kol* 'furnace, forge' *bhaTa* 'worshipper' rebus: *bhaTa* 'furnace'.

Seated person in penance. Wears a scarf as pigtail and curved horns with embedded stars and a twig.

mēḍha The polar star. (Marathi) Rebus: *meḍ* 'iron' (Ho.) *dula* 'pair' (Kashmiri); Rebus: *dul* 'cast (metal)'(Santali) *ḍabe, ḍabea* 'large horns, with a sweeping upward curve, applied to buffaloes' (Santali) Rebus: *ḍab, ḍhimba, ḍhompo* 'lump (ingot?)', clot, make a lump or clot, coagulate, fuse, melt together (Santali) *kūṭī* = bunch of twigs (Skt.) Rebus: *kuṭhi* = (smelter) furnace (Santali) The narrative on this metalware catalog is thus: (smelter) furnace for iron and for fusing together cast metal. *kamaḍha* 'penance'.Rebus 1: *kaṇḍ* 'stone (ore) metal' *kaṇḍa* 'implements' Rebus 2: *kampaṭṭa* 'mint'.

m453B 1629 Pict-82 Person seated on a pedestal flanked on either side by a kneeling adorant and a hooded serpent rearing up.

mēḍa 'platform' rebus: *meḍ* 'iron' *meḍ* 'copper' (Slavic) *kamaḍha* 'penance' rebus: *kammaṭa* 'mint, coiner, coinage' *eragu* 'bow' rebus: *erako* 'moltencast, copper' *kulā* 'serpent hood' rebus: *kol* 'working in iron' 'furnce, forge' *kolhe* 'smelter' *bhaṭa* 'worshipper' rebus: *bhaṭa* 'furnace'.

Thus, the message expands on th message conveyed on side A of m453 tablet with additional semantic determinative specifications on side B hypertexts: metal casting blacksmith & supercargo, a representative of the ship's owner on board a merchant ship, responsible for overseeing the cargo and its sale PLUS additional specifications on side B: smelter, furnace/forge for iron, copper mint, and bronze workshop.

These examples demonstrate hypertexts of orthographed Harappa Script hieroglyph to document mint-work with a *kol* 'furnace, forge' (Kuwi).

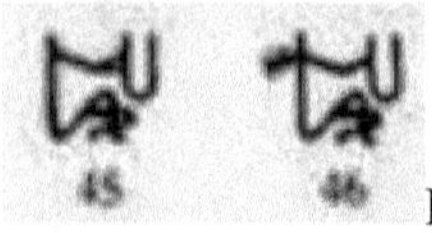
Ligatures: Worshipper + rimless pot + scarf (on pigtail)

Signs 45, 46: A variant of 'adorant' hieroglyph sign is shown with a 'rimless, broad-mouthed pot' which is *baṭa* read rebus: *bhaṭa* 'furnace'. If the 'pot' ligature is a phonetic determinant, the gloss for the 'adorant' is *bhaṭa* 'worshipper'. If the 'kneeling' posture is the key hieroglyphic representation, the gloss is *eragu* 'bow' Rebus: *erako* 'moltencast copper'. Thus moltencast copper furnace. + *dhaṭu* m. (also dhaṭhu) m. 'scarf' (Western Pahari) (CDIAL 6707) Rebus*:* *dhatu* 'minerals' (Santali). Thus Sign 46 read rebus: moltencast copper minerals furnace.

Arbour, canopy: మండ [maṇḍa] *manḍa*. [Tel.] n. A twig with leaves on it. చెట్టుకొమ్మ. A small branch, ఉపశాఖ.MAṆḌ ' adorn '. [Scarcely < *mr̥ndati ' rubs '; nor is P. Thieme's derivation (ZDMG 93, 133) as MIA. < **mr̥ṁṣṭē* (√mr̥j) phonet. convincing. Prob. with J. Bloch BSOS v 741 ← Drav. (Tam.*maṇṇu* ' to decorate ' 9736 maṇḍa2 m. ' ornament ' lex. [√maṇḍ]Pk. *maṁḍaya* -- ' adorning '; Ash. *mōṇḍa, mōnda, mūnda* NTS ii 266, *mōṇə* NTS vii 99 ' clothes '; G. *mā̃ḍ* m. ' arrangement, disposition, vessels or pots for decoration ', *māṇ* f. ' beautiful array of household vessels '; Si. *maḍa -- ya* ' adornment, ornament '.(CDIAL 9736) maṇḍa6 ' some sort of framework (?) '. [In *nau -- maṇḍé* n. du. ' the two sets of poles rising from the thwarts or the two bamboo covers of a boat (?) ' ŚBr. (as illustrated in BPL p. 42); and in BHSk. and Pa. *bōdhi -- maṇḍa* -- n. perh. ' thatched cover ' rather than ' raised platform ' (BHS ii 402).(CDIAL 9737) N. *maṛher, maṛer* ' one who carries ornaments &c. in the marriage procession '.(CDIAL 9738) maṇḍana n. ' adorning ' MBh., *maṇḍaná* -- adj. Pāṇ. [√maṇḍ] Pa. *maṇḍana* -- n., Pk. *maṁḍaṇa* -- n. and adj.; OMarw. *māṁḍaṇa* m. ' ornament '; G. *mā̃ḍaṇ* n. ' decorating foreheads and cheeks of women on festive occasions '.(CDIAL 9739) maṇḍapa m.n. ' open temporary shed, pavilion ' Hariv., °*pikā* -- f. ' small pavilion, customs house ' Kād. 2. maṇṭapa -- m.n. lex. 3. *maṇḍhaka -- . [Variation of *ṇḍ* with *ṇṭ*supports supposition of non -- Aryan origin in Wackernagel AiGr ii 2, 212: see EWA ii 557. -- Prob. of same origin as maṭha -- 1 and maṇḍa -- 6 with which NIA. words largely collide in meaning and form] 1. Pa. *maṇḍapa* -- m. ' temporary shed for festive occasions '; Pk. *maṁḍava* -- m. ' temporary erection, booth covered with creepers ', °*viā* -- f. ' small do. '; Phal. *maṇḍau* m. ' wooden gallery outside a house '; K. *manḍav* m. ' a kind of house found in forest villages '; S. *manahũ* m. ' shed, thatched roof '; Ku. *mā̃ṛyā, manyā* ' resthouse '; N. *kāṭhmā̃ṛau* ' the city of Kathmandu ' (*kāṭh* -- < kāṣṭhá --); Or. *maṇḍuā̃* ' raised and shaded pavilion ', *paṭā -- maṇḍoi* ' pavilion laid over with planks below roof ', *muṇḍoi*, °*ḍei* ' raised unroofed platform '; Bi. *mā̃ṛo* ' roof of betel plantation ', *mā̃ṛuā, maṛ°, malwā* ' lean -- to thatch against a wall ', *maṛaī* ' watcher's shed on ground without platform '; Mth. *māṛab* ' roof of betel plantation ', *maṛwā* ' open erection in courtyard for festive occasions '; OAw. *māṁḍava* m. ' wedding canopy '; H. *mā̃ṛwā* m., °*wī* f., *maṇḍwā* m., °*wī* f. ' arbour, temporary erection, pavilion ', OMarw. *maṁḍavo, māḍhivo* m.; G.*mā̃ḍav* m. ' thatched open shed ', *mā̃ḍvɔ* m. ' booth ', *mā̃ḍvī* f. ' slightly raised platform before door of a house, customs house ', *mā̃ḍaviyɔ* m. ' member of bride's party '; M. *mā̃ḍav* m. ' pavilion for festivals ', *mā̃ḍvī* f. ' small canopy over an idol '; Si. *maḍu -- va* ' hut ', *maḍa* ' open hall ' SigGr ii 452.2. Ko. *māṁṭav* ' open pavilion '.3. H. *mā̃ḍhā, māṛhā, mā̃ḍhā* m. ' temporary shed, arbour ' (cf. OMarw. *māḍhivo* in 1); -- Ku. *mā̃ṛā* m.pl. ' shed,

resthouse ' (or < maṇḍa -- 6?]*chāyāmaṇḍapa -- .Addenda: maṇḍapa --
: S.kcch. *māṇḍhvo* m. ' booth, canopy '.(CDIAL 9740) maṇḍáyati ' adorns, decorates ' Hariv., *máṇḍatē*, °*ti* Dhātup. [√maṇḍ]Pa. *maṇḍēti* ' adorns ', Pk. *maṁḍēi*, °*ḍaï*; Ash. *mū̃ṇḍ* -- , *moṇ* -- intr. ' to put on clothes, dress ', *muṇḍaā´* -- tr. ' to dress '; K. *manḍun* 'to adorn', H. *maṇḍnā*;
(CDIAL 9741) G. *mā̃ḍāṇ* n. ' wooden frame on a well for irrigation bucket '?(CDIAL 9745) *Ta.* maṇṇu (maṇṇi-) to do, make, perform, adorn, beautify, decorate, polish, perfect, finish; maṇṇ-uṟu to polish as a gem; maṉai (-v-, -nt-) to make, create, form, fashion, shape. *Ma.*manayuka, maniyuka to fashion, form earthenware, make as a potter. (DEDR 4685) మండనము [maṇḍanamu] *manḍanamu*. [Skt.] n. Adorning, dressing, decorating, decoration. An ornament, jewel, భూషణము, అలంకరణము. మండనుడు *manḍanuḍu*. n. One who is dressed or ornamented. "ఏకాంతభక్తి మహితమండనుడు" he who is adorned with faith. BD. v. 1.

మండపము [maṇḍapamu] *manḍapamu*. [Skt.] n. A porch, a portico, స్తంభములమీద కట్టిన కట్టడము. A bower, pavilion, చావడి, సభాభేదము, నాలుగు కాళ్లమండపము a four pillared portico. ముఖమండపము a porch of a temple. మండపి or గర్భమండపి *manḍapi*. n. A shrine, a sanctuary. గర్భగృహము. A small portico. చిన్నమండపము. "గర్భమండపి గడిగిన కలశజలము." A. vi. 7.

మందాడు [mandāḍu] *manḍ-āḍu*. [Tel.] v. a. To beg, beseech, pray. బతిమాలుకొను, గో□రాడు, దైన్యముతో యాచించు. "ద్వి ఆవేళభయకంపితాత్ముడైనాడు. చండికి నీశ్వరేశ్వరునకునెరగి. మండాడబోయిన మరియొండుతగిలె. "పండి" ప్ర. i. మండాటము *manḍ-āṭamu*. n. The act of begging with great humulity. దైన్యముతో యాచించుట.

మండి [maṇḍi] or మండీ *manḍi*. [Tel.] n. Kneeling down with one leg, an attitude in archery, ఒక కాలితో నేలమీద మోకరించుట, ఆలీఢపాదము.

మండము [maṇḍamu] or మండాము *manḍamu*. [Skt.]An ornament, భూషణము.

मंडन (p. 626) [maṇḍana] *n* (S) corruptly मंडण *n* Ornament or decoration: also the adorning material; jewels, trinkets &c. 2 Adorning, dressing out, bedecking. 3 In disputation; as opp. to खंडन. Establishing, proving, maintaining (of a position). 4 A festive occasion in general. 5 (For मेघमंडन) Overspreading (of clouds); canopy. *v* घाल. मंडप (p. 626) [maṇḍapa] *m* (S) An open shed or hall adorned with flowers and erected on festive occasions, as at marriages &c.: also an arched way of light sticks for the vine &c. to climb and overspread. 2 An open building consecrated to a god. 3 fig. A canopy of clouds. Ex. पावसानें मं0 घातला. मंडपी (p. 626) [maṇḍapī] *f* (Dim. of मंडप) A canopy of light framework (to suspend over an idol &c.) Ku. *mā̃ṛā* m. pl. ' shed, resthouse '(CDIAL 9737)

maṇḍū´ka m. ' frog ', *maṇḍūkī´* -- f. RV., °*kíkā* -- f. Suparṇ., *marūka* -- m. lex. 2. *maṇḍukka -- . 3. maṇḍūra -- m. lex. 4. maṇḍa -- 5 m. lex. 5. *maṇṭrakka -- or *maṭrakka -- . [The many aberrant forms in NIA. are due to taboo (EWA ii 561 with lit.: see also dardurá --) as well as onom. influences (as, e.g., **maṭrakka* -- ~ Gk. ba/traxos). P. Thieme's derivation (ZDMG 93, 135) as MIA. < **mṛṁṣṭa* -- is phonet. unacceptable. -- → Orm. *maṛyūg* ' frog ' IIFL i 401]1. Pa. *maṇḍūka* -- m., °*kī* -- f. ' frog ', Pk. *maṁḍū̆ka* -- , °*ḍūa* -- , °*ḍuga* -- m., WPah.bhiḍ. *maḍõ*, pl. °*ḍū* n., bhal. *mā´ṇū* n. (+ *go* < gōdhā´ -- in *mango* f. ' large frog '), khas.*mn/aḍū*, marm. *mā̃ḍū*, Si. *maḍu* -- *vā*, *mäňḍi*, *mäḍi* -- *yā* (< *maṇḍūkī´* --).2. Pk. *maṁḍukka* --

m., °*kiyā* -- , °*kaliyā* -- f., Ḍ. *minik* m., Ash. *muṇḍúk*, Wg. *āvmeḍák*, *āmə́ṛk* (*āv* -- , *ā* -- < *ā'paḥ* s.v. áp --), Kt. *muṇúk*, (Kamdesh) *ṍmaṇuk*, Pr. *mā'ṇḍux*, *māṇḍuk*, *mā̃ḍək*, Paš.kuṛ. chil. *marák*, °*rék*, Gaw. *muṇḍā'ka*, *miṇ*°, Bshk. *mänā'k* (< *maṇḍ* -- or *mandr* -- AO xviii 244), Sv. *miṇḍā'ka*, Sh. *măṇū'kụ* m., K. *miñĕmŏnḍukh*, dat. °*dakas* m. (see 4), P. *mē̃ḍuk*, °*ḍak*,*mī̃ḍuk*, °*ḍak* m., WPah.rudh. *mínku*, (Joshi) *minkā* m.; Ku. *munki* -- *ṭaulo* ' tadpole '; OMarw. *mīḍako* m. ' frog ', *mīṁḍakī* f. ' small frog ', G. *me_ḍak*, *meḍ*° m., *me_ḍkī*, *meḍ*° f.; M. *mē̃ḍūk* -- *mukh* n. ' frog -- like face '.3. Pk. *maṁḍūra* -- m.4. K. *main*, *mōn* m., *miñ* f., *miñĕ* -- *mŏnḍukh* m. (orig. ' female and male frog '?).5. Wg. *āwmaṭrakōg*, Dm. *maṭrak*, Paš.lauṛ. *máṭrax*, uzb. *máṭrōk*, *katrṓx*, nir. kch. *maṭeṅ*, dar. *maṭḗx*, weg. *maṭék*, ar. *matrek*, Shum. *maṭərok*, Kal.rumb. *manḍrák*, urt. *maḍrák*, Phal. *maṭrōk* m..*matíya -- ' harrow ' see matyà -- .Addenda: maṇḍū'ka -- . 2. *maṇḍukka -- : WPah.kṭg. (kc.) *miṇḍkɔ* m. ' frog ', J. *minkā* m.3. Read *maṇḍūra -- 1: Pk. *maṁḍūra* -- m.(CDIAL 9746)

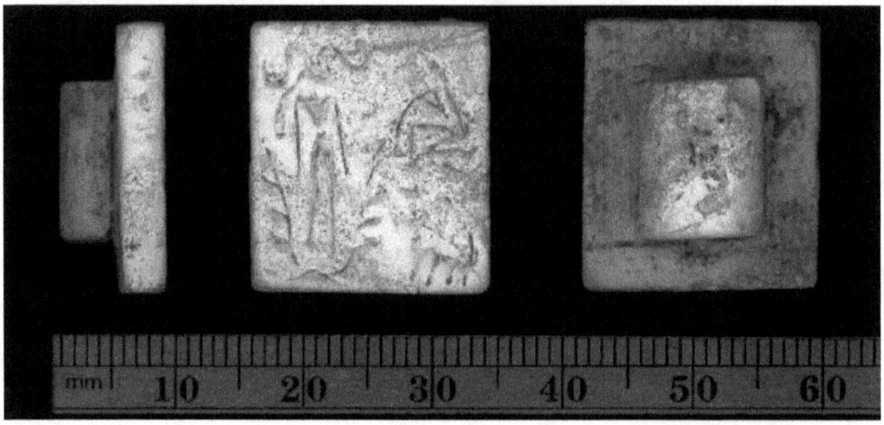

Fig. 8.11: Example of seal from Stage III and IV/V

http://bharatkalyan97.blogspot.in/2015/04/dholavira-1-signboard-and-2-stone.html
Dholavira report details 225 seals, 60 sealings." The report covers 225 seals and 60 sealings. Majority of seals are of steatite. The inscriptions are thematically and technologically are comparable to the inscriptions found in other sites of Sarasvati-Sindhu Civilization. While Bisht attempts to find thematic changes over time from Stage I to Stage VI of the stratigraphy of th archaeological site, no significant patterns of differences in the media or content of inscriptions have been found. Of these 225 seals and 60 sealings, a sequential growth in terms of sigillography is given as: Stage IIIA. Geometric and mythological motif with no inscription; square with rudimentary perforated boss; Stage IV&V usual Harappa motifs, inscription present; square with classical and sub-classical boss; rectangular ones in upper levels; Stage VI NO motif present, only inscription; Plano-convex with rectangular face; convex, rounded, triangulated or wagon-vaulted back with a perforation. (p.233: Section 8.2) "Another evidence of literate Harppans is gleaned from several examples of graffiti from pottery, terracotta cakes, stoneware bangles, etc. These graffitti belong to the typical Harappa signs and in a few cases complete inscriptions in the form of two or more signs have been depicted together. An interesting example of graffitti is from a stoneware bangle fragment, which might indicate that it could be a kind of ownership record." (Section 8.1.3, p.231). No evidence of seals sealings and tablets or evidence of writing was found during Stages I, II and VII so far. However, potter's marks are occasionally present in the first two. First appearance of seals occurred in Stae II with only one tiny specimen seal...the script had evolved as evidenced from a potsherd bearing three Harappa signs written in black pigment. The seal is depicted with a mythological scene which is closely similar to the one depicted on Mohenjodaro seal (M-1186A, CISI, Vol. 2). The scene exhibits an iconographic elaboration of the same

theme that occurs on the Dholavira example its early evolutionary stage. The same theme has been repeated on seals and terracotta tablets at Mohenjo-daro and Harappa. In Stage IV and V (Harappa), there is a phenomenal increase in seals, bearing iconography and inscriptions, and usually executed deftly showing all such features which mark the Harappa sigillography everywhere else in the mature phase at a number of contemporary sites.(p.233)".

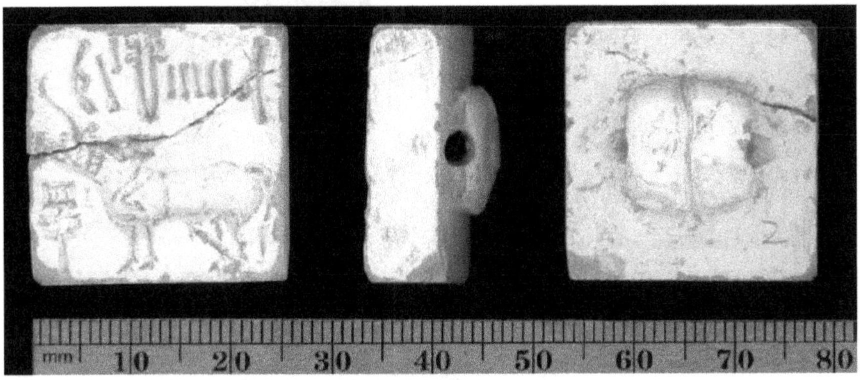

Fig. 8.12: Example of seal from Stage III and IV/V

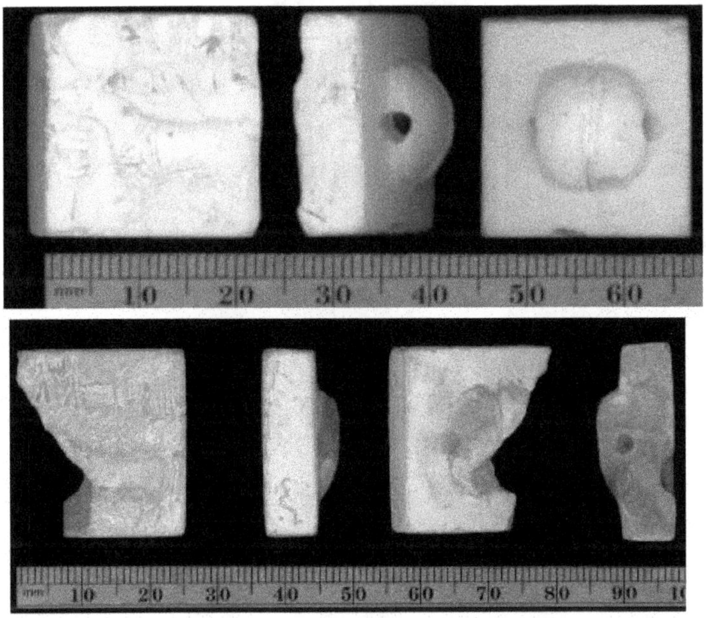

Fig. 8.13: Example of seal from Stage IV/V

Fig. 8.14: Example of seals from Stage IV/V

Fig. 8.18: Harappa seals and impressions

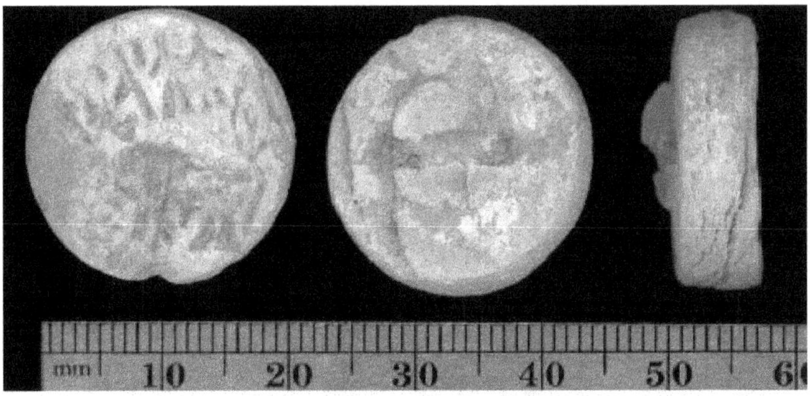

Fig. 8.15: Example of round seal from Stage IV/V

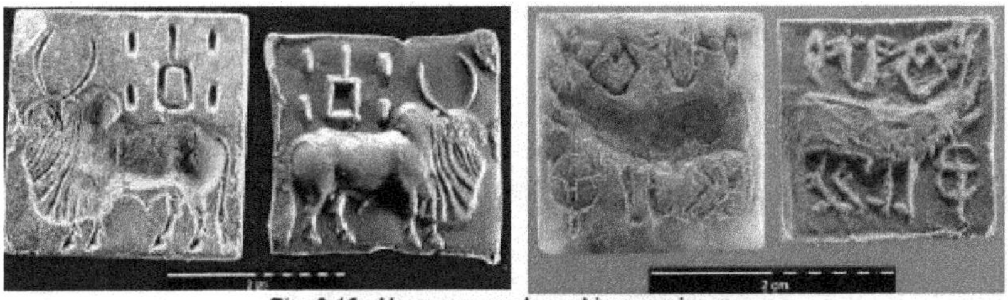

Fig. 8.16: Harappan seals and impressions

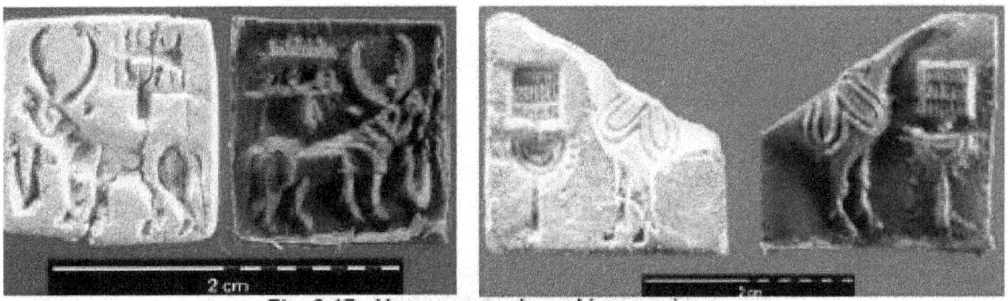

Fig. 8.17: Harappan seals and impressions

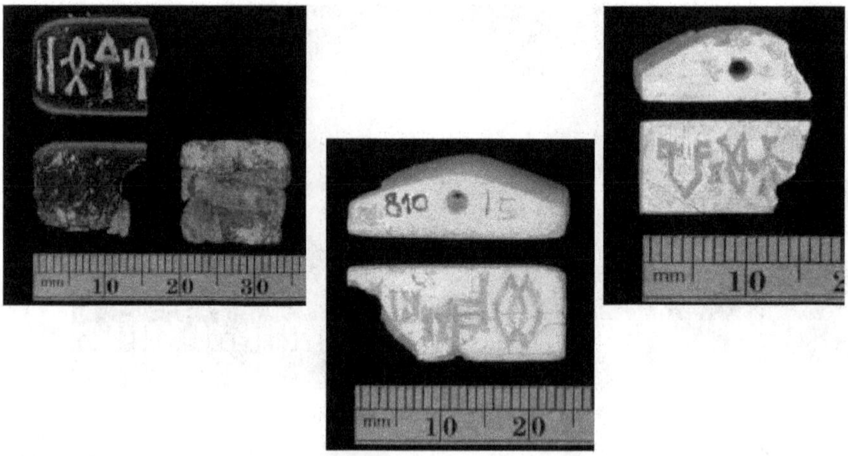

Fig. 8.19: Example of seals from Stage VI

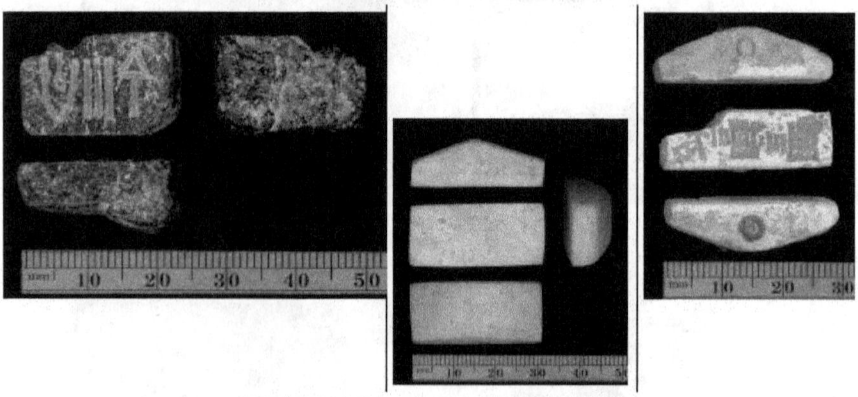

Fig. 8.20: Example of seals from Stage VI

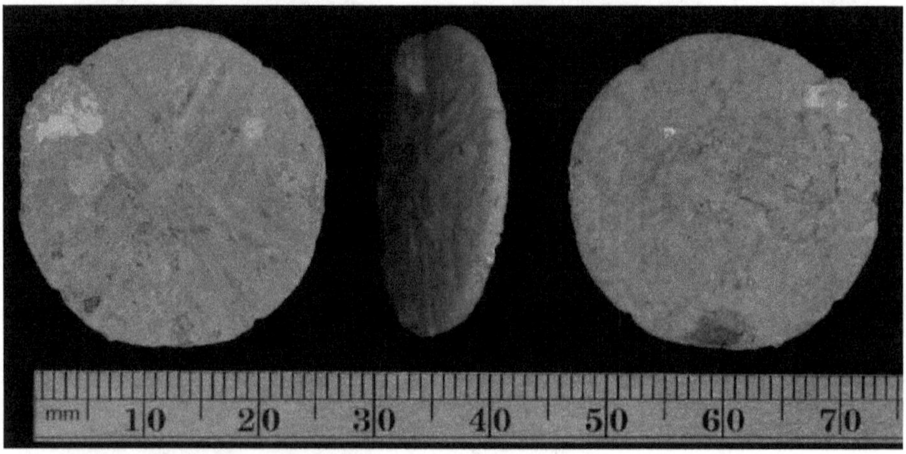

Fig. 8.21: Example of copper seal from Stage VI

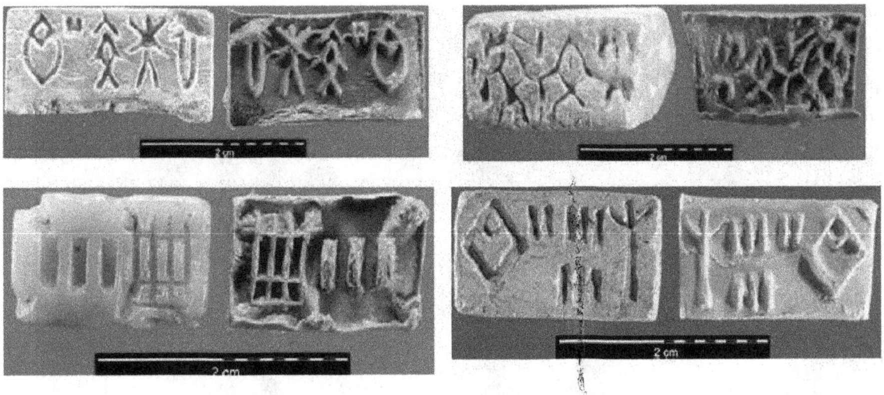

Fig. 8.22: Seals of Stage VI and their impressions

Bailey and castle are a single unit which dominate the total number of seal findings with 85 seals (41.7%), while seals have also been found in middle town and lower town. It appears that the nature of manufacturing of seals, and trading control was mainly exercised by the castle, bailey and middle town. (p. 243) The dominant motifs are unicorn (one-horned young bull), bos taurus; other motifs included buffalo, elephant, rhinoceros, scorpion, tiger, composite animals, geometric motifs. (p. 240: Section 8.2.1)

Fig. 8.28, 8.29, 8.30 Sealings from Dholavira excavation

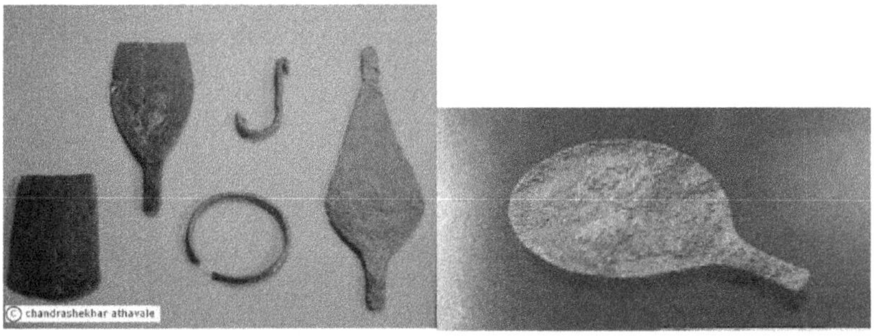

Dholavira. Bronze/coper artefacts. Copper mirror. http://akshardhoolstories.blogspot.in/p/amazing-world-of-dholavira.html

Dholavira2. Seal.

kōnṭa corner (Nk.); tu. kōṇṭu angle, corner (Tu.); rebus: kõdā 'to turn in a lathe' (Bengali)

aṭar 'a splinter' (Ma.) aṭaruka 'to burst, crack, sli off,fly open; aṭarcca ' splitting, a crack'; aṭarttuka 'to split, tear off, open (an oyster) (Ma.); aḍaruni 'to crack' (Tu.) (DEDR 66) Rebus: aduru 'native, unsmelted metal' (Kannada) aduru 'gan.iyinda tegadu karagade iruva aduru', that is, ore taken from the mine and not subjected to melting in a furnace (Kannada). Vikalpa: sal 'splinter'; rebus: sal 'workshop' (Santali) An order of men. Ex. गोसाव्यांचे अठरा अखाडे आहेत.(M.)

khaḍā 'circumscribe' (M.); Rebs: khaḍā 'nodule (ore), stone' (M.)

Thus, the three glyphs together read: *khaḍā* 'stone ore' + *aduru* 'native, unsmelted metal' + *kõdā* 'to turn in a lathe'; that is, stone- and mineral-ore turner.

Dholavira1 Seal. *kōnṭa* corner (Nk.); tu. kōṇṭu angle, corner (Tu.) Rebus: *kõdā* 'to turn in a lathe' (Bengali) *sal* 'splinter'; rebus: *sal* 'workshop' (Santali) Thus, together, 'turner workshop'.

koḍa 'in arithmetic, one' (Santali); rebus: *koḍ* 'artisan's workshop' (Kuwi) loa ‘ficus religiosa’ (Santali) rebus: *loh* ‘metal’ (Skt.) Rebus: lo ‘copper’. khāṇḍā ‘notch’ Marathi: खांडा [khāṇḍā] *m* A jag, notch, or indentation (as upon the edge of a tool or weapon). Rebus: *khāṇḍā* ‘metal tools, pots and pans’.

kuṭi ‘woman water carrier’ (Te.); *kuṭhi* ‘smelter furnace’ (Santali)

Thus, together, the text message reads: *kõdā sal* 'turner's workshop' + *koḍ* ‘artisan’s workshop’+ *loh khāṇḍā* 'copper tools, pots and pans' + kuṭhi 'smelter furnace' That is, the seal described the metalware repertoire: artisan's turner workshop for copper tools, pots and pans (with) smelter furnace.

Dholavira. Seals.

Two seals on top row showing a three-headed animal:

kõdā खोंड [khōṇḍa] m A young bull, a bullcalf. (Marathi) Rebus: *kõdā* ‘to turn in a lathe’ (Bengali) mẽḍha ‘antelope’; krammara ‘looking back’; meḍ ‘iron’; 'merchant's helper'; kamar ‘blacksmith (artisan)’ (Santali) *ḍaṅgara1 ‘ cattle ’rebus: ḍhangar ‘blacksmith’ (Hindi)

The composite animal motif is thus a professional calling card of *ḍhangar kõdā meḍ kamar* 'blacksmith, turner, merchant (artisan)'

Not far from Dholavira is the site of Bet Dwaraka.

Bet Dwaraka 1 śankha (turbinella pyrum) seal. This shows the composite animal motif: One-horned young bull, short-horned bull looking down and an antelope looking backward. This combination is read rebus as: *ḍhangar kõdā meḍ kamar* 'blacksmith, turner, merchant (artisan)'

kondh, 'young bull' *khōṇḍī* 'pannier sack' Rebus: *kōnda* 'engraver, lapidary'

Hieroglyph of 'looking back' is read rebus as *kamar* 'artisan': క్రమ్మరు [krammaru] *krammaru*. [Tel.] v. n. To turn, return, go back. మరలు. క్రమ్మరించు or క్రమ్మరుచు *krammarinṭsu*. V. a. To turn, send back, recall. To revoke, annul, rescind.క్రమ్మరజేయు. క్రమ్మర *krammara*. Adv. Again. క్రమ్మరిల్లు or క్రమరబడు Same as క్రమ్మరు. krəm back'(Kho.)(CDIAL 3145) Kho. Krəm ' back ' NTS ii 262 with (?) (CDIAL 3145)[Cf. Ir. *kamaka – or *kamraka -- ' back ' in Shgh. Čůmč ' back ', Sar. Čomǰ EVSh 26] (CDIAL 2776) cf. Sang. kamak ' back ', Shgh. Čomǰ (< *kamak G.M.) ' back of an animal ', Yghn. Kama ' neck ' (CDIAL 14356). Kár, kãr 'neck' (Kashmiri) Kal. Gřä ' neck '; Kho. Goḷ ' front of neck, throat '. Gala m. ' throat, neck ' MBh. (CDIAL 4070) Rebus: *karmāra* 'smith, artisan' (Skt.) *kamar* 'smith' (Santali)

meḍ 'body' Rebus: meḍ 'iron' (Mu.) Vikalpa: *kāḍ* 2 काड् a man's length, the stature of a man (as a measure of length); rebus: *kāḍ* 'stone'; Ga. (Oll.) *kanḍ* , (S.) *kanḍu (pl. kanḍkil)* stone

tagaraka 'tabernae montana' Rebus: tagaram 'tin' (Malayalam)

Thus, the two seals show:

1. *meḍ kāḍ kamar* 'Iron stone blacksmith' +*kõdā* 'turner' + *kāḍ meḍ* 'stone merchant's helper'

2. tagara kamar 'tin smith' +*kõdā* 'turner' + *kāḍ meḍ* 'stone merchant's helper'

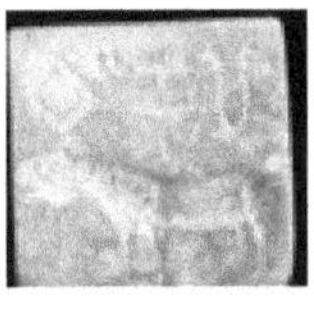

Glyph 342 'rim of jar': *kaṇḍ kanka* 'rim of jar'; Rebus: karṇaka 'scribe'; kaṇḍ 'furnace, fire-altar'. Thus the ligatured Glyph is decoded: *kaṇḍ karṇaka* 'furnace scribe

G. kā̃gsī f. ' comb ', with metath. kā̃sko m., °kī f.; WPah. khaś. kāgśī, śeu. kāśkī ' a comblike fern ' kāmsako, kāmsiyo = a large sized comb (G.) Rebus: kaṁsa= bronze (Te.) dula 'pair' Rebus dul 'cast (metal)'. Thus the composite glyph reads: *dul kaṁsa* 'cast bronze'.

sal 'splinter'; rebus: sal 'workshop' (Santali)

kōnṭa corner (Nk.); tu. kōṇṭu angle, corner (Tu.) Rebus: *kõdā* 'to turn in a lathe' (Bengali)

Thus, together, the text of the inscription reads: *kõdā* 'turner' + *dul kaṁsa* 'cast bronze' +*karṇaka*'scribe', that is, cast bronze turner scribe.

 Dholavira3 Seal.

kõdā 'young bul' Rebus: *kõdā* 'to turn in a lathe' (Bengali) *sangaḍa* 'pair' (Marathi) Rebus: jaṅgaḍ 'entrustment articles'.

kaṇḍ kanka 'rim of jar'; Rebus: karṇaka 'scribe'; kaṇḍ 'furnace, fire-altar'. Thus the ligatured Glyph is decoded: *kaṇḍ karṇaka* 'furnace scribe'

koḍa 'in arithmetic, one' (Santali); rebus: *koḍ* 'artisan's workshop' (Kuwi)

kōnṭa corner (Nk.); tu. kōṇṭu angle, corner (Tu.) Rebus: *kõdā* 'to turn in a lathe' (Bengali)

ayo 'fish' Rebus: ayas 'iron, metal'

ḍagar f. ' little hill, slope ' (Marathi) Rebus: damgar 'merchant' (Akkadian)

keṇṭai carp (Ta.) Rebus: *kẽṛẽ* bell-metal, brass.

Glyph: phala 'what is split' Rebus: P. N. *phal* ' blade ', B. *phal*, *°lā*; Or. *phaḷā* ' blade' (CDIAL 9052).

Thus the text message reads: *phal* 'blade' + *kõdā* 'to turn in a lathe' +*kẽṛẽ* bell-metal, brass + *damgar*'merchant'+ *kõdā* 'to turn in a lathe'+ *koḍ* 'artisan's workshop' + *karṇaka* 'furnace scribe'. The professional calling card of the artisan reads: scribe, turner, merchant (with) workshop for blade and bell-metal.

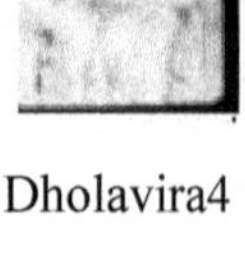

Dholavira4 Seal.

khaḍā 'circumscribe' (M.); Rebs: khaḍā 'nodule (ore), stone' (M.)

kolmo 'paddy plant'; rebus: kolimi 'smithy' (Te.Ka.)

ranku 'liquid measure'; rebus: ranku 'tin' (Santali)

sal stake, spike, splinter, thorn, difficulty (H.); Rebus: sal 'workshop' (Santali) *kōnṭa* corner (Nk.); tu. kōṇṭu angle, corner (Tu.) Rebus: *kõdā* 'to turn in a lathe' (Bengali)

Thus the message reads: *kõdā* 'to turn in a lathe'+ *khaḍā* 'nodule (ore), stone'+ *kolimi* 'smithy'+ *ranku* 'tin'+ *sal*'workshop'+ *kõdā* 'to turn in a lathe'. The professional calling card: stone-work (lapidary), smithy, turner, tin workshop,

Dholavira5 Seal with one-horned young bull + standard device.

kõdā 'young bul' Rebus: *kõdā* 'to turn in a lathe' (Bengali) *sangaḍa* 'pair' (Marathi) Rebus: jaṅgaḍ 'entrustment articles'.

kōnṭa corner (Nk.); tu. kōṇṭu angle, corner (Tu.) Rebus: *kõdā* 'to turn in a lathe' (Bengali)

sal stake, spike, splinter, thorn, difficulty (H.); Rebus: sal 'workshop' (Santali)

khaḍā 'circumscribe' (M.); Rebs: khaḍā 'nodule (ore), stone' (M.) kolmo 'paddy plant'; rebus: kolimi 'smithy' (Te.Ka.)

G. kā̃gsī f. ' comb ', with metath. kā̃sko m., °kī f.; WPah. khas'. kāgśī, śeu. kāśkī ' a comblike fern ' kāmsako, kāmsiyo = a large sized comb (G.) Rebus: *kaṁsa*= bronze (Te.) dula 'pair' Rebus dul 'cast (metal)'. Thus the composite glyph reads: *dul kaṁsa* 'cast bronze'.

ayo 'fish' Rebus: ayas 'iron, metal'

Combined glyph: khāṇḍā 'notch' Marathi: खांडा [khāṇḍā] *m* A jag, notch, or indentation (as upon the edge of a tool or weapon). Rebus: *khāṇḍā* 'metal tools, pots and pans'. *kōnṭa* corner (Nk.); tu. kōṇṭu angle, corner (Tu.) Rebus: *kõdā* 'to turn in a lathe' (Bengali)

kaṇḍ kanka 'rim of jar'; Rebus: karṇaka 'scribe'; kaṇḍ 'furnace, fire-altar'. Thus the ligatured Glyph is decoded: *kaṇḍ karṇaka* 'furnace scribe'

gaṇṭa = bat (Telugu) Rebus: *kaṇḍ* 'fire-altar, furnace' (Santali) The last glyph may be a variant of water-carrier. kuṭi 'woman water carrier' (Te.); *kuṭhi* 'smelter furnace' (Santali) Thus, both a furnace and a smelter are referenced.

Thus the entire text of the message reads: *khaḍā kolimi* stone (workshop/smithy), i.e. lapidary; workshop (with) *kõdā* 'lathe'.; *kaṁsa* 'bronze' and *ayas* 'alloy (metal)' *khāṇḍā* 'tools, pots and pans'; *kaṇḍ kanka* fire-altar, *kuṭhi* 'smelter' scribe.

Dholavira7 Seal. ḍagar f. ' little hill, slope ' (Marathi) Rebus: damgar 'merchant' (Akkadian) *kāṇḍa* 'arrow' *khāṇḍā* 'tools, pots and pans' (Marathi)

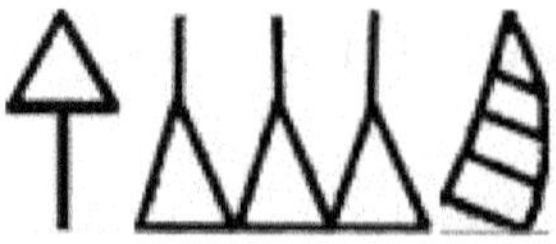

Dholavira6 Seal. One-horned young bull + standard device.

kõdā 'young bul' Rebus: *kõdā* 'to turn in a lathe' (Bengali) *sangaḍa* 'pair' (Marathi) Rebus: jaṅgaḍ 'entrustment articles'.

Glyph: potramu = snout of a hog Rebus: *pot* = jeweller's polishing stone (Bi.)

ḍagar f. ' little hill, slope ' (Marathi) Rebus: damgar 'merchant' (Akkadian)

kāṇḍa 'arrow' *khāṇḍā* 'tools, pots and pans' (Marathi)

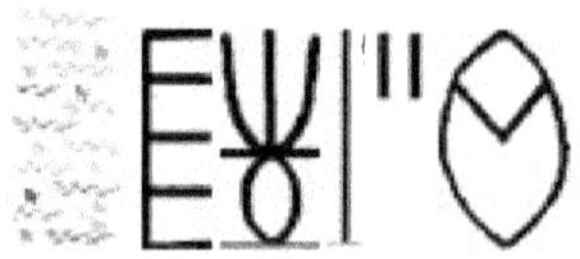

Dholavira8 Seal. Gharial (Crocodile).

karā 'crocodile' Rebus: khār 'blacksmith' (Kashmiri)

kōnṭa corner (Nk.); kōṇṭu angle, corner (Tu.) Rebus: *kõdā* 'to turn in a lathe' (Bengali) sal 'splinter' Rebus: sal 'workshop'.

koḍa 'in arithmetic, one' (Santali); rebus: *koḍ* 'artisan's workshop' (Kuwi) *khaḍā*'circumscribe' (M.); Rebus: *khaḍā* 'nodule (ore), stone' (M.) *koḍ* 'horn'; *koḍ* 'artisan's workshop' (Kuwi)

sal stake, spike, splinter, thorn, difficulty (H.); Rebus: sal 'workshop' (Santali)

Composite glyph with modifying elements: *ḍhālako* = a large metal ingot (G.) *ḍālakī* = a metal heated and poured into a mould; a solid piece of metal; an ingot (G.) *ḍabu* 'an iron spoon' (Santali) Rebus: *ḍab, ḍhimba, ḍhompo* 'lump (ingot?)', *baṭa* = wide-mouthed pot; Rebus: *baṭa* = kiln (Te.) That is, *baṭa ḍab* .); Rebus: sal 'workshop' (Santali) Composite glyph with modifying elements reads: *baṭa ḍab ḍhālako* 'kiln for lump ingot, large metal ingot'.

G. kā̃gsī f. ' comb ', with metath. kā̃sko m., °kī f.; WPah. khas'. kāgśī, śeu. kāśkī ' a comblike fern ' kāmsako, kāmsiyo = a large sized comb (G.) Rebus: *kaṁsa* = bronze (Telugu)

Thus, the entire text of the message on the Dholavira8 tablet reads: *baṭa ḍab ḍhālako* 'kiln for lump ingot, large metal ingot' (for) *kaṁsa* 'bronze' + *koḍ* 'artisan's workshop' + *kõdā* 'to turn in a lathe'; that is, a lathe workshop.

Dholavira9 Tablet

kolmo 'three' Rebus: *kolimi* 'smithy, forge'.

kāṇḍa 'arrow' *khāṇḍā* 'tools, pots and pans' (Marathi)

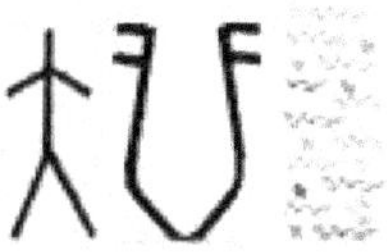

Dholavira 10 Tablet

kāḍ 2 काड् a man's length, the stature of a man (as a measure of length); rebus: *kāḍ* 'stone'; Ga. (Oll.) *kanḍ*, (S.) *kanḍu (pl. kanḍkil)* stone

kaṇḍ kanka 'rim of jar'; Rebus: karṇaka 'scribe'; kaṇḍ 'furnace, fire-altar'. Thus the ligatured Glyph is decoded: *kaṇḍ karṇaka* 'furnace scribe'

Dholavira20 Seal.

kāḍ 2 काड् a man's length, the stature of a man (as a measure of length); rebus: *kāḍ* 'stone'; Ga. (Oll.) *kanḍ*, (S.) *kanḍu (pl. kanḍkil)* stone. *khāṇḍā* 'notch' Marathi: खांडा [khāṇḍā] *m* A jag, notch, or indentation (as upon the edge of a tool or weapon). Rebus: *khāṇḍā* 'metal tools, pots and pans'. Thus, the composite glyph reads: *kāḍ khāṇḍā* 'stone tools, pots and pans'.

ḍhālako = a large metal ingot (G.) *ḍālakī* = a metal heated and poured into a mould; a solid piece of metal; an ingot (G.) *khaḍā* 'circumscribe' (M.); Rebus: *khaḍā* 'nodule (ore), stone' (M.) Thus, the composite glyph reads: *khaḍā ḍhālako* 'stone (mould) (for) large metal ingot'.

Dholavira11 Seal.

ḍabu 'an iron spoon' (Santali) Rebus: *ḍab, ḍhimba, ḍhompo* 'lump (ingot?)', *baṭa* = wide-mouthed pot; Rebus: *baṭa* = kiln (Te.) That is, *baṭa ḍab* kiln for lump ingot.

Ku. *khuṭo* ' leg, foot ', °*ṭī* ' goat's leg '; N. *khuṭo* ' leg, foot '(CDIAL 3894). S. *khuṛī* f. ' heel '; WPah. paṅ. *khūṛ* ' foot '. khura m. ' hoof ' Rebus: *khũṭ* 'community, guild' (Santali) *kūṭa*'workshop'

Fig leaf *'loa'*; rebus: loh '(copper) metal' *kamaḍha* = ficus religiosa (Skt.); *kamaṭa* = portable furnace for melting precious metals (Te.); *kampaṭṭam* = mint (Ta.)

kuṭi 'water-carrier' (Te.); Rebus: *kuṭhi* 'smelter' (Santali) *kaṇḍ kanka* 'rim of jar'; Rebus: karṇaka 'scribe'; kaṇḍ 'furnace, fire-altar'. Thus the ligatured, composite glyph is decoded: *kuṭhi kaṇḍ karṇaka* 'furnace, fire-altar scribe'.

The entire text of Dholavira11 Seal reads: *kampaṭṭam* 'mint' + *kuṭhi kaṇḍ karṇaka* 'furnace, fire-altar scribe'+ *baṭa ḍab* 'kiln for lump ingot' + *kūṭa* 'workshop'. That is, mint with furnace, fire-altar and ingot, engraving workshop.

Dholavira16 Seal.

ranku 'liquid measure' Rebus: *ranku* 'tin' (Cassiterite)

tagaraka 'tabernae montana' Rebus: *tagaram* 'tin'

bhaṭa 'warrior' Rebus: *baṭa* = kiln (Te.)

kaṇḍ kanka 'rim of jar'; Rebus: *karṇaka* 'scribe'; kaṇḍ 'furnace, fire-altar'.

The entire message reads: *ranku* 'cassiterite (unfurnace)', *tagaraka* 'tin (furnaced)' + *baṭa* 'kiln' + *karṇaka* 'scribe'.

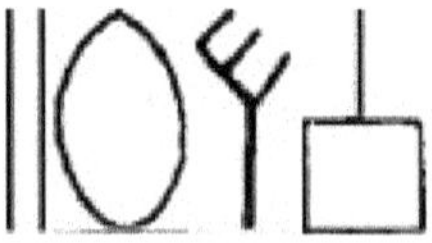

Dholavira12 Seal.

ranku 'liquid measure' Rebus: *ranku* 'tin' (Cassiterite)

tagaraka 'tabernae montana' Rebus: *tagaram* 'tin'

khaḍā 'circumscribe' (M.); Rebs: *khaḍā* 'nodule (ore), stone' (M.) *ḍhālako* = a large metal ingot (G.) *ḍālakī* = a metal heated and poured into a mould; a solid piece of metal; an ingot (G.)

dula 'two, pair' Rebus: *dul* 'cast (metal)'. Thus the message reads: cassiterite (unfurnace), tin (furnaced) nodule stone (ore), cast metal large ingot. Thus, the seal announces the availability of cassiterite (tin) ore and cast tin ingot.

Dholavira13 Seal.

kōnṭa corner (Nk.); tu. kōṇṭu angle, corner (Tu.) Rebus: *kõdā* 'to turn in a lathe' (Bengali) sal 'splinter' Rebus: sal 'workshop'.

bhaṭa 'six'; rebus: *bhaṭa* 'furnace' *bhaṭa* 'iron' (Gujarati)

kolmo 'paddy plant' Rebus: *kolimi* 'smithy, forge'.
Thus the entire message reads: *kolimi* 'smithy,forge'; *bhaṭa* 'iron, furnace'; *kõdā sal* 'turner workshop'.

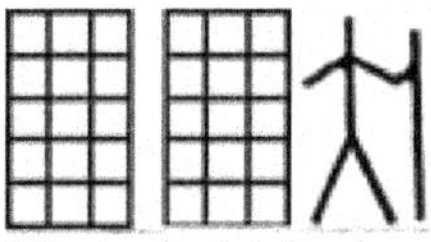

Dholavira14 Seal.

kāḍ 2 काड् a man's length, the stature of a man (as a measure of length); rebus: *kāḍ* 'stone'; Ga. (Oll.) *kanḍ* , (S.) *kanḍu (pl. kanḍkil)* stone

koḍa 'in arithmetic, one' (Santali); rebus: *koḍ* 'artisan's workshop' (Kuwi)

खांडा [*khāṇḍā*] A division of a field. (Marathi) *khāṇḍā* 'tools, pots and pans' (Marathi) dula 'pair' Rebus: dul 'cast (metal)'.
Thus, the entire message reads: *dul khāṇḍā* 'cast metal tools, pots and pans' + *kāḍ* 'stone' + *koḍ* 'artisan's workshop'. It is a lapidary's workshop and a smithy forge.

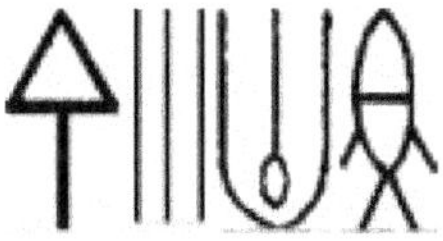

Dholavira15 Seal.

ayo 'fish' Rebus: *ayo* 'metal' + inclined stroke: *dhāḷ* 'a slope'; 'inclination of a plane' (G.); *ḍhāḷiyum* = adj. sloping, inclining (G.) Rebus: *ḍhālako* = a large metal ingot (G.) *ḍhālakī* = a metal heated and poured into a mould; a solid piece of metal; an ingot (Gujarati) Thus the composite glyph reads: *ayo ḍhālako* 'a large alloy metal ingot'

ḍabu 'an iron spoon' (Santali) Rebus: *ḍab, ḍhimba, ḍhompo* 'lump (ingot?)', *baṭa* = wide-mouthed pot; Rebus: *baṭa* = kiln (Te.) That is, *baṭa ḍab* kiln for lump ingot.

kolmo 'three' Rebus: *kolimi* 'smithy, forge'.

kāṇḍa 'arrow' *khāṇḍā* 'tools, pots and pans' (Marathi)

Thus the entire message reads: *khāṇḍā* 'tools, pots and pans' + kolimi 'smithy, forge'+ *baṭa ḍab* kiln for lump ingot + *yo ḍhālako* 'a large alloy metal ingot'.

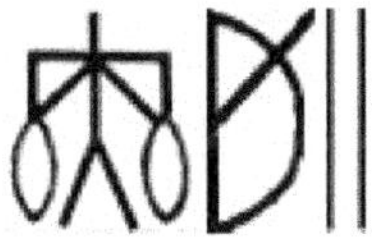

Dholavira17 Seal.

dula 'pair' Rebus: *dul* 'cast (metal)'

kamāṭhiyo = archer; *kāmaṭhum* = a bow; *kāmaḍ, kāmaḍum* = a chip of bamboo (G.) *kāmaṭhiyo* a bowman; an archer (Skt.lex.) Rebus: *kammaṭi* a coiner (Ka.); *kampaṭṭam* coinage, coin, mint (Ta.) *kammaṭa* = mint, gold furnace (Te.)

kuṭi 'water-carrier' (Te.); Rebus: *kuṭhi* 'smelter' (Santali)

Thus the message reads: *dul* 'cast (metal)' *kampaṭṭam* 'mint' *kuṭhi* 'smelter'

Dholavira18 Seal. 'One-horned young bull'.

kõdā 'young bull' Rebus: 'to turn in a lathe' That is, 'lathe turner'.

L. *nõ*∨, khet. *naũ*, awāṇ. *naɔ̃*, Ku. *nau*, gng. *nɔ*, náva2 ' nine ' RV. Kal.rumb. *nō*, Kho. *nyoh* (whence *y*? -- *h* from Pers.? BelvalkarVol 94), Pa. *nava*, Pk. *ṇava*, Ḍ. *nau*, Ash. *no*, *nū*, Wg. *nū̃*, Pr. *nū*, Dm. *nȭ*, Tir. *nāb*, Paš.lauṛ. *nā´wa*, ar. *nāu*, dar. *nō*, Shum. *nū*, Niṅg. *nū̃*, Woṭ. *nau*, Gaw. *nū̃*, Bshk. *nab*, *num*, Tor. *nom*, Kand. *nāũ*, Mai. *naũ*, Sv. *nōu*, Phal. *nau*, *nū*, *nū̃*, Sh.gil. *náŭ*, pales. *nāũ*, K. *nav*,*nau*, *nam*, pog. *nāu*, rām. kash. ḍoḍ. *nau*, S. *nãvã*, P. *naũ*, bhaṭ. *nau*, WPah.bhal. paṅ. cur. *nao*, N. *nau*, A. B. *na*, Or.*na*, *naa*, Bi. Mth. Aw.lakh. *nau*, H. *nau*, *nam*, OMarw. *nova*, G. *nav*, M. *nav*, *naũ*, Ko. *nav*, OSi. *nava*, Si. *namaya*, Md. *nuva*.(CDIAL 6984). Rebus: rebus: *loa* 'copper' (Santali); loha 'copper' (Skt.)

kuṭi 'water-carrier' (Te.); Rebus: *kuṭhi* 'smelter' (Santali) *kaṇḍ kanka* 'rim of jar'; Rebus: karṇaka 'scribe'; kaṇḍ 'furnace, fire-altar'. Thus the ligatured, composite glyph is decoded: *kuṭhi kaṇḍ karṇaka* 'furnace, fire-altar scribe'.

Thus the message reads: *lo* 'copper' + *kuṭhi* 'smelter'.

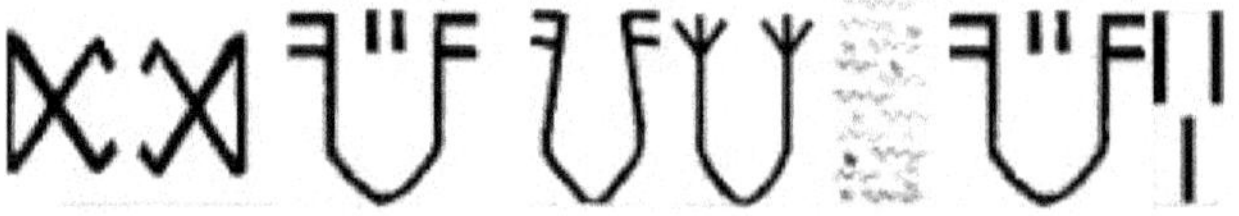

Dholavira19 Seal.

Segment 1: blade workshop scribe

Glyph: *phala* 'what is split' Rebus: P. N. *phal* ' blade ', B. *phal*, *°lā*; Or. *phaḷā* ' blade' (CDIAL 9052).

sal 'splinter' Rebus: *sal* 'workshop'. *kaṇḍ kanka* 'rim of jar';
Rebus: *karṇaka* 'scribe'; kaṇḍ 'furnace, fire-altar'. Thus the complex glyph reads: *sal karṇaka* 'workshop scribe'.

Segment 2: metal casting smithy scribe

kolmo 'paddy plant' Rebus: *kolimi* 'smithy, forge' *dula* 'pair' Rebus: *dul* 'cast (metal). Together, the compound glyph reads: *dul kolimi* 'metal casting smithy, forge'.

kaṇḍ kanka 'rim of jar'; Rebus: *karṇaka* 'scribe'

Segment 3: cast bronze workshop scribe

sal 'splinter' Rebus: *sal* 'workshop'. *kaṇḍ kanka* 'rim of jar';
Rebus: *karṇaka* 'scribe'; kaṇḍ 'furnace, fire-altar'. Thus the complex glyph reads: *sal karṇaka* 'workshop scribe'.

Ta. *koṭiṟu* pincers. Ma. koṭil tongs. Ko. *koṛ* hook of tongs. / Cf. Skt. (P. 4.4.18) kuṭilikā- smith's tongs.(DEDR 2052). Rebus: kuṭi
'smelter furnace' (Santali) *kuṭila, katthīl* = bronze (8 parts copper and 2 parts tin)(CDIAL 3230). *dula* 'pair' Rebus: *dul* 'cast (metal). Thus the complex glyph reads: *dul kuṭila* 'cast bronze with copper 8 parts and tin 2 parts'.

The name of the Dholavira village is koTDa. Sign 244 and variants could be a representation of a warehouse (granary) with three rows of pillars to hold storage planks to stock metal/stone artefacts. See the photos of a number of warehouses in Harappa; and of what is called a "granary room" in Mohenjodaro. These structures compare with the Sign 244. These structural remains have also been interpreted by many archaeologists as a granary.

Excavations at Rakhigarhi, 1997-2000 ASI Report by Dr. Amarendra Nath (Full text, 396 pages). Lead ingot inscription: metalwork Meluhha hieroglyphs.

Reading the Harappa Script writing inscriptions on both sides of bun-shaped lead ingots of Rakhigarhi

The Harappa Script writing inscriptions relate to cataloging of metalwork as elaborated by the following rebus-metonymy cipher and readings in Meluhha (Bharata *sprachbund*):

Hieroglyphs (from l.): body, linear stroke, notch, corner, U plus notch, rim of jar

meḍ 'body' *kATi* 'body stature' Rebus: meḍ 'iron' *kATi* 'fireplace trench'. Thus, iron smelter.

koDa 'one' Rebus: *koD* 'workshop'

खांडा [*khāṇḍā*] m A jag, notch, or indentation (as upon the edge of a tool or weapon). (Marathi) Rebus: *khāṇḍā* 'tools, pots and pans, metal-ware'.

kanac 'corner' Rebus: *kancu* 'bronze'
baTa 'rimless pot' Rebus: *baTa* 'furance'
kanka, karNika 'rim of jar' Rebus: *karNi* 'supercargo'; *karNika* 'account'.

Hieroglyphs: rhombus (as circumgraph) + spoked wheel PLUS a pair of 'bodies' (twins)
dula 'pair' Rebus: *dul* 'cast metal'; *meḍ* 'body' *kATi* 'body stature' Rebus: *meḍ* 'iron' *kATi* 'fireplace trench'. Thus, iron smelter.

A spoked wheel is ligatured within a rhombus: kanac 'corner' Rebus: kancu 'bronze'; eraka 'nave of wheel' Rebus: eraka 'copper, moltencast'[275]

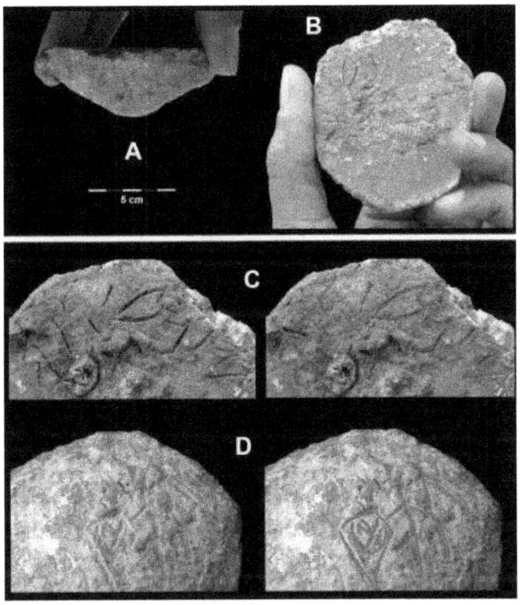

Figure 14: Side (A) and top (B) views of a lead ingot inscribed with Harappa characters. Detailed images of the top (C) and bottom (D) inscriptions.

There are many examples of the depiction of 'human face' ligatured to animals:

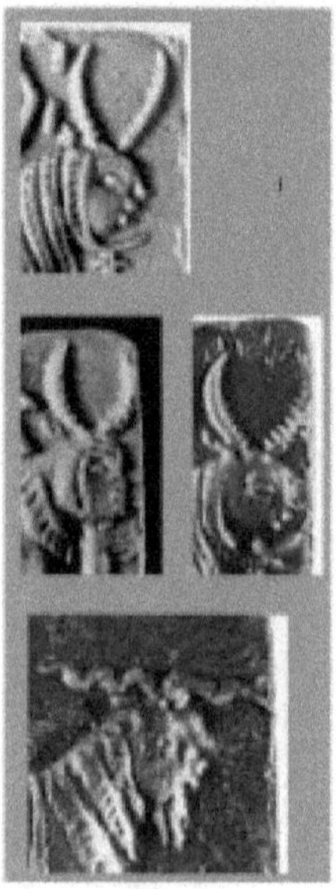

Ligatured faces: some close-up images.
The animal is a quadruped: pasaramu, pasalamu = an animal, a beast, a brute, quadruped (Te.)Rebus: pasra 'smithy' (Santali) Allograph: panǰā̃r 'ladder, stairs'(Bshk.)(CDIAL 7760) Thus the composite animal connotes a smithy. Details of the smithy are described orthographically by the glyphic elements of the composition.

Rebus reading of the 'face' glyph: mũhe 'face' (Santali) mũh opening or hole (in a stove for stoking (Bi.); ingot (Santali)mũh metal ingot (Santali) mũhã = the quantity of iron produced at one time in a native smelting furnace of the Kolhes; iron produced by the Kolhes and formeḍ like a four-cornered piece a little pointed at each end; mūhā mẽṛhẽt = iron smelted by the Kolhes and formeḍ into an equilateral lump a little pointed at each of four ends; kolhe tehen mẽṛhẽt ko mūhā akata = the Kolhes have to-day produced pig iron (Santali.lex.) kaula mengro 'blacksmith' (Gypsy) mleccha-mukha (Skt.) = milakkhu 'copper' (Pali) The Sanskrit loss mleccha-mukha should literally mean: copper-ingot absorbing the Santali gloss, mũh, as a suffix.

A remarkable phrase in Sanskrit indicates the link between mleccha and use of camels as trade caravans. This is explained in the lexicon of Apte for the lexeme: auṣṭrika 'belonging to a camel'. The lexicon entry cited *Mahābhārata*: औष्ट्रिक a. Coming from a camel (as milk); Mb.8. 44.28; -कः An oil-miller; मानुषाणां मलं म्लेच्छा म्लेच्छाना-मौष्ट्रिका मलम् । औष्ट्रिकाणां मलं षण्ढाः षण्ढानां राजयाजकाः ॥ Mb.8.45.25. From the perspective of a person devoted to śāstra and rigid disciplined life, Baudhāyana thus defines the word म्लेच्छः *mlēcchḥ* : -- गोमांसखादको यस्तु विरुद्धं बहु भाषते । सर्वाचारविहीनश्च म्लेच्छ इत्यभिधीयते ॥ 'A person who eatrs meat, deviates from traditional practices.'

The 'face' glyph is thus read rebus: *mleccha mũh* 'copper ingot'.

It is significant that Vatsyayana refers to crptography in his lists of 64 arts and calls it mlecchita-vikalpa, lit. 'an alternative representation -- in cryptography or cipher -- of mleccha words.'

The glyphic of the hieroglyph: tail (serpent), face (human), horns (*bos indicus*, zebu or ram), trunk (elephant), front paw (tiger),

Annex F

Multiple tablets with same inscription in Harappa signify work-in-process in circular platforms

Many multiple (duplicated) hypertexts on Harappa tablets are metalwork descriptions, catalogues related to works in process in smithy/forge guild-organized workshops, NOT names.

Such duplicated inscriptions on tablets indicates that work was assigned in the guild to artisans functioning on many circular platforms which constituted the workshops of smithy/forge.

Data mining of Harappa Script Corpora (about 7000 objects with inscriptions) yields a remarkable feature of Harappa tablets (i.e. sealings as multiples and tablets both on tiny steate tablets and other multi-sided tablets). The feature is occurrence of multiple hypertexts (strings of hieroglyph-multiplexes). This feature of duplication confirms the decipherment of product descriptions of the Bronze Age and confirn that the inscriptions are NOT names of artisans. The set of Harappa tablets with inscriptions are metalwork catalogues.

Out of 985 inscribed objects published in Mahadevan Concordance (1997, p.7), 288 are 'sealingś (i.e. tablets creating multiples or duplicates)' and 272 are 'miniature stone, terracotta or faience tablets'. Thus, 288+272 = 560 objects (i.e. 57%) of Mahadevan corpora are multiples to record works in process. The information conveyed by these tablets (both sealings and miniatures) are compiled into seals for shipment of supercargo as demonstrated.

h1827A

h1827B

Rebus reading of h1827A: *khāreḍo* = a currycomb (G.) Rebus: *khārādī* ' turner' (G.) *karṇika, kanka* 'rim of jar' rebus: kaṇḍa kanka 'smelting furnace account (scribe), *karNI,* supercargo' *baraDo* 'spine' Rebus: भरत 'alloy of pewter, copper, tin'.(Frequency of occurrence 41) Note: Frenquency is in reference to Mahadevan corpus. The occurrences will be more if HARP discoveries are reckoned. The string of three hieroglyphs signifies भरत 'alloy of pewter, copper, tin' ready as supercargo (for seafaring merchants) and for turners in smithy. Side h1827B: *kanac* 'corner' rebus: *kancu* 'bronze' *koḍi* 'flag' rebus: *koḍ* 'workshop' *dATu* 'crosś rebus; *dhatu* 'mineral' *dula* 'pair' rebus: *dul* 'cast metal' baṭa 'rimless pot' rebus: *bhaṭa* 'furnace'. Thus, bronze workshop mineral casting out of furnace.

This hypertext string of 3 hieroglyphs has some variants in messaging by replacing the third hieroglyph (Sign 176 in this case). Such variant strings are 8 copper tablets with raised script which replaces Sign 176 with a dotted oval (like an ingot) or h2200A where Sign 176 is replaced by fish+fin hieroglyph with a linear stroke added

h2200A

fish fins *khambharā* 'fin' rebus: *kammaṭa* 'mint' PLUS *baraDo* 'spine' rebus: *bharata* 'alloy of pewter, copper, tin' PLUS *karṇaka* 'rim of jar' rebus: *karṇī* 'supercargo' PLUS *koḍa* 'one' rebus: *koḍ* 'workshop'

Dotted ovarl hieroglyph: gōṭā 'round' rebus: khōṭa 'ingot' PLUS baraDo 'spine' rebus: bharata 'alloy of pewter, copper, tin' PLUS karṇī 'supercargo' PLUS third hieroglyph (illegible, could be karṇaka 'rim of jar' rebus: karṇī 'supercargo').

Many tiny steatite inscised tablets also, as prism tablets add on one side three dotted circles, tridhAtu 'three strandś rebus: tri-dhAtu 'three minerals' to confirm that the product descriptions relate to baraDo 'an alloy of three minerals, copper, pewter and perhaps zinc'. On h979, for example, the rebus readings are: Side C: *tridhAtu* 'three dotted circles' rebus: *tridhAtu* 'three minerals' PLUS Side A *khāreḍo* = a currycomb (G.) Rebus: *khārādī* ' turner' (G.) *karṇika, kanka* 'rim of jar' rebus: *kaṇḍa kanka* 'smelting furnace account (scribe), *karNI,* supercargo' *baraDo* 'spine' Rebus: भरत 'alloy of pewter, copper, tin'.(Frequency of occurrence 41) *kolmo* 'three' rebus: *kolimi* 'smithy, forge' PLUS baṭa 'rimless pot' rebus: bhaṭa 'furnace'.

Note: Frenquency of hypertext string Signs 176, 342 and 48 (centre-piece oval in venn diagram) is in reference to Mahadevan corpus. The occurrences will be more if HARP discoveries are reckoned. The string of three hieroglyphs signifies भरत 'alloy of pewter, copper, tin' ready as supercargo (for seafaring merchants) and for turners in smithy.

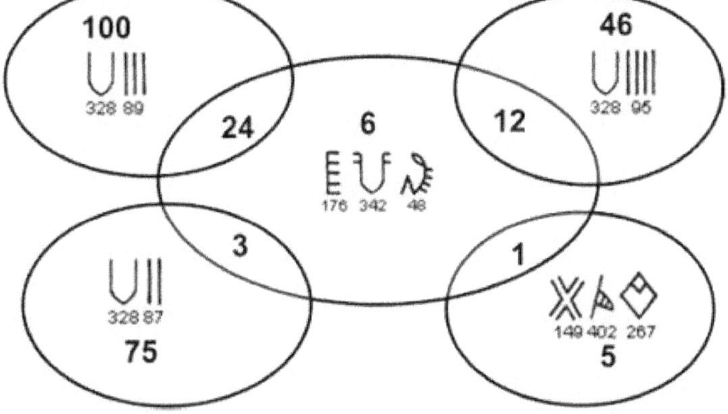

Figure 12. Venn diagram of the four most frequent texts in M77. The number of times a pair of texts appears on different sides of objects is marked in the overlapping region of the Venn diagram.

 h978Ait 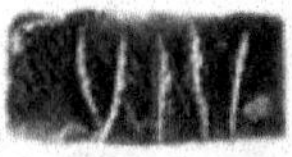 h978Bit  h978Cit  5412

 h979Ait  h979Bit  h979Cit

 h980Ait  h980Bit 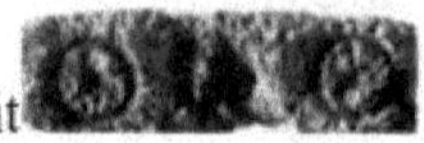 h980Cit

*khāreḍo* = a currycomb (G.) Rebus: *khārādī* ' turner' (G.) *karṇika, kanka* 'rim of jar' rebus: *kaṇḍa kanka* 'smelting furnace account (scribe), *karNI,* supercargo' *baraDo* 'spine' Rebus: भरत 'alloy of pewter, copper, tin' (Frequency of occurrence 41) Note: Frenquency is in reference to Mahadevan corpus. The occurrences will be more if HARP discoveries are reckoned. The string of three hieroglyphs signifies भरत 'alloy of pewter, copper, tin' ready as supercargo (for seafaring merchants) and for turners in smithy.

Examples of 22 duplicates steatite triangular tablets h-2218 to h-2239

Many examples of such smultiple inscriptions on Harappa tablets have been noted by Meadow and Kenoyer.[276]

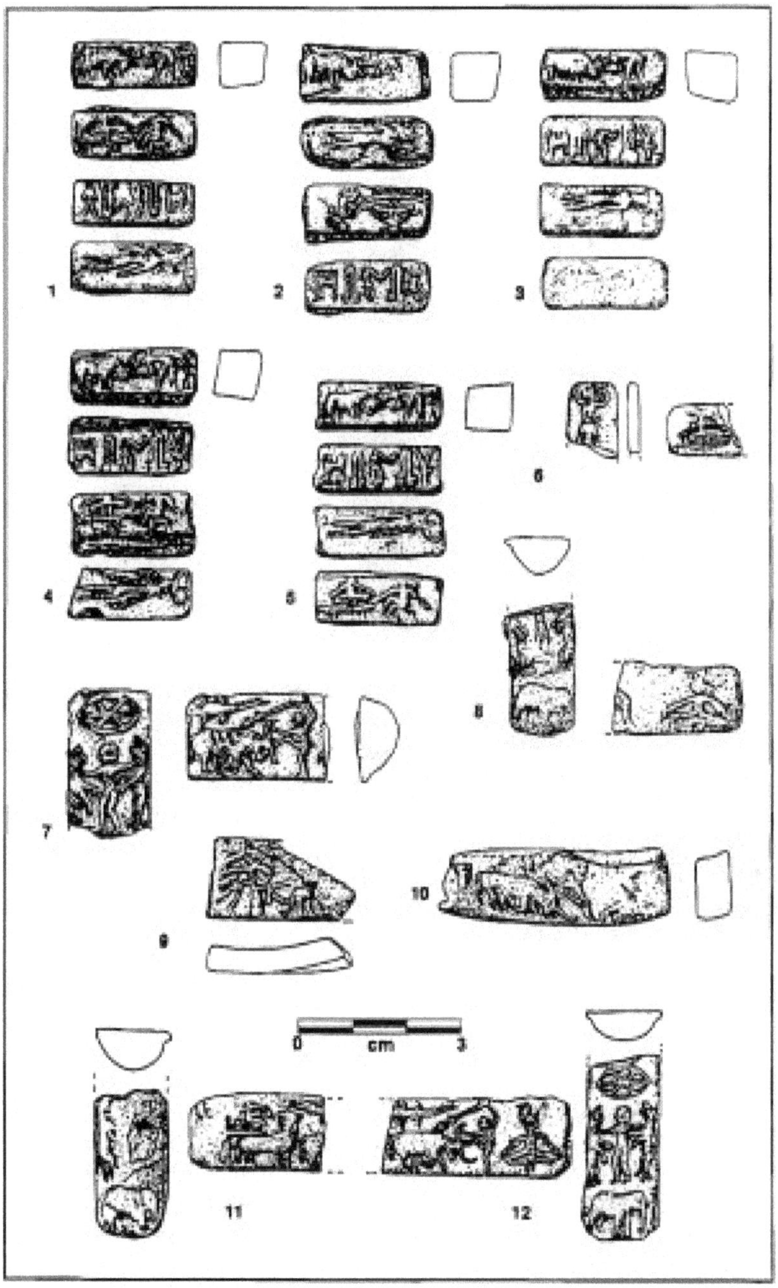

h252Ah253N

h1155 A&B two-sided tablet (which is one of the 31 duplicates). Tablets in bas relief. The first sign looks like an arch around a pillar with ring-stones. Obverse: One-horned bull.

The inscription on these 31 multiples or duplicates can be read rebus in three parts:

1. Composite glyph of arch-around-a-pillar with ring-stones: anvil, storehouse

2. unsmelted native metal

3. furace (with)a quantity of iron, excellent iron (metal) from stone ore

h739B & A (Standard device; obverse: tree)

A variant glyph comparable to the 'pillar with ring-stones' which is part of the composite glyph with an arch over the glyph is provided by one side of a Harappa tablet: h739B Obverse: H739A: glyph: kuṭi 'tree'; rebus: kuṭhi 'smelter furnace'

(Santali)

If this comparison of glyphs is valid, the 'pillar with ring-stones' may, in fact, represent a churning motion of a lathe-drill: Allograph: A sack slung on the front shoulder of the young bull is *khōṇḍā, khōṇḍī, kothḷɔ Rebus: B. kõdā 'to turn in a lathe'; Or. kū̆nda 'lathe', kũdibā, kū̃d 'to turn' (→ Drav. Kur. kū̃d 'lathe')* (CDIAL 3295) Rebus: *koṭṭil 'workshop' (Ma.)(DEDR 2058). koṭe 'forged metal' (Santali) koḍ* 'artisan's workshop' (Kuwi) Vikalpa: *saṅgaḍa,* portable brazier and lathe; rebus: *sanga* 'guild (of turners)'. Rebus: *samgraha, samgaha* 'assembler, manager'

Circular platforms (Harappa): **prastarapaṭṭa* ' stone slab '. [*prastará* -- , *paṭṭa* -- 1] Ku. *pathrauṭī* f. ' pavement of slates and stones '.(CDIAL 8858) *Ta. paṭṭaṭai, paṭṭaṟai* anvil, smithy, forge. *Ka. paṭṭaḍe, paṭṭaḍi* anvil, workshop. *Te. paṭṭika, paṭṭeḍa* anvil; *paṭṭaḍa* workshop. (DEDR 3865) ***Ta.*** paṭṭai flatness; paṭṭam flat or level surface of anything, flat piece (as of bamboo). *Ko.* paṭ flatness (of piece of iron, of head); paṭm (*obl.paṭt-)* ground for house. *To.* poṭ site of dairy or house. ? *Koḍ.* paṭṭi space before house, spreading space; maṇa-paṭṭi sandbank. *Nk.* paṛ place. *Pa.*paḍ place, site. *Pe.* paṭ kapṛa top of the head. *Manḍ.* paṭ kapṛa id. *Malt.* paṭa numeral classifier of flat objects.(DEDR 3878)

paṭṭaṭai , n. prob. படு¹- +அடை¹-. 1. [*Ta. paṭṭika, Ka. paṭṭaḍe.*] Anvil Rebus: *pattar* 'guild of goldsmiths'. *Ta. paṭaṅku* tent, awning, curtain; *paṭaṅkam* tent. *Ma. paṭaṅṅu* tent, awning (DEDR 3839)

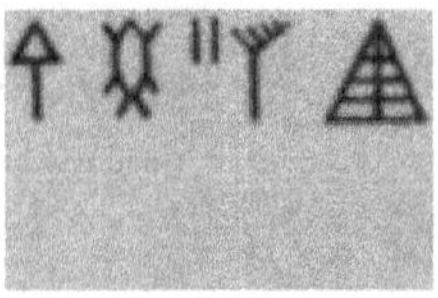

Text 5207 etc. (From 2-sided tablets h859-870, samples of the 31 duplicated)...Copies of incised tablets and duplicates of molded tablets have been found in large numbers in two noteworthy instances at Harappa: (1) script copies incised into 22 rectangular steatite tablets, triangular in section, from secondary deposits of Period 3B on the outside of the perimeter wall in Trench 11 on East side of Mound E (Meadow & Kenoyer 2000, fig. 4; this volume: H-2218 through H-2239) and (2) 31 duplicates bearing iconography and script, made of regular molded terracotta, biconvex in section, from the northern portion of Trench II in Area G (Vats 1940: 195; CISI 1: H-252 through H-265 and H-276 & H-277; CISI 2: H-859 through H-870; this volume: H-1155). Other copies and duplicates have been found scattered across the site where, like the multiples above, they are always found in trash, fill, or street deposits. Why tablets were made, how they were used, and why they were discarded remain intriguing unanswered questions. Their intrinsic interest lies not only in the script that they often bear, but even more so in the iconography, which provides an important glimpse, however fragmentary, into details of Harappa ideology, particularly for the time frame from ca.2400 to ca. 2000 BC (Harappa Period 3B through much of Period 3C). For a more detailed discussion see Meadow & Kenoyer 2000."[277] In the referenced Kenoyer & Meadow 2000, it is noted: "The tablets (or tokens) are common at Harappa, and multiple copies were often produced. In 1997, HARP excavators found 22 three-sided steatite tablets, all with the same inscriptions, from the middle Harappa Phase (about 2300 BC). Sixteen were discovered in a single group, as if they had been in a perishable container that was thrown over the city wall with other trash. In a street deposit of similar age just inside the wall, a seal was found with two of the same characters as seen on one side of the tablets. Why were these intact seals or tablets discarded? They were individually manufctured by craftsmen from models or molds at the demand of an individual or group. They were used for a time, then discarded. Unlike coins, they apparently had value only in relation to the individual or group permitted to employ them. They have never been found in graves -- either the grave of a seal-owning individual has not been excavated, or the seals were not integral to n individual's identity. Perhaps a change in an individual's status made a specific seal or tablet invalid. Or perhaps the use of a seal or tablet was validated only when competent authority used it, otherwise, it was worthless."[278]

Thus, the arch over the drill glyph may connote a turner's workshop. This is a vikalpa reading, if the 'arch' is not to be read as roof of a 'storehouse'. The arch over the drill-lathe glyph may connote semantics of a guild: *pattar*. (Tamil); *battuḍu* 'guild of goldsmiths'. This may be consistent with the semant. *patthar* 'stones' (Hindi) *pattar* 'trough'; rebus: *patthara* -- m. ' stone; *pattar* 'merchants, guild (smiths)' (The word may, thus, denote a lapidary)(CDIAL 8857).

Glyph and rebus decoding: *prastará* m. ' anything strewn, grass to sit on ' RV., ' flat surface ' Mn., ' (v.l. prastāra --) plain ' Hariv., ' rock, stone ' Hit. [√stṛ] K. *pathur*, °*thuru* (dat. °*tharas*, °*tharis*) m. ' levelled area, bare floor ', *pathürü* f. ' level piece of ground, plateau, small village '; S. *patharu* m. ' rug, mat '; Or. *athuripathuri* ' bag and baggage '; Bi. *pāthar* ' outside of edge of felly when flat (not bevelled), sowing wide apart '; G. *pāthrɔ* m. ' cut grass lying in a field '; M. *pāthrā* m. ' a line (of plants &c.) set out to dry '; Si. *patara* ' anything that spreads itself ' (or < prastāra --); -- Pa. Pk. *patthara* -- m. ' stone ', S. *patharu* m., L. (Ju.) *pathar* m., khet. *patthar*, P. *patthar* m. (→ forms of Bi. Mth. Bhoj. H. G. below with *atth*or *ath*), WPah.jaun. *pātthar*; Ku. *pāthar* m. ' slates, stones ', gng. *pāth**l*r* ' flat stone '; A. B. *pāthar* ' stone ', Or. *pathara*; Bi. *pāthar*, *patthar*,*patthal* ' hailstone '; Mth. *pāthar*, *pathal* ' stone ', Bhoj. *pathal*, Aw.lakh. *pāthar*, H. *pāthar*, *patthar*, *pathar*, *patthal* m., G. *patthar*, *pathrɔ* m.; M. *pāthar* f. ' flat stone '; Ko. *phāttaru* ' stone '; Si. *patura* ' chip, fragment '; -- S. *pathirī* f. ' stone in the bladder '; P. *pathrī* f. ' small stone '; Ku. *patharī* ' stone cup '; B. *pāthri* ' stone in the bladder, tartar on teeth '; Or. *pathurī* ' stoneware '; H. *patthrī* f. ' grit ', G. *pathrī* f. *prastarapaṭṭa -- , *prastaramṛttikā -- , *prastarāsa -- .Addenda: *prastará* -- : WPah.ktg. *pátthər* m. ' stone, rock '; *pəthreuṇõ* ' to stone '; J. *pāthar* m. ' stone '; OMarw. *pātharī* ' precious stone '. (CDIAL 8857)

Rebus: *paṭṭarai* 'workshop' (Ta.) *pattharika [fr. patthara]* a merchant Vin ii.135 (kaŋsa°).(Pali) cf. *Pattharati* [pa+tharati] to spread, spread out, extend J i.62; iv.212; vi.279; DhA i.26; iii.61 (so read at J vi.549 in cpd °*pāda* with spreading feet, v. l. patthaṭa°). -- pp. patthaṭa (q. v.). பத்தர்&sup5; *pattar*, n. perh. *vartaka*. Merchants; வியாபாரிகள். (W.) battuḍu. n. The caste title of all the five castes of artificers as vaḍla b*, carpenter.

Thus, the seal inscription shows the pattern of tally accomplished by bringing into the storehouse 1. unsmelted native metal; and 2. (output from) furnace of worker in wood and iron. The assumption made is that the the two categories brought into the storehouse would have been tallied using tablets with inscriptions denoting: 1. unsmelted metal; and 2. (output from) stone iron (metal) ore furnace.

Hypertext: *mūdh* ' ridge of roof ' (Assamese)(CDIAL 10247)

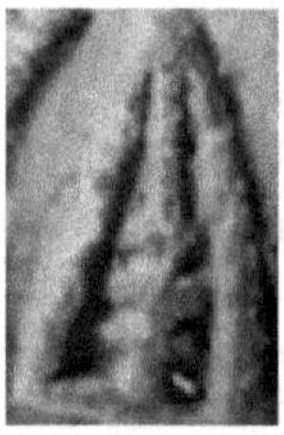

Rebus: *mund* 'iron' PLUS 'pillar with ringstones': -waṭh -वठ् । आघाताधारशिला m. (sg. dat. -waṭas -वटि), the large stone used by a blacksmith as an anvil.(Kashmiri)

பட்டடை[1] *paṭṭaṭai* , *n.* prob. படு[1]- + அடை[1]-. 1. [T. *paṭṭika*, K. *paṭṭaḍe*.] Anvil; அடைகல். (பிங்.) சீரிடங்காணி னெறிதற்குப் பட்ட டை (குறள், 821). 2. [K. ***paṭṭaḍi***.] Smithy, forge; கொல்லன் களரி. 3. Stock, heap, pile, as of straw, firewood or timber; குவியல். (W.) Alternative: *Ir.* bärī roof. *ĀlKu. bari* thatched roof. *Ko. varj- (varj-)* to wrap, wind; *vayr* roof. *To. pary* roof of hut. Rebus: *baḍhi* 'worker in wood and iron' (Santali) *bāṛaï* 'carpenter' (Bengali) *bari* 'merchant' *barea* 'merchant' (Santali) *vāḍhī*, 'one who helps a merchant (Hemacandra Desinamamamala).

Hieroglyph: hand: *karā̃* n. pl. ' wristlets, bangles '(Gujarati)(CDIAL 2779)
Rebus: khār 1 खार् । लोहकारः m. (sg. abl. khāra 1 खार; the pl. dat. of this word is khāran 1 खारन्, which is to be distinguished from khāran 2, q.v., s.v.), a blacksmith, an iron worker (cf. bandūka-khār, p. 111*b,* l. 46; K.Pr. 46; H. xi, 17); a farrier (El.). This word is often a part of a name, and in such case comes at the end (W. 118) as in Wahab khār, Wahab the smith (H. ii, 12; vi, 17).khāra-basta khāra-basta खार-बस्ꠃत । चर्मप्रसेविका f. the skin bellows of a blacksmith. -büṭhü -ब&above;ठू&below; । लोहकारभित्तिः f. the wall of a blacksmith's furnace or hearth. -bāy -बाय् । लोहकारपत्नी f. a blacksmith's wife (Gr.Gr. 34). -dŏkuru -द्वकुरु&below; । लोहकारायोघनः m. a blacksmith's hammer, a sledge-hammer. । लोहकारचुल्लिः f. a blacksmith's furnace or hearth. -hāl -हाल् । लोहकारकन्दुः f. a blacksmith's smelting furnace; cf. hāl 5. -kūrü -कूरू&below; । लोहकारकन्या f. a blacksmith's daughter. । लोहकारपुत्रः m. the son of a blacksmith, esp. a skilful son, who can work at the same profession. -लोहकारकन्या f. a blacksmith's daughter, esp. one who has the virtues and qualities properly belonging to her father's profession or caste. - । लोहकारमृत्तिका f. (for 2, see [khāra 3]), 'blacksmith's earth,' i.e. iron-ore. । लोहकारात्मजः m. a blacksmith's son. -nay -नय् । लोहकारनालिका f. (for khāranay 2, see [khārun]), the trough into which the blacksmith allows melted iron to flow after smelting लोहकारशान्ताङ्गाराः f.pl. charcoal used by blacksmiths in their furnaces. -wān वान् । -- 48 -- लोहकारापणः m. a blacksmith's shop, a forge, smithy (K.Pr. 3). -waṭh -वठ् । आघाताधारशिला m. (sg. dat. -waṭas -वटि), the large stone used by a blacksmith as an anvil (Kashmiri)

Hieroglyph: kolmo 'seedling, paddy plant'; rebus: kolimi 'forge, smithy' (Te.)Vikalpa: pajhaṛ = to sprout from a root (Santali); Rebus: pasra 'smithy, forge' (Santali)[It is possible that two variants of the glyph: one with three pronged

representation of seedling; and the other with five-pronged representation of seedling might have been intended to decode the fine distinction between the two lexemes: kolmo, pajhaṛ perhaps denoting two types of forge].
Glyph: aṭar 'a splinter' (Ma.)aṭaruka 'to burst, crack, sli off,fly open; aṭarcca ' splitting, a crack'; aṭarttuka 'to split, tear off, open (an oyster) (Ma.); aḍaruni 'to crack' (Tu.) (DEDR 66) Rebus: aduru 'native, unsmelted metal' (Kannada)aduru = gan.iyinda tegadu karagade iruva aduru = ore taken from the mine and not subjected to melting in a furnace (Ka. Siddha_nti Subrahman.ya' Śastri's new interpretation of the Amarakośa, Bangalore, Vicaradarpana Press, 1872, p. 330)Viklpa: sal 'splinter'; rebus: sal 'workshop' (Santali)

Thus the two glyphs of the text of the tablet inscription showing arch-around a pillar with ring-stones + paddy plant + splinter glyph may connote, rebus: kolimi koḍ aduru, 'forge unsmelted metal workshop'.

Glyph: Fish + scales *aya ãs* (*amśu*) 'metllic stalks of stone ore'279 Vikalpa: *badhoṛ* 'a species of fish with many bones' (Santali) Rebus: badhoria 'expert in working in wood'(Santali)

Glyph: *kāṇḍa* 'arrow' (Skt.) rebus: *kāṇḍa* 'fire-altar, furnace'.

The two glyphs together are furnace of a worker in wood and iron: *aya ãs (amśu)* 'metallic stalks of stone ore' *aya ãs kanḍa* 'furnace (with)a quantity of iron, excellent iron (metal) from stone ore' Vikalpa: *badhor kanḍa* 'furnace (of) worker in wood and iron'. *ayaskanḍa* is a lexeme attested in: Paan.gan.

Circular platforms in the southwestern part of Mound F excavated by M.S. Vats in the 1920s and 1930s, as conserved by the Department of Archaeology and Museums, Government of Pakistan.

The circular platforms parallel to the street of houses seem to be workspots or workshops of a guild of artisans. Such a workshop is called *paTTaDa* 'smith's workplace'.

Examples of 'trough' hieroglyph are seenn front of wild, domesticated and composite animals. Signifying 'troughs' in front of even wild undomesticated animals is evidence that 'trough' is a hieroglyph read rebus, with the rebus reading of 'animal' hieroglyph.

Maybe, the 19 circular working platforms of Harappa were used for assembling 19 'types' of forged products -- the 'trough' glyph denoting the working platform and the 'animal' glyph denoting the product type (e.g. copper, gold, metal alloy, output of furnaces (of various types), minerals). Ku. *pathrauṭī* f. ' pavement of slates and stones '.(CDIAL 8858) Ta. *paṭṭaṭai, paṭṭaṟai* anvil, smithy, forge. Ka. *paṭṭaḍe, paṭṭaḍi* anvil, workshop. Te. *paṭṭika, paṭṭeḍa* anvil; *paṭṭaḍa* workshop.(DEDR 3865). *pathürü* f. ' level piece of ground, plateau, small village '; S. *patharu* m. ' rug, mat '; Or. *athuripathuri* ' bag and baggage '; M. *pāthar* f. ' flat stone '; OMarw. *pātharī* ' precious stone '.(CDIAL 8857)

ಪಟ್ಟಡಿ paṭṭu 2-aḍi 4. = ಪಟ್ಟಡೆ, q. v. (My.; Ś. 399). 2, = ಪಟ್ಟಡಿಮನೆ (My.). — ಪಟ್ಟಡಮನೆ. A workshop (ಚದೆಸ್ಥಳ, ಚಿಟ್ಟಸಾಲೆ Śl. 108; My.).

ಪಟ್ಟಳೆ paṭṭaḷĕ. A district, a community. (R.).

The circular platforms could have served as prastara for the articles taken for display from out of the storage pots. "During excavations of the circular platform area on Mound F numerous Cemetery H-type sherds and some complete vessels were recovered in association with pointed base goblets and large storage vessels that are usually associated with Harappa Period 3C." South fo the platforms was a furnace. "A large kiln was also found just below the surface of the mound to the south of the circular platforms."

Circular platforms as guild trade platforms for artisans of forge/smithy and lapidaries Pattharati [pa+tharati] to spread, spread out, extend J i.62; iv.212; vi.279; DhA i.26; iii.61 (so read at J vi.549 in cpd °pāda with spreading feet, v. l. patthaṭa°). -- pp. patthaṭa (q. v.). -- Caus. patthāreti with pp. patthārita probably also to be read at Th 1, 842 for padhārita. (Pali)

[An allograph pattara 'trough' is a glyph used in front of many types of animals including wild animals and composite animal glyphs. pātra 'trough'; patthar 'merchant'. It also connotes a 'guild'.] पात्र pātra, (l.) s. Vessel, cup, plate; receptacle. [lw. Sk. id.] (Nepali) pātramu A utensil, ఉపకరణము. Hardware. metal vessels. (Telugu) பத்தல் pattal, n. பத்தர்[1] pattar 1. A wooden bucket; மரத்தாலான நீரிறைக்குங் கருவி. தீம்பிழி யெந்திரம் பத்தல் வருந்த (பதிற்றுப். 19, 23).

Ceramic stoneware badge of the type worn on the forehead badge and the shoulder badge of 'Priest-king' of Mohenjodaro. Rebus: Ta. *paṭṭaṭai, paṭṭaṟai* anvil, smithy, forge. Ka. *paṭṭaḍe, paṭṭaḍi* anvil, workshop. Te. paṭṭika, *paṭṭeḍa* anvil; *paṭṭaḍa* workshop. (DEDR 3865) Cf. 86 Ta. *aṭai.* Rebus: *paṭṭaḍa* workshop (Telugu) I suggest that the circular workplatforms were *paṭṭaḍa* 'workshops'.[280]

The script stands fully unraveled in an archaeological context of 19 circular platforms found in Harappa some with Harappa Script tablets -- close to a furnace/kiln. Thanks to the work of Randall Law, Kenoyer, Meadow, HARP recent Harappa excavations and Susa pot reported by Maurizio Tosi (with a 'fish' glyph painted on the pot which yielded metal artifacts from Meluhha?)-- all who have raised thoughtful questions and provided the archaeological finds which complete the picture of the ancient work of ancient bronze age artisans of Indus-Sarasvati civilization. Ku. pathrauṭī f. ' pavement of slates and stones '.(CDIAL 8858) Ta. *paṭṭaṭai, paṭṭaṟai* anvil, smithy, forge. Ka. paṭṭaḍe, paṭṭaḍi anvil, workshop. Te. *paṭṭika, paṭṭeḍa* anvil; *paṭṭaḍa* workshop.(DEDR 3865). *pathürü* f. ' level piece of ground, plateau, small village '; S. *patharu* m. ' rug, mat '; Or. *athuripathuri* ' bag and baggage '; M. *pāthar* f. ' flat stone '; OMarw. *pātharī* ' precious stone '(CDIAL 8857) Allograph Harappa Script glyph: pātra 'trough' in front of wild/domesticated/composite animals. pattar 'trough' (DEDR 4079) 4080 Ta. cavity, hollow, deep hole; pattar (DEDR 4080) Rebus: பத்தர்[2] *pattar* , n. < T. *battuḍu.* A caste title of goldsmiths. It was a smiths' guild at work on circular platforms of Harappa using tablets as category 'tallies' for the final shipment of package with a seal impression.

'Each platform is 11 feet in diameter and consists of a single course of four continuous concentric rings of brick-on-edge masonry with a hollow at the centre equal to the length of three bricks. The mortar used in them is mud but the pointing is of gypsum. (Pl. XIII, c) (Picture 26.4) Their purpose is not clear. While digging the hollow of P8 there was found a small quantity of burnt wheat and husked barley and about two pounds of animal bones. Some bits of bones were also found in two or three others. As, however, the bones etc., lay about a foot below the central hollow, that is to say distinctly below the brickwork of these platforms, and similar fragments of bones were also found sticking at the same level among the edges of the platforms, it appears certain that they were merely a part of the debris and by no means the contents of the hollow.' (Vats, MS, 1940, Excavation at Harappa, Delhi, ASI, p. 182).

Note: HARP excavators surmised the possible production of indigo. An alternative explanation is possible and deserves further investigation in the context of metalwork on the circular working platforms.

HARP excavations of one of the circular brick floors in mound F at Harappa revealed a deep depression containing greenish layers of clay. The greenish layers may have been caused by the presence of zinc particles which have a bluish green color. Zinc dust is flammable when exposed to heat and burns with a bluish-green flame. In an identification of the corrosion minerals identified on the Great Buddha, Kamakura, Japan it is noted that "some of the compounds found on the Buddha were mixed copper-zinc salts...and schulenbergite, a mixed copper-zinc basic sulfate, that is rhombohedral with a pearly, light green-blue color."[281]

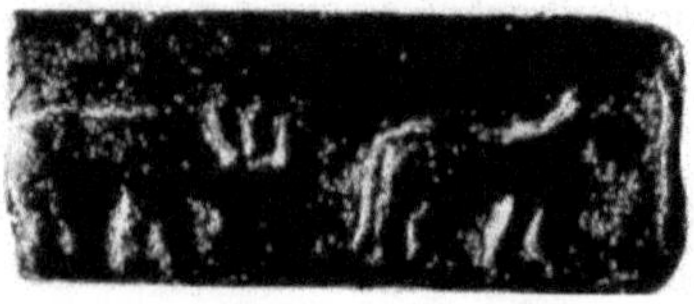

m1405 B

m1405A Pict-97 Person standing at the centre pointing with his right hand at a bison facing a trough, and with his left hand pointing to the Sign 15. This tablet is a clear and unambiguous example of the fundamental orthographic style of Harappa Script inscriptions that: both signs and pictorial motifs are integral components of the message conveyed by the inscriptions. Attempts at 'deciphering' only what is called a 'sign' in the concordances of Parpola or Mahadevan will result in an incomplete decoding of the complete message of the inscribed object.

Water-carrier glyph *kuṭi 'water-carrier' (Telugu); Rebus: kuṭhi 'smelter furnace' (Santali) kuṛī f. 'fireplace' (H.); krvṛi f. 'granary (WPah.); kuṛī, kuṛo house, building'(Ku.)(CDIAL 3232) kuṭi 'hut made of boughs' (Skt.) guḍi temple (Telugu)*

The most frequently occurring glyph -- rim of jar -- ligatured to Glyph 12 becomes Glyph 15 and is thus explained as a kanka, karṇaka: 'furnace scribe' and is consistent with the readings of glyphs which occur together with this glyph. *kan-ka* may denote an artisan working with copper, *kaṉ* (Ta.) *kaṉṉār* 'coppersmiths, blacksmiths' (Ta.) Thus, the phrase kaṇḍ karṇaka may be decoded rebus as a brassworker, scribe. *karṇaka* 'scribe, accountant' *karNI* 'supercargo'.

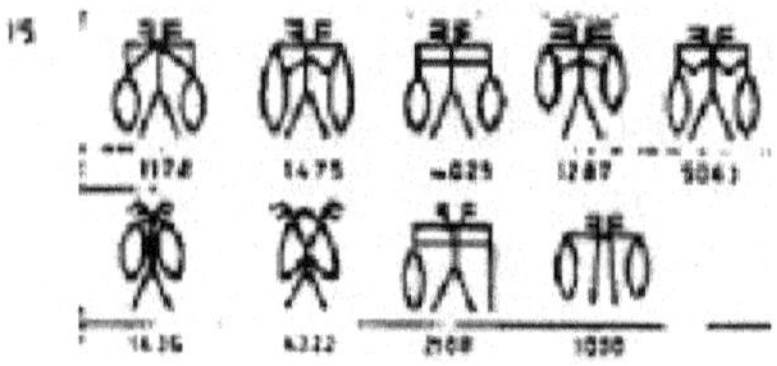

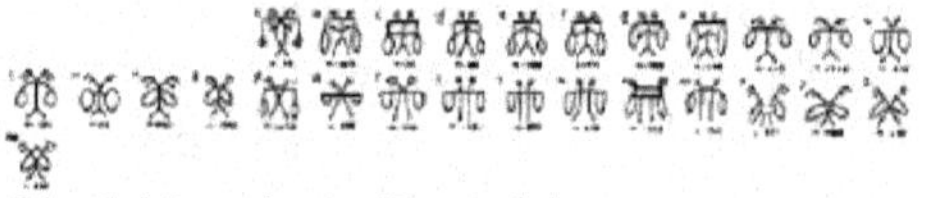

Glyph15 variants (Parpola)

The inscription of this tablet is composed of four glyphs: bison, trough, shoulder (person), ligatured glyph -- Glyph 15(rim-of-jar glyph ligatured to water-carrier glyph).

barad, barat 'ox' Rebus: भरत (p. 603) [*bharata*] *n* A factitious metal compounded of copper, pewter, tin &c.(Marathi)
pattar 'trough'; rebus *pattar, vartaka* 'merchant, goldsmith' (Tamil) பத்தர்[2] ***pattar***
, *n.* < *T. battuḍu.* A caste title of goldsmiths; தட்டார் பட்டப்பெயருள் ஒன்று.
eraka 'raised arm' Rebus: *eraka* 'metal infusion' (Kannada. Tulu)
Sign 15: *kuṭhi kaṇḍa kanka* 'smelting furnace account (scribe)'.
Thus, the hieroglyph multiplex on m1405 is read rebus from r.: *kuṭhi kaṇḍa kanka eraka bharata pattar*'goldsmith-merchant guild -- smelting furnace account (scribe), molten cast metal infusion, alloy of copper, pewter, tin.'
Sign 13 is a composition of hieroglyph component Sign 12 *kuṭi* 'woman water-carrier' PLUS
Sign ' which signifies hieroglyph: 'notch'. Reading the two hieroglyph components together Sign 13 reads: *kuṭi* 'woman water-

carrier' rebus: *kuṭhi* 'smelter' furnace for iron/*kuṭila,* 'tin metal'.PLUS khāṇḍā 'notch' Marathi: खांडा [*khāṇḍā*] *m* A jag, notch, or indentation (as upon the edge of a tool or weapon). Rebus: *khāṇḍā* 'metal tools, pots and pans'. Thus, the reading is: *kuṭhi khāṇḍā*'smelter metal tools, pots and pans'.

Sign 14 add the hieroglyph component *kōla* 'arrow' or kāṇḍa ;'arrow-head' to Sign 12. This Sign 14 is deciphered as *kuṭhi kāṇḍa* 'smelter metal tools, pots and pans' (Thus, a synonym of Sign 13*)* OR *kuṭhi kola* 'smelter, working in iron' or *kuṭhi kole.l* 'smelter, smithy'.

Hieroglyph: *eraka* 'raised arm' (Telugu) Rebus: *eraka* 'copper' (Telugu); 'moltencast' (Gujarati); metal infusion (Kannada.Tulu

Annex G

kulā 'hood of snake' as tail and Harappa Script hypertext

Hieroglyph: *nāga* ‘serpent’ Rebus: *nāga* ‘lead’

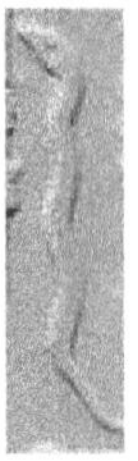

This hieroglyph appears on Jasper Akkadian cylinder seal. *kulā* hood of snake Rebus: *kolle* 'blacksmith' *kol* ‘furnace, forge’ A pronunciation varian is: Kur. *xolā* tail. Malt. *qoli* id. (DEDR 2135)

This is a defining hieroglyph component of many hypertexts, exemplified by the orthography of many animal parts combined together to yield a Harappa Script message.[282]

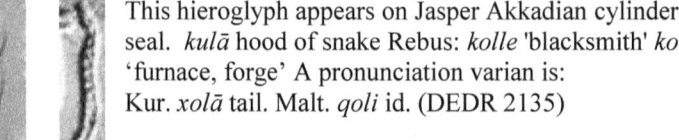

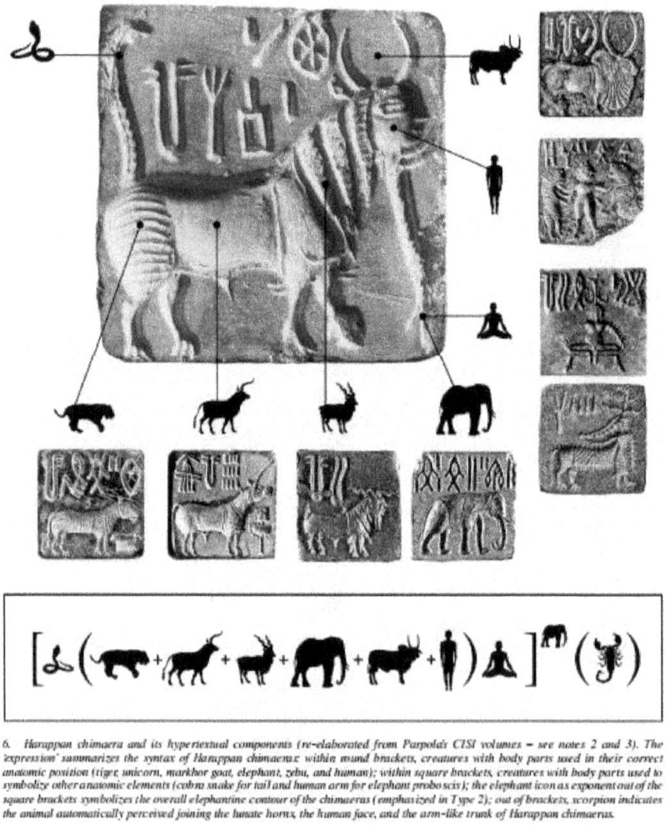

6. Harappan chimaera and its hypertextual components (re-elaborated from Parpola's CISI volumes – see notes 2 and 3). The 'expression' summarizes the syntax of Harappan chimaeras: within round brackets, creatures with body parts used in their correct anatomic position (tiger, unicorn, markhor goat, elephant, zebu, and human); within square brackets, creatures with body parts used to symbolize other anatomic elements (cobra snake for tail and human arm for elephant proboscis); the elephant icon as exponent out of the square brackets symbolizes the overall elephantine contour of the chimaeras (emphasized in Type 2); out of brackets, scorpion indicates the animal automatically perceived joining the lunate horns, the human face, and the arm-like trunk of Harappan chimaeras.

m1186 (DK6847) [Pleiades, scarfed, framework, *ficus religiosa* , scarfed person, worshipper, twigs (on head), horn, markhor, human face ligatured to markhor, stool, ladle, frame of a building]

Mohenjo-daro seal. Ligaturing components: horns of zebu, human face, tail-hood of serpent, elephant tusk, scarves on neck, bovine forelegs, feline hind legs.

The hypertext principle is demonstrated effectively by Dennys Frenez and Massimo Vidale for Harappa Script, identifying pictorial components which constitute a composite orthographic construction as in the example of a composite animal orthographed by various parts of various animals on m0300 Mohenjo-daro seal. Orthographic components are identified and explained by Dennys Frenez and Massimo Vidale.

Metalwork provides a framework for defined meaning of words used in the vernacular and continued use of such words in writing systems using what Frenez and Vidale call 'symbolic hypertexts as on Harappa Script provide the evidence for Harappa Script decipherment of Harappa Script Corpora as catalogus catalogorum of metalwork.[283]

miṇḍāl 'markhor' (Tōrwālī) meḍho a ram, a sheep' Rebus: meḍ 'iron'

Mĕṛhĕt́. **Iron.**
Mĕṛhĕt́ iĉena. The iron is rusty.
Ispat mĕṛhĕt́. Steel.
Dul mĕṛhĕt́. Cast iron.
Mĕṛhĕt́ khanḍa. Iron implements. Santali glosses for 'iron'

On meḍ 'copper' in Eurasian languages:

Wilhelm von Hevesy wrote about the Finno-Ugric-Munda kinship, like "Munda-Magyar-Maori, an Bharata link between the antipodes new tracks of Hungarian origins" and "Finnisch-Ugrisches aus Indien". (DRIEM, George van: Languages of the Himalayas: an ethnolinguistic handbook. 1997. p.161-162.) Sumerian-Ural-Altaic language affinities have been noted. Given the presence of Meluhha settlements in Sumer, some Meluhha glosses might have been adapted in these languages. One etyma cluster refers to 'iron' exemplified by meḍ (Ho.). The alternative suggestion for the origin of the gloss meḍ 'copper' in Uralic languages may be explained by the word meḍ (Ho.) of Munda family of Meluhha language stream:

Sa. <i>mE~R~hE~'d</i> `iron'. ! <i>mE~RhE~d</i>(M).

Ma. <i>mErhE'd</i> `iron'.

Mu. <i>mERE'd</i> `iron'.

~ <i>mE~R~E~'d</i> `iron'. ! <i>mENhEd</i>(M).

Ho <i>meḍ</i> `iron'.

Bj. <i>merhd</i>(Hunter) `iron'.

KW <i>mENhEd</i>

@(V168,M080)[284]

— Slavic glosses for 'copper'

Мед [Meḍ]Bulgarian

Bakar Bosnian

Медзь [meḍz']Belarusian

Měď Czech

Bakar Croatian

KòperKashubian

Бакар [Bakar]Macedonian

Miedź Polish

Медь [Meḍ']Russian

Meď Slovāk

BakerSlovenian

Бакар [Bakar]Serbian

Мідь [mid'] Ukrainian[unquote]

http://www.vanderkrogt.net/elements/element.php?sym=Cu

Miedź, meḍ' (Northern Slavic, Altaic) 'copper'.

One suggestion is that corruptions from the German "Schmied", "Geschmeide" = jewelry. Schmied, a smith (of tin, gold, silver, or other metal)(German) result in meḍ 'copper'.

I suggest that the lanuages which use Meḍ 'copper, metal, iron' are cultural contact areas of Meluhha and in particular, Meluhha metalworkers.

paṭa 'hood of snake'. *Rebus: padm* 'tempered, sharpness (metal)'. nāga 'serpent' Rebus: nāga 'lead (alloy)'

mũh 'face' Rebus: *mũhe* 'ingot'. *khũṭ* 'zebu'.khũṭ 'community, guild' (Munda)

ibha 'elephant' Rebus: ib 'iron'. Ibbo 'merchant' (Gujarati).

ḍhangar 'bull' Rebus: *dhangar* 'blacksmith' (Maithili) *ḍangar* 'blacksmith' (Hindi)

kol 'tiger' Rebus: kol 'working in iron'.

dhaṭu m. (also *dhaṭhu*) m. 'scarf' (WPah.) Rebus: *dhatu* 'mineral (ore)'

Rebus reading of the 'face' glyph: mũhe 'face' (Santali) mũh opening or hole (in a stove for stoking (Bi.); ingot (Santali) mũh metal ingot (Santali) mũhã = the quantity of iron produced at one time in a native smelting furnace of the Kolhes; iron produced by the Kolhes and formeḍ like a four-cornered piece a little pointed at each end; mūhā mẽṛhẽt = iron smelted by the Kolhes and formeḍ into an equilateral lump a little pointed at each of four ends; kolhe tehen mẽṛhẽt ko mūhā akata = the Kolhes have to-day produced pig iron (Santali.lex.) kaula mengro 'blacksmith' (Gypsy) mleccha-mukha (Skt.) = milakkhu 'copper' (Pali) The Sanskrit loss mleccha-mukha should literally mean: copper-ingot absorbing the Santali gloss, mũh, as a suffix

The composite animal (bovid) is re-configured by Huntington. http://huntington.wmc.ohio-state.edu/public/index.cfmIn a scintillating study of the orthography of Harappa Script, Dennys Frenez & Massimo Vidale provide an insight comparing two hieroglyph components on Harappa Script corpora: 1. elephant trunk and 2. hand of a person seated in penance

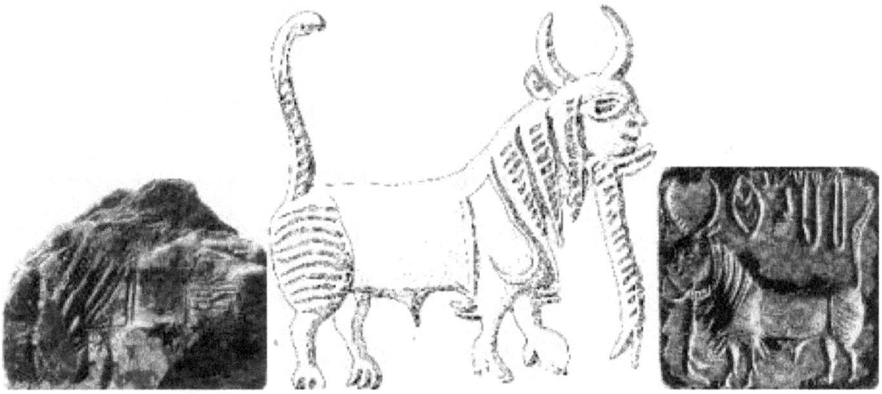

m1177, m1175, m300

7. Different personages and creatures depicted on Indus seals and tablets with both arms entirely covered by bangles: male deity or man in yogic position over a throne with bovine hoofs, centaur-like creature with tiger body and human fore-body and deity or man/woman standing within a pipal tree (from Parpola's CISI volumes – see notes 2 and 3; not to scale).

One Proto-Prakritam word signifies both 'tail' and 'hood of serpent'. The word is: *xolā* 'tail' of antelope and *ulā* hooded snake as tail. A similar sounding word signifies a blacksmith or smelter, furnace, forge: *kolle* 'blacksmith' *kolhe* 'smelter' *kol* 'furnace, forge'. These can be cited as 'signature' tunes of the writing system, to convey the semantics of a metalworker -- a smith or a smelter.

Rebus: *kol* 'pañcalōha' (Ta.) கொல் kol, n. 1. Iron; இரும்பு. மின் வெள்ளி பொன் கொல்லெனச் சொல்லும் (தக்கயாகப். 550). 2. Metal; உலோகம். (நாமதீப. 318.) கொல்லன் *kollaṉ*, n. < T. *golla*. Custodian of treasure; கஜானாக்காரன். (P. T. L.) கொல்லிச்சி *kollicci*, n. Fem. of கொல்லன். Woman of the blacksmith caste; கொல்லச் சாதிப் பெண். (யாழ். அக.) The gloss *kollicci* is notable. It clearly evidences that *kol* is a blacksmith. *kola* 'blacksmith' (Ka.); Koḍ. *kollë* blacksmith (DEDR 2133). Ta. *kol* working in iron, blacksmith; *kollaṉ* blacksmith. Ma. *kollan* blacksmith, artificer. Ko. *kole·l* smithy, temple in Kota village. To. *kwala·l* Kota smithy. Ka. *kolime, kolume, kulāme, kulime, kulume, kulme* fire-pit, furnace; (Bell.; U.P.U.) *konimi* blacksmith; (Gowda) *kolla* id. Koḍ. *kollë* blacksmith. Te. *kolimi* furnace. Go. (SR.) *kollusānā* to mend implements; (Ph.) *kolstānā, kulsānā* to forge; (Tr.) *kōlstānā* to repair (of ploughshares); (SR.) *kolmi* smithy (Voc. 948). Kuwi (F.) *kolhali* to forge (DEDR 2133) கொல்² *kol* Working in iron; கொற்றொழில். Blacksmith; கொல்லன். (Tamil).

mũhe 'face' (Santali); Rebus: *mũh* '(copper) ingot' (Santali); *mleccha-mukha* (Samskrtam) = *milakkhu* 'copper' (Pali) mũh opening or hole (in a stove for stoking (Bi.); ingot (Santali) mũh metal ingot (Santali) mũhã̄ = the quantity of iron produced at one time in a native smelting furnace of the Kolhes; iron produced by the Kolhes and formeḍ like a four-cornered piece a little pointed at each end; mūhā mẽṛhẽt = iron smelted by the Kolhes and formeḍ into an equilateral lump a little pointed at each of four ends; kolhe tehen mẽṛhẽt ko mūhā akata = the Kolhes have to-day produced pig iron (Santali.lex.) kaula mengro 'blacksmith' (Gypsy) The Samskritam loss mleccha-mukha should literally mean: copper-ingot absorbing the Santali gloss, mũh, as a suffix.

karã̄ n. pl. ' wristlets, bangles ' (Gujarati)(CDIAL 2779) Rebus: *khār* 1 खार् । लोहकारः m. (sg. abl. *khāra* 1 खार; the pl. dat. of this word is *khāran* 1 खारन्, which is to be distinguished from *khāran* 2, q.v., s.v.), a blacksmith, an iron worker (Kashmiri)

கோடு *kōṭu* : •நடுநிலை நீங்குகை. கோடிறீக் கூற் றம் (நாலடி, 5). 3. [K. *kōḍu*.] Tusk; யானை பன்றிகளின் தந்தம். மத்த யானையின் கோடும் (தேவா. 39, 1). 4. Horn; விலங்கின் கொம்பு. கோட்டிடை யாடினை கூத்து (திவ். இயற். திருவிருத். 21). Ko. *kṛ* (obl. kṭ-) horns (one horn is *kob*), half of hair on each side of parting, side in game, log, section of bamboo used as fuel, line marked out. To. *kwṛ* (obl. *kwṭ-)* horn, branch, path across stream in thicket. Ka. *kōḍu* horn, tusk, branch of a tree; *kōṟ* horn. Tu. *kōḍů, kōḍu* horn. Te. *kōḍu* rivulet, branch of a river. Pa. *kōḍ* (pl. *kōḍul*) horn (DEDR 2200) Rebus: *koḍ* = the place where artisans work (G.)

h175B Pict-87

Pict-85

h714At

h714Bt

m1224e

1224 Pict-88

Pict-90:

Pict-89 (Copper plate)

Pict-103

eṛaka 'upraised arm' (Tamil); rebus: *eraka* = copper (Kannada) *erako* 'molten cast' (Tulu) *ḍhangar* 'bull' Rebus: *dhangar* 'blacksmith' (Maithili) *ḍangar* 'blacksmith' (Hindi)
dhaṭu m. (also *dhaṭhu*) m. 'scarf' (WPah.) Rebus: *dhatu* 'mineral (ore)'

kamaDha 'archer' 'penance' (person seated in this posure) Rebus: *kampaTTa* 'mint'

kul 'tiger' (Santali); *kōlu* id. (Te.) kōlupuli = Bengal tiger (Te.) Pkt. *kolhuya* -- , *kulha* -- m. ' jackal ' < **kōḍhu* -- ; H. *kolhā, °lā* m. ' jackal ', adj. ' crafty '; G. *kohlũ, °lũ* n. ' jackal ', M. *kolhā, °lā* m. *krōṣṭŕ̥* ' crying ' BhP., m. ' jackal ' RV. = *krṓṣṭu* -- m. Pāṇ. [√kruś] Pa. *koṭṭhu --, °uka* m. ' jackal ', Pk. *koṭṭhu* -- m.; Si. *koṭa* ' jackal ', *koṭiya* ' leopard ' GS 42 (CDIAL 3615). कोल्हा [*kōlhā*] कोल्हें [*kōlhēṃ*] A jackal (Marathi) Rebus: *kol* 'furnace, forge' (Kuwi) *kol* 'alloy of five metals, pañcaloha' (Ta.) Allograph: *kōla* = woman (Nahali) [The ligature of a woman to a tiger is a phonetic determinant; the scribe clearly conveys that the gloss represented is *kōla*]

karibha 'trunk of elephan' rebus: *karba* 'iron' (Ka.)(DEDR 1278) as in *ajirda karba* 'iron' (Ka.) *kari, karu* 'black' (Ma.)(DEDR 1278) *karbura* 'gold' (Ka.) *karbon* 'black gold, iron' (Ka.) *kabbiṇa* 'iron' (Ka.) *karum pon* 'iron' (Ta.); *kabin* 'iron' (Ko.)(DEDR 1278) ibha 'elephant' rebus: *ib* 'iron' (Santali) [cf. Toda gloss below: *ib* 'needle'.] Ta. Irumpu iron, instrument, weapon. a. irumpu,irimpu iron. Ko. ibid. To. Ib needle. Koḍ. *Irïmbï* iron. Te. *Inumu* id. Kol. (Kin.) *inum* (pl. *inmul*) iron, sword. Kui (Friend-Pereira) *rumba vaḍi* ironstone (for *vaḍi*, see 5285). (DEDR 486) Allograph: *karibha* -- m. ' *Ficus religiosa* (?) [Semantics of *ficus religiosa* may be relatable to homonyms used to denote both the sacred tree and rebus gloss: *loa*, ficus (Santali); *loh* 'metal' (Skt.)]

Hieroglyph: *rā̃go* 'buffalo': raṅku m. ' a species of deer ' Vās., *°uka* -- m. Śrīkaṇṭh.Ku. N. *rā̃go* ' buffalo bull '? (CDIAL 10559)

raṅga3 n. ' tin ' lex. [Cf. nāga -- 2, vaṅga -- 1]Pk. *raṁga* -- n. ' tin '; P. *rā̃g* f., *rā̃gā* m. ' pewter, tin ' (← H.); Ku. *rāṅ* ' tin, solder ', gng. *rā̃k*; N. *rāṅ, rāṅo* ' tin, solder ', A. B. *rāṅ*; Or. *rāṅga* ' tin ', *rāṅgā* ' solder, spelter ', Bi. Mth. *rā̃gā*, OAw. *rāṁga*; H. *rā̃g* f., *rā̃gā* m. ' tin, pewter '; Si. *raṅga* ' tin '.(CDIAL 10562

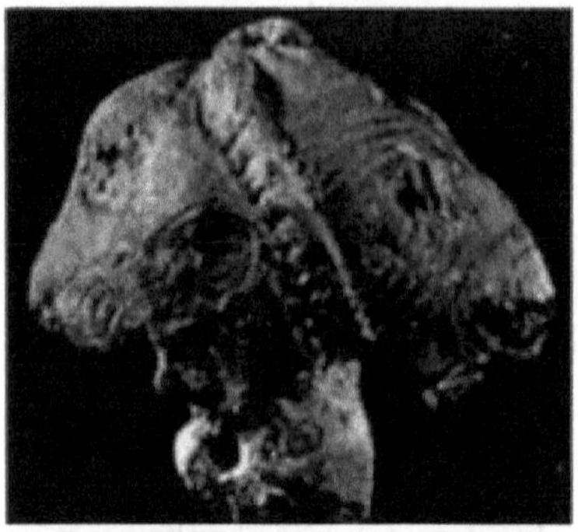

Terracotta. Tiger, bovine, elephant, Nausharo NS 92.02.70.04 h. 6.76 cm; w. 4.42; l. 6.97 cm. Centre for Archaeological Research Indus Balochistan, Musée Guimet, Paris

Three-headed: elephant, buffalo, bottom jaw of a feline. NS 91.02.32.01.LXXXII.

Dept. of Archaeology, Karachi. EBK 7712 Hieroglyph: karabha 'trunk of elephant' (Pali) ibha 'elephant' (Samskritam) Rebus: karba 'iron' rango 'buffalo bull' Rebus: ranga 'pewter, solder' kola 'tiger' Rebus: kol 'working in iron'

Hieroglyphs and rebus readings: mũh 'face' Rebus: mũhe 'ingot' kola 'woman' kola 'tiger' Rebus: kol 'working in iron' Nahali (kol 'woman') and Santali (kul 'tiger'; kol 'kolhe, smelter')

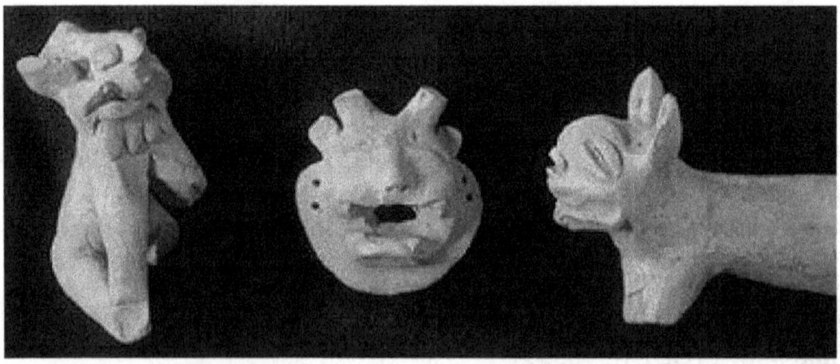

harappa.com

"Slide 88. Three objects (harappa.com) Three terra cotta objects that combine human and animal features. These objects may have been used to tell stories in puppet shows or in ritual performances. On the left is a seated animal figurine with female head. The manner of sitting suggests that this may be a feline, and a hole in the base indicates that it would have been raised on a stick as a standard or puppet. The head is identical to those seen on female figurines with a fan shaped headdress and two cup shaped side pieces. The choker with pendant beads is also common on female figurines. Material: terra cotta Dimensions: 7.1 cm height, 4.8 cm length, 3.5 cm width Harappa, 2384 Harappa Museum, HM 2082 Vats 1940: 300, pl. LXXVII, 67 In the center is miniature mask of horned deity with human face and bared teeth of a tiger. A large mustache or divided upper lip frames the canines, and a flaring beard adds to the effect of rage. The eyes are defined as raised lumps that may have originally been painted. Short feline ears contrast with two short horns similar to a bull rather than the curving water buffalo horns. Two holes on either side allow the mask to be attached to a puppet or worn as an amulet.

Material: terra cotta Dimensions: 5.24 height, 4.86 width Harappa Harappa Museum, H93-2093 Meadow and Kenoyer, 1994 On the right is feline figurine with male human face. The ears, eyes and mouth are filled with black pigment and traces of black are visible on the flaring beard that is now broken. The accentuated almond shaped eyes and wide mouth are characteristic of the bearded horned deity figurines found at Harappa and Mohenjo-daro (no. 122, 123). This figurine was found in a sump pit filled with discarded goblets, animal and female figurines and garbage. It dates to the final phase of the Harappa occupation, around 2000 B. C.

Harappa, Lot 5063-1 Harappa Museum, H94-2311 Material: terra cotta Dimensions: 5.5 cm height, 12.4 cm length, 4.3 cm width[285]

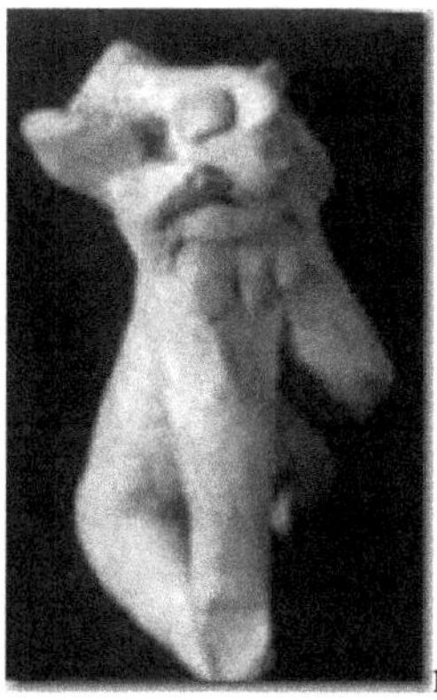
masks/amulets and

Slide72. Two composite anthropomorphic / animal figurines from Harappa. Whether or not the attachable water buffalo horns were used in magic or other rituals, unusual and composite animals and anthropomorphic/animal beings were clearly a part of Indus ideology. The ubiquitous "unicorn" (most commonly found on seals, but also represented in figurines), composite animals and animals with multiple heads, and composite anthropomorphic/animal figurines such as the seated quadruped figurines with female faces, headdresses and tails offer tantalizing glimpses into a rich ideology, one that may have been steeped in mythology, magic, and/or ritual transformation. Approximate dimensions (W x H(L) x D) of the larger figurine: 3.5 x 7.1 x 4.8 cm. (Photograph by Richard H. Meadow)

Ligatured glyph on copper tablet. m571B (serpent-like tail, horns, body of ram, elephant trunk, hindlegs of tiger). Hieroglyph: miṇḍāl 'markhor' (Tōrwālī) meḍho a ram, a sheep' Rebus: meḍ 'iron' पोळ *pōḷa,* 'zebu' rebus: पोळ *pōḷa*, 'magnetite, ferrite ore' *paTam* 'snake hood' Rebus: *padm* 'sharpness' *kulA* 'hood of serpent' rebus: *kol* 'metal, furnace, forge' *karabha* 'trunk of elephant' (Pali) Rebus: *karba* 'iron'

Annex H

Black ant hieroglyph and *cīmara kāra* ‘coppersmith’

h151 5057Text

h144 4280Text

h131 4271Text

h260A,B 4345Text

చీమ [cīma] *chīma.* [Tel.] n. An ant. కొండచీమ.

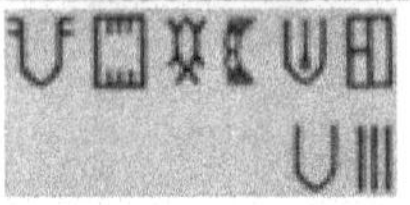

4345

the forest ant. రెక్కలచీమ a winged ant. పారేచీమను వింటాడు he can hear an ant crawl, i.e., he is all alive.చీమదూరని అడవి a forest impervious even to an ant. చలిచీమ a black ant; పై పారేపక్షి కిందపారే చీమ (proverb) The bird above, the ant below, i.e., I had no chance with him. చీమంత of the size of an ant. **చీమపులి** *chīma-puli*. n. The ant lion, an ant-eater.

చీముంత [cīmunta] *chīmunta*.. [Tel.] n. A metal vessel. చెంబు.

cīmara -- ‘ copper ’ in *cīmara* -- *kāra* -- ‘ coppersmith ’ in Saṁghāṭa -- sūtra Gilgit MS. 37 folio 85 verso, 3 (= *zaṅs* -- *mkhan* in Tibetan Pekin text Vol. 28 Japanese facsimile 285 a 3 which in Mahāvyutpatti 3790 renders *śaulbika* -- BHS ii 533. But the Chinese version (Taishō issaikyō ed. text no. 423 p. 971 col. 3, line 2) has *t'ie* ‘ iron ’: H. W. Bailey 21.2.65). [The Kaf. and Dard. word for ‘ iron ’ appears also in Bur. *čhomār*, *čhumər*. Turk. *timur*

(NTS ii 250) may come from the same unknown source. Semant. cf. lōhá --]Ash. *ċímä*, *ċimə* ‘ iron ’ (*ċiməkára* ‘ blacksmith ’), Kt. *čimé;*, Wg. *čümā´r*, Pr. *zíme*, Dm. *čimár(r)*, Paš.lauṛ. *čimā´r*, Shum. *čímar*, Woṭ. Gaw. *ċimár*,Kal. *čĩmbar*, Kho. *čúmur*, Bshk. *čimer*, Tor. *čimu*, Mai. *sẽwar*, Phal. *čímar*, Sh.gil. *čiměr* (adj. *čĭmārī*), gur. *čimăr* m., jij. *čimer*, K. *ċamuru* m. (adj.*ċamaruwu*).(CDIAL 14496) [Cf. Shgh. *čindōn* ‘ furnace for smelting iron ’ perh.

← Dardic or Kafiri e.g. Kt. *čimə* in cmpds. like *čim -- dur* ' saucepan '] Md. *timara* ' lead, tin '.(CDIAL 4842a)

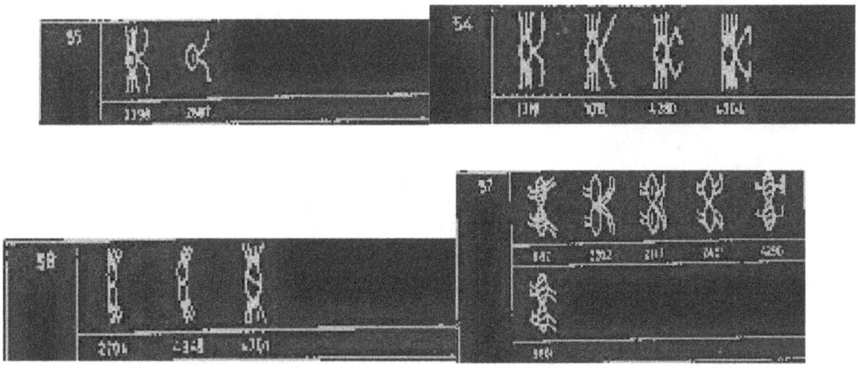

Tablet Mohenjo-daro m1430

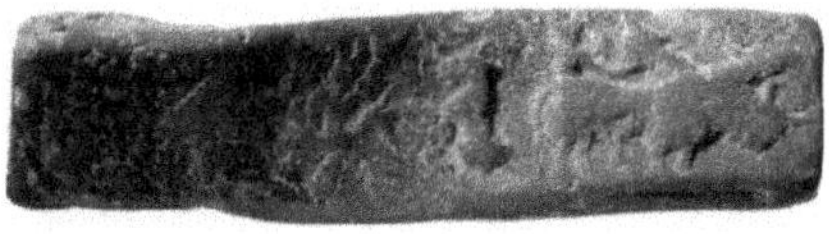

m1430B m1430C m1430A

Pict-101: Person throwing a spear at a buffalo and placing one foot on its head; three persons standing near a tree at the center. Hieroglyph: kick *kolsa* 'to kick' Rebus: *kol* working in iron, blacksmith *kol* 'furnace, forge' *kuTi* 'tree' rebus: *kuThi* 'smelter' *tagad.o* = [Skt. *trika* a group of three] the figure three (3)(Gujarati) [Note. Three persons shown next to a tree on a tablet].

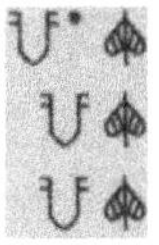

2819 Pict-60: Composite animal with the body of an ox and three heads [one each of one-horned bull (looking forward), antelope (looking backward) and bison (looking downwards)] at right; a goat standing on its hindlegs and browsing from a tree at the center. *ḍhangar* 'bison' rebus: *ḍhangar* 'blacksmith' melh 'antelope' rebus: *milakkhu* 'copper' PLUS *krammara* 'look back' rebus: *kamar* 'artisan' *kondh*, 'young bull' *khōṇḍī* 'pannier sack'
Rebus: *kōnda* 'engraver, lapidary'. Thus, the hypertext of a bovine with three animal heads reads: lapidary, smith working in copper. The text message repeated on three sides of the tablet: *loa* 'ficus religiosa' rebus: *loha* 'copper' PLUS *kanka* 'rim of jar' rebus: *karNI* 'supercargo' *karNika* 'scribe, account'. Thus m1430 seal inscription signifies: supercargo for smelter, blacksmith's work in copper, engraver work artifacts.

This is a flat square double sided seal. On one side, four script symbols are inscribed in reverse, above a bison with head lowered to the feeding trough. A swastika motif turning counter clockwise is carved on the reverse. The seal is perforated from the side along the axis of the animal motif. Material: gray brown unfired steatite Dimensions: 2.04 x 2.04 cm, 0.74 cm thickness Mohenjo-daro, HR 4503 Mohenjo-daro Museum, 50.258, MM 487 Marshall 1931: pl. CX, 311 Text message: *cīmara* 'black ant' Rebus: *cīmara* 'copper'. *cīmara kāra* -- 'coppersmith'. dhAtu '**strands** of rope' Rebus: *dhAtu* 'mineral, metal, ore' . खांडा [*khāṇḍā*] m A jag, notch, or indentation (as upon the edge of a tool or weapon). (Marathi) Rebus: *khāṇḍā* 'tools, pots and pans, metalware' *kāru* 'artisan'. *kolom* 'three' rebus: *kolimi* 'smithy, forge' PLUS *dula* 'two' rebus: *dul* 'metalcasting' PLUS *kõdā* 'one' rebus: *kõd* **'**workshop**'**; also, *tagar.*'trough' rebus: *tagara* 'tin'; thus, metalcasting, smithy in copper and tin. Inscription hieroglyphs: *barad, balad* 'ox' rebus: *bharata* 'alloy of pewter, copper, tin' PLUS *pattar* 'trough rebus: *pattaharaka* 'merchant', *pattar* 'guild of goldsmiths'*tagar.* = a trough; *tagar.re surti ar cunko sipia* they mix surti and lime in a trough (Santali.lex.) *taga_rum* [Pers. *tagarih*] a bricklayer's trough; a hod (Gujarati)

Hieroglyph (allograph): *tagara* = antelope (Skt.) Rebus: *tagara, tavara* [Tbh. of *tamara* or *trapu*] tin (Ka.Te.Ta.M.)(Kannada) *takaram* tin, white lead, metal sheet, coated with tin (Ta.); tin, tinned iron plate (Ma.); *tagarm* tin (Ko.); *tagara, tamara, tavara* id. (Ka.) *tamaru, tamara, tavara id. (Ta.): tagaramu, tamaramu, tavaramu id. (Te.); t.agromi* tin metal, alloy (Kuwi); tamara id. (Skt.)(DEDR 3001). *trapu* tin (AV.); *tipu (Pali); tau, taua* lead (Pkt.); *tu~_* tin (P.); *t.au* zinc, pewter (Or.); *taru_aum* lead (OG.); *tarvu~ (G.); tumba* lead (Si.)(CDIAL 5992).

The inscription on the seal is *dharma samjna,* 'respolnsibility indicators' of: artisan (working in) tin, copper ores, metal casting workshop.

Kalibangan 080 Seal impression 8120 Text

Kalibangan080A

8120

m0143

2002

m0143 Mohenjo-Daro seal 2002 Text

A cylinder seal made in Susa with inscription in Harappa script

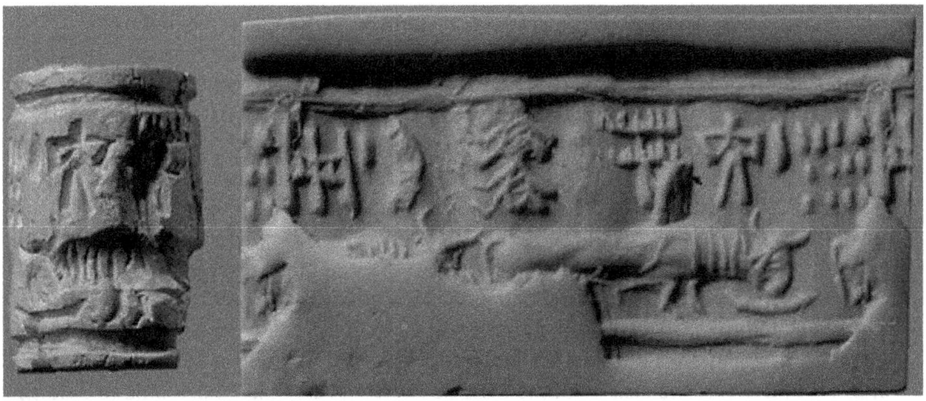

Sceau-cylindre : buffle très étiré et inscription harapéenne (It ain't a buffalo, but a bull)

Stéatite cuite H. 2.3 cm; Diam. 1.6 cm Fouilles J. de Morgan Sb 2425

Near Eastern Antiquities Richelieu wing Ground floor Iran and Susa during the 3rd millennium BCE Room 8 Vitrine 4 : Importations exotiques à Suse, 2600 - 1700 avant J.-C. Suse IVB (2340 - 2100 avant J.-C.). Courtesy: Louvre Museum

The discovery in Susa, of a cylinder seal (now in Louvre museum) with Harappa Script inscription (shown below) is a landmark event in historical studies.

A seal made in Meluhha. The language of the inscription on this cylinder seal found in Susa reveals that it was made in Harappa in the Indus Valley. In antiquity, the valley was known as Meluhha. The seal's chalky white appearance is due to the fired steatite it is made of. Craftsmen in the Indus Valley made most of their seals from this material, although square shapes were usually favored. The animal carving is similar to those found in Harappa works. The animal is a bull with no hump on its shoulders, or possibly a short-horned gaur. Its head is lowered and the body unusually elongated. As was often the case, the animal is depicted eating from a feeding trough, a woven wicker manger.[286]

Marshall comments on the Susa cylinder seal: "...the occurrence of the same form of manger on a cylinder-seal of bone found at Susa leaves no doubt, I think, that this seal either came from India in the first instance, or, as is suggested by its very rough workmanship, was engraved for an Bharata visitor to Susa by an Elamite workman...One of these five (Mesopotamian seals with Harappa Script) is a bone roll cylinder found at Susa, apparently in the same strata as that of the tablets in Proto-Elamitic script of the second period of painted ware. Scheil, in Delegation en Perse, vol. xvii, assigns this group of tablets and painted pottery to the period of Sargon of Agade, twenty-eighth century BCE, and some of the tablets to a period as late as the twenty-fourth century. The cylinder was first published by Scheil in Delegation en Perse ii, 129, where no precise field data by the excavator are given. The test is there given as it appears on the seal, and consequently the text is reversed. Louis Delaporte in his Catalogue des Cylindres Orientaux...du Musee du Louvre, vol. I, pl. xxv, No. 15, published this seal from an impression, which gives the proper representation of the inscription. Now, it will be noted that the style of the design is distinctly pre-Sargonic: witness the animal file and the distribution of the text around the circumference of the seal, and not parallel to its axis as on the seals of the Agade and later periods...It is certain that the design known as the animal file motif is extremely early in Sumerian and Elamitic glyptic; in fact is among the oldest known glyptic designs. But the two-horned bull standing over a manger was a design unknown in Sumerian glyptic, except on the small round press seal found by De Sarzec at Telloh and published by Heuzey, Decouvertes en Chaldee, pl. xxx, fig. 3a, and by Delaporte, Cat. I, pl. ii, t.24. The Indus seals frequently represent this same bull or bison with head bent towards a manger…Two archaeological aspects of the Susa seal are disturbing. The cylinder roll seal has not yet been found in the Indus Valley, nor does the Sumero-Elamitic animal file motif occur on any of the 530 press seals of the Indus region. It seems evident, therefore, that some trader or traveler from that country lived at Susa in the pre-Sargonic period and made a roll seal in accordance with the custom of the seal-makers of the period, inscribing it with his own native script, and working the Indian bull into a file design after the manner of the Sumero-Elamitic glyptic. The Susa seal clearly indicated a period ad quem below which this Indian culture cannot be placed, that is, about 2800 BCE. On a roll cylinder it is frequently impossible to determine where the inscription begins and ends, unless the language is known, and that is the case with the Susa seal. However, I have been able to determine a good many important features of these inscriptions and I believe that this text should be copied as follows:

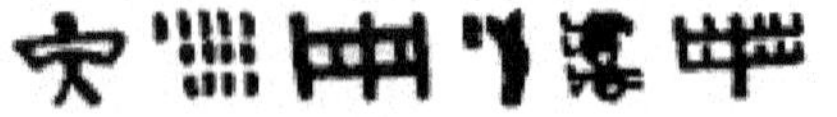

The last sign is No. 194 of my list, variant of No. 193, which is a post-fixed determinative, denoting the name of a profession, that is 'carrier, mason, builder', and invariably stands at the end. (The script runs from right to left.)"[Catalogue des cylinders orient, Musee du Louvre, vol. I, pl. xxv, fig. 15. See also J. de Morgan, Prehistoric Man, p. 261, fig. 171; Mem. Del. En Perse, t.ii, p. 129.loc.cit.,John Marshall, 1931, Mohenjo-daro and the Indus Civilization, Delh, AES, Repr., 2004, p.385; pp. 424-425 Note: Five cylinder seals have since been found at Mohenjo-daro and Kalibangan.] The seal's chalky white appearance is due to the fired steatite it is made of. Craftsmen in the Indus Valley made most of their seals from this material, although square shapes were usually favored. The animal carving is similar to those found in Harappa works. The animal is a bull with no hump on its shoulders, or possibly a short-horned gaur. Its head is lowered and the body unusually elongated. As was often the case, the animal is depicted eating from a woven wicker manger."

Marshall's transcription of the Susa cylinder seal requires some modifications, based on a sharper rolling of the cylinder and a photograph of the seal impression.

Hieroglyph: barad, barat 'ox' Rebus: भरत (p. 603) [bharata] n A factitious metal compounded of copper, pewter, tin &c.(Marathi)

Hieroglyph: pattar 'feeding trough' rebus: pattharika 'merchant'; pattar 'guild, goldsmith'. Susa, Iran; steatite cylinder seal.Cylinder seal carved with an elongated buffalo and a Harappa inscription circa 2600-1700 BCE; Susa, Iran; F

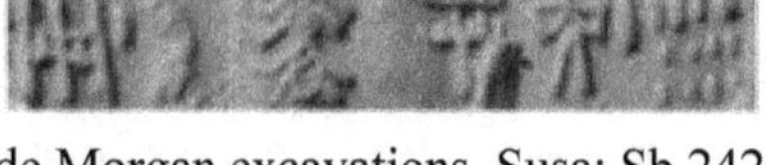

ired steatite; H. 2.3 cm; Diam. 1.6 cm; Jacques de Morgan excavations, Susa; Sb 2425; Near Eastern Antiquities; Richelieu wing; Ground floor; Iran and Susa during the 3rd millennium BC; Room 8.

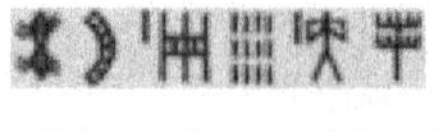

ad.ar 'harrow'; rebus: *aduru* 'native metal'. *aduru = gan.iyinda tegadu karagade iruva* aduru = ore taken from the mine and not subjected to melting in a furnace (Kannada)

dula 'pair' rebus: *dul* 'metal casting'

कर्णक *kárṇaka, kannā* 'legs spread', rebus: *karaṇī* 'scribe, supercargo', *kañi-āra* 'helmsman' PLUS खाडा [*khāṇḍā] 'A jag, notch, or indentation (as upon the edge of* *a tool or weapon)' Rebus: khaṇḍa 'implements (Santali). *lōhōpaskara ' iron tools '. [lōhá -- , upaskara -- 1] N. lokhār ' bag in which a barber keeps his tools '; H. lokhār m. ' iron tools, pots and pans '; -- X lauhabhāṇḍa -- : Ku. lokhaṛ ' iron tools '; H. lokhaṇḍ m. ' iron tools, pots and pans '; G. lokhā̃ḍn. ' tools, iron, ironware '; M. lokhā̃ḍ n. 'iron'(CDIAL 11171)*

baroṭi 'twelve' Rebus: bharata 'alloy of copper, pewter, tin'

śrēṣṭrī 'ladder' Rebus: seṭh ' head of a guild' PLUS dula 'pair' rebus: metal casting'. Hence, metal casting guild.

खाडा [khāṇḍā] 'A jag, notch, or indentation (as upon the edge of a tool or weapon)' Rebus: kāṇḍa 'implements (Santali).

kuṭi 'curve; rebus: कुटिल kuṭila, katthīl bronze (8 parts copper, 2 parts tin) PLUS dula 'pair' rebus: dul 'metal casting. Hence, bronze metal casting. PLUS khaṇḍa 'divisions' rebus: kāṇḍa 'implements'. Hence, bronze metal casting implements.

cīmara 'black ant' Rebus: cīmara 'copper'. cīmara kāra -- 'coppersmith'.

Annex I

Hieroglyphs of animal clusters. Mohenjo-daro m0304 (Reconstructed) Seal. A person is shown seated in 'penance' may signify *Triśiras*, son of *Tvaṣṭā*, कुबेर

Germanic people are divided into three large branches, the Ingaevones, the Herminones and the Istaevones. Their ancestry is derived from three sons of Mannus, son of Tuisto, their common forefather. (Publius Cornelius Tacitus, *Germania*, 98 CE). Tuisto is equated to the Vedic Tvaṣṭṛ.287 It is possible that the three branches of people associated with Tuisto may explain the metaphor of three heads, *triśiras* remembered from Rigvedic tradition: त्रि--शिरस् [p= 460,3] *mfn.* three-headed (त्वाष्ट्र, author of RV.x,8) Ta1n2d2yaBr. xvii Br2ih. KaushUp. MBh. Ka1m. (ज्वर) BhP. x , 63 , 22 कुबेर L (Monier-Williams). The *kāraṇī or kāraṇīka*, 'helmsman' signified on Seal m0304 may also relate to karnonou (Cernunnos) on the Pillar of Boatmen of 1st cent., CE.

Harappa Script hieroglyphs with 3 heads
-- Tuisto, Father of Germanic people, tatara 'smelter' (Japanese) ṭhaṭherā 'brassworker' (Sindhi) Kubera ~Triśiras, son of Tvaṣṭā

Tuisto, Father of Germanic people (ca. 1st cent. BCE), is seen in the tradition of *ṭhaṭherā* 'brassworker' of Harappa Script Corpora (ca. 3500 to 1900 BCE).

Triśiras 'three heada is a Rigveda metaphor linked to Tvaṣṭā, the divine artificerr. Calling Triśiras a son of Tvaṣṭā on a Harappa Script inscription may be a metaphorical expression connoting the continuity of Rigveda artificer tradition. Triśiras as a hieroglyph-multiplex (hypertext) is deciphered as metalwork of Sarasvati - Sindhu civilization. The evidence from Harappa Script Corpora for such hieroglyph-multiplexes are presented in this monograph.;

The spread of Tvaṣṭā tradition to Germanic people is a surmise.

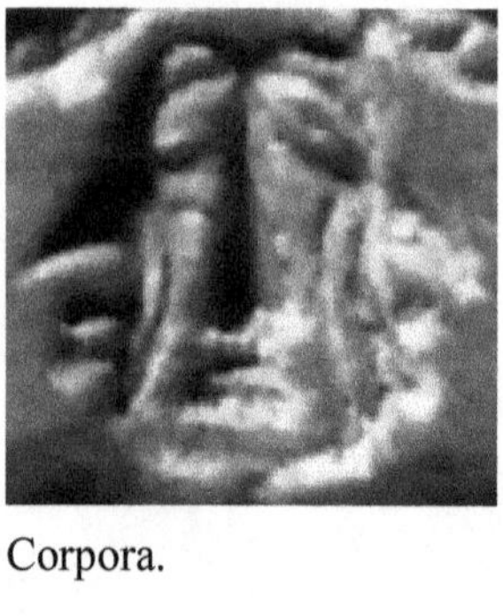

Triśiras 'three heads' of person seated in penance Seal m0304

A possibility is that the three heads signified on seal m0304 may relate to Kubera ~Triśiras,son of Tvaṣṭā of Rigveda. One meaning of *tvāṣṭra* त्वाष्ट्र is 'copper'.

A remarkable concordance between Rigveda metaphor of Triśiras associated with Tvaṣṭā occurs in the orthography of three-headed animals on Harappa Script Corpora.

Rebus reading of glyphic elements of the 'bristled (tiger's mane) face':

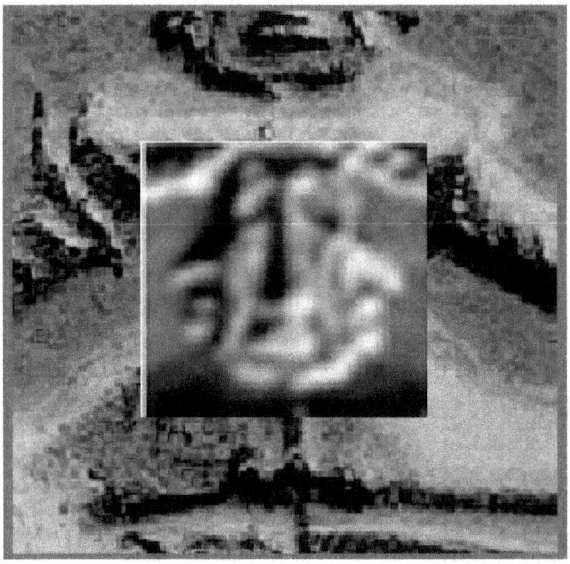

There are two glyphic elements denoted on the face. *mũh* 'face'; rebus: metal ingot (Santali) *mũhã̄* = the quantity of iron produced at one time in a native smelting furnace of the Kolhes; iron produced by the Kolhes and formeḍ like a four-cornered piece a little pointed at each end; *mũhā mẽṛhẽt* = iron smelted by the Kolhes and formeḍ into an equilateral lump a little pointed at each end; *kolhe tehen me~ṛhe~t mũhā akata* = the Kolhes have to-day produced pig iron (Santali.lex.)

Shoggy hair; tiger's mane. *sodo bodo, sodro bodro* adj. adv. Rough, hairy, shoggy, hirsute, uneven; *sodo [Persian. sodā,* dealing] trade; traffic; merchandise; marketing; a bargain; the purchase or sale of goods; buying and selling; mercantile dealings

(Gujarati) *sodagor* = a merchant, trader; *sodāgor* (P.B.) (Santali) The face is depicted with bristles of hair, representing a tiger's mane. *cūḍā, cūlā, cūliyā* tiger's mane (Pkt.)(CDIAL 4883).Rebus: *cūḷai* 'furnace, kiln, funeral pile' (Te.)(CDIAL 4879; DEDR 2709). Thus the composite glyphic composition: 'bristled (tiger's mane) face' is read rebus as: *sodagor mũh cūḷa* 'furnace (of) ingot merchant'.

In the hypertext of such three-headed animals, one-horned young bull signifies an engraving, enchasing artisan: Hieroglyph. खोंड (p. 216) [*khōṇḍa*] m A young bull, a bullcalf. Rebus: खोदणी (p. 216) [*khōdaṇī*] f (Verbal of खोदणें) Digging, engraving &c. 2 fig. An exacting of money by importunity. v लाव, मांड. 3 An instrument to scoop out and cut flowers and figures from paper. 4 A goldsmith's die. खोदणें (p. 216) [khōdaṇēṃ] v c & i (H) To dig. 2 To engrave.खोदींव (p. 216) [khōdīṃva] p of खोदणें Dug. 2 Engraved, carved, sculptured. खोदणावळ (p. 216) [*khōdaṇāvaḷa*] f (खोदणें)

barad, barat, ‘ox’ rebus: *bharata* भरत (p. 603) [*bharata*] n A factitious metal compounded of copper, pewter, tin &c भरती (p. 603) [*bharatī*] a Composed of the metal भरत, *baran, bharat* ‘mixed alloys (5 copper, 4 zinc and 1 tin)’.

Cipher device of combining body parts -- hieroglyph-multiplexes -- सांगड *sāṅgaḍa* 'joined animal parts to saṅ-kīrṇa encrypt blended figure of speech: *saṅgaha* संग्रह 'catalogue' an archive for data mining

Amri06 The cipher device is: सांगड *sāṅgaḍa* 'joined animal', rebus *saṅgaha* संग्रह 'catalogue' . Hieroglyph components combined are: *barad, balad* 'ox' rebus: *bharata* 'alloy of pewter, copper, tin' PLUS खोंड (p. 216) [*khōṇḍa*] m A young bull, a bullcalf.rebus: *kũdār*

'turner, sculptor, engraver' PLUS *mēlh (Brahui), mṛēka (Telugu)* 'goat' rebus: milakkhu 'copper'. Thus specific functional responsibilities of the metalworker are signified on this catalogue, Amri Seal.

Banawali 2 has an added set of hieroglyphs: Ligature: rim of jar Rebus: kaṇḍa kanka 'fire-trench

account, karṇi supercargo' karṇika 'helmsman, merchantman' Hieroglyphs: backbone + four short strokes

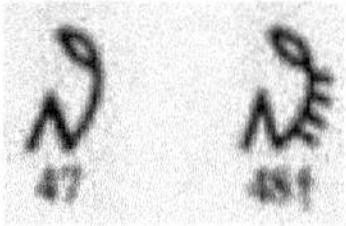

Signs 47, 48: baraḍo = spine; backbone (Tulu) Rebus: baran, bharat ‘mixed alloyś (5 copper, 4 zinc and 1 tin) (Punjabi) +

gaṇḍa ‘four’ Rebus: *kaṇḍ* ‘fire-altar’; *hkaṇḍa* ‘implements’. Thus, Sign 48 reads rebus: bharat kaṇḍ ‘fire-altar’, furnace for mixed alloy called bharat(copper, zinc, tin alloy), Pk. *karaṁḍa* -- m.n. ‘ bone shaped like a bamboo ’, *karaṁḍuya* -- n. ‘ backbone ’.((CDIAL 2670) rebus: *karaḍā* 'hard alloy'. Thus, on this Banawali seal, the inscription is a catalogue of collected hard alloy supercargo to be handed to the helmsman, as karṇi, seafaring merchandise.

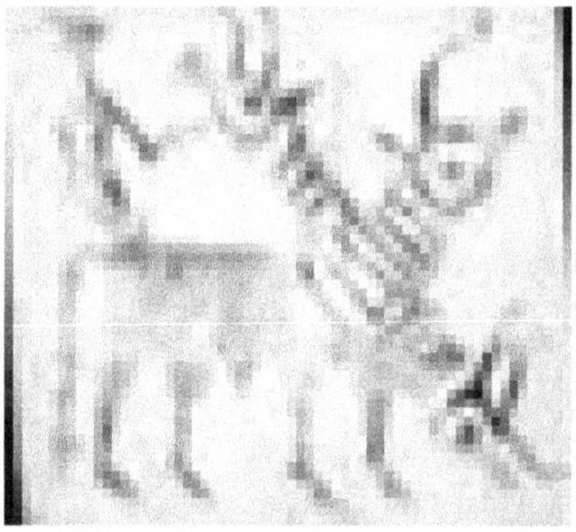

Harappa Script seals. Dholavira, Dwaraka (śankhaseal), Mohenjodaro 1171,

Dwaraka seal is made of turbinella pyrum śankha shell with three heads of animals (antelope, young bull, bull) joined to a bovine body. This is a सांगड *sāṅgaḍa* rebus:

sangara 'proclamation'of ranku 'antelope' Rebus: ranku 'tin' Alternative: mē<u>lh</u> (Brahui), mr̤ēka (Telugu) 'antelope, goat' Rebus: milakkha 'copper' PLUS kōnda 'young bull' Rebus: कोंद kōnda 'engraver, lapidary setting or infixing gemś PLUS barad 'ox' rebus: भरत bharat, bharan or toul 'alloy of copper, pewter, tin'. सं-ग्रह *saṁgraha* 'a guardian , ruler , manager , arranger' <u>R. BhP.</u>

Hieroglyph on Dholavira seal includes: *karṇika* 'spread legś rebus: *karṇika* 'helmsman', together with *pasara* 'domestic animals rebus: *pasra* 'smithy, forge'.

Together, the *triśiras*, 'three-headed' is read as Tvaṣṭā (father of Triśiras) rebus 1: त्वाष्ट्र 'copper' rebus 2: *ṭhaṭṭhāra* 'brass worker' (Prakritam) *K. ṭhö̃thur m., S. ṭhā̃ṭhāro m., P. ṭhaṭhiār, °rā m.2. P. ludh. ṭhaṭherā m., Ku. ṭhaṭhero m., N. ṭhaṭero, Bi. ṭhaṭherā, Mth. ṭhaṭheri, H. ṭhaṭherā* m (CDIAL 5473).

In Rigveda narrative, Triśiras is Kubera and also a son of Tvaṣṭā (cognate, Tuisto, Father of Germanic People). In Harappa Script Corpora, this Rigveda metaphor of a three-headed person gets signified orthographically as three-headed animals which are hieroglyph-multiplexes (hypertexts). In Samskritam lexis, tvaṣṭiḥ त्वष्टिः is a reference to such community of artisans engaged in carpentry. Some synonyms in Pali, Kashmiri, Pashto, Telugu: Thapati [Vedic sthapati, to sthā+pati] 1. a builder, master carpenter M i.396=S iv.223; M iii.144, <-> 2. officer, overseer S v.348.Tacchaka=taccha1. (a) a carpenter Dh 80 (cp. DhA ii.147); Miln 413. magga° a road-- builder J vi.348. -- (b)=taccha-- sūkara J iv.350. -- (c) a class of Nāgas D ii.258. Taccha1 [Vedic takṣan, cp. taṣṭṛ, to takṣati (see taccheti), Lat. textor, Gr. te/ktwn carpenter (cp. architect), te/xnh art] a carpenter, usually as °ka: otherwise only in cpd. °sūkara the carpenter-- pig (=a boar, so called from felling trees), title & hero of Jātaka No. 492 (iv.342 sq.). Cp. vaḍḍhakin. (Pali) tŏrka त्वर्क in tŏrka-chān त्वर्क-छान् । कौटतक्षः m. a private carpenter, a village carpenter who works on his own account, a cabinet maker (H. vii, 17, 2); cf. chān 1.-chān-bāy -छान्-बाय् । स्वतन्त्रतक्षस्त्री f. his wife.-chönil -छा&above;निल् । कौटतक्षता f.(Kashmiri) तक्षक <u>(p. 372)</u> [takṣaka] carpenter वाढया <u>(p. 746)</u> [vāḍhayā] m (वर्द्धकि S through H) A carpenter. 2 An affix of honor to the names of carpenters.(Marathi) tarkā<u>rrn</u> ترکانڑ tarkā<u>rrn</u>, s.m. (5th) A carpenter. Pl. ترکانڑان tarkā<u>rrn</u>ān. (Panjābī). darūz-gar دروزگر darūz-gar, s.m. (5th) A carpenter, a joiner. Pl. دروزگران darūzgarān (corrup. of P درود گر).(Pashto) త్వష్ట [tvaṣṭa] tvashṭa. [Skt.] n. A carpenter, వడ్లవాడు. The maker of the universe. విశ్వకర్త. One of the 12 Adityas, ద్వాదశాదిత్యులలో నొకడు.(Telugu) தட்டான்[1] taṭṭāṉ 'golsdmith' (Tamil. Malayalam) தட்டான்[1] taṭṭāṉ , n. < தட்டு-. [M. taṭṭān.] Gold or silver smith, one of 18 kuṭimakkaḷ, q. v.; பொற்கொல்லன். (திவா.)தட்டாக்குடி taṭṭā-k-kuṭi , n. < தட்டான்[1] +. Goldsmiths' quarters; தட்டார்கள் குப்பிடம். Loc.தட்டாத்தி taṭṭātti , n. Fem. of தட்டான்[1]. Woman of goldsmith caste; தட்டாரச்சாதிப் பெண்.தட்டார்பாட்டம் taṭṭār-pāṭṭam , n. < தட் டான்[1] +. Profession tax on goldsmiths; தட்டார் இறுக்கும் அரசிறைவகை. (S. I. I. ii, 117.)தட்டாரப்பாட்டம் taṭṭāra-p-pāṭṭam , n. < தட்டார் +. See தட்டார்பாட்டம். (S. I. I. iii, 115.) தரிப்புத்தட்டான் tarippu-t-taṭṭāṉ , n. < தரிப்பு[1] +. Monied man; பணக்காரன். (W.)பஞ்சகம்மாளர் pañca-kammāḷar , n. < pañcantaṭṭā<u>ṉ</u>, ka<u>ṉṉā</u>ṉ, ci<u>rpa</u>ṉ, tacca<u>ṉ</u>, kolla<u>ṉ</u>; தட்டான், கன்னான், சிற்பன், தச்சன் கொல்லன் என்ற ஐவகைப் பட்ட கம்மாளர். (சங். அக.) குடிமக்கள் kuṭi-makkaḷ , n. < id. +. 1. Sub-castes rendering service in a village, being 18 in number, viz., வண்ணான், நாவிதன், குயவன், தட்டான், கன்னான், கற்றச்சன், கொல்லன், தச்சன், எண்ணெய்வாணிகன், உப்புவாணிகன், இலைவாணிகன், பள்ளி, பூமாலைக்காரன், பறையன், கோவிற்குடியான், ஒச்சன், வலையன், பாணன்; பணிசெய்தற்குரிய பதி னெண்வகைக் கிராமக்குடிகள். (W.)

त्वष्टृ[p=<u>464</u>,1] m. a carpenter , maker of carriages (= त्/अष्टृ) <u>AV.</u> xii , 3 , 33" creator of living beings " , the heavenly builder , N. of a god (called सु-क्/ऋत् , -पाण्/इ , -ग्/अभस्ति , -ज्/अनिमन् ,स्व्-/अपस् , अप्/असाम् अप्/अस्तम , विश्व्/अ-रूप &c <u>RV.</u> ; maker of divine implements , esp. of इन्द्र's thunderbolt and teacher of the ऋभुs i , iv-vi , x <u>Hariv.</u> 12146 f. <u>R.</u> ii , 91 , 12 ; former of the bodies of men and animals , hence called " firstborn " and invoked for the sake of offspring , esp. in the आप्री hymns <u>RV. AV.</u> &c <u>MBh.</u> iv , 1178 <u>Hariv.</u> 587 ff.<u>Ragh.</u> vi , 32 ; associated with the similar deities धातृ , सवितृ , प्रजा-पति , पूषन् , and surrounded by divine females [ग्न्/आस् , जन्/अयस् , देव्/आनाम् प्/अत्नीस् ; cf. त्व्/अष्टा-व्/अरूत्री] recipients of his generative energy <u>RV. S3Br.</u> i

<u>Ka1tyS3r.</u> iii ; supposed author of <u>RV.</u> x , 184 with the epithet गर्भ-पति <u>RAnukr.</u> ; father of सरण्यू [सु-रेणु <u>Hariv.</u> ; स्व-रेणु <u>L.</u>] whose double twin-children by विवस्वत् [or वायु ?

<u>RV.</u> viii , 26 , 21 f.] are यमयमी and the अश्विन्s x , 17 , 1 f. <u>Nir.</u> xii , 10 <u>Br2ih.Hariv.</u> 545 ff. <u>VP.</u> ; also father of त्रि-शिरस् or विश्वरूप ib. ; overpowered

by इन्द्र who recovers the सोम [RV. iii f.] concealed by him because इन्द्र had killed his son विश्व-रूप TS. ii S3Br. i , v , xii ; regent of the नक्षत्र चित्रा

TBr.S3a1n3khGr2. S3a1ntik. VarBr2S. iic , 4 ; of the 5th cycle of Jupiter viii , 23 ; of an eclipse iii , 6 ; त्वष्टुर् आतिथ्य N. of aसामन् A1rshBr.)a form of the sun MBh. iii , 146 Hariv. 13143 BhP. iii , 6 , 15of an आदित्य MBh. i Hariv. BhP. vi , 6 , 37 VP. i , 15 , 130 ; ii , 10 , 16. आदित्य a. [अदितेरपत्यं ण्य P.IV.1.85.] 1 Solar, belonging to, or born in, the solar line; आदित्यैर्यदि विग्रहो नृपतिभिर्धन्यं ममैतत्ततो U.6.18. -2 Devoted to, or originating from, Aditi; आदित्यं चरुं निर्वपेत् Yaj. Ts.2.2.6.1. -3 Belonging to, or sprung from, the Ādityas. -त्यः 1 A son of Aditi; a god, divinity in general. (The number of Ādityas appears to have been originally seven, of whom Varuṇa is the head, and the name Āditya was restricted to them (देवा आदित्या ये सप्त Rv.9.114.3.). In the time of the Brāhmaṇas, however, the number of Ādityas rose to 12, representing the sun in the 12 months of the year; धाता मित्रो$र्यमा रुद्रो वरुणः सूर्य एव च । भगो विवस्वान् पूषा च सविता दशमः स्मृतः ॥ एकादशस्तथा त्वष्टा विष्णुर्द्वादश उच्यते ।); आदित्यानामहं विष्णुः Bg.1.21; Ku. 2.24. (These 12 suns are supposed to shine only at the destruction of the universe; cf. Ve.3.8; दग्धुं विश्वं दहनकिरणैर्नोदिता द्वादशार्काः). -2 The sun; Vāj.4.21. -3 A name of Viṣṇu in his fifth or dwarf-incarnation; स्वयंभूः शंभुरादित्यः V. Sah.

त्वष्टृ m. [त्वक्ष्-तृच्] 1 A carpenter, builder, workman, त्वष्ट्रेव विहितं यन्त्रम् Mb.12.33.22. -2 Viśvākarman, the architect of the gods. [Tvaṣṭri is the Vulcan of the Hindu mythology. He had a son named Triśiras and a daughter called संज्ञा, who was given in marriage to the sun. But she was unable to bear the severe light of her husband, and therefore Tvaṣṭṛi mounted the sun upon his lathe, and carefully trimmed off a part of his bright disc; cf. आरोप्य चक्रभ्रमिमुष्णतेजास्त्वष्ट्रेव यत्नो- ल्लिखितो विभाति R.6.32. The part trimmed off is said to have been used by him in forming the discus of Viṣṇu, the Triśūla of Śiva, and some other weapons of the gods.] पर्वतं चापि जग्राह क्रुद्धस्त्वष्टा महाबलः Mb.1.227. 34. -3 Prajāpati (the creator); यां चकार स्वयं त्वष्टा रामस्य महिषीं प्रियाम् Mb.3.274.9. -4 Āditya, a form of the sun; निर्भिन्ने अक्षिणी त्वष्टा लोकपालो$विशद्विभोः Bhāg.3.6.15.

त्वाष्ट्र tvāṣṭra त्वाष्ट्र a. Belonging or coming from त्वष्टृ; त्वाष्ट्रं यद् दस्रावपिकक्ष्यं वाम् Rv.1.117.22. -ष्ट्रः Vṛitra; येनावृता इमे लोकास्तमसा त्वाष्ट्रमूर्तिना । स वै वृत्र इति प्रोक्तः पापः परमदारुणः ॥ Bhāg.6.9.18;11.12.5. -ष्ट्री 1 The asterism Chitra. -2 A small car. -ष्ट्रम् 1 Creative power; तपःसारमयं त्वाष्ट्रं वृत्रो येन विपाटितः Bhāg.8.11.35. -2 Copper.

tvaṣṭiḥ त्वष्टिः f. Carpentry; Ms.1.48. पिश् piśपिश् 6 U. (पिंशति-ते) To shape, fashion, form; त्वष्टा रूपाणि पिंशतु Rv.1.184.1.- रूपम् rūpam -आश्रय a. exceedingly beautiful; त्वष्टा रूपाश्रयं रथम् Bhāg.4.15.17.

tvaṣṭiḥ त्वष्टिः f. Carpentry. -m. N. of a mixed tribe (?).त्वाष्ट्र tvāṣṭra त्वाष्ट्र a. [त्वष्टा देवता अस्य अण्] Belonging to Tvaṣṭṛi; U.6.3. (v. l.). -ष्ट्री 1 The asterism चित्रा. -2 A small car. -ष्ट्रम् The creative power.

Ta. *taṭṭumuṭṭu* furniture, goods and chattels, utensils, luggage. Ma. *taṭṭumuṭṭu* kitchen utensils, household stuff. Tu. *taṭṭimuṭṭu* id.(DEDR 3041) *ṭhaṭṭh ' strike '. [Onom.?] N. *ṭhaṭāunu* ' to strike, beat ', *ṭhaṭāi* ' striking ', *ṭhaṭāk -- ṭhuṭuk* ' noise of beating '; H. *ṭhaṭhānā* ' to beat ', *ṭhaṭhāī f. ' noise of beating '.(CDIAL 5490) *ṭhaṭṭhakāra ' brass worker '. 2. *ṭhaṭṭhakara -- . [*ṭhaṭṭha -- 1, kāra -- 1]1. Pk. ṭhaṭṭhāra -- m., K. ṭhȫṭhur m., S. ṭhā̃ṭhāro m., P. ṭhaṭhiār, °rā m.2. P.*

ludh. ṭhaṭherā m., Ku. ṭhaṭhero m., N. ṭhaṭero, Bi. ṭhaṭherā, Mth. ṭhaṭheri, H. ṭhaṭherā m.(CDIAL 5493) Ta. *taṭṭu (taṭṭi-) to knock, tap, pat,* strike against, dash against, strike, beat, hammer, thresh; n. knocking, patting, breaking, striking against, collision; *taṭṭam* clapping of the hands; *taṭṭal* knocking, striking, clapping, tapping, beating time; *taṭṭāṉ* gold or silver smith; *fem. taṭṭātti.* Ma. *taṭṭu* a blow, knock; *taṭṭuka* to tap, dash, hit, strike against, knock; taṭṭān goldsmith; fem.

taṭṭātti; taṭṭāran washerman; *taṭṭikka* to cause to hit; taṭṭippu beating. Ko. *taṭ- (tac-)* to pat, strike, kill, (curse) affects, sharpen, disregard (words); *taṭ a·ṛ- (a·c)* to stagger from fatigue. To. *toṭ* a slap; *toṭ- (toṭy-)* to strike (with hammer), pat, (sin) strikes; *toṛ- (toṭ-)* to bump foot; toṭxn, toṭxïn goldsmith; fem. *toṭty, toṭxity; toṭk* ïn- (ïḏ-) to be tired, exhausted. Ka. *taṭṭu* to tap, touch, come close, pat, strike, beat, clap, slap, knock, clap on a thing (as cowdung on a wall), drive, beat off or back, remove; n. slap or pat, blow, blow or knock of disease, danger, death, fatigue, exhaustion. Koḍ. *taṭṭ- (taṭṭi-)* to touch, pat, ward off, strike off, (curse)
effects; *taṭṭë* goldsmith; fem. *taṭṭati* (Shanmugam).

Tu. *taṭṭāvuni* to cause to hit, strike. Te. *taṭṭu* to strike, beat, knock, pat, clap, slap; n. stripe, welt; *taṭravā̃ḍu* goldsmith or silversmith. Kur. *taṛnā (taṛcas)* to flog, lash, whip. Malt. *taṛceto* slap. Cf. 3156 Ka. *tāṭu*. / Cf. Turner, CDIAL, no. 5490, **ṭhaṭṭh-* to strike; no. 5493, **ṭhaṭṭhakāra-* brassworker; √ *taḍ*, no. 5748, *tā'ḍa-* a blow; no. 5752, *tāḍáyati* strikes(DEDR 3039).

Mleccha rebus decoding Seal m0304:

ibha 'elephant' (Skt.) Rebus: ib 'iron'; *ibbho* 'merchant' (cf. Hemacandra, Desinamamala, *vaṇika*) *kol* 'tiger'; *kolla* 'smith'; *kamaḍha* 'penance' (Pkt.); Rebus: *kammaṭa* = mint, gold furnace (Te.) *tāttāru* 'buffalo horns' (Munda); Rebus: *ṭhaṭhero* 'brassworker'(Ku.) *cūḍā, cūlā, cūliyā* tiger's mane (Pkt.)(CDIAL 4883) *sodo bodo, sodro bodro* adj. adv. rough, hairy, shoggy, hirsute, uneven; Rebus: *sodo* [Persian. sodā, dealing] trade; traffic; merchandise; marketing; a bargain; the purchase or sale of goods; buying and selling; mercantile dealings (G.lex.) *sodagor* = a merchant, trader; *sodāgor* (P.B.) (Santali) *sal* 'bos gauruś; rebus: *sal* 'workshop'. *rango* 'buffao' rebus: *rango* 'pewter'

kola 'tiger' Rebus: Ta. *kol* working in iron, blacksmith; *kollan̠* blacksmith. Ma. *kollan* blacksmith, artificer. Ko. *kole·l* smithy, temple in Kota village; *kolhali* to forge (DEDR 2133)(Kuwi).

kūrda m. ' jump ', *gūrda* -- m. ' jump ' Kāṭh. [√kūrd] S. *kuḏu* m. ' leap ', N. *kud*, Or. *kuda*, °*dā*, *kudā* -- *kudi* ' jumping about '. *kū́rdati* ' leaps, jumps ' MBh. [*gū́rdati*, *khū́rdatē* Dhātup.: prob. ← Drav. (Tam. kuṭi, Kan. gudi ' to spring ') T. Burrow BSOAS xii 375]S. *kuḏaṇu* ' to leap '; L. *kuḏaṇ* ' to leap, frisk, play '; P. *kuddṇā* ' to leap ', Ku. *kudṇo*, N. *kudnu*, B. *kũdā*, *kõdā*; Or. *kudibā* ' to jump, dance '; Mth. *kūdab* ' to jump ', Aw. lakh. *kūdab*, H. *kūdnā*, OMarw. *kūdaï*, G. (CDIAL 3411, 3412) Rebus: *kunda* 'turner' *kundār* turner (A.) Vikalpa: ஏறு *ēṟu* Pouncing upon, as an eagle; பருந்தின் கவர்ச்சி. பரிந்தி னேறுகுறித் தொரீஇ (புறநா. 43, 5). Rebus: *eruvai* 'copper' (Ta.); ere dark red (Ka.)(DEDR 446). कोल्हा [*kōlhā*] कोल्हें [*kōlhēṃ*] tiger, jackal.

Pouncing tiger glyph is read rebus: *kũdā kol* 'jumping tiger' rebus: 'turner smith'.

The four animal glyphs surrounding the seated person thus connote: merchant (ibbho), carpenter (baḍhoe), turner-smith (*kũdā kol*), 'turner, smith (with) furnace, forge'.

Hieroglyphs on platform: *mēṭu, mēṭa, mēṭi* stack of hay; (Inscr.) (Telugu) *meṛā* m. (Bihari) *meṇḍa* -m. ' ram ' (Pali) Rebus: *meḍ* 'iron' *krammara* 'look back' rebus: *kamar* 'artisan, smith' Thus, ironsmith. Addendum with glyphs and inscriptions consistent with the themes depicting repertoire of artisan-smiths of the civilization: A lexeme which may explain the 'mountain' or 'haystack' glyphs; Rebus: Rebus: *mẽṛhẽt, meḍ* 'iron' (Mu.Ho.): *kunda* 'hayrick'; rebus: *kundār* turner (A.)

kamaḍha 'penance' (Pkt.) Rebus: *kammaṭi* a coiner (Ka.); *kampaṭṭam* coinage, coin, mint (Ta.) *kammaṭa* = mint, gold furnace (Te.) Thus, the over-arching message of the inscription composed of many hieroglyphs (of glyphic elements) thus is a description of the offerings of a 'mint or coiner (workshop with a gold furnace)'.

kūtī = bunch of twigs (Skt.) Rebus: *kuṭhi* = furnace (Santali) Vikalpa: clump between the two horns: *kuṇḍa* n. ' clump ' e.g. *darbha—kuṇḍa*—Pāṇ.(CDIAL 3236). *kundār* turner (A.)(CDIAL 3295). : *kundār* turner (A.); *kũdār, kũdāri (B.); kundāru (Or.);* kundau to turn on a lathe, to carve, to chase; *kundau dhiri* = a hewn stone; *kundau murhut* = a graven image (Santali) *kunda* a turner's lathe (Skt.)(CDIAL 3295) Vikalpa: kudī, kūṭī 'bunch of twigś (Skt.) Rebus: *kuṭhi* 'smelter furnace' (Santali)

Reading the glyphic elements on the chest of the person and arms:

kamarasāla = waist-zone, waist-band, belt (Te.) *karmāraśāla* = workshop of blacksmith (Skt.) *kamar* 'blacksmith' (Santali) *kamarasa_la* = waist-zone, waist-band, belt (Te.) *kammaru* = the loins, the waist (Ka.Te.M.); *kamara* (H.); *kammarubanda* = a leather waist band, belt (Ka.H.) *kammaru* = a waistband, belt (Te.) *kammarincu* = to cover (Te.) *kamari* = a woman's girdle (Te.) *komor* = the loins; *komor kat.hi* = an ornament made of shells, resembling the tail of a tortoise, tied round the waist and sticking out behind worn by men sometimes when dancing (Santali) *kambra* = a blanket (Santali) Rebus: *kamarsa_ri_* smithy (Mth.) kamba_r-ike, *kamma_r-ike* = a blacksmith's business (Ka.Ma.)(DEDR 1236).

sekeseke, sekseke covered, as the arms with ornaments; Rebus: *sekra* those who work in brass and bell metal; *sekra sakom* a kind of armlet of bell metal (Santali) Vikalpa:

bāhula n. armour for the arms (Skt.) Rebus: బంగల *bangala*. [Tel.] n. An oven. కుంపటి. (Telugu) bagala 'dhow, seafaring vessel' Vikalpa: *cūri* 'bangles' (H.) Rebus: *cūḷai* 'furnace, kiln, funeral pile' (Te.)(CDIAL 4879; DEDR 2709). *karA* 'wristlets, bangles' rebus: *khAr* 'blacksmith'

Thus, together, the glyphic elements on the chest of the person and arms are read rebus: *sekra karmāraśāla* 'brass/bell-metal workshop of smith (with) furnace'.

Glyphic compositions on the base on which the person is seated; hence, the rebus readings of glyphics: stool, pair of hayricks, pair of antelopes.

Kur. *kaṇḍō* a stool. Malt. *kanḍo* stool, seat. (DEDR 1179) Rebus: *kaṇḍ* = a furnace, altar (Santali) khāṇḍa 'implements'.

Three hieroglyphs, namely, platform, stack of hay, antelope seem to signify the same rebus reading: meḍ 'iron' (Mu.Ho.)

Platform: *Ta. mēṭai* platform, raised floor, artificial mound, terraced house. *Ma. mēṭa* raised place, tower, upper story, palace. Cf. Skt. (*lex.*) *meṭa-* whitewashed storied house; Pkt. *meḍaya-* id. (DEDR 4796)

Antelope: *minḍāl* 'markhor' (Tōrwālī) m*eḍho* a ram, a sheep (G.)(CDIAL 10120); rebus: *mẽṛhẽt, meḍ* 'iron' (Mu.Ho.)

Alternative: *tagara* 'antelope' Rebus: *tagara* 'tin'; damgar 'merchant'. *mēṭu, mēṭa, mēṭi* stack of hay (Te.)(DEDR 5058). Rebus: *meḍ* 'iron' (Ho.) Thus, a pair of haystacks can be read as phonetic determinatives of a pair of antelopes. Vikalpa: *kuntam* 'haystack' (Te.)(DEDR 1236) Rebus: *kuṇḍamu* 'a pit for receiving and preserving consecrated fire' (Te.) Vikalpa: *kundavum* = manger, a hayrick (G.) Rebus: *kundār* turner (A.*); kũdār, kũdāri (B.); kundāru (Or.); kundau* to turn on a lathe, to carve, to chase; *kundau dhiri* = a hewn stone; *kundau murhut* = a graven image (Santali) *kunda* a turner's lathe (Skt.)(CDIAL 3295)

Decoding a pair: dula दुल । युग्मम् m. a pair, a couple, esp. of two similar things (Rām. 966) (Kashmiri); *dol* 'likeness, picture, form' (Santali) Rebus: *dul* 'to cast metal in a mould' (Santali) *dul meṛeḍ* cast iron (Mundari. Santali)

Glyph: *krammara* 'look back' (Te.); Rebus: *kamar* 'smith' (Santali) Vikalpa 1: *mē̄lh* (Brahui), *mṛēka* (Telugu) 'antelope'(Br.); *milakkhu* 'copper' (Pali) Vikalpa 2: kala stag, buck (Ma.) Rebus: *kallan* mason (Ma.); *kalla* glass beads (Ma.); *kalu* stone (Konḍa); xal id., boulder (Br.)(DEDR 1298). Rebus: *kallan* 'stone-bead-maker'. Vikalpa: Rebus: *meḍ* 'iron' (Ho.)

Thus, together, the glyphs on the base of the platform are decoded rebus:*meḍ kamar* dul *meṛeḍ* (vikalpa: *kũdār*),'iron (metal) smith, casting (metal) (Vikalpa: *kũdār* 'turner').

Animal glyphs around the seated person, glyphics: buffalo (rango, sal), boar (rhinoceros, *baḍhoe*), elephant (ib), tiger (jumping, *kūdā kol*).

The four animal glyphs surrounding the seated person thus connote, rebus: workshop (sal), worker in both iron and wood (*baḍhi*), *rango* 'pewter, tin' merchant *(ibbho)*, turner-smith (kūdā kol),

sal 'bos gauruś; rebus: *sal* 'workshop' (Santali) Vikalpa 1: *ran:gā* 'buffalo'; *ran:ga* 'pewter or alloy of tin (ran:ku), lead (*nāga*) and antimony (*añjana*)'(Santali) Vikalpa 2: *kaṭamā* 'bison' (Ta.)(DEDR 1114) Rebus: *kaḍiyo* [Hem. Des. *kaḍa-i-o* = (Skt. Sthapati, a mason) a bricklayer, mason (G.)]

kaṇḍa 'rhinoceros' rebus: *khāṇḍa* 'implements' *baḍhia* = a castrated boar, a hog (Santali) Rebus: *baḍhi* 'a caste who work both in iron and wood' (Santali) *baḍhoe* 'a carpenter, worker in wood'; *badhoria* 'expert in working in wood'(Santali)

ibha 'elephant' (Skt.) Rebus: *ibbho* 'merchant' (cf.Hemacandra, Desinamamala, vaṇika). ib 'iron' (Santali) *karibha* 'elephant' (Skt.); rebus: *karba* 'iron' (Ka.)

kolo, koleā 'jackal' (Kon.Santali); *kola kukur* 'white tiger' (A.); कोल्हा [*kōlhā*] कोल्हें [kōlhēṃ] (Marathi) Rebus: *kol* pañcaloha 'five metals'(Ta.); *kol* 'furnace, forge' (Kuwi) Ta. *kol* working in iron, blacksmith; *kollaṉ* blacksmith. Ma. *kollan* blacksmith, artificer. Ko. *kole·l* smithy, temple in Kota village; *kolhali* to forge (DEDR 2133) kū*rda* m. ' jump ', *gūrda* -- m. ' jump ' Kāṭh. [√*kūrd*] S. *kuḏu* m. ' leap ', *N. kud, Or. kuda, °dā, kudā -- kudi* ' jumping about '.*kū´rdati* ' leaps, jumps ' MBh. [*gū´rdati, khū´rdatē* Dhātup.: prob. ← Drav. (Tam. *kuṭi*, Kan. *gudi* ' to spring ') T. Burrow BSOAS xii 375]S. *kuḏaṇu* ' to leap '; L. *kuḏaṇ* ' to leap, frisk, play '; P. kudd*ṇā* ' to leap '*, Ku. kudṇo, N. kudnu, B. kũdā, kõdā; Or. kudibā* ' to jump, dance '; Mth. *kūdab* ' to jump ', Aw. lakh. *kūdab, H. kūdnā, OMarw. kūdaï*, G. (CDIAL 3411, 3412) Rebus: *kunda* 'turner' *kundār* turner (A.) Vikalpa: puṭi 'to jump'; puṭa 'calcining of metals'. Pouncing tiger glyph is read rebus: *kũdā kol* 'turner smith'. Allograph: ஏறு *ēṟu* Pouncing upon, as an eagle; பருந்தின் கவர்ச்சி.

பரிந்தி னேறுகுறித் தொரீஇ(புறநா. 43, 5). Rebus: *eruvai* 'copper' (Ta.); *ere* dark red (Ka.)(DEDR 446).

Thus, together, the set of animals surround the seated person are decoded rebus: *ran:ga baḍhi karb kol dhātu puṭi kaṇḍa '(*worker in) pewter, iron & wood, iron(metal) forge/furnace for calcining metals, implements.

Decoding the text of the inscription

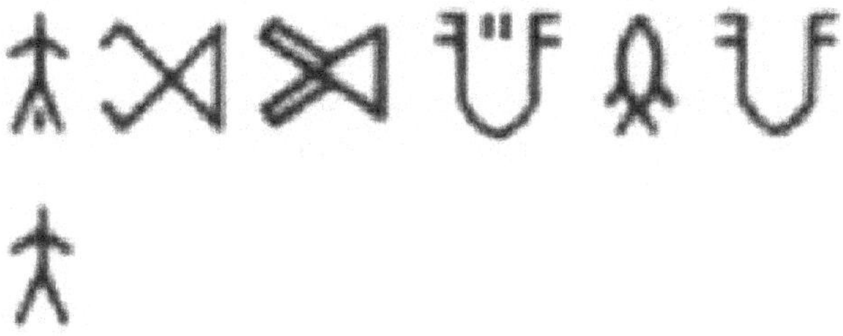

Text 2420 on m0304

Line 2 (bottom): 'body' glyph. *mēd* 'body' (Kur.)(DEDR 5099); *meḍ* 'iron' (Ho.) karNaka 'spread legs' rebus: karNaka 'helmsman'

Line 1 (top):

'Body' glyph plus ligature of 'splinter' shown between the legs: *mēd* 'body' (Kur.)(DEDR 5099); *meḍ* 'iron' (Ho.) *sal* 'splinter'; Rebus: *sal* 'workshop' (Santali)

Thus, the ligatured glyph is read rebus as: *meḍ sal* 'iron (metal) workshop'. Alternative: खांडा [*khāṇḍā*] m a jag, notch, or indentation (as upon the edge of a tool or weapon); rebus: *khāṇḍā* 'metal tools, pots and pans'. Thus the body hieroglyph ligatured with the splinter hieroglyph is read: *meḍ khāṇḍā* 'iron tools, pots and pans'.

Sign 216 (Mahadevan). *ḍato* 'claws or pincers (chelae) of crabś; ḍaṭom, ḍiṭom to seize with the claws or pincers, as crabs, scorpions; *ḍaṭkop* = to pinch, nip (only of crabs) (Santali) Rebus: *dhatu* 'mineral' (Santali) Vikalpa: erā 'clawś; Rebus: era 'copper'. Allograph: *kamaṛkom* = fig leaf (Santali.lex.) *kamarmaṛā (*Has.), *kamaṛkom* (Nag.); the petiole or stalk of a leaf (Mundari.lex.) *kamat.ha* = fig leaf, religiosa (Skt.) *kammata* 'mint, coiner, coinage' *kAru* 'pincers' rebus: *kAru* 'artisan' *khAr* 'blacksmith'.

Vikalpa: Sign 229. *Sannī, sannhī* = pincers, smith's vice (P.) *śannī* f. ' small room in a house to keep sheep in ' (Wpah.) Bshk. *Šan*, Phal.*šān* 'roof' (Bshk.)(CDIAL 12326). *seṇi* (f.) [Class. Sk. *Śreṇi* in meaning "guild"; Vedic= row] 1. A guild Vin iv.226; J i.267, 314; iv.43; Dāvs ii.124; their number was eighteen J vi.22, 427; VbhA 466. ° -- pamukha the head of a guild J ii.12 (text *seni* --). — 2. A division of an army J vi.583; *ratha* -- ° J vi.81, 49; *seṇimokkha* the chief of an army J vi.371 (cp. *Senā and seniya*). (Pali)

Together, Sign 229 and Sign 216 may be read as: *dhatu seṇi* 'mineral (products) guild (of artisans)'

Fish glyph: *ayo* 'fish' Rebus: *ayas* 'metal' (Vedic.Samskrtam)

Sign 342. *kaṇḍa kanka* 'rim of jar' (Santali): *karṇaka* rim of jar'(Skt.) Rebus: *karṇaka* 'scribe, accountant' (Te.); *gaṇaka* id. (Skt.) (Santali) copper fire-altar scribe (account)(Skt.) Rebus: *kaṇḍ* 'fire-altar' (Santali) Thus, the 'rim of jar' ligatured glyph is read rebus: fire-altar (furnace) scribe (account)

Sign 344. Ligatured glyph: 'rim of jar' ligature + splinter (infixed); 'rim of jar' ligature is read rebus: *kāṇḍa karṇaka* 'furnace scribe (account)' PLUS *sal* stake, spike, splinter, thorn, difficulty (H.); Rebus: *sal* 'workshop' (Santali) *ஆலை[3] *ālai,* n. < *šālā.* 1. Apartment, hall; சாலை. ஆலைசேர் வேள்வி (தேவா. 844. 7). 2. Elephant stable or
stall; யானைக்கூடம். களிறு சேர்ந்தல்கிய வழுங்க லாலை (புறநா. 220, 3).ஆலைக்குழி *ālai-k-kuḻi*, n. < ஆலை[1] +. Receptacle for the juice underneath a sugar-cane
press; கரும்பாலையிற் சாறேற்கும் அடிக்கலம்.*ஆலைத்தொட்டி āla i-t-toṭṭi, n. < id. +. Cauldron for boiling sugar-cane
juice; கருப்பஞ் சாறு காய்ச்சும்

சால். ஆலைபாய்-தல் *ālai-pāy-,* v. intr. < id. +. 1. To work a sugar-cane mill; ஆலையாட்டுதல். ஆலைபாயோதை (சேதுபு. நாட்டு. 93). 2. To move, toss, as a ship; அலைவுறுதல். (R.) 3. To be undecided, vacillating; மனஞ் சுழலு

தல். நெஞ்ச மாலைபாய்ந் துள்ளமழிகின்றேன் (அருட்பா,) Thus, together with the 'splinter' glyph, the entire ligature 'rim of jar + splinter/splice' is read rebus as: furnace scribe (account workshop). Sign 59. *ayo, hako* 'fish'; *a~s* = scales of fish (Santali); rebus: a*y*a = iron (G.); *ayah, ayas* = metal (Samskrtam) *khambhaṛā* 'fish **fin' rebus:** *kammaTa* **'mint, coiner, coinage'. Thus,** *ayo kammaTa* 'iron mint'. Sign 342. *kāṇḍa karṇaka* 'rim of jar'; rebus: 'furnace scribe (account)'.

Thus the inscription reads rebus: iron, iron (metal) workshop, mint, copper (mineral) guild, fire-altar (furnace) scribe (account workshop), metal furnace scribe (account).

As the decoding of m0304 seal demonstrates, the Harappa Script hieroglyphs are the professional repertoire of an artisan (miners"/metalworkers") guild detailing the stone/mineral/metal resources/furnaces/smelters of workshops (smithy/forge/turners" shops).

Vikalpa: *kuntam* 'haystack' (Te.)(DEDR 1236) Rebus 1: *kuṇḍamu* 'a pit for receiving and preserving *consecrated fire' (Te.) khaṇḍ 'tools, pots and pans and metal-ware' (Gujarati).Rebus 2: kunda* a turner's lathe (Skt.)(CDIAL 3295). Rebus: *kundan* 'pure gold'. *kuṇḍamu* 'a pit for receiving and preserving consecrated fire' (Te.)

Vikalpa: *krammara*. Adv. Again. క్రమ్మరిల్లు or క్రమరబడు Same as క్రమ్మరు. *krəm* back'(Kho.)(CDIAL 3145) Rebus: *karmāra* 'smith, artisan' (Samskrtam) *kamar* 'smith' (Santali) t*agara* 'antelope' Rebus 1: *tagara* 'tin' Rebus 2: *damgar* 'merchant' (Akkadian)

Vikalpa: *kuṇḍī* = crooked buffalo horns (L.) Rebus: *kuṇḍī* = chief of village. *kuṇḍi-a* = village headman; leader of a village (Pkt.lex.) i.e., *śreṇi jeṭṭha* chief of metal-worker guild.

The entire hieroglyph composition of seal m0304 is thus the metalware catalog of a chief of metal worker, mineral worker, kundan 'pure gold' merchant (*damgar*) guild.

Together with *meḍ* 'body', rebus: *meḍ* 'iron', the rebus reading of the 'body with spread feet' karNaka 'spread legs' rebus: karNaka 'helmsman'. may read rebus: *meḍ khāṇḍā karNaka* 'iron implements (cargo) helmsman'.

This Sign 1 hieroglyph ligatured with a notch-glyph, the reading is: *meḍ khāṇḍā* 'iron guild tools pots and pans'. खांडा [khāṇḍā] m A jag, notch, or indentation (as upon the edge of a tool or weapon). Rebus: *khāṇḍa* 'tools, pots and pans, and metal-ware'.

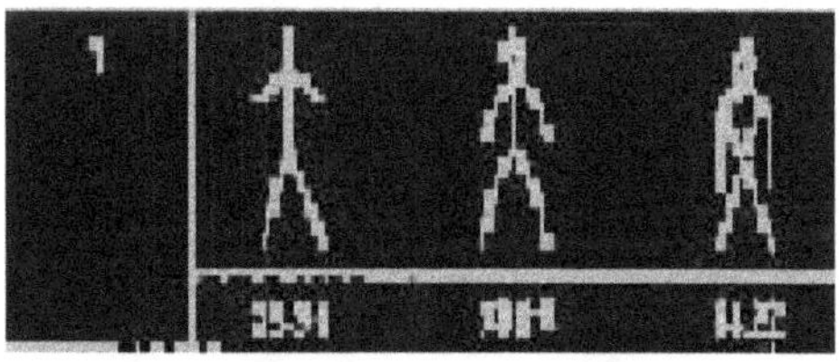

Alternative:

dhaṛu 'body' (Sindhi) rebus: *dhatu* 'ore' (Santali) *kāḍ* 2 काड् a man's length, the stature of a man (as a measure of length) Rebus: *kāḍ* 'stone'. Ga. (Oll.) kanḍ, (S.) *kanḍu (pl. kanḍkil)* stone

Listed by Koskenniemi and Parpola and cited by Kiwiyana Ligatured glyph of three sememes: 1. *meḍ* 'body' (Mu.); rebus: 'iron' (Ho.); 2. *kuṭi* 'water carrier' (Te.)

Rebus: *kuṭhi* 'smelter furnace' (Santali); 3. खांडा [khāṇḍā] m a jag, notch, or indentation (as upon the edge of a tool or weapon); rebus: *khāṇḍā* 'metal tools, pots and pans. The hypertext may be read as: *kuṭhi meḍ khāṇḍā karNaka* 'smelter (cargo)+ iron implements (cargo) helmsman'

The uniqueness of Harappa Script as a writing system is in the device of combining animals or parts of animals and forming a composite hieroglyph-multiplex. There is a word in Bharata sprachbund to denote this device. The word is:
सांगड sāṅgaḍa f A body formeḍ of two or more (fruits, animals, men) linked or joined together. सांग [sāṅga] a (S स & अंग) That is with all its members, parts, wings, appendages, and appertaining particulars; complete, entire, full, perfect;--as a ceremony, rite, work, act. (Marathi) ஸங்கரம்[1] saṅkaram, n. . (Rhet.) A composite figure of speech. See சங்கீரணம், caṅkīraṇam

, n. < saṅ-kīrṇa. 1. Mixing, commingling, coalescing; கலப்பு. 2. (Rhet.) A composite figure of speech in which several figures of speech are blended; கலவையணி. (தண்டி. 87.) 3. See சங்கீர்ணசாதி. (பரத. தாள. 47.) 4. A kind of mattaḷam; மத்தளவகை. (பரத. ஒழிபி. 13.) सं-
कीर्ण a [p= 1125,3]mfn. poured together , mixed , commingled &c f. a kind of riddle (of a mixed character) Ka1vya7d. iii , 105 (Samskrtam) वाक्यसंकीर्ण Jumbling of the different parts of a sentence so as to confound the subjects and the predicates (e. g. Give not....unto the dogs, lest they trample them under their feet, neither cast....before swine, lest they turn again and rend you) संकीर्ण [saṅkīrṇa] p S Mixed or mingled; esp. in a tumultuous or confused manner. 2 Crowded; covered or filled with a confused assemblage--a room or place. 3 Compressed, contracted, shortened, narrowed, reduced within small compass. Ex. किं कृष्ण वेणी मूळ सं0 ॥ पुढें होत विशाळ पैं ॥(Marathi)An orthographic variant of signifying three-heads of three animals is to incorporate selected body parts of selected animals as shown on the following seals m1175 to m1177. Additional animals added to the composition are: elephant, snake-hood, zebu (horn) and tiger (paws). On thse compositions, the horns of a zebu (पोळ *pōḷa*, 'zebu' rebus: पोळ *pōḷa*, 'magnetite, ferrite ore') PLUS trunk of elephant (*kariba* 'trunk of elephant' rebus: *karba*'iron') PLUS hood of serpent (*kulā* 'hood of serpent' rebus: *kolhe* 'smelter' *kol* 'furnace, forge') PLUS *dhatu* 'scarf' rebus *dhatu* 'mineral' PLUS body of bovine (perhaps, one-horned young bull (*konda* 'young bull' rebus *konda* 'engraver, sculptor'). Thus, the materials collected are *dhatu* 'minerals': *pōḷa*, 'magnetite, ferrite ore', *karba* 'iron ore', *mẽṛhẽt, meḍ* 'iron/copper (maybe, pyrites)', *mũh* 'metal ingot' (produced and formeḍ using *kol*, 'furnace, forge').

sā̃gaha arranger of minerals, ores for metalwork, seafaring merchandise, सांगड *sāṅgaḍa* 'joined animal, lathe, brazier', rebus *saṅgaha*

Ligatured faces: some close-up images. These are some examples of combined parts: human face, horn, body of animal, scarf on animal's neck. Each of these components is a hieroglyph. For example, *mũhe* 'face' rebus: *mũh* 'metal ingot' *dhatu* 'scarf' rebus: *dhatu* 'mineral'. *miṇḍāl* 'markhor' (Tōrwālī) *meḍho* a ram, a sheep'

Rebus: *mẽṛhẽt, meḍ* 'iron' (Munda.Ho.) *meḍ* 'iron' *meḍ* 'copper' (Slavic) *koḍ* 'horn' rebus: *koḍ* 'workshop'; see expression: *koṭe meṛed* = forged iron, in contrast to dul meṛed, cast iron (Mundari) Thus, by the device of hieroglyph-multiplexing, a catalogue has been created of metalwork: iron or copper ingot from mineral forged or cast in workshop. The hieroglyph-multiplex of markhor's horns can be read as *koḍ* 'horn' PLUS *miṇḍāl* 'markhor' read together rebus as: *kote meṛed* = forged iron, By combining body parts in a सांगड sāṅgaḍa 'joined animal', a *vākyapadIya* has been constructed, a meaningful sentence has been formeḍ, वाक्य--पदीय [p=936,2]n. N. of a celebrated wk. on the science of grammar by भर्तृ-हरि (divided into ब्रह्म-काण्डor आगम-समुच्चय , वाक्य-काण्ड , पद-काण्ड or प्रकीर्णक).

mũhe 'face' (Santali) Rebus: *mũh* opening or hole (in a stove for stoking (Bi.); ingot (Santali) *mũh* metal ingot (Santali) mũhā̃= the quantity of iron produced at one time in a native smelting furnace of the Kolhes; iron produced by the Kolhes and formeḍ like a four-cornered piece a little pointed at each end; *mũhā mẽṛhẽt* = iron smelted by the Kolhes and formeḍ into an equilateral lump a little pointed at each of four ends; kolhe tehen mẽṛhẽt ko mũhā akata = the Kolhes have to-day produced pig iron (Santali) *kaula mengro* 'blacksmith' (Gypsy) *mleccha-mukha* (Skt.) = *milakkhu* 'copper' (Pali) The Samskritam gloss *mleccha-mukha* should literally mean: copper-ingot absorbing the Santali gloss, mũh, as a suffix.

Hypertext: *sãghāṛɔ* 'lathe' (Gujarati. Desi) सांगड [*sāṅgaḍa*]That member of a turner's apparatus by which the piece to be turned is confined and steadied. सांगडीस धरणें To take into linkedness or close connection with, lit. fig.(Marathi) *sangaḍ* 'lathe/portable furnace': *sanghāḍo, saghaḍī* (G.) = firepan; *saghaḍī, śaghaḍi* = a pot for holding fire (Gujarati) 2. *sãghāṛɔ* lathe 3. *śaghaḍi* portable furnace [4].

This hieroglyph-multiplex can be read rebus as: 1. **guardian, ruler, manager, arranger, collection**: The arrangement relates to hieroglyph 'dotted circle': dhAu 'strand' rebus: dhAtu 'mineral, ore'. Thus, *saṅgaha* is responsible for arranging, collecting the 'building materials': minerals, ores for metalwork. *saṁgraha* m. ' collection ' Mn., 'holding together' MBh. [√*grah*] Pa. *saṅgaha* -- m. 'collection ', *Pk. saṁgaha -- m.; Bi. sãgah* 'building materials'; *Mth. sãgah* 'the plough and all its appurtenances', *Bhoj. har -- sãga; H. sãgahā* collection of materials (e.g. for building)'; <-> Si. *saṅgaha* 'compilation' ← Pa. सं-ग्रह [p=1129,2] complete enumeration or collection , sum , amount , totality (एण , " completely " , "entirely") Ya1jn5. MBh. &c a compendium, summary , catalogue , list , epitome , abridgment , short statement (एण orआत् , " shortly " , " summarily " , " in few words ") Kat2hUp. MBh. &c a guardian, ruler, manager, arranger R. BhP.(CDIAL 12852) *sáṁgr̥hṇāti* 'seizes' RV. 2. **saṁgrahati. 3. saṁgrāhayati* 'causes to be taken hold of, causes to be comprehended' BhP. [√*grah*]1. Pa. *saṅgaṇhāti* 'collects', *Pk. saṁgiṇhaï; Or. saṅghenibā* 'to take with, be accompanied by'. 2. *Pa. fut. saṅgahissati, pp. saṅgahita* -- ; *Pk. saṁgahaï* ' collects, chooses, agrees to '; Si. *haṅginavā ' to think ', hãṅgenavā, ãṅg°* 'to be convinced, perceive', *haṅgavanavā, aṅg°* 'to make known'.3. Or. *saṅgāibā* 'to keep'(CDIAL 12850) *sangāha* (adj. -- n.) [fr. *saŋ+grah*] 1. collecting, collection, Mhvs 10, 24. -- 2. restraining, self -- restraint A ii.142. *sangāhaka* (adj. -- n.) [fr. *sangāha*] 1. compiling, collection, making a recension J i.1; Miln 369; VvA 169 (dhamma°). -- 2. treating kindly, compassionate, kind (cp. *sangaha* 5) A iv.90; J i.203; iii.262. -- 3. (m.) a charioteer D ii.268; J i.203; ii.257; iv.63. sung; uttered, proclaimeḍ, established as the text Vin ii.290; J i.1; DA i.25 (of the Canon, said to have been rehearsed inseven months). -- (nt.) a song, chant, chorus D ii.138; J vi.529. *sangaha1 [fr. saŋ+grah*] 1. collecting, gathering, accu-mulation Vin i.253; Mhvs 35, 28. -- 2. comprising, collection, inclusion, classification Kvu 335 sq. (*°kathā*), cp. Kvu. trsln 388 sq.; Vism 191, 368 (*eka°*); *°ŋ gacchati* to be comprised, included, or classified SnA 7, 24, 291. -- 3. inclusion, i. e. constitution of consciousness, phase Miln 40. -- 4. recension, collection of the Scriptures Mhvs 4, 61; 5, 95; 38, 44; DA i.131. -- 5. (appld) kind disposition, kindliness, sympathy, friendliness, help, assistance, protection, favour D iii.245; Sn 262, 263; A i.92; J i.86 sq.; iii.471; vi.574; DA i.318; VvA 63, 64; PvA 196 (°ŋ karoti). The 4 sangaha -- vatthūni or objects (characteristics) of sympathy are: dāna, peyyavajja, atthacariyā, samānattatā, or liberality, kindly speech, a life of usefulness (Rh. D. at Dial. iii.145: sagacious conduct; 223: justice), impartiality (? better as state of equality, i. e. sensus communis or feeling of common good). The BSk. equivalents (as *sangrahavastūni) are dāna, priyavākya, tathārthacaryā, samānasukha -- duḥkatā* MVastu i.3; and d., p., *arthakriyā, samānārthatā (=samāna+artha+tā)* Lal. Vist. 30. Cp. Divy 95, 124, 264. The P. refs. are D iii.152, 232; A ii.32, 248; iv.219, 364; J v.330; SnA 236, 240. See also Kern, Toev. ii.67 s. v. (Pali) *saṅgaha* संग्रह 'catalogue' *sãgah* 'building materials' collection of mateials; sangāṭh संगाठ् । सामग्री m. (sg. dat. *sangāṭas* संगाटस्), a collection (of implements, tools, materials, for any object), apparatus, furniture, a collection of the things wanted on a journey, luggage, and so on. -- karun -- करुन् । सामग्रीसंग्रहः m.inf. to collect the ab. (L.V. 17)(Kashmiri). Catalogue or संगाटस् 'collection of implements, tools' saṁghāṭa m. ' fitting and joining of timber '

R. [√ghaṭ](CDIAL 12859) संगत saṅgata Assembled, collected, convened, met together.संगतिः saṅgatiḥ Company, society, association, intercourse (Samskritam. Apte) Sangata [pp. of sangacchati] 1. come together, met Sn 807, 1102 (=samāgata samohita sannipātita Nd2 621); nt. sangataŋ association Dh 207. -- 2. compact, tightly fastened or closed, well -- joined Vv 642 (=nibbivara VvA 275). *sangati* (f.) [fr. *sangacchati]* 1. meeting, intercourse J iv.98; v.78, 483. In defn of yajati (=service?) at Dhtp 62 & Dhtm 79. -- 2. union, combination M i.111; Sii.72; iv.32 sq., 68 sq.; Vbh 138 (=VbhA 188). <-> 3. accidental occurrence D i.53; DA i.161. (Pali)
5. *sanghāta* adamantine glue; *vajra sanghāta* 'binding together': Mixture of 8 lead, 2 bell-metal, 1 iron rust constitute adamantine glue. *saṁghaṭayati* ' strikes (a musical instrument) ' R., ' joins together ' Kathās. [√*ghaṭ*]Pa. *saṅghaṭita* -- ' pegged together '; Pk. *saṁghaḍia*<-> ' joined ', caus. *saṁghaḍāvēi;* M. *sā̃gaḍṇẽ* ' to link together . Addenda: *saṁghaṭayati:* A. *sāṅoriba* (phonet. x --) ' to yoke together ' AFD 333, *sāṅor* (phonet. x --) ' yoking together ' 223.(CDIAL 12855) सांगडणें (p. 840) [*sāṅgaḍaṇēṃ*] v c (सांगड) To link, join, or unite together (boats, fruits, animals). 2 Freely. To tie or bind up or unto (Marathi) 6. *sangara,* 'proclamation' sangara [fr. saŋ+gṛ] promise, agreement J iv.105, 111, 473; v.25, 479 (Pali) 7. . सांगड double-canoe or float, catamaran; सांगड [*sāṅgaḍa*] m f (संघट्ट S) A float composed of two canoes or boats bound together: also a link of two pompions &c. to swim or float by. (Marathi) सांगाडा (p. 840) [*sāṅgāḍā*] m The skeleton, box, or frame (of a building, boat, the body &c.), the hull, shell, compages. सांकाटा (p. 839) [*sāṅkāṭā*] m (Commonly सांगाडा) The skeleton, box, or frame (of a building, boat, cart, the body). 2 A frame or texture of sticks (as for the covering of a मंडप or shed, for the flooring of a loft &c.); a crate, a hurdle, or similar thing. सं-ग्रह *saṁgraha* 'a guardian , ruler , manager , arranger' R. BhP.

Trade caravan, *utsava bera* (utsava murti carried on processions)

Inscribed Tablets. Pict-91
(Mahadevan) m0490At m0490B Mohenjodaro Tablet showing Meluhha combined standard of three standards carried in a procession, comparable to Tablet m0491. The hieroglph multiplex: *sā̃gaḍ* 'lathe, portable furnace' सं-ग्रह *saṁgraha* 'a guardian , ruler , manager , arranger' R. BhP. PLUS a standing person with upraised arm: *eraka* 'upraised arm'

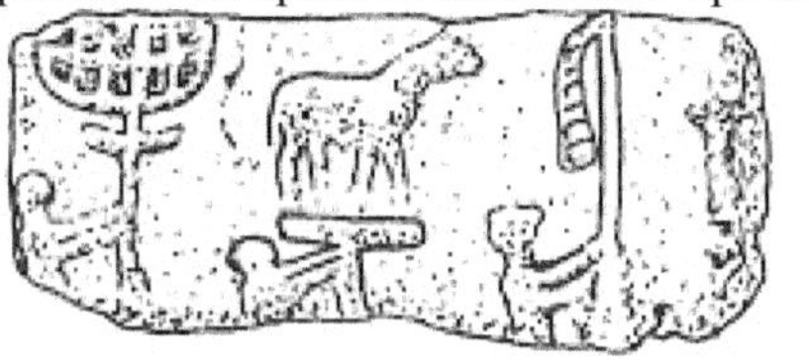

rebus: *eraka* 'moltencast (metal)'.

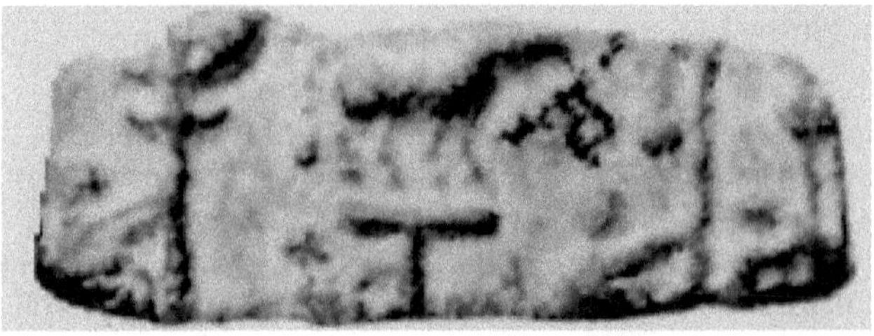 m0490, m0491

Two Mohenjo-daro tablets showing a procession of four standard bearers; the four standards are: lathe, one-horned young bull; scarf; spoked-circle (knave + spokes). All four are hieroglyphs in procession, read rebus related to lapidary/smith turner work on metals and minerals (*eraka* 'copper', *āra* 'brass', *dhatu* 'ores') *eraka* 'nave of wheel' rebus: *erako* 'moltencast, copper' *dhatu* 'scarf' rebus: *dhatu* 'mineral' *kundar* 'one-horned young bull' rebus: *kundar* 'turner' koḍiya 'young bull' rebus: *koTiya* 'dhow, seafaring vessel' *sangaDa* 'lathe, brazier' rebus: सं-ग्रह *saṁgraha* 'a guardian , ruler , manager , arranger' R. BhP. *sangar* 'fortification'. The procession of four banners has been read rebus as mineral (stones) and metal alloys transacted on जांगड [*jāṅgaḍa*] 'goods on approval' basis.

A turner uses a lathe for turning. A turner is also a lapidary, a person who cuts, polishes, or engraves gems. In the context of metalwork, a turner is a blacksmith who forges and fabricates tools, implements, pots and pans. Tvastr of Rigveda is Visvākarma the smith. *Tuatha Dé* among the celts and *Tuisto* the founder of Germanic people may be related to this expression Tvastr of Rigveda.

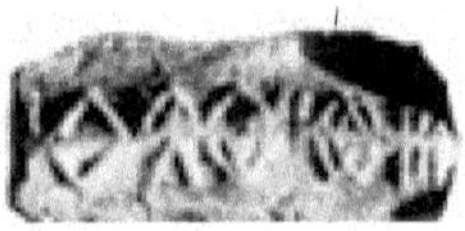

Text 1605 on m0490 and m0491 tablets. The hieroglyphs read rebus denote the following specialist functions of the artisan guild: workshop (for) casting metals, gemstones, smithy working with alloys, kiln, guild.

1. *dula* 'pair' (i.e., two long linear strokes). Rebus: *dul* 'to cast metal in a mould' (Santali)

2. *karā̃* n. pl. 'wristlets, bangles' (Gujarati) Rebus: खडा [*khaḍā*] the gem or stone of a ring or trinket: a lump of hardened fæces or scybala: a nodule or lump gen. (Marathi)

3. *sal* stake, spike, splinter, thorn, difficulty (Hindi) Rebus: *sal* 'workshop' (Santali)

4. *kolmo* 'seeding, rice-plant'(Munda) Rebus: *kolimi* 'smithy' (Telugu) खोट [khōṭa] 'ingot, wedge'. Rebus: alloy (Marathi) That is, a smithy working with alloys.

5. *bhaṭa* -- m. 'soldier' (Pali) Rebus: *baṭa* = kiln (Santali); *baṭa* = a kind of iron (Gujarati) *bhaṭṭhī* f. 'kiln, distillery' (Gujarati)

6. *kanac* 'corner' Rebus: *kañcu* 'bronze' Altenative: *khū̃ṭ* f. 'corner, side') (Punjabi) Rebus: *khū̃ṭ* 'community, guild' (Mu.)

1. *dula* 'pair' (Kashmiri); *dula* दुल । युग्मम् m. a pair, a couple, esp. of two similar things (Rām. 966) *dul* 'cast (metal)' (Santali). *dul* 'to cast metal in a mould' (Santali) *dul meṛeḍ* cast iron (Mundari. Santali) Alternative: *taṭṭe* 'a thick bamboo or an areca-palm stem, split in two' (Ka.) (DEDR 3042) Rebus: *toṭxin, toṭ.*xn goldsmith (To.); *taṭṭāṉ* 'gold- or silver-smith' (Ta.); *taṭṭaravāḍu* 'gold- or silver-smith' (Te.); **ṭhaṭṭakāra* 'brass-worker' (Skt.)(CDIAL 5493). Thus, the glyph is decoded: *taṭṭara* 'worker in gold, brass'. Alternative: S. *jāṛo* m. ' twin ', L. P. *jāṛā* m.;

M.*jā̃ḍī* f. ' a double yoke '. (CDIAL 5091) Rebus: **jaḍati* ' joins, sets '. 1. Pk.*jaḍia* -- ' set (of jewels), joined '; K.*jarun* ' to set jewels ' (← Ind.); S.*jaṛaṇu* ' to join, rivet, set ',*jaṛa* f. ' rivet, boundary between two fields '; P.*jaṛāuṇā* ' to have fastened or set '; A. *zarāiba* ' to collect '; B.*jaṛāna* ' to set jewels, wrap round, entangle ',*jaṛ* ' heaped together '; Or.*jaṛibā* ' to unite '; OAw.*jaraï* ' sets jewels, bedecks '; H.*jaṛnā* ' to join, stick in, set ' (→ N.*jaṛnu* ' to set, be set '); OMarw.*jaṛāū* ' inlaid '; G.*jaṛvũ* ' to join, meet with, set jewels '; M.*jaḍṇẽ* ' to join, connect, inlay, be firmly established ',*jaṭṇẽ* ' to combine, confederate '. (CDIAL 5091)

2. *karā̃* n. pl. 'wristlets, bangles (Gujarati); S. karāī f. 'wrist' (CDIAL 2779). Rebus: *khār* खार् 'blacksmith' (Kashmiri) खडा [*khaḍā*] the gem or stone of a ring or trinket: a lump of hardened fæces or scybala: a nodule or lump gen. (Marathi)

3. *sal* stake, spike, splinter, thorn, difficulty (H.); Rebus: *sal* 'workshop' (Santali) Alternative: *aḍar* = splinter (Santali); rebus: *aduru* = native metal (Ka.) aduru = *gan.iyinda tegadu karagade iruva* aduru = ore taken from the mine and not subjected to melting in a furnace (Kannada. *Siddha_nti Subrahman.ya' Śastri's new interpretation of the Amarakośa,* Bangalore, Vicaradarpana Press, 1872, p. 330)

4. *kolmo* 'seeding, rice-plant'(Munda) rebus: *kolimi* 'smithy' (Telugu)

san:ghāḍo, saghaḍī (G.) = firepan; *saghaḍī, śaghaḍi* = a pot for holding fire (G.)[*cula_ sagaḍi_* portable hearth (G.)] *aguḍe* = brazier (Tu.) *san:gaḍa,* 'lathe, portable furnace'; Rebus: सं-ग्रह *saṁgraha* 'a guardian , ruler , manager , arranger' R. BhP. sãgo m. 'caravan' (S.) *sangath* संगथ् association, living together, partnership (Kashmiri); battle; *jangaḍiyo* 'military guard who accompanies treasure into the treasury'; *san:ghāḍiyo*, a worker on a lathe (Gujarati) sangar 'fortification'.

eraka 'nave of wheel' Rebus: moltencast copper
dhatu 'scarf' Rebus: mineral ore dhāū, dhāv m.f. 'a partic. soft red stone' (Marathi) (whence *dhā̆vaḍ* m. 'a caste of iron -- smelters', *dhāvḍī* ' composed of or relating to iron ')
kōnda 'young bull' Rebus: turner
sãgaḍ 'lathe' Rebus: *sangara* 'proclamation'. सं-ग्रह *saṁgraha* 'a guardian , ruler , manager , arranger' R. BhP.

kanga 'portable brazier' Rebus: fireplace, furnace

The procession seen on m0491 tablet is emphatic evidence linking the brazier hieroglyph with the *dhā̆vaḍ* m. 'a caste of iron -- smelters', *dhāvḍī* ' composed of or relating to iron ').

Two Mohenjo-daro tablets showing a procession of four standard bearers; the four standards are: lathe, one-horned young bull; scarf; spoked-circle (knave + spokes). All four are hieroglyphs read rebus related to lapidary/smith turner work on metals and minerals (*eraka* 'coppr', *āra* 'brass', *dhatu* 'ores')

Rakhigarhi seal and bronze metal implements

Supercargo consignment documented by this metalwork catalogue on Rakhigarhi seal is: metal (alloy) swords, metal cast ingots, metal (alloy) implements कुटिल *kuṭila, katthīl* (8 parts copper, 2 parts tin), i.e. bronze implements.

Rakhigarhi seal

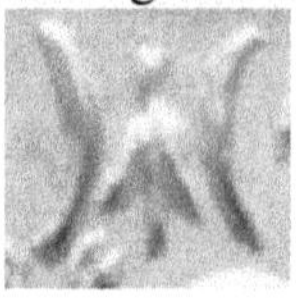

Hieroglyph-multiplex on Rakhigarhi seal.

On the Rakhigarhi seal, a fine distinction is made between two orthographic options for signifying an arrow with fine pronunciation variants, to distinguish between an arrowhead and an arrow: *kāṇḍa, kāṇḍa*. The word kāṇḍa is used by Panini in an expression ayaskāṇḍa to denote a quantity of iron, excellent iron (Pāṇ.gaṇ) i.e., metal (iron/copper alloy). This expression *ayas+ kāṇḍa* अयस्--काण्ड is signified by hieroglyphs: *aya* 'fish' PLUS *kāṇḍa*, 'arrow' as shown on Kalibangan Seal 032. An allograph for this hieroglyph 'arrowhead' is *gaṇḍa* 'four' (short strokes) as seen on Mohenjo-daro seal M1118.

Rebus: *ayaskāṇḍa* 'a quantity of iron, excellent iron' (Pāṇ.gaṇ) aya = iron (G.); ayah, ayas = metal (Skt.)

Thus, the arrowhead is signified by the hieroglyph which distinguishes the arrowhead as a triangle attached to a reedpost or handle of tool/weapon.

As distinct from this orthographic representation of 'arrowhead' with a triangle PLUS attached linear stroke, an arrow is signified by an angle ^ (Caret; Circumflex accent; Up arrow) with a linear stroke ligatured, as in the Rakhigarhi seal. To reinforce the distinction between 'arrow' and 'arrowhead' in Harappa script orthography, a notch is added atop the tip of the circumflex accent. Both the hieroglyph-components are attested in Bharata sprachbund with a variant pronunciation: *khaṇḍa*. खाडा [*kāṇḍā*] m A jag, notch, or indentation (as upon the edge of a tool or weapon) (Marathi)

It is thus clear that the morpheme kāṇḍa denotes an arrowhead, while the ^ circumflex accent hieroglyph is intended to signify rebus: *kāṇḍā* 'edge of tool or weapon' or a sharp edged implement, like a sword. In Bharata sprachbund, the word which denotes a sword is *khaṁḍa* -- m. 'sword'(Prakritam).

Two parenthesis: *dula* 'two' rebus: *dul* 'metal casting' PLUS *kuṭi* '**curve**; rebus: कुटिल *kuṭila, katthīl* bronze alloy (8 parts copper, 2 parts tin).

In the hieroglyph-multiplex of Rakhigarhi seal inscription, the left and right parentheses are used as circumscript to provide phonetic determination of the gloss: *khaṁḍa* -- m. 'sword' (Prakritam), while the ligaturing element of 'notch' is intended to signify खाडा [*kāṇḍā*] 'A jag, notch, or indentation (as upon the edge of a tool or weapon)' Rebus: *kāṇḍa* 'implements, furnace' (Santali).

Thus, the hieroglyph-multiplex is read rebus as *kāṇḍa* 'implements, furnace' PLUS *khaṁḍa* 'sword'. The supercargo is thus catalogued on the seal as: 1. arrowheads; 2. metal implements and ingots; 3. swords.

The hieroglyph 'rhinoceros is: *kāṇḍa* rebus: *kāṇḍa* 'implements/weapons'.
The entire inscription or metalwork catalogue message on Rakhigarhi seal can be deciphered:

kāṇḍa 'implements/weapons' (Rhinoceros) PLUS खाडा [*kāṇḍā*] 'weapons' PLUS mūhā 'cast ingots' (Left and Right parentheses as split rhombus or ellipse).

Guild, community of smiths and masons evolves into Harosheth Hagoyim, 'a smithy of nations'

Bharata-standard coinage of Menander I with an eight-spoked wheel and a palm of victory on the reverse (British Museum). The 'palm' evokes the spike shown on Tukulti-Ninurta fire-altar frieze (which is a rebus) of his ancestor's worship of fire-god *karaṇḍa,* 'fire-god' (Remo spoken by Bonda people of Odisha).

Votive altar depicting King Tukulti-Ninurta I in prayer between two gods holding wooden standards. Assyrian civilization, 13th century BCE. I suggest that the first hieroglyph carried on Mohenjo-daro standard of professionals in procession is a post with a spoked-wheel.

This flagpost topped by a spoked-wheel (as on Tukulti Ninurta altar) could be the first flagpost carried on the procession of Mohenjo-daro artisans. *āra* 'spokes' Rebus: *āra* 'bronze', *eraka* 'nave of wheel' Rebus: *eraka* 'copper', *eraka* 'moltencast'(Tulu). Thus, signifying 'metalcaster'

Safflower hieroglyph adorns one side of Tukulti-Ninurta I

altar: करडी [*karaḍī*] f (See करडई) Safflower: also its seed. Rebus: *karaḍa* 'hard alloy' of arka 'copper'. Rebus: fire-god: Remo <*karandi* ``fire-god".(Munda). The safflower hieroglyph shown on Tukulti-Ninurta altar is also found on flower ornament of jewellery.

Kunal, silver ornaments. Safflower-shaped hieroglyph is shown on the top left. safflower *karaḍī* as fire-god *karandi.*

From the stone reliefs of Ashurnasirpal II. Wrist with a safflower bracelet: safflower *karaḍī* as fire-god *karandi*

The Sumerian Princess

Pu'abi or Shab'ad "The Sumerian princess" : Jewelry and headdress of gold and imported precious stones such as carnelian and lapis lazuli from India and Afghanistan. From the Royal Cemetery of Ur. Early Dynastic, ca. 2400 BC. The National Museum of Iraq – Baghdad

Head-dress found in the tomb of Puabi: safflower *karaḍī* as fire-god *karandi*

Uruk seal impression showing safflower hieroglyph: safflower *karaḍī* as fire-god *karandi*

A goat standing on its hind legs eating the leaves of a tree. safflower *karaḍī* as fire-god *karandi*

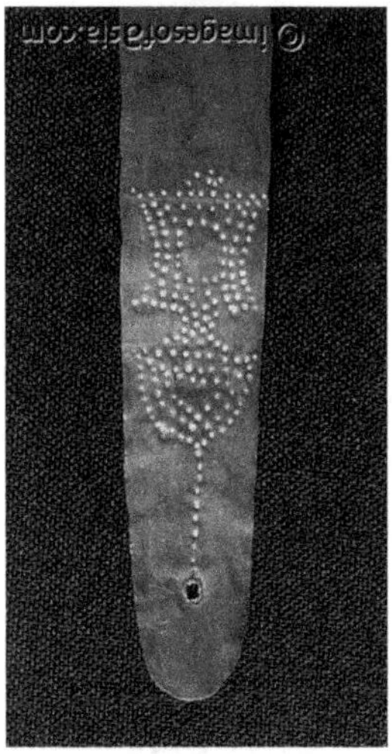 

Pict-91 (Mahadevan) m0490At m0490B Mohenjodaro Tablet showing Meluhha combined standard of three standards carried in a procession, Gold fillet. Punctuated design on both ends. Mohenjodaro.288

Carved ivory standard in the middle

  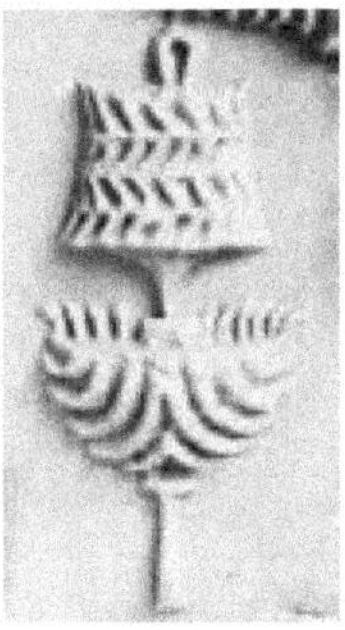 

Mohenjo-daro seal m008 and variants of flagposts on Meluhha standard.

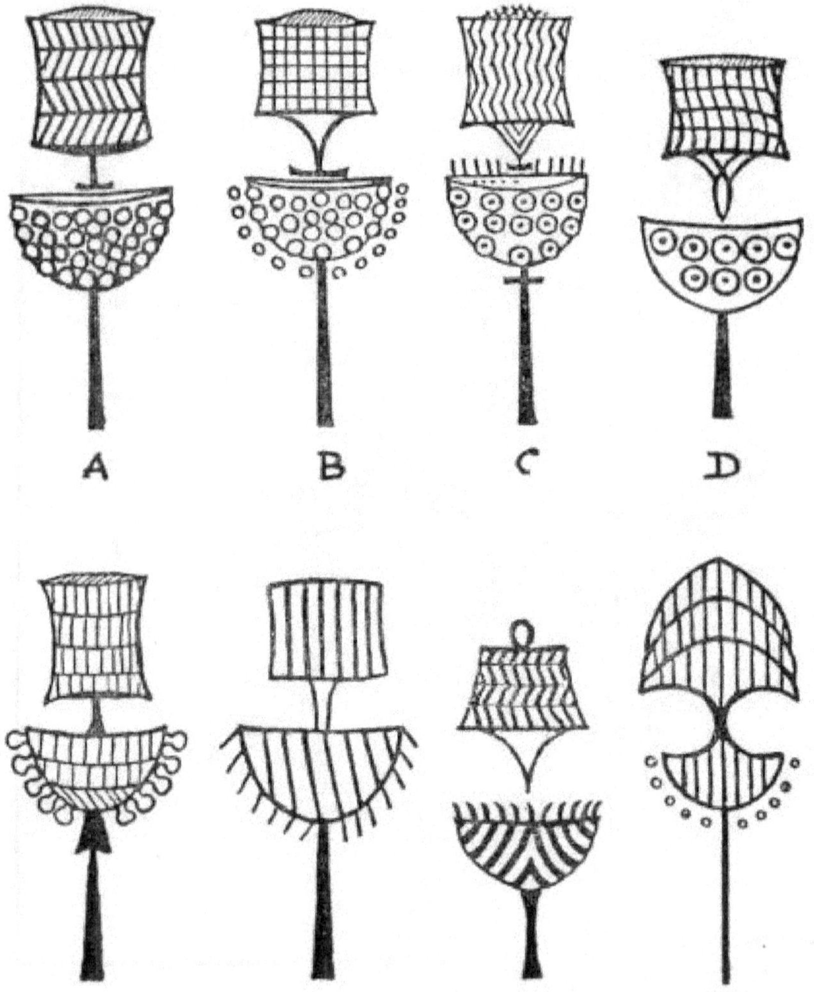
A
B
C
D
E
F
G
H

h739B & A (Standard device; obverse: tree)

Chalcolithic scepter with ibex and ram's heads. The standard has a hole at the top of the tube.

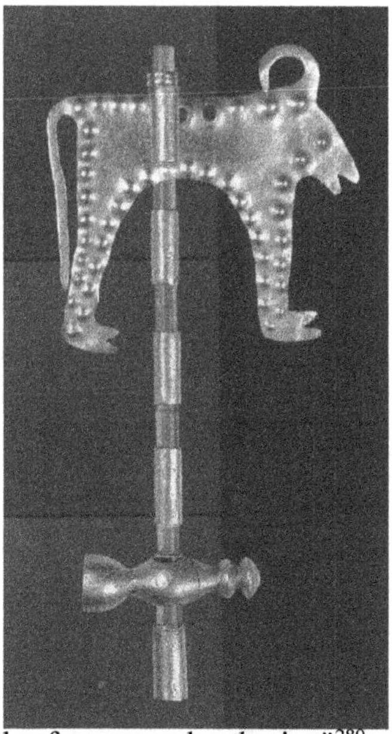

Veneration of ancestors (Varna), Processions of metalware

A remarkable object from Varna indicates the possible function served by the 'scepters" of Nahal Mishmar. Possibly, the scepters were held aloft by standard bearers as shown on Mohenjo-daro procession of standards. "In 1972, during excavations at the Chalcolithic necropolis of a settlement dating to the end of the fifth millennium BC near the present-day city of Varna on the Black Sea coast, archaeologists revealed traces of a civilization equal to that of Egypt and Mesopotamia. During the digs many tombs were found with over 300 objects made of pure gold - scepters, axes, bracelets, other decorative pieces, bull-shaped plates. Most amazing is the sepulcher of a ruler/high priest with a gold scepter and a set of gold regalia, symbols of power and authority."[289]

Hollow scepters. Copper. Nahal Mishmar hoard. Such hollow scepters could have held the standards shown on a processio on Mohenjo-daro tablets.

sangaḍa 'lathe' Rebus: *jangaḍa* 'entrustment articles'. Rebus 2: *samgara* 'living in the same house, guild', *sangar* 'fortified place' (Pushto). L. *sãgaṛh* m. 'line of entrenchments, stone walls for defence '.(CDIAL 12845) Hence, smith guild in a fortification, which is a characteristic architectural feature of hundreds of civilization sites. सं-ग्रह *saṁgraha* 'a guardian , ruler , manager , arranger' R. BhP.

khoṇḍ 'young bull-calf' read rebus *khuṇḍ* '(metal) turner'. Rebus 1: *kǒṇḍu, konḍu* कुण्डम् m. a hole dug in the ground for receiving consecrated fire (Kashmiri) Rebus 2*: A. kundār, B. kũdār, °ri, Or. kundāru; H.* kũderā m. ' one who works a lathe, one who scrapes ', °rī f., *kũdernā* ' to scrape, plane, round on a lathe '.(CDIAL 3297).

dhatu 'scarf'; rebus: 'cast mineral' (Santali); (cf. H. *dhāṛnā* 'to send out, pour out, cast metal)

eraka 'nave-of-wheel', 'moltencast, copper'; *arā* 'spokes', *āra* 'brass'. Rebus: *eraka, era, era* = syn. *erka,* 'copper, weapons' (Kannada). This hieroglyph also occurs on Tikulti-Ninurta altar, together with another hieroglyph, 'safflower' karaḍa (Allograph: करण्ड m. a sort of duck L. కారండవము (p. 274) [*kāraṇḍavamu*] *kāraṇḍavamu.* [Skt.] n. A sort of duck. (Telugu) karaṭa1 m. ' crow ' BhP., °aka -- m. lex. [Cf. *karaṭu* -- , *karkaṭu* -- m. ' Numidian crane ', *karēṭu* -- , *°ēṭavya* -- , *°ēḍuka* -- m. lex., *karaṇḍa2* -- m. ' duck ' lex: see kāraṇḍava --]Pk. *karaḍa* -- m. ' crow ', *°ḍā* -- f. ' a partic. kind of bird '; S. *karaṛa -- ḍhĩgu* m. ' a very large aquatic bird '; L. *karṛā* m., °ṛī f. ' the common teal'(CDIAL 2787) Rebus: *karaḍā* 'hard alloy'

Later 4th millennium BCECrown, copper, lost wax technique, from the Cave of the Treasure (Nahal

Mishmar) Judean Desert.

Crown of Nahal Mishmar hoard with Harappa Script hieroglyphs. 4th millennium BCE. *kole.l* 'temple' Rebus: kole.l 'smithy'. ***karaḍā*** 'aquatic bird' Rebus: *karaḍā* 'hard alloy of copper, tin, zinc'.

khuṇṭa 'peg'; *khũṭi* = pin (M.) rebus: *kuṭi*= furnace (Santali) *kūṭa* 'workshop' kuṇḍamu 'a pit for receiving and preserving consecrated fire' *khũṭ* 'community, guild' (Mu.)

The hoard was made up mainly of copper objects, 240 mace heads, 80 sceptres and 10 crowns, probably from the sanctuary at Ein Geddi. Collections of IDAM.[290]

Were the 240 maceheads carried on staff to signify maces? I suggest that almost all Nahal Mishmar metal artifacts are utsava bera, hieroglyphs carried in processions to proclaim the metallurgical competence of the guild of artisans indicating the types of metal products available for barter, trade exchanges.

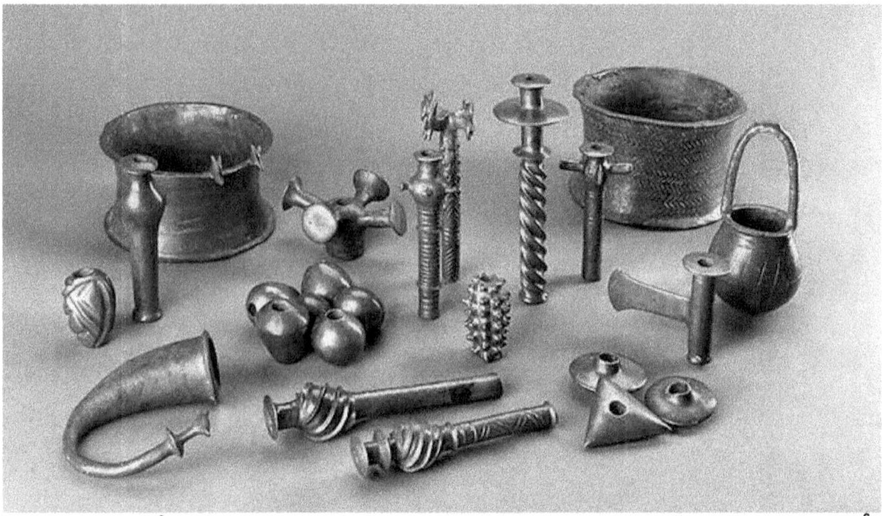

Hieroglyphs: బేరము [*bēramu*] *bēramu* [Skt.] n. An image. ప్రతిమ. "పంకములోని హైమబేరము." పర. v.பேரம்[2] *pēram,* n. < *bēra*. 1. Form, shape; வடிவம். (நன். 273, மயிலை.) 2. Body; உடம்பு. 3. Idol; விக்கிரகம். உத்ஸவபேரம் *uṟcava-pēram*, n. < *ut-sava* + *bēra*. Idol taken out in processions; உற்சவ விக்கிரகம். Loc. யாகபேரம் *yāka-pēram*, n. < id. + *bēra.* The idol that presides over the sacrificial hall of a temple; கோயிலுள் யாகசாலைக்குரிய மூர்த்தி. Loc.

Rebus: బేరము *[bēramu] bēramu*. [Tel.] n. Trade, dealing, a bargain, బేరముసారము

or బేరసారము trade, &c. (సారము being a mere expletive.) బేరకాడు *bēra-kāḍu*. n. One who makes a bargain, a purchaser, buyer. కొనువాడు, బేరమాడువాడు. బేరకత్తె *bēra-katte*. n. A woman who bargains or purchases. బేరమాడు or బేరముచేయు *bēram-āḍu*. v. n. To bargain. బేరముపోవు to go on a trading journey. బేరి *bēri.* n. A man of the Beri or merchant caste. பேரம்[1] *pēram*, n. < Pkt. *bēra*. [*T. bēramu, K. bēra*.] 1. Sale, trade; விற்பனை. 2. Bargaining, higgling and haggling; ஒப்பந்தத்திற்குமுன் பேசும் விலைப்பேச்சு. பேரஞ்சொல்லாமற்கறாராகச் சொல்லு. 3. High value; கிராக்கி.

Susa panels.

These Susa panels of molded bricks were used to decorate the facade of the exterior temple on the Susa hill. This monument, dedicated to royal worship under the

Shutrukid dynasty, was commissioned by the kings of this dynasty. Begun by Kuṭir-Nahunte (c. 1710 BCE), the work was completed by Shilhak-Inshushinak. The panels feature alternating figures of bull-men protecting a palm tree and Lama goddesses, also considered as protective divinities. *khōli* f. ' quiver ' lex.P. *khol* f. ' sheath, case '; Ku. *khol* ' covering '; N. *khol* ' sheath ', B. *khol*, °*lā*; Or. *khoḷi* ' quiver ', °*ḷā* ' sheath ', H. *khol* m.; -- G. *khoḷiyũ* n. ' quilt '; M. *khoḷ* m.f. ' pillowcase, mattress cover '.(CDIAL 3944) rebus: kol 'working in iron'. ढांगर [*ḍhāṅgara*] n 'A stout stake or stick as a prop to a Vine or scandent shrub]' (Marathi); rebus: *ḍhaṅgar* 'smith' (Maithili. Hindi)

Panels of molded bricks Mid 12th century BCE Apadana mound, Susa Baked clay

H. 1.355 m; W. 0.375 m Excavations led by Roland de Mecquenem 1913¿21; panels sb19575¿19577 were restored thanks to the Philip Morris Jury Prize, 1991

Sb 2732, Sb 2733, Sb 2734, Sb 2735, Sb 14390, Sb 14391, Sb 19575, Sb 19576, Sb 19577

A Meluhha village was locted in Lagash (Southwestern Mesopotamia) with a port city Guabba which had the temple of Nin-mar.[291]

crocodile, buffalo, elephant, rhinoceros in procession.

Processions of animals shown on Ancient Near East artifacts and Harappa Script inscriptions.

गौरीर्मिमाय सलिलानि तक्षत्येकपदी द्विपदी सा चतुष्पदी |
अष्टापदी नवपदी बभूवुषी सहस्राक्षरा परमे व्योमन् || **41** ||
तस्याः समुद्रा अधि वि क्षरन्ति तेन जीवन्ति प्रदिशश्चतस्रः |
ततः क्षरत्यक्षरं तद्विश्वमुप जीवति || **42** ||

Griffith translation: RV 1.164.41-42: 41 Forming the water-floods, the buffalo hath lowed, one-footed or two-footed or fourfooted, she, Who hath become eight-footed or hath got nine feet, the thou sand-syllabled in the sublimest heaven. [42] From her descend in streams the seas of water; thereby the world's four regions have their being, Thence flows the imperishable flood and thence the universe hath life.

karā 'crocodile' (Telugu). Rebus: *khāra* 'blacksmith' (Kashmiri) rango, 'buffalo' rebus: rango 'pewter'; karba, ibha 'elephant' rebus: karba, ib 'iron' kaṇḍa 'rhinoceros' rebus: khāṇḍa 'implements'.

h1973B h1974B Two tablets. One side shows a person seated on a tree branch, a tiger looking up, a crocodile on the top register and other animals in procession in the bottom register.

Glyph: seven: *eae* 'seven' (Santali); rebus: *eh-ku* 'steel' (Ta.)

खांडा [*khāṇḍā*] m A jag, notch, or indentation (as upon the edge of a tool or weapon). Rebus: *khāṇḍa* 'tools, pots and pans, and metal-ware'. Alternative: *aṭar* 'a splinter' (Ma.) *aṭaruka* 'to burst, crack, sli off,fly open; *aṭarcca* ' splitting, a crack'; *aṭarttuka* 'to split, tear off, open (an oyster) (Ma.); *aḍaruni* 'to crack' (Tu.) (DEDR 66) Rebus: *aduru* 'native, unsmelted metal' (Kannada)

Alternative: *sal* 'splinter' Rebus: sal 'artisan's workshop'. *kanac* 'corner' rebus: *kancu* 'bronze'

dAl 'slant' rebus: *dhALa* 'ingot' *PLUS ayo* 'fish' Rebus: *ayas* 'metal' PLUS *kāṇḍa* 'arrow' Rebus: *khāṇḍa* 'tools, pots and pans, and metal-ware'. ayaskāṇḍa is a compounde word attested in Panini. The compound or glyphs of fish + arrow may denote ingots, metalware tools, pots and pans. gaṇḍa 'four' rebus: knda 'fire-altar' PLUS kolom 'three' rebus: kolimi 'smithy, forge'. Thus a smithy furnace.

Thus the message conveyed by the text is that the metalware -- ayaskāṇḍa -- is of guild, bronze workshop -- kancu sal.
Hieroglyphs on side B: *karā* 'crocodile' (Telugu). Rebus: *khāra* 'blacksmith' (Kashmiri)

Lion and Bull, Iran, 1500-1000 BC. bronze, cast, Cleveland Museum of Art. Combining the strength of the lion and the fertility of the bull, this creature must have served as an object of worship in a temple or shrine. kola 'tiger' rebus: kol 'working in iron' barad, balad 'ox' rebus: bharata 'alloy of copper, pewter, tin'.[292]

m0308 Mohenjodaro seal. Person grappling with two flanking tigers standing and rearing on their hindlegs. Comparable to the Mesopotamian cylinder seal (BM 89538), this Indus seal depicts a person with six hair-knots. kaṇṇahāra -- m. 'helmsman, sailor'. (काण *kāṇa* 'one-eyed', *āra* 'six', 'rings of hair' symbolic forms). *kannār* 'coppersmiths'; kan 'copper'. baTa 'six' rebus: bhaTa 'furnace'

Set 1: crocodile + person with foot on head of animal + spearing + bison + horned (with twig) seated person in penance

Plano convex molded tablet showing an individual spearing a water buffalo with one foot pressing the head down and one arm holding the tip of a horn. A gharial is depicted above the sacrifice scene and a figure seated in yogic position, wearing a horned headdress, looks on. The horned headdress has a branch with three prongs or leaves emerging from the center.

h1971B Harappa. Three tablets with identical glyphic compositions on both sides: h1970, h1971 and h1972. Seated figure or deity with reed house or shrine at one side. Left: H95-2524; Right: H95-2487.

Harappa. Planoconvex molded tablet found on Mound ET. A. Reverse. a female deity battling two tigers and standing above an elephant and below a six-spoked wheel; b. Obverse. A person spearing with a barbed spear a buffalo in front of a seated horned deity wearing bangles and with a plumeḍ headdress. The person presses his foot down the buffalo's head. An alligator with a narrow snout is on the top register. "We have found two other broken tablets at Harappa that appear to have been made from the same mold that was used to create the scene of a deity battling two tigers and standing above an elephant. One was found in a room located on the southern slope of Mount ET in 1996 and another example comes from excavations on Mound F in the 1930s. However, the flat obverse of both of these broken tablets does not show the spearing of a buffalo, rather it depicts the more well-known scene showing a tiger looking back over its shoulder at a person sitting on the branch of a tree. Several other flat or twisted rectangular terracotta tablets found at Harappa combine these two narrative scenes of a figure strangling two tigers on one side of a tablet, and the tiger looking back over its shoulder at a figure in a tree on the other side." (JM Kenoyer, 1998, Ancient cities of the Indus Valley, Oxford University Press, p. 115.)

Set 2: crocodile + person seated on branch of tree + tiger looking back and up + rhinoceros + tiger in processio

Molded terracotta tablet (H2001-5075/2922-01) with a narrative scene of a man in a tree with a tiger looking back over its shoulder.

Comparable are hieoroglyphs of jackals appear where tigers are normally shown on a tablet h1971B Harappa. Three tablets with identical glyphic compositions on both sides: h1970, h1971 and h1972. Seated figure or deity with reed house or shrine at one side. Left: H95-2524; Right: H95-2487. Planoconvex molded tablet found on Mound ET. Reverse. a female deity battling two tigers and standing above an elephant and below a six-spoked wheel.

h1973B h1974B Harappa Two tablets. One side shows a person seated on a tree branch, a tiger looking up, a crocodile on the top register and other animals in procession in the bottom register. Obverse side (comparable to h1970, h1971 and h1972) shows an elephant, a person strangling two tigers (jackals or foxes) and a six-spoked wheel.

Stone vase from Mesopotamia

Late Uruk period, about 3400-3200 BCE. Ht. 1.2 cm. It shows a bull, goat and ram.

dhangar 'bull' rebus: *dhangar* 'blacksmith'

meNDha 'ram' rebus: meḍ 'iron'

melh 'goat' rebus: milakkhu 'copper'.

Akkadian cylinder seal, showing kneeling heroes. Around 2200 BCE.Cylinder seal with kneeling nude heroes, ca. 2220–2159 b.c.; Akkadian Mesopotamia Red jasper H. 1 1/8 in. (2.8 cm), Diam. 5/8 in. (1.6 cm) Metropolitan Museum of Art - USA

Red jasper H. 1 1/8 in. (2.8 cm), Diam. 5/8 in. (1.6 cm) cylinder Seal with four hieroglyphs and four kneeling persons (with six curls on their hair) holding flagposts, c. 2220-2159 B.C.E., Akkadian (Metropolitan Museum of Art) Cylinder Seal (with modern impression). The four hieroglyphs are: from l. to r. 1. crucible PLUS storage pot of ingots, 2. sun, 3. narrow-necked pot with overflowing water, 4. fish A hooded snake is on the edge of the composition. (The dark red color of jasper reinforces the semantics: eruvai 'dark red, copper' Hieroglyph: *eruvai* 'reed'; see four reedposts held. Six culs: meḍh 'curl' rebus: meḍ 'iron' baTa 'six' rebus: bhaTa 'furnace'. Thus, iron furnace (artisan). *koThAri* 'crucible' Rebus: *koThAri* 'treasurer, warehouse'

The leftmost hieroglyph shows ingots in a conical-bottom storage jar (similar to the jar shown on Warka vase (See Annex: Warka vase), delivering the ingots to the temple of Inanna). Third from left, the overflowing pot is similar to the hieroglyph shown on Gudea statues. Fourth from left, the fish hieroglyph is similar to the one shown on a Susa pot containing metal tools and weapons. (See Susa pot hieroglyphs of bird and fish: Louvre Museum) Hieroglyph: meṇḍā 'lump, clot' (Oriya)

If the hieroglyph on the leftmost is moon, a possible rebus reading: قمر ḳamar

A قمر *ḳamar,* s.m. (9th) The moon. Sing. and Pl. See سپوږمي or سپوګمي (Pashto) Rebus: *kamar* 'blacksmith'

Four flag-posts(reeds) with rings on top held by the kneeling persons define the four components of the iron smithy/forge. This is an announcement of four shops, पेढी (Gujarati. Marathi). पेंढें 'rings Rebus: पेढी 'shop'. *āra* 'serpent' Rebus; *āra* 'brass'. *karaḍa* 'double-drum' Rebus: *karaḍa* 'hard alloy'.

Specific materials offered for sale/exchange in the shop are: hard alloy brass metal (*ayo*, fish); *lokhaṇḍ* (overflowing pot) 'metal tools, pots and pans, metalware'; *arka* 'sun' rebus: *arka/erka* 'copper'; *kammaṭa* (a portable furnace for melting precious metals) 'coiner, mint' Thus, the four shops are: 1. brass alloys, 2. metalware, 3. copper and 4. mint (services).

erãguḍu bowing, salutation (Telugu) iṟai (-v-, -nt-) to bow before (as in salutation), worship (Tamil)(DEDR 516). Rebus: *eraka, eṟaka* any metal infusion (Kannada.Tulu) *eruvai* 'copper' (Tamil); *ere* dark red (Kannada)(DEDR 446).

puṭa Anything folded or doubled so as to form a cup or concavity; crucible. Alternative: ḍhālako = a large metal ingot (G.) ḍhālakī = a metal heated and poured into a mould; a solid piece of metal; an ingot (Gujarati)

Allograph: ढाल [*ḍhāla*] f (S through H) The grand flag of an army directing its march and encampments: also the standard or banner of a chieftain: also a flag flying on forts &c. ढालकाठी [*ḍhālakāṭhī*] f ढालखांब m A flagstaff; esp.the pole for a grand flag or standard. 2 fig. The leading and sustaining member of a household or other commonwealth. 5583 *ḍhāla* n. ' shield ' lex. 2. **ḍhāllā* -- . 1. Tir. (Leech) "*dàl*" ' shield ', *Bshk. ḍāl, Ku. ḍhāl, gng. ḍhāw, N. A. B. ḍhāl, Or. ḍhāḷa, Mth. H. ḍhāl m.2.* Sh. *ḍal (pl. °lẹ)* f., *K. ḍāl f., S. ḍhāla, L. ḍhāl (pl. °lā) f., P. ḍhāl f., G. M. ḍhāl f. WPah.kṭg. (kc.) ḍhā`l f. (obl. -- a) ' shield ' (a word used in salutation), J. ḍhāl* f. (CDIAL 5583).

kamaṭha m. ' bamboo ' lex. 2. *kāmaṭha -- . 3. *kāmāṭṭha -- . 4. *kammaṭha -- . 5. *kammaṭṭha -- . 6. *kambāṭha -- . 7. *kambiṭṭha -- . [Cf. kambi -- ' shoot of bamboo ', *kārmuka* -- 2 n. ' bow ' Mn., ' bamboo ' lex. which may therefore belong here rather than tokr̥múka -- . Certainly ← Austro -- as. PMWS 33 with lit. -- See kāca -- 3]
1. Pk. *kamaḍha* -- , *°aya* -- m. ' bamboo '; Bhoj. *kōro* ' bamboo poles '.
2. N. *kāmro* ' bamboo, lath, piece of wood ', OAw. *kāṁvari* ' bamboo pole with slings at each end for carrying things ', H. *kā̃war*, *°ar*, *kāwaṛ*,*°ar* f., G. *kāvaṛ* f., M. *kāvaḍ* f.; -- deriv. Pk. *kāvaḍia* -- , *kavvāḍia* -- m. ' one who carries a yoke ', H. *kā̃waṛī*, *°ṛiyā* m., G. *kāvaṛiyɔ* m.3. S. *kāvāṭhī* f. ' carrying pole ', *kāvāṭhyo* m. ' the man who carries it '.
4. Or. *kāmaṛā*, *°muṛā* ' rafters of a thatched house '; G. *kāmṛũ* n., *°ṛī* f. ' chip of bamboo ', *kāmaṛ -- koṭiyũ* n. ' bamboo hut '. 5. B. *kāmṭhā* ' bow ', G. *kāmṭhũ* n., *°ṭhī* f. ' bow '; M. *kamṭhā*, *°ṭā* m. ' bow of bamboo or horn '; -- deriv. G. *kāmṭhiyɔ* m. ' archer '.6. A. *kabāri* ' flat piece of bamboo used in smoothing an earthen image '.
7. M. *kā̃bīṭ*, *°baṭ*, *°bṭī*, *kāmīṭ*, *°maṭ*, *°mṭī*, *kāmṭhī*, *kāmāṭhī* f. ' split piece of bamboo &c., lath '. (CDIAL 2760). *kambi* f. ' branch or shoot of bamboo ' lex. *Pk. kaṁbi -- , °bī -- , °bā -- f. ' stick, twig ', OG. kāṁba; M. kā̃b* f. ' longitudinal division of a bamboo &c., bar of iron or other metal '. (CDIAL 2774). कंबडी [*kambaḍī*] f A slip or split piece (of a bamboo &c.)(Marathi) Rebus: kammata 'mint, coiner, coinage'.

The rings atop the reed standard: पेंढें [*pēṇḍhēṃ*] पेंडकें [*pēṇḍakēṃ*] n Weaver's term. A cord-loop or metal ring (as attached to the गुलडा of the बैली and to certain other fixtures). पेंडें [*pēṇḍēṃ*] n (पेड) A necklace composed of strings of pearls. 2 A loop or ring. Rebus: पेढी (Gujaráthí word.) A shop (Marathi) Alternative: *koṭiyum* [*koṭ, koṭī* neck] a wooden circle put round the neck of an animal (Gujarati) Rebus: *ācāri koṭṭya*

= forge, kammārasāle (Tulu) koTiya 'dhow, seafaring vessel'.

The four hieroglyphs define the four quarters of the village smithy/forge: alloy, metalware, turner's lathe-work, crublc (or, ingot).

ayo 'fish' Rebus: ayo 'metal, alloy'

కాండము [*kāṇḍamu] kāṇḍamu.* [Skt.] n. Water. నీళ్లు (Telugu) *kaṇṭhá* -- : (b) ' water -- channel ': Paš. *kaṭā́* ' irrigation channel ', Shum. *xãṭṭä*. (CDIAL 14349). *lokhãḍ* 'overflowing pot' Rebus: 'tools, iron, ironware' (Gujarati)

*arká*1 m. ' flash, ray, sun ' RV. [√arc] Pa. Pk. *akka* -- m. ' sun ', *Mth. āk; Si. aka* ' lightning ', inscr. *vid -- äki* ' lightning flash '.(CDIAL 624) அருக்கன் *arukkaṉ, n.* < *arka*. Sun; சூரி யன். அருக்க னணிநிறமுங் கண்டேன் (திவ். இயற்.

3, 1).(Tamil) *agasāle* 'goldsmithy' (Kannada) *arkaasāli* = అగసాలి [*agasāli*] or అగసాలెవాడు *agasāli*. n. A goldsmith. కంసాలివాడు. (Telugu) *erka* = *ekke (Tbh. of arka) aka (Tbh. of arka)* copper (metal); crystal (Kannada) cf. eruvai = copper (Tamil) *eraka, er-aka* = any metal infusion (Ka.Tu.); *erako* molten cast (Tulu) Rebus: *eraka* = copper (Ka.) *eruvai* = copper (Ta.); *ere* - a dark-red colour (Ka.)(DEDR 817). *eraka, era, er-a* = *syn. erka*, copper, weapons (Ka.) erka = ekke (Tbh. of arka) aka (Tbh. of arka) copper (metal); crystal (Kannada) *akka, aka* (Tadbhava of *arka*) metal; *akka* metal (Te.) a*rka* = copper (Skt.) *erako* molten cast (Tulu)

Alternative: *kunda* 'jasmine flower' Rebus: *kunda* 'a turner's lathe'. *kundaṇa* pure gold.

The image could denote a crucible or a portable furnace: *kammaṭa* 'coiner, mint, a portable furnace for melting precious metals (Telugu) On some cylinder seals, this image is shown held aloft on a stick, comparable to the bottom register of the 'standard device' normally shown in front of a one-horned young bull.

Late Uruk and Jemdet Nasr seal; ca. 3200-3000 BC; serpentine; cat.1; boar and bull in procession; terminal: plant; heavily pitted surface beyond plant. *kaṇḍa* 'rhinocros' rebus: *khāṇḍa* 'implements' *ḍhangar* 'bull' rebus: *ḍhangar* 'smith' (Maithili. Hindi)

Unpierced cylindere seal with horned animals. Heulandite H. 1 7/8 in. (4.9 cm); dia. 1 1/8 in. (3 cm) Proto-Elamite period, ca. 3100-2900 BCE. Sb 2429 Holly Pittman notes: "The two files of creatures on this beautiful seal (Delaporte, 1920, pl. 26:7) include two types of horned mountain animals, probably goats, and mountain sheep, walking in a field of flowers."[293]

Hieroglyphs and rebus readings are: markhor, antelope, twigs. On the top register, between the two antelopes, a tiger is also signified.

Tor. miṇḍā'l 'markhor'. Rebus: meḍ 'copper'

ranku 'antelope' Rebus: *ranku* 'tin'

*dala*3 n. ' leaf, petal ' MBh. [Same as dala -- 2 EWA ii 24? -- √dal1?]
Pa. Pk. *dala* -- n. ' leaf, petal ', G. M. *daḷ* n. rebus: dhALa 'ingot'

kola 'tiger' Rebus: kol 'working in iron' kolle 'blacsmith' kol 'furnace, forge'

kuṭhI 'bunch of twigś Rebus: *kuṭh*i 'iron smelter'.

The U sign infixed within Sign 242 (which becomes Sign 243), could be bat.i 'broad-mouthed, rimless metal vessel'; rebus: bat.i 'smelting furnace'. The structural form within which this sign is enclosed may represent a temple: *kole.l* 'temple, smithy' (Ko.);*kolme* smithy' (Ka.)
Thus, the ligatured Sign 243 may be read as: *kolme bat.i*= smithy furnace.

kole.l smithy, temple in Kota village (Ko.); kwala.l Kota smithy (To.) (DEDR 2133).

m0295 Mohenjo-daro seal
cāli 'Interlocking bodies' (IL 3872) Rebus: *sal* 'workshop' (Santali) Hieroglyph of joined, interlocked bodies: *ca_li* (IL 3872); rebus: *śa_lika* (IL) village of artisans. cf. *sala_yisu* = joining of metal (Ka.)

Pict-61: Composite motif of three tigers

1386
kõdā 'to turn in a lathe' (Bengali) *sal* 'splinter'; sal 'workshop' (Santali)

kāḍ 2 काड् a man's length, the stature of a man (as a measure of length); rebus: kāḍ 'stone'; Ga. (Oll.) kanḍ , (S.) kanḍu (pl. kanḍkil) stone
kuṇḍ kanka 'rim of jar'; Rebus: karṇaka 'scribe'; *kaṇḍ* 'furnace, fire-altar'. Thus the ligatured Glyph is decoded: kaṇḍ*karṇaka* 'furnace scribe'
kole.l 'temple' rebus: smithy, in Kota village (Ko.) *kol* 'furnace, forge'

Thus, the message on the seal reads: *kõdā* sal 'turner's lathe '; *kāḍ* 'stone workshop'; *karṇaka* 'furnace scribe'; *kole.l*smithy, temple.

Obverse of m1395 and m0441 had the following images of a multi-headed tiger.

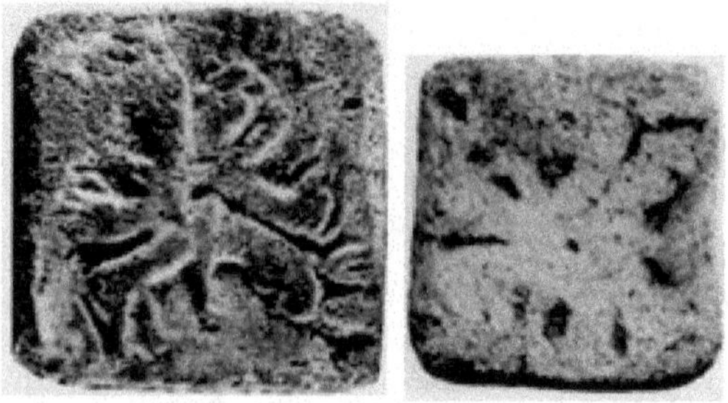

m2015, m0295

kola 'tiger' rebus: *kol* 'furnace, forge' *cāli* 'Interlocking bodies' (IL 3872) Rebus: *sal* 'workshop' (Santali) Hieroglyph of joined, interlocked bodies: *ca_li* (IL 3872); rebus: *śa_lika* (IL) village of artisans. cf. *sala_yisu* = joining of metal (Ka.)

Terracotta sealing from Mohenjo-daro depicting a collection of animals and some script

Hieroglyphs. Centrepiece is a scorpion, surrounded by a pair of oxen (bulls), rhinoceros, monkey, elephant, a tiger looking back, a stan

m1393t

m1394t

m440A

m0439t

m1395Bt t

m0441Bt ding person with spread legs. This hieroglyph cluster is duplicated on a six tablets.

m02015 A,B, m2016, m1393, m1394, m1395, m0295, m0439, m440, m0441 A,B On some tablets, such a glyphic composition (hypertext) is also accompanied (on obverse side, for example, cf. m2015A and m0295) with a glyphic of two or more joined tiger heads to a single body. In one inscription (m0295), the text inscriptions are also read.

bica 'scorpion' rebus: *bica* 'haematite, ferrite ore' *kola* 'tiger' rebus: *kol* 'furnace, forge' *kol* 'metal' PLUS *krammara* 'look back' rebus: *kamar* 'smith' *karabha* 'trunk of elephant' *ibha* 'elephant' rebus: karba 'iron' *ib* 'iron' ibbo 'merchant' *kaṇḍa* 'rhinoceros' rebus; *kaṇḍa* 'implements' *kuThAru* 'monkey' rebus: *kuThAru* 'armourer' *dula* 'two' rebus: *dul* 'metal casting' *dhangar* 'bull' rebus; *dhangar* 'blacksmith'.

Mohenjo-daro seal m417 six heads from a core.

Allographs to signify sangaḍa, 'lathe-brazier' rebus: सं-ग्रह *saṁgraha* 'a guardian , ruler , manager , arranger' R. BhP. *sangar* 'fortification' are: 1. *sangaḍa*, 'joined parts of animals and ' 2. *śãgal, śãgaḍ* 'chain' signified on m417 by using a chain to join six heads of animals. The hypertext added to this orthographic 'linking by a chain' six heads of animals is 'warrior' hieroglyph: *bhaṭa* 'warrior' Rebus: *bhaṭa* 'furnace.

Three heads of animals identified on m417 are: पोळ *pōḷa* 'zebu' rebus: पोळ *pōḷa* 'magnetite (a ferrite ore)'; barad, balad 'ox' rebus: *bharata* 'alloy of pewter, copper, tin'; *konda* 'young bull' rebus: *kõdār*, 'turner' – all rebus renderrings related to metalwork and work with furnace..

A phonetic determinant is the number of animal heads signified; the number is six: *bhaṭa* 'six' Rebus: *bhaṭa* 'furnace.

śãgal, śãgaḍ 'chain' (WPah.) *śr̥ṅkhala* m.n. ' chain ' MārkP., °lā -- f. VarBr̥S., *śr̥ṅkhalaka* -- m. ' chain ' MW., ' chained camel ' Pāṇ. [Similar ending in mḗkhalā --]Pa. *saṅkhalā* -- , *°likā* -- f. ' chain '; Pk. *saṁkala -- m.n., °lā* -- , *°lī* -- , *°liā* -- , *saṁkhalā* -- , *siṁkh°, siṁkalā* -- f. ' chain ', *siṁkhala* -- n. ' anklet '; Sh. *šăṅāḷi̯* f., (Lor.) *š*lṅāli, šiṅ°* ' chain ' (lw .with *š* -- < śr̥ --), K. hŏ̃kal f.; S. *saṅgharu* m. ' bell round animal's neck ', *°ra* f. ' chain, necklace ', *saṅghāra* f. ' chain, string of beads ' *saṅghirī* f. ' necklace with double row of beads '; L. *saṅglī* f. ' flock of bustard ', awāṇ. *saṅgul* ' chain '; P. *saṅgal* m. ' chain ', ludh. *suṅgal* m.; WPah.bhal. *śaṅgul* m. ' chain with which a soothsayer strikes himself ', *śaṅgli* f. ' chain ', *śiṅkhal* f. ' railing round a cow-stall ', (Joshi) *śãgaḷ* ' door -- chain ', jaun. *śãgal, śãgaḍ* ' chain '; Ku. *sãglo* ' doorchain ', gng. *śãṅaw* ' chain '; N. *sãṅlo* ' chain ', °li ' small do. ', A. *xikali*, OB. *siṅkala, B. sikal, sikli, chikal, chikli,* (Chittagong) *hĩol* ODBL 454, Or. *sãṅk(h)uḷā, °ḷi, sãṅkoḷi, sikaḷã̄, °ḷi, sikuḷā, °ḷi;* Bi. *sĩkaṛ* ' chains for pulling harrow ', Mth. sĩkaṛ; Bhoj. sĩkar, *sĩkarī* ' chain ', OH. sāṁkaḍa, sīkaḍa m., H. *sãkal, sãkar, °krī, saṅkal, °klī, sikal, sīkar, °krī* f.; OG. *sāṁkalu* n., G. *sãkaḷ, °kḷī* f. ' chain ', *sãkḷũ* n. ' wristlet '; M. *sãk(h)aḷ, sāk(h)aḷ, sãk(h)ḷī* f. ' chain ', Ko. *sāṁkaḷ*; Si. *säkilla, hä°, ä°* (st. *°ili* --) ' elephant chain '. *śr̥ṅkhalayati*. Addenda: *śr̥ṅkhala* -- : WPah.ktg. (kc.) *śáṅgəḷ* f. (obl. -- i) ' chain ', J. *śãgaḷ* f., Garh. *sãgaḷ. śr̥ṅkhalayati* ' enchains ' Das'. [*śr̥ṅkhala* --]

Ku.gng. *śãṅaī* ' intertwining of legs in wrestling ' (< *śr̥ṅkhalita* --); Or. *sāṅkuḷibā* ' to enchain '.(CDIAL 12580, 12581)சங்கிலி[1] *caṅkili,* n. < *šr̥ṅkhalā*. [M. *caṅ- kala.*] 1. Chain, link; தொடர். சங்கிலிபோ லீர்ப்புண்டு (சேதுபு. அகத். 12). 2. Land-measuring chain, Gunter's chain 22 yards long; அளவுச் சங்கிலி. (C. G.) 3. A superficial measure of dry land=3.64 acres; ஓர் நிலவளவு. (G. Tn. D. I, 239). 4. A chain-ornament of gold, inset with diamonds; வயிரச்சங்கிலி என்னும் அணி. சங்கிலி நுண்டொடர் (சிலப். 6, 99). 5. Hand-cuffs, fetters; விலங்கு.

Rebus: *Vajra Sanghāta* 'binding together': Mixture of 8 lead, 2 bell-metal, 1 iron rust constitute adamantine glue. (Allograph) Hieroglyph: *sãghāṛɔ* 'lathe'.(Gujarati) The chain hieroglyph component is a semantic determinant of the stylized 'standard device' *sā̃gaḍa*, 'lathe, portable brazier' used for making, say, crucible steel. Hence the circle with dots or blobs/globules signifying ingots. सं-ग्रह *saṁgraha* 'a guardian , ruler , manager , arranger' R. BhP.

Hieroglyphs chained:

1. Glyph: 'one-horned young bull': *kondh* 'heifer'. *kũdār* 'turner, brass-worker'.

kōḍu horn (Kannada. Tulu. Tamil) खोंड [*khōṇḍa*] m A young bull, a bullcalf. (Marathi) Rebus: कोंड [*kōṇḍa*] A circular hamlet; a division of a मौजा or village, composed generally of the huts of one caste. खोट [*khōṭa*] Alloyed--a metal (Marathi).

2. Glyph: 'bull': *ḍhangra* 'bull'. Rebus: *ḍhangar* 'blacksmith'.

3. Glyph: 'ram': *meḍh* 'ram'. Rebus: *meḍ* 'iron'

4. Glyph: 'antelope': *mr̤eka* 'goat'. Rebus: *milakkhu* 'copper'. Vikalpa 1: *meluhha* 'mleccha' 'copper worker'. Vikalpa 2: *meṛh* 'helper of merchant'.

5. pōḷa'zebu' rebus: pōḷa 'magnetite, ferrite ore'

6. The sixth animal can only be guessed. Perhaps, a tiger (A reasonable inference, because the glyph 'tiger' appears in a procession on some Harappa Script inscriptions. Glyph: 'tiger?': *kol* 'tiger'. Rebus: *kol* 'working in iron' 'furnce, forge'. Vikalpa (alternative): perhaps, rhinoceros. *gaṇḍa* 'rhinoceroś; rebus: *khaṇḍa* 'tools, pots and pans and metal-ware'.

Thus, the entire glyphic composition of six animals on the Mohenjo-daro seal m417 is semantically a representation of a *śrḗṇi,* 'guild', a khũṭ , 'community' of smiths and masons. पोळ *pōḷa*, 'zebu' rebus: पोळ *pōḷa*, 'magnetite, ferrite ore'

gōtrá n. ' cowpen, enclosure ' RV., ' family, clan ' ChUp., *gōtrā* -- f. ' herd of cows ' Pāṇ. 2. *gōtraka* -- n. ' family ' Yājñ. [gṓ --] 1. Pa. *gotta* -- n. ' clan ', Pk. *gotta* -- , *gutta* -- , amg. *gōya* -- n.; Gau. *gū* ' house ' (in Kaf. and Dard. several other words for ' cowpen ' > ' house ': *gōśrayaṇa -- , gōṣṭhá -- , *gōstha -- (?), ghōṣa --); Pr. *gū´ṭu* ' cow '; S. *goṭru* m. ' parentage ', L. *got* f. ' clan ', P. *gotar, got* f.; Ku. N. *got* ' family '; A. *got -- nāti* ' relatives '; B. *got* ' clan '; Or. *gota* ' family, relative '; Bhoj. H. *got* m. ' family, clan ', G. *got* n.; M. *got* ' clan, relatives '; -- Si. *gota* ' clan, family ' ← Pa.
2. B. H. *gotā* m. ' relative '.gōtrin -- ; sagōtra -- , *sāgōtriya -- ; *gōtragharaka -- ; mātr̥gōtra -- , *mātr̥ṣvasr̥gōtra -- .Addenda: *gōtrá* -- **:** Garh. *got* ' clan '; -- A. *goṭāiba* ' to collect '(CDIAL 4279).

This guild, community of smiths and masons evolves into Harosheth Hagoyim, 'a smithy of nations'.

It appears that the Meluhhas were in contact with many interaction areas, Dilmun and Susa (elam) in particular. There is evidence for Meluhha settlements outside of Meluhha. It is a reasonable inference that the Meluhhas with bronze-age expertise of creating arsenical and bronze alloys and working with other metals constituted the 'smithy of nations', Harosheth Hagoyim.

Pa. kōḍ (pl. kōḍul) horn; Ka. kōḍu horn, tusk, branch of a tree; kōr horn Tu. kōḍů, kōḍu horn Ko. kṛ (obl. kṭ-)((DEDR 2200) Paš. kōṇḍā 'bald', Kal. rumb. kōṇḍa 'hornless'.(CDIAL 3508). Kal. rumb. khōṇḍ a 'half' (CDIAL 3792).

Rebus: *koḍ* 'workshop' (Gujarati) Thus, a horned crocodile is read rebus: *koḍ khār* 'blacksmith workshop'. *khār* 'blacksmith' (Kashmiri) *kāruvu* 'crocodile' Rebus: kAru 'artisan, blacksmith'.

Hieroglyph: Joined animals (tigers): *sangaḍi* = joined animals (M.) Rebus: *sãgaṛh* m. ' line of entrenchments, stone walls for defence ' (Lahnda)(CDIAL 12845) *sang* संग् m. a stone (Kashmiri) *sanghāḍo* (G.) = cutting stone, gilding; *sangatarāśū* = stone cutter; *sangatarāśi* = stone-cutting; *sangsāru karan.u* = to stone (S.), *cankatam* = to scrape (Ta.), sankaḍa (Tu.), *sankaṭam* = to scrape (Skt.) *samgraha, samgaha* 'assembler, guardian, manager' *kol* 'tiger' Rebus: *ko*l 'working in iron''furnace, forge'. Thus, the multi-headed tiger is read rebus: *kol sangaḍi* 'fortified place for metal (& ore stone) workers".

Ancient Near East 'scarf' hieroglyph on Warka vase, cyprus bronze stand and on Harappa Script writing

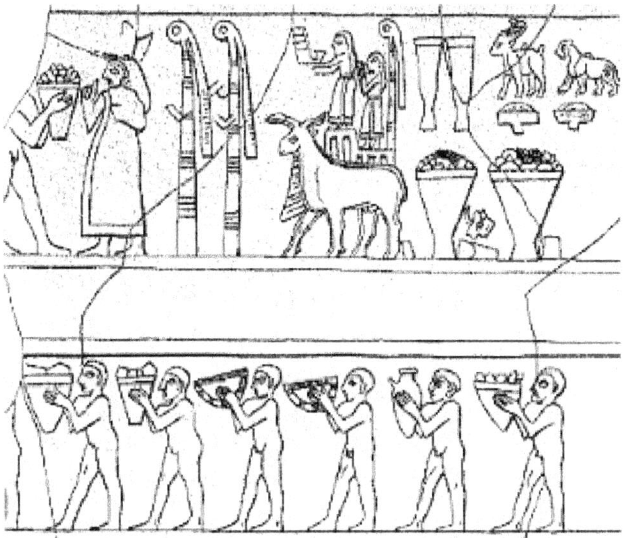

Sketching made of the side of the Warka Vase...

dhatu 'scarf' Rebus: *dhatu* 'mineral; *eruvai* 'reed' Rebus: 'copper'.

Focus is on the'scarf' hieroglyph ligatured to the reed posts on Warka vase.
The narrative of the vase is that ingots of tin and iron are conveyed into the treasury (of minerals and metal ingots) from smithy/forge.
Reed

Reeds on Susa ritual basin. Compare with the reed posts PLUS scarves of Warka vase *eruva*i 'reed' + *dhatu* 'scarf' + *dula* 'pair' Rebus: *eruvai* 'copper' + *dhatu* 'mineral' + *dul* 'cast metal'.

Hieroglyph: *eruvai* 'European reed' European bamboo reed. See கொறுக்கச்சி. (குறிஞ்சிப். 68, உரை.) Species of Cyperus. See பஞ்சாய்க்கோரை. எருவை செருவிளை மணிப்பூங் கருவிளை (குறிஞ்சிப். 68). Straight sedge tuber; கோரைக்கிழங்கு. மட் பனை யெருவைதொட்டி (தைலவ. தைல. 94).

Rebus: *eruva* 'copper' எருவை eruvai Copper; செம்பு. எருவை யுருக்கினா லன்ன குருதி (கம்பரா. கும்பக. 248).

Meluhha brassworker's artisanal repertoire on al-Sabah Kuwait gold disc with Harappa Script hieroglyphs

"Gold disc. al-Sabah Collection, Kuwait National Museum. 9.6 cm diameter, which was obviously from the Indus Valley period in India. Typical of that period, it depicts zebu, bulls, human attendants, ibex, fish, partridges, bees, pipal free an animal-headed standard."[294]

Kuwait Museum gold disc can be read rebus:

1. A pair of tabernae montana flowers tagara 'tabernae montana' flower; rebus: tagara 'tin'

2. A pair of rams tagara 'ram'; rebus: damgar 'merchant' (Akkadian) Next to one ram: kuṭi 'tree' Rebus: kuṭhi 'smelter' Alternative: kolmo 'rice plant' Rebus: kolimi 'smithy, forge'.

3. Ficus religiosa leaves on a tree branch (5) loa 'ficus leaf'; rebus: loh 'metal'. kol in Tamil means pancaloha'alloy of five metals'. PLUS flanking pair of lotus flowers: tAmarasa 'lotuś Rebus: tAmra 'copper' dula 'pair' Rebus: dul 'cast metal' thus, denoting copper castings.

4. A pair of bulls tethered to the tree branch: barad, barat 'ox' Rebus: bharata 'alloy of copper, pewter, tin' (Marathi) PLUS kola 'man' Rebus: kolhe 'smelter' kur.i 'woman' Rebus: kol 'working in iron' Alternative: ḍhangar 'bull'; rebus ḍhangar 'blacksmith' pōḷa 'zebu' Rebus: pōḷa 'magnetite'.

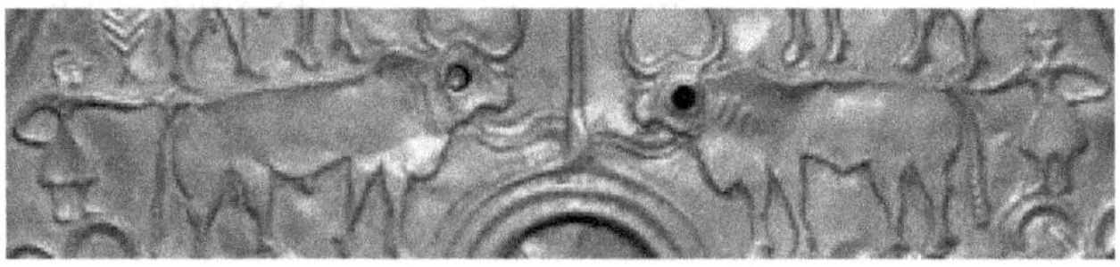

Two persons touch the two bulls: *meḍ* 'body' (Mu.) Rebus: *meḍ* 'iron' (Ho.) Thus, the hieroglyph composition denotes ironsmiths.

5. A pair of antelopes looking back: *krammara* 'look back'; rebus: *kamar* 'smith' (Santali); *tagara* 'antelope'; rebus: damgar 'merchant' (Akkadian) Alternative: melh, *mr..eka* 'goat' (Brahui. Telugu) Rebus: *milakkhu* 'copper' (Pali), *mleccha-mukha* 'copper' (Samskritam)

6. A pair of antelopes *mẽḍh* 'antelope, ram'; rebus: *mẽḍ* 'iron' (Mu.)

7. A pair of combs *kāṅga* 'comb' Rebus: *kanga* 'brazier, fireplace'

káṅkata m. ' comb ' AV., n. lex., °*tī* -- , °*tikā* -- f. lex. 2. **kaṅkaṭa* -- *2. 3. *kaṅkaśa* -- . [Of doubtful IE. origin WP i 335, EWA i 137: aberrant -- *uta* -- as well as -- *aśa* -- replacing -- *ata* -- in MIA. and NIA.]1. Pk. *kaṁkaya* -- m. ' comb ', *kaṁkaya* -- , °*kaï* -- m. ' name of a tree '; Gy. eur. *kangli* f.; Wg. *kuṇi* -- *přũ* ' man's comb ' (for *kuṇi* -- cf. *kuṇälíkbeside kuṅälík* s.v. kr̥muka -- ; -- *přũ* see prapavaṇa --); Bshk. *kēṅg* ' comb ', Gaw. *khēṅgī'*, Sv. *khēṅgiā*, Phal. *khyḗṅgia*, *kēṅgī* f., *kāṅga* ' combing ' in *ṣiṣ k*° *dūm* ' I comb my hair '; Tor. *kyäṅg* ' comb ' (Dard. forms, esp. Gaw., Sv., Phal. but not Sh., prob. ← L. P. type < **kaṅgahiā* -- , see 3 below); Sh. *kōṅyị* f. (→ Ḍ. *k**l*ṅi* f.), gil. (Lor.) *kōĩ* f. ' man's comb ', *kōũ* m. ' woman's comb ', pales. *kōgō* m. ' comb '; K. *kanguwu* m. ' man's comb ', *kangañ* f. ' woman's '; WPah. bhad. *kã'kei* ' a comb -- like fern ', bhal. *kãkei* f. ' comb, plant with comb -- like leaves '; N. *kāṅiyo*, *kāĩyo* ' comb ', A. *kãkai*, B. *kãkui;* Or. *kaṅkāi*, *kaṅkuā* ' comb ', *kakuā* ' ladder -- like bier for carrying corpse to the burning -- ghat '; Bi. *kakwā* ' comb ', *kakahā*, °*hī*, Mth. *kakwā*, Aw. lakh. *kakawā*, Bhoj. *kakahī* f.; H. *kakaiyā* ' shaped like a comb (of a brick) '; G. (non -- Aryan tribes of Dharampur) *kākhāī* f. ' comb '; M. *kaṅkvā* m. ' comb ', *kãkaī* f. ' a partic. shell fish and its shell '; -- S. *kaṅgu* m. ' a partic. kind of small fish ' < **kaṅkuta* -- ? -- Ext. with -- *l* -- in Ku. *kãgilo*, *kāĩlo* ' comb '.2. G. (Soraṭh) *kãgaṛ* m. ' a weaver's instrument '? 3. L. *kaṅghī* f. ' comb, a fish of the perch family ', awāṇ. *kaghī* ' comb '; P. *kaṅghā* m. ' large comb ', °*ghī* f. ' small comb for men, large one for women ' (→ H. *kaṅghā* m. ' man's comb ', °*gahī*, °*ghī* f. ' woman's ', *kaṅghuā* m. ' rake or harrow '; Bi. *kãgahī* ' comb ', Or. *kaṅgei*, M.*kaṅgvā*); -- G. *kãgsī* f. ' comb ', with metath. *kãsko* m., °*kī* f.; WPah. khas. *kāgśī*, śeu. *kāśkī* ' a comblike fern ' or < **kaṅkataśikha* -- .*kaṅkatakara -- , *kaṅkataśikha -- .Addenda: **káṅkata -- :** WPah.kṭg. *kaṅgi* f. ' comb '; J. *kāṅgṛu* m. ' small comb '(CDIAL 2598) ***kaṅkatakara** ' comb -- maker '. [káṅkata -- , kará -- 1]H. *kãgherā* m. ' caste of comb -- makers ', °*rī* f. ' a woman of this caste '.(CDIAL 2599) ***kaṅkataśikha** ' comb -- crested '. [káṅkata -- , śíkhā --] WPah. khaś. *kāgśī*, śeu. *kāśkī* ' a comb -- like fern ', or < **kaṅkaśa* -- s.v. káṅkata -- (CDIAL 2600)

Rebus: large furnace, fireplace: *kang* कंग् । आवसथ्यो &1;ग्निः m. the fire-receptacle or fire-place, kept burning in former times in the courtyard of a Kāshmīrī house for the benefit of guests, etc., and distinct from the three religious domestic fires of a Hindū; (at the present day) a fire-place or brazier lit in the open air on mountain sides, etc., for the sake of warmth or for keeping off wild beasts. *nāra-kang*, a fire-receptacle; hence, met. a shower of sparks (falling on a person) (Rām. 182). *kan:gar* `portable furnace' (Kashmiri)Cf. *kãgürü*, which is the fem. of this word in a dim. sense (Gr.Gr. 33, 7). *kãgürü* कॉँगु़्ऱ or kãgürü कॉँग or *kãgar* कॉँगु़र्ऱ । हसब्तिका f. (sg. dat. *kãgrĕ* कॉँग्र्य or *kãgarĕ* कॉँगर्य, abl. *kãgri* कॉँग्रि), the portable brazier, or *kāngrī*, much used in Kashmīr (K.Pr. *kángár*, 129, 131, 178; *káṅgrí*, 5, 128, 129). For particulars see El. s.v. *kángri;* L. 7, 25, *kangar*; and K.Pr. 129. The word is a fem. dim. of kang, q.v. (Gr.Gr. 37). *kãgri-khŏphürü* कॉँग्रि-ख्वफ़ु । भग्ना काष्ठाङ्गारिका f. a worn-out brazier. काष्ठाङ्गारिकार्धभागः m. the outer half (made of woven twigs) of a brazier, remaining after the inner earthenware bowl has been broken or removed;

हसन्तिकापात्रम् m. the circular earthenware bowl of a brazier, which contains the burning fuel. -köñü - हसन्तिकालता f. the covering of woven twigs outside the earthenware bowl of a brazier.

It is an archaeometallurgical challenge to trace the Maritime Tin Route from the tin belt of the world on Mekong River delta in the Far East and trace the contributions made by seafaring merchants of Meluhha in reaching the tin mineral resource to sustain the Tin-Bronze Age which was a revolution unleashed ca. 5th millennium BCE.

8. A pair of fishes *ayo* 'fish' (Mu.); rebus: *ayo* 'metal, iron' (Gujarati); *ayas* 'metal' (Samskrtam)

9.A pair of buffaloes tethered to a post-standard kāṛā 'buffalo' கண்டி *kaṇṭi* buffalo bull (Tamil); rebus: *kaṇḍ* 'stone ore'; *kāṇḍa* 'tools, pots and pans and metal-ware'; *kaṇḍ* 'furnace, fire-altar, consecrated fire'. Alternative: *rango* 'buffalo' rebus: *rango* 'pewter'

10. A pair of birds *dula* 'two' rebus: *dul* 'metal casting' 1: *kōḍi.* [Tel.] n. A fowl, a bird. (Telugu) Rebus: *khōṭ* 'alloyed ingots'. Rebus 2: *kol* 'the name of a bird, the Bharata cuckoo' (Santali) *kol* 'iron, smithy, forge' 'furnace, forge' Rebus 3: *baṭa* = quail (Santali) Rebus: *baṭa* = furnace, kiln (Santali) *bhrāṣṭra* = furnace (Skt.) *baṭa* = a kind of iron (G.) *bhaṭa* 'furnace' (Gujarati)

11. The buffaloes, birds flank a post-standard with curved horns on top of a stylized 'eye' PLUS 'eyebrowś with one-horn on either side of two faces

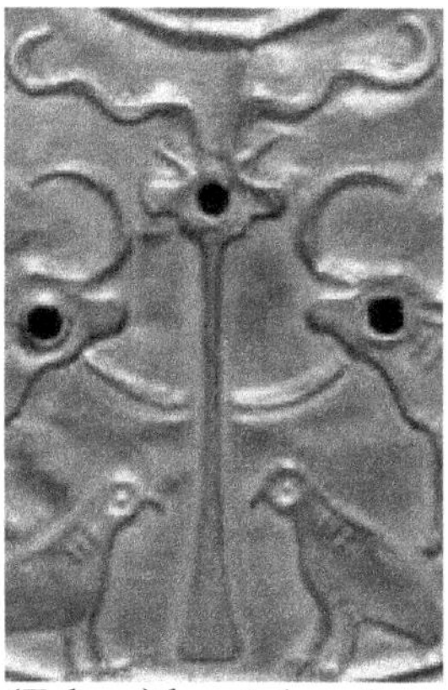

mũh 'face'; rebus: *mũh* 'ingot' (Mu.)

ṭhaṭera 'buffalo horns'. *ṭhaṭerā* 'brass worker' (Punjabi)

Pe. *kaṇga* (pl. -ŋ, kaṇku) eye. Rebus: *kanga* ' large portable brazier, fire-place' (Kashmiri).

Thus the stylized standard is read rebus: Hieroglyph components: *kanga* + *ṭhaṭerā* 'one eye + buffalo horn' Rebus: *kanga* 'large portable barzier' (Kashmiri) + *ṭhaṭerā* 'brass worker' (Punjabi)

करण्ड m. a sort of duck L. కారండవము (p. 274) [*kāraṇḍavamu*] *kāraṇḍavamu.* [Skt.] n. A sort of duck. (Telugu) karaṭa1 m. ' crow ' BhP., °aka -- m. lex. [Cf. *karaṭu* -- , *karkaṭu* -- m. ' Numidian crane ', *karēṭu* -- , °*ēṭavya* -- , °*ēḍuka* -- m. lex., *karaṇḍa*2 -- m. ' duck ' lex: see kāraṇḍava --]Pk. *karaḍa* -- m. ' crow ', °*ḍā* -- f. ' a partic. kind of bird '; S. *karaṛa* -- *ḍhĩgu* m. ' a very large aquatic bird '; L. *karṛā* m., °ṛī f. ' the common teal'(CDIAL 2787) Rebus: *karaḍā* 'hard alloy'

Ta. *kaṇ* eye, aperture, orifice, star of a peacock's tail. Ma. *kaṇ, kaṇṇu* eye, nipple, star in peacock's tail, bud. Ko. *kaṇ* eye. To. *koṇ* eye, loop in string.Ka. *kaṇ* eye, small hole, orifice. Koḍ. *kaṇṇï* id. Tu. *kaṇṇů* eye, nipple, star in peacock's feather, rent, tear. Te. *kanu, kannu* eye, small hole, orifice, mesh of net, eye in peacock's feather. Kol. *kan* (pl. *kanḍl*) eye, small hole in ground, cave. Nk. *kan* (pl. *kanḍḷ*) eye, spot in peacock's tail. Nk. (Ch.) *kan* (pl. -l) eye. Pa. (S. only) *kan* (pl. *kanul*) eye. Ga. (Oll.) *kaṇ* (pl. *kaṇkul*) id.; *kaṇul maṭṭa* eyebrow; *kaṇa* (pl. *kaṇul*) hole; (S.) kanu (pl. *kankul*) eye. Go. (Tr.) *kan* (pl. *kank*) id.; (A.) *kaṛ (pl. kaṛk)* id. Konḍa *kaṇ* id. Pe. *kaṇga (pl. -ŋ, kaṇku)* id. Manḍ. *kan (pl. -ke)* id. Kui *kanu (pl. kan-ga),* (K.) *kanu (pl. kaṛka)* id. Kuwi(F.) *kannū (pl. karnka),* (S.) *kannu* (pl. *kanka*), (Su. P. Isr.) *kanu (pl. kaṇka)* id. Kur. *xann* eye, eye of tuber; *xannērnā (*of newly born babies or animals) to begin to see, have the use of one's eyesight Malt. *qanu* eye.

Br. *xan* id., bud. (DEDR 1159) *kāṇá* ' one -- eyed ' RV.Pa. Pk. *kāṇa* -- ' blind of one eye, blind '; Ash. *kā̃ṛa*, *°ṛī* f. ' blind ', Kt. *kā̃ŕ*, Wg. *kŕā̃macr;*, Tir. *kā'na*, Kho. *kāṇu*NTS ii 260, *kánu* BelvalkarVol 91; K. *kônu* ' one -- eyed ', S. *kāṇo*, L. P. *kāṇā̃*; WPah. rudh. śeu. *kāṇā* ' blind '; Ku. *kāṇo*, gng. *kā̃&rtodtilde;* ' blind of one eye ', N. *kānu;* A. *kanā* ' blind '; B. *kāṇā* ' one -- eyed, blind '; Or. *kaṇā*, f. *kāṇī* ' one -- eyed ', Mth. *kān*, *°nā*, *kanahā*, Bhoj. *kān*, f.*°ni*, *kanwā* m. ' one -- eyed man ', H. *kān*, *°nā*, G. *kāṇũ*; M. *kāṇā* ' one -- eyed, squint -- eyed '; Si. *kaṇa* ' one -- eyed, blind '. -- Pk. *kāṇa* -- ' full of holes ', G. *kāṇũ* ' full of holes ', n. ' hole ' (< ' empty eyehole '? Cf. *ā̃dhḷũ* n. ' hole ' < andhala --).*kāṇiya -- ; *kāṇākṣa -- .Addenda: kāṇá -- : S.kcch. *kāṇī* f.adj. ' one -- eyed '; WPah.kṭg. *kaṇɔ* ' blind in one eye ', J. *kāṇā*; Md. *kanu* ' blind '.(CDIAL 3019) Ko. kāṇso ' squint -- eyed '(Konkani) Paš. ainċ -- *gánik* ' eyelid '(CDIAL 3999) Phonetic reinforcement of the gloss: Pe. *kaṇga* (pl. -ŋ, *kaṇku*) eye.
See also: *nimišta kanag* 'to write' (SBal): **nipēśayati* ' writes '. [√piś] Very doubtful: Kal.rumb. Kho. *nivḗš* -- ' to write ' more prob. ← EPers. Morgenstierne BSOS viii 659. <-> Ir. pres. st. **nipaiš* -- (for **nipais* -- after past **nipišta* --) in Yid. nuviš -- , Mj. *nuvuš* -- , Sang. Wkh. *nəviš* -- ; -- *Aś. nipista*<-> ← Ir. **nipista* -- (for **nipišta* -- after pres. **nipais* -) in SBal. novīsta or nimišta kanag ' to write '.(CDIAL 7220) Alternative: *dol* 'eye'; Rebus: *dul* 'to cast metal in a mould' (Santali)Alternative: *kandi* 'hole, opening' (Ka.)[Note the eye shown as a dotted circle on many Dilmun seals.]; *kan* 'eye' (Ka.); rebus: *kandi* (pl. –l) necklace, beads (Pa.); *kaṇḍ* 'stone ore' Alternative: *kā̃gsī* f. 'comb' (Gujarati); rebus 1: *kangar* 'portable furnace' (Kashmiri); rebus 2: *kamsa* 'bronze'. *khuṇḍ* 'tethering peg or post' (Western Pahari) Rebus: *kūṭa* 'workshop'; kuṭi= smelter furnace (Santali); Rebus 2: *kuṇḍ* 'fire-altar'

Why are animals shown in pairs?

dula 'pair' (Kashmiri); rebus: dul 'cast metal' (Mu.)

Thus, all the hieroglyphs on the gold disc can be read as Harappa Script writing related to one bronze-age artifact category: metalware catalog entries.

Annex J

Crocodile, scorpion, disheveled hair in Harappa Script hieroglyphs signify work in *bica* 'haematite stone ore'

Rakhigarhi *kāru* a wild crocodile or alligator (Te.) Rebus: *khār* a blacksmith, an iron worker (cf. *bandūka-khār)* (Kashmiri)

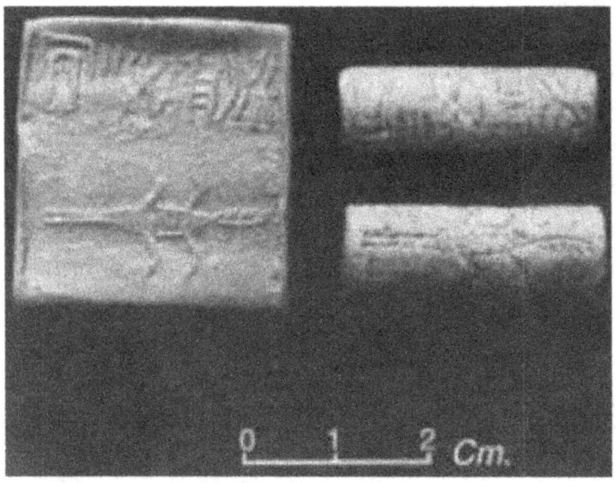

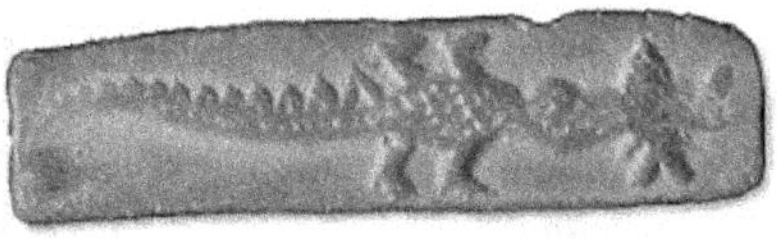

m1429C

ayo 'fish' (Mu.); rebus: aya '(alloyed) metal' (G.) kāru a wild crocodile or alligator (Te.) Rebus: khār a blacksmith, an iron worker (cf. bandūka-khār) (Kashmiri) ayakāra 'blacksmith' (Pali) kāru 'artisan'.

Crocodile hieroglyph in combination with other animal hieroglphs also appears on a Mohenjo-daro seal m0489 in the context of an erotic Meluhha hieroglyph: a tergo copulation hieroglyph.

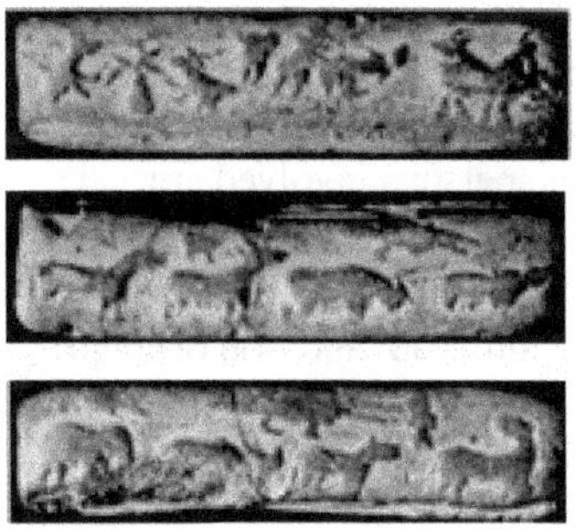

m0489a,b,c Mohenjo-daro prism tablet

A standing human couple mating (a tergo) *r-anku, ranku* = fornication, adultery (Telugu); rebus: *ranku* 'tin' (Santali); one side of a prism tablet from Mohenjo-daro (m489b). Other motifs on the inscribed object are: two goats eating leaves on a platform; a cock or hen (?) and a three-headed animal (perhaps antelope, one-horned bull and a short-horned bull). The leaf pictorial connotes on the goat composition connotes *loa* 'ficus religiosa'; hence, the reading is of this pictorial component is: *lohar kamar* = a blacksmith, worker in iron, superior to the ordinary kamar (Santali.) *melh* 'goat' rebus: *milakkhu* 'copper'

Hieroglhyphs: elephant (ibha), boar/rhinoceros [*kāṇḍā mṛga* 'rhinoceroś (Tamil)], tiger (kol), tiger face turned (*krammara*), young bull calf (*khōṇḍa*) खोंड m A young bull, a bullcalf. (Marathi)], antelope, *ḍangur 'bullock', melh* 'goat' (Brahui)

Rebus mleccha glosses: Ib 'iron' *ibbo* 'merchant'; *kāṇḍā,* 'tools, pots and pans, metalware'; *kol* 'worker in iron, smithy'; *krammara, kamar* 'smith, artisan', *kõdā* 'lathe-turner' [B. *kõdā* 'to turn in a lathe'; Or. *kū̃nda* 'lathe', *kū̃dibā, kū̃d* 'to turn' (→ Drav. Kur. *kū̃d* 'lathe') (CDIAL 3295)], *khũṭ* 'guild, community', *ḍāṅro* 'blacksmith' (Nepalese) *milakkhu* 'copper' (Pali) [*Meluhha!] pōḷa* 'zebu' Rebus: *pōḷa* 'magnetite, ferrite ore'.

Phoneme *karba* has two hieroglyph components which are semantic determinatives:

kari 'elephant' *ibha*'elephant'

Hieroglyph: *karabha* 'trunk of elephant' (Pali) 2803 *karin* m. ' elephant '. [See karabhá --]*Pa. karin -- m., Pk. kari -- , °iṇa -- m., °iṇī -- , °iṇiyā -- f.;* <-> *Si. kiriyā* ← Pa.(CDIAL 2803)

Hieroglyph: hand: *kará*1 ' doing, causing ' AV., m. ' hand ' RV. [√kr̥1]

Pa. Pk. *kara* -- m. ' hand '; S. *karu* m. ' arm '; Mth. *kar* m. ' hand ' (prob. ← Sk.); Si. kara ' hand, shoulder ', inscr. *karā* ' to ' < karāya. -- Deriv. S. *karāī* f. ' wrist '; G. *karā̃* n. pl. ' wristlets, bangles '.(CDIAL 2779)

Rebus: *karba* 'very hard iron' (Tulu) Tu. *kari* soot, charcoal; *kariya* black; karṅka state of being burnt or singed; *karṅkāḍuni* to burn (tr.); k*arñcun*i to be burned to cinders; *karñcāvuni* to cause to burn to cinders; *kardů* black; *karba* iron; *karvāvuni* to burn the down of a fowl by holding it over the fire; karṇṭuni to be scorched; karguḍe a very black man; fem. karguḍi, kargi. Kor. (T.) *kardi* black. *kabbiṇa* iron (Kannada) *kabïn* iron (Toda) *karum poṉ* iron (Tamil)(DEDR 1278)

Allograph: pot with narrow neck: Koḍ. *karava* clay pot with narrow neck. Go. (Ma.) *karv*i narrow-mouthed earthen vessel for oil or liquor (DEDR 1273A)

Hieroglyph: *ibha* 'elephant' Rebus: *ib* 'iron' (Santali). *kāṇḍā* 'rhinoceroś Rebus: *khāṇḍa* 'tools, pots and pans, and metal-ware'. *karā* 'crocodile' Rebus: *khār* 'blacksmith' (Kashmiri) Note*: Ib* is the name of a station between Howrah and Nagpur. The Railway station is in the iron ore belt, close to Rourkela steel plant.

bicha 'scorpion' rebus: *bicha* 'sand stone ore, haematite ore'.

The text on m0489 tablet: *loa* 'ficus religiosa' Rebus: *loh* 'copper'. *kolmo* 'rice plant' Rebus: kolimi 'smithy, forge'. *dula* 'pair' Rebus: *dul* 'cast metal'. Thus the display of the metalware catalog includes the technological competence to work with minerals, metals and alloys and produce tools, pots and pans. The persons involved are *krammara* 'turn back' Rebus: *kamar* 'smiths, artisans'. *kola* 'tiger' Rebus: *kol* 'working in iron, working in pancaloha alloyś. పంచలోహము *pancha-lōnamu*. n. A mixed metal, composed of five ingredients, viz., copper, zinc, tin, lead, and iron (Telugu). Thus, when five *svastika* hieroglyphs are depicted, the depiction is of satthiya 'svastika' Rebus: *satthiya* 'zinc' and the totality of 5 alloying metals of copper, zinc, tin, lead and iron.

Hieroglyph: Animals in procession: खांडा [khāṇḍā] A flock (of sheep or goats) (Marathi) கண்டி[1] *kaṇṭi* Flock, herd (Tamil) Rebus: *khāṇḍā* 'tools, pots and pans, and metal-ware'. Glyphs: కారుమొసలి a wild crocodile or alligator (Telugu). crocodile + fish *ayo* 'fish' rebus: *aya* 'iron' + *kāruvu* 'crocodile' rebus: *kāru* 'artisan' *khār* 'blacksmith' (Kashmiri) Rebus: *ayakāra* 'blacksmith' (Pali)

Glyph of a crocodile and a lying-in woman. This glyph is part of one side of h180 Harappa tablet. A sequence of signs is repeated on both sides of the tablet.

Harappa tablets h180, h705B, h172B

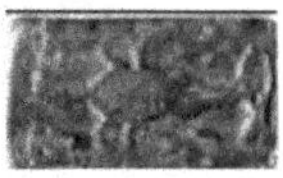

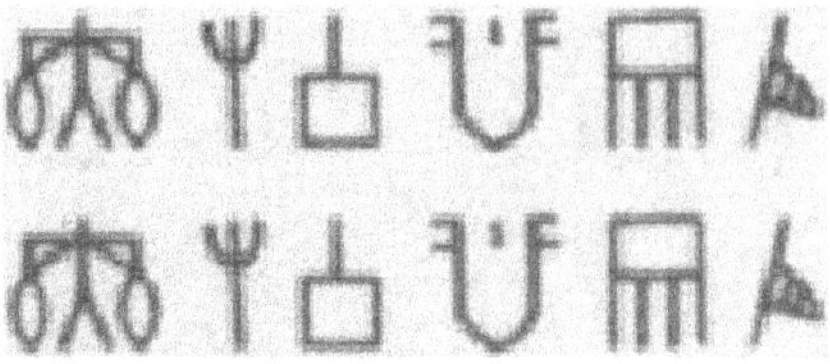

h705B, h172B Harappa tablets show variants of crocodile hieroglyph.

Text 4340 Inscription on h180 tablet. kuTi 'water-carrier' rebus: kuThi 'smelter' kolmo 'rice plant' rebus: kolimi 'smithy, forge' ranku 'liquid measure' rebus: ranku 'tin' kanka 'rim of jar' rebus: karNI 'supercargo' PLUS khāṇḍa 'notch' rebus: kaṇḍa 'implements' kole.l 'temple' rebus: kole.l 'smithy, forge' kol 'furnace, forge' koDi 'flag' rebus: koD 'workshop'. Thus the text message is: tin smelter smithy implements workshop. The person standing in front of the seated person with disheveled hair carries a sickle and a disc; he is kuThAru 'armourer' kAru, 'artisan', maker of weapons and worker with rAca 'stone ore' *sanga* 'stone', hence, *sangatarAsu* 'stone worker'. Side B of h180 tablet shows two narratives: woman with spread legs + crocodile and two standing tigers: kudi 'jump' rebus: kuThi 'smelter' PLUS kola 'tiger' rebus: kol 'furnace, forge'. *dula* 'pair' rebus: *dul* 'metal casting' Thus, artisan in metalcasting with smelter, furnace, forge.

The object between the outspread legs of the woman lying upside down is comparable orthography of a crocodile holding fiish in its jaws shown on tablets h705B and h172B. The snout of the crocodile is shown in copulation with the lying-in woman (as seen from the enlarged portion of h180 Harappa tablet).*ranku* 'fornication, adultery' rebus: *ranku* 'tin' PLUS *kāruvu* 'crocodile' rebus: *kāru* 'artisan'. Thus, tinsmith'. *kola* 'woman'; rebus: *kol* 'iron'. *kola* 'blacksmith' (Ka.); *kollë* 'blacksmith' (Koḍ) Thus, tinsmith working with iron. *kamḍa, khamḍa* 'copulation' (Santali) Rebus: *kammaṭi* a coiner (Ka.); *kampaṭṭam* coinage, coin, mint (Ta.) *kammaṭa* = mint, gold furnace (Te.) Thus a tinsmith working in iron in a mint.

Glyph: vagina: *kuṭhi* 'vagina'; *kuṭhi* 'pudendum muliebre' (Mu.) *khoḍu* m. 'vulva' (CDIAL 3947). rebus: *kuṭhi* 'smelting furnace'. Rebus: *kuṭhi* 'smelter furnace' (Mu.) *khŏḍ* m. 'pit', *khŏḍü* f. 'small pit' (Kashmiri. CDIAL 3947)

Narrative from Harappa tablet h180: Woman with disheveled hair: <raca>(D) {ADJ} ``^dishevelled'' (Munda) *rasāṇẽ* n. 'glowing embers' (Marathi). *rabca* 'dishevelled' Rebus: రాచ *rāca* (adj.) Pertaining to a stone (ore).

Women with flowing hair and scorpions, Samarra, Iraq. After Ernst Herzfeld, Die Ausgrabungen von Samarra V: Die vorgeschichtischenTopfereien, Univ. of Texas Press, pl. 30. Courtesy Dietrich Reimer. This image is discussed in Denise Schmandt-Besserat, When writing met art, p.19. “The design features six humans in he center of the bowl and six scorpions around the inner rim. The six identical anthropomorphic figures, shown frontally, are generally interpreted as females because of their wide hips, large thighs, and long, flowing hair…Six identical scorpions, one following after the other in a single line, circle menacingly around the women.”

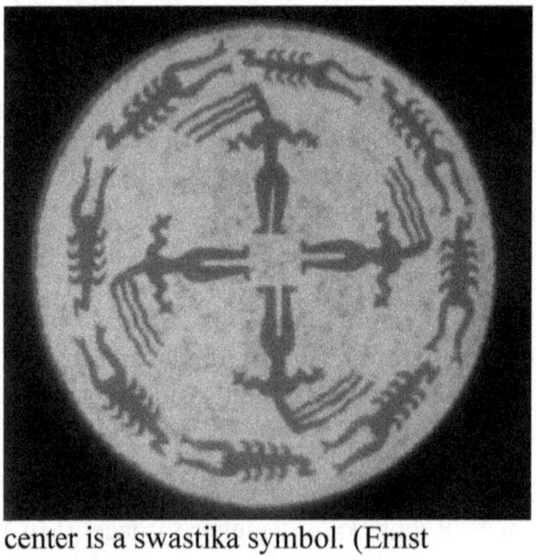

Four women with disheveled hair surrounded by 8 scorpions. The Samarra bowl (ca. 4000 BC) at on exhibit at the Pergamon museum, Berlin. The bowl was excavated as Samarra by Ernst Herzfeld in the 1911-1914 campaign, and described in a 1930 publication. The design consists of a rim, a circle of eight fish, and four fish swimming towards the center being caught by four birds. At the center is a swastika symbol. (Ernst Herzfeld, Die vorgeschichtlichen Töpfereien von Samarra, Die Ausgrabungen von Samarra 5, Berlin 1930.)

Four women with disheveled hair on a potsherd together with sun and dotted circles hieroglyphs PLUS markhor hieroglyph. Harappa. *dhAu* ‘strand’ rebus: *dhAtu* ‘mineral, ore’ *arka* ‘sun’ rebus: *arka, eraka* ‘moltencast, copper’ meḍha ‘ram’ rebus: meḍ ‘iron’ <raca>(D) {ADJ} ``^dishevelled'' (Munda) *rasāṇẽ* n. ‘glowing embers’ (Marathi). *rabca* ‘dishevelled’ Rebus: రాచ *rāca* (adj.) Pertaining to a stone (ore). The stone ore is: bica ‘scorpion’ rebus: bica ‘haematite ore, stone ore’. The suffix -rAsu in: *sangatarAsu* 'stone cutter' may relate to రాచ *rāca* (adj.) Pertaining to a stone (ore)

(Telugu). Thus, by signifying disheveled hair together with scorpions, the scribe signifies *bica* ‘scorpion’ rebus: ‘haematite, ferrite ore, stone ore’ worker. The prefix sangata- in: *sangatarAsu* is related rebus, to the word *samgaha , samgraha* ‘manager, assembler’. Thus, the pictorial narrative signifies smelter worker working in haematite stone ore.

Comparable narratives signifying vagina, scorpion occur on other Harappa script inscriptions and on seals of Ancient Near East.

Seal impession from Ur showing a squatting female. L. Legrain, 1936, Ur excavations, Vol. 3, Archaic Seal Impressions. [cf. Nausharo seal with two scorpions flanking a similar glyph with legs apart – also looks like a frog]. *kuṭhi* ‘pudendum muliebre’ (Mu.) *khoḍu* m. ‘vulva’ (CDIAL 3947). Rebus: *kuṭhi* ‘smelter furnace’ (Mu.) *khŏḍ* m. ‘pit’, *khŏḍü* f. ‘small pit’ (Kashmiri. CDIAL 3947),

Rahman-dheri seal. Obverse: Two scorpions. Two holes. One T glyph. One frog in the middle. Reverse: two rams.
1. *mūxā* ‘frog’. Rebus: *mũh* ‘(copper) ingot’ (Santali) Allograph: mũhe ‘face’ (Santali)
2. *bica* 'scorpion' (Assamese) Rebus: *bica* 'stone ore' as in: *meṛed-bica* = 'iron stone ore', in contrast to *bali-bica*, 'iron sand ore' (Munda).

3. *tagaru* ‘ram’ (Tulu) Rebus: *tagarm* ‘tin’ (Kota). *damgar* ‘merchant’ (Akk.)
4. T-glyph may denote a fire altar like the two fire-altars shown on Warrka vase below two animals: antelope and tiger. kand ‘fire-altar’ (Santali)
5. Two holes may denote ingots. dula ‘pair’ Rebus: dul ‘cast’ (Santali)

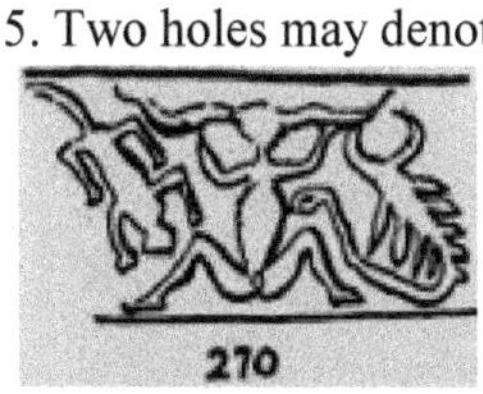

270

kola ‘woman’ Rebus: *kol* ‘working in iron’
kuṛī f. ‘ girl’ Rebus: *kuṭhi* ‘smelter’.
The glyphic elements shown on the tablet are: copulation, vagina, crocodile. h180 tablet.

269

The squatting woman on the Ur cylinder seals 269 and 270 impression may be showing dishevelled hair. <raca>(D) {ADJ} ``^dishevelled'' (Munda) *rasāṇẽ* n. ‘glowing embers’ (Marathi). *rabca* ‘dishevelled’ Rebus: రాచ *rāca* (adj.) Pertaining to a stone (ore).

Note on smelter: *kolheko kuṭhieda* koles smelt iron (Santali) kuṭhi, kuṭi (Or.; Sad. koṭhi) (1) the smelting earthen furnace of the blacksmith; *kuṭire bica duljad.ko talkena*, they were feeding the furnace with ore; (2) the name of *ēkuṭi* has been given to the fire which, in lac factories, warms the water bath for softening the lac so that it can be spread into sheets; to make a smelting furnace; *kuṭhi-o* of a smelting furnace, to be made; the smelting furnace of the blacksmith is made of mud, cone-shaped, 2’ 6” dia. At the base and 1’ 6” at the top. The hole in the centre, into which the mixture of charcoal and iron ore is poured, is about 6” to 7” in dia. At the base it has two holes, a smaller one into which the nozzle of the bellow is inserted, as seen in fig. 1, and a larger one on the opposite side through which the molten iron flows out into a cavity (Mundari) *kuṭhi* = a factory; *lil kuṭhi* = an indigo factory (koṭhi - Hindi) (Santali.Bodding) *kolheko do kuṭhi benaokate baliko dhukana*, the Kolhes build an earthen furnace and smelt iron-ore, blowing the bellows; *tehen:ko kuṭhi yet kana*, they are working (or building) the furnace to-day (H. *koṭhī*) (Santali. Bodding) *kuṭṭhita* = hot, sweltering; molten (of tamba, cp.*uttatta*)(Pali.lex.) uttatta (ut + tapta) = heated, of metals: molten, refined; shining, splendid, pure (Pali.lex.) *kuṭṭakam, kuṭṭukam* = cauldron (Ma.); *kuṭṭuva* = big copper pot for heating water (Kod.)(DEDR 1668). *gudgā* to blaze; gud.va flame (Man.d); *gudva, gūdūvwa, guduwa id.* (Kuwi)(DEDR 1715). *dāntar-kuṭha* = fireplace (Sv.); *kōti* wooden vessel for mixing yeast (Sh.); *kōlhā* house with mud roof and walls, granary (P.); *kuṭhī* factory (A.); *koṭhā* brick-built house (B.); *kuṭhī* bank, granary (B.); *koṭho* jar in which indigo is stored, warehouse (G.); *koṭhī* lare earthen jar, factory (G.); *kuṭhī* granary, factory (M.)(CDIAL 3546). *koṭho* = a warehouse; a revenue office, in which dues are paid and collected; *koṭhī* a store-room; a factory (Gujarat) *koḍ* = the place where artisans work (Gujarati) *kōṣṭhāgāra* n. ' storeroom, store ' Mn. [kṓṣṭha -- 2, agāra --]

Pa. *koṭṭhāgāra* -- n. ' storehouse, granary '; Pk. *koṭṭhāgāra* -- , *koṭṭhāra* -- n. ' storehouse '; K. *kuṭhār* m. ' wooden granary ', WPah. bhal. *kóṭhār* m.; A. B. *kuṭharī* ' apartment ', Or.*koṭhari*; Aw. lakh. *koṭhār* ' zemindar's residence '; H. *kuṭhiyār* ' granary '; G. *koṭhār* m. ' granary, storehouse ', *koṭhāriyũ* n. ' small do. '; M. *koṭhār* n., *koṭhārẽ* n. ' large granary ', --°*rī* f. ' small one '; Si. *koṭāra* ' granary, store '. kōṣṭhāgārika -- .Addenda: *kōṣṭhāgāra* -- : WPah.ktg. *kəṭhā́r*, kc. *kuṭhār* m. ' granary, storeroom ', J. *kuṭhār*, *kṭhār* m.; -- Md. *kořāru* ' storehouse ' ← Ind. (CDIAL 3550).

Annex K

Structure, form, function and significance of *caṣālḥ* चषालः on Yūpa in a *yajna* and carburization

Snout of a boar as a Harappa script hieroglyph: *caṣālḥ* चषालः (चशाल) S3Br. &c *n.* the snout of a hog MaitrS. i , 6 , 3. (Monier-Williams)

A further elaboration --an explanatory process related to the function -- of *Yūpa* occurs from Vedic times, with चषालः *caṣāla,* wheat-chaff as *vajra.* This semantic elaboration (which bristles with metaphors) signifies pyrolysis to carburize hard alloy metal. The infusion of carbon is explained by the *kangar* 'brazier' which uses charcoal:

**kāṅgārikā* ' poor or small brazier '. [Cf. *kāgni* -- m. ' a small fire ' Vop.: ka -- 3 or kā -- , aṅgāri --]K. *kã̄gürü, kã̄gar* f. ' portable brazier ' whence *kangar* m. ' large do. ' (or < **kāṅgāra* -- ?); H. *kã̄grī* f. ' small portable brazier '.(CDIAL 3006)

áṅgāra m. n. ' glowing charcoal ' RV., °*aka* -- lex. 2. *iṅgāra -- , *iṅgāla* -- m. Vāsav. com.1. Pa. *aṅgāra* -- m. ' charcoal ', Pk. *aṁgāra* -- , °*aya* -- , *aṁgāla* -- , °*aya* -- m., Gy. eur. *angár* ' charcoal ', wel. *vaṅār* m. (*v* -- from m. article), germ. *yangar* (*y* -- from *yag*, s.v. agní -- 1); Ash. *aṅā´* ' fire ', Kt. *aṅā́*, Gmb. *aṅā´*, Pr. *anéye*, Dm. *aṅgar* (*a* < *ā* NTS xii 130), Tir. Chilis Gau. K. *nār* (*n* < *ṅ* -, not ← Psht. *nār* ← Ar. AO xii 184), Paš. *aṅgā´r*, Shum. *ã̄r* (← Paš. NOGaw 59), Gaw. Kal. Kho. *aṅgā´r*, Bshk. *äṅgā´r*, Tor. *aṅā*, Mai. *agār*, Phal. *aṅgŏ́r*, Sh. *agā´r*, *ha*° m.; S. *aṅaru* m. ' charcoal ' (*a* < *ā* as in Dm.), L. *aṅgār* m., P. *aṅgyār*, °*rā* m., EP. *ãgeār* (*y* or *e* from MIA. *aggi* < agní --1?), WPah. bhid. *aṅgā´rõ* n., pl. -- *ã*, Ku. *aṅār* (*ḍaṅār* id. X *ḍājṇo* < dahyátē), N. *aṅār*, A. *āṅgār*, *eṅgār*, B. *āṅgār*, *āṅrā*, Or. *aṅgāra*; Bi. *ãgarwāh* ' man who cuts sugar -- cane into lengths for the mill ' (=*pakwāh*); OMth. *aṁgāra*, Mth. *ãgor*, H. *ãgār*, °*rā* m., G. *ãgār*, °*rɔ* m., M. *ãgār* m., Si. *aňgura*. -- Wg. *ãř*, *ã̄ī´* ' fire ' (as opp. to *aṅarī´k* ' charcoal ', see *aṅgāryā´* --) poss. < agní -- 1, Morgenstierne NTS xvii 226.2. Pa. *iṅghāḷa* -- ' glowing embers (?) ', Pk. *iṁgāra* -- , *iṁgāla*, °*aya* -- ; K. *yĕṅgur* m. ' charcoal ', *yĕṅguru* m. ' charcoal -- burner '; M. *ĩgaḷ*, *ĩgḷā* m., Ko. *ĩgḷo*. -- Deriv. M. *ĩgḷā* m. ' a kind of large ant ', *ĩgḷī* f. ' a large black deadly scorpion *'aṅgāraka* -- , *aṅgāri* -- , *aṅgāryā´* -- ; *aṅgāradhānī* -- , **aṅgāravarta* -- , **aṅgārasthana* -- , **aṅgr̥ṣṭha* -- .Addenda: *áṅgāra* -- : Md. *aňguru* ' charcoal '.(CDIAL 125)

The hardening of ores in a smelter/furnace is an awe-inspiring phenomenon which explains the ancient enquiry in *Atharva Veda Skambha Sukta* (AV X.7,8) which follows up on the *Nasadiya Sukta of Rigveda* (RV 10.129) to enquire into the creation of the universe and consciousness as ordering linking the *aatman* with the *paramaatman. ná ásat āsīt ná u sátāsīt tadânīm... ná mr̥tyúḥ āsīt amŕtam ná tárhi* "not the non-existent existed, nor did the existent exist then" "then not death existed, nor the immortal" *ânīt avātám svadháyā tát ékam* "breathing without breath, of its own nature, that one" (*tápasaḥ tát mahinâ ajāyata ékam* "from heat (tapas) was born that one" "That One (*tad ekam*)" which is, "Spaceless, timeless, yet in its own way dynamic and the Sole Force, this Absolute..."[295] *Atharva Veda Skambha Sukta* sees the 'Support', as the first principle which is both the material and efficient cause of the universe, to Prāna, the 'Breath of Life', to Vāc, the 'Word'.[296]

Skambha as th octagonal Yūpa results in the aniconic Siva linga with three parts: *Vishnu bhAga* (quadrangular base), *Rudra bhAga* (octagonal middle) and *Brahma bhAga* (circular top) as an endless, infinite cosmic pillar. A *lingodbhava* representation of Mahes'vara is shown in Airavatesvara temple with the metaphors of *varAha* as *Vishnu* searching for the roots of this *skambha* and *Hamsa* as *Brahma* searching for the end of the *skambha* in the skies and heavens. The seeds of *adhyatmika* philosophical enquiries into this cosmic ordering recognized the foundations of the *weltanschauung* of *dharma-dhamma.*

The data mining process of this civilization treasure of over 7000 Harappa Script inscriptions matched with 10,800 *rica-s* of Rigveda.Rigveda is a very ancient text resonant with a particular view of life and cosmic phenomena. The world-view or *weltanschauung* is given in extraordinary metaphors ज्ञानम् *jñānam* of cosmic-consciousness enquiries rendered in prosodic Chandas. This matching of two databases results in knowledge discovery of relationships with ancient knowledge documentation, dissemination systems. Discovery relates to a broad spectrum of multidisciplinary knowledge systems: Vedic culture continuum in Bharata *sprachbund* (language union), formation and evolution of ancient languages, metallurgical advances connected to the Bronze Age Revolution of alloying metals/*cire perdue* techniques of metal castings, production of metal implements and weapons, related technological advances in many aspects of life which transformed cultures and social interactions in civilization areas, formation of artisan/trade guilds, monetary systems connected with ancient mints, and state formation in ancient Harappa civilization, seafaring trade contact areas extending from Ancient Near East to Ancient Far east.

Lingam, grey sandstone *in situ*, Harappa, Trench Ai, Mound F, Pl. X (c) (After Vats). "In an earthenware jar, No. 12414, recovered from Mound F, Trench IV, Square I... in this jar, six lingams were found along with some tiny pieces of shell, a unicorn seal, an oblong grey sandstone block with polished surface, five stone pestles, a stone palette, and a block of chalcedony..."[297]

చషాలము (p. 407) *caṣālamu chashālamu*. [Skt.] n. A chalice, or cup used in sacrifice. A ring attached to the sacrificial post in a horse sacrifice. రాజ మాయము నందు యూపస్తంభమునకు అడుగున తగిలించే కడియము. రాజ మాయము నందు యూపస్తంభమునకు అడుగున తగిలించే
కడియము. యూపస్తంభమునకు అడుగున తగిలించే కడియము.

caṣālḥ चषालः 1 A wooden ring on the top of a sacrificial post; चषालं ये अश्वयूपाय तक्षति Rv.1.162.6; चषालयूपत- च्छन्नो हिरण्यरशनं विभुः Bhāg.4.19.19. -2 An iron ring at the base of the post. -3A hive. pracaṣālam प्रचषालम् A particular ornament on a sacrificial post; चषालं प्रचषालं च यस्य यूपे हिरण्मये Mb.7.61.6. (Apte) RV. i , 162 , 6 TS. vi Ka1t2h. xxvi ,

चषालः, पुं, (चष्यते वध्यतेऽस्मिन् । चष + "सानसिवर्णसीति ।" उणां । ४ । १०७ । इति आल प्रत्ययेन निपातनात् साधुः ।) यूपकटकः । इत्यमरः । २ । ७ । १८ ॥ यज्ञसमाप्तिसूचकं पशुबन्धनाद्यर्थं यज्ञभूमौ यत् काष्ठमारोप्यते स यूपः तस्य शिरसि वलयाकृतिर्डमरुकाकृतिर्व्वा

यःकाष्ठविकारः सः । यूपमूलेविहितलोहवलयश्च ।इति केचित् । इति भरतः ॥ मधुस्थानम् । इतिसंक्षिप्तसारे उणादिवृत्तिः ॥ https://sa.wikisource.org/wiki/शब्दकल्पद्रुमः चषाल पु० न० चष--आलच् अर्द्धर्च्चादि । यूपकटके यज्ञियपशुबन्धनार्थे यूपमध्येदेये बलयाकारे काष्ठमये लौहमये वा पदार्थे अमरः । तल्लक्षणादिकमुक्तं का० श्रौ०६ । १ । २८ । सूत्रादौ"अग्राच्चषालं पृथमात्रमष्टाश्रि मध्यसंगृहीतम्" २८ सू०"यूप परिवासनानन्तरं यदवशिष्टं पृथक्कृतमग्रम् ततश्चषालं कर्त्तव्यम् प्रसारिताङ्गुलिः पाणिरामणिवन्धनान् पृथक् इत्युच्यते चषालमिति संज्ञा सं व्यवहारार्था "आ चषालेक्षणात्" इत्यादौ । अष्टाश्रि अष्टकोणम् तदपि तक्षणेनाष्टकोणं कुर्य्यात् तक्षैव । उलूखलवन्मध्ये संकुचितम्" कर्कः ।"ऊर्द्धमग्रे प्रतिमुञ्चति" २९ सू० "तच्चषालं यूपस्याग्रे ऊर्द्ध्वं प्रतिमुञ्चति अतएवोर्द्धप्रतिमोकविधानाच्चषालस्य तथा बेधः कार्यः । प्रतिमुञ्चतीति वचनाच्च चूड़ाग्रो यूपः चषालं च ससुषिरमिति गम्यत इति हरिस्वामिनः तथा चाहापस्तम्बः "मूलतोऽतष्टमुपरम् अष्टाश्रिरनु पूर्वोऽग्रतोऽणीयान् प्रज्ञाताष्टाश्रिरिति" कर्क० "द्व्यङ्गुलं त्र्यङ्गुलं वां तर्द्मातिक्रान्तं यूपस्य" ३० सू० "यूपस्य यूपाग्रस्य द्व्यङ्गुलं त्र्यङ्गुलं वा चषालं तर्द्माति क्रान्तं चषालच्छिद्राग्रवेधादतिक्रान्तं भवति अतिक्रम्योर्द्ध्वं निःसृतं भवति तथा चषालस्योर्द्धं प्रवयणं कर्त्तव्यम् यथा चषालो यूपाग्रादधो द्व्यङ्गुले त्र्यङ्गुले वा तिष्ठतीत्यर्थः" कर्कः "भूश्चषालतुलिताङ्गुलीयकम्" माघः https://sa.wikisource.org/wiki/वाचस्पत्यम्

?Rebus: சவளை *cavaḷai n. Lead sand;* வங்கமணல். (மூ. அ.)

ಚವುಳು (= ಚೌಳು) k. n. Brackishness. -ಉಪ್ಪು, ಚವುಳುಪ್ಪು, -ಕಾರ. Soda-saltpetre-

Knowledge system of carburization of metal conveyed in Hindu Art tradition: hieroglyph, चषालः *caṣāla* 'boar snout' rebus: चषालः *caṣāla* 'godhuma, wheat chaff, earth smoke' atop Yūpa

caṣāla चषाल This is a Rigveda word which signifies the top-piece of the Yūpa.

चषालः *caṣāla* on Yūpa, made of wheat straw, an Harappa script hieroglyph, signifies pyrolysis/carburization in smelting ores into steel/hard alloys

चषालः *caṣāla* is made of wheat straw according to Satapatha Brāhmana. This is a knowledge system of the times that the wheat straw, *godhuma*, constituted *annam*, food for the process of hardening of metal. In modern metallurgical jargon, this is carburization or pyrolysis to explain the process of infusing carbon into metal to harden the mineral-complex That, this was seen as a knowledge system is evident from the use of चषालः *caṣāla* 'snout of boar' to signify the knowledge system by deploying the symbol of *Vākdevi Sarasvati* on a monolithic sculptural metaphor of monolithic venerated statue of Khajuraho *VarAha.*

Sarasvati sculptural frieze on the *caṣāla* चषाल 'snout of boar', i.e. of varAha, divine boar.चषाल 'the snout of a hog'(MaitrS. i , 6 , 3).Nandsa Yūpa which had an inscription evidencing performance *of a soma samsthA* yajna, shows an octagonal चषालः caṣāla atop the Yūpa which is metaphored as locks of hair of Rudra on ekamukhalinga of JaiyA.

jaṭa जट *a.* [जट्-अच्; जन् उणा° टन् अन्त्यलोपश्च] Wearing twisted locks of hair. -टा [Uṇ.5.3] 1 The hair matted and twisted together, matted or clotted hair; जटाधरणसंस्कारं द्विजातित्वमवाप्य च Mb.12.61.3. अंसव्यापि शकुन्तनीडनिचितं बिभ्रज्जटामण्डलम् Ś.7.11; जटाश्च बिभृयान्नित्यम् Ms.6.6; Māl.1.2. -2 A fibrous root; यत्र मुञ्जावटे रामो जटाहरणमादिशत् Mb.12.122.3. -3 A particular manner of reciting Vedic texts; thus the word रुद्रेभ्यः repeated in this manner would stand thus :-- नमो रुद्रेभ्यो रुद्रेभ्यो नमो नमोरुद्रेभ्यः

जट [p=409,1] *mfn.* wearing twisted locks of hair g. अर्श-आदि; जटा *f.* the hair twisted together (as worn by ascetics , by शिव , and persons in mourning) Pa1rGr2. ii , 6 Mn. vi , 6 MBh. (ifc. *f.*(आ). , iii , 16137) &*cf.;* a fibrous root , root (in general) Bhpr. v , 111 S3a1rn3gS. i , 46 and 58; *f.* N. of a पाठ or arrangement of the Vedic text (still more artificial than the क्रम , each pair of words being repeated thrice and one repetition being in inverted order) Caran2.

In this semantic structure, the जटा is orthographed to signify fibrous roots of the wheat straw which constitute the *annam* in pyrolysis for the smelting process. Pyrolysis is a thermochemical decomposition of organic material to caburize -- to produce hard alloy metal, to transform wrought iron into steel by infusing carbon through the fumes, *godhuma* from the smoke of burning wheat straw set up in the form of a ring atop the *yajna Yūpa*. That the reference to animals in yajna is ONLY a metaphor is evident from the Kalibangan terracotta cake which shows an archer dragging a tiger tied with a rope. The tiger and tied rope are rebus Harappa Script rebus renderings of *meḍhi* 'rope' rebus: *meḍ* 'iron' and *kola* 'tiger' rebus: *kol* 'metal'.

The structure and form of *Yūpa* and *caSAla* explains the *sthApatya* millennial tradition to consecrate linga.

Rigveda text on Rudra, *vajrabāho and Śatapatha Brāhmaṇa signifiers* चतुर्श्रि, अष्टाश्रि quadrangular, octagonal Yūpa

Reference to a thunderbolt weapon made of metal occurs in Rigveda:

(15)	33	(म.2, अनु.4)
ऋषिः गृत्समदः भार्गवः शौनकः	छन्दः त्रिष्टुप्	देवता रुद्रः

आ ते पितर्मरुतां सुम्नमेतु मा नः सूर्यस्य संदृशो युयोथाः ।
अभि नो वीरो अर्वति क्षमेत प्र जायेमहि रुद्र प्रजाभिः ॥ 1 ॥
त्वादत्तेभी रुद्र शंतमेभिः शतं हिमा अशीय भेषजेभिः ।
व्यस्मद्द्वेषो वितरं व्यंहो व्यमीवाश्चातयस्वा विषूचीः ॥ 2 ॥
श्रेष्ठो जातस्य रुद्र श्रियासि तवस्तमस्तवसां वज्रबाहो ।
पर्षि णः पारमंहसः स्वस्ति विश्वा अभीती रपसो युयोधि ॥ 3 ॥

Rigveda describes Rudra is *vajrabāho*, wielder of the thunderbolt weapon signified by *Yūpa* which is चतुर्श्रि, अष्टाश्रि quadrangular, octagonal with a चषालः caṣāla on top of the *Yūpa* post.

The metaphors of Rigveda point to a metallurgical process.

Soma Yaga is signified by a *Yūpa* – an octagonal pillar. All 19 *Yūpa* inscriptions are on pillars which are octagonal shaped and refer to *Soma Yaga* (of specific descriptions). An account of *Yūpa* inscriptions, most of which were found on sites on the banks of Vedic River Sarasvati mostly in Rajasthan has been compiled. *Yūpa* inscriptions were also found in Indonesia ascribed to the reign of King Mulavarman in Kutai kingdom.[298]
Tvastr maker of instruments, *vajra*

त्वष्टा वज्रम् अतक्षद आयसम् मयि देवासो वृजन्नपि क्रतुम्

मामानीकम् सूर्यस्ये वादुष्टरम् माम् आर्यन्ति कृत्येन कर्त्वेनच

Translation. Griffith: 3 For me hath Tvastar forged the iron thunderbolt: in me the Gods have centred intellectual power.

Translation: Sayana, Wilson: 10.048.03 For me *TvashTA* fabricated the metal thunderbolt; in me the gods have concentrated pious acts; my lustre is insurmountable, like that of the Sun; men acknowledge me as lord in consequence of what I have done, and of what I shall do. [My lustre is the Sun: my army is hard to overcome, like the sun's lustre; *anIka* = lit., face].

He slew the Dragon lying on the mountain: his heavenly bolt of thunder *Tvastr* fashioned. (RV 1.32.2).
Even for him hath *Tvastr* forged the thunder, most deftly wrought, celestial, for the battle (RV 1.61.6)
When *Tvastr* deft of hand had turned the thunderbolt, golden, with thousand edges, fashioned (RV 1.85.9)

Yea, Strong One! *Tvastr* turned for thee, the Mighty, the bolt with thousand spikes and hundred (RV 6.17.10)

Tvastr is the maker of divine instruments."*Tvastr* made it for him from the bones of the seer *Dadhica*: it is hundred-jointed, thousand-pointed. ..." (Rigveda)[299]

It appears that the orthographic shapes chosen during the Bronze Age to denote a metallic thunderbolt weapon use the wavy lines or streaks of lightning as a metaphor. Now that it is evident that iron forging is dated to the 3rd millennium BCE, the use of hardened or carbide ferrous metal weapons cannot be ruled out. The ancient word which denoted such a metallic weapon is *vajra* in Rigveda, specifically described as*Ayasam vajram*, metallic weapon or metallic thunderbolt.

I suggest that the association of the gloss *vajra* with lightning becomes a metaphor to further define *vajrasanghAta* 'adamantine glue' which creates a steel metallic form with nanotubes or cementite. I also suggest the person with three faces, seated in penance surrounded by animals on seal m0304 (so-called Pasupati seal) is likely to be *triśiras Tvastr*.

The *samAsa* used by Varahamihira is *vajrasanghAta*, an adamantine glue. In archaeometallurgical terms, this is defined as a mixture consisting of eight parts of lead, two of bell-metal and one of iron dust.

Vajra with octagonal bases. Indra. Visvantara Jataka. Great Stupa. Northern Torana, Sanchi, 1st half of 1st cent. CE (After Marshall, J. & A. Foucher, 1940, The monuments of Sanchi, Calcutta, vol. .II, pl. 29)

Vajra with octagonal base.Relief fragment. Dipamkara Jataka with Buddha & Vajrapani. Butkara, Swat, 1st-2nd cent. CE c., Museo Nazionale d'Arte Orientale 'Giuseppe Tucci', Roma, dep. IsIAO, Inv. MNAOR 1127, MAI B 65;79 (after Bussagli, M.,1984, L'Arte del Gandhara, Torino, p.146) Note: Vajrapani holds a *Vajra* of eight-angles.

चतुश्रि, अष्टाश्रि quadrangular, octagonal Sivalinga

Sivalinga, Lelei, Dist.Sundergarh. A full (Square base the (brahmabhaga), octagonal in the middle (vishnubhaga), cylindrical on top (rudrabhaga signifying the projecgting flame of the fiery pillar of light). I suggest that this is a signifier of wealth, nidhi, padma nidhi: *tAmarasa* 'lotuś rebus: *tAmra* 'copper'.

Sivapurana explains Lingodbhava in a variant narrative with Brahma (Hamsa) searching for the end of the pillar and Vishnu (*VarAha*) searching for bottom of the endless pillar of light, so depicted in the Mahes'vara temple, Tiruvatturai. Lotus is the centerpiece on the top decorative ring. bloomed lotus is carved as yonipitha, on the base of Sivalinga. *tAmarasa* 'lotuś rebus: *tAmra* 'copper'

NM-ALH-70357 Allahabad Museum. Sivalinga has preserved the plain octagonal section Visnu-bhaga surmounted by the circular Rudrabhaga from which projects Siva s head, wearing an elaborate jatajuta tied in the middle, karnatakundalas and ekavali. The third eye is marked vertically on the forehead.
Lingodbhava as Mahadeva, on the west side of the *Vimana*. Airavatesvara temple. Darasuram. *Hamsa* (flying paramahamsa). varAha.

Paramesvara tempe, Tiruvatturai. Lingodbhava. Somaskāṇḍa. Carries a paraśu (axe) and antelope (like Shu-ilishu who carries an antelope on an Akkadian cylinder seal): *melh* 'goat' rebus: *milakkhu* 'copper' (Pali).

Nāga worshippers of fiery pillar, Amaravati stupa Smithy is the temple of Bronze Age: *stambha, thãbharā* fiery pillar of light, Sivalinga. Rebus-metonymy layered Harappa script cipher signifies: *tamba, tā̃bṛā, tambira* 'copper'[300]

Ekamukha linga

Gupta, Linga with One Face of Shiva, India, early 5th century CE
Ekamukhalinga, 600s-800s East India, Bihar,

Sandstone Mukhalingam Pre-Angkor period, 7th century, Cambodia Height: 69 cm 27.17 inches; Width 21.7 cm 8.54 inches301

Muha. The quantity of iron at one time in a native smelting furnace.

(Santali dictionary, Campbell, p. 420). The ligature of a face on the linga is a Meluhha hieroglyph denoting: *mũh* 'face' is: *mũh* 'ingot' (Santali).mũh opening or hole (in a stove for stoking (Bi.); ingot (Santali) mũh metal ingot (Santali) mũhã = the quantity of iron produced at one time in a native smelting furnace of the Kolhes; iron produced by the Kolhes and formeḍ like a four-cornered piece a little pointed at each end; mūhā mẽṛhẽt = iron smelted by the Kolhes and formeḍ into an equilateral lump a little pointed at each of four ends; kolhe tehen mẽṛhẽt ko mūhā akata = the Kolhes have to-day produced pig iron (Santali)

Rudra, in his fiery matted hair has been depicted beautifully in the Ekamukha linga of Lord Shiva at Udayagiri in the 4th cent. CE? This artistry of showing wavy lines denotes that linga is a pillar of light, pillar of fire. Rudra was a Rigvedic asura, a form of Agni and associated with the 'roar' of wind or storm.

Ekamukha linga. Nui Ba The, An Giang, 6th-7th century CE Museum of Vietnamese History, Ho Chi Minh City, Vietnam

Linga, cổ vật được khai quật tại Ba Thê, thị trấn Óc Eo, huyện Thoại Sơn, tỉnh An Giang (Bảo tàng An Giang, Long Xuyên).

Jean-Pierre Dalbéra from Paris, France - Jatalinga sur cuve à ablution (musée Guimet)

Jatalinga sur cuve à ablution Vietnam, Thap Banh It (Tours d'argent), province de Binh Dinh (?) Style de Thap Mam, XIIème siècle Or et argent repoussé Salle sur la culture Cham (Vietnam).[302] Image abstraite d'origine phallique, le linga est la forme la plus sacrée du dieu Shiva. Il est ici marqué par le dessin stylisé du chignon d'ascète dont ce dieu est habituellement coiffé. La rigole qui l'entoure, munie d'un canal d'écoulement, est destinée à recueillir l'eau lustrale dont le linga est ondoyé lors du culte qui lui est rendu" extrait du cartel du musée

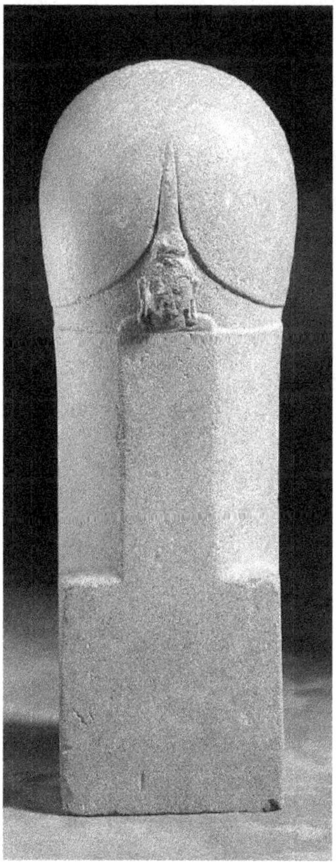

Guimet.[303]

Jatalinga période de Tra Kieu Xè siècle Grès gris Ce linga posé sur la cuve à ablations est lié au culte de Shiva Construit par l'École Française d'Extrême-Orient en 1915, le musée fut initialement baptisé Musée Henri Parmentier (nom de l'un des premiers explorateurs des sites du Royaume du Champa). Les oeuvres sont classées par provenance et par période, ce qui permet de suivre, de salle en salle, l'évolution de l'art cham au niveau de la sculpture. La majorité des objets proviennent des sites de Tra Kieu (ancienne capitale administrative du Royaume du Champa), de My Son, de Dong Duong (centre bouddhiste) et de Thap Man.

Ekamukhalinga, c. 700

Cambodia: Pre-Angkor period, 675-725 Sandstone 14-1/4 x 4-3/8 x 4-3/8 in. (36.2 x 11.1 x 11.1 cm) Norton Simon Art Foundation, from the Estate of Jennifer Jones Simon M.2010.1.202.S

Mukhalinga, Oc Eo, An Giang, 6th-7th century CE, sandstone

Large Khmer Shiva, Koh Ker, 10th Century

The Harran Inscriptions of Nabonidus

C. J. Gadd

Anatolian Studies

Vol. 8 (1958), pp. 35-92

Published by: British Institute at Ankara304

Stone. Cambodia. 67.0 x 18.4 x 18.4 cm, 55.73 kg.305

Mukhalinga được đề nghị công nhận Bảo vật Quốc gia đang được lưu giữ tại Disarn Văn hóa thế giới Mỹ Sơn. (Ảnh: Đoàn Hữu Trung/Vietnam)

Mukhalinga có trang trí hình tượng thần, chất liệu đá (Thế kỷ 6-7).306

Cambodia khmer, mukha-linga,7th-8th c. Art Gallery, New South Wales.

A

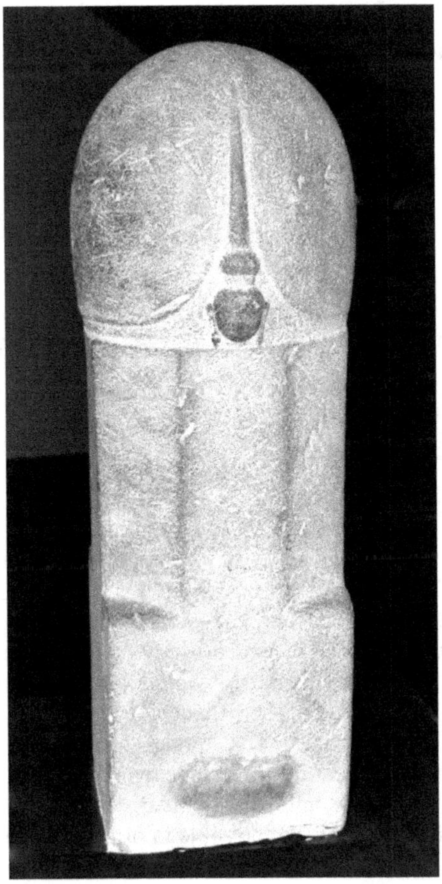

remarkable evidence is provided by a 6 ft. tall Phetchabun Province, Si Thep, Thailand Śivalinga which combines both चतुर्श्रि,अष्टाश्रि quadrangular and octagonal components with a चषालः caṣāla topping the aniconic sculpture with a 'face' hieroglyph: *mũh* 'face' (Hindi) rebus: *mũhe* 'ingot' *mũhā̃* = the quantity of iron produced at one time in a native smelting furnace of the Kolhes; iron produced by the Kolhes and formed like a four-cornered piece a little pointed at each end; *mũhā mẽṛhẽt* = iron smelted by the Kolhes and formed into an equilateral lump a little pointed at each of four ends; *kolhe tehen mẽṛhẽt ko mũhā akata* =

the Kolhes have to-day produced pig iron (Santali). Thus, the चतुर्श्रि,अष्टाश्रि *śivalinga* is a metalwork catalogue recording the iron smelted in a smelter. मेढ्या (p. 665) [*mēḍhyā*] *a* (मेढ Stake or post) Rebus: *meḍ, mẽṛhẽt* 'iron' (Ho. Santali) अश्रि [p= 114,2]*f.* the sharp side of anything , corner , angle (of a room or house) , edge (of a sword) S3Br.Ka1tyS3r._often ifc. e.g.

अष्टा*श्रि , त्रिर्-/अश्रि , च्/अतुर्-श्रि , शता*श्रि q.v. (cf. अश्र) ;
([cf. Lat. acies , acer ; Lith.assmu3]). (Monier-Williams) अस्रिः asriḥअस्रिः 1 An angle; अष्टास्रयः सर्व एव श्लक्ष्णरूपसमन्विताः Rām.1.14.26.-2 Ten million; see अश्रि. -अश्र, -अस्र *a.* (for अश्रि-स्रि) 1 four cornered, quardran- gular; R.6.1. A quality of gems; Kau. A.2.11. -2 symmetrical, regular or handsome in all parts; बभूव तस्याश्चतुरस्रशोभि वपुः Ku.1.32. (-श्रः, स्रः) 1 a square. -2 a quardrangular figure. -3 (in astr.) N. of the fourth and eighth lunar mansions अश्रिः aśriḥ श्री śrīअश्रिः श्री *f.* [अश्यते संहन्यते अनया अश् वङ्क्यादि° क्रि; cf. Uṇ.4.137] 1 A corner, angle (of a room, house &c. changed to अश्र at the end of comp. with चतुर्, त्रि, षट् and a few other words; see चतुरस्र); अष्टाश्रिर्वै वज्रः Ait. Br. -2 The sharp side or edge (of a weapon &c.); वृत्रस्य हन्तुः कुलिशं कुण्ठिताश्रीव लक्ष्यते Ku.2.2. -3 The sharp side of anything. अश्रिमत् *a.* Cornered, angular. (Apte. Samskritam)-

Linga with One Face of Shiva (Ekamukhalinga), Mon–Dvāravati period, 7th–early 8th century Thailand (Phetchabun Province, Si Thep) Stone; H. 55 1/8 in. (140 cm)

Ekamukhalinga from JaiyA. National Museum, Bangkok

Ekamukhalinga from Vat Sak Sampou. Ecole Francaise d'extreme-orient

(ekamukhalinga)...is divided into three parts in accodance with the prescriptions in the Siva Agamas. The base, the BrahmabhAga, is cubic in form and is 47.8 cms. High. The middle section, the ViSNubhAga, is octagonal in shape and is approximately 43 cms. High. The topmost section, the RudrabhAga, is cylindrical and is approximatey 51 cms. High, while the superimposed face measures 29.5 cms from the bottom of the chin to the top of the jaTA...Professor Malleret would date the most realistic lingas from the Transbassac area from the end of the fifth century to the beginning of the sixth century... It would thus seem that some Gupta ekamukhalinga, such as the early fifth century and very simple emblem from the cave temple at Udayagiri, is the ultimate prototype behind the JaiyA emblem and other somewhat similar ekamukhalingas of Cambodia and Borneo...It is not possible to offer an exact date for the JaiyA emblem but seventh through the eighth centuries would seem a reasonable guess."[307]

Ekamukhalinga. Jammu and Kashmir or Logar district, Afghanistan. Shahi period. ca. 7th or 9th cent. Royal Ontario Museum.Toronto, Canada. Note. the motif of 'flames' in the hairdo and on the wavy hairs of flames behind the ears..

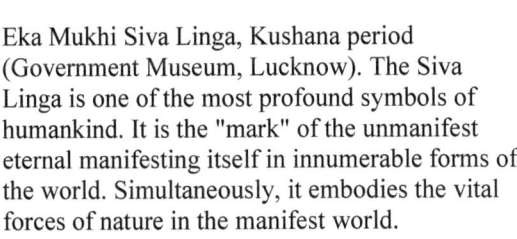

Eka Mukhi Siva Linga, Kushana period (Government Museum, Lucknow). The Siva Linga is one of the most profound symbols of humankind. It is the "mark" of the unmanifest eternal manifesting itself in innumerable forms of the world. Simultaneously, it embodies the vital forces of nature in the manifest world.

Ekamukhalinga, 600s-800s East India,

Bihar, Medieval Period, Pala Dynasty, 7th-8th Century[308] Ekamukhalinga Northwestern India 6th-7th century White marble Height: 32 cm[309] Galagesvara temple of Galaganatha. An octagonal pillar -- *Yūpa.*

It is possible that the quadrangular segment of the Yūpa is below the surface level of the circumambulating prAkAra of the Rudra-Siva temple.

Hoysala carving of a deity Shiva from a Belur-Halebid temple. Is he shown carrying a *Yūpa.* with चषालः *caṣāla* on his left hand? This explains why चषालः *caṣāla* is

orthographed as the जटा as seen in the JaiyA śivalinga. *caṣāla* चषाल This is a Rigveda word which signifies the top-piece of the *Yūpa.* (RV 1.162)

(22) **162** (म. 1, अनु. 22)

ऋषिः दीर्घतमाः औचथ्यः	छन्दः त्रिष्टुप् 1-2, 4-5, 7-22, जगती 3, 6	देवता अश्वः

मा नो मित्रो वरुणो अर्यमायुरिन्द्र ऋभुक्षा मरुतः परि ख्यन् ।
यद्वाजिनो देवजातस्य सप्तेः प्रवक्ष्यामो विदथे वीर्याणि ॥ 1 ॥
यन्निर्णिजा रेक्णसा प्रावृतस्य रातिं गृभीतां मुखतो नयन्ति ।
सुप्राङ्जो मेम्यद्विश्वरूप इन्द्रापूष्णोः प्रियमप्येति पाथः ॥ 2 ॥
एष च्छागः पुरो अश्वेन वाजिना पूष्णो भागो नीयते विश्वदेव्यः ।
अभिप्रियं यत्पुरोळाशमर्वता त्वष्टेदेनं सौश्रवसाय जिन्वति ॥ 3 ॥
यद्धविष्यमृतुशो देवयानं त्रिर्मानुषाः पर्यश्वं नयन्ति ।
अत्रा पूष्णः प्रथमो भाग एति यज्ञं देवेभ्यः प्रतिवेदयन्नजः ॥ 4 ॥
होताध्वर्युरावया अग्निमिन्धो ग्रावग्राभ उत शंस्ता सुविप्रः ।
तेन यज्ञेन स्वरंकृतेन स्विष्टेन वक्षणा आ पृणध्वम् ॥ 5 ॥
यूपव्रस्का उत ये यूपवाहाश्चषालं ये अश्वयूपाय तक्षति ।
ये चार्वते पचनं संभरन्त्युतो तेषामभिगूर्तिर्न इन्वतु ॥ 6 ॥

Griffith translation: RV 1.162.1-6

1. SLIGHT us not Varuna, Aryaman, or Mitra, Rbhuksan, Indra, Ayu, or the Maruts, When we declare amid the congregation the virtues of the strong Steed, God-descended. 2 What time they bear before the Courser, covered with trappings and with wealth, the grasped oblation, The dappled goat goeth straightforward, bleating, to the place dear to Indra and to Pusan. 3 Dear. to all Gods, this goat, the share of Pusan, is

first led forward with the vigorous Courser, While Tvastar sends him forward with the Charger, acceptable for sacrifice, to glory. 4 When thrice the men lead round the Steed, in order, who goeth to the Gods as meet oblation, The goat precedeth him, the share of Pusan, and to the Gods the sacrifice announceth. 5 Invoker, ministering priest, atoner, fire-kindler Soma-presser, sage, reciter, With this well ordered sacrifice, well finished, do ye fill full the channels of the rivers. 6 The hewers of the post and those who carry it, and those who carve the knob to deck the Horse's stake; Those who prepare the cooking-vessels for the Steed,-may the approving help of these promote our work.

Satapatha Brāhmana describes this as made of wheaten dough (gaudhūma).

गौधूम [p= 369,3] *mf*(ई *g.* बिल्वा*दि)*n.* made of wheat MaitrS. i Hcat. i , 7 (*f*(आ).) made of wheat straw S3Br. v , 2 , 1 , 6 Ka1tyS3r. xiv , 1 , 22 and 5 , 7.

गो--धूम a [p= 365,1] *m.* (√गुध् Un2.) " earth-smoke " , wheat (generally pl.) VS. TBr. i S3Br. v (sg.) , xii , xiv S3a1n3khS3r. Mn. &c गो--धूमी*f.* = -लोमिका L. गो *mf.* the thunderbolt Sa1y. on RV. v , 30 , 7

amṛtā abhūmeti 'we have become immortal'

--*Śatapatha Brāhmaṇa* elucidates the process using wheat chaff as चषालः caṣāla, the metaphor is ascent on Yūpa to heaven.

5.2.1.[9]*atha niśrayaṇo niśrayati | sa dakṣiṇata udaṅ roheduttarato vā dakṣiṇā dakṣiṇatastvevodaṅ rohettathā hyudagbhavati*

5:2:1:99. He then leans a ladder (against the post). He may ascend either from the south northwards, or from the north southwards; but let him rather ascend from the south northwards (udak), for thus it goes upwards (udak).

5.2.1.[10]*sa rokṣyanjāyāmāmantrayate | jāya ehi svo rohāveti rohāvetyāha jāyā tadyajjāyāmāmantrayate 'rdho ha vā eṣa ātmano yajjāyā tasmādyāvajjāyāṃ na vindate naiva tāvatprajāyate 'sarvo hi tāvadbhavatyatha yadaiva jāyāṃ vindate 'tha prajāyate tarhi hi sarvo bhavati sarva etāṃ gatiṃ gacānīti tasmājjāyāmāmantrayate*

5:2:1:1010. Being about to ascend, he (the Sacrificer) addresses his wife, 'Come, wife, ascend we the sky!'--'Ascend we!' says the wife. Now as to why he addresses his wife: she, the wife, in sooth is one half of his own self; hence, as long as he does not obtain her, so long he is not regenerated, for so long he is incomplete. But as soon as he obtains her he is regenerated, for then he is complete. 'Complete I want to go to that supreme goal,' thus (he thinks) and therefore he addresses his wife.

5.2.1.[11]*sa rohati | prajāpateḥ prajā abhūmeti prajāpaterhyeṣa prajā bhavati yo vājapeyena yajate*

5:2:1:1111. He ascends, with, 'We have become Pra*j*âpati's children;' for he who offers the Vâgapeya indeed becomes Pra*j*âpati's child:

5.2.1.[12]*atha godhūmānupaspṛśati | svardevā aganmeti svarhyeṣa gacati yo vājapeyena yajate*

5:2:1:1212. He then touches the wheat (top-piece) 2, with, 'We have gone to the light, **O** ye gods!' for he who offers the Vâ*j*apeya, indeed goes to the light.
5.2.1.[13] *tadyadgodhūmānupaspṛśati | annaṃ vai godhūmā annaṃ vā eṣa ujjayati yo*

vājapeyena yajate 'nnapeyaṃ ha vai nāmaitadyadvājapeyaṃ tadyadevaitadannamudajaiṣīttenaivaitadetāṃ gatiṃ gatvā saṃspṛśate tadātmankurute tasmādgodhūmānupaspṛśati

5:2:1:1313. And as to why he touches the wheat: wheat is food, and he who offers the Vâgapeya, wins food, for vâga-peya is the same as anna-peya (food and drink): thus whatever food he has thereby won, therewith now that he has gone to that supreme goal, he puts himself in contact, and possesses himself of it--therefore he touches the wheat (top-piece).

5.2.1.[14]*atha śīrṣṇā yūpamatyujjihīte | amṛtā abhūmeti devalokamevaitenojjayati*

5:2:1:1414. He then rises by (the measure of) his head over the post, with, 'We have become immortal!' whereby he wins the world of the gods.

5.2.1.[15] *atha diśo 'nuvīkṣamāṇo japati | asme vo astvindriyamasme nṛmṇamuta kraturasme varcāṃsi santu va iti sarvaṃ vā eṣa idamujjayati yo vājapeyena yajate prajāpatiṃ hyujjayati sarvamu hyevedam prajāpatiḥ so 'sya sarvasya yaśa indriyaṃ vīryaṃ saṃvṛjya tadātmandhatte tadātmankurute tasmāddiśo 'nuvīkṣamāṇo japati*

5:2:1:1515. Thereupon, while looking in the different directions, he mutters (Vâg. S. IX, 22), 'Ours be your power, ours your manhood and intelligence ours be your energies!' For he who offers the Vâgapeya wins everything here, winning as he does Pra*j*âpati, and Pra*j*âpati being everything here;--having appropriated to himself the glory, the power, and the strength of this All, he now lays them within himself, makes them his own: that is why he mutters, while looking in the different directions.

5.2.1.[16] *athainamūṣapuṭairanūdasyanti | paśavo vā ūṣā annaṃ vai paśavo 'nnaṃ vā eṣa ujjayati yo vājapeyena yajate 'nnapeyaṃ ha vai nāmaitadyadvājapeyaṃ tadyadevaitadannamudajaiṣīttenaivaitadetāṃ gatiṃ gatvā saṃspṛśate tadātmankurute tasmādenamūṣapuṭairanūdasyanti*

5:2:1:1616. They throw up to him bags of salt; for salt means cattle, and cattle is food; and he who offers the Vâgapeya wins food, for vâga-peya is the same as anna-peya: thus whatever food he thereby has gained, therewith now that he has gone to the supreme goal, he puts himself in contact, and makes it his own,--therefore they throw bags of salt up to him.

5.2.1.[17]*āśvattheṣu palāśeṣūpanaddhā bhavanti | sa yadevādo 'śvatthe tiṣṭhata indro maruta upāmantrayata tasmādāśvattheṣu palāśeṣūpanaddhā bhavanti viśo 'nūdasyanti viśo vai maruto 'nnaṃ viśastasmādviśo 'nūdasyanti saptadaśa bhavanti saptadaśo vai prajāpatistatprajāpatimujjayati*

5:2:1:1717. They (the pieces of salt) are done up in a*s*vattha (ficus religiosa) leaves: because Indra on that (former) occasion called upon the Maruts staying on the A*s*vattha tree 1, therefore they are done up in a*s*vattha leaves. Peasants (vi*s*) throw them up to him, for the Maruts are the peasants, and the peasants are food (for the nobleman): hence peasants throw them up. There are seventeen (bags), for Pra*j*âpati is seventeenfold: he thus wins Pra*j*âpati.

5.2.1.[18]*athemāmupāvekṣamāṇo japati | namo mātre pṛthivyai namo mātre pṛthivyā itibṛhaspaterha vā abhiṣiṣicānātpṛthivī bibhayāṃ cakāra mahadvā ayamabhūdyo 'bhyaṣeci yadvai māyaṃ nāvadṛṇīyāditi bṛhaspatirha pṛthivyai bibhayāṃ cakāra yadvai meyaṃ nāvadhūnvīteti tadanayaivaitanmitradheyamakuruta na hi mātā putraṃ hinasti na putro mātaram*

5:2:1:1818. Thereupon; while looking down upon this (earth), he mutters, Homage be to the mother Earth! homage be to the mother Earth!' For when B*ri*haspati had been consecrated, the Earth was afraid of him, thinking, 'Something great surely has he become now that he has been consecrated: I fear lest he may rend me asunder 2!' And B*ri*haspati also was afraid of the Earth, thinking, 'I fear lest she may shake me off!' Hence by that (formula) he entered into a friendly relation with her; for a mother does not hurt her son, nor does a son hurt his mother.

5.2.1.[19]*bṛhaspatisavo vā eṣa yadvājapeyam | pṛthivyu haitasmādbibheti mahadvā ayamabhūdyo 'bhyaṣeci yadvai māyaṃ nāvadṛṇīyādityeṣa u hāsyai bibheti yadvai meyaṃ nāvadhūnvīteti tadanayaivaitanmitradheyaṃ kurute na hi mātā putraṃ hinasti na putro mātaram*

5:2:1:1919. Now the B*ri*haspati consecration 3 is the same as the Vâgapeya; and the earth in truth is afraid of that (Sacrificer), thinking, 'Something great surely has he become now that he has been consecrated: I fear lest he may rend me asunder!' And he himself is afraid of her, thinking, 'I fear lest she may shake me off!' Hence he thereby enters into a friendly relation with her, for a mother does not hurt her son; neither does a son hurt his mother.

5.2.1.[20]*atha hiraṇyamabhyavarohati | amṛtamāyurhiraṇyaṃ tadamṛta āyuṣi pratitiṣṭhati*

5:2:1:2020. He then descends (and treads) upon a piece of gold;--gold is immortal life: he thus takes his stand on life immortal.

5.2.1.[21]*athājarṣabhasyājinamupastṛṇāti | taduparistādrukmaṃ nidadhāti tamabhyavarohatīmāṃ vaiva*

5:2:1:2121. Now (in the first place) he (the Adhvaryu) spreads out the skin of a he-goat, and lays a (small) gold plate thereon: upon that--or indeed upon this (earth) itself--he (the Sacrificer) steps.

5.2.1.[22]*athāsmā āsandīmāharanti | uparisadyaṃ vā eṣa jayati yo jayatyantarikṣasadyaṃ tadenamuparyāsīnamadhastādimāḥ prajā upāsate tasmādasmā āsandīmāharanti*

5:2:1:2222. They then bring a throne-seat for him; for truly he who gains a seat in the air 1, gains a seat above (others): thus these subjects of his sit below him who is seated above,--this is why they bring him a throne-seat.

5.2.1.[23]*audumbarī bhavati | annaṃ vā ūrgudumbara ūrjo 'nnādyasyāvaruddhyai tasmādaudumbarī bhavati tāmagreṇa havirdhāne jaghanenāhavanīyaṃ nidadhāti*

5:2:1:2323. It is made of udumbara wood,--the Udumbara tree being sustenance, (that is) food,--for his obtainment of sustenance, food: therefore it is made of udumbara wood. They set it down in front of the Havirdhâna (cart-shed), behind the Âhavanîya (fire).

5.2.1.[24]*athājarṣabhasyājinamāstṛṇāti | prajāpatirvā eṣa yadajarṣabha etā vai prajāpateḥ pratyakṣatamāṃ yadajāstasmādetāstriḥ saṃvatsarasya vijāyamānā dvau trīniti janayanti tatprajāpatimevaitatkaroti tasmādajarṣabas yājinamāstṛṇāti*

5:2:1:2424. He then spreads the goat-skin thereon; for truly the he-goat is no other than Pra*j*âpati, for they, the goats, are most clearly of Pra*j*âpati (the lord of generation or creatures);--whence, bringing forth thrice in a year, they produce two or three 2:

thus he thereby makes him (the Sacrificer) to be Prajâpati himself,--this is why he spreads the goat-skin thereon.

5.2.1.[25]*sa āstṛṇāti | iyaṃ te rāḍiti rājyamevāsminnetaddadhātyathainamāsādayati yantāsi yamana iti yantārameva inametadyamanamāsām prajānāṃ karoti dhruvo 'si dharuṇa iti dhruvamevainametaddharuṇamasmiṃloke karoti kṛṣyai tvā kṣemāya tvā rayyai tvā poṣāya tveti sādhave tvetyevaitadāha*

5:2:1:2525. He spreads it, with, 'This is thy kingship 1!' whereby he endows him with royal power. He then makes him sit down, with, Thou art the ruler, the ruling lord!' whereby he makes him the ruler, ruling over those subjects of his Thou art firm, and steadfast!' whereby he makes him firm and stedfast in this world;--'Thee for the tilling!--Thee for peaceful dwelling!--Thee for wealth!--Thee for thrift!' whereby he means to say, '(here I seat) thee for the welfare (of the people).'[310]

Yūpa is a kunda, a pillar of bricks. This kunda signifies a fire-alter or agnikunda in Vedic tradition. A signifier of the pillar is a चषालः caṣāla as its top piece. This चषालः caṣāla (Rigveda) is made of wheat straw for pyrolysis to convert firewood into coke to react with ore to create hard alloys, e.g. iron reacting with coke to create crucible steel or carburization of wrought iron in a crucible to produce steel.[311]

A skambha linking heaven and earth, a fiery pillar of light. The following three ricas of Rigveda also refer to and explain the metaphor of skambha as a prop which upholds heaven and earth; RV 9.89.6 places it in the context of purification of Soma, reinforcing the possibility that the Skambha signified the impeller of the purification process of yajna -- a process which is replicated in the purification of metals in a smelter/funace/fire-altar:

इन्द्रो॑ः दि॒वः प्र॑ति॒मानं॑ पृथि॒व्या विश्वा॑ वेद॒ सव॑ना॒ हन्ति॒ शुष्ण॑म्
म॒हीं चि॒द्द्यामात॑नो॒त्सूर्ये॑ण चा॒स्कम्भ॑ चि॒त्कम्भ॑नेन॒ स्कभी॑यान् ॥

10.111.05 Indra, the counterpart of heaven and earth, is cognizant of all sacrifices, he is the slayer of Śus.n.a; he spread out the spacious heaven with the sun (to light it up); best of proppers, he propped up (the heaven) with a prop. [Propped up the heaven with a prop: Satyata_ta_ = that which is stretched out by the true ones, the gods; or, ta_ti as a suffix, that which is true, i.e., heaven].

दि॒वो यः स्क॒म्भो ध॒रुण॒ः स्वा॑तत॒ आपू॑र्णो अं॒शुः प॒र्येति॑ वि॒श्वतः॑
सेमे म॒ही रोद॑सी यक्षदा॒वृता॑ समीची॒ने दा॑धार॒ समिषः॑ क॒विः ॥

9.074.02 The supporter of heaven, the prop (of the earth), the Soma-juice who, widely spreading, filling (the vessels), flows in all directions-- may he unite the two great worlds by his own strength; he has upheld them combined; (may he) the sage (bestow) food upon (his worshippers). [The prop of the earth: cf. RV. 9.089.06; may he unite: yaks.at = sam.yojayatu; a_vr.ta = by its own unaided strength].

वि॒ष्ट॒म्भो दि॒वो ध॒रुण॑ः पृथि॒व्या विश्वा॑ उ॒त क्षि॒तयो॒ हस्ते॑ अस्य
अस॑त्त॒ उत्सो॑ गृण॒ते नि॒यत्वा॒न्मध्वो॑ अं॒शुः प॑वत इन्द्रि॒याय॑

9.089.06 The prop of heaven, the support of earth-- all beings (are) in his hands; may (Soma) the fountain (of desires) be possessed of horses for you (his) adorer; the filament of the sweet-flavoured (Soma) is purified for (the sake of winning) strength.

Harappa Script in Bharhut, Sanchi proclaims sculptors architectural-metallurgical competence

Harappa Script hieroglyph on a Bharhut frieze is *sippī* 'bivalve shell' rebus: architect, *sippi, śilpin, viśvákarman* 'the divine creator'.

There are many hieroglyphs of Harappa Script at Bharhut and Sanchi which are proclamations of metal products made by artisans, sculptors with competence to work with metals.

Bharhut and Sanchi sculptors in metal had the competence to build and consecrate a Lohapasada, 'lofty copper mansion' (pace *Mahavamśa*).

**skambha2* ' shoulder -- blade, wing, plumage '. [Cf. **skapa* -- *s.v.* **khavāka* -- *]S. khambhu, °bho* m. ' plumage ', *khambhuṛi f. ' wing '; L. khabbh m., mult. khambh* m. ' shoulder -- blade, wing, feather ', khet. *khamb* ' wing ', mult. *khambhaṛā* m. ' fin '; P. *khambh* m. ' wing, feather '; *khā̃m f., khabhɔ* m. ' shoulder'(CDIAL 13640).

The flagpost is shaped like a pillar (phonetic determinant): *skambha* 'pillar' rebus: *kampaTTa* 'mint'. The sculptural expression can be read as: *sippi kammaTa* 'metal sculptor mint'.

The person with wings (carried on a flagpost by a rider with a snail on his headgear) may also signify a KINNARA but one with *khambhuṛi* f. ' wing '(Sindhi) rebus: *kampaTTa, kammaṭa* 'mint, coinage, coiner'. He is embellished with outflowing molluscs: *sippi* 'snail' rebus: *śilpi, sippi* 'sculptor, artificer, artisan'. He may thus signify memory of an ancestral image of a *viśvākarma* or *tvaSTr* or *Tuisto*, the divine architect.

Kinnara (male), Kinnari (female), Apsara, and Devata guarding Kalpataru, the divine tree of life. 8th century Pawon temple, Java, Indonesia. *kuṭi* 'tree' rebus: *kuṭhi* 'smelter'. The epic Mahabharata and the Puranas describe, regions north of the Himalayas as the abode of Kinnaras. This region was also the abode of a tribe of people called Kambojas.[312]

Kāṇḍari and Kinnara. Kāṇḍari-Jataka, Bharhut.[313]

Selected hieroglyphs as signifiers of metalwork (Bharhut Harappa Script hieroglyphs):
tAmarasa 'lotuś rebus: *tAmra* 'copper' Hieroglyph: pine-cone: *kaṇṭal* 'pine-cone'; maraka 'peacock' Rebus: मारक *loha* 'a kind of calcining metal' (Samskritam) *khaṇḍa, kaṇṭa* 'temple front' *smāraka*, 'memorial for ancestors"., n. < *khaṇḍa.* A portion of the front hall, in a temple; கோயில் முக மண்டபப்பகுதி. (S. I. I. v, 236.)Ash. piċ -- *kandə* ' pine ', Kt. pūċi,

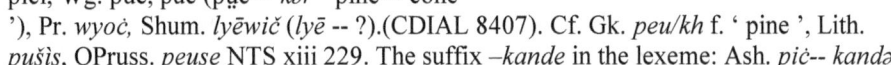

piċi, Wg. puċ, püċ (pūċ -- *kəŕ* ' pine -- cone '), Pr. *wyoċ,* Shum. *lyēwič* (*lyē* -- ?).(CDIAL 8407). Cf. Gk. *peu/kh* f. ' pine ', Lith. *pušìs*, OPruss. *peuse* NTS xiii 229. The suffix *–kande* in the lexeme: Ash. *piċ-- kandə*

' pine ' may be cognate with the bulbous glyphic related to a mangrove root: Koḍ. *kaṇḍe* root-stock from which small roots grow; ila·ti kaṇḍe sweet potato (ila·ti England). Tu. kaṇḍe, gaḍḍè a bulbous root; Ta. *kaṇṭal* mangrove, *Rhizophora mucronata*; dichotomous mangrove, Kandelia rheedii. Ma. *kaṇṭa* bulbous root as of lotus, plantain; point where branches and bunches grow out of the stem of a palm; *kaṇṭal* what is bulb-like, half-ripe jackfruit and other green fruits; R. *candel.* (DEDR 1171). Rebus: *khaṇḍa, kaṇṭa* 'temple front'. Rebus: *khānḍa* 'tools, pots and pans, metal-ware'. Rebus 2: kaṇḍ 'fire-altar' (Santali)

Brj. *dā̃u* m. ' tying '; H. *dā̃wrī* f. ' id., rope, string '; M. *dāvẽ* n.; Si. *dama* ' chain, rope ', (SigGr) *dam* ' garland ' Pk. *dāvaṇa -- n., dāmaṇī --* f. ' tethering rope '(CDIAL 6283) rebus: *dhAvaD* 'smelter'; *dhAtu* 'element, ore': *dhā́tu* n. ' substance ' RV., m. ' element ' MBh., ' metal, mineral, ore (esp. of a red colour) ' Mn., 'ashes of the dead' lex., ' *strand of rope' (cf. *tridhā́tu --* ' threefold ' RV., *ayugdhātu --* ' having an uneven number of strands ' KātyŚr.). [√*dhā*] Pa. *dhātu --* m. ' element, ashes of the dead, relic '; KhārI. *dhatu* 'relic'; Pk. *dhāu --* m. ' metal, red chalk '; N. *dhāu* ' ore (esp. of copper) '; Or. *ḍhāu* 'red chalk, red ochre' (whence *ḍhāuā* ' reddish '; M. *dhāū, dhāv* m.f. ' a partic. soft red stone ' (whence *dhā̆vaḍ* m. ' a caste of iron -- smelters ', *dhāvḍī* ' composed of or relating to iron '); -- Si. *dā* ' relic '; -- S. *dhāī* f. 'wisp of fibres added from time to time to a rope that is being twisted', L. *dhāī̃* f.(CDIAL 6773)

Procession on Horseback Bharhut, c. 100 BCE Indian Museum, Calcutta

Site Name: Bharhut Monument: Bharhut vedika Alternate Name: Railing from the stupa at Bharhut Subject of Photo: Figure on horseback Locator Info. of Photo: Vedika pillar, overview. Dynasty/Period: Sunga Date: 100-80 BCE, 100 BCE - 80 BCE Material: red sandstone Architecture: structural Dimensions: H - ca. 300.00 cm Current Location: Indian Museum, Calcutta, West Bengal, India Copyright Holder: Huntington, John C. and Susan L. Scan Number: 0052996

Bharhut. Vedica. Hieroglyph-multiplex: fish-fin, snail, elephant, crocodile. The Harappa Script hieroglyphs read rebus are: *khambhaṛā* 'fin' rebus: *kampaṭṭa* 'mint, coiner, coinage'; *sippi* 'snail' rebus: *sippi* 'sculptor'; *kariba* 'trunk of elephant' *ibha* 'elephant' rebus: *karba* 'iron' ib 'iron'; *karA* 'crocodile' rebus: *khār* 'blacksmith', kAru 'artisan'.

The flagpost carried on an elephant has the hieroglyphs: elephant, fish-fin, lotus, mollusc (snail): *kariba* 'elephant trunk' *ibha* 'elephant' rebus: *karba* 'iron' *ib* 'iron'. *aya* 'fish' rebus: *aya* 'iron' *ayas* 'metal'. *sippi* 'snail, spathe' rebus: *sippi* 'artisan, sculptor. *tAmarasa* 'lotuś rebus: *tAmra* 'copper'.

The Bharhut and Sanchi toranas are architectural splendour. The hieroglyphs which constituted proclamations on the gateways are recognizable as Harappa Script hieroglyph-multiplexes (hypertexts).

Tatsama (cognates) and *tadbhava* (common root) words in a comparative lexicon of Bharatiya languages (e.g. *Indian Lexicon*), establish the reality of Bharatiya *sprachbund.* It appears *mlecchita vikalpa* wass based on artificer-lapidary-metalwork lexis of Prakrtam (i.e., *vāk,* spoken form of Samskrtam).

1. *tAmarasa* 'lotuś (*tAmra*); *sippi* 'palm spathe, mollusc' (*śilpi* 'sculptor'); *eraka* (*arka* 'copper, gold'); *aya* 'fish' (*aya, ayas* 'iron') *khambhaṛā* 'fin' (*kammaṭa* 'coiner, coinage, mint (Kannada); *kariba* 'trunk of elephant' *ibha* 'elephant' (*ib* 'iron' *karba* 'iron' Santali.Turu). Hence the proclamation is explained as an advertisement hoarding by the Begram dantakara (ivory carvers) who moved to Bhilsa topes. There is an epigraph in Sanchi stupa which records the donations of *dantakara* 'ivory carvers' to the venerated *dhAtugarbha* (*dagoba*, stupa).

śilpin ' skilled in art ', m. ' artificer ' Gaut., *śilpika*<-> ' skilled ' MBh. [śílpa --] Pa. *sippika* -- m. ' craftsman ', NiDoc. *śilpiǵa*, Pk. *sippi* -- , *°ia* -- m.; A. *xipini* ' woman clever at spinning and weaving '; OAw. *sīpī* m. ' artizan '; M. *śīpī* m. ' a caste of tailors '; Si. *sipi -- yā* ' craftsman '.(CDIAL 12471) शिल्प [*śilpa*] n (S) A manual or mechanical art, any handicraft.

शिल्पकर्म [*śilpakarma*] n (S) Mechanical or manual business, artisanship. शिल्पकार [*śilpakāra*] m or शिल्पी m (S) An artisan, artificer, mechanic. शिल्पविद्या [*śilpavidyā*] f (S) Handicraft or art: as disting. from science. शिल्पशाला [*śilpaśālā*] f (S) A manufactory or workshop. शिल्पशास्त्र [*śilpaśāstra*] n (S) A treatise on mechanics or any handicraft. शिल्पी [*śilpī*] a (S) Relating to a mechanical profession or art.(Marathi) శిల్పము [*śilpamu*] *ṣilpamu.* [Skt.] n. An art, any manual or mechanical art. చిత్తరువు వ్రాయడము మొదలైనపని. శిల్పి or శిల్పకారుడు ṣilpi. n. An artist, artisan, artificer, mechanic, handicraftsman. పనివాడు. A painter, ముచ్చి. A carpenter, వడ్లంగి. A weaver, సాలెవాడు. (Usually) a stonecutter, a sculptor, కాసెవాడు. శిల్పిశాస్త్రము ṣilpi-ṣāstramu. n. A mechanical science; the science of Architecture. చిత్రాదికర్మలను గురించిన విధానము.(Telugu) சிப்பம்[3] *cippam, n. < šilpa.* Architecture, statuary art, artistic fancy work; சிற்பம். கடி மலர்ச் சிப்பமும் (பெருங். உஞ்சைக். 34, 167).சிப்பியன் *cippiyaṉ,n. < šilpin. [T. cippevāḍu, K. cippiga, Tu. cippige.*] 1. Fancy- worker, engraver; கம்மியன். (W.) 2. Tailor; தையற்காரன். (யாழ். அக.)சில்பி *šilpi , n. < šilpin.* See சிற்பி.சிலாவி[3] cilāvi, n. prob. *šilpin.* Artisan; சிற்பி. சிற்பர் *ciṟpar, n. < šilpa.* Mechanics, artisans, stone-cutters; சிற்பிகள். (W.) சிற்பி *ciṟpi, n. < šilpin.* Mechanic, artisan, stone-cutter; கம்மியன். (சூடா.)

khambhaṛā 'fin' (kammaṭa 'coiner, coinage, mint (Kannada): the Prakrtam word for 'fin' *khambhaṛā* has related phonemes and allographs (as Harappa Script hieroglyphs):

**skambha2* ' shoulder -- blade, wing, plumage '. [Cf. **skapa -- s.v. *khavāka --]*
S. khambhu, °bho m. ' plumage ', *khambhuṛi* f. ' wing '; L. *khabbh* m.,
mult. *khambh* m. ' shoulder -- blade, wing, feather ', khet. *khamb* ' wing ',
mult. *khambhaṛā* m. ' fin '; P. *khambh* m. ' wing, feather '; G. *khā̆m f., khabhɔ* m. ' shoulder '.(CDIAL 13640).

*skambhá*1 m. ' prop, pillar ' RV. 2. ' *pit ' (semant. cf. kū´pa -- 1). [√*skambh*]
1. Pa. *khambha* -- m. ' prop '; Pk. *khaṁbha* -- m. ' post, pillar '; Pr. *iškyöp, üšköb* ' bridge ' NTS xv 251; L. (Ju.) *khabbā* m., mult. *khambbā* m. ' stake forming fulcrum for oar '; P. *khambh, khambhā,khammhā* m. ' wooden prop, post ';
WPah.bhal. *kham* m. ' a part of the yoke of a plough ', (Joshi) *khāmbā* m. ' beam, pier '; Ku. *khāmo* ' a support ', gng. *khām* ' pillar (of wood or bricks) '; N. *khā̃bo* ' pillar, post ', B. *khām, khāmbā*; Or. *khamba* ' post, stake '; Bi. *khāmā* 'post of brick -- crushing machine', *khāmhī* 'support of betel -- cage roof', *khamhiyā* 'wooden pillar supporting roof '; Mth. *khāmh, khāmhī* ' pillar, post ', *khamhā* ' rudder -- post ';
Bhoj. *khambhā* ' pillar ', *khambhiyā* ' prop '; OAw. *khāṁbhe* m. pl. ' pillars ',
lakh. *khambhā*; H. *khām* m. ' post, pillar, mast ', *khambh* f. ' pillar, pole '; G. *khām* m. ' pillar ', *khā̃bhi, °bi* f. ' post ', M. *khā̃b* m., Ko. *khāmbho, °bo,* Si. *kap (< *kab);* --
X *gambhīra -- , sthāṇú -- , sthū´ṇā* -- qq.v.2. K. *khambürü* f. ' hollow left in a heap of grain when some is removed '; Or. *khamā* ' long pit, hole in the earth ', *khamiā* ' small hole '; Marw. *khā̃baṛo* ' hole '; G. *khā̃bhũ* n. ' pit for sweepings and manure (CDIAL 13639).

These semantic clusters indicate that the *skambha* 'pillar' and *skambha* 'wing' are also hieroglyphs and so depicted in Harappa Script Corpora. This leads to a reasonable inference that the *Atharva Veda Skambha Sukta* (AV X.7,8) -- an extraordinary philosophical enquiry into the Ruda hieroglyph as *linga, śivalinga* is also embellished with a चषाल: *caṣāla* (wheatchaff *godhUma*, snout of boar, *varAha*) is an intervention to explain the phenomenon of pyrolysis (thermachemical decomposition) and carburization which infuse carbon into soft metal (e.g. wrought iron) to create hard metal. The snout of boar is also called *pota*, evoking the *potR* 'purifier' of Rigveda and hence the abiding metaphor of Bharatiya tradition venerating *varAha* as *yajna purusha* personifying the Veda.

Annex L

List of Harappa Script 'text signs'

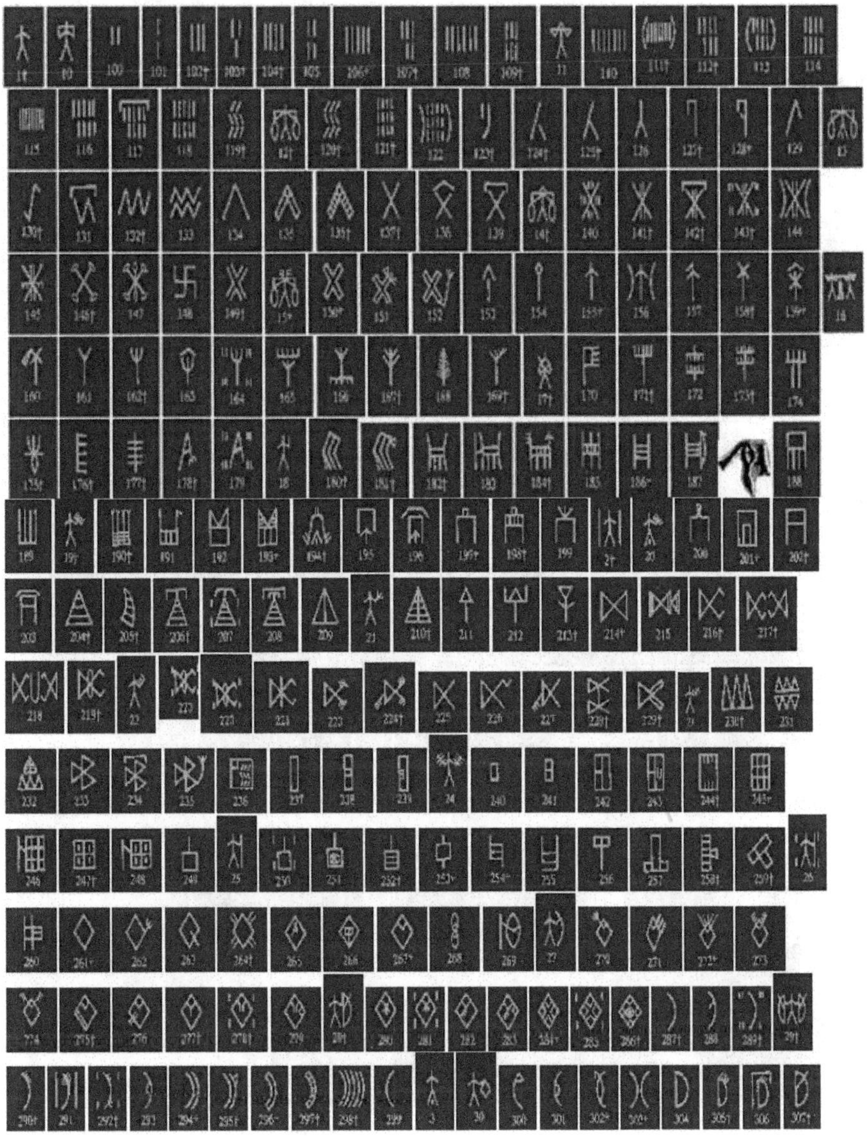

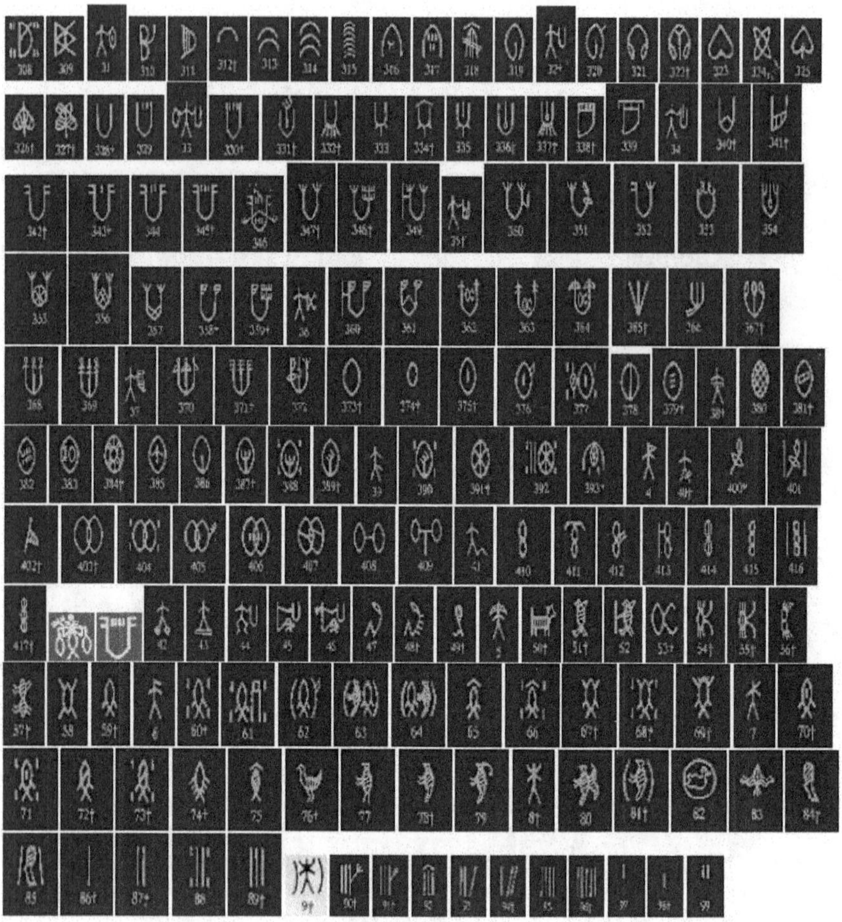

Sign Variants

 V001 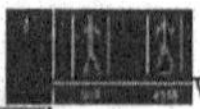 V002 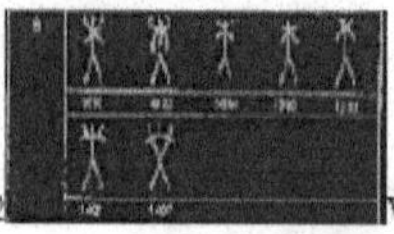 V008  V009

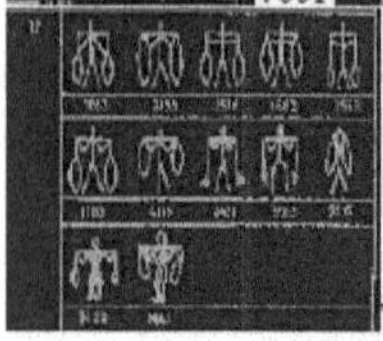 V012  V014 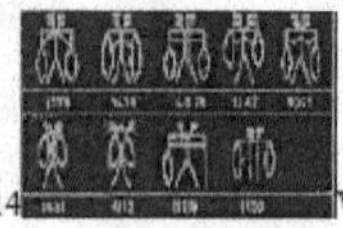 V015

V017
V019
V028
V029
V032
V035
V038
V039
V040
V048
V049
V050
V051
V053
V054
V055
V056
V057
V059
V060
V067
V068
V069
V070
V072
V073
V074
V076
V078
V081
V084
V086
V087
V089
V090
V091
V094
V096
V089
V090
V091
V094
V096
V098
V102
V103
V104
V106
V107
V109
V111
V112
V119
V120
V121
V123
V124
V125
V127
V128
V130
V132
V136
V137
V141
V142
V143
V146
V149
V150
V155
V158
V159
V162
V167
V169
V171

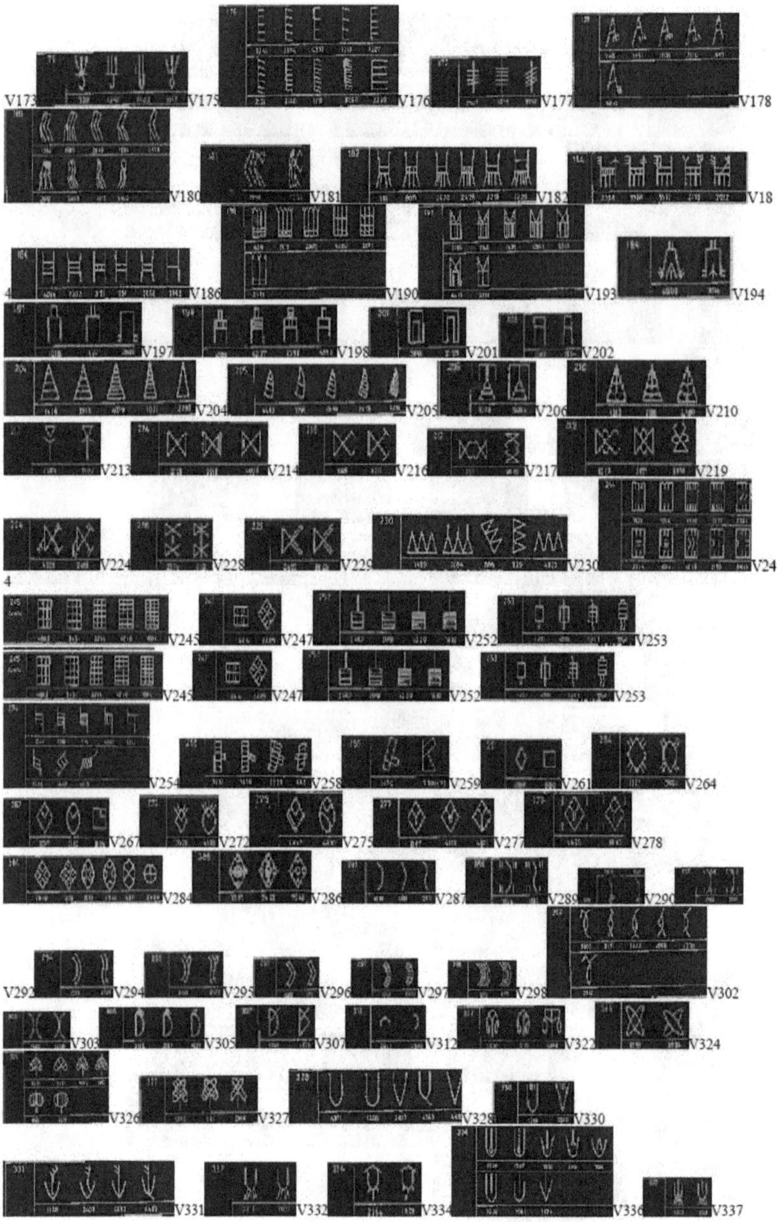
V173 V175 V176 V177 V178
V180 V181 V182 V18
4 V186 V190 V193 V194
V197 V198 V201 V202
V204 V205 V206 V210
V213 V214 V216 V217 V219
V224 V228 V229 V230 V24
4
V245 V247 V252 V253
V245 V247 V252 V253
V254 V258 V259 V261 V264
V267 V272 V275 V277 V278
V284 V286 V287 V289 V290
V292 V294 V295 V296 V297 V298 V302
V303 V305 V307 V312 V322 V324
V326 V327 V328 V330
V331 V332 V334 V336 V337

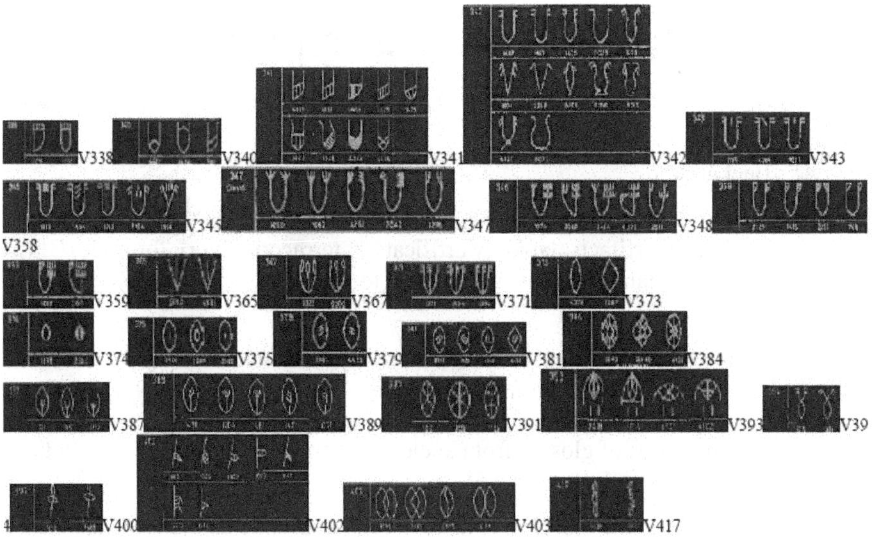
V338 V340 V341 V342 V343
V345 V347 V348
V358
V359 V365 V367 V371 V373
V374 V375 V379 V381 V384
V387 V389 V391 V393 V39
V400 V402 V403 V417

Select inscriptions of Harappa Script Corpora

Background

Seafaring Meluhha merchants used Harappa writing in trade transactions; artisans created metal artifacts, lapidary artificats of terracotta, ivory for trade. Glosses of the Proto-Indic or Harappa language are used to read rebus the Harappa Script inscriptions.

The glyphs of the Harappa script or Harappa writing include both pictorial motifs and signs and both categories of glyphs are read rebus. As a first step in delineating the Harappa language, an *Indian lexicon*[314] provides a resource, compiled semantically cluster over 1240 groups of glosses from ancient Indian languages as a Proto-Indic substrate dictionary.

The evidence is remarkable that many single glyphs or glyptic elements of the Harappa writing can be read rebus using the repertoire of artisans (lapidaries working with precious shell, ivory, stones and terracotta, mine-workers, stone-masons, metal-smiths working with a variety of minerals, furnaces and other tools) who created the inscribed objects and used many of them to authenticate their trade transactions. Many of the inscribed objects are seen to be calling cards of the professional artisans, listing their professional skills and repertoire. Many are veritable mining- and metal-work catalogs.

Continuing legacies of glyptic art noted by Huntington: "There is a continuity of composite creatures demonstrable in Indic culture since Kot Diji ca. 4000 BCE."315

The identification of glosses from the present-day languages of India on Sarasvati river basin is justified by the continuation of culture evidenced by many artifacts evidencing civilization continuum from the Vedic Sarasvati River basin, since language and culture are intertwined, resulting in a unique, logo-semantic writing system. .

Harappa writing in Ancient Near East is a tribute to the Meluhha artisans who have established an expansive contact area in Eurasia and left for posterity the bronze-age *harosheth hagoyim*, 'the smithy of nations.'

Concordance lists for epigraphs

Abbreviations and references to heiroglyphs and text transcripts

m-Mohenjodaro

h-Harappa

ABCDE at the end of a reference number indicate side numbers of an inscribed object. Multiple seal impressions on the same object are numbered 1 to 4.

At the end of the reference number:

'a' sealing; 'bangle' inscription on bangle or bangle fragment; other objects: shell, ivory stick, ivory plaque, ivory cube, faience ornament, steatite ornament; 'ct' copper tablet; 'Pict-'Pictorial motifs (0 to 145) described as illustrations of field-symbols in Appendix III of Mahadevan corpus (pp. 793 to 813); 'it' inscribed tablet; 'si' seal impression; 't' tablet.

Illegible inscribed objects are excluded in the following tabulations. Many potsherds Rahmandheri and Nausharo are excluded since the 'signs' are considered to be potters' marks; only those inscriptions which appear to have parallels of field symbols or 'signs' in the corpora are included.

Based on a number of resources and from the collections of inscribed objects held in many museums of the world, such as the Metropolitan Museum of Art, the Harappa writing Corpora include Sarasvati heiroglyphs, representing many facets of glyptic art of Sarasvati Civilization. The corporas also includes many texts of inscriptions, corresponding to the epigraphs inscribed on objects. The compilation is based mostly on published photographs in archaeological reports right from the days of Alexander Cunningham who discovered a seal at Harappa in 1875, of Langdon at Mohenjodaro (1931) and of Madhu Swarup Vats at Harappa (1940). The corpus includes objects collected in India, Pakistan, other countries and the finds of the excavations at Harappa by Kenoyer and Meadow during the seasons 1994-1995 and 1999-2000.

Framework for decoding epigraphs of Sarasvati Sindhu Civilization

This is also intended to serve as a pictorial and text index to Mahadevan Concordance and to the three volumes published so far of pictorial corpus of Parpola et al.

Many texts are indexed to the text numbers of Mahadevan concordance. The choice of this concordance is based on four factors: (a) the concordance is priced at a reasonable cost; (b) it is a true concordance for every sign of the corpus to facilitate an analysis of the frequency of occurrence of a sign and the context of other sign clusters/ sequences in relation to a sign and for researchers to cross-check on the basic references for the inscribed objects; (c) the exquisite nature of orthography is notable and 'readings' are authentic, even for very difficult to read inscriptions; and (d) signs and variants of signs have been delineated with cross-references to selected text readings.

Mahadevan concordance excludes inscribed objects which do not contain 'texts'; for example, this concordance excludes about 50 seals inscribed with the 'svastikā' pictorial motif and a pectoral which contains the pictorial motif of a one-horned bull with a device in front and an over-flowing pot. Parpola concordance has been used to present such objects which also contain valuable orthographic data which may assist in decoding the inscriptions. Many broken objects are also contained in Parpola concordance which are useful, in many cases, to count the number of objects with specific 'field symbols', a count which also provides some valuable clues to support the decoding of the messages conveyed by the 'field symbols' which dominate the object space.

Cross-references to excavation numbers, publications, photographs and the museum numbers based on which these texts have been compiled are provided in Appendix V: List of Inscribed Objects (pages 818 to 829) in Iravatham Mahadevan, 1977, *The Indus Script: Texts, Concordance and Tables*, Memoirs of the Archaeological Survey of India No. 77, New Delhi, Archaeological Survey of India, Rs. 250. In most cases, these text numbers are matched with the inscribed objects after Asko Parpola concordance [Two volumes: Rs. 21,000: 1. Jagat Pati Joshi and Asko Parpola, eds., 1987, *Corpus of Indus Seals and Inscriptions: 1. Collections in India*, Memoirs of the Archaeological Survey of India No. 86, Helsinki, Suomalainen Tiedeakatemia; 2. Sayid Ghulam Mustafa Shah and Asko Parpola, eds., 1991, *Corpus of Indus Seals and Inscriptions: 2. Collections in Pakistan*, Memoirs of the Department of Archaeology and Museums, Govt. of Pakistan, Vol. 5, Helsinki, Suomalainen Tiedeakatemia]. *Memoir of ASI No. 96 Corpus of Indus Seals and Inscriptions, Vol. II* by Asko Parpola, B.M. Pande and Petterikoskikallio (containing copper tablets) is in press (December 2001).

The debt owed to Iravatham Mahadevan, Asko Parpola, Archaeological Survey of India, Department of Archaeology and Museums, Govt. of Pakistan and Finnish Academy for making this presentation possible is gratefully acknowledged. I am grateful to Iravatham Mahadevan who made available to me his annotated personal copy of a document which helped in collating the texts with the pictures of inscribed objects. [Kimmo Koskenniemi and Asko Parpola, 1980, Cross references to Mahadevan 1977 in: *Documentation and Duplicates of the Texts in the Indus Script, Helsinki*, pp. 26-32].

Four epigraphs from Bhirrana from ASI website http://asi.nic.in and five epigraphs from Bagasra (Gola Dhoro) reported by VH Sonawane in *Puratattva*, Number 41, 2011 have also been included.

Pitfalls of normalising orthography of some glyphs

Parpola (1994) identifies 386 (+12?) signs (or graphemes) and their variant forms. Mahadevan (1977) identifies 419 graphemes; out of these 179 graphemes have variants totalling 641 forms.

Parpola observes: "...the grapheme count might be as low as 350...The total range of signs once present in the Indus script is certain to have been greater than is observable now, for new signs have kept turning up in new inscriptions. The rate of discovery has been fairly low, though, and the new signs have more often been ligatures of two or more signs already known as separate graphemes than entirely new signs." (Parpola, 1994, p. 79)

Many 'signs' are ligatures of two or more 'signs'.

In the process of normalizing the orthography of some glyphs to identify the core 'signs' of the script, some information is lost and at times, the process itself impedes the possibility of decoding the writing system. This can be demonstrated by (1) the 'identification' of a 'squirrel' glyph and (2) the failure to identify 'dotted circle' or 'stars' as glyphs.

It is, therefore, necessary to view the inscribed object as a composite message composed of glyphs: pictorial motifs and signs alike. Many scholars have noted the contacts between the Mesopotamian and Sarasvati Sindhu (Indus) Civilizations, in terms of cultural history, chronology, artefacts (beads, jewellery), pottery and seals found from archaeological sites in the two areas.

An outstanding contribution to the study of the script problem is the publication of the Corpus of Indus Seals and Inscriptions (CISI) Three volumes have been published so far:

> *Corpus of Indus Seals and Inscriptions, 1. Collections in India, Helsinki, 1987 (eds. Jagat Pati Joshi and Asko Parpola)*
>
> *Corpus of Indus Seals and Inscriptions, 2. Collections in Pakistan, Helsinki, 1991 (eds. Sayid Ghulam Mustafa Shah and Asko Parpola)*
>
> *Corpus of Indus Seals and Inscriptions, 3. 1 Supplement to Mohenjo-daro and Harappa, 2010 (eds. Asko Parpola, B.M. Pande and Petteri Koskikallio) in collaboration with Richard H. Meadow and Jonathan Mark Kenoyer. (Annales Academiae Scientiarum Fennicae, B. 239-241.) Helsinki: Suomalainen Tiedeakatemia.*

These volumes in which Asko Parpola is the co-author constitute the photographic corpus. The CISI contains all the seals including those without any inscriptions, for e.g. those with the geometrical motif called the 'svastika'. Parpola's initial corpus (1973) included a total number of 3204 texts. After compiling the pictorial corpus, Parpola notes that there are approximately 3700 legible inscriptions (including 1400 duplicate inscriptions, i.e. with repeated texts). Both the concordances of Parpola and Mahadevan complement each other because of the sort sequence adopted. Parpola's concordance was sorted according to the sign following the indexed sign. Mahadevan's concordance was sorted according to the sign preceding the indexed sign. The latter sort ordering helps in delineating signs which occur in final position. With the publication of CISI Vol. 3, Part 1, the total number of inscriptions from Mohenjo-daro totals 2134 and from Harappa totals 2589; thus, these two sites alone accounting for 4,723 bring the overall total number of inscriptions to over 6,000 from all sites (even after excluding comparable inscriptions on 'Persian Gulf type' circular seals from the total count).

Compendia of the efforts made since the discovery by Gen. Alexander Cunningham, in 1875, of the first known Indus seal (British Museum 1892-12-10, 1), to decipher the script appear in the references listed in he Bibliography.:

Alamgirpur Late Harappan pottery, a three-legged chakala_(After YD Sharma)

Alamgirpur Agr-1 a(2) graffiti

9062

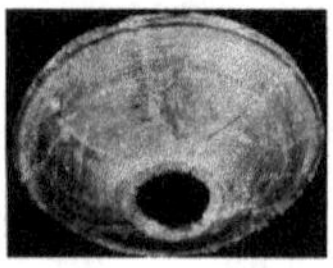

9063

Alamgirpur: Late Harappan pottery (After YD Sharma)

Alamgirpur2

Allahdino (Nel Bazaar)01

Allahdino (Nel Bazaar)02

Allahdino (Nel Bazaar)03

Allahdino (Nel Bazaar)04

Allahdino (Nel Bazaar)05

Allahdino (Nel Bazaar)06

Allahdino (Nel Bazaar)07

Allahdino (Nel Bazaar)08

Allahdino (Nel Bazaar)09

Allahdino (Nel Bazaar)11

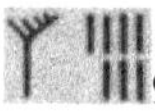
9061

Amri

9084

Amri

9085

Amri06

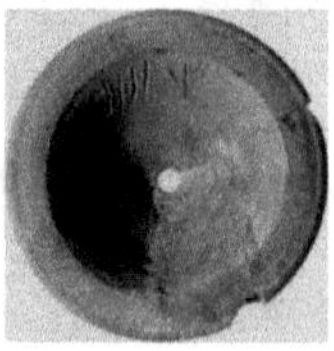

Amri07

Bagasra1 (Gola Dhoro)

Bagasra2 (Gola Dhoro)

Bagasra3 (Gola Dhoro)

Bagasra4 (Gola Dhoro)

Bagasra5 (Gola Dhoro)

Balakot01

Balakot 02

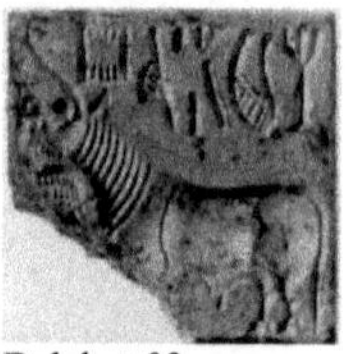

Balakot 03

Balakot 04

Balakot 05

Balakot 06 bangle

Balakot 06bangle

Balakot 06C

Banawali1

Banawali10
9204

Banawali11

Banawali12

Banawali13a

Banawali14

Banawali15 

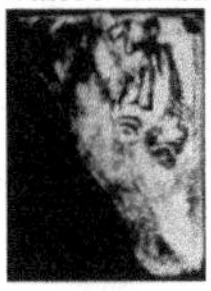
9203

Banawali16

Banawali 17

9201

Banawali 18a

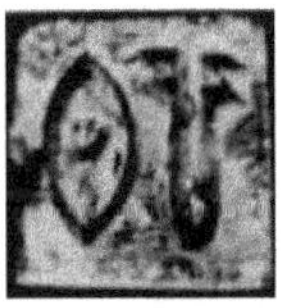

Banawali19

Banawali2

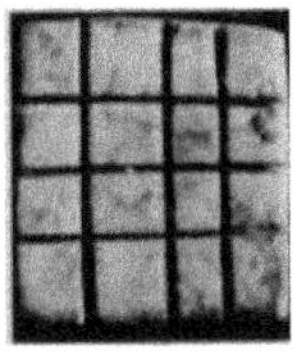

Banawali 20

Banawali 21a

9205

Banawali 23A

Banawali 23B

Banawali 24t
9211

Banawali 26A

Banawali0026a

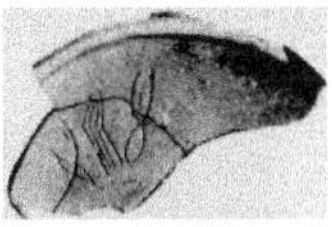
Banawali 28A

9221

Banawali 3

Banawali30

Banawali 4

Banawali 5

9203

Banawali 6

Banawali 7

Banawali 8

Banawali 9C

Bet Dwaraka 1

S'ankha seal. One-horned bull, short-horned bull looking down and an antelope looking backward.

Bhirrana1

Bhirrana2

Bhirrana3

Bhirrana4

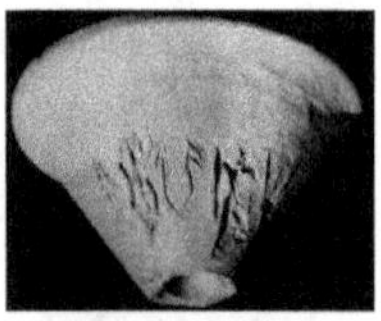

Chandigarh01

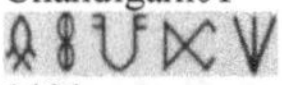

9101

Chandigarh02

9102

Chandigarh

9103

Chandigarh

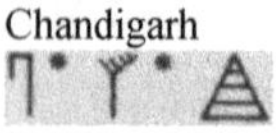

9104

Chanhudaro10

6129

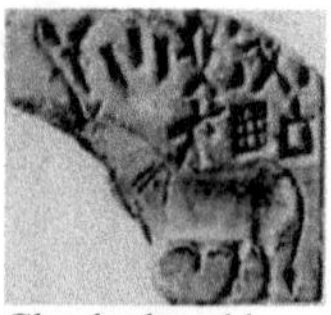

Chanhudaro 11

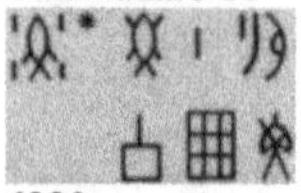

6220

Chanhudaro12a

6231

Chanhudaro13

6221

Chanhudaro14a

6108

Chanhudaro15a

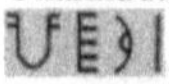

6213

Chanhudaro16a

6222

Chanhudaro17a

6122

Chanhudaro18a

6216

Chanhudaro1a

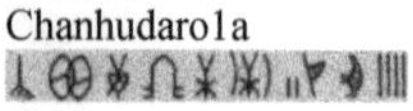

6125

Chanhudaro2

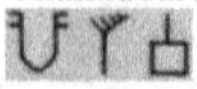

6128

Chanhudaro20

6210

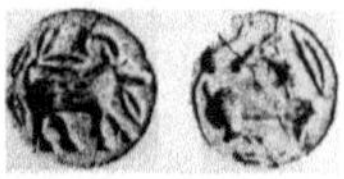

Chanhudaro Seal obverse and reverse. The oval sign of this Jhukar culture seal is comparable to other inscriptions. Fig. 1 and 1a of Plate L. After Mackay, 1943.

Chanhudaro21a

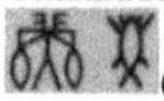

6209

Chanhudaro22a

6115

Chanhudaro23

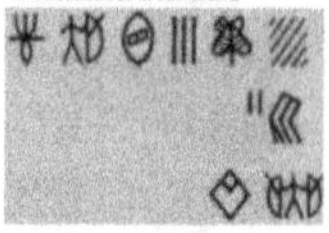

6402 Goat-antelope with a short tail.

The object in front of the goat-antelope is a double-axe.

Chanhudaro24a

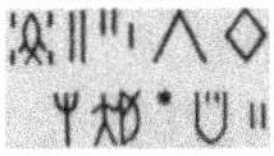

6116

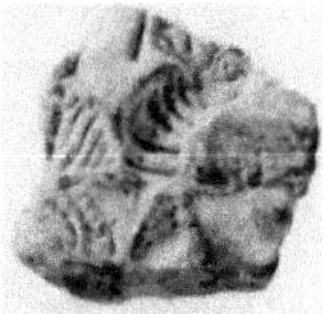

Chanhudaro25

Chanhudaro26

6405

Chanhudaro27

Chanhudaro28

Chanhudaro29

6403

Chanhudaro3

6230

Chanhudaro30

6111

Chanhudaro32a

6123

Chanhudaro33a

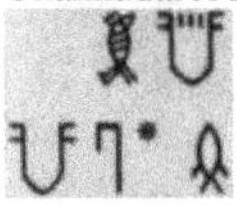

6104

Chanhudaro. Tablet. Obverse and reverse. Alligator and Fish. Fig. 33 and 33a. of Plate LII. After Mackay, 1943.

6233 Pict-67: Gharial, sometimes with a fish held in its jaw and/or surrounded by a school of fish.

6303

6304

6301

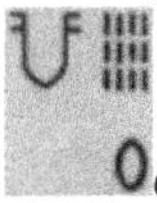6305

6109

6112

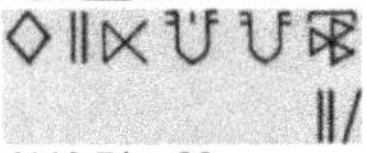

6113 Pict-98

It is seen from an enlargement of the bottom portion of the seal impression that the ‘prostrate person’ may not be a person but a ligature of the neck of an antelope with rings on its necks or of a post with ring-stones. The head of the ‘person’ is not shown. So, I would surmise that this is an artist's representation of an act of copulation (by an animal) + a ligatured neck of another bovine or alternatively, a pillar with ring-stones ligatured to the bottom portion of a body. It is not uncommon in the artistic tradition to ligature bodies to the rump of, for example, a bull's posterior ligatured to a horned woman (Pict. 103 Mahadevan) or standing person with horns and bovine features (hoofed legs and/or tail) -- Pict. 86-88 Mahadevan.

Bison (gaur) trampling a prostrate person (?) underneath. Impression of a seal from Chanhujodaro (Mackay 1943: pl. 51: 13). The prostrate ‘person’ is seen to have a very long neck, possibly with neck-rings, reminiscent of the rings depicted on the neck of the one-horned bull normally depicted in front of a standard device.

6114

Pict-108

Person kneeling under a tree facing a tiger. [*Chanhudaro Excavations*, Pl. LI, 18]

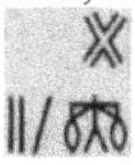

6118

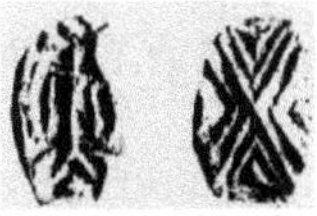

Chanhudaro Seal obverse and reverse. The ‘water-carrier’ and X signs of this so-called Jhukar culture seal are comparable to other inscriptions. Fig. 3 and 3a of Plate L. After Mackay, 1943.

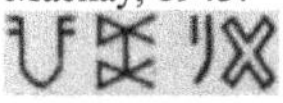

6120 Pict-40

Ox-antelope with a long tail; a trough in front.

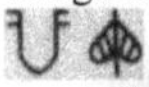 6121

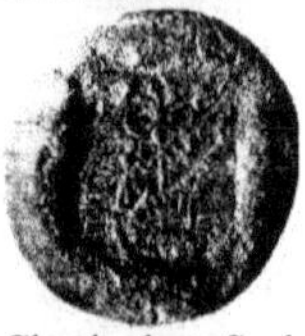

Chanhudaro. Seal impression. Fig. 35 of Plate LII. After Mackay, 1943.

6124

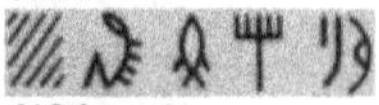

6126

6130

6131

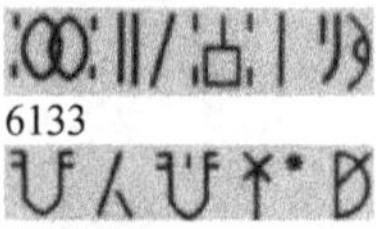

6133

6201

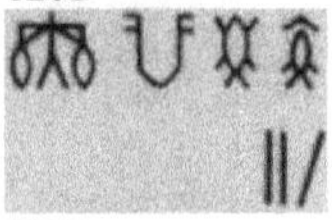

6202

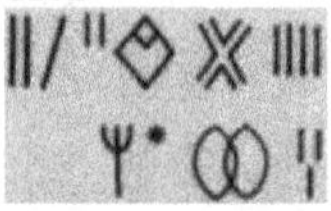

6203

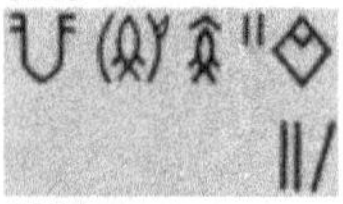

6204

6208

6211

6214

6215

6217

6218

6219

6223

6224

6225

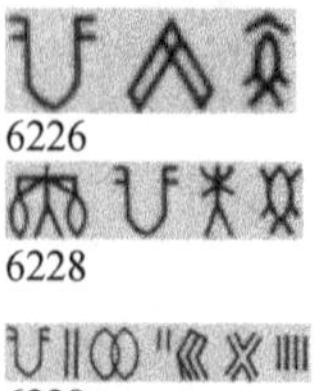

6226

6228

6229

 6232

Chanhudaro. Tablet. Fig. 34 of Plate LII. After Mackay, 1943.

 6234

Chanhudaro. Seal impression. Fig. 35 of Plate LII. After Mackay,

1943. 

6235

Chanhudaro38A

Chanhudaro

39A1

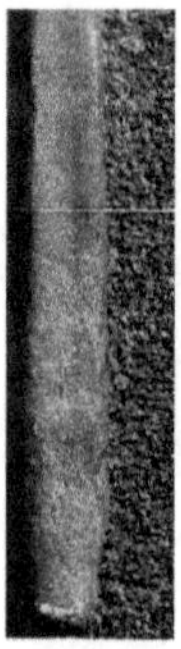

Chanhudaro

39A2

Chanhudaro4

6206

Chanhudaro40A

6306

Chanhudaro40B

Chanhudaro41a

Chanhudaro42

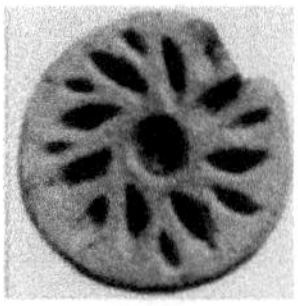

Chanhudaro43

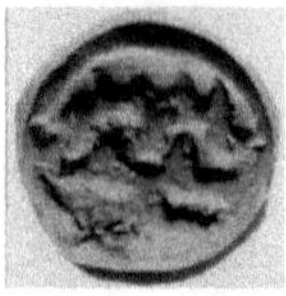

Chanhudaro46a

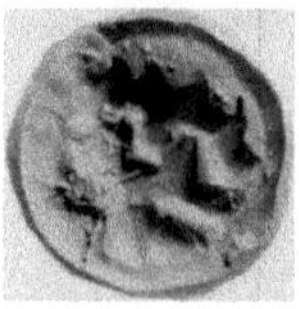

Chanhudaro46b

Chanhudaro47

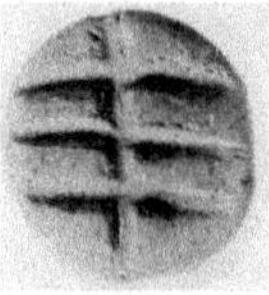

Chanhudaro 48

Chanhudaro49A

Chanhudaro49B

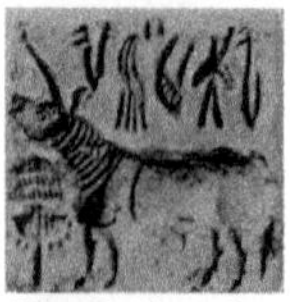

Chanhudaro 5

6132

Chanhudaro50A

Chanhudaro50B

Chanhudaro 6

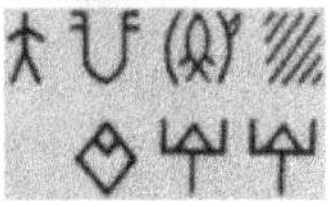

6205

Chanhudaro 7

6207

Chanhudaro 8
6227

Chanhudaro 9

6127

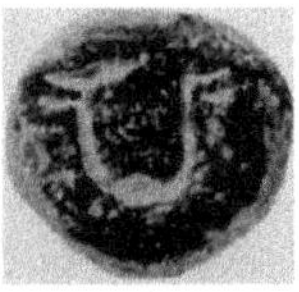

Daimabad1
Sign342

Daimabad 2a

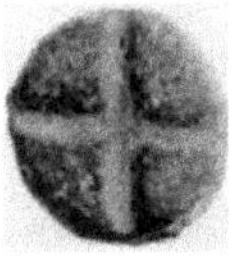
Daimabad 3A

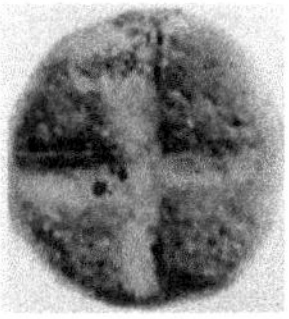
Daimabad 3B

Daimabad 4

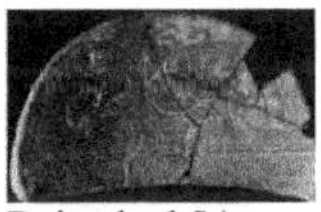
Daimabad 5A

Daimabad 5B

Desalpur1a

9071Desalpur2

esalpur3

9073

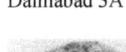

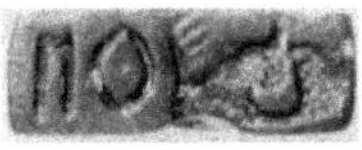

Dholavira Sign-board mounted on a gateway.

Dholavira (Kotda) on Kadir island, Kutch, Gujarat; 10 signs inscription found near the western chamber of the northern gate of the citadel high mound (Bisht, 1991: 81, Pl. IX).

Dholavira: Seals (Courtesy ASI)

Dholavira1a

9121

Dholavira 2a

Gharo Bhiro
(Nuhato) 01

Gumla10a

Gumla8a

h001a

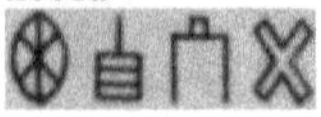

4010

h002

4012

h003

4002

h004

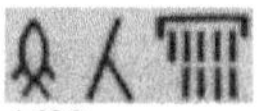

4693

h005

4004

h006a

4006

h007

4008

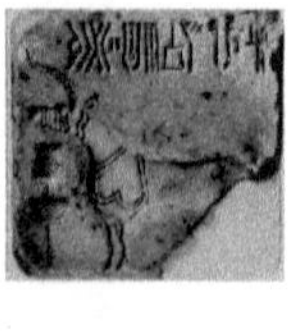

h008 4001

h009

4009

h010a

4003

h011a

4038

h012

4005

h013

5055

h014

4106

h015

4053

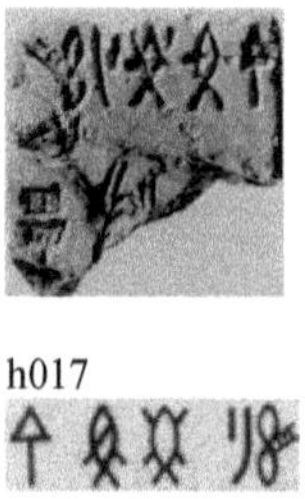

h017

4052

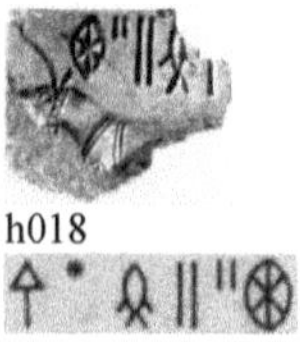

h018

4071

h019

4694

h020

4019

h021

4022

h022

4023

h023

4047

h024

4013

h025

4081

h026

4016

h027

4017

h028

4040

h029

4042

h030

4049

h031

4103

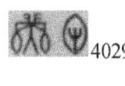

h032 4018

h033

5059

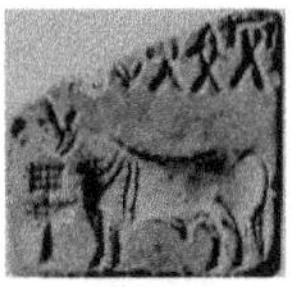

h035

5083

h036

4113

h037 4031

h038

4029

h039

h040

4072

h041

4178

h042

**4057

h043

4077

h044

4028

h045

4043

h046

4076

h047

4030

h048 4091

h049

4133

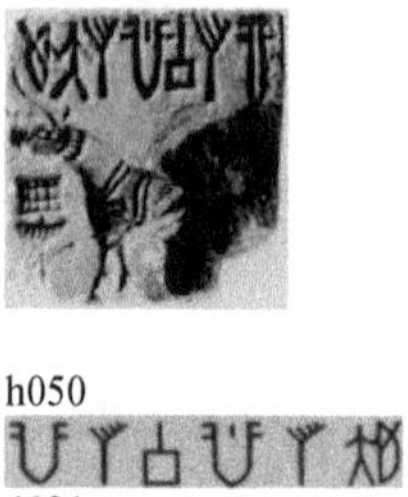

h050

4131

h051

4090

h052

4109

h053 5089

h054 4085

h055

4107

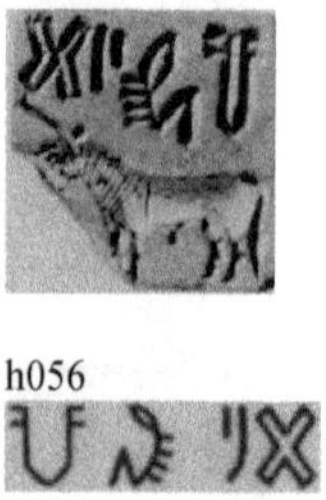

h056

4110

h057 4086

h058

4105

h059 5120

h060

5119

h061

4118

h062

4128

h063 4142

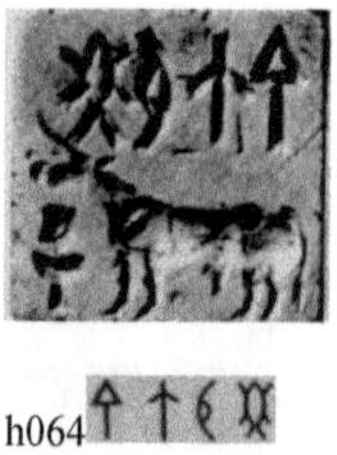

h064

h065 4094

h066

4130

h067 4115

h068

4141

h069 4146

h070 4122

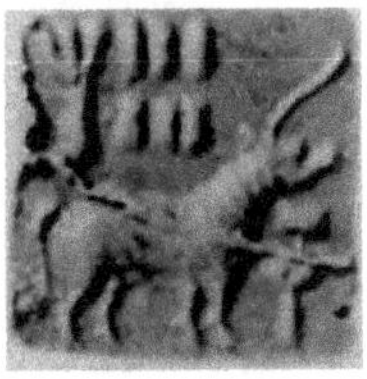
h071 5054

h072

4120

h073 4617 [An orthographic representation of a water-carrier].

h074

4135

h075
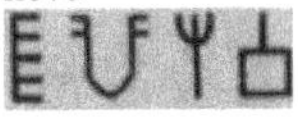
4161

h076

4241

h077

h078

4244

h079

5060

h080
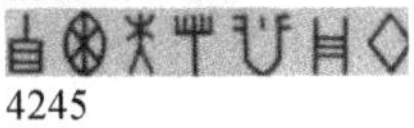
4245

h081 5063

h082a Text 4238

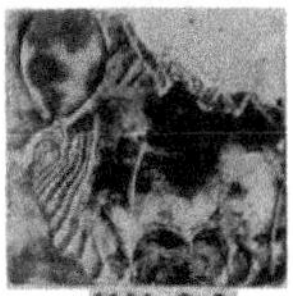
h083
4236

h084

h085

4232

h086

4233

h087

4240

h088

4253

h089

090

227

h091

4230

h092

4229

h093a 4231

h094 4246

h095

h096

4249

h097 Pict-95: Seven robed figures (with pigtails, twigs)

4251

h098

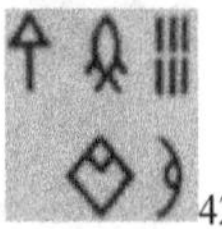
4256

Pict-122 Standard device which is normally in front of a one-horned bull.

h099 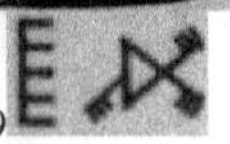

4223

h100  4258

One-horned bull.

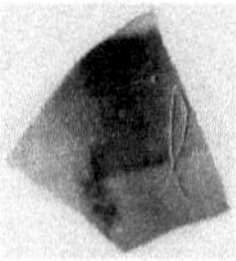

h1002

h1007

h101 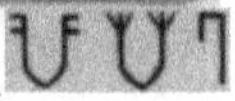

5069

h1010bangle

h1011cone 

5103

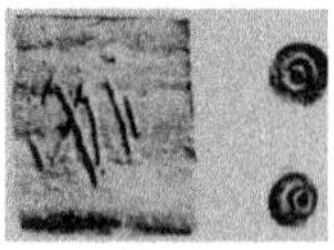

h1012cone

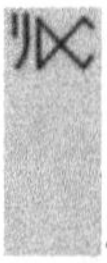

h1017ivorystick

4561

h1018copperobjec t Head of one-horned bull ligatured with a four-pointed star-fish (Gangetic octopus?)

h102A*

h102B

h102D

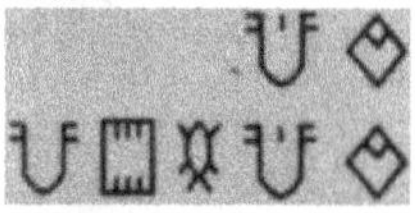

5056

h103

4254

h104

h105

h106

h107

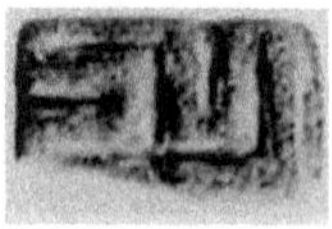

h108

h109

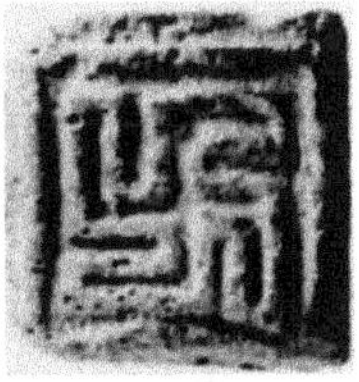

h110

h111

h112

h113

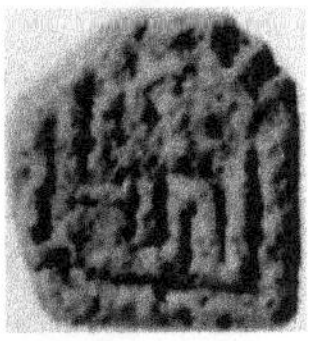

h114

h115

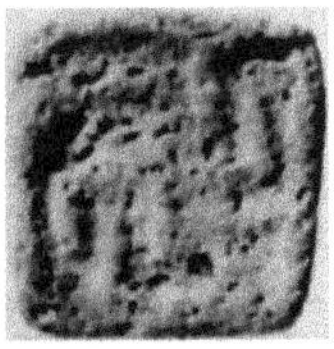

h116

h117

h118

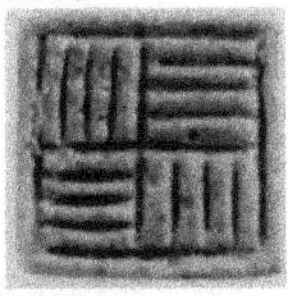

h119

h120

h121

h122

h123

h124

h125

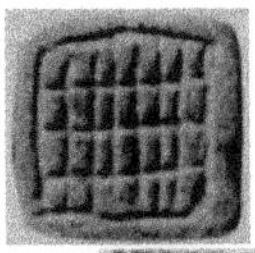

h126
h127

h130

5096

h131 4271

h128

h129A

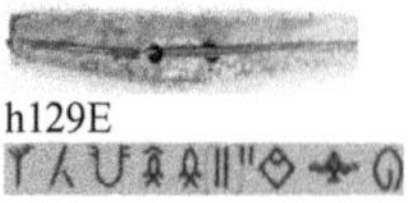
h129E
4269

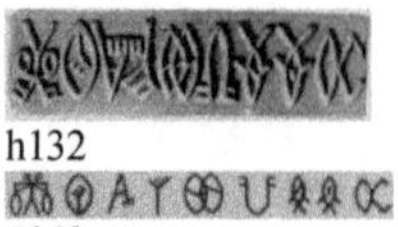
h132
5052

h133
4261

h134
4264

h135
4270

h136
4288

h137a
5058

h138a
5072

h139

4267

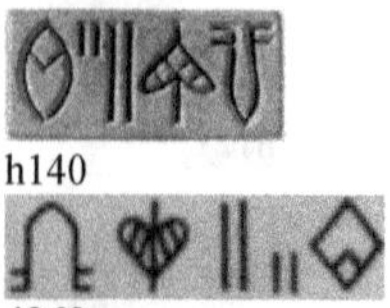
h140
4268

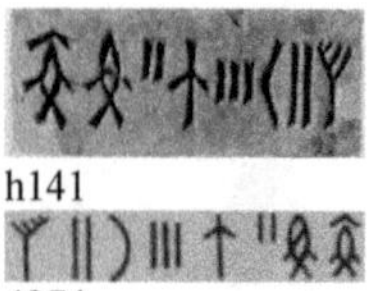
h141
4274

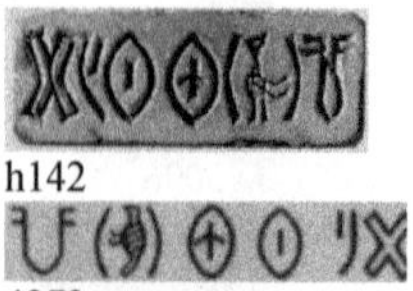
h142
4272

h143a
5101

h144
4280

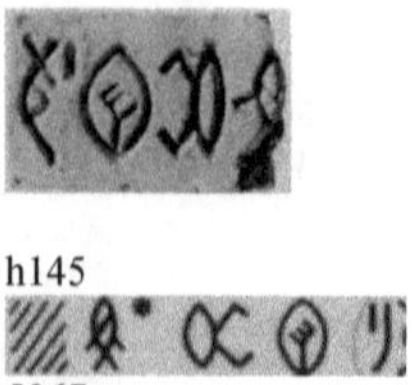
h145
5067

h146
4628

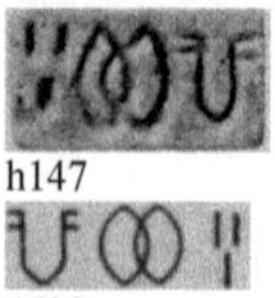
h147
4629

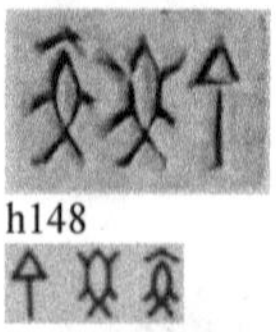
h148
4285

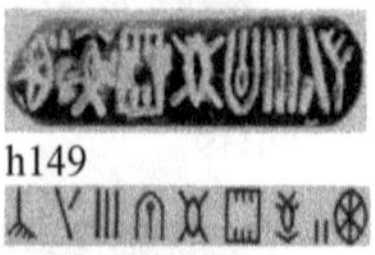
h149
4275

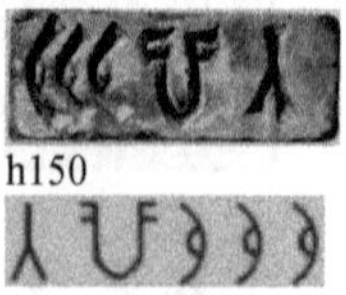
h150
4283

h151
5057

h152
5016

h153

4627

h154
4282

h155
4630

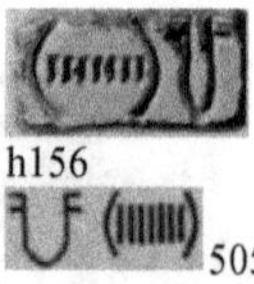
h156
5051

h157
4284

h158
4297

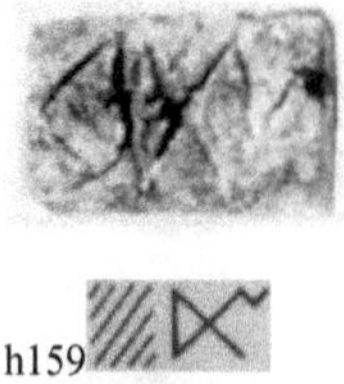
h159
4633

h160A

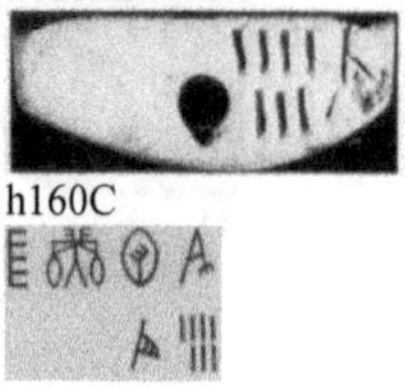
h160C
4276

h161

4262

h162

4294

h163

h164

5046

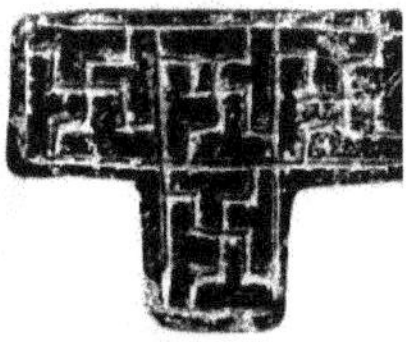

h165

h166A

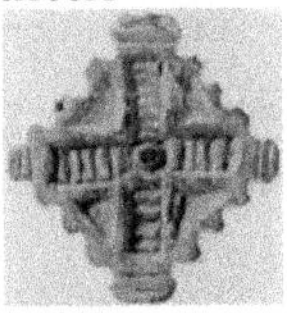

h166B

h167A

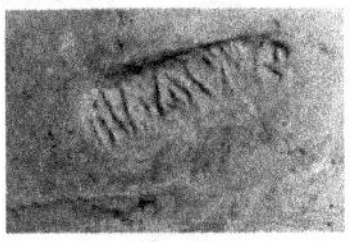

h167A2

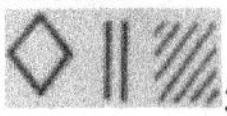

5225

h168

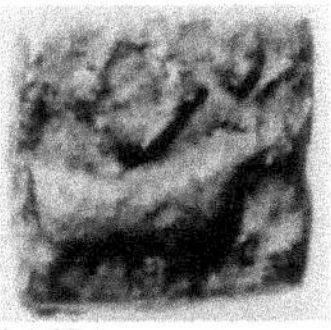

h169A

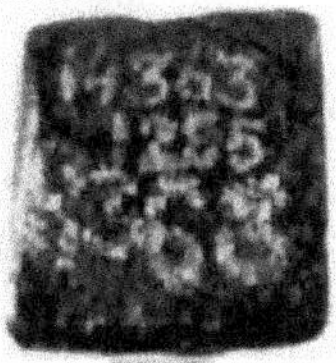

h169B

5298

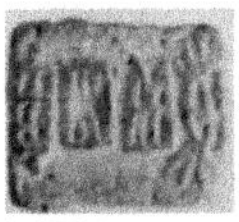

h170A

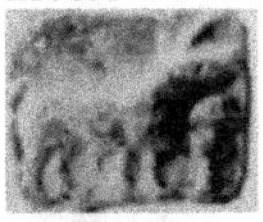

h170B

4701

h171A

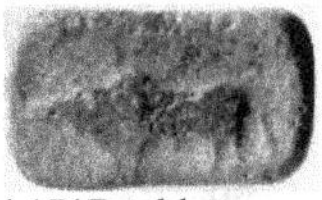

h171B tablet

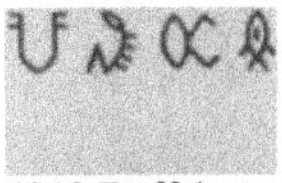

4312 Buffalo.

h172A

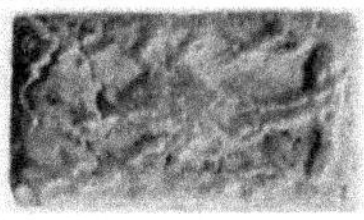

h172B

5305 Pict-66: Gharial, sometimes with a fish held in its jaw and/or surrounded by a school of fish.

h173A

h173B

4333

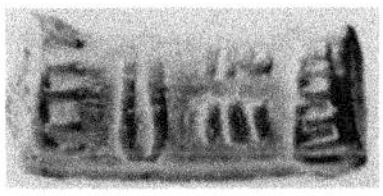

h174A

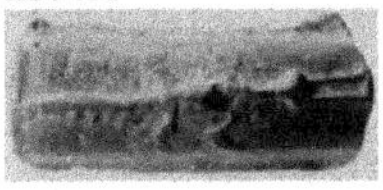

h174B

4338

h175A

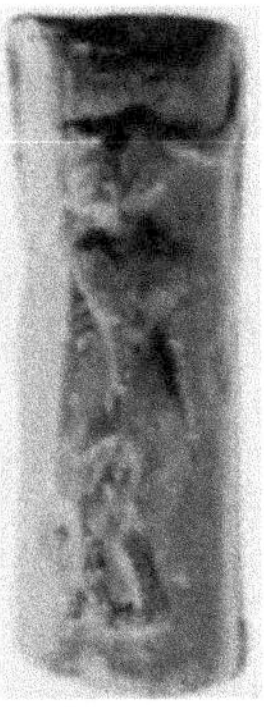

h175B Pict-87

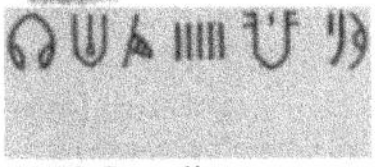

4319 Standing person with horns and bovine features (hoofed legs and/or tail).

h176A

h176B

h176bb

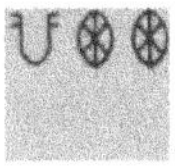

4303

Tablet in bas-relief h176a Person standing at the centerbetween a two-tiered structure at R., and a short-horned bull (bison) standing near a trident-headed post at L. h176b From R.—a tiger (?); a seated, pigtailed person on a platform; flanked on either side by a person seated on a tree with a tiger, below, looking back. A hare (or goat?) is seen near the platform.

h177A

h177B

4316 Pict-115: From R.—a person standing under an ornamental arch; a kneeling adorant; a ram with long curving horns.

h178A

h178B

4318

Pict-84: Person wearing a diadem or tall head-dress (with twig?) standing within an arch or two pillars?

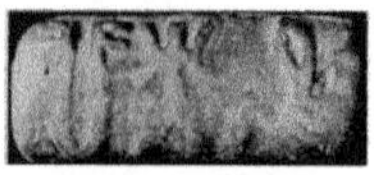

h179A

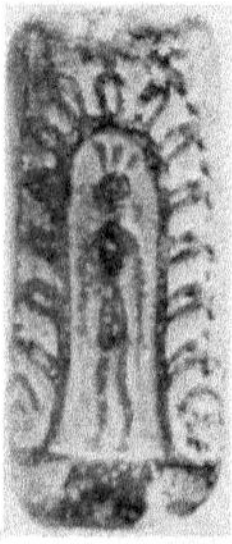

h179B

4307 Pict-83: Person wearing a diadem or tall head-dress standing within an ornamented arch; there are two stars on either side, at the bottom of the arch.

h180A

h180B

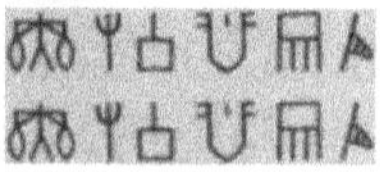

4304 Tablet in bas-relief h180a Pict-106: Nude female figure upside down with thighs drawn apart and crab (?) issuing from her womb; two tigers standing face to face rearing on their hindlegs at L.

h180b

Pict-92: Man armed with a sickle-shaped weapon on his right hand and a cakra (?) on his left hand, facing a seated woman with disheveled hair and upraised arms.

h181A

h181B

h182A

h182B

4306Tablet in bas-relief

h182a Pict-107: Drummer and a tiger.

h182b Five svastika signs alternating right- and left-handed.

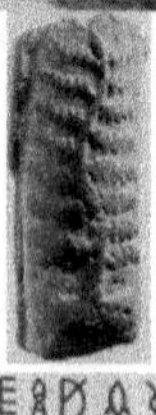

h183A

h183B

4327

h184A

h184B

h185A

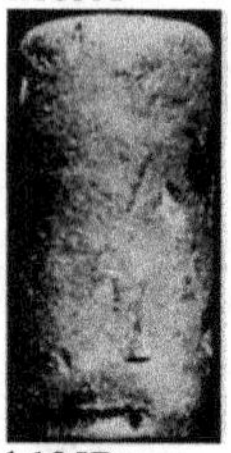

h185B

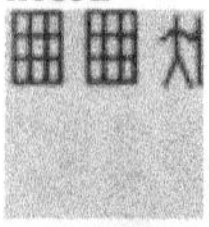

5279

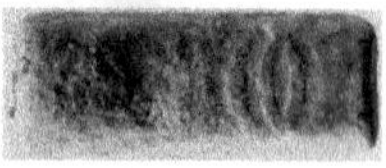

h186A

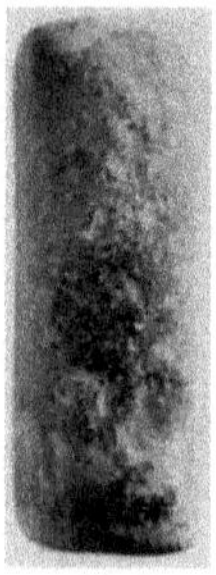

h186B

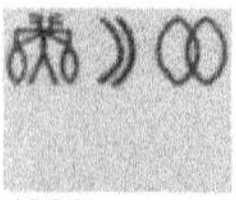

4329

h187A

h187B

5282 Pict-75: Tree, generally within a railing or on a platform.

h188A

h188B

4325

h189A

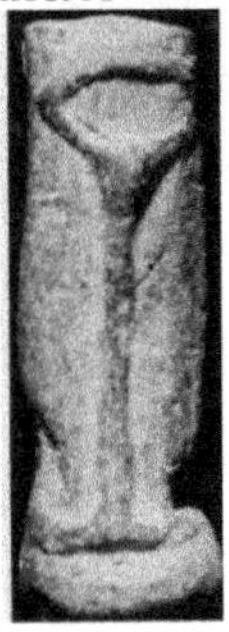

h189B

4341 Pict-126: Anchor?

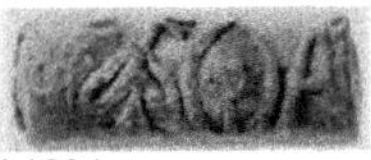

h190A

h190B

4323

h191A

h191B

4332

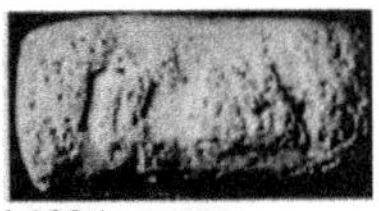

h192A

h192B

5340

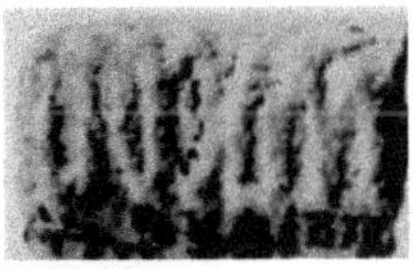

h193A

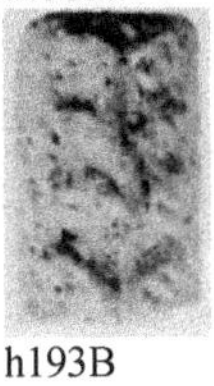

h193B

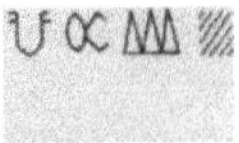

5332

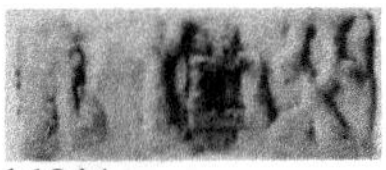

h194A

h194B

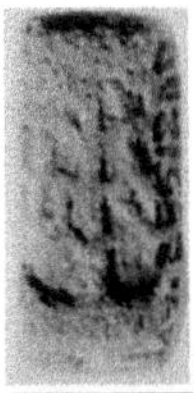

h195A

h195B

h196A

h196B

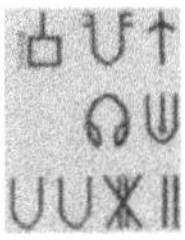

4309 Tablet in bas-relief h196b

Pict-91: Person carrying the standard. h196a The standard.

h197A

h197B 5333

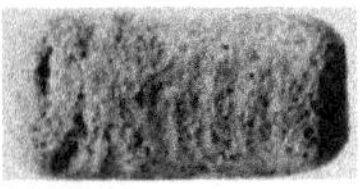

h198A

h198B

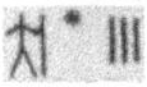

5331

h199A

h199B

5252

h200A

h200B

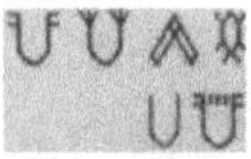

4321

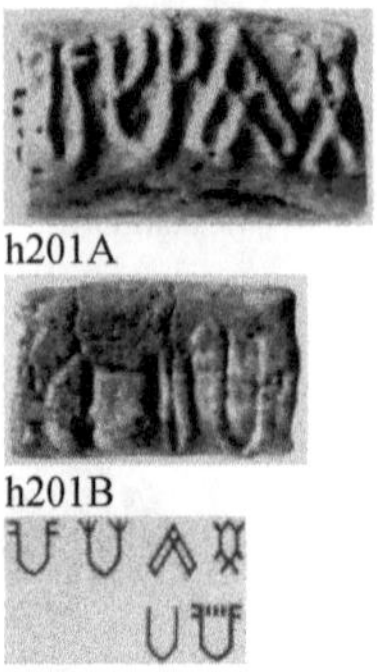

h201A

h201B

5289

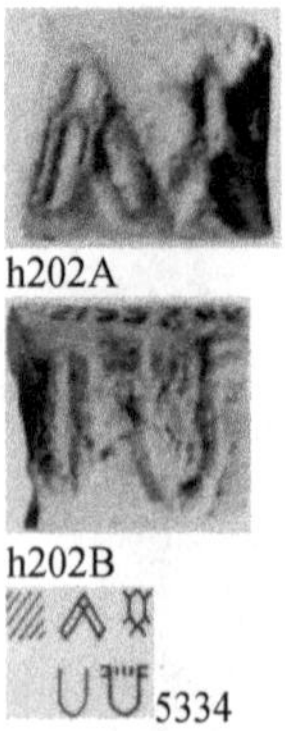

h202A

h202B

5334

h203A

5226

5236

h204A

h204B

5211

h205A

h205B

5254

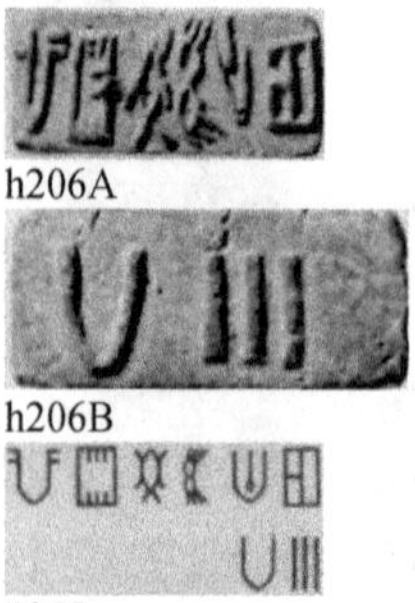

h206A

h206B

4345

h207A

5297

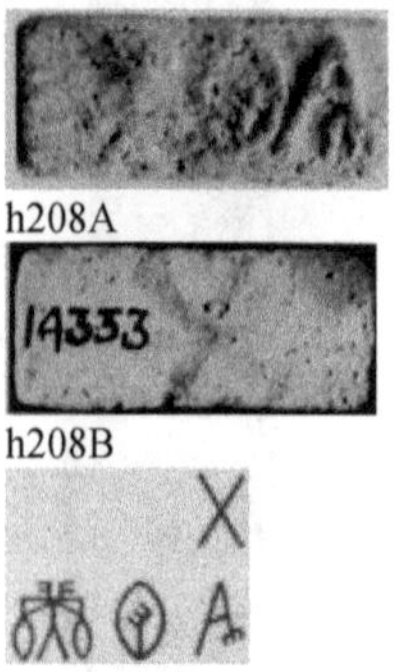

h208A

h208B

5296

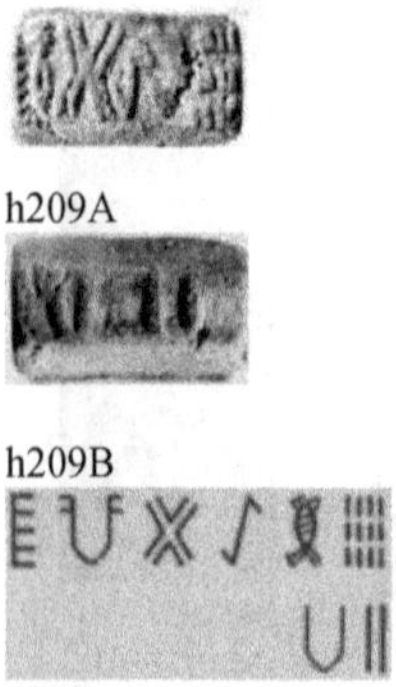

h209A

h209B

4348

h210A

h210B

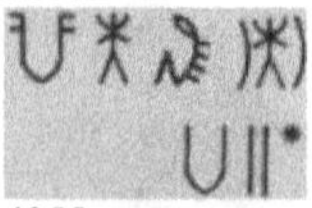

4355

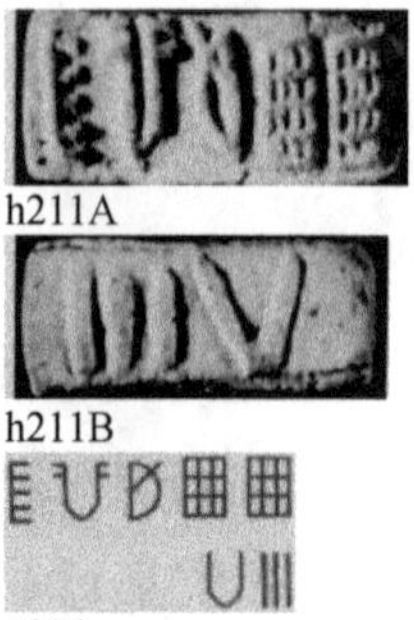

h211A

h211B

5274

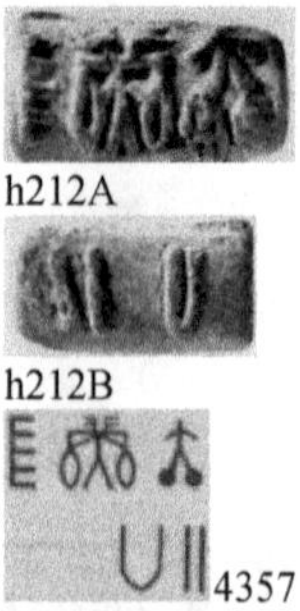

h212A

h212B

4357

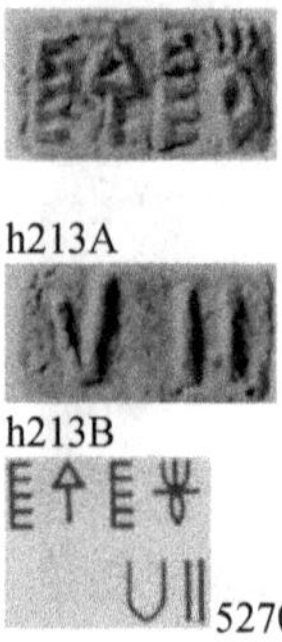

h213A

h213B

5270

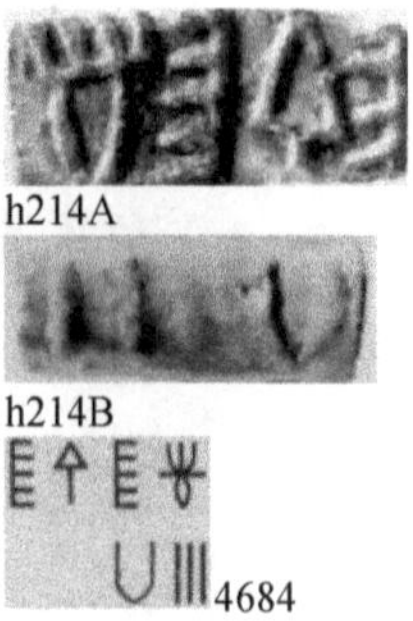

h214A

h214B

4684

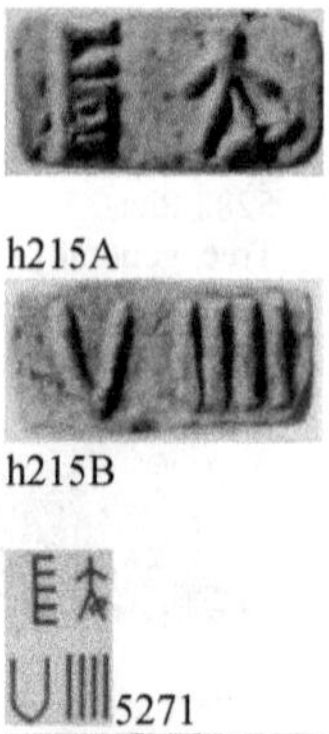

h215A

h215B

5271

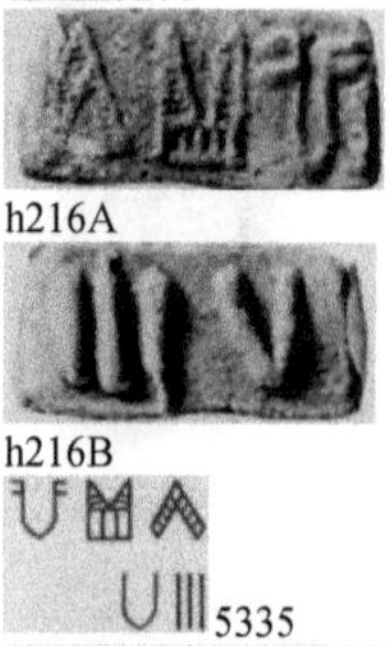

h216A

h216B

5335

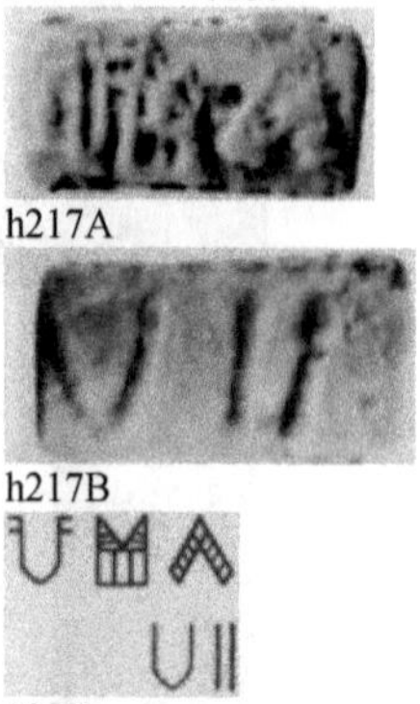

h217A

h217B

5336

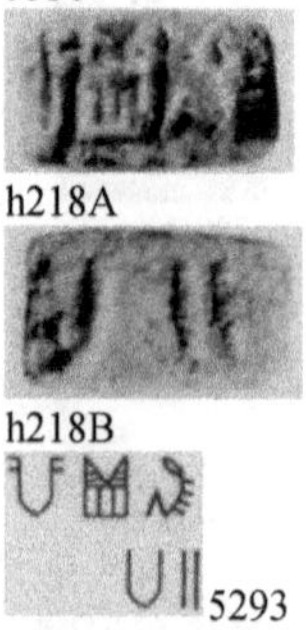

h218A

h218B

5293

h219A

h219B

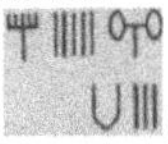

5269

h220A

5267

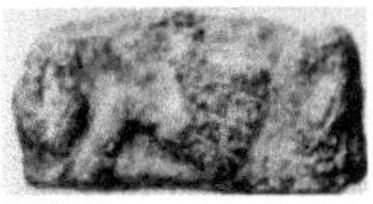

h221A

h221B

5265

h222A

h222B

5339

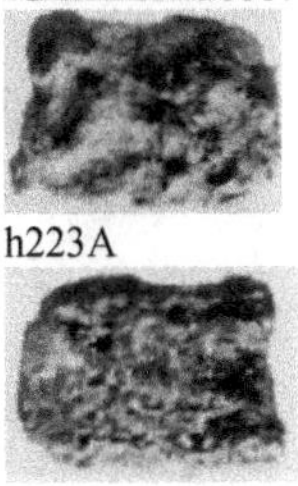

h223A

h223B

5221

h225A

h226A

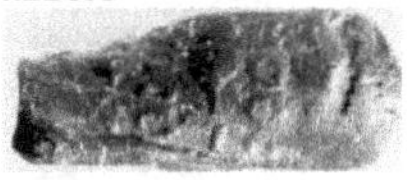

h226B

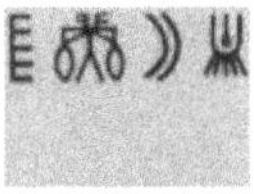

5243 Standard.

h227A

h227B

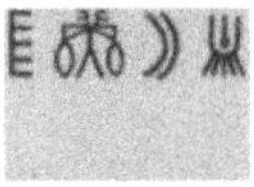

4322 Standard.
Pict-123

Standard device which is normally in front of a one-horned bull. The device is flanked by columns of dotted circles.

h228A

h228B

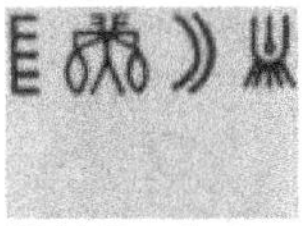

5244 Standard.

h229A

h229B

4674

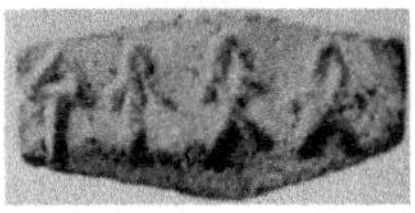

h230A

h230B

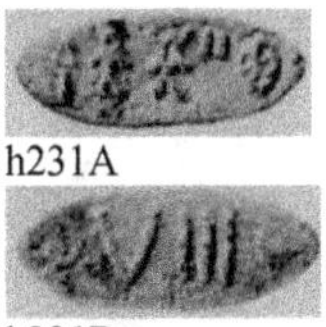

h231A

h231B

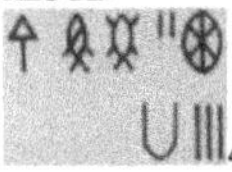

4673

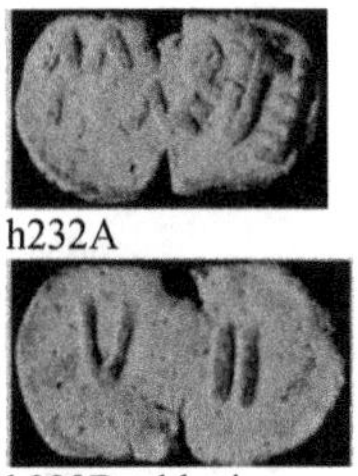

h232A

h232B tablet in bas relief

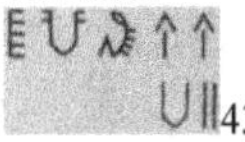

4368

Inscribed object in the shape of a double-axe.

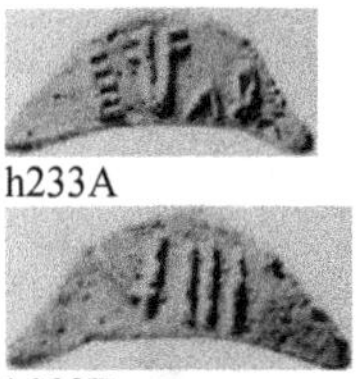

h233A

h233B

4387

Tablct in bas-relief. Sickle-shaped. Pict-131: Inscribed object in the shape of a crescent?

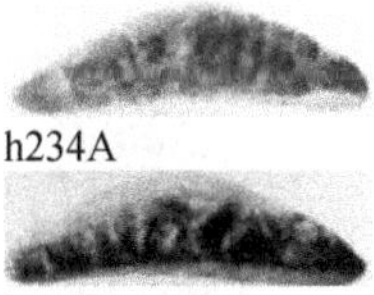

h234A

h234B

4717

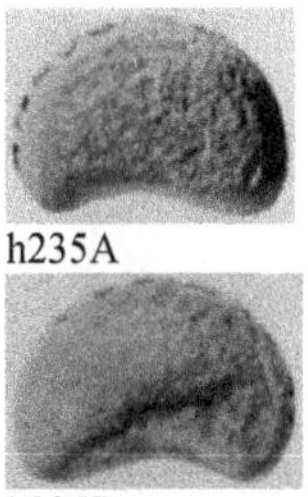

h235A

h235B

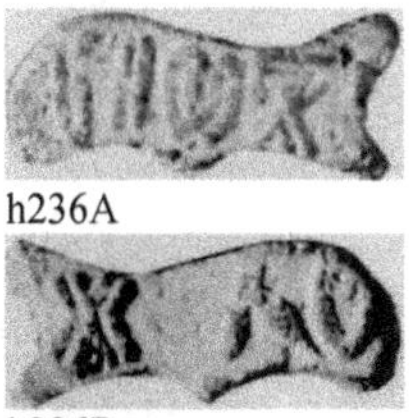

h236A

h236B

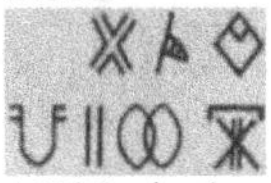

4658 Incised miniature tablet. Object shaped like fish or sickle? h825A h8 25B

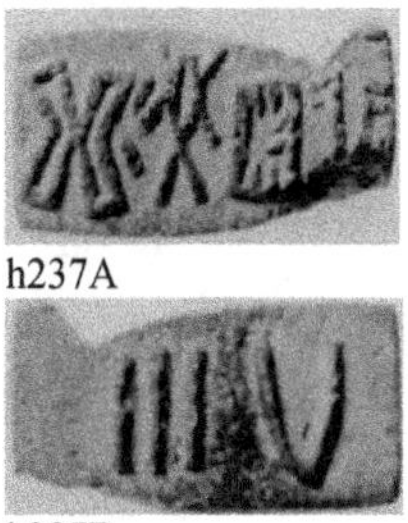

h237A

h237B

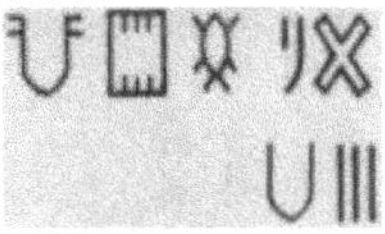

5337

h238A

h239A

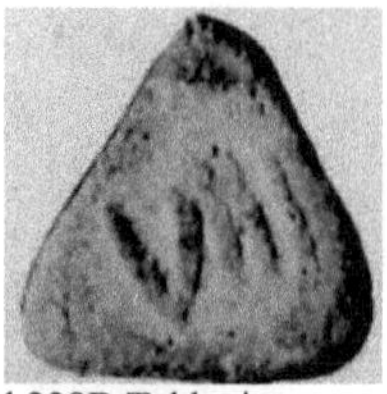

h239B Tablet in bas relief

4386

h240

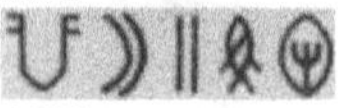

4657

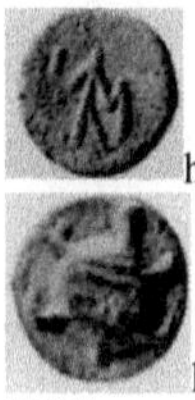

h241A

h241B

4663

Pict-69: Tortoise.

h242A

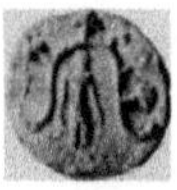

h242B

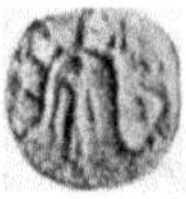

Pict-84

4317

2863

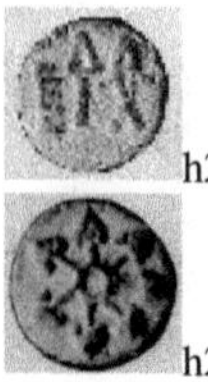

h243A

h243B

Tablet in bas-relief

Pict-78: Rosette of seven pipal (?) leaves.

4664

For  See inscription: 4466

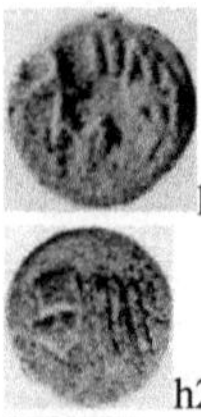

h244A

h244B

4665

h245A

h245B

4702

h246A

h246B

5283

h247A

h247B Tablet in bas-relief

4372

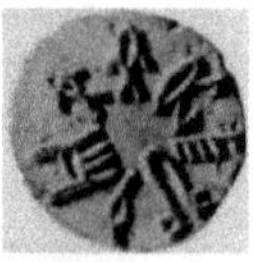

h248A

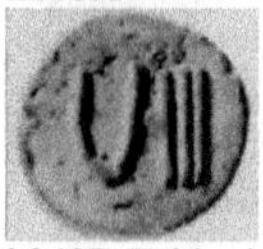

h248B Tablet in bas-relief

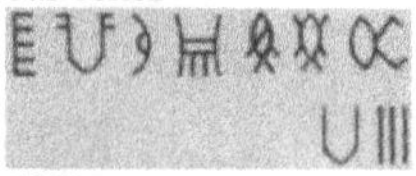

4371

See 3354.

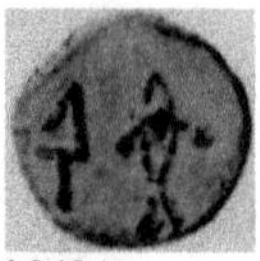

h249A

h249B Tablet in bas-relief 

4374

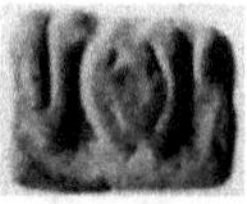

h250A

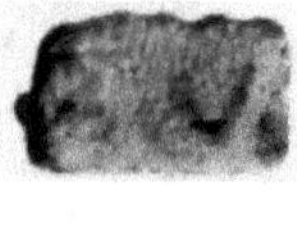

h250B

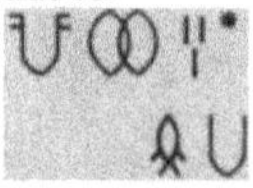

5250

h251A

h251B

h251C

4342

Tablet in bas-relief. Prism. Bison (short-horned bull).

h252A

h252B
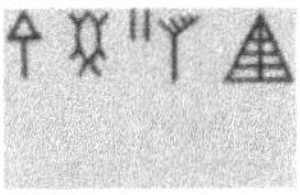
5215

h253A
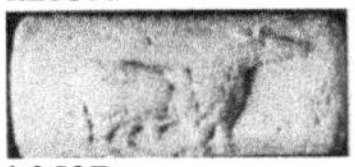
h253B
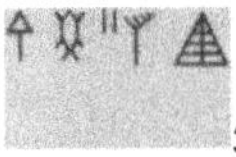
5219

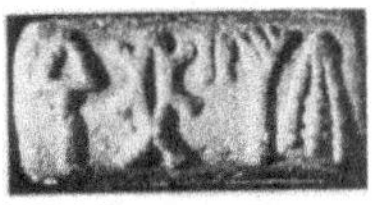
h254A

h254B
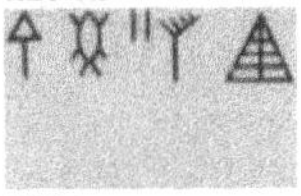
5214

h255A
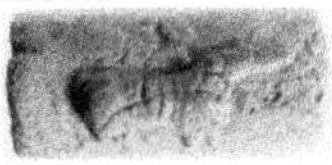
h255B
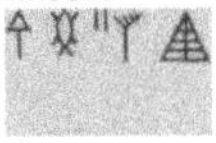
5208

h256A
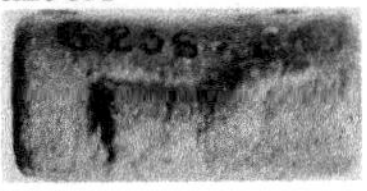

h256B
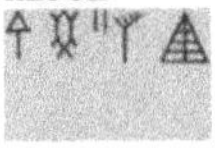
5213

h257A

h257B
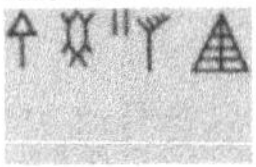
5216

h258A

h258B
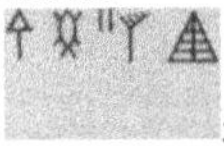
5217

h259A
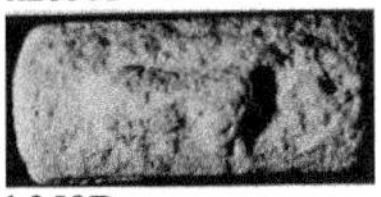
h259B
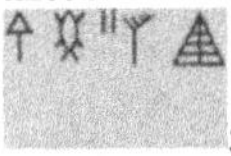
5218

h260A
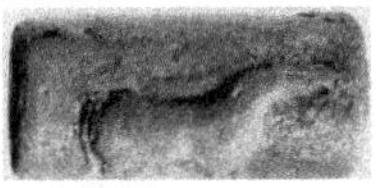
h260B

h261
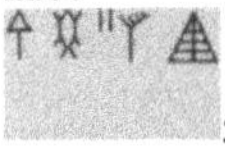
5212

h262
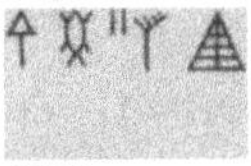
5220

h263
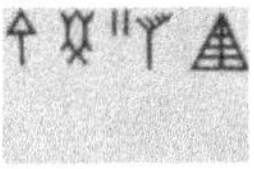
5262

h264
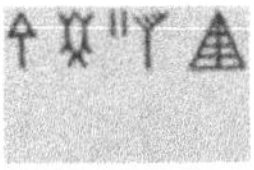
4315
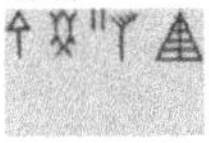

5207, 5208, 5209, 5210, 5212, 5213, 5214,5215, 5216, 5217, 5218,5219, 5220, 5262 Tablets in bas relief. The first sign looks like an arch around a pillar with ring-stones. One-horned bull. h252, h253, h255, h256, h257, h258, h259, h260,h261, h262, h263, h264, h265, h276, h277, h859, h860, h861, h862,h863, h864, h865, h866,h867, h868, 869, 870

h266

4011

h267
4007

h268

4020

h269

h270

4014

h271

4069

h272
4619

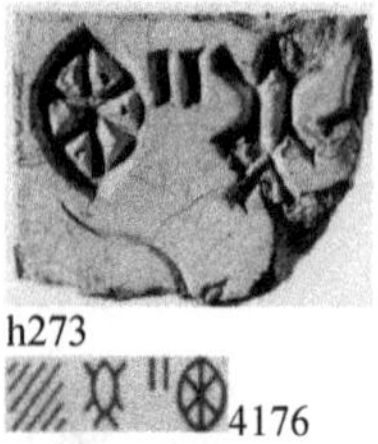
h273
4176

h274

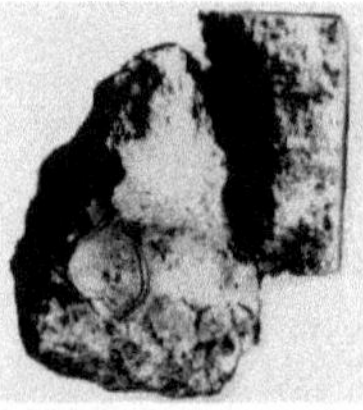
h275

h276A
h276B

h277A
h277B
5207

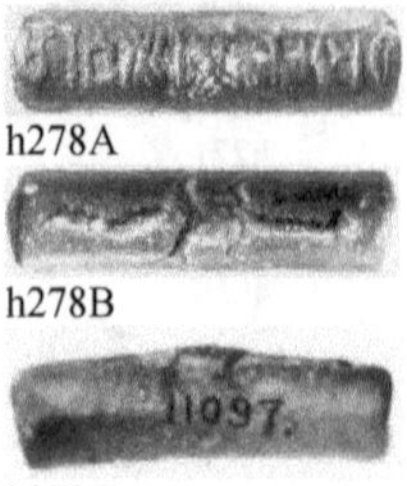
h278A
h278B
h278C

5205

h279A
h279B
5256

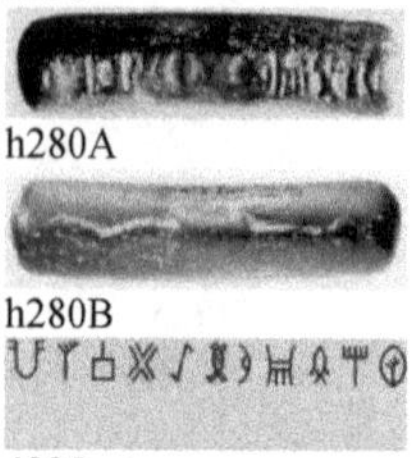
h280A
h280B
4335

h281A
h281B
4336

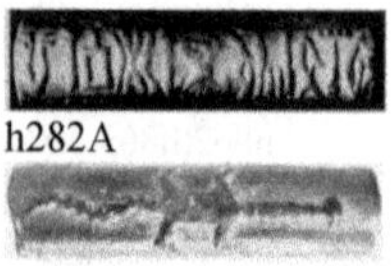
h282A
h282B

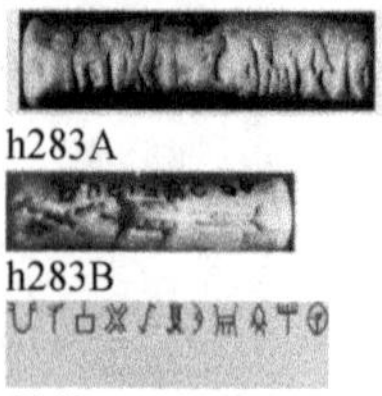
h283A
h283B
5253

h284A
h284B
5229

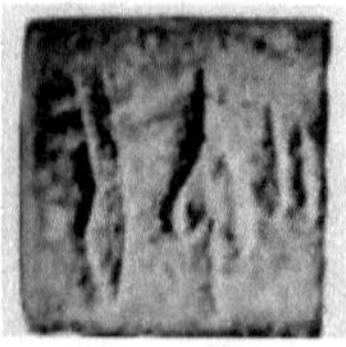

h285A

h285B

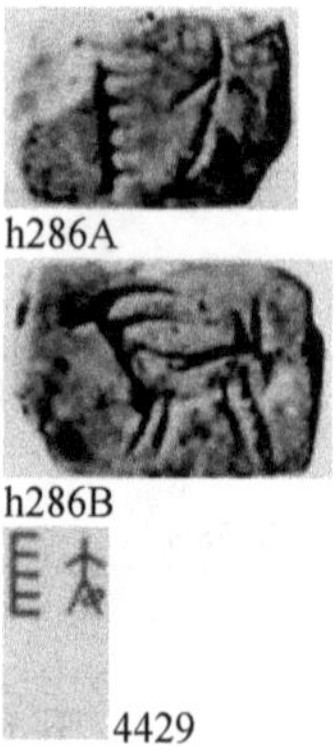
h286A
h286B
4429
Incised miniature tablet
Goat-antelope with a short tail

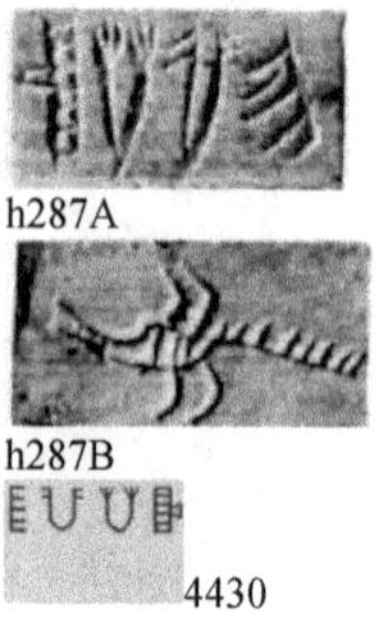
h287A
h287B
4430

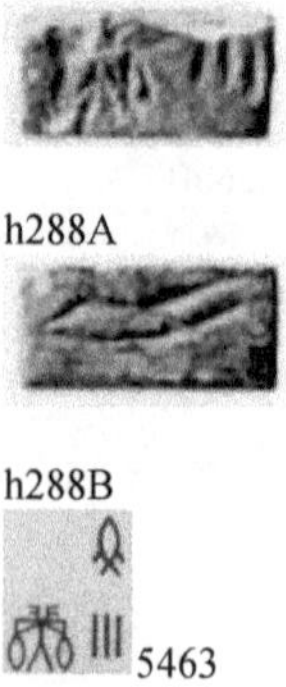
h288A
h288B
5463

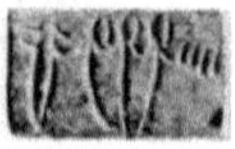
h289A

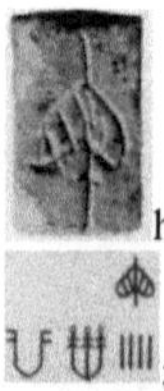
h289B
5467

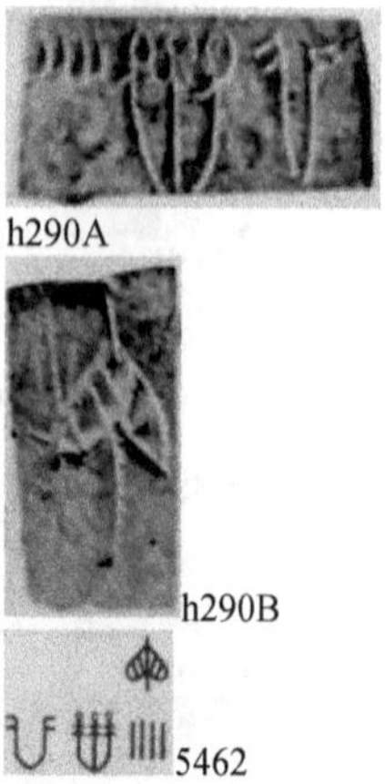
h290A
h290B
5462

h291A
h291B
4440
Standard.

h292A

h292B
4443 Standard.

h293A

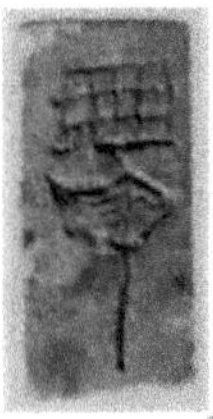

h293B
4441 Standard.

h294A

h294B

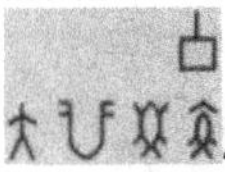

4442

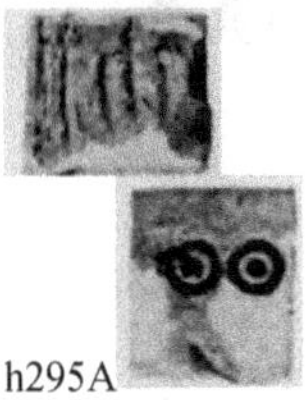

h295A

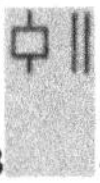

h295B 4505

h296A
h296B

4457

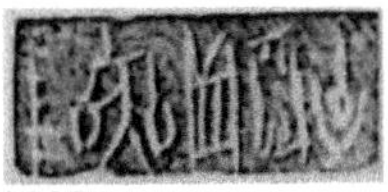

h297A

h297B

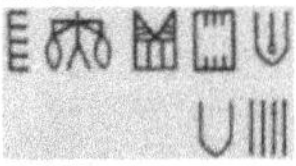

5497

h298A
h298B

5473

h299A

h299B

4478

h300A

h300B

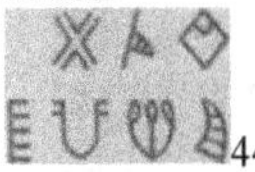

4454

h301A
h301B

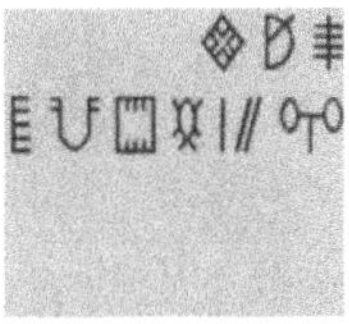

4450

h302A
h302B

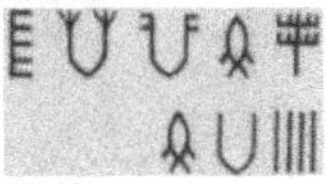

5460

h303A
h303B

4444

h304A
h304B

5401

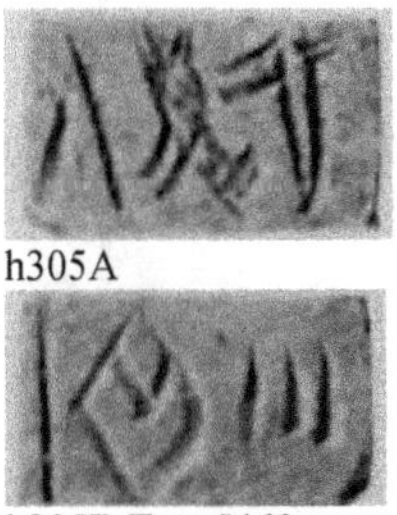

h305A
h305B Text 5460

h306A

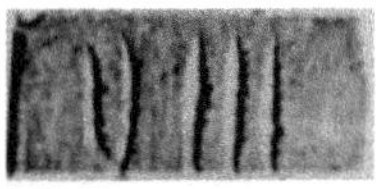

h306B

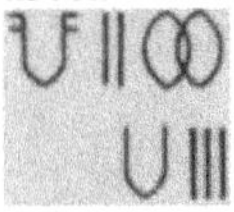

5474

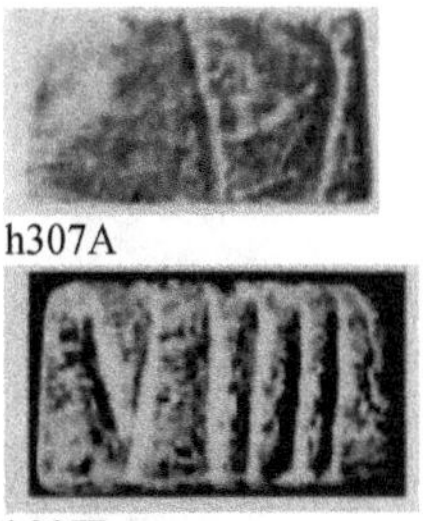

h307A
h307B

h308A
h308B

5427

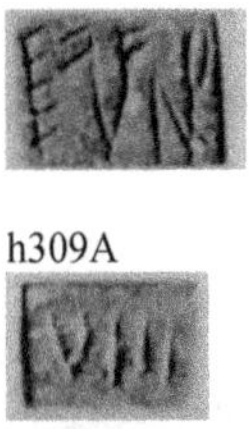

h309A
h309B

4403
4405, 4509, 4543, 5419, 5421, 5422, 5423, 5425, 5442, 5449

Incised miniature tablets
h309, h311, h317, h932, h959, h935, h960

h310A

h310B

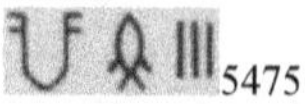
5475

h311A

h311B

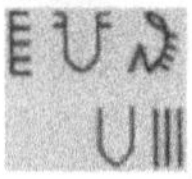
5421

h312B

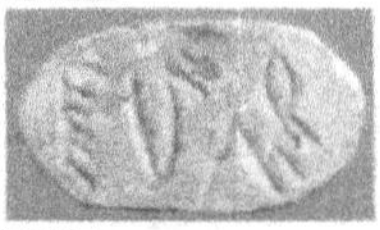

h312Ac

5426

h313A

h313B

5432

5433

h314A

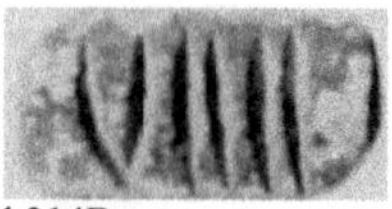

h314B

5447

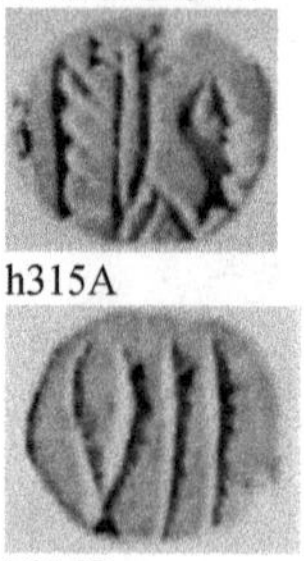

h315A

h315B

5464

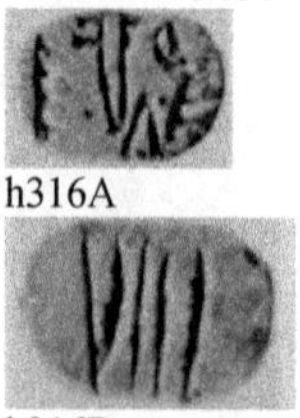

h316A

h316B

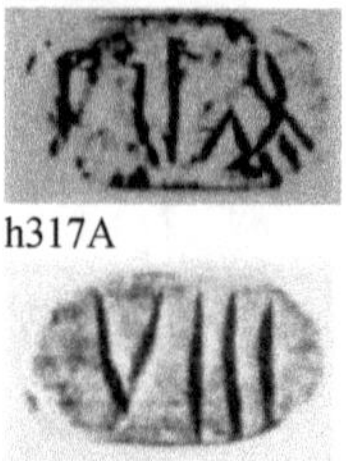

h317A

h317B

5442

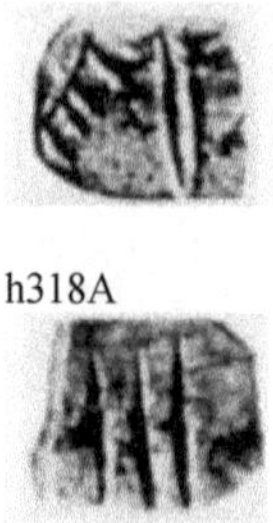

h318A

h318B

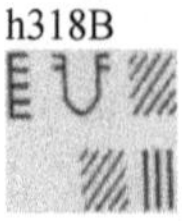
5451

h319A

h319B

4544

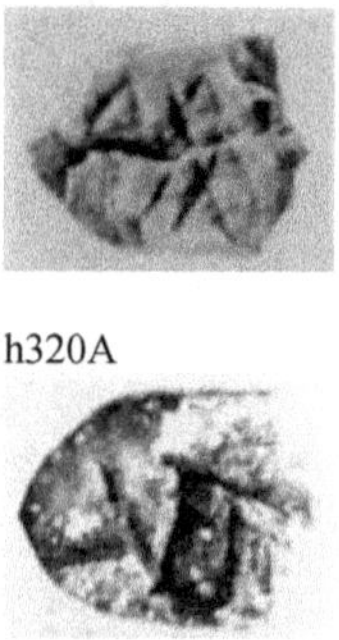

h320A

h320B

5450

h321A

h321B

5402

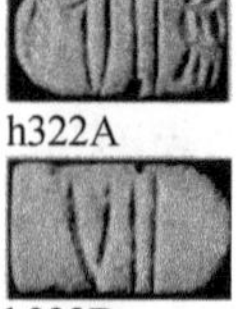

h322A

h322B

5498

h323A

h323B

4497

h324A

h324B

4484

h325A

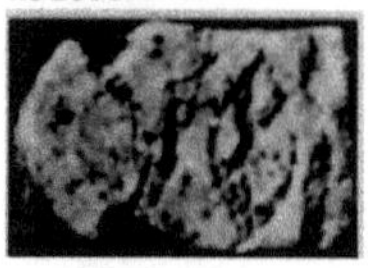

h325B

4416

Pict-130: Inscribed object in the shape of a writing tablet (?)

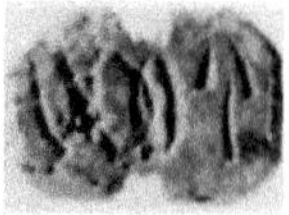

h326A

h326B

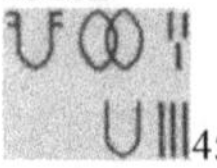
4564

Double-axe?

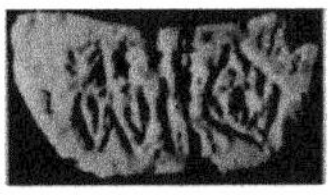

h327A

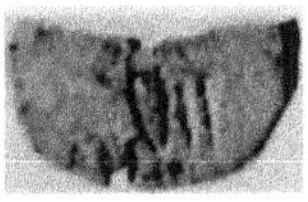

h327B

5472
5483 Shape of object: Blade of a weapon?

h328a

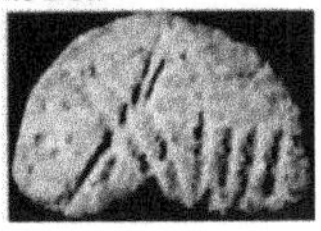

h328B

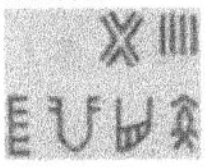
4415 Shape of object: Bladeof weapon?

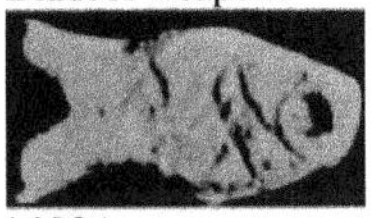

h329A

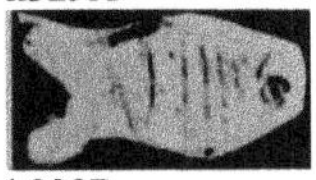

h329B

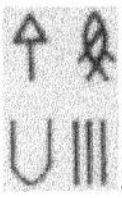
5496 Pict-68: Inscribed object in the shape of a fish.

h330A

h330B  4560

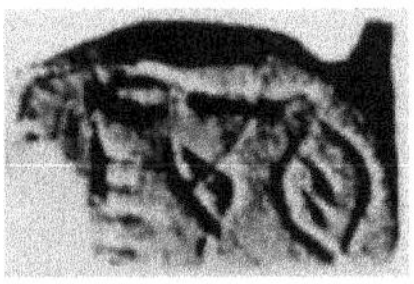

h331A Incised miniature tablet.

4421, 4422, 4423

h332C 4885

h333A

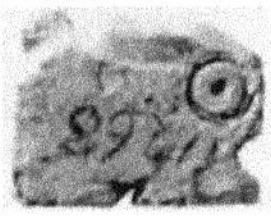

h333B

4421

h334A

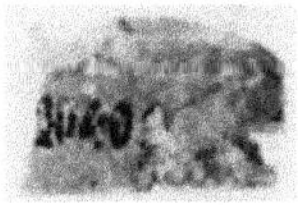

h334B 4423

h335a

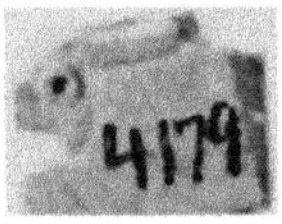

h335B
4425

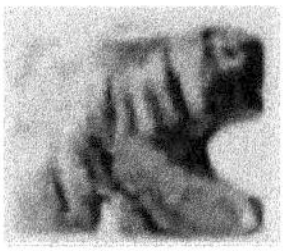

h336A

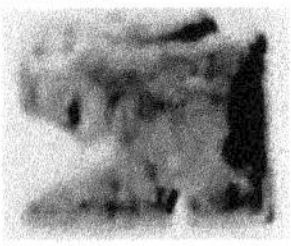

h336B

4424

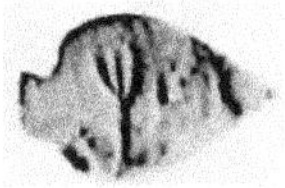

h337A

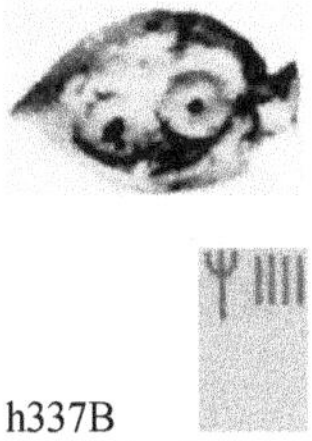

h337B
4417 Pict-79: shape of a leaf. Dotted circle on obverse.

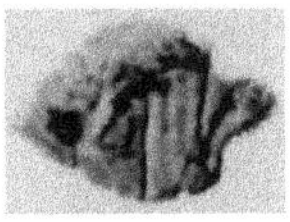

h338A

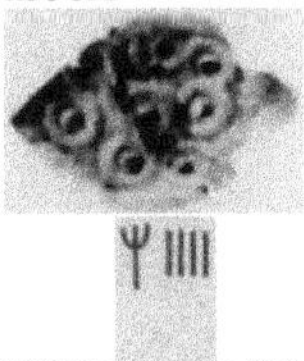

h338B 4426
Pict-39: Inscribed object in the shape of a tortoise (?) or leaf (?). Dotted circles on obverse.

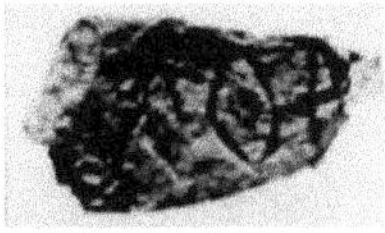

h339A

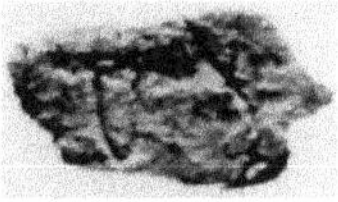

h339B

4559

h340A

h340B

4420

h341A

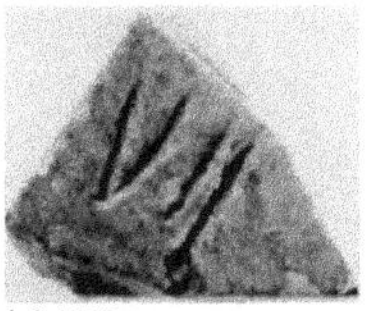

h341B

4419

h342A

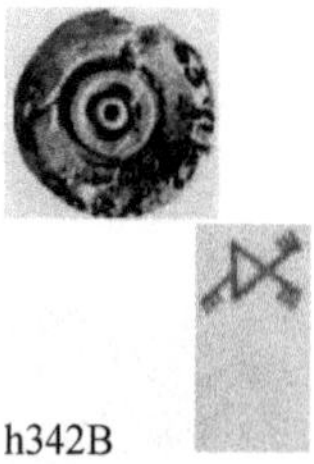

h342B
4413

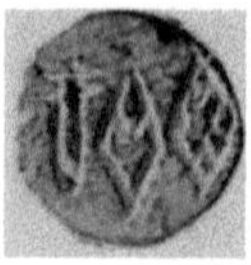

h343A

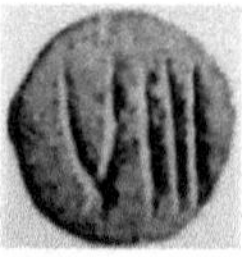

h343B

4549

h344A

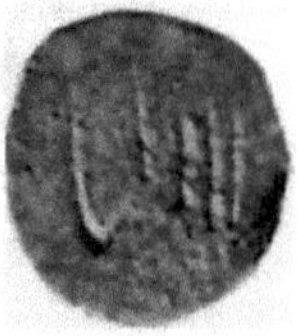

h344B

4410

h345A

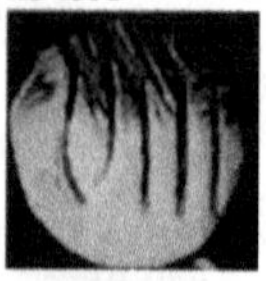

h345B

4550

h346A

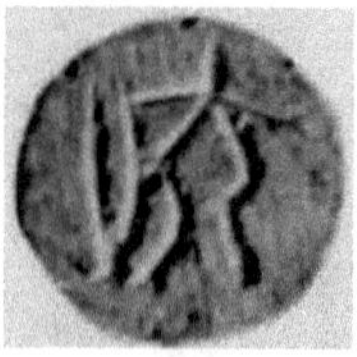

h346B Incised miniature tablet.

4412

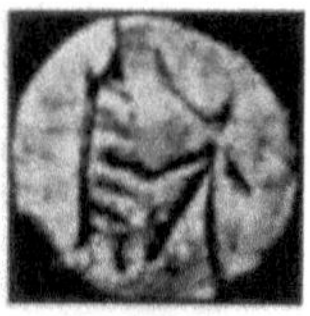

h347A 4414

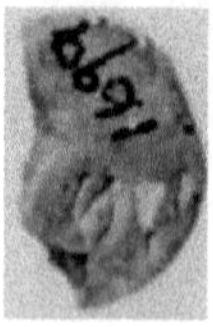

h348A

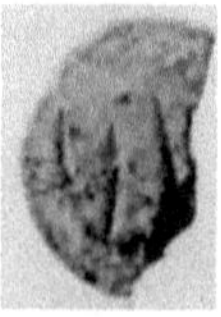

h348B

4552

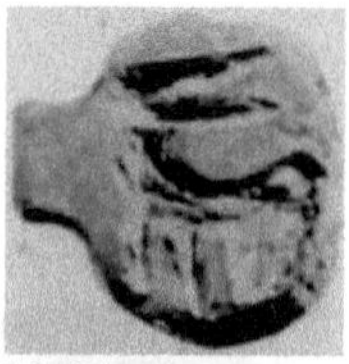

h349A

h349B

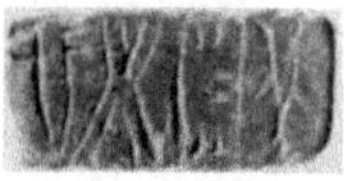

h350A

h350B

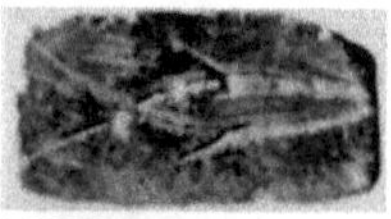

h350C

4576

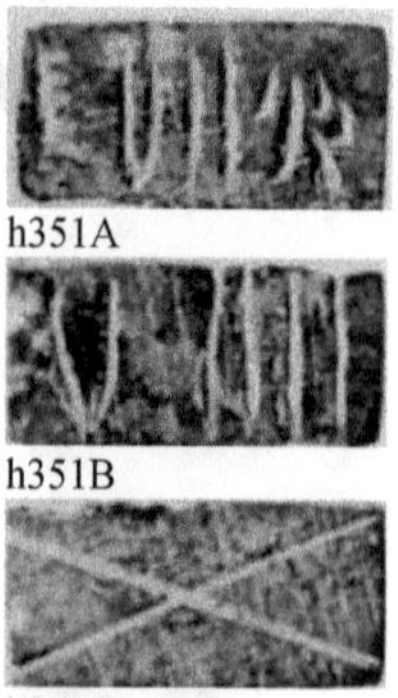

h351A

h351B

h351C

4581

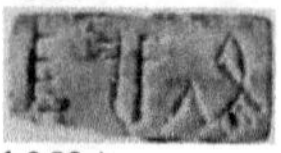

h352A

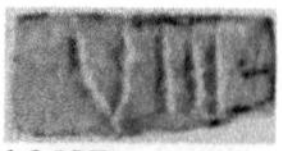

h352B

h352C

4575

Pict-120: One or more dotted circles.

h353A

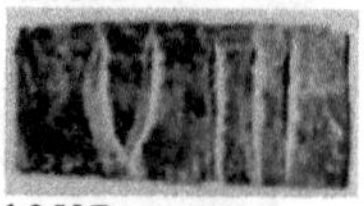

h353B

h353C

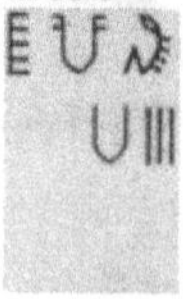

5416

h354A

h354B

h354C

5499

h355A

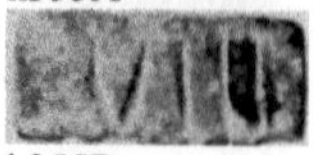

h355B

h355C

5413

h356

h357

h358A

h358B

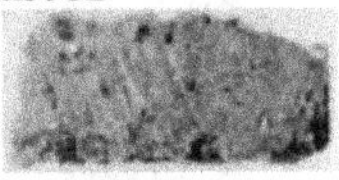

h358C

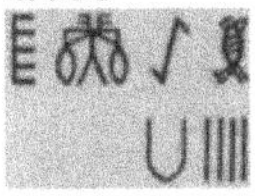

4579

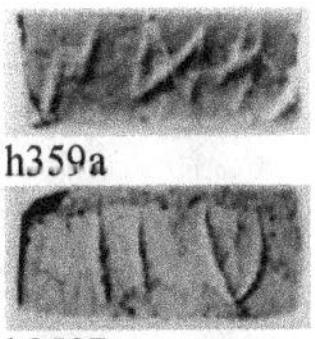

h359a

h359B

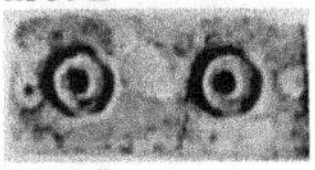

h359C

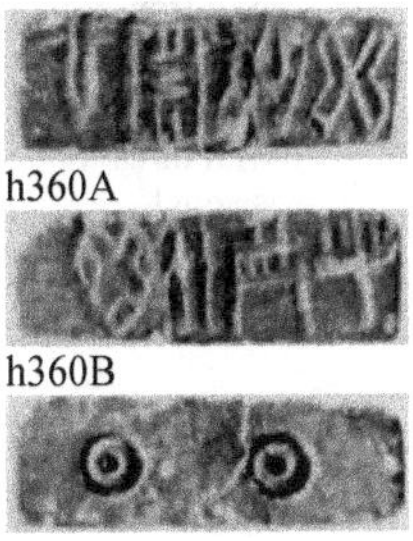

h360A

h360B

h360C

4584

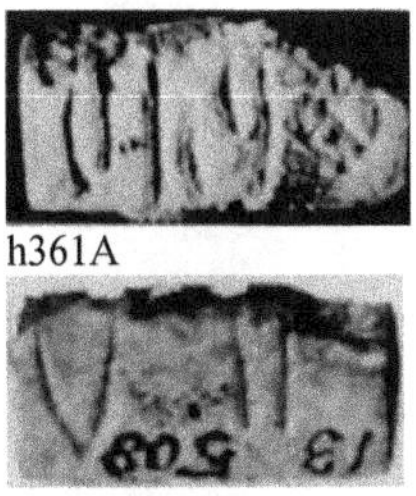

h361A

h361B

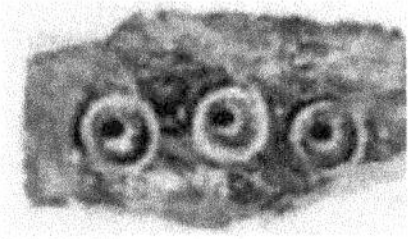

h361C

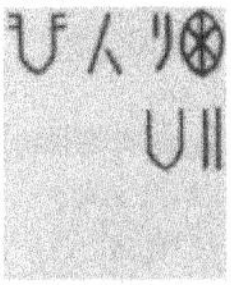

5476

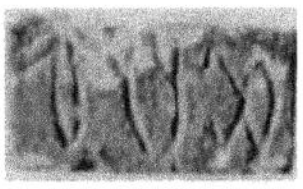

h362A

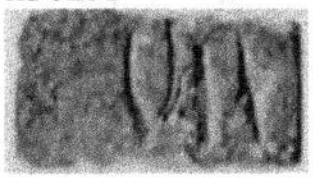

h362B

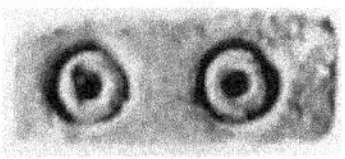

h362C

5466

h363A

h363B

h363C

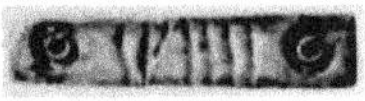

h363E Pict-

86

Pict-85
Standing person with horns and bovine features (hoofed legs and/or tail).

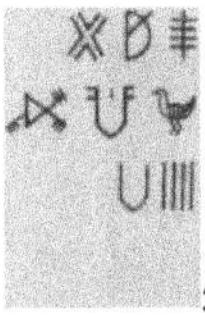

5471

h364A

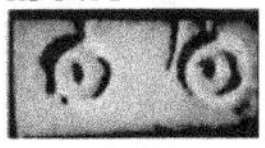

h364B

h364C

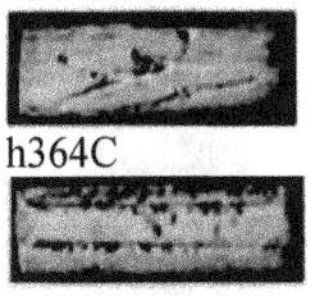

h364E

4635

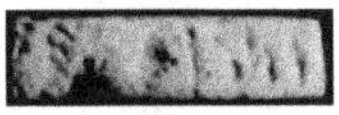

h365A

h365B

h365C

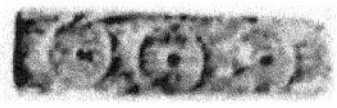

h365E

h366C

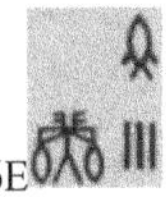

h366E 4590

h367A

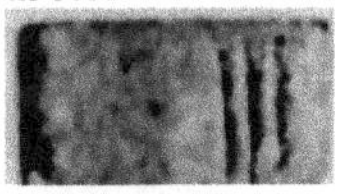

h367B

h367C

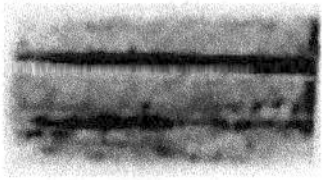

h367E 4401

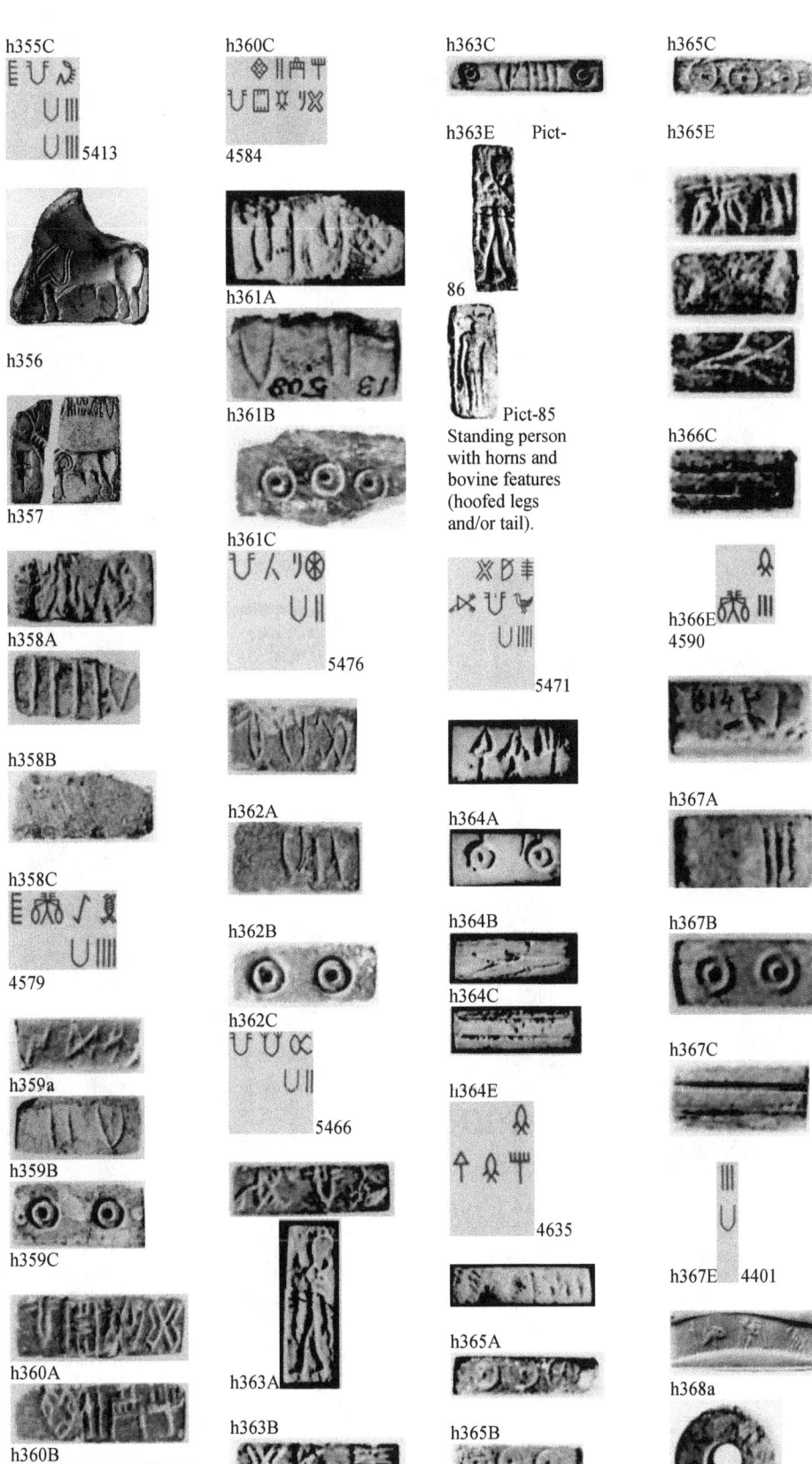

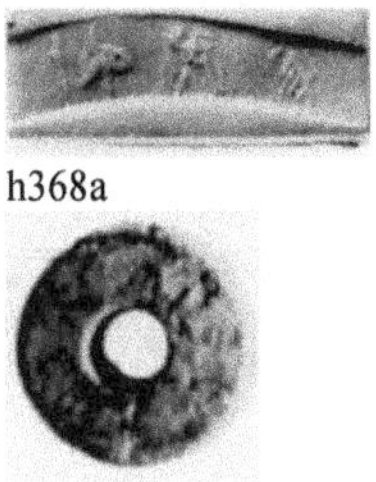

h368a

h368E

4409

h369a

h369C

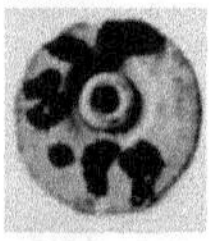

h369E

4718

h370A

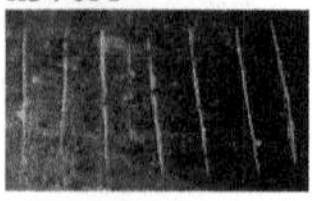

h370A2

h371A

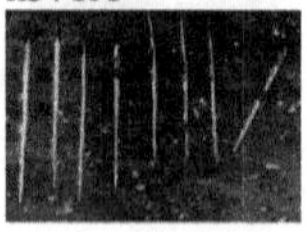

h371A2

h372A

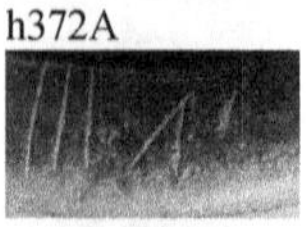

h372A2

h374 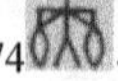 4815

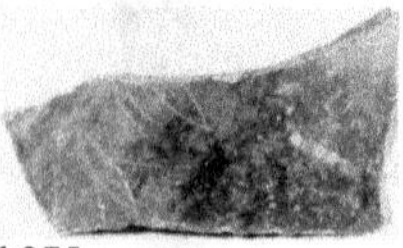

h375

4812

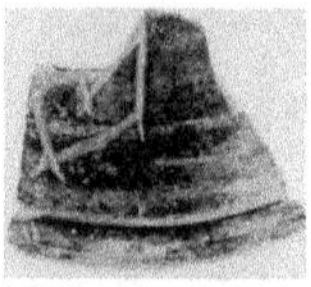

h377

h378

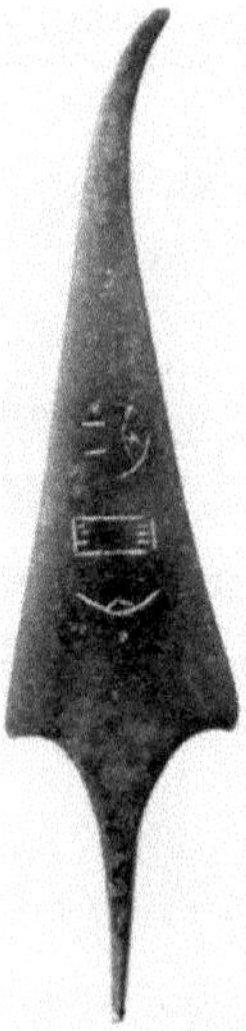

h380

4902 Bronze dagger

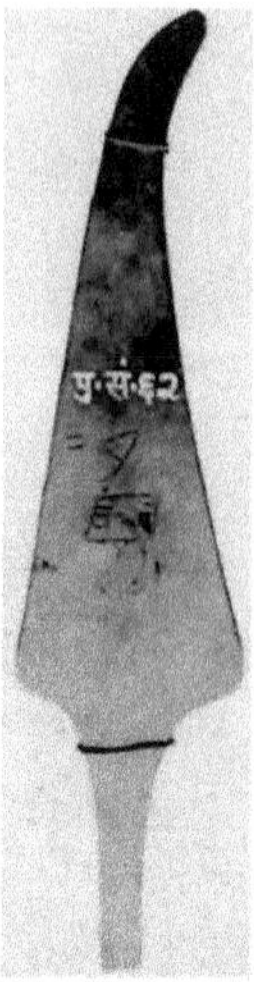

h381

 4901

Bronze dagger

h382

4818

h383 (Not shown).

4021

h384

h385

4045

h386

4025

h387

h388

5062

h389

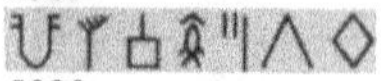

5090

h390

4024 [The second sign from right appears like a weaver's loom with three looped strings].

h391

5064

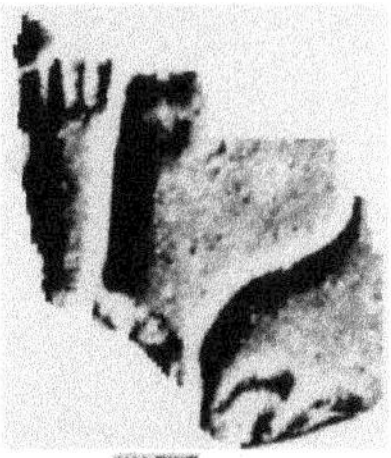
h392a  4207

h393

h394a
 5003

h395a

h396

4027

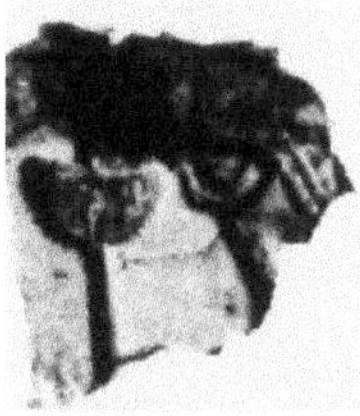
h397

h398

h399

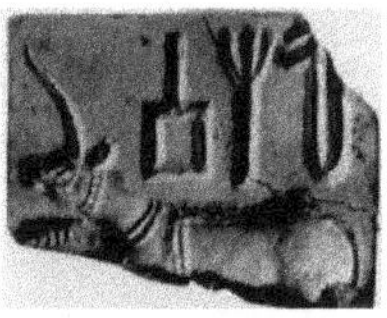
h400

h401

4168

h402

h403

h404

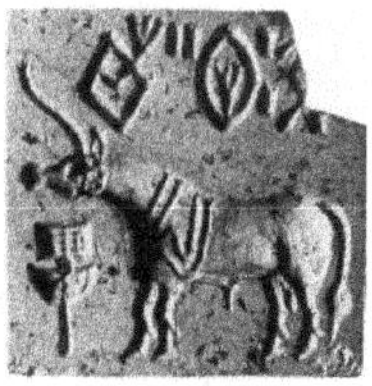
h405
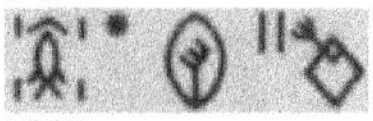
5091

h406  5034

h407
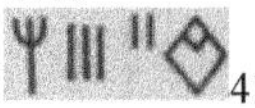 4126

h408
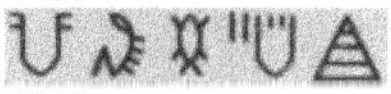
4079

h409

h410

4080

h411

4078

h412

4036

h413 
4032

h414

h415

4204

h416

 4059

h417

4051

h418

h419

5092

[ The first sign may be a squirrel as in Nindowaridamb 01 Seal].

h420

4614

h421

4026

h422

4185

h423

4056

h424

h425

h426

4153

h427

 4217

h428

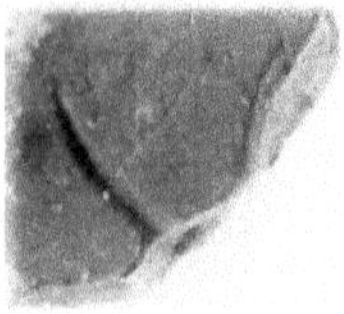

h429

h430

h431

5068

h432

4616

h433

h434

h435

h436

h437

h438

h439

h440 

4615

h441
4074

h442
4095

h443 4121

h444

h445
5110

h446
4034

h447 4089

h448 4054

h449
4082

h450
4084

h451 4137

h452a 4124

h453
4061

h454
4132

h455
4055

h456
4083

h457
5080

h458
4050

h459
4092

h460

h461
4037

h462
4620

h463
h464a
4100

h465
4181

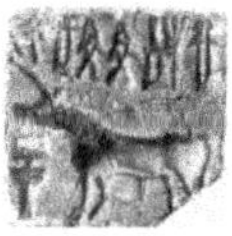

h466
4111

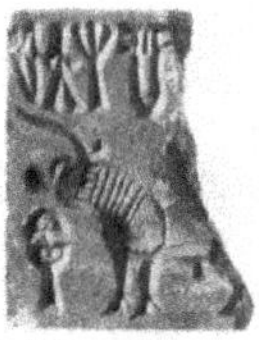

h467
4624

h468

4087

h469

4138

h470

4186

h471

4145

h472

4152

h473

4096

h474

4188

h475 4093

h476

4102

h477

h478

4088

h479

4099

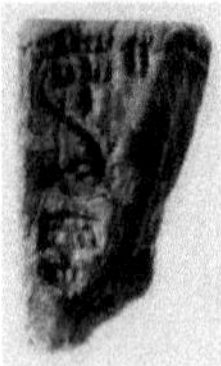

h480 4180

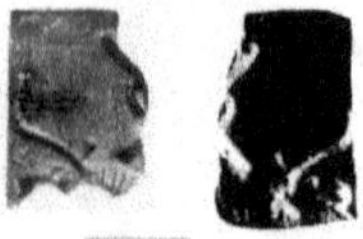

h482 4208

h483

h484

4154

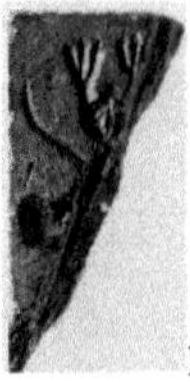

h485

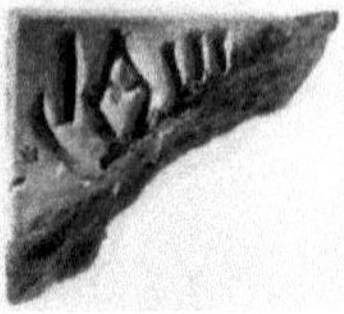

h486

h488

4198

h489

4189

h490

h492

h493

h494

h495

h497

h498

h499 5093

h500

h501

4112

h502
4143

h503 4129

h504
4183

h505 5094

h506
4097

h507 4159

h508

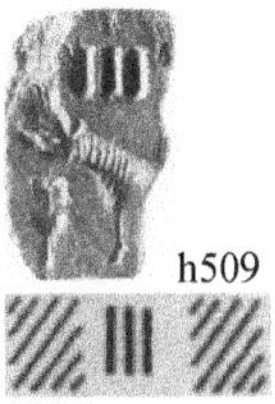
h509
4206

h510
4139

h511 4165

h512a
4618

h513
4163

h514
4116

h515
4162

Text 4166
h516a

h517

h518 4160

h519
4147

h520 4127

h521 4155

h522

h523

5071

h524
4150

h525
4149

h526

h527

h528

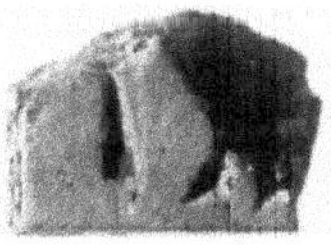
h529

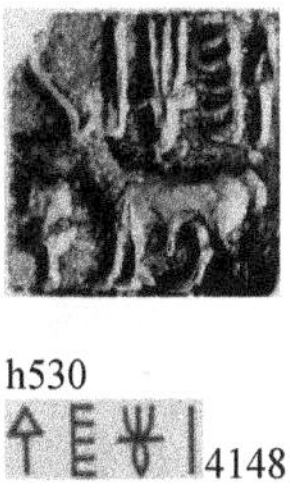
h530
4148
[May have to be arranged from right to left?]

h531
4172

h532

h533
4625

h534

h535

h536

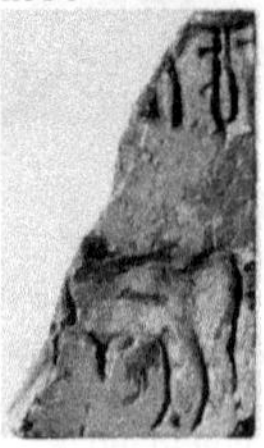

h537
4170

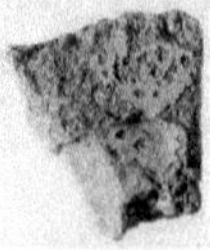
h538

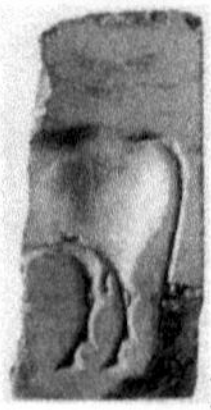
h539

h541

h542

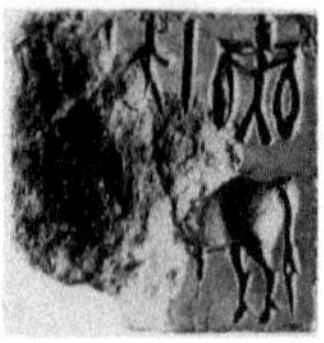
h543
4177

h544
4144

h545 4622

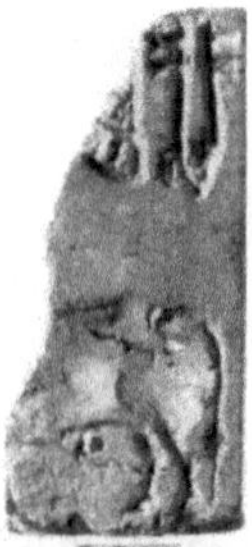
h546 4697

h547

h548

h549

h550
4211

h551 4197

h552

h553

h554

h555

h556

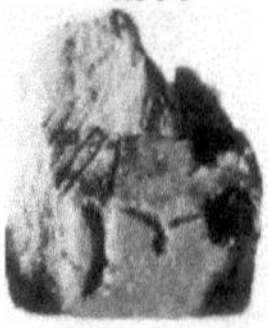
h557

h558 4220

h559 4290

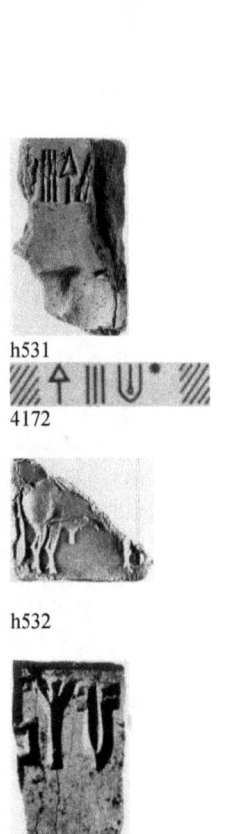

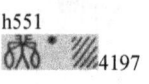

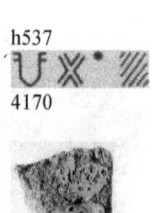

h561

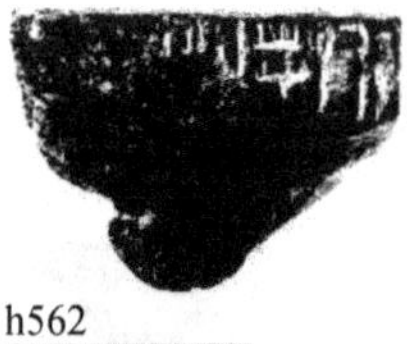

h562

5066

h563

5065

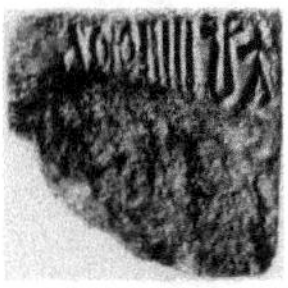

h565

4621

h566

4277

h567

h568

h569

4263

h570

4212

h571

h572

4695

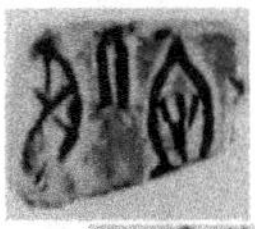

h574

4696

h575

h576

h577

4243

h578

h579

5109

h580

h581

h582

h583

h584 4235

Bison.

h585

h586

4237

h587

h588

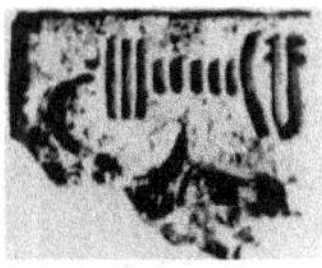

h589

4239

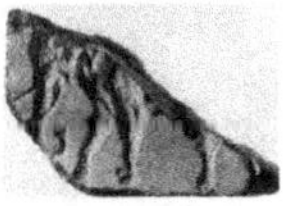

h590

h591

4228

h592

5081

h593

4250 [Composite animal].

h594 [Composite animal].

h595

4623

h596a

4382 [One-horned bull].

h597A

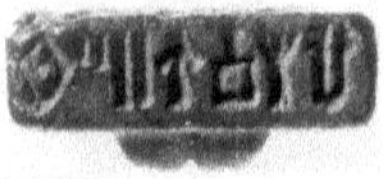

h597D

4075

h598A

h598D

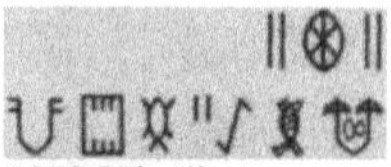

5073 [The ligature in-fixed on the last sign of the second line may be Sign 54 ]

h599A

h599D

5076

h600

4156 [The last sign may be a variant of Sign 51 ]

h601

4044

h602a

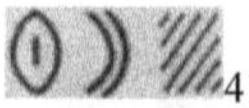
4169

h603

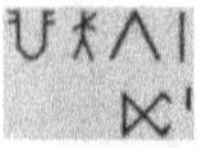
4224

h604

h605

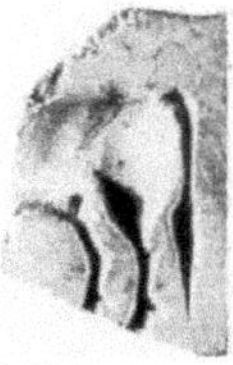

h606

4167

h608 

4225

h609

4060

h610

4098

h611

4260 One-horned bull.

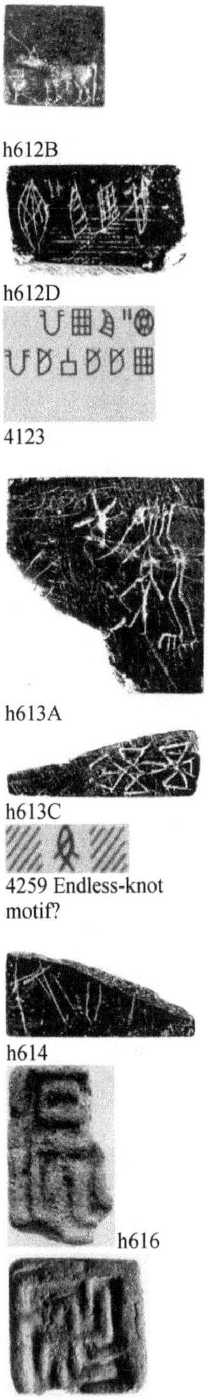

h612A

h612B

h612D

4123

h613A

h613C

4259 Endless-knot motif?

h614

h616

h617

h618

h619

h620 h621

h622

h623

h624

h625

h626

h627

h628

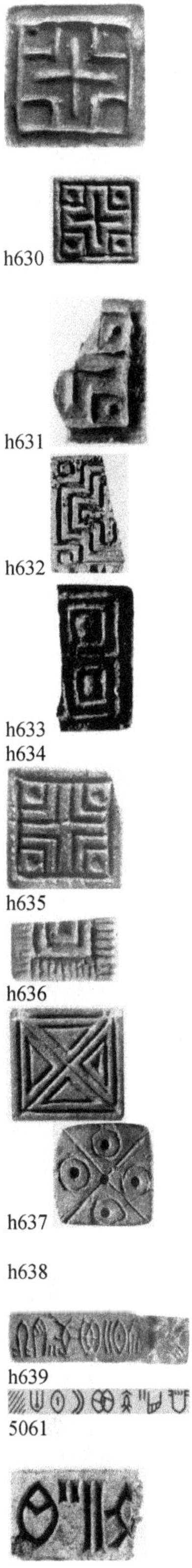

h629

h630

h631

h632

h633

h634

h635

h636

h637

h638

h639

5061

h640

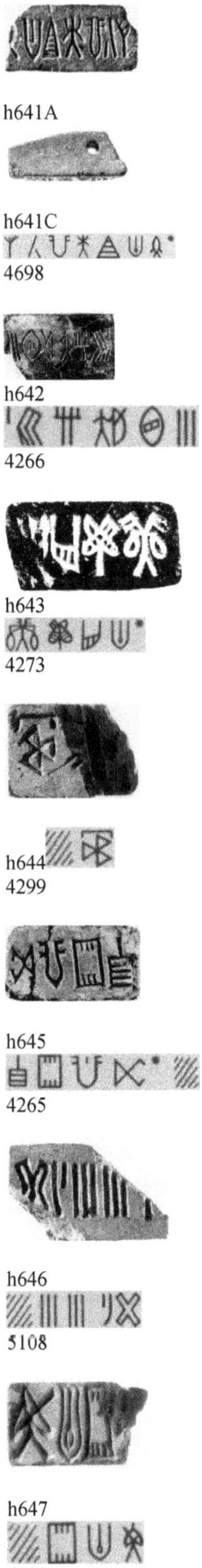

h641A

h641C

4698

h642

4266

h643

4273

h644

4299

h645

4265

h646

5108

h647

4291

h648

h649

4281

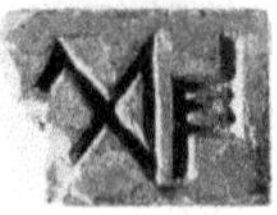

h650A

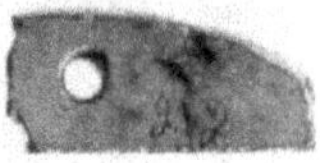

h650C

h651

4295

h652

h653

4301

h654

5035

h655AC

4300

h656

4286

h657

4287

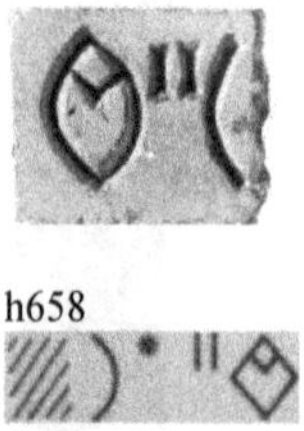

h658

4293

h659

5074

h660

5114

h661

4279

h662a

h663A

h663C

5006

h664A

h664E

5010

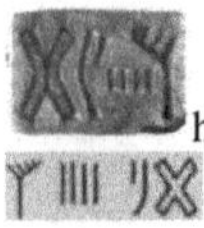

h665

5100

h666

4631

h667A

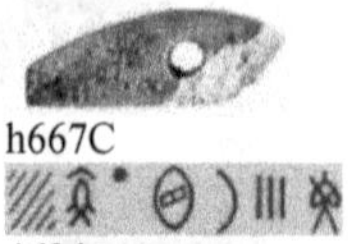

h667C

4634

h668

5266

h669

4289

h670

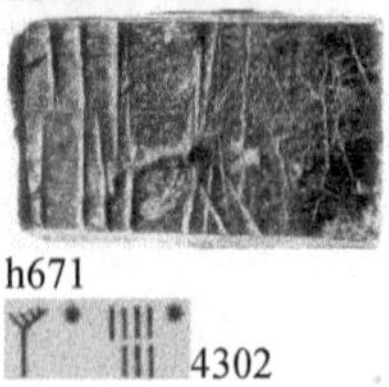

h671

4302

h679

4298

h680

5099

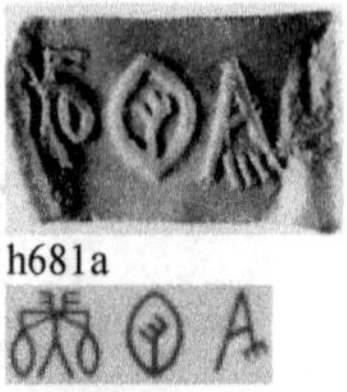

h681a

5105

h682

5078

h683

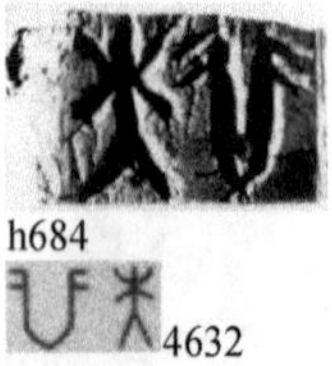

h684

4632

h685

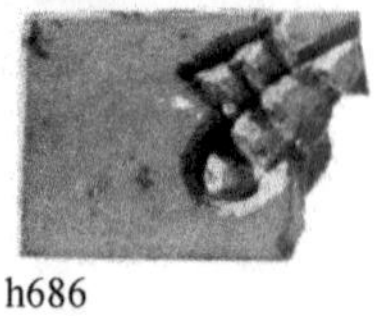

h686

h688A

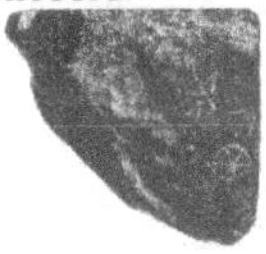

h688F

h689A

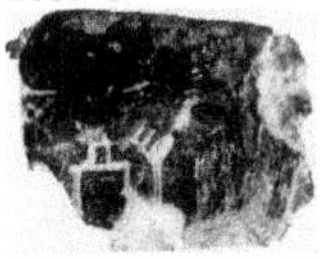

h689B

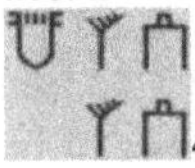

4222

h690si

5304

h691A1si

h691A2si

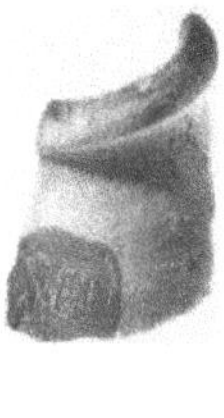

h692A1si

h692A2si

h693t

4707

h694t

h695t

h696At

h696Bt

4677

h697At

h697Bt

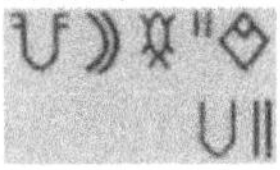

4314

h698At

h698Bt

4659

h699At

h699Bt

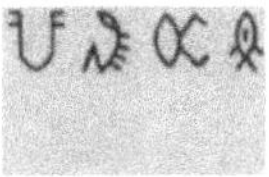

5288

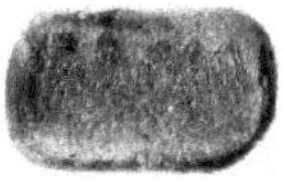

h700At

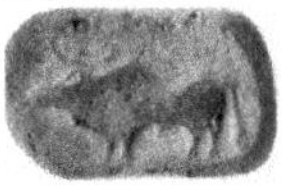

h700Bt

h701At

h701Bt

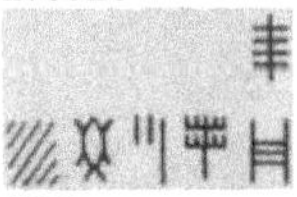

5329

h702At

h702Bt

4601

h703At

h703Bt

4595

h704At

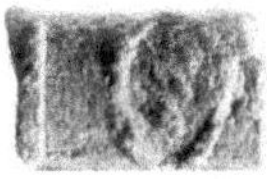

h704Bt

h705At

h705Bt

4337

h706At

h706Bt

4340

h707At

h707

4339

h708At

h708Bt

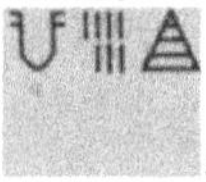

5280

h709 Text

5260

h710 Text

5249

h711 Text

4715

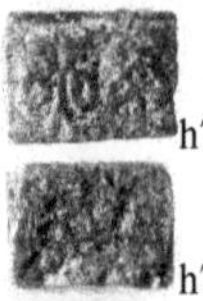

h713At

h713Bt

h714At

h714Bt

Standing person with horns and bovine features (hoofed legs and/or a tail) Icon of a person has bull's legs and a raised club.

h715At

h715Bt

5299

h716At

h716Bt

h717At

h717Bt

h718At

h718Bt

4328

h719At

h719Bt

4326

h720At

h720Bt

h722At

h722Bt

h723At

h723Bt

h724At

h724Bt

5255

h725At

h725Bt

h726At

h726Bt

h727At

h727Bt

h728At

h728Bt

h729At

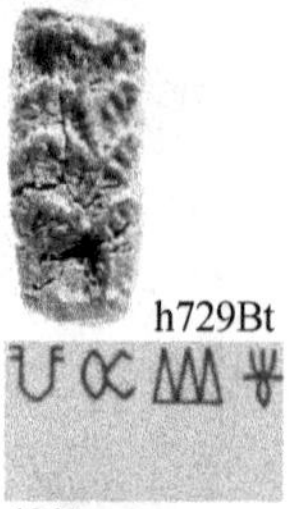

h729Bt

4331

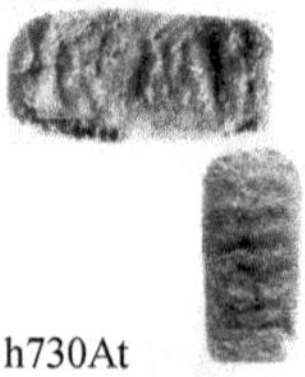

h730At

h730Bt

h731At

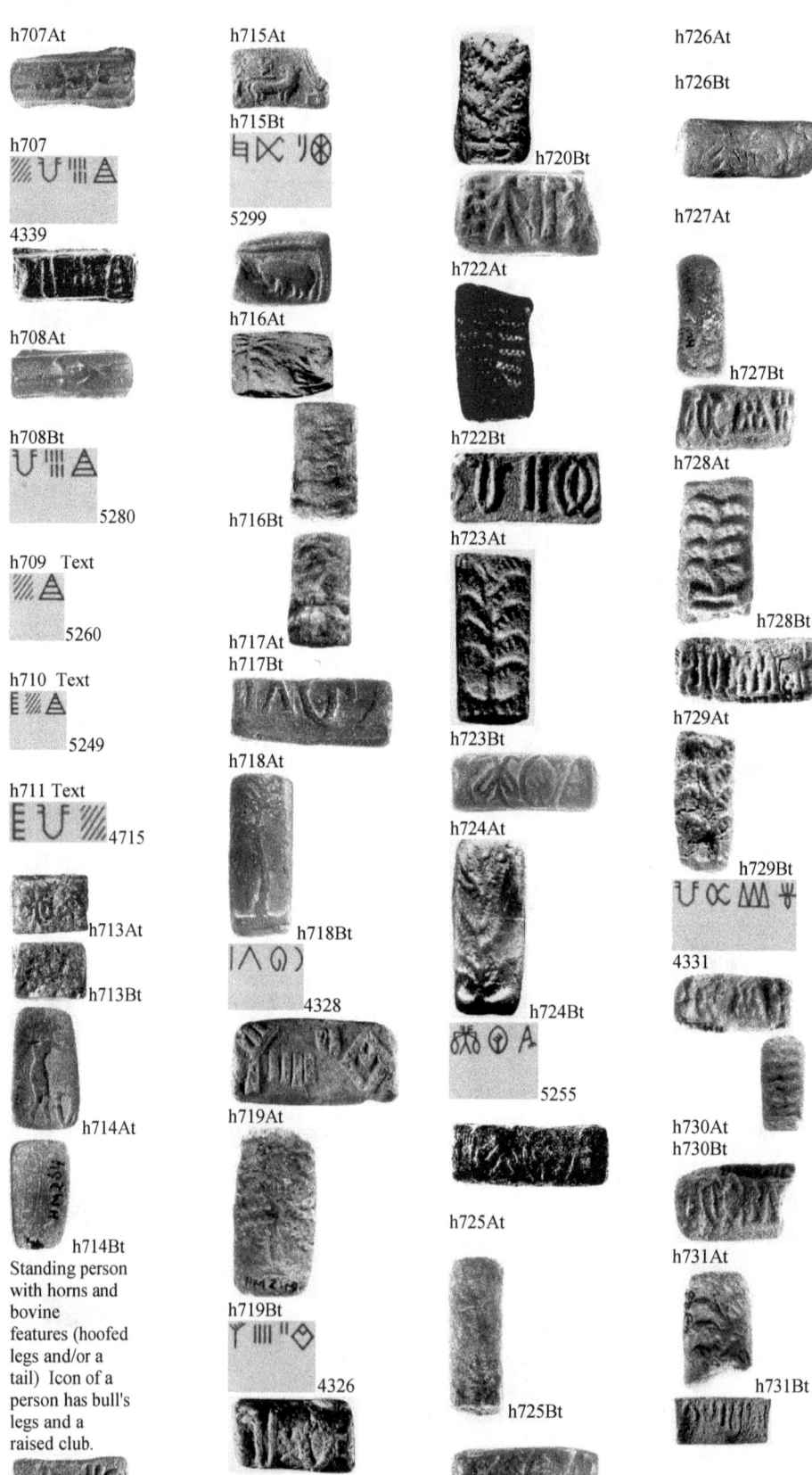

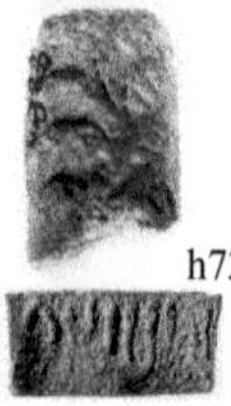

h731Bt

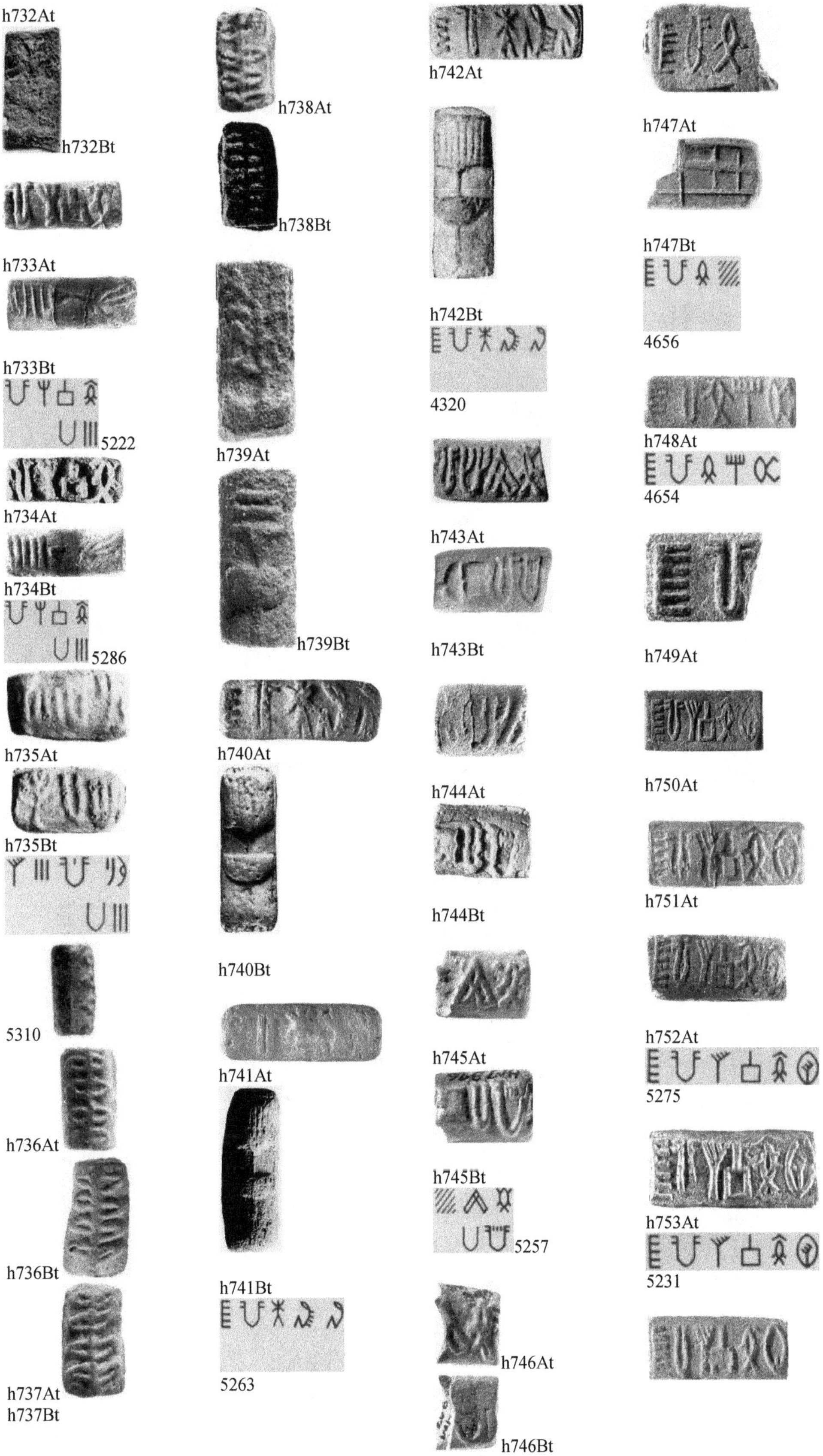

h732At
h732Bt
h733At
h733Bt
5222
h734At
h734Bt
5286
h735At
h735Bt
5310
h736At
h736Bt
h737At
h737Bt

h738At
h738Bt
h739At
h739Bt
h740At
h740Bt
h741At
h741Bt
5263

h742At
h742Bt
4320
h743At
h743Bt
h744At
h744Bt
h745At
h745Bt
5257
h746At
h746Bt

h747At
h747Bt
4656
h748At
4654
h749At
h750At
h751At
h752At
5275
h753At
5231

h754At

4716

h755At

5287

h756At

4669

h757At

4655

h758At

h759At

h760At

h760Bt

h761At

h761Bt

h762At

h762Bt Tablet in bas-relief.

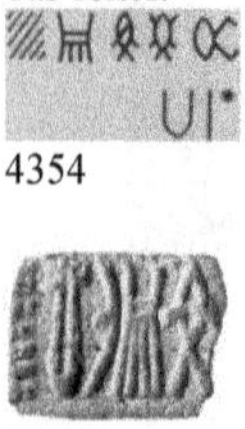

4354

h763At

h763Bt

4661

h764At

h764Bt

h765At

h765Bt

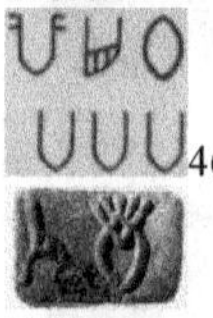

4653

h766At

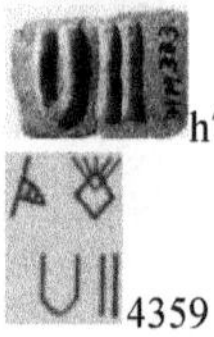

h766Bt

4359

h767At

h767Bt

4352

h768At

h768Bt

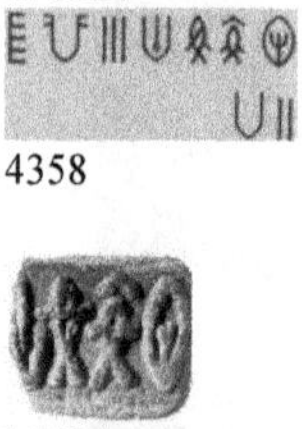

4358

h769At

h769Bt

4667

h770At

h770Bt

4353

h771At

h771Bt

4678

[The second sign on line 1 is a squirrel ].

h772At

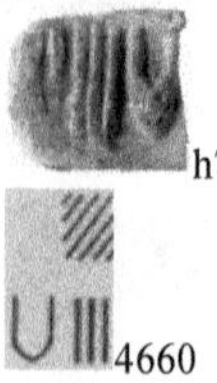

h772Bt

4660

h773At

h773Bt

4351

h774At

h774Bt

4672

h775At

h776At

h776Bt

4350

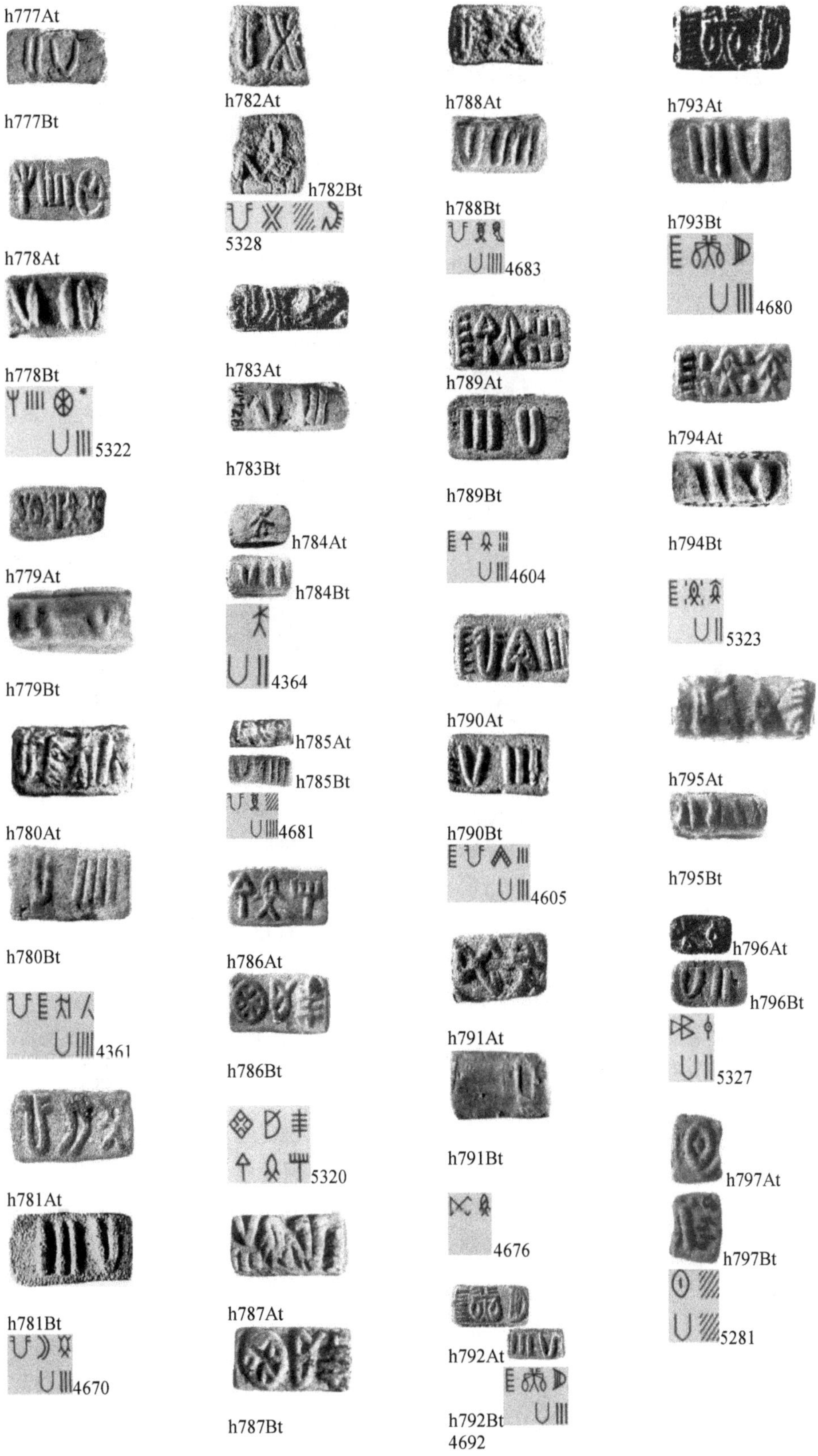

h777At
h777Bt
h778At
h778Bt
5322
h779At
h779Bt
h780At
h780Bt
4361
h781At
h781Bt
4670

h782At
h782Bt
5328
h783At
h783Bt
h784At
h784Bt
4364
h785At
h785Bt
4681
h786At
h786Bt
5320
h787At
h787Bt

h788At
h788Bt
4683
h789At
h789Bt
4604
h790At
h790Bt
4605
h791At
h791Bt
4676
h792At
h792Bt
4692

h793At
h793Bt
4680
h794At
h794Bt
5323
h795At
h795Bt
h796At
h796Bt
5327
h797At
h797Bt
5281

h798At
h798Bt

4607

h799At
h799Bt

4603

h800At
h800Bt

4689

h801At
h801Bt

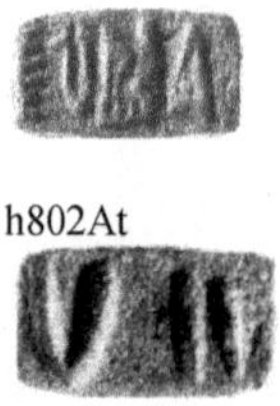
h802At
h802Bt

4679

h804At

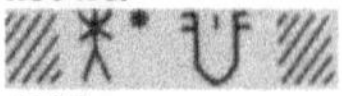
5233

h806At

h806Bt

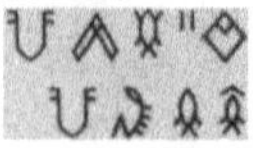
5237

h807At
h807Bt

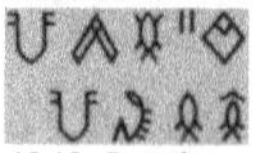
4343 One-horned bull.

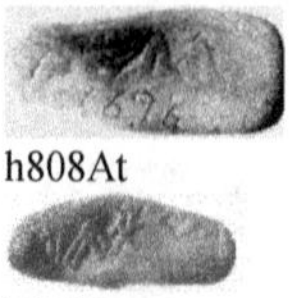
h808At
h808Bt

5238

h810At

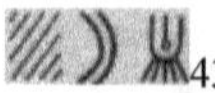
4366

h811At
h811Bt

4349

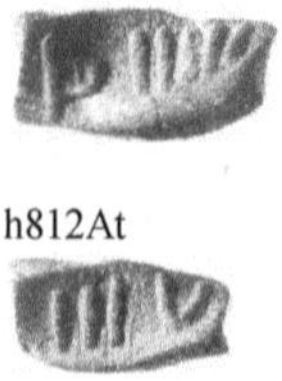
h812At
h812Bt

4686

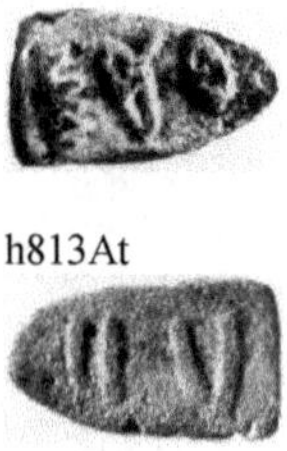
h813At
h813Bt

4682

h814At
h814Bt

4606

h815At
h815Bt

h816At
h816Bt

4602

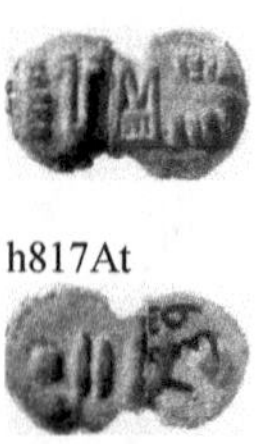
h817At

h817Bt Inscribed object in the shape of a double-axe.One or more dotted circles.

h818At

h818Bt Inscribed object in the shape of a double-axe.

4376

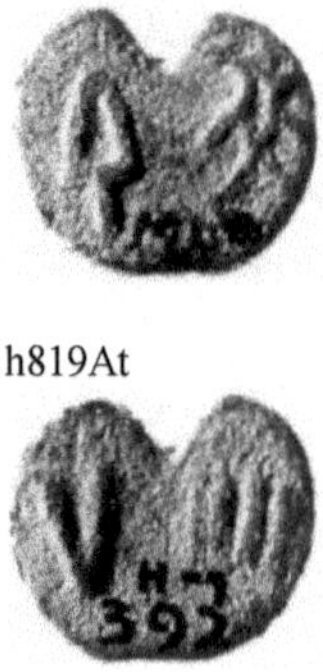
h819At

h819Bt Shape of object: Blade of a weapon?

5302

h820At
h820Bt

h821At

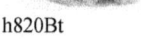

h821Bt Shape of object: axe.

h822At

h822Bt Shape of object: axe.

5319

h823At

h823Bt

4346
h824At
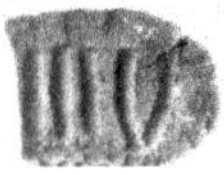
h824Bt
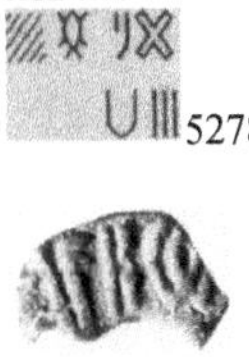
5278
h825At

h825Bt Shape of object: sickle?

5324

h827At

h827Bt Shape of object: axe?

h829At
h829Bt
5303
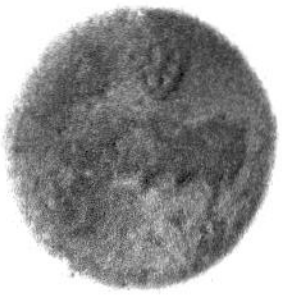
h830At
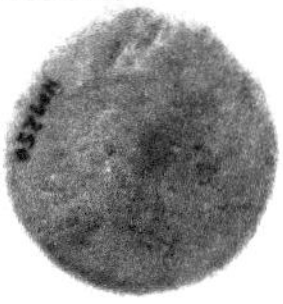
h830Bt Tablet in bas-relief. Bovid.
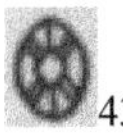
4311
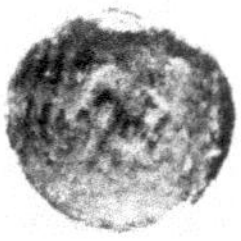
h832At
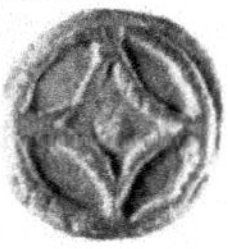
h832Bt Tablet in bas-relief
Pict-121: Lozenge within a circle with a dot in the center.

4377

h833At
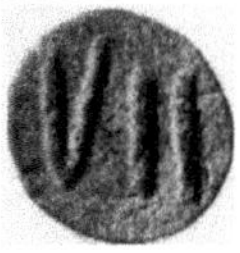
h833Bt

4370
h834At
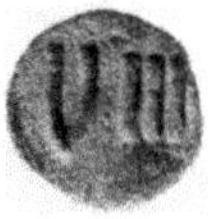
h834Bt

4666
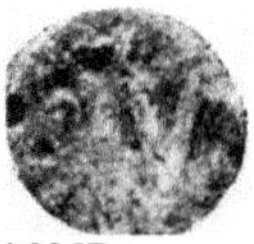
h835Bt

h836At

h837At

h837Bt
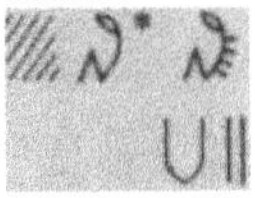
4381
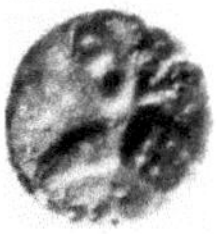
h838At

h838Bt
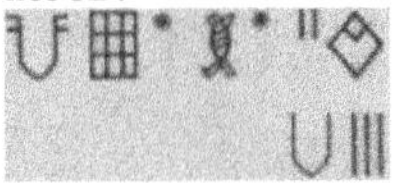

4375
h839At
h839Bt
4378

h840At
4380

h841At

4379
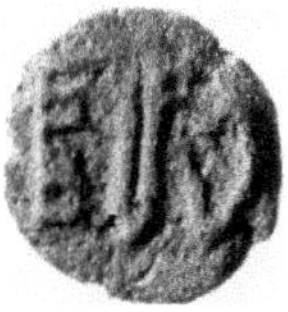
h842At

h843At
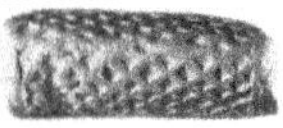
h843Ct

5326
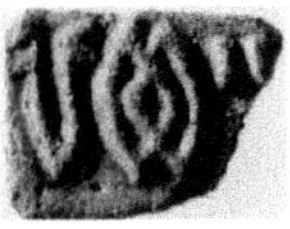

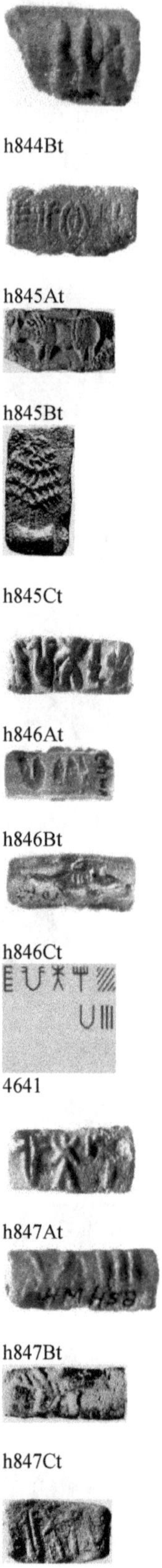

h844At
h844Bt
h845At
h845Bt
h845Ct
h846At
h846Bt
h846Ct
4641
h847At
h847Bt
h847Ct

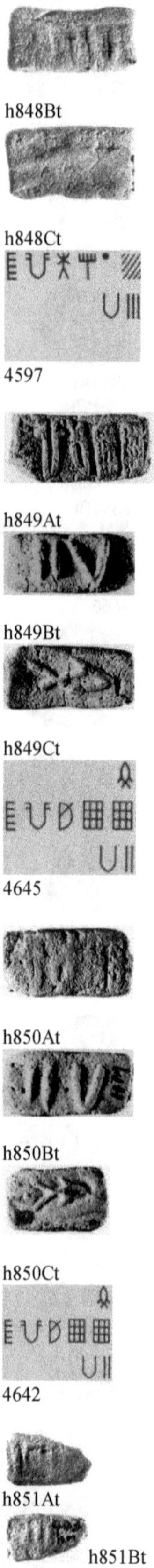

h848At
h848Bt
h848Ct
4597
h849At
h849Bt
h849Ct
4645
h850At
h850Bt
h850Ct
4642
h851At
h851Bt

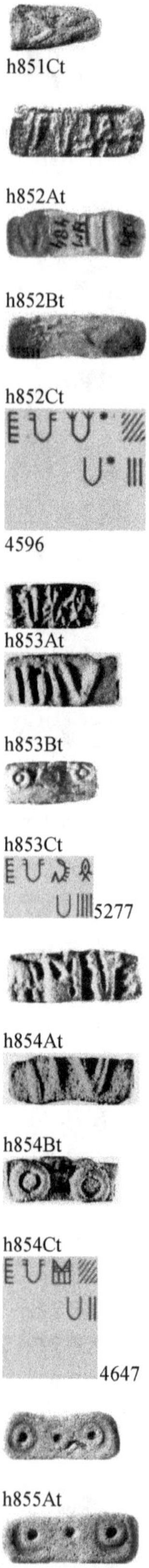

h851Ct
h852At
h852Bt
h852Ct
4596
h853At
h853Bt
h853Ct
5277
h854At
h854Bt
h854Ct
4647
h855At

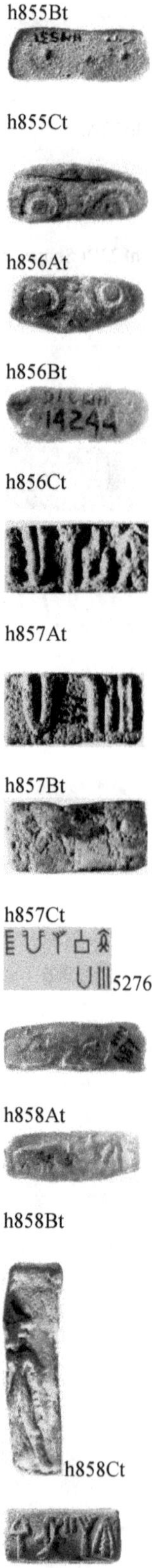

h855Bt
h855Ct
h856At
h856Bt
h856Ct
h857At
h857Bt
h857Ct
5276
h858At
h858Bt
h858Ct

h859At

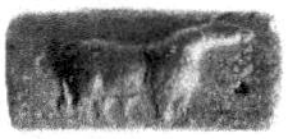

h859Bt

h859Ct

h860At

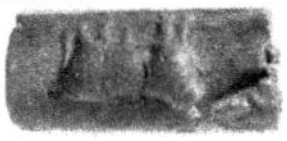

h860Bt

h861At

h861Bt

h862At

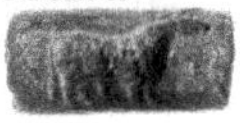

h862Bt

h863ABt

h864ABt

h865ABt

h866ABt

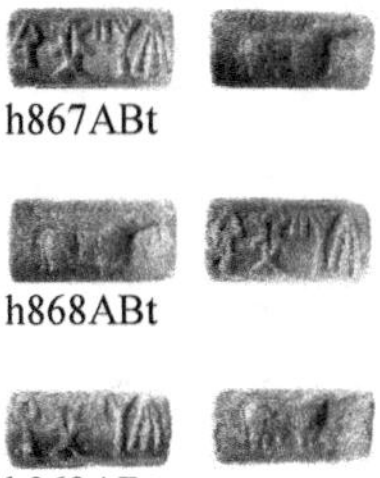

h867ABt

h868ABt

h869ABt

h870ABt

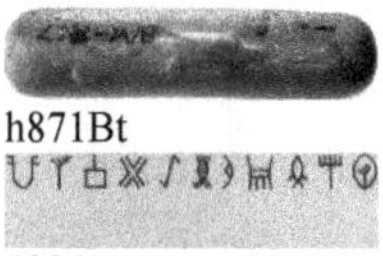

h871Bt

5234

h872Bt

5230

h873At

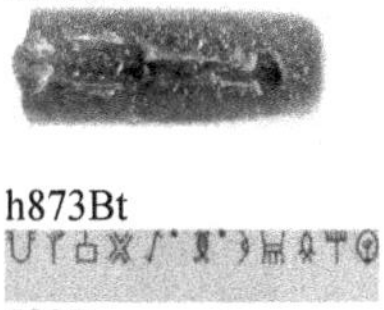

h873Bt

5227

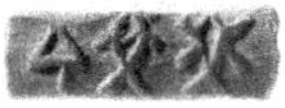

h874At

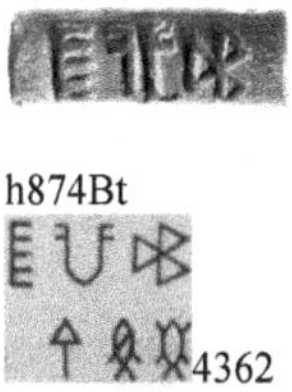

h874Bt

4362

h875At

h875Bt

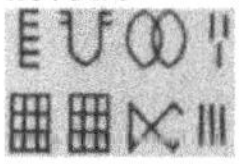

4651

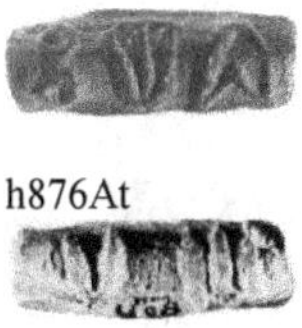

h876At

h876Bt

4675

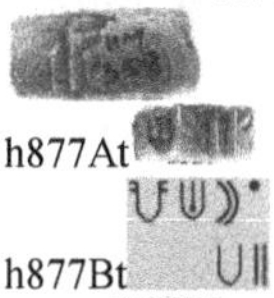

h877At

h877Bt

4594

h878At

h878Bt

4687

h879Abit

h880ABit

4433

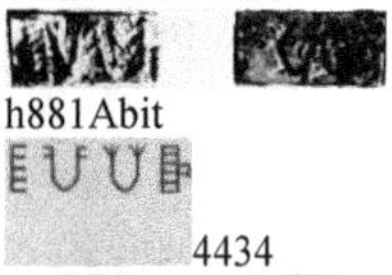

h881Abit

4434

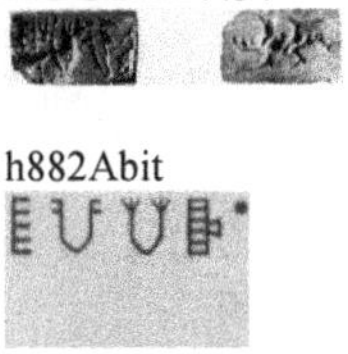

h882Abit

4436

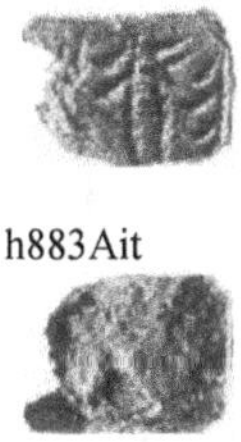

h883Ait

h883Bit

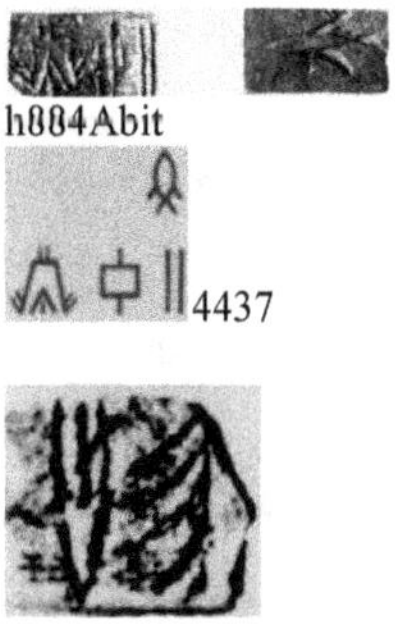

h884Abit

4437

h885Ait

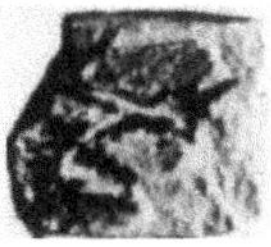

h885Bit

4530 Fish.

h887Ait

h887Bit

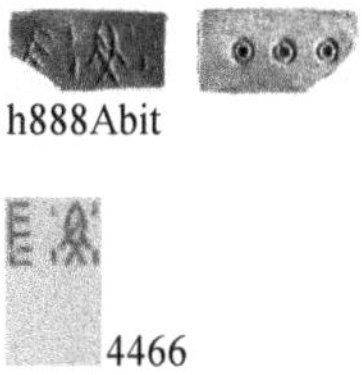

h888Abit

4466

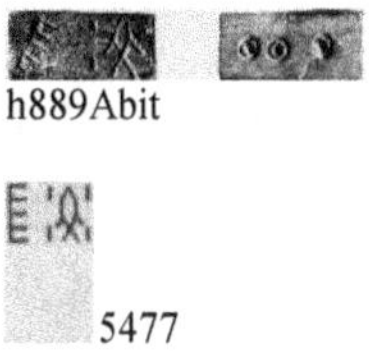

h889Abit

5477

h890ABit

4446

h891ABit

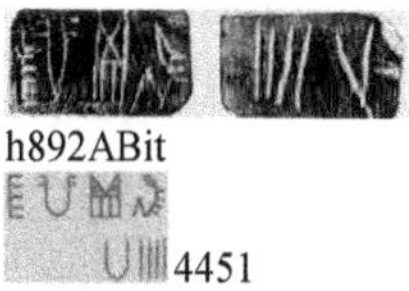

h892ABit

4451

h893Ait

h893Bit

4522

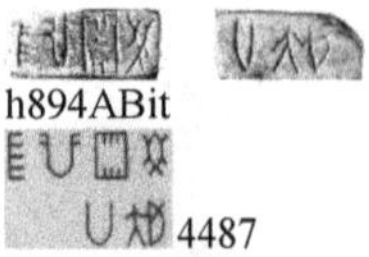
h894ABit
4487

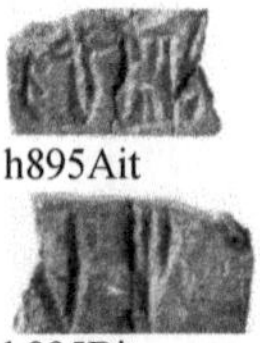
h895Ait
h895Bit

h896ABit
4480

h897ABit

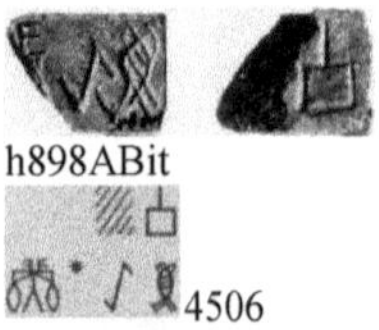
h898ABit
4506

h899Ait
h899Bit
4471

h900Ait
h900Bit
4455

h901Ait
h901Bit
4460

h902Ait
h902Bit
4535

h903Ait
h903Bit
4485

h904Ait
h904Bit
4477

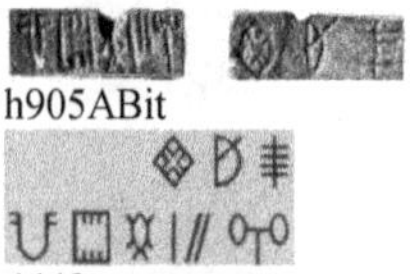
h905ABit
4449

h906Ait
h906Bit

5494

h907Ait
h907Bit
4537 The second sign on h907Ait may be a ligatured fish?

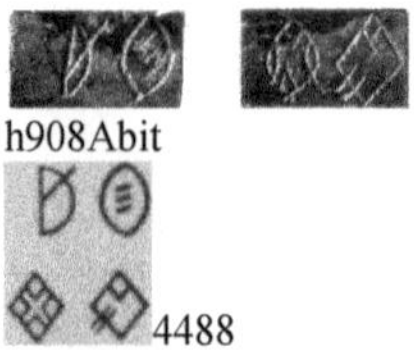
h908Abit
4488

h909ABit
5325

h910ABit
4470

h911Ait
h911Bit
4486

h912Abit

5461

h913Ait
h913Bit

h914Ait
h914Bit
4483

h916Ait
h916Bit
4456

h917Ait
h917Bit
4472

h918Ait
h918Bit
4481

h919Ait

h919Bit

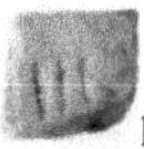

h920Ait

h920Bit
4527

h921ABit

4514

h922Abit
4518

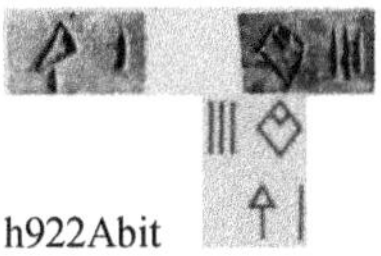

h923Abit
4474

h924ABit

h925Abit

4512

h926Abit

4519

h927Ait

h927Bit 4502

h928Ait

h928Bit

h929Ait

h929Bit

h930Ait

h930Bit

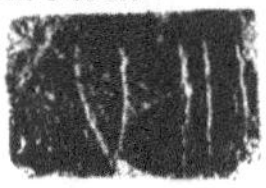

4520

h931Ait

h931Bit

4511

h932Ait

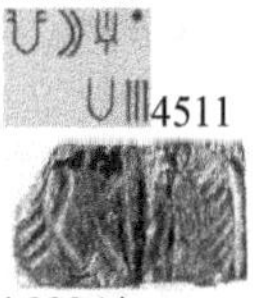

h932Bit

4403

h933Ait

h933Bit

4516

h934Ait

h934Bit

h935Ait

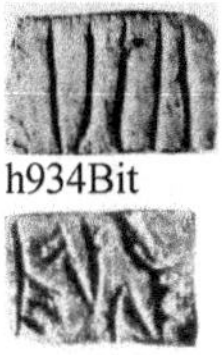

h935Bit

4509

h936Ait

h936Bit

5405

h937Ait

h937Bit

5458

h938Ait

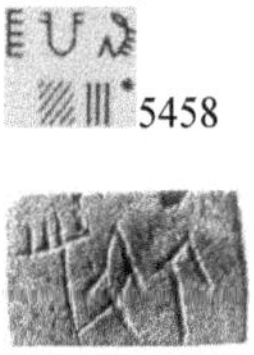

h938Bit

h939Ait

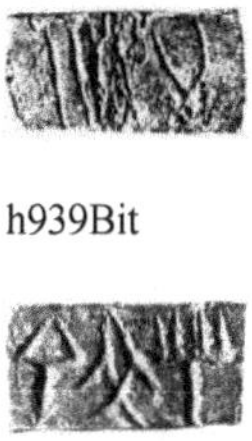

h939Bit

h940Ait

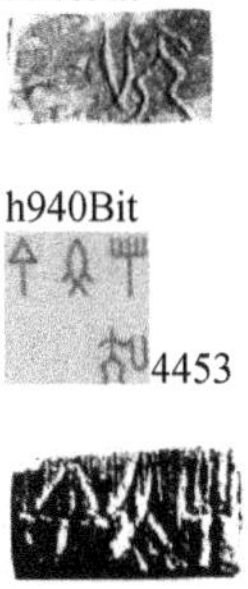

h940Bit

4453

h941Ait

h941Bit

4464

h942Ait

h942Bit

4490

h943Ait

h943Bit

4461

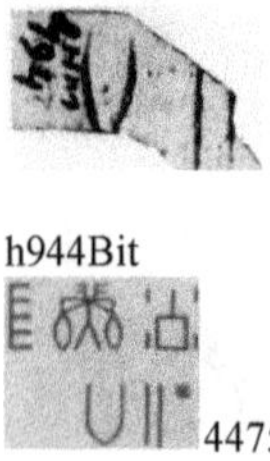
h944Ait
h944Bit
4475

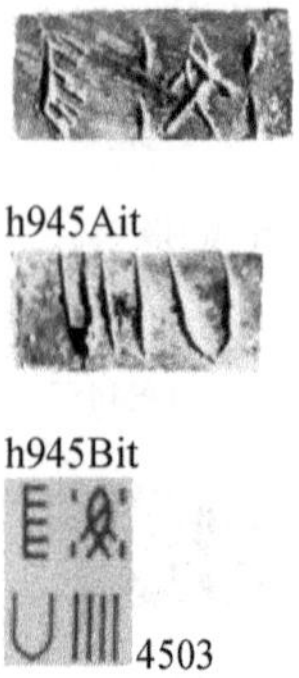
h945Ait
h945Bit
4503

h946Ait
h946Bit
4501

h947Ait
h947Bit
4493

h948Abit
4489

h949Abit
4479

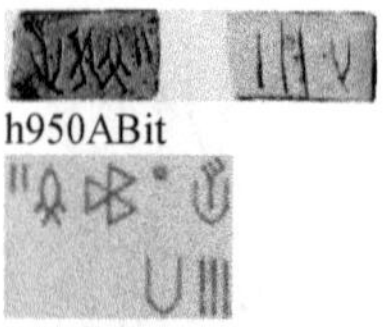
h950ABit
4463

h951Ait
h951Bit
4498

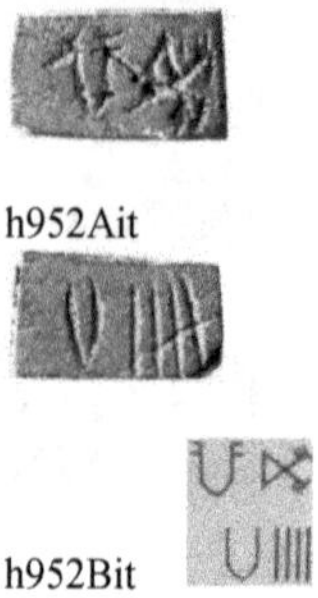
h952Ait
h952Bit
4469

h953Ait
h953Bit

h954Ait
4467

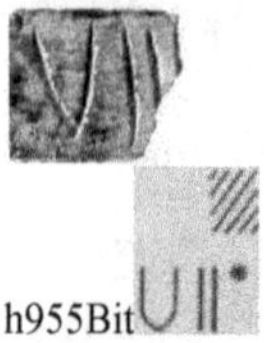
h955Bit
5429

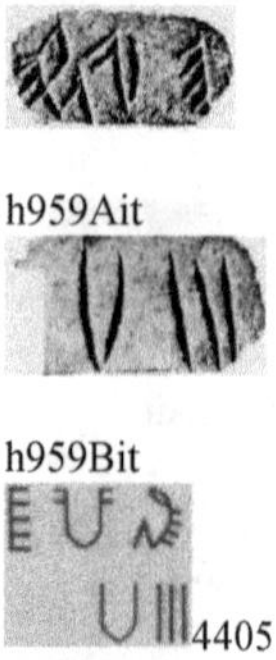
h959Ait
h959Bit
4405

h960Ait
h960Bit
4543

h961Ait
h961Bit
5449

h962Ait
h962Bit
4548

h963Ait
h963Bit
5420

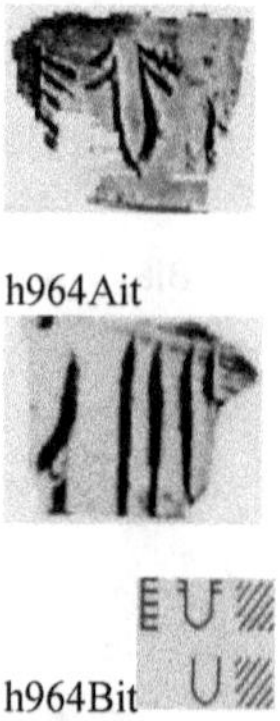
h964Ait
h964Bit
5456

h965Ait
h965Bit
4562

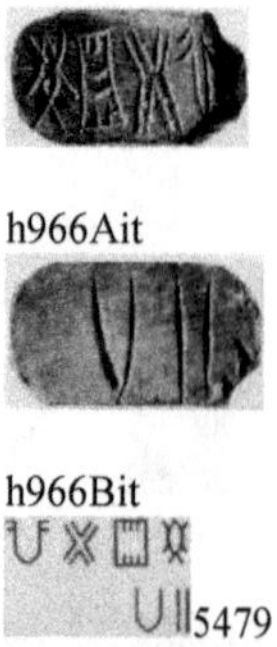
h966Ait
h966Bit
5479

h967Ait
4563

h968Ait
h968Bit

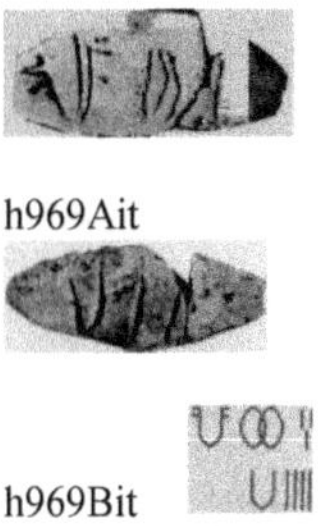

h969Ait

h969Bit

4555

h970Ait

h970Bit

4553

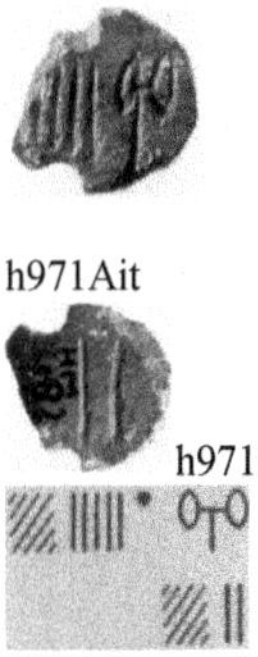

h971Ait

h971Bit

4557 Shape of object: double-axe?

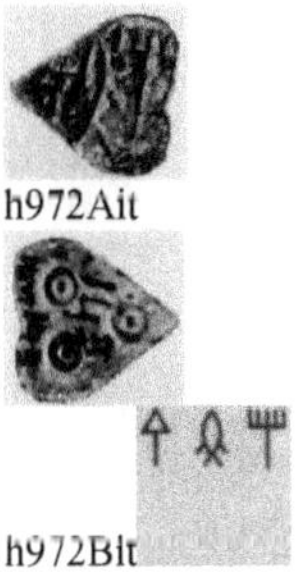

h972Ait

h972Bit

4418 Pict-128: Inscribed object in the shape of a leaf? Dotted circles on obverse.

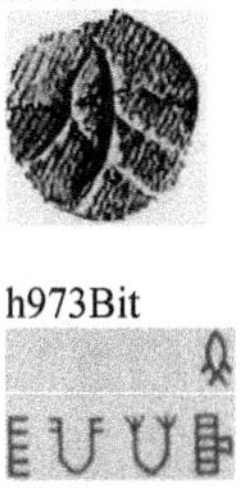

h973Ait

h973Bit

4411

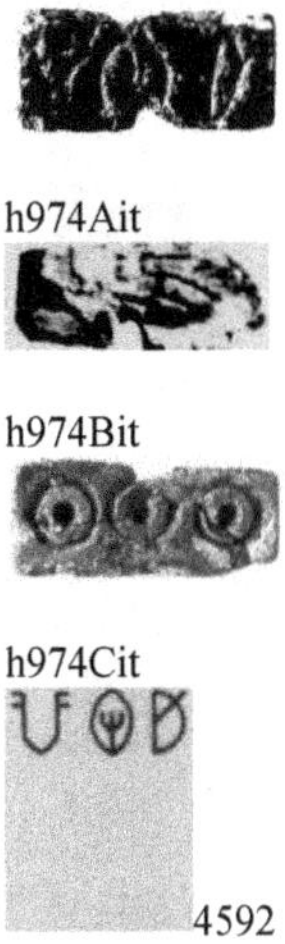

h974Ait

h974Bit

h974Cit

4592

h975Ait

h975Bit

h975Cit

4402

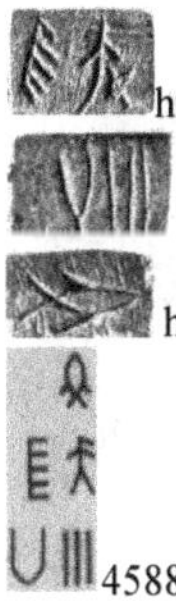

h976Ait

h976Bit

h976Cit

4588

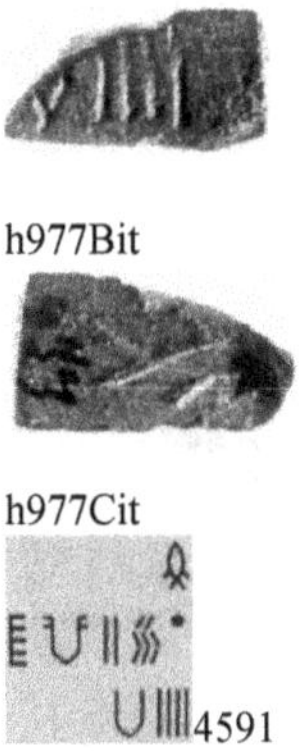

h977Ait

h977Bit

h977Cit

4591

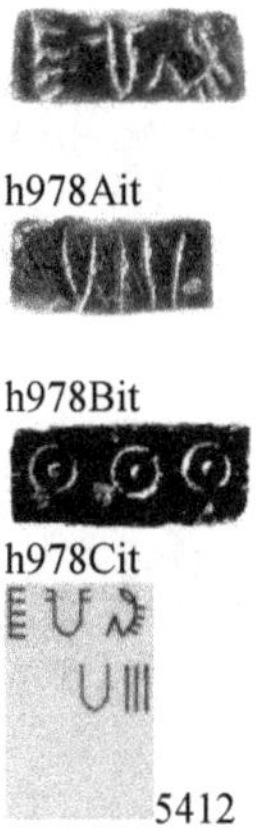

h978Ait

h978Bit

h978Cit

5412

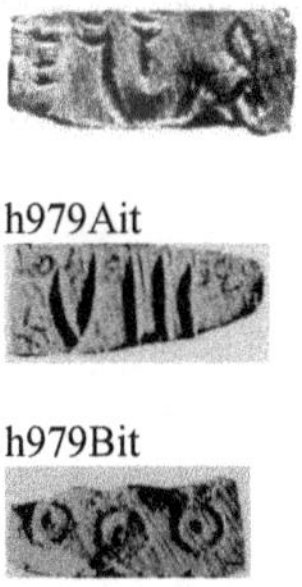

h979Ait

h979Bit

h979Cit

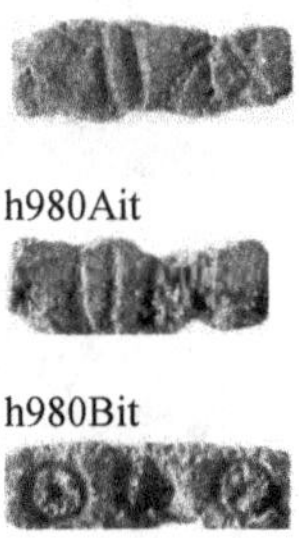

h980Ait

h980Bit

h980Cit

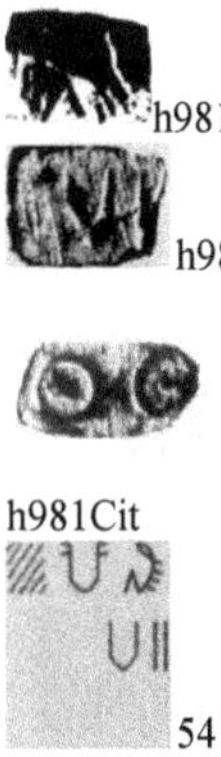

h981Ait

h981Bit

h981Cit

5415

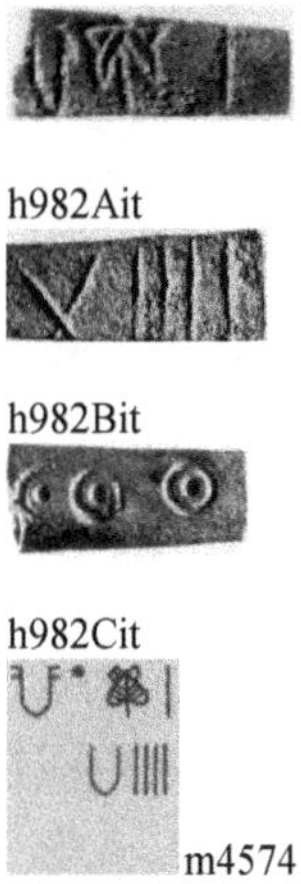

h982Ait

h982Bit

h982Cit

m4574

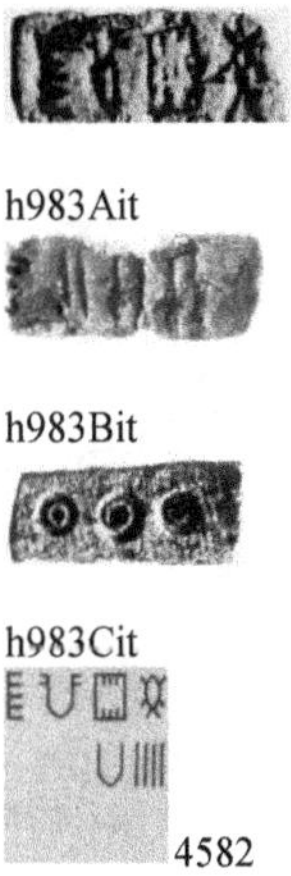

h983Ait

h983Bit

h983Cit

4582

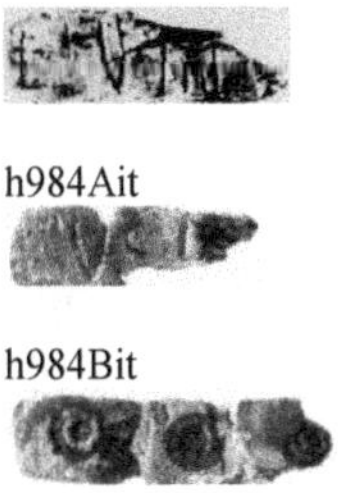

h984Ait

h984Bit

h984Cit

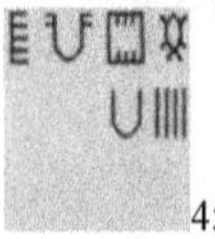

4587

h985Ait

h985Bit

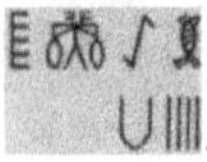

4577

h987Ait

h987Bit

h987Cit

4586

h988Ait

h988Bit

h988B2it

h988Cit

h988Eit

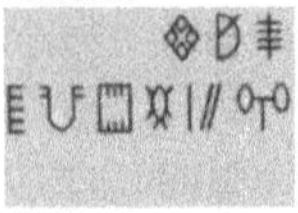

4573

h990

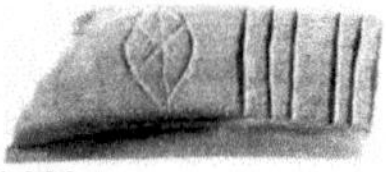

h992

h994

h1020

h1021

h1022

h1023

h1024

h1025a

h1027a

h1028

h1029a

h1030a

h1031

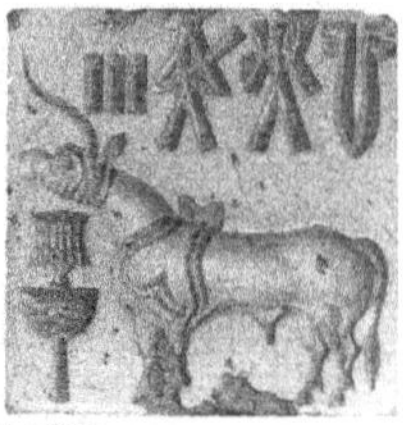

h1032a

h1033a

h1035

h1036

h1037

h1038

h1042a

h1043a

h1044a

h1045a
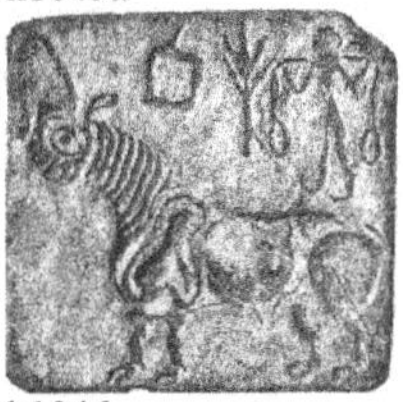
h1046

h1047a

h1048

h1049a

h1050

h1051

h1052

h1053a

h1056a

h1058a

h1059
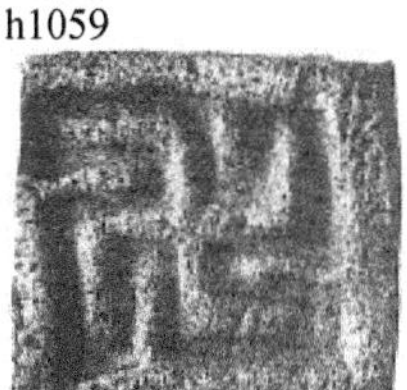
h1064

h1065

h1066a

h1067a

h1068

h1071
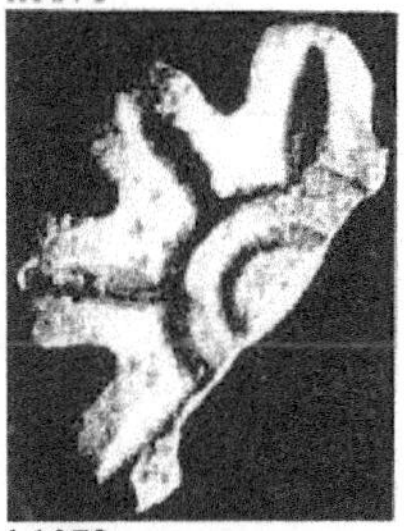
h1072
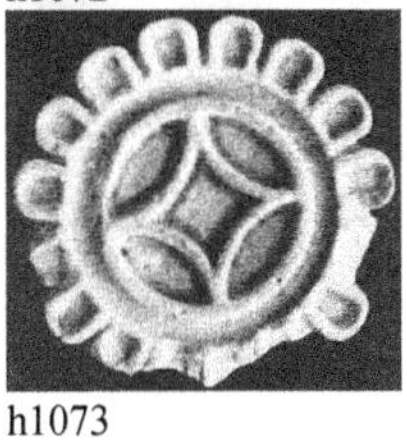
h1073

h1075

h1076

h1077

h1079a

h1080a
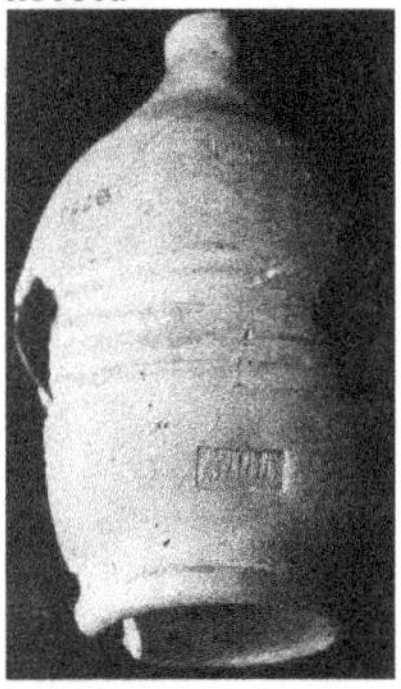
h1081

h1082

h1083

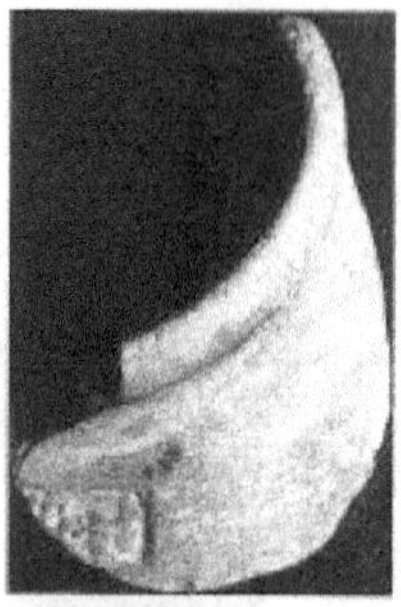
h1084

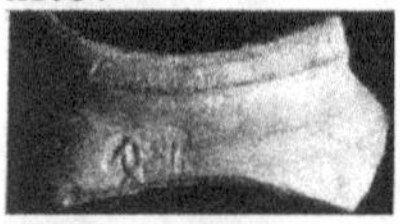
h1085

h1086

h1087

h1091

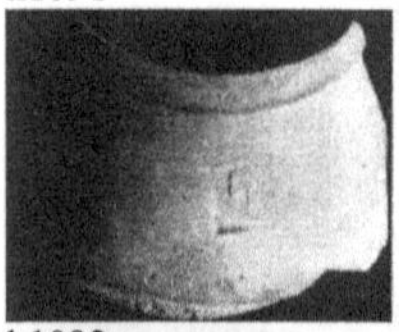
h1092

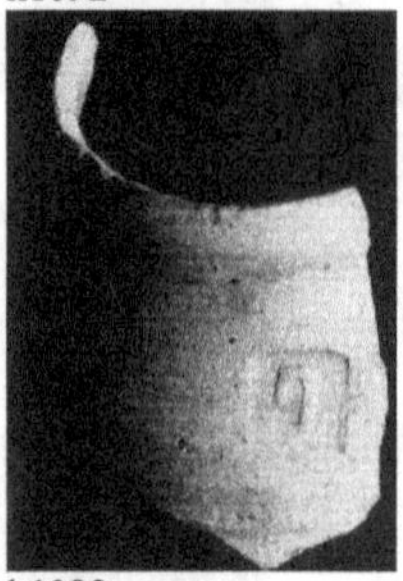
h1093

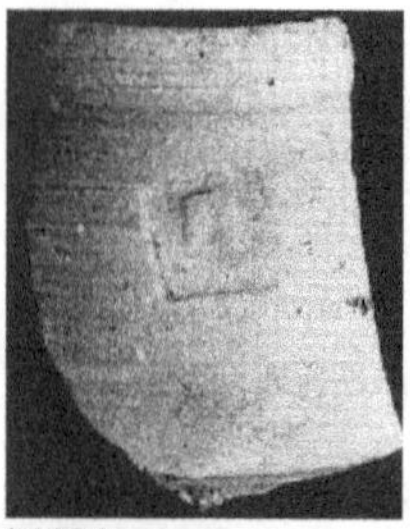
h1094

h1097

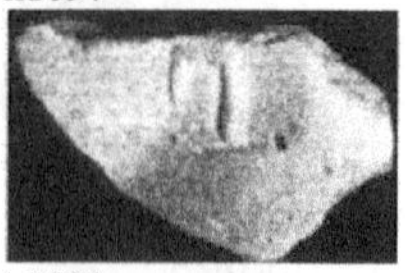
h1098

h1100A

h1100B

h1101A

h1101B

h1102A

h1102B

h1103A

h1103B

h1104A

h1104B

h1105A

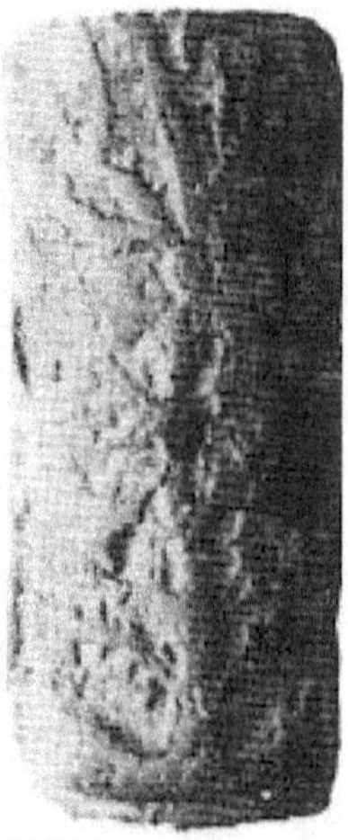
h1105B

h1107A

h1107B

h1108A

h1108B

h1109A

h1109B

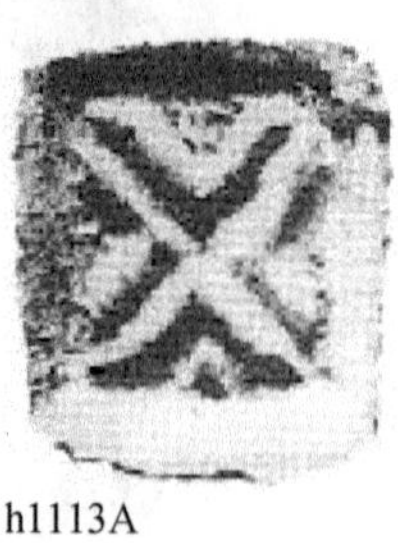
h1113A

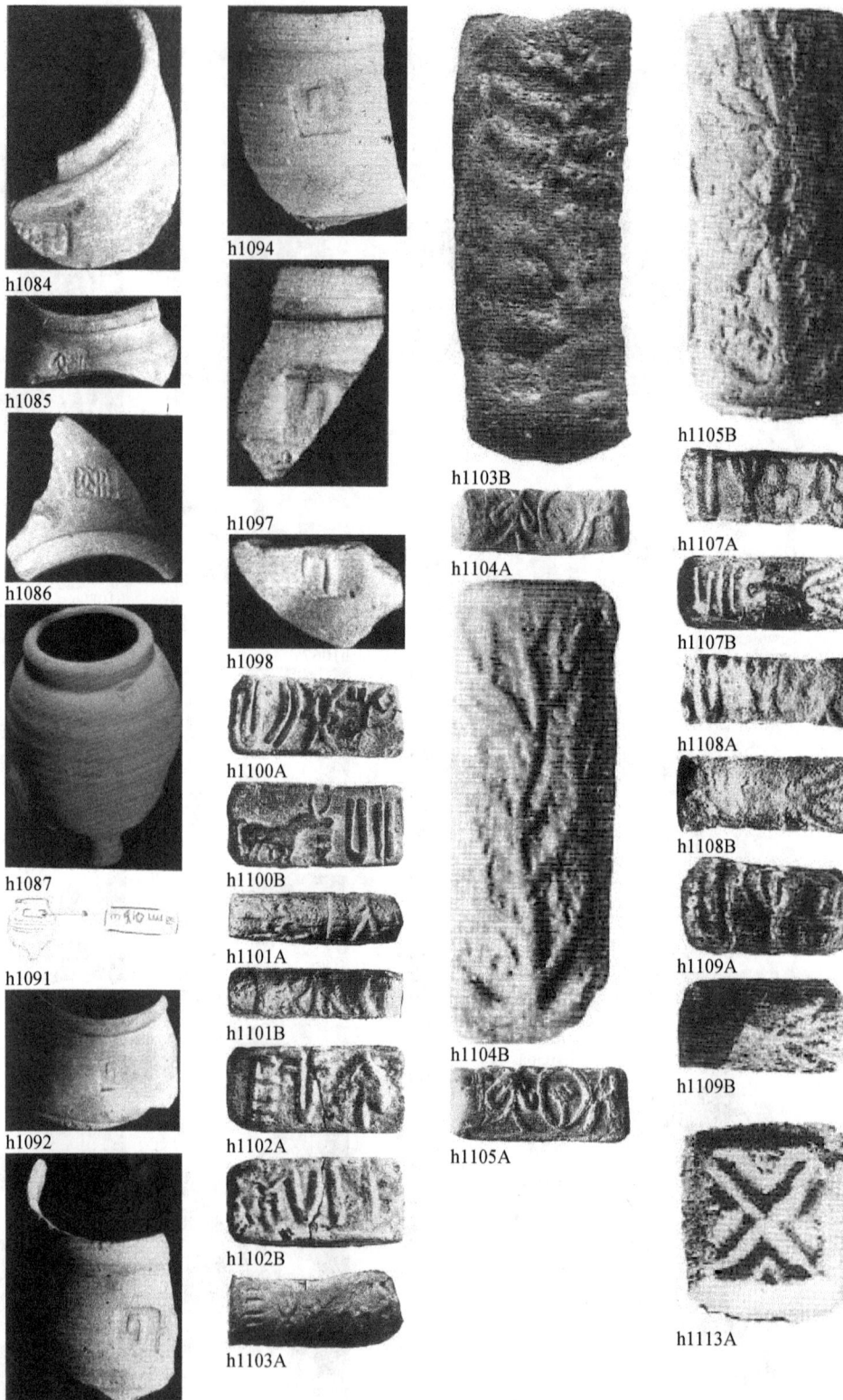

h1113B h1114B h1115A h1116A h1116B h1117A h1121A h1121B h1122A

h1122B h1123A h1123B h1124A h1124B h1126A h1126B h1130A h1130B h1131A h1131B h1133A

h1133B h1134A h1134B h1137A h1138A h1138B h1139A h1139B h1140A h1140B h1141A h1141B h1142A h1142B

h1144A h1144B h1146A h1146B h1148A h1149A h1150ABC h1151A

h1151C
h1152A
h1152B
h1155A
h1155B
h1158A
h1158B
h1159A
h1159B

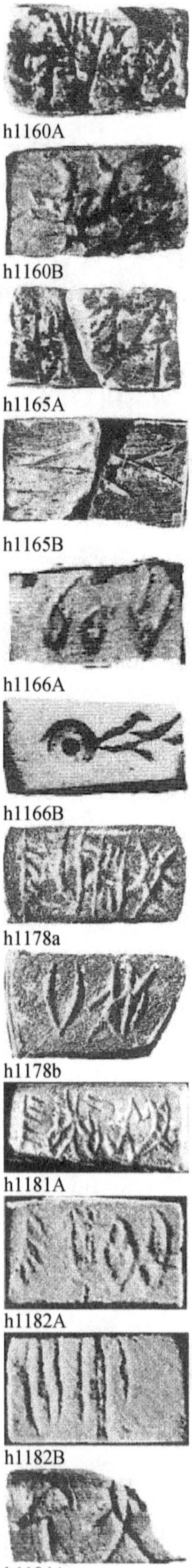

h1160A
h1160B
h1165A
h1165B
h1166A
h1166B
h1178a
h1178b
h1181A
h1182A
h1182B
h1184A

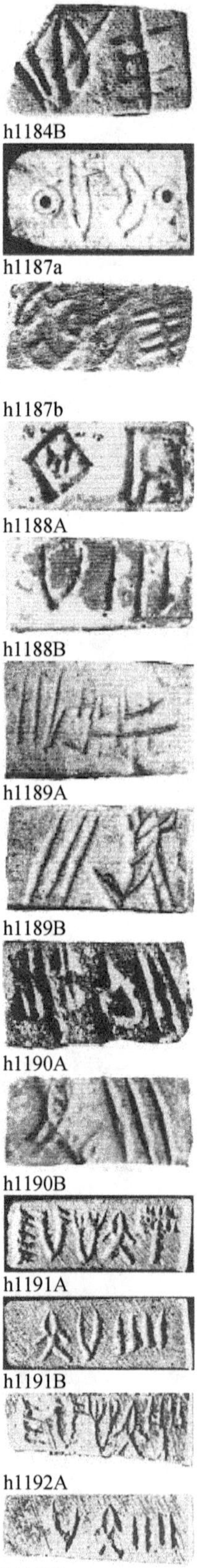

h1184B
h1187a
h1187b
h1188A
h1188B
h1189A
h1189B
h1190A
h1190B
h1191A
h1191B
h1192A
h1192B

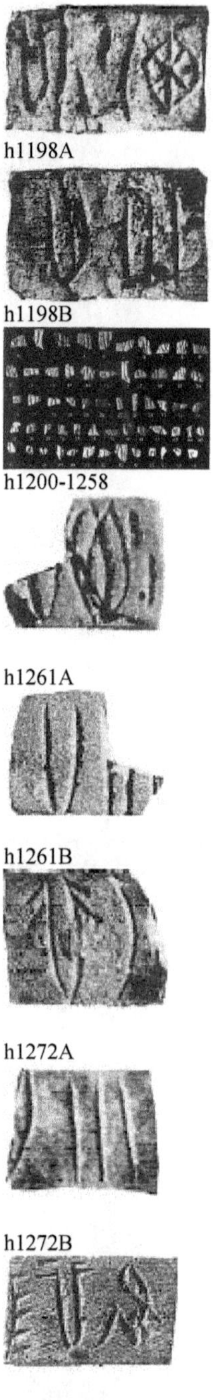

h1198A
h1198B
h1200-1258
h1261A
h1261B
h1272A
h1272B
h1273A
h1273B

h1274A
h1274B

h1275A
h1275B

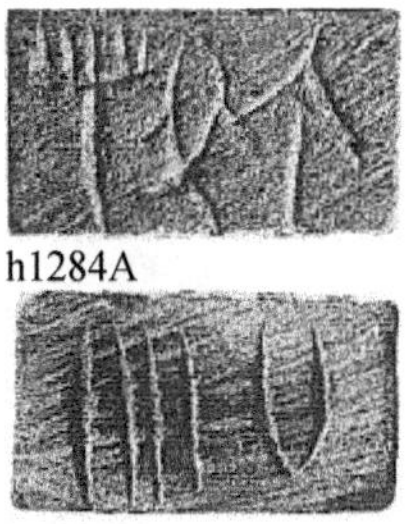
h1284A
h1284B

h1287A
h1287B

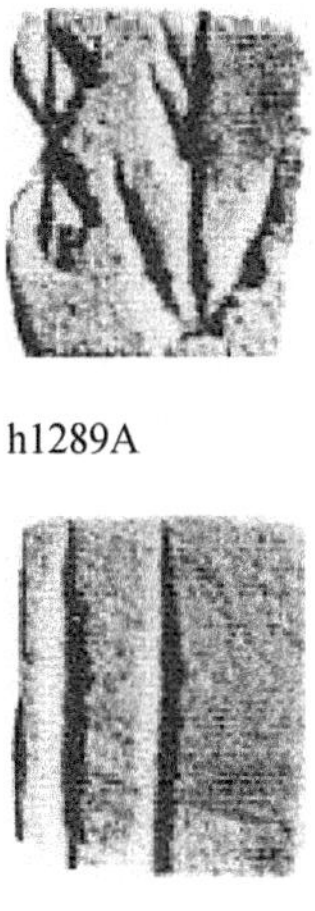
h1289A
h1289B

h1293A
h1293B

h1294A
h1294B

h1302A
h1302B

h1303A
h1303B

h1304A
h1304B

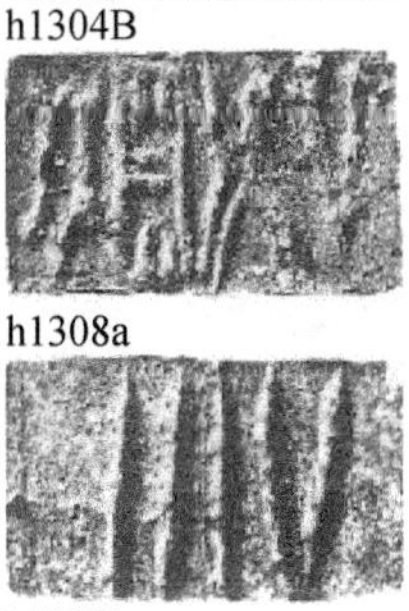
h1308a
h1308b

h1309A
h1309B

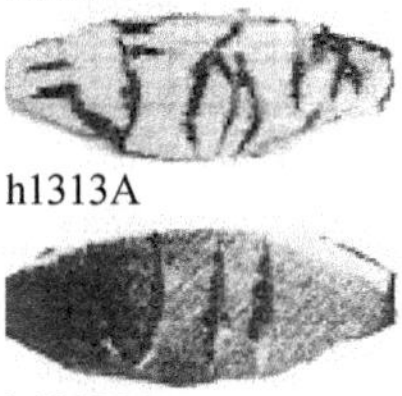
h1313A
h1313B

h1319A
h1319B

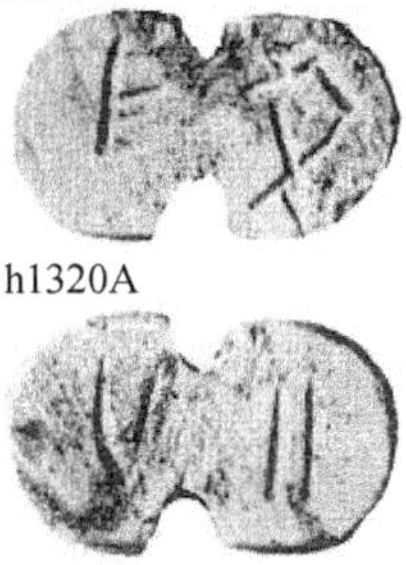
h1320A
h1320B

h1321A
h1321B

h1325A
h1325b

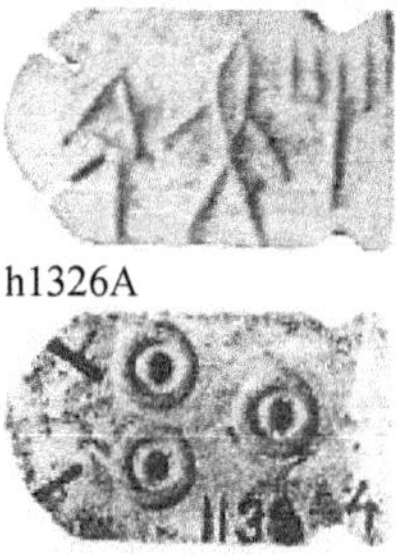
h1326A
h1326B

h1329A
h1329B

h1330A
h1330B

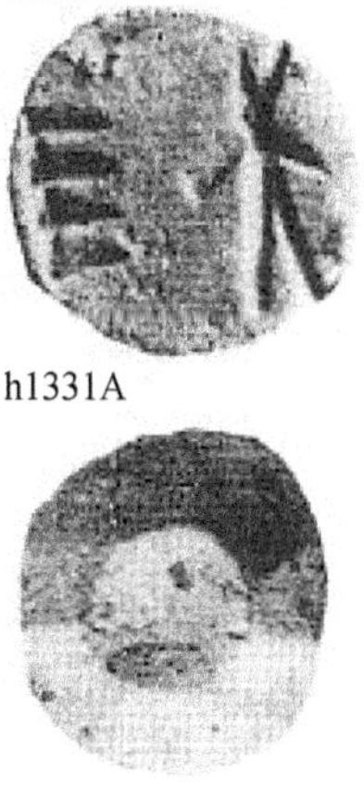
h1331A

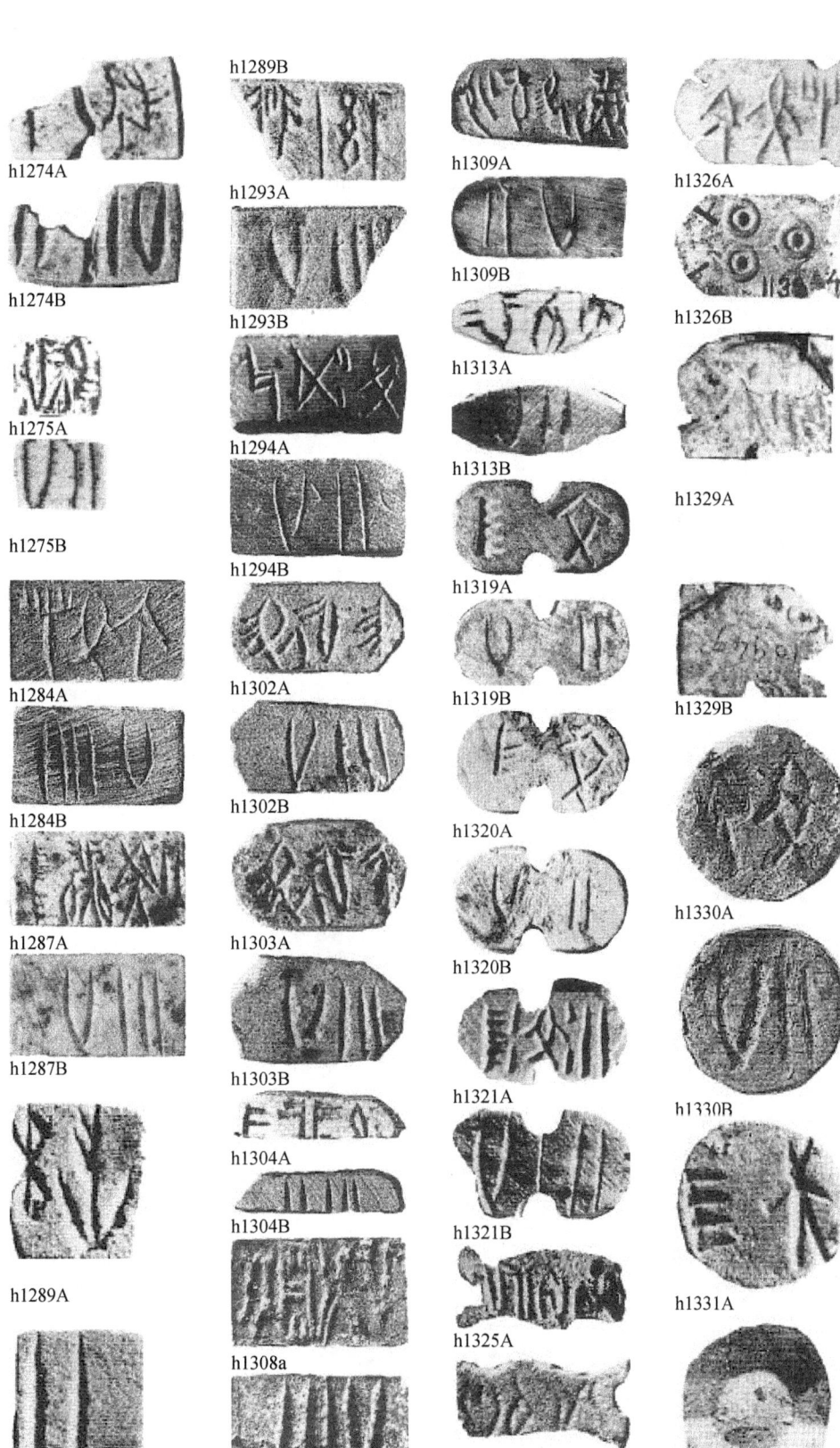

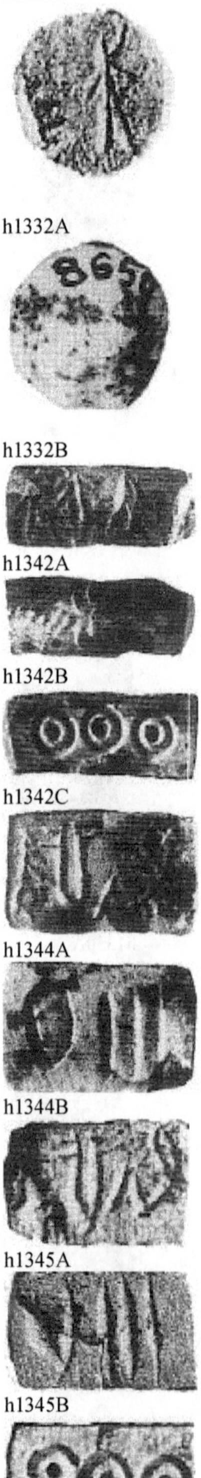

h1331B
h1332A
h1332B
h1342A
h1342B
h1342C
h1344A
h1344B
h1345A
h1345B
h1345C

h1347A
h1347B
h1347C
h1348A
h1348B
h1348C
h1350A
h1350B
h1350C
h1353a
h1353b
h1353c
h1354A
h1354B
h1354C

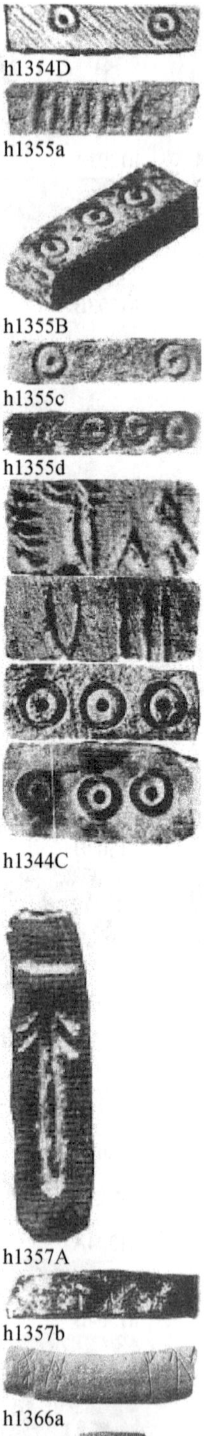

h1354D
h1355a
h1355B
h1355c
h1355d
h1344C
h1357A
h1357b
h1366a
h1388A

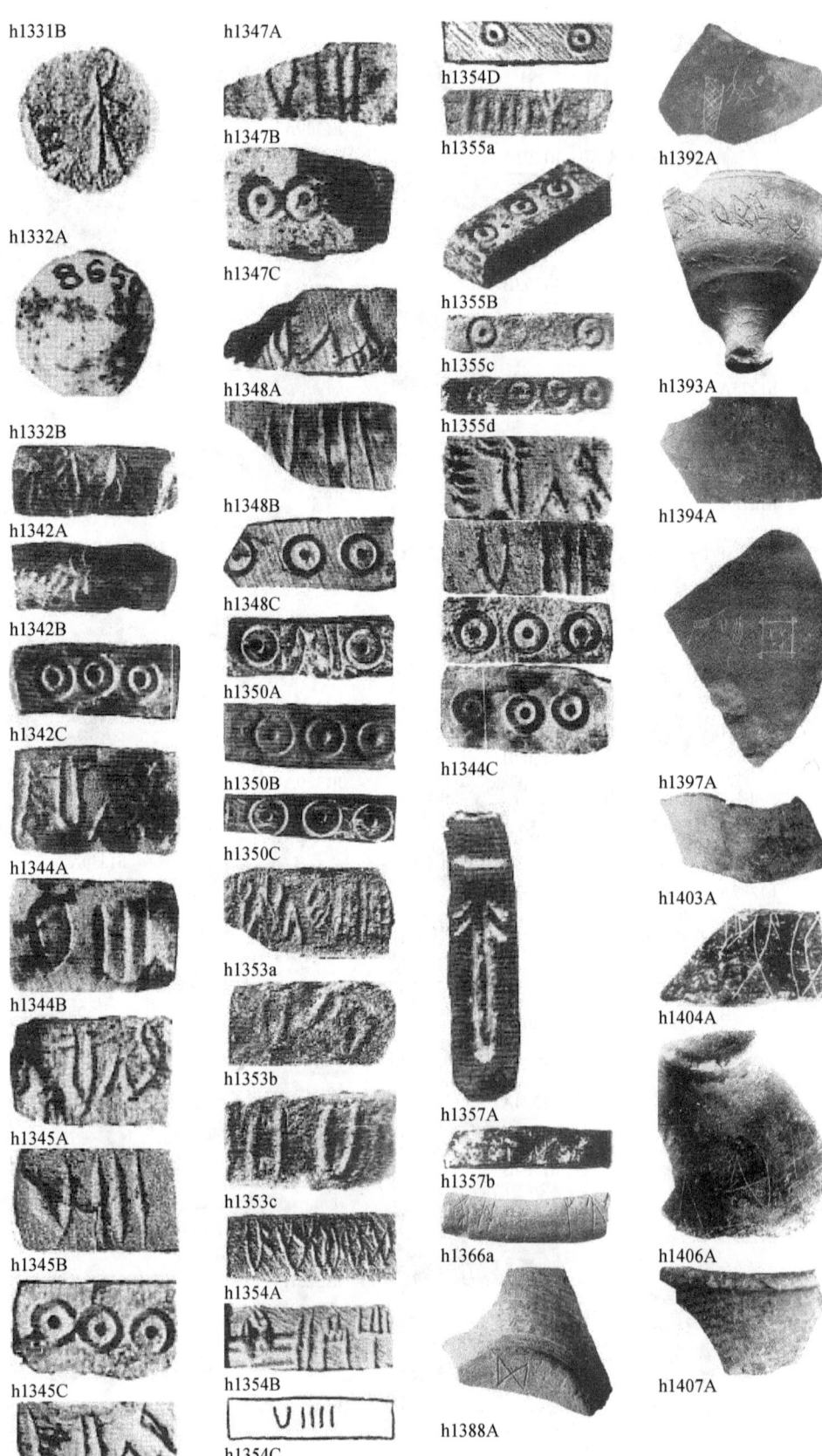

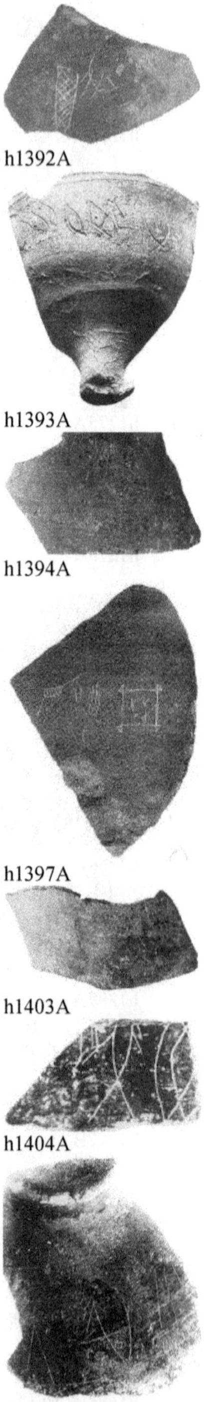

h1392A
h1393A
h1394A
h1397A
h1403A
h1404A
h1406A
h1407A

h1408A

h1410A

h1411A

h1412A

h1421A

h1422A

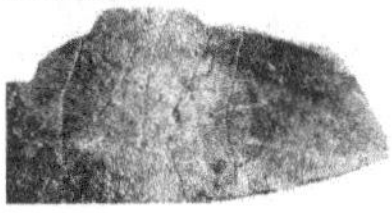
h1424A

h1431A

h1433A

h1434A

h1441A

h1444A

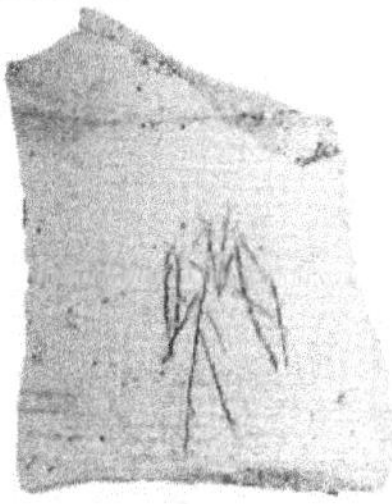
h1461A

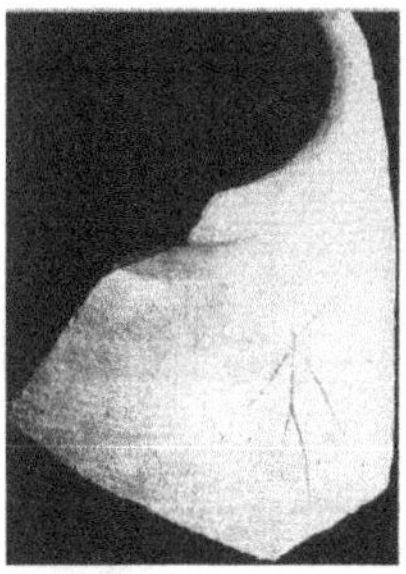
h1462A

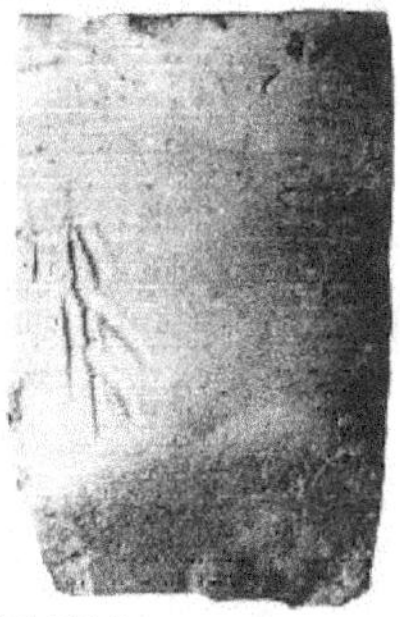
h1464A

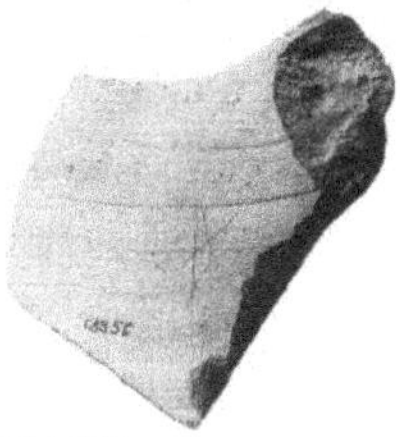
h1467A

h1468A

h1471A

h1481A

h1487A

h1491A

h1501A

h1506A

h1507A

h1513A

h1516A

h1517A

h1518copperaxe

h1522A

h15533A
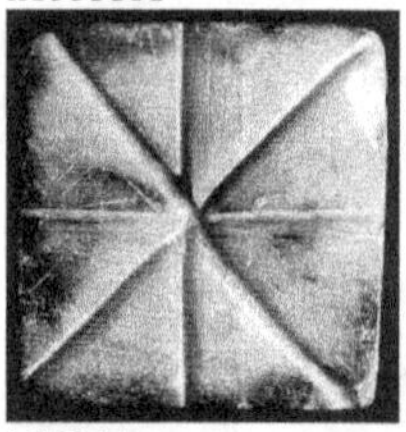
h1534A

h1535A

h1536A
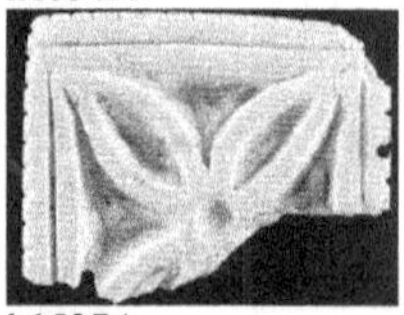
h1537A
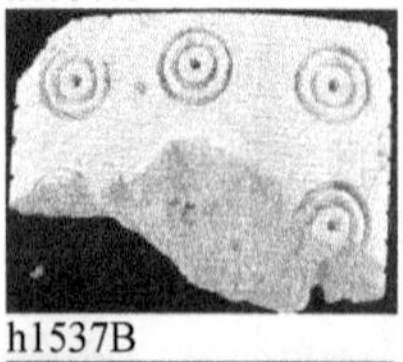
h1537B
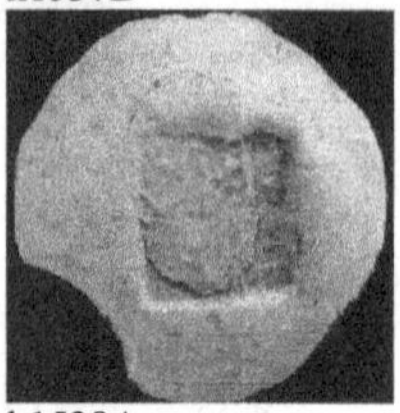
h1538A
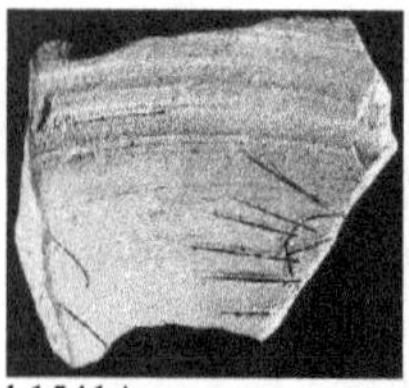
h1541A

h1544A
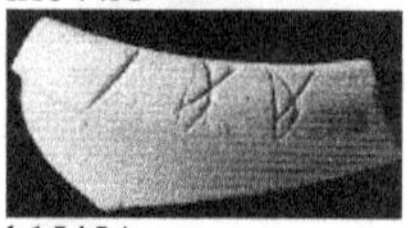
h1545A

h1547A
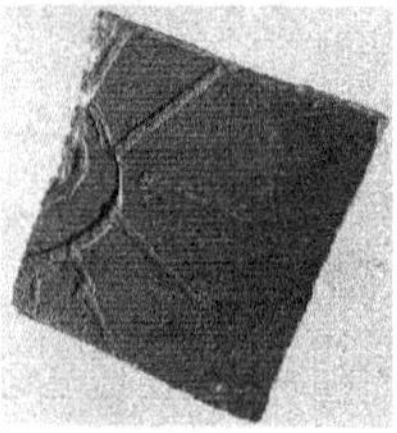
h1559A

h1586A
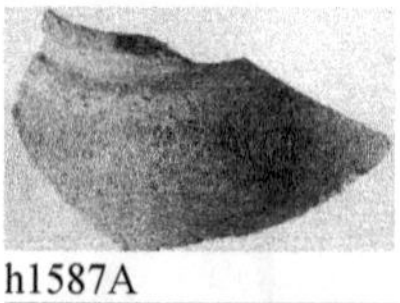
h1587A

h1657A

h1662A
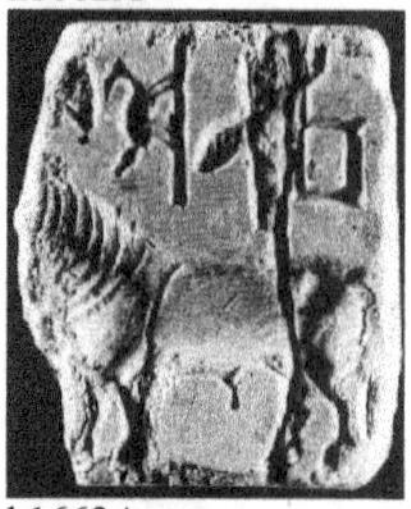
h1663A

h1664A

h1666A

h1667A

h1669A
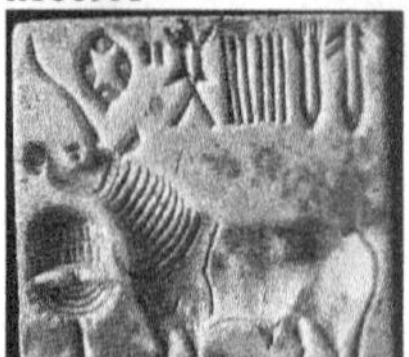
h1670A

h1671A

h1672A

h1673A

h1676A
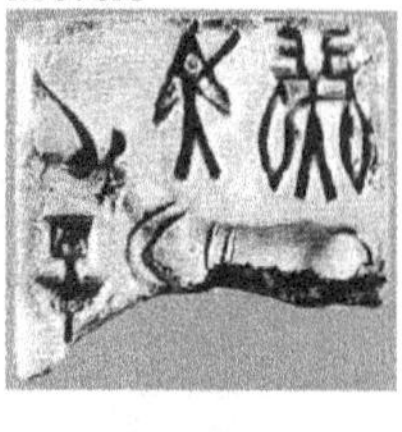
h1677A

h1678A

h1679A

h1680A

h1681A

h1682A

h1684A

h1685A

h1687A

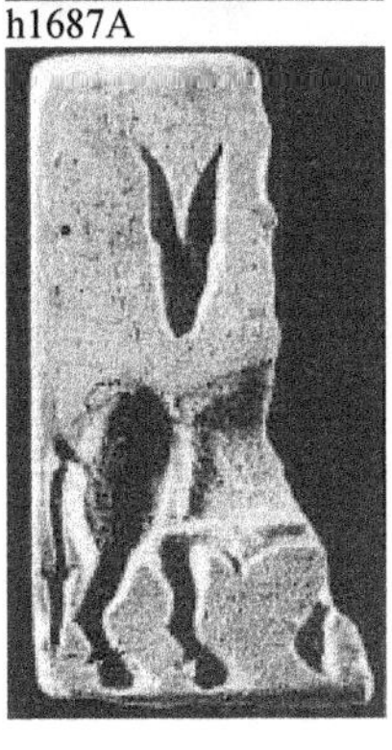

h1688A

h1690A

h1691A

h1692A

h1694A

h1695

h1696

h1697

h1698

h1699

h1700

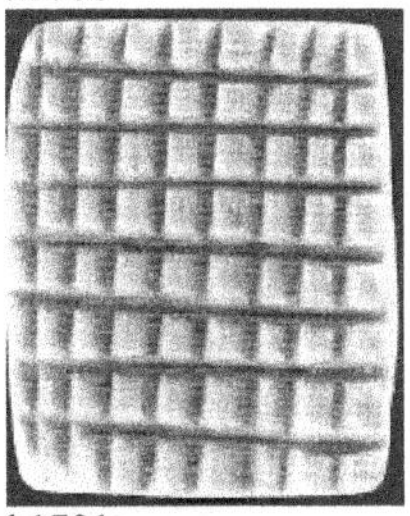

h1701

h1702

h1703

h1704

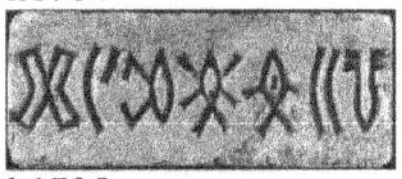

h1705

h1706

h1707

h1708

h1709

h1710

h1711

h1712

h1713

h1714

h1715

h1716

h1719A

h1719B

h1720A

h1720B

h1721A

h1721B

h1722A

h1723

h1724

h1725A

h1726

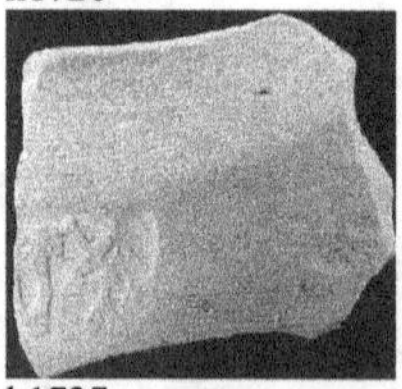
h1727

h1728

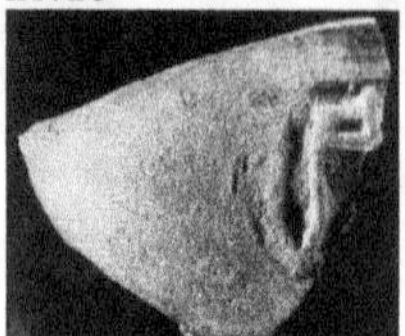

h1729

h1731

h1732

h1733

h1734

h1735

h1736

h1737

h1739

h1740

h1742

h1743

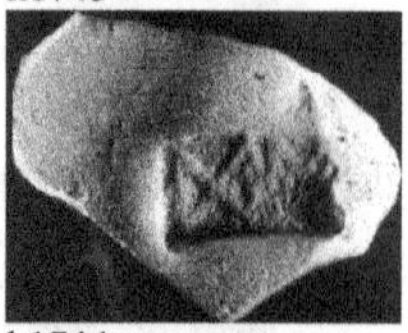
h1744

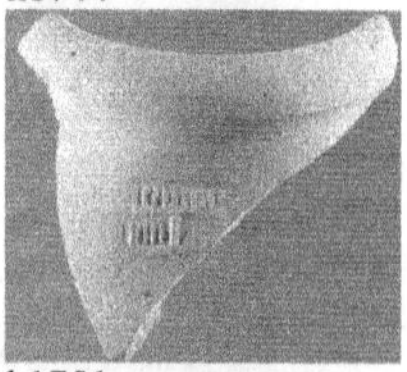
h1751

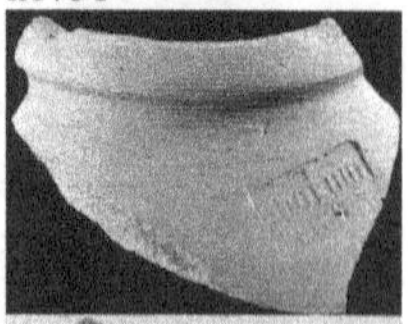

h1753

h1756

h1757

h1758

h1759

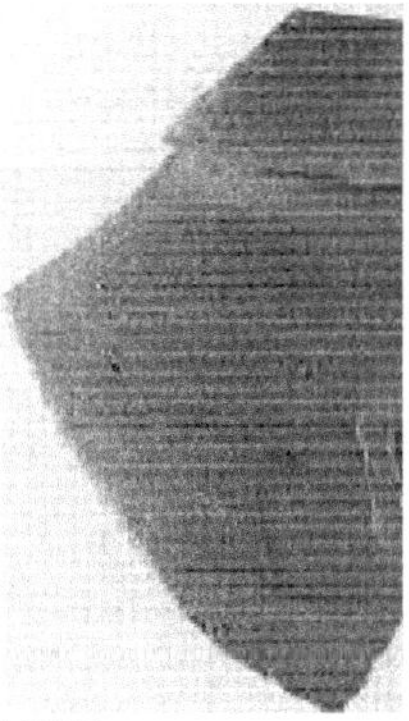
h1760

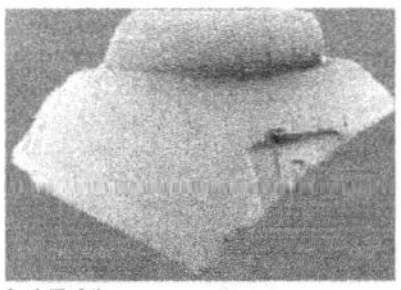
h1761

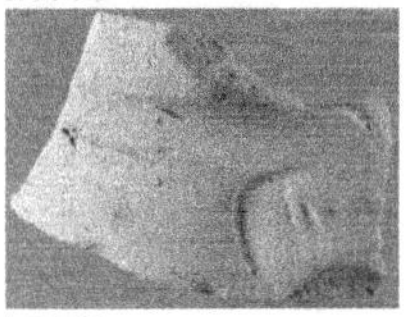
h1762

h1767A

h1767B

h1768A

h1768B

h1770A

h1770B

h1771A

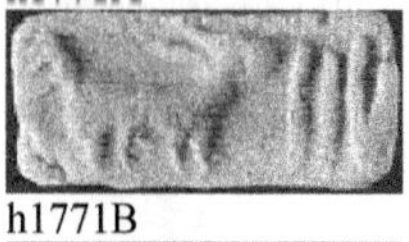
h1771B

h1772A

h1772B

h1773A

h1773B

h1774A

h1774B

h1775A

h1775B

h1776A

h1776B

h1777A

h1777B

h1778A

h1778B

h1779A

h1779B

h1780A

h1780B

h1781A

h1781B

h1782A

h1783A

h1783B

h1785A

h1785B

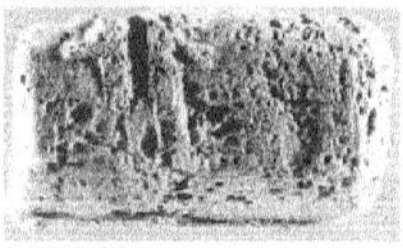
h1786A

h1786B

h1787A

h1787B

h1788A

h1788B

h1791A

h1791B

h1792A
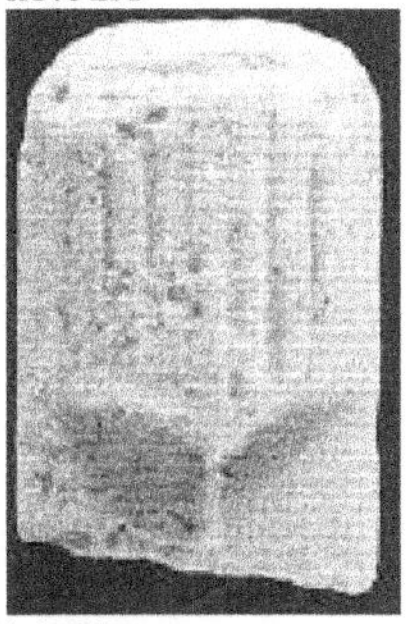
h1792B

h1793A

h1793B

h1796A

h1796B

h1797A

h1797B

h1799A

h1800A
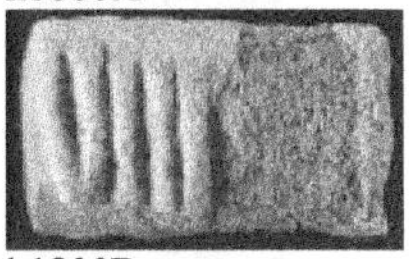
h1800B

h1801A

h1801B

h1802A

h1802B

h1803A

h1803B

h1804A

h1804B

h1805A
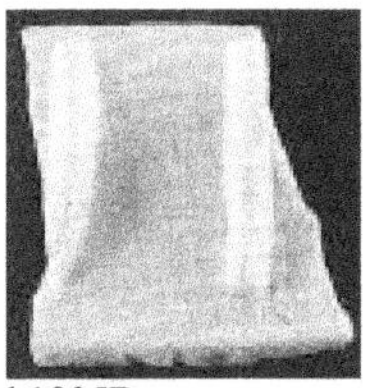
h1805B

h1806A

h1806B

h1807A

h1807B
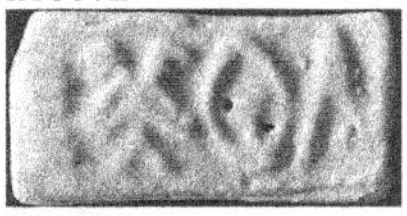
h1808A

h1809A

h1810A

h1810B

h1811A

h1811B

h1812A

h1812B

h1813A
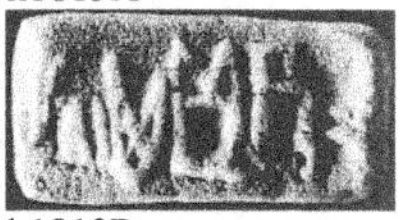
h1813B

h1815A

h1815B

h1816A

h1816B
h1817A
h1817B
h1818A
h1818B
h1819A
h1819B
h1820A
h1820B
h1821A
h1821B
h1822A

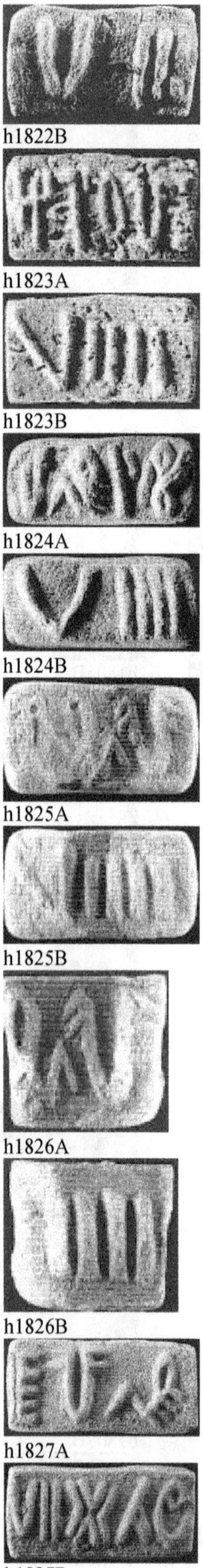

h1822B
h1823A
h1823B
h1824A
h1824B
h1825A
h1825B
h1826A
h1826B
h1827A
h1827B

h1829A
h1829B
h1830A
h1830B
h1831A
h1831B
h1832A
h1832B
h1833A
h1833B
h1834A

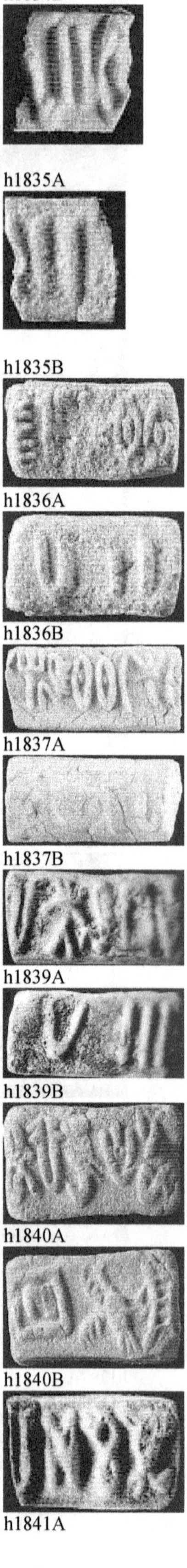

h1834B
h1835A
h1835B
h1836A
h1836B
h1837A
h1837B
h1839A
h1839B
h1840A
h1840B
h1841A

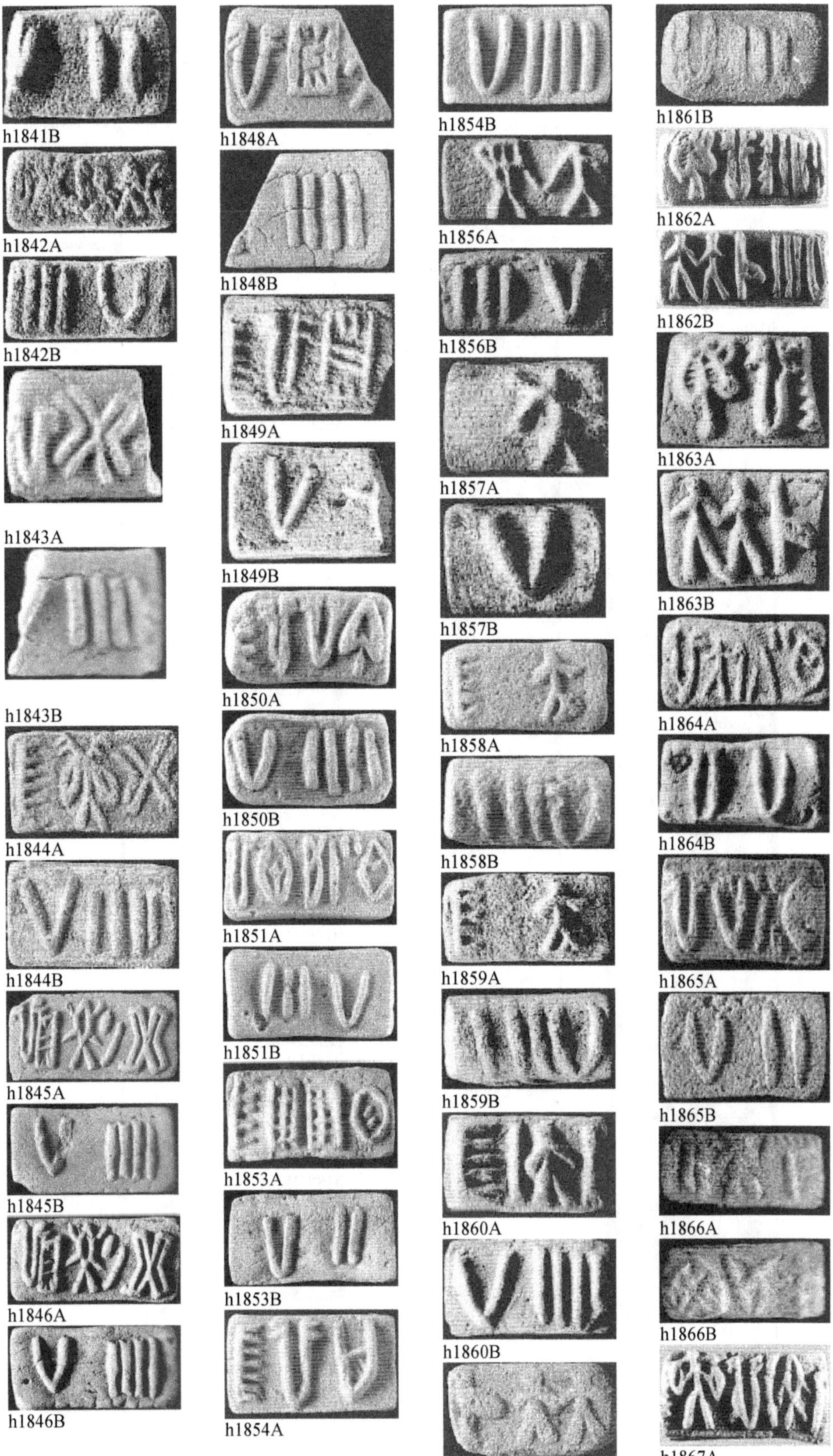

h1841B
h1842A
h1842B
h1843A
h1843B
h1844A
h1844B
h1845A
h1845B
h1846A
h1846B
h1848A
h1848B
h1849A
h1849B
h1850A
h1850B
h1851A
h1851B
h1853A
h1853B
h1854A
h1854B
h1856A
h1856B
h1857A
h1857B
h1858A
h1858B
h1859A
h1859B
h1860A
h1860B
h1861A
h1861B
h1862A
h1862B
h1863A
h1863B
h1864A
h1864B
h1865A
h1865B
h1866A
h1866B
h1867A

h1867B

h1868A

h1868B

h1869A

h1869B

h1870A

h1870B

h1871A

h1871B

h1872A

h1872B

h1873A

h1873B

h1874A

h1874B

h1875A

h1875B

h1876A

h1876B

h1877A

h1877B

h1878A

h1878B

h1879A

h1879B

h1880A

h1880B

h1881A

h1881B

h1882A

h1882B
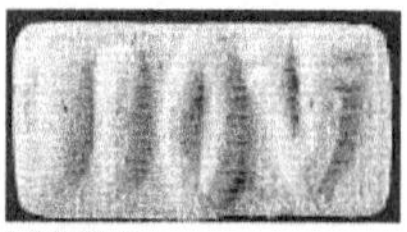
h1883A

h1883B

h1886A

h1886B

h1887A

h1887B
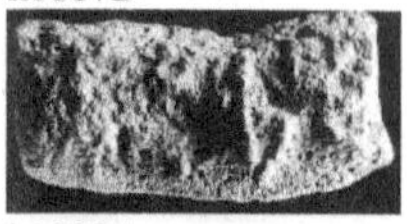
h1892A

h1892B

h1893A
h1893B

h1895A

h1895B

h1896A

h1896B

h1897A

h1897B

h1898A

h1898B

h1899A

h1899B

h1900A

h1900B

h1901A
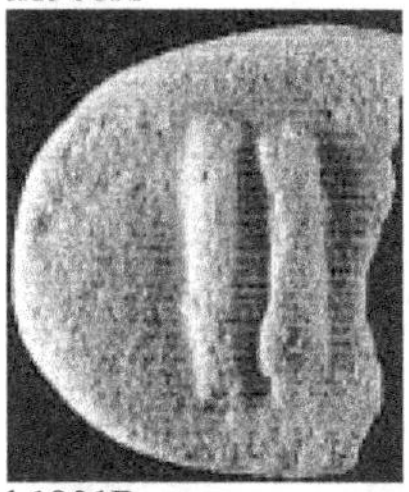
h1901B

h1902A

h1902B

h1903A

h1903B

h1904A
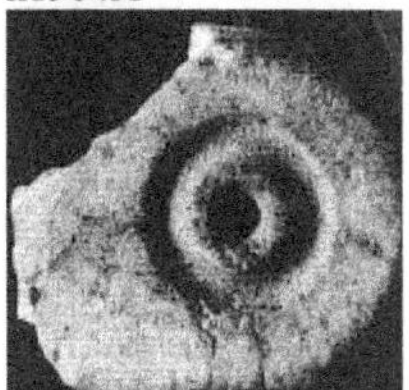
h1904B
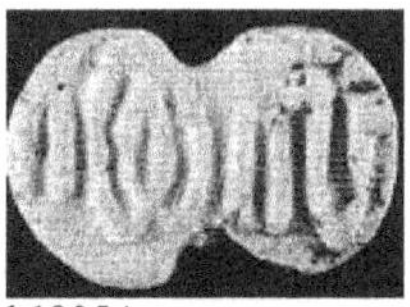
h1905A

h1905B

h1906A

h1907A

h1907B
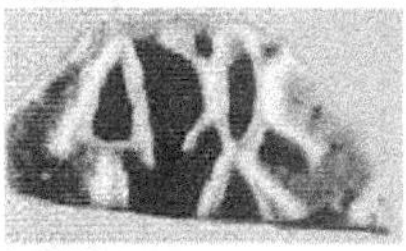
h1908A

h1908B

h1909A

h1909B

h1910A

h1910B

h1911A
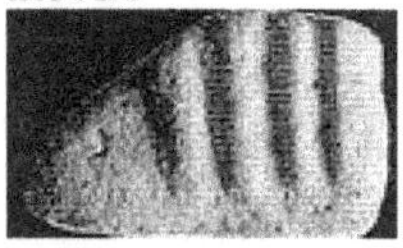
h1911B

h1912A
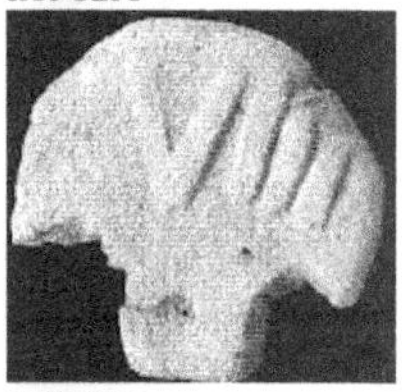
h1912B
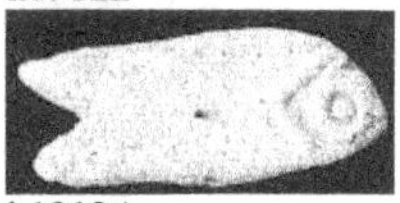
h1913A
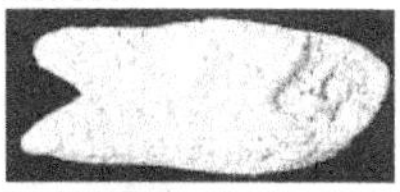
h1913B

h1914A

h1914B

h1915A

h1915B

h1916A

h1916B

h1917A

h1917B

h1918A
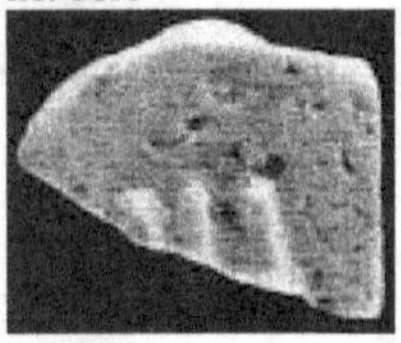
h1918B

h1920A
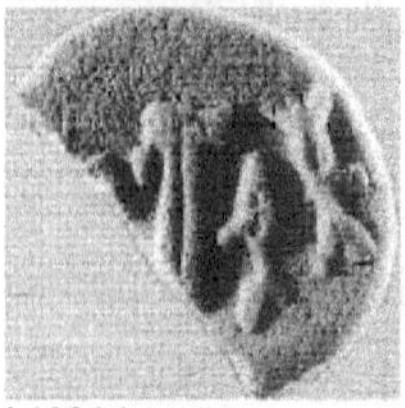
h1921A
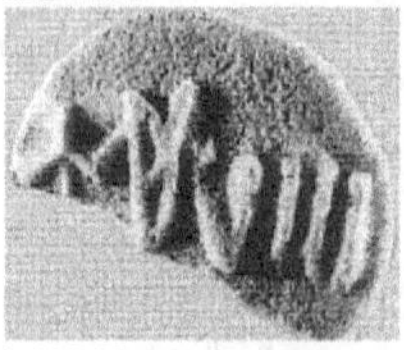
h1921B

h1922A

h1922B

h1923A

h1923B

h1924A

h1924B

h1925A

h1925B

h1926A

h1927A

h1929A

h1929B

h1929C

h1930A

h1930B

h1930C

h1931A
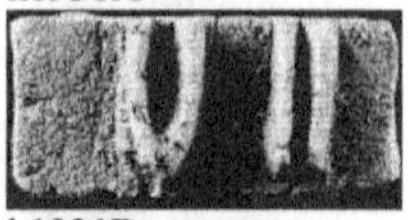
h1931B
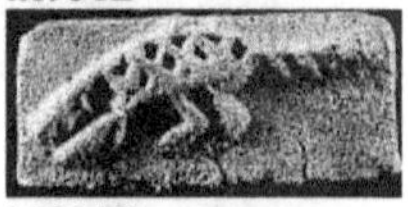
h1931C

h1932A

h1932B

h1932C

h1933A

h1933B

h1933C

h1934A

h1934B

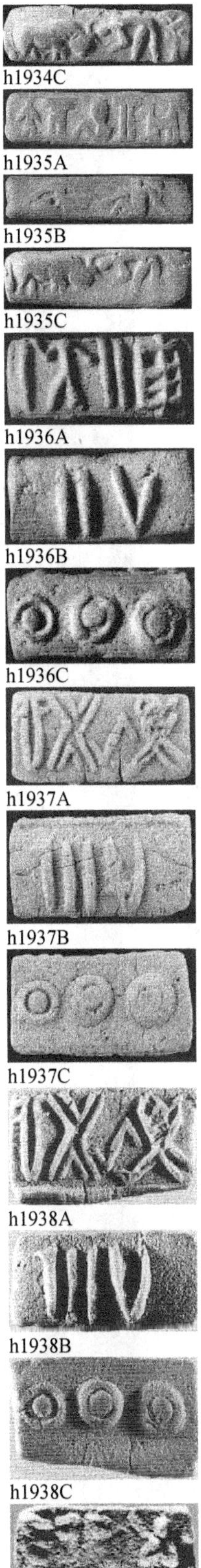

h1934C
h1935A
h1935B
h1935C
h1936A
h1936B
h1936C
h1937A
h1937B
h1937C
h1938A
h1938B
h1938C
h1939A

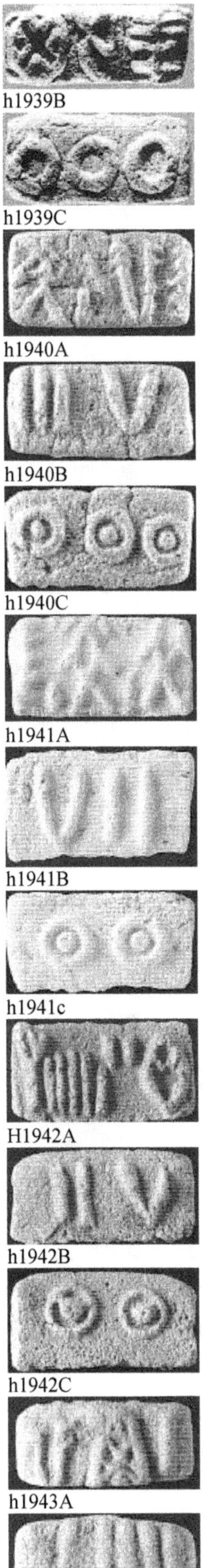

h1939B
h1939C
h1940A
h1940B
h1940C
h1941A
h1941B
h1941c
H1942A
h1942B
h1942C
h1943A
h1943B

h1943C
h1944A
h1944B
h1944C
h1945A
h1945B
h1945C
h1946A
h1946B
h1946C
h1947A
h1947B
h1947C

h1950A
h1950B
h1950C
h1950E
h1951A
h1951B
h1953A
h1953B

h1955A

(bird+fish)

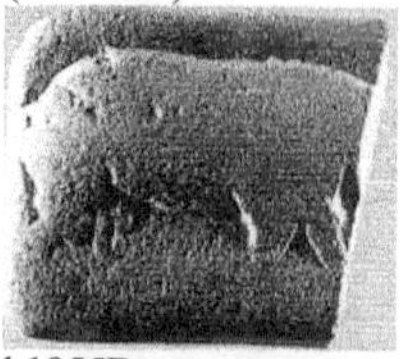

h1955B

h1958A

h1958B

h1959

h1961A

h1961B

h1962A

h1962B

h1963A

h1963B

h1964A

h1964B

h1966A

h1966B

h1967A

h1967B

h1968A

h1968B

h1969A

h1969B

h1970A

h1970B

h1971A

h1971B

h1972A

h1972B

h1973A

h1973B

h1974A

h1974B

h1975A

h1975B

h1976A

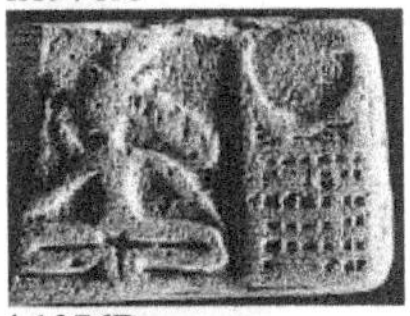
h1976B

h1977A

h1977B

h1978A

h1978B

h1979A

h1979B

h1980A

h1981B

h1981A

h1981B

h1985A

h1985B

h1987A

H1987B

h1988A, h1989A, h1990A

h1988B, h1989B, h1990B

h1991A

h1991B

h1992B

h1993A

h1993B

h1994A

h1994B

h1995A

h1995B

h1997A

h1997B

h1999A

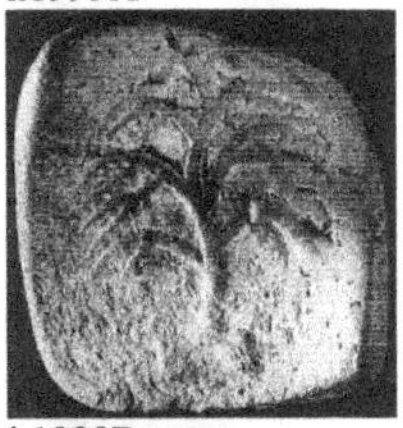
h1999B

h2002A

h2003Ah

h2003B

h2005A

h2005B

h2006A

h2006B

h2010A
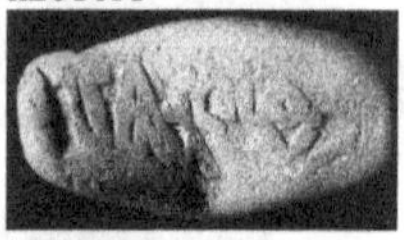
h2010B
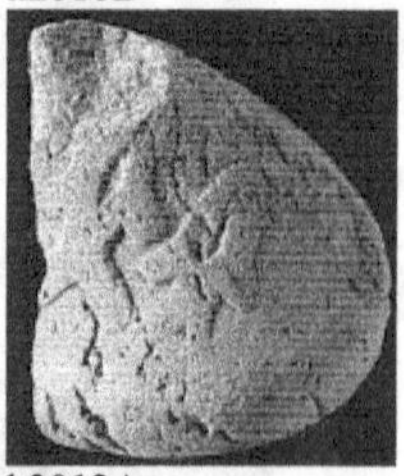
h2012A

h2012B

h2013A

h2014A

h2014B

h2015A

h2015B

h2016A
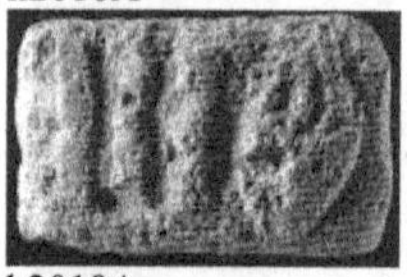
h2018A
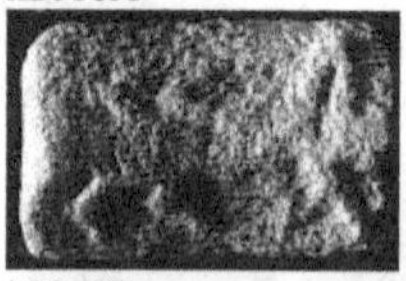
h2018B

h2019A

h2019B

h2019C

h2020A

h2020C

h2021A

h2021B

h2021C

h2022A

h2022B
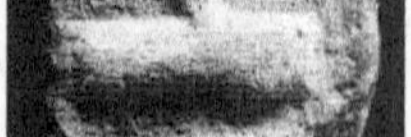

h2022C

h2023A

h2023B

h2023C

h2024A

h2024B

h2024C

h2025C

h2026A

h2026B
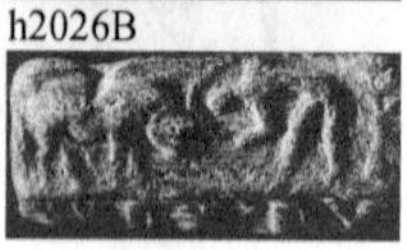

h2026C

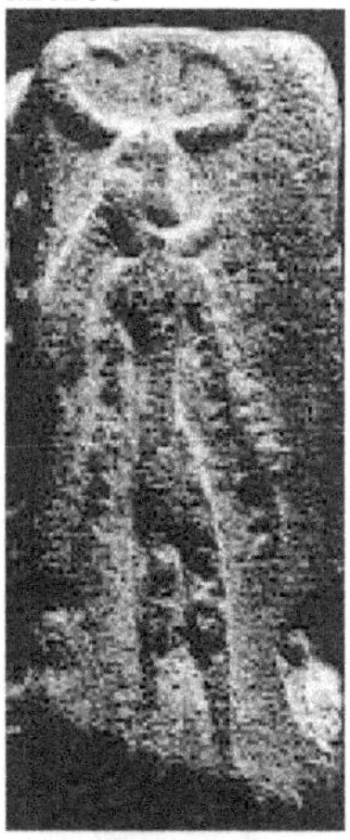

h2026D

h2027A

h2027B

h2027C

h2027D

h2028A

h2028B

h2028C

h2028A

h2029A

h2029B

h2029C

h2029D

h2030A

h2030C

h2030D

h2031A

h2031B

h2031C

h2031D

h2032B

h2032D

h2033A

h2033B

h2034A

h2034B

h2035A

h2035B

h2036A

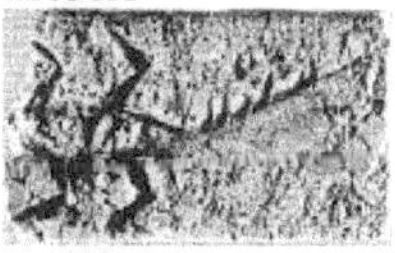

h2036B

h2308A

h2038iB

h2039A

h2039B

h2040A

h2040B

h2041A

h2041B

h2043A
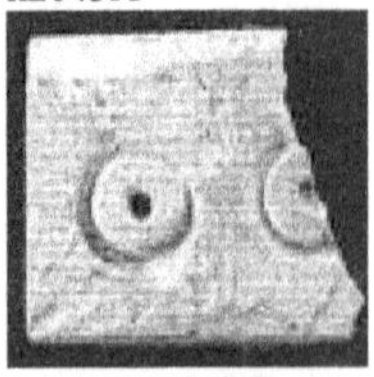
h2043B
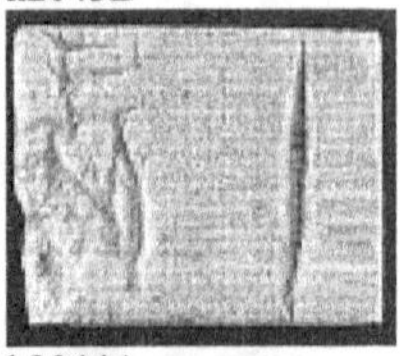
h2044A

h2044B

h2045A

h2045B

h2046A
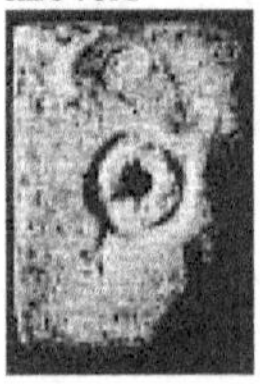
h2046B

h2047A
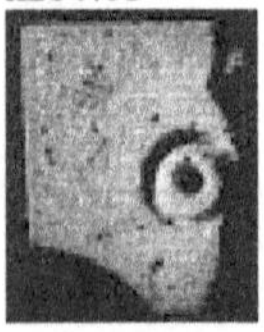
h2047B

h2048A

h2048B

h2049A

h2049B
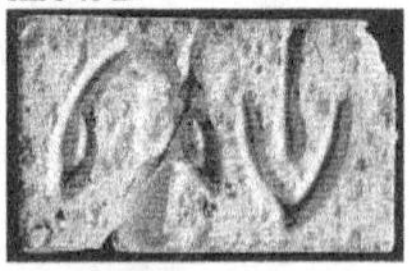
h2050A

h2050B

h2051A

h2052A

h2053A
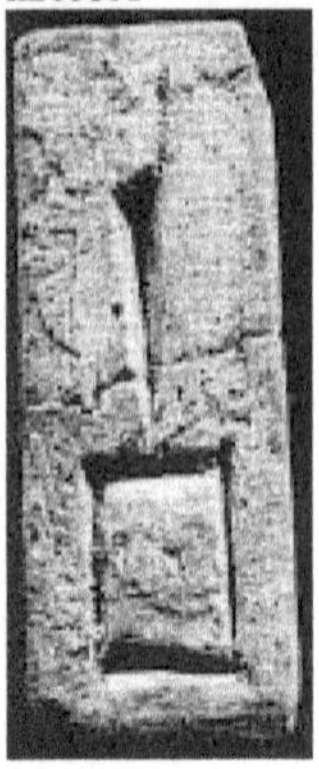
h2054B

h2055A
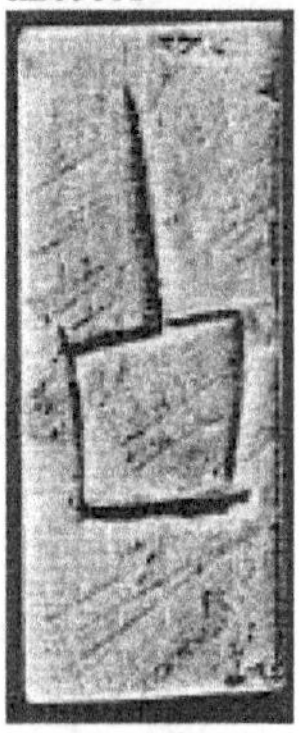
h2055B

h2056A
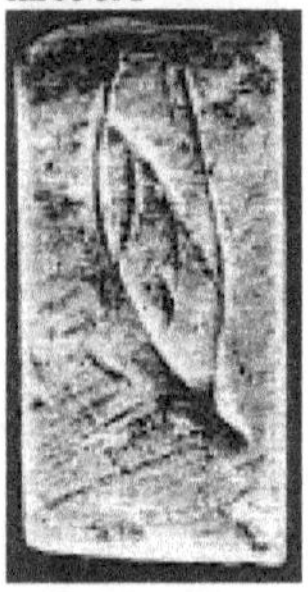
h2056B
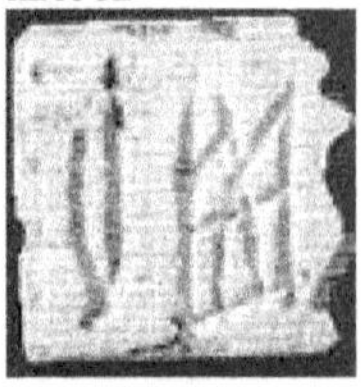
h2057A
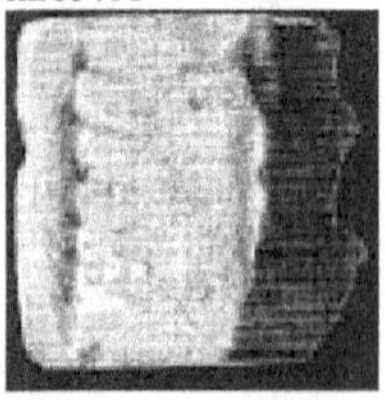
h2057B

h2058A

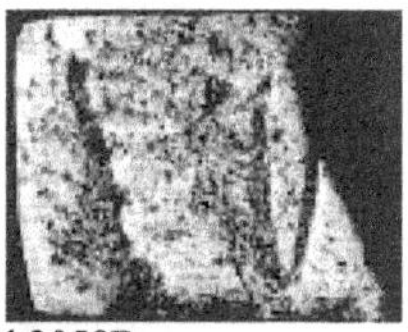

h2058B

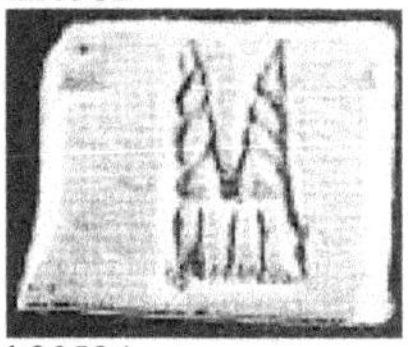

h2059A

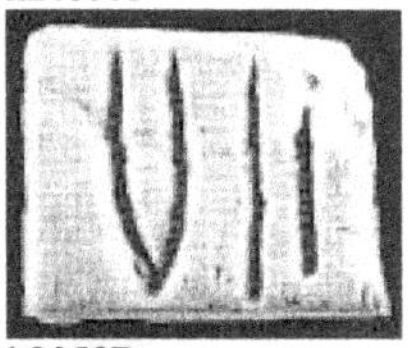

h2059B

h2062A

h2062B

h2063A

h2063B

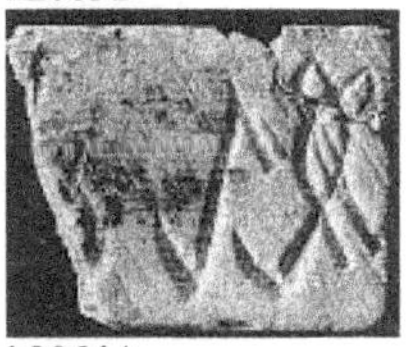

h2064A

h2064B

h2065A

h2065B

h2066A

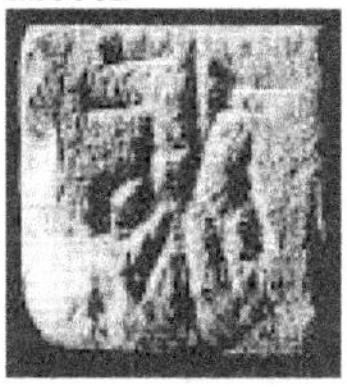

h2066B

h2067A

h2067B

h2068A

h2068B

h2069A

h2069B

h2070A

h2070B

h2071A

h2071B

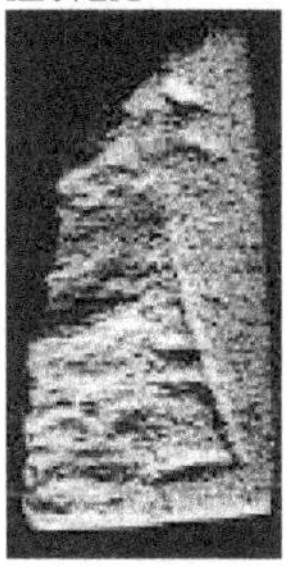

h2072A

h2072B

h2073A

h2073B

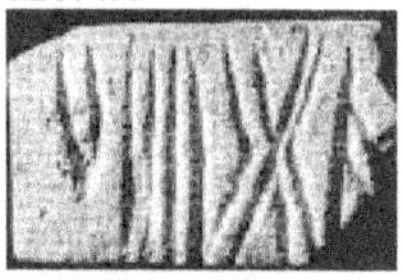

h2074A

h2074B

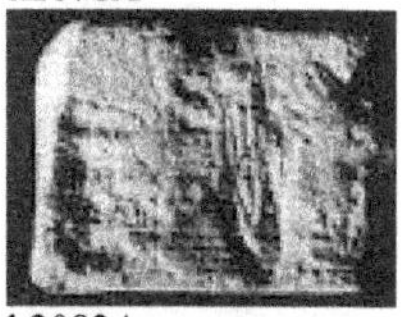

h2076A

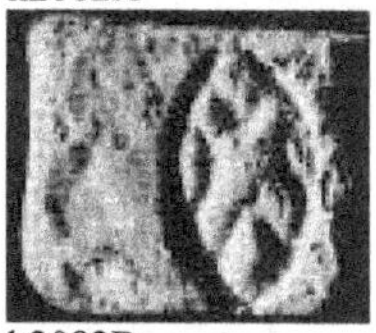

h2082A

h2082B

h2083A

h2083B

h2084A

h2084B

h2085A

h2085B

h2086A

h2086B

h2089A

h2089B

h2090A

h2090B

h2091A

h2091B

h2092A

h2092B

h2093A

h2093B

h2094A

h2094B

h2095A

h2095B

h2096A

h2096B

h2097A

h2097B

h2098A

h2098B

h2099A

h2099B

h2102A

h2102B

h2104A

h2104B

h2105A

h2105B

h2106A

h2106B

h2107A

h2107B

h2108A

h2108B

h2109A1B2

h2109B1A2

h2110A

h2110B

h2111B

h2112A

h2112B

h2113A

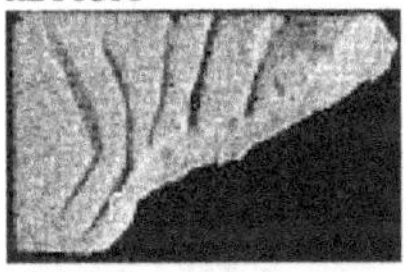

h2113B

h2114A

h2114B

h2115A

h2115B

h2119A

h2119b

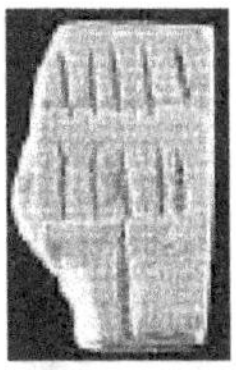

h2120A

h2120B

h2121A

h2121B

h2123A

h2123B

h2125A

h2125B

h2127A

h2127B

h2128A

h2128B

h2129A

h2129B

h2130A

h2130B

h2131A

h2131B

h2132A

h2132B

h2133A

h2133B

h2134A

h2134B

h2135A

h2136A

h2137A

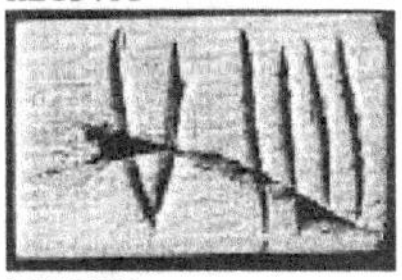

h2137B

h2138A

h2138B

h2139A

h2139B

h2140A

h2140B

h2141A

h2141B

h2142A

h2142B

h2143A

h2143B

h2144A

h2144B

h2145A

h2145B

h2146A

h2146B

h2147A

h2147B

h2148A

h2148B

h2149A

h2149B

h2150A

h2150B

h2151A

h2151B

h2152A

h2152B

h2153A

h2153B

h2154A

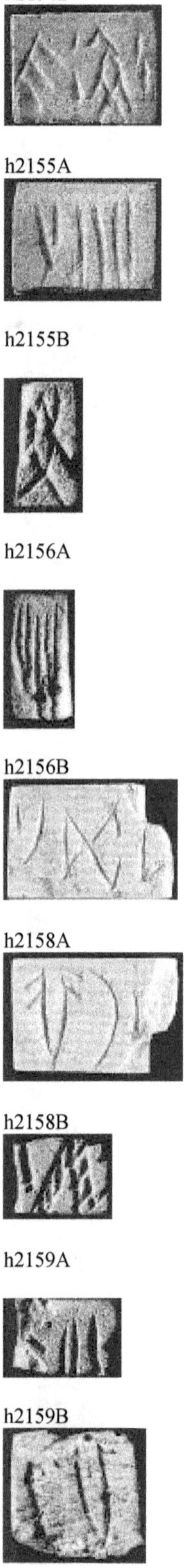

h2154B

h2155A

h2155B

h2156A

h2156B

h2158A

h2158B

h2159A

h2159B

h2160A

h2160B

h2173A

h2173B

h2174A

h2174B

h2175A

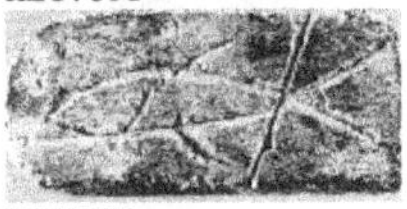

h2175B

h2176A

h2176B

h2177A

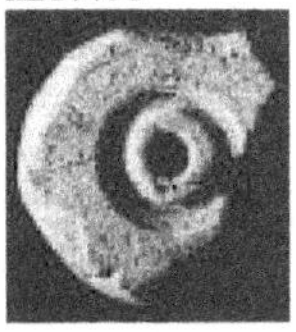

h2177B

h2178A

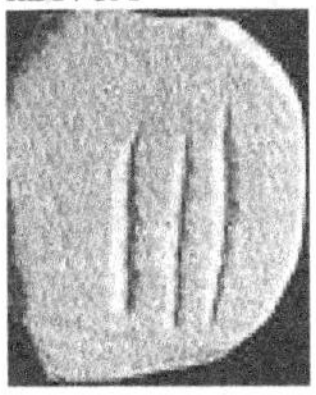

h2178B

h2180A

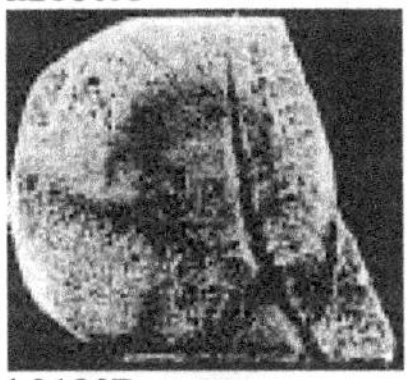

h2180B

h2181A

h2181B

h2182A

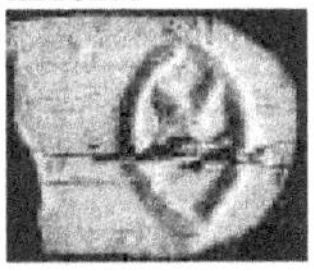

h2182B

h2183A

h2183B

h2184A

h2184B

h2185A

h2185B

h2186A

h2186B

h2187A

h2187B

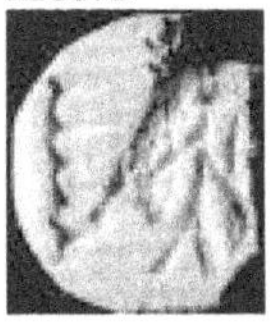

h2188A

h2188B

h2189A

h2189B

h2190A

h2190B

h2192A

h2192B

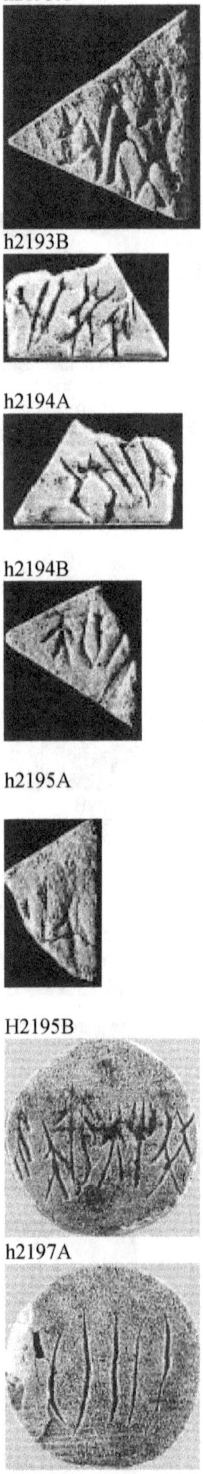

h2193A
h2193B
h2194A
h2194B
h2195A
H2195B
h2197A
h2197B

h2198A
h2198B
h2200A
h2200B
h2200C
h2201A
h2201B
h2201C
h2204A
h2204B
h2204c
h2205A

h2205B
h2205C
h2207A
h2207B
h2207C
h2208A
h2208B
h2208C
h2209A
h2209B
h2209C
h2210A

h2210B
h2210C
h2211A
h2211B
h2211C
h2212A
h2212B
h2212C
h2213A
h2213B
h2213C
h2214A
h2214N

h2214C
h2215B
h2215C
h2217A
h2217B
h2217C
h2218A
h2218B
h2218C
h2219A
h2219B

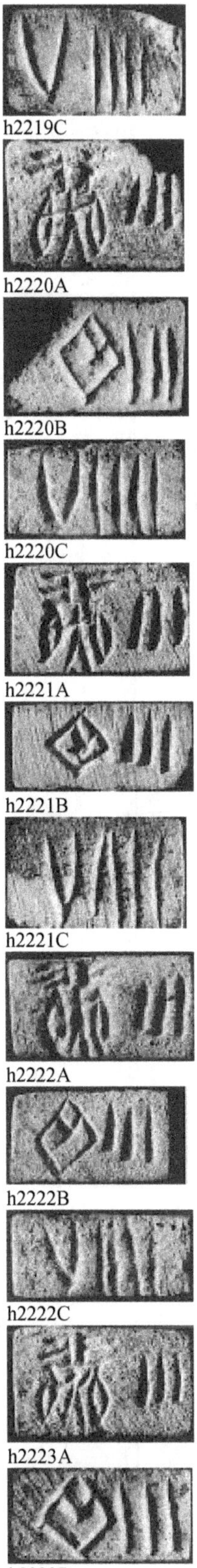

h2219C
h2220A
h2220B
h2220C
h2221A
h2221B
h2221C
h2222A
h2222B
h2222C
h2223A
h2223B

h2223C
h2224A
h2224B
h2224C
h2225A
h2225B
h2225C
h2226A
h2226B
h2226C
h2227A

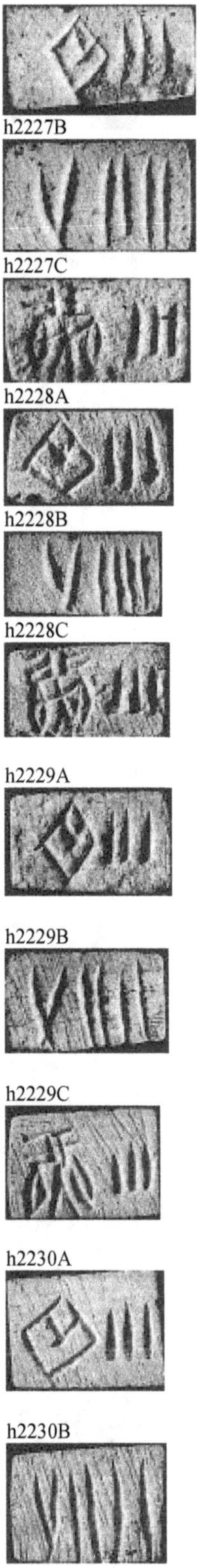

h2227B
h2227C
h2228A
h2228B
h2228C
h2229A
h2229B
h2229C
h2230A
h2230B

h2230C

h2231A

h2231B

h2231C

h2232A

h2232B

h2232C

h2233A

h2233B

h2233C

h2234A

h2234B

h2234C

h2235A

h2235B

h2235C

h2236A

h2236B

h2236C

h2237A

h2237B

h2237C

h2238A

h2238B

h2238C

h2240A

h2240B

h2240C

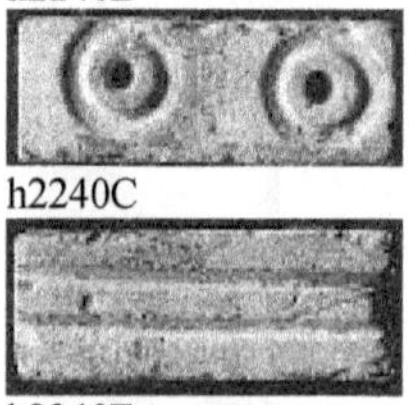

h2240E

h2241A

h2241B

h2241C

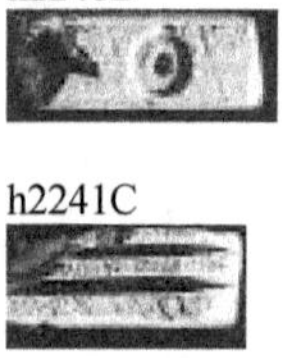

h2241E

h2243A

h2243B

h2244A

h2244B

h2244E

h2245A

h2245B

h2245E

h2246A

h2246B

h2246C

h2246E

h2247A

h2247B

h2249Acopper

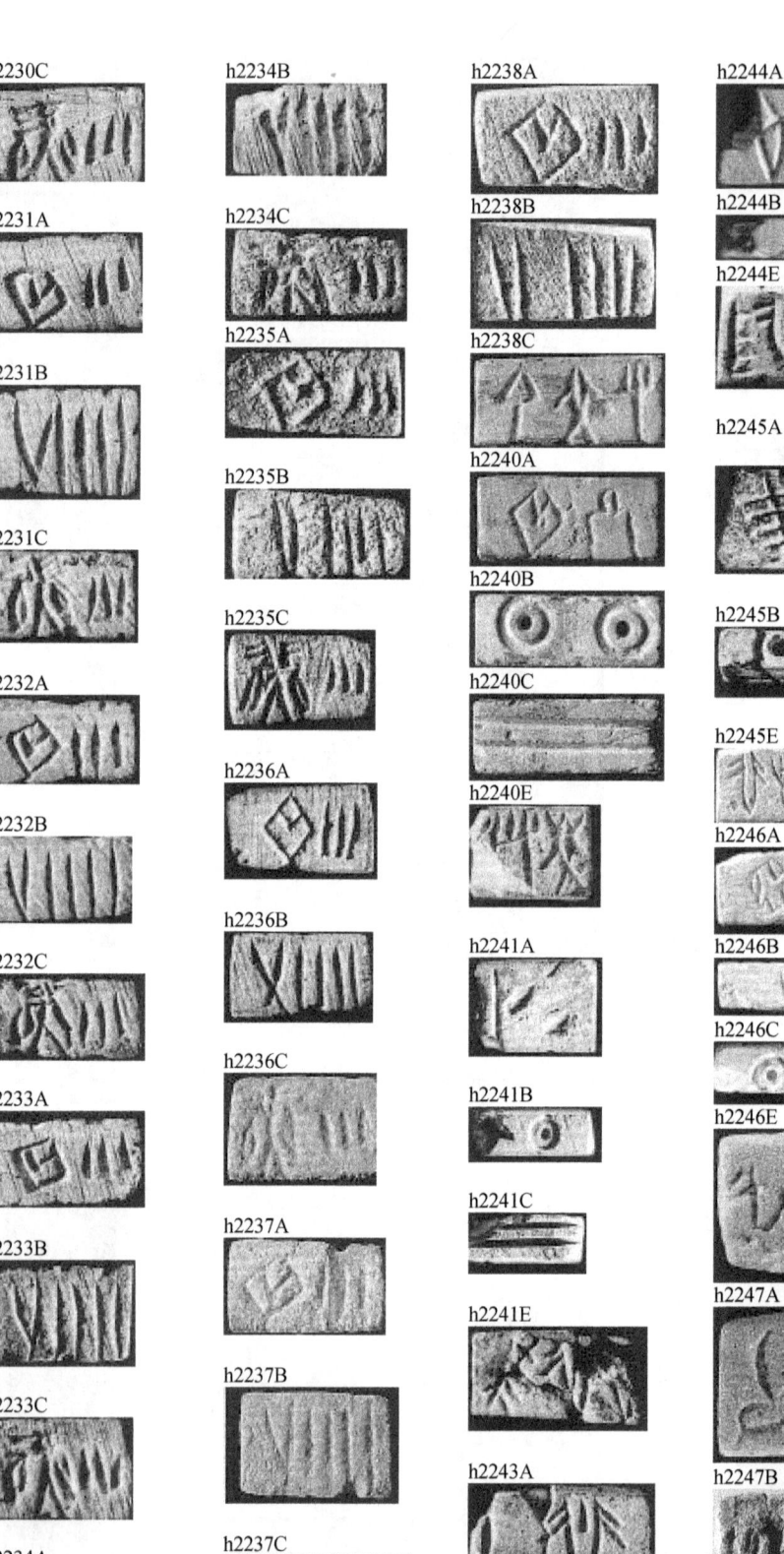

h2250Acopper

h2251Acopper

h2252Acopper

h2253Acopper

h2254Acopper

h2255Acopper

h2256Acopper

h2257Acopper

h2264A

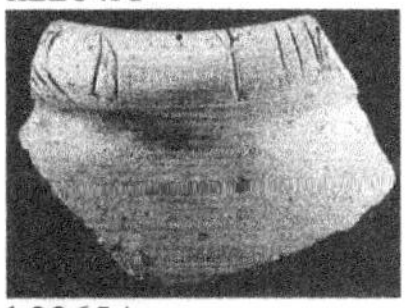

h2265A

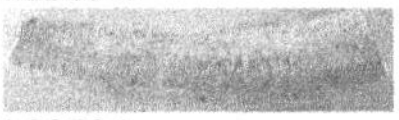

h2270A

h2334A

h2339A

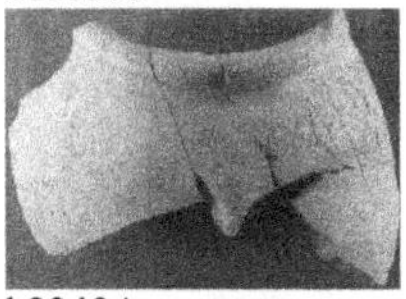

h2340A

h2341A

h2345A

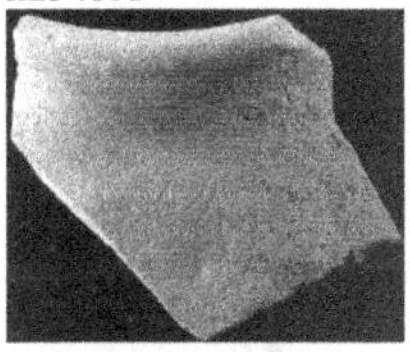

h2353A

h2354A

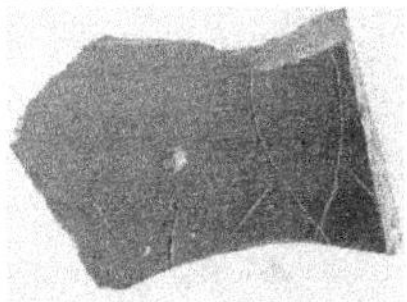

h2357A

h2358A

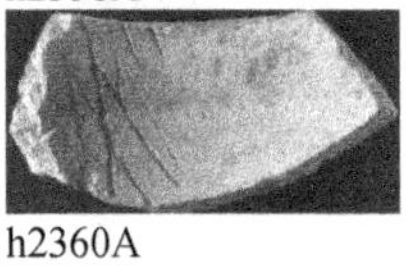

h2360A

h2367A

h2368A

h2373A

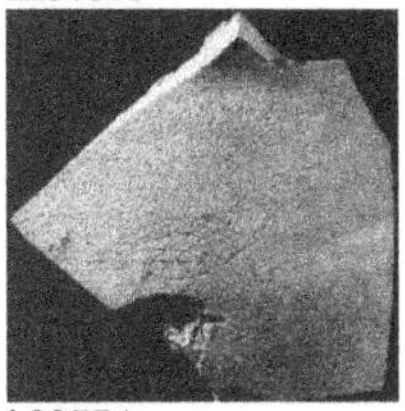

h2377A

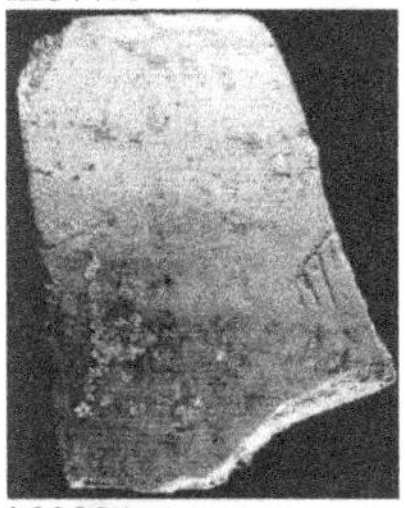

h2380A

h2383A

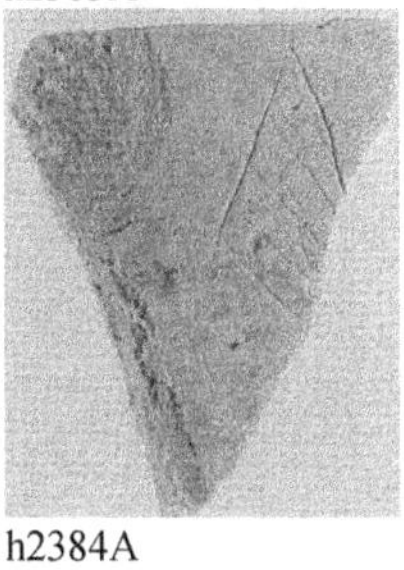

h2384A

h2390A

h2397A

j2398A

h2399A

h2400A

h2403A

h2405A

h2548A

h2549A

h2586A

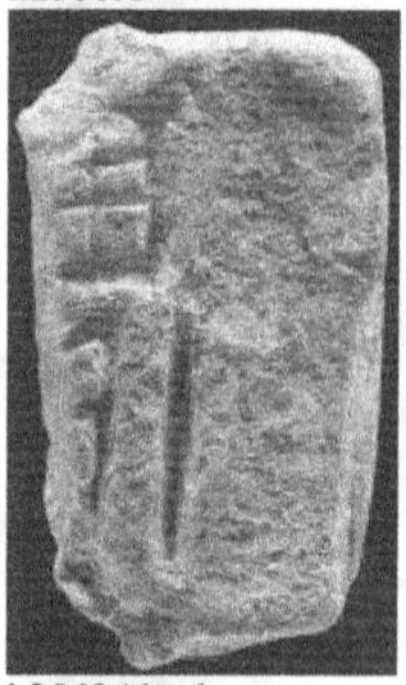
h2569Alead

h2570Abone

h2576Abangle

h2590

Harappa Texts (Either unmatched with inscribed objects or objects not illustrated)

4015

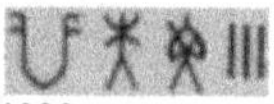
4033

4035

4046

4067

4073

4101

4108

4114

4117

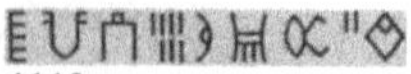
4119

4134

4136

4140

4158

4164

4292

4296

4305

Pict-90: Standing person with horns and bovine features holding a staff or mace on his shoulder.

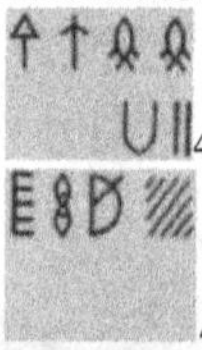
4324

4330

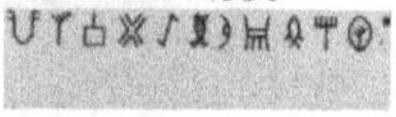
4334

Pict-63: Gharial, sometimes with a fish held in its jaw and/or surrounded by a school of fish.

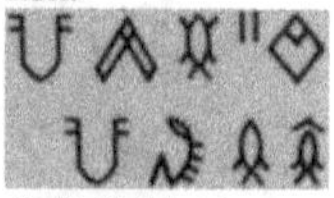
4343 Tablet in bas-relief One-horned bull

4344

4347

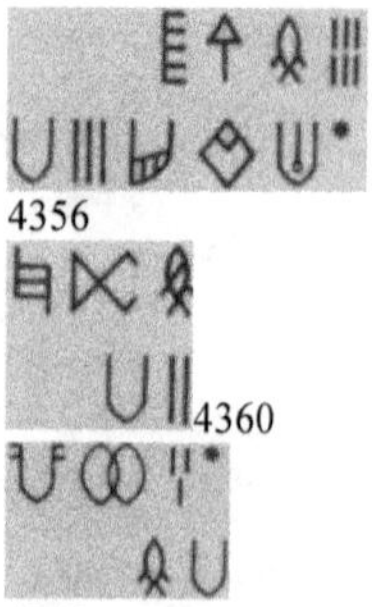
4356

4360

4363

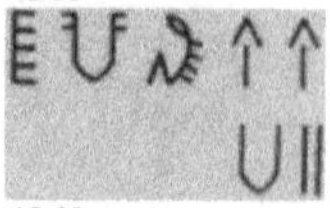
4369

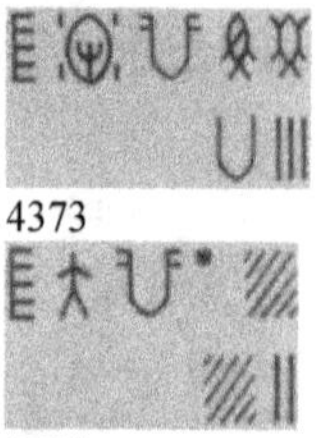
4373

4384

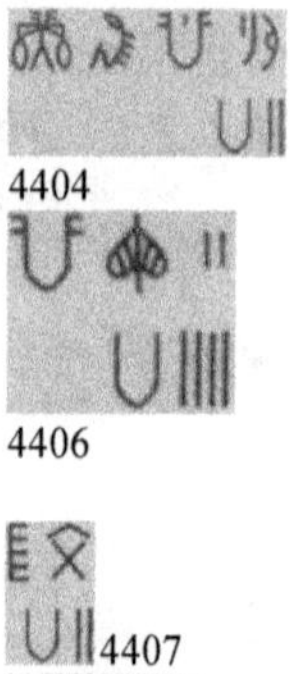
4404

4406

4407

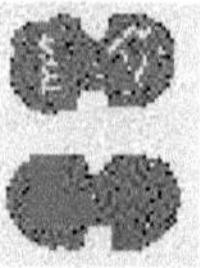
Pict-129: Inscribed object in the shape of a double-axe or double-shield?

4408

4422

4427

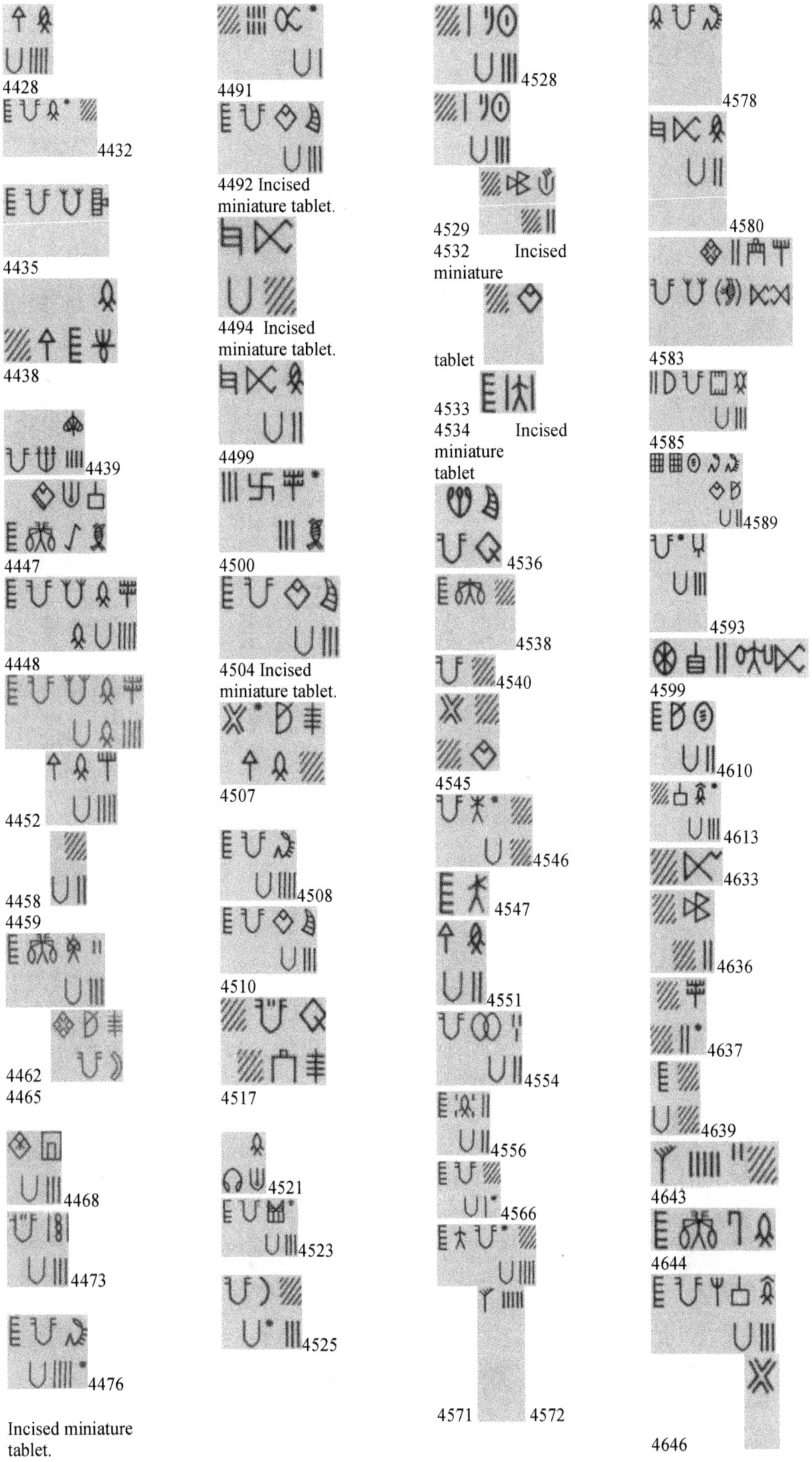
4428
4432
4435
4438
4439
4447
4448
4452
4458
4459
4462
4465
4468
4473
4476
Incised miniature tablet.
4491
4492 Incised miniature tablet.
4494 Incised miniature tablet.
4499
4500
4504 Incised miniature tablet.
4507
4508
4510
4517
4521
4523
4525
4528
4529
4532 Incised miniature tablet
4533
4534 Incised miniature tablet
4536
4538
4540
4545
4546
4547
4551
4554
4556
4566
4571
4572
4578
4580
4583
4585
4589
4593
4599
4610
4613
4633
4636
4637
4639
4643
4644
4646

4648

4649

4650 4652

4658

4668 4671

4685

4690

4691

4699

4700

4703

4704

4709 4710

4712

4713

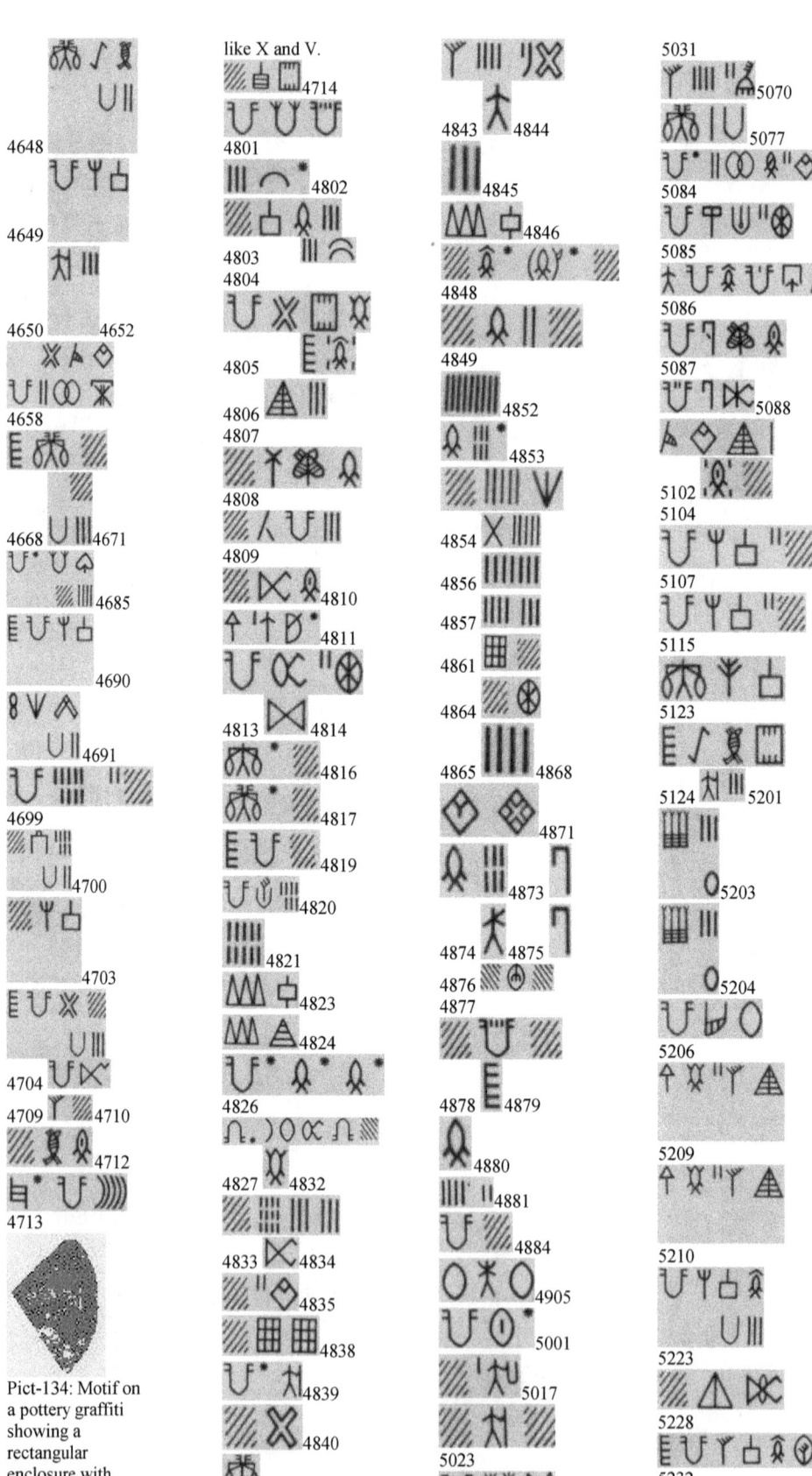

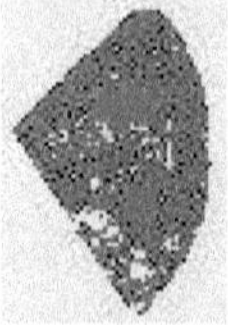

Pict-134: Motif on a pottery graffiti showing a rectangular enclosure with four marks within; the marks looks like X and V.

4714

4801

4802

4803

4804

4805

4806

4807

4808

4809

4810

4811

4813 4814

4816

4817

4819

4820

4821

4823

4824

4826

4827 4832

4833 4834

4835

4838

4839

4840

4841

4843 4844

4845

4846

4848

4849

4852

4853

4854

4856

4857

4861

4864

4865 4868

4871

4873

4874 4875

4876

4877

4878 4879

4880

4881

4884

4905

5001

5017

5023

5031

5070

5077

5084

5085

5086

5087

5088

5102

5104

5107

5115

5123

5124 5201

5203

5204

5206

5209

5210

5223

5228

5232

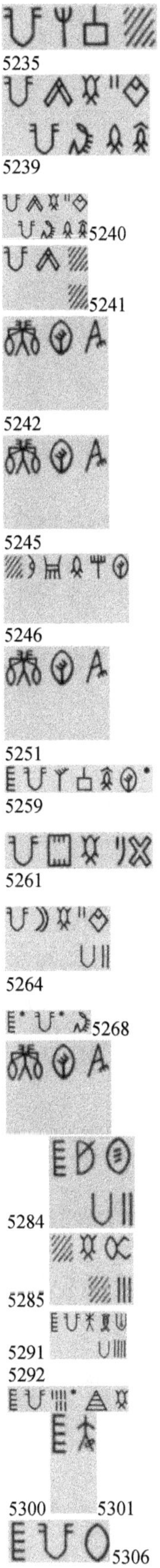

5235
5239
5240
5241
5242
5245
5246
5251
5259
5261
5264
5268
5284
5285
5291
5292
5300
5301
5306

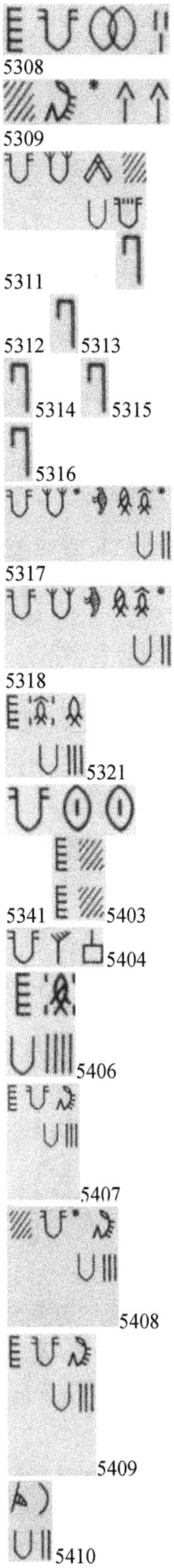

5308
5309
5311
5312
5313
5314
5315
5316
5317
5318
5321
5341
5403
5404
5406
5407
5408
5409
5410

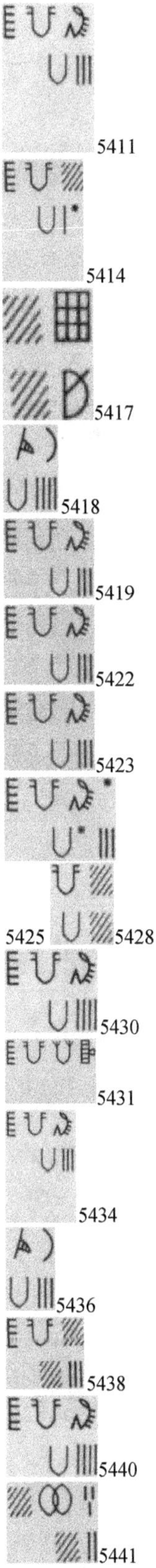

5411
5414
5417
5418
5419
5422
5423
5425
5428
5430
5431
5434
5436
5438
5440
5441

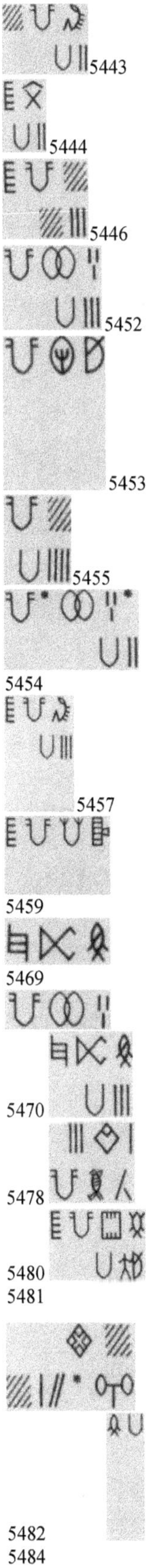

5443
5444
5446
5452
5453
5455
5454
5457
5459
5469
5470
5478
5480
5481
5482
5484

5485
5486
5487
5488
5489
5490
5492
5495
5501 5504
5505
5506
5507
5508
5510
5511 5513
5514
5515
5516 5517

5518
5519
5601

hd06

hulas

jhukar1

jhukar2
9001

jhukar3
8009
8036
8048
8060
8061
8062
8202
8214
8215
8217

Kalibangan002

8019

Kalibangan003
8030

Kalibangan004
8026

Kalibangan005
8017

Kalibangan006
8020

Kalibangan007
8043

Kalibangan008
8041

Kalibangan009
8021

Kalibangan010
8006

Kalibangan011
8034

Kalibangan012

Kalibangan013
8051

Kalibangan014
8012

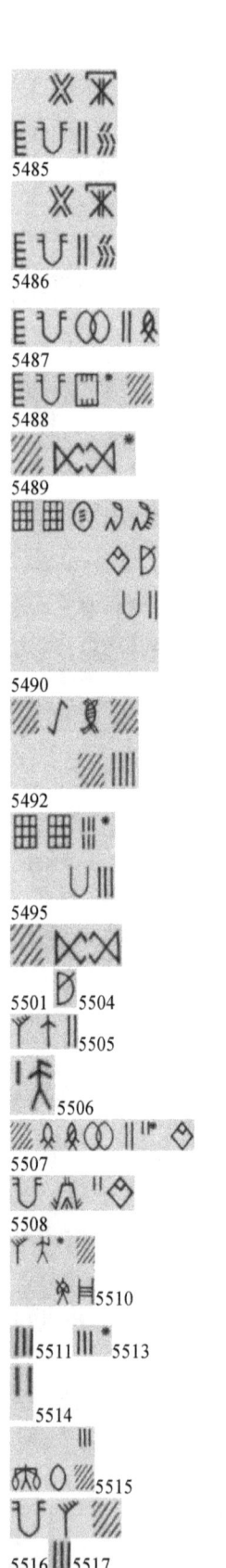

Kalibangan015

8056

Kalibangan016

8044

Kalibangan017

8027

Kalibangan018

8040

Kalibangan019

8058

Kalibangan020

8047

Kalibangan021

Kalibangan022

8008

Kalibangan023

8029

Kalibangan024

Kalibangan025

8037

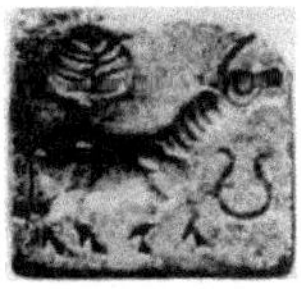

Kalibangan026

8071

Kalibangan027

8022

'Unicorn' with two horns! "Bull with two long horns (otherwise resembling the 'unicorn')", generally facing the standard. That it is the typical 'one-horned bull' is surmised from two ligatures: the pannier on the shoulder and the ring on the neck.

Kalibangan028

8038

Kalibangan029

8018

Kalibangan030

8002

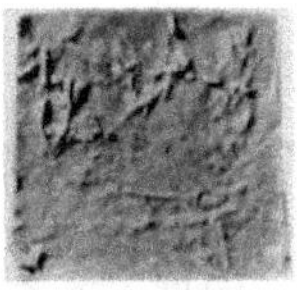

Kalibangan031a

8007

Kalibangan032a

Kalibangan033

8025

Kalibangan034

8052

Kalibangan035

Kalibangan036

Kalibangan037

8042

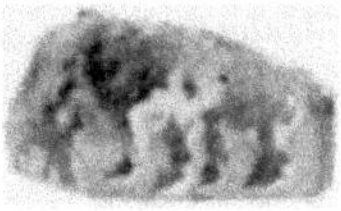

Kalibangan038

Kalibangan039

8011

Kalibangan040

8072

Kalibangan041

Kalibangan042a

Kalibangan043

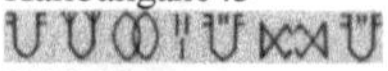

8039 Pict-59:Composite motif: body of an ox and three heads: of a one-horned bull (looking forward), of antelope (looking backward), and of short-horned bull (bison) (looking downward).

Kalibangan044

8045

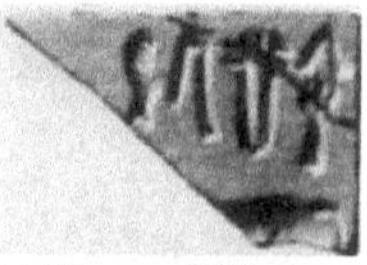

Kalibangan045

8054

Kalibangan046

8053

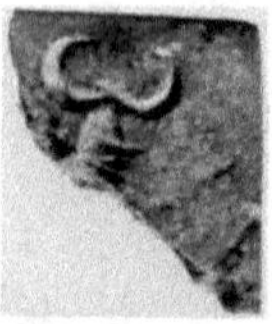

Kalibangan047

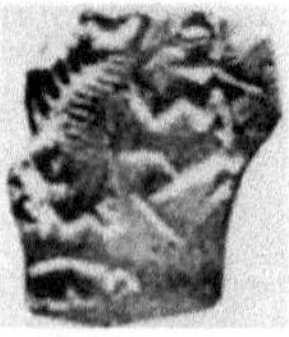

Kalibangan048

Kalibangan049

8013

Kalibangan050c

8031 Pict-53: Composition: body of a tiger, a human body with bangles on arm, a pig-tail, horns of an antelope crowned by a twig.

Kalibangan051

8003

Kalibangan052

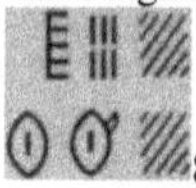8015

Kalibangan053

Kalibangan054

8033

Kalibangan055a

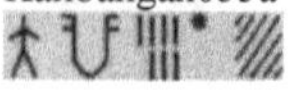

8035

Kalibangan056

8004

Kalibangan057

Kalibangan058

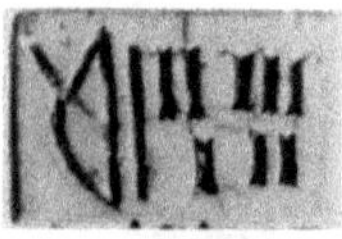

Kalibangan059

8016

Kalibangan060

8059

Kalibangan061

8001

Kalibangan062

8023

Kalibangan063

8055

Kalibangan064

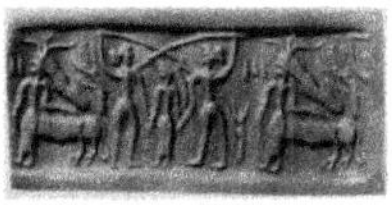

Kalibangan065a

Kalibangan065A6

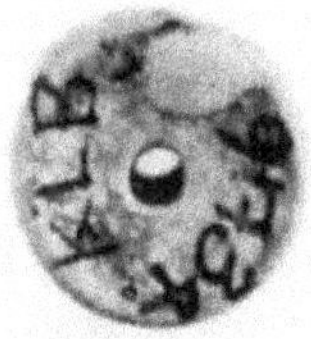

Kalibangan065E

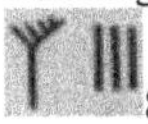

8024

Pict-104: Composition: A tree; a person with a composite body of a human (female?) in the upper half and body of a tiger in the lower half, having horns, and a trident like head-dress, facing a group of three persons consisting of a woman (?) in the middle flanked by two men on either side throwing a spear at each other (fencing?) over her head.

Kalibangan066

8102

Kalibangan067

8121 Ox-antelope with a long tail; sometimes with a trough in front.

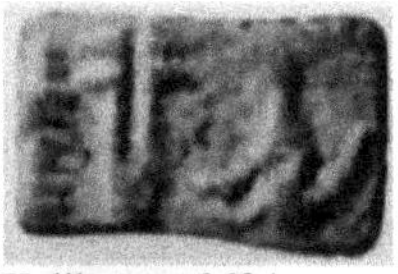

Kalibangan068A

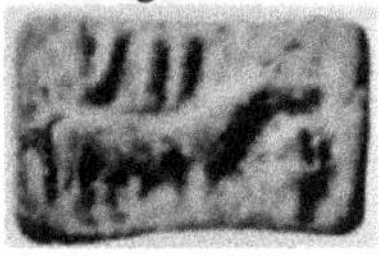

Kalibangan068B

8117 [Is it a bird or an India River Otter? Could be a scorpion, a model for Signs 51 and 52 ?

See variant in Text 9845 West Asia find]

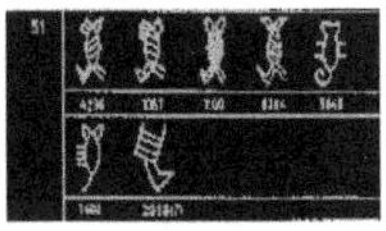

Kalibangan069A

8109

Kalibangan070A

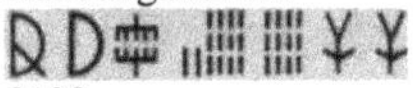

8108

Kalibangan071

8110

Kalibangan072

8111

Kalibangan073

8112

Kalibangan074

8115

Kalibangan075

8113

Kalibangan076A

Kalibangan076B

Kalibangan077A

Kalibangan077B

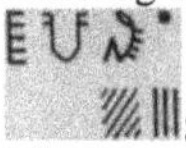

8118

Kalibangan078A

Kalibangan078B

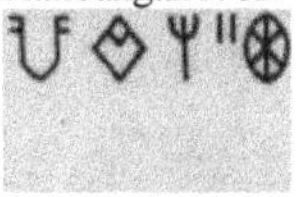

8104

Kalibangan

079AB

Kalibangan080A

8120

Kalibangan081A

8105

Kalibangan082A

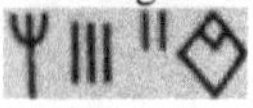

8122

Kalibangan

083A12

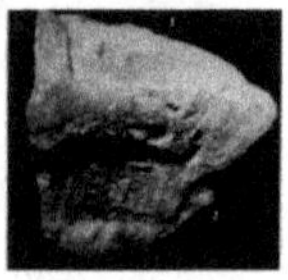

Kalibangan

084A12

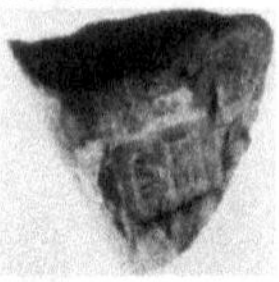

Kalibangan

084A2 

8103

Kalibangan

085A12

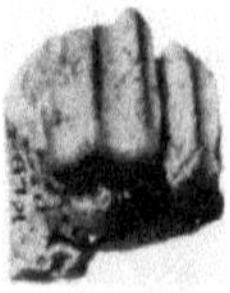

Kalibangan085B

8106

Kalibangan086A1
4

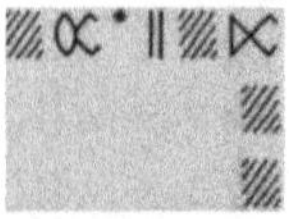

8114

Kalibangan087A1
2

8116

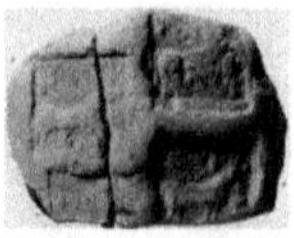

Kalibangan

088A14

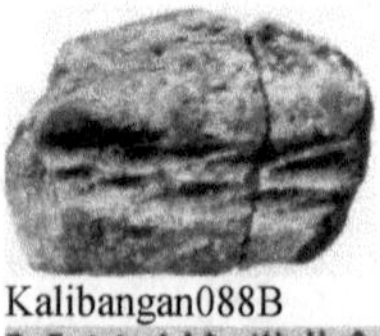

Kalibangan088B

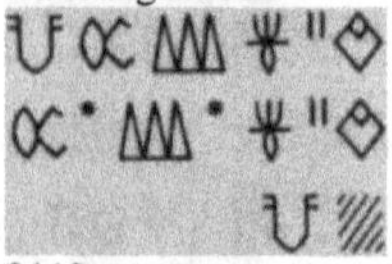

8119

Kalibangan089A1
4c

8101

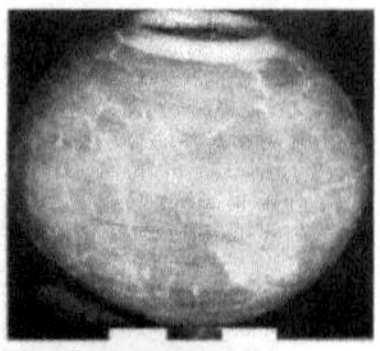

Kalibangan090A

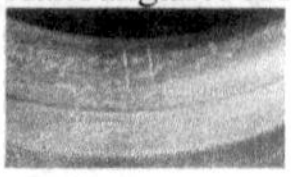

Kalibangan

090A1

Kalibangan

090A2

 8202

Kalibangan091A

 8212

Kalibangan092A

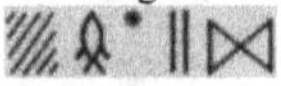

8210

Kalibangan093A

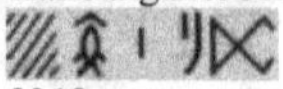

8219

Kalibangan094A

Kalibangan095A

Kalibangan096c

8221

Kalibangan097A

 8213

Kalibangan098A

8201

Kalibangan099A

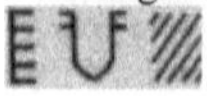 8208

Kalibangan100A

Kalibangan101A

8205

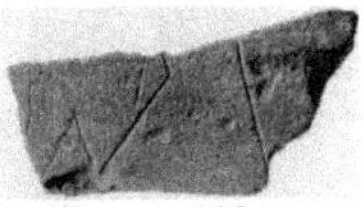

Kalibangan102A

8207

Kalibangan103A

8209

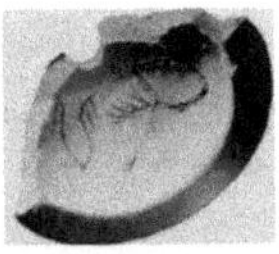

Kalibangan104A

8218

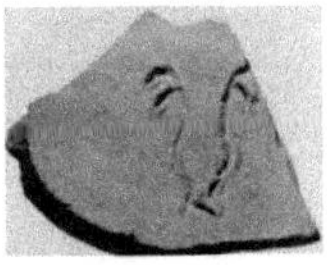

Kalibangan105A

8216

Kalibangan106A

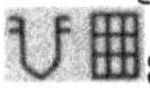8204

Kalibangan107A

Kalibangan108A

8206

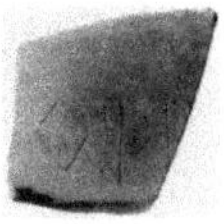

Kalibangan109A

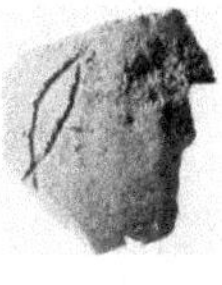

Kalibangan110A

8211

Kalibangan111A

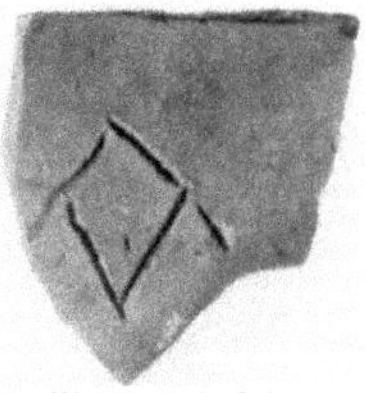

Kalibangan112A

Kalibangan118

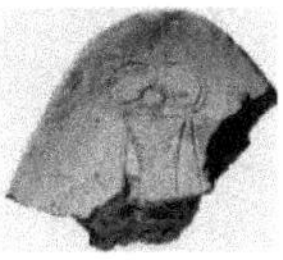

Kalibangan119A

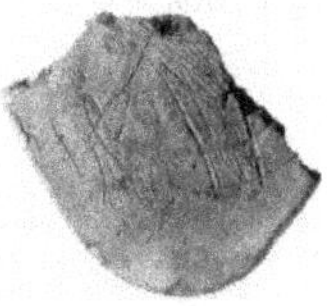

Kalibangan119B

Kalibangan120A

8220

Kalibangan122B

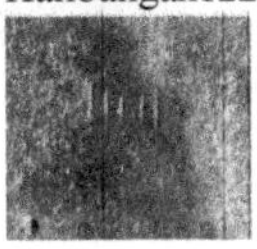

Kalibangan

122B2

Kalibangan

121A, B

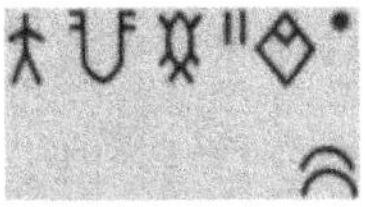

8302

Kalibangan122A

Kalibangan

122A2

8301

Kalako-deray 01

Kalako-deray 05
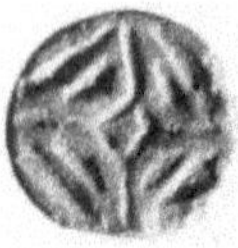
Kalako-deray 06

Kalako-deray 07

Kalako-deray 08
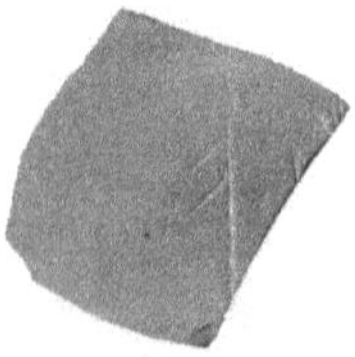
Kalakoderay10

Khirsara1a

Khirsara2a

9051 Kot-diji

Lewandheri01

Loebanr01

Lohumjodaro1a

9011

Lothal001

7015

Lothal002

7031
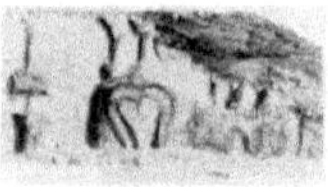
Lothal003

Lothal004a

7080

Lothal005

7044

Lothal006a

7038

Lothal007a
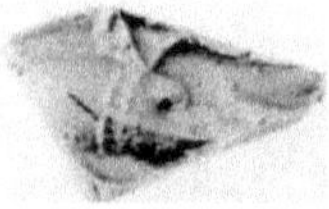
Lothal008a

Lothal009

7022
Lothal010

7009

Lothal011

7026

Lothal012a
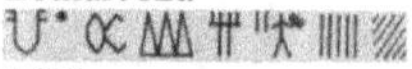
7089
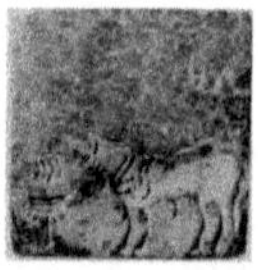
Lothal013

7050

Lothal014a
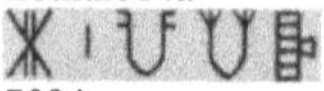
7094

Lothal015
 7086

Lothal016
7002

Lothal017
7008

Lothal018
7096

Lothal019a
7092

Lothal020
7078

Lothal021
7047

Lothal022a
7035

Lothal023a
7043

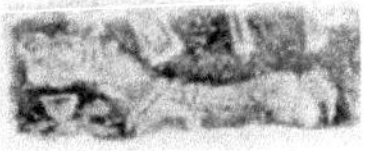

Lothal024

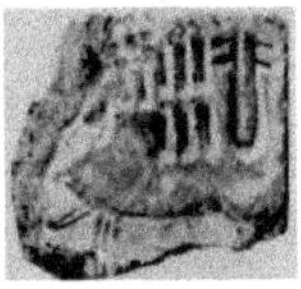

Lothal025
7104

Lothal026
7024

Lothal027
7036

Lothal028
7045

Lothal029
7005

Lothal030a

Lothal031
7076

Lothal032a

Lothal033a

Lothal035
7101

Lothal036a
7081

Lothal037
7034

Lothal038a
7053

Lothal039
7102

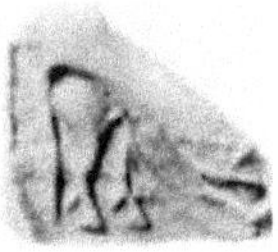

Lothal040a

Lothal041
7066

Lothal042

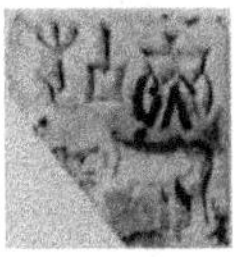

Lothal043
7049

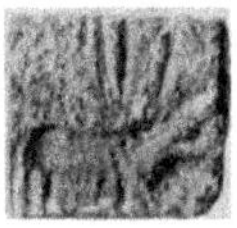

Lothal044

Lothal045
7028

Lothal046

7107

Lothal047a

7074

Lothal048

7025

Lothal049

Lothal050

Lothal051a

7057 Pict-127: Upper register: a large device with a number of small circles in three rows with another row of short vertical lines below; the device is horned. A seed-drill? [Is this an orthographic model for Sign 176?]

Lothal052

7011

Lothal054a

7099

Lothal055

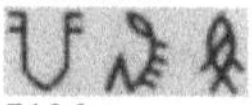

7106

Lothal056

7100

Lothal057

7095

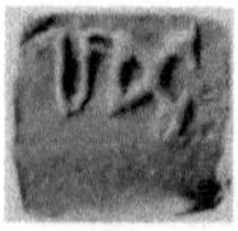

Lothal058a

7029

Lothal059

7097

Lothal060

7039

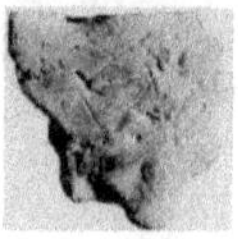

Lothal061

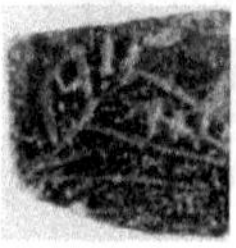

Lothal062

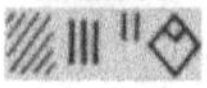

7054

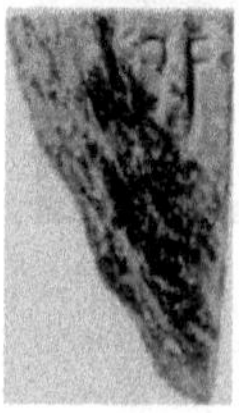

Lothal063

Lothal064

7030

Lothal065

7103

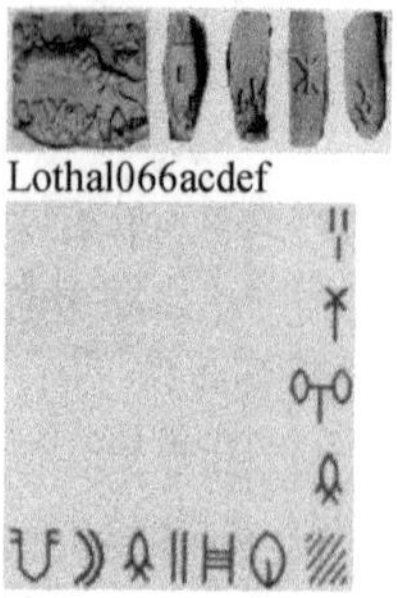

Lothal066acdef

7048

Lothal068

7070

Lothal069

Lothal070

Lothal071

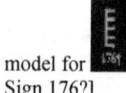

Lothal072

Lothal075

Lothal076a

Lothal077

Lothal078
7077

Lothal079
7063

Lothal080a

Lothal081
7093

Lothal082
7105

Lothal083
7068

Lothal084
7112

Lothal085

Lothal086
7007

Lothal087
7021

Lothal088
7017

Lothal089
7090

Lothal090
7032

Lothal091
7111

Lothal092
7062

Lothal093
7064

Lothal094a
7073

Lothal095
7042

Lothal096
7023

Lothal097
7072

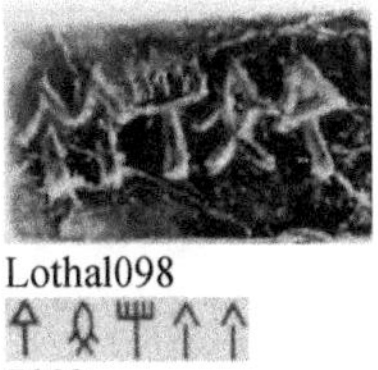
Lothal098
7082

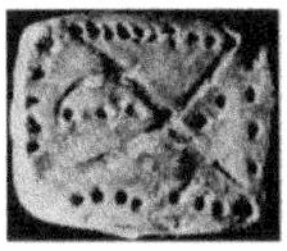
Lothal099

Lothal100a

Lothal100B
7055

Lothal101
7001

Lothal102
7040

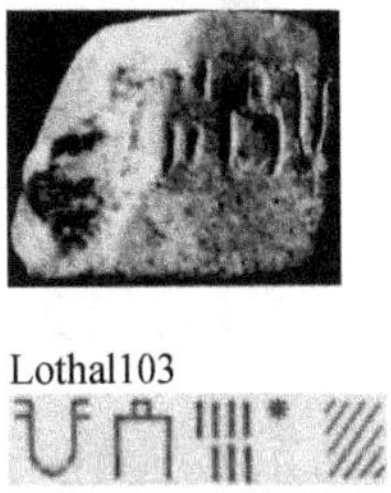
Lothal103
7018

Lothal104
7085

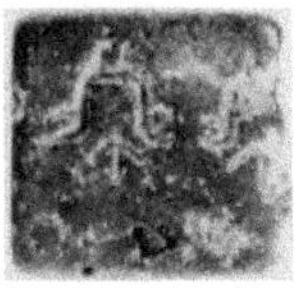

Lothal105

7016

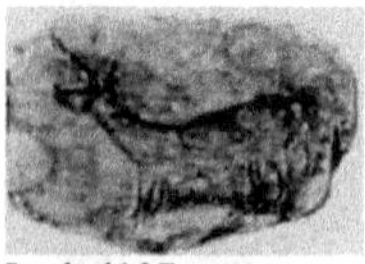

Lothal107

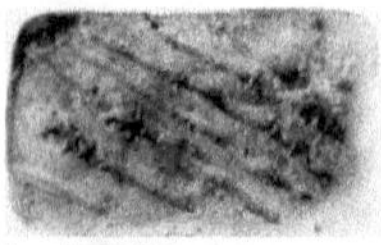

Lothal108

Lothal109a

7046

Lothal110

7006

Lothal111

7056

Lothal112

7020

Lothal113a

7004

Lothal114a

7013

Lothal115

7065

Lothal116

7027

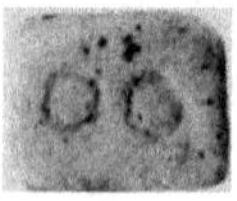

Lothal117

7075

Lothal118

7019

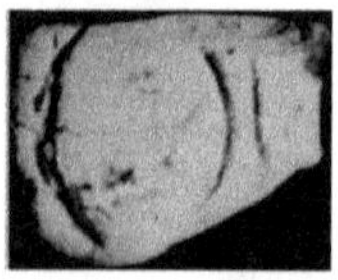

Lothal119

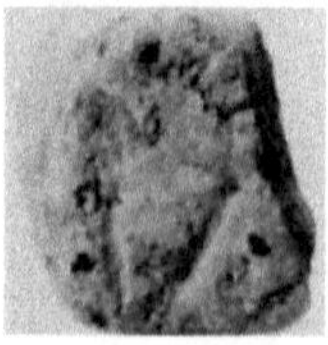

Lothal120

Lothal121

Lothal122

7069

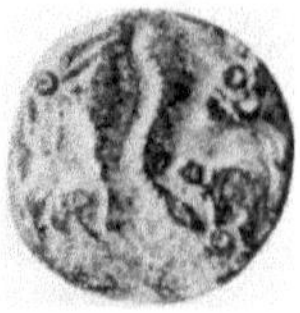

Lothal123A

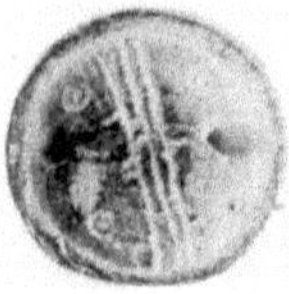

Lothal123B

Lothal124A

7224

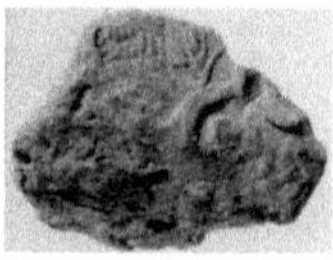

Lothal125A

7241

Lothal126A

7242

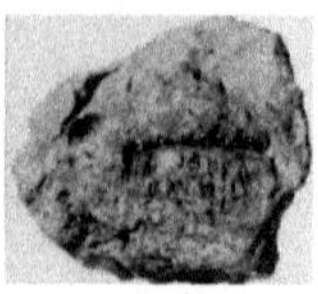

Lothal127A

7221

Lothal128A

7239

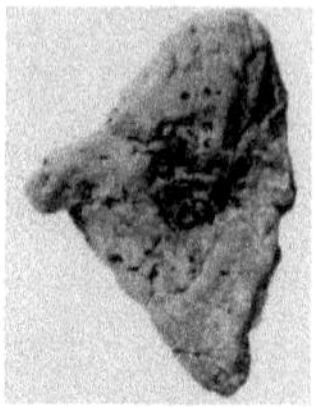

Lothal129A

Lothal130A

Lothal131A

7255

Lothal132A

7213

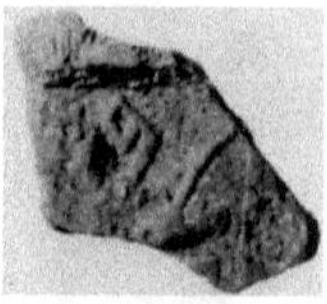

Lothal133A

7245

Lothal134A

7252

Lothal135A

7220

Lothal136A

7225

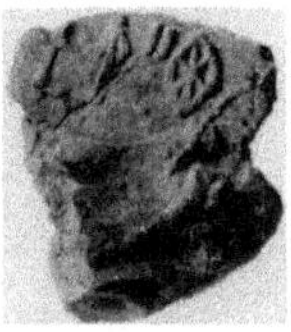

Lothal137A

7257

Lothal138A

Lothal138B

7214

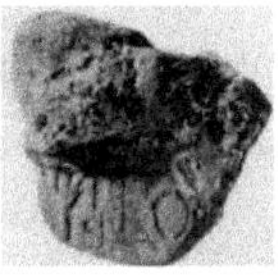

Lothal139A

7223

Lothal140A

7244

Lothal141A1

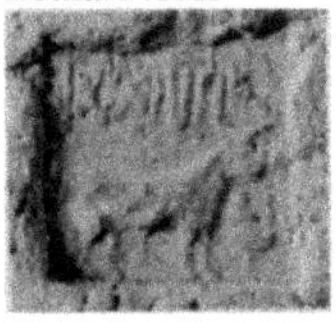

Lothal141A2

7280

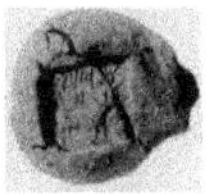

Lothal142A

Lothal142B

7204

Lothal143A

Lothal143B

7243

Lothal144A

7274

Lothal145A

Lothal146AB

7279

Lothal147A

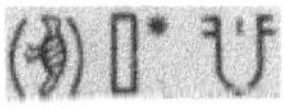

7260

Lothal148A

7270

Lothal149A

7272

Lothal150A

7268

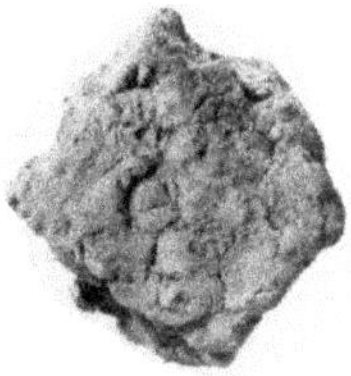

Lothal151A

7266

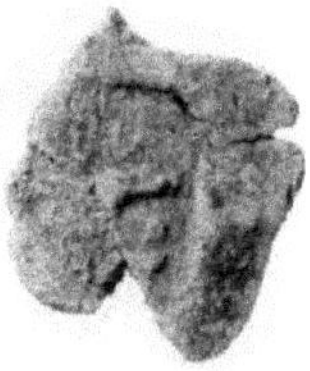

Lothal152A

7222

Lothal153A

7271

Lothal154A

Lothal155A

Lothal156A

Lothal157A

Lothal158A

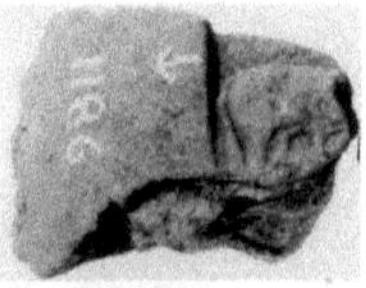

Lothal159A

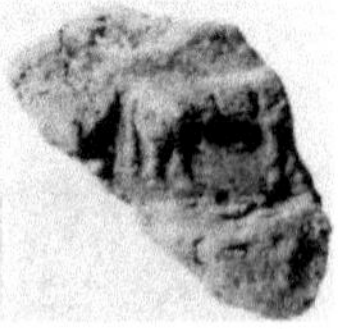

Lothal160A

Lothal161A

7205

Lothal162A

Lothal162B

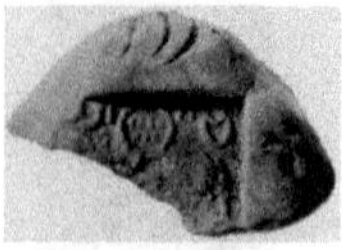

Lothal163A

Lothal163C

7228

Lothal164A

7230

Lothal165A

7203

Lothal166A

7206

Lothal167A

7231

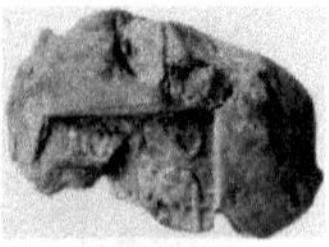

Lothal168A

7234

Lothal169A

7235

Lothal170A

7229

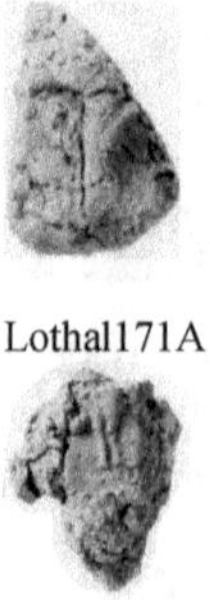

Lothal171A

Lothal172A

Lothal173A

Lothal174A

Lothal175A

Lothal176A

7216

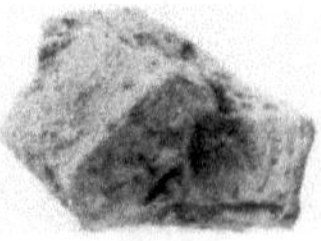

Lothal177A

7211

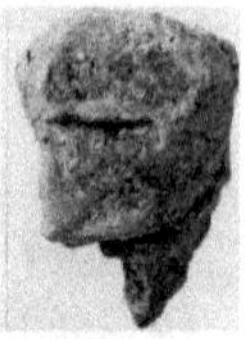

Lothal179A

Lothal180A

7240

Lothal181A

7273

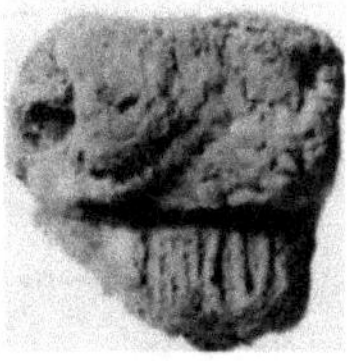

Lothal182A

7238

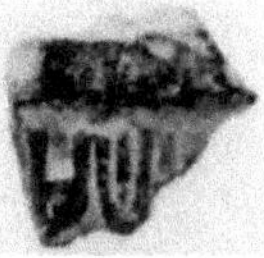

Lothal183A

Lothal184A

Lothal185A

Lothal186A

7259

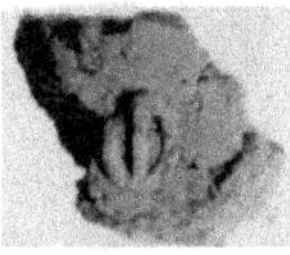

Lothal187A

7209

Lothal188A

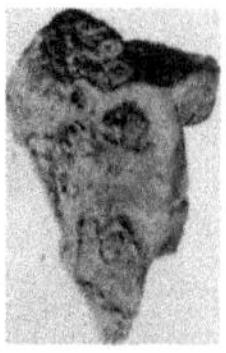

Lothal189A12

Lothal189A34

7217

Lothal190A13

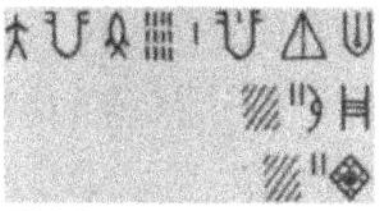

7236

Lothal191A12

7249

Lothal192A12

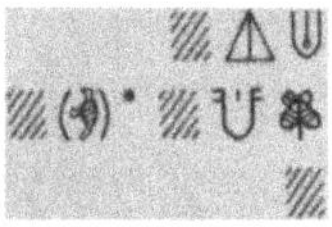

7227

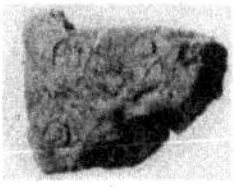

Lothal193A12

Lothal193A3

7253

Lothal194A1

Lothal194A2

7251

Lothal195A12

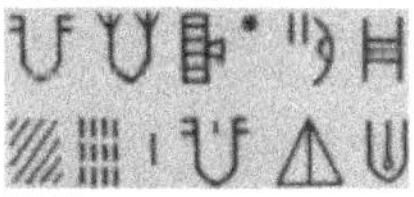

7258

Lothal196A12

7248

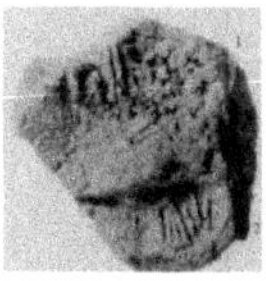

Lothal197A12

7237

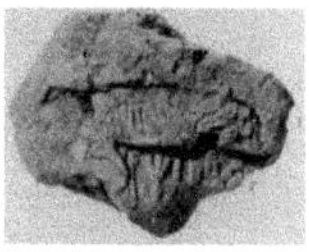

Lothal198A12

7215

Lothal199A12

7247

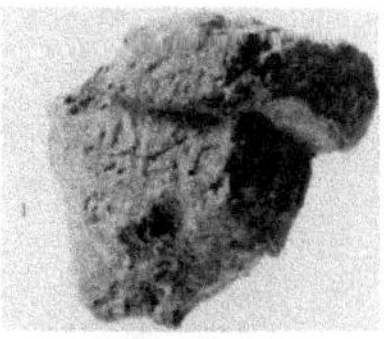

Lothal200A1

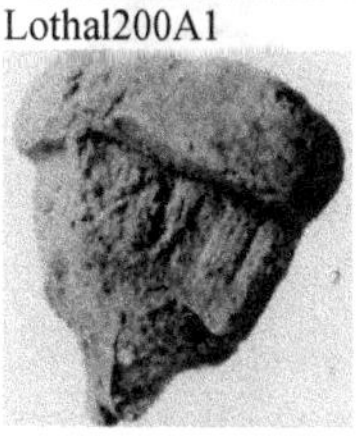

Lothal200A2

7219

Lothal201A12
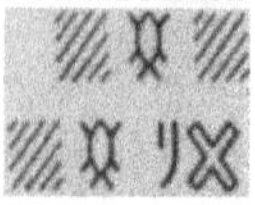
7263

Lothal202A12
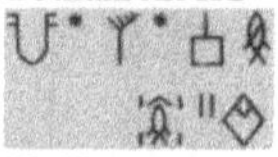
7267

Lothal203A12

7246

Lothal204A
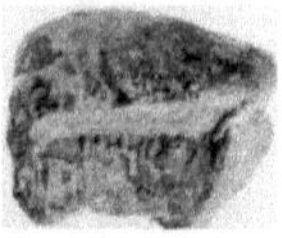
Lothal204F
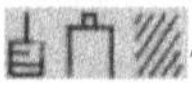
7275

Lothal205A12

7218

Lothal206A12

7265

Lothal207A12

7281

Lothal208A12

Lothal209A12
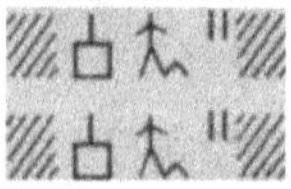
7262

Lothal210A12

7201

Lothal211A13

7277

Lothal212A12
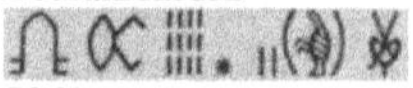
7261

Lothal213A2

7207

Lothal214A12

Lothal216D12

Lothal216E
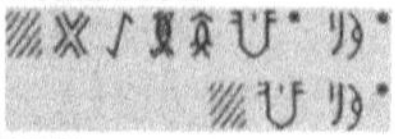
7283

Lothal217A

Lothal217B

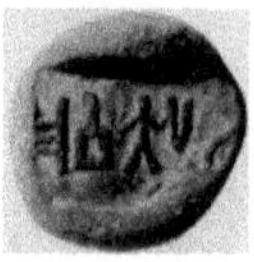
Lothal218A

7202

Lothal219A

7282

Lothal220A

7278

Lothal221A

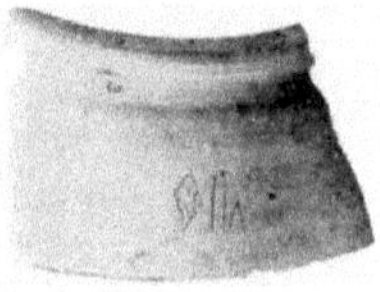
Lothal222A

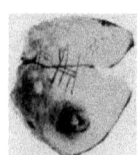

Lothal223A

Lothal224A

Lothal225A

Lothal227A

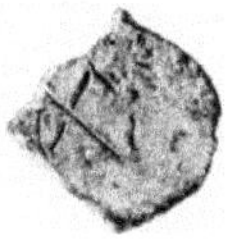

Lothal229A

Lothal230A

Lothal233A

Lothal246A

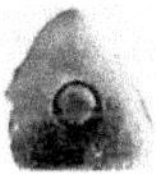

Lothal269A

Lothal270A

Lothal272A

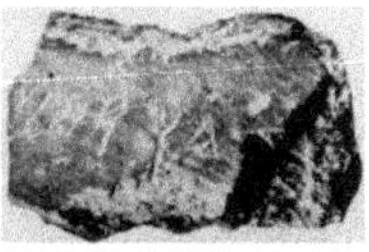

Lothal273A

7301

Lothal277A

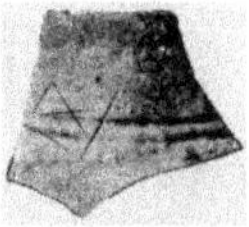

Lothal280A

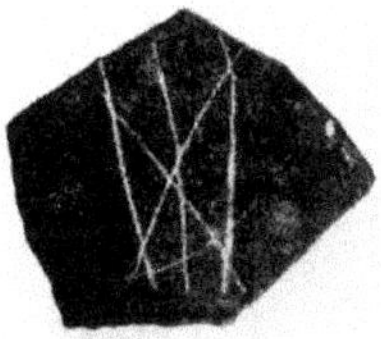

Lothal281A

7088

7098

7212

7232

7233

7269

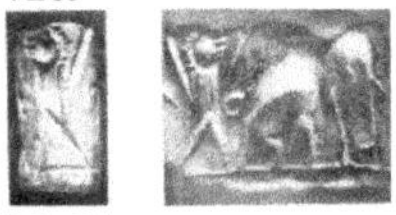

Maski

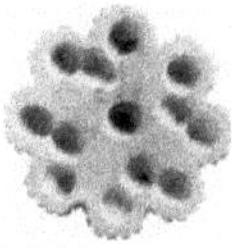

Mehi

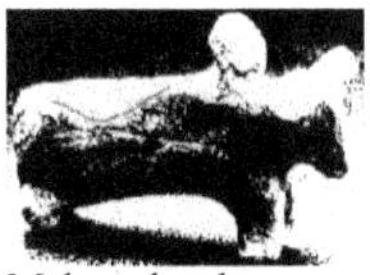

Mehrgarh zebu

Mehrgarh01

Mehrgarh04

Mehrgarh05

Mehrgarh08

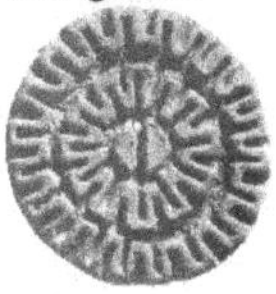

Mehrgarh10

Mehrgarh11

Mehrgarh12

Mehrgarh13

Mehrgarh14

Mehrgarh15

Mehrgarh16

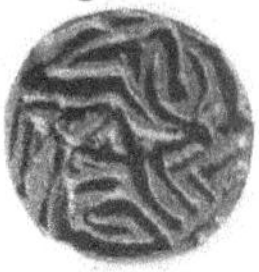

Mehrgarh17

Mehrgarh18

m0001a

1067

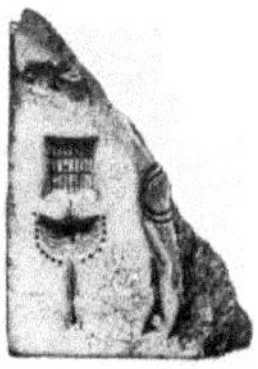

m0002a

m0003a

2225

m0004a

3109

m0005
2247

m0006a
2422

m0007
1011

m0008a
1038

m0009a
2616

m0010
1006

m0011

m0012
3031

m0013
1069

m0014
1022

m0015
2177

m0016a
1037

m0017
1035

m0018Ac
1548

m0019a
1085

m0020a
1054

m0021a
2103

m0022a
1023

m0023a
2398

m0024
2694

m0025
1056

m0026a
2074

m0027a
2084

m0028a

2178

m0029a

2033

m0030a

2396

m0031

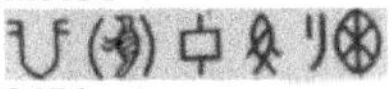

2576

m0032a

2180

m0033a

1042

m0034a

1058

m0035a

2333

m0036a

2455

m0037a

3103

m0039a

1544

m0040

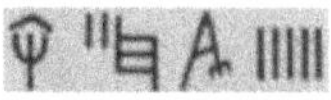

1051

m0038a

1087

m0041

2271

m0042a

1096

m0043

2584

m0044a

3110

m0045a

1552

m0046a

3089

m0047a

1098

m0048a

1186

m0049a

1047

m0050a

1557

m0051a

1555

m0052a

1540

m0053a

2128

m0054

2307

m0055a

2511

m0056

2406

m0057a

2340

m0058a

2680

m0059a

1029

m0060a

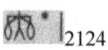

2124

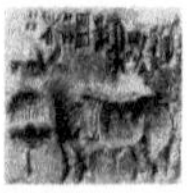

m0061

m0062

3112

m0063

3068

m0064

2524

m0065

2440

m0066AC

1052

m0067

2264

m0068

3108

m0069

1095

m0070

1048

m0071a

3083 [The second sign from left is an orthographic representation of the thigh of a bovid, perhaps a bull].

m0072a

2085

m0073

1046

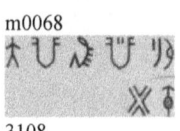

m0074

2353

m0075
1019

m0076

m0077

3111

m0078
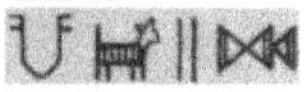
3118

m0079a
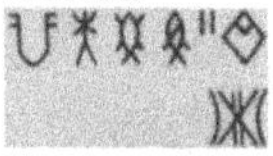
2083

m0080

2635

m0081a

1180

m0082

2451

m0083a

2267

m0084a

1108

m0085a

2365

m0086

2208

m0087

2148

m0088
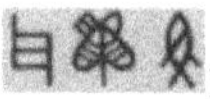
1075

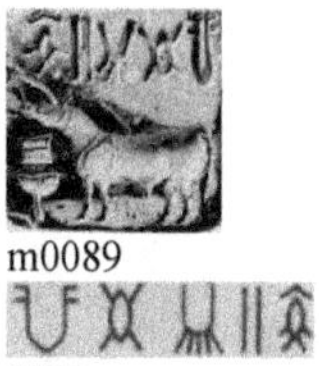
m0089
3116

m0090
3039

m0091
2429

m0092
2407

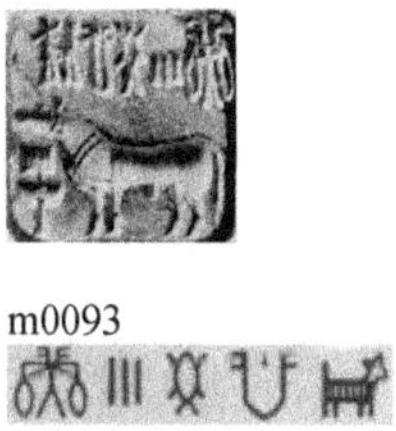
m0093
2305

m0094
2594

m0095
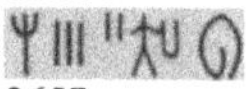
2657

m0096
2698

m0097
2549

m0098
2012

m0099
2475

m0100
1115

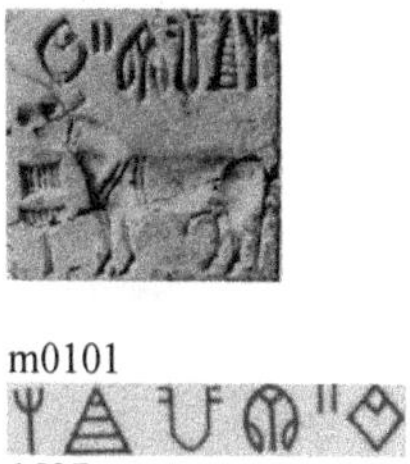
m0101
1537

m0102

1129

m0103

1076

m0104

2574

m0105

2337

m0106

2459

m0107

2593

m0108

1110

m0109

1151

m0110

2031

m0111

2029

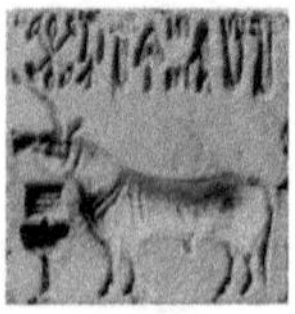

m0112

2099

m0113

2115

m0114

2166

m0115

3087

m0116

2481

m0117

1105

m0118

1104

m0119a

2018

m0120a

1099

m0121a

1188

m0122a

2015

m0123a

2702

m0124

1120

m0125

m0126

2311

m0127

1119

m0128a

2284

m0129

2193

m0130a

2285

m0131

2263

m0132

2082

m0133a

2052

m0134

2187

m0135

1168

m0136

2233

m0137

2261

m0138

2381

m0139

2185

m0140

2563

m0141

2543

m0142

2630

m0143

2002

m0144

2048

m0145

1118

m0146

1100

m0147

3097

m0148

1245

m0149

1233

m0150

1236

m0151

2323

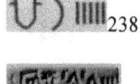

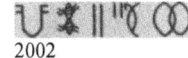

m0152

2102

m0153

2361

m0154

2373

m0155

1187

m0156

m0157

2022

m0158

2198

m0159

2355

m0160

2286

m0161

2088

m0162

2486

m0163

1543

m0164

2403

m0165

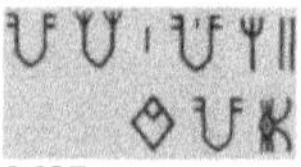

2687

m0166

1080

m0167.

1297

m0168a [The second sign may be an orthographic variant for a thigh of a bovid?]

2442

m0169

1113

m0170

2237

m0171

1149

m0172

1071

m0173

1161

m0174

1114

m0175

1291

m0176

1193

m0177

m0178

2354

m0179

m0180

2014

m0181

2490

m0182

2154

m0183

3113

m0184

2634

m0185

m0186

2161

m0187

2382

m0188

1287

m0189

1195

m0190

1205

m0191

1288

m0192

1206

m0193

2113

m0194

2254

m0195

2415

m0196

2474

m0197

2371

m0198

2363

m0199

2647

m0200

1148

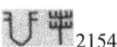

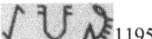

m0201

2678

m0202

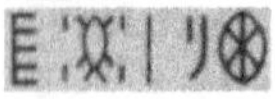
2625

m0203

1556

m0204

2623

m0205

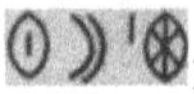1221

m0206

m0207

2458

m0208

2047

m0209

2375

m0210

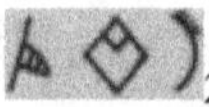2656

m0211

1214

m0212

2577

m0213

1150

m0214

2571

m0215

3081

m0216

3036

m0217

2087

m0218

2175

m0219

2433

m0220a

3093

m0221a

3164

m0222

1194

m0223

1167 [The sign in front of the one-horned bull may be Sign 162

]

m0224

2215

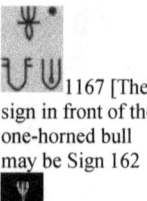

m0225

2199

m0226

2152

m0227 2226

m0228

2502

m0229

3075

m0230.

1295

m0231

2444

m0232

2234 'Unicorn' with two horns! "Bull with two long horns (otherwise resembling the 'unicorn')", generally facing the standard. That it is the typical 'one-horned bull' is surmised from two ligatures: the pannier on the shoulder and the ring on the neck.

m0233

m0234.

1321

m0235

2689

m0236

2123

m0237

m0238AC

2534

m0239

2238

m0240.

1324

m0241

1536

m0242

2216

m0243

2390

m0244

2399

m0245

2290

m0246.

1317

m0247

2298

m0248.

1310

m0249

2378

m0250.

 1308

m0251

2370

m0252

2423

m0253

2701

m0254

2090

m0255

2409
[The second sign is diamond-shaped?]

m0256

1332

m0257

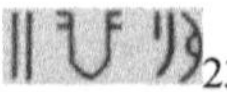 2314

m0258a.

1340

m0259

2132

m0260

2567

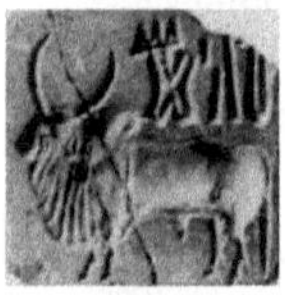

m0261

2535

m0262 Zebu

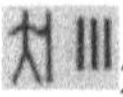 2249

m0263

1336

m0264

 2607

m0265

2155

m0266.

1306

m0267 Water-buffalo

2257

m0268 Water-buffalo

2445

m0269

2663

m0270

m0271 Goat-antelope with horns turned backwards and a short tail

m0272 Goat-antelope with horns bending backwards and neck turned backwards
2554

m0273 2673

m0274

1342

m0275

2131

m0276AC

3122

m0277

2309

m0278

2648

m0279

3060

m0280

1373

m0281

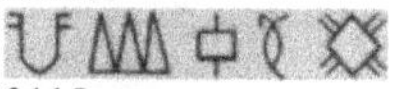

3115

m0282

2304

m0283

2127

m0284

2195

m0285

1367

m0286

2517

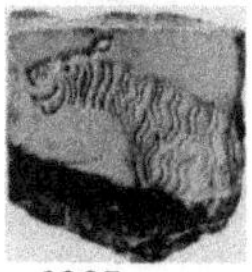

m0287

m0288

2518

m0289

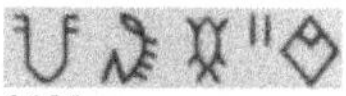

3121

m0290

2527

m0291 Tiger

3069

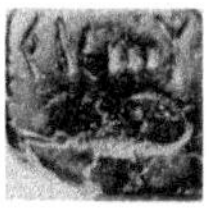

m0292 Gharial

1361

m0293 Gharial

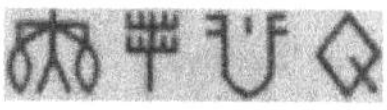

1360

m0294 One-horned bull?; elephant

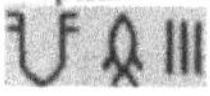

1376

m0295 Pict-61: Composite motif of three tigers joined together.

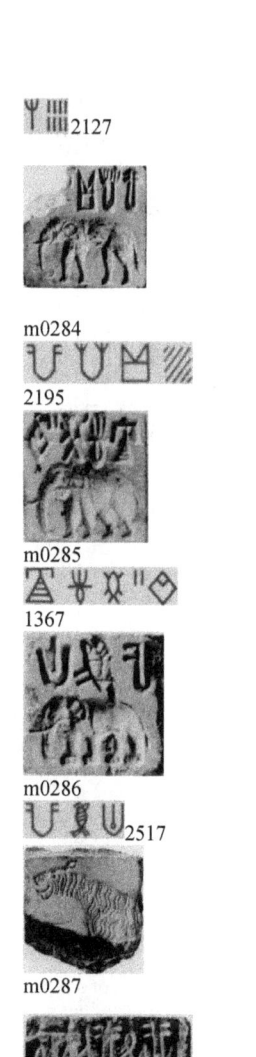

1386

m0296 Two heads of one-horned bulls with neck-rings, joined end to end (to a standard device with two rings coming out of the top part?), under a stylized pipal tree with nine leaves.

1387

m0297a Head of a one-horned bull attached to an undentified five-point symbol (octopus-like?)

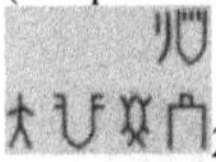
2641

m0298

m0299 Composite animal with the body of a ram, horns of a bull, trunk of an elephant, hindlegs of a tiger and an upraise serpent-like tail.

1381

m0300 Pict51: Composite animal: human face, zebu's horns, elephant tusks and trunk, ram's forepart, unicorn's trunk and feet, tiger's hindpart and serpent-like tail.

2521

m0301 Composite motif: human face, body or forepart of a ram, body and front legs of a unicorn, horns of a zebul, trunk of an elephant, hindlegs of a tiger and an upraised serpent-like tail.

2258

m0302 Composite animal with the body of a ram, horns of a bull, trunk of an elephant, hindlegs of a tiger and an upraise serpent-like tail.

1380

m0303 Composite animal.

2411

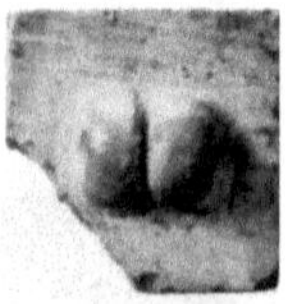

m0304B

m0304AC Pict-81: Person (with three visible faces) wearing bangles and armlets seated on a platform (with an antelope looking backwards) and surrounded by five animals: rhinoceros, buffalo, antelope, tiger and elephant.

2420

m0305AC

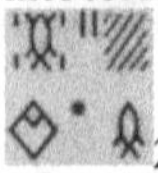
2235

Pict-80: Three-faced, horned person (with a three-leaved pipal branch on the crown with two stars on either side), wearing bangles and armlets.

m0306 Person grappling with two tigers standing on either side of him and rearing on their hindlegs.

2086

m0307 Person grappling with two tigers standing on either side of him and rearing on their hindlegs.

2122

m0308AC Pict-105: Person grappling with two tigers standing on either side of him and rearing on their hindlegs.

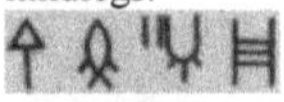

2075 [The third sign from left may be a stylized 'standard device'?]

m0309 Pict-109: Person with hair-bun seated on a tree branch; a tiger looks at the person with its head turned backwards.

2522

m0310AC

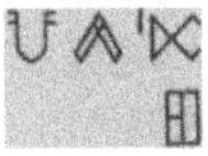
1355

m0311 Pict-52: Composite motif: body of a tiger, a human body with bangles on arms, antelope horns, tree-branch and long pigtail.

2347

m0312 Persons vaulting over a water-buffalo.

m0313

2637

m0314

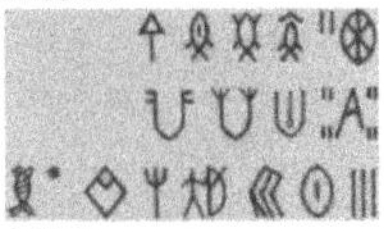
1400

m0315

1395

m0316

2408

m0317silver

2016

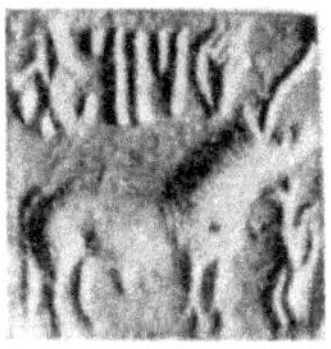

Mohenjodaro FEM, Pl. LXXXVIII, 316

2316

Mohenjodaro MIC, Pl. CVI,93

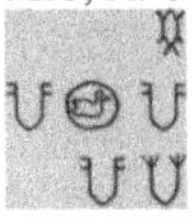
1093

Mohenjo-daro. Copper seal. National Museum, New Delhi. [Source: Page 18, Fig. 8A in: Deo Prakash Sharma, 2000, *Harappan seals, sealings and copper tablets*, Delhi, National Museum].

m0318

m0318B

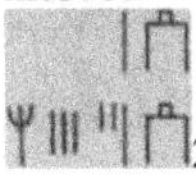
2626

m0319

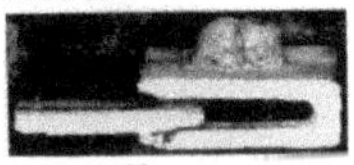

m0319C

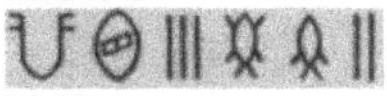
2260

m0320

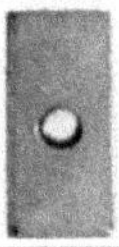

m0320D

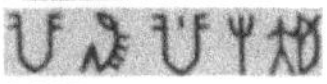
2449

m0321

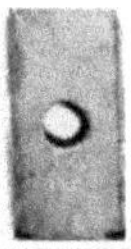

m0321D

2173

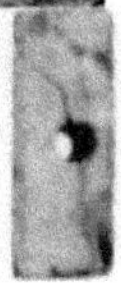

m0322
m0322D

1192

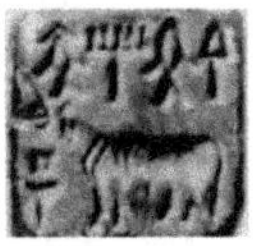

m0323

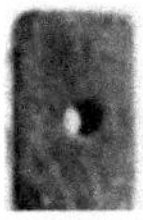

m0323D

1277

m0324A

m0324B

m0324D

1252

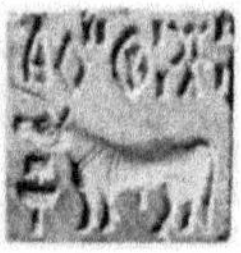

m0325A

m0325B

m0325F

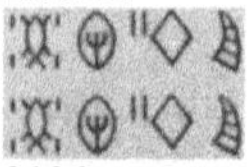

3106

m0326A

m0326B

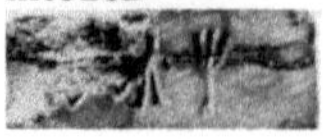

m0326C

m0326D

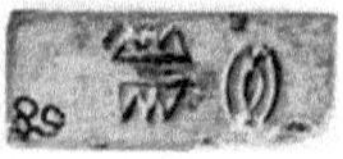

m326E

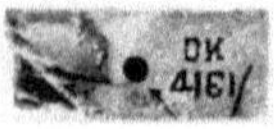

m0326F

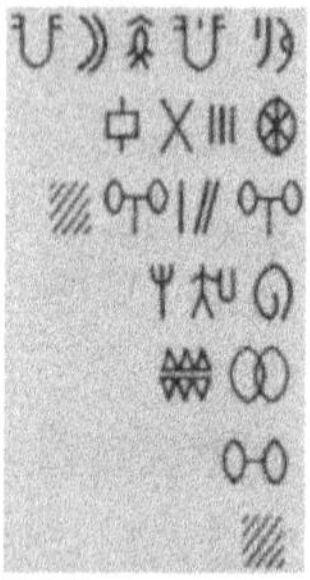

2405

m0327

2631

m0328

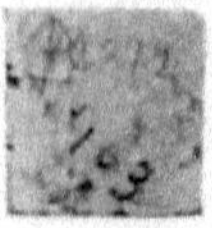

m0328B

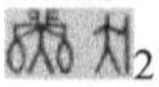

2108

m0329

1477

m0330A

m0330B Perforated through the narrow edge of a two-sided seal

1475

m0331A

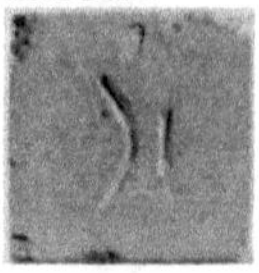

m0331B

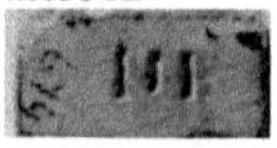

m0331D

m0331F Cube seal

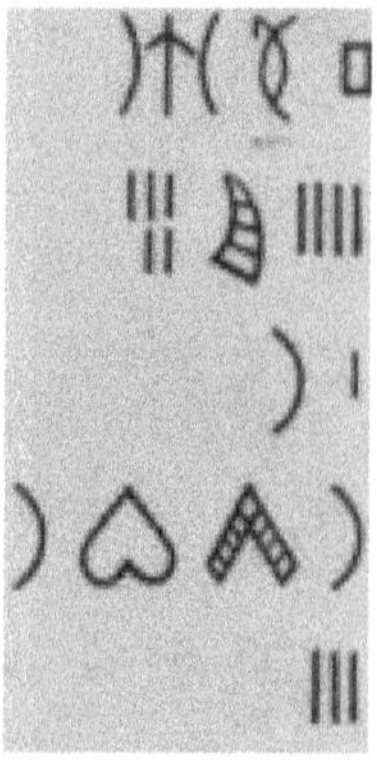

1471

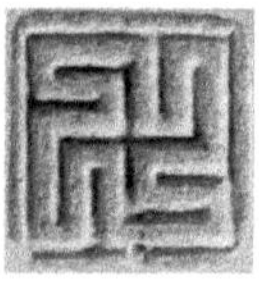

m0332AC

m0333

m0334

m0335

m0336

m0337

m0338

m0339

m0340

m0341

m0342

m0343

m0344

m0345

m0346

m0347

m0348

m0349

m0350
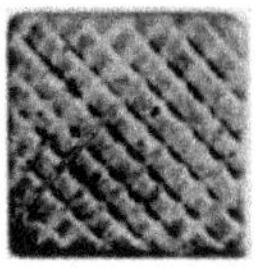
m0351
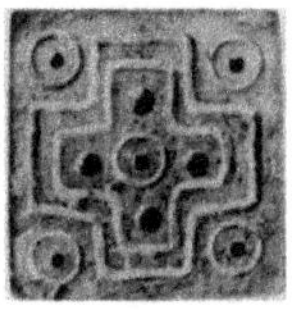
m0352A

m0352C
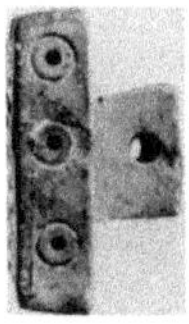
m0352D

m0352E
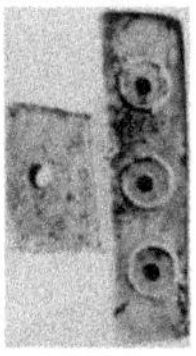
m0352F
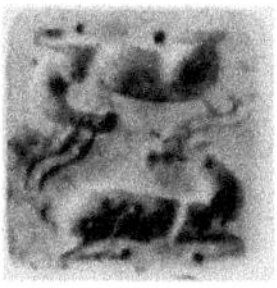
m0353

m0354

1403

m0356

1406

m0357

1401

m0358

2297

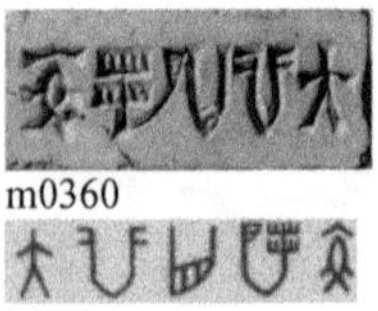
m0360
3102

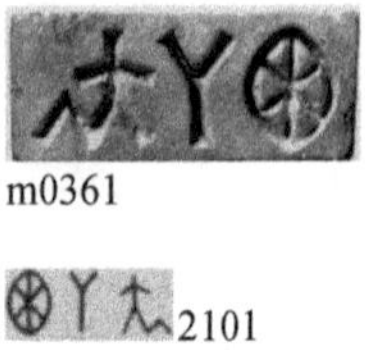
m0361
2101

m0362
1466

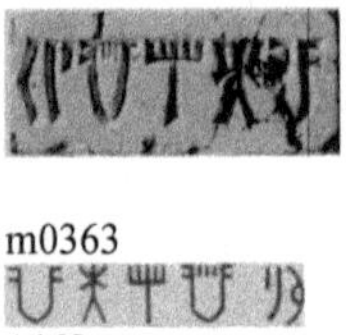
m0363
1469

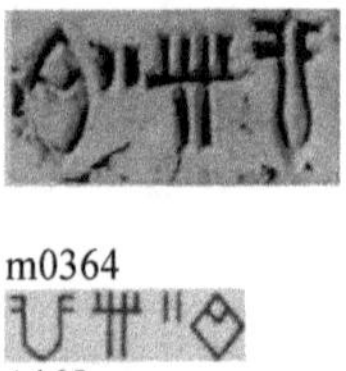
m0364
1465

m0365
2273

m0366
2077

m0367

2044

m0368
2336

m0370
2138

m0371
2461

m0372
1438

m0373
2043

m0374
2097

m0375
m375AC

m0376
1426

m0377
3120

m0378
1402

m0379
2159

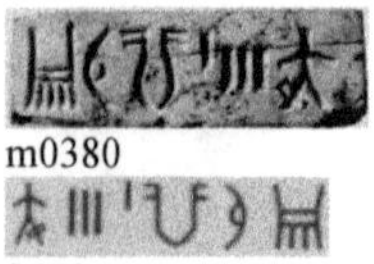
m0380
2470

m0381
2162

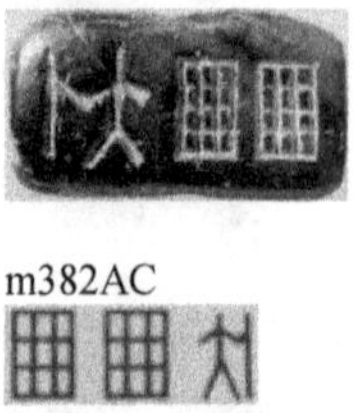
m382AC
1437

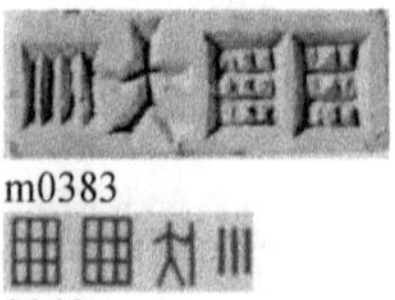
m0383
2240

m0384
2302

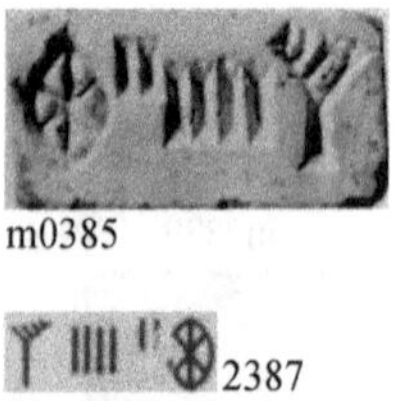
m0385
2387

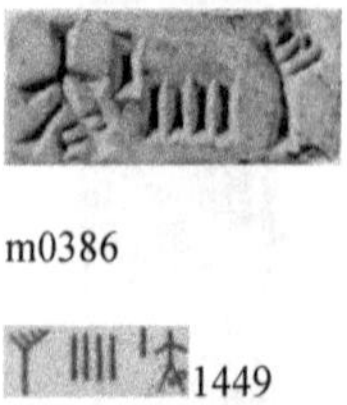
m0386
1449

m0387
2041

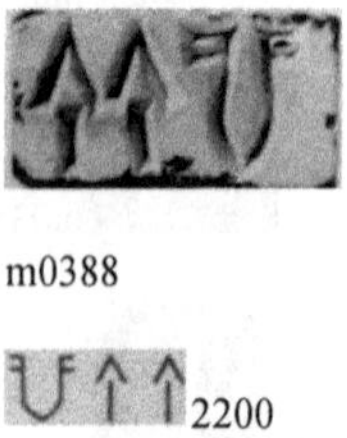
m0388
2200

m0389
2397

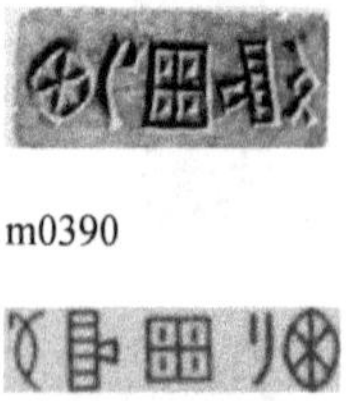
m0390
1444

m0392
2046

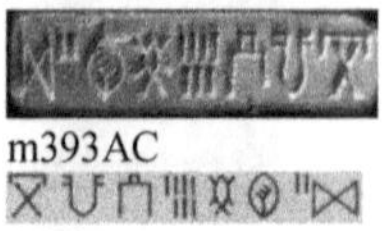
m393AC
2120

m0394

2213

m0395

2183

m0396

1421

m0397

1415

m0398

2308

m399AC

1414

m0400

3088

m0401

2346

m0402

2395

m0403

1410

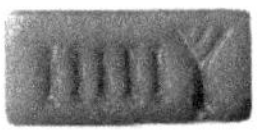

m404AC

1422

m0405

2221

m0406

1399

m0407

2643

m0408

2100

m0409

2699

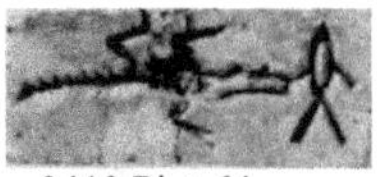

m0410 Pict-64: Gharial snatching, with its snout, the fin of a fish

2133

m0411

1431

m0412

1450

m0413

2319

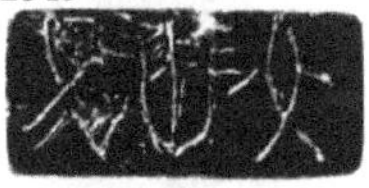

m0414A

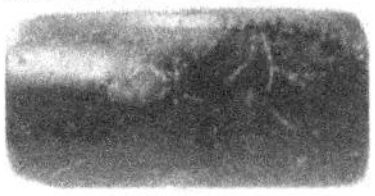

m0414B Seal with incision on obverse

2004

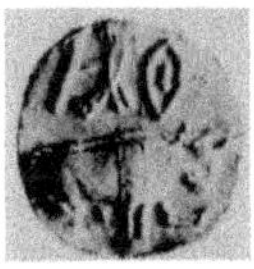

m0415a Bison

2500

m0416 Bison .

1309

m417AC Pict-62: Composition: six heads of animals: of unicorn, of short-horned bull (bison), of antelope, of tiger, and of two other uncertain animals) radiating outward from a hatched ring (or 'heart' design).

1383

m0418acyl

m0419acyl

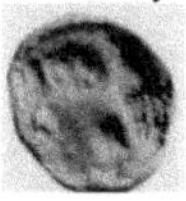

m0419dcyl

m0419fcyl

m0420A1si

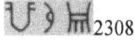

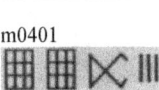

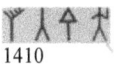

m0420A2si

3236

m0421A1si

m0421A2si

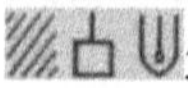3237

m0422A1si

m0422A2si

m0423A1si

m0423A2si

3221

m0424A1si

m0424A2si

m0425A1si

m0425A2si

m0426Asi

m0426Bsi

2809

m0427t

1630

m0428At

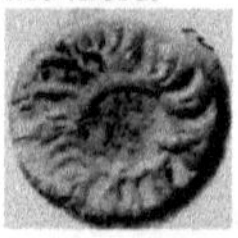

m0428Bt

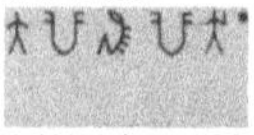

1607 Pict- 132: Radiating solar symbol.

m0429 Text

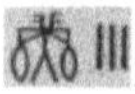2862

m0430At

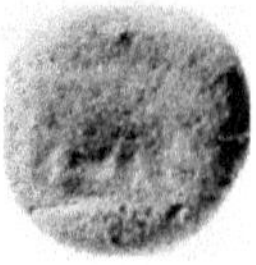

m0430Bt

2862

m0431At

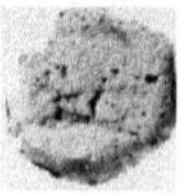

m0431Bt

3239

m0432At

m0432Bt

1624

m0433At

m0433Bt

3233

m0434At

m0434Bt

3248

m0435t

m0436At

m0436Bt

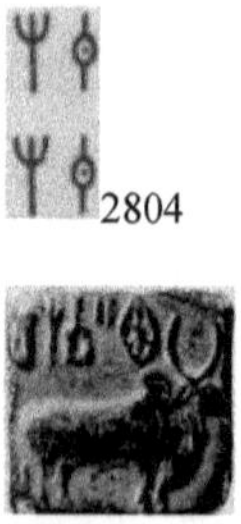2804

m0437t

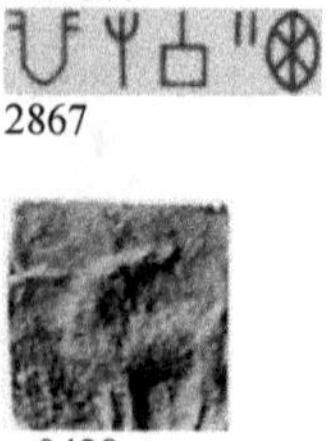

2867

m0438atcopper

m0439t

m440AC

m0441At

m0441Bt

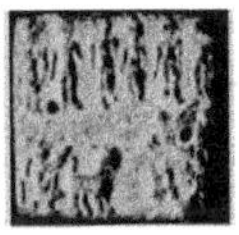
m0442At

m0442Bt

m443At

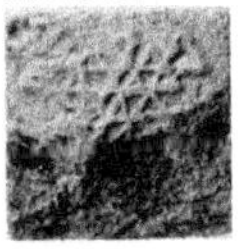
m443Bt

m444At

3223

m445Bt

m445AC

2821

m446At

m446Bt

2854

m447At

m447Bt

m448t

m449Bt

m449AC

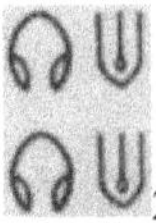
2836

m450At

m450Bt

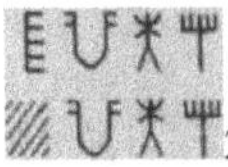
2864

m0451At

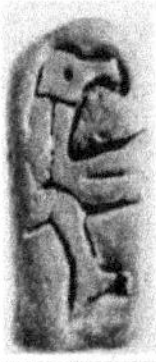
m0451Bt

3235

m0452At
m0452Bt

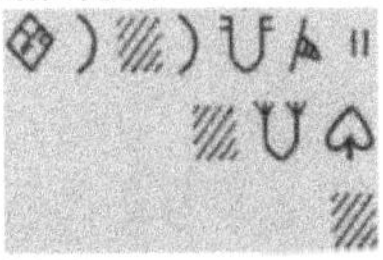
2855

m0453At

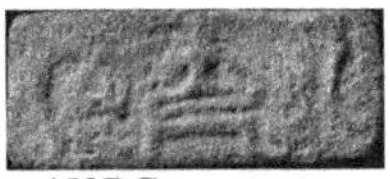
m453BC

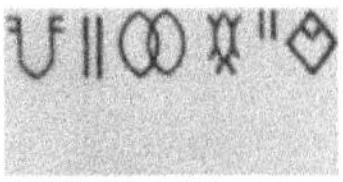
1629 Pict-82
Person seated on a pedestal flanked on either side by a kneeling adorant and a hooded serpent rearing up.

m0455At

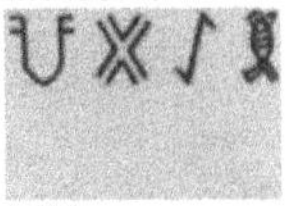
1619

m0456At

3219

m0457At

m0457Bt

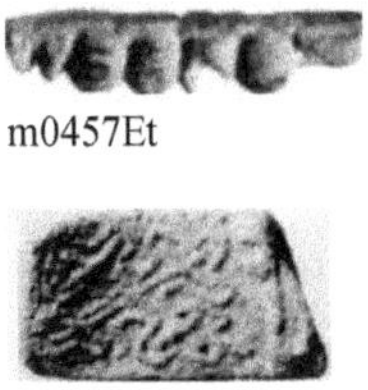
m0457Et

m0458At

m0458Bt

 3227

m0459At

m0459Bt

 3225

m0460At

m0460Bt

 3228

m0461At

m0461Bt

 2806 Pict-73: Alternative 1. Serpent (?) entwined around a pillar with capital (?); motif carvd in high-relief. Alternative 2. Ring-stones around a pillar with coping stones in a building-structure as at Dholavira?

m0462At

m0462Bt

 3215

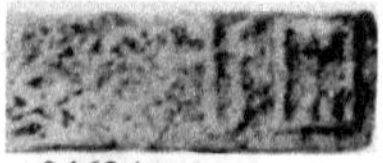

m0463At

m0463Bt

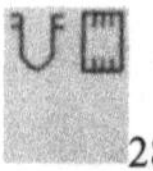 2813

m0464At

m0464Bt

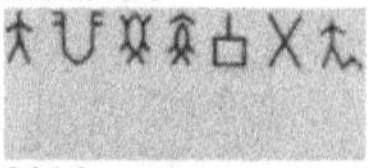

3216

m0465At

m0465Bt

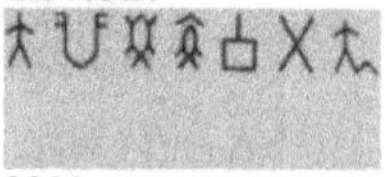

3220

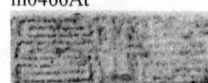

m0466At

m0466Bt

m0467At

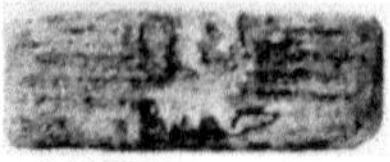

m0467Bt

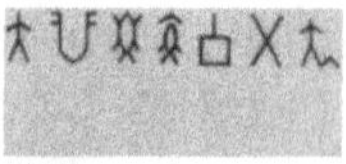

3209

m0468At

m0468Bt

3249

m0469At

m0469Bt

2830

m0470At

2810

m0471At

m0471Bt

3232

m0472At

1615

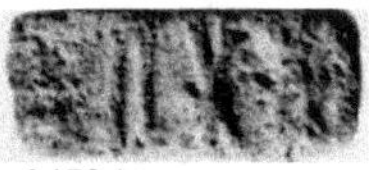
m0473At

2848

m0474At

3243

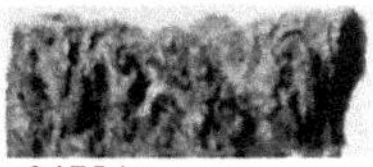
m0475Atcopper

3247

m0476At

m0476Ct

m0477At

m0477Bt

m0477Ct

2844

Two rhinoceroses, one at either end of the text (Pict-29).

m0478At

m0478Bt

m0479At

m0479Bt

3224

m0480At

m0480Bt Tablet in bas-relief. Side a: Tree Side b: Pict-111: From R.: A woman with outstretched arms flanked by two men holding uprooted trees in their hands; a person seated on a tree with a tiger below with its head turned backwards; a tall jar with a lid.

Is the pictorial of a tall jar the Sign 342 with a lid? Sign 45 seems to be a kneeling adorant offering a pot (Sign 328)

2815 Pict-77: Tree, generally within a railing or on a platform.

3230

m0481At

m0481Bt

m0481Ct

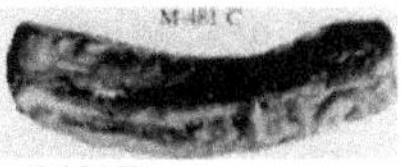
m0481Et

2846 Pict-41: Serpent, partly reclining on a low platform under a tree

m0482At

m0482Bt

1620

Pict-65: Gharial, sometimes with a fish held in its jaw and/or surrounded by a school of fish.

m0483At

m0483Bt

m0483Ct

m0483Et

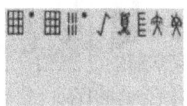

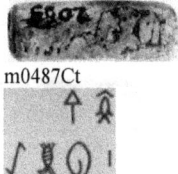

2866

Pict-145: Geometrical pattern.

m0484At

m0484Bt

2861

m0486at

m0486bt

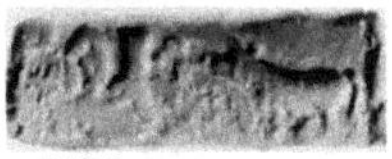
m0486ct

1625

m0487At

m0487Bt

m0487Ct

2852

m0488At

m0488Bt

m0488Ct

2802 Prism: Tablet in bas-relief. Side b: Text +One-horned bull + standard. Side a: From R.: a composite animal; a person seated on a tree with a tiger below looking up at the person; a svastika within a square border; an elephant (Composite animal has the body of a ram, horns of a zebu, trunk of an elephant, hindlegs of a tiger and an upraised serpent-like tail). Side c: From R.: a horned person standing between two branches of a pipal tree; a ram; a horned person kneeling in adoration; a low pedestal with some offerings.

m0489At

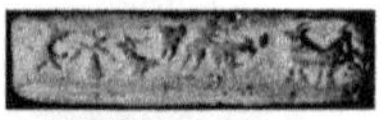

m0489Bt

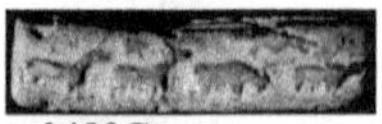

m0489Ct

m0490At

m0490BCt

1605

m0491At

m0491BCt

1608 Pict-94: Four persons in a procession, each carrying a standard, one of which has the figure of a one-horned bull on top.

m0492At

m0492Bt Pict-14: Two bisons standing face to face.

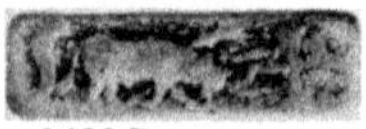

m0492Ct

2835 Pict-99: Person throwing a spear at a bison and placing one foot on the head of the bison; a hooded serpent at left.

m0493At

m0493Bt Pict-93: Three dancing figures in a row.

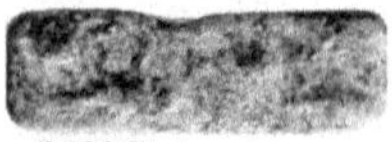

m0493Ct

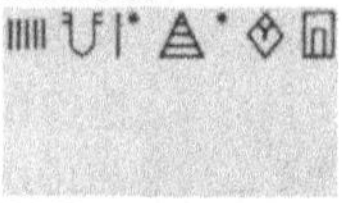

2843

m0494At

m0494BGt Prism Tablet in bas-relief.

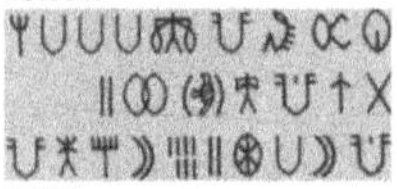

1623

m0495At

m0495Bt

m0495gt

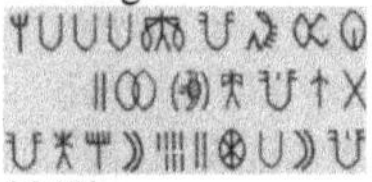

2847b

m0496At

m0496Bt

m0496Dt

m0497At

m0497Bt

m0498At

m0498Bt

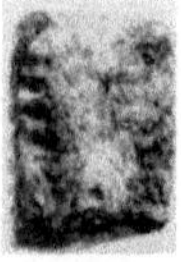

m0498Dt

m0499At

m0500at

m0500bt

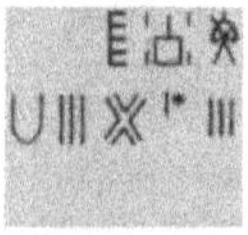

2604 Pict-76: Tree, generally within a railing or on a platform.

m0501At

m0501Bt

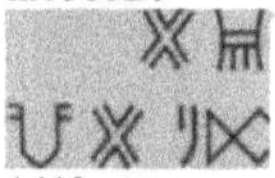

1412

m0502At

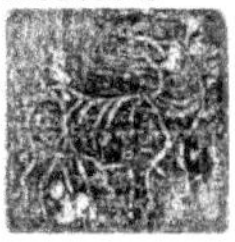

m0502Bt

3345

m0503 Text

3346

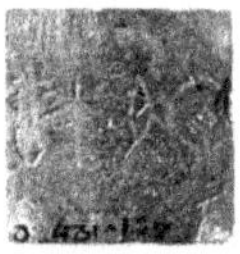

m0504At

m0504Bt

3323

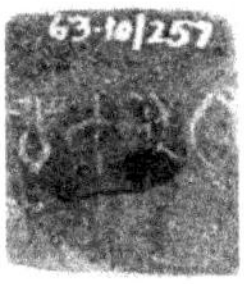

m0505At

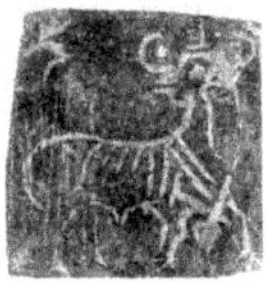

m0505Bt

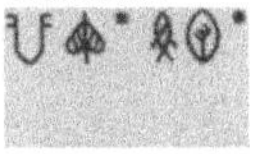

1702

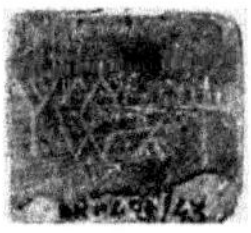

m0507At

m0507Bt

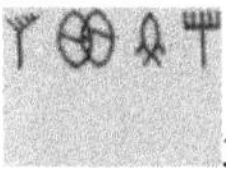

3350

m0508At

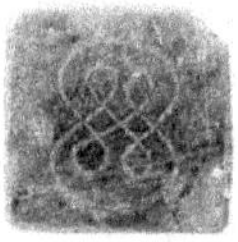

m0508Bt

3352

m0509At

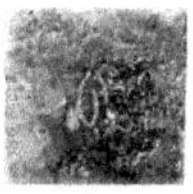

m0509Bt

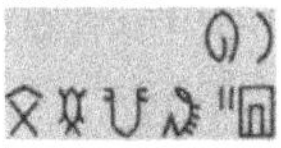

3320

m0510At

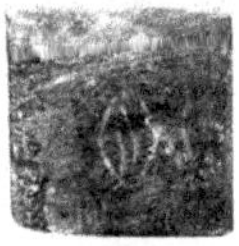

m0510Bt

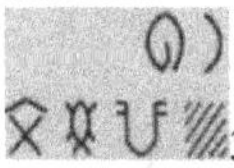

3319

m0511At

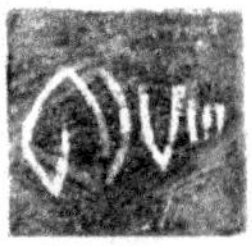

m0511Bt

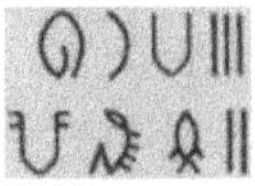

2905

m0512At

m0512Bt

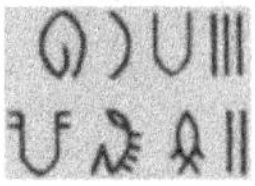

2906

m0513At

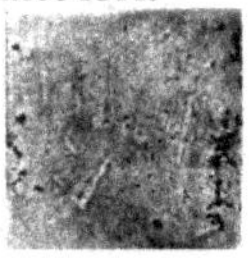

m0513Bt

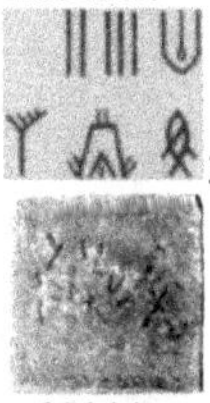

3364

m0514At

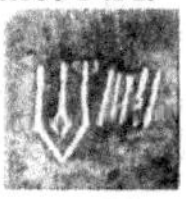

m0514Bt

3302

m0515 Text

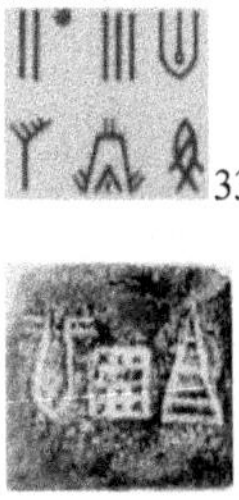

3335

m0516At

m0516Bt

3398

m0517At

m0517Bt

3334

m0519At

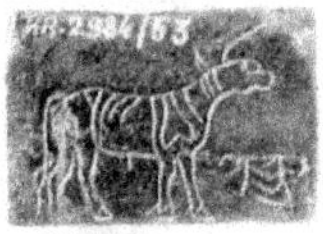

m0519Bt

1710

m0520 At, Bt

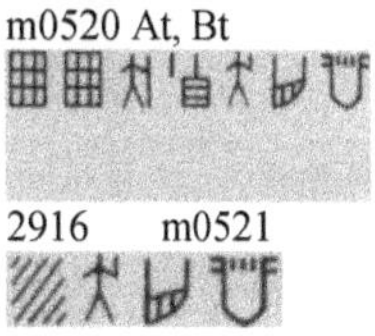

2916 m0521

3407

m0522At

m0522Bt

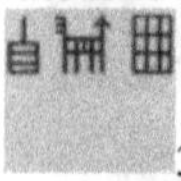

3378

m0523At

m0523Bt

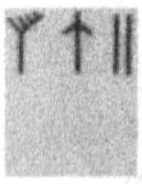

1714

m0524At

m0524Bt

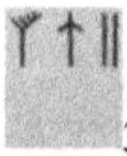

3391

m0525At

m0525Bt

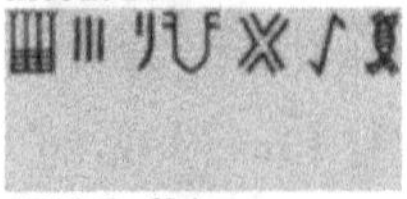

1713 Buffalo

m0526At

m0526Bt

3329

Buffalo

m0527At

m0527Bt

3336

m0528At

m0528Bt

3368

m0529At

m0529Bt

3392

m0530At

m0530Bt

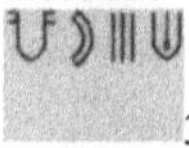

3356

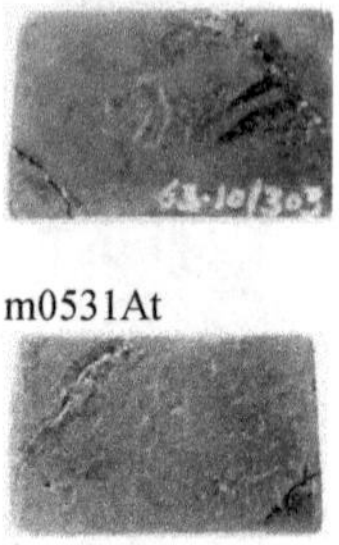

m0531At

m0531Bt

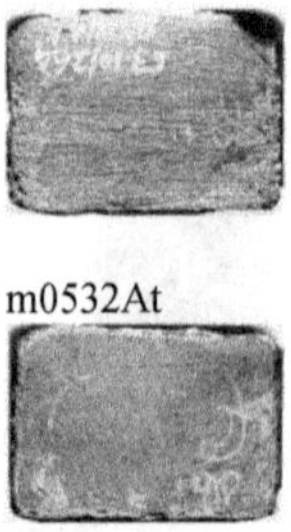

m0532At

m0532Bt

3349

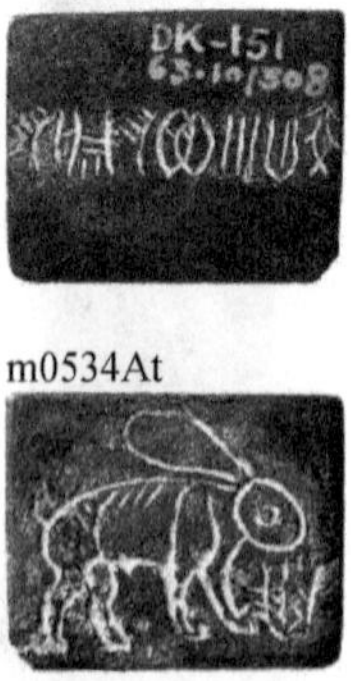

m0534At

m0534Bt

3304

m0535At

m0535Bt

3355

m0536At

m0536Bt

3312

m0537At

m0537Bt

1705

m0538At

m0538Bt

3384

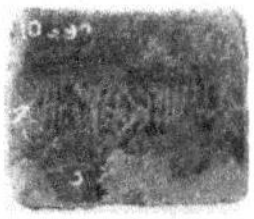
m0539At

m0539Bt

m540t
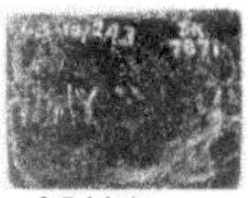
m0541At
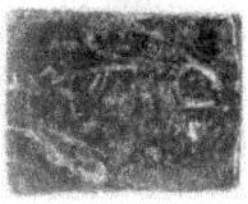
m0541Bt
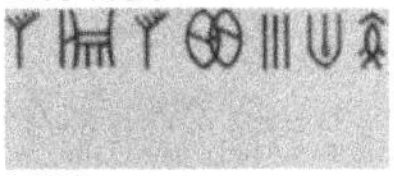
3331

m0542At

m0542Bt

3326 Hare?

m0543At

m0543Bt

3363 [Note the 'heart' orthograph on the body of the antelope. This is comparable to

Sign 323 ]

m0544At

m0544Bt

3357
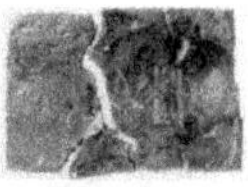
m0545At

m0545Bt
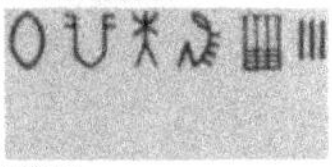
3301

m0546At
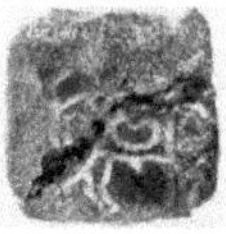
m0546Bt

3383
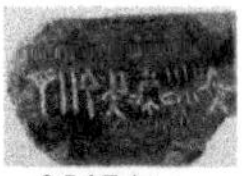
m0547At
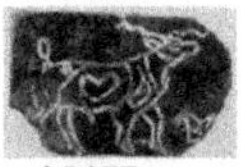
m0547Dt

3303

m0548At
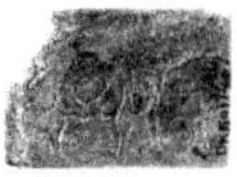
m0548Bt
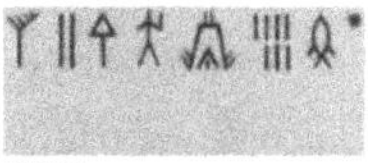
3305

m0549At

m0549Bt
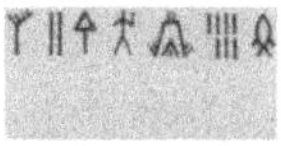
3373

m0550At
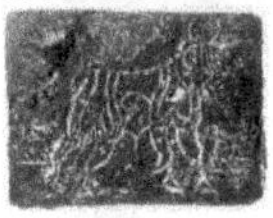
m0550Bt

3351

m0551At

m0551Bt

1708
Ox-antelope with long tail.

m0552At

m0552Bt
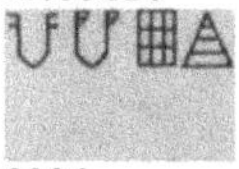
3306
m0553At
m0553Bt
3353
m0554At
m0554Bt
1712
m0555At
m0555Bt
3314
m0556At
m0556Bt
3404

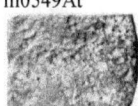

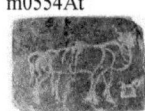

m0557At
m0557Bt

3341

m0558At
m0558Bt

3342

m0559At
m0559Bt

2909

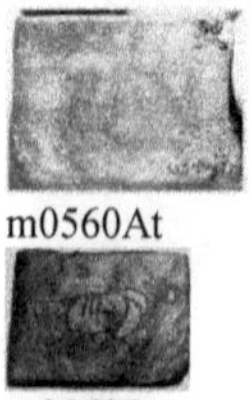
m0560At
m0560Bt

3386

m0561At

m0561Bt

3339

m0562At
m0562Bt

3361

m0563At
m0563Bt

3379

m0564At
m0564Bt

3371

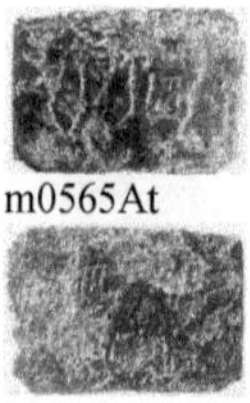
m0565At
m0565Bt

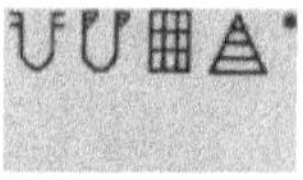
3403

m0566At
m0566Bt

3359

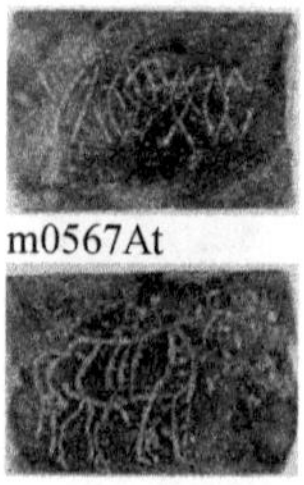
m0567At
m0567Bt
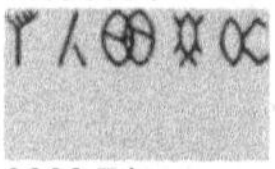
3322 Bison.

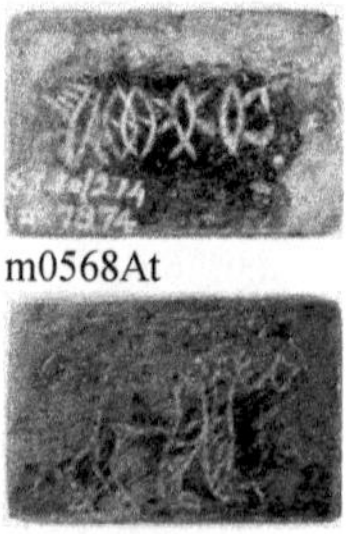
m0568At
m0568Bt
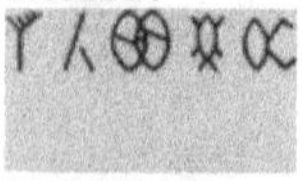
3332 Tiger.

m0569At
m0569Bt

3372

m0571At
m0571Bt

2913

Horned elephant. Almost similar to the composition: Body of a ram (with inlaid 'heart' sign), horns of a bull, trunk of an elephant, hindlegs of a tiger and an upraised serpent-like tail

m0572At
m0572Bt

3317

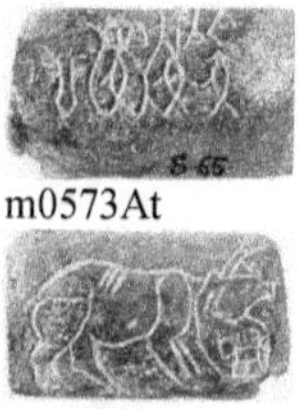
m0573At
m0573Bt

3415

m0574At

m0574Bt

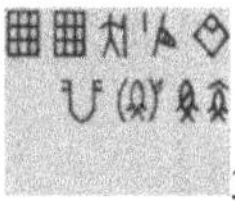

3318

m0575At

m0575Bt

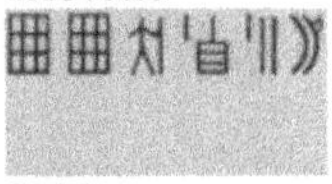

3316

m0576At

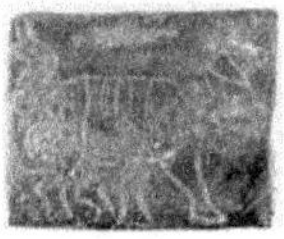

m0576Bt

3344

m0577At

m0577Bt

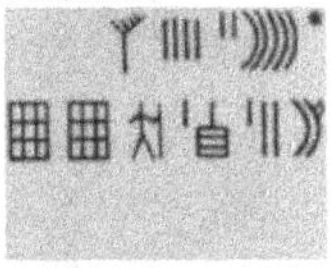

3347

m0578At

m0578Bt

2908

m0580At

m0580Bt

3321

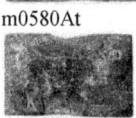

m0581At

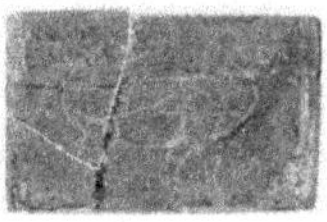

m0581Bt

3340

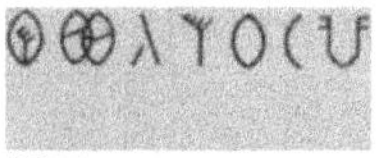

2914

Pict-89: Standing person with horns and bovine features, holding a bow in one hand and an arrow or an uncertain object in the other.

m0582At

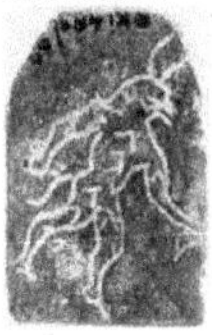

m0582Bt

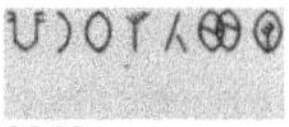

3358

m0583At

m0583Bt

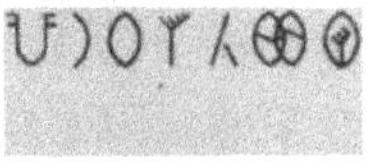

3387

m0584At

m0584Bt

m0585At

m0585Bt

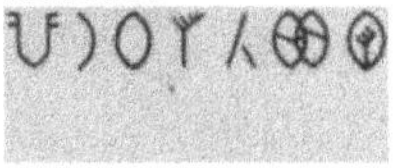

3369

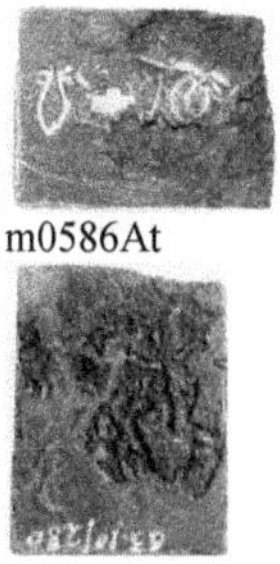

m0586At

m0586Bt

3406

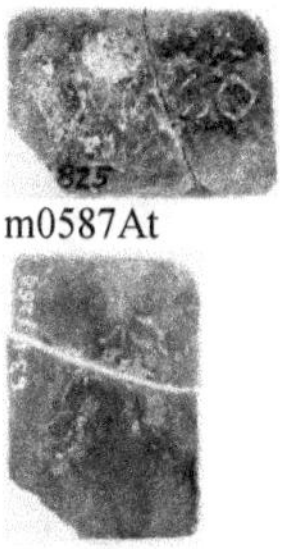

m0587At

m0587Bt

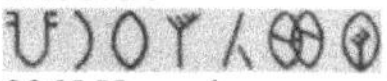

3365 Horned Archer?

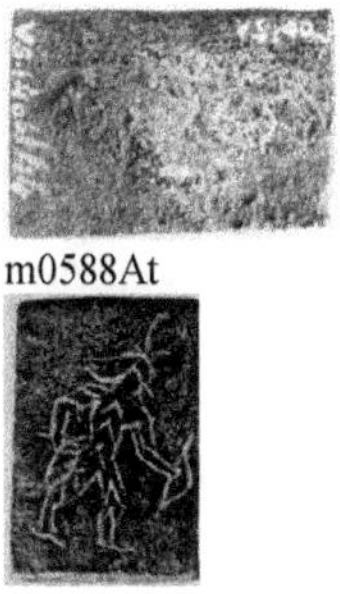

m0588At

m0588Bt Horned archer.

m0592At

m0592Bt

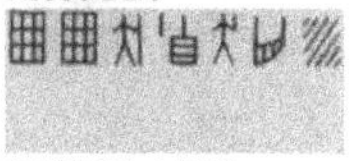

3413 Pict-133: Double-axe (?) without shaft. [The sign is comparable to the sign which appears on the text of a Chanhudaro seal: Text 6402, Chanhudaro Seal 23].

m0593At
m0593Bt

3337

m0594At
m0594Bt

m0595A
m0595B

1010

m0596At
m0596Bt

3313

m0598 Text

3410

m0599At
m0599Bt

3360

m0600At
m0600Bt

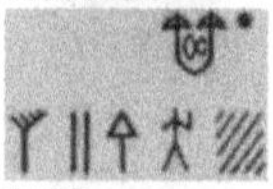
3375

m0601At
m0601Bt

m0602At
m0602Bt

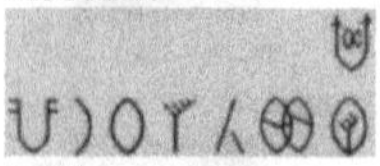
3414

m0604At
m0604Bt

3315

m0605At
m0605Bt

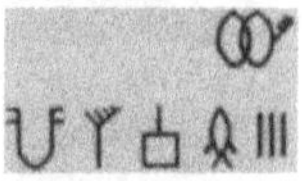
2902

m0606At
m0606Bt

2918

m0608At
m0608Bt

m0614

1904

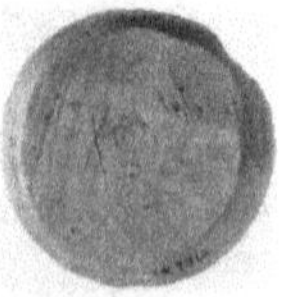
m0615

m0618

m0619

2939

m0620

m0621

2367

m0622

m0623

m0624

1015

m0625

1027

m0626

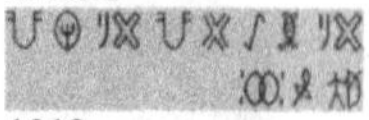
1012

m0627

1004

m0628

1033

m0629

m0630A

m0631

1008

m0632

1017

m0633

1016

m0634

2069

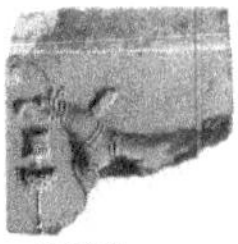
m0635a

m0636

2019

m0637

1034

m0638 One-horned bull

1404

m0639

m0640

m0641

m0642

m0643

m0644

1553

m0645

m0646A1

m0646a12

m0646A2

2653

m0647

1024

m0648

3104

m0649

2530

m0650

1032

m0651

2578

m0652

m0653

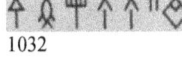

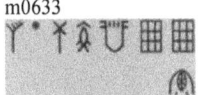

1057

m0654
2561

m0655
2098

m0656

m0657

 2026

m0658
1039

m0659

m0661
2207

m0662

1061

m0663

2597

m0664

2628

m0665

1139

m0666

2243

m0667

1111

m0668

2032

m0669
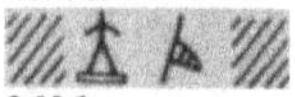
2686

m0670

1030

m0671

1021

m0672

1040

m0673
1025

m0674

1068

m0675

2197

m0676

m0677

m0678

1066

m0679

m0680A1

m0681

2182

m0682

m0682A2

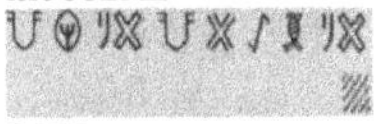

2690

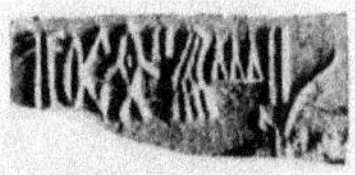

m0683a

m0683A1

m0683A2

2174

m0684

m0685

1276

m0686

2324

m0687

m0688

m0689

m0690

m0691

m0692

1031

m0693

m0694

m0695

m0696

m0697

m0698

m0699

1050

m0700

m0701

1059

m0702

2206

m0703

2438

m0704

2351

m0705

2272

m0706

1097

m0707

m0708

2666

m0709

2071

m0710

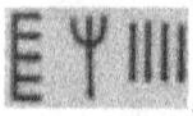
3159

m0711

1166

m0712

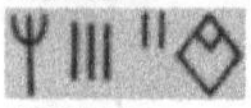
1091 Note Sign391 ligatured on the animal's neck; this may be a logonym (i.e. two heiroglyphs – rings and spoked circle -- representing the same lexeme) for the rings on the neck?

m0713

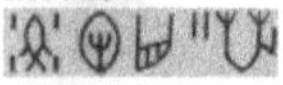
2432

m0715

2681

m0716

2076

[Are there signs following these two signs?]

m0717

1078

m0714

2446

m0718

2209

m0719

2137

m0720

1082

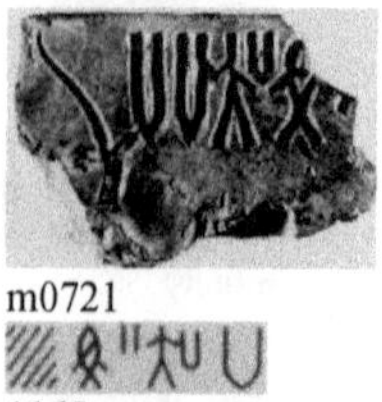
m0721

1165

m0722

1014

m0723

2054

m0724

m0725

m0726

m0727a

m0727A1

m0727A2

2168

m0728

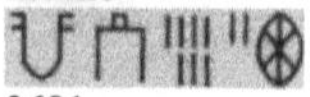
2691

m0729

1177

m0730

m0732

2674

m0733
2519

m0734
1539

m0735
1060

m0736
2562

m0737
1112

m0738
2644

m0739

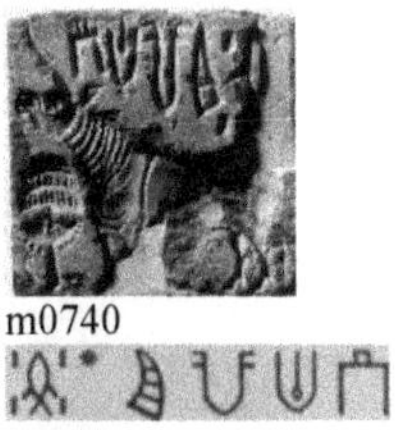
m0740
1090

m0741
2421

m0742
2595

m0743

m0744

m0745
1175

m0746

1081

m0747
2471

m0748
1135

m0749
2008

m0750
2065

m0751
1102

m0752a

m0753a

m0753A1

m0753A2
2589

m0754
1145

m0755

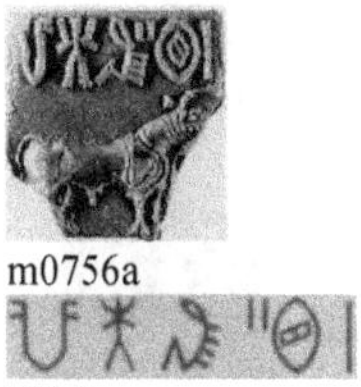
m0756a
1028

m0757
2507

m0758a
2184

m0759 One-horned bull.

2384

m0760

m0761 One-horned bull.

1417

m0762a

2645

m0763

m0764

m0765

m0766

m0767

m0768

1176

m0769

2034

m0770a

1138

m0771

2676

m0772

2453

m0773

m0774

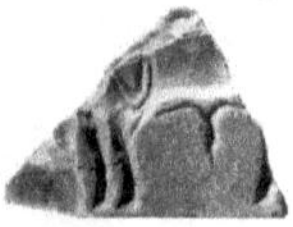
m0775

m0776

1146

m0777

2536

m0778

2425

m0779

2622

m0780

1178

m0781

2251

m0782

1122

m0783

1127

m0784

1128

m0785

1181

m0786

1107

m0787

2503

m0788

m0789

1185

m0790

m0791

m0792

2013

m0793

m0794

2067

m0795

1228

m0796

2105

m0797

m0798

1084

m0799 3015 or 3147

m0800

m0801

2104

m0802

1182

m0803

1131

m0804

2570

m0805

3041

m0806

m0807

2669

m0808

2146

m0809

2548

m0810

2364

m0811

2211

m0812

2629

m0813

m0814

2426

m0815
2555

m0816
2424

m0817
2435

m0818
1089

m0819
2081

m0820

m0821
1238

m0822
1249

m0823
1086

m0824
1164

m0825
1239

m0826

m0827

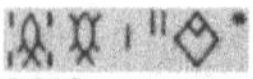
2513

m0828
2114

m0829

m0830
2274

m0831
2546
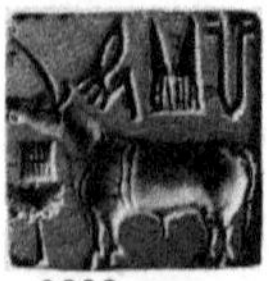
m0832

m0833
2281

m0834
2569b

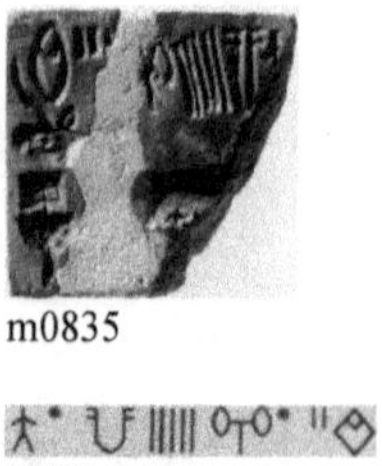
m0835
2179

m0836

m0837
3085

m0838
2368

m0839
2476

m0840
2617

m0841

m0842

2704

m0843

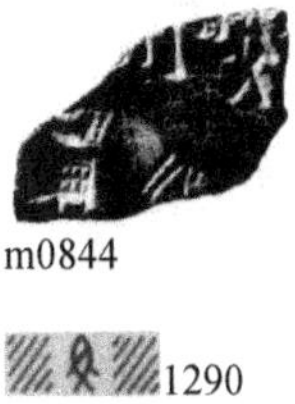

m0844

1290

m0845

2202

m0846

1005

m0847

1156

m0848

2241

m0849

1121

m0850

2533

m0851

2660

99933333m0852a

2413

m0853

2255

m0854

2501

m0855

2473

m0856

1211

m0857

2091

m0858a

2189

m0859

2063

m0860

m0861

1123

m0862

2253

m0863

2621 Is the 'stubble' ligatured glyph a variant of

Sign 162  ?]

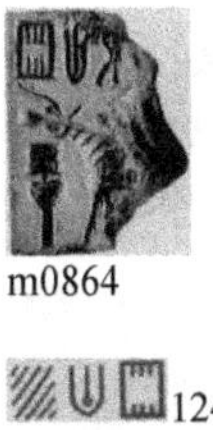

m0864

1240

m0865

1109

m0866

2646

m0867

m0868

3160

m0869

m0870

1160

m0871

m0872

m0873

1170

m0874
3092

m0875
1189

m0876

m0877

m0878

1092

m0879

2121

m0880

m0881
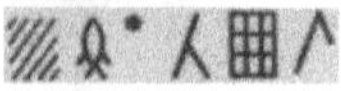
1242

m0882

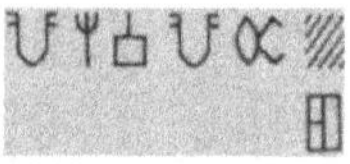
2312

m0883

m0884

3158

m0885

m0886
3072

m0887a

1169

m0888

1155

m0889

1126

m0890
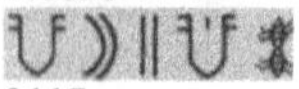
2117

m0891

1073

m0892
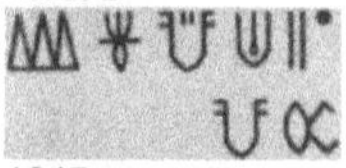
1247

m0893

2659
One-horned bull.

m0894

2393

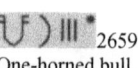

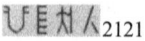

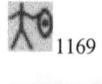

m0895

2262

m0896

2134

m0897

2545

m0898 
2167

m0899

 2242

m0900

2335

m0901

2276

m0902a

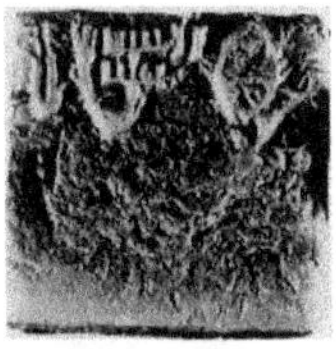
m0903a.

1294

m0904

m0905

m0906

m0907

2192

m0908

m0909

3028

m0910

m0911

m0914

2143

m0915

 1218

m0916

 1204

m0917
1224

m0918

m0919

2343

m0920

1219

m0921

m0922
1282

m0923

m0924
2591

m0925

1292

m0926

2219

m0927

1171

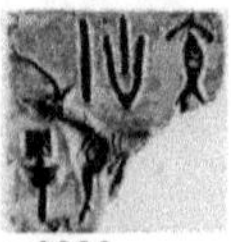
m0928

1202

m0929a

1144

m0930

3020

m0931

3091

m0932

3022

m0933

2160

m0934

1158

m0935

2144

m0936

1197

m0937

2066

m0938

2158

m0939a

2652

m0940a

2060

m0941

2256

m0942

1296

m0943

2282

m0944

2419

m0945

1208

m0946

2358

m0947

2404

m0948

2250

m0949A

m0949C

1271

Also, Sign 141

m0950a

1013

m0951

1263

m0952

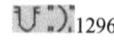

2265

m0953
2582

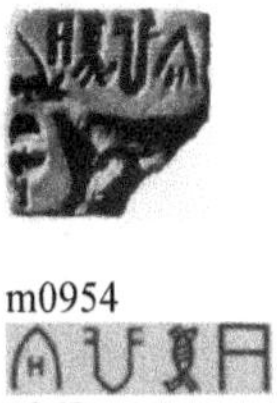
m0954
1262

m0955
2547

m0956
1251

m0957
1026

m0958
2348

m0959
1147

m0960
1388

m0961
1163

m0962
3074

m0963
1232

m0964
2010

m0965
1222

m0966
2070

m0967
2460

m0968
2300

m0969
2239

m0970a
2116

m0971
1234

m0972a
2557

m0973a
2585

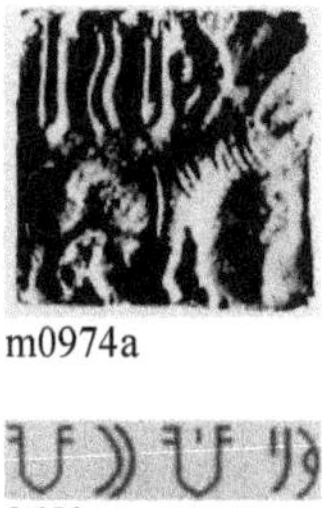
m0974a
2650

m0975
2295

m0976
1203

m0977
3152

m0978

m0979
2564

m0980
2317

m0981

m0982a

2021

m0983

m0984
1143

m0985

m0986a
2341

m0987a

1007

m0988

m0989

m0990

2472
One-horned bull.

m0991
2203

m0992

2464

m0993a

1267

m0994a
2165

m0995

m0996

2299
One-horned bull.

m0997a
3105

m0998

2176

m0999

2452

m1000a

1487 One-horned bull.

m1001a
1283

m1002

m1003
1275

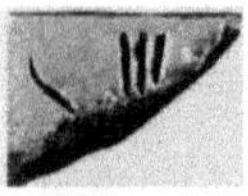
m1004

m1005
1001

m1006

1499
Bovid.

m1007

m1008

m1009
2627

m1010
2672 Bovid.

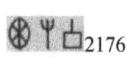

m1011

m1012

m1013

m1014 One-horned bull?

1397

m1015

m1016.

1348

m1017.

1300

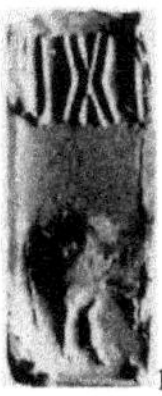
m1018a

2483 Bovid.

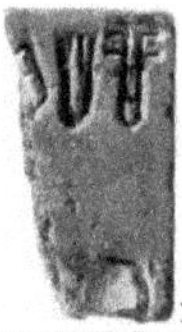
m1019.

1298

m1020

2496

m1021a.

1299

m1022

m1023

m1024

m1025a

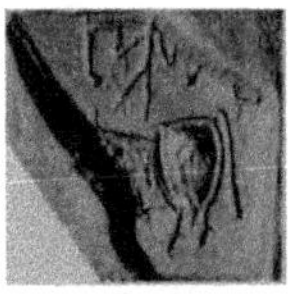
m1026a.

1307

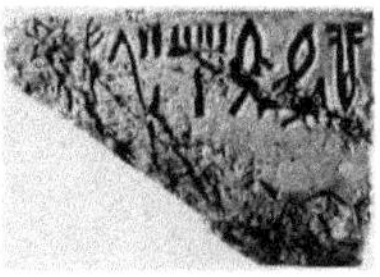
m1027

m1028

2671 Bovid.

m1029

1265

m1030

3145

m1031

2053

m1032

2217

m1033

m1034

2467

m1036

m1037

m1038

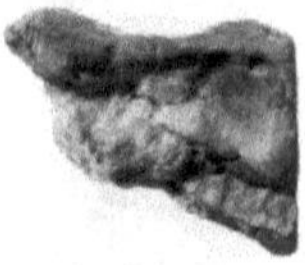
m1039

m1040

m1041

m1042

m1043

m1044a
1551
Bovid.

m1045
2447 Bovid.

m1046

3058

m1047
1281

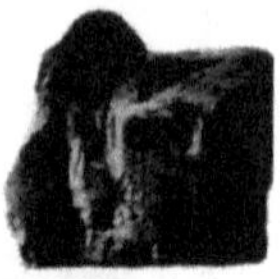
m1048

m1049
3032

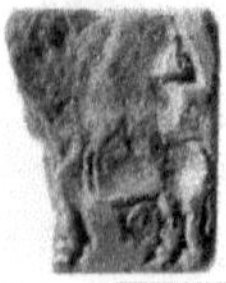
m1050

1196

m1051

m1052
3100

m1053
2163

m1054

2448

m1055
2529

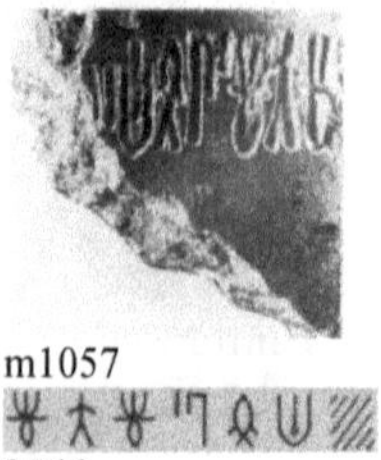
m1057
2566

m1058a

1392

m1059

m1060

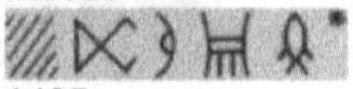
1497

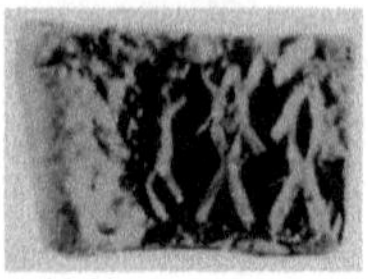
m1061a

1379

m1062
2089

m1063

2357

m1064

1492

m1065

2151

m1066

1547

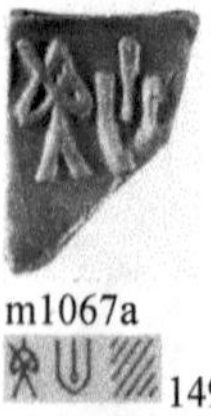
m1067a
1496

m1068

m1069

1390

m1070

2040

m1071

1488

m1072a

1443

m1073

1489

m1074

m1075a

1479

m1076

m1077a

2359

m1078

m1079

2655

m1080

1542

m1081a

2129

m1082.

1349

m1083

m1084 1316

Bison.

m1085.

1322

m1086a

3070

m1087a.

1319

m1088

2268

m1089a.

1315

m1090

2675

m1091

m1092

1312

m1093

m1094

m1095

2495 Bison

m1096

2410

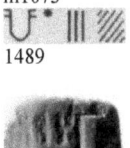

m1097

2313

m1098

1301

m1099

1313

m1100

2201
Bison

m1101

2431
Zebu.

m1102

m1103.

1337

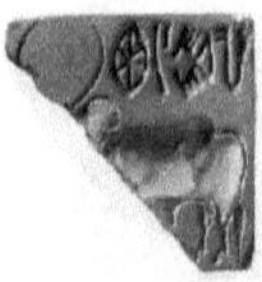
m1104

1335

m1105

m1106

2331
Zebu

m1107a

2306

m1108

1339

m1109

1327 Zebu

m1110

1334

m1111.

1333

m1112

2366
Zebu.

m1113

2441

m1114.

1331

m1115

1328 Zebu

m1116.

1329

m1117a

2615

m1118

3157

m1119

2463

m1120

2362

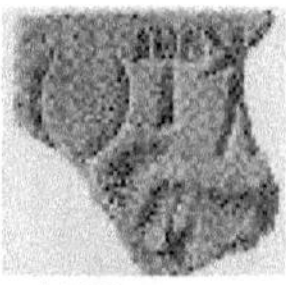
m1122

2610

m1126

2332

m1127

2696

m1128a

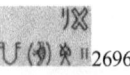

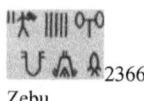

3163

m1129a .

1302 Markhor.

m1130

m1131

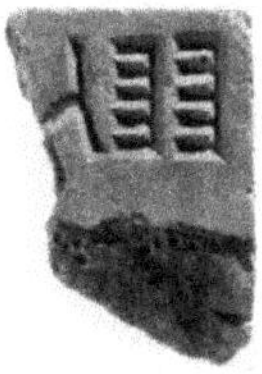

m1132

1545

Rhinoceros.

m1133

1343

m1134

2651

m1135

2140 Pict-50

Composite

animal: features of an ox and a rhinoceros facing the standard device.

m1136

m1137

2531

Rhinoceros.

m1138.

1344

m1139.

1341

m1140a

2188 Rhinoceros.

m1141

2169

m1142

m1143

m1144

m1145

m146a

1374 Elephant

m1147

m1148

2590

m1149

1368 Elephant.

m1150

1534

m1151

1535

m1152

1369

m1154

1362 Elephant.

m1155

2573

m1156

1370

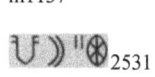

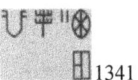

m1157a

2110

m158

m1159

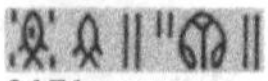
2171

m1160

2057

m1161

2504

m1162

2058

m1163

2640

Tiger.

m1164

2665 Tiger.

m1165a

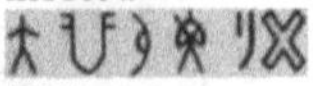
2064

m1166.

1351

m1167

2484 Tiger.

m1168

2360

Seal showing a horned tiger. Mohenjodaro. (After Scala/Art Resource).

Tiger with long (zebu's) horns?

1385

Pict-49 Uncertain animal with dotted circles on its body.

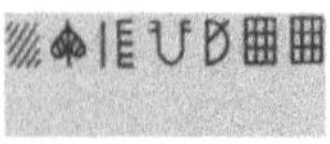
1626

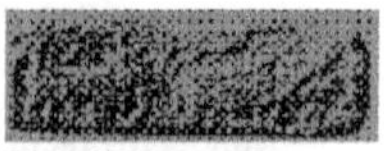
Pict-47 Row of uncertain animals in file.

m1169a

2024

Pict-58: Composite motif: body of an ox and three heads: of a one-horned bull (looking forward), of antelope (looking backward), and of short-horned bull (bison) (looking downward).

m1170a

1382 Composite animal

m1171 Composite animal

m1172

m1173

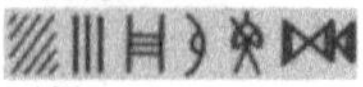
1191

m1175a

2493 Composite animal: human face, zebu's horns, elephant tusks and trunk, ram's forepart, unicorn's trunk and feet, tiger's hindpart and serpent-like tail.

m1176

m1177

2450 Composite animal: human face, zebu's horns, elephant tusks and trunk, ram's forepart, unicorn's trunk and feet, tiger's hindpart and serpent-like tail.

m1178

2559

m1179

2606

Human-faced markhor with long wavy horns, with

neck-bands and a short tail.

m1180a .

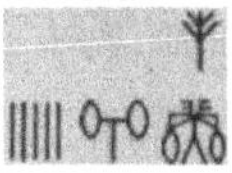
1303

Human-faced markhor

m1181A

2222 Pict-80: Three-faced, horned person (with a three-leaved pipal branch on the crown), wearing bangles and armlets and seated on a hoofed platform

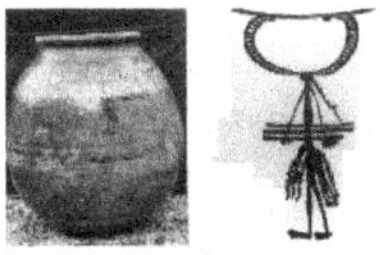
Padri . Head painted on storage jar from Padri, Gujarat (c. 2800 BCE). Details of body with multiple hands (?) Similar horned-heads painted on jars are found at Kot Diji, Burzhom and Kunal (c. 3rd millennium BCE), [Source: Page 21, Figs. 10A and B in: Deo Prakash Sharma, 2000, *Harappan seals, sealings and copper tablets*, Delhi, National Museum].

m1182a

m1183a

m1184

m1185

Pict-103 Horned (female with breasts hanging down?) person with a tail and bovine legs standing near a tree fisting a horned tiger rearing on its hindlegs.

1357

m1186A

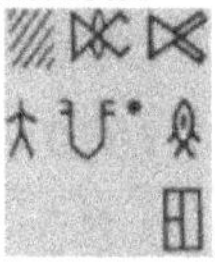
2430

Composition: horned person with a pigtail standing between the branches of a pipal tree; a low pedestal with offerings (? or human head?); a horned person kneeling in adoration; a ram with short tail and curling horns; a row of seven robed figures, with twigs on their pigtails.

m1187

m1188

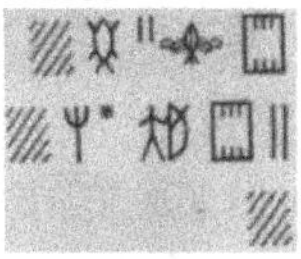
2228

m1189

1396

m1190

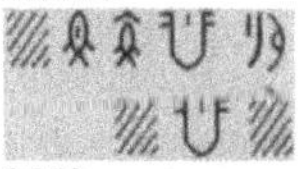
2558

m1191

1389

m1192

1495

m1193a

2401

m1194a

3066

m1195

2181

m1196

m1197

m1198

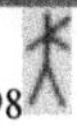
1482

Silver m1199A

2520

m1200A

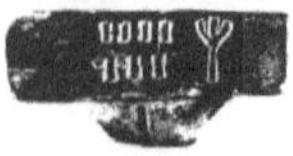

m1200C

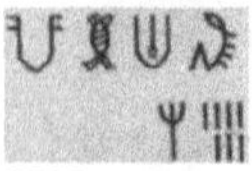

3078

m1201

m1202A

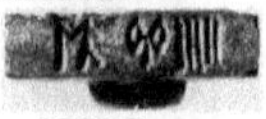

m1202C.

1325 Space on the side of the seal was used to inscribe a third line

m1203A

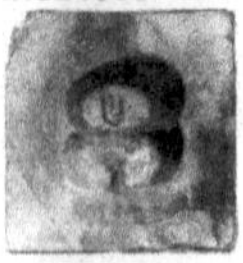

m1203B

1018

m1204

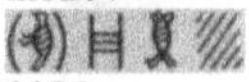

2095

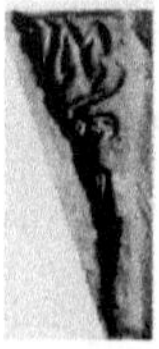

m1205a

m1205c

m1205f

1293 + Two signs on the sides of the seal.

m1206AE

m1206e1

m1206F

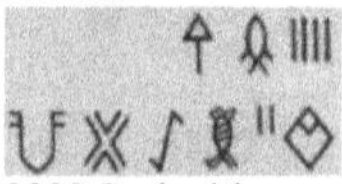

2229 Seal with a projecting knob containing the top three signs; m1206e is inscribed on the top edge of the lower indented frame which depicts the bison.

m1208

m1221

m1222

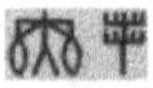

1268

m1223

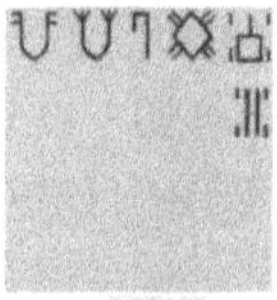

2045 Pict-40: Frog.

2565

Pict-37 Goat-antelope with a short tail

m1224A

m1224B

1224

m1224e

Pict-88

1227 Standing person with horns and bovine features (hoofed legs and/or tail).

m1225A

m1225B.

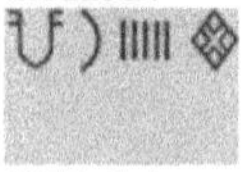

1311 Cube seal with perforation through the breadth of the seal Pict-118: svastika_, generally within a square or rectangular border.

m1226A.

1326 Unfinished seal.

m1227

m1228a

1394

m1230a

1358

m1231

2321
Unfinished seal?

m1232a

2497
Unfinished seal

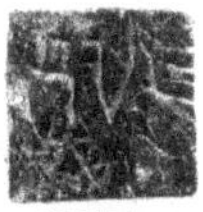
m1233A

m1233B

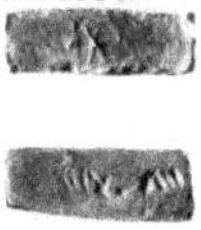
m1233cd

2352

m1234a

m1234b

m1234d

m1234e

m1235a

m1235bc

2394
Unfinished seal

m1236

1483
Unfinished seal?

m1239

m1240

m1241

m1242

m1243

m1244

m1245

m1246

m1247

m1248

m1249

m1250

m1251

m1252

m1253

m1254

m1255

m1256

m1257

m1258

m1259

m1260

m1261

m1262

2301

m1263

1391

m1264a

1405

m1265

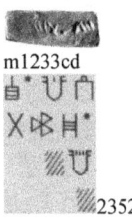

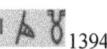

2227

m1266

1470

m1267

1494

m1268

2288

m1269

m1270

1464

m1271

2603

m1272

m1273

2679

m1274

2106

m1275

3161

m1276

2428

m1277

m1278

2028

m1280a

1462

m1281

2266

m1282

m1283

m1284a

2477

m1285a

2204

m1286

1455

m1287

1454

m1288

3086

m1289

1452

m1290

1463

m1291a

2688

m1292

1461

m1293a

2388

m1294

2291

m1295

1458

m1296a

3144

m1297

1445

m1298

3037

m1299a

1456

m1300

2350

m1301

m1302a

1432

m1303a

1398

m1304

1423

m1305

2289

m1306

1430

m1307

m1308

2697

m1309

2579

m1310

1418

m1311

2485

m1312

2318

m1313

2093

m1314a

1439

m1315

2345

m1316a

m1317

3095

m1318

1416

m1319

m1320

1447

m1321

1446

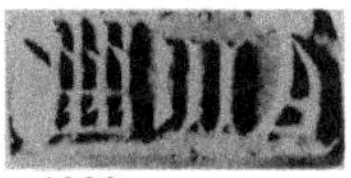

m1322a

3079

m1323

2006

m1324

2682

m1325

2118

m1326

3143

m1327

1408

m1328

2392

m1329A

m1329C

2439

m1330

1409

m1331a

2303

m1332

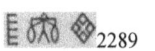

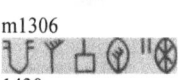

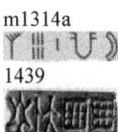

m1333

1434

m1334a

2170

m1335a

2072

m1336a

2515

m1337

2055

m1338a

2020

m1339

2025

m1340

2369

m1341

2092

m1342a

1393

m1343

1433

m1344

2315

m1346a

m1349B

m1349A

m1350

2599

m1351

2142

m1353

1459

m1354a

1498

m1355a

2568

m1356

m1357

2356

m1358

m1359

2575

m1360

1442

m1361a

1474

m1362A

m1362C

2230

m1363

2372

m1364A

m1364C

2542

m1365A

m1365B

2658 Cricket, spider or prawn?

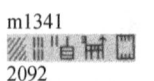

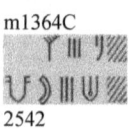

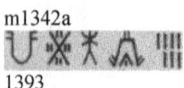

m1366

2094

m1367a 
2661 Two bisons standing face-to-face

m1368

1460

m1369

1478

m1370a

2509
Cylinder seal; tree branch

m1371A1

m1371A2

m1372A1

m1372A2

m1373A1

m1373A2

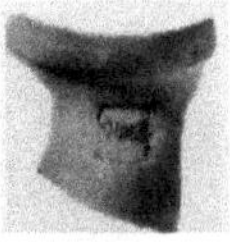

m1374A1

m1374A2

m1375A1

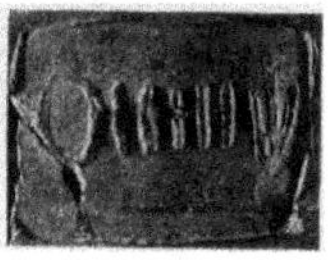

m1375A2

1560
Seal impression on pot

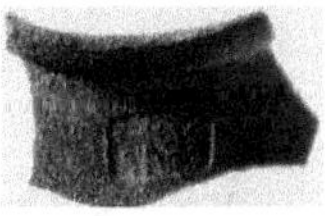

m1376A1

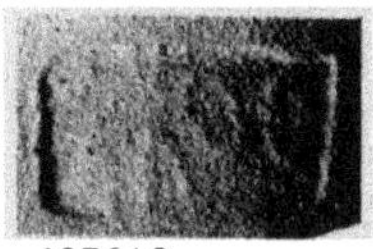

m1376A2

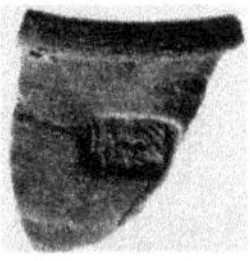

m1378A1

m1378A2

m1379A2

m1380A2

m1381A1

m1381A2

1559
Seal Impression on a pot

m1382A1

m1382A2 Seal impression on a potsherd

3244

m1383

m1384si

m1385A14

m1385A2

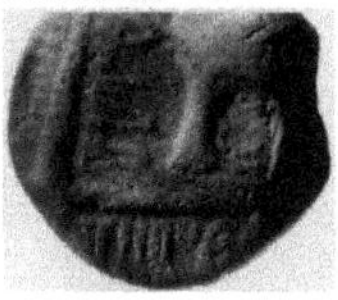

m1385A3

m1386si

m1387t

m1388t

2856

m1389t

m1390At

m1390Bt

2868
Pict-74: Bird in flight.

m1391t

2826

m1392t

2837

m1393t

m1394t

m1395At

m1395Bt

m1396t

m1397At

m1397Bt

m1398t

2807

m1400At

m1400B

2851

m1401t

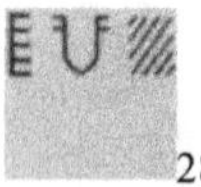

2822

m1402At

m1402Bt

m1403At

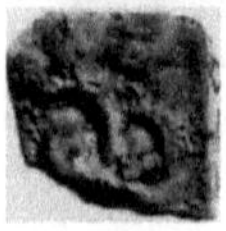

m1403Bt

m1405At Pict-97: Person standing at the center pointing with his right hand at a bison facing a trough, and with his left hand pointing to the

sign
Obverse: A tiger and a rhinoceros in file.

m1405Bt Pict-48 A tiger and a rhinoceros in file

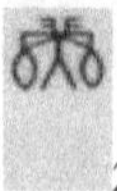

2841

m1406At

m1406B

2827 Pict-102: Drummer and people vaulting over? An adorant?

m1407At

m1407Bt

m1408At

m1409At

m1409Bt Serpent (?) entwined around a pillar with capital (?) or ring-stones stacked on a pillar?; the motif is carved in high relief on the reverse side of the inscribed object.

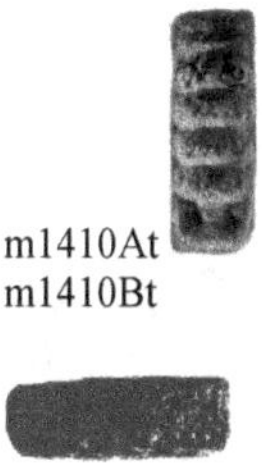

m1410At
m1410Bt

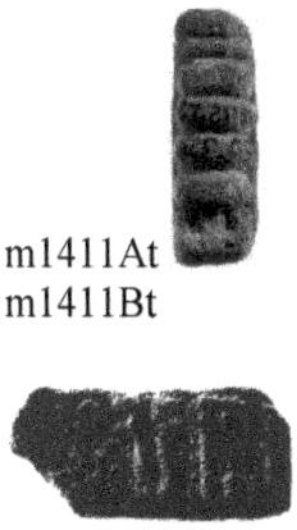

m1411At
m1411Bt

m1412At

m1412Bt

m1413At

m1413Bt

m1414At

m1414Bt

m1415At

m1415Bt

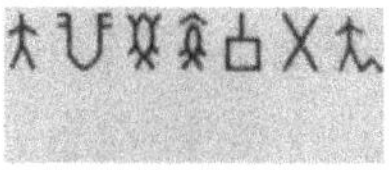

2825

m1416At

m1416Bt

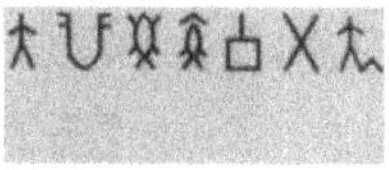

2818

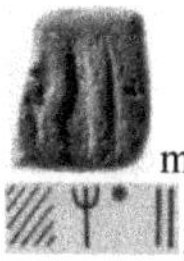

m1417t

3242

m1418At

m1418Bt

m1419At

m1419Bt

2812

m1420At

2865

m1421At

m1421Bt

m1422At

2845

m1423At

m1423Bt
Elephant shown on both sides of the tablet.

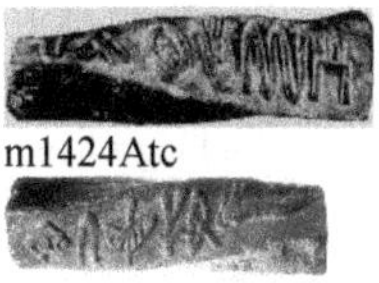

m1424Atc

m1424Btc

3234

m1425At

m1425Bt

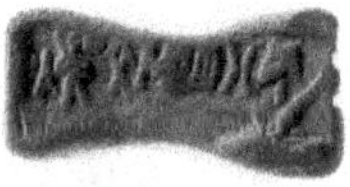

m1427At

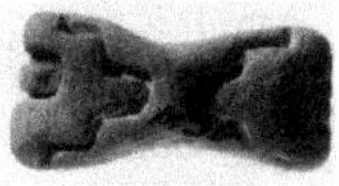

m1427Bt

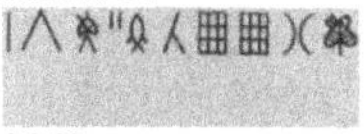

2860

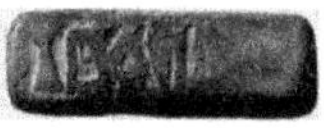

m1428At

m1428Bt

m1428Ct

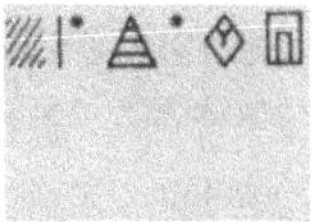

2842

m1426

1621

m1429At

m1429Bt Pict-125: Boat.

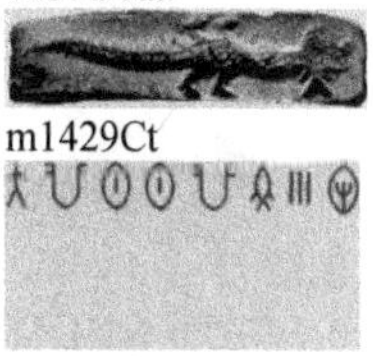

m1429Ct

3246 Gharial holding a fish in its jaws.

Pict-100

Person throwing a spear at a buffalo and placing one foot on the head of the buffalo.

2279

m1430Bt

m1430C

m1430At Pict-101: Person throwing a spear at a buffalo and placing one foot on its head; three persons standing near a tree at the center.

2819

Pict-60: Composite animal with the body of an ox and three heads [one each of one-horned bull (looking forward), antelope (looking backward) and bison (looking downwards)] at right; a goat standing on its hindlegs and browsing from a tree at the center.

m1431A

m1431B

m1431C

m1431E

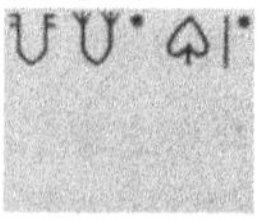
2805 Row of animals in file (a one-horned bull, an elephant and a rhinoceros from right); a gharial with a fish held in its jaw above the animals; a bird (?) at right. Pict-116: From R.—a person holding a vessel; a woman with a platter (?); a kneeling person with a staff in his hands facing the woman; a goat with its forelegs on a platform under a tree. [Or, two antelopes flanking a tree on a platform, with one antelope looking backwards?]

m1432At

m1432Bt

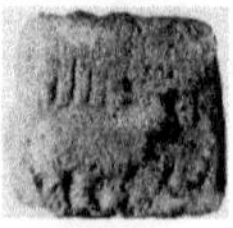
m1432Ct

m1433At

m1433Bt

m1433Ct

m1436it

m1438it

m1439it

3132

m1440 it

2374

m1441it

m1442it

m1443it

3213

m1444Ait

m1444Bit

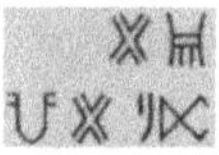
2339

m1445Ait

m1445Bit

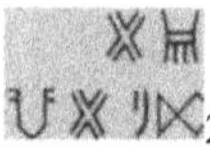
2505

m1447Ait

m1448Act

m1448Bct

m1449Act

m1449Bct (obverse of inscription) Incised copper tablet (two sides) Markhor with head turned backwards

1801

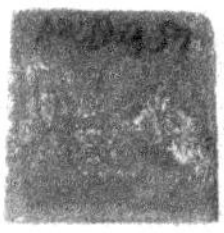

m1450Act

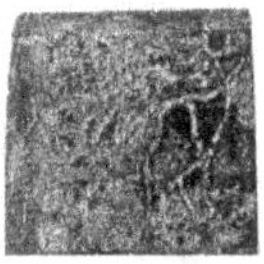

m1450Bct

1701

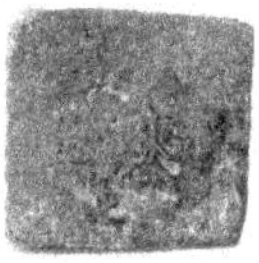

m1451Act

m1451Bct

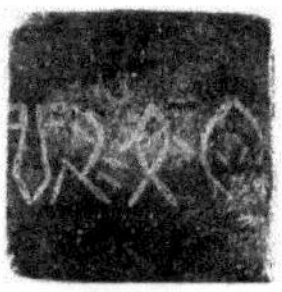

m1452Act

m1452Bct

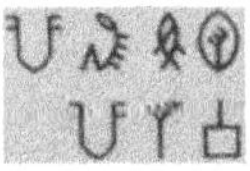

2912

m1453Act

m1453Bct

m1456Act

1805

m1457Act

m1457Bct

2904 Pict-124: Endless knot motif.

m1458Act

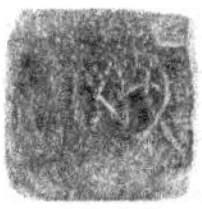

m1461Act

m1462Act

m1463ABct

2919

m1465Act

2921

m1470Act

m1472Bct

m1474Act

m1474Bct

m1475Act

m1475Bct

m1476Bct

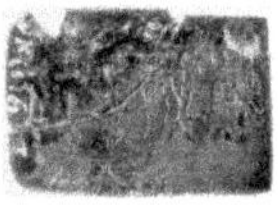

m1477Act

m1477Bct

m1482Act

m1482Bct

m1483Act

m1483Bct

m1484Act

m1484Bct

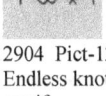

m1485Bct

m1486Act

m1486Bct

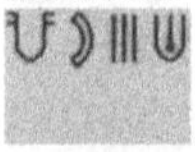

1711

Incised copper tablets.Elephant

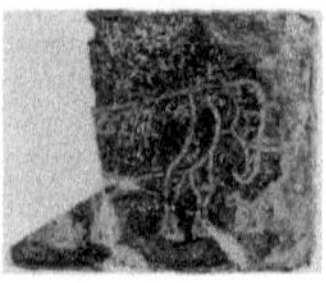

m1488Bct

m1491Act

m1491Bct

m1492Act

m1492Bct

m1493Bct

m1494

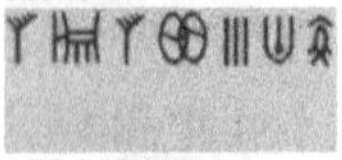

1706 Hare

Pict-42

m1497Act

m1498Act

m1498Bct

2917

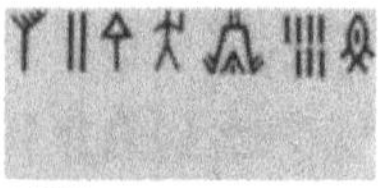

1803

Pict-30

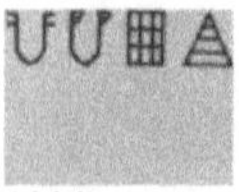

1804

Pict-39 Ox-antelope with a long tail; a trough in front.

m1501Bct

m1502Bct

m1503Act

m1503Bct

m1505Act

m1505Bct

m1506Act

m1506Bct

m1508Act

m1508Bct

1708

m1511Act

m1511Bct

m1512Act

m1512Bct

m1513

1712

m1514

1715

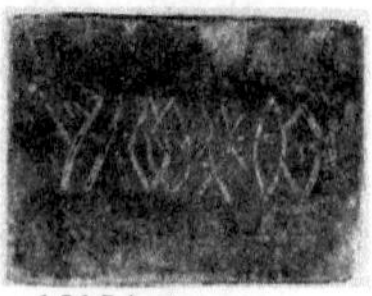

m1515Act

m1515Bct

2910

m1516Act

m1516Bct

m1517Act

m1517Bct

m1518

1709

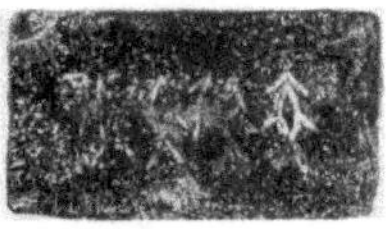
m1520Act

m1520Bct

2907

m1521Act

m1521Bct

m1522Act

m1522Bct

m1523Act

m1523Bct

m1524

3396

m1528Act

m1529Act
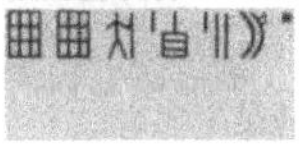
2920

m1529Bct

m1532Act

m1532Bct

m1534Act

m1534Bct

1703
Composition:

Two horned heads one at either end of the body. Note the dottings on the thighs which is a unique artistic feature of depicting a rhinoceros (the legs are like those of a rhinoceros?). The body apparently is a combination of two rhinoceroses with heads of two bulls attached on either end of the composite body.

m1535Act

m1535Bct

m1540Act
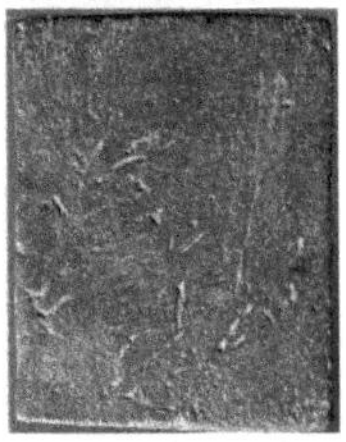
m1540

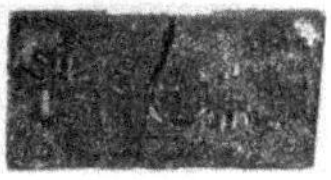
m1547Act

1547Bct

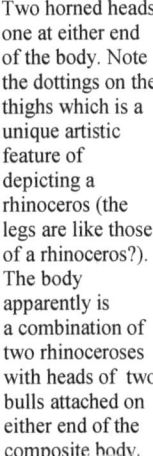

m1548A

m1548Bct

m1549Act

m1549Bct

m1563Act

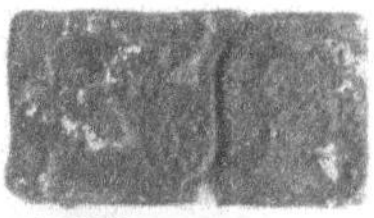
m1563Bct

m1566Bct

m1568Act

m1568Bct

m1569
3333

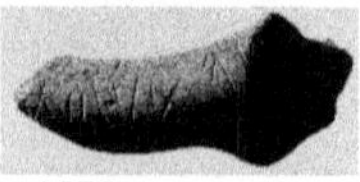
m1575

m1576

m1578
3251

m1591

1592

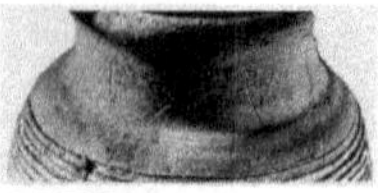
m1597

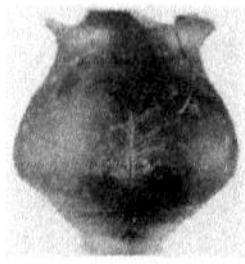
m1598

m1601

3252

m1603

m1609

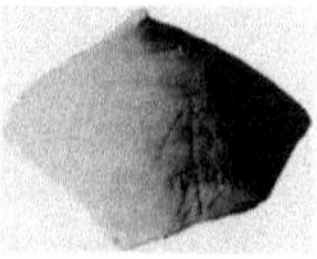
m1611

m1626
3245

m1629bangle

m1630bangle

m1631bangle

m1632bangle

m1633bangle

m1634bangle

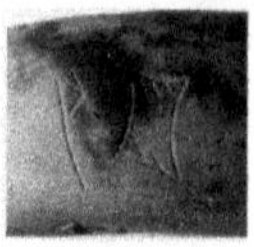
m1635bangle

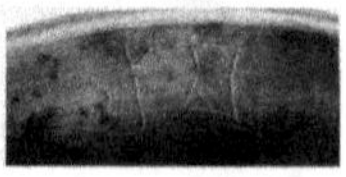
m1636bangle

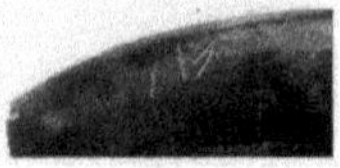
m1637bangle

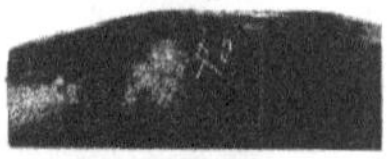
m1638bangle

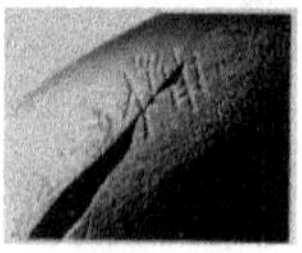
m1639bangle

m1640bangle

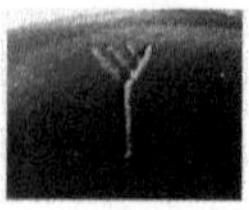
m1641bangle

m1643bangle

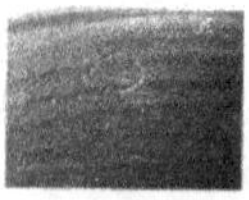
m1645bangle

m1646bangle

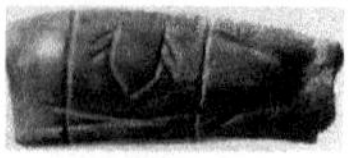
m1647bangle

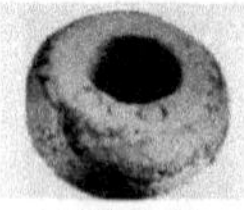
m1648shell

m1649Acone

m1649Bcone
3253

m1650ivory stick
3505

Pict-144: Geometrical pattern.

Pict-141: Geometrical pattern.

2942

Pict-142: Geometrical pattern.

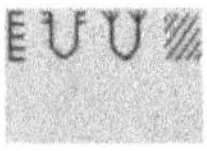

2943
Ivory or bone rod

Pict-143: Geometrical pattern.Ivory stick

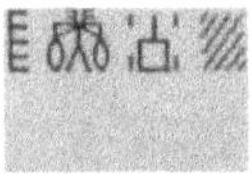

2948

Ivory rod, ivory plaque with dotted circles. Mohenjodaro. [Musee National De Arts Asiatiques Guimet, 1988-1989, *Les cites oubliees de l'Indus Archeologie du Pakistan*.]

m1652A ivory stick

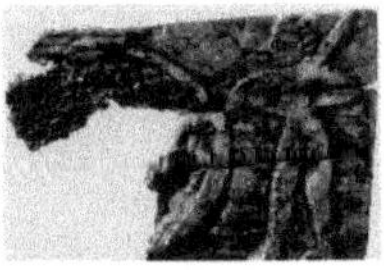

m1653 ivory plaque

1905

m1654A ivory cube

m1654B ivory cube

m1654D ivory cube

m1655faience ornament

m1656 steatite ornament

m1657A steatite

m1657B steatite

m1658AB etched bead

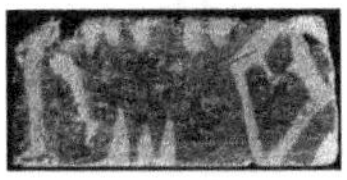

m1658

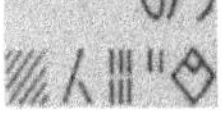

2952 Etched Bead

m1659 bangle

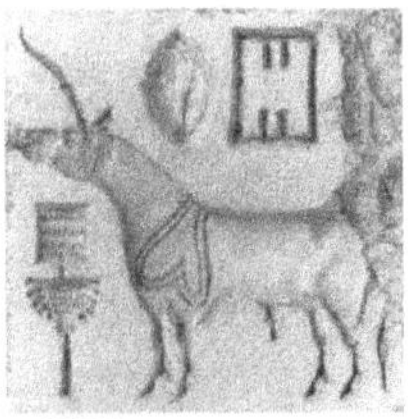

m1660

m1661a

m1662

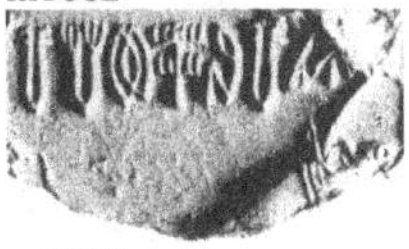

m1663a

m1664a

m1665a

m1666a

m1667

m1668a

m1669a

m1670a

m1671a

m1672

m1673a

m1674a

m1675a

m1676a

m1677a

m1678a

m1679a

m1680a

m1681a

m1682a

m1683a

m1684a

m1685a

m1686a

m1687a

m1688a

m1689a

m1690a

m1691a

m1692a

m1693a

m1694a

m1695a

m1696a

m1697

m1698

m1699a

m1700a

m1701a

m1702a

m1703a

m17054

m1705a

m1706a

m1707a

m1708a

m1709a

m1710a

m1711a

m1712a

m1713a

m1714a

m1715a

m1716a

m1717a

m1718

m1719a

m1720

m1721

m1722a

m1723a

m1724a

m1725a

m1726a

m1727

m1728a

m1729a

m1730a

m1731a

m1732

m1733a

m1734

m1735

m1736a

m1737a

m1738

m1739a

m1740

m1741a

m1742

m1743

m17441

m1745a

m1746

m1747a

m1748

m1749a

m1750a

m1751a

m1752a

m1753a

m1754a

m1755a

m1756a

m1757a

m1758a

m1759a

m1760

m1761a

m1762a

m1763a

m1764a

m1765

m1766a

m1767

m1768a

m1769a

m1770a

m1771a

m1772a

m1773

m1774a

m1775a

m1776

m1777a

m1778

m1779a

m1780a

m1781a

m1782

m1783a

m1784a

m1785a

m1786a

m1787a

m1788a

m1789a

m1790a

m1791a

m1792a

m1793a

m1794

m1795a

m1796a

m1797

m1798a

m1799

m1800

m1801a

m1802

m1803a

m1804a

m1805a

m1806a

m1807a

m1808a

m1809a

m1810a

m1811a

m1812a

m1813a

m1814

m1815a

m1816a

m1817a

m1818

m1819

m1820

m1821a

m1822a

m1823

m1824a

m1825a

m1826

m1827

m1828a

m1829a

m1830

m1831a

m1832a

m1833a

m1834a

m1835a

m1836

m1837a

m1838a

m1839a

m1840

m1841a

m1842a

m1843a

m1844

m1845a

m1846a

m1847a

m1848

m1849

m1850a

m1851

m1852

m1853a

m1854a

m1855a

m1856a

m1857

m1858

m1860a

m1863a

m1864

m1865a

m1866

m1868a

m1869
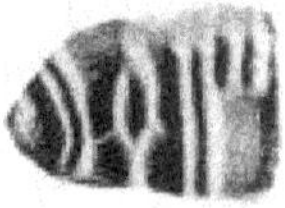
m1872a

m1876a

m1877

m1878a

m1879a

m1880a

m1881

m1882

m1883

m1884a

m1885a

m1886a

m1887

m1888a

m1889

m1890

m1891a

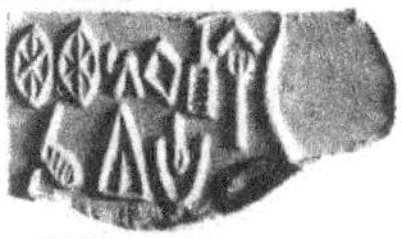
m1892a

m1893

m1894

m1895a

m1896a

m1897

m1898a

m1899a

m1900a

m1901

m1092a

m1903a

m1904a

m1905a

m1906

m1907a

m1909

m1910

m1911a

m1912

m1912

m1913

m1914

m1915a

m1916a

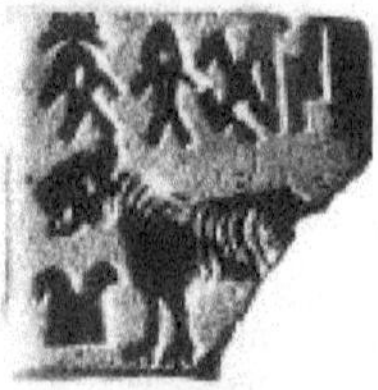
m1917

m1918a

m1919

m1920a

m1921a

m1922a

m1923a

m1923c

m1923d

m1923e

m1927a

m1927b

m1928a

m1928b

m1930A

m1930B

m1931

m1932

m1933

m1934a

m1935

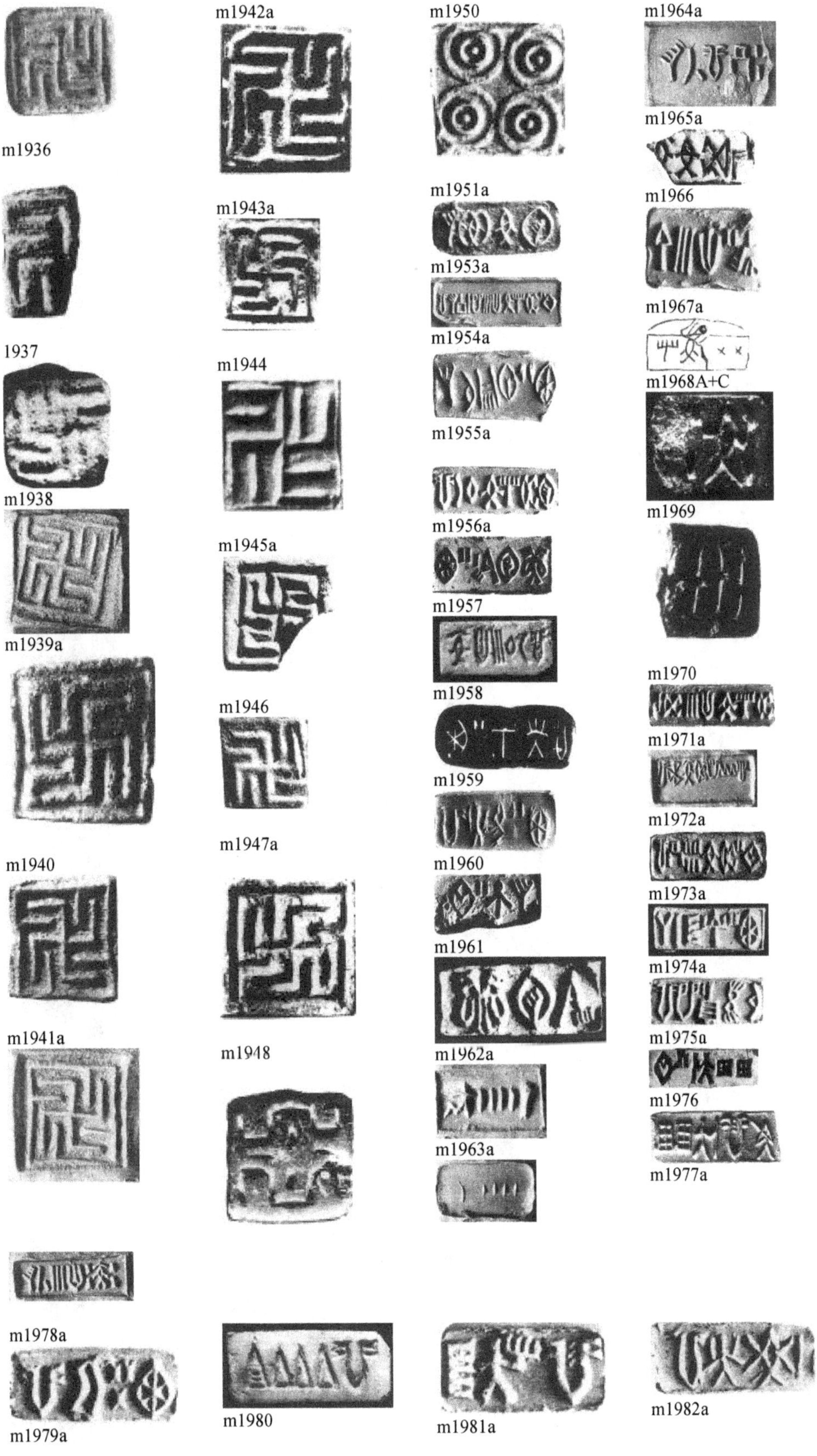

m1936
1937
m1938
m1939a
m1940
m1941a
m1942a
m1943a
m1944
m1945a
m1946
m1947a
m1948
m1950
m1951a
m1953a
m1954a
m1955a
m1956a
m1957
m1958
m1959
m1960
m1961
m1962a
m1963a
m1964a
m1965a
m1966
m1967a
m1968A+C
m1969
m1970
m1971a
m1972a
m1973a
m1974a
m1975a
m1976
m1977a
m1978a
m1979a
m1980
m1981a
m1982a

m1983a

m1984a

m1985a

m1986a

m1987a

m1988a

m1989a

m1989b

m1990a

m1990b

m1991a

m1992a

m1993a

m1994A
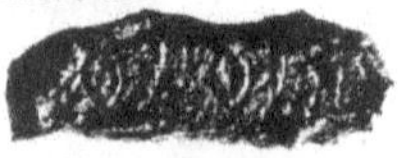
m1995A

m1996A
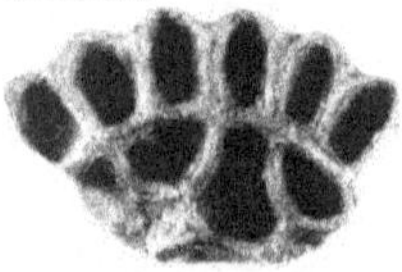
m1997A
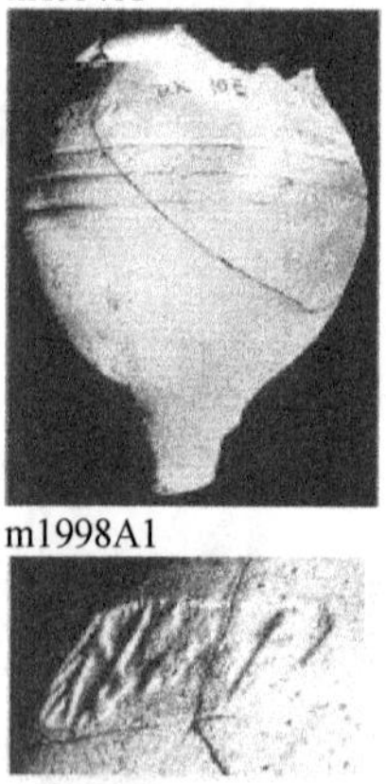
m1998A1
m1998A2
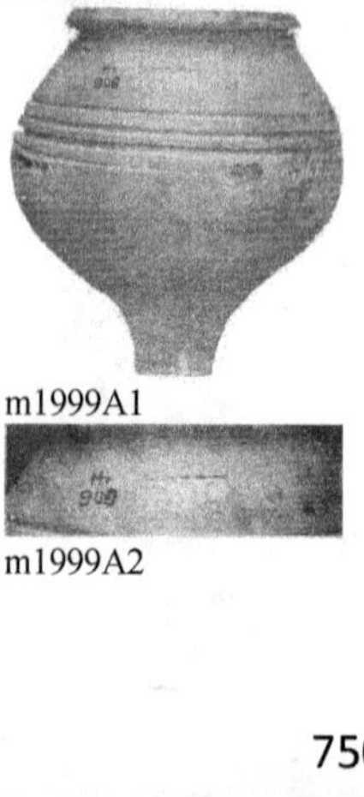
m1999A1
m1999A2
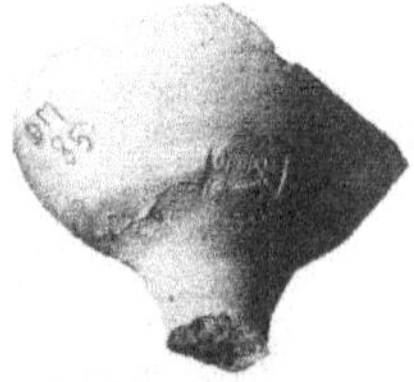
m2000A1

m2000A2
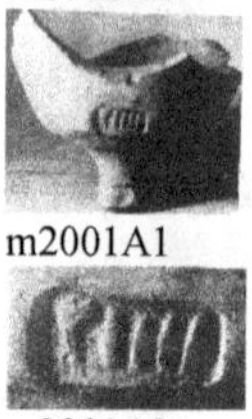
m2001A1
m2001A2

m2002

m2003

m2004

m2005

m2006
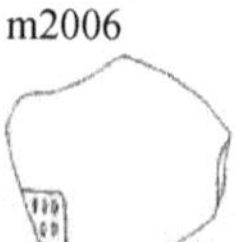
m2007

m2008

m2008B

m2009A

m2009B

m2010A
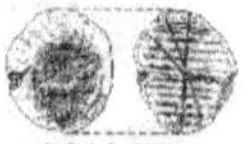
m2010AB
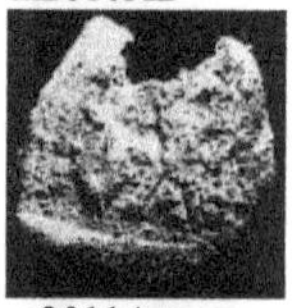
m2011A

m2012A

m2013B

m2014A

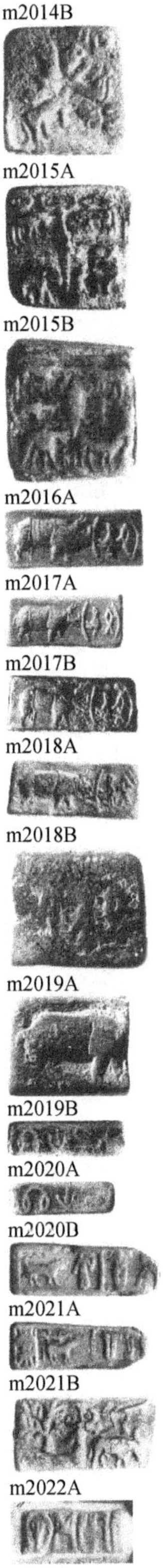

m2014B
m2015A
m2015B
m2016A
m2017A
m2017B
m2018A
m2018B
m2019A
m2019B
m2020A
m2020B
m2021A
m2021B
m2022A
m2024a

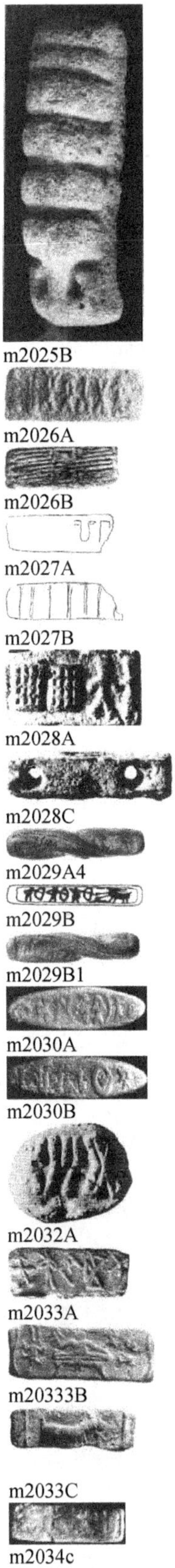

m2025B
m2026A
m2026B
m2027A
m2027B
m2028A
m2028C
m2029A4
m2029B
m2029B1
m2030A
m2030B
m2032A
m2033A
m20333B
m2033C
m2034c

m2035A
m2035B
m2035d
m2036A
m2036F
m2037A
m2038F
m2039a
m2039B
m2040a

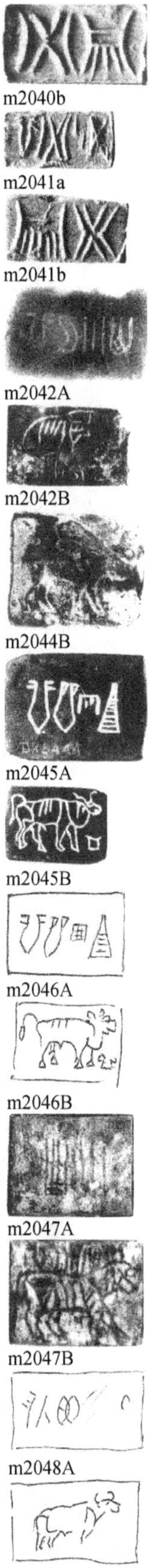

m2040b
m2041a
m2041b
m2042A
m2042B
m2044B
m2045A
m2045B
m2046A
m2046B
m2047A
m2047B
m2048A
m2048B

m2049A
m2049B

m2050A

m2050B

m2053A
m2053B

m2054A
m2054B

m2055A

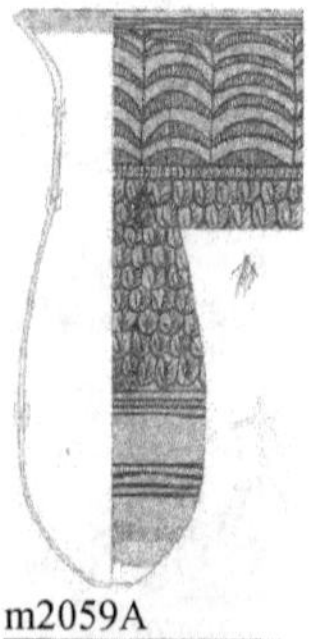
m2059A

m2060A

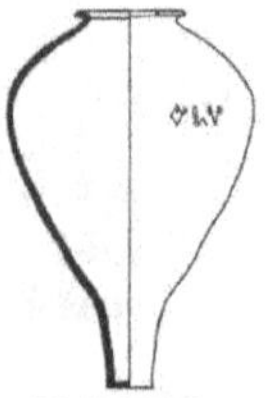
m2060A1+2

m2060b

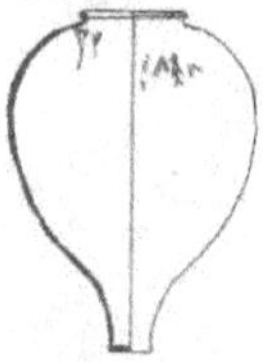
m2061A1+2

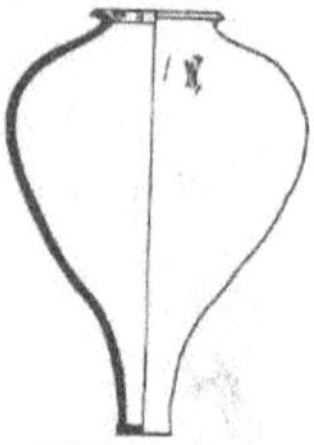
m2062A1+2

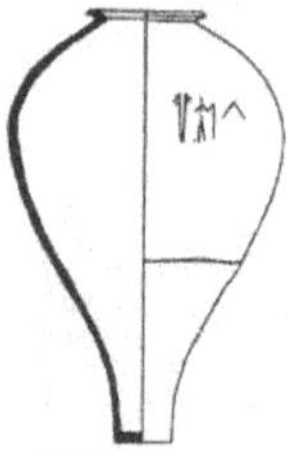
m2063

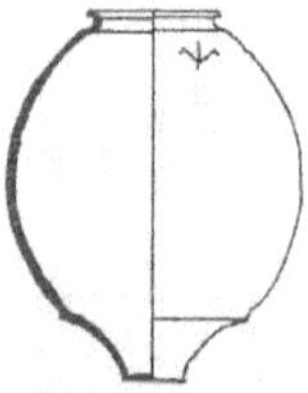
m2065

m2065

m2078

m2079
m2080

m2086

m2089A

m2089BC

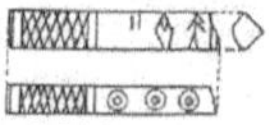
m2090

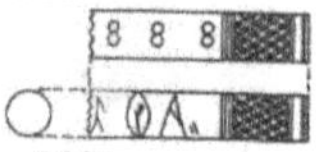
m2091

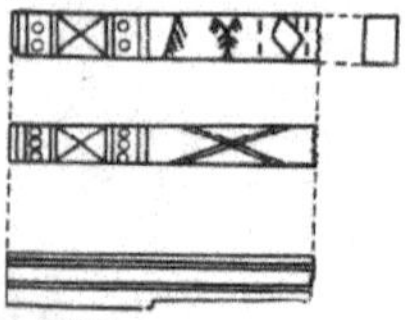
m2092

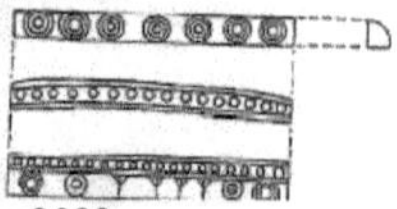
m2093

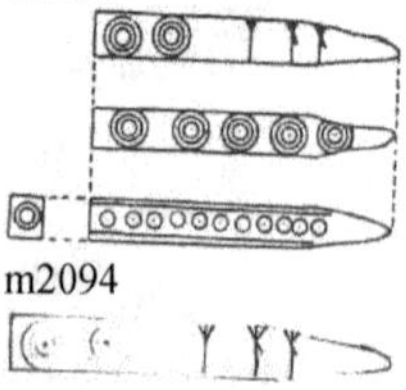
m2094
m2094A

m2095

m2096

m2097a

m2098a

m2099

m2102a

m2103a

m2104a
m2105

m2106D
m2107a

m2108a
m2109a

m2110
m2111

m2112a

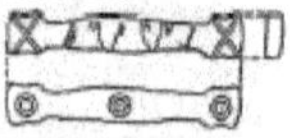
m2113ABD

m2114
m2115

m2116

m2118a

m2118B

m2121A

m2121B

m2123

m2124

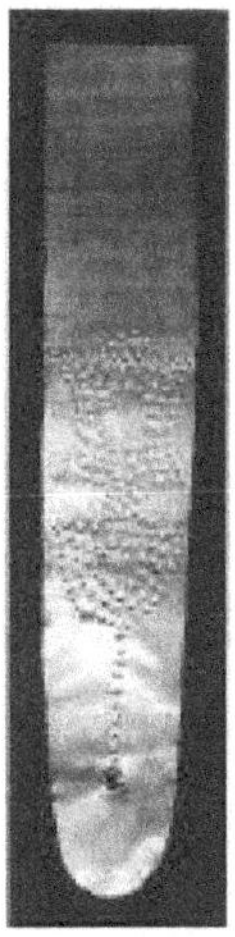

m2125

m2125A1

m2128A1

m2129A1

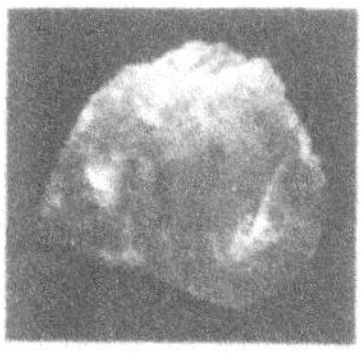

M-2131 A

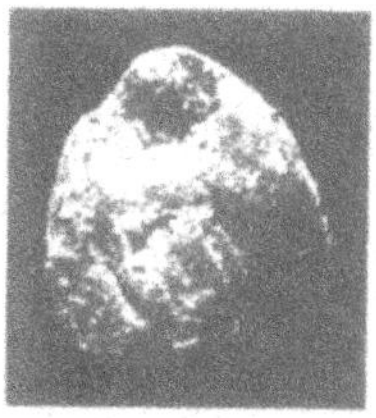

M-2131 B

Photograph from ASI: Sindh series Photo archive of ASI, Janpath, New Delhi. Si. 5:6639, 5:6640. Rattle? Bulla?

Mohenjodaro Texts either not illustrated or not linked with inscribed objects:

1002

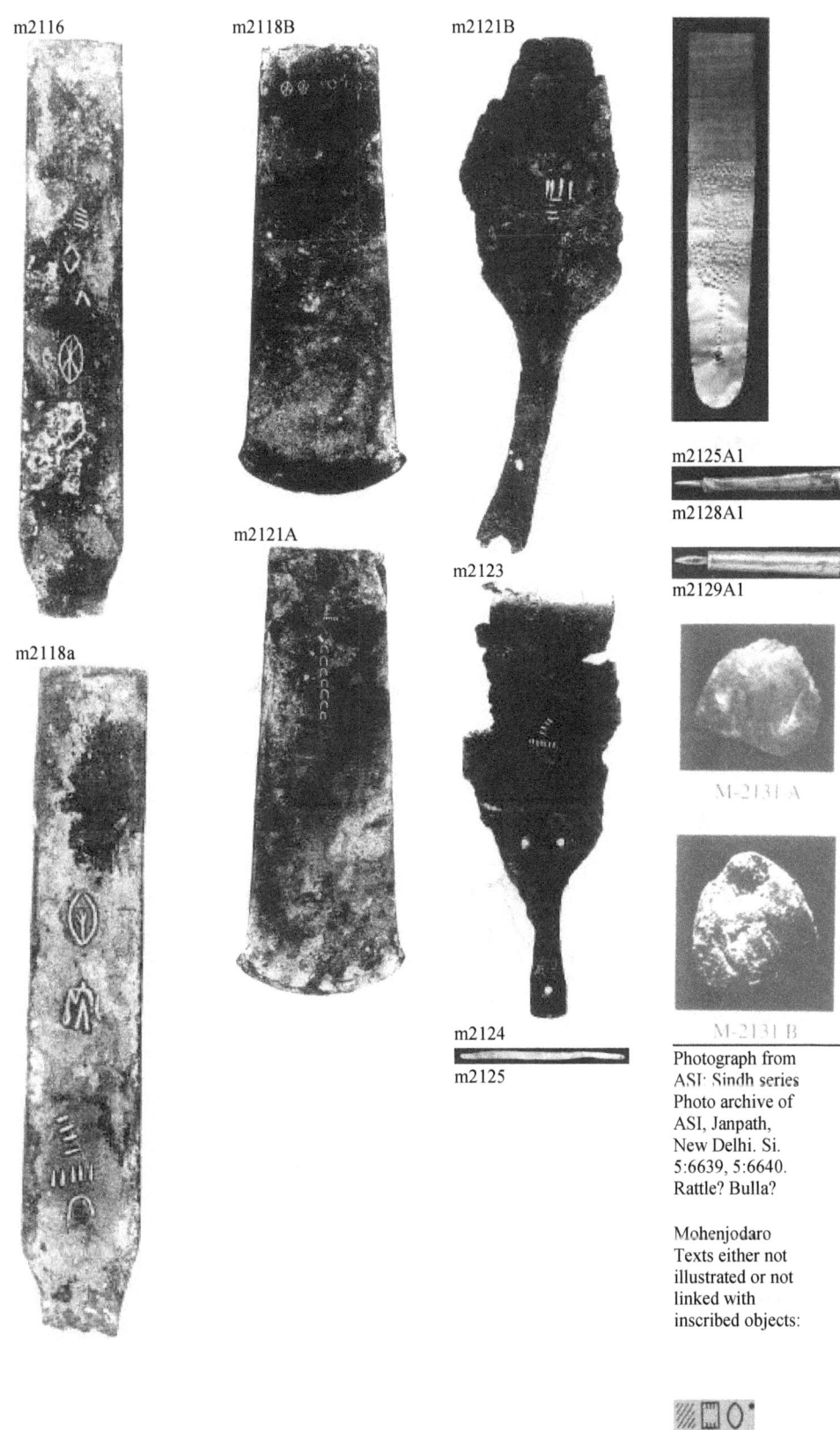

1003

1020

1036

1041

1043 1044

1045

1049

1053 1055

1065

1070

1072

1074

1077

1079

1083

1088

1094

1101

1103

1106

1116

1117

1125

1130

1429

m1651Aivory stick

m1651D

m1651F

2947

1132

1133

1134

1136

1137

1141

1142

1154

1157

1159

1162

1172

1173

1174

1179

1183

1190

1198

1199

1200

1201

1207

1209

1212

1213

1215

1217

1220

1225

1226

1229

1231

1235

1237

1243

1244

1246

1248

1253

1254

1255

1257

1260

1261

1266

1269

1270

1272

1273

1274

1278

1279

1285

1286

1289

1305

1314

1318

1320

1323

1330 zebu bull

1338

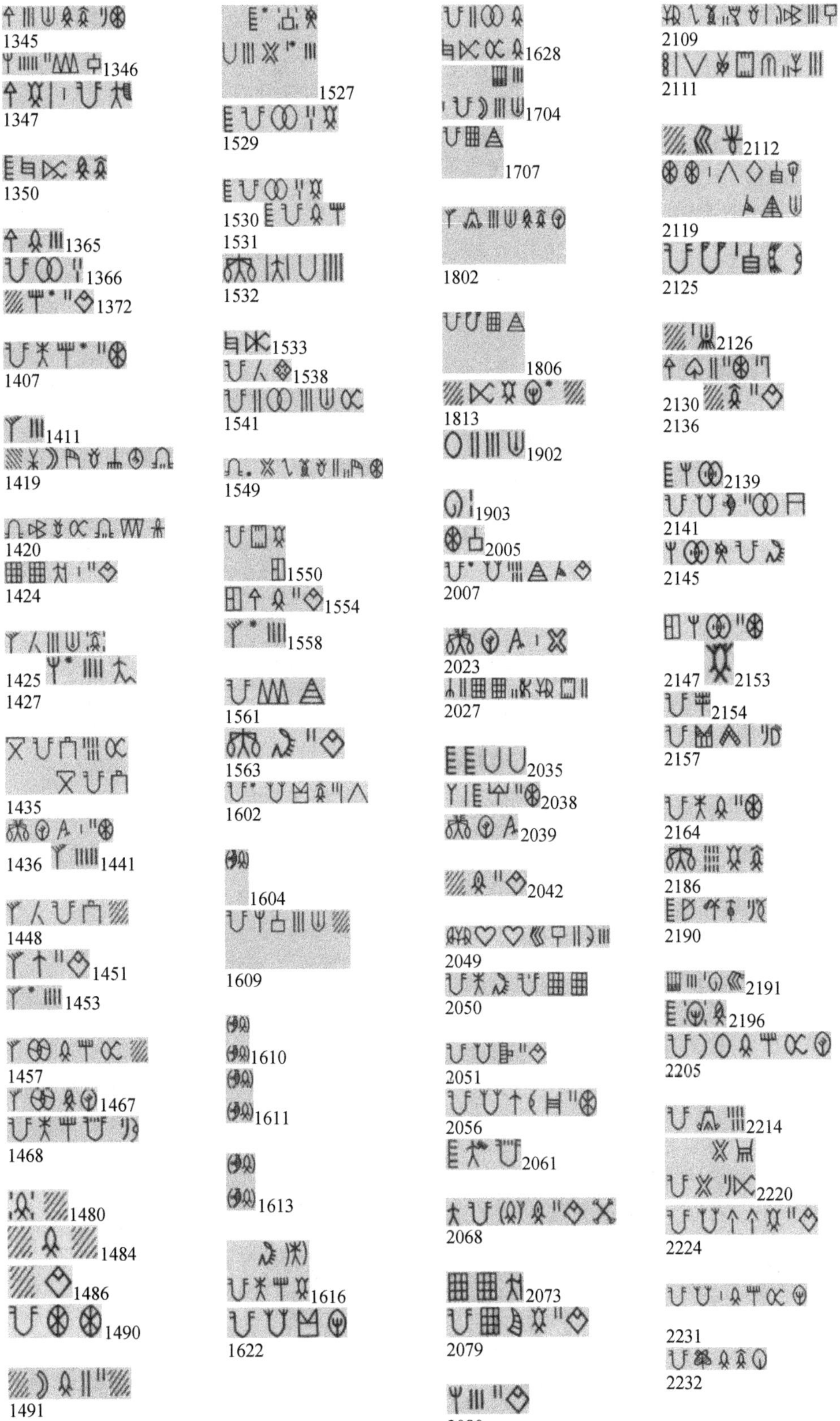
1345
1346
1347
1350
1365
1366
1372
1407
1411
1419
1420
1424
1425
1427
1435
1436
1441
1448
1451
1453
1457
1467
1468
1480
1484
1486
1490
1491
1527
1529
1530
1531
1532
1533
1538
1541
1549
1550
1554
1558
1561
1563
1602
1604
1609
1610
1611
1613
1616
1622
1628
1704
1707
1802
1806
1813
1902
1903
2005
2007
2023
2027
2035
2038
2039
2042
2049
2050
2051
2056
2061
2068
2073
2079
2080
2107
2109
2111
2112
2119
2125
2126
2130
2136
2139
2141
2145
2147
2153
2154
2157
2164
2186
2190
2191
2196
2205
2214
2220
2224
2231
2232

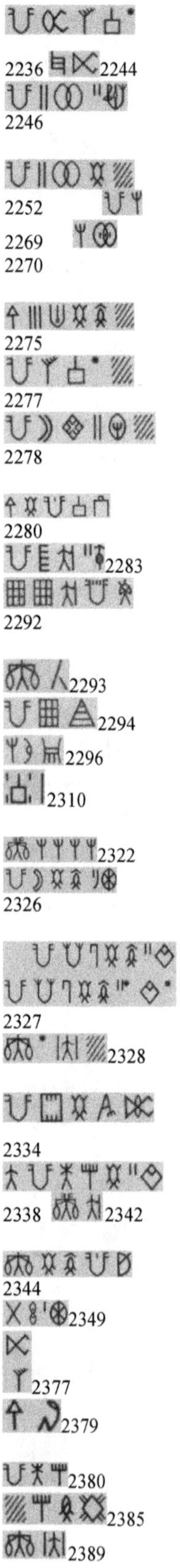

2236 2244
2246
2252
2269
2270
2275
2277
2278
2280
2283
2292
2293
2294
2296
2310
2322
2326
2327
2328
2334
2338 2342
2344
2349
2377
2379
2380
2385
2389

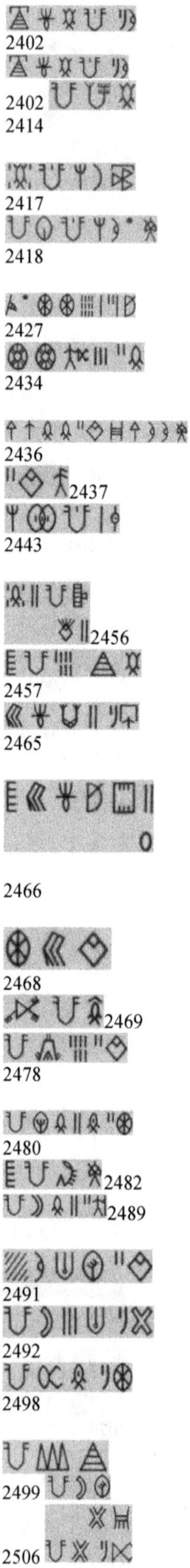

2402
2402 2414
2417
2418
2427
2434
2436
2437
2443
2456
2457
2465
2466
2468
2469
2478
2480
2482
2489
2491
2492
2498
2499
2506
2508

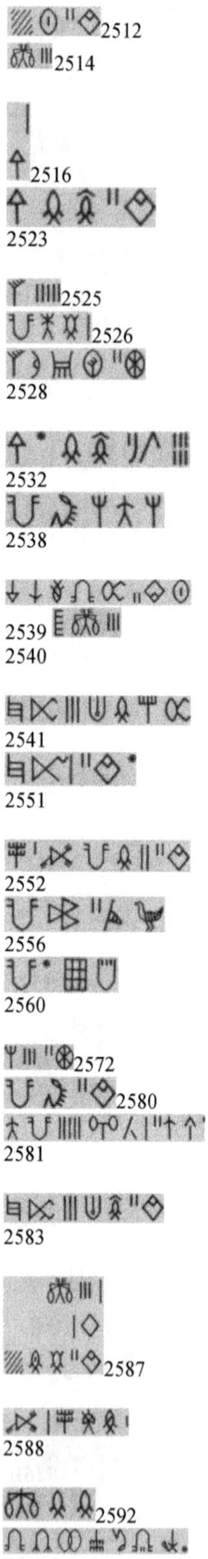

2512
2514
2516
2523
2525
2526
2528
2532
2538
2539
2540
2541
2551
2552
2556
2560
2572
2580
2581
2583
2587
2588
2592
2596

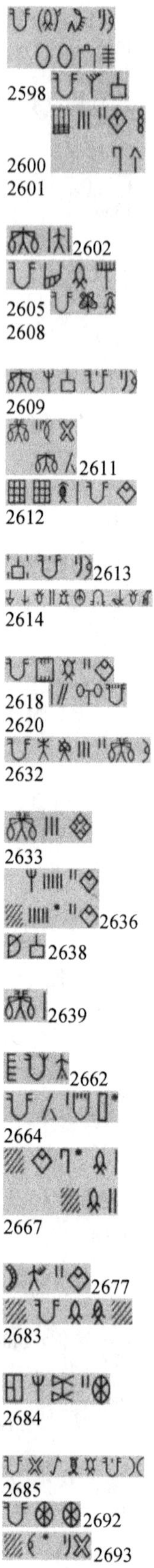

2598
2600
2601
2602
2605
2608
2609
2611
2612
2613
2614
2618
2620
2632
2633
2636
2638
2639
2662
2664
2667
2677
2683
2684
2685
2692
2693

2695

2700 2705

2706

2808

2814

2820

2824

2831

2839

2849

2857

2858

2901
Incised copper tablet

2903 Incised copper tablet

2911 Incised copper tablets. Markhor.

2915

2923
Inscribed bronze implement (MIC Plate CXXVI-2)

2924
Inscribed bronze implement (MIC Plate CXXVI-3)

2925
Inscribed bronze implement (MIC Plate CXXVI-5)

2926
Inscribed bronze implement (MIC Plate CXXVII-1)

2928
Inscribed bronze implement (MIC Plate CXXXIII-1)

2929 Incised on pottery

2930 Graffiti on pottery

2931 Graffiti on pottery

2934 Graffiti on pottery

2935 Graffiti on pottery

2936 Graffiti on pottery

2937 Seal impression on pot

2938Mohenjodaro , Pottery graffiti. Boat.

2940 Ivory or bone rod

2941 Ivory or bone rod Geometrical patterns followed by inscription.

2944
Ivory or bone rod

2945 Ivory or bone rod

2947

2949 Dotted circles

2950

2951

3001

3002

3010

3016

3019

3021

3023

3024

3035

3038

3042

3044

3051

3052

3056

3063

3064

3067

3069

3080

3090

3094

3096

3098

3099

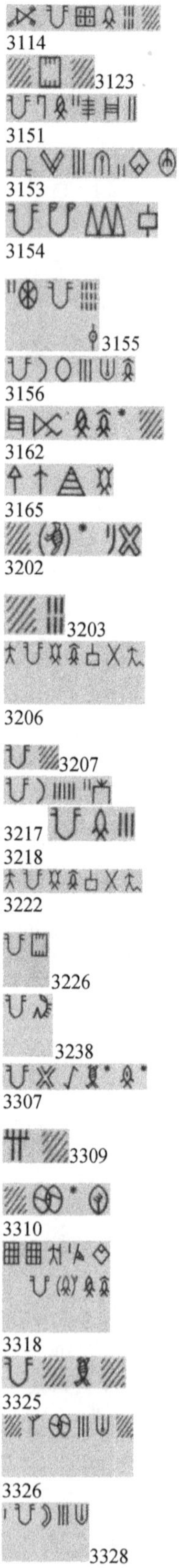

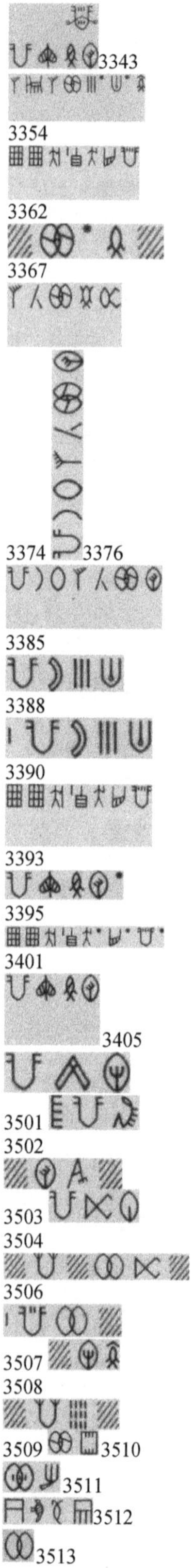

Nindowari-

damb01
Squirrel sign

Nindowari-damb02

Nindowari-damb03

Nausharo01

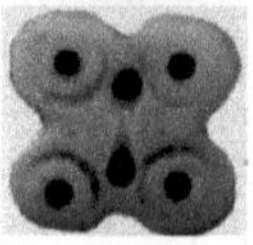

Nausharo02

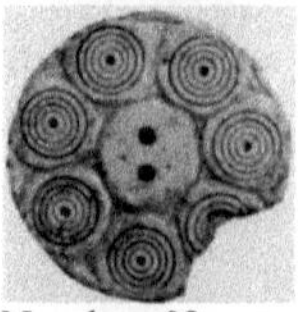

Nausharo03

Nausharo04

Nausharo05

Nausharo06

Nausharo07

Nausharo08

Nausharo09

Nausharo10

Naro-Waro-dharo01

Naro-Waro-dharo02

Naro-Waro-dharo03

Pabumath

Prabhas Patan (Somnath) 1A

Prabhas Patan (Somnath)1B

Pirak1

Pirak12

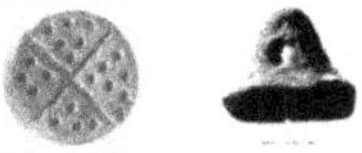

Pirak13

Pirak15

Pirak16

Pirak17

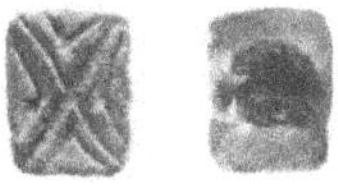

Pirak18

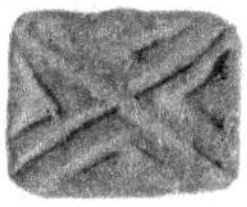

Pirak18A

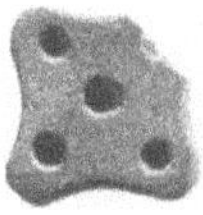

Pirak19

Pirak2

Pirak20

Pirak24

Pirak26Ac

Pirak27

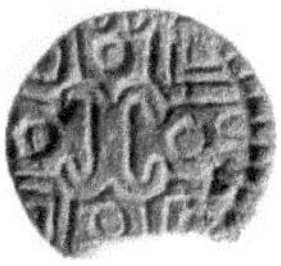

Pirak28

Pirak35

Pirak38

Pirak3 post-harappan

Pirak40

Pirak4

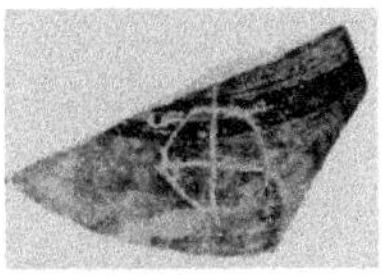

Rangpur

Rakhigarhi1

Rakhigarhi 2

9111

Rakhigarhi 65

Rahman-dheri01A

Rahman-dheri01B

Rahman-dheri120

Rahman-dheri126

Rahman-dheri127

Rahman-dheri150

Rahman-dheri153

Rahman-dheri156

Rahman-dheri158

Rahman-dheri216

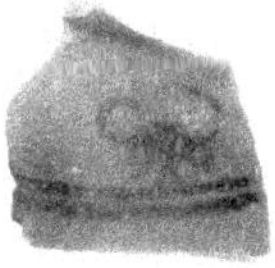

Rahman-dheri241

Rahman-dheri242

Rahman-dheri243

Rahman-dheri254

Rahman-dheri255

Rahman-dheri257

Rahman-dheri258

Rahman-dheri259

Rahman-dheri260

Rahman-dheri90

Rahman-dheri92

Rohira1

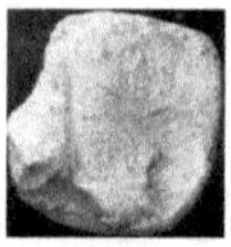

Rohira2

Rojdi

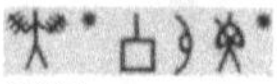

9041

9042

Rupar1A

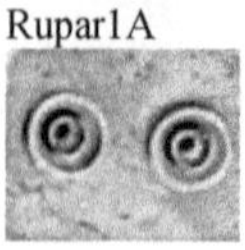

Rupar1B

9021

9022

Shahi-tump

Sibri-damb01A

Sibri-damb01B

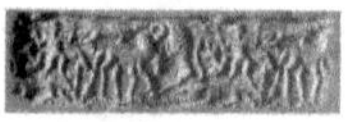

Sibri-damb02a

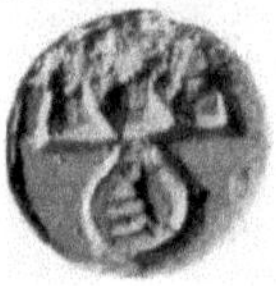

Sibri-damb02E

Sibri-damb03a

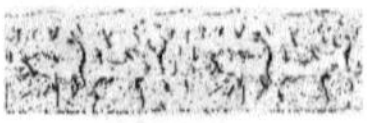

sibri cylinder seal
zebu

Surkotada1

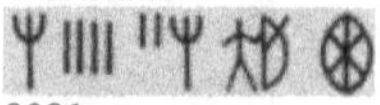

9091

Surkotada 2

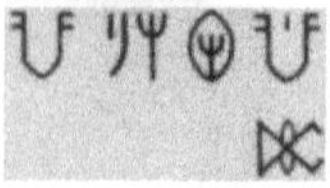

9092

Surkotada3c

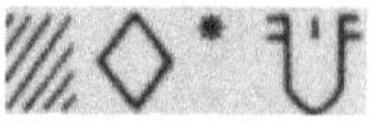

9093

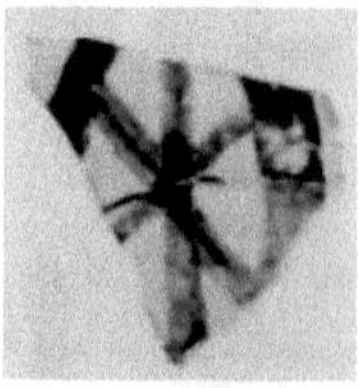

Surkotada 4
9094

Surkotada 6

9095

Surkotada 7

Tarkhanewala-
dera1AB

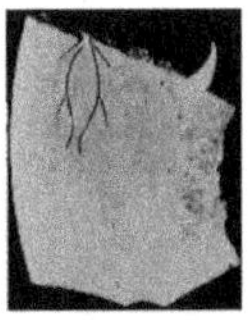

Tarkhanewala-
dera 3

 9031

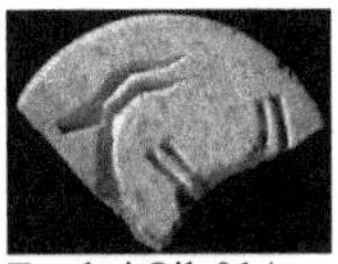

Tarakai Qila01A

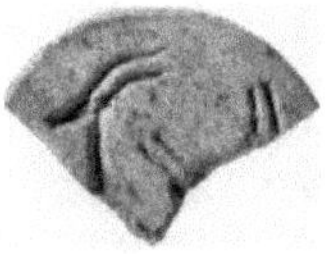

Tarakai Qila01B

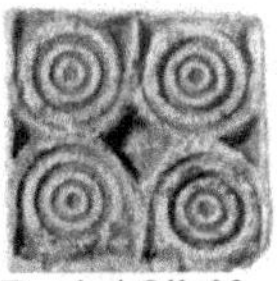

Tarakai Qila02

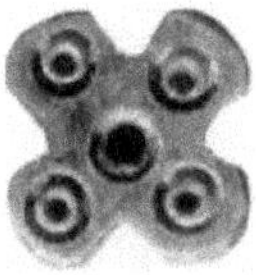

Tarakai Qila03

Tarakai Qila04

Tarakai Qila06

(provenance)
unkn01

Lakhonjodaro

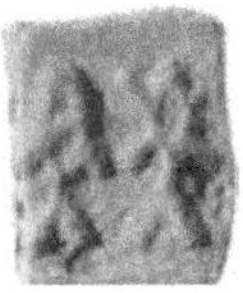

unkn02

*****

unkn03

unkn04 unkn05A unkn06

Seau l'nde. Musee des Arts Asiatique, Guimet, France

Mohenjo-daro. Copper tablet DK 11307 (SC 63.10/262).

Mohenjodaro; limestone; Mackay, 1938, p. 344, Pl. LXXXIX:376.

Mohenjodaro; Pale yellow enstatite; Mackay 1938, pp. 344-5; Pl. XCVI:488; Collon, 1987, Fig. 607.

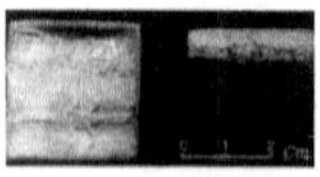

Rakhigarhi: Cylinder Seal (ASI), Lizard or gharial?

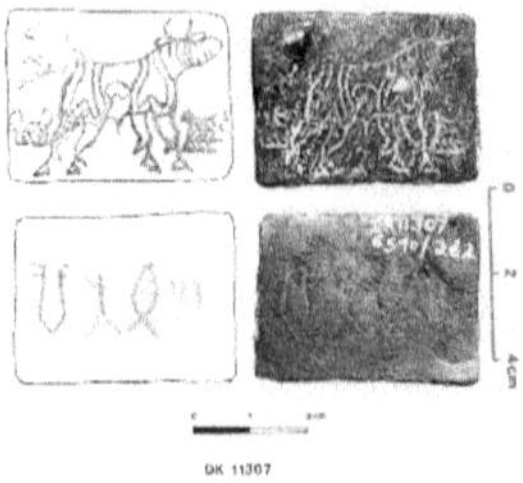

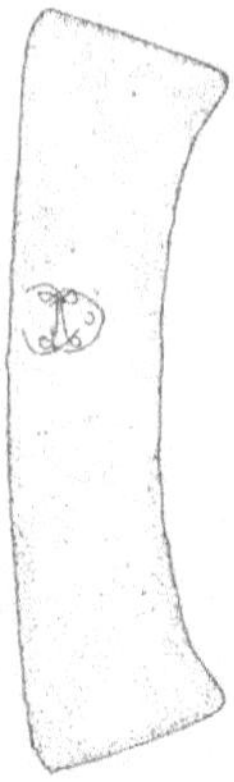

Rojdi. Ax-head or knife of copper, 17.4 cm. long (After Possehl and Raval 1989: 162, fig. 77

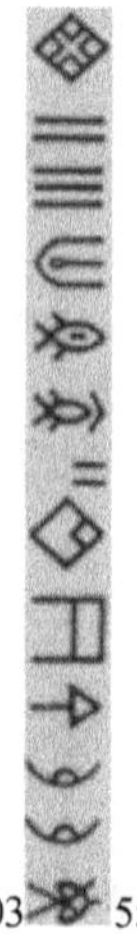

m03 552654

m0359

2325

m0369

2537

m0391

310

Bibliography

A number of concordances and sign lists have been compiled, by many scholars, for the 'Indus' script:

Dani, A.H., *Indian Palaeography*, 1963, Pls. I-II

Gadd and Smith, *Mohenjodaro and the Indus Civilization*, London,1931,vol. III, Pls. CXIX-CXXIX

Hunter, G.R., *JRAS*, 1932, pp. 491-503

Hunter, G.R., *Scripts of Harappa and Mohenjodaro*, 1934, pp. 203-10

Langdon, in:John Marshall, *Mohenjodaro and the Indus Civilization*, London, 1931, vol. II, pp. 434-55

Koskenniemi, Kimmo and Asko Parpola, *Corpus of texts in the Indus script*, Helsinki, 1979; *A concordance to the texts in the Indus script*, Helsinki, 1982

Mahadevan, I., *The Indus Script: Texts, concordance and tables*, Delhi, 1977, pp. 32-35

Parpola et al., *Materials for the study of the Indus script, I: A concordance to the Indus Inscriptions*, 1973, pp. xxii-xxvi

Vats, *Excavations at Harappa*, Calcutta, 1940, vol. II, Pls. CV-CXVI

Amiet, P., Age of inter-Iranian Trade, Paris: Meeting of National Museums, 1986, p.125-126; Fig. 96, 1-9, (Notes and documents of the Museums of France).

Amiet, P., Susa 6000 years of history, Paris: Meeting of National Museums, 1988, p.64-65; Fig. 26.

Benoit, A., The Civilizations of the former Prochre East Paris: Ecole du Louvre, 2003, p.252-253; Fig. 109 (Manuals Ecole du Louvre, Art and Archaeology).

Corpus of Indus Seals and Inscriptions, 1. Collections in India, Helsinki, 1987 (eds. Jagat Pati Joshi and Asko Parpola)

Corpus of Indus Seals and Inscriptions, 2. Collections in Pakistan, Helsinki, 1991 (eds. Sayid Ghulam Mustafa Shah and Asko Parpola)

Corpus of Indus Seals and Inscriptions 3.1 supplement to Mohenjoo-daro and Harappa, Helsinki, Suomalainen Tiedeakatemia Paropola, Asko, BM Pande and Petteri Koskikallio, 2010.

Kalyanaraman, S., 1988, Harappa Script: A bibliography, Manila.

Kalyanaraman, S, 1995, SarasvatiSindhu civilization: evidence from the veda, archaeology, geology and satellite, 10th Wold Sanskrit Conference, Bangalore.

Kalyanaraman S. 1997, A project to revive the Sarasvati river: Role of GIS, National Seminar on Geographic Information Systems for Development Planning, Chennai, 10-12 January, 1997, Renganathan Centre for Information Studies

Kalyanaraman S, 1999, SarasvatiRiver, Godess and Civilization, in: Memoir 42, Vedic Sarasvati, Geological Survey of India, Bangalore, pp. 25-29.

Kalyanaraman, S, 2000, River Sarasvati: Legend, Myth and Reality, All India Sarasvat Association, Mumbai

Kalyanaraman S., 2001, Sarasvati, Babasaheb Apte Smarak Samiti, Bangalore (1100 pages, 600 illustrations); part of 6 vol. Encyclopaedia on Sarasvati (Other 5 vols. in press).

Kalyanaraman, S., 2003, National River Network, An overview, Bangalore, Rashtrotthana Research and Communication Centre

Kalyanaraman S, 2004, Indian Alchemy: Soma in the Veda, Munshiram Manoharlal, Delhi

Kalyanaraman S., 2004, Sarasvati (an encyclopaedic work in 7 volumes: Civilization, River, Bharati, Technology, Epigraphs, Language), Bangalore, Babasaheb Apte Smarak Samiti, Bangalore

Kalyanaraman S., 2007, Rama Setu, Chennai, Rameswaram Ramsetu Protection Movement

Kalyanaraman S., 2008, Harappa Script encodes mleccha speech (5 vols.: Language, Writing, Epigraphica Sarasvati, Dictionary, Indian Lexicon), Chennai, Jayalakshmi Book Stores, 6 Apparsami Koil St., Mylapore, Chennai 600004

Kalyanaraman, S., 2010, Harappa Script Cipher: Hieroglyphs of Indian Linguistic Area, Amazon.

Kalyanaraman, S., 2011, Rastram – Hindu history in United Indian Ocean States, Amazon.

Kalyanaraman, S., 2012, Indian Hieroglyphs – Invention of Writing, Amazon.

Kalyanaraman, S., 2013 Indus writing in Ancient Near East – Corpora and a Dictionary, Amazon.

Kalyanaraman, S., 2011, Rastram – Hindu history in United Indian Ocean States, Amazon.

Kalyanaraman, S., 2012, Indian Hieroglyphs – Invention of Writing, Amazon.

Kalyanaraman, S., 2013 Indus writing in Ancient Near East – Corpora and a Dictionary, Amazon.

Kalyanaraman, S., 2014, Sagan finds Saravati (Novel), Amazon.

Kalyanaraman, S., 2014, A theory for Wealth of nationa, Amazon.

Kalyanaraman, S., 2014, Indian Ocean Community, Amazon.

Kalyanaraman, S., 2014, Harosheth Hagoyim, Amazon.

Kalyanaraman, S., 2015, Outrage for Dharma, Amazon.

Kalyanaraman, S., 2015, Akkadian Rising sun (Novel) , Amazon

Kalyanaraman, S., 2015, Harappa Script Deciphered, Amazon.
Kalyanaraman, S., 2015, Philosophy of Symbolic Forms in Meluhha, Amazon.

Kalyanaraman, S., 2015, Meluhha, a Visible language, Amazon.

Kalyanaraman, S., 2015, Meluhha, tree of life (Novel), Amazon.

http://groups.yahoo.com/group/hinducivilization

Kalyanaraman, S., 2016, 642 monographs/papers at https://independent.academia.edu/SriniKalyanaraman

Mahadevan, I., 1986, A Computer Study of the Harappa Script by I. Mahadevan, International Association of Tamil Research. Madras. (Residence: Vyjayanthi. 112. Chamit!'s Road. Nandanam. Madras 600035. Indio)in: Current Science, January 20, 1986, Vol.55, No.2, pp. 77-79.

Pande, BM, 'Inscribed copper tablets from Mohenjo-daro: a preliminary analysiś in: D. Agrawal/A. Ghosh eds., Radiocarbon and Indian Arcaheology, Bombay 1973, tablet no. 38.

Pande, B. M. 1979 Inscribed Copper Tablets from Mohenjo daro: A Preliminary Analysis. In Ancient Cities of the Indus, edited by G. L. Possehl, pp. 268-288. New Delhi, Vikas Publishing House PVT LTD.

Pande, B. M. 1991 Inscribed Copper Tablets from Mohenjo-daro: Some Observations.Puratattva (21): 25-28.

Parpola, A. 1992 Copper Tablets from Mohenjo-daro and the study of the Harappa Script. In: Proceedings of the Second International Conference on Moenjodaro, edited by I. M. Nadiem, pp. Karachi, Department of Archaeology.

Asko Parpola, 2008, Copper tablets from Mohenjo-daro and the study of the Harappa Script, pp. 132-139 in: Eri Olijdam & Richard H Spoor (eds.), Intercultural relations between south and southwest Asia: Studies in commemoration of ECL During Caspers (1234-1996). BAR Interntional Series 1826. Oxford: Archaeopress.

Shinde, V. & Willis, R.J., (2014). A New Type of Inscribed Copper Plate from Indus Valley (Harappa) Civilisation. Ancient Asia. 5, p.Art. 1. http://www.ancient-asia-journal.com/articles/10.5334/aa.12317/ The paper analyzes a group of nine Indus Valley copper plates (c. 2600–2000 BC), discovered from private collections in Pakistan

Yule, Paul, 1988, A new copper tablet from Mohenjo-daro (DK 11307), in: M. Jansen and G. Urban (eds.), *Reports on field work carried out at Mohenjo-daro, Interim Reports, Vol.2,Pakistan 1983-84*, German Research Project Mohenjo-daro RWTH Aachen, Istituto Italiano per ilmedio ed estremo oriente, Roma https://www.academia.edu/737300/A_New_Copper_Tablet_from_Mohenjo-daro_DK_11307_ Paul Yule analyses the stratigraphic and archaeological context of this find.

agate........................33, 56, 108, 170, 239
Akkadian... 33, 52, 60, 79, 80, 88, 91, 107, 113, 114, 115, 117, 120, 148, 167, 176, 182, 206, 209, 265, 446, 447, 448, 470, 495, 516, 525, 526, 541, 765
Alamgirpur..............................52, 65, 570
Allahdino (Nel Bazaar) 570
alligator..........24, 153, 166, 514, 529, 530
allograph.......31, 148, 264, 315, 325, 336, 407, 467, 480, 502
alloy6, 9, 23, 24, 25, 34, 36, 38, 43, 58, 59, 60, 61, 64, 66, 67, 74, 78, 80, 84, 86, 87, 88, 90, 92, 97, 108, 109, 110, 112, 115, 118, 121, 122, 126, 127, 128, 136, 139, 140, 141, 151, 169, 171, 172, 181, 184, 188, 189, 195, 196, 197, 203, 204, 205, 207, 210, 213, 231, 232, 236, 263, 270, 275, 294, 302, 308, 309, 310, 311, 320, 321, 327, 347, 357, 358, 370, 372, 373, 375, 378, 379, 381, 382, 384, 386, 389, 394, 395, 398, 399, 403, 404, 406, 407, 413, 415, 423, 424, 431, 447, 451, 458, 459, 460, 466, 468, 473, 475, 480, 483, 486, 487, 493, 500, 501, 502, 503, 508, 513, 516, 517, 521, 525, 527, 535, 538
alloying . 50, 127, 165, 186, 195, 199, 345, 388, 530, 536
Amri..486, 570
Ancient Near East6, 9, 10, 14, 18, 21, 39, 53, 63, 64, 65, 67, 74, 86, 104, 110, 119, 121, 129, 143, 159, 162, 170, 182, 242, 260, 511, 523, 533, 536, 566, 765, 780
angle. 26, 40, 56, 203, 352, 443, 446, 447, 448, 450, 502, 546
antelope 5, 6, 7, 28, 52, 60, 61, 65, 82, 88, 129, 132, 149, 165, 169, 187, 188, 232, 385, 393, 394, 395, 396, 411, 428, 444, 445, 474, 479, 480, 487, 492, 495, 519, 522, 526, 529, 533, 541, 572, 573, 574, 592, 662, 663, 686, 687, 688, 689, 693, 701, 724, 726, 734, 736
antelope looking back.82, 445, 572, 688, 734
archer . 5, 42, 61, 120, 146, 359, 365, 376, 377, 396, 407, 408, 451, 475, 517, 538, 703
arrow25, 31, 32, 63, 65, 74, 110, 125, 144, 147, 177, 180, 187, 206, 207, 228, 293, 294, 299, 303, 304, 336, 339, 352, 371, 374, 377, 396, 398, 406, 447, 448, 449, 451, 465, 469, 502, 512, 703
artifact........................7, 87, 171, 528, 780
artifacts 7, 9, 10, 14, 33, 52, 63, 64, 65, 86, 87, 97, 100, 105, 106, 119, 140, 143, 159, 162, 165, 170, 175, 176, 186, 239, 243, 315, 367, 428, 467, 479, 509, 511, 566, 780
artisan 6, 10, 24, 26, 30, 33, 40, 60, 64, 79, 82, 83, 85, 94, 96, 97, 105, 110, 121, 132, 139, 143, 146, 154, 170, 171, 196, 210, 219, 234, 239, 254, 259, 294, 299, 300, 302, 303, 304, 305, 310, 331, 353, 365, 375, 376, 385, 393, 395, 399, 401, 404, 406, 407, 408, 413, 419, 422, 423, 430, 431, 432, 443, 444, 445, 446, 448, 451, 462, 468, 479, 480, 485, 491, 494, 495, 500, 512, 516, 523, 529, 530, 531, 536, 556, 559
artisan guild 105, 143, 239, 305, 500
artisan guilds 143, 239, 305
Austro-Asiatic 163, 182
awl..21
axe 7, 26, 87, 117, 232, 245, 246, 247, 248, 254, 337, 395, 396, 397, 421, 541, 572, 589, 594, 614, 615, 621, 656, 703
ayas . 2, 6, 20, 25, 30, 31, 32, 33, 34, 37, 46, 60, 68, 74, 78, 81, 112, 120, 122, 134, 137, 147, 153, 172, 177, 178, 183, 193, 231, 248, 275, 293, 294, 299, 302, 303, 304, 309, 311, 321, 324, 327, 335, 346, 365, 369, 370, 371, 372, 373, 375, 380, 388, 394, 399, 402, 403, 404, 406, 410, 411, 412, 419, 432, 433, 446, 447, 494, 502, 512, 527, 559
ayo .. 2, 6, 20, 25, 29, 30, 31, 32, 37, 42, 46, 60, 68, 74, 81, 83, 110, 112, 120, 122, 134, 137, 147, 153, 172, 177, 178, 183, 231, 234, 248, 293, 294, 299, 302, 303,

304, 309, 311, 321, 324, 327, 335, 346, 365, 369, 370, 371, 372, 373, 374, 375, 386, 388, 419, 432, 433, 446, 447, 451, 494, 512, 516, 517, 527, 529, 530
backbone.... 152, 188, 189, 294, 320, 321, 322, 380, 381, 382, 384, 386, 403, 404, 406, 486
Banawali.............125, 207, 233, 486, 571
bangle .. 15, 55, 67, 69, 151, 315, 316, 317, 318, 326, 331, 332, 333, 334, 436, 566, 571, 739
baran50, 80, 141, 188, 189, 219, 320, 321, 380, 382, 384, 386, 403, 404, 406, 430, 486
bat 44, 46, 237, 239, 447, 519
BB Lal 55
bead 108, 185, 291, 306, 355, 492, 739
beads...... 17, 32, 35, 36, 55, 146, 165, 185, 216, 233, 290, 306, 316, 355, 476, 492, 521, 528, 568
bell-metal.... 148, 206, 413, 414, 418, 446, 492, 499, 522, 540
Bhirrana.... 16, 55, 93, 104, 192, 193, 568, 780
Binjor................ 56, 57, 58, 75, 76, 78, 229
bird ...23, 24, 34, 37, 38, 45, 58, 60, 78, 95, 106, 120, 123, 139, 142, 161, 171, 195, 238, 239, 245, 302, 308, 372, 391, 478, 508, 516, 527, 642, 663, 734
Bisht....................................388, 436, 576
bison 112, 150, 260, 468, 479, 480, 482, 493, 513, 585, 662, 693, 698, 724, 726, 732, 734
blacksmith 6, 13, 24, 25, 29, 32, 42, 43, 60, 61, 66, 73, 82, 83, 85, 94, 96, 97, 100, 105, 112, 120, 121, 127, 129, 135, 137, 139, 141, 147, 149, 151, 153, 166, 173, 177, 180, 193, 198, 203, 230, 234, 239, 245, 246, 247, 255, 260, 269, 276, 277, 294, 295, 299, 310,314, 315, 325, 328, 335, 346, 365, 367, 371, 373, 375, 385, 386, 387, 393, 395, 396, 399, 400, 401, 407, 408, 409, 411, 419, 423, 426, 429, 432, 434, 444, 445, 448, 457, 464, 470, 473, 474, 475, 478, 479, 491, 493, 494, 497, 500, 501, 512, 515, 516, 521, 522, 523, 525, 529, 530, 531, 533, 559
boar. 5, 150, 178, 179, 180, 245, 246, 247, 294, 307, 309, 310, 311, 336, 338, 339, 411, 412, 413, 488, 493, 518, 529, 535, 537, 538, 560
boat..... 20, 22, 23, 66, 124, 171, 179, 225, 254, 260, 291, 311, 339, 353, 424, 428, 430, 434, 499
body..2, 6, 10, 20, 59, 72, 90, 99, 105, 117, 125, 135, 141, 146, 148, 149, 167, 169, 183, 187, 188, 206, 208, 219, 220, 225, 233, 235, 239, 245, 248, 262, 274, 280, 281, 291, 292, 298, 300, 307, 310, 319, 322, 323, 324, 331, 334, 335, 337, 365, 375, 376, 377, 378, 379, 380, 386, 397, 399, 403, 405, 406, 410, 412, 419, 422, 423, 430, 431, 445, 454, 455, 477, 479, 481, 482, 486, 487, 493, 495, 496, 499, 520, 526, 573, 662, 663, 688, 689, 698, 701, 724, 725, 734, 737
bos indicus............................32, 142, 457
bovine6, 94, 125, 169, 206, 407, 471, 476, 479, 487, 496, 573, 585, 597, 610, 656, 703, 725, 726
bracelet.... 60, 86, 145, 151, 379, 430, 504
branch. 18, 24, 82, 97, 143, 151, 153, 167, 182, 204, 237, 238, 300, 318, 351, 423, 430, 434, 474, 512, 514, 515, 517, 523, 525, 688, 725, 731
brass 12, 26, 44, 60, 61, 63, 64, 66, 83, 85, 90, 109, 114, 118, 120, 123, 126, 127, 128, 137, 147, 148, 151, 192, 197, 204, 207, 209, 210, 213, 238, 254, 303, 310, 311, 326, 327, 328, 372, 375, 377, 380, 389, 400, 401, 402, 404, 408, 409, 415, 425, 432, 446, 487, 489, 491, 500, 501, 508, 516, 522, 527
bronze..7, 9, 12, 14, 15, 26, 35, 36, 39, 42, 43, 50, 51, 63, 64, 65, 66, 67, 68, 69, 71, 86, 90, 92, 93, 96, 109, 112, 115, 116, 122, 129, 134, 137, 140, 141, 143, 146, 147, 148, 154, 155, 160, 161, 162, 165, 170, 173, 175, 176, 177, 183, 189, 195, 196, 200, 210, 213, 231, 232, 238, 239, 240, 241, 242, 246, 247, 248, 254, 255, 259, 260, 261, 262, 263, 266, 269, 294, 295, 299, 300, 301, 303, 307, 309, 311, 326, 330, 347, 352, 353, 360, 367, 370, 372, 373, 377, 380, 382, 386, 388,

389, 390, 392, 394, 395, 396, 400, 401, 402, 403, 408, 409, 410, 411, 412, 415, 419, 424, 425, 426, 427, 428, 431, 432, 433, 434, 446, 447, 448, 452, 455, 458, 467, 483, 500, 501, 502, 503, 512, 513, 523, 528, 566, 757
bucket............................99, 346, 435, 467
buffalo... 5, 6, 9, 10, 60, 65, 109, 110, 112, 113, 114, 115, 117, 118, 125, 126, 140, 142, 149, 187, 206, 207, 310, 375, 398, 441, 475, 476, 477, 479, 481, 482, 490, 493, 495, 511, 512, 514, 527, 686, 688, 689, 733, 734, 780
bull..6, 8, 12, 15, 29, 31, 41, 44, 45, 46, 58, 60, 64, 72, 78, 83, 93, 95, 99, 100, 102, 109, 110, 113, 114, 119, 120, 124, 125, 126, 133, 135, 137, 141, 142, 143, 144, 145, 146, 147, 151, 152, 153, 162, 169, 173, 178, 180, 181, 187, 203, 205, 206, 207, 209, 228, 231, 232, 235, 236, 245, 246, 247, 248, 254, 259, 293, 309, 310, 330, 339, 344, 348, 349, 350, 351, 353, 356, 397, 403, 431, 441, 444, 445, 447, 448, 452, 461, 462, 473, 475, 476, 479, 481, 482, 485, 486, 487, 496, 500, 501, 507, 508, 511, 513, 515, 518, 521, 522, 525, 527, 529, 567, 572, 573, 582, 585, 589, 590, 591, 606, 610, 614, 656, 661, 662, 678, 684, 685, 687, 688, 693, 697, 698, 702, 705, 710, 714, 718, 719, 724, 734, 754, 780
bullcalf..... 44, 83, 119, 124, 133, 137, 143, 144, 146, 148, 205, 210, 254, 259, 293, 310, 344, 350, 351, 353, 356, 444, 485, 486, 522, 529
Burrow...... 45, 71, 95, 118, 136, 161, 175, 309, 338, 373, 378, 491, 493
bush...275, 401
Campbell.. 542
canal....................................26, 173, 543
carnelian.................36, 56, 116, 239, 504
carpenter 58, 78, 150, 170, 179, 245, 247, 294, 295, 301, 309, 310, 311, 336, 337, 346, 411, 412, 413, 421, 425, 426, 464, 487, 489, 491, 493, 559
carpenters... 488
Caspian Sea....................................... 65
cast..11, 25, 26, 29, 39, 43, 48, 63, 64, 71, 82, 85, 86, 87, 90, 92, 93, 95, 96, 98, 99, 109, 110, 121, 124, 126, 127, 128, 129, 135, 138, 139, 141, 148, 149, 160, 162, 171, 177, 188, 189, 196, 204, 205, 207, 219, 238, 245, 246, 275, 276, 289, 303, 308, 309, 322, 324, 326, 327, 330, 347, 350, 355, 360, 372, 373, 374, 376, 377, 378, 379, 380, 382, 384, 394, 397, 398, 399, 400, 401, 402, 403, 404, 405, 406, 407, 408, 409, 411, 412, 413, 414, 419, 423, 427, 428, 432, 433, 446, 447, 450, 451, 452, 455, 458, 468, 475, 492, 496, 497, 500, 501, 502, 508, 513, 518, 524, 525, 528, 530, 533
casting.....6, 24, 26, 29, 30, 42, 43, 46, 50, 63, 66, 67, 81, 82, 86, 87, 88, 91, 92, 93, 94, 95, 96, 97, 98, 112, 118, 121, 129, 131, 140, 141, 147, 159, 162, 165, 171, 195, 225, 250, 293, 294, 295, 298, 299, 300, 301, 302, 303, 304, 307, 311, 322, 355, 360, 365, 367, 372, 373, 374, 378, 380, 384, 386, 394, 395, 396, 399, 401, 402, 406, 408, 409, 410, 411, 412, 413, 414, 418, 419, 420, 422, 426, 428, 432, 433, 452, 458, 480, 482, 483, 492, 500, 502, 521, 527, 531
chalcedony...536
cipher...12, 19, 41, 63, 65, 66, 68, 80, 129, 174, 345, 360, 388, 454, 457, 486, 541
circumgraph...............................374, 455
cire perdue 6, 9, 39, 43, 50, 51, 59, 61, 63, 64, 66, 68, 86, 87, 92, 93, 94, 96, 97, 129, 162, 165, 171, 175, 250, 311, 365, 367, 403, 418, 428, 536
citadel...................................74, 278, 576
comb 5, 113, 122, 195, 196, 231, 299, 300, 301, 303, 346, 410, 421, 424, 425, 426, 431, 446, 447, 448, 526
community...... 61, 75, 100, 165, 176, 274, 331, 397, 407, 411, 426, 449, 473, 487, 500, 503, 508, 522, 523, 529
composite animal.. 10, 65, 105, 187, 431, 441, 444, 445, 456, 466, 467, 471, 473, 477, 698
conch...69, 170
copper...... 15, 16, 566, 567, 689, 725, 734, 736, 757, 762

copper tablet 2, 15, 16, 20, 50, 51, 68, 186, 188, 189, 232, 234, 242, 255, 260, 322, 365, 367, 382, 383, 384, 406, 413, 418, 458, 477, 566, 567, 689, 725, 734, 736, 757, 766
coppersmith 30, 83, 87, 147, 247, 255, 260, 365, 367, 385, 393, 395, 396, 408, 409, 415, 478
copulation 61, 234, 332, 529, 531, 533, 573
corner 26, 56, 112, 147, 183, 184, 189, 240, 248, 254, 280, 292, 295, 300, 330, 335, 352, 377, 382, 386, 396, 409, 411, 412, 427, 432, 433, 443, 446, 447, 448, 450, 454, 455, 458, 500, 512, 546
crab 5, 26, 30, 295, 299, 300, 302, 365, 376, 399, 404, 406, 408, 409, 410, 430, 586
crocodile 5, 13, 24, 83, 94, 96, 97, 105, 153, 166, 167, 336, 339, 373, 407, 448, 511, 512, 513, 514, 515, 523, 529, 530, 531, 533, 558
Cunningham 14, 15, 17, 20, 181, 236, 567, 569
currycomb 32, 112, 122, 195, 219, 231, 299, 300, 301, 303, 346, 357, 358, 378, 386, 410, 422, 424, 425, 431, 458, 459, 460
curve 42, 96, 137, 240, 294, 326, 380, 394, 400, 402, 409, 410, 419, 426, 428, 433, 483, 502
curved ... 71, 123, 124, 130, 196, 205, 274, 308, 327, 380, 400, 401, 405, 408, 430, 431, 433, 527
dagger 60, 117, 240, 257, 258, 598
daggers 86, 117, 231
dance . 43, 64, 65, 192, 221, 379, 491, 493
data mining 2, 4, 14, 19, 20, 27, 68, 71, 129, 367, 370, 486, 536
decoded 51, 169, 355, 356, 360, 446, 447, 449, 452, 468, 492, 493, 500, 519
decryption 175
deer 39, 149, 400, 408, 475
Dholavira .. 11, 12, 25, 26, 92, 94, 96, 423, 436, 442, 443, 444, 449, 453, 487, 576, 578, 696
dotted circle 5, 6, 16, 31, 32, 33, 43, 47, 67, 147, 165, 214, 281, 288, 289, 290, 302, 303, 357, 459, 498, 528, 532, 568, 589, 596, 614, 724, 739
drill 462, 463, 668
drum 63, 129, 154, 160, 161, 204, 205, 322, 337, 381, 516
drummer 5, 126, 127, 204, 205, 206
Egyptian 18, 19, 21, 22, 27, 29, 30, 64, 86, 150, 373, 390
Emeneau 53, 56, 175, 176
engraver ..6, 10, 26, 41, 44, 58, 66, 67, 78, 82, 83, 115, 138, 145, 146, 147, 178, 187, 234, 254, 259, 293, 300, 301, 307, 309, 310, 311, 318, 322, 323, 330, 331, 336, 344, 351, 353, 398, 445, 479, 486, 487, 496, 559
epigraph 237, 408, 409, 559
eraka 12, 26, 29, 60, 61, 82, 83, 85, 96, 118, 147, 148, 150, 161, 172, 209, 260, 263, 303, 310, 327, 377, 400, 401, 406, 423, 424, 431, 455, 468, 469, 475, 499, 500, 501, 503, 508, 516, 518, 532, 559
Fabri 27
Failaka 7, 29, 107, 165, 780
Farmana 104, 780
ficus religiosa. 5, 30, 40, 44, 82, 129, 379, 396, 406, 419, 423, 424, 427, 428, 432, 444, 449, 471, 475, 479, 529, 530, 551
field symbol 15, 16, 18, 29, 41, 50, 188, 567, 780
fin 693
fish 2, 5, 6, 20, 21, 24, 25, 29, 30, 31, 32, 33, 34, 37, 41, 42, 46, 58, 60, 65, 68, 74, 78, 81, 83, 85, 86, 105, 110, 112, 120, 122, 123, 134, 137, 147, 149, 151, 167, 172, 178, 183, 193, 195, 221, 223, 225, 228, 231, 233, 234, 248, 254, 259, 263, 274, 293, 294, 299, 302, 303, 304, 307, 308, 309, 310, 311, 321, 324, 327, 335, 336, 344, 346, 365, 367, 369, 370, 371, 372, 373, 374, 375, 386, 388, 394, 399, 402, 403, 404, 406, 410, 411, 412, 413, 419, 429, 432, 433, 446, 447, 451, 458, 465, 467, 494, 502, 512, 516, 517, 525, 526, 527, 529, 530, 532, 558, 559, 573, 582, 585, 589, 595, 618, 642, 656, 693, 697, 733, 734, 780
fishes 83, 223, 407, 527

flag .. 58, 78, 188, 380, 407, 412, 419, 458, 516, 517, 531
forge.12, 25, 30, 42, 43, 44, 45, 46, 59, 60, 63, 64, 66, 73, 82, 83, 84, 85, 94, 96, 109, 110, 112, 120, 124, 127, 128, 129, 132, 135, 137, 139, 147, 149, 151, 177, 183, 186, 188, 193, 195, 203, 206, 221, 240, 248, 254, 263, 269, 276, 277, 278, 282, 293, 294, 295, 297, 300, 301, 302, 305, 306, 311, 325, 328, 347, 353, 357, 360, 364, 366, 374, 375, 380, 386, 394, 395, 396, 398, 399, 400, 401, 403, 404, 405, 406, 409, 410, 411, 413, 419, 422, 423, 426, 427, 428, 429, 431, 433, 434, 448, 450, 451, 452, 458, 459, 462, 464, 465, 466, 467, 470, 474, 475, 477, 479, 480, 487, 491, 493, 495, 496, 512, 516, 517, 519, 520, 521, 522, 523, 524, 525, 527, 530, 531
frog 5, 35, 65, 161, 172, 435, 533
Gadd 764
Gharo Bhiro (Nuhato) 578
gimlet 12, 31, 146, 147
gloss.... 115, 127, 142, 198, 208, 214, 228, 344, 345, 351, 369, 374, 380, 425, 434, 457, 472, 473, 474, 475, 497, 502, 528, 540
glosses . 11, 14, 34, 50, 52, 115, 127, 128, 142, 146, 176, 182, 199, 208, 214, 221, 230, 335, 363, 370, 375, 388, 472, 529, 566
glyph 14, 16, 25, 50, 74, 126, 127, 135, 136, 137, 143, 144, 150, 151, 172, 174, 189, 196, 213, 215, 223, 225, 231, 238, 308, 310, 322, 323, 352, 355, 359, 388, 420, 424, 446, 447, 448, 449, 451, 452, 456, 461, 462, 463, 464, 465, 466, 467, 468, 473, 477, 491, 493, 494, 495, 500, 522, 530, 533, 566, 568, 713
glyptic 14, 15, 20, 114, 145, 146, 148, 149, 150, 151, 152, 154, 205, 235, 237, 308, 481, 566, 567
goat 5, 60, 61, 65, 80, 82, 88, 92, 108, 109, 128, 130, 131, 132, 138, 169, 173, 187, 194, 231, 255, 260, 274, 276, 379, 396, 398, 401, 423, 449, 479, 486, 487, 504, 515, 522, 526, 529, 541, 549, 552, 572, 586, 734
goats 87, 88, 128, 169, 518, 529, 530, 552
Gola Dhoro 16, 104, 568, 570
gold ..5, 7, 8, 23, 29, 32, 35, 41, 47, 48, 50, 53, 56, 64, 65, 83, 90, 92, 99, 107, 109, 110, 115, 117, 146, 149, 150, 151, 154, 161, 162, 165, 171, 183, 184, 185, 208, 209, 230, 245, 246, 249, 260, 270, 291, 306, 314, 318, 323, 324, 329, 338, 367, 390, 392, 401, 415, 420, 430, 451, 466, 473, 475, 490, 491, 495, 500, 504, 507, 518, 522, 525, 528, 531, 552, 559
gold pendant.... 5, 8, 41, 53, 65, 183, 185, 367
grapheme..................................... 16, 568
guild .10, 12, 31, 41, 50, 51, 53, 60, 61, 62, 66, 67, 74, 100, 105, 110, 140, 175, 185, 193, 196, 248, 277, 293, 294, 295, 305, 310, 311, 314, 319, 320, 327, 331, 347, 356, 366, 375, 384, 395, 397, 398, 399, 400, 402, 403, 405, 407, 412, 413, 426, 449, 458, 462, 463, 466, 467, 468, 473, 480, 482, 483, 494, 495, 500, 507, 508, 509, 512, 522, 523, 529
Haifa 5, 9, 11, 38, 51, 52, 60, 63, 64, 68, 104, 129, 162, 163, 175, 230, 331, 780
hair-knot 193, 513
hare 586
Hare 701, 736
harrow..... 5, 299, 378, 386, 399, 420, 436, 482, 521, 526
haystack 491, 492, 495
head-dress 59, 73, 150, 167, 586, 663
heifer.................... 148, 210, 355, 356, 522
hieroglyph .2, 5, 6, 7, 9, 10, 12, 19, 20, 21, 23, 29, 30, 31, 32, 34, 38, 40, 41, 42, 45, 47, 48, 58, 64, 67, 68, 72, 78, 79, 83, 84, 93, 99, 108, 115, 118, 119, 124, 126, 127, 128, 129, 131, 142, 146, 147, 161, 162, 169, 171, 172, 178, 182, 188, 195, 197, 198, 199,205, 206, 210, 213, 214, 215, 216, 219, 221, 228, 230, 264, 270, 274, 288, 299, 302, 306, 307, 308, 309, 310, 311, 312, 314, 315, 319, 322, 325, 326, 327, 330, 344, 345, 357, 366, 367, 369, 370, 371, 372, 373, 375, 376, 377, 378, 379, 380, 381, 386, 387, 388, 393, 394, 396, 397, 398, 399, 400, 402, 405, 406, 407, 408, 409, 410, 411, 412,

413, 414, 422, 423, 424, 425, 429, 434, 457, 458, 459, 466, 468, 469, 470, 473, 478, 484, 486, 487, 494, 495, 496, 497, 498, 501, 502, 503, 504, 508, 516, 520, 521, 522, 523, 524, 526, 529, 530, 531, 532, 535, 537, 542, 545, 554, 559, 560
hieroglyphic...... 11, 30, 65, 142, 205, 380, 425, 430, 434
hill 61, 82, 100, 109, 149, 151, 181, 236, 392, 395, 407, 414, 446, 447, 448, 510
homophone 22
horn31, 46, 73, 74, 97, 101, 130, 143, 145, 146, 187, 215, 234, 248, 254, 259, 344, 351, 353, 359, 373, 375, 387, 399, 405, 407, 412, 413, 414, 419, 430, 432, 446, 447, 448, 471, 474, 496, 500, 501, 514, 517, 522, 523, 527
horns. 48, 59, 73, 105, 115, 123, 125, 130, 148, 149, 150, 167, 171, 178, 185, 187, 206, 207, 307, 351, 423, 427, 429, 431, 433, 457, 471, 474, 476, 477, 490, 491, 495, 496, 527, 573, 585, 586, 597, 610, 656, 661, 662, 663, 685, 686, 687, 688, 689, 698, 702, 703, 724, 725, 726
Hunter 11, 205, 208, 308, 428, 472, 764
ibex............ 61, 88, 90, 133, 247, 507, 525
Indo-European.............55, 174, 175, 182
ingot ...6, 11, 22, 24, 25, 29, 30, 38, 42, 43, 50, 60, 61, 66, 72, 74, 82, 85, 94, 110, 112, 121, 122, 127, 134, 147, 148, 149, 161, 172, 174, 181, 188, 189, 203, 204, 205, 232, 236, 237, 274, 293, 294, 295, 301, 303, 304, 311, 318, 319, 323, 326, 328, 329, 336, 345, 373, 375, 379, 380, 382, 386, 388, 394, 396, 397, 398, 399, 400, 401, 402, 404, 409, 410, 413, 419, 420, 423, 426, 427, 428, 430, 432, 433, 448, 449, 450, 451, 453, 455, 457, 458, 459, 473, 474, 476, 485, 496, 500, 512, 517, 519, 527, 533, 542, 545
intercourse 332, 499
inventory.....................145, 165, 420, 421
iron .2, 6, 10, 13, 20, 23, 24, 25, 28, 29, 30, 31, 32, 33, 34, 37, 40, 42, 43, 44, 46, 47, 48, 51, 56, 58, 59, 60, 61, 64, 66, 67, 68, 70, 72, 73, 74, 78, 81, 82, 83, 84, 85, 88, 90, 93, 94, 95, 96, 97, 101, 109, 110, 112, 114, 115, 118, 120, 122, 124, 126, 127, 128, 129, 131, 132, 134, 135, 137, 138, 139, 140, 141, 147, 148, 149, 150, 151, 152, 153, 161, 165, 166, 171, 172, 173, 174, 177, 178, 179, 180, 182, 183, 186, 189, 192, 193, 194, 195, 196, 198, 199, 202, 203, 204, 205, 206, 207, 208, 209, 210, 211, 213, 214, 215, 216, 217, 219, 221, 229, 230, 231, 239, 245, 247, 248, 263, 269, 274, 275, 276, 277, 281, 288, 289, 291, 292, 293, 294, 295, 298, 299, 300, 302, 303, 304, 307, 308, 309, 310, 311, 315, 319, 321, 322, 323, 324, 325, 327, 328, 330, 335, 336, 346, 350, 360, 365, 367, 369, 370, 371, 372, 373, 374, 375, 376, 377, 378, 379, 380, 385, 386, 387, 388, 393, 394, 395, 396, 397, 398, 399, 400, 401, 402, 403, 404, 405, 406, 407, 408, 410, 411, 412, 413, 419, 420, 422, 423, 424, 425, 427, 428, 429, 430, 431, 432, 433, 434, 444, 445, 446, 447, 448, 449, 450, 451, 454, 455, 457, 462, 464, 465, 469, 471, 472, 473, 474, 475, 476, 477, 478, 479, 480, 483, 485, 490, 491, 492, 493, 494, 495, 496, 499, 500, 501, 502, 511, 512, 513, 515, 516, 517, 519, 521, 522, 523, 524, 525, 526, 527, 529, 530, 531, 532, 533, 536, 538, 539, 540, 542, 545, 553, 558, 559, 560
iron ore 140, 141, 193, 195, 196, 211, 239, 281, 300, 373, 376, 378, 496, 530, 533
ironsmith. 24, 83, 147, 219, 269, 367, 374, 379, 491
jackal84, 88, 152, 203, 346, 423, 475, 491, 493
jar 5, 6, 7, 8, 25, 30, 34, 35, 42, 44, 46, 50, 65, 83, 96, 102, 109, 110, 112, 118, 122, 124, 127, 137, 169, 189, 196, 203, 231, 237, 238, 248, 266, 294, 295, 299, 300, 301, 303, 318, 323, 330, 334, 351, 352, 357, 358, 377, 386, 394, 395, 397, 398, 399, 400,403, 404, 406, 407, 409, 410, 411, 412, 415, 419, 420, 422, 423, 424, 425, 426, 429, 432, 446, 447, 449, 450, 452, 454, 455, 458, 459, 460, 468, 479, 486, 494, 501, 516, 519, 531, 534, 536, 697, 725
Jhukar..572, 573

joined .. 6, 12, 13, 105, 146, 147, 169, 232, 254, 259, 307, 331, 332, 335, 353, 394, 403, 409, 410, 413, 486, 487, 496, 497, 499, 501, 519, 520, 521, 523, 687, 688
jump 95, 491, 493, 531
Kalyanaraman 1, 764, 765, 766
kamaḍha..... 376, 377, 404, 406, 407, 410, 414, 424, 425, 433, 449, 490, 491, 517
Kanmer 104
Kazanas 55
Kenoyer 15, 17, 20, 33, 183, 185, 189, 195, 234, 334, 347, 348, 349, 350, 354, 358, 460, 463, 467, 477, 514, 567, 569
Kish 29, 30, 172, 780
Kot-diji 666
kūdār 486, 508
Kuiper 53, 56, 182
kundau 96, 491, 492
ladder 314, 326, 456, 483, 526, 550
lapidaries 14, 65, 366, 466, 566
lapidary . 12, 14, 25, 26, 44, 58, 60, 69, 78, 82, 83, 137, 143, 145, 146, 147, 148, 178, 254, 259, 293, 309, 310, 331, 349, 351, 353, 367, 398, 445, 447, 451, 463, 479, 487, 500, 501, 559, 566
lapis lazuli... 32, 35, 36, 56, 107, 116, 233, 239, 504
leafless tree... 82
ligature .. 31, 139, 188, 336, 373, 380, 401, 412, 425, 434, 475, 493, 494, 542, 573, 606
ligatured.... 12, 25, 30, 31, 40, 71, 84, 124, 152, 174, 178, 189, 203, 215, 223, 228, 232, 248, 254, 259, 274, 307, 308, 309, 323, 344, 352, 353, 367, 375, 379, 394, 403, 410, 411, 430, 431, 446, 447, 449, 452, 455, 468, 471, 494, 495, 502, 519, 524, 573, 582, 618, 708, 713
linear stroke . 42, 131, 219, 299, 320, 355, 364, 374, 394, 403, 411, 454, 458, 500, 502
linga 11, 69, 70, 71, 72, 73, 266, 271, 274, 408, 536, 539, 542, 543, 544, 545, 560
lion7, 60, 61, 106, 113, 114, 120, 123, 139, 148, 181, 209, 224, 236, 246, 478, 513
lizard 153, 166, 407, 420
logographic 8, 9
logo-semantic 14, 566
Luristan...36, 116
Mackay........................572, 573, 574, 762
Mahābhārata 457
Mahadevan 15, 16, 17, 31, 176, 188, 241, 259, 308, 319, 327, 357, 358, 407, 414, 458, 459, 460, 468, 494, 499, 505, 566, 567, 568, 569, 573, 764, 766, 780
makara 105, 780
markhor 2, 5, 7, 20, 42, 61, 88, 90, 101, 114, 130, 131, 161, 165, 172, 178, 180, 194, 247, 307, 309, 310, 311, 371, 396, 406, 422, 423, 427, 428, 430, 432, 471, 477, 492, 497, 519, 532, 724, 725
Marshall 93, 167, 176, 183, 280, 288, 297, 298, 299, 480, 481, 482, 540, 764
Masica 53, 56
Meadow...... 15, 17, 20, 79, 185, 189, 347, 348, 349, 350, 354, 358, 460, 463, 467, 477, 567, 569
Meluhha ..4, 5, 6, 9, 10, 11, 12, 13, 14, 18, 19, 22, 30, 31, 32, 33, 36, 38, 41, 47, 49, 50, 52, 56, 60, 63, 66, 79, 80, 88, 92, 94, 96, 100, 105, 106, 107, 108, 113, 115, 116, 118, 127, 128, 129, 131, 139, 144, 145, 146, 162, 169, 175, 179, 182, 188, 193, 195, 197, 200, 202, 206, 208, 214, 263, 293, 331, 345, 349, 350, 367, 373, 388, 398, 453, 454, 467, 472, 473, 481, 499, 505, 511, 523, 525, 527, 529, 542, 566, 766
merchant .6, 23, 40, 45, 46, 49, 52, 60, 66, 67, 83, 93, 96, 101, 110, 129, 165, 166, 169, 178, 179, 180, 230, 231, 234, 245, 247, 248, 259, 277, 282, 295, 305, 307, 309, 310, 311, 314, 318, 325, 327, 329, 336, 349, 371, 375, 379, 380, 396, 399, 411, 421, 423, 424,425, 428, 431, 432, 434, 444, 445, 446, 447, 448, 464, 467, 468, 473, 480, 482, 485, 490, 491, 492, 493, 495, 510, 521, 522, 525, 526, 529, 533
metal 14, 566
metalsmith 30, 83, 97, 181, 236, 311, 373, 408
mineral.....6, 12, 25, 26, 29, 32, 33, 38, 39, 40, 42, 43, 48, 50, 51, 56, 59, 60, 61, 63, 67, 68, 70, 85, 88, 89, 94, 110, 115, 117, 127, 134, 146, 175, 183, 186, 195,

196, 197, 198, 205, 207, 209, 210, 219, 231, 275, 281, 289, 292, 294, 295, 300, 301, 302, 303, 305, 320, 323, 329, 374, 376, 387, 393, 398, 404, 408, 411, 422, 429, 430, 432, 433, 443, 458, 473, 475, 480, 494, 495, 496, 498, 500, 501, 508, 524, 527, 532, 537, 558
mine-worker 14, 566
mleccha 31, 50, 52, 53, 56, 63, 79, 80, 86, 88, 145, 173, 174, 182, 183, 202, 206, 248, 255, 260, 363, 457, 473, 474, 497, 522, 526, 529, 765
monkey 61, 129, 130, 187, 520, 521
mountain....... 5, 36, 61, 82, 120, 139, 150, 180, 181, 236, 237, 339, 380, 395, 401, 407, 419, 491, 518, 526, 539
Munda... 25, 34, 52, 53, 71, 83, 88, 90, 93, 114, 115, 118, 119, 131, 133, 138, 162, 163, 165, 170, 172, 174, 175, 176, 177, 178, 180, 182, 192, 195, 198, 199, 202, 204, 208, 214, 247, 263, 274, 289, 308, 309, 311, 329, 335, 369, 370, 371, 372, 379, 380, 396, 404,422, 423, 428, 472, 473, 490, 497, 500, 501, 503, 531, 532, 533
Narmer.................................... 19, 21, 143
native metal.... 26, 31, 42, 58, 78, 96, 100, 153, 165, 173, 177, 203, 231, 234, 299, 300, 304, 336, 359, 360, 369, 375, 377, 378, 399, 412, 413, 423, 431, 462, 464, 482, 501
Nausharo.... 15, 31, 41, 69, 142, 146, 476, 533, 567
neck 31, 41, 110, 145, 146, 147, 148, 178, 185, 245, 254, 259, 288, 291, 351, 445, 471, 497, 517, 521, 530, 573, 661, 685, 687, 688, 708, 725
Nindowari-damb 758
numeral... 5, 127, 183, 188, 329, 359, 360, 364, 462
offering 2, 20, 42, 132, 150, 219, 277, 322, 346, 381, 387, 422, 427, 429, 430, 697
on all fours 96
ore 2, 6, 8, 9, 12, 13, 21, 25, 26, 31, 32, 33, 40, 43, 47, 58, 59, 60, 61, 64, 67, 70, 78, 83, 85, 93, 94, 95, 96, 100, 110, 117, 122, 126, 139, 140, 141, 147, 152, 153, 173, 177, 178, 180, 186, 189, 193, 195, 196, 197, 198, 199, 203, 204, 205, 207, 211, 214, 215, 219, 231, 236, 239, 247, 275, 281, 288, 289, 292, 293, 294, 300, 301, 302, 303, 304, 323, 329, 335, 336, 346, 369, 370, 371, 373, 375, 376, 378, 379, 382, 384, 387, 399, 402, 404, 405, 409, 410, 411, 413, 424, 429, 430, 431, 433, 443, 446, 447, 448, 449, 450, 462, 464, 465, 473, 475, 477, 480, 482, 495, 496, 498, 501, 521, 522, 523, 527, 528, 529, 530, 531, 532, 533, 553, 558
oval 572
Pabumath... 758
pace 18, 56, 373, 554
Pande 16, 17, 382, 384, 567, 569, 764, 766
Pāṇini... 31
pannier . 31, 145, 147, 344, 379, 398, 445, 479, 661, 685
Parpola 11, 15, 16, 17, 30, 31, 94, 95, 125, 167, 176, 311, 334, 349, 365, 382, 468, 495, 567, 568, 569, 764, 766, 780
pectoral.............. 8, 15, 145, 170, 567, 780
penance . 2, 5, 21, 61, 146, 185, 375, 407, 414, 424, 425, 433, 473, 475, 484, 490, 491, 513, 540
Persian Gulf... 6, 9, 17, 18, 26, 29, 39, 51, 65, 76, 104, 107, 115, 205, 230, 569, 780
pewter..6, 9, 10, 50, 60, 80, 109, 110, 112, 114, 115, 118, 121, 122, 126, 127, 128, 170, 172, 188, 189, 197, 207, 213, 232, 263, 294, 310, 326, 327, 328, 357, 358, 372, 375, 382, 384, 386, 388, 394, 395, 398, 399, 400, 402, 403, 404, 406, 407, 408, 409, 415, 431, 458, 459, 460, 468, 475, 476, 480, 482, 483, 486, 487, 491, 493, 512, 513, 521, 525, 527
phonetic.....2, 6, 18, 19, 21, 27, 41, 45, 65, 70, 71, 79, 86, 127, 133, 135, 176, 177, 182, 210, 219, 302, 314, 325, 353, 367, 370, 378, 380, 399, 405, 412, 425, 434, 475, 492, 502, 521, 556
pictograph 65
pictorial motif . 8, 9, 11, 13, 14, 15, 17, 18, 21, 22, 27, 29, 30, 41, 50, 51, 65, 80, 94, 96, 170, 188, 309, 353, 395, 407, 429, 468, 566, 567, 568, 780

pig-tail....................................430, 586, 662
Pinault..56, 373
pipal 70, 429, 431, 525, 590, 688, 698, 725
platform....... 5, 70, 82, 140, 183, 186, 238, 266, 269, 365, 366, 404, 407, 424, 426, 433, 434, 466, 467, 491, 492, 529, 586, 587, 688, 697, 698, 725, 734
Pleiades..........................23, 427, 430, 471
portable furnace 6, 12, 23, 31, 41, 47, 145, 146, 153, 172, 186, 195, 196, 221, 233, 234, 293, 306, 346, 353, 359, 403, 407, 408, 413, 414, 420, 428, 431, 449, 498, 499, 501, 516, 518, 526, 528
Possehl.. 18, 140, 199, 280, 762, 766, 780
Prakrit 32, 52, 61, 182, 224, 300, 401
present 14, 15, 16, 566, 567, 568, 780
Priest......................47, 286, 288, 289, 467
Proto-Elamite..............................131, 518
Proto-Indo-European.......................... 55
pun 47, 86, 89, 90, 260
punch-marked.... 9, 11, 27, 28, 50, 51, 53, 71, 181, 237, 239
Rakhigarhi.. 124, 453, 454, 501, 502, 529, 759, 762, 780
ram ...5, 49, 60, 61, 79, 88, 90, 95, 99, 101, 114, 130, 131, 138, 161, 165, 171, 172, 178, 180, 194, 231, 247, 276, 307, 309, 311, 339, 371, 396, 405, 423, 427, 428, 429, 430, 431, 432, 457, 471, 477, 491, 492, 497, 507, 515, 522, 525, 526, 532, 533, 586, 688, 698, 702, 724, 725
Rāmāyaṇa... 92
Rampurva......................50, 180, 181, 236
rat203
rebus...14, 566
rebus method..........................18, 44, 182
reduplicated 7, 192, 355
reduplication 9, 175
rhinoceros 5, 6, 83, 117, 140, 149, 150, 162, 166, 167, 187, 188, 309, 399, 412, 441, 493, 502, 511, 512, 514, 520, 521, 522, 529, 688, 723, 732, 734, 737
Rigveda .. 9, 33, 34, 45, 47, 49, 50, 54, 55, 56, 58, 60, 62, 63, 64, 67, 79, 80, 110, 127, 175, 177, 183, 193, 210, 275, 289, 367, 484, 487, 500, 535, 536, 537, 539, 540, 549, 553, 560
rim of jar ..5, 6, 7, 8, 25, 30, 42, 44, 46, 50, 65, 83, 96, 109, 110, 112, 122, 127, 137, 169, 189, 196, 203, 231, 237, 248, 294, 295, 299, 300, 301, 303, 318, 323, 330, 351, 352, 357, 358, 377, 386, 394, 395, 397, 398, 399, 400, 403, 404, 406, 407, 409, 410, 411, 412, 419, 420, 422, 423, 424, 425, 426, 429, 432, 446, 447, 449, 450, 452, 454, 455, 458, 459, 460, 468, 479, 486, 494, 519, 531
rimless pot...... 5, 30, 43, 74, 82, 124, 181, 195, 196, 219, 236, 238, 293, 294, 295, 298, 300, 301, 304, 321, 322, 324, 330, 357, 379, 380, 396, 400, 401, 403, 407, 410, 413, 419, 422, 425, 427, 428, 429, 434, 455, 458, 459
rings on neck 31, 145, 146, 147, 254, 259
road................ 64, 183, 203, 331, 335, 487
Rojdi....................................199, 760, 762
Ropar...50
Sarasvati1, 2, 7, 11, 13, 14, 15, 17, 18, 33, 39, 50, 52, 53, 54, 56, 65, 71, 74, 75, 76, 78, 79, 92, 93, 106, 143, 145, 182, 206, 229, 231, 237, 238, 239, 331, 346, 424, 436, 467, 484, 537, 538, 539, 566, 567, 568, 764, 765
Sarasvati river basin................14, 331, 566
scarf...... 5, 12, 59, 61, 134, 193, 194, 275, 300, 375, 380, 425, 430, 432, 433, 434, 473, 475, 496, 500, 501, 508, 523, 524
scorpion.... 2, 21, 40, 48, 60, 83, 102, 105, 173, 196, 231, 399, 410, 411, 431, 441, 520, 521, 529, 530, 532, 533, 535, 663, 780
scribe .6, 10, 25, 44, 45, 46, 49, 50, 83, 85, 109, 110, 114, 122, 124, 127, 129, 169, 178, 189, 196, 203, 214, 294, 295, 299, 300, 301, 303, 323, 336, 344, 347, 350, 351, 352, 353, 357, 358, 377, 386, 394, 395, 397, 399, 400, 406, 407, 409, 410, 411, 412, 419, 420, 424, 425, 426, 429, 432, 446, 447, 449, 450, 452, 458, 459, 460, 468, 475, 479, 482, 494, 519, 533
semantic......2, 6, 14, 19, 20, 48, 53, 73, 74, 130, 134, 135, 173, 176, 211, 230, 289, 336, 365, 372, 433, 522, 530, 535, 538, 560, 566
semantic clusters 176, 560

serpent.... 5, 112, 139, 148, 152, 276, 337, 431, 433, 457, 470, 471, 473, 474, 477, 496, 516, 688, 695, 698, 702, 724
serpent hood.......................... 5, 139, 433
shawl.......... 5, 47, 199, 280, 289, 291, 305
Shortugai.................................... 65, 116
signboard 11, 12, 53, 436
silver. 23, 34, 35, 50, 53, 59, 61, 64, 86, 88, 92, 99, 107, 109, 115, 133, 139, 145, 149, 151, 165, 171, 208, 209, 210, 231, 235, 239, 245, 246, 247, 270, 302, 308, 323, 329, 372, 373, 378, 386, 390, 473, 488, 490, 500, 504
śivalinga 546, 549, 560
slope 90, 110, 126, 380, 388, 414, 419, 446, 447, 448, 451, 514
sloping 167, 189, 336, 380, 451
smelt 533
smelter.... 6, 10, 11, 26, 27, 29, 32, 42, 47, 48, 59, 60, 61, 65, 66, 67, 70, 72, 73, 82, 85, 94, 95, 118, 120, 121, 128, 136, 139, 165, 180, 185, 193, 198, 203, 205, 206, 214, 219, 237, 245, 246, 247, 265, 266, 274, 277, 281, 288, 289, 294, 295, 298, 299, 301, 302,303, 304, 305, 310, 311, 318, 323, 344, 346, 347, 349, 351, 363, 375, 377, 387, 398, 399, 400, 401, 407, 408, 410, 413, 422, 423, 427, 431, 433, 434, 444, 447, 449, 451, 452, 454, 455, 462, 468, 469, 474, 476, 479, 484, 491, 495, 496, 519, 525, 528, 531, 533, 535, 546, 553, 557, 558
smelting.. 6, 11, 29, 48, 50, 51, 56, 59, 63, 66, 68, 69, 72, 85, 95, 96, 109, 126, 148, 161, 165, 173, 174, 197, 198, 216, 219, 221, 237, 239, 274, 311, 319, 322, 347, 350, 352, 353, 357, 358, 378, 407, 430, 457, 458, 459, 460, 464, 468, 473, 474, 478, 485, 497, 519, 531, 533, 537, 538, 542, 545
smith ..6, 25, 30, 40, 50, 51, 53, 74, 82, 83, 96, 123, 129, 132, 135, 145, 151, 152, 175, 177, 209, 232, 261, 315, 319, 320, 325, 328, 336, 347, 351, 371, 385, 393, 395, 408, 421, 423, 431, 445, 452, 464, 466, 473, 474, 479, 488, 490, 491, 492, 493, 494, 495, 500, 501, 507, 511, 518, 521, 526, 529
smiths 14, 68, 93, 145, 186, 237, 305, 310, 366, 463, 467, 491, 503, 522, 523, 530, 566
smithy 12, 15, 25, 30, 34, 42, 43, 46, 50, 51, 59, 63, 64, 66, 68, 73, 82, 96, 105, 109, 112, 120, 124, 127, 128, 129, 133, 135, 137, 147, 149, 151, 183, 188, 193, 195, 202, 206, 221, 231, 240, 248, 254, 263, 269, 276, 277, 278, 282, 293, 294, 295, 297, 300, 301, 302, 305, 306, 311, 325, 328, 331, 347, 349, 350, 352, 353, 355, 357, 358, 359, 360, 364, 374, 375, 380, 385, 386, 387, 394, 395, 396, 398, 399, 400, 401, 403, 404, 405, 406, 409, 410, 411, 413, 419, 420, 421, 423, 426, 427, 428, 429, 430, 431, 446, 447, 448, 450, 451, 452, 456, 458, 459, 460, 462, 464, 466, 467, 469, 474, 480, 487, 491, 493, 495, 500, 501, 503, 508, 512, 516, 517, 519, 523, 524, 525, 527, 529, 530, 531, 566
Sohgaura....... 50, 181, 237, 238, 239, 240
Southworth.................................... 52, 56
spade... 366
spear. 23, 59, 60, 112, 151, 237, 238, 351, 479, 514, 663, 698, 733, 734
spinner....................................... 193, 780
splinter.... 42, 96, 112, 126, 137, 152, 153, 183, 240, 248, 254, 293, 294, 299, 300, 302, 304, 326, 327, 329, 336, 359, 364, 366, 375, 394, 396, 404, 419, 432, 433, 443, 446, 447, 448, 450, 452, 465, 493, 494, 500, 501, 512, 519
spokes 83, 90, 98, 118, 147, 254, 303, 377, 500, 501, 503, 508
spotted....................................... 108, 149
sprachbund.. 9, 10, 13, 19, 30, 44, 47, 49, 51, 52, 53, 54, 56, 58, 60, 66, 79, 80, 146, 162, 173, 175, 176, 177, 182, 193, 206, 208, 221, 230, 288, 360, 363, 367, 370, 373, 398, 454, 496, 502, 536, 559
spy 82, 83, 84, 423, 430, 431
squirrel.... 16, 41, 293, 294, 311, 312, 314, 315, 325, 568, 600, 612
śreṇi.. 320, 495
śrivatsa...................................... 221, 223
standard device. 8, 12, 31, 41, 47, 58, 64, 78, 144, 145, 205, 221, 228, 233, 293,

348, 355, 356, 447, 448, 518, 522, 573, 688, 723
star 11, 28, 32, 61, 68, 114, 117, 118, 162, 181, 195, 205, 221, 222, 236, 248, 254, 259, 263, 363, 375, 433, 527, 582
steel 9, 31, 96, 172, 183, 204, 234, 404, 424, 512, 522, 530, 537, 538, 540, 553
step 14, 43, 64, 93, 192, 379, 566
stone 2, 6, 12, 14, 21, 25, 32, 33, 34, 40, 42, 43, 44, 47, 48, 58, 60, 61, 64, 65, 69, 70, 71, 72, 78, 83, 93, 96, 99, 107, 109, 119, 121, 126, 140, 141, 147, 149, 153, 162, 167, 171, 177, 178, 180, 183, 195, 196, 197, 203, 204, 207, 209, 217, 219, 231, 240, 247, 270, 276, 277, 279, 281, 286, 288, 289, 291, 293, 305, 315, 323, 329, 334, 335, 336, 345, 366, 371, 373, 375, 379, 399, 404, 407, 410, 411, 430, 431, 433, 436, 443, 445, 446, 447, 448, 449, 450, 451, 453, 458, 462, 463, 464, 465, 466, 467, 491, 492, 495, 500, 501, 504, 507, 519, 523, 527, 528, 529, 530, 531, 532, 533, 536, 558, 559, 566
stool 2, 5, 20, 42, 138, 193, 202, 376, 407, 422, 424, 427, 429, 430, 432, 471, 492
stump 152, 239
substrate 14, 52, 174, 176, 566
substrates 106
Sumerian .. 33, 36, 92, 106, 108, 128, 134, 136, 138, 144, 167, 174, 176, 197, 214, 230, 276, 472, 481, 504
summit 63, 100, 237, 239, 380
Surkotada 760
Susa 33, 34, 35, 36, 37, 41, 132, 179, 193, 260, 261, 263, 274, 275, 307, 308, 467, 480, 481, 482, 510, 511, 516, 523, 524, 764, 780
svastika. 5, 9, 17, 126, 127, 128, 172, 195, 196, 213, 214, 215, 221, 223, 225, 226, 228, 388, 391, 392, 393, 431, 530, 569, 586, 698, 726
swastika 172, 393, 480, 532
tablet 15, 566, 585, 589, 592, 594, 595, 596, 657, 733, 734, 757, 762
tail 2, 21, 94, 129, 135, 137, 139, 152, 173, 187, 221, 222, 225, 228, 385, 393, 394, 395, 396, 398, 401, 411, 420, 427, 429, 430, 431, 457, 470, 471, 474, 477, 491, 527, 572, 573, 574, 585, 592, 597, 610, 662, 663, 686, 688, 698, 701, 702, 724, 725, 726, 736
tantra yukti 1, 2, 4, 5, 8, 10, 11, 395
Tarkhanewala-dera 761
Tello 209
Tepe Yahya 107, 117, 245, 420
terracotta 14, 69, 71, 73, 74, 96, 125, 188, 189, 229, 239, 315, 316, 318, 333, 334, 356, 358, 407, 436, 458, 463, 514, 515, 538, 566
Theobald 27, 50
throat 72, 445
tiger 5, 6, 13, 18, 42, 59, 60, 65, 73, 82, 83, 84, 85, 88, 94, 97, 127, 132, 139, 149, 150, 151, 152, 153, 162, 167, 187, 193, 194, 203, 213, 229, 233, 234, 245, 246, 247, 309, 345, 346, 399, 400, 423, 431, 441, 457, 473, 475, 476, 477, 484, 485, 490, 491, 493, 496, 512, 513, 514, 515, 519, 520, 522, 523, 529, 530, 531, 533, 538, 573, 585, 586, 662, 663, 688, 689, 693, 697, 698, 702, 724, 725, 732
tin 6, 9, 22, 28, 36, 38, 39, 42, 50, 51, 59, 60, 61, 64, 67, 68, 79, 80, 86, 88, 92, 93, 96, 109, 110, 112, 115, 116, 121, 122, 126, 129, 131, 132, 137, 141, 146, 151, 162, 163, 170, 172, 174, 175, 177, 188, 189, 207, 209, 210, 219, 231, 232, 240, 243, 247, 263, 294, 301, 303, 310, 311, 320, 321, 322, 326, 331, 357, 358, 360, 372, 375, 380, 381, 382, 384, 385, 386, 394, 395, 397, 398, 399, 400, 401, 402, 403, 404, 406, 407, 408, 409, 410, 411, 419, 425, 426, 428, 430, 431, 445, 446, 447, 450, 452, 458, 459, 460, 468, 469, 473, 475, 479, 480, 482, 483, 486, 487, 492, 493, 495, 501, 502, 508, 513, 519, 521, 524, 525, 527, 529, 530, 531, 533, 780
tin ingot 22, 38, 51, 162, 231, 450, 780
Tocharian 56, 373
trader 482, 485, 491
tree ... 18, 23, 24, 27, 32, 42, 59, 61, 70, 82, 83, 94, 97, 102, 120, 121, 147, 153, 154, 165, 167, 172, 178, 180, 203, 204, 219, 237, 238, 239, 262, 263, 266, 274, 276, 282, 294, 300, 318, 335, 337, 339,

346, 369, 407, 408, 422, 423, 426, 429, 431, 462, 474, 475, 479, 504, 507, 511, 512, 514, 515, 523, 525, 526, 551, 557, 573, 586, 663, 688, 689, 697, 698, 725, 731, 734, 766
trefoil .. 11, 47, 48, 199, 277, 289, 315, 318
trough.... 11, 110, 134, 138, 153, 276, 309, 345, 346, 366, 375, 384, 395, 397, 398, 400, 403, 405, 407, 412, 413, 463, 464, 466, 467, 468, 480, 481, 482, 574, 663, 732, 736
Turkmenistan 245
turner .6, 12, 14, 30, 32, 43, 45, 58, 59, 60, 78, 82, 88, 94, 96, 113, 122, 139, 145, 148, 150, 170, 178, 196, 210, 219, 226, 231, 232, 299, 300, 301, 303, 307, 308, 310, 331, 335, 344, 345, 346, 349, 350, 353, 355, 356, 357, 358, 367, 372, 378, 386, 403, 410, 422, 424, 425, 431, 443, 444, 445, 446, 447, 450, 452, 458, 459, 460, 463, 486, 491, 492, 493, 495, 498, 500, 501, 508, 517, 518, 519, 521, 522, 529
tusk. 97, 136, 355, 373, 419, 471, 474, 523
twig 586, 662
unsmelted metal 373, 378, 386, 402, 410, 412, 413, 420, 443, 464, 465, 512
upraised arm.........96, 406, 475, 499, 586
Ur 11, 32, 35, 36, 50, 107, 108, 114, 205, 344, 504, 533, 780
Uruk .. 36, 79, 99, 132, 133, 134, 135, 137, 138, 171, 276, 504, 515, 518
Vats.. 15, 20, 141, 242, 255, 295, 321, 354, 356, 365, 463, 465, 467, 476, 536, 567, 764
Vātsyāyana 66, 174
Veda............... 72, 264, 265, 535, 560, 765
Vedic..9, 11, 14, 18, 19, 49, 52, 53, 54, 55, 56, 58, 59, 60, 63, 66, 68, 69, 71, 72, 74, 75, 76, 78, 80, 106, 182, 239, 264, 274, 275, 305, 306, 311, 319, 320, 331, 336, 369, 388, 484, 487, 494, 535, 536, 538, 539, 553, 566, 765
vessel.... 11, 14, 23, 30, 35, 40, 41, 44, 45, 46, 50, 66, 71, 73, 80, 82, 83, 85, 88, 97, 102, 110, 118, 119, 137, 143, 144, 145, 147, 148, 170, 178, 180, 193, 203, 205, 213, 230, 231, 245, 248, 311, 314, 318, 325, 326, 329, 335, 346, 351, 352, 353, 370, 372, 386, 389, 400, 402, 403, 404, 406, 408, 409, 415, 425, 427, 428, 429, 430, 478, 492, 500, 517, 519, 530, 534, 734
vice..............................123, 319, 320, 494
Vidale..................... 10, 315, 332, 471, 473
vikalpa . 60, 63, 66, 80, 457, 463, 492, 559
waist-zone..491
warehouse . 143, 254, 260, 351, 363, 428, 430, 453, 516, 534
water-carrier 11, 42, 65, 205, 239, 310, 344, 352, 377, 427, 447, 449, 451, 452, 468, 469, 531, 573, 581
weights 51, 204, 233, 292, 404
wheel .. 12, 26, 85, 98, 118, 147, 154, 208, 224, 290, 303, 323, 327, 334, 377, 400, 401, 455, 500, 501, 503, 508, 514, 515
wide-mouthed pot 353, 408, 448, 449, 451
wing. 61, 78, 132, 148, 149, 193, 195, 209, 245, 399, 481, 482, 556, 560
workshop.... 10, 12, 14, 26, 42, 58, 64, 66, 67, 73, 78, 82, 85, 87, 96, 97, 110, 112, 121, 126, 137, 143, 146, 147, 151, 171, 183, 188, 210, 219, 234, 237, 240, 248, 254, 259, 294, 299, 300, 301, 302, 303, 304, 305, 311, 319, 320, 321, 324, 325, 326, 327, 328, 329, 331, 344, 349, 350, 353, 355, 356, 359, 360, 364, 366, 375, 378, 380, 387, 394, 395, 396, 397, 399, 404, 405, 406, 407, 409, 412, 413, 419, 422, 423, 427, 428, 430, 432, 433, 434, 443, 444, 446, 447, 448, 449, 450, 451, 452, 454, 458, 462, 463, 464, 465, 466, 467, 480, 491, 493, 494, 497, 500, 501, 508, 512, 519, 520, 523, 528, 531, 559
writer...8, 61, 129
zebu5, 8, 9, 13, 31, 32, 41, 48, 65, 83, 100, 101, 102, 105, 137, 139, 142, 152, 153, 172, 173, 180, 203, 232, 242, 255, 309, 319, 346, 387, 431, 457, 471, 473, 477, 496, 521, 522, 525, 529, 675, 688, 698, 724, 754, 760, 780
zinc...... 9, 50, 80, 109, 115, 127, 128, 141, 172, 184, 186, 188, 189, 195, 196, 197, 198, 210, 213, 214, 215, 219, 225, 243, 320, 321, 327, 357, 360, 380, 381, 382,

End Notes

1 The terminology and citations are from M. Jayaraman, The doctrine of tantrayukti https://www.academia.edu/12132105/Tantrayukti
2 Set Theory was propounded by Cantor. (Cantor, Georg (1874), "Ueber eine Eigenschaft des Inbegriffes aller reellen algebraischen Zahlen", J. *Reine Angew. Math.* 77: 258–262. Wittgenstein critiques Set Theory annexas 'fictitious symbolism' and notes that it is nonsense to talk about all numbers. (Wittgenstein, Ludwig (1975). *Philosophical Remarks*, §129, §174. Oxford: Basil Blackwell).
3 Also called Indus Script. Decipherment demonstrates that an apt expression will be Dharma saṁjñā or Bharatiya hieroglyphs.
4 The total number of Harappa script inscriptions now total over 7,000. The initial corpus of Parpola (and associates)(1973) includes a total number of 3204 texts. After compiling the pictorial corpus, Parpola notes that there are approximately 3700 legible inscriptions (including 1400 duplicate inscriptions, i.e. with repeated texts). Two subsequent volumes of the pictorial corpus include a total of inscriptions as collections from India and Pakistan (e.g., Harappa 2590, Mohenjo-daro 2129, Lothal 281, Chanhudaro 50). Additional inscriptions have been discovered which are not included in the three volumes of Corpus of Inscriptions of Parpola et al.: e.g. Khirsara, Farmana, Gilund, Bhirrana, Kunal, Garo Biro, Rakhigarhi). Mahadevan concordance (1977) with only 2906 artifacts, excludes inscribed objects which do not contain 'texts; for example, this concordance excludes about 50 seals inscribed with the 'svastikā' pictorial motif and a pectoral which contains the pictorial motif of a one-horned bull with a device in front and an over-flowing pot. Parpola concordance has been used to present such objects which also contain valuable orthographic data which may assist in decoding the inscriptions. Many broken objects are also contained in Parpola concordance which are useful, in many cases, to count the number of objects with specific 'field symbolś, a count which also provides some valuable clues to support the decoding of the messages conveyed by the 'field symbolś which dominate the object space. Along the Persian Gulf, in sites such as Failaka, Bahrain, Saar, nearly 2000 Harappa script inscriptions (so-called Dilmun or Persian Gulf seals) have been found on seals and sealings. These are in addition to the Gadd seals of Ancient Near East (Gadd, CJ, Seals of Ancient Indian Style found in Ur in: Possehl, GL, ed. 1979, *Ancient Cities of the Indus*, Delhi, Vikas Publishing House, p.119). In many sites of Ancient Near East such as Shahdad, Susa (lady spinner artifact with Harappa script hieroglyphs, pot containing metal implements with Harappa script hieroglyphs of fish, quail, flowing water), Tepe Hissar, Haifa (three tin ingots with Harappa script found in a shipwreck), Anau, Altyn Depe (also spelt as Altin Tepe), caravan routes from Ashur and Mari to Kish, Anatolia. Many cylinder seals with cuneiform inscriptions also contain uniquely characteristic Harappa script hieroglyphs such as 'overflowing pot', sun's rays, safflower, pine-cone, fish, scorpion, zebu, buffalo, hair-styles with six curls.

5 http://www.scribd.com/doc/2232617/lexicon linked at http://sites.google.com/site/kalyan97/indus-writing
6 [http://huntingtonarchive.osu.edu/Makara%20Site/makara

7 The earliest inscription in Harappa script was discovered on a potsherd by (Harappa Archaeological Research Project of Harvard University) (HARP) team and dated to ca. 3300 BCE

8 Harappa script hieroglyphs were seen together with an inscription in Brahmi on Sohgaura copper plate dated to pre-Mauryan times, ca. 600 BCE. On thousands of punch-marked and cast coins of mints from Takshasila to Karur to Anuradhapura signify Harappa Script hieroglyphs attesting to the significance of the hieroglyphs in mintwork (e.g. kuTi 'tree' rebus: kuThi 'smelter' karibha 'elephant' rebus: karba 'iron' ayo, aya 'fish' rebus: aya 'iron' satthiya 'svastika hieroglyph glyph' rebus: sattva, jasta 'zinc')

9 George Coedes, *Histoire ancienne des Etats hindouises d'Extreme-Orient*,1944 (*Ancient History of the Hinduised States of Ancient Far East*)

10 http://arabian-archaeology.com/images/ic-007.jpg

11 Possehl, Gregory L. (1996). *Indus Age: The Writing System*. University of Pennsylvania Press.

12 A phrase used by linguist MB Emeneau

13 http://www.dictionary.com/browse/data--mining

14 Internet access: https://drive.google.com/file/d/0B4BAzCi4O_l4bHpvVTNRa2U5R00/view?usp=drive_web

15 After I.Mahadevan, 1977, opcit.

16 Cf. Parpola, Asko (2005) *Study of the Harappa Script*. 50th ICES Tokyo Session. Phonetic representation of Narmer's name is seen as central serekhs at the top of both sides of the Palette bearing the rebus symbols *n'r* (catfish) and *mr* (chisel) inside.

17 Gunther Dreyer. A Hundred Years at Abydos.

18 Elise V. Macarthur, "The Concept and Development of the Egyptian Writing System" IN: Woods (ed), *Visible Language. Inventions of Writing in the Middle East and Beyond* [2010] 120; the book illustrates many of the objects from Tomb U-j; see also 138-143

19 "The ship's principal cargo was copper ingots, of which no less than 345 have been recovered. Three hundred and seventeen of these were "ox-hide" shape with four legs or handles for easy lifting. The rest were similar two-handled ingots as well as a few flat, pillow-shaped and oval "bun" ingots...Each of the oxhide ingots... weighed about 23 kilograms. The ore for the ingots came from Cyprus (ancient Alashiya) though the only known casting mould for such shapes was one excavated near the city of Ugarit (modern Ras Shamra) on the North- Syrian coast. A letter in the form of a clay tablet from the king of Alashiya to an Egyptian pharaoh found at Amarna in Egypt dated around 1370 BC reads: "I will bring to thee as a present 200 talents of copper". Was this the promised shipment, a gift that ended up on the sea floor off the point known today as Uluburun? We can only speculate ... the estimated six tons of copper on the Uluburun ship was enough (when mixed with tin) to manufacture a total of 300 bronze helmets, 300 bronze corselets, 3000 spearheads, and 3000 bronze swords...During the early stages of the excavation a grayish, brittle material was discovered – samples showed it to be pure tin. Tin ingots were also found later. It is possible that the tin could have come from modern-day Afghanistan. The approximately one ton of tin eventually excavated is the oldest ever discovered in its raw form. Alloyed with copper this would yield 11 tons of bronze." (Fawcett. N & JC Zietsman, 2001, "Uluburun - the discovery and excavation of the world's oldest

known shipwreck". *Akroterion*, Vol. 46 (2001): 5 - 20. , http://akrolerion.journals.za)
20 *Siddhānti Subrahmaṇya' śāstri's new interpretation of the Amarakośa*, Bangalore, Vicaradarpana Press, 1872, p. 330
21 For detailed Meluhha (Indian sprachbund) readings, see:
http://bharatkalyan97.blogspot.in/2015/04/dholavira-1-signboard-and-2-stone.html
Meluhha is parole (vāk) Prakritam of Indian sprachbund.
22 Witzel, Michael, Central Asian Roots and Acculturation in South Asia. Linguistic and Archaeological Evidence from Western Central Asia, the Hindukush and Northwestern South Asia for Early Indo-Aryan Language and Religion. In: T. Osada (ed.), Linguistics, Archaeology and the Human Past (Kyoto : Indus Project, Research Institute for Humanity and Nature 2005), pp. 87-211.
23 .Lubotsky, A., The Indo-Iranian Substratum, in: Early Contacts between Uralic and Indo-European: Linguistic and Archaeological Considerations, ed. Chr. Carpelan, A. Parpola, P.Koskikallio (Helsinki, Suomalais- Ugrilainen Seura 2001), pp. 301-317.
24 D.W. Anthony, *The Horse, the Wheel and* Language (2007), pp. 455-6.
25 Fabri, CL, The punch-marked coins: a survival of the Indus Civilization, 1935, *Journal of the Royal Asiatic Society of Great Britain and Ireland*, Cambridge University Press. pp.307-318. A comparison of Punch-marked hieroglyphs with Harappa Script inscriptions:
26 W. Theobald, 1890, Notes on some of the symbols found on the punch-marked coins of Hindustan, and on their relationship to the archaic symbolism of other races and distant lands, *Journal of the Asiatic Society of Bengal, Bombay Branch (JASB),* Part 1. History , Literature etc., Nos. III & IV, 1890, pp. 181 to 184) W. Theobald, Symbols on punch-marked coins of Hindustan (1890,1901).
27 Source for the tables of symbols on punchmarked coins: Savita Sharma, 1990, *Early Indian Symbols, Numismatic Evidence*, Delhi, Agam Kala Prakashan.
28 https://indiacoinsmarks.wordpress.com/tag/punch-marks/
29 After Durrani, FA, et al., 1994-95, Seals and inscribed sherds in: *Excavations in the Gomal valley: Rehman Dheri report No.2 ed.* Taj Ali. Ancient Pakistan 10, Peshawar: Department of Archaeology, University of Peshawar: Pp. 198-223.
30 After C. Jarrige et al., 1995, Mehrgarh Field Reports 1974-1985: From neolithic times to the Indus civilization, Karachi: Sind Culture Department: 160.
31 Dennys Frenez and Massimo Vidale, 2012*, Harappa Chimaeras as 'Symbolic Hypertexts'. Some Thoughts on Plato, Chimaera and the Indus Civilization*
http://a.harappa.com/content/harappan-chimaeras
32 After Fig. 11 in Parpola

http://www.thehindu.com/multimedia/archive/00133/_A_Dravidian_Soluti_133901a.pdf

33 Donkin, R.A., 1998, Beyond price: pearls and pearl-fishing: origins to the age of discoveries, Philadelphia, American Philosophical Society, Memoir Volume 224, pp.49-50)Full text at http://tinyurl.com/y9zpb5n Note 109. For Sumerian words, see Delitzch, 1914: pp.18-19 (igi, eye), 125 (ku, fish), 195 (na, stone); and cf. Chicago Assyrian Dictionary I/J: 1960: pp.45 (iga), 153-158 (Akk. i_nu), N(2), 1980: p.340 (k), 'fish-eye stoneś.Note 110. A.L. Oppenheim, 1954: pp.7-8; Leemans, 1960b: pp.24 f. (IGI-KU6). Followed by Kramer, 1963a: p.113, 1963b: p.283; Bibby, 1970: pp.189, 191-192: Ratnāgar, 1981: pp.23-24,79, 188; M. Rice, 1985: p.181.Note 111. A.L. Oppenheim, 1954: p.11; Leemans, 1960b: p.37 (NA4 IGI-KU6, 'fish-eye stoneś.Note 112. Leemans, 1968: p.222 ('pearls from Meluhha'. Falkenstein (1963: pp.10-11 [12]) has '*augenformigen Perlen aus Meluhha*'.(lit. shaped eyes beads from Meluhha).

34 loc.cit. Donkin, RA, 1998, Beyond price: pearls and pearl-fishing: origins to the age of discoveries, Vol. 224, American Philosophical Society, p.50; Berlin, ed., 1947, *Fragmentos desconocidos del codice de Yanbuiltan y otras investigaciones mixtecos*, Mexico, p.31; Humboldt, 1811, 1966, *Political essay on the Kingdom of New* Spain (1811), 4 volumes, London, Vol. 3: p.80

35 Role of shell in Mesopotamia: evidence for trade exchange with Oman and Indus valley - T.R. Gensheimer (1984)
36 http://www.louvre.fr/oeuvre-notices/vase-la-cachette
37 Moorey, Peter Roger Stuart, 1999, Ancient Mesopotamian Materials and industries: the archaeological evidence, Eisenbrauns, p.245

38 Potts, Daniel T., 1997, *Mesopotamian civilization: the material foundations*, A&C Black, pp.266-269
39 S. Kalyanaraman, 2010, The Bronze Age Writing System of Sarasvati Hieroglyphics as Evidenced by Two "Rosetta Stones" in: *Journal of Indo-Judaic Studies* Volume 1: Number 11 (2010), pp. 47-74
http://bharatkalyan97.blogspot.in/2015/04/ox-hide-ingots-of-tin-and-one-third.html
Fig. 4 Inscribed tin ingot with a moulded head, from Haifa (Artzy, 1983: 53). (Michal Artzy, 1983, Arethusa of the Tin Ingot, Bulletin of the American Schools of Oriental Research, BASOR 250, pp. 51-55). https://www.academia.edu/5476188/Artzy-1983-Tin-Ignot

40 http://bharatkalyan97.blogspot.in/2016/08/tin-bronze-age-revolution-on-maritime.html Tin-Bronze Age Revolution on Maritime Tin Route from Hanoi to Haifa & matching revolution of Harappa Script writing system
41 Stamp seal with unicorn and ritual offering stand, ca. 2000-1900 B.C.; Harappa. Indus Valley, Harappa, 8796-01. Harappa Script (Indus) inscription. Steatite; L. 5.2 cm (2 in.); W. 5.2 cm (2 in.). Harappa Museum, Harappa H99-4064. Courtesy of the Department of Archaeology and Museums, Ministry of Minorities, Culture, Sports, Tourism, and Youth Affairs, Government of Pakistan www.metmuseum.org
42 http://bharatkalyan97.blogspot.in/2016/04/karani-helmsman-scribe-supercargo-of.html kāraṇī 'helmsman, scribe, supercargo' of Harappa Script~~Kernunno of maritimePilier des Nautes
43 Bernard Maier, *Dictionary of Celtic Religion and Culture* (Alfred Kröner, 1994; Boydell, 2000), p. 69.The website of Ceisiwr Serith is at http://www.ceisiwrserith.com/therest/Cernunnos/cernunnospaper.htm
44 Modification of a photograph by Malene Thyssen, published under a Creative Commons licence
45 http://bharatkalyan97.blogspot.in/2015/06/tvastr-meluhha-of-bharatam-janam.html
46 Schaller, Helmut W, Roman Jakobson's conception of 'sprachbund' in: Cahiers de l'ILSL, No. 9, 1997, p.200, 202
47 Emeneau, MB, India as a Lingustic Area M. B. Emeneau *Language* Vol. 32, No. 1 (Jan. - Mar., 1956), pp. 3-16

48 cf. Emeneau, Murray; Dil, Anwar (1980), Language and Linguistic Area: Essays by Murray B. Emeneau, Palo Alto: Stanford University Press. Kuiper, FBJ, 1967, 'The genesis of a linguistic area' in: Indo-Iranian Journal 10: 81-102
49 Kazanas, Nicholas, 2015, Vedic and Indo-European Studies, Delhi, Aditya Prakashan, p.xxxi

50 *The Rigvedic People, 'Invaders"? 'Immigrants? or Indigenous? -- Evidence of Archaeology and Literature*, 2015, Aryan Books International
51 Ibid., BB Lal, 2015, pp. 50-52

52 Note on *(amśu)* 'metallic stalks of stone ore'. An uncertain meaning of *soma* in Rigveda though the entire samhita holds the processing of soma in a nutshell, can be resolved in the context of modifers to 'fish' hieroglyph to denote 'fins or scaleś.The vedic texts provide an intimation treating *amśu* as a synonym of *soma.*George Pinault has found a cognate word in Tocharian, *ancu* which means 'iron'. I have argued in my book, *Indian alchemy, soma in the Veda*, that *Soma* was an allegory, 'electrum' (gold-silver compound). See: http://bharatkalyan97.blogspot.in/2011/10/itihasa-and-eagle-narratives.html for Pinault's views on *ancu, amśu* concordance.The link with the Tocharian word is intriguing because *Soma* was supposed to come from Mt. Mujavant. A cognate of Mujavant is Mustagh Ata of the Himalayan ranges in Kyrgystan.Is it possible that the *ancu* of Tocharian from this mountain was indeed *Soma*? The referemces to *Anzu* in ancient Mesopotamian tradition parallels the legends of *śyena* 'falcon' which is used in Vedic tradition of *Soma yajña* attested archaeologically in Uttarakhand with a *śyenaciti*, 'falcon-shaped' fire-altar.

http://bharatkalyan97.blogspot.in/2011/11/syena-orthography.html śyena, orthography, Sasanian iconography. Continued use of Harappa Script hieroglyphs. Comparing the allegory of soma and the legend of Anzu, the bird which stole the tablets of destiny, I posit a hypothesis that the tablets of destiny are paralleled by the Harappa Script writing corpora which constitute a veritable catalog of stone-, mineral- and metal-ware in the bronze age evolving from the chalcolithic phase of what constituted an 'industrial' revolution of ancient times creating ingots of metal alloys and weapons and tools using metal alloys which transformed the relation of communities with nature and resulted in the life-activities of lapidaries transforming into miners, smiths and traders of metal artefacts.
I suggest that ayas of bronze age created a revolutionary transformation in the lives of people of these bronze age times. Maybe, Tocharian ancu had the same meaning as Rigvedic gloss, *amśu.* If so, *ancu* might have denoted electrum, 'gold-silver compound' which was subjected to reduction, by oxidation of impurities, by incessant firing for five days and nights to create the shining wealth of gold. The old Egyptian gloss for electrum was*assem*, cognate *soma.*
53 http://bharatkalyan97.blogspot.in/2016/07/having-eight-corners-vedic-yupa-in_35.html
54 Robert S. Wicks, 1992, Money, markets and trade in early Southeast Asia: the development of indigenous monetary systems to AD 1400, SEAP Publications, Cornell, Ithaca, NY, p.245; loc. Cit. Mulavarman's First Yūpa Inscription; FH van Naerssen, and RC longh, *The economic and administrative history of early Indonesia,* Leiden: Brill, 1977), p. 20; J. Ph. Vogel, 'The Yūpa inscription of Mulavarman from Koelei (East Borneo)', Bijdragen tot de Taal-, *Land-en Volkenkunde* 79, 1918: 213; Mulavarman's Second Yūpa Inscription, Vogel, 'Yūpa Inscriptionś, p. 214; Mulavarman's Third Yūpa Inscription; Vogel, '*Yūpa Inscriptions*', p. 215.
55 Occurs in the Atharvaveda(AV 5.19.12) and KauśikaSūtra (Bloomsfield's edn, xliv. cf. Bloomsfield, *American Journal of Philology*, 11, 355; 12,416; Roth, Festgruss anBohtlingk, 98) denotes it as a twig. This is identified as that of Badarī, the jujube tied to the body of the dead to efface their traces. (See *Vedic Index*, I, p. 177).

56 Davey. CJ, 2009, *The early history of lost wax casting. Metallurgy and Civilisation*, J. Mei and Th. Rehren eds. Archetype, London, 147-154
57 https://www.scribd.com/doc/219986780/Davey-Christopher-J-The-early-history-of-lost-wax-casting-in-J-Mei-and-Th-Rehren-eds-Metallurgy-and-Civilisation-Eurasia-and-Beyond-Archety
58 http://bharatkalyan97.blogspot.in/2016/04/dharma-samjna-corporate-badges-of-indus.html
59 1. "Data Mining"ACM SIGKDD. 2006-04-30.2. Clifton, Christopher (2010). Encyclopaedia Britannica; definition of Data Mining. 3.Hastie, Trevor; Tibshirani, Robert; Friedman, Jerome (2009). "The elements of statistical learning: Data mining, inference, and prediction"
60 After Fig. 2.19, Kenoyer, JM,1998, *Ancient cities of the Indus Valley*, Oxford U. Press
61 After Fig. 7.44, Kenoyer, 1998 National Museum, Karachi. 54.3554. HM 13828. Seal, Bet Dwaraka 20 x 18 mm of conch shell. Seven shell bangles from burial ofan elderly woman, Harappa; worn on the left arm; three on the upper arm and four on the forearm; 6.3 X 5.7 cm to 8x9 cm marine shell, *Turbinella pyrum* (After Fig. 7.43, Kenoyer, 1998) Harappa museum. H87-635 to 637; 676 to 679.

62 After Mackay 1938: I, 411; II, pl. 107:35; Parpola, 1994, p. 218.

63 http://bharatkalyan97.blogspot.in/2015/05/smithy-is-temple-of-bronze-age-stambha_14.html Srivastava, AK, 1999, Catalogue of Saiva sculptures in Government Museum, Mathura: 47, GMM 52.3625
64 https://en.wikipedia.org/wiki/Shiva
65 Kalibangan Excavation report, p. 31
66 http://bharatkalyan97.blogspot.in/2015/12/binjor-seal-with-indus-script.html http://www.asi.nic.in/nmma_reviews/Indian%20Archaeology%201963-64%20A%20Review.pdf

67 Denise Schmandt-Besserat, *How Writing Came About*, University of Texas Press 1996
68 DEDR – , by Burrow, T. and MB Emeneau, 2nd edn., Oxford, Clarendon Press, 1984
69 Source: Elements of Indian Archaeology Bharatiya Puratatva,in Hindi) by Shri Krishna Ojha, published by Research Publications in Social Sciences, 2/44 Ansari Riad, Daryaganj, New Delhi-2, pp.119-120. (The fifth chapter summarizes the excavation report of Kalibangan in 11 pages.
70 https://en.wikipedia.org/wiki/Course_in_General_Linguistics
71 Gregory L. Possehl,Shu-ilishu's cylinder seal, *Expedition*, Vol. 48, Number 1, pp. 42-43).http://www.penn.museum/documents/publications/expedition/PDFs/48-1/What%20in%20the%20World.pdf
72 http://bharatkalyan97.blogspot.in/2016/08/proclamations-of-sanchi-torana-and.html?view=mosaic
73 Joshi and Parpola, Corpus of Indus Seals and Inscriptions, Vol. 1, M 306-8 http://bharatkalyan97.blogspot.in/2016/03/indus-script-hieroglyphs-of-prakrtam.html

74 http://www.fhw.gr/chronos/02/islands/en/technology/metallurgy/index.html

75 https://www.academia.edu/4614800/The_early_history_of_lost-wax_casting Davey, Christopher J., 2009, The early history of lost-wax casting in: Mei and Th. Rehren (eds*), Metallurgy and Civilisation: Eurasia and Beyondrchetype,* London 2009. Davey, C.J. (1988) 'Tell edh-Dhiba'i and the southern Near Easternmetalworking tradition', in R. Maddin (ed.),
The Beginning ofthe Use of Metals and Alloys, 63–8. Cambridge, MA: MIT Press.

76 Bernabò-Brea, L., 1964, *Poliochni, citta preistorica nell' isola di Lemnos, Vol.1.* Rome: L'Erma di Bretschneider.B: 64, 591, pl. 85(d); de Jesus, P.S. (1980)*The Development of Prehistoric Mining and Metallurgy in Anatolia* . BAR International Series 4. Oxford:BAR: 41, Fig. 15; Branigan, K.
(1974) *Aegean Metalwork of the Early and Middle Bronze Age*. Oxford: Clarendon Press: 82, Fig. 4).
77 Mille, B., 2006, 'On the origin of lost-wax casting and alloying in the Indo-Iranian world', in *Metallurgy and Civilisation: 6th Inter-national Conference on the Beginnings of the Use of Metals*
and Alloys, University of Science and Technology, Beijing, BUMAVI).
78 http://bharatkalyan97.blogspot.in/2016/08/soma-in-rigveda-allegory-for-metalwork.html Soma is an allegory in Rigveda. Metaphorical expressions have to be unraveled to identify the material, wealth-giving resource of ancient Vedic times.
79 Alchemical treatise: Rudrayamala Tantra, cited in P.Ray, History of Chemistry in Ancient and Medieval India, p.157

80 Hunt, L.B., 1980, The long history of lost wax casting, Over five thousand years of art and craftsmanship, in: *Gold Bull* (1980) 13: 63.

81 Scheel, B. (1989). *Egyptian Metalworking and Tools*. Shire Publications.
82 Kuppuram, Govindarajan (1989). *Ancient Indian Mining, Metallurgy, and Metal Industries*. Sundeep Prakashan; Krishnan, M.V. (1976). *Cire perdue casting in India*. Kanak Publications. *Vishnu Purana*, chapter XIV attests the lost-wax technique of castingmetal "if an image is to be made of metal, it must first be made of wax."
http://bharatkalyan97.blogspot.in/2015/10/indus-script-corpora-of-lost-wax.html
http://bharatkalyan97.blogspot.in/2014/04/revisiting-cire-perdue-in.html
83 Mille, B., Bessenval, R. and Bourgarit, D. Early 'lost-wax casting' in Balochistan (Pakistan): the "Leopards Weight " from Shahi-Tump. Persiens antike Pracht, Bergbau-Handwerk-Archäologie, T. Stöllner, R. Slotta and A. Vatandoust (eds). Der Anschnitt Beiheft 12: Deutsches Bergbau Museum, Bochum (2004): 274- 280.
84 Higham, C. *"Prehistoric Metallurgy in Southeast Asia: Some New Information from the Excavation of Ban Na Di"* in: Robert, ed. (1988). *The beginning of the use of metals and alloys: papers from the Second International Conference on the Beginning of the Use of Metals and Alloys, Zhengzhou, China, 21–26 October 1986*; Agrawal, D. P. (2000). *Ancient Metal Technology and Archaeology of South Asia. A Pan-Asian Perspective.* New Delhi: Aryan Books International

85 Parpola, Asko, 2013, Beginnings of Indian astronomy (Asko Parpola, 2013) With reference to a parallel development in China. in: *History of Science in South Asia* 1 (2013), pp. 21-78)
86 After Parpola 2011: 41 fig. 48 (sketch AP). 'Crocodile in the Indus civilization and later south Asian traditions. In Linguistics, archaeology and the human past: occasional paper 12, ed. Toshiki Osada & Hitoshi Endo. Pp. 1-58. Kyoto: Indus Project, Research Institute for Humanity and Nature.

87 http://www.iranicaonline.org/articles/jiroft-iv-iconography-of-chlorite-artifacts

88
https://www.academia.edu/5689136/Reflections_Upon_Accepted_Dating_of_the_Prestige_Items_of_Nahal_Mishmar

89
https://www.academia.edu/5689136/Reflections_Upon_Accepted_Dating_of_the_Prestige_Items_of_Nahal_Mishmar
90 http://www.hermitagemuseum.org/html_En/04/b2003/hm4_2_013_1.html

91 http://www.pinterest.com/pin/429250026721301O3/
92
https://www.academia.edu/5689136/Reflections_Upon_Accepted_Dating_of_the_Prestige_Items_of_Nahal_Mishmar
93 http://www.pinterest.com/pin/236439667668243761/
94 .http://www.metmuseum.org/toah/works-of-art/55.137.5

95 http://www.iranicaonline.org/articles/jiroft-iv-iconography-of-chlorite-artifacts
Jean Perrot, 2008, Jiroft: Iconography of chlorite artifacts

96 http://www.iranicaonline.org/articles/jiroft-iv-iconography-of-chlorite-artifacts
97 Gods, caves, and scholars: Chalcolithic Cult and Metallurgy in the Judean Desert by Yuval Goren Near Eastern Archaeology Vol. 77, No. 4 (December 2014), pp. 260-266Published by: The American Schools of Oriental Research http://www.jstor.org/stable/10.5615/neareastarch.77.4.0260
98 http://bharatkalyan97.blogspot.in/2013/07/location-of-marhashi-and-cheetah-from.html
99 W.F.Albright, The Mouth of the Rivers, AJSL, 35 (1919): 161-195

100 http://www.bibleorigins.net/DilmunMaganMeluhhaBahrainFailakaCrawford.jpg
101 http://www.hindunet.org/hindu_history/sarasvati/lapis/lapis_lazuli.htm
102 Total prestation in marhashi-ur relations (DT Potts, 2002, Iranica Antiqua, Vol.XXXVII)

103 http://www.scribd.com/doc/156872759/Total-prestation-in-marhashi-ur-relations-DT-Potts-2002-Iranica-Antiqua-Vol-XXXVII

104
https://commons.wikimedia.org/wiki/Category:Bead_dedicated_to_the_Moon_god-AO_27622
105 http://www.tf.uni-kiel.de/matwis/amat/iss/kap_a/backbone/ra_1_5.html
106 Skeat, Walter William (1893), An etymological dictionary of the English language (2nd ed.), Clarendon Press, pp. 438–439. https://en.wikipedia.org/wiki/Spelter
107 Ripley, George; Dana, Charles Anderson (1861). The New American Cyclopaedia: A Popular Dictionary of General Knowledge 3. D. Appleton and Co. p. 729.
108 https://en.wikipedia.org/wiki/French_Bronze (Watt, Alexander (1887). Electro-Metallurgy Practically Treated. D. Van Nostrand. pp. 211–212.)
109 Funerary crozier of the Bishops of St Davids, on display at St David's Cathedral, West Wales https://en.wikipedia.org/wiki/Latten

110 http://www.metmuseum.org/toah/works-of-art/1999.325.4 (Bos gaurus shown with greater clarity) http://art.thewalters.org/viewwoa.aspx?id=33263
111
https://archive.org/details/sealcylindersofw00warduoft http://www.scribd.com/doc/221054125/The-cylinder-seals-of-western-Asia-Carnegie-Institute-of-Washington-Publication-No-100-Ward-William-Hayes-1910

112 http://www.louvre.fr/en/oeuvre-notices/cylinder-seal-ibni-sharrum
113 Burney, 1977, 86; Muhly, 1973, 306-7, 449 note 542; Muhly, J.D., 1973, Tin trade routes of the Bronze Age, *Scientific American*, 1973, 61, 404-13.
114 . Wheeler, R.E.M., 1953, The Indus Civilization, CUP, 58.

115 Lamberg-Karlovsky, C.C., 1967, Archaeology and metallurgy in prehistoric Afghanistan, India and Pakistan, American Anthropologist, 1967, 69, 145-62). The rarity of the metal is seen at Mohenjo-daro where, of 64 artifacts examined, only nine were of tin bronze. (Tylecote, R.F., 1976, A History of Metallurgy, The Metals Society, p.11.
116 Caley, E.R., 1972, Results of an examination of fragments of corroded metal from the 1962 excavation at Snake Cave, Afghanistan, Trans. American Phil. Soc., New Ser. , 62, 43-84
117 Shaffer, J.G., in Allchin F.R. and N. Hammond (eds.), 1979, The Archaeology of Afghanistan, Academic Press, 91, 141-4
118 Lyonnet, B., 1977, Decouverte des sites de l'age du bronze dans le N.E. de l'Afghanistan: leurs rapports avec la civilisation de l'Indus, Annali Instituto Orientali di Napoli, 37, 19-35.
119 Lamberg-Karlovsky, C.C. and M., 1971, An early city in Iran, Scientific American, 1971, 224, No. 6, 102-11; Muhly, 1973, Appendix 11, 347
120 Burney, C., 1975, From village to empire: an introduction to Near Eastern Archaeology, 1977, Phaidon
121 Lamberg-Karlovsky, 1973, reviewing Masson and Sarianidi (1972) in Antiquity, 43-6
122 Penhallurick, R.D., 1986, Tin in Antiquity, London, Institute of Metals, pp.18-32

123 Drawing after Huntington.
http://huntingtonarchive.osu.edu/resources/downloads/webPresentations/HarappaSeals.pdf
124 Human face, stars, buffalo horn. Drawing after Huntington.
http://huntingtonarchive.osu.edu/resources/downloads/webPresentations/HarappaSeals.pdf
125 Molesworth, J. T. (James Thomas). *A dictionary, Marathi and English.* 2d ed., rev. and enl. Bombay: Printed for government at the Bombay Education Society's press, 1857.
126 http://host.themorgan.org/collections/collections.asp?id=628

127 Porada, CANES, p.
3http://www.themorgan.org/collections/collections.asp?id=789
128 Bloomsfield's ed.n, xliv. Cf. Bloomsfield, *American Journal of Philology*, 11, 355; 12,416; Roth, Festgruss an Bohtlingk, 98) denotes it as a twig. This is identified as that of *Badarī*, the jujube tied to the body of the dead to efface their traces. (See Vedic Index, I, p. 177.

129 http://www.arthistory.upenn.edu/spr03/422/April22/4.JPG

130 After Fig. 46, Prudence O Harper et al, opcit., p.78.cf. Amiet, Pierre, 1972, Glyptique susienne: Des origins a l'epoque des Perses achemenides. MDP 43

131 Percy S.P.Handcock, 1912, Mesopotamian Archaeology, London, Macmillan and Co., p. 256

132 After figure d. Barthel Hrouda. Editor. *Der Alte Oriente, Geschichte und Kultur des alten Vorderasien.* Munchen. C. Bertelsmann Verlag GmbH. 1998, p.360

133 After Moorey, PRS, 1999, Ancient materials and industries: the archaeological evidence, Eisenbrauns.

134 Beck, Pirhiya, Notes on the style and iconography of the chalcolithic hoard from Nahal Mishmar (Chapter 3) in:Albert Leonard, Jr., & Bruce Beyer Williams, ed., 1989, Essays in ancient civilization presented to Helene J. Kantor, Studies in ancient oriental civilization No. 47, Oriental Institute of the University of Chicago, pp. 39-54 http://oi.uchicago.edu/pdf/saoc47.pdf

Ziffeer, Irit, 2007, A note on the Nahal Mishmar crown, in: Jack Cheng, Marian H. Feldman, eds., Ancient near eastern art in context: studies in honor of Irene J. Winter by her students, BRILL., pp. 47-67 Irit Ziffeer presents motifs comparable to the architectural model of Naham Mishmar crown:

135 https://aryaninvasionmyth.wordpress.com/2012/10/01/3/

136 http://www.waa.ox.ac.uk/XDB/tours/indus6.asp

137 https://en.wikipedia.org/wiki/Pola_(festival)

138 http://bharatkalyan97.blogspot.in/2016/01/pola-festival-in-bharatam-buffalo-in.html

139 http://bharatkalyan97.blogspot.in/2013/06/ancient-near-east-art-indus-writing.html

http://bharatkalyan97.blogspot.in/2013/06/ancient-near-east-bronze-age-legacy_6.html

140 http://www.tf.uni-kiel.de/matwis/amat/

141 Mirrored at http://spaces.msn.com/members/sarasvati97 Entry: Meluhhan smithś Gundestrup cauldron, together with an album of photographs/figures.

142 Taylor, T. 1992. "The Gundestrup cauldron." *Scientific American* 266(March): 84-89.

143 Dr. Tim Taylor (University of Bradford). Univ. of Birmingham, Archaeology and World Religions, Session held on 19 December 1998. http://www.bham.ac.uk/TAG98/pages/abs

144 http://bharatkalyan97.blogspot.in/2015/05/dating-tin bronze-culture-of-ancient_15.html

145 . http://www.visual-arts-cork.com/site/about.htm

146 http://bharatkalyan97.blogspot.in/2015/02/archaeometallurgy-of-cire-perdue-lost.html

147 Riccio et al. (2011), *The Austroasiatic Munda population from India and Its enigmatic origin: a HLA diversity study* Language Gulper, *Austroasiatic Languages Donegan,* Patricia; David Stampe (2002). South-East Asian Features in the Munda Languages: Evidence for the Analytic-to-Synthetic Drift of Munda. In Patrick Chew, ed., *Proceedings of the 28th Annual Meeting of the Berkeley Linguistics Society*, Special Session on Tibeto-Burman and Southeast Asian Linguistics, in honor of Prof. James A. Matisoff. 111-129. Berkeley, CA: Berkeley Linguistics Society." The paper considers the vexing issues of the homeland and dispersal of the Austroasiatic languages. A critical analysis finds little firm support for nested sub-groupings among a dozen recognised branches, while lexical analyses suggest a long-term pattern of contact and convergence within mainland Southeast Asia. These facts are interpreted as consistent with a stable long-term presence in Indo-China, probably centred on the Mekong River. The most geographically distant branch — the Munda of India — is treated as a highly innovative outlier, and the evolution of Munda root structure is reconstructed, consistent with this theory." (Paul Sidwell, 2010, 'The Austroasiatic central riverine hypothesis' in: *Journal of Language Relationship*, 4 (2010), pp. 117-134.
148 After Fig. 8.1 in: Charles Higham, 1996, *The Bronze Age of Southeast Asia*, Cambridge University Press].Some Bronze Age sites, Far East. (After Fig. 2.2 in Higham, Charles, 1996, *The bronze age of Southeast Asia*, Cambridge Univ. Press
149 http://www.ling.hawaii.edu/faculty/stampe/aa.html
150 Poul Kjaerum, The Dilmun Seals as evidence of long distance relations in the early second millennium BC, pp. 269-277.
151 loc.cit. Bronze in pre-Islamic Iran, Encyclopaedia Iranica, http://www.iranicaonline.org/articles/bronze-i Negahban, 1977

152 Frankfort, Henri: Stratified Cylinder Seals from the Diyala Region. Oriental Institute Publications 72. Chicago: University of Chicago Press, no. 642. Museum Number: IM14674 3.4 cm. high. Glazed steatite. ca. 2250 - 2200 BCE.
153 Parpola, Asko, 1994, *Deciphering the Harappa Script,* Cambridge Univ. Press, p. 253.

154 Ernest J. Mackay, *The Indus Civilization,* 1935, p. 193.

155 H. Frankfort, Cylinder Seals, Macmillan and Co., 1939, p. 304-305.
156 John *Marshall, Mohenjo-daro and the Indus Civilization*, p. 371
157 After Fig. 1 in Thomas et al) Thomas, R., Tengberg, M., Moulhérat, C. et al. Archaeol Anthropol Sci (2012) 4: 15.
158 B. Mille, R. Besenval, D. Bourgarit, 2004, Early lost-wax casting in Balochistan (Pakistan); the 'Leopards weight' from Shahi-Tump. in: *Persiens antike Pracht, Bergbau-Handwerk-Archaologie*, T. Stollner, R Slotta, A Vatandoust, A. eds., pp. 274-280. Bochum: Deutsches Bergbau Museum, 2004.
Mille, B., D. Bourgarit, JF Haquet, R. Besenval, From the 7th to the 2nd millennium BCE in Balochistan (Pakistan): the development of copper metallurgy before and during the Indus Civilisation, South Asian Archaeology, 2001, C. Jarrige & V. Lefevre, eds., *Editions Recherches sur les Civilisations*, Paris, 2005.
159 Gensheimer, TR, 1984, The role of shell in Mesopotamia: evidence for trade exchange with Oman and the Indus Valley, in: *Paleorient*. Annee 1984. Volume 10. Numero 1, pp. 65-73).

http://discover.odai.yale.edu/ydc/Record/3373589

160 http://bharatkalyan97.blogspot.in/2016/04/dharma-samjna-corporate-badges-of-indus.html 21 functional allocations of responsibilitie of artisans delineated in a Vedic village on stoneware bangles with Harappa Script hieroglyphs; references in parethesis are inscription in the Harappa Script Corpora:

1. iron smelting, furnace work (m1659)
2. metal casting, engraving, documenting supercargo (m1647)
3. bronze (casting)(m1646)
4. *gōṭā* (laterite) (m1641)
5. Seafaring merchant, magnetite ingot workshop (m1643)
6. Smithy, forge (m1641)
7. Moltencast copper, brass (m1640)
8. Alloy metal mint, weapons, implements workshop, guild master workshop (m1639)
9. Bronze ingots, implements, magnetite ingots (m1638)
10. Metalcasting workshop (cire perdue?)(m1637)
11. Metal implements, weapons, smithy, forge (m1636)
12. Blacksmith, seafaring merchant (m1634)
13. Helman for supercargo boat, iron furnace work, metals workshop (m1633)
14. Metal casting, alloy mixing workshop (m1632)
15. *dhā̆vaḍ* 'smelter', supercargo of implements (m1631)
16. Magnetite ingots, furnace work, supercargo engraver (m1630)
17. Iron furnace work, metal casting of tin, helmsman supercargo of metals, *bharat* 'mixed alloyś metalworker (m1629)
18. Minerals workshop guild (h2576)
19. Magnetite ingots, smelter (h1010)
20. *dhā̆vaḍ* 'smelter' tri-dhAtu, "three minerals (H98-3516/8667-01)
21. Seafaring merchant, supercargo engraver(Blkt-6)

161 LB Hunt, 1980, The long history of lost wax casting, over five thousand yers of art and craftsmanship, *Gold Bulletin*. June 1980, Volume 13, pp. 62-79

162
https://www.academia.edu/5689136/Reflections_Upon_Accepted_Dating_of_the_Prestige_Items_of_Nahal_Mishmar

163 Ernst Herzfeld, Die vorgeschichtlichen Töpfereien von Samarra, *Die Ausgrabungen von Samarra* 5, Berlin 1930.

164 Kannada. Siddhānti Subrahmaṇya Śastri's new interpretation of the *Amarakośa*, Bangalore, Vicaradarpana Press, 1872, p.330

165 F.B.J. Kuiper, Aryans in the Rigveda, (Amsterdam-Atlanta: Rodopi 1991) from which some of these examples are taken.

166 Natya Shastra of Bharata Muni in English THE NATYASASTRA A Treatise on Hindu Dramaturgy and Histrionics Ascribed to B H A R A T A - M r X I Vol. I. (Chapters I-XXVII) Completely translated for the first tune from the original Sanskrit. Introduction and Various Notes, Royal Asiatic Society of Bengal, Calcutta

http://archive.org/stream/NatyaShastraOfBharataMuniVolume1/NatyaShastraOfBharataMuniVolume1_djvu.txt See S. K. Chatterji, Origin and Development of the Bengali Language,Calcutta,1926 pp. 42,178'

167 Parpola, Parpola and Brunswig 1977: 155-159
168 Brunswig et al, 1983, p. 110
169 Trubetzkoy, NS, 1928, 'Proposition 16' in Actes du premier congres international des linguistes, Leiden, p. 17-18
170 Emeneau, Murray (1956), "India as a Linguistic Area", Language, 32 (1): 3–16
171 The evolution of sentential complementation, Oxford University Press, p. 20-21
172 MB Emeneau, India as a Linguistic Area, Lg. 32:1.3-16 (1956); see p. 16, fn. 28
173 cf. Southworth, FC 2005;Emeneau, MB 1980; Masica, CP 1993; Kuiper, FBJ 1967, Indo-Iranian Journal 10: 81-102
174 cf. Sarasvati – Vedic River and Hindu Civilization by S. Kalyanaraman (2008)]
175
https://drive.google.com/file/d/0B4BAzCi4O_l4bHpvVTNRa2U5R00/view?usp=drive_web (Access on internet) Dr. Kalyanaraman's *Indian Lexicon* - A comparative study of the 'semanticś of lexemes of all the languages of India (which may also be referred to, in a geographical/ historical phrase, as the Indian linguistic area).

The objective of the lexicon is to discover the semantic repertoire of India ca. 3000 B.C. to further facilitate efforts at deciphering the inscriptions and Harappa script of the Sarasvati-Sindhu civilization.
176 Eric Olijdam, Additional Evidence of Late Second Millennium Lapis Lazuli Route,the Fulllol Hoard in: Maurizio Taddei and Giuseppe de Marco, ed., *South Asian Archaeology, Vol. I,* Rome, Istituto Italiano per L'afria e l'oriente, pp.403-404
177 F.R. Allchin, 1959, Upon the contextual significance of certain groups of ancient signs, Bulletin of the School of Oriental and African Studies, London.

178 Fleet, J.F., The inscription on the Sohgaura Plate, JRAS, 1907, pp. 509-532; B.M. Barua, Sohgaura copper plate, Indian Historical Quarterly, Vol. X, 41.
179 Trubetzkoy, 1928: 18]Trubetzkoy, N. S., 1928, 17-18.Leiden: A. W. Sijthoff's Uitgeversmaatschappij.
180 F.B.J. Kuiper, Proto-Munda Words in Sanskrit, Amsterdam, Verhandeling der Koninklijke Nederlandsche Akademie Van Wetenschappen, Afd. Letterkunde, Nieuwe Reeks Deel Li, No. 3, 1948
http://www.hindunet.org/hindu_history/sarasvati/dictionary/9MUNDA.HTM

181 . After Fig. 4.17a, b in: JM Kenoyer, 1998, p. 196

182 http://www.metmuseum.org/exhibitions/listings/2009/cinnabar
183 https://en.wikipedia.org/wiki/Rosasite
184 http://www.galleries.com/Rosasite
185 http://www.mineralgallery.co.za/rosasite.htm
186 Indus valley mystery (Kenoyer & Meadow, 2000)

Ernest Mackay, Chapter XXI. Seals and seal impressions, copper tablets, with tabulation (pp.370-405).
187 http://www.scribd.com/doc/32303649/Indus-Writing-on-Metal

188 Source: http://www.harappa.com/indus4/351.html

189 http://bharatkalyan97.blogspot.in/2015/03/a-tribute-to-rick-willis-who.html

190 http://www.harappa.com/indus4/print.html

191 http://bharatkalyan97.blogspot.in/2016/06/indus-script-data-archive-knowledge.html
192 http://cdli.ucla.edu/search/search_results.php?SearchMode=Text&ObjectID=P010670

193 http://cdli.ucla.edu/pubs/cdlb/2015/cdlb2015_006.html#fn1

194 http://www.dli.gov.in/rawdataupload/upload/insa/INSA_1/20005afd_33.pdf

195 http://www.iranicaonline.org/img/v4/v4f5a012_f1_300.jpg

196 http://www.mrmaheri.com/page.php?id=1-5-1)
197 Shah, SGM & Parpola, A., 1991, Corpus of Indus Seals and Inscriptions 2: Collections in Pakistan, Helsinki: Suomalainen Tiedeakatemia, MR-17.

198 http://www.penn.museum/documents/publications/expedition/PDFs/48 1/What%20in %20the%20World.pdf Shu-ilishu's cylinder seal, Expedition, Vol. 48, No. 1

199 http://www.ling.hawaii.edu/austroasiatic/AA/Munda/ETYM/Pinnow&Munda

200 http://www.vanderkrogt.net/elements/element.php?sym=Cu
201 Image source for Brahmi: vocalized consonant http://www.ancientscripts.com/brahmi.html See also:

http://www.payer.de/exegese/exeg03.htm#5.2.2.

202 https://en.wikipedia.org/wiki/Spelter
203 http://www.fouman.com/Y/Image/History/Gilan_Gold_Rhyton_Lion.jpg
204 http://www.coinnetwork.com/profiles/blogs/swastika-on-indian-coins
205 https://en.wikipedia.org/wiki/Rope
See: Thomas R., Tengberg M., Moulhérat C., Marcon V. & Besenval R. – 2012. Analysis of a Protohistoric net from Shahi Tump, Baluchistan (Pakistan).Archaeological and Anthropological Sciences, 4 (1) : 15-23.

See: http://www.mae.u-paris10.fr/arscan/IMG/article_PDF/article_a1412.pdf

See: https://www.academia.edu/2557263/A_Late_Neolithic_fishing_net_from_Kurdistan_Northern_Iraq

206 http://puratattva.in/2012/03/21/sanchi-buddham-dhammam-sangahm-5-1484
207 books.google.com/books?id=evtIAQAAIAAJ&q=In+the+image...
208 http://www.cristoraul.com/ENGLISH/readinghall/UniversalHistory/INDIA/Cambridge/I/CHAPTER_XXVI.html
209 http://www.bl.uk/onlinegallery/onlineex/apac/photocoll/a/largeimage58906.html

210 http://www.bl.uk/onlinegallery/onlineex/apac/photocoll/a/largeimage58907.html
211 https://www.academia.edu/11522244/A_temple_at_Sanchi_for_Dhamma_by_a_k%C4%81ra%E1%B9%87ik%C4%81_sanghin_guild_of_scribes_in_Indus_writing_cipher_continuum
212 http://bharatkalyan97.blogspot.in/2016/01/data-mining-techniques-decipherment-of.html

213 .http://www.ancient-asia-journal.com/articles/10.5334/aa.12317/
214 Kenoyer, J. M. (1998). Ancient cities of the Indus Valley Civilization. Oxford: Oxford University Press. p.159
215 Source:Encyclopaedia Biblica/Trade and Commerce http://en.wikisource.org/wiki/Encyclopaedia_Biblica/Trade_and_Commerce
216 http://press.princeton.edu/chapters/s9006.pdf (Page 12).Michael Hudson, Entrepreneurs: from the Near Eastern Takeoff to the Roman collapse July 19, 2010 http://michael-hudson.com/2010/07/entrepreneurs-from-the-near-eastern-takeoff-to-the-roman-collapse/
217 see: Pettersson, JS, 1999, *Indian Journal of Historyh of Science*, 34(2): 89-108http://www.new.dli.ernet.in/rawdataupload/upload/insa/INSA_2/20005a61_89.pdf

218 loc.cit. VK Agnihotri, 2005, Indian History, Delhi, Allied Publishers, p. A-60
219 Excerots from: http://www.antiqueprints.com/Info/engraving.php http://bharatkalyan97.blogspot.in/2014/10/copper-plates-of-indus-script-and-rebus.html

220 F.R. Allchin, 1959, Upon the contextual significance of certain groups of ancient signs, Bulletin of the School of Oriental and African Studies, London.
221 Fleet, JRAS, 63, 1894 proceedings, 86, plate, IA 25. 262; cf. Sohgaura copper plate/B.M. Barua. The Indian Historical Quarterly, ed. Narendra Nath Law. Reprint. 41
222 Fleet, J.F., The inscription on the Sohgaura Plate, JRAS, 1907, pp. 509-532; B.M. Barua, Sohgaura copper plate, Indian Historical Quarterly, Vol. X, 41
223 BM Barua, 1929, The Sohgaura copper-plate inscription, ABORI, vol. 11, 1929, pp. 31-48.
224 Ananda K. Coomaraswamy, Indian Architectural Terms, *Journal of the American Oriental Society*, Vol. 48, no. 3, SEPT 1928, pp.250-275

225 http://www.royalathena.com/PAGES/NearEasternCatalog/Bronze/CLT168.html
226
http://www.lessingimages.com/search.asp?a=L&lc=202020207EE6&ln=Collection+George+Ortiz%2C+Geneva%2C+Switzerland&p=1
227 R. Maxwell-Hyslop, 'British Museum “axe” no. 123628: a Bactrian bronze', *Bulletin of the Asia Institute*, NS I (1987), pp. 17-26
Curator's comments: See RL file 6616 (29/6/1995); also Research Lab file 4992 of 12/09/1983 where XRF analysis of surface indicates composition as tin bronze with approx 10% tin and traces of arsenic, nickel, silver and lead. Dalton's inclusion in the 'Catalogue of the Oxus Treasure' among a small group of comparative items has unfortunately led to recurrent confusion over the date and provenance of this piece. It was first believed to be Achaemenid in date (Dalton, 'Catalogue of the Oxus Treasure', p. 48), labelled as such in 1975 in the former Iranian Room and thus suggested to be an Achaemenid scabbard chape (P R S Moorey CORRES 1975, based on an example said to have been excavated by P. Bernard at Ai Khanoum or seen by him in Kabul Bazaar, cf. P. Bernard CORRES 1976). It has also been assigned a 4th-5th century AD Sasanian date (P. Amiet, 1967, in 'Revue du Louvre' 17, pp. 281-82). However, its considerably earlier - late 3rd mill. BC Bronze Age - date has now been clearly demonstrated following the discovery of large numbers of objects of related form in south-east Iran and Bactria, and it has since been recognised and/or cited as such, for instance by H. Pittmann (hence archaeometallurgical analysis in 1983; R. Maxwell-

Hyslop, 1988a, "British Museum axe no. 123628: a Bactrian bronze", 'Bulletin of the Asia Institute' 1 (NS), pp. 17-26; F. Hiebert & C.C. Lamberg-Karlovsky 1992a, "Central Asia and the Indo-Iranian Borderlands",' Iran' 30, p. 5; B. Brentjes, 1991a, "Ein tierkampfszene in bronze", 'Archäologische Mitteilungen aus Iran' 24 (NS), p. 1, taf. 1).
http://www.britishmuseum.org/research/collection_online/collection_object_details.aspx?objectId=367862&partId=1
228 http://www.imagesofasia.com/html/mohenjodaro/gold-fillet.html
229 https://en.wikipedia.org/wiki/Nabu-apla-iddina
See: The Sun-God Tablet of Nabû-apla-iddina Revisited Christopher E. Woods Journal of Cuneiform Studies Vol. 56 (2004), pp. 23-103 Published by: American Schools of Oriental Research http://www.jstor.org/stable/3515920

230 http://www.louvre.fr/sites/default/files/imagecache/940x768/medias/medias_images/images/louvre-maquette-d039un-lieu-culte.jpg

231 Epoque médio-élamite Suse Calcaire H. 62.8 cm; W. 92 cm Fouilles J. de Morgan 1904 – 1905 Sb 19 http://www.louvre.fr/en/oeuvre-notices/ritual-basin-decorated-goatfish-figures

232 http://www.louvre.fr/en/oeuvre-notices/stele-untash-napirisha-king-anshan-and-susa

233 http://www.sumscorp.com/new_models_of_culture/terms/?object_id=150959
234 http://bharatkalyan97.blogspot.in/2015/08/bharhut-stupa-torana-announces.html?view=classic

235 https://www.academia.edu/10640140/distribution_and_features_of_the_Indus_Civilization
236 Jansen, Michael, 1986, *Die Indus-Zivilisation: Wiederentdeckung einer fruhen Hochkultur*, Cologne, 200f., fig. 125
237 John Marshall, 1931, *Mohenjo-daro and the Indus Civilization*, London, Arthur Probsthain, p. 371
238 https://www.harappa.com/sites/default/files/pdf/stoneware_bangles.pdf
239 After Fig.3, 4, 5, 7 in Massimo Vidale, 1986, Stoneware industry of the Indus civilization: an evolutionary dead-end in the history of ceramic technology, in: In: WD Kingery, ed., Vol. V, Ceramics and civilization. The changing roles of ceramics in society: 26000 BP to the present, Westerville, OH, The American Ceramic Society, Inc.
240 J.M. Blackman, M. Vidale, 1992, The Production and Distribution of Stoneware Bangles at Mohenjo-Daro and Harappa as Monitored by Chemical Charachterization Studies, in: Catherine Jarrige, ed., 1992, *South Asian Archaeology 1989*, Prehistory Press,
p.38See: shttps://www.academia.edu/5597400/J.M._Blackman_M._Vidale_The_Production_and_Distribution_of_Stoneware_Bangles_at_Mohenjo-Daro_and_Harappa_as_Monitored_by_Chemical_Charachterization_Studies

241 Massimo Vidale, in: Jansen and Urban, 1987, p. 109 Jansen, M. 1987 Preliminary results on the "forma urbis" research at Mohenjo-Daro. In Interim Reports Vol. 2:

Reports on Field Work Carried out at Mohenjo-Daro, Pakistan 1983-84 by IsMEO-Aachen University Mission., edited by M. Jansen and G. Urban, pp. 9-21. Aachen, IsMEO/ RWTH.
242 Massimo Vidale, in:Jansen and Urban, 1987, p. 111
243 https://www.harappa.com/sites/default/files/pdf/KenoyerMeadow%202010%20Inscribed%20Objects%20from%20Harappa.pdf Kenoyer, J. Mark and Richard H. Meadow, 2010, Inscribed objects from Harappa excavations 1986 to 2007 https://www.scribd.com/doc/311112457/The-tinysteatite-seals-incised-steatite-tablets-of-Harappa-Some-observations-ontheir-context-and-dating-Meadow-Richard-H-and-Jonathan-Kenoyer Meadow, Richard H. & Jonathan Mark Kenoyer, 2000, in: I.Maurizio Taddei & Giuseppe de Marco, South Asian Archaeology, 1997, Vol. I, Rome, Istituto Italiano per l'aafrica e l'oriente,
244 After Asko, 1994. Deciphering the Harappa Script. Cambridge: Cambridge University Press.,p. 234, fig. 13.13.
245 https://www.harappa.com/blog/ringstones
246 Root / lemma: *ai̯os-* (Pokorny)

247 References: WP. I 4, WH. I, 19, 20, Feist 31. http://dnghu.org/indoeuropean.html Indo-European Etymological Dictionary - Indogermanisches Etymologisches Woerterbuch (JPokorny)

248 http://bharatkalyan97.blogspot.in/2015/05/composite-copper-alloy-anthropomorphic.html
249 Korvink, Michael, 2007, The Harappa Script: A Positional-statistical Approach, Gilund Press.
250 http://bharatkalyan97.blogspot.in/2013/07/legend-of-anzu-which-stole-tablets-of.html
251 Shinde, V. & Willis, R.J., (2014). A New Type of Inscribed Copper Plate from Indus Valley (Harappa) Civilisation. *Ancient Asia* 5, p. Art. 1. http://www.ancient-asia-journal.com/articles/10.5334/aa.12317/
252 H. Sarkar & BM Pande, 1999, Symbols and Graphic Representations in Indian Inscriptions, Delhi: Aryan,
253 https://en.wikipedia.org/wiki/Spelter
254 http://www.gutenberg.org/files/40812/40812-h/images/img196.jpg

255 http://www.gutenberg.org/files/40812/40812-h/images/img188.jpg

256 Goodyear, "Grammar of the Lotus," pl. 60, fig. 9

257 http://www.gutenberg.org/files/40812/40812-h/images/img187.jpg

258 Athens. Birch, "History of Ancient Pottery," quoted by Waring in "Ceramic Art in Remote Ages," pl. 41, fig. 15; Dennis, "The Cities and Cemeteries of Etruria," i, p. 91.

259 http://www.gutenberg.org/files/40812/40812-h/images/img179.jpg

260 http://www.gutenberg.org/files/40812/40812-h/images/img171.jpgFig. 158. (After T Wilson opcit)

261 Goodyear, "Grammar of the Lotus," pl. 60, fig. 15261.

262 http://www.gutenberg.org/files/40812/40812-h/images/img214.jpg (After Fig. 201, T. Wilson, p.864) Spearhead with svastika (croix swasticale) and triskelion. Brandenburg. Germany. Waring, 'Ceramic art in remote age,' p. 44. fig. 21 and 'Viking age' I, fig. 336

263 http://www.gutenberg.org/files/40812/40812-h/images/img215.jpg
264 http://www.gutenberg.org/files/40812/40812-h/images/img228.jpg After Fig. 220 (T. Wilson opcit.) Stone altar with svastika on pedestal. France museum of Toulouse De Mortillet. 'Musee Prehistorique', fig. 1267

265 http://www.gutenberg.org/files/40812/40812-h/images/img239.jpg After Figs. 231 to 234 T. Wilson, opcit..
266 http://www.gutenberg.org/files/40812/40812-h/images/img240.jpg
http://www.gutenberg.org/files/40812/40812-h/images/img052.jpg

267 http://www.gutenberg.org/files/40812/40812-h/images/img047.jpg

268 Source: Wilson, Thomas, 1894, *The Swastika, the earliest known symbol and its migration. Annual Report,* US National Museum, pages 757-1011. Washington, DC. Govt. Printing Office. http://www.gutenberg.org/files/40812/40812-h/40812-h.htm
269
http://www.gutenberg.org/files/40812/40812-h/40812-h.htm (Photo from an obituary written by OT Mason, 1902. After Fig. 10 in:
http://www.sil.si.edu/smithsoniancontributions/Anthropology/pdf_hi/SCtA-0048.pdf
270 After Fig. 21.14 in Asko Paropla, 2015 opcit. After Fig. 13.13
in: Parpola, Asko, 1994. *Deciphering the Harappa Script*. Cambridge: Cambridge University Press., p. 232

271 http://en.wikipedia.org/wiki/World-Turtle

272 http://frontiers-of-anthropology.blogspot.in/2011/11/giant-turtle-that-bears-world-on-its.html

273 http://frontiers-of-anthropology.blogspot.in/2011/11/giant-turtle-that-bears-world-on-its.html http://en.wikipedia.org/wiki/Colossochelys

274 http://en.wikipedia.org/wiki/Giant_tortoise

275 See many variants of 'body' hieroglyph and ligatures at
https://www.academia.edu/8408578/Stature_of_body_Meluhha_hieroglyphs_48_in_Indus_writing_catalogs_of_metalwork_processes

276 Meadow, Richard H. and Jonathan Kenoyer, 1997, The 'tinysteatite seals (incised steatitetablets) of Harappa: Some observations ontheir context and dating in: Taddei, Maurizio and Giuseppe de Marco, 2000, South Asian Archaeology, 1997, Rome, Istituto Italiano per l'Africa e l'Oriente.After Fig. 3, p.12 Harappa 1995-1997: Mounds E and ET; molded terracotta tablets)
277 Kenoyer, J.Mark & Richard H. Meadow, 2010, Inscribed objects from Harappa excavations 1986-2007 in: Asko Parpola, B.M. Pande and Petteri Koskikallio (eds.), Corpus of Indus seals and inscriptions, Volume 3: New material, untraced objects and collections outside India and Pakistan, Part 1: Mohenjo-daro and Harappa,

Helsinki, Suomalainen Tiedeakatemia, pp. xlix-l) http://www.harappa.com/indus/Kenoyer-Meadow-2010-HARP.pdf

278 Richard H. Meadow and Jonathan Mark Kenoyer, 2000, The Indus valley mystery, one of the world's first great civilizations is still a puzzle, in: Scientific American Discovering Archaeology, March/April 2000, p. 41

Richard H. Meadow and Jonathan Mark Kenoyer, 2000, The Indus Valley Mystery in: Scientific American, Discovery Archaeology, March/April 2000, pp. 38-43

Source: http://www.anthropology.wisc.edu/pdfs/Kenoyer%20Articles/The%20Indus%20Valley%20Mystery.pdf

279 (Seehttp://bharatkalyan97.blogspot.com/2011/11/decoding-longest-inscription-of-indus.html)
280 See also:http://docslide.us/documents/antelope-hieroglyphs-1.html (embedded) See: http://bharatkalyan97.blogspot.in/2015/03/indus-script-tablets-are-workshop.html It is suggested that tablets are workshop product tokens to aggregate supercargo for shipment (with a seal impression documenting product specifications).

http://bharatkalyan97.blogspot.in/2015/05/contributions-of-bharatam-janam-to.html On Indian alchemy of historical periods

281 David A. Scott, Getty Conservation Institute, 2002, Copper and Bronze in Art: corrosion, colorants, conservation, Getty Publications, p. 162
282 Dennys Frenez & Massimo Vidale, 2012, *South Asian Studies*, Vol. 28, No. 2, September 2012, p.115

283 Dennys Frenez & Massimo Vidale, 2012, Harappa Chimaeras as 'Symbolic Hypertexts. Some Thoughts on Plato, Chimaera and the Indus Civilization in: *South Asian Studies* Volume 28, Issue 2, pp. 107-130
284 http://www.ling.hawaii.edu/austroasiatic/AA/Munda/ETYM/Pinnow&Munda

285 http://www.harappa.com/indus/88.html

286 http://tinyurl.com/bq3xul5
287 https://en.wikipedia.org/wiki/Tuisto
288 http://www.imagesofasia.com/html/mohenjodaro/gold-fillet.html
289 http://old.omda.bg/engl/history/varna_necropolis_treasure.htm

290 Israel Museum(IDAM), Jerusalem, Israel

291 Charles Keith Maisels, *The emergence of civilization* (Taylor & Francis, 1990).
292 http://www.persiangulfstudies.com/userfiles/images/prehistory-museum-04.jpg
293 After Fig. 43, Prudence O. Harper et al, opcit., p.73
294 Benoy K. Behl https://www.facebook.com/BenoyKBehlArtCulture See: Cultural relationships Beyond the iranian plateau: The Helmand civilization, Baluchistan and the Indus Valley in the 3rd millennium bce -- E. Cortesi, M. Tosi, A. Lazzari and M. Vidale (2008) https://www.harappa.com/sites/default/files/pdf/Indus-helmand2.pdf
295 Werner, Karel (1977). "Symbolism in the Vedas and Its Conceptualisation". *Numen*. **24** (3): 223–240

296 Zaehner, R. C. (1966), *Hindu Scriptures,* London: Everyman's Library.
297 Vats,MS, *Excavations at Harappa*, p. 370

298 http://bharatkalyan97.blogspot.in/2015/12/yupa-inscriptions-document-yajna-s-fire.html

http://bharatkalyan97.blogspot.in/2015/12/binjor-indus-script-seal-mulavarman.html

http://bharatkalyan97.blogspot.in/2016/01/a-note-on-yupa-pillars-of-rajasthan-dr.html

299 http://bharatkalyan97.blogspot.in/2015/06/vajra-ayasam-vajram-metal-weapon-rv.html
300 http://bharatkalyan97.blogspot.in/2015/12/kalibangan-terracotta-cake-hieroglyphs.html
301 http://www.ajspeelman.com/details.php?sid=448

302 www.flickr.com/photos/dalbera/sets/72157623402022149/
303 www.guimet.fr/spip.php?page=recherche&recherche=linga... voir une autre cuve à ablution : www.flickr.com/photos/dalbera/2416473091/
304 http://www.jstor.org/stable/3642415
305 http://www.artgallery.nsw.gov.au/collection/works/477.1996/
306 http://laodong.com.vn/lao-dong-cuoi-tuan/vuong-quoc-phu-nam-qua-co-vat-77529.bld

307 O'Connor, SJ, 1961, *An ekamukhalinga from Peninsular Siam, The Journal of the Siam Society*. The Siam Society. pp. 43-49
308 http://www.asianart.com/exhibitions/mukhalinga/mukhalingas.html
309 http://www.asianart.com/exhibitions/boaf2010/anninos.html
310 http://gretil.sub.uni-goettingen.de/gretil/1_sanskr/1_veda/2_bra/satapath/sb_05_u.htm (Text)
http://www.sacred-texts.com/hin//sbr/sbe41/sbe4108.htm (Translation)
http://bharatkalyan97.blogspot.in/2016/01/wheat-earth-smoke-of-casala-of-yupa.html
311 https://en.wikipedia.org/wiki/Crucible_steel
312 They were fierce warriors skilled in horse riding and horse warfare. "Kinnaras are mentioned as half-men and half-horses at (1.66) where they are described as kinsmen of other tribes. Kinnaras were mentioned along with other exotic tribes like the Nāgas, Uragas, Pannāgas, Suparnas, Vidyadharas, Siddhas, Charanas, Valikhilyas, Pisachas, Gandharvas, Apsaras, Kimpurushas, Yakshas, Rakhsasas, Vanaras etc. at various places. (1-18,66), (2-10), (3-82,84,104,108,139,200,223,273) (4-70), (5-12), (7-108,160), (8-11), (9-46), (12- 168,227,231,302,327,334,(13-58,83,87,140), (14-43,44,88,92)."
313 http://www.ignca.nic.in/coilnet/asp/showbig.asp?projid=jtk2
314 IndianLexicon.pdf (file://HP-PC/Users/HP/Google%20Drive/IndianLexicon.pdf)
315 http://huntingtonarchive.osu.edu/Makara%20Site/makara

www.ingramcontent.com/pod-product-compliance
Lightning Source LLC
Chambersburg PA
CBHW062136160426
43191CB00014B/2297